THE LEGAL ENVIRONMENT OF BUSINESS

McGraw-Hill Book Company

New York
St. Louis
San Francisco
Auckland
Bogotá
Hamburg
Johannesburg
London
Madrid
Mexico
Milan
Montreal
New Delhi
Panama
Paris
São Paulo
Singapore
Sydney
Tokyo
Toronto

Seventh Edition

THE LEGAL ENVIRONMENT OF BUSINESS

Robert N. Corley

Distinguished Professor of Legal Studies
University of Georgia

O. Lee Reed

Professor of Legal Studies
University of Georgia

With the assistance of
Russell L. Welch
North Texas State University

This book was set in Baskerville by Better Graphics, Inc.
The editor was Sam Costanzo; the cover was designed by Joan Greenfield;
the production supervisor was Diane Renda.
Project supervision was done by The Total Book.
R. R. Donnelley & Sons Company was printer and binder.

THE LEGAL ENVIRONMENT OF BUSINESS

Library of Congress Cataloging-in-Publication Data

Corley, Robert Neil.
  The legal environment of business.

  "The appendixes include the United States
Constitution and excerpts from the antitrust laws
and labor laws"—P.
  1. Trade regulation—United States.   I. Reed, O.
  Lee (Omer Lee)   II. Welch, Russell L.   III. Title.
KF1600.C6   1987   346.73'07   86-15171
ISBN 0-07-013256-9   347.3067

1 2 3 4 5 6 7 8 9 0   DOCDOC   8 9 4 3 2 1 0 9 8 7 6

ISBN 0-07-013256-9

ABOUT THE AUTHORS

Robert N. Corley is currently Distinguished Professor of Legal Studies at the Universiy of Georgia. He received J.D. and B.S. degrees from the University of Illinois, where he taught for eighteen years. He was admitted to the Illinois Bar in 1956. Professor Corley is past president of the American Business Law Association and a past member of the editorial board of the *American Business Law Journal.* Winner of numerous teaching awards at both the undergraduate and graduate levels, he also teaches in three national executive development programs. Since 1964 he has been senior author of *The Legal Environment of Business.* In important respects his contributions have shaped the content of the entire legal environment of business field.

O. Lee Reed holds a J.D. degree from the University of Chicago and a B.A. degree from Birmingham-Southern College. Presently, he is Professor of Legal Studies at the University of Georgia. The author of many scholarly articles, he is former editor-in-chief of the *American Business Law Journal.* He also has served as president of the Southeastern Regional Business Law Association. Professor Reed has received teacher-of-the-year awards from both undergraduate and graduate student organizations. He has been co-author of the *Legal Environment of Business* since 1977.

CONTENTS

PART ONE
INTRODUCTION

Chapter 1   THE LAW AND LAWYERS   2

Chapter 2   THE POWERS AND FUNCTIONS OF COURTS   22

PART TWO
PRIVATE LAW PRINCIPLES

Chapter 5   CONTRACT LAW AND PRIVATE ENTERPRISE   110

Chapter 6   TORTS IN THE BUSINESS ENVIRONMENT   136

Chapter 7   PRODUCTS AND SERVICE LIABILITY   174

PART 3
PUBLIC LAW AND BUSINESS

Chapter 12   LIABILITY OF BUSINESS ORGANIZATIONS AND MANAGERS   345

Chapter 13   INTERNATIONAL TRANSACTIONS   375

PART FIVE
PROTECTING THE INDIVIDUAL

Chapter 16 INVESTOR PROTECTION   462

PART SIX
PROTECTING GROUPS

PART SEVEN
PROTECTING SOCIETY

Chapter 22   ENVIRONMENTAL LAWS AND POLLUTION CONTROL   691

LIST OF CASES

PREFACE

One oil company has recently been ordered to pay nearly $2 billion under federal environmental clean-up law. A jury has returned a verdict of $10.5 billion against another oil company for interfering with a merger. In March 1986 over a thousand manufacturers traveled to Washington and lobbied Congress to federalize product liability law. Now more than ever, students preparing for careers in the business community need to grasp the significance of law and its potential impact on their lives.

Beginning around 1960, the impact of law on the business community grew significantly. Important changes in the law brought new rights to employees, investors, consumers, and others that were often enforced by regulatory action. In 1963 we wrote *The Legal Environment of Business*, the first textbook responding to the great changes taking place in the law. In it we developed an approach to law that focuses on public law, the regulation of business, and legal trends rather than on detailed private law rules. We are gratified that this aproach has come to define the *legal environment of business*, the required law course of the American Assembly of Collegiate Schools of Business. The majority of new collegiate law textbooks being published have adopted this approach. With the seventh edition of *The Legal Environment of Business*, we now continue our leadership in the teaching of law that was begun more than two decades ago.

GUIDING PRINCIPLE

In preparing these materials for an environmental course in law, a basic principle has guided us: the materials should actively prepare students for decision making in business rather than merely summarize for them the course content of various law school subjects. This is the heart of our instructional approach, and it ensures that we have treated law as an important institution of society and as a tool for generating policy. Only students who appreciate these dynamics of law will be able to go beyond the commonly held lay concept of law as a series of rules and to understand it most effectively for business decision making. At the same time we have not neglected important substantive legal rules.

CASE TREATMENT

The materials in this book include text discussions, summaries of imporatnt legislation, articles, and decided cases. We have deleted most of the procedural issues from the cases and have omitted case references and footnotes. Since we believe that students should be required to study judicial language and reasoning on substantive issues, we include those portions of each case that show the arguments of the parties and the court's resolution of the issues raised. We have shortened long cases without deleting the heart of the opinions.

NEW FEATURES

The seventh edition of the *Legal Environment of Business* contains several new features. Among the most important are:

1 The chapter arrangement has been completely reorganized. We have grouped twenty-two chapters into seven basic categories: (1) Introduction (the working of the legal system), (2) Private Law principles, (3) Public Law and Business, (4) Conducting Business, (5) Protecting the Individual, (6) Protecting Groups, and (7) Protecting Society.

2 Since contracts form the basis for economic exchanges, and since much government regulation affects contracts, a new chapter covers principles of contract law. This chapter also introduces contracts to students who will not take additional, specialized courses in private law subjects.

3 To emphasize the importance of international law, we have added an entire chapter on that topic. The chapter was prepared by Russell Welch of North Texas State University. We are delighted to bring to students Professor Welch's special expertise in international law since exporting and importing by multinational corporations are of steadily growing significance to American economic life.

4 An explanation of limitations on the employment-at-will doctrine forms part of a new chapter on worker protection. Other subjects include unemployment compensation, the Fair Labor Standards Act, workers' compensa-

tion, and pension plans. Understanding worker protection law is vital in a system where a great majority of the labor force is employed by corporations.

5 A full 60 percent of the cases in the seventh edition are new. Over 70 percent were decided since 1980. These figures reflect our conviction that judicial interpretation of the law is best impressed upon students as a currently relevant, ever-evolving process. Of course, a certain number of landmark decisions are also covered.

6 Where appropriate, we have added material treating the ethical issues of public and social policy that underlie legal rules. This material meets AACSB standards for coverage of business ethics.

STUDENT AIDS

The text continues to include a glossary that defines legal terms used throughout the text so that students will not require access to a legal dictionary while reading. The appendixes include the United States Constitution and excerpts from the antitrust laws and labor laws for student reference. We feel that students often benefit from reading the exact language of the Constitution and of some of the major statutes that furnish the basic legal principles for substantial portions of the text.

Following this preface, there is a special section addressed to students. In this section we provide step-by-step instructions on how to study this textbook. We include as a part of the instructions a written example of the case briefing system so that students will know how to brief a case if the instructor asks them to do so.

For the first time the text now places important terms in bold type. This innovation should also aid students in their study.

SUPPLEMENTARY MATERIALS

To supplement the text's coverage, a comprehensive instructor's manual and test bank are available to adopters. The test bank was prepared by Robert J. Aalberts, Louisiana State University.

For students there is a study guide prepared by Professor O. Lee Reed. As one of the co-authors of the text, his special insight has enabled him to prepare a study guide that complements the text. As a teaching tool, it should aid in understanding the more difficult subjects of the text. If the study guide is not available to students, it may be ordered for them by their bookstores on a rush basis directly from the publisher.

ACKNOWLEDGMENTS

The authors express their gratitude to the Yale University press for permission to reprint excerpts from Cardozo, *The Nature of the Judicial Process;* and the *Harvard Business Review* for permission to reprint two articles. We are also grateful to the Caterpillar Tractor Company of Peoria, Illinois, for permission to quote extensively throughout the text from its Code of World-wide Business Conduct and Operating Principles.

The authors also acknowledge the assistance of the following professors who reviewed the manuscript and provided many helpful suggestions: Jack Manders, Drake University; and John Norwood, University of Arkansas.

Finally, we thank Sue Hoy of the University of Georgia for her many contributions to the manuscript.

Robert N. Corley
O. Lee Reed

TO THE STUDENT

To gain the most from this textbook, you should learn how to study written material effectively. You can achieve effective study through use of the SQ3R method, a method widely taught by study-skills psychologists for learning textual material.

SQ3R stands for **survey, question, read, recite,** and **review.** As a study method, it has dramatically improved the grade-point averages of most students who have practiced it. It is based upon the concept that active study of written material improves memory and comprehension of information far better than passive reading. Unfortunately, many students have not recognized the difference between active study and mere passive reading.

Students often read a textbook chapter exactly as they would read a novel or a magazine article. They begin with the first sentence of the chapter and read straight through the material, pausing only to underline occasionally. This way of reading may be suitable for a novel, but it is quite inappropriate for a textbook. Psychologists insist that an active study method must begin with a **survey** of the material to be read. If you plan to spend two hours studying a thirty-page chapter, take three-to-five minutes in the beginning and survey the chapter. First, read the boldtype section headings; (each chapter of this book is divided into numbered sections). Second, read a sentence or two from the text of each section. The purpose of this survey is to familiarize you with the topics covered in the chapter. Fight the tendency to stop your surveying process in order to comprehend all of the concepts you are surveying. Comprehension is not the goal of surveying.

Following the survey of all the sections, go back to the beginning of the chapter. Ask yourself a **question** before reading each section. Ask it aloud, if possible, but silently if circumstances demand. The important thing is actually to "talk to yourself." Normally, each section heading can easily be turned into a question. If the section heading reads **Stare Decisis,** ask yourself the question, "What does stare decisis mean?"

Only after asking a question are you finally ready to **read** a chapter section. In reading keep your question in mind. By so doing you will be reading for a purpose: to discover the answer to your question.

Upon finishing each section, stop and **recite** the answer to your question. As an example, at the end of the section on stare decisis say to yourself, "Stare decisis refers to the legal tradition that a judge in a given case will follow the precedent established in similar cases decided by courts in that jurisdiction." According to psychologists, to recite this way greatly aids memory. Recitation also lets you know whether or not you have understood the material just read.

The last step of the SQ3R method is **review.** When devoting two hours to the study of a chapter, take the final fifteen minutes of that time to review the material. Review the questions taken from the headings of each chapter section and recite the answers to them, rereading material if necessary to answer accurately.

While the SQ3R method may be used effectively to study any subject, the **case briefing system** is uniquely designed to aid in the study of court decisions. In studying law, students frequently write up case briefs of each decision they read. Whether you are required to write up every decision is up to your individual instructor. However, the case briefing system provides an excellent framework for comprehending complicated judicial reasoning processes, and you should brief cases whether required to do so or not.

To avoid getting lost in a maze of judicial terminology, you should ask yourself a standard set of questions about each case decision and read to discover the answers to these questions. These standard questions lie at the heart of the case briefing system. They are:

1   Who is the plaintiff and who is the defendant?

2   What are the facts of the case? (Who did what to whom? What is the behavior complained of?)

3   Did the plaintiff or the defendant win in the lower court(s), and which party is appealing? (All decisions in this textbook come from appellate courts.)

4   What was the legal issue or issues appealed?

5   Does the plaintiff or the defendant win on the appeal?

6   What rules of law and reasoning does the appellate court use in deciding the issue?

Here is an illustration of a written case brief. It is a brief on the first case in the book, which is found on page 51. Before looking at the brief you should now read that case. To understand the case you need to know that the term "diversity jurisdiction" refers to the power of the federal courts to try cases on subjects of state law. Such jurisdiction is appropriate only when there is complete "diversity of citizenship," i.e., when every plaintiff is from a different state than every defendant.

Case Brief

NAVARRO SAV. ASS'N v LEE, 100 S.Ct. 1779 (1980) [The notation following the name of the case indicates that the case may be found in volume 100 of the Supreme Court Reporter, starting at page 1779. The case was decided in 1980.]

Plaintiff and Defendant

The plaintiffs are eight individual trustees of Fidelity Mortgage Investors. The defendant is the Navarro Savings and Loan Association.

Facts

In 1971, the trustees who controlled Fidelity Mortgage Investors, a real estate investment trust organized under Massachusetts law, loaned $850,000 to a Texas firm in return for a promissory note. The note was secured in part by the commitment letter of Navarro Savings and Loan Association to loan the Texas firm the money necessary to repay the note. In 1973, the trustees demanded that Navarro honor its commitment, but Navarro refused. The trustees (none of whom were from Texas) sued Navarro (a Texas S & L) in federal district court, alleging that the court had diversity jurisdiction.

Lower Courts

The district court dismissed the case for lack of proper jurisdiction. When the U.S. court of appeals reversed the district court's decision, Navarro (called the *petitioner*) petitioned the Supreme Court to decide the issue. (The trustees are called the *respondents* because they respond to the petition.) The Supreme Court agreed to hear the case (the proper phrase is *granted certiorari*).

Issue Appealed

In a case involving a business trust is diversity of citizenship determined by the states of citizenship of the trustees or by those of the trust's beneficiaries?

Who Wins

The plaintiff.

Reasoning

Prior Supreme Court cases establish that the trustees of business trusts may bring diversity of citizenship cases based on their own states of citizenship. In the present case this applies even though some beneficiaries of the trust are citizens of Texas, as is the defendant Navarro. The trustees have complete legal power over the investment monies they control, and the trust beneficiaries have no say-so over investment decisions. [*The judgment of the court of appeals is affirmed.*]

As with the SQ3R method, the case briefing system assists you best when you pause after reading each case to recite answers to the questions raised by the system. These questions should either be memorized or written down for easy reference while reading case material.

Regular use of the SQ3R method and the case briefing system will substantially raise the grades of most students. The secret to your own success, however, is for you to continue to practice these methods despite an initial awkwardness in their use. The temptation to slide back into a passive reading of the material must be overcome.

Robert N. Corley
O. Lee Reed

Part One
INTRODUCTION

Chapter
1

The Law and Lawyers

1. The Law and Business

The subject matter of this text is the law as it defines and prescribes the environment in which business is conducted in the United States. Since the focus of the book is law, much of the discussion concerns litigation and lawyers. In a real sense, litigation has replaced baseball as our national pastime. Today, our courts are filled with cases involving every conceivable controversy that may arise. Whenever people have a disagreement, there is a distinct possibility that they may resolve it with a lawsuit.

Whether it is a cause or an effect of our litigious society, a significant development in recent years is the explosion in the number of lawyers in this country. In 1970, there were about 350,000 lawyers. By the mid-1980s, there were 650,000, and in the 1990s the number will reach 1 million. Two-thirds of the world's lawyers practice in the United States, and more lawyers were admitted to practice in the 1970s than in the previous 100 years. Law and lawyers are involved in almost every aspect of our daily lives and in almost every business decision. An understanding of the law and the role of lawyers in conducting business is essential to an understanding of the legal environment.

The increase in litigation and in the number of lawyers is consistent with another trend in our society—increased regulation of business. We have experienced an explosion in regulating laws in recent years in response to public demands for protection from an unhealthy environment, for safer products and workplaces, and for equal employment opportunity. This text discusses these regulatory laws as a major component of the legal environment of business.

The basic role of law in business decisions is readily apparent. It constrains business in its decisions and in its selection of alternative courses of action. Certain conduct is illegal, and individuals or businesses who commit acts or omissions declared to be illegal are subject to sanctions. There may be fines or imprisonment if the conduct is declared a crime. The sanctions may include liability for dollar damages if the conduct is tortious (involving a wrongful act) or a breach of contract. In addition, the law and legal sanctions may be used to prevent certain conduct or to require that certain things be done. Business decisions must be made within the law, or sanctions will be imposed. The law is the foundation for the regulations of all business conduct and decisions. Throughout this text, we will attempt to acquaint you with some of the more important laws controlling business decisions and individual behavior.

2. Definitions of Law

Before we classify various legal subjects, you should recognize several definitions of the word "law." No word of such common usage is so hard to define precisely or is used to express a variety of concepts so well as is the word "law." For example, "law" is used to describe specific statutory enactments and also to denote a general system of rules for governing conduct. Popular uses of the terms "law," "legal," and "illegal" are limitless. The meaning of these words in any particular situation must be determined from the context in which they are used. For example, the use of the word "illegal" to describe a forward pass in a football game differs significantly from the use of "illegal" to describe a contract. The force of the law generally is not involved in a football game, but since the game must be played by rules, the use of legal terminology is to be expected. An illegal contract is similar to an illegal forward pass in that both may result in penalties. However, the legality of a contract is determined by our courts and the legal system. To date, the legality of a forward pass has been left up to the referees to decide.

Law is often considered to be a command: You shall do this or you shall not do that. As a command, it is prescribed by a superior, and the inferior is bound to obey. Law is a rule of conduct commanding what is right and prohibiting what is wrong. The criminal law is essentially a body of commands flowing from the people as a whole to people as individuals telling them what they may or may not do.

Many areas of our law, such as those involving contracts and torts, do not "command compliance" in the technical sense. They are so constructed that an aggrieved party is given a remedy against one who violates accepted legal principles in these areas. Civil courts, except in unusual situations, do not require compliance but instead impose liability for noncompliance.

LAW AS PRINCIPLES USED BY COURTS

Law has also been defined as the body of principles and rules which the courts apply in the decision of controversies. Law is made up of three elements: (1) formulated legislation, including constitutions, statutes, treaties, ordinances, and codes; (2) rules of law announced by the courts in deciding cases; and (3) the system of legal concepts and techniques which forms the basis of judicial action.

Justice Oliver Wendell Holmes said, "Law is a statement of the circumstances in which the public force will be brought to bear through courts." Law is simply what the courts will or will not order in any particular case. Other judges have stated that law is "a rule of reason applied to existing conditions," that "it is an expression of the public will," and that it is "that which must be obeyed and followed by citizens subject to sanctions or legal consequences."

LAW AS A SCHEME OF SOCIAL CONTROL

Law is a scheme for controlling the conduct of people; it deals with social interests. Whereby social interests recognize a right in one person, courts create machinery to assist the person with this right in obtaining redress against the person with the duty or obligation, if the duty is not performed or if the obligation is unfulfilled. By this concept, law has four characteristics:

1 It is a scheme of social control.

2 It protects social interests.

3 It accomplishes its purpose by recognizing a capacity in persons to influence the conduct of others.

4 It provides courts and legal procedures to help the person with this capacity.

This definition of law supports the position of judges as social engineers. This role is present in decisions such as those allowing abortions, prohibiting prayer in school, and requiring busing of school children to achieve racial balance in education.

LAW AS JUSTICE

All the foregoing definitions convey the concept that law regulates human conduct and that through courts it resolves controversies. The goal of law is justice, but law and justice are not synonymous, just as legal justice and social justice are not synonymous. Justice has been defined as that which is founded in equity, honesty, and righteousness. It is the attempt of honorable men to do that which is fair. Justice is the purpose and end of government and civil society. Apparently, the achievement of justice depends upon the concept of right and wrong in the society involved. The purpose of justice in our society, as stated in the Declaration of Independence, is to secure for all men "life, liberty, and the pursuit of happiness."

Social justice recognizes more rights and duties than does legal justice, although the trend of the law is toward equating these concepts. Perfect justice would require that all persons discharge all their obligations and duties so that all other persons may enjoy all their rights and privileges. Our society through law determines which rights and duties will be protected and strives through its judicial system for perfect justice. Of course, the law is incapable of perfect justice because it is in the hands of imperfect men and operates with imperfect procedures. As law approaches perfect justice, legal justice and social justice tend to merge.

Dean Roscoe Pound of the Harvard Law School attempted to define law in terms of justice when he said that the science of law is "that organized body of knowledge that has to do with the administration of justice by public or regular tribunals in accordance with principles or rules of general character and more or less uniform application."

3. The Rule of Law

Justice Felix Frankfurter in his opinion in *United States v. Mine Workers,* 330 U.S. 258 (1947), began with these words: "The historic phrase 'a government of laws and not of men' epitomizes the distinguishing character of our political society. When John Adams put that phrase into the Massachusetts Declaration of Rights, he was not indulging a rhetorical flourish. He was expressing the aim of those who, with him, framed the Declaration of Independence and founded the Republic." Adams's statement, which recognizes the role of the rule of law in our society, had its origin in England prior to the Magna Charta. The Magna Charta used the term "per legem terrae"—the law of the land. English history is filled with numerous statements proclaiming that even the royal power is subject to the rule of law.

The concept of the rule of law has been the cornerstone of our society and government from the beginning, and it is simply accepted as part of our heritage. As President Lincoln said, it is the "political religion" of the country.

In our society, it is the law which is used to decide disputes, not the wishes or ideas of any mere mortal, irrespective of his or her position. Moreover, the parties for the most part accept the fact that the dispute will be decided by a rule of law and that the winner and the loser alike will accept the determination without resorting to another method of resolution, such as force.

The role of the rule of law as the basic ingredient in ordered liberty is obvious from even a cursory examination of the matters before the Supreme Court in any term. The issues presented involve due process of law, equal protection of the laws, and the power of the governors over the governed. To a substantial extent, the failures of our society can be directly attributed to the failure of people to accept and abide by application of rules of law. In a real sense, the subject matter of this text is the rule of law as it applies to business.

The study of law essentially concerns "rules of law." A rule of law, using Holmes's definition, is a statement that if certain facts exist, then the judicial branch of government will take certain action or refuse to take certain action at the request of someone involved. In other words, a rule of law is a prediction as to what a court will or will not do in a given factual situation. It is then obvious that facts create legal issues which are resolved by using rules of law. You should therefore be aware of the tremendous importance of facts to the law. A majority of our legal procedures are designed to discover the facts. For instance, the function of the jury is fact finding.

4. General Classifications of Legal Subjects

The law has often been described as "a seamless web" in which principles of law are hopelessly and endlessly intertwined with each other. For this reason, any attempted classification or description of the many and varied legal subjects is necessarily inaccurate.

One means of classifying the law is to divide it into matters of public law and matters of private law. *Public law* includes **constitutional law**, **administrative law**, and **criminal law**. In each of these areas, society or "the people" are directly involved. Their interests are represented by a governmental agency, officer, or official whose obligation it is to see that justice is accomplished and the ends of society fulfilled. Public law provides a major portion of the legal environment of business. For this reason, much of the material in subsequent chapters deals with constitutional and administrative areas of public law and their application to business.

Private law encompasses those legal problems and relationships which exist between individuals, as contrasted with those in which society is involved. Private law is traditionally separated into *the law of contracts, the law of torts,* and *the law of property.*

Another important classification or distinction in law is the one between substance and procedure. **Substantive law** defines the legal relationship of people with other people, or as between them and the state. Thus, the rules of contract law are substantive in nature. **Procedural law** deals with the method and means by which substantive law is made and administered. In other words, substantive rules of law define rights and duties, while procedural rules of law provide the machinery for enforcing those rights and duties. Every social institution has rules by which it conducts its affairs or "proceeds." There are rules of law relating to legislative procedure which govern the steps that must be taken for a statute to be valid. A typical rule of legislative procedure might require that all bills be read to the assembly twice before adoption. Failure to follow this rule of procedure might void the legislature's attempt to create rights or duties in the statute.

Judicial procedures involve the method of conducting lawsuits, appeals, and the enforcement of judgments. The rules for conducting civil trials are different from those for criminal trials. For example, each party may call the other party to the witness stand for cross-examination in a civil trial, but the defendant may not be required to testify in a criminal case. Procedural problems sometimes arise concerning papers filed in lawsuits, the admission of evidence, and various other techniques involved in trying the case. They are the rules of the game. Many rules classified as procedural in character might be just as easily classified as substantive because they actually affect rights and duties. Chapter 4 deals with the procedural aspects of law in greater depth.

A classification similar to that of public versus private contrasts civil law cases with criminal cases. For administrative purposes courts usually separate criminal actions from other lawsuits, with the latter known as civil cases. Such cases include (1) suits for breach of contract, (2) torts, and (3) other actions in which the remedy sought is not punishment of the defendant but a remedy such as dollar damages.

5. The Criminal Law

A crime is a public wrong against society. Criminal cases are brought by the government on behalf of the people. When a person is convicted of a crime, one of the following punishments is imposed by society: (1) death, (2) imprisonment, (3) fine, (4) removal from office, or (5) disqualification from holding and enjoying any office or from voting. Among the purposes of such punishment are to protect the public and to deter persons from wrongful conduct. Conduct involved in murder and kidnapping is considered criminal in order to protect individuals from harm. Arson and embezzlement are terms used to describe crimes relating to the protection of property. Some conduct is criminal in order to protect government and the public interest. For example, bribery of a public official is a wrong against society as is price-fixing or selling pornography. Punishment is also imposed simply for the sake of punishment, as well as the isolation and suppression of the criminal element of society.

Although criminal conduct often or usually involves acts of violence or the wrongful use of physical force, other criminal conduct involves non-violent, illegal acts committed by guile, deceit, or concealment, or through simple contracts. Such wrongful conduct as obtaining money by false pretenses or obtaining a business advantage by agreeing with a competitor to fix the price of goods or services is criminal.

Although business crime does not depend on force or violence, physical injury and even death can be caused by it. Defective products sold in violation of applicable statutes frequently cause injuries. Building code violations may result in fire and injury to persons and property. Some businesses, in order to compete, buy stolen merchandise or employ illegal aliens. The maintenance of a dangerous workplace may be a crime.

Criminal law is generally subdivided into **felonies** and **misdemeanors**. This classification is based on the punishment imposed in the event of a conviction. Felonies are punishable by fine or imprisonment in a penitentiary for a period of one year or more, whereas misdemeanors are punishable by a fine or a jail sentence of less than one year. Table 1-1 lists typical offenses under each classification.

TABLE 1-1 Criminal Law

Typical Felonies (Imprisonment for More than One Year and/or Fine)	Typical Misdemeanors (Jail for Less than One Year and/or Fine)
Aggravated assault	Battery
Arson	Gambling
Bribery	Larceny (petty)
Burglary	Littering
Embezzlement	Prostitution
Forgery	Public disturbance
Kidnapping	Simple assault
Larceny (grand)	Traffic offenses
Manslaughter	Trespass
Mayhem	
Murder	
Price-fixing	
Rape	
Robbery	

Violations of traffic ordinances, building codes, and similar municipal ordinances are sometimes termed *petty offenses*. A person guilty of such an offense may be fined or put in jail or both.

WHITE-COLLAR CRIME

Criminal law includes many crimes that may be committed by a business enterprise as well as those that may be committed by individuals. Some of these, such as violating the antitrust laws, will be discussed later in this book. These crimes are often referred to as *white-collar crimes*. The amount of white-collar crime concerns the business community greatly. Losses from embezzlement and employee theft, including theft through manipulation of computers, not only exceed losses from burglary and larceny, but also are growing at an alarming rate. Theft of technology caused an international furor in 1983 when agents of a Japanese firm admitted purchasing secrets stolen from IBM. There is evidence that losses from shoplifting by employees exceed losses from shoplifting by customers. The cost of crime is a cost of doing business which results in higher prices for consumers. Costs include higher insurance premiums as well as the cost of the property stolen. The total cost of business-related crime amounts to several billion dollars annually.

One reason sometimes advanced for the increase in white-collar crime is that historically the risk of being caught and sent to prison has been slight. For example, bribery of local officials frequently was considered a legitimate cost of doing business, especially overseas. In addition, employers are often hesitant to prosecute employees for crimes such as embezzlement because disclosure would adversely affect the image of the business. Discharge without prosecution has been a common action taken against employees committing such crimes.

Legal scholars are suggesting new approaches in an attempt to reverse the trend. The most common suggestion is to impose stiff penalties for white-collar crime. Another is to improve the internal controls of businesses, so that internal theft and wrongdoing are more likely to be discovered. Finally, there is a trend toward punishing corporate officials for the crimes of their corporations. A corporate official who fixes prices with competitors in violation of the Sherman Antitrust Act is more likely to go to jail now than in the past, and the fine for such conduct has been greatly increased. In one recent case corporate officials were convicted of homicide when an employee died from job-related poisoning.

PROBLEMS

The criminal justice system is a subject of great debate today. For example, the acquittal of President Reagan's attempted assassin on the ground of temporary insanity has prompted a reexamination of the insanity defense. The public attitude that "justice" was not achieved in so significant a case has fueled the continuing debate about an individual's responsibility for his or her conduct. In addition, the dockets of the criminal courts are overcrowded in many areas of the country. Many persons convicted of criminal conduct appeal their convictions to higher courts, creating a heavy case load and congestion in those courts. Although the number of judges hearing criminal cases has been greatly increased in recent years, delay and the many problems associated with it still exist.

The criminal law system in this country often fails to provide swift and sure punishment of criminals. It has apparently failed to deter many criminal acts or to rehabilitate a significant portion of those persons convicted of crimes. We have overcrowded jails and unworkable probation systems. As a result, many experts are seeking changes in our criminal law system. For example, some people propose eliminating many offenses commonly regarded as victimless crimes. Alcoholism and drug addiction, for example, would no longer be considered wrongs against society if such people had their way. The same may be true of adultery, sodomy, and other sex crimes between consenting adults, as well as many forms of gambling. Those who propose these changes contend that far too much police effort is spent on these nonviolent crimes, which became part of criminal law in an earlier era when there were different views on morality.

In late 1981, a federal task force on violent crime made sixty-four recommendations to improve the criminal justice system. Among the more significant were to:

1 Permit judges to deny bail to persons rated a danger to the community.

2 Eliminate parole of federal inmates, forcing them to serve the entire sentence imposed.

3 Allow verdicts of "guilty but mentally ill," thus blocking release of many now considered not guilty because of insanity.

4   Make illegally seized evidence admissible in trials if police thought they were complying with the law.

5   Bar lawsuits challenging convictions unless filed within three years.

As a result of these and other recommendations, it is likely that there will be major changes in the criminal justice system in this decade.

6. The Law of Contracts

Contract law concerns the legal relationships created between individuals by their own agreement. The purpose of contract law is to make promises enforceable by courts. It contains several subbodies of law which are frequently treated as separate legal subjects. For example, there is a special body of law relating to contracts for the sale of goods, and there is another covering the subject of commercial paper such as checks and notes. Although the general principles of contract law developed in the common law in case-by-case decisions, the specialized areas are usually covered to a substantial degree by a statute known as the Uniform Commercial Code.

The detailed subject matter of contracts is covered in Chapter 5. Throughout this text we refer to contracts and to contractual obligations. Many of the chapters contain discussions directly related to contracts. For example, most of the laws that protect consumers relate to the contractual obligations of consumers. Debtor protection, a part of contract law, protects debtors in their borrowing contracts. Much of the discussion about business organizations finds its basis in the law of contracts. The conduct of business is primarily a series of contracts, and one of the major functions of lawyers is to assist with the contracts. Lawyers draft contracts and review those drafted by others prior to their execution. These duties are a part of the "preventive law" function of attorneys—to avoid disputes and controversies through legal advice. Large corporations usually retain "house counsel" to perform these functions, and other businesses frequently retain outside counsel for this purpose.

As we refer to contracts throughout this text, remember that the law of contracts provides the basis whereby persons can create legal rights and impose legal duties on themselves by their own agreement. Such agreements may be expressed orally or in writing, or they may be implied from the conduct of the parties. The force of organized society, exerted by the courts and the appropriate executive agencies, stands behind a valid contract and provides machinery for its enforcement. Whenever a contract is breached, the injured party can obtain money damages equivalent to the economic loss which he or she can prove was suffered because of the breach. If a breach by one party is serious enough, the other party may be permitted to rescind or cancel the contract. In some circumstances, the remedy of an injured party may be a decree of specific performance, or an order of a court of equity commanding the defendant actually to perform the bargain as agreed.

Many of the legal problems arising in contract law can be described as language issues. Such cases involve "contract interpretation," or a search for the intention of the parties. This is especially true in contracts drafted by the parties themselves without the assistance of legal counsel.

7. The Law of Torts

A **tort** is a wrong other than a breach of contract committed against persons or their property for which the law gives a right to recover damages. It differs from a crime, which is a wrong against society, although the same act may be both a wrong against a person and against society, as for example, an assault.

Tort liability is based on two premises: that in a civilized society persons will not intentionally injure others or their property, and that all persons will exercise reasonable care and caution in their activities. The first premise has resulted in a group of torts usually labeled *intentional torts*. These include such traditional wrongs as assault and battery, false imprisonment, libel, slander, trespass, and conversion of personal property. It also includes relatively new torts such as interference with contractual relationships and invasion of privacy. The second premise has led to the general field of tort liability known as **negligence.** Negligence is frequently further broken down into degrees, depending on the extent of carelessness involved and the extent of the duty owed. For example, a grocery store's operator owes a higher standard of care to customers than to trespassers. Each of these premises creates liability for wrongful conduct because a party is at fault. Our legal system in effect says: "If you are at *fault* and cause injury to another or his property, you shall compensate the injured party for the loss with money."

A major area of tort litigation today deals with malpractice suits against professionals such as physicians, dentists, accountants, lawyers, architects, and engineers. Malpractice actions are a special form of negligence action based on the alleged failure of the professional person to perform services in accordance with professional standards. The law of torts is covered in detail in Chapter 6.

For many years tort claims have been the single largest source of civil litigation in this country. Most of these controversies have resulted from automobile collisions. In addition to automobile accident and other negligence cases, business is often involved in tort actions arising out of the sale of a product which has caused harm. Product liability suits involve injuries such as those resulting from deleterious food or defective drugs. Although such suits have contractual aspects, they usually seek damages for injuries caused by the product. Therefore, product liability, a major subject of the law of torts, is covered in a separate chapter—Chapter 7.

8. The Law of Property

The law of property concerns the rights and duties of ownership and possession of real estate and personal property. These rights and duties are frequently created by contract and enforced by the law of contracts and torts.

Thus, some legal scholars do not consider property to be a separate classification. Perhaps no legal concept has been as important in American history, and as significant for our cultural and economic development, as that of private property. As one might expect, the vast majority of statutes and decisions rendered by both the courts and administrative agencies deals in some way with issues involving the ultimate determination of property rights.

Property is usually classified, according to the nature of the subject matter which is owned, as **real** or **personal property**, and the latter is further classified as **tangible** or **intangible**. Real property is land or any interest in land and includes things permanently attached thereto, such as timber and buildings, which are called *fixtures*. Personal property encompasses chattels or things such as livestock, an automobile, clothing, or a television set. These and real property are referred to as tangible property because the property owned has physical existence. Personal property also includes intangible property such as stocks, bonds, accounts receivable, and patent rights. Frequently intangible property is associated with a document, such as a stock certificate. The document itself is not the property interest, or rights owned, but merely evidence of them. Even if the document is destroyed, the property may still exist.

The concept of property is frequently described in terms of ownership, title to, and possession of corporeal objects. Ownership has to do with the extent of a person's rights in property and is usually synonymous with title. Title itself is a confusing term because it is frequently associated with a document of title, such as that to an automobile. Because of this, people frequently think of title in terms of a document labeled "title." Yet persons usually have "title" to the clothes they wear and to their other property without a document of title. Possession is a term which often indicates physical control or dominion. However, in law, possession must be defined in terms of the assistance that the law gives a person in controlling property. For example, it is easy to physically possess a book, but impossible to physically possess a 1,000-acre tract of land. However, one may be in legal possession of a 1,000-acre tract because of sanctions provided by law to keep others out.

The term **ownership** includes, besides the right to possess objects, the right to dispose of them by sale, gift, or will; the right to use, possess, and enjoy them; the right to change their nature; and probably the right to destroy them. These rights are creatures of the law which are backed by legal sanctions. Thus, without law, property is nonexistent. Although most people tend to think of property as the thing owned itself, this approach is inaccurate. More correctly, it consists of a bundle of legal rights, such as those listed previously, with respect to a thing. With this concept of property it is viewed as a series of legal relationships between the owner and all other persons in which the owner has many rights, and the others, each individually, owe him or her many duties which are often negative in character. For example there is a duty not to take or use another's property.

Ownership also encompasses a series of limitations imposed by law on the owner and often carries with it duties owed by the owner to other persons.

Ownership does not include a complete bundle of rights. It is always subject to the rights of government such as the right of government to take private property for public purposes (eminent domain), the power to tax, and so on. When it is viewed in this manner, technically all property is intangible, consisting of specific legal rights and duties, but may exist *with regard to* a physical, tangible object. Nevertheless, it is generally accepted in legal terminology to refer to the property rights associated with corporeal things as being tangible property.

The reader knows the more common rights associated with ownership. Clearly, the owner of farmland generally has the right to sow crops on it, harvest and sell them, and keep the proceeds for personal use (unless, of course, the owner has contracted that right away by leasing the land to a tenant). Also, the owner of a farm has the right, as a rule, to sell it and then use the proceeds of sale as he or she sees fit. And, by a properly executed will, the owner can, subject to some limitations, dispose of the farm at death as he or she wishes. Fundamental to the concept of property are the rights to exclude others from its possession and use.

9. Sources of Law

The total body of law by which we are governed comes from four basic sources: (1) constitutions, (2) legislation, (3) judicial decisions, and (4) the rules, regulations, and decisions of administrative agencies. If it is assumed that administrative agencies are part of the executive branch of government, then our body of law comes from all three branches.

Under our constitutional system, the constitution of the governmental unit is its basic and supreme law. All other laws, written or unwritten, must be in harmony with it, or they are void. By and large, state constitutions are modeled after the federal Constitution and, as such, provide the same general organization for government, dividing it into executive, legislative, and judicial branches, giving each branch checks and balances on the others. In addition to providing a government's organization, constitutions define the powers and functions of the various branches. Historically, there was a distinction in this respect between the federal and state constitutions. The federal Constitution when ratified was a delegation of authority from the states, which were the basic sovereigns, to the federal government. All powers not contained therein were retained by the states. In other words, the federal Constitution contains grants of power to the federal government, which was established by the states. On the other hand, state governments have all other powers not denied them by the federal or their own constitution. State constitutions, therefore, generally contain limitations on the power of state government.

Most of our laws are found in some form of legislation. Legislative bodies exist at all levels of government, as the term includes not only Congress but also state general assemblies, city councils, and many other local government bodies that adopt or enact laws. The term *legislation* in its broad sense includes treaties entered into by the executive branch of government and ratified by the Senate.

Legislation enacted by Congress or a state legislature is usually referred to as a **statute**. Laws passed by local governments are frequently called **ordinances**. Compilations of legislation at all levels of government are called **codes**. For example, we have local traffic codes covering such matters as speed limits, and state laws such as the Uniform Commercial Code which covers all aspects of commercial transactions. The statutes of the United States are known as the U.S. Code.

Judicial decisions provide us with our third major source of laws, often referred to as the common law. Courts "make law" as part of the process of deciding cases and controversies before them. The case law created in this process is based on a doctrine known as "stare decisis," the principle that prior decisions provide precedents which should be followed in subsequent cases involving the same question of law. In other words, where a rule of law has been announced and followed by courts so that the rule has become settled by judicial decision, a precedent is established for future cases. Judicial decisions create precedent where there is no legislation as well as by interpreting legislation. This precedent is found by studying cases.

When a court decides a case, particularly upon an appeal from a lower court decision, the court writes an opinion setting forth, among other things, the reasons for its decision. From these written opinions, rules of law can be deduced, and these make up the body of what is called case law or common law. The decisions set forth later in the text are cases that have been decided by courts of review. All cases that have been decided are available to interested persons for use in legal research, as are the statutory enactments of legislatures.

The common law system, which originated in England, is contrasted with civil law systems such as those in France and Spain. Civil law systems rely primarily on statutes for the law. Issues not covered by specific statutes are decided by courts on their merits in civil law systems without the use of precedent. With the exception of Louisiana, the states of the United States have used the common law system rather than the civil law system as a model. Many state constitutions specifically adopt the common law of England except where changed by statute.

Stare decisis arose from the desire of courts as well as society for certainty and predictability in the law. In addition, following precedent was expedient. The common law, through precedent, settled many legal issues and brought stability into many areas of the law, such as contracts. Individuals could then act in reliance upon prior decisions with reasonable certainty as to the results of their conduct.

As you read further, remember that the judicial system has established a general priority among the various sources of law. Constitutions prevail over statutes, and statutes prevail over common law principles established in court decisions. Courts will not turn to case decisions for law if a statute is directly in point.

The fourth source of law is generally referred to as administrative law. This source gives us rules and regulations similar to statutes as well as case decisions. Administrative law will be discussed in detail in Chapter 10. The role of courts in interpreting legislation and the problems associated with case law are discussed later in this chapter.

10. Lawyers

Before we begin our examination of various legal topics, it is helpful to have an understanding about lawyers and the legal profession. As members of the legal profession, lawyers usually play a major role in the application of rules of law and legal principles. Liberty and justice are abstractions that can only be realized when individuals operate a system in such a manner as to achieve them. The law can only work through individuals; it is not self-enforcing. Although couts and juries constitute the decision makers in our judicial system, lawyers play an integral role in our legal system.

The practice of law is a profession. It involves a dedication to society in which the service performed is more important than any remuneration received for the service. The individual practitioner assumes duties and responsibilities which extend to the courts, to the public, and to the client.

A lawyer's first duty is to the administration of justice. As an officer of the court, he or she should see that proceedings are conducted in a dignified and orderly manner and that issues are tried on their merits only. The practice of law is not a game or mere battle of wits, but a means to promote justice. The lawyer's duties to each client require the highest degree of fidelity, loyalty, and integrity.

To engage in the practice of law is not a natural or constitutional right but a privilege conferred because one knows the law and possesses good moral character. The latter involves a proper conception of the nature and duties of the office of attorney and also of the ethics of the profession. It has sometimes been described as absolute obedience to the unenforceable. Absolute honesty and integrity are minimum standards for the profession.

Sometimes the conduct of some lawyers has not met the high professional standards of the profession. Conflicts of interest and activities such as "ambulance chasing" have occurred, contrary to professional ethics. The courts and bar associations try to eliminate such activities by disbarring or suspending such persons from the practice of law. The code of ethical standards for lawyers undergoes periodic review and updating in order that the profession may effectively serve the public interest.

A lawyer serves in essentially three capacities—counselor, advocate, and public servant. As a counselor, a lawyer by the very nature of the profession knows his or her client's most important secrets and affairs. A lawyer is often actively involved in the business and personal lives of clients, ranging from their business affairs and family matters such as divorce to their alleged violations of the criminal law. These relationships dictate that a lawyer meet the highest standards of professional and ethical conduct.

As an advocate, a lawyer is not only a "fighter" in court but a negotiator of compromise. Lawyers spend most of their efforts seeking solutions to differences between adversaries. Advocacy is practiced not only before courts and juries but also before opposing counsel and with one's own client as well.

As public servants, lawyers serve in all capacities at all levels of organized society. Their formal education, training, and experience leave them better equipped than most to render valuable public service.

It is obvious that if a lawyer is to give competent advice and adequate representation, he or she must know to the fullest extent possible all the facts involved in any legal problem presented by the client. In attempting to ensure that a lawyer may be fully advised of a client's problems and all matters affecting them, the rules of evidence provide that confidential communications to a lawyer are privileged. The law does not permit a lawyer to reveal such facts and testify against a client, even if called to the stand to do so at a trial. This is called the attorney-client privilege, and it may extend to communications made to the lawyer's employees in certain cases. This is especially important today because law firms frequently use paralegals to gather facts and assist attorneys. This privilege extends to corporations as well as to individuals. The corporate privilege protects communications by corporate employees with corporate counsel.

11. Other Influences on Behavior

One definition of law noted in the previous section is a scheme of social control. Law is not the only method of controlling society, however. Factors other than law influence and regulate the behavior of individuals and business organizations. Among the more important are economic principles, individual and institutional ethical standards, and a company's or firm's view of its responsibility to society. The law interacts with economics, ethics, and social responsibility to influence decisions.

The forces or factors which influence business decisions and individual conduct are often compatible and consistent with each other. The law provides the foundation for ethical standards in that it often distinguishes right from wrong. However, the goals and principles of law and economics, of law and ethical standards, or of economics and ethical standards are sometimes in conflict. For example, the economics of a situation may indicate that a price-fixing agreement among competitors would be desirable, but the law and perhaps ethical values would dictate that such an agreement not be made. These factors have different weights at different times and under different conditions. The law is often said to provide the foundation for the operation of the other factors.

It is apparent that our competitive economic system provides both incentives and constraints on individual and business decisions and the conduct that flows from them. Indeed, most decisions to do or not to do a certain thing are based on the economic consequences of the contemplated course of action. The profit motive and cost considerations play as great a role in most decisions as do legal aspects. Our competitive economic system is based upon millions of people and thousands of businesses making numerous daily decisions in their own self-interest. Indeed, there are those who believe that economic considerations and the profit motive are the best means of regulating business conduct.

Ethical standards are also very important in business decision making and in controlling human behavior. *Ethics* has been defined as the name given to our concern for good behavior. It is our commitment to what is right and our rejection of what is wrong. Ethics provides a system of values beyond what the law requires or prohibits. Ethical values are required if people are to live together in a free society. It is not enough to have laws. People and businesses must have values because a free society depends upon the trust and confidence of people. High ethical standards are the foundation upon which trust and confidence are built.

Today, many business associations as well as professional groups such as the American Bar Association or the American Institute of Certified Public Accountants have adopted ethics codes. In addition, many companies have established their own codes of ethics. There is also a federal ethics code for government service. Although these codes do not have the force of law, employees of these firms and members of the professions and government employees are expected to obey them. This "obedience to the legally unenforceable" in a real sense is the hallmark of a profession. If business persons desire professional status, a commitment to a positive code of ethical values is essential.

Although most of this text concerns laws and the legal environment in which business operates, it also deals with several aspects of economics and with business ethics and social responsibility. For example, the material on antitrust laws is the portion that deals most heavily with economic theory. The legal environment is so closely interconnected with our economic system that one of its major concerns is ensuring that our competitive economic system actually works. Materials on business ethics and businesses' responsibility to society are discussed throughout the text where appropriate because ethical standards which become generally accepted frequently are enacted into law. In a sense, the law follows society's view of what is right and wrong. Any examination of trends in the law requires reference to contemporary ethical standards that may become law.

12. Law and Ethics

Defining ethics as "good behavior" and "a recognition of the rights and interests of others as well as society as a whole" means that ethical standards go beyond the law. It is often said that ethics leads the law and is ahead of or above the law. Morality must exist above the law if it is to advance. If the goal of the law is justice, including social justice, then the ethics of society plays a major role in the search for that goal.

The basis of most ethical standards is honesty. Honesty is also required in our legal system. Witnesses testify under oath and are cross-examined as a part of the search for truth. We assume that juries will be able to ascertain the truth. Thus, both the law and ethics are founded on the same fundamental principles and goals. Yet their standards are not always the same.

Although the law and ethics are not identical, each influences the other. Traditional ethical values have often changed the law as moral standards usually are developed and generally accepted prior to becoming law. The law also influences ethical values as it provides a sense of what is right and what is wrong. Ethical values are also affected by economic considerations. Economic principles and ethics are compatible most of the time. Profits cannot be considered unethical most of the time if our competitive system is to survive.

As previously noted, all professions, government, and many businesses have adopted codes of ethics. These value systems of the organizations serve as internal laws for persons subject to them. These codes of ethics are codes of conscience based on fairness, honesty, courtesy, self-restraint, and consideration for others. Such codes may only require disclosure of facts to superiors in certain situations. At other times they may dictate decisions and conduct. They are based on a collective sense of right and wrong. This in turn is influenced by the time frame and by the cultural background of society with special input from religions and philosophy. Many codes are general statements, because the more specific the code, the more difficult it is to obtain agreement to the principles. Most codes are written in positive rather than negative terms.

Ethical business conduct often requires behavior at a level well above the minimum required by law. Ethical conduct may be thought of as doing more than the law requires or less than it allows. An individual's or society's sense of ethics may actually condemn that which the law allows. Ethical codes often recognize that the interests of society are paramount to those of the individual.

For purposes of illustrating a typical code of business conduct we have selected the one developed by the Caterpillar Tractor Company of Peoria, Illinois. Its code was selected because Caterpillar is a company conducting business worldwide in a basic industry employing thousands of people. The company has been very successful in obtaining acceptance of and compliance with its operating principles and ethical standards. Excerpts from its Code of Worldwide Business Conduct and Operating Principles will be found throughout this text to demonstrate the close connection between law, ethics, and corporate responsibility.

Caterpillar's code recognizes that the company is subject to the law of many countries and that what is legal in some countries may be illegal in others. Its code requires adherence to local laws but goes further and contains a commitment to work for constructive change where desirable. The code states:

OBSERVANCE OF LOCAL LAWS

A basic requirement levied against any business enterprise is that it know and obey the law. This is rightfully required by those who govern; and it is well understood by business managers.

However, a corporation operating on a global scale will inevitably encounter laws which vary widely from country to country. They may even conflict with each other. And laws in some countries may encourage or require business practices which—based on experience elsewhere in the world—we believe to be wasteful or unfair. Under such conditions it scarcely seems sufficient for a business manager merely to say; we obey the law, whatever it may be!

We are guided by the belief that the law is not an end but a means to an end—the end presumably being order, justice, and, not infrequently, strengthening of the governmental unit involved. If it is to achieve these ends in changing times and circumstances, law itself cannot be insusceptible to change or free of criticism. The law can benefit from both.

Therefore, in a world characterized by a multiplicity of divergent laws at international, national, state, and local levels, Caterpillar's intentions fall in two parts: (1) to obey the law; and (2) to offer, where appropriate, constructive ideas for change in the law.

The Caterpillar Code's Statement on Business Ethics also recognizes that complying with the law is only the beginning of what is necessary for ethical business conduct. Its comment on business ethics provides:

BUSINESS ETHICS

The law is a floor. Ethical business conduct should normally exist at a level well above the minimum required by the law.

One of a company's most valuable assets is a reputation for integrity. If that be tarnished, customers, investors, suppliers, employees, and those who sell our products will seek affiliation with other, more attractive companies. We intend to hold to a single high standard of integrity everywhere. We will keep our word. We won't promise more than we can reasonably expect to deliver; nor will we make commitments we don't intend to keep.

The goal of corporate communication is the truth—well and persuasively told. In our advertising and other public communications, we will avoid not only untruths, but also exaggeration, overstatement, and boastfulness.

Caterpillar employees shall not accept costly entertainment or gifts (excepting mementos and novelties of nominal value) from dealers, suppliers, and others with whom we do business. And we won't tolerate circumstances that produce, or reasonably appear to produce, conflict between personal interests of an employee and interests of the company.

We seek long-lasting relationships—based on integrity—with all whose activities touch upon our own.

The ethical performance of the enterprise is the sum of the ethics of the men and women who work here. Thus, we are all expected to adhere to high standards of personal integrity. For example, perjury or any other illegal act ostensibly taken to "protect" the company is wrong. A sale made because of deception is wrong. A production quota achieved through questionable means or figures is wrong. The end doesn't justify the means.

Finally, the code acknowledges the importance of employees' compliance by requiring regular reporting. Note the specific request that the reports go to the legal counsel:

REPORTING CODE COMPLIANCES

Each officer, subsidiary head, plant or parts department manager, and department head shall prepare a memorandum by the close of each year: (1) affirming a full knowledge and understanding of this Code; and (2) reporting any events or activities which might cause an impartial observer to conclude that the Code hasn't been fully followed. These reports should be sent directly to the company's General Counsel; General Offices; Peoria, Illinois.

REVIEW QUESTIONS

1 Law is defined in a variety of ways. Give three definitions of law, and contrast law with justice.

2 Blackstone defined laws as "that rule of action which is prescribed by some superior and which the inferior is bound to obey." Explain how this definition ails to accurately describe the United States' legal system of today.

3 Classify the following subjects as public law or private law: (a) constitutional law; (b) contract law; (c) administrative law; (d) criminal law; (e) property law; (f) tort law.

4 Compare and contrast the following:
   a Public law and private law
   b Civil law and criminal law
   c Tort and crime
   d Felony and misdemeanor
   e Substance and procedure
   f Personal property and real property
   g Title to property and possession of property

5 Which of the following are generally considered to be white-collar crimes?
   a Arson
   b Bribery
   c Burglary
   d Embezzlement
   e Forgery
   f Obstruction of justice
   g Price-fixing
   h Rape
   i Robbery
   j Securities fraud

6 List three of the changes in the criminal law system that have been proposed by the federal task force on violent crime and give the common thread of each proposal.

7 Which body of civil law results in the most litigation in the United States? What is the usual legal theory asserted in such cases? Why was this theory developed in law

8 Ranch owners in west Texas brought suit against the owners and operators of airplanes

and equipment used in a "weather modification program" by which they engaged in cloud seeding. The trial court issued an injunction commanding the defendants to refrain from seeding the clouds or in any other way interfering with the natural conditions of the air, atmosphere, and air space over and in the area of plaintiff's lands, and to refrain from affecting or modifying the weather conditions on or about said lands in any degree or way. What theory of property was used by the court?

9 Lawyers serve in three capacities and owe duties and obligations to three groups or institutions. Identify the three capacities and groups.

10 Contrast the approach of the federal Constitution from the approach of the constitutions of the various states.

11 Name factors other than the law which have significant influence on individual and business behavior.

12 What is the relationship between law and ethics?

Chapter
2

The Powers and Functions of Courts

1. Introduction

As was noted before, law comes from constitutions, legislation, decided cases, and administrative rulings. Courts play a major role in the development of the law as it comes from each of these sources. Courts have the function not only to interpret the Constitution but also to decide whether a law is in violation of the Constitution. This latter function is known as the power of judicial review.

When legislation is enacted, courts are frequently called upon to interpret its language and to apply it to a specific controversy. Statutes usually are written in general language. Since cases deal with specific problems, interpretation is necessary to fill in the gaps of the legislation and to eliminate the ambiguities caused by the general language statutes. Judicial interpretation gives much of the substance to legislation, and thus courts have a "legislative" function to perform.

The common law system has several aspects which tend to increase the cost of litigation and which fail to give it the desired level of certainty and predictability. Case law is sometimes difficult to find, and it is not always followed. The sections which follow discuss the doctrine of judicial review, the interpretation of legislation, and the problems of the common law system. Chapter 10 discusses administrative law including the role of courts in reviewing decisions of administrative agencies.

2. Judges and Justices

Before we look at the powers and functions of courts, some background and understanding of the people who operate our courts are helpful. The persons who operate our courts are usually called judges at the trial court level and justices at the reviewing court level. The judge is the trial court, and the court is the judge. The terms are synonymous.

In all cases being tried before a judge, the function of the court is to determine the applicable rules of law to be used to decide the case before it. Such rules may be **procedural** or **substantive**. In cases tried without a jury, the court is also responsible for finding the facts. In cases tried before a jury, the function of the jury is to decide questions of fact.

Trial judges are the main link between the law and the citizens it serves. The trial judge renders decisions which deal directly with people in conflict. These judges bear the burden of upholding the dignity of the courts and maintaining respect for the law. They have the primary duty to observe and to apply constitutional limitations and guarantees. They should not be swayed by public clamor or consideration of personal popularity nor fear unjust criticism. They should not improperly interfere in the conduct of a trial. They should be mindful of the general law and administer justice with due regard for the integrity of the legal system. Trial judges are responsible for conducting the "search for truth."

The roles of justice and judge differ substantially. Whereas a trial judge has direct contact with the litigation and litigants, a justice rarely has any contact with them. Justices do more than simply decide an appeal—they give reasons for their decisions in written form so that they will become precedent and a part of our body of law. Thus, decisions by justices may affect society as a whole as well as the litigants. In deciding cases before them, justices must consider not only the result between the parties but also the total effect of the decision on the law. In this sense, their role is similar to that of legislators. On review, justices are essentially concerned with issues of *law*. Issues of *fact* are resolved at the trial court level.

For the foregoing reasons, the personal characteristics required for a justice are somewhat different from those of a trial judge. The manner of performing duties and the methodology also vary between trial and reviewing courts. A trial judge who has observed the witnesses is able to use knowledge gained from participation as an essential ingredient in his or her decision. A justice must spend most of the time in the library studying the briefs, the record or proceedings, and the law in reaching decisions.

The judicial power is perhaps the most extensive power possessed by any branch of government. Lower court judges may be reviewed by a reviewing court, but they have almost total personal immunity from legal actions against them based on their judicial acts. Judicial immunity extends to court personnel such as prosecutors and police officers who testify, as well. The system works only if such persons can act without fear of reprisal. The judicial immunity of judges applies even when the judge acts maliciously, exceeds his or her authority, or commits grave procedural errors. A judge can be sued only if she or he acts in clear absence of jurisdiction or is to be prevented from doing so. For example, the Supreme Court in 1984 held that a judge may be enjoined by another court from doing an illegal act, but even then, he or she has no liability for damages flowing from the illegal act. In such cases, the only liability is for the attorney's fees and court costs involved in the injunction suit.

3. The Jury

Before we turn to a discussion of the judicial functions, we should understand the role of the jury as a fact-finding body. Since litigation involves questions of law and fact, the distinction between such questions and the limited role of the courts in cases tried before a jury must be recognized.

The function of the jury in criminal cases is to prevent government oppression and, in both criminal and civil cases, to ascertain the facts. This contrasts with the function of the court, which is to ascertain the law applicable to a case. Remember that in cases tried without a jury, the court also is the finder of the facts.

The jury system was adopted as a matter of right in the Constitution of the United States. The Sixth and Seventh Amendments to the U.S. Constitution guarantee the right of trial by jury in both criminal and civil cases. The Fifth Amendment provides for indictment by a grand jury for capital offenses and infamous crimes. A grand jury differs from a petit jury. A grand jury determines whether there is sufficient evidence of guilt to warrant a trial. The petit jury is the jury that determines actual guilt or innocence. Indictment is the term used to describe the decision of a grand jury. In civil cases the right to trial by a jury is preserved in suits at common law when the amount in controversy exceeds $20. State constitutions have like provisions guaranteeing the right of trial by jury in state courts.

Historically, a jury consisted of twelve persons. Today many states and some federal courts have rules of procedure which provide for smaller juries in both criminal and civil cases. Such provisions are constitutional since the Constitution does not specify the *number* of jurors—only the *types* of cases which may be brought to trial before a jury at common law. There is no discernible difference between results reached by a six-person jury and those reached by a twelve-person jury. As a result, many cases are tried before six-person juries today.

In most states, a jury's decision must be unanimous, or a total assertion. It is believed that the truth is more nearly to be found and justice rendered if the jury acts only on one common conscience. Statutes and constitutions specify the number of jurors who must concur for a verdict. In some states less than a unanimous verdict is constitutionally permissible for a jury of twelve. However, less than unanimous verdicts are not permissible for six-person juries.

Recognizing that a jury's function is to determine the facts, a relatively new technique of a "mock" trial is being used by attorneys in very significant cases. The attorneys assemble a group of citizens and present their evidence. The jury then deliberates and makes findings. This dress rehearsal gives attorneys insight on jury reaction to the evidence and points up weaknesses in the case. Sometimes issues are tested without introducing evidence. Lawyers argue the case on the basis of assumed facts to "the jury" for a few hours and the jury returns a verdict. The verdicts often cause plaintiffs to take a more realistic view of their damages and almost always prompt a negotiated settlement.

The jury system has been subject to much criticism. It has been contended that many jurors are not qualified to distinguish fact from fiction, that they vote their prejudices, and that their emotions are too easily swayed by skillful trial lawyers. However, most members of the bench and bar feel the "right to be tried by a jury of his peers" in criminal cases is as fair and effective a method of ascertaining the truth and giving an accused his or her "day in court" as has been devised.

As Jeremiah Black, the attorney for the defendant in the famous case of *Ex Parte Milligan,* said:

> I do not assert that the jury trial is an infallible mode of ascertaining truth. Like everything human, it has its imperfection. I only say, that it is the best protection for innocence and the surest mode of punishing guilt that has yet been discovered. It has borne the test of longer experience, and borne it better than any other legal institution that ever existed among men.

Jurors do not take notes as a general rule and do not give reasons for their decision. Judges often feel that a jury does not understand the court's instructions on the law of the case to be decided. Actually, it would be almost impossible for the jury to agree as to the reasons for its verdict. A jury may agree as to the result but disagree on some of the facts, and different jurors may have different ideas on the significance of various items of testimony.

Many, if not most, people attempt to avoid jury duty. Some lose money because of time away from a job or profession. Others may feel great "pressure" in helping to make important decisions affecting the lives of many people. As a result of people coming forth with multiple excuses for avoiding jury duty, courts are often forced either to go with juries consisting of the unemployed and retired, or they must excuse only a few persons from jury duty. Because of the desire to have juries that are a cross-section of society, most courts tend toward the latter.

To alleviate problems associated with jury service, many states are expanding the rolls of people eligible for service and are reducing the list of occupations that exempt a person from jury duty. For example, lawyers and the police are exempt in most states, but firefighters are usually not exempt. In addition some states are limiting the service of each juror to one case, and if a juror is called for duty and not assigned to a case, that juror is excused for at least one year.

One of the most difficult issues facing the judicial system is the right to a trial by jury in very complex and complicated cases which frequently take a long time to try. For example, many antitrust cases involve economic issues that baffle economists, and such cases may last for several months. The average juror cannot comprehend the meaning of much of the evidence, let alone remember it when the time to reach a verdict arrives. Long trials also may cause financial hardship for many jurors. As a practical matter, many persons cannot serve on a jury for several weeks or even months. For these and other reasons, some people recommend that the right to a trial by jury be abolished in very complex and time-consuming cases.

4. Judicial Review

The most significant of the powers of the judiciary is known as **judicial review**. The doctrine of judicial review empowers courts to review laws passed by the legislative body and to declare them to be unconstitutional and thus void. It also allows the courts to review actions taken by the executive branch and to declare them to be unconstitutional. Although the Constitution does not expressly provide that the judiciary shall be the overseer of the government, the net effect of this doctrine is to make it so. Chief Justice John Marshall in *Marbury v. Madison*[1] announced the doctrine of judicial review, using the following language and reasoning:

> The question, whether an act, repugnant to the constitution, can become the law of the land, is a question deeply interesting to the United States; but, happily, not of an intricacy proportioned to its interest. . . .

> It is a proposition too plain to be contested, that the constitution controls any legislative act repugnant to it; or that the legislature may not alter the constitution by an ordinary act. . . .

> Certainly, all those who have framed written constitutions contemplate them as forming the fundamental and paramount law of the nation, and consequently, the theory of every such government must be, that an act of the legislature, repugnant to the constitution, is void. . . .

> If an act of the legislature, repugnant to the constitution, is void, does it, notwithstanding its invalidity, bind the courts, and oblige them to give it effect? Or, in other words, though it be not law, does it constitute a rule as operative as if it was a law? This would be to overthrow, in fact, what was established in theory; and would seem, at first view, an absurdity too gross to be insisted on. It shall, however, receive a more attentive consideration.

> It is, emphatically, the province and duty of the judicial department, to say what the law is. Those who apply the rule to particular cases, must of necessity

---

[1] U.S. (1 Cranch) 137 (1803).

expound and interpret that rule. If two laws conflict with each other, the courts must decide on the operation of each. So, if a law be in opposition to the constitution; if both the law and the constitution apply to a particular case, so that the court must either decide that case, conformable to the law, disregarding the constitution; or conformable to the constitution, disregarding the law; the court must determine which of these conflicting rules governs the case: this is of the very essence of judicial duty. If then, the courts are to regard the constitution, and the constitution is superior to any ordinary act of the legislature, the constitution, and not such ordinary act, must govern the case to which they both apply.

The doctrine of judicial review as a component of the concept of separation of powers was subjected to a severe test during the mid-1970s. As a part of the so-called "Watergate affair," a special prosecutor sought to subpoena certain documents and tape recordings from the President of the United States. The President claimed executive privilege and stated that he was the final authority on the issue. The application of judicial review to the executive branch was the basic issue in this historic confrontation. Chief Justice Warren Burger, in speaking for a unanimous court in the case of *United States v. Nixon,* stated in part:[2]

> . . . [W]e turn to the claim that the subpoena should be quashed because it demands "confidential conversations between a President and his close advisors that it would be inconsistent with the public interest to produce." The first contention is a broad claim that the separation of powers doctrine precludes judicial review of a President's claim of privilege. . . .
>
> In the performance of assigned constitutional duties each branch of the Government must initially interpret the Constitution, and the interpretation of its powers by any branch is due great respect from the others. The President's counsel . . . reads the Constitution as providing an absolute privilege of confidentiality for all presidential communications. Many decisions of this Court, however, have unequivocally reaffirmed the holding of Marbury v. Madison, that "it is emphatically the province and duty of the judicial department to say what the law is." . . .
>
> Our system of government "requires that federal courts on occasion interpret the Constitution in a manner at variance with the construction given the document by another branch." . . . Notwithstanding the deference each branch must accord the others, the "judicial power of the United States" vested in the federal courts by Art. III, § 1 of the Constitution can no more be shared with the Executive Branch than the Chief Executive, for example, can share with the Judiciary the veto power, or the Congress share with the Judiciary the power to override a presidential veto. Any other conclusion would be contrary to the basic concept of separation of powers and the checks and balances that flow from the scheme of a tripartite government. We therefore reaffirm that it is "emphatically the province and the duty" of this Court "to say what the law is" with respect to the claim of privilege presented in this case.

---

[2]94 S. Ct. 3090 (1974).

5. Attitudes toward Judicial Review

As individual jurists exercise the power of judicial review, they do so with varying attitudes and philosophies. Some judges believe that the power should be used very sparingly, although others are willing to use it more often. Those who believe that the power should not be used except in unusual cases are said to believe in **judicial restraint**. Those who think that the power should be used whenever the needs of society justify its use believe in **judicial activism**. All members of the judiciary believe in judicial restraint and all are activists to some extent. Often a jurist may be an activist in one area of the law and a firm believer in judicial restraint in another. Both judicial restraint and judicial activism describe attitudes or tendencies by matters of degree. Both terms also are used to describe general attitudes toward the exercise of the power of judicial review.

JUDICIAL RESTRAINT

The philosophy of judicial restraint developed naturally from the recognition that, in exercising the power of judicial review, the courts are overseeing their co-equal branches of government. When the power of judicial review is used to set aside decisions by the other branches of government, the courts are wielding great power. Logic and a commitment to the constitutional system dictate that this almost unlimited power be exercised with great restraint, say those jurists who follow the judicial restraint philosophy.

Those who believe in such a philosophy think that constitutional issues are too important to be decided unless absolutely necessary and are to be avoided if there is another legal basis for a decision. They believe that the proper use of judicial power demands that courts refrain from determining the constitutionality of an act of Congress unless it is absolutely necessary to a decision of a case. This modest view of the role of the judiciary is based upon the belief that litigation is not the appropriate technique for bringing about social, political, and economic change.

The philosophy of judicial restraint is sometimes referred to as *judicial abstention* or *strict construction*. Strict constructionists believe that the Constitution should be interpreted in light of what the founding fathers intended. They place great weight on the debates of the constitutional convention and in the language of the Constitution. "Judicial abstention" means that courts will decide only those matters which they must in order to resolve actual cases and controversies before them. Courts should abstain from deciding issues whenever possible, and doubts about the constitutionality of legislation should be resolved in favor of the statute. Cases should be decided on the facts if possible and on the narrowest possible grounds.

Those who believe in judicial restraint feel that social, political, and economic change in society should result from the political process rather than from court action. Justice John Marshall Harlan in *Reynolds v. Sims*, 84 S. Ct. 1362 (1964), epitomized this philosophy when, in dissenting from a reapportionment decision, he stated in part:

The vitality of our political system, on which in the last analysis all else depends, is weakened by reliance on the judiciary for political reform. . . . These decisions give support to a current mistaken view of the Constitution and the constitutional function of this Court. This view, in a nutshell, is that every major social ill in the country can find its cure in some constitutional 'principle,' and that this Court should 'take the lead' in promoting reform when other branches of government fail to act. The Constitution is not a panacea for every blot upon the public welfare, nor should this Court, ordained as a judicial body, be thought of as a general haven for reform movements. The Constitution is an instrument of government, fundamental to which is the premise that in a diffusion of governmental authority lies the greatest promise that this nation will realize liberty for all its citizens. This Court, limited in function in accordance with that premise, does not serve its high purpose when it exceeds its authority, even to satisfy justified impatience with the slow working of the political process.

Judges who identify with judicial restraint give great deference to the political process and to the other branches of government. They believe that the courts, especially the federal courts, ought to defer to the actions of the states and of the coordinate branches of government unless these actions are clearly unconstitutional. They allow the states and the federal legislative and executive branches wide latitude in finding solutions to the nation's problems.

Judicial restraint jurists have a deep commitment to precedent. They overrule cases only when the prior decision is clearly wrong. Persons who follow this belief do not believe that they should attempt to write their own personal convictions into the law. They do not view the role of the lawyer and the practice of law as that of social reform. To them, this is the function of the political process.

Followers of judicial restraint often take a pragmatic approach to litigation. Whenever possible, decisions are based on the facts rather than a principle of law. Reviewing courts exercising judicial restraint tend to accept the trial court decisions unless they are clearly wrong in the facts or the law. If there is any reasonable basis for the lower court decision, it will not be reversed if this philosophy dominates the thinking of the reviewing court. Such courts often engage in a balancing approach to their decisions. They weigh competing interests. For example, justices who adhere to judicial restraint often weigh he rights of the person accused of crime with the interests of the victim and of society in determining the extent of the rights of the accused in criminal cases.

JUDICIAL ACTIVISM

Throughout most of our history, judicial restraint has been the dominant philosophy. Today, a majority of the justices of the U.S. Supreme Court usually follow this philosophy, but all courts to some degree are activists. Indeed, many argue that today's Supreme Court is significantly activist. They point to decisions such as those allowing abortions to prove their point.

Those who believe in the philosophy of judicial activism believe that courts have a major role to play in correcting wrongs in our society. To them, courts must provide leadership in bringing about social, political, and economic change because the political system is often too slow or unable to bring about those changes which are necessary to improve society. Activists tend to be innovative and less dependent on precedent for their decisions. They are value-oriented and policy-directed. Activist jurists believe that constitutional issues must be decided within the context of contemporary society and that the meaning of the Constitution is relative to the times in which it is being interpreted. To activists, the courts, and especially the Supreme Court, sit as a continuing constitutional convention to meet the needs of today.

During the 1950s and 1960s, there was an activist majority on the Supreme Court. This activist majority brought about substantial changes in the law, especially in such areas as civil rights, reapportionment, and the criminal law. For example, the activist court of this period ordered desegregation of public schools and gave us the one-man, one-vote concept in the distributing of legislative bodies. Earl Warren, Chief Justice during this period, used to request that lawyers appearing before the Court address themselves to the effect of their clients' positions on society. "Tell me why your position is 'right' and that of your opponent is 'wrong' from the standpoint of society," was a common request to lawyers arguing cases before him.

Activist courts tend to be more result-conscious and place less reliance on precedent. Activists are often referred to as liberals, but that description is too narrow to explain their belief in the role of the judiciary as an instrument of change. They also believe that justices must examine for themselves the great issues facing society and then decide them in light of contemporary standards. Otherwise, we are governed by the dead or by people who were not aware of all of the complexities of today's problems.

Tables 2-1 and 2-2 illustrate typical activist and judicial restraint decisions. Those labeled "judicial restraint" have been decided by other branches of government and the political process. Those labeled "activist" are examples of decisions in which the judiciary has imposed its will on society.

TABLE 2-1   Typical Activist Decisions

1. Busing is a valid technique to achieve school desegregation.
2. Legislative apportionment must be based on population and not area.
3. No prayer is to be permitted in school.
4. The Miranda warning shall be given to all criminal suspects prior to interrogation.
5. Abortion is not a crime.
6. Female pensions must be the same as male pensions, even though females live longer.
7. There shall be equal pay for comparable worth.
8. Legislative veto of decisions of governmental agencies is unconstitutional.
9. Residency requirement for public assistance violates equal protection.
10. OSHA inspectors must have a search warrant if a business objects to inspection.
11. Aliens are entitled to be notary publics.
12. Certain public employees, such as a public defender, cannot be fired because of political affiliation.

6. The Interpretation of Legislation

The second major function of the courts is to interpret legislation. Most legislation is by its very nature stated in general language. It usually purports to cover a multitude of factual situations and is often ambiguous and imprecise. It is up to the judiciary to find the meaning of general language in a statute and apply it to the limited facts of a case. The purpose of statutory construction is to determine the intent of the legislature when the statute was enacted.

One technique of statutory interpretation is to examine the *legislative history* of an act to determine the purpose of the legislation or the evil it was designed to correct. Courts try to find the legislative intent by examining the debates of the legislative body, the committee reports, amendments that were rejected, and other matters that transpired prior to the adoption of the statute. Legislative history may supply the legislative intent, but many of the questions of interpretation which confront courts were never even visualized by the legislature. The real problem often is to determine what the legislature *would have* intended had it considered the question.

Resort to legislative history is not the only means for ascertaining the legislative intent. Courts have developed rules of statutory construction which are frequently followed in determining the legislative intent. These rules in effect recognize that the courts do not actually know what the legislature intended. Therefore, by following the rule of construction it is assumed that the legislature intended a certain meaning. Many of these rules are based on the type of law being interpreted. For example:

1   Taxing laws *shall be* strictly *construed.*

2   Criminal laws *shall be* strictly *construed.*

3   Statutes in derogation of the common law *shall be* strictly *construed.*

4   Remedial statutes *shall be* liberally *construed.*

TABLE 2-2 Typical Judicial Restraint Decisions

---

1. Male-only draft is not a denial of equal protection of the law.
2. States can regulate nuclear power.
3. States can tax the foreign income of multinational corporations.
4. Prayer in the legislature does not violate the First Amendment.
5. Unanimous verdicts are not required, and juries may consist of fewer than twelve persons.
6. Communal living may be prohibited.
7. Homosexuality can be a crime.
8. Class action suits require actual notice to members of the class.
9. Plaintiffs must have direct interest in a lawsuit in order to have standing to sue.
10. Seniority has preference over affirmative action in layoffs.
11. A city-erected Nativity scene does not violate the First Amendment.
12. Factory surveys by the Immigration and Naturalization Service looking for illegal aliens do not violate the Fourth Amendment.

The first two rules mean that doubts about the applicability of a taxing law or criminal law *will be resolved* in favor of the taxpayer or the defendant, respectively. The third rule means that statutes which change the common law will be interpreted as doing so only to the extent that the lawmakers intended and specified. Such a statute will change the common law only to the extent necessary to carry out legislative intent. The fourth rule recognizes that many laws provide a legal remedy for victims of a violation of the law. Such statutes *are described* as remedial because of the remedy given. As a general rule, a *remedial statute* is given a broad or liberal *interpretation*. Doubts about meaning *are* usually *resolved* in favor of the remedy created for the injured party. What happens if a remedial statute is in derogation of the common law? Courts have an obvious choice of alternative rules that allow the desired interpretation.

There are rules of law which aid in finding the meaning of words used in statutes. Some words are simply given their plain or usual meaning. Technical words *are* usually *given* their technical meaning. Others *are interpreted* by the context in which they are used. For example, if a general word in a statute follows particular and specific words of the same nature, the general words take their meaning from the specific words and are presumed to be restricted to the same genus as those words. For example, a statute that said that indigent persons were not required to pay filing fees, sheriff's fees, or "other court costs" was construed to include the cost of publishing notice of a lawsuit in the newspaper. The language "other court costs" takes its meaning from the words preceding it.

There are other rules of statutory construction that are not based on the type of statute or the words used. For example, if a statute contains both specific and general provisions, the specific provisions control. However, courts also attempt to give effect to all the provisions of a statute, if possible, so the purpose of the act will be accomplished. Exemptions from statutes are construed strictly against the party claiming the exemption. Repeal by implication is not favored. If two statutes purport to cover the same topic, they will be construed as consistent with each other if possible, and effect will be given to both. However, if two statutes so clearly conflict that they cannot stand together upon any reasonable construction of both, the legislature is presumed to have repealed the earlier statute while it enacted the latter one.

A frequently cited rule provides: "A thing may be within the letter of the statute and yet not within the statute because not within its spirit nor within the intention of the makers." This rule allows a court to have a great deal of flexibility and to give an interpretation contrary to the plain meaning.

The meaning of a statute may also be established indirectly. A legislative body may fail to act in an area in which the meaning of a law has already been established. The meaning may have been based on judicial decision or on interpretation by the executive branch of government charged with its administration. When an established interpretation is present and not changed, it becomes the accepted one because presumably the legislature would pass a new law if the meaning were not correct. Many people question the validity of this reasoning.

The role of courts in interpreting statutes is very important. The power of courts to interpret legislation means that, in the final analysis, it is what the court says a statute means that determines its effect.

7. Uniform Statutes

Each state has its own constitution, statutes, and body of case law. As a result, there are substantial differences in the law among the various states. In many cases, it does not matter that the law is not uniform. If the parties to a dispute are citizens of the same state and if the controversy has all of its contacts with that state, the law of that state is used to resolve the dispute. However, if citizens of different states are involved in a transaction (perhaps a buyer in one state contracts with a seller in another), many difficult questions may arise if the law in one state differs from the law in another. Although a body of law called "conflict of laws" (see page 37) has been developed to cover such cases, more uniformity may be desirable.

Uniformity in the law may be achieved either by federal legislation or by the enactment of the same law by all states. The latter method has been attempted by a legislative drafting group known as the National Conference of Commissioners on Uniform State Laws. These commissioners endeavor to promote uniformity by drafting model acts. When approved by the National Conference, proposed uniform acts are recommended to the state legislatures for adoption.

More than 100 uniform laws have been drafted and presented to the various state legislatures. Most of these relate to business; the response has varied. A few of the uniform laws have been adopted by all the states. Sometimes a state adopts the uniform law in principle but changes some of the provisions to meet local needs. As a result, we often have "nonuniform uniform state laws."

The most significant uniform law for business is the Uniform Commercial Code. It was prepared for the stated purpose of collecting in one body the law that "deals with all the phases which may ordinarily arise in the handling of a commercial transaction from start to finish. . . ." Thus it covers the law as it relates to the sale of goods, the use of commercial paper to pay for them, and the giving of security to ensure that the purchase price will be paid. The Uniform Commercial Code is not applicable to contracts for the sale of real estate or to contracts for personal services. It is limited to commercial transactions involving personal property.

CASE LAW

8. Inherent Problems

The third major function of courts is to create law when deciding cases and controversies. Precedent is a byproduct of judicial decisions. Several aspects of case law must be understood if we are to understand the role of law and lawyers in the decision-making process. First, notwithstanding the fact that common law arose out of a desire for certainty, and is designed to create it, common law creates a great deal of uncertainty in the law. The sheer volume of judicial decisions, each possibly creating precedent, makes "the law" beyond the comprehension of lawyers and judges, let alone the rest of us. Large law firms employ lawyers whose sole task is to search the case reports for "the law" to be used in lawsuits and in advising their clients. Access to hundreds of volumes of cases is required. Since the total body of ruling case law is beyond the grasp of lawyers, it is obvious that laypersons who are supposed to know the law and govern their conduct accordingly do not know the law and are somewhat bewildered by it. Case law does not give the level of certainty and predictability intended by its creators. Moreover, in many cases the law is not clear. It is not found by searching cases. The law used to decide many cases is being made in the process. Many years ago a legal scholar in discussing this aspect of case law observed:

> It is the judges that make the common law. Do you know how they make it? Just as a man makes laws for his dog. When your dog does anything you want to break him of, you wait till he does it, and then beat him for it. This is the way you make laws for your dog: and this is the way the judges make laws for you and me. They won't tell a man beforehand what it is he should not do—they won't so much as allow of his being told: they lie by till he has done something which they say he should not have done, and then they hang him for it. What way, then, has any man of coming at this dog-law? Only by watching their proceedings: by observing in what cases they have hanged a man, in what cases they have sent him to jail, in what cases they have seized his goods, and so forth.[3]

The common law system of reliance on precedent is not very efficient. Conflicting precedents are frequently cited to a court by the parties of litigation. One of the major tasks of the courts in such cases is to determine which of the precedents cited is applicable. In addition, even today, many questions of law arise on which there has been no prior decision, or in areas where the only authority is by implication.

The problem of finding the law in a case law system is compounded in a

---

[3] 5 Bentham, *Works* 235, quoted in 1 Steffen and Levi, *Cases and Materials on the Elements of the Law* 207 (3d ed., 1946).

country which consists of fifty sovereign states, because each of these creates its own body of common law. The law as it develops on a case-by-case basis in different states varies from state to state. Moreover, the federal legal system is superimposed on the state systems, thus creating additional bodies of judge-made laws. The methods of determining the applicable precedent where conflicts exist between the laws of different jurisdictions are discussed later in Section 10.

There is an important distinction between **precedent** and mere **dicta**. A judicial decision, as authority for future cases, is limited by the facts upon which it is founded and the rules of law upon which the decision actually is based. Frequently courts make comments on matters not necessary to the decision reached. Such expressions, called "dicta," lack the force of a judicial settlement; they, strictly speaking, are not precedent which courts will be required to follow within the rule o stare decisis. However, dicta may be followed if sound and just, and dicta which have been repeated frequently are often given the force of precedent. Moreover, even though a statement by a court is not pure precedent, it does express the court's opinion, and to the extent that the court is knowledgeable about the subject matter, the court's opinion is entitled to some weight.

One of the major reasons that the case law system leads to uncertainty is that a precedent may be changed or reversed. Since case law is susceptible to change, absolute reliance on it is not possible. This problem is discussed further in the next section.

9. The Weight to Be Given Precedent

Case law created by the judiciary can be changed by the judiciary. The common law is not set in stone to be left unchanged for decades and centuries. As Justice William O. Douglas observed:

> Inherent in the common law is a dynamic principle which allows it to grow and to tailor itself to meet changing needs within the doctrine of stare decisis, which, if correctly understood, was not static and did not forever prevent the courts from reversing themselves or from applying principles of common law to new situations as the need arose. If this were not so, we must succumb to a rule that a judge should let others "long dead and unaware of the problems of the age in which he lives, do his thinking for him."

Courts usually hesitate to reject a precedent or to change case law. The assumption is made that a principle or rule of law announced in a former judicial decision, if unfair or contrary to public policy, will be changed by legislation. Precedent has more force in trial courts than in courts of review, which have the power to make precedent in the first instance. However, stare decisis does not mean that former decisions *always* will be followed, even by trial courts. A former ruling may have been erroneous, or the conditions upon which it was based may have changed or may no longer exist. The doctrine does not require courts to multiply their errors by using former mistakes as authority and support for new errors. Thus just as legislatures change the law by new legislation so also do courts change the law, from time to time, by reversing or modifying former precedents.

Judges are subject to social forces and changing circumstances just as are legislatures. The personnel of courts changes, and each new generation of judges has a responsibility to reexamine precedents and to adapt them to changing conditions. This responsibility is especially present in cases involving constitutional issues. A doctrine known as "constitutional relativity" stands for the proposition that the meaning of the language found in the Constitution is relative to the time in which it is being interpreted. The doctrine has been used rather frequently by the Supreme Court to give effect to society's attitudes. Under this concept great weight is attached to social forces and needs, as the court sees them, in formulating judicial decisions. As the attitudes and problems of society change, precedent changes.

Some quotes from justices indicate their attitude toward precedent. For example, Justice Wanamaker in the case of *Adams Express Co. v. Beckwith,* 100 Ohio St. 348, said that "A decided case is worth as much as it weighs in reason and righteousness, and no more. It is not enough to say 'thus saith the court.' It must prove its right to control in any given situation by the degree in which it supports the rights of a party violated and serves the cause of justice as to all parties concerned." Or as Justice Musmanno stated in the case of *Bosley v. Andrews,* 393 Pa. 161 (1958):

> Stare decisis is the viaduct over which the law travels in transporting the precious cargo of justice. Prudence and a sense of safety dictate that the piers of that viaduct should be examined and tested from time to time to make certain that they are sound, strong and capable of supporting the weight above. . . . A precedent, in law, in order to be binding, should appeal to logic and a genuine sense of justice. What lends dignity to the law founded on precedent is that, if analyzed, the particularly cited case wields authority by the sheer force of its self-integrated honesty, integrity, and rationale. A precedent cannot, and should not, control, if its strength depends alone on the fact that it is old, but may crumble at the slightest probing touch of instinctive reason and natural justice.

The extent to which precedent is followed varies a great deal depending on the subject matter of the litigation. If the dispute involves subject areas of private law, such as torts, contracts, or property, there is much greater deference to precedent than if the subject area is constitutional law. The fact that precedent is to be given great weight in the areas of private law does not mean that courts will continue to follow a rule of private law where the reasoning behind the rule no longer exists. Even here, precedents are reversed as the needs of society change. The belief that the meaning of the Constitution is relative to the times in which it is being interpreted results in less deference to precedent in constitutional law cases. To the extent that courts provide leadership in bringing about social, political, and economic change, they are likely to give less weight to precedent and more weight to other factors which influence judicial decisions.

10. Selecting the Applicable Case Law

Each state has its own statutory laws and its own body of judge-made precedent. These laws cover both matters of substance and matters of procedure. Generally, the decisions of one state are considered to be applicable precedent only in that state. The decisions of other states, however, may be considered by way of analogy when there are no previous decisions on the point in question in the state where a case is being heard. For example, precedent of other states is frequently referred to in cases involving the construction of statutes such as the Uniform Acts, where each state has adopted the same statute. Where there is no precedent, a case is one of "first impression." In such cases, each state is free to decide for itself questions concerning its common law and interpretation of its own constitution and statutes.

In addition to this system of fifty distinct bodies of state precedent, there is the federal legal system. The federal courts have thei own body of procedural law and substantive law o questions arising under the federal Constitution, codes, statutes, or treaties. Decisions of the federal courts are binding on state courts in federal question cases. In federal court suits based on diversity of citizenship, the federal courts use the substantive law of the states in which they are sitting to determine the rights and duties of the parties. However, in such cases, the federal courts use their own rules of procedure. Thus, just as state courts are bound by federal precedent in certain situations, so also are federal courts bound by state precedent in others.

The problem of determining the applicable case law is sometimes difficult because of conflicting precedents within the same court system. When a case or controversy involves more than one state, the difficulty is compounded when the precedents of each state differ. Differences in case law between the states are quite common. The law of torts varies from state to state as does the law of contracts. For example, in some states the plaintiff in an auto accident case must allege and prove freedom from negligence that contributed to the accident. In other states, a defendant must prove that the accident was the fault of the plaintiff if liability is to be avoided. Similar differences exist in every area of the law because there is no uniformity in case law.

In cases involving transactions or occurrences with contact with more than one state, the question must always be asked: Which state law applies? To answer this question a body of law has developed primarily through judicial decisions, which is generally referred to as "conflict of laws." The decisions that comprise this body of law simply determine which state's substantive law is applicable to any given question when more than one state is involved. This usually arises where all or some of the facts occur in one state and the trial is held in another. For example, the conflict-of-laws rules for tort actions are, in most cases, that the law of the place of injury is applicable. Thus, if a car accident occurred in Missouri but suit was brought in an Illinois state court, the judge would apply the law of Missouri in determining the rights of the parties. There are several different views held by courts about which law to select in resolving issues involving contracts. Some favor the law of the state where the contract was made, others the law of the place of performance, and still others have adopted the "grouping of contacts" theory which uses the law of the state with the most substantial contact with the contract. This latter theory has also been applied in a few tort cases. In the criminal law, the law of the place of the crime is the applicable substantive law. Table 2-3 illustrates typical conflict of laws principles.

In a multistate situation, the first problem confronting the court is, therefore, to select the appropriate state to turn to for legal precedent on substantive issues. Once a determination has been made of which state is appropriate, the court's business then is to review the citations of authority advanced by the opposing attorneys to determine which of that state's case decisions to apply in following the doctrine of stare decisis.

Therefore, it must be recognized that there is a body of law used to decide conflicts between the precedent of the various states. This is especially significant in our modern society with its ease of communication and transportation. The trend toward uniform statutes and codes has tended to decrease these conflicts, but many of them still exist. So long as we have a federal system and fifty separate state bodies of substantive law, the area of conflict of laws will continue to be of substantial importance in the application of the doctrine of stare decisis.

11. The Judicial Process

In deciding cases and in examining the powers discussed in the prior sections, courts are often faced with several alternatives. They may decide the case by use of existing statutes and precedents. This will often be the case as courts must have a deep commitment to the common law system. However, as previously noted, they may refuse to apply existing case law or may declare a statute to be void as unconstitutional. Also, if there is no statute or case law, the court may decide the case and create law in the process. However, case law as a basis for deciding controversies often provides only the point of departure from which the difficult labor of the courts begins. Courts must examine and compare cases cited as authority to them, to determine not only which is correct, but whether the principles or rules of law contained there should be followed or rejected as no longer valid. In reaching and preparing its decision, the court must consider whether the law as announced will provide justice in the particular case and whether it will establish sound precedent for future cases involving similar issues.

The foregoing alternatives raise several questions: Why do courts reach one conclusion rather than another in any given case? What formula, if any, is used in deciding cases and in determining the direction of the law? What forces tend to influence judicial decisions when the public interest is involved?

There is, obviously, no simple answer to these questions. Many persons

TABLE 2-3 Sample Conflict of Laws Principles

Substantive Law Issue	Law to Be Applied
1. Liability for injury caused by tortious conduct	1. State in which injury was inflicted
2. Validity of a contract	2. State in which contract was made or State in which it is to be performed or State with most significant contacts with the contract or State specified in the contract
3. Inheritance of real property	3. State of situs of real property
4. Inheritance of tangible personal property	4. State of domicile of deceased
5. Validity of a marriage	5. State of celebration
6. Child custody	6. State of domicile of child
7. Workers' compensation	7. State of employment or State in which injury was received

assume that logic is the basic tool of the judicial decision. But Justice Holmes stated "the life of the law has not been logic; it has been experience."[4] Other persons argue that courts merely reflect the predominant attitude of the times and that they simply follow the more popular course in decisions where the public is involved.

Justice Benjamin Cardozo, in a series of lectures on the judicial process[5] discussed the sources of information judges utilize in deciding cases. He stated that if the answer were not clearly established by statute or by unquestioned precedent, the problem was twofold: "He [the judge] must first extract from the precedents the underlying principle, the *ratio decidendi;* he must then determine the path or direction along which the principle is to work and develop, if it is not to wither and die."[6] The first part of the problem is separating legal principles from dicta so that the actual precedent is clear. Commenting on the second aspect of the problem, Cardozo said: "The directive force of a principle may be exerted along the line of logical progression; this I will call the rule of analogy or the method of philosophy; along the line of historical development; this I will call the method of evolution; along the lines of the customs of the community; this I will call the method of tradition; along the lines of justice, morals and social welfare, the *mores* of the day; and this I will call the method of sociology."[7]

---

[4]Holmes, *The Common Law* 1 (1938).

[5]Cardozo, *The Nature of the Judicial Process* (1921). Excerpts are used by permission from the Yale University Press.

[6]Id. at 28.

[7]Id. at 30–31.

In Cardozo's judgment, the rule of analogy was entitled to certain presumptions and should be followed if possible. He believed that the judge who molds the law by the method of philosophy is satisfying humanity's deep-seated desire for certainty. History, in indicating the direction of precedent, often illuminates the path of logic and plays an important part in decisions in areas such as real property. Custom or trade practice has supplied much of the direction of the law in the area of business. All judicial decisions are at least in part directed by the judge's viewpoint on the welfare of society. The end served by law must dictate the administration of justice, and ethical considerations, if ignored, will ultimately overturn a principle of law.

Noting the psychological aspects of judges' decisions, Cardozo observed that it is the subconscious forces which keep judges consistent with one another. In so recognizing that all persons, including judges, have a philosophy which gives coherence and direction to their thought and actions whether they admit it or not, he stated:[8]

> All their lives, forces which they do not recognize and cannot name, have been tugging at them—inherited instincts, traditional beliefs, acquired conviction; and the resultant is an outlook on life, a conception of social needs, . . . which when reasons are nicely balanced, must determine where choice shall fall. In this mental background every problem finds its setting. We may try to see things as objectively as we please. None the less, we can never see them with any eyes except our own. To that test they are all brought—a form of pleading or an act of parliament, the wrongs of paupers or the rights of princes, a village ordinance or a nation's charter.

In the following comments, Cardozo summarized his view of the judicial process.

FROM THE NATURE OF THE JUDICIAL PROCESS[9]
Benjamin N. Cardozo

. . . My analysis of the judicial process comes then to this, and little more: logic, and history, and custom, and utility, and the accepted standards of right conduct are the forces which singly or in combination shape the progress of the law. Which of these forces shall dominate in any case must depend largely upon the comparative importance or value of the social interests that will be thereby promoted or impaired. One of the most fundamental social interests is that law shall be uniform and impartial. There must be nothing in its action that savors of prejudice or favor or even arbitrary whim or fitfulness. Therefore in the main there shall be adherence to precedent. There shall be sym-

---

[8]Id. at 12–13.
[9]Id. at 112–115.

metrical development, consistently with history or custom when history or custom has been the motive force, or the chief one, in giving shape to existing rules, and with logic or philosophy when the motive power has been theirs. But symmetrical development may be bought at too high a price. Uniformity ceases to be a good when it becomes uniformity of oppression. The social interest served by symmetry or certainty must then be balanced against the social interest served by equity and fairness or other elements of social welfare. These may enjoin upon the judge the duty of drawing the line at another angle, or staking the path along new courses, of marking a new point of departure from which others who come after him will set out upon their journey.

If you ask how he is to know when one interest outweighs another, I can only answer that he must get his knowledge just as the legislator gets it, from experience and study and reflection; in brief, from life itself. Here, indeed, is the point of contact between the legislator's work and his. The choice of methods, the appraisement of values, must in the end be guided by like considerations for the one as for the other. Each indeed is legislating within the limits of his competence. No doubt the limits for the judge are narrower. He legislates only between gaps. He fills the open spaces in the law. How far he can go without traveling beyond the walls of the interstices cannot be staked out for him upon a chart. He must learn it for himself as he gains the sense of fitness and proportion that comes with years of habitude in the practice of an art. Even within the gaps, restrictions not easy to define, but felt, however impalpable they may be, by every judge and lawyer, hedge and circumscribe his action. They are established by the traditions of the centuries, by the example of other judges, his predecessors and his colleagues, by the collective judgment of the profession, and by the duty of adherence to the pervading spirit of the law. . . . None the less, within the confines of these open spaces and those of precedent and tradition, choice moves with a freedom which stamps its action as creative. The law which is the resulting product is not found, but made. The process, being legislative, demands the legislator's wisdom. . . .

REVIEW QUESTIONS

1 Contrast the duties and functions of a trial judge with those of a reviewing court justice.

2 The Supreme Court held that the Selective Service law is constitutional, notwithstanding the fact that only males are subject to the draft. It also allowed courts in the state of Florida to televise criminal proceedings, over the objection of a defendant.
What judicial philosophy is reflected in these decisions? Explain.

3 A Supreme Court justice made the following observations:
   a It is the business of a judge to decide cases on the narrowest grounds possible and not to reach out for constitutional questions. As a judge, you don't have the freedom to substitute your own views for the law.
   b A judge should try to obey and not go beyond the intent of Congress in interpreting federal laws. A judge must be most reluctant to depart

from prior precedent. A judge is not a legislator, and the Supreme Court should not be used as an instrument of policy.

c Judicial power can be exercised only as to matters that were the traditional concern of the courts at Westminster, and only if they arise in ways that lawyers, in their expert opinion, think constitute "cases" or "controversies." Even as to questions that were the staple of judicial business, it is not for the courts to pass upon them unless they are indispensably involved in a conventional litigation—and then, only to the extent that they are involved.

What judicial philosophy do the foregoing illustrate? Explain.

4   The jury system is sometimes criticized by litigants and jurists. Give reasons for settling cases and avoiding a decision by a jury.

5   A government employee who had been fired by the President of the United States sued the President for wrongful discharge. The President moved to dismiss the case. He contended that as President he could not be sued for actions performed as part of his official duties. Who decides this issue? Why?

6   In recent years, courts have halted construction of a dam to preserve an endangered species of fish, ruled that females must be allowed to compete with males in athletics, banned school dress codes, and blocked suspension of public school students without a hearing. Courts have operated the schools in Boston, Massachusetts, and the prisons in Alabama. Which judicial philosophy is present in these decisions? Explain.

7   Courts are frequently called upon to interpret the Constitution and legislation. This function is performed in the context of applying legislation to a factual situation. Answer the following questions relative to statutory interpretation.

a Why is it necessary for courts to interpret legislation?

b List two techniques that are used to perform this function.

c List three rules of statutory construction based on the type of law involved.

d List two rules of statutory construction based on the words used in the statute.

8   A state statute provided that "every person who, at the request of the owner of any real property . . . rents, leases or otherwise supplies equipment . . . for clearing, grading, filling in, or otherwise improving any real property . . . has a lien upon such real property for the value of the services rendered for such purposes."

A wrecking company supplied trucks and drivers for removal of debris, which resulted from the demolition of a building on certain premises. The owner failed to pay the cost of removal, and the wrecking company filed a lien under the statute mentioned above. There was no such lien at common law. What rules of statutory construction could be used by a court to decide the validity of the lien?

9   What is the function of the Commissioners on Uniform State Laws?

10   What are some of the advantages of a precedent-oriented legal system? What are some of the disadvantages?

11   Ann, a resident of Iowa, purchased some auto parts by mail from RST Company in Illinois. The contract called for the seller to deliver the parts to Ann. Ann wishes to return some of the parts she received, but RST refuses to accept returns. Iowa has a law requiring sellers of consumer goods to refund the purchase price if the goods are returned within ten days. Illinois has no such law. What law will be applied regarding the return of the merchandise? Explain.

12 George was on a coast-to-coast trip by automobile. While passing through Ohio, he had a flat tire. It was fixed by Al's Turnpike Service Station, and later, while George was driving in Indiana, the tire came off and George was injured. George was hospitalized in Indiana, so he sued Al in Indiana for his injuries. What rules of substantive law will the Indiana court use to determine if Al is at fault? Explain.

13 Justice Cardozo, in his comments about the judicial process, described four forces which, singly or in combination, shaped the progress of the law. Name or describe these four forces, and give an example of each.

14 Stare decisis is less likely to be followed in the area of public law than in the area of private law. Why?

Chapter
3

The Court System

1. Introduction

This chapter examines our court system. It is a dual system consisting of state courts and federal courts. The system at the federal level and in most states contains three levels—trial courts, intermediate reviewing courts, and final reviewing courts. Lawsuits are commenced at the trial court level, and the results are reviewed at the other two levels.

For a court to hear and decide a case at any level it must have **jurisdiction**. Jurisdiction is power over the subject matter of the case and over the parties. Some state trial courts have general jurisdiction; others have limited jurisdiction. They may be limited as to subject matter, amount in controversy, or area in which the parties live. For example, small-claims courts have jurisdiction only if the amount in controversy does not exceed a certain sum. Even a court of general jurisdiction has geographical limitations. As we shall see in this chapter, all federal courts have limited jurisdiction.

Courts, especially those of limited jurisdiction, may be named according to the subject matter with which they deal. Probate courts deal with wills and the estates of deceased persons; juvenile courts, with juvenile crime and dependent children; criminal and police courts, with violators of state laws and municipal ordinances; and traffic courts, with traffic violations. For an accurate classification of the courts of any state, the statutes of that state must be examined.

Even courts of general jurisdiction cannot attempt to resolve every dispute or controversy that may arise. Some issues are simply nonjusticiable as the following case illustrates.

WOODRUFF v. GEORGIA STATE UNIVERSITY

304 S.E.2d 697 (Ga. 1983)

WELTNER, J.: Woodruff brought this action against the Board of Regents, Georgia State University and certain Georgia State University professors alleging state and federal constitutional violations, tort, and breach of contract claims. The trial court granted summary judgment and Woodruff appeals.

Woodruff was admitted to a master's degree program in the music department of Georgia State University in 1972. In the fall of 1973, she received an "F" on the basis of plagiarism, and appealed that grade to an appeals committee within the university. The committee changed the grade to an "incomplete." She alleges that thereafter her professors were "hostile and sarcastic" to her, refusing to help her with course work and thesis preparation, changing course requirements prior to graduation, placing damaging information about her in an open file, and giving her undeservedly low grades in an attempt to block her graduation.

In 1979, after seven years in a program which normally takes two or three years to complete, Woodruff was awarded the degree of Master of Arts in Music. She then applied for admittance into a doctoral program at the University of Georgia in Athens, which required recommendations from former professors. Woodruff's former professors either refused or ignored her request for recommendations. In their depositions, several professors testified that Woodruff was an "argumentative and troublesome" student who was erratic in her studies and not academically qualified to proceed to a doctoral program. They offered academic reasons for withholding their recommendations. . . .

. . . [T]he central issue is whether or not a dispute concerning academic decisions of a public educational institution is a justiciable controversy.

In the general realm of educational institutions, we have reviewed standards of dismissals and student discipline. We have examined the denial of student eligibility to participate in sports, and we have refused to permit the judiciary to referee high school football games. The Court of Appeals has upheld the authority of a local board of education to impose proficiency requirements as a prerequisite to graduation from high school. School financing was considered in *Deriso v. Cooper*, 246 Ga. 540 (1970). *Deriso v. Cooper* raised, as well, questions concerning the adequacy of school curriculum and physical facilities, "and various others relating to the manner in which educational services shall be provided and student progress shall be monitored."

We have not thus far, however, entertained an individual student's complaint seeking money damages for alleged impropriety in academic assessment of her work.

"This court traditionally has been reluctant to embark upon courses of judicial action which would require continuing supervision of the official conduct of public officers. . . . Courts are ill-equipped to make such fundamental, legislative and administrative policy decisions as how much local supplement to teachers' salaries should be paid in order to attract qualified teachers, how many levels of English or math should be taught, whether a system of pupil ability grouping shall or shall not be used, whether buildings shall be constructed and, if so, where, and the myriad other matters involved in the everyday administration of a public school system which the courts would face were they to embark upon the course of judicial activism desired by the school patrons. *Resolutions of these discretionary policy determinations best can be made by other branches of government* (Emphasis supplied)."

In *McDaniel v. Thomas,* we declined to tell the General Assembly precisely how it must allocate state funds among school systems. In *Deriso v. Cooper,* we declined to tell a local school board the manner in which it must perform its responsibilities. In *Georgia High School Assn. v. Waddell,* we declined to review the call of a football referee.

We now decline to review a teacher's academic assessment of a student's work.

This is clearly consistent with the authorities we have mentioned. It is restraint which stems from confidence that school authorities are able to discharge their academic duties in fairness and with competence. It is born alike of the necessity for shielding the courts from an incalculable new potential for lawsuits, testing every Latin grade and every selection for the Safety Patrol.

It protects every teacher from the cost and agony of litigation initiated by pupils and their parents who would rely upon the legal process rather than the learning process.

It protects every school system—all of them laboring under pressures of financing, personnel problems and student discipline, academic performance, taxpayer revolt and patron unrest, and a rising tide of recalls—from an added and unbearable burden of continuous legal turmoil. . . . [*Judgment affirmed.*]

2. The State Court System

Government in the United States is based on dual sovereignty; that is, the judicial branch is an essential element of government at both the state and federal levels. Both the state and federal court systems are created and their operations governed from three sources. First, constitutions provide the general framework for the court system. Second, the legislature, pursuant to constitutional authority, enacts statutes which add body to the framework. This legislation provides for various courts; establishes their jurisdiction, or an area of authority; and deals with such problems as the tenure, selection, and duties of judges. Other legislation may establish the general rules of procedure to be used by these courts. Third, each court sets forth its own rules of procedure within the statutory bounds set. These rules are detailed and may specify, for example, the form of a summons or the times when various documents must be filed with the court clerk. Thus, a study of the court system for any particular state must refer to its constitution, such legislation as Civil Practice Acts, and the rules of the various courts. Each state has its own terminology and arrangement for its courts. Figure 3-1 is representative of the courts of a typical state.

TRIAL COURTS

The general jurisdiction trial court is frequently known as the "circuit court," deriving its name from earlier times when the judge "rode the circuit," or in

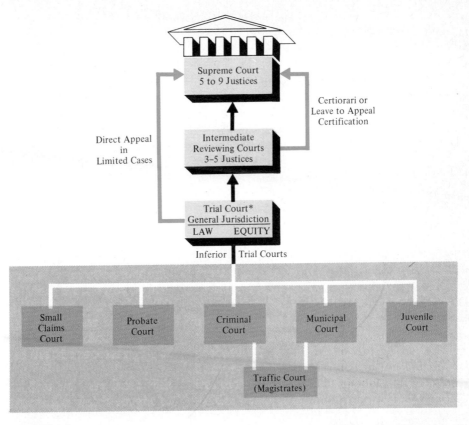

FIGURE 3-1
Typical State Court System.

other words traveled from town to town in a certain territory over which his court had jurisdiction, hearing and deciding cases. Some states call the basic trial court the "superior court," while others call it the "district court" or "court of common pleas." In New York it is known as the "supreme court." The term "general jurisdiction" means that the court has the power to hear any type of case. The courts below this trial court in Figure 3-1 are limited to the types of cases which they may hear and thus are referred to as "inferior courts," or courts of limited jurisdiction. For example, probate courts are involved with the administration of the estates of deceased persons or those of incompetents. Juvenile courts deal with criminal offenses committed by children below a stated age.

At one time the basic trial courts were divided into two branches, one known as a "court of law" and the other a "court of chancery or equity," but this is no longer the case in most states. The distinction between law and equity is discussed in section 9 of this chapter.

Some states do not have intermediate reviewing courts between the trial court and the court of final resort; however, intermediate reviewing courts are usually found in the more heavily populated states. Some states call their court of last resort "Supreme Court of Appeals" or "Court of Appeals."

REVIEWING COURTS

In states with two levels of reviewing courts, most appeals are taken to the lower of the two courts, and the highest court of the state reviews only very important cases. Courts of review are essentially concerned with questions of law. Although a party is entitled to one trial and one appeal, he or she may obtain a second review if the higher reviewing court, in the exercise of its discretion, agrees to such a review. The procedure for requesting a second review is to file what is called in some states a "petition for leave to appeal" and in others a "petition for a writ of certiorari."

Since this request for a second review must be acted upon by the higher court, the party requesting it actually obtains a second review, although it is a limited one. The case is examined to see whether it is one that the highest court wishes to hear. Deciding such requests is a major function of the Supreme Court of the United States and of the highest court in each state. As a practical matter, less than 5 percent of all such requests are granted.

3. Small-Claims Courts

One court of limited jurisdiction is especially important to the business community. This court, usually known as **small-claims court**, handles the majority of litigation between business and its customers. Small-claims courts are used by businesses to collect accounts and by customers to settle disputes with the business community that are relatively minor from a financial standpoint. Such suits are often quite important from the standpoint of principle, however. For example, many persons use small-claims courts to sue for damages caused by defective merchandise or by services poorly performed. Landlord-tenant disputes are another example of controversies decided in these courts.

Small-claims courts have low court costs and simplified procedures. The informality of the proceedings speeds up the flow of cases. The services of a lawyer are not usually required, but if one side uses a lawyer, the other side probably needs one also. Some states do not allow lawyers to participate in these proceedings. Such courts usually are subject to a dollar limitation over the suits which may be filed. In some states this amount may be as low as $500, whereas in others it may be as high as $5,000. A typical jurisdictional amount is $2,000. Most states have raised this jurisdictional limitation, as inflation has taken its toll here also.

As small-claims courts have grown in number and their case loads have expanded, numerous problems have arisen. In large cities, there is often a need for a bilingual court. In addition, night sessions are frequently required so that litigants need not miss work. As a practical matter, the judge often serves as mediator of the dispute, and many cases are settled by agreement with the court. For many people, the chance to complain to some third party is all they really seek in filing a lawsuit. Any financial recovery is secondary. One continuing problem, however, is that many successful litigants are unable to collect their judgments because the decision of the small-claims court is not self-enforcing. A recent study in New York City found that 44 percent of successful litigants in small-claims court did not collect any money.

The sections which follow examine the state and federal court systems. They demonstrate the difference between trial courts and reviewing courts and distinguish between courts of law and courts of equity. Finally, we discuss some of the problems that exist today in the system.

4. The Federal Court System

Article III of the Constitution (see Appendix 1) provides that judicial power be vested in the Supreme Court and such lower courts as Congress may create. The judicial power of the federal courts is limited. Essentially, it extends to matters involving questions of federal law (federal question cases), to matters in which the United States is a party, to controversies among the states, and to cases involving *diversity of citizenship* (suits between citizens of different states). The federal judicial power does not extend to cases involving a state law between citizens of the same state. Such cases will be dismissed by federal courts, because they lack the power to hear them.

In order for a claim to arise under the Constitution, laws, or treaties of the United States (federal question), a right or immunity created by said Constitution or laws must be an essential element of the plaintiff's cause of action. Thus, federal question cases may be based on issues arising out of the U.S. Constitution or out of federal statutes. Any amount of money may be involved in such a case, and it need not be a suit for damages. For example, a suit to enjoin a violation of a constitutional right can be filed in the federal courts as a federal question case. These civil actions may involve matters such as bankruptcy or suits based on patents, copyrights, trademarks, taxes, elections, the rights guaranteed by the Bill of Rights, and those rights secured to individual citizens by the Fourteenth Amendment. In addition, by statute the federal district courts have original jurisdiction to try tort cases involving citizens who suffer damages caused by officers or agents of the federal government.

The district courts are the trial courts of the federal judicial system. They have original jurisdiction, exclusive of the courts of the states, over all federal crimes; that is, all offenses against the laws of the United States. The accused is entitled to a trial by jury in the state and district where the crime was committed.

If a case affects ambassadors or other public ministers and consuls, or is one in which a state is a party, the Supreme Court has original jurisdiction. In all other cases, the Supreme Court has appellate jurisdiction unless Congress creates an exception.

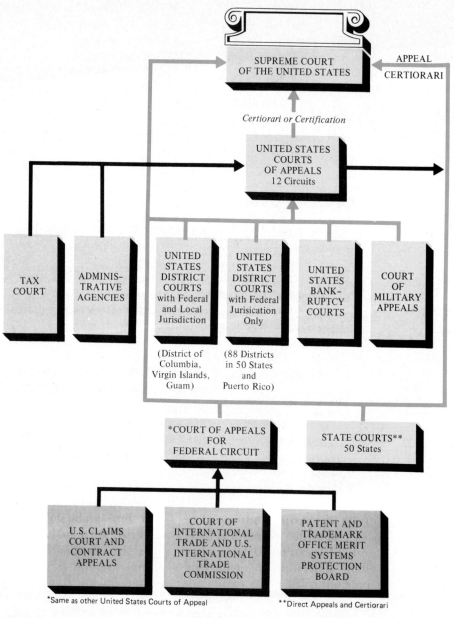

FIGURE 3-2
The federal court system

Under its constitutional authorization, Congress has enacted legislation providing for various inferior federal courts; it has also defined their jurisdiction. Congress has created twelve U.S. Courts of Appeals plus a special Court of Appeals for the Federal Circuit. This special reviewing court, located in Washington, D.C., hears appeals from special courts such as the U.S. Claims Court and Contract Appeals, as well as from administrative decisions such as those by the Patent and Trademark Office. Congress has also created the U.S. district courts (at least one in each state) and other courts, such as the Court of Military Appeals, to handle special subject matter. Figure 3-2 illustrates the federal court system and shows the relationship of state courts and administrative agencies for review purposes. The U.S. Code also contains provisions concerning such matters as appellate procedure and the review of actions by administrative agencies. The Federal Rules of Civil Procedure provide the details concerning procedures to be followed in federal court litigation.

5. Diversity of Citizenship Cases

There are several problems related to the jurisdiction of federal courts based on diversity of citizenship. Diversity of citizenship does not extend to domestic relations cases. The fact that a husband and wife may live in different states does not justify the federal courts to hear their divorce case. In addition, diversity of citizenship requires that all plaintiffs be citizens of different states from all defendants. If a case involves several parties on one or more sides of the case, and if a party on one side is a citizen of the same state as a party on the other, there will then be no diversity of citizenship and thus no federal jurisdiction. In some types of cases where some parties actually represent others, deciding if total diversity exists is sometimes difficult.

NAVARRO SAV. ASS'N v. LEE
100 S. CT. 1779 (1980)

POWELL, J.: The question is whether the trustees of a business trust may invoke the diversity jurisdiction of the federal courts on the basis of their own citizenship, rather than that of the trust's beneficial shareholders.

The respondents are eight individual trustees of Fidelity Mortgage Investors, a business trust organized under Massachusetts law. They hold title to real estate investments in trust for the benefit of Fidelity's shareholders. The declaration of trust gives the respondents exclusive authority over this property "free from any power and control of the Shareholders, to the same extent as if the Trustees were the sole owners of the Trust Estate in their own right. . . ." The respondents have power to transact Fidelity's business, execute documents, and "sue and be sued in the name of the Trust or in their names as Trustees of the Trust." They may invest the funds of the trust, lend money, and initiate or compromise lawsuits relating to the trust's affairs.

In 1971, respondents lent $850,000 to a

Texas firm in return for a promissory note payable to themselves as trustees. The note was secured in part by a commitment letter in which petitioner Navarro Savings and Loan Association agreed to lend the Texas firm $850,000 to cover its obligation to the respondents. In 1973, respondents called upon Navarro to make the "takeout" loan. Navarro refused, and this action followed. . . . Federal jurisdiction was premised upon diversity of citizenship. The complaint asserted—and the parties agree—that Navarro was a Texas citizen and that each respondent was a citizen of another State. The parties have stipulated, however, that some of Fidelity's beneficial shareholders were Texas residents.

The District Court dismissed the action for want of subject matter jurisdiction. Concluding that a business trust is a citizen of every State in which its shareholders reside, the court held that the parties lacked the complete diversity. . . . The Court of Appeals for the Fifth Circuit reversed. It held that the respondent trustees were real parties in interest because they had full power to manage and control the trust and to sue on its behalf. Since complete diversity existed among the actual parties to the controversy, the Court of Appeals directed the District Court to proceed to trial on the merits. We granted certiorari. . . .

Federal courts have jurisdiction over controversies between "citizens of different States" by virtue of 28 U.S.C. § 1332(a)(1) and U.S. Const., Art. III, § 2. Early in its history, this Court established that the "citizens" upon whose diversity a plaintiff grounds jurisdiction must be real and substantial parties to the controversy. Thus, a federal court must disregard nominal or formal parties and rest jurisdiction only upon the citizenship of real parties to the controversy.

The early cases held that only persons could be real parties to the controversy. Artificial or "invisible" legal creatures were not citizens of any State. Although corporations suing in diversity long have been "deemed" citizens, unincorporated associations remain more collections of individuals. When the "persons composing such association" sue in their collective name, they are the parties whose citizenship determines the diversity jurisdiction of a federal court.

Navarro contends that Fidelity's trust form masks an unincorporated association of individuals who make joint real estate investments. Navarro observes that certain features of the trust's operations also characterize the operations of an association: centralized management, continuity of enterprise, and unlimited duration. Arguing that this trust is in substance an association, Navarro reasons that the real parties to the lawsuit are Fidelity's beneficial shareholders.

We need not reject the argument that Fidelity shares some attributes of an association. In certain respects, a business trust also resembles a corporation. But this case involves neither an association nor a corporation. Fidelity is an express trust, and the question is whether its trustees are real parties to this controversy for purposes of a federal court's diversity jurisdiction.

As early as 1808, this Court stated that trustees of an express trust are entitled to bring diversity actions in their own names and upon the basis of their own citizenship. Fed. Rule Civ. Proc. 17(a) now provides that such trustees are real parties in interest for procedural purposes. Yet similar principles governed diversity jurisdiction long before the advent of uniform rules of procedure. In 1870, the Court declared that jurisdiction properly founded upon the diverse citizenship of individual trustees "is not defeated by the fact that the parties whom they represent may be disqualified." "[T]he citizenship of those who may have the equitable interest" is simply irrelevant. . . . A trustee is a real party to the controversy for purposes of diversity jurisdiction when he possesses certain customary powers to hold, manage, and dispose of assets for the benefit of others. The trustees in this case have such powers. At all relevant times, Fidelity operated under a declaration of trust that authorized the trustees to take legal title to trust assets, to invest those assets for the benefit of the shareholders, and to sue and be sued in their capacity as trustees. Respondents filed this lawsuit in that capacity. They seek damages for breach of an obligation running to the holder of a promissory note held in their own names. Fidelity's 9,500 beneficial shareholders had no voice in the initial investment decision. They can neither control the disposition of this action nor intervene in the affairs of the trust except in the most extraordinary situations.

We conclude that these respondents are active trustees whose control over the assets held in their names is real and substantial. That the trust may depart from conventional forms in other respects has no bearing upon this determination. Nor does Fidelity's resemblance to a business enterprise alter the distinctive rights and duties of the trustees. There is no allegation of sham or collusion. The respondents are not "naked trustees" who act as "mere conduits" for a remedy flowing to others. They have legal title; they manage the assets; they control the litigation. In short, they are real parties to the controversy. For more than 150 years, the law has permitted trustees who meet this standard to sue in their own right, without regard to the citizenship of the trust beneficiaries. We find no reason to forsake that principle today. [*The judgment of the Court of Appeals is affirmed.*]

The fact that business corporations are frequently incorporated in one state and have their principal place of business in another state also causes problems in determining when diversity of citizenship exists. A corporation is a citizen of the state of incorporation and also a citizen of the state in which it has its principal place of business, for purposes of diversity jurisdiction. Thus, a Delaware corporation with its principal place of business in Illinois is a citizen of both Delaware and Illinois for purposes of diversity. If any party on the other side of a lawsuit with such a corporation is a citizen of either Illinois or Delaware, there is then no diversity and no federal jurisdiction. Questions as to the state in which a corporation has its principal place of business often arise. The total activity of the corporation is examined to determine its principal place of business. This test incorporates both the "place of activities" and the "nerve center" tests. The nerve center test places general emphasis on the locus of the managerial and policy-making functions of the corporations. The place of activities test focuses on production or sales activities. The "total activity" test is not an equation that can provide a simple answer to the question of a corporation's principal place of business. Each case necessarily involves somewhat subjective analysis.

In diversity of citizenship cases, the federal courts have a jurisdictional amount of more than $10,000. If a case involves multiple plaintiffs with separate and distinct claims, *each* claim must satisfy the jurisdictional amount. Thus, in a class action suit, the claim of each plaintiff must meet the $10,000 minimum, unless changed by statute.

6. Federal Reviewing Courts

Direct appeals from the district courts to the U.S. Supreme Court may be taken in three situations: (1) in criminal cases when the district court holds invalid the statute upon which the indictment or information was based, (2) when the district court holds an act of Congress unconstitutional in a case in which a government agency is a party, and (3) when the district court consisting of three judges has either granted or denied an injunction. In most cases appeals are taken from the U.S. district court to the Courts of Appeals. Since litigants are entitled to one review as a matter of right, parties may obtain additional review of decisions only if the Court of Appeals holds a state statute to be unconstitutional or contrary to federal law, or upon the granting of a writ of **certiorari** by the Supreme Court.

A petition for a writ of certiorari is a request by the losing party to a higher court for permission to file an additional appeal. In such cases, the Supreme Court has discretion as to whether or not it will grant the petition and allow another review. The review is not a matter of right. Writs of certiorari are granted only in cases of substantial federal importance or where there is an obvious conflict between decisions of two or more Circuit Courts of Appeals in an area of the law which needs clarification. Certiorari may be granted before or after the decision of the Circuit Court of Appeals. When the Supreme Court of the United States reviews petitions for a writ of certiorari, the writ is granted if four of the nine justices vote to take the case. The net result of this procedure is that the Supreme Court spends a great deal of time and effort in deciding which cases it will hear. It is able to pick and choose those issues with which it will be involved.

In addition to cases on appeal and accepted by writ of certiorari, the Supreme Court will review questions of law certified to it for decision by the Court of Appeals. The federal court system is thus limited in the types of cases it decides.

The U.S. district courts and the Courts of Appeals cannot review, retry, or correct the judicial errors charged against a state court. Final judgments or decrees rendered by the highest court of a state are reviewed only by the Supreme Court of the United States. State cases appealed to the U.S. Supreme Court must concern the validity of a treaty or statute of the United States or must present a question involving the validity of a state statute on the grounds that the statute is repugnant to the Constitution, treaties, or laws of the United States and that the state decision is in favor of the statute's validity. When a case involves the constitutionality of a state statute or treaty or when a citizen's rights, privileges, or immunities under the constitution or laws are impaired, the case may be brought to the Supreme Court by writ of certiorari. In all other cases the decision of the highest state court is not subject to review.

7. Transfer from the States to the Federal System

It is possible to transfer a case from the state court system to the federal court system under three circumstances. First, a defendant sued in a state court may have the case removed to the federal system if it meets the requirements of those cases which first could have been brought into the federal system. In other words, if the case involves a *federal question,* or if there is diversity of citizenship and the requisite amount is involved, the case may be transferred by a defendant to the federal district court.

In addition, there is a special statute dealing with civil rights cases. If a defendant is denied or cannot enforce in the courts of a state a right under any law providing for the equal civil rights of citizens of the United States, the case may be removed from the state courts to the appropriate federal district court.

Whenever a separate and independent claim or cause of action, which would be removable if sued upon alone, is joined with one or more otherwise nonremovable claims or causes of action, the entire case may be removed. The district court may determine all issues in the case, or, in its discretion, may send all matters not otherwise within its original jurisdiction back to the state court.

Second, a party has the right to appeal a decision of the highest court of a state to the Supreme Court of the United States if (1) the case involves the validity of a treaty or statute of the United States, and the decision is against its validity; or if (2) the case involves the validity of a state statute which allegedly violates the U.S. Constitution, and the decision is in favor of its validity.

Third, a party may seek review of the decision of a state's highest court by writ of certiorari where a federal question is involved. Each year there are several thousand such petitions filed. Almost all of them are denied.

8. The Law in the Federal Courts

As a general proposition, each court system uses its own rules of procedure. Thus, in the federal courts, the Federal Rules of Procedure (both civil and criminal) are followed. For state court proceedings, each state has adopted applicable rules of procedure.

The problem as to the applicable substantive law is far more complex. In federal question cases, the controlling statutes and judicial decisions are those of the federal courts by definition. However, if the case is in the federal courts because of diversity of citizenship, what is the applicable substantive law? Is there a federal common law? The case which follows is a landmark decision answering these questions.

ERIE RAILROAD v. TOMPKINS
304 U.S. 64 (1938)

BRANDEIS, J.: The question for decision is whether the oft-challenged doctrine of *Swift v. Tyson* shall now be disapproved.

Tompkins, a citizen of Pennsylvania, was injured on a dark night by a passing freight train of the Erie Railroad Company while walking along its right of way at Hughestown in that state. He claimed the accident occurred through negligence in the operation, or maintenance, of the train; that he was rightfully on the premises as a licensee because he was on a commonly used beaten footpath which ran for a short distance alongside the tracks; and that he was struck by something which looked like a door projecting from one of the moving cars. To enforce that claim he brought an action in the federal court for Southern New York, which has jurisdiction because the company is a corporation of that state. It denied liability; and the case was tried by a jury.

The Erie insisted that its duty to Tompkins was no greater than that owed to a trespasser. It contended, among other things, that its duty to Tompkins, and hence its liability, should be determined in accordance with the Pennsylvania law; that under the law of Pennsylvania, as declared by its highest court, persons who use pathways along the railroad right of way—that is, a longitudinal pathway as distinguished from a crossing—are to be deemed trespassers; and that the railroad is not liable for injuries to undiscovered trespassers resulting from its negligence, unless it be wanton or willful. Tompkins denied that any such rule had been established by the decisions of the Pennsylvania courts; and contended that, since there was no statute of the state on the subject, the railroad's duty and liability is to be determined in federal courts as a matter of general law.

The trial judge refused to rule that the applicable law precluded recovery. The jury brought in a verdict of $30,000; and the judgment entered thereon was affirmed by the Circuit Court of Appeals, which held that it was unnecessary to consider whether the law of Pennsylvania was as contended, because the question was one not of local but of general law, and that

. . . upon questions of general law the federal courts are free, in absence of a local statute, to exercise their independent judgment as to what the law is; and it is well settled that the question of the responsibility of a railroad for injuries caused by its ervants is one of general law. . . . Where the public has made open and notorious use of a railroad right of way for a long period of time and without objection, the company owes to persons on such permissive pathway a duty of care in the operation of its trains. . . . It is likewise generally recognized law that a jury may find that negligence exists toward a pedestrian using a permissive path on the railroad right of way if he is hit by some object projecting from the side of the train.

The Erie had contended that application of the Pennsylvania rule was required, among other things, by section 34 of the Federal Judiciary Act which provides: "The laws of the several States, except where the Constitution, treaties, or statutes of the United States otherwise require or provide, shall be regarded as rules of decision in trials at common law, in the courts of the United States, in cases where they apply."

Because of the importance of the question whether the federal court was free to disregard the alleged rule of the Pennsylvania common law, we granted certiorari. . . .

First, *Swift v. Tyson*, 16 Pet. 1, 18, 10 L.Ed. 865, held that federal courts exercising jurisdiction on the ground of diversity of citizenship need not, in matters of general jurisprudence, apply the unwritten law of the state as declared by its highest court; that they are free to exercise an independent judgment as to what the common law of the state is—or should be. . . .

Doubt was repeatedly expressed as to the correctness of the construction given section 34, and as to the soundness of the rule which it introduced. But it was the more recent research of a competent scholar, who examined the original document, which established that the construction given to it by the Court was erroneous; and that the purpose of the section was merely to make certain that, in all matters except those in which some federal law is controlling, the federal courts exercising jurisdiction in diversity of citizenship cases would apply as their rules of decision the law of the state, unwritten as well as written. . . .

Second. Experience in applying the doctrine of *Swift v. Tyson* had revealed its defects, political and social; and the benefits expected to flow from the rule did not accrue. Persistence of state courts in their own opinions on questions of common law prevented uniformity, and the impossibility of discovering a satisfactory line of demarcation between the province of general law and that of local law developed a new well of uncertainties.

On the other hand, the mischievous results of the doctrine had become apparent. Diversity of citizenship jurisdiction was conferred in order to prevent apprehended discrimination in state courts against those not citizens of the state. *Swift v. Tyson* introduced grave discrimination by noncitizens against citizens. It made rights enjoyed under the unwritten "general law" vary according to whether enforcement was sought in the state or in the federal court; and the privilege of selecting the court in which the right should be determined was conferred upon the noncitizen. Thus, the doctrine rendered impossible equal protection of the law. In attempting to promote uniformity of law throughout the United States, the doctrine had prevented uniformity in the administration of the law of the state. . . .

Third. Except in matters governed by the Federal Constitution or by acts of Congress, the law to be applied in any case is the law of the state. And whether the law of the state shall be declared by its Legislature in a statute or by its highest court in a decision is not a matter of federal concern. There is no federal general common law. Congress has no power to declare substantive rules of common law applicable in a state whether they be local in their nature or "general," whether they be commercial law or a part of the law of torts. And there is no clause in the Constitution that purports to confer such a power upon the federal courts. . . .

The fallacy underlying the rule declared in *Swift v. Tyson* is made clear by Mr. Justice Holmes. The doctrine rests upon the assumption that there is "a transcendental body of law outside of any particular State but obligatory that federal courts have the power to use their judgment as to what the rules of common law are; and that in the federal courts "the parties are entitled to an independent judgment on matters of general law":

. . . But law in the sense in which courts speak of it today does not exist without some definite authority behind it. The common law so far as it is enforced in a State, whether called common law or not, is not the common law generally but the law of that State existing by the authority of that State without regard to what it may have been in England or anywhere else. . . .

The authority and only authority is the State,

and if that be so, the voice adopted by the State as its own (whether it be of its Legislature or of its Supreme Court) should utter the last word.

Thus the doctrine of *Swift v. Tyson* is, as Mr. Justice Holmes said, "an unconstitutional assumption of powers by the Courts of the United States which no lapse of time or respectable array of opinion should make us hesitate to correct." In disapproving that doctrine we do not hold unconstitutional section 34 of the Federal Judiciary Act of 1789 or any other act of Congress. We merely declare that in applying the doctrine this Court and the lower courts have invaded rights which in our opinion are reserved by the Constitution to the several states.

Fourth. The defendant contended that by common law of Pennsylvania as declared by its highest court, the only duty owed to the plaintiff was to refrain from willful or wanton injury. The plaintiff denied that such is the Pennsylvania law. In support of their respective contentions the parties discussed and cited many decisions of the Supreme Court of the state. The Circuit Court of Appeals ruled that the question of liability is one of general law; and on that ground declined to decide the issue of state law. As we hold this was error, the judgment is reversed and the case remanded to it for further proceedings in conformity with our opinion. [*Reversed.*]

One further complicating factor should be noted in the process of a *federal* court in selecting the law of the state's precedent it has decided to follow. The federal court will look at the total body of law of the state in which it is sitting, *including the state's conflict of laws principles.* Thus, in using the law of state X, it may, in turn, look to the law of some other state for the actual precedent. For example, assume that a citizen of the state of Illinois sues a citizen of the state of Indiana in the federal district court in Indiana for personal injuries received in an automobile accident which occurred in the state of Kentucky. The federal district court sitting in Indiana will use federal procedure and the substantive law of the state of Indiana. The substantive law of the state of Indiana includes the conflict of laws principle that the applicable tort law is the law of the place of injury. The federal court in Indiana will use the Kentucky tort law since that is the law which would be used by an Indiana state court.

Subsequent to the *Erie* case, in diversity of citizenship cases many federal decisions have been concerned with whether a given issue is one of substantive law, in which case the applicable state law will be followed, or one of procedure, in which case the federal practice will be followed. If the state rule of law, whether created by statute or case decision, will affect the *result* of the controversy, the rule is treated as substantive and will be followed by the federal court in diversity cases.

As a result of the doctrine of *Erie Railroad v. Tompkins,* federal courts are sometimes presented with a dilemma when there is no state decision or statute on the issue involved in a diversity case. In such situations, the federal court under a doctrine known as "abstention" may hold its case in abeyance and direct the litigants to try their case in the state court. This is also true if a federal question is involved with a question of state law. The doctrine is invoked to allow the state to decide state issues prior to the federal court's deciding federal issues, especially where the state decision may end the litigation. The doctrine allows federal courts to eliminate guesswork on the meaning of local laws and is designed to further harmoniou relations between state and federal courts. The state court may decide the federal question if the parties so desire, or it may leave the federal question to the federal courts. In the event the state court decides the federal question, the losing party may appeal to the U.S. Supreme Court.

9. Law and Equity

Courts having general jurisdiction in the United States have traditionally been divided into courts of law and courts of equity. Some states historically had two separate courts, and others simply had one court with one side known as law and the other side known as equity or chancery.

Courts of law were developed early in English jurisprudence to handle cases such as the various forms of trespass, other torts, and breach of contract. These courts dealt with legal disputes where one party was seeking dollar damages from another. Courts of law were not equipped to give remedies such as requiring a person to do or not to do something.

When courts of law were inadequate to furnish the desired relief, a practice developed of petitioning the king of England for such relief. As the number of such petitions grew, the king delegated his authority in granting or denying petitions to his chancellor. The name **chancery** is derived from this practice. Since the action taken was originally taken by the king, results were not a matter of right but in each case rested in the grace and favor of the king; or, by modern terminology, the decisions were strictly discretionary.

The concept of equity did not originate in England, however. Aristotle had defined equity as the "correction of the law, where, by reason of its universality, it is deficient." The purpose of equity has always been to remedy defects in the law. As courts of chancery grew and developed in England, the need for supplemental legal procedures where courts of law were inadequate assisted the steady growth of equity, although the courts of law strenuously objected.

Courts of chancery or equity were firmly entrenched in English jurisprudence by the time the American court system was developed. Those who established our courts recognized the need for resort to natural principles to define and interpret positive law and to remedy its defects, and they therefore provided for equity jurisprudence.

In recent years, federal law and many state laws have attempted to abolish the distinctions between law and equity. These attempts have affected procedural aspects of the distinction but have not changed its substantive aspects. These attempts have combined the procedures of law and equity into one action known as a "civil action." In civil actions, equitable concepts have been generally utilized and adopted for actions at law. The influence of equity has predominated over law where the procedures have been combined.

Notwithstanding statements that the distinctions between law and equity have been abolished, since the historical substantive distinctions are still important, it is usually necessary to decide whether an action would have been "at law" or "in chancery." Many states require that the pleading so indicate.

Many matters depend on whether an action is legal or equitable in nature. For example, cases in chancery, with a few exceptions such as will contests, are not tried before a jury. The court, or in a few states a person appointed by it, known as a "master in chancery," serves as the trier and finder of the facts. Thus, whether a party has a right to a trial by jury depends on the nature of the action.

Equity jurisdiction is used in cases where the remedy at law is deemed inadequate. That is, where dollar damages are not an adequate remedy, a court of chancery will hear the case. Such cases as suits for an accounting; cancellation, rescission, or reformation of a contract; injunctions; partition suits; suits to quiet title; and suits for specific performance are litigated in chancery. If a case is filed in equity and if the remedy at law, such as dollar damages for breach of contract, is an adequate remedy, the suit in equity will be dismissed.

BECKMAN v. VASSALL-DILLWORTH LINCOLN-MERCURY
468 A.2d 784 (Pa. Super. 1983)

On December 14, 1978, Beckman signed a contract with the Vassall-Dillworth Lincoln-Mercury dealership for the purchase of a 1979 Lincoln Continental. Four weeks later Beckman inquired about the car. He was told that the purchase order agreement was lost, so no car was ordered. The dealer offered to order a 1979 Lincoln Continental, but at a price higher than the price originally agreed upon. Beckman sued the dealership for specific performance of the original contract. The trial court dismissed the suit.

MONTGOMERY, J. . . . Beckman contends the trial court incorrectly held he was not entitled to specific performance because he failed to show that he had no adequate remedy at law. It is clear that an order for specific performance is inappropriate where the moving party has an adequate remedy at law. Our Court has held that specific performance is a proper remedy when the subject matter of an agreement is an asset that is unique or one such that its equivalent cannot be purchased on the open market. In this case, the record shows that the Appellant was given an opportunity by the dealer to purchase the automobile he wanted, but at a higher price. It may not be ignored that the Appellant could also have sought to purchase the same vehicle from another source. His remedy in such circumstances was to seek damages for any difference between the original order price and the actual purchase price he paid. Because the subject matter of the contract was not unique, and because it is obvious that an adequate remedy at law was available, we agree with the lower court's rejection of the Appellant's demand for specific performance. [*Affirmed.*]

10. Equitable Procedures

Courts of equity use *maxims* instead of rules of law. Strictly speaking, there are no legal rights in equity, for the decision is based on moral rights and natural justice. A court of equity is a court of conscience in which precedent is secondary to natural justice.

Some of the typical maxims of equity are:

1 "Equity will not suffer a right to exist without a remedy."

2 "Equity regards as done that which ought to be done."

3 "Where there is equal equity, the law must prevail."

4 "He who comes into equity must do so with clean hands."

5 "He who seeks equity must do equity."

6 "Equity aids the vigilant."

7 "Equality is equity."

These maxims serve as guides for the chancellor to use in exercising his or her discretion. The following case illustrates some of the foregoing maxims.

ALBER v. STANDARD HEATING AND AIR CONDITIONING
476 N.E.2d 507 (Ind. App. 3 Dist. 1985)

HOFFMAN, J.: . . .
On July 8, 1968, appellant Dale Alber purchased a heating and air-conditioning business from the H.B. Shank family. As condition to the purchase agreement, Alber was permitted to use the trade name H.B. Shank & Sons, Inc. for a period of six years. Without permission, Alber continued to use this trade name after his contractual right expired. In 1975, Alber sold out to appellee

Ronald Mitchell and warranted unlimited use of the H.B. Shank & Sons, Inc., trade name.

In 1977, Mitchell was contacted by the Shank family attorney and advised that he could no longer use the family trade name. Alber intervened, insuring Mitchell continued use of the trade name while promising the Shanks that he would clear matters up. In September of 1981, the Shanks sued Mitchell to prohibit further use of their trade name. Mitchell joined Alber as a third-party defendant, alleging breach of contract. [The trial court enjoined further use of name and relieved second buyer of remaining liability on its purchase contract, and first buyer appealed.]

Alber first contends the trial court erred in refusing to bar the Shanks' suit under the doctrine of laches. He specifically maintains the Shanks waited for an inexcusable period of time before asserting any rights to their trade name.

The doctrine of laches is based upon the legal maxim, equity aids the vigilant, not those who slumber on their rights. The defense of laches is a determination which rests within the sound discretion of the trial court and will be reversed on appeal only in the event of a clear abuse of discretion. The following three elements comprise the defense of laches:

1   inexcusable delay in asserting a right;

2   implied waiver arising from knowing acquiescence in existing conditions; and

3   circumstances causing prejudice to the adverse party.

The evidence most favorable to the judgment does not indicate an abuse of discretion. Alber's license to use the trade name ran until July of 1974. In 1975 he conveyed the business to Mitchell with a warranty that the trade name was free to use. The Shanks assumed Alber ceased using the name in 1974, and first became aware that he had not in 1977. They took immediate action to prevent further use when Alber convinced them he would resolve this matter with Mitchell. In 1981 the Shanks again discovered illegal use of their name and promptly sued Mitchell. Under these circumstances, the Shanks' delay is neither unreasonable, nor does it imply acquiescence from which waiver arises. The trial court properly refused to bar this suit under the doctrine of laches. . . .

In reference to Alber's preceding arguments based upon principles of equity, an independent basis exists to affirm the judgment. It is universally accepted that he who seeks equity, must do equity. A party petitioning for equitable relief must come before the court with clean hands. Alber was well aware of the contractual restriction on the use of the trade name but continued to use it after the right expired. He later warranted unlimited use of this name to Mitchell. When Mitchell and the Shanks learned that the name was being improperly used, Alber convinced both sides that he would resolve the problem most favorable to their interests. These actions constitute a substantial misrepresentation of the truth tantamount to actual or constructive fraud. Alber is in no position to request equitable relief. . . . [*Affirmed.*]

The decision of the court of equity is called a decree, as contrasted with a judgment in a court of law which is measured in damages. A decree of a court of equity is said to be in personam; that is, it directs the defendant to do or not to do some specific thing.

Decrees are either final or interlocutory. A decree is final when it disposes of the issues in the case, reserving no question to be decided in the future. A decree is interlocutory when it reserves some question to be determined in the future. A decree granting a temporary injunction would be interlocutory.

Failure of the defendant to obey a decree of a court of equity is contempt of court. Any person in contempt of court may be placed in jail or fined.

Equity has played a significant role in our system of jurisprudence, and it will continue to do so. In moving toward social justice the courts will rely more on equitable maxims and less on rigid rules of law. This will also contribute further to the decay of the doctrine of stare decisis.

11. Contemporary Problems

A recent headline in *The Wall Street Journal* read "Too Much Law, Too Many Lawyers, Not Enough Justice." The president of Harvard, Derek Bok, observed that "there is far too much law for those who can afford it and far too little for those who cannot." Such articles and observations are strong evidence that there are numerous problems facing the court system. Delay and the high cost of operating the system are two major problems. Court dockets have expanded with resultant delays in recent years because of the litigious nature of our society and increases in population. The high cost of litigation has priced most minor disputes either out of the court system or to small-claims court, where the matter can be resolved without legal counsel. It is no longer economically feasible to litigate such matters as consumer claims for shoddy merchandise or poor services with the aid of an attorney. The costs of transmitting property on death are unsatisfactorily high for many Americans. It has been estimated that it costs up to 100 times as much to transfer property on death in this country as it does in England. Probate costs often run 2½ to 3 times funeral expenses.

"Justice delayed is justice denied." That often-quoted cliché sums up the most obvious defect in our court system—court congestion and the delay that results therefrom. In many large cities, the backlog of civil cases is so great that a period of five or more years elapses between the transaction or occurrence in question and a jury trial. Such delays tend to force unsatisfactory settlements upon many plaintiffs. They also cause other serious problems for the parties and adversely affect the search for truth. The thousands of criminal cases awaiting trials or pending on appeal at all times raise many serious consequences for society. Not the least of these is that an accused person free on bond is free to commit more crimes while the case is awaiting trial.

The high cost of legal services, especially of litigation, greatly concerns clients and the organized bar. Litigation is expensive, not only for the parties to the dispute, but also for society as a whole. Society pays the cost of providing judges, court officials, and juries. The current trend is to have more and longer jury trials, thus greatly increasing the cost of the system. Much of jurors' time is unproductively spent, since they must frequently wait for the lawyers and the court to proceed. Since jurors are paid by the day, inefficiency adds to society's costs.

Adequate legal advice is priced out of the reach of many low- and middle-income persons. The wealthy can afford the best legal talent. Public defender programs provide free legal service to indigents charged with crime, and legal aid projects have generally made legal service available to poor persons with civil problems. However, the cost of legal services for the average person is often prohibitive. As a result, many people either do not have legal advice when it is needed or often turn to other lay persons for legal advice. Although the increase in the number of lawyers and the resulting competition have helped alleviate this problem, the cost of adequate legal assistance has made it unavailable to many Americans.

12. Delay: Some Solutions

Many state legislatures and court authorities are implementing several changes designed to eliminate and reduce court congestion and the backlog of court cases. Among the changes to reduce court congestion which have partial acceptance to date are: (1) six-person juries instead of twelve; (2) requiring only majority verdicts instead of unanimous ones; (3) elimination of oral argument on appeal whenever possible; (4) application of management techniques to the system by designating someone other than a judge to assign cases, court rooms, and juries so that all judicial personnel are utilized more effectively; and (5) elimination of jury trials in certain types of cases. In addition, the number of judges has been expanded in many jurisdictions.

Several suggestions have been made to reduce the case load of the federal courts. Perhaps the most radical idea is to abolish diversity of citizenship jurisdiction in the federal courts or to deny jurisdiction if the plaintiff is from the same state as the court in which the case is filed. It is argued that there is no rational basis today for putting an automobile accident case in a federal court simply because litigants are citizens of different states, especially if the plaintiff is from the state from which the jury will be selected.

It has also been proposed that a special court be created to hear petitions for writs of certiorari. This would free the Supreme Court to spend its time deciding cases before it rather than requiring it to spend a significant portion of its time deciding which cases it wants to hear. Each year the Supreme Court must review over 5,000 petitions for writs of certiorari. This new court would probably consist of Courts of Appeals justices on a rotating basis.

Another technique for reducing delay caused by court congestion is to standardize the "plea-bargaining" process in criminal cases. The criminal law as currently organized requires plea bargaining. The case load is too great to try all criminal cases. Definite rules and regulations relating to plea bargaining are needed. For example, perhaps pleas that are bargained should be published so that at least the victims of the crimes involved could comment to the court before the plea and bargain are accepted and implemented.

Attempts are being made to reduce the quantity of civil litigation. Most legal scholars feel mechanisms other than litigation may resolve many disputes and controversies that arise. For example, arbitration clauses are included in many contracts. Many other controversies are submitted to binding arbitration by the parties. Arbitration is less expensive and much quicker than litigation as a dispute-resolving technique. It creates less hostility and allows issues to be submitted to experts for decision. Arbitration will be discussed further in the next chapter.

13. High Cost: Some Solutions

Historically, the parties to a lawsuit have been required to pay their own attorney's fees. Thus, the winner of a lawsuit is actually a loser to the extent of the cost of legal counsel. Some people advocate that the loser in a civil lawsuit should be required to pay the winner's legal costs. This would encourage many people to settle claims rather than run the risk of the additional expense of paying the other party's attorney. In a few cases, such as divorce proceedings, attorney's fees have been awarded, and it is felt by some that this policy may have advantages in other cases.

Many authorities advocate a change in the traditional policy on fees in cases affecting the public interest, because the plaintiff in such cases acts as a sort of private attorney general. They argue that if the plaintiff is entitled to collect attorney's fees in public interest cases, such litigation will be encouraged. However, such a policy has mixed benefits. Many frivolous claims could be brought by lawyers seeking only relatively nominal damages for their clients but substantial attorney's fees. On the other hand, allowing the successful party's counsel to be paid will encourage attorneys to bring to court attention many serious problems of society that might otherwise not be the subject of litigation.

Adequate legal services are usually available to personal injury and other damage claim litigants irrespective of the client's ability to pay. The poorest person in the country can obtain the best legal talent in a personal injury case because of a method of compensation known as the **contingent fee system**. In cases handled under the contingent fee arrangement, the attorney's fee is a fixed percentage of the total recovery. In a typical case, the attorney receives one-third of the net amount collected for the client.

The contingent fee system gives everyone equal access to the courts and to legal talent. However, it often does so at a high cost to the client. Assume that a person loses both legs as the result of the negligent conduct of another, and that the issue of negligence is not debatable. Assume that the jury awards the victim $3 million as damages. It is difficult to believe that the attorney earned a fee of $1 million in such a case. Of course, if the liability or the extent of injury is not clear, then the attorney certainly would "earn" more of the fee for his or her efforts.

Contingent fee arrangements also have a negative impact in that they encourage solicitation or "ambulance chasing" of cases with potential for a large recovery. Personal injury litigation has such potential for large fees that unethical conduct is not uncommon and cases tend to gravitate to a few lawyers, adding to court congestion.

Some states have limited contingent fees on a sliding scale basis by which lawyers receive a lower percentage the higher the recovery. Steps have also been taken to prevent ambulance chasing and to discipline attorneys found guilty of such unethical conduct.

In order to make legal services available to more people, many lawyers (especially young lawyers) are opening legal clinics. Some legal clinics are funded by government or private foundations. However, in recent years federal funding has been reduced significantly and may be eliminated altogether as attempts are made to reduce federal deficits.

Employer plans for prepaid legal services are another recent development. Under these plans, a relatively small fixed fee is paid each year by the employee, and whenever a legal problem crops up, it is handled without additional charge. Legal insurance programs similar to those for health insurance also are being suggested. Prepaid legal fees together with the attacks on fee schedules are tending to lower the cost of legal services and make them more available.

The high cost of the law is not limited to poor or middle-income people, however. Many corporations today have found that they too are confronted with soaring legal costs. Much of this cost is required for dealings with government. The Equal Employment Opportunity Act, the Occupational Safety and Health Administration (OSHA), and the National Environmental Policy Act have all contributed substantially to higher legal costs for major corporations. As a result, more and more corporations have hired ever greater numbers of lawyers as regular employees and have turned less to outside counsel.

14. The Competency of Lawyers

The issue as to the competency of lawyers is most frequently raised in connection with litigation. Chief Justice Burger has commented that at least half the lawyers in the country are not qualified to try a case in court. He believes that higher qualifications must be required for the trial bar and that unqualified lawyers should not be allowed to engage in trial practice. He argues that significant experience at the state court level should be a prerequisite to practice in the federal courts.

Inadequate performance by trial attorneys adds to court congestion and delays. Poorly trained lawyers take longer to try a case and often fail to settle cases that experienced lawyers would settle. In addition, many cases are filed that experienced, able lawyers would reject. These cases often have some nuisance value because of the cost of defending the case. If litigation were limited to lawyers with special licenses, many of these nuisance cases might be eliminated because higher ethical standards could be enforced. It is noted that in one recent case, the court ordered a plaintiff's lawyer and his client to pay $50,000 to a defendant who had been subjected to a baseless lawsuit. Such actions would cause lawyers to review cases before filing lawsuits, ensuring that the cases have some merit.

15. Advertising and Competition

Perhaps the most significant change in the practice of law in recent years is the discarding of the prohibition on advertising. Historically, a lawyer could not advertise and could not claim to be a specialist in any area other than patent or admiralty law. However, such prohibitions ran afoul of the First Amendment protection of freedom of speech. Truthful advertising by lawyers is protected by the First Amendment as a form of commercial speech. This will be discussed further in Chapter 9.

A significant impetus to advertising by lawyers is the desire to lower the cost of legal services through "price" competition. Today the classified advertisements sections of most newspapers contain ads for such routine legal services as divorces and bankruptcy proceedings. Many lawyers advertise their hourly rate for office consultations. These practices have significantly lowered the cost of legal services since such advertising commenced in the late 1970s.

Although there are some ethical limits on the type of ads that lawyers may use, the fact that it is no longer unethical to advertise has had a significant impact on the legal profession. The practice of law demands so much knowledge and expertise that specialization is not only desirable but necessary. The public is entitled to know which lawyers possess expertise in a given area just as they know the specialties of the medical profession. In addition, a lawyer claiming expertise should be required to actually possess it. It is now recognized that higher standards of performance will result if lawyers are allowed to specialize and advertise their specialty. The public is better served by such specialists whose background and continuing education keep them fully informed on a limited area of the law.

While price competition among lawyers is probably in the public interest, especially in routine matters, it must be recognized that price should not be the factor determining the selection of professional persons in many situations. A patient seeking a surgeon to do open-heart surgery is not likely to be guided primarily by the fee to be charged. Likewise, there are many considerations other than cost in selecting a lawyer. The quality of the service may or may not be affected by the price. The fees for a lawyer with great skill in a certain area are likely to be relatively unaffected by the fees charged by less skilled competitors.

16. Other Policy Trends and Ethical Considerations

There are numerous other questions facing our court system and the legal profession. For example, whether or not we should televise trials is hotly debated today. Proponents of television in the courtroom contend that the people are entitled to know what goes on in our courtrooms. They argue that televising criminal trials would serve as a deterrent to crime and would aid in the education of the public. Proponents would especially like to televise arguments before the Supreme Court.

Those who object to television in the courtroom point out that trials are not entertainment and that the public's viewing of the proceedings would not be particularly educational. Trials that take several weeks are basically dull with only a few dramatic moments. Most people would not watch all the proceedings and the net effect would be negative. In addition, most people would not understand many of the legal points discussed before the Supreme Court. Television could tend to encourage lawyers and judges to "ham it up" before the camera, with the search for truth hampered by theatrics.

To date, a few states have permitted television of judicial proceedings. The cameras used are small and unobtrusive. It is too early to tell whether or not such practices will become common. However, the Supreme Court has held that the decision is up to the states. States need not televise trials, but may do so over the objection of the defendant if they so desire.

The ethical standards of the profession are another cause of concern to those seeking to improve the quality of legal services in this country. Whereas advertising of fees is now permissible, solicitation by lawyers is still generally unethical. Solicitation is most common in personal injury cases. To discourage such activities, courts can suspend or disbar any lawyer found to be guilty of solicitation for pecuniary gain. The solicitation of business by lawyers through direct in-person communications is inconsistent with the attorney-client relationship and is deemed likely to cause harm to the client. An exception to the solicitation rule exists for not-for-profit corporations that engage in litigation as a form of political expression and political association. Such solicitation has been held to be protected by the constitutional guarantees of freedom of expression. The collective activity of the organization provides access to the courts and tends to protect the public. For example, a lawyer for a not-for-profit corporation who sought out persons and advised them of their right to litigate threatened sterilization under a medicaid program could not be guilty of unethical solicitation.

Several states today have special agencies to investigate and prosecute the misconduct of lawyers. Historically the bar was slow to start disbarment proceedings, and many unethical activities, such as ambulance chasing, were common. Today, bar associations are actively attempting to restore the profession to a desirable level from the ethics standpoint. Substantial progress has been made, and the public is benefiting from these efforts.

Another important ethical question which needs resolving in the near future concerns lawyer-client confidences and clients' misconduct. To what extent does the bond between lawyer and client require the lawyer to hold in confidence what a client has said? A lawyer usually should hold in confidence information about a client's past misconduct. However, a lawyer certainly should not assist any present or future illegal conduct by the client. In fact, the lawyer should try to deter such conduct. But is a lawyer allowed or required to disclose the client's confidences and thereby "blow the whistle" on the client to prevent a crime? Currently, "whistle-blowing" is permitted in such a case, but is not required.

The American Bar Association is considering a clarification of the professional standard which would require a lawyer to disclose facts "necessary to prevent" assisting a client in a present or future criminal or fraudulent transaction. The lawyer's duty of disclosure to third parties might arise, for example, in business negotiations where the lawyer *knows* a fraud is intended by the client, or in trial where the lawyer *knows* a client has perjured himself or herself and refuses to correct the testimony. The lawyer would be assisting in a violation of the law not to disclose the facts in these circumstances. However, the proposed rules would not require disclosure or investigation of *suspicions* the lawyer might have. In some situations, a lawyer might be able to withdraw from representing a client if that is all that is "necessary to prevent" assisting criminal or fraudulent conduct.

New ethical rules would also permit, but not mandate, disclosing of a client's confidences if it was necessary to prevent serious personal or economic harm caused by the client even though the lawyer has no part in assisting the client. Prospective crimes and frauds of lesser consequences could not be disclosed to third persons by the lawyer under the suggested standards. If the lawyer was uninvolved in completed crimes or frauds, they could not be disclosed either.

A lawyer representing a corporation would be permitted to disclose prospective misconduct to those outside the corporation only in very limited circumstances. It has been suggested that this is an inconsistent exception to such proposed ethical rules, given the great potential for harm if a corporation markets unsafe products, dumps hazardous wastes, or engages in bribery, for example. However, an attorney for an individual or corporate client would not be obliged, or even permitted, to make such disclosures if the misconduct is prevented by the lawyer's advice. The internal corporate hierarchy may indeed give a corporation's lawyer more opportunities to prevent unlawful conduct without the need for disclosure to outsiders.

It is argued that these proposed changes could discourage open communication between lawyer and client by destroying their relationship of trust. If so, this could hinder a lawyer's ability to counsel against unlawful conduct. On the other hand, the proposed changes do recognize that a lawyer cannot be morally blind. The lawyer has obligations to the courts and legal system as well as to the client. The integrity of the lawyer and the adversary process are important values to protect.

REVIEW QUESTIONS

1 An attorney filed a $10 million class action suit against the National Football League for allowing a players' strike. The league moved to dismiss the suit. What was the result? Why?

2 A tort action was filed in the state court of Illinois by an Illinois limited partnership. The general partner was a citizen of Illinois, and the limited partners were citizens of Illinois and a Delaware corporation. The defendant was a Delaware corporation. The defendant requests that the case be removed from the Illinois court to a federal district court. Should it be? Explain.

3 For diversity of citizenship purposes, a corporation is a citizen of two states. Identify them. What is the jurisdictional amount in the federal courts in diversity of citizenship cases?

4 Vince agreed to sell his house to Pat, but he later changed his mind. Pat sued Vince for specific performance. Vince demanded a jury trial. Is he entitled to it? Explain.

5 Henry, a resident of Nevada, sued Adam, a resident of Oregon, in a state court in California. He sought $20,000 damages for personal injuries arising out of an automobile accident which occurred in Los Angeles while both parties were attending the 1984 Olympics.

    a Can Adam have the case transferred to the federal court system? Why, or why not?

    b What rules of procedure will the California court use? Why?

    c If the case is transferred to the federal court, what rules of procedure will the court use? Why?

    d If the case is tried in the state court of California, what rules of substantive law will the court use? Why?

    e If the case is tried in the federal district court, what rules of substantive law will the court use? Why?

6 Susan sues Alice in a state court, seeking damages for personal injuries. The trial court finds for Alice. Susan announces that she will appeal "all the way to the Supreme Court of the United States if necessary" to change the decision. Assuming that Susan has the money to do so, will she be able to obtain review by the Supreme Court of the United States? Explain.

7 The trial courts of different states are given different names. List three names used to describe trial courts, and indicate which is used in your state.

8 Explain the function of a petition for a writ of certiorari or a petition for leave to appeal.

9 Joe College deposited $300 with his landlord to secure his lease and to pay for any damages to the apartment which he had rented. At the end of the school year he vacated the apartment and requested the return of his deposit. Although the landlord admitted that the apartment was in good shape, the landlord refused to return the deposit. What should Joe College do? Explain.

10 Paula, a citizen of Georgia, was crossing a street in New Orleans when she was struck by a car driven by David, a citizen of Texas. The car was owned by David's employer, a Delaware corporation, which has its principal place of business in Atlanta, Georgia. Paula sues both David and the corporation in the federal district court in New Orleans. Paula's complaint alleges damages in the amount of $100,000. Does this court have jurisdiction? Why, or why not?

11 Describe four proposed changes in the

judicial system which are designed to reduce the amount of time between the filing of a lawsuit and its final decision.

12 Plaintiff, a Pennsylvania citizen and resident, filed suit for personal injuries sustained by the alleged negligence of defendant, Chemical Leaman Tank Lines, Inc., a Delaware corporation. After the state statute of limitations had run, the defendant filed a motion to dismiss, claiming that its principal place of business is in Pennsylvania. The plaintiff admitted that Pennsylvania was the principal place of business and argued that a gross unfairness will result if the case is dismissed. Plaintiff noted that the defendant answered the complaint and engaged in discovery prior to filing its motion. Should the case be dismissed? Why, or why not?

13 Walker, a resident of Oklahoma, was injured on August 22, 1975, in Oklahoma City, Oklahoma, while pounding a sheffield nail into a cement wall. Defendant, a nonresident of Oklahoma, was the manufacturer of the nail. Walker claimed that the nail contained a defect which caused its head to shatter and strike him in the right eye, resulting in permanent injuries.

The complaint was filed on August 19, 1977. Although a summons was issued that same day, service of process was not made until December 1, 1977. Defendant contended that the action was barred by the Oklahoma two-year statute of limitations. Oklahoma does not deem an action "commenced" until service of the summons on the defendant. However, if the complaint is filed within the limitations period, the action is not barred if the defendant is served within sixty days. Plaintiff admitted that his case would be foreclosed in state court, but he argued that under Rule 3 of the Federal Rules of Civil Procedure, the filing of the complaint tolled the statute of limitations.

Does the federal rule or the state rule apply? Explain.

14 Adam and Eve were not married. By contract they had agreed to live together and to divide all property evenly on death of either party or separation. They separated and began to live in separate states. Adam sued Eve in federal court to collect all of the proceeds of the sale of their apartment. Eve moved to dismiss, alleging it was a domestic relations suit and thus an exception to diversity jurisdiction. What was the result? Why?

15 Give five examples of cases that would be filed in a court of chancery in those states which have not abolished the distinction between law and equity.

Chapter
4

Litigation and Other Methods for Resolving Disputes

1. Introduction

The law as a means to an ordered and civilized society seeks to avoid controversy and disputes. It also provides techniques for resolving them when they arise. While a judicial decision ending litigation among parties to a controversy is the most obvious legal technique for resolving disputes, other methods exist which have their basis in law. These legal methods have replaced naked force as a solution to controversy.

Although statistics are not kept which would prove the point, it is generally accepted that most disputes in our society are resolved by mutual agreement without resort to litigation. In addition, more than 90 percent of all lawsuits filed are settled by the parties and their attorneys without a court decision.

The law plays a major role in encouraging such settlements. It is the framework within which the parties evaluate their positions and contains many procedures designed to encourage settlement. The high cost of litigation, both financially and in time, is a major force in many settlements. Since both parties are usually required to pay their own attorneys (the losing party usually pays court costs only), financial considerations weigh heavily even for wealthy parties and large corporations. The high cost of litigation often results in payments to plaintiffs with very weak cases because such cases have nuisance value. The amount of the nuisance value is often the cost of a successful defense.

The law also contains other procedures and techniques for settling disputes without formal litigation. Many of these techniques are included within the body of law known as administrative law. As a practical matter, more problems and controversies are submitted to administrative agencies for decision than are submitted to courts. Several later chapters deal with the role of administrative agencies. Other procedures such as mediation and arbitration are used to encourage settlement and to decide disputes. These will be briefly discussed in this chapter.

2. Parties to Litigation

In a criminal case the people of the state or the people of the United States, depending on whether or not the alleged crime is a state offense or a federal offense, bring action against the named defendant. Whereas most civil cases use the term *plaintiff* to describe the party bringing the lawsuit, and the term *defendant* to describe the party against whom it is brought, there are some cases, especially in courts of equity, in which the parties are described as the *petitioner* and the *respondent*. When a counterclaim is filed, most jurisdictions use the term *counter-plaintiff* and *counter-defendant* to describe the parties to the counterclaim. Thus, the plaintiff also becomes a counter-defendant and the defendant also becomes a counter-plaintiff when a counterclaim is filed.

When the result at the trial court level is appealed, the party appealing is usually referred to as *appellant*, and the successful party in the trial court is called the *appellee*. Many jurisdictions, in publishing decisions of reviewing courts, list the appellant first and the appellee second, even though the appellant may have been the defendant in the trial court. As a result, the names used in a case are somewhat misleading. Since the party first named is not always the plaintiff, in studying cases in this text it should be recognized that the first-named party in the case title may be the defendant-appellant.

In most state jurisdictions and in federal courts, the law allows all persons to join in one lawsuit as plaintiffs if the causes of action arise out of the same transaction or series of transactions and involve common questions of law or fact. In addition, plaintiffs may join as defendants all persons who are necessary to a complete determination or settlement of the questions involved. It is not necessary that each defendant be interested in every claim. In addition, if a defendant alleges that there cannot be a complete determination of a controversy without the presence of other parties, such a defendant may bring in new third parties as third-party defendants. This procedure is usually followed when there is someone who may have liability to a defendant if the defendant has liability to the plaintiff.

There are two problem areas or issues relating to the parties to a lawsuit which frequently arise in litigation. The first of these issues is generally described as "standing to sue," which is discussed in the next section. The second problem area relating to the parties is class action suits. These suits, which involve one or more individuals suing on behalf of all who may have the same grounds for suit, are discussed more fully in section 4.

3. Standing to Sue

The question in **standing to sue** is whether a litigant is entitled to have the court decide the dispute. This issue has two aspects: (1) Does the court have jurisdiction, and (2) if the answer is yes, should the court in the exercise of its discretion assume jurisdiction? Both questions recognize the limited role of courts in our society.

The Constitution requires that a plaintiff must allege a case or controversy between himself or herself and the defendant if the court is to have jurisdiction. The "standing" question is whether the plaintiff has alleged such a personal stake in the outcome of the controversy to warrant his or her invocation of the court's jurisdiction and to justify its exercise in his or her behalf.

Standing requires an allegation of a present or immediate injury in fact; the party requesting standing must allege such a personal stake in the outcome of the controversy as to assure concrete adverseness, which sharpens the presentation of issues. There must be some causal connection between the asserted injury and the challenged action, and the injury must be of the type likely to be redressed by a favorable decision.

Additional limitations on standing may exist even though the foregoing requirements are met, because the judiciary seeks to avoid deciding questions of broad social import where no individual rights would be vindicated; it also seeks to limit access to the federal courts to those litigants best suited to assert a particular claim. One of these limits on standing is that a litigant must normally assert her or his own legal interests rather than those of third parties. Without the requirement of standing, courts would be called upon to decide abstract questions of wide public significance. Such questions are best resolved by the political process.

When the asserted harm is a generalized grievance shared in substantially equal measure by all or a large class of citizens, that harm alone normally does not warrant the exercise of jurisdiction by a court. For example, individual radio listeners do not have standing to obtain review of a decision canceling a radio station's license. Likewise, a plaintiff must assert her or his own legal rights and not those of a third party. For example, a citizen objected to surveillance of civilians by the Army. The case was dismissed without a showing that the plaintiff was one of the civilians under surveillance.

Standing to sue is often an issue in cases brought by organizations on behalf of their members. An association may have standing to assert claims for its members even if it suffers no injury. Representational standing requires that: (1) the association have members with standing to sue in their own right; (2) the interest the association seeks to protect must be fundamental to the organization's purpose; and (3) the claim asserted and the relief requested must not require individual participation in the litigation. This last requirement was used to prevent a college-student organization from challenging the constitutionality of the Selective Service Act provision making students who failed to register for the draft ineligible for federal financial assistance. The court held that there was no organizational standing because individual participation is required. It held that it is in the financial interests of many students to defend the constitutionality of the statute and their individual participation is required.

Standing to sue does not depend upon the merits of the plaintiff's contention that particular conduct is illegal. The presence of standing is determined by the nature and source of the plaintiff's claim. The basic question in such a case is whether the constitutional or statutory provision on which the claim rests can be understood as granting the plaintiff a right to judicial relief. Congress may grant an express right of action to persons who otherwise would lack standing if the plaintiff has sustained a personal injury, even if the injury is shared by a large class.

As a general rule, "standing" requires that a complaining party have a very personal stake in the outcome of the controversy to ensure adversity in the proceedings; that will result in all aspects of the issues being presented for decision. A complainant must present facts showing that his or her individual needs require the remedy being sought. A plaintiff must show that he or she has sustaind or is immediately in danger of sustaining a direct injury as a result of a governmental action involved in the lawsuit. In civil rights cases and in cases involving environmental threats, the courts have been rather liberal in finding a personal stake in a plaintiff bringing an action. In such cases, standing to sue still requires a specific injury in fact to the plaintiff.

HAVENS REALTY CORP. v. COLEMAN
102 S. Ct. 1114 (1982)

The Fair Housing Act of 1968 outlaws discrimination in housing and Section 812 authorizes civil suits to enforce the law. Suit was filed against the defendant operator of two apartment complexes alleging "racial steering" in violation of the law. The suit was filed by a black tester (Coleman) and a white tester (Willis). The black plaintiff was told that no apartments were available but the white tester was told that there were vacancies. The District Court held that the plaintiffs lacked standing and dismissed the suit. The Court of Appeals reversed.

BRENNAN, J.: . . . Our inquiry with respect to the standing issues raised in this case is guided by our decision in *Gladstone Realtors v. Village of Bellwood,* 441 U.S. 91 (1979). There we considered whether six individuals and the Village of Bellwood had standing to sue under the Fair Housing Act, to redress injuries allegedly caused by the racial steering practices of two real estate brokerage firms. Based on the complaints, we concluded that the Village and four of the individual plaintiffs did have standing to sue under the Fair Housing Act. In reaching that conclusion, we held that . . . the sole requirement for standing to sue under § 812 is the Article III minima of injury-in-fact: that the plaintiff alleges that as a result of the defendant's actions he had suffered "a distinct and palpable injury." With this understanding, we proceed to determine whether each of the respondents in the present case has the requisite standing.

The Court of Appeals held that Coleman and Willis have standing to sue . . . as "testers."

In the present context, "testers" are individuals who, without an intent to rent or purchase a home or apartment pose as renters or purchasers for the purpose of collecting evidence of unlawful steering practices. Section 804(d) states that it is unlawful for an individual or firm covered by the Act "[t]o represent to *any person* because of race, color, religion, sex, or national origin that any dwelling is not available for inspection, sale, or rental when such dwelling is in fact so available," a prohibition made enforceable through the creation of an explicit cause of action in § 812(a) of the Act. Congress has thus conferred on all "persons" a legal right to truthful information about available housing.

This congressional intention cannot be overlooked in determining whether testers have standing to sue. As we have previously recognized, "[t]he actual or threatened injury required by Art. III may exist solely by virtue of 'statutes creating legal rights, the invasion

of which creates standing. . . .'" Section 804(d), which, in terms, establishes an enforceable right to truthful information concerning the availability of housing, is such an enactment. A tester who has been the object of a misrepresentation made unlawful under § 804(d) has suffered injury in precisely the form the statute was intended to guard against, and therefore has standing to maintain a claim for damages under the Act's provisions. That the tester may have approached the real estate agent fully expecting that he would receive false information, and without any intention of buying or renting a home, does not negate the simple fact of injury within the meaning of § 804(d). . . .

In the instant case, respondent Coleman—the black tester—alleged injury to her statutorily created right to truthful housing information. As part of the complaint, she averred that petitioners told her on four different occasions that apartments were not available in the Henrico County complexes while informing white testers that apartments were available. If the facts are as alleged, then respondent has suffered "specific injury" from the challenged acts of petitioners and the Article III requirement of injury-in-fact is satisfied.

Respondent Willis' situation is different. He made no allegation that petitioners misrepresented to him that apartments were unavailable in the two apartment complexes. To the contrary, Willis alleged that on each occasion that he inquired he was informed that apartments were available. As such, Willis has alleged no injury to his statutory right to accurate information concerning the availability of housing. We thus discern no support for the Court of Appeals' holding that Willis has standing to sue in his capacity as a tester. More to the point, because Willis does not allege that he was a victim of a discriminatory misrepresentation, he has not pleaded a cause of action under § 804(d). We must therefore reverse the Court of Appeals' judgment insofar as it reversed the District Court's dismissal of Willis' "tester" claims. [*So ordered.*]

---

4. Class Action Suits

A **class action suit** is one in which a person files suit on his or her own behalf and on behalf of all other persons who may have a similar claim. For example, all sellers of real estate through a broker were certified as a class in an antitrust suit against Atlanta, Georgia, realtors. All persons suing a drug company, alleging injuries from a product, also were considered a class in that case. Class action suits may also be filed on behalf of all shareholders of a named corporation. The number of people comprising a class is frequently quite large. Class action suits are popular because they often involve matters in which no one member of the class would have a sufficient financial interest to warrant litigation. However, the combined interest of all members of the class not only makes litigation feasible, it quite often makes it very profitable for the lawyer who brings the suit. In addition, such litigation avoids a multiplicity of suits involving the same issue, especially when the issues are complex and the cost of preparation and defense is very substantial. Many of the cases involve millions of dollars. In one recent case, the recovery was $310 million and the attorney's fees were $25 million.

Class action suits are often considered a form of harassment by many defendants. It has been alleged that some lawyers have on occasion sought out a member of a class and encouraged him or her to file suit. Courts cannot prevent lawyers for a class from contacting members of the class even though this increases the danger of abuse.

At the federal level, the Supreme Court has tended to discourage class action suits. First, federal cases require that all members of the class be given actual notice of the pendency of the lawsuit—individual notice and not merely public notice. This notice must be given to all members of the class whose names and addresses can be found through reasonable efforts. In addition, those plaintiffs seeking to bring the class action suit must pay all court costs of the action, including the cost of compiling the names and addresses of those in the class. If the trial court denies the plaintiff a right to represent the class, that decision cannot be appealed until a final decision in the lawsuit itself. Denial of class action status making it impractical to continue the litigation does not give grounds for an immediate appeal of the denial.

If a class action suit is in federal court because of diversity of citizenship, the claim of each member of the class must meet the jurisdictional amount of

$10,000. This requirement, together with the requirement of notice to each member of the class, has greatly reduced the number of class action suits in federal courts. However, the practice of consumers' and plaintiffs' lawyers of combining a single grievance into a lawsuit on behalf of every possible litigant is quite common in state courts. There are numerous state class action statutes which allow consumers and others to file suit in state courts on behalf of all citizens of that state. For some claims suitable to class action, there may be as many as fifty class action suits at once. Although the Supreme Court has attempted to reduce class action cases, it is apparent that public companies are still subject to this type of claim.

The notice in class action suits typically includes a form for persons to sign indicating that they desire to be a part of the class. However, some state procedures are "opt-out" rather than "opt-in." In these states, a person is a member of the class unless affirmative action is taken to be excluded. Either procedure satisfies due process, as the case which follows illustrates.

PHILLIPS PETROLEUM CO. v. SHUTTS
105 S. Ct. 2965 (1985)

During the 1970s, Phillips Petroleum Co., petitioner, produced or purchased natural gas from leased land located in eleven states. Respondents, royalty owners possessing rights to leases from which petitioner produced the gas, brought a class action suit against petitioner in a Kansas state court, seeking to recover interest on royalty payments that had been delayed by petitioner. The trial court certified a class consisting of 33,000 royalty owners. Respondents provided each class member with a notice by first-class mail describing the action and informing each member that he or she could appear in person or by counsel, that otherwise they would be represented by respondents, and that class members would be included in the class and bound by the judgment unless they "opted out" of the action by returning a "request for exclusion." The final class consisted of some 28,000 members, who reside in all fifty states,

the District of Columbia, and several foreign countries. The average claim of each member of the class was $100.

Petitioner asserted that the Kansas trial court did not possess personal jurisdiction over absent plaintiff class members as required by *International Shoe Co. v. Washington*, 326 U.S. 310, (1945), and similar cases. Related to this first claim was petitioner's contention that the "opt-out" notice to absent class members, which forced them to return the request for exclusion in order to avoid the suit, was insufficient to bind class members who were not residents of Kansas or who did not possess "minimum contacts" with Kansas.

The Supreme Court of Kansas held that the absent class members were plaintiffs, not defendants, and thus the traditional minimum contacts test of *International Shoe* did not apply. The court held that nonresident class action plaintiffs were only entitled to adequate notice, an opportunity to be heard, an opportunity to opt out of the case, and adequate representation by the named plaintiffs.

REHNQUIST, J.: . . . Reduced to its essentials, petitioner's argument is that unless out-of-state plaintiffs affirmatively consent, the Kansas courts may not exert jurisdiction over their claims. Petitioner claims that failure to execute and return the "request for exclusion" provided with the class notice cannot constitute consent of the out-of-state plaintiffs; thus Kansas courts may exercise jurisdiction over these plaintiffs only if the plaintiffs possess the sufficient "minimum contacts" with Kansas as that term is used in cases involving personal jurisdiction over out-of-state defendants. Since Kansas had no prelitigation contact with many of the plaintiffs and leases involved, petitioner claims that Kansas has exceeded its jurisdictional reach and thereby violated the due process rights of the absent plaintiffs.

In *International Shoe* we were faced with an out-of-state corporation which sought to avoid the exercise of personal jurisdiction over it as a defendant by Washington state court. We held that . . . the Due Process Clause did not permit a State to make a binding judgment against a person with whom the State had no contacts, ties, or relations. If the defendant possessed certain minimum contacts with the State, so that it was "reasonable and just, according to our traditional conception of fair play and substantial justice" for a State to exercise personal jurisdiction, the State could force the defendant to defend himself in the forum, upon pain of default, and could bind him to a judgment. . . . [P]etitioner claims that the same analysis must apply to absent class-action plaintiffs. . . .

We think petitioner's premise is in error. The burdens placed by a State upon an absent class-action plaintiff are not of the same

order or magnitude as those it places upon an absent defendant. An out-of-state defendant summoned by a plaintiff is faced with the full powers of the forum State to render judgment *against* it. The defendant must generally hire counsel and travel to the forum to defend itself from the plaintiff's claim, or suffer a default judgment. The defendant may be forced to participate in extended and often costly discovery, and will be forced to respond in damages or to comply with some other form of remedy imposed by the court should it lose the suit. The defendant may also face liability for court costs and attorney's fees. These burdens are substantial and the minimum contacts requirement of the Due Process Clause prevents the forum State from unfairly imposing them upon the defendant.

A class-action plaintiff, however, is in quite a different posture. . . . The class action was an invention of equity to enable it to proceed to a decree in suits where the number of those interested in the litigation was too great to permit joinder. The absent parties would be bound by the decree so long as the named parties adequately represented the absent class and the prosecution of the litigation was within the common interest.

Modern plaintiff class actions follow the same goals, permitting litigation of a suit involving common questions when there are too many plaintiffs for proper joinder. Class actions also may permit the plaintiffs to pool claims which would be uneconomical to litigate individually. For example, this lawsuit involves claims averaging about $100 per plaintiff; most of the plaintiffs would have no realistic day in court if a class action were not available.

In sharp contrast to the predicament of a defendant haled into an out-of-state forum, the plaintiffs in this suit were not haled anywhere to defend themselves upon pain of a default judgment. . . . Unlike a defendant in a civil suit, a class-action plaintiff is not required to fend for himself. The court and named plaintiffs protect his interests. . . .

Besides this continuing solicitude for their rights, absent plaintiff class members are not subject to other burdens imposed upon defendants. They need not hire counsel or appear. They are almost never subject to counterclaims or cross-claims, or liability for fees or costs. Absent plaintiff class members are not subject to coercive or punitive remedies. Nor will an adverse judgment typically bind an absent plaintiff for any damages, although a valid adverse judgment may extinguish any of the plaintiff's claim which was litigated.

Unlike a defendant in a normal civil suit, an absent class-action plaintiff is not required to do anything. He may sit back and allow the litigation to run its course, content in knowing that there are safeguards provided for his protection.

Petitioner contends, however, that the "opt out" procedure provided by Kansas is not good enough, and that an "opt in" procedure is required to satisfy the Due Process Clause of the Fourteenth Amendment. Insofar as plaintiffs who have no minimum contacts with the forum State are concerned, an "opt in" provision would require that each class member affirmatively consent to his inclusion within the class.

. . . In this case we hold that a forum State may exercise jurisdiction over the claim of an absent class-action plaintiff, even though that plaintiff may not possess the minimum contacts with the forum which would support personal jurisdiction over a defendant. . . . The plaintiff must receive notice. . . . The notice should describe the action and the plaintiff's rights in it. Additionally, we hold that due process requires at a minimum that an absent plaintiff be provided with an opportunity to remove himself from the class by executing and returning an "opt out" or "request for exclusion" form to the court. . . .

We reject petitioner's contention that the Due Process Clause of the Fourteenth Amendment requires that absent plaintiffs affirmatively "opt in" to the class, rather than be deemed members of the class if they do not "opt out." . . .

We therefore hold that the protection afforded the plaintiff class members by the Kansas statute satisfies the Due Process Clause. . . .

We conclude that the Kansas court properly asserted personal jurisdiction over the absent plaintiffs and their claims against petitioner. . . . [*Affirmed*]

5. Jurisdiction of Courts

Jurisdiction refers to the power of a court to hear a case. To have the power to hear a case, the court must have jurisdiction over the subject matter of the case and the parties to the case. Jurisdiction over the subject matter exists if the case is of the type which the court is authorized to hear. This is not a problem with state courts of general jurisdiction. It may be in cases before the inferior state courts and can be an issue in all federal cases, because, as previously noted, all federal courts are courts of limited jurisdiction. For example, a federal court would not have jurisdiction over a breach of contract suit for $5,000 damages between citizens of different states because it doesn't meet the jurisdictional amount. If the amount were $15,000 and the parties were citizens of the same state, the federal court would still have no power to hear the case because of lack of diversity of citizenship. Similarly, a state probate court would lack the power to hear a murder case.

Jurisdiction over the plaintiff is obtained by plaintiff's filing the suit. Such action indicates voluntary submission to the power of the court. Jurisdiction over the defendant is usually obtained by the service of a **summons**, or notice to appear in court, although in some cases it is obtained by the publication of notice and mailing a summons to the last known address. Service of summons on the defendant usually is valid if it is served upon any member of the household above a specified age, and if another copy addressed to the defendant is mailed to the home. This procedure recognizes the practical difficulties which may exist in finding the defendant, and at the same time accomplishes the goal of the summons, which is simply to give the defendant fair notice of the suit.

For many years, it was felt that a summons could not be properly served beyond the borders of the state in which it was issued. However, this concept has changed, and most states now have **long-arm statutes** which provide for the service of process beyond their boundaries. Such statutes are valid and constitutional if they provide a defendant with due process of law. Due process requires only that if a defendant is not present within the forum state, he or she must have certain minimum contacts with it so that maintenance of the suit does not offend "traditional notions of fair play and substantial justice."

The typical long-arm statute allows a court to obtain jurisdiction over a defendant even though the process is served beyond its borders if the defendant has (1) committed a tort within the state; (2) owns property within the state, which property is the subject matter of the lawsuit; or (3) entered into a contract within the state or transacted the business which is the subject matter of the lawsuit within the state.

Long-arm statutes do not authorize extraterritorial service of process in all cases. It is only where requiring a defendant to appear and defend does not violate due process that jurisdiction is obtained under long-arm statutes. The case which follows illustrates the extent of constitutional limitations on modern long-arm statutes which allow extraterritorial service of process to obtain jurisdiction.

WORLD-WIDE VOLKSWAGEN CORP. v. WOODSON
100 S. Ct. 559 (1980)

Plaintiff-respondent filed a product liability suit in a state court of Oklahoma to recover for personal injuries sustained in an automobile accident. The automobile had been purchased from the defendants in the state of New York. The defendants were a New York corporation that did no business in Oklahoma. They were served under the Oklahoma long-arm statute and they objected to the Court's jurisdiction.

WHITE, J.: . . . The issue before us is whether, consistently with the Due Process Clause of the Fourteenth Amendment, an Oklahoma court may exercise in personam jurisdiction over a nonresident automobile retailer and its wholesale distributor in a products liability action, when the defendants' only connection with Oklahoma is the fact that an automobile sold in New York to New York residents became involved in an accident in Oklahoma. . . .

As has long been settled, and as we reaffirm today, a state court may exercise personal jurisdiction over a nonresident defendant only so long as there exist "minimum contacts" between the defendant and the forum State. The concept of minimum contacts, in turn, can be seen to perform two related, but distinguishable, functions. It protects the defendant against the burdens of litigating in a distant or inconvenient forum. And it acts to ensure that the States through their courts, do not reach out beyond the limits imposed on them by their status as coequal sovereigns in a federal system.

The protection against inconvenient litigation is typically described in terms of "reasonableness" or "fairness." We have said that the defendant's contacts with the forum State must be such that maintenance of the suit "does not offend 'traditional notions of fair play and substantial justice.'" The relationship between the defendant and the forum must be such that it is reasonable . . . to require the corporation to defend the particular suit which is brought there. Implicit in this emphasis on reasonableness is the understanding that the burden on the defendant, while always a primary concern, will in an appropriate case be considered in light of other relevant factors, including the forum State's interest in adjudicating the dispute, the plaintiff's interest in obtaining convenient and effective relief, . . . the interstate judicial system's interest in obtaining the most efficient resolution of controversies; and the shared interest of the several States in furthering fundamental substantive social policies.

The limits imposed on state jurisdiction by the Due Process Clause, in its role as a guarantor against inconvenient litigation, have been substantially relaxed over the years. . . .

Nevertheless, we have never accepted the proposition that state lines are irrelevant for jurisdictional purposes, nor could we and remain faithful to the principles of interstate federalism embodied in the Constitution. . . .

Hence, even while abandoning the shibboleth that "[t]he authority of every tribunal is necessarily restricted by the territorial limits of the State in which it is established," we emphasized that the reasonableness of asserting jurisdiction over the defendant must be assessed "in the context of our federal system of government," and stressed that the Due Process Clause ensures, not only fairness, but also the "orderly administration of the laws."

Thus, the Due Process Clause "does not contemplate that a state may make binding a judgment in personam against an individual or corporate defendant with which the state has no contacts, ties, or relations." Even if the defendant would suffer minimal or no inconvenience from being forced to litigate before the tribunals of another State; even if the forum State has a strong interest in applying its law to the controversy; even if the forum State is the most convenient location for litigation, the Due Process Clause, acting as an instrument of interstate federalism, may sometimes act to divest the State of its power to render a valid judgment.

Applying these principles to the case at hand, we find in the record before us a total absence of those affiliating circumstances that are a necessary predicate to any exercise of state-court jurisdiction. Petitioners carry on no activity whatsoever in Oklahoma. They close no sales and perform no services there. They avail themselves of none of the privileges and benefits of Oklahoma law. They solicit no business there either through salespersons or through advertising reasonably calculated to reach the State. Nor does the record show that they regularly sell cars at wholesale or retail to Oklahoma customers or residents or that they indirectly, through others, serve or seek to serve the Oklahoma market. In short, respondents seek to base jurisdiction on one, isolated occurrence and whatever inferences can be drawn therefrom: the fortuitous circumstance that a single Audi automobile, sold in New York to New York residents, happened to suffer an accident while passing through Oklahoma.

It is argued, however, that because an automobile is mobile by its very design and purpose it was "foreseeable" that the Robinsons' Audi would cause injury in Oklahoma. Yet "foreseeability" alone has never been a sufficient benchmark for personal jurisdiction under the Due Process Clause. . . .

If foreseeability were the criterion, . . . every seller of chattels would in effect appoint the chattel his agent for service of process. His amenability to suit would travel with the chattel. . . . This is not to say, of course, that foreseeability is wholly irrelevant. But the foreseeability that is critical to due process analysis is not the mere likelihood that a product will find its way into the forum State. Rather, it is that the defendant's conduct and connection with the forum State are such that he should reasonably anticipate being haled into court there. The Due Process Clause, by ensuring the "orderly administration of the laws," gives a degree of predictability to the legal system that allows potential defendants to structure their primary conduct with some minimum assurance as to where that conduct will and will not render them liable to suit.

When a corporation "purposefully avails itself of the privilege of conducting activities within the forum State," it has clear notice that it is subject to suit there, and can act to alleviate the risk of burdensome litigation by procuring insurance, passing the expected costs on to customers, or, if the risks are too great, severing its connection with the State. Hence if the sale of a product of a manufacturer or distributor such as Audi or Volkswagen is not simply an isolated occurrence, but arises from the efforts of the manufacturer or distributor to serve directly or indirectly, the market for its product in other States, it is not unreasonable to subject it to suit in one of those States if its allegedly defective merchandise has there been the source of injury to its owner or to others. The forum State does not exceed its powers under the Due Process Clause if it asserts personal jurisdiction over a corporation that delivers its products into the stream of commerce with the expectation that they will be purchased by consumers in the forum State.

But there is no such or similar basis for Oklahoma jurisdiction over World-Wide or Seaway in this case. . . . [*Because we find that petitioners have no "contacts, ties, or relations" with the State of Oklahoma, the judgment of the Supreme Court of Oklahoma is Reversed.*]

Occasionally, process may be served upon a defendant who has no minimum contacts with the state in which a court sits. For example, a bankruptcy court may order process served nationwide. It may be required to do so in order to settle the affairs of a bankrupt corporation such as Braniff Airlines. All citizens of the United States have sufficient contact to justify this jurisdiction by United States courts.

It was previously noted that jurisdiction may sometimes be obtained by publication of notice of the suit in a general circulation newspaper and by mailing a copy of the summons to the defendant. This method is often used in cases involving title to real estate and in divorce actions. Such cases proceed **in rem** (against the thing) rather than **in personam** (against the person). The judgments or decrees in such cases affect the property involved or the status (marriage) but do not operate against the defendant individually. Marital status or title to property may be changed, but no personal liability results. Service by publication must also meet due process standards. For example, a Kentucky law which authorized posting of a notice of eviction of a tenant on the premises rather than by mail was held to be a denial of due process. Notice by publication must be reasonably calculated to ensure that the defendant learns of the suit.

The foregoing discussion of jurisdiction related to civil suits. In criminal suits, the crime must have been committed within the state for the court to have jurisdiction of the case. Jurisdiction of the person of the defendant is obtained by arrest. In the event of arrest in a state other than that in which the crime was committed, extradition is necessary. This is obtained by the governor of the state of arrest voluntarily turning the prisoner over to the governor of the requesting state.

6. Venue

A question similar to jurisdiction refers to the place or court in which the lawsuit should be brought, or what is the proper **venue**. Although jurisdiction determines if a court has the *power* to hear a case, venue determines whether a court *should* hear the case when any one of several courts technically might have jurisdiction. A typical venue statute specifies that suit must be brought in the county of residence of any defendant who is joined in good faith and not solely for the purpose of fixing venue in that county. Suits may also be brought in the county where the transaction or some part thereof occurred out of which the cause of action arose. Actions against nonresidents can usually be commenced in any county which has jurisdiction, with jurisdiction being obtained under a long-arm statute. Corporations are usually considered to be residents of any county in which they have a registered office or are doing business. Corporations not authorized to do business in a state are usually treated as nonresidents. Similar rules usually exist for partnerships. They are generally considered to be residents of any county in which a partner resides, in which there is a partnership office, or in which the partnership does business. Thus, venue statutes provide, as one of two possibilities for the proper forum for a lawsuit, the place of residence of the defendant, and define where this is.

Most venue statutes have special provisions for suits involving real estate which require the suit to be brought in the county where the real estate is located. Special provisions frequently allow suits against insurance companies in the county where the plaintiff resides.

A defendant may object to the venue for several reasons. First of all, he or she may complain that the requirements of the venue statute as discussed above are not met. This will not usually be the case because, as noted, the statutes are specific and relatively clear. Venue may also be objected to because of prejudice of either the judge or, in some cases, the probable jury to be selected. The latter objection is frequently made in a criminal trial which has had substantial publicity. Motions for a change of venue based on the prejudice of the trial judge must usually be supported by affidavit but are granted as a matter of right if in proper form. Failure to object to the venue is a *waiver*, and the trial may proceed if the court where the suit was brought has jurisdiction, in spite of the provisions of the venue statute, or constitutional requirements of due process.

Another ground for a change of venue is the doctrine of **forum non conveniens**, which literally means that the place of trial is not convenient. The defendant may attempt to invoke this principle in cases in which the plaintiff has attempted to have the suit tried in a country which produces juries known for large verdicts. For example, a plane crash killed a citizen of Scotland. The crash was in Scotland. When suit was filed in the United States, the case was dismissed for being brought in the wrong venue. The plaintiff had filed in the United States expecting a larger verdict.

7. Pleadings

Most lawsuits begin by a plaintiff's filing a pleading called a "complaint" with the court clerk. (In this section, for convenience, we refer to judge, plaintiff, and defendant as if they are male; obviously, however, both sexes may be represented by these terms.) The complaint contains allegations by the plaintiff and a statement of the relief sought. The clerk issues a summons which, together with a copy of the complaint, is served on the defendant by leaving it either with him personally or with some member of his family, if the law so provides. The summons notifies the defendant of the date he is required to file his **pleading**, usually called an "answer," or his appearance in the suit. Failure to file an appearance is considered a default which may result in the court's awarding the plaintiff the relief sought. The defendant's answer will either admit or deny each allegation of the plaintiff's complaint and may contain affirmative defenses, such as payment of the obligation, which will defeat the plaintiff's claim. The answer may also contain causes of action the defendant has against the plaintiff, called "counterclaims." After receiving the defendant's answer, the plaintiff will, unless the applicable rules of procedure do not so require, file a reply which specifically admits or denies each allegation of the defendant's answer. The factual issues of a lawsuit are thus formed by one party making an allegation and the other party either admitting it or denying it. Pleadings give notice of each party's contentions and serve to set the boundary lines of the litigation.

8. Motions

Not all lawsuits involve questions of fact. In many cases the parties may be in complete agreement as to the facts, in which case the issue to be decided is the legal effect of these facts. Such cases involve only questions of law. Questions of law may be raised at several stages of the lawsuit.

First of all, the defendant may, instead of filing an answer, file a pleading which at common law was called a "general demurrer." Today we usually call this a "**motion** to dismiss for failure to state a cause of action or a claim for relief." By this pleading the defendant, in effect, says to the court: "Even if everything the plaintiff says in his complaint is true, he is not entitled to the relief he seeks." For example, in a state where mental cruelty is not a ground for divorce, a complaint seeking a divorce on such grounds would be dismissed. The litigation would end unless the plaintiff then filed an amended complaint. It would have to properly allege a ground on which a divorce might be granted.

In addition, a defendant may also move to dismiss a suit for reasons which as a matter of law prevent the plaintiff from winning his suit. Such matters as a discharge in bankruptcy, lack of jurisdiction of the court to hear the suit, or expiration of the time limit during which the defendant is subject to suit may be raised by such a motion. This latter ground is usually referred to as the "statute of limitations." Each state has proscribed a time limit after which you cannot file suit. For example, suits for breach of a contract for the sale of goods must be filed within four years of the breach. These are matters of a technical nature which raise questions of law for the court's decision.

Most states and the federal courts will allow either party to submit a case for final decision through procedures known as "motions for **summary judgment**" or "motions for judgment on the pleadings." In such hearings, the court examines all papers on file in the case, including affidavits that may have been filed with the motion or in opposition to it, to see if a genuine material issue of fact remains. If there is no such question of fact, the court will then decide the legal question raised by the facts and find for one party or the other.

Remember that the above discussion refers to matters occurring prior to any trial of the case. As the trial itself proceeds, questions of fact raised by the pleadings may be resolved, leaving only questions of law. If the case is being tried by a jury, a party moves to take the case from the jury by asking the judge to **direct a verdict**. The court can only direct a verdict for one party if the evidence taken in the light most favorable to the other party establishes as a matter of law that the party moving is entitled to a verdict. Either party may make such a motion, although it is usually used by defendants to argue that the plaintiff has failed to prove each allegation of his complaint. Just as a plaintiff must *allege* certain facts or have the complaint dismissed by motion to dismiss, he must have some *proof* of each essential allegation or lose the case on a motion for a directed verdict, as the following case illustrates.

MAY v. HALL COUNTY LIVESTOCK IMP. ASS'N
344 N.W.2d 629 (Neb. 1984)

CAMBRIDGE, J.: This is an appeal in a slip and fall case. The trial court sustained the defendant's motion for a directed verdict at the close of the plaintiff's case.

The plaintiff has appealed, contending that the evidence presented by her was sufficient at law to sustain a jury verdict against the defendant for damages.

As we must, we assume the truth of the material and relevant evidence presented by the plaintiff, find every controverted fact in her favor, and give her the benefit of every reasonable inference deducible from the evidence.

On April 12, 1977, the plaintiff attended the horseraces at Fonner Park Racetrack, Grand Island, Nebraska. The defendant owned and operated the park. The plaintiff, in addition to paying the general charge for admission into the grandstand, paid for admittance into a reserved area thereof, enclosed by metal railings, where there were tables and chairs from which the races could be observed. The area had a cement floor. Food, soft drinks, and beer, purchased either at concession stands located in the area or from waitresses who served the tables, were consumed in the area. The plaintiff sat at one of those tables, and on various trips from and to the table she saw "slippery places" and liquid on the cement in the areas around her table but not near her table; she never looked under her own table before the accident to see if there was any liquid under the table or

around her chair. The plaintiff stood up most, if not all, of the sixth race, and when she saw that the horse she had bet was going to win, she started to take steps to go, and her left foot slipped; she tried to break her fall by catching the leg of the table with her right foot, but did not succeed. After regaining consciousness the plaintiff recalled that the bottom or lower part of her right pantleg was wet. According to the food concession manager, who arrived on the scene while the plaintiff was still lying on the floor and who remained there until the plaintiff had left, there were no spills, liquids, or debris of any kind on the floor where the plaintiff had fallen, and the floor was dry; and when spills did occur, there was a procedure for cleaning them up. As a result of the fall, the plaintiff sustained head injuries and a broken right hip with complications in the healing of that fracture.

The defendant was not an insurer of the safety of business invitees on its premises. It is well-established law in this state that a possessor of premises is under a duty to use reasonable care to make his premises safe for a business visitor or to give him adequate warning to enable him to avoid harm when certain conditions are true. . . .

The plaintiff contends in her brief to this court that something wet on the floor caused her to slip and fall, but the bill of exceptions in this case simply does not support that claim. It is apparent from the foregoing recital of facts that the plaintiff failed to produce any evidence which could have reasonably satisfied the jury that the physical harm suffered by the plaintiff was caused by a condition or activity on the defendant's premises. Giving full weight to all of the plaintiff's evidence and all inferences reasonably deducible therefrom, it can be concluded that such conditions and activities did in fact exist on the defendant's premises at the time in question, but there is literally no evidence in the record establishing that any one of them was the proximate cause or a proximately contributing cause of the plaintiff's slip and fall and the physical harm which resulted therefrom.

Where the facts presented to sustain an issue are such that but one conclusion can be drawn when related to the applicable law, it is the duty of the court to decide the question as a matter of law and not submit it to a jury. . . .[*Affirmed.*]

In cases tried without a jury, either party may move for a finding in his favor. Such a motion will be allowed during the course of the trial if the result is not in doubt. Although judges on such motions weigh the evidence, they may end the trial only if there is no room for a fair difference of opinion as to the result.

Finally, questions of law may be raised after the trial is completed by motions seeking a new trial or a judgment, notwithstanding the verdict of the jury. A motion seeking a new trial may be granted if the judge feels that the jury's verdict is contrary to the manifest weight of the evidence. The court may enter a judgment opposite to that of the jury verdict if the judge finds that the jury verdict is, as a matter of law, erroneous. To reach such a conclusion, the court must find that reasonable persons viewing the evidence could not have reached the jury verdict returned. For example, a verdict for the plaintiff may be based on sympathy instead of evidence. Thus, the results of lawsuits may turn on procedural questions of law raised by the pleadings or evidence. These issues of law are the sole province of the court to resolve.

9. Discovery Procedures

Modern law has procedures commonly referred to as "discovery procedures." These are used when the parties are filing their pleadings and before the trial itself. These procedures are designed to take the "sporting aspect" out of litigation and ensure that the results of lawsuits are based on the merits of the controversy and not on the ability, skill, or cunning of counsel. Historically, an attorney who had no case on the facts or law could win a lawsuit through surprise by keeping silent about a fact or by concealing his or her true case until the trial. Lawsuits should not be based on the skill or lack thereof of counsel, but on the relative merits of the controversy. Discovery practice is designed to ensure that each side is fully aware of all the facts involved in the case and of the intentions of the parties, prior to trial. One of its purposes is to encourage settlement of suits, avoiding actual trial.

Discovery practices include the taking of the **deposition** of other parties and witnesses, the serving of written questions to be answered under oath by the opposite party, compulsory physical examinations by doctors chosen by the other party, orders requiring the production of exhibits, documents, maps, photographs, and so on, and the serving by one party on another of demands to admit facts under oath. (Some courts, those of Illinois for example, have even allowed the discovery of the amount of insurance coverage possessed by the defendant in a personal injury case.) These procedures allow a party to learn not only about matters that may be used as evidence, but also about matters that may lead to the discovery of evidence.

Just prior to the trial, a pretrial conference between the lawyers and the judge will be held in states with modern rules of procedure. At this conference the pleadings, results of the discovery process, and probable evidence are reviewed in an attempt to settle the suit. The issues may be further narrowed, and the judge may even predict the outcome in order to encourage settlement.

On occasion, a party may fail to comply with the discovery rules. When this occurs, a party may actually lose a case or facts sought may be considered proved.

10. Conduct of a Trial

In addition to questions of law, most lawsuits involve questions of fact. Such cases as automobile negligence actions and criminal proceedings are essentially questions of fact. Suits at law and criminal actions have traditionally been tried before a jury, while suits in equity have been considered too complicated for juries; as a general rule the questions of fact have been found by the courts. It should be noted that juries are sometimes used in chancery cases to serve as the trier of the facts.

JURY SELECTION

For purposes of examining a trial, we shall use a typical suit for dollar damages either in tort or contract being tried before a jury. As the case is called, the first order of business is to select a jury. Prior to the calling of the case, the court clerk will have summoned prospective jurors. Their names will be drawn at random from lists of eligible citizens, and the number of jurors required, usually twelve, will be selected or called into the jury box for the conduct of **voir dire** examination. Voir dire examination is simply a method by which the court and the attorneys for each party examine jurors as to their qualifications and ability to hear the case. A party to a lawsuit is entitled to fair and impartial jurors in both civil and criminal cases. Due process requires that a party be allowed to inquire into a prospective juror's biases and prejudices.

Each side in the lawsuit may challenge or excuse a prospective juror for cause. In addition, each side will be given a certain number of challenges known as **peremptory challenges** for which no cause need be given. Each side has an opportunity to examine the jurors and either to accept them or to reject them until the challenges are exhausted. Prospective jurors are sworn to give truthful answers to the questions on voir dire. The processes continue until the full jury is selected.

OPENING STATEMENTS

After selecting jurors to hear the case, the attorneys then make their opening statements. An opening statement is not evidence but is only used to familiarize the jury with the essential facts in the case which each side expects to prove. It is similar to the prologue of a book. In order that the jury may understand the overall picture of the case and the relevancy of each bit of evidence as presented, each side informs the jury of the facts she or he expects to prove and of the witnesses she or he expects to call to make such proof. After the opening statements are made, the party with the burden of proof, which is usually the plaintiff, presents his or her evidence. The term "burden of proof" is explained more fully in the next section.

INTRODUCING EVIDENCE

Evidence is normally presented in open court by examination of witnesses and production of documents and other exhibits. The person calling a witness has a right to examine that witness and ask questions to establish the facts with which the witness is familiar about the case. As a general rule, a party calling a witness is not permitted to ask "leading questions." After the party calling the witness has completed direct examination, the other party is given the opportunity to cross-examine the witness. Matters inquired into on cross-examination are limited to those matters raised on direct examination. Cross-examination is an art, and the well-prepared lawyer will usually not ask a question on cross-examination to which he or she does not already know the answer.

After the cross-examination, the party calling the witness again has the opportunity of examining the witness. This examination is called "redirect examination." It is limited to those matters gone into on cross-examination and is used to clarify matters raised on cross-examination. After redirect examination, the opposing party is allowed recross-examination, with the corresponding limitation as to the scope of the questions. Witnesses may be asked to identify exhibits. Expert witnesses may be asked to give their opinion, within certain limitations, about the case. Sometimes, experts are allowed to answer hypothetical questions. For example, a doctor in a personal injury case may be given all the evidence surrounding the accident and then be asked hypothetically whether such an occurrence might have or could have caused the injury which the plaintiff suffers.

After the party with the burden of proof has presented his or her evidence, the opposing party usually makes the motion for a directed verdict, as heretofore mentioned. If the motion for directed verdict is overruled, the defendant then presents his or her evidence. The order of examination of these witnesses is the same as those for the plaintiff. The party calling a witness vouches for his or her credibility. The party is not allowed to impeach witnesses whom he or she has called. After the defendant has presented all his or her evidence, the original party may bring in rebuttal evidence. When neither party has any additional evidence, the attorneys and the judge retire for a conference to consider the instructions to be given the jury.

JURY INSTRUCTIONS

Jury instructions serve to acquaint the jury with the law applicable to the case. As previously stated, the function of the jury is to find the facts, and the function of the court is to determine the applicable law. The purpose of jury instructions is to bring the facts and the law together in an orderly manner that will result in a decision. At the conference, each attorney submits to the court instructions which he or she feels should be given to the jury. The court examines these instructions and confers with the attorneys, then decides which instructions will be given to the jury. A typical jury instruction follows:

> The plaintiff in his complaint has alleged that he was injured as the proximate cause of the negligence of the defendant. If you find from the evidence that the defendant was guilty of negligence, which proximately caused plaintiff's injuries, then your verdict should be for the plaintiff.

In this instruction, the court is in effect saying that the plaintiff must prove that the defendant was at fault. Thus, the jury is instructed as to the result to be returned if they find certain facts.

CLOSING ARGUMENT

After the conference on jury instructions, the attorneys argue the case to the jury. The party with the burden of proof, usually the plaintiff, is given an opportunity to open the argument and to close it. The defendant's attorney is only allowed to argue after the plaintiff's argument and is only allowed to argue once. After the arguments are completed, the court reads the instructions to the jury, and the jury retires to deliberate. Upon reaching a verdict, the jury returns from the jury room and announces its verdict, and judgment is entered. Thereafter, the losing party starts the procedure of posttrial motions and appeals. Any final decision of the court, whether on a motion made before trial, during the trial, or after the trial, or on the court's judgment or decree, may be appealed within certain prescribed time limits. If the appeal is perfected according to law, the right of review is absolute.

11. The Burden of Proof

The term **burden of proof** has two distinct meanings depending on the context in which it is used. It may describe the person with the burden of coming forward with evidence on a particular issue. The party alleging the existence of a certain fact usually has the burden of coming forward with evidence to establish the fact.

The more common usage of the term is to identify the party with the *burden of persuasion*. The party with this burden must convince the trier of fact on the issue involved. If a party with the burden of persuasion fails to do so, that party loses the lawsuit.

The extent of proof required to satisfy the burden of persuasion varies, depending upon the issue and the type of case. There are three distinct levels of proof recognized by the law. For criminal cases, the burden of proof is described as "beyond a reasonable doubt." This means that the prosecution in a criminal case has the burden of convincing the trier of fact, usually a jury, that the defendant is guilty of the crime charged and that the jury has no reasonable doubt about the defendant's guilt. This burden of proof does not require evidence beyond any doubt, but only beyond a reasonable doubt. A reasonable doubt is one that a reasonable person viewing the evidence might reasonably entertain. This standard is not used in civil cases.

In civil cases the party with the burden of proof will be subject to one of two standards—the **clear and convincing proof** standard, or the **preponderance of the evidence** standard. The latter standard is used most frequently. It requires that a party convince the jury by a preponderance of evidence that the facts are as he or she contends. By preponderance of evidence we mean there is greater weight of evidence in support of the proposition than there is against it. In terms of the scales of justice, it means that they tilt more one way than the other.

The clear and convincing proof requirement is used in certain situations where the law requires more than a simple preponderance of the evidence but less than proof beyond a reasonable doubt. For example, in a securities law case, proof of fraud usually requires clear and convincing evidence if a plaintiff is to succeed. The scales of justice must tilt heavily one way. A slight preponderance of evidence in favor of the party asserting the truth of a proposition is not enough. Unless the evidence clearly establishes the proposition, the party with the burden of proof fails to sustain it and loses the lawsuit.

12. Rules of Evidence

In the conduct of a trial, the rules of evidence govern the admissibility of testimony and exhibits and establish which facts may be presented to the jury and which facts may not. The lawyer is concerned with specific rules of evidence, but an understanding of the areas in which these rules operate will give us some insight into the workings of our judicial system.

PRIVILEGED COMMUNICATIONS

One of the major rules for excluding evidence is based on what the law calls "privileged communications" or **privilege**. Nearly everyone is aware that the Fifth Amendment contains a privilege against compulsory self-incrimination. In addition, communications between an attorney and client are considered privileged by the law in order that such communications can be made without fear of their subsequent use against the client. Fair play requires that an attorney not be required to testify as to matters told in confidence by a client. Some matters are privileged, such as the existence of insurance coverage of a party, because of the great effect that knowledge of the existence of insurance would have on a jury. Matters which are privileged are matters which by the rules of fair play should not be admitted into evidence.

HEARSAY RULE

Another basic concept of our judicial system is the right of confrontation, or the right to be confronted by the witnesses against you and to cross-examine them about their allegations or contentions. Cross-examination in open court, as a fundamental right, provides the background for the rule of evidence known as the **hearsay rule**. Hearsay is an out-of-court statement which is being offered to prove the truth of the matter contained in the statement. For example, if the issue of the case was whether certain stock had been purchased, the testimony of a witness that her broker had *told* her the stock had been purchased would be hearsay. The statement is offered to prove the purchase of the stock when the *broker* is not available for cross-examination. The lack of cross-examination establishes that hearsay evidence should not be admitted. There are many exceptions to the hearsay rule. For example, if the party *herself* had made the statement, she could hardly object to the fact that she was not able to cross-examine herself, and thus we have the exception for admissions against interest by a party to the suit. Testimony at a former trial at which the party was able to cross-examine and subsequent unavailability of the witness create another exception to the hearsay rule. Business entries made in the ordinary course of business constitute still another exception. They may be introduced as evidence of the facts they represent. In a criminal case a dying declaration by the victim of murder is an exception, because the effect of impending death is considered by the courts to give sufficient credibility to the truthfulness of the testimony to eliminate the need for cross-examination. There are many other exceptions to the hearsay rule, but each of them is based on the fact that cross-examination has either been had at a former time or is not required for a fair trial in the present case.

RELEVANCY

There are other rules of evidence, such as the rule requiring that all evidence be relevant to the matter involved in the litigation. If a person is involved in a suit for breach of contract for the sale of goods, wares, or merchandise, the fact that he has been divorced five times should have no effect on the litigation and would not be admissible evidence. It might, if presented, influence some member of the jury who particularly disliked divorced persons. In cases where direct testimony as to what happened is not available, evidence of habit or practice is sometimes admitted to show what probably happened, and this is considered relevant.

DOCUMENTS

Another rule of evidence concerns the requirement of producing the best evidence available as proof in a lawsuit. The "best evidence rule," as it is commonly called, pertains only to written documents. There are many other rules of evidence concerning written documents, such as the "parol evidence rule," which prevents the proof of modification or change of a written document by the use of oral evidence.

It can be seen from this short examination of these elementary rules of evidence that they specify the rules of the game, so to speak, to ensure a fair trial and that each party has ample opportunity to present his or her contentions and case without unduly taking advantage of the other party. These rules were not created to serve as a stumbling block to meritorious litigants or to create unwarranted roadblocks to justice. On the contrary, the rules of evidence were created and should be applied to ensure fair play and to aid in the goal of having controversies determined on their merits.

FEDERAL RULES

In order to reduce the cost of litigation and to speed up the search for truth, the Supreme Court has adopted rules of evidence for civil and criminal trials in the federal courts which greatly expand the admissibility of evidence and eliminate many of the traditional technical rules of evidence. For example, (1) cross-examination of a witness is not limited to the scope of direct examination; (2) a lawyer calling a witness does not vouch for the witness's credibility, which may be attacked by any party, including the party calling the witness; (3) expert testimony requires much less groundwork in that the facts or data upon which an expert bases his or her opinion need not be admissible in evidence; (4) opinion testimony on the ultimate issue to be decided by the jury is admissible; and (5) an expanded list of exceptions may be applied to the hearsay rule. This list of hearsay exceptions includes any statement having some inherent guarantee of trustworthiness if the statement has more bearing on the point for which it is offered than the other evidence reasonably available.

These rules of evidence have reduced the expense of litigation as well sped up the trial process. In addition, more evidence is presented to juries for their factual determination. As a result of these rules, evidence is often admissible in federal cases that would not be admissible if the case were tried in state courts.

13. Appellate Procedure

The previous chapter discussed the structure of the court system, including courts of review. Each state prescribes its own appellate procedure and determines the jurisdiction of its various reviewing courts. Although the procedure followed in an appeal is essentially a problem for the lawyer, certain aspects of this procedure assist us in understanding our judicial system.

Courts of review deal with the record of the proceedings in lower court. All the pleadings, testimony, and motions are reduced to a written record, which is filed with the court of review. The court of review studies the issues, testimony, and proceedings to determine whether prejudicial errors occurred or whether the lower court reached an erroneous result. In addition to the record, each party files a **brief** (the appellant may file a reply brief on receipt of the appellee's brief) which contains a short description of the nature of the case, the factual situation, the points and authorities on which the party relies, and his or her argument for reversing or affirming the decision of the lower court, depending on whether the party is an appellant or appellee. The points and authorities contain the statutes and judicial decisions relied upon as precedent in the argument.

In addition to the brief, the reviewing court is often given the benefit of oral argument in deciding the case. The attorneys are given a specified amount of time to explain orally to the court their position in the case. This also gives the court of review an opportunity to question the attorneys about various aspects of the case.

After oral argument, an impression vote is usually taken, and the case is assigned to one justice to prepare an opinion. Each justice has a staff of clerks assisting in the preparation of opinions. The intellectual backgrounds of these clerks have some influence on the decisions. The opinion as prepared by the clerks and the justice may not follow the impression vote. After the opinion is prepared, it will be circulated among the other members of the court. If a majority approve the opinion, it is adopted. Those who disagree may prepare a dissenting opinion. Thereafter the opinion is announced, and the losing party may ask for a rehearing on points stated in the opinion which he or she believes to be erroneous. Such rehearings are rarely granted. If the rehearing is denied or none is requested, the decision then becomes final. The mandate of the reviewing court is then forwarded to the trial court for appropriate proceedings either by way of enforcement of the decision or new proceedings, if required.

Courts of review are essentially concerned with questions of law. However, a reviewing court may be asked to grant a new trial on the ground that the decision in the lower court is contrary to the manifest weight of the evidence found in the record. Thus, questions of fact may be examined. In the federal courts and in many states, reviewing courts are not allowed to disturb factual findings unless they are clearly erroneous. This limitation recognizes the unique opportunity afforded the trial judge in evaluating the credibility of witnesses and weighing the evidence. Because of the deference due the trial judge, unless an appellate court is left with the "definite and firm conviction that a mistake has been committed," the reviewing court must accept the trial court's findings of fact. Determining the weight and credibility of the evidence is the special province of the trial court. An appellate court cannot substitute its interpretation of the evidence for that of the trial court simply because the reviewing court might give the facts another construction or resolve the ambiguities differently.

ANDERSON v. CITY OF BESSEMER CITY, N.C.
105 S. Ct. 1504 (1985)

Bessemer City (respondent) decided in 1975 to hire a new recreation director. A committee of four men and one woman was responsible for choosing the director. Eight persons applied for the position, including Anderson (petitioner), the only woman applicant. At the time, she was a 39-year-old schoolteacher with college degrees in social studies and education. The committee chose a 24-year-old male applicant, who had recently graduated from college with a degree in physical education. The four men voted to offer the job to him, and only the woman voted for petitioner. Petitioner then filed discrimination charges with the Equal Employment Opportunity Commission (EEOC). When conciliation efforts failed, Anderson filed suit under Title VII of the Civil Rights Act of 1964. After a trial in which testimony from petitioner, the applicant who was hired, and members of the selection committee was heard, the court issued a memorandum announcing its finding that petitioner was entitled to judgment because she had been denied the position on account of her sex. The court's finding that petitioner had been denied employment because of her sex was based on findings of fact that petitioner was the most qualified candidate, that she had been asked questions during her interview regarding her spouse's feelings about her application for the position that other applicants were not asked, and that the male committee members were biased against hiring a woman. The reasons given for the decisions were a pretext. The Court of Appeals reversed, holding that the district court's findings were clearly erroneous and that the court had therefore erred in finding that pe-

titioner had been discriminated against on account of sex.

WHITE, J.: . . . Because a finding of intentional discrimination is a finding of fact, the standard governing appellate review of a district court's finding of discrimination is that set forth in Federal Rule of Civil Procedure 52(a): "Findings of fact shall not be set aside unless clearly erroneous, and due regard shall be given to the opportunity of the trial court to judge of the credibility of the witnesses." The question before us, then, is whether the Court of Appeals erred in holding the District Court's finding of discrimination to be clearly erroneous.

Although the meaning of the phrase "clearly erroneous" is not immediately apparent, certain general principles governing the exercise of the appellate court's power to overturn findings of a district court may be derived from our cases. The foremost of these principles . . . is that "a finding is 'clearly erroneous' when although there is evidence to support it, the reviewing court on the entire evidence is left with the definite and firm conviction that a mistake has been committed." This standard plainly does not entitle a reviewing court to reverse the finding of the trier of fact simply because it is convinced that it would have decided the case differently. The reviewing court oversteps the bounds of its duty under Rule 52 if it undertakes to duplicate the role of the lower court. In applying the clearly erroneous standard to the findings of a district court sitting without a jury, appellate courts must constantly have in mind that their function is not to decide factual issues *de novo*. If the District

Court's account of the evidence is plausible in light of the record viewed in its entirety, the court of appeals may not reverse it even though convinced that had it been sitting as the trier of fact, it would have weighed the evidence differently. Where there are two permissible views of the evidence, the factfinder's choice between them cannot be clearly erroneous. . . .

The rationale for deference to the original finder of fact is not limited to the superiority of the trial judge's position to make determinations of credibility. The trial judge's major role is the determination of fact, and with experience in fulfilling that role comes expertise. . . .

In addition, the parties to a case on appeal have already been forced to concentrate their energies and resources on persuading the trial judge that their account of the facts is the correct one; requiring them to persuade three more judges at the appellate level is requiring too much. As the Court has stated in a different context, the trial on the merits should be "the 'main event' . . . rather than a 'tryout on the road.'" For these reasons, review of factual findings under the clearly-erroneous standard—with its deference to the trier of fact—is the rule, not the exception.

When findings are based on determinations regarding the credibility of witnesses, Rule 52 demands even greater deference to the trial court's findings; for only the trial judge can be aware of the variations in demeanor and tone of voice that bear so heavily on the listener's understanding of and belief in what is said. This is not to suggest that the trial judge may insulate his findings from review by denominating them credibility determinations, for factors other than demeanor and inflection go into the decision whether or not to believe a witness. Documents or objective evidence may contradict the witness' story; or the story itself may be so internally inconsistent or implausible on its face that a

reasonable factfinder would not credit it. Where such factors are present, the court of appeals may well find clear error even in a finding purportedly based on a credibility determination. But when a trial judge's finding is based on his decision to credit the testimony of one of two or more witnesses, each of whom has told a coherent and facially plausible story that is not contradicted by extrinsic evidence, that finding, if not internally inconsistent, can virtually never be clear error.

Application of the foregoing principles to the facts of the case lays bare the errors committed by the Fourth Circuit in its employment of the clearly-erroneous standard. In detecting clear error in the District Court's finding that petitioner was better qualified than Mr. Kincaid, the Fourth Circuit improperly conducted what amounted to a *de novo* weighing of the evidence in the record. The District Court's finding was based on essentially undisputed evidence regarding the respective backgrounds of petitioner and Mr. Kincaid and the duties that went with the position of Recreation Director. The District Court, after considering the evidence, concluded that the position of Recreation Director in Bessemer City carried with it broad responsibilities for creating and managing a recreation program involving not only athletics, but also other activities for citizens of all ages and interests. The court determined that petitioner's more varied educational and employment background and her extensive involvement in a variety of civic activities left her better qualified to implement such a rounded program than Mr. Kincaid, whose background was more narrowly focused on athletics.

The Fourth Circuit, reading the same record, concluded that the basic duty of the Recreation Director was to implement an athletic program, and that the essential qualification for a successful applicant would be either education or experience specifically related to athletics. Accordingly, it seemed evident to the Court of Appeals that Mr. Kincaid was in fact better qualified than petitioner.

Based on our own reading of the record, we cannot say that either interpretation of the facts is illogical or implausible. Each has support in inferences that may be drawn from the facts in the record; and if either interpretation had been drawn by a district court on the record before us, we would not be inclined to find it clearly erroneous. The question we must answer, however, is not whether the Fourth Circuit's interpretation of the facts was clearly erroneous, but whether the District Court's finding was clearly erroneous. The District Court determined that petitioner was better qualified, and, as we have stated above, such a finding is entitled to deference notwithstanding that it is not based on credibility determinations. When the record is examined in light of the appropriately deferential standard, it is ap-

parent that it contains nothing that mandates a finding that the District Court's conclusion was clearly erroneous. . . .

Our determination that the findings of the District Court regarding petitioner's qualifications, the conduct of her interview, and the bias of the male committee members were not clearly erroneous leads us to conclude that the court's finding that petitioner was discriminated against on account of her sex was also not clearly erroneous. The District Court's findings regarding petitioner's superior qualifications and the bias of the selection committee are sufficient to support the inference that petitioner was denied the position of Recreation Director on account of her sex. Accordingly, we hold that the Fourth Circuit erred in denying petitioner relief under Title VII. . . .

Accordingly, the judgment of the Court of Appeals is. . . . [*Reversed.*]

---

14. Enforcement of Judgments and Decrees

After a judgment in a court of law or a decree in a court of equity has become final, either because the decision is on appeal or because the losing party failed to perfect an appeal within the proper time, it may become necessary for the successful party to obtain judicial assistance in enforcing the court decision. For example, the judgment debtor may not voluntarily pay the amount of the judgment to the judgment creditor.

In such a case, the judgment creditor may levy execution on the property of the judgment debtor, cause any property which is not exempt from execution by statute to be sold at public sale, and have the proceeds applied on the judgment. The judgment creditor may also garnishee the wages of the judgment debtor, subject to the amount that is exempt, or attach any property which may be due him or her. Modern statutes give the judgment creditor the right to question the judgment debtor in open court to discover assets that might be applied to the debt. All states allow a debtor to keep certain items of property and a certain amount of wages free from his or her debts. In addition, the federal bankruptcy law provides exemptions. The debtor may exempt significant amounts of property from the proceedings. The net effect of this law is to allow bankrupt judgment debtors to avoid the judgment and at the same time retain many of their assets.

15. Res Judicata

Once a decision of the court has become final, it is said to be "res judicata"—"the thing has been decided"—meaning that a final decision is conclusive on all issues between the parties whether raised in the litigation or not. Res judicata means that a cause of action finally determined by a competent court cannot be litigated by the parties in a new proceeding by the same court or in any other court. By final decision, we mean that either the case has been finally decided on appeal or that the time for appeal has expired. This prevents successive suits involving the same question between the same parties and brings disputes to a final conclusion. A matter once litigated and legally determined is conclusive between the parties in all subsequent proceedings. The case which follows illustrates this concept.

CUMMINGS v. DRESHER
218 N.E.2d 688 (N.Y. 1966)

DESMOND, J.: There was a collision between an automobile owned by Martin Cummings and driven by Mary Cummings and an automobile driven by Bernard Dresher. The car driven by Bernard Dresher was owned by Standard Electric Co., Inc., and in it Henry Dresher was a passenger. Driver Bernard Dresher and passenger Henry Dresher as coplaintiffs sued driver Mary Cummings and owner Martin Cummings in the Federal District Court for damages for personal injuries sustained by the two Dresher brothers. The issues up for determination in that *Dresher v. Cummings* suit included, therefore, questions as to the negligence of either or both the Dreshers and either or both of the defendants Cummings. Returning their verdict, the jury told the Federal Judge that it found in favor of the passenger Henry Dresher

against defendants Cummings and found also that Mrs. Cummings was "guilty of negligence" and the "plaintiff" (apparently meaning driver Bernard Dresher) "was guilty" of contributory negligence to a very minor degree. The Judge, to "complete" the verdict, instructed the Clerk to ask the jury whether it intended a verdict of no cause of action in Bernard Dresher's suit. The jurors replied that such was their intention. Judgment was thereupon entered in favor of Mr. and Mrs. Cummings dismissing the complaint of Bernard Dresher, and the judgment was affirmed by the Federal Court of Appeals 325 F. 2d 156 (2d Cir.). At the close of these Federal court proceedings it was completely clear that the jury had found that driver Mary Cummings had been found guilty of negligence and that, therefore, she as driver and her husband as owner had to pay damages to passenger Henry Dresher. Equally clear was the Federal court jury's finding that driver Bernard Dresher had been guilty of contributory negligence and so, notwithstanding the found negligence of driver Mary Cummings, Bernard Dresher could not recover against the defendants Cummings.

Despite this definite and unmistakable Federal court jury finding as to both drivers being at fault, driver Mary Cummings and her husband brought the present suit against driver Dresher and the corporate owner of the Dresher car. The courts below, for inscrutable reasons, held that the Federal court judgment was not determinative here. We do not understand why in a reasonable, prompt and nonrepetitious judicial system the negligence or not of these two drivers must be decided all over again, after having once been settled after a jury trial in which all these same people were parties and all the same issues tried and decided. "One who has had his day in court should not be permitted to litigate the question anew. . . ." Under such circumstances the judgment is held to be conclusive upon those who were parties to the action in which the judgment was rendered. Where a full opportunity has been afforded to a party to the prior action and he has failed to prove his freedom from liability or to establish liability or culpability on the part of another, there is no reason for retrying these issues. . . . [*Reversed.*]

16. Mediation and Arbitration

The term **mediation** describes a process in which a third party is brought into a controversy to help settle the dispute. The mediator brings to the discussions an unbiased viewpoint and skill in effecting compromise. Although a mediator cannot impose a solution upon the parties, her or his viewpoint as to what would constitute a fair and reasonable settlement is usually given significant weight. This is especially true in labor-management disputes, because the public usually accepts the mediator's viewpoint as a reasonable solution.

Arbitration proceedings are a nonjudicial means for submitting a controversy to a third person or persons for a binding decision. Arbitration may result either from agreement of the parties to the controversy or from legislation which requires that certain disputes be decided by that process.

Arbitration has several advantages over litigation as a means for resolving disputes. Arbitration procedures generally are much quicker and less expensive than litigation. The arbitrators selected do not have a crowded docket and other disputes to decide, and thus there is little or no delay. In most arbitration proceedings, formal pleadings and other procedural steps which tend to prolong litigation are not required.

Arbitration also has the advantage of submitting many disputes to experts for solution. For example, if the issue involves whether or not a building has been properly constructed, the matter could be submitted to an architect for resolution. If it involves a technical accounting problem, it could be submitted to a certified public accountant. The Securities and Exchange Commission (SEC) has approved an arrangement where investors with complaints against securities dealers may submit them for arbitration. The arbitration is handled by arbitrators assigned by the various stock exchanges and the National Association of Securities Dealers. They possess the special knowledge required to determine if a customer of a brokerage house has a legitimate complaint.

Arbitration as a substitute for litigation is very important to business, especially in international business transactions. It is used not only in labor-management relations but also to solve disputes in many contracts. In international business transactions it avoids turning a dispute over to the courts of any one country and allows the parties in advance to agree upon the person or persons to resolve any controversies that may arise.

17. Arbitration Proceedings

Arbitration almost always results from an agreement of the parties, but it may result from legislation. Agreement may come before the dispute or controversy, or it may come after the controversy has developed. In other words, the parties by contract may agree to submit all issues that may arise in the future, or they may agree to submit a particular dispute to arbitration after it has arisen. The term *submission* is used to describe the act of referring a matter to the arbitration process.

The decision in arbitration is known as an *award*. It is final on all issues submitted, and it will be enforced by the courts just as if it were a judgment of a court. Awards are not subject to judicial review on the merits of the decision.

Arbitrators are the final judges of both the facts and the law, and mistakes of either will not justify a court to change the decision. Arbitration is viewed favorably by the law, and every doubt is resolved in favor of the award. However, a court may review whether there was, in fact, a submission of the issue to arbitration or whether the arbitrator exceeded his or her authority. Arbitrators must act within the authority conferred by the submission. In addition, a party may obtain judicial review of allegations of fraud or other misconduct by the arbitrator amounting to corruption. Short of fraud or other gross errors, courts do not reexamine the facts and substitute their view for that of the arbitrator.

TAYLOR v. FITZ COAL COMPANY, INC.
618 S.W.2d 432 (Ky.) 1981

LUKOWSKY, J.: The parties had a dispute over the amount of money due as "minimum royalties" under a mineral lease. They submitted the dispute to arbitration pursuant to the provisions of the lease. The arbitrators awarded the lessor $37,214.67. The Floyd Circuit Court enforced the award. The Court of Appeals held that there was no substantial evidence in the record to support an award of less than $75,000.00 and directed entry of a judgment for that amount. We reverse the Court of Appeals and affirm the circuit court.

Generally, an arbitrator's award is not reviewable by a court. The rationale for this principle is inherent in the concept of arbitration. The decision by the arbitrator is considered an extension of the parties' voluntary agreement to arbitrate, and is final and binding. In fact, the finality of decision has long been recognized as one of the objects of arbitration.

Logically included in this limitation on a court's scope of review is the nonreviewability of the sufficiency of the evidence supporting the award. This is so because when a court examines the evidence and imposes its view of the case it substitutes the decision of another tribunal for the arbitration upon which the parties have agreed, and in effect sets aside their contract. As early as 1855 the Supreme Court of the United States, assuming the absence of statutory or contractual provisions to the contrary, put it this way in *Burchell v. March*, 17 How. 344 (1855).

If the award is within the submission, and contains the honest decision of the arbitrators, after a full and fair hearing of the parties, a court of equity will not set it aside for error, either in law or fact. A contrary course would be a substitution of the judgment of the chancellor in place of the judges chosen by the parties, and would make an award the commencement, not the end, of litigation.

The scope of review by a court of an arbitrator's award is similarly strictly limited in this Commonwealth. Our expression of the rule is that an award may be set aside if there has been a "gross mistake of law or fact constituting evidence of misconduct amounting to fraud or undue partiality." Neither party here suggests fraud or undue partiality on the part of the arbitrators. An arbitrator's award in absence of such misconduct is not reviewable by our judiciary, and, a fortiori, the evidence supporting that award may not be evaluated by our courts. The Court of Appeals exceeded its authority when it sifted the evidence presented during the arbitration hearings. Consequently, its decision to increase the amount of the award based on insufficiency of the evidence can not stand. [*The decision of the Court of Appeals is reversed and the judgment of the Floyd Circuit Court is affirmed.*]

Generally, arbitrators are under no obligation to explain the reasons for their award or the findings of fact and conclusions of law on which that award is premised. However, disclosure of findings and the reasons therefore must be given if the applicable statute, arbitration agreement, or submission so requires. In addition, it should always be recognized by those agreeing to arbitration that in so doing a party necessarily accepts the more summary, informal, and less structured procedures which characterize arbitration as compared with judicial litigation.

Most states have enacted statutes covering arbitration procedures, and these statutes have changed the common law. Most statutes cover all aspects of the submission, the award, and its enforcement. Under statutory arbitration, an agreement to submit an issue to arbitration is irrevocable, and a party who senses that the process is not going as well as expected cannot withdraw and resort to litigation. Most arbitration statutes require a written agreement to arbitrate.

If a party who has agreed to submit an issue to arbitration refuses to do so, the court will order the parties to proceed with arbitration according to the agreement. After the award is made by the arbitrator, it is usually filed with the clerk of an appropriate court. If no objections to the award are filed within a statutory period, it becomes final and enforced as if a judgment of the court.

Although many arbitration proceedings are conducted by one arbitrator, it is common to use three. In such a case, the parties to the dispute each select one arbitrator and the two arbitrators so selected name a third. Since the parties themselves are selecting two of the arbitrators, it is not a ground to remove an arbitrator that the arbitrator is biased or has an interest in the subject matter of the dispute. Many arbitrators are not lawyers. They are not required to use the usual rules of evidence and are not bound by the rules of substantive law. Arbitrators are free to fashion their own rules of procedure and to determine the facts of the dispute as they see them.

18. Policy Trends and Ethical Considerations

An important element of any dispute resolution process is its fairness to the parties involved. The legitimacy and usefulness of any such process will greatly depend on the equitable treatment of the parties and the impartiality of any decisions or recommendations by judge, jury, arbitrator, mediator, or others.

A growing area for increased arbitration and mediation is consumer complaints. Most consumer complaints do not involve enough money to warrant litigation other than through small-claims courts or class action suits. Except for small claims litigation, consumer lawsuits against a company tend to be very costly, not only in money but in goodwill for the corporation. As a result, many corporations desire to settle such complaints quickly and easily through some kind of arbitration or mediation process.

To build consumer confidence and goodwill, many corporations have established arbitration or mediation procedures to handle customer complaints. A Better Business Bureau frequently serves as arbitrator or mediator in such cases. In this case, the submission is made to an expert with a general reputation for fairness to both sides. The disadvantage to the consumer in using the Better Business Bureau to arbitrate is that the decision, as with traditional commercial arbitration, is binding on both parties and cannot normally be appealed to a court. Other third-party arbitration services often reach decisions which are binding on the manufacturer or dealer only if the consumer is satisfied with the decision and elects to accept it. If dissatisfied, the consumer is free to sue in court. This is also the case with arbitration panels established by manufacturers or trade associations.

For example, defective automobiles have been the focus of innumerable consumer complaints. Several U.S. manufacturers have recently experimented with panels to handle consumer complaints on a voluntary basis. Often called AUTOCAPs (Automobile Consumer Action Programs), the panels attempt to resolve disputes involving both sales and service. They are composed of industry members and a majority of consumer representatives. A panel's decision in any dispute, while binding on the dealer or manufacturer if the consumer accepts it, may be rejected by the consumer. Although the companies say the panels have worked well, consumer groups have complained of delays, difficult access, and general dissatisfaction. At least one company has been criticized by a consumer representative for not heeding the advice of consumer members in creating a program truly fair to consumers. An industry-sponsored program does run a greater risk of being partial to the industry, especially if the industry chooses the consumer representatives. The ethical dangers and practical disadvantages of any voluntary process stacked against the consumer would ultimately undermine it, throwing the consumer back to more traditional litigation or arbitration.

Connecticut and California have recently passed automobile "lemon laws" requiring a consumer to use any mediation or nonbinding arbitration procedures established by auto manufacturers to try to settle complaints before going to court to seek a refund or replacement. If such laws become common throughout the country, the impartiality and fairness of such dispute resolution procedures would be crucial, as the consumer would be required to use them before seeking certain remedies in court. The California law, for example, ensures that these informal dispute settlement procedures will be impartial. The law requires that the procedures meet the Federal Trade Commission's minimum fairness standards, including the consumer's right to make an informal settlement binding only if he or she is satisfied.

Some critics favor using governmental agencies for mediation rather than industry-run or industry-sponsored groups. Local and state consumer protection offices and special agencies such as state motor vehicle bureaus have become more involved in mediation but normally lack the power to force a settlement or to arbitrate. Private or industry-supported mediation and arbitration can be effective if precautions are taken to ensure objectivity and fair treatment.

REVIEW QUESTIONS

1 For each term in the left-hand column, match the most appropriate description in the right-hand column:

(1) Brief

(2) Beyond a reasonable doubt

(3) Preponderance of the evidence

(4) Hearsay

(5) Voir dire examination

(6) Peremptory challenge

(7) Clear-and-convincing proof standard

(8) Cross-examination

(9) Mediation

(10) Jury instruction

(a) The burden-of-proof standard in criminal cases

(b) The usual burden-of-proof standard in civil cases

(c) A document used in the appeal process to set forth the grounds on which the appeal is based

(d) The removal of a prospective juror for which no cause need be given

(e) Questioning a witness under oath by the attorney on the opposing side

(f) An out-of-court statement offered to prove a point which is not subject to cross-examination

(g) A process in which a third party attempts to help settle a dispute.

(h) The questioning of prospective jurors as to their qualifications to be fair and impartial

(i) A method of informing the jury as to the law applicable to the case.

(j) A burden-of-proof standard used in limited situations in which the law requires more proof than usual

2 Kay was injured when a pool table collapsed on her foot. The manufacturer was a Missouri corporation which sold the pool table to a wholesaler in Nebraska. The wholesaler sold to an Iowa pool hall where the injury occurred. Kay sued the manufacturer in Iowa, and summons was served on the manufacturer in Missouri. The defendant challenged the jurisdiction of the court. Decide the challenge. Give reasons for your answer.

3 The Minnesota Public Interest Research Group is a college-student-directed, non-profit corporation; it purports to represent the interests of college students on issues of public importance. This group filed suit to challenge the constitutionality of the Selective Service Act provision making students who failed to register for the draft ineligible for federal financial assistance. The government moved to have the suit dismissed. Rule on the motion, and give reasons for your ruling.

4 Plaintiff, a resident of New York, brought a libel suit against defendant magazine publisher, an Ohio corporation, in federal district court in New Hampshire alleging jurisdiction by reason of diversity of citizenship. The statute of limitations had run in all other states. Defendant's contacts with New Hampshire consist of monthly sales of some 10,000 to 15,000 copies of its nationally published magazine. Defendant moved to dismiss because the plaintiff had never been to New Hampshire. What was the result? Why?

5 The plaintiff alleged that the defendant caused pharmacists to mislabel drugs by marketing drugs with the similar appearance to those sold by the plaintiff. The trial court found for the defendant. It found that a technical violation of federal law had occurred but found no proof of intent. The Court of Appeals reversed, holding that the trial court failed to give sufficient weight to the evidence of a violation.
Did the reviewing court act within its proper role? Explain.

6 An action was brought in federal court by a realtor against the Real Estate Commission challenging a regulation relating to advertising by real estate dealers. The court found for the defendants. A subsequent action was brought in state court by the same plaintiff against the same defendants. They moved to dismiss the suit. How should the court rule on the motion? Explain.

7 A class action suit was filed on behalf of certain odd-lot traders against brokerage firms and a stock exchange for alleged violations of the antitrust and securities laws. Plaintiffs asked the court to order defendants to furnish the names and addresses of all members of the class because defendants could easily gather the information and because plaintiffs had limited funds. Should the court grant the plaintiffs' request? Explain.

8 A paving contractor, incorporated in Delaware with its principal place of business being in Georgia, was hired to oil and chip streets in a mobile-home park located in Florida. Heavy winds developed during the spraying of oil on the street, and a light film of oil was sprayed on thirty-six mobile homes, doing approximately $500 damage to each. A class action suit was filed in federal court seeking $18,000 damages. Does the court have jurisdiction? Explain.

9 Geraldine's car had been illegally repossessed in Texas by the Baker Bank, a federally chartered national bank located in the state of Tennessee. The National Bank Act requires that suits against national banks be brought in the county in which the bank is located. Geraldine sued the bank in Texas, and the Texas court moved to dismiss. What was the result? Why?

10 What is the basic distinction between jurisdiction and venue? Give three reasons for granting a motion for a change of venue.

11 What is the function of the pleading stage of a lawsuit? Explain how this function is accomplished.

12 What is the function of discovery procedures? Illustrate three such procedures, and indicate the sanctions available to a court for noncompliance.

13 Give three reasons for the use of arbitration rather than litigation as a means of resolving disputes.

14 Plaintiffs and defendant were parties to

a lease which contained a provision requiring arbitration of all disputes. A dispute arose, and the matter was submitted to arbitration before three arbitrators. By a 2-to-1 vote, the arbitrators found for the plaintiffs. In a suit brought to enforce the decision, the defendant contended that the award was unlawful because it was not unanimous. Is he correct? Why, or why not?

15   What element is necessary to ensure the viability of informal consumer dispute-resolution procedures established by companies or industries?

Part Two
PRIVATE LAW PRINCIPLES

Chapter 5

Contract Law and Private Enterprise

1. Introduction

When is the last time you entered a contract? Was it last month when you signed an apartment or dorm lease? If so, you must be very hungry. This is because one enters a contract when buying a meal or a snack from the vending machine. Actually, most people contract daily for a great variety of goods and services that they purchase or lease. The rules of contract law underlie the private enterprise system at every turn.

A **contract** is a *legally enforceable promise*. It need not usually be a formal, written document, and those who make a contract do not have to use the word "contract" nor recognize that they have made a legally enforceable promise. Still, the rules of contract law apply. If the expectations of the parties to a contract are not met, these rules affect legal negotiations or a lawsuit. For instance, contract law says that a restaurant "promises" that its food is fit to eat. Should the restaurant serve a meal that gives the buyer food poisoning, it would now be liable for the injury caused by breaking its promise.

Contract law enables people to make private agreements legally enforceable. Enforceability of agreements is desirable because it gives people the certainty they need to rely on promises contained in agreements. For instance, a shirt manufacturer in Los Angeles must know that it can rely on the promise of a store in Boston to pay for a thousand specially manufactured shirts. The manufacturer is more likely to agree to sew the shirts if it can enforce payment from the buyer, if necessary, under the law of contracts.

Millions of new contracts are formed daily in the United States. Both business persons and consumers alike make contractual agreements. Over the years no other area of the law has been as important as the law of contracts in supporting the private enterprise system.

The making of contracts is basic to the understanding of the legal environment of business. Labor unions and managers make collective-bargaining agreements, which are contracts (Chapter 18). Antitrust law prohibits contracts that restrain trade (Chapters 20–21). Corporations can act only through contracts made by their agents (Chapters 8–9). In securities law (Chapter 16) and in consumer protection (Chapter 15), the government regulates the contractual process. A major cause of action in product liability cases is breach of contract (Chapter 7). Even the Constitution has a clause that prohibits the states from "impairing the Obligation of Contracts" (Chapter 11).

A special area of contract law covers the sale of goods. Goods are tangible, movable personal property, a category that covers everything from airplanes to flea collars. It does not, however, include services and real estate. Contracts for the sale of goods are covered by the Uniform Commercial Code, a special body of law adopted in every state except Louisiana. This chapter recognizes many instances in which the law treats sales of goods differently from other types of contracts.

2. Classification of Contracts

We use a number of terms to help classify contracts. Mastery of these terms provides an important basis for further understanding of the topic. For instance, an **executory contract** (or term of a contract) is one which the contracting parties have not yet performed. An **executed contract** (or term) is one which the parties have performed.

Many contracts arise from discussions in which parties actually discuss the promised terms of their agreement. These are called **express contracts**. A negotiated purchase of land for construction of a manufacturing plant is an example of an express contract. There are also **implied in fact contracts** which arise from the conduct or actions of the parties, rather than by words. For instance, seeking professional services at a doctor's office implies a contractual agreement too pay the going rate for services even though no express promise to pay is made.

One classification of contracts concerns those that are unilateral and those that are bilateral. A **unilateral contract** involves a present act given in return for a promise of future performance. A loan of money in return for a promise to repay at interest is an example of a unilateral contract. Another example is catching a bank robber in return for the promise of a reward. In

bilateral contracts each party makes a promise to perform for the other. For instance, Greshman promises to deliver a deed to land on October 31; Gomez promises to pay Greshman $50,000 for the land on that date. When it is unclear whether the parties to an agreement intend a unilateral or a bilateral contract, courts usually presume that the contract is bilateral.

Void contracts are really not contracts at all. They are agreements which lack an essential contractual element. Often this element is legality of purpose. For example, in states where gambling is illegal, a bet on a football game is void. This usually means that a court will take no action when parties do not live up to the betting agreement. The opposite of a void contract is a **valid** one, which contains all the proper elements of a contract.

A *voidable contract* binds one of the parties to the agreement but gives the other party the option of withdrawing from it. Contracts based on fraud or misrepresentation are voidable. **Fraud** involves an intentional misstatement of material (important) fact which induces one to rely justifiably to his or her injury. Intentionally calling a zircon a diamond and persuading someone to purchase it on that basis is a fraud. The defrauded party can withdraw from the contract. **Misrepresentation** is simply a misstatement without intent to mislead. However, a contract entered into through misrepresentation is still voidable by the innocent party.

Other examples of voidable contracts are those induced by duress or undue influence. *Duress* means force or threat of force. The force may be physical or, in some instances, economic. *Undue influence* occurs when one is taken advantage of unfairly through a contract by a party who misuses a position of relationship or legal confidence. Contracts voidable because of undue influence often arise when persons weakened by age or illness are persuaded to enter into a disadvantageous contract by a family member or other person.

When one party is unjustly enriched at the expense of another, the law may imply a duty on the first party to pay the second, even though there is no contract between the two parties. The doctrine which requires this result is **quasi-contract**.

If a debtor overpays a creditor $5,000, the debtor can force the creditor to return that amount by suing under quasi-contract. It would be an unjust enrichment to allow the creditor to keep the $5,000. Likewise, when John has paid taxes on land, thinking that he owns it, and Mary comes along with a superior title (ownership) to the land and has John evicted, quasi-contract requires that Mary reimburse John for the taxes paid.

Note that quasi-contract is not an answer to every situation in which no contract exists. Over the years courts have come to apply quasi-contract in a fairly limited number of cases based on unjust enrichment.

3. Remedies for Breach of Contract

A party who does not live up to the obligation of contractual performance is said to *breach* the contract. There are several remedies available for a breach

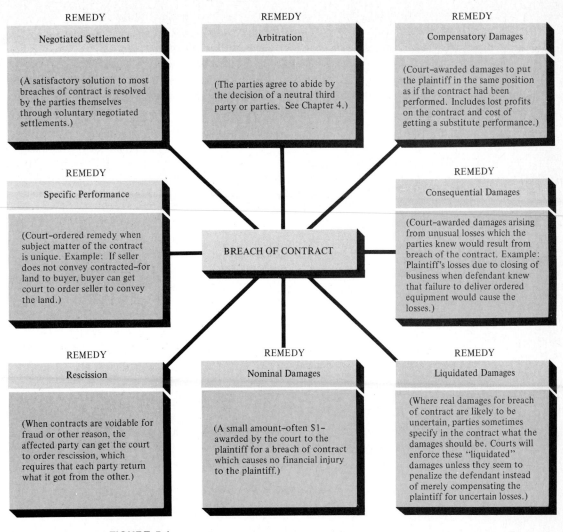

FIGURE 5-1
Remedies for Breach of Contract.

of contract. Figure 5-1 summarizes these remedies, which include the negotiated settlement, arbitration, various damage awards, specific performance, and rescission.

Trial litigation for breach of contract is fairly rare. By far the most common remedy for breach of contract is the *negotiated settlement*. The parties voluntarily reach an agreement to resolve the breach of contract. There are several reasons for this fact. First, trial litigation is time-consuming and very expensive. No matter who ultimately wins a lawsuit, both sides will lose the valuable productive effort of employees required to participate in the litigation. If at all possible, it is better to reach a mutual settlement of a breach of contract and to avoid trial litigation. Second, litigation inevitably causes hard feelings between parties and can destroy valuable business relationships. Since the parties may need to continue to do business with each other, it is best to settle a breach of contract rather than litigate it. Finally, in a trial situation one party wins and the other loses. When millions of dollars are at stake, it may be better to compromise and settle a breach of contract rather than risk losing everything in a trial. The wisdom of compromise and settlement in such situations is emphasized by the fact that juries are often ignorant of business practices, which tends to make their verdicts in business matters unpredictable.

In the mid-1970s, Westinghouse Electric Corp. failed to honor contracts calling for it to deliver uranium to a number of utility companies operating nuclear reactors. A sudden, worldwide tripling of prices by uranium producers caused Westinghouse to be unable to afford uranium to supply to the utility companies. When more than fifteen companies sued Westinghouse, Westinghouse reached settlements totaling over $700 million. Not one of the cases ever went to trial.

4. Offer to Contract

The contractual agreement begins with an offer made to an offeree (the person to whom the offer is made). An *offer* contains a specific promise and a specific demand. "I will pay $15,000 for that electrical transformer" promises $15,000 and demands a specific transformer in return. An offeror (person making the offer) must intend to make the offer, but courts measure intent objectively, that is, by how others reasonably see it rather than by what the offeror thinks he or she means. Still, as the following case illustrates, there can be confusion over what is and what is not an offer.

PIONEER REALTY AND LAND CO. v. MORTGAGE PLUS, INC.

346 N.W. 286 (N.D. 1984)

Prospective homebuyers applied for mortgages with Mortgage Plus. At the time of application, Kocourek, the Mortgage Plus loan officer, told the home buyers that its interest rate was 11½ percent. While the applications were being processed, Mortgage Plus raised its rate and refused to honor the 11½ percent rate. The homebuyers then got their loans elsewhere and had to pay more than 11½ percent. They sued Mortgage Plus, claiming that Mortgage Plus breached its offer to lend money to qualified buyers at 11½ percent. The trial court determined that Mortgage Plus and the homebuyers did not enter into any agreements binding Mortgage Plus to provide the loans at the 11½ percent interest rate.

VANDE WALLE, J.: On appeal, the plaintiffs raised a number of issues of which we conclude our answer to the following single issue is dispositive: Whether or not the district court erred by failing to find that a binding obligation to lend money at a specified interest rate and discount points existed between Mortgage Plus and the loan applicants.

The district court determined that Mortgage Plus and the loan applicants represented in this lawsuit did not enter into any oral or written agreements binding Mortgage Plus to provide home-loan funding at a specified interest rate and discount point fee.

Having reviewed the record in this case, we conclude that there is sufficient evidence to support the trial court's finding that Mortgage Plus did not enter binding agreements with the loan applicants to provide home-loan funding at a specified interest rate and discount point fee. It is undisputed that Kocourek quoted home-loan funding to be available, at the time the loan applications were submitted, at an interest rate of 11½ percent together with a fee of two or three discount points. However, there is evidence upon which the district court could find, as it did, that Kocourek's quotations did not constitute a binding agreement or commitment to provide funds at the quoted rates.

Kocourek testified that, in his opinion, at no time did he commit, orally or in writing, to provide home-loan money to any applicant at a specified interest rate or discount points.

The substance of the loan applicant's testimony was that Kocourek quoted the interest rate and discount points in effect at the time the loan applications were filed, but not necessarily the rates that would be in effect when the loans closed. In that regard, Jean Foltz [a plaintiff] testified:

"Q. When you met with him [Kocourek], did you discuss interest rates and points?

"A. Yes, we did.

"Q. What did Mr. Kocourek say to you at that time?

"A. The rate at that time was eleven-and-a-half, and three points."

Each of the loan applicants signed the following written statement during the time that their loan applications were being processed by Mortgage Plus:

I/We the undersigned who have applied for the mortgage loan on the above property do agree that the loan will bear the maximum interest rate in effect at the time of closing but in no event will the interest rate be less than that in effect at the time of application.

At no time did any of the loan applicants receive a written commitment from Mortgage Plus relative to the interest, discount points, or date of closing on the loan application requests. . . . [*Affirmed.*]

Under the common law of contracts, contractual terms must be definite and specific. An offer to employ at a "reasonable salary" cannot be the basis for a contract because of *indefiniteness*. Most advertisements and catalog price quotes are considered too indefinite to form the basis for a contract unless they are specific about the quantity of goods being offered.

However, under the Uniform Commercial Code (UCC), contracts for the sale of goods can leave open nonquantity terms to be decided at a future time. An agreement for the sale of 500 cameras will bind the parties even though they leave open the price to be decided on delivery in six months.

Once an offer is made, when does it terminate if the offeree does not accept it? Table 5-1 lists several common instances showing when an offer may terminate.

5. Acceptance of Offer

Acceptance of an offer is necessary to a binding contract. An offer to enter into a bilateral contract is accepted by the offeree's making the required promise. When Toni offers Aaron certain widgets for $2,500 to be delivered by November 30 on ninety-day credit terms, and Aaron accepts, Aaron is promising to pay $2,500 on ninety-day credit terms.

Unilateral contracts are accepted by performing a requested act, not by making a promise. A company's offer of a $2,500 reward for information leading to the conviction of anyone vandalizing company property is not accepted by promising to provide the information. Only the act of providing information accepts such an offer.

When does the acceptance become binding on the offeror? Unless the offer itself specifies a particular moment, the acceptance usually binds the parties when the offeree dispatches it. Since the offeree frequently mails the acceptance, the acceptance becomes binding when it is "deposited" with the postal service—hence, the *deposited acceptance rule.*

The importance of the deposited acceptance rule is that the offeror cannot revoke the offer once the offeree has accepted it. An added significance is that an offeror's revocation is not effective until the offeree actually receives it. Thus, a deposited acceptance creates a binding contract even though a revocation is also in the mail.

TABLE 5-1   When an Offer Terminates

1. By provision in the offer: "This offer terminates at noon Friday."
2. By lapse of a reasonable period of time if the offer fails to specify a time: What is "reasonable" depends on the circumstances.
3. By rejection of the offer: "Thank you, but I do not want the widgets you are offering." A *counteroffer* is also a rejection: "Your offer of $10,000 for the land is too low. I will sell it to you for $12,500."
4. By revocation of the offer: "I regret to inform you that I am withdrawing my offer."
5. By destruction of the subject matter: The widgets are destroyed by fire before the offer of their sale has been accepted.
6. By the offeror's death or insanity: Offeror dies before the offer has been accepted.
7. By the contractual performance becoming illegal: The State Department declares that sales of certain computers to the Soviet Union are illegal. This terminates an offer to sell the computers to a Soviet trading company.

MIRROR IMAGE RULE

In order for an acceptance to create a binding contract, standard contract law requires that the acceptance must "mirror" the offer, that is, must match it exactly. If the acceptance changes the terms of the offer or adds new terms, it is not really an acceptance. It is a counteroffer.

The UCC has changed the *mirror image rule* with regard to merchants contracting for the sale of goods. An acceptance between merchants creates a binding contract even though it proposes new or different terms. The new or different terms become part of the contract unless (1) the offer expressly limits acceptance to the original terms; (2) the proposed terms materially (importantly) alter the contract; or (3) the offeror rejects the proposed terms.

SILENCE NOT ACCEPTANCE

In general, an offeror's failure to reject an offer does not imply acceptance. Another way to say this is that silence is not acceptance. The offeree has no usual duty to reply to the offer, even if the offer states that the offeror will treat silence as acceptance.

There are major exceptions to this rule. For instance, parties may have a contract that specifies that future shipments of goods be made automatically unless the offeree expressly rejects them. Many book and record-club contracts operate in this manner.

A related doctrine looks at the parties' prior *course of dealing*—the way they have done business in the past. Silence may well imply acceptance if the parties previously dealt with each other by having the buyer take shipments from the seller unless the buyer notified the seller in advance not to ship.

Finally, the UCC says that a contract may arise from the *conduct* of a buyer and seller of goods. Emphasis is placed on how the parties act rather than on a formal offer and acceptance of terms.

6. Voluntary Consent to Contracts

To be enforceable, a contract must be voluntarily made. The previously discussed doctrines of fraud, misrepresentation, duress, and undue influence show that a contract is voidable when both parties do not reach it through a voluntary, knowing consent.

What happens when each party misunderstands something very basic and material about a contract? Such a situation goes right to the heart of whether there has been a "voluntary" consent to a contract. The doctrine of **mutual mistake** allows either party to a contract to void and rescind it when there has been a material mutual misunderstanding.

There is a difference between a mutual or bilateral mistake and a unilateral mistake. A *unilateral mistake* arises when only one of the parties to a contract is wrong about a material fact. Suppose that Royal Carpet Co. bids $8.70 per yard for certain carpet material instead of $7.80 per yard as it had intended. If the seller accepts Royal Carpet's bid, a contract results even though there was a unilateral mistake.

The party that has entered a contract and made a unilateral mistake cannot legally withdraw from it in most instances. Only if the other party knew or should have known of the mistake, can the mistaken party withdraw.

7. Consideration in the Contract

Courts will not enforce contractual promises unless they are supported by **consideration**. Before Robert can enforce a promise made by Peter, Robert must have given consideration, that is, assumed a legal obligation to Peter or surrendered a legal right. In a bilateral contract, each party promises something to the other. The binding promises are the consideration. In a unilateral contract, the consideration of one party is a promise; the consideration of the other party is performance of an act.

When it is not clear whether there is consideration to support a promise, a court will often examine a transaction as a whole. The next case illustrates this point.

FILES v. SCHAIBLE
445 So.2d 257 (Ala. 1984)

Plaintiff Schaible purchased a restaurant from defendant Files. The sale contained two written agreements. First, Files agreed to sell and deliver the restaurant equipment. Second, he agreed not to operate a restaurant in competition with Schaible within a 5-mile radius of the restaurant being sold for a five-year period. The next year Files opened a new restaurant across the street from Schaible. At trial, Files argued that the noncompetition clause was unenforceable because it lacked consideration. The jury returned a verdict for Schaible in the amount of $50,000, and Files appealed.

EMBRY, J.: . . . Files contends that because the written agreement, containing his agreement not to compete, does not express consideration specifically for the covenant not to compete, that covenant is not enforceable.

Adequate consideration exists, or is implied, if it arises from any act of the plaintiff from which the defendant derived a pecuniary benefit (i.e., the profitable sale of the restaurant business), if such act was performed by the plaintiff to the desired end, with the expressed or implied assent of the defendant. That which creates and carries a benefit to the party promising, or causes trouble, injury, inconvenience, prejudice, or detriment to the other party, is sufficient consideration.

The written agreement signed by Files can be interpreted, as Files urges, as two separate contracts. However, contrary to Files' assertion, each is supported by adequate consideration. That Schaible would not have entered the agreement for the sale of the restaurant equipment absent the covenant not to compete supplies sufficient considera- tion to support the obligation in that Schaible has thereby suffered a legal detriment. . . . [*Affirmed*].

An important part of consideration is that it must be *bargained for*. Sometimes the parties to an agreement specify an insignificant consideration in return for a great one, for example, a promise of $1 in return for a promise to convey 40 acres of land. In such situations a court must decide whether the party promising to convey the land really bargained for the $1 or merely promised to make a gift. Promises to make gifts are not binding, because no bargained-for consideration supports the promise.

Similarly, *prior consideration* is no consideration. For instance, after many years of working at Acme Co., Bigman retires as vice president for financial planning. The company's board of directors votes him a lifetime pension of $3,000 per month "for services rendered." One year later the board termi- nates his pension. If Bigman sues for breach of contract, he will lose. He gave no consideration to support the promise of a pension. The past years of service were not "bargained for" by the company's board when they granted the pension. The board merely promised to give an unenforceable gift to Bigman.

AGREEMENT NOT TO SUE IS CONSIDERATION

Where reasonable grounds for a lawsuit exist, an agreement not to sue is consideration to support a promise. If First Bank agrees not to sue Maria, who has failed to repay a student loan, in return for the promise of Maria's parents to repay the loan, First Bank has given consideration. It has promised to surrender its legal right to sue Maria.

Likewise, suppose that a consulting firm bills a client $5,000 for fifty hours' work at $100 per hour. The client disputes the bill and contends that the consulting firm worked only twenty-five hours and should get only $2,500. If the two parties compromise the bill at $3,500 for thirty-five hours, this agreement binds them both. Each has surrendered the right to have a court determine exactly what amount is owed. Such an agreement and the payment of the $3,500 is an *accord and satisfaction*.

PERFORMANCE OF PRE-EXISTING OBLIGATION IS NOT CONSIDERATION

A party to an agreement does not give consideration by promising to do something which he or she is already obligated to do. For example, suppose a warehouse owner contracts to have certain repairs done for $20,000. In the middle of construction, the building contractor demands an additional $5,000 to complete the work. The owner agrees, but when the work is finished he gives the contractor only $20,000. If the contractor sues, he will lose. The owner's promise to pay an extra $5,000 is not supported by consideration.

The contractor is under a pre-existing obligation to do the work for which the owner promises an additional $5,000.

If the contractor promised to do something he was not already obligated to do, there would be consideration to support the promise of the additional $5,000. Promising to modify the repair plans illustrates such new consideration.

WHEN NO CONSIDERATION IS NECESSARY

The pre-existing obligation rule discussed above does not apply to a sale of goods contract. The UCC states that parties to a sale of goods contract may make binding modifications to it without both parties giving new consideration. If a buyer of widgets agrees to pay a seller an additional $5,000 over and above the amount already promised, the buyer is bound, although the seller gives only the consideration (widgets) which she is already obligated to give.

Under the UCC, the rules of consideration also do not apply to a **firm offer**. A firm offer exists when a merchant offering goods promises in writing that the offer will not be revoked for a period not to exceed three months. This promise binds the merchant, although the offeree buyer gives no consideration to support it. With offers not involving sales of goods by a merchant, a promise not to revoke an offer must be supported by the offeree's consideration to be binding. Such an arrangement is called an *option*.

An important exception to the rule requiring consideration to support a promise is the doctrine of **promissory estoppel**. This doctrine arises when an offeree justifiably relies on the offeror's promise to his or her injury in a situation in which the promise has been revoked before the offeree can accept it. The offeror must also know that the offeree is likely to rely on the promise. In such situations, courts treat the offeror's revocation as if the offeror had breached a contract. For instance, suppose that a building subcontractor bids (offers) to do certain plumbing work for $90,000. The offeree, a general contractor, relies on this bid and includes it in a $400,000 general bid to construct an office building. The general contractor's bid is accepted, but before the general contractor can accept the subcontractor's bid, the subcontractor revokes it. It costs the general contractor $120,000 to get another subcontractor to do the plumbing work. Because the first subcontractor knew that the general contractor would rely on the $90,000 bid, the general contractor can sue and recover $30,000 from the first subcontractor under the doctrine of promissory estoppel.

8. Capacity of Parties to Contract

Capacity refers to a person's ability to be bound by a contract. Courts have traditionally held three classes of persons to lack capacity to be bound by contractual promises: minors (also called "infants"), intoxicated persons, and mentally incompetent persons.

In most states a *minor* is anyone under age 18. Minors can usually not be legally bound to contractual promises unless they involve *necessaries of life* such as food, clothing, shelter, medical care, and—in some states—education. Even for necessaries, minors often cannot be sued for the contract price, only for a "reasonable" value. In a number of states, courts will hold a minor who has misrepresented his or her age to contractual promises.

A contract into which a minor has entered is voidable at the election of the minor. The minor can *disaffirm* the contract and legally recover any consideration which has been given an adult, even if the minor cannot return the adult's consideration. On the other hand, the adult is bound by the contract unless the infant elects to disaffirm it.

A minor may disaffirm a contract anytime before reaching the age of majority (usually 18) and for a reasonable time after reaching majority. If the minor fails to disaffirm within a reasonable time after reaching majority, the minor is said to *ratify* the contract. Upon ratification, the minor loses the right to disaffirm.

Except when an adult has been judged by the court to be mentally incompetent, she or he does not lose capacity to contract simply because of intoxication or mental impairment. In most cases involving adult capacity to contract, courts measure capacity by whether the adult was capable of understanding the nature and purpose of the contract. Obviously, the more complex a contractual transaction gets, the more likely a court is to decide that an intoxicated or mentally impaired person lacks capacity to contract.

9. Illegal Contracts

A basic requirement of a valid contract is legality of purpose. A "contract" to murder someone is hardly enforceable in a court of law. Contracts which require commission of a crime or tort or which violate accepted standards of behavior ("public policy") are void. Table 5-2 gives common examples of illegal contracts.

TABLE 5-2 Examples of Illegal Contracts

1. Gambling agreements (except where permitted)
2. Certain contracts made on Sunday (in about half the states)
3. Contracts for usurious interest (see Chapter 15)
4. Professional contracts made by unlicensed persons in which a regulatory statute requires licensing
5. Contracts which unreasonably restrain trade (see Chapters 20–21)
6. Many contracts which attempt to limit negligence liability of a seller of goods or services to the public (called "exculpatory" contracts)
7. *"Unconscionable"* contracts involving a sale of goods under the UCC (usually applied when a difference in bargaining power or education leads a merchant to take unreasonable advantage of a consumer)
8. Other contracts prohibited by statute or against *"public policy"*

Illegality makes a contract void. Courts will generally take no action on a void contract, and they will leave the parties to the contract where they have put themselves. As the next case shows, this fact means that a plaintiff can get no damages for breach of an illegal contract.

MASON v. HOSTA
199 Cal. Rptr. 859 (1984)

Plaintiff Mason, a hospital administrator, made an agreement with defendant Hosta, a medical doctor. Mason agreed to contact other medical hospital administrators on behalf of Hosta and try to persuade them to use Hosta's emergency room services. For each hospital client Mason referred to Hosta, Hosta was to pay Mason $250. After three years, Hosta stopped making referral payments to Mason because he claimed the contract violated the Business and Professions Code. Mason sued under the contract for the unpaid amount owed for his referrals on behalf of the defendant. The trial court denied the plaintiff's motion for summary judgment. On appeal, the California Court of Appeal determined that the contract was illegal under the Business and Professions Code.

MERRICK, J.: The subject contract provides for payments to [Mason] by [Hosta] as compensation for [Mason's] soliciting, referring and procuring clients on [Hosta's] behalf. It is precisely this sort of referral fee to which the prohibition of Business and Professions Code section 650 is directed. Performance of the subject contract violates the statute. "It is well established in California that a contract which

requires the performance of unlawful acts is unenforceable." Civil Code section 1550 provides that a lawful object is essential to the very existence of a valid contract. Similarly, Civil Code section 1607 states that the consideration for a promise must be lawful. Civil Code section 1608 provides that if any part of a single consideration for one or more objects, or of several considerations for a single object, is unlawful, the entire contract is void. Lastly a purported agreement in direct violation of the terms of the express prohibition in a statute is void.

No matter how subtly disguised, or ingeniously interpreted, the subject contract, by its terms, and the performance required of defendant/respondent thereunder, violates section 650 of the Business and Professions Code. Further it is an attempt to thwart the legislative design and public policy to proscribe illegal and unethical contracts providing for the payment by licensed physicians of consideration as compensation and inducement to non-licensees for the referral of patients, clients or customers.

We find the trial court correctly granted [Hosta's] Motion for Summary Judgment. [*Its judgment is affirmed.*]

There are several exceptions to the general rule that courts will take no action on an illegal contract. A contract may have both legal and illegal provisions to it. In such a case, courts will often enforce the legal provisions and refuse to enforce the illegal ones. For instance, a contract providing services or leasing goods sometimes contains a provision excusing the service provider or lessor from liability for negligently caused injury. Courts usually will not enforce this provision but will enforce the rest of the contract.

Often, courts will allow an innocent party to recover payment made to a party who knows (or should know) that a contract is illegal. For example, courts will allow recovery of a payment for professional services made by an innocent person to a person who is unlicensed to provide such services.

Finally, in some cases courts may allow a person to recover compensation under quasi-contract for services performed on an illegal contract. Recovery may be allowed where an otherwise qualified professional lets his or her license expire and provides services to a client before renewing the license.

10. When Contracts Should Be in Writing

Some people have the impression that contracts have to be in writing to be enforceable. In most instances this is not so. However, it is true that certain contracts must be in writing (or at least evidenced by writing) to be enforceable.

The law requiring that certain contracts be in writing is the **statute of frauds**. Designed to prevent frauds arising from oral contracts, the original English statute is more than 300 years old. Today, every state has its own statute of frauds. Business-related provisions require writing for the following contracts: (1) contracts for the sale of an interest in land, (2) collateral contracts to pay the debt of another person, (3) contracts which cannot be performed within one year, and (4) sale of goods contracts for $500 or more.

CONTRACTS FOR THE SALE OF AN INTEREST IN LAND

Sales of interests in land are common contracts covered by the statute of frauds. Although "sales of interests in land" covers a contract to sell land, it includes much more. Interests in land include contracts for mortgages, mining rights, easements (rights to use another's land, such as the right to cross it with electrical power wires), and leases of longer than one year. However, a contract to insure land or to erect a building is not an interest in land.

The doctrine of *part performance* creates an exception to the requirement that sales of interests in land must be in writing. When a buyer of land has made valuable improvements in it or where the buyer is in possession of it and has paid part of the purchase price, even an oral contract to sell is enforceable.

COLLATERAL CONTRACTS TO PAY THE DEBT OF ANOTHER

A collateral contract is a secondary one. It is not Janet's promise to pay Joan's debt, which is a primary promise. A collateral or secondary contract arises only from Janet's promise to pay Joan's debt if Joan does not. Only collateral contracts must be in writing under the statute of frauds.

Collateral contracts are often called "suretyship contracts." A **surety** is a person who guarantees that he or she will pay a debt if a debtor does not. Contracts made by bonding companies are common examples of collateral contracts.

The *main purpose doctrine* provides an exception to the statute of frauds rule about collateral contracts. If the main purpose of making a collateral contract to answer for another's debt is to benefit one's own self, the contract need not be in writing. An oral contract to guarantee the debt of a corporation which one wholly owns falls under the main purpose doctrine. It is enforceable.

CONTRACTS WHICH CANNOT BE PERFORMED WITHIN ONE YEAR

The statute of frauds applies to a contract which the parties cannot perform within one year after its making. Courts usually interpret the one-year requirement to mean that the contract must specify a period of performance longer than one year. Thus, an oral contract for services which last twenty months is not enforceable. But an oral contract for services to be completed "by" a date twenty months away is enforceable. The difference is that the latter contract can be performed within one year, even if it actually takes longer than that to perform it.

As interpreted by the courts, the statute of frauds applies only to executory contracts which the parties cannot perform within a year. Once one of the parties has executed her performance for the other, she can enforce an oral multiyear contract.

SALE OF GOODS OF $500 OR MORE

Under the UCC, the statute of frauds covers sales of goods of $500 or more. Modifications to such contracts are also included. Table 5-3 lists exceptions to the writing requirement for sale of goods contracts.

In addition to the basic contracts covered by the statute of frauds, other contracts must be in writing in various states. Most states require insurance policies to be written. Several states demand written estimates in contracts for automobile repair. And, as the next case makes clear, some states specify that contracts not to compete must be in writing.

TABLE 5-3   Exceptions to Statute of Frauds Requirement for Oral Sale of Goods Contracts

1. Contract for goods specially manufactured for the buyer in which the seller has begun performance
2. Contract for goods for which payment has been made and accepted or which have been received and accepted
3. Contract for goods in which the party being sued admits in court or pleadings that the contract has been made
4. Contract for goods between merchants in which the merchant sued has received a written notice from the other merchant confirming the contract and in which merchant sued does not object to the confirmation within ten days

NORLIN INDUSTRIES, INC. v. MUSIC ARTS, INC.
313 S.E.2d 166 (N.C. 1984)

The plaintiff is the national distributor of Lowrey Organs. After Lowrey delivered organs to the defendant, Music Arts, Inc., for six years, Music Arts defaulted by failing to pay for the organs sold and delivered to it by Lowrey. Lowrey sued to recover the outstanding balance under the contract. Music Arts counterclaimed that Lowrey had breached an oral agreement not to compete by opening a new store in the exclusive area granted to Music Arts. At trial, Lowrey argued that no such oral agreement was made and if it did exist, it could not be enforced since the statute of frauds required an agreement not to compete to be in writing.

BRASWELL, J.: The defendants also sought leave of court to amend their answer in order to assert two additional alternative counterclaims. . . .

The second of the additional alternative counterclaims alleges that the defendants have been damaged by the opening of another Lowrey store by the plaintiff in 1979 in violation of its alleged oral "franchise agreement. . . ." [T]he assertion of the oral "franchise agreement" in which the plaintiff allegedly gave Music Arts an exclusive area in which to sell is barred by the statute of frauds pursuant to G.S. 75-4. This statute states in part that:

No contract or agreement hereafter made, limiting the rights of any person to do business anywhere in the State of North Carolina shall be enforceable unless such agreement is in writing duly signed by the party who agrees not to enter into any such business within such territory. . . .

The oral franchise agreement allegedly prohibited the plaintiff from distributing Lowrey organs within a certain territory, including all of Pitt County, to any of Music Arts' competitors or from opening any new stores of its own. This oral contract substantially limited the plaintiff's right to do business in this area, except through the defendant as its exclusive distributor. Through G.S. 75-4, "[t]he General Assembly has declared that no contract whereby a person limits and restricts his legal right to do business in the State shall be valid and enforceable unless in writing and signed by the party so contracting." Because under G.S. 75-4, the alleged oral contract is void and unenforceable, we hold that the trial court correctly denied the defendants' motion to amend their answer in order to assert this counterclaim. [*Affirmed.*]

In some states the statute of frauds requires that the actual contract between the parties must be in writing. However, most states merely require that the contract be *evidenced* by writing and be signed by the party to be held. This requirement means that the party being sued must have signed a note, memorandum, or another written form short of a formal contract which describes with reasonable certainty the terms of the oral agreement. As Table

5-3 indicates with regard to a sale of goods between merchants, the writing need not be by the party sued. It may be by the suing party under certain circumstances.

11. The Parol Evidence Rule

Like the statute of frauds, the **parol evidence rule** influences the form of contracts. This rule states that parties to a complete and final written contract cannot introduce oral evidence in court which changes the intended meaning of the written terms.

The parol evidence rule applies only to evidence of oral agreements made at the time of or prior to the written contract. It does not apply to oral modifications coming after the parties have made the written contract (although the statute of frauds may apply).

Suppose that Chris Consumer wants to testify in court that a merchant of an Ultima Washing Machine gave him an oral six-month warranty on thhe machine, even though the $450 written contract specified "no warranties." If the warranty was made after Chris signed the contract, he may testify about its existence. Otherwise, the parol evidence rule prevents him from testifying about an oral agreement which changes the terms of the written contract.

An exception to the parol evidence rule allows evidence of oral agreement which merely explains the meaning of written terms, without changing the terms. Also, oral evidence which changes the meaning of written terms can be given if necessary to prevent fraud.

12. Interpretation of Contracts

If each party is satisfied with the other's performance under a contract, there is no problem with interpreting the contract's terms. But when disagreement about contractual performance exists, often interpretation of the terms becomes necessary. Courts have devised several rules to assist in interpreting contracts.

Common words are given their usual meaning. "A rose is a rose is a rose," said the poet, and a court will interpret this common word to refer to a flower. However, if the word has a particular *trade usage,* courts will give it that meaning. In a contract in the wine trade, the term "rose" would not refer to a flower at all but to a type of wine.

Some words have special legal meanings. A party to a contract had best appreciate that courts give legal terms their legal meaning. The buyer of radios may think that a contractual phrase calling for "delivery to the buyer on November 20" means that the seller will take the radios to the buyer's place of business, but it does not.

"Delivery" is a legal term referring to the transfer of possession from the seller to the buyer. It does not make the seller responsible for "shipping" the radios to the buyer. Furthermore, the UCC says that when the contract states no place for delivery, the place of delivery is the seller's place of business. The buyer will have to take delivery of the radios at the seller's place of business on November 20. Because some terms have both common and legal meanings, a person should have an attorney examiine contracts drawn up by others.

Many businesses today use printed form contracts. Sometimes the parties to one of these printed contracts type or handwrite additional terms. What happens when the typed or handwritten terms contradict the printed terms? What if the printed terms of a contract state "no warranties," but the parties have written in a ninety-day warranty? In such a case, courts interpret handwritten terms to control typed terms and typed terms to control printed ones. The written warranty will be enforced since the writing is the best evidence of the parties' true intention.

Another rule is that when only one of the parties drafts (draws up) a contract, courts will interpret ambiguous or vague terms against the party who drafts them. As the following case shows, courts often apply this rule to insurance contracts.

STATE FARM MUTUAL AUTOMOBILE INSURANCE COMPANIES v. QUEEN
688 P.2d 935 (Mont. 1984)

Rhonda R. Queen was sued for injuries received in an accident by the passenger of an automobile she was driving. Queen was insured by State Farm Mutual Automobile Insurance Company, and she demanded that the company defend her under the insurance policy. State Farm asked the court to order that Queen's accident was not covered by her insurance policy since (1) she did not own the automobile involved in the accident, (2) the policy covered only the first-named insured in nonowned automobiles, and (3) she was the second-named insured under the policy. Agreeing with State Farm, the court so ordered. The order was appealed.

MORRISON, J.: The following issue was certified to this Court by the Circuit Court of Appeals: Must this policy be construed to provide coverage for Rhonda Queen while driving a non-owned automobile, on the ground that the policy is ambiguous as to whether Gary Queen, Rhonda Queen, or both, are the first-named insured?

The policy question affords coverage for the use of "non-owned automobiles" to "the first person named in the declaration." The policy declaration lists the following as insureds:

Queen, Gary A. and Rhonda R.
Box 145
Rt. 2
Ronan, MT 59864

The insurer is responsible for the language which the policy contains. Whenever a contract of insurance is drawn so that it is fairly susceptible to two constructions, one favorable to the insured and the other favorable to the insurer, the one favorable to the insured will be adopted.

There are several different ways that State Farm could have listed the persons in the declaration so that the first person listed would present no ambiguity. The names could have been listed as: Gary Queen, Rhonda Queen. Less clear but perhaps sufficient to avoid an ambiguity would be: Gary Queen and Rhonda Queen. Though the names are here coupled, Gary Queen's name does appear first. However, in the instant policy, the first-named is simply "Queen." Following the last name the names Gary and Rhonda are coupled. This would seem to indicate an intention on the part of State Farm to grant no preference to one of the individuals as a first-named insured entitled to coverage on non-owned automobiles.

One test for determining whether a policy is capable of more than one construction is whether different persons looking at the writing in light of its purpose cannot agree upon its meaning. This case is a perfect illustration. The dissenters think the policy clearly shows Gary Queen as the first person named in the declaration. The three members of the Court signing this opinion think that the last name of the couple is the first name listed in the declaration and the first two names are coupled together making both parties first named in the declaration. We have seven Supreme Court Justices, who frequently review insurance policy language, closely divided in interpretation. What more need be said?

In conclusion, the declaration sheet of the insurance policy contains an ambiguity which must be construed against the maker of the policy. We find there is coverage for Rhonda Queen. [*Reversed and remanded.*]

---

13. Assignment of Contracts

Electronics, Inc., sells 250 radios on credit at $20 apiece to Radio Land Retail. Electronics then sells its rights under the contract to Manufacturers' Credit Co. When payment is due, can Manufacturers' Credit legally collect the $5,000 owed to Electronics by Radio Land? This transaction is controlled by the law of *assignment,* which is a transfer (generally a sale) of rights under a contract. Figure 5-2 shows the transaction and introduces important terms.

There is an important exception to the rule that assignees are subject to assignors' defenses. Under the UCC, an assignee called a *holder in due course* who takes an assignment of rights through a *negotiable instrument or document* will not be subject to the personal contract defenses of an assignor. To be negotiable, an instrument or document must be signed by the obligor (the party bound by legal obligation) and must contain certain language.

When an assignor assigns rights, he or she makes an implied warranty that the rights are valid. If the assignee is unable to enforce the rights against the obligor because of illegality, incapacity, or breach of contract, the assignee can sue the assignor. But the assignor does not guarantee that the obligor is able to pay the claim.

When an assignment is made, an assignee should notify the obligor immediately. Otherwise, the obligor may perform for the obligee-assignor. If

FIGURE 5-2
Assignment Diagram.

Radio Land pays Electronics before being notified of the assignment by Manufacturers' Credit, Radio Land cannot be held liable to Manufacturers' Credit.

A dishonest or careless assignor may assign the same contract rights to two different assignees. Notification of the obligor is especially important in this situation. In most states the law says that the first assignee to give notice has priority no matter which assignee first receives the assignment of rights.

Although most contracts can be assigned, certain ones cannot. An assignment that increases the burden of performance to the obligor cannot be assigned. For instance, a right to have goods shipped to the buyer's place of business cannot be assigned by an Atlanta buyer to a Miami buyer if a New York seller has to ship the goods to Miami instead of Atlanta. Similarly, a *requirements contract* to supply a retail buyer with all the radios needed cannot be assigned because it depends upon the buyer's personal situation.

Most states regulate the assignment of wages. They limit the amount of wages which a wage earner can assign. This protects wage earners and their families.

A party to a contract cannot assign (delegate) performance of duties under a contract when performance depends on the character, skill, or training of that party. Otherwise, duties under a contract can be assigned as well as rights.

14. Contracts Benefiting a Third Party

The performance of a contract may benefit persons who are not parties to the contract. Such persons are called *third-party beneficiaries*. In general, persons who are not parties to a contract have no rights to sue to enforce the contract or to obtain damages for breach of contract. As the next case illustrates, however, a third-party beneficiary can sue if the parties to the contract intended to benefit that person.

SPEEDEE OIL CHANGE NO. 2, INC. v. NATIONAL UNION FIRE INSURANCE CO.
444 So.2d 1304 (La. 1984)

An attorney contracted to provide legal services to secure a lease with the promoters of a corporation that was in the process of being incorporated. On August 18, 1980, the attorney sent a letter to the promoters advising them that notice to renew the lease must be given thirty-one days *after* the termination of the lease. This advice was wrong, and the lease expired without any notice that the promoters wished to exercise their option to renew the lease. The corporation sued for the amount of the increase in lease payments due to the failure to exercise the option. The trial court decided in favor of the corporation and awarded $54,800 damages.

REDMANN, C.J.: A legal malpractice insurer appeals from a judgment in this direct action for $54,800 damages from failure to timely exercise an option to extend a lease. The attorney at law insured by defendant had advised one of plaintiff corporation's promoters in writing that the option to extend could be exercised until 31 days after the termination of the lease.

The basic issue [is] whether the corporation has any right to recover for the attorney's mistaken advice to the promoter. . . .

We conclude that the corporation as an intended third-party beneficiary may recover from the attorney upon his contract with its promoters. . . .

Defendant correctly states the basic principle that a corporation not yet in existence cannot be a party to a contract, because not then "legally capable of contracting."

But "[a]ll things, in the most extensive sense of the expression, . . . to which rights can legally be acquired, may become the object of contracts," including future things. . . . Although a promoter may ordinarily bind only himself, one "may contract, in his own name, that another shall ratify or perform the stipulation which he makes," so that a promoter may oblige *himself* that his intended corporation will perform a stipulated obligation, such as to pay an attorney for pre-incorporation services. More pertinent to our case, "A person may also, in his own name, make some advantage for a third person the condition or consideration of a commutative contract . . .; and if such third person consents to avail himself of the advantage stipulated in his favor, the contract can not be revoked," so that a promoter may stipulate for the benefit of his intended corporation. The third-party beneficiary need not exist at the time of a contract in his favor by others.

By the time of the attorney's August 18 letter he understood that his legal advice on the option was intended for the use and benefit of the future corporation that he was in the process of forming. He had to know and intend that not the individual promoters but the future corporation would use his advice in respect to exercising the option to extend. The other party to the contract, the promoters, also knew and intended that. The future corporation was therefore the intended third-party beneficiary of the parties' contract for the lawyer's advice; and the corporation accepted the stipulation in its favor by (as the trial court found, supported by sufficient evidence) acting upon the advice.

As the intended and accepting third-party beneficiary of the contract, the corporation has the right to sue for damages from its breach. . . . [*Affirmed.*]

If Susan owes Bob $1,000 and she performs services for Frank, she may contract to have Frank pay Bob $1,000. In such an instance, Bob is a third-party *creditor beneficiary* of the contract between Susan and Frank. Bob can sue Frank if there is a breach of the contract and can also sue Susan, since she still owes him $1,000.

When the performance under a contract is meant as a gift to a third party, that person is a *donee beneficiary*. Donee beneficiaries can sue the party that owes them a performance under a breached contract, but cannot sue the party that contracted to make them a gift. The beneficiary of a life insurance policy is usually a donee beneficiary.

An *incidental beneficiary* is a third party that unintentionally benefits from a contract. The incidental beneficiary has no rights under a contract.

15. Performance of Contracts

At the time parties reach agreement under a contract, the *duty of performance* becomes binding. Each party must perform the consideration promised to the other. Failure to perform breaches the contract.

Parties often put conditions in a contract that affect its performance. If something must take place in the future before a party has a duty to perform, it is called a *condition precedent*. For example, a building developer may contract to buy certain land "when the city of Euphoria annexes it." The annexation is a condition precedent to the developer's duty to purchase the land.

A *condition subsequent* excuses contractual performance if some future event takes place. A marine insurance policy that terminates shipping loss coverage "if war is declared" contains a condition subsequent.

Under *concurrent conditions* each party's contractual performance is triggered by the other party's tendering (offering) performance. In a contract for the purchase of land, the performing obligations of the seller and buyer are concurrent conditions. The significance of a concurrent condition is that a party must offer to perform before legally holding the other party for non-performance. The land buyer must offer to pay for the land before suing the seller for failing to perform.

The conditions discussed above may be express or implied. Express conditions are set forth in the contract. Implied conditions do not appear in the contract, but are implied by law.

A party to a contract may not always perfectly perform duties under it. The more complex a contract is, the more difficult it is for a party to complete every aspect of performance. Courts generally recognize three levels of contract performance.

Complete performance recognizes that a contracting party has fulfilled every duty required by the contract. Payment of money, for example, is a contractual duty of performance which a party can perform completely. A party that performs completely is entitled to a complete performance by the other party and may sue to enforce this right.

Substantial performance represents a less-than-complete performance. A contracting party has honestly attempted to perform but has fallen short. Because of the complexity of building contractors' work, they often are able to reach substantial performance but not complete performance. One who substantially performs is entitled to the price promised by the other less that party's damages.

Material breach is a level of performance below what is reasonably acceptable. A party that has materially breached a contract cannot sue the other party for performance and is liable for damages arising from the breach.

16. Discharge of Contracts

A party to a contract is *discharged* when the party is released from all further obligation of performance. Of course, complete performance discharges a party to a contract. Table 5-4 also lists other events which create discharge.

One event which discharges a party's obligation of performance deserves special attention. A party is discharged because of *impossibility of performance.*

If the subject matter of the contract is destroyed, the contract becomes impossible to perform. When a contract exists for the sale of a building, and the building burns, the seller is discharged from performance. Likewise,

TABLE 5-4   Events Which Discharge a Party to a Contract

1. Complete performance
2. Occurrence of a condition subsequent
3. Nonoccurrence of a condition precedent
4. Material breach by the other party
5. Legal surrender of the right to enforce performance (waiver)
6. Mutual agreement to rescind
7. Expiration of the statute of limitations for enforceability
8. Novation (the substitution by agreement of one party for another on a contract)
9. Impossibility of performance

when there is a contract for personal services, and the party promising the services becomes ill or dies, the party receives discharge from performance.

The party that promised performance that becomes illegal is also discharged due to impossibility of performance. Mere increased difficulty or reduced profitability, however, does not constitute impossibility of performance.

Finally, under the UCC a party to a sale of goods contract receives discharge from performance due to *commercial impracticability*. The "impracticability" standard is not as difficult to meet as the "impossibility" standard. What constitutes impracticabillity of performance depends upon the circumstances of the situation. For instance, a manufacturer may be discharged from an obligation to make goods for a buyer when the manufacturer's major source of raw materials is unexpectedly interrupted. But if the raw materials are reasonably available from another supplier, the manufacturer may not receive discharge because of impracticability.

17. Trends in Contract Law

This chapter has given you an appreciation of the influence of contract law on private commercial transactions. The discussion has centered on the rules of contract law. Legal enforceability of contractual agreements provides an important framework for promoting certainty and efficiency in commercial dealings.

In general, however, trends in contract law do not affect the basic rules discussed in this chapter. Other chapters in the book develop many of the trends that affect contract law today. They deal with specific types of contracts or the use of contracts in particular situations. Still, several trends which are not mentioned elsewhere deserve attention here.

As commercial transactions have grown increasingly complex, courts and legislatures have created more and more exceptions to traditional, fairly inflexible requirements of contract formation. These exceptions reflect an attempt to accommodate law to the actual reality of business dealings. For instance, UCC provisions on modification of contracts without consideration, opened-ended contract terms, and contract formation by course of dealing are exceptions to traditional rules.

Similarly, courts have demonstrated greater willingness in recent years to grant damages based on one party's reasonable reliance on another's promises instead of merely on the party's expectations under a formal contract. This development reflects attempts to conform law to actual behavior in a complicated business world.

Finally, as previously mentioned, many contracting parties do not seek legal enforcement of breached agreements. With ever greater frequency, parties use arbitration, mediation, and negotiation when business problems arise under contracts. They avoid the time-consuming, expensive, and uncertain litigation process.

A major trend in contract law has been the passage of many statutes affecting contracts between businesses and consumers. Government has stepped in both at the federal and state levels to protect consumers as they make contracts with businesses. Chapter 15 discusses protection of consumers and debtors.

One recent development affecting business and consumer contracts has been enactment of "plain English" statutes in several states. These statutes require that standard business and consumer form contracts be written in a clearly understandable way. Drafters of such contracts must avoid legal expressions not ordinarily comprehended by consumers. More than thirty states have related statutes directed specifically at insurance contracts. A number of federal laws affecting readability also apply to specific types of contracts.

REVIEW QUESTIONS

1   How does a contract differ from an unenforceable promise? Explain.

2   Why is the law of contracts vital to the private enterprise system?

3   Nina goes to work for Classic Realty as a sales agent. She is promised a "reasonable salary" in addition to a sales commission. After three months and no sales, Nina leaves Classic to accept another job. She demands that Classic pay her the promised salary. If Classic refuses, can Nina recover damages for breach of contract? For quasi-contract? Discuss.

4   Most contractual disputes are resolved by negotiated settlement. Explain why.

5   Womack Widget Co. offers 1,000 widgets to Lowery Hardware at $1.25 per widget. Two days later Lowery sends a letter accepting the offer. While the letter is in the mail, Womack calls Lowery and revokes his offer. Has a contract been formed? Discuss.

6   Fielding Bros. offers to ship six furnaces to Central City Heating and Cooling Co. for $4,500 cash. Central City accepts on the condition that Fielding give 120 days' credit. Has a contract resulted? Explain.

7   Farley and Gutman enter a contract for the sale of 5 acres of land at $8,000 per acre. Later, Gutman, the buyer, asks if Farley will agree to modify the contract to $7,000 per acre. Farley agrees. Is Farley's promise legally binding on him? Would the answer be different if five used cars were sold instead of 5 acres of land?

8   What does it mean to say that a contract which attempts to disclaim liability for negligence is against "public policy"?

9   Under what legal circumstances does a contract for the sale of goods of $500 or more not have to be in writing to be enforceable?

10   Gus contracts to buy a used car from Cars Galore, Inc. The printed contract specifies "no warranties." But Gus and the sales manager of Cars handwrite into the contract a ninety-day guarantee on the transmission. If the transmission fails after sixty days, is there a warranty protecting Gus or not?

11   What does it mean to say that an assignee of contract rights has no greater rights than the assignor had?

12   The Store Owners Association at the Clearcreek Mall hires City Security Service to patrol the mall's parking lot after dark. Nancy Boggins, owner of the Shoe Attic at the mall, is mugged one night while the security guard is making an unauthorized visit to a friend's house. Can Nancy successfully sue City Security? Does it change your answer if Nancy is not a member of the Store Owners Association?

13   Explain the difference between a condition precedent and a condition subsequent.

14   Ace Contracting constructs an office building for Realty Enterprises. Realty's tenants quickly find a number of minor problems with the plumbing and insulation of the new building. When Realty contacts Ace about bringing its work up to standard, Ace promises to correct the problems but never does. Can Realty rescind the contract? What are Realty's legal remedies?

15   In the mid-1970s, a tripling of prices by an illegal cartel of uranium producers caused Westinghouse Electric Corp. to default on uranium delivery contracts to a number of utility companies. The companies sued, and Westinghouse settled. If the case had gone to trial, what defense might Westinghouse have raised to excuse its nonperformance under the contracts?

Chapter 6

Torts in the Business Environment

1. Introduction

The escape of toxic chemical fumes at a Union Carbide plant in Bhopal, India, leaves over 2,000 persons dead. Getty Oil decides to merge with Texaco rather than with Pennzoil. The *Washington Post* publishes a story alleging that the president of Mobil Oil used his position to gain company business for his consultant son. What do these situations have in common? They have all led to legal claims based upon the various theories of tort.

A **tort** is a legal wrong to a person or property, one for which a court will provide a remedy. In a sense, breaches of contract are also legal wrongs, so we must qualify the concept of tort by emphasizing that it does not include breaches of contract. Breaches of contract happen because people fail to honor specific, binding promises they make to one another. Torts arise when people do not live up to duties of action and behavior society imposes upon them. Tort duties may be general—such as the duty to use reasonable care toward others—or they may be as specific as the duty of the commercial seller not to sell defective products.

Historically, a principal aim of tort law has been to provide persons injured by legal wrongs with *corrective justice*. The idea of corrective justice is an old one. It is that the preservation of order in society demands that tortfeasors (those who commit wrong) compensate their innocent victims. The alternative to corrective justice is personal feuding and, ultimately, the breakdown of civilized order. In addition to soothing moral outrage and financial loss through compensation, corrective justice punishes intentional or wanton wrongdoing by imposing special punishment (punitive) damages. It also deters future wrongdoing.

From its beginnings, however, tort law themes went beyond corrective justice to face issues of *distributive justice*. As used here, distributive justice concerns the specific way the law allocates losses caused by accidents. Should losses lie where they fall, or should the law distribute them in some other fashion? Although there is certainly an overlap between these two types of justice, corrective justice focuses on restoring order between the parties to a dispute. The scope of distributive justice looks past the immediate parties and considers how best to spread economic losses through the parties, given the resources of society as a whole.

The legislation and case law which address distributive justice issues have pointed generally toward shifting loss from injured accident victims and placing it on those sued, especially when insurance or increased prices ultimately can spread the loss to society as a whole. This trend is most visible in business-related accidents involving injured employees or defective products, when no one may have been negligent. "There is a strong and growing tendency," wrote Roscoe Pound in 1914, "where there is blame on neither side, to ask, in view . . . of social justice, who can best bear the loss and hence to shift the loss by creating liability where there has been no fault." In recent years this "tendency" has become more evident and encompasses even those situations where some blame is present.

The complexities of technology and contemporary economic life may make it difficult at best, however, to achieve distributive justice through application of tort law. As an example, consider the following facts: A hotel employee, angry at being dismissed by his employer, sets a small fire in the hotel kitchen. The flames quickly ignite some highly combustible electrical insulation and spread into the hotel halls. Alarm and sprinkler systems, which fail to meet city fire codes, are ineffective to warn hundreds of sleeping guests of the growing danger and to control the spread of the fire. When awakened by wailing fire engines, some guests are quickly overcome by clouds of highly toxic smoke from burning plastics and synthetic fabrics. Other guests race from their rooms, only to be unable to find poorly located and marked fire exits. Some reach exits and find them locked. Some enter unlocked exits and face choking smoke because hotel employees improperly have left several exit doors propped open. When firefighters finally bring the fire under control, hundreds are dead or injured.

Who is liable under these facts, and how shall the losses be spread? The arsonist is liable, but he has no money. What should be the hotel's liability for failing to protect its guests properly from the fire? Does the architectural firm which designed the hotel have liability? How about the construction firm and the electrical subcontractor? Are there any others who should share the losses? Consider the manufacturers of fabrics and plastics used in the hotel whose products when burned released deadly fumes.

In the illustration here, which is based on actual fact, the tort system will spread much of the injury loss through insurance payments first, then by raised premium prices for insurance, and finally by increased prices for goods and services. In the final analysis society will bear much of the financial burden of the fire. But many question the fairness and efficiency of the court system and tort law as methods for allocating losses under such complicated circumstances.

This chapter divides torts into three main categories: intentional torts, negligence torts, and strict liability torts. Intentional torts involve deliberate actions which cause injury. Negligence torts involve injury following a failure to use "reasonable care." Strict liability torts impose legal responsibility for injury even though a liable party neither intentionally nor negligently causes the injury. In studying these categories try to determine where tort law is changing and affecting issues of distributive justice. By doing so, you will get a deeper understanding of the controversy surrounding tort law today.

2. The Development of Tort Law

Prior to 1800 much of the law of personal property injury was founded on the doctrine of **trespass**. When we think of trespass now, we think mainly of trespass to land. In the past, however, the doctrine was used by any plaintiff who had sustained an injury to person or property due to the act of the defendant. And the trespass doctrine was a strict liability one. The fact that the defendant was not at fault or could not have reasonably avoided the accident was usually irrelevant.

The trespass doctrine as applied to personal injury, however, was the doctrine of an uncomplicated age and of a simple people. At that time, any injury done by another invited swift revenge if the law did not impose itself between the actor and the injured. But in the 1800s, as populations expanded and social and economic life became more complex, values and attitudes grew more sophisticated. The law changed to meet these changing conditions, and the doctrine of **negligence** emerged. No longer was one liable for reasonably unavoidable injury inflicted upon the person of another. Instead, liability would be imposed only when the actor was at fault and had failed to act as a "reasonable man."

Economic realities in the 1800s help explain the widespread acceptance of the new negligence doctrine. Many judges apparently considered that the strict liability of trespass would threaten the struggling infant industries of the time, putting an end to the socially valuable production of machined goods. The courts thus extended negligence law and defenses into areas of employer-employee relations, products liability, and accidents arising from business activity.

The nineteenth-century negligence doctrine is sometimes viewed as achieving a type of distributive justice which removed legal liability from nonnegligent behavior on the injured victims of such behavior, providing a type of "subsidy" for business development. Although this view prevails today among legal scholars, it is not the only one. Many economics-inclined scholars disagree. They argue that in cases developing negligence doctrine the courts simply were allocating accident losses and property rights in the most economically efficient manner possible.

Whichever view is most accurate, it remains undeniable that courts in the 1800s fashioned numerous tort principles which left injury losses on accident victims. In addition to negligence doctrine, the courts created the defense of **contributory negligence**, which barred plaintiffs from any recovery if their own fault contributed to their injuries. Another court-created doctrine, the **assumption of risk** defense, barred plaintiffs from recovery when they knowingly submitted themselves to hazardous conditions created by the carelessness of others.

Another barrier courts placed in the way of plaintiff recovery was the doctrine of **proximate causation**. Not only did plaintiffs have to prove that their injuries actually were caused by negligence, they also had to establish that their injuries "foreseeably" arose from (were proximately caused by) the negligence (see section 17). Courts regarded questions of proximate cause as "matters of law." Judges dismissed many negligence claims upon the basis that the alleged facts showed no proximate cause.

Beginning in the twentieth century, the pendulum started to swing back. The courts (and legislatures) acted in many situations to distribute accident losses away from injured victims. In the workplace, the passage of workers' compensation statutes accomplished this goal (see Chapter 14). In product-related accidents, the courts arrived at tort reform through a series of developments which culminated in strict tort liability—which requires no proof of fault—for the sale of defective products (see Chapter 7). Also, the harsh application of contributory negligence has been eased (see section 18).

Even the application of negligence doctrine has changed. Today, many courts consider questions of proximate cause as issues which plaintiff-sympathetic juries, rather than judges, should resolve. Also, in recent years courts have expanded the scope of "duty," which defines those to whom one owes reasonable care (nonnegligence) (see section 14).

What has caused these changes in tort law in the twentieth century? Economic conditions are chiefly responsible. The infant industries of the nineteenth century have grown into healthy maturity. Business no longer needs the liability protection it required a hundred years ago. Courts and legislatures also follow the mood of the country. To a significant extent, the public has demanded that tort laws be reformed tto relieve injured individuals of potentially catastrophic accident losses.

Note that the rapid development of tort law has chiefly concerned negligence and strict liability. Changes in intentional tort law have been more gradual, although they have also taken place.

INTENTIONAL TORTS

An important element in the following torts is *intent,* as we are dealing with *intentional* torts. Intent is usually defined as the "desire" to bring about certain results. But in some circumstances the meaning is even broader, including not only desired results but also results which are "substantially likely" to result from an action. Recently, employers who knowingly exposed employees to toxic substances without warning them of the dangers have been sued for committing the intentional tort of battery. The employers did not desire their employees' injuries, but these injuries were "substantially likely" to result from the failure to warn.

The following sections explain the basic types of intentional torts. Table 6-1 lists these torts.

3. Assault and Battery

An **assault** is the placing of another in immediate apprehension for his or her physical safety. "Apprehension" has a broader meaning than "fear." It includes the expectation that one is about to be physically injured. The person who intentionally creates such apprehension in another is guilty of the tort of assault. Many times a battery follows an assault. A **battery** is an illegal touching of another. As used here, "illegal" means that the touching is done without justification and without the consent of the person touched. The touching need not cause injury.

A store manager who threatens an unpleasant customer with a wrench is probably guilty of assault. Actually hitting the customer with the wrench would constitute battery.

4. Intentional Infliction of Mental Distress

Intentional **infliction of mental distress** is a battery to the emotions. It arises from outrageous, intentional conduct which carries a strong probability of causing mental distress to the person at whom it is directed. Usually, one who sues on the basis of an intentional infliction of mental distress must prove that the defendant's outrageous behavior caused not only mental distress, but also physical symptoms, such as headaches or sleeplessness.

In the business world, many examples of this tort come about from the efforts of creditors to extract payment from their debtors. Frequent, abusive, threatening phone calls by creditors might provide the basis for a claim of intentional infliction of mental distress. As torts go, this tort is of fairly recent origin. It is a judge-made tort which furnishes a good example of how the courts are becoming increasingly sensitive to the range of injuries for which

TABLE 6-1 Types of Intentional Torts

Assault and battery
Intentional infliction of mental distress
Invasion of privacy
False imprisonment
Trespass
Conversion
Defamation
Common law business torts
Statutory competitive torts
Constitutional torts

compensation is appropriate. In some states, courts have gone so far as to establish liability for carelessly inflicted mental distress, such as the distress of a mother who sees her child negligently run down by a delivery truck.

5. Invasion of Privacy

The tort of **invasion of privacy** is one that is still in the early stages of legal development. As the statutes and court cases recognize it, the tort at present comprises three principal invasions of personal interest. An invasion of any one of these areas of interest is sufficient to trigger liability.

Most commonly, liability will be imposed on a defendant who appropriates the plaintiff's name or likeness for his or her own use. Many advertisers and marketers have been required to pay damages to individuals when pictures of them have been used without authorization to promote products, or when their names and identities have been used without permission for promotional purposes. Before using anyone's picture or name, an advertiser must obtain a proper release from that person to avoid possible liability. Appropriating another's name and identity in order to secure credit is an additional example of this invasion of privacy tort.

A second invasion of privacy is the defendant's intrusion upon the plaintiff's physical solitude. Illegal searches or invasions of home or possessions, illegal wiretapping, and persistent and unwanted telephoning can provide the basis for this invasion of privacy tort. In one case, a woman even recovered damages against a photographer who entered her sickroom and snapped a picture of her. Employers who enter their employees' homes without permission have also been sued successfully for invasions of privacy. If the invasion of privacy continues, it may be enjoined by the court. Jacqueline Kennedy Onassis sought and obtained an injunction which forbade a certain photographer from getting too close to her and her children. Under this tort, the invasion of physical solitude must be highly objectionable to a reasonable person.

The third invasion of personal interest which gives rise to the invasion of privacy tort is the defendant's public disclosure of highly objectionable, private information about the plaintiff. A showing of such facts can be the basis for a cause of action, even if the information is true. Thus, publishing in a newspaper that the plaintiff does not pay his or her debts has been ruled to create liability for the defendant creditor. Communicating the same facts to a credit reporting agency or the plaintiff's employer usually does not impose liability, however. In these cases there has been no disclosure to the public in general. Also, the news media are protected under the First Amendment when they publish information about public officials and other public figures.

6. False Imprisonment and Malicious Prosecution

Claims of **false imprisonment** stem most frequently in business from instances of shoplifting. This tort is the intentional unjustified confinement of a nonconsenting person. Although most states have statutes which permit merchants or their employees to detain customers suspected of shoplifting, this detention must be a reasonable one. The unnecessary use of force, lack of reasonable suspicion of shoplifting, or an unreasonable length of confinement can cause the merchant to lose the statutory privilege. The improperly detained customer is then able to sue for false imprisonment. Allegations of battery are also usually made if the customer has been touched.

The tort of **malicious prosecution** is often called "false arrest." Malicious prosecution arises from causing someone to be arrested criminally without proper grounds. It occurs, for instance, when the arrest is accomplished simply to harass someone. In 1984 in Albany, New York, a jury awarded a man $200,000 for malicious prosecution. His zipper had broken, leaving open his fly, and a store security guard had him arrested for indecent exposure even after he explained that he had not noticed the problem.

7. Trespass

To enter another's land without consent or to remain there after being asked to leave constitutes the tort of **trespass**. A variation on the trespass tort arises when something (such as particles of pollution) is placed on another's land without consent. Although the usual civil action for trespass asks for an injunction to restrain the trespasser, the action may also ask for damages.

Union pickets walking on company property (in most instances), customers refusing to leave a store after being asked to do so, and unauthorized persons entering restricted areas are all examples of trespass. Note that trespass is often a crime as well as a tort. Intentional wrongdoing is frequently criminal.

8. Conversion

Conversion is the wrongful and unlawful exercise of dominion (power) and control over the personal property of another. Conversion deprives the proper owner of lawful rights in the property. The deprivation may be either temporary or permanent, but it must constitute a serious invasion of the owner's rights. Abraham Lincoln once convinced an Illinois court that a defendant's action in riding the plaintiff's horse for fifteen miles was not sufficiently serious to be a conversion since the defendant had returned the horse in good condition. The plaintiff had left the horse with the defendant to be stabled and fed.

Conversion arises often in business situations. Stealing property or purchasing stolen property (even innocently) is a conversion. Failing to return properly acquired property at the designated time, delivering property to the wrong party, and destruction and alteration of property are all conversions if the deprivation of ownership rights is serious or long-lasting. Even if she or he intends to return it, one who converts is absolutely liable for any damage done to property. A warehouse operator who improperly transfers stored goods from a designated to a nondesignated warehouse is absolutely liable when a tornado destroys the goods, or when a thief steals them.

9. Defamation

Defamation is the publication of untrue statements about another which hold up that individual's character or reputation to contempt and ridicule. "Publication" means that the untruth must be made known to third parties. If defamation is oral, it is called **slander**. Written defamation, or defamation published over radio or television, is termed **libel**.

False accusations of dishonesty or inability to pay debts frequently bring on defamation suits in business relationships. Sometimes, such accusations arise during the course of a takeover attempt by one company of another through an offering to buy stock. In a recent instance, the chairman of one company called the chairman of a rival business "lying, deceitful, and treacherous" and charged that he "violated the standards by which decent men do business." If untrue, these remarks provide a good example of defamation of character. Punitive or punishment damages, as well as actual damages, may be assessed in defamation cases.

Individuals are not the only ones who can sue for defamation. A corporation can also sue for defamation if untrue remarks discredit the way the corporation conducts its business. Untruthfully implying that a company's entire management is dishonest or incompetent defames the corporation.

Because of the First Amendment, special rules regarding defamation apply to the news media. These media are not liable for the defamatory untruths they print about public officials and public figures unless plaintiffs can prove that the untruths were published with "malice" (evil intent, that is, the deliberate intent to injure) or with "reckless disregard for the truth." Public figures are those who have consciously brought themselves to public attention.

Despite the difficulty of proving malice or reckless disregard, defamed persons can successfully sue news media. In 1984 *The Wall Street Journal* agreed to pay two federal prosecutors $800,000 after the prosecutors sued the newspaper for alleging that they improperly harassed a prisoner to force his cooperation with an investigation they were conducting. As of this writing the *Washington Post* is still appealing a $2 million judgment for libeling the president of Mobil Oil Co.

Does the malice standard apply to nonmedia as well as media defendants? The Supreme Court faced this issue in the following case. NO

DUN & BRADSTREET, INC. v. GREENMOSS BUILDERS, INC.
105 S. Ct. 2939 (1985)

Dun & Bradstreet issued a false credit report to plaintiff's creditors indicating that the plaintiff had filed a voluntary petition for bankruptcy. The report grossly misrepresented plaintiff's assets and liabilities. Dun & Bradstreet thereafter issued a corrective notice, but the plaintiff was dissatisfied with the notice and filed a defamation suit in Vermont State Court alleging injury to reputation. When the jury awarded compensatory and punitive damages to the plaintiff, the trial court granted Dun & Bradstreet's motion for a new trial. The Vermont Supreme Court reversed the trial court. The United States Supreme granted certiorari on the issue of whether or not the Constitution requires a showing of "actual malice" before damages can be awarded against a nonmedia defendant.

POWELL, J.: In *New York Times Co. v. Sullivan* . . . the Supreme Court for the first time held that the First Amendment limits the reach of state defamation laws. That case concerned a public official's recovery of damages for the publication of an advertisement criticizing police conduct in a civil rights demonstration. As the Court noted, the ad-

vertisement concerned "one of the major public issues of our time." Noting that "freedom of expression upon public questions is secured by the First Amendment," and that "debate on public issues should be uninhibited, robust, and wide-open," the Court held that a public official cannot recover damages for defamatory falsehood unless he proves that the false statement was made with " 'actual malice'—that is, with knowledge that it was false or with reckless disregard of whether it was false or not." In later cases, all involving public issues, the Court extended this same constitutional protection to libels of public figures, and in one case suggested in a plurality opinion that this constitutional rule should extend to libels of any individual so long as the defamatory statements involved a "matter of public or general interest." . . .

In *Gertz v. Robert Welch, Inc.,* we held that the fact that expression concerned a public issue did not by itself entitle the libel defendant to the constitutional protections of *New York Times.* These protections, we found, were not "justified solely by reference to the interest of the press and broadcast media in immunity from liability." Rather, they represented "an accommodation between [First

Amendment] concerns[s] and the limited state interest present in the context of libel actions brought by public persons." In libel actions brought by private persons we found the competing interests different. Largely because private persons have not voluntarily exposed themselves to increased risk of injury from defamatory statements and because they generally lack effective opportunities for rebutting such statements, we found that the State possessed a "strong and legitimate . . . interest in compensating private individuals for injury to reputation." Balancing this stronger state interest against the same First Amendment interest at stake in *New York Times*, we held that a State could not allow recovery of presumed and punitive damages absent a showing of "actual malice." Nothing in our opinion, however, indicated that this same balance would be struck regardless of the type of speech involved.

We have never considered the *Gertz* balance obtains when the defamatory statements involve no issue of public concern. To make this determination, we must employ the approach approved in *Gertz* and balance the State's interest in compensating private individuals for injury to their reputation against the First Amendment interest in protecting this type of expression. This state interest is identical to the one weighed in Gertz. There we found that it was "strong and legitimate." . . .

The First Amendment interest, on the other hand, is less important than the one weighed in *Gertz*. We have long recognized that not all speech is of equal First Amendment importance. It is speech on "matters of

public concern" that is "at the heart of the First Amendment's protection." [S]peech on matters of purely private concern is of less First Amendment concern. As a number of state courts, including the court below, have recognized, the role of the Constitution in regulating state libel law is far more limited when the concerns that activated *New York Times* and *Gertz* are absent. In such a case, [t]here is no threat to the free and robust debate of public issues; there is no potential interference with a meaningful dialogue of ideas concerning self-government; and there is no threat of liability causing a reaction of self-censorship by the press. The facts of the present case are wholly without the First Amendment concerns with which the Supreme Court of the United States has been struggling.

While such speech is not totally unprotected by the First Amendment, its protections are less stringent. In *Gertz*, we found that the state interest in awarding presumed and punitive damages was not "substantial" in view of their effect on speech at the core of First Amendment concern. This interest however, is "substantial" relative to the incidental effect these remedies may have on speech of significantly less constitutional interest. . . . In light of the reduced constitutional value of speech involving no matters of public concern, we hold that the state interest adequately supports awards of presumed and punitive damages—even absent a showing of "actual malice." [*The court then decided that Dun & Bradstreet's credit report did not concern a public issue. Affirmed.*]

There are two basic defenses to a claim of defamation. One defense is that the statements made were true. *Truth* is an absolute defense. The second defense is that statements arose from *privileged communications*. For example, statements made by legislators, judges, attorneys, and those involved in lawsuits are privileged under many circumstances.

10. Business Torts

The label *business torts* is admittedly a vague one. It embraces several different kinds of torts which involve intentional interference with business relations.

INJURIOUS FALSEHOOD

Injurious falsehood, sometimes called *trade disparagement,* is a common business tort. It consists of the publication of untrue statements which disparage the plaintiff's ownership of property or its quality. General disparagement of the plaintiff's business may also provide basis for liability. As a cause of action, injurious falsehood is similar to defamation of character. It differs, however, in that it usually applies to the plaintiff's property or business rather than character or reputation. The requirements of proof are also somewhat different. Defamatory remarks are presumed false unless the defendant can prove their truth. But in disparagement cases the plaintiff must establish the falsity of the defendant's statements. In disparagement cases, the plaintiff must also show actual damages arising from the untrue statements.

As an example of injurious falsehood, consider the cases filed by a major home products company. The complaints alleged that the defendants had distributed handouts which associated the company's familiar emblem of moon and stars with satanism—the worship of the devil. At the heart of this tort is the interference with the company's future sales.

INTENTIONAL INTERFERENCE WITH CONTRACTUAL RELATIONS

A second type of business tort is intentional **interference with contractual relations**. Inducing employees to breach contracts with their employers can bring liability to third parties. Recently, a jury awarded Pennzoil $10.53 billion against Texaco for inducing Getty Oil to breach an agreement of merger with Pennzoil. Although Texaco has appealed, the judgment emphasizes the seriousness of this tort.

Lawsuits for interfering with contractual relations are not limited to those involving employee contracts. As the following case shows, however, suits to recover damages for such interference are not always successful.

WELCH v. BANCORP MANAGEMENT ADVISORS, INC.
675 P.2d 172 (Or. 1984)

The plaintiff executed a contract with a real estate investment trust (the Trust). The Trust agreed to finance a real estate development plan by the plaintiff. In return it would re-ceive interest on the money borrowed and half of the net profit when the property sold. An Investment Committee comprised of employees of the banks that supplied the Trust with funds for such ventures had an agreement with the Trust to act as an agent for the Trust by providing investment advice. Upon advice from the Investment Committee, the Trust breached the contract with the plaintiff and refused to loan him any money. The plaintiff sued the Investment Committee in tort for intentional interference with a contractual relationship between the Trust and the plaintiff. He argued that the Investment Committee was primarily motivated by the interest of the banks involved instead of the interest of the Trust.

CARLSON, J.: We hold that the privilege of a financial adviser is analogous to the qualified privilege of a corporate officer or employee. An agent acting as financial adviser is thus privileged to interfere with or induce breach relations with third parties, as long as the agent's actions are within the scope of his employment and taken with an intent to further the best interests of the principal. If this two-prong test is met, it is immaterial that the agent or another principal also profits by the advice. However, where an agent-financial adviser acts against the best interests of the principal or acts solely for his own benefit, he is liable in tort for harm done to the other contracting party.

We turn now to the facts of this case. Applying the two-prong test set out above, there is no evidence that the Investment Committee acted outside the scope of its authority in advising the Trust. In fact, in paragraph XI of the first count of plaintiff's Fifth Amended Complaint, he asserts that defendant's actions were within the scope of their actual and apparent authority.

As for the second prong, we find that there is no genuine issue of material fact to dispute that the advice given by the Investment Committee to the Trust was given with the intent to benefit the Trust. . . .

The evidence in defendant's exhibits was enough for the trial judge to determine that the Investment Committee was acting in the best interests of the Trust. The evidence when viewed in the light most favorable to plaintiff, shows that defendants did meet their burden of proving that they acted within the scope of their authority as advisers to the Trust and that they acted to benefit the Trust, even if they benefited the banks as well. The trial judge applied the correct legal analysis. . . . [*Reversed.*]

OBTAINING TRADE SECRETS

Another variety of business tort arises from wrongfully obtaining a rival's trade secrets. The Fifth Circuit Court of Appeals has defined a *trade secret* as "any formula, pattern, device, or compilation of information which is used in one's business, and which gives him an opportunity to obtain an advantage over competitors who do not know or use it." Information which is general knowledge cannot be a trade secret.

Many times employees who leave their employment to go into competition with their employers are accused of misappropriating trade secrets. In 1985, Apple Computer, Inc., filed suit against its founder Steven Jobs on this basis when he left the company. An employee may draw upon the general knowledge, skills, and experience he or she has gained in working for a former employer, but it is a tort for the employee to use specific customer lists, documents, or other trade secrets gained through previous employment. In addition to obtaining provable damages, someone whose trade secrets have been misappropriated will usually ask the court to enjoin the defendant from using trade secrets in competition with the plaintiff.

In order for a trade secret to remain a trade secret, a business must take active steps to keep the information confidential. A major soft-drink manufacturer once withdrew from a consumer market of 400 million people in India rather than reveal the secret of its cola-based mixture, as demanded by the Indian government.

A final common law business tort involves *unfair competition*. It includes "palming off" a competitor's goods as one's own, and misappropriating trademarks. In addition to being a common law tort, unfair competition also includes several statutory torts. A statutory tort is, of course, one created by statute. For instance, violation of the antitrust laws is a tort under the Clayton Act (see Chapter 21). The next two sections discuss statutory torts of unfair competition involving trademarks, false advertising, patents, and copyrights.

11. Trademarks and False Advertising: The Lanham Act

TRADEMARKS

The law of trademarks covers trademarks, service marks, certification marks, and collective marks. A *trademark* is any mark, word, picture, or design that attaches to goods to indicate their source. If the mark is associated with a service, it is a *service mark*. A *certification mark* is used by someone other than its owner to certify the quality, point of origin, or other characteristic of goods or services. Use of a *collective mark* represents membership in a certain organization or association. McDonald's golden arches, the words and design of Coca-Cola, the Good Housekeeping Seal of Approval, the prancing horse of Ferrari, and the "union label" are all marks of one kind or another. In the discussion that follows, all marks are termed trademarks.

The common law protects the use of trademarks, but since the *Lanham Act* of 1946, the principal protection has come from federal law. Trademark law recognizes that property rights extend beyond ownership of actual goods to the intangible aspects of goodwill which trademarks represent. In forbidding misappropriation of trademarks, the law prevents misappropriation of a company's goodwill and reputation. It protects both the company that owns the mark and the buyer of goods or services who relies upon it.

To acquire the protection of the Lanham Act, a trademark must be registered on the Principal Register. Only a mark in current use on goods and services in interstate commerce may be registered. In addition, the mark must be uniquely distinctive and nondescriptive. A mark that merely describes a use or characteristic of the product cannot generally be registered. A quick-order restaurant could not register the trademark "Fast Food."

Unauthorized use of a registered trademark constitutes the competitive tort of *infringement.* Infringement exists not only when the exact trademark is copied but also when the mark used resembles the protected trademark enough to confuse the public. For instance, Vernors, Inc., sued the Coca-Cola Co. for trademark infringement for using the slogan "It's One of a Kind." The Vernors' trademarked slogan was "The One of a Kind Soft Drink." The Lanham Act provides that any person who infringes on another's registered trademark in selling or advertising goods or services is liable for damages and subject to injunction. In instances of willful infringement, a court may award triple damages. Wendy's International, Inc. forced dozens of retailers to remove thousands of "Where's the beef?" t-shirts from their shelves. The shirts' manufacturer lacked the fast-food chain's permission to use the trademarked slogan.

A growing problem in recent years has been the deliberate counterfeiting of products. Levi jeans, Rolex watches, and other well-known brand products have been copied and sold. The U.S. International Trade Commission estimated that the volume of counterfeiting tripled between 1978 and 1983.

Now Congress has made deliberate counterfeiting a felony, punishable by jail terms and substantial fines. It is also a federal crime to traffic knowingly in goods containing a counterfeit mark.

To maintain a trademark, the owner must prevent its misuse and unauthorized use. If the public comes to think that a registered trademark represents a general class of goods, rather than a single brand, registration and the right to sue for trademark infringement may be lost. For instance, employees of a popular cola beverage have been instructed always to ask for it at a restaurant by its famous trademarked name. If the restaurant brings a competitor's cola beverage instead of the one ordered, the employees are instructed to object strenuously to the substitution for the trademarked brand. It is all part of the attempt to preserve the uniqueness of the trademark. Table 6-2 gives examples of trademarks which have lost their uniqueness due to general use.

FALSE ADVERTISING

A tort related to but different from trademark infringement is the competitive tort of *false advertising.* Section 43(a) of the Lanham Act establishes an action for civil damages for any false description or representation of one's goods or services which may damage a competitor. This action need not involve trademarkk infringement.

There are many different kinds of false advertising which are actionable

TABLE 6-2 Trademarks Lost Due to General Use

Aspirin
Cellophane
Thermos
Monopoly (the game)
Escalator

under the Lanham Act. For an advertiser to represent its product as "California redwood" when the wood is actually red oak might invite a tort action by anyone legitimately associated with the redwood industry. To portray a picture of a competitor's product as one's own, as in an advertisement, is actionably false if the two products are not identical. Altering a competitor's product as shown in one's advertisement also violates Section 43(a). In 1985 a federal court awarded $40 million to U-Haul International against Jartran. Jartran admitted reducing the size of U-Haul trucks in advertising pictures in order to make the Jartran trucks appear larger.

Section 43(a) applies only to false representations made about the defendant's own goods or services. It does not apply to false statements made about the plaintiff's goods or services. Falsehooods of the latter kind are actionable under the common law tort of disparagement.

12. Patents and Copyrights

PATENTS

In the last century a government official urged that the Patent Office be closed because there was nothing left to invent. Today, however, inventors file approximately 100,000 new patent applications every year. When granted, **patents** give their holders a seventeen-year legal monopoly over the use and licensing of new processes, products, machines, and other combinations of matter. Design patents can be obtained for shorter time periods. Underlying the grant of patents is the belief that the law should encourage invention by granting inventors exclusive rights for a limited duration to the profits of their efforts.

To be patentable, inventions must be *nonobvious, novel,* and *useful.* They also must be tangible applications of an idea. Discovery of a new fact about the universe does not in itself allow the discoverer to patent all future uses of that fact. Only when that fact is specifically applied through design of a new machine or process may it be patented.

Federal patent law permits the holder of a patent to bring a statutory tort action against anyone who infringes on the patent. The principal issues in most patent cases are (1) whether or not the patent is valid, and (2) whether or not the defendant has infringed the patent. The plaintiff in patent cases usually seeks remedies of injunction and damages. For instance, a feederal court recently awarded Hughes Tool Co. $121 million against Dresser Industries for infringing on Hughes tool patents. Another court enjoined Eastman Kodak Co. from marketing instant cameras and film because of a patent infringement suit by the Polaroid Corporation. Interestingly, having a patent properly registered with the Patent Office does not conclusively establish its validity. It creates only a presumption of validity. In over half the cases involving patents, courts find the patents either invalid or otherwise unenforceable.

New technologies lead to new issues of patent law. Of special current concern is the patentability of computer programs. In *Diamond v. Diehr and Lutton*, the Supreme Court held that a process for curing rubber did not become unpatentable simply because it incorporated a computer program. On the other hand, computer applications of mathematical formulas are not patentable. Another issue of present significance to patent law involves the extent to which new "genetically engineered" life forms can be patented. The Supreme Court has ruled that under some circumstances patent law does apply to protect the inventors of such life forms.

COPYRIGHTS

Copyright law protects authors rather than inventors. An author creates works of a literary, dramatic, musical, graphic, choreographic, audio, or visual nature. Ranging from printed material to photographs to records and motion pictures, these works receive automatic federal protection under the Copyright Act of 1976 from the moment the author creates them. The copyright allows the holder to control the reproduction, display, distribution, and performance of a protected work. The copyright runs for the author's lifetime, plus fifty additional years.

Although copyright protection is automatic, a tort action for copyright infringement cannot be begun unless the author has properly filed copies of the protected work with the Copyright Office. And one who infringes on a copyright cannot be held liable for actual or statutory damages unless a copyright symbol or notice accompanies the protected work. When the author has observed the proper formalities, however, she or he may recover actual or statutory damages, attorney's fees, and any profits which the infringer has made. Illegally reproduced copies may also be seized, and willful copyright violations are criminal offenses.

The law permits a fair use of copyrighted work for teaching, research, and reporting purposes. In the next case, the Supreme Court considers whether video-taping television programs for home use violates the copyright laws.

SONY CORP. OF AMERICA v. UNIVERSAL CITY STUDIOS, INC.

104 S. Ct. 774 (1984)

Sony Corporation manufactures home videotape recorders (VTRs). Universal City Studios owns the copyrights on some of the television programs that are broadcast on the public airwaves. Universal brought an action against Sony Corp. alleging that VTR customers had recorded some of Universal's work that infringed on their copyrights, and

Universal claimed that Sony was liable for this infringement because it marketed the VTRs. The federal district court denied relief, holding that noncommercial home use was not a copyright infringement. The Court of Appeals reversed the district court decision, and Sony appealed.

STEVENS, J.: The respondents and Sony both conducted surveys of the way the Betamax machine was used by several hundred owners during a sample period in 1978. Although there were some differences in the surveys, they both showed that the primary use of the machine for most owners was "time-shifting"—the practice of recording a program to view it once at a later time, and thereafter erasing it. Time-shifting enables viewers to see programs they otherwise would miss because they are not at home, are occupied with other tasks, or are viewing a program on another station at the time of a broadcast that they desire to watch. . . .

[U]nauthorized uses of a copyrighted work are not necessarily infringing. An unlicensed use of the copyright is not an infringement unless it conflicts with one of the specific exclusive rights conferred by the copyright statute. Moreover, the definition of exclusive rights in section 106 of the present Act is prefaced by the words "subject to sections 107 through 118." Those sections describe a variety of uses of copyrighted material that "are not infringements of copyright notwithstanding the provisions of section 106." The most pertinent in this case is section 107, the legislative endorsement of the doctrine of "fair use."

That section identifies various factors that enable a Court to apply an "equitable rule of reason" analysis to particular claims of infringement. Although not conclusive, the first factor requires that "the commercial or nonprofit character of an activity" be weighed in any fair use decision. If the Betamax were used to make copies for a commercial or profit-making purpose, such use would presumptively be unfair. The contrary presumption is appropriate here, however, because the District Court's findings plainly establish that time-shifting for private home use must be characterized as a noncommercial, nonprofit activity. Moreover, when one considers the nature of a televised copyrighted audiovisual work, and that timeshifting merely enables a viewer to see such a work which he had been invited to witness in its entirety free of charge, the fact that the entire work is reproduced, does not have its ordinary effect of militating against a finding of fair use.

This is not, however, the end of the inquiry because Congress has also directed us to consider "the effect of the use upon the potential market for or value of the copyrighted work." The purpose of copyright is to create incentives for creative effort. Even copying for noncommercial purposes may impair the copyright holder's ability to obtain the rewards that Congress intended him to have. But a use that has no demonstrable effect upon the potential market for, or the value of, the copyrighted work need not be prohibited in order to protect the author's incentive to create. The prohibition of such noncommercial uses would merely inhibit access to ideas without any countervailing benefit.

Thus, although every commercial use of copyrighted material is presumptively an unfair exploitation of the monopoly privilege that belongs to the owner of the copyright, noncommercial uses are a different matter. A challenge to a noncommercial use of a copyrighted work requires proof either that the particular use is harmful, or that if it should become widespread, it would adversely affect the potential market for the copyrighted work. Actual present harm need not be shown; such a requirement would leave the copyright holder with no defense against predictable damage. Nor is it necessary to show with certainty that future harm will result. What is necessary is a showing by a preponderance of the evidence that some meaningful likelihood of future harm exists. If the intended use is for commercial gain, that likelihood may be presumed. But if it is for a noncommercial purpose, the likelihood must be demonstrated.

In this case, respondents failed to carry their burden with regard to home time-shifting. The District Court described respondents' evidence as follows:

Plaintiffs' experts admitted at several points in the trial that the time-shifting without librarying would result in "not a great deal of harm." Plaintiffs' greatest concern about time-shifting is with "a point of important philosophy that transcends even commercial judgment." They fear that with any Betamax usage, "invisible boundaries" are passed: "the copyright owner has lost control over his program."

Later in its opinion, the District Court observed: "Most of plaintiffs' predictions of harm hinge on speculation about audience viewing patterns and ratings, a measurement system which Sidney Sheinberg, MCA's president, calls a 'black art' because of the significant level of imprecision involved in the calculations."

There was no need for the District Court to say much about past harm: "Plaintiffs have admitted that no actual harm to their copyrights has occurred to date."

On the question of potential future harm from time-shifting, the District Court offered a more detailed analysis of the evidence. It rejected respondents' "fear that persons 'watching' the original telecast of a program will not be measured in the live audience and the ratings and revenues will decrease," by observing that current measurement technology allows the Betamax audience to be reflected. It rejected respondents' prediction "that live television or movie audiences will decrease as more people watch Betamax tapes as an alternative," with the observation that "[t]here is no factual basis for [the underlying] assumption." It rejected respondents' "fear that time-shifting will reduce audiences for telecast reruns," and concluded instead that "given current market practices, this should aid plaintiffs rather than harm them." And it declared that respondents' suggestion "that theater or film rental exhibition of a program will suffer because of time-shift recording of that program" lacks merit.

When these factors are all weighed in the "equitable rule of reason" balance, we must conclude that this record amply supports the District Court's conclusion that home time-shifting is fair use. In light of the findings of the District Court regarding the state of the empirical data, it is clear that the Court of Appeals erred in holding that the statute as presently written bars such conduct. [*Reversed.*]

Recently, Congress has granted copyright protection to the designs of integrated circuits. These circuits are designed into silicon chips used in computers and other electronic equipment. The new law gives ten years of copyright protection to any chips designed since July 1, 1983.

13. Constitutional Torts

Section 1983 of the Civil Rights Act of 1871 creates tort liability for any public official or employee who injures a person by depriving him or her of constitutionally guaranteed rights. Through interpretation, the Supreme Court has extended this liability to municipal (city) governments that support such behavior by "custom, practice, or policy." An example of constitutionally guaranteed rights—called "civil rights"—is the Fourteenth Amendment's right not to be deprived of life, liberty, or property without due process.

Most Section 1983 cases have involved police misconduct—usually false arrest, physical abuse, or failure to protect prisoners in custody. However, other areas of potential liability exist (see Table 6-3). Injured persons may sue municipal governments and their employees for actual damages and attorneys' fees. Employees may have to pay *punitive* (punishment) *damages* as well.

As with many other types of tort cases, the number of Section 1983 cases is increasing rapidly. Between 1977 and 1983, the number of cases filed annually doubled. Even judges are not immune from the reach of Section 1983. In 1984, the Supreme Court ruled that it applied to a judge who wrongfully jailed two men who were unable to post bond for misdemeanors, which were not jailable offenses.

NEGLIGENCE

The second major field of tort liability involves behavior which causes an unreasonably great risk of causing injury. This field of tort is called negligence. In the United States more lawsuits allege negligence than any other single cause of action.

A complaint for negligence must show four elements (see Table 6-4). The following sections discuss these elements.

14. Duty of Care

A critical element of the negligence tort is **duty**. Without a duty to another person, one does not owe that person reasonable care. Accidental injuries

TABLE 6-3 Areas of Potential Liability Involving Section 1983

1 Unfavorable recommendations of former government employees
2 Use of zoning for political or discriminatory purposes
3 Failure to award contracts to lowest bidders (in some instances)
4 Discharge of government employees
5 Failure to train and supervise public employees
6 Use of permit, inspection, or licensing procedures for political, harassing, or discriminatory purposes

TABLE 6-4   Elements of Negligence

1 Existence of a duty of care owed by the defendant to the plaintiff
2 Unreasonable behavior which breaches the duty
3 Causation of the plaintiff's injury by the defendant's behavior:
   a. Cause in fact
   b. Proximate causation
4 An actual injury

occur daily for which people other than the victim have no responsibility, legally or otherwise.

Duty usually arises out of a person's conduct or activity. A person doing something has a duty to use reasonable care and skill around others to avoid injuring them. Whether one is driving a car or manufacturing a product, she or he has a duty not to injure others by unreasonable conduct.

Usually, a person has no duty to avoid injuring others through nonconduct. There is no general duty requiring a sunbather at the beach to warn a would-be surfer that a great white shark is lurking offshore, even if the sunbather has seen the fin. There is moral responsibility but no legal duty present.

Where there is a special relationship between persons, the situation changes. A person in a special relationship with another may have a duty to avoid unreasonable nonconduct. A business renting surfboards at the beach would probably be liable for renting a board to a customer who was attacked by a shark if it knew the shark was nearby and failed to warn the customer. The "special business relationship" between the two parties creates a duty to warn and makes the business potentially liable for nonconduct (failing to warn).

In recent years negligence cases against businesses for nonconduct have grown dramatically. Most of these cases have involved failure to protect customers from crimes. The National Crime Prevention Institute estimates that such cases have increased tenfold since the mid-1970s. In probably the most famous case to date, singer Connie Francis settled with a Long Island motel for $1.475 million. She alleged that the motel was negligent for failing to protect her from an attack she suffered in her room.

15. Unreasonable Behavior

At the core of negligence is the unreasonable behavior which breachees the duty of care that the defendant owes to the plaintiff. The problem is how do we separate reasonable behavior which causes accidental injury from unreasonable behavior which causes injury? Usually a jury determines this issue, but negligence is a mixed question of law and fact. Despite the trend for judges to let juries decide what the standard of reasonable care is, judges also continue to be involved in the definition of negligence. A well-known definition by Judge Learned Hand states that negligence is determined by "the likelihood that the defendant's conduct will injure others, taken with the seriousness of the injury if it happens, and balanced against the interest which he must sacrifice to avoid that risk."

In some negligence cases there is a strong suspicion that the defendant failed to use reasonable care, but the plaintiff may have great difficulty in proving exactly what the defendant did. Suppose that a barrel rolled off an upper story of the defendant's warehouse and struck the plaintiff on the head. No one seems to know how the barrel came to fall from the warehouse. A negligence doctrine that aids a plaintiff in situations such as these is called *res ipsa loquitur.* Meaning "the thing speaks for itself," res ipsa loquitur applies when a plaintiff can show that the item that caused the injury was within the sole control of the defendant and that the injury typically would not have occurred unless the defendant were negligent.

When the plaintiff's case shows these circumstances, the burden of proof shifts from the plaintiff to the defendant. Instead of the plaintiff having to prove that the defendant's conduct was unreasonable, the defendant must now prove that he or she followed reasonable standards. In our hypothetical case, the barrel was in the sole control of the defendant, and barrels do not normally roll off buildings unless someone is negligent. Res ipsa loquitur is appropriate for this case.

A special type of aggravated negligence is "willful and wanton" negligence. Although this negligence does not reveal intent, it does show an extreme lack of due care. Negligent injuries inflicted by drunk drivers show willful and wanton negligence. The significance of this type of negligence is that in many states the injured plaintiff can recover punitive damages as well as actual damages.

16. Cause in Fact

Before a person is liable to another for negligent injury, the person's failure to use reasonable care must actually have "caused" the injury. This observation is not so obvious as it first appears. A motorist stops by the roadside to change a tire. Another motorist drives past carelessly and sideswipes the first as he changes the tire. What caused the accident? Was it the inattention of the second motorist or the fact that the first motorist had a flat tire? Did the argument that the second motorist had with her boss before getting in the car cause the accident, or was it the decision of the first motorist to visit one more client that afternoon? In a real sense, all these things caused the accident. Chains of causation stretch out infinitely.

Still, in a negligence suit the plaintiff must prove that the defendant actually caused the injury. The courts term this *cause in fact.* In light of the many possible ways to attribute accident causation, how do courts determine if a plaintiff's lack of care in fact caused a certain injury? They do so very practically. Courts leave questions of cause in fact almost entirely to juries as long as the evidence reveals that a defendant's alleged carelessness could have been a substantial, material factor in bringing about an injury. Juries then make judgments about whether a defendant's behavior in fact caused the harm.

A particular problem of causation arises where the carelessness of two or more tortfeasors contributes to cause the plaintiff's injury, as when two persons are wrestling over control of the car which strikes the plaintiff. Tort law handles such cases by making each tortfeasor *jointly and severally* liable for the entire judgment. The plaintiff can recover only the amount of the judgment, but may recover it wholly from either of the tortfeasors, or get a portion of the judgment from each.

A variation of the joint tortfeasor situation occurs when two or more persons are guilty of negligence and the plaintiff cannot identify which one. In the next case, the Michigan Supreme Court faces this problem.

ABEL v. ELI LILLY AND CO.
343 N.W.2d 164 (Mich. 1984)

Plaintiffs brought suit against several companies that had previously manufactured diethylstilbestrol (DES), a drug taken by the mothers of the plaintiffs to prevent miscarriages during pregnancy. The plaintiffs, all women, developed cancer, usually while in their twenties, and claimed it was the result of the DES taken by their mothers. The plaintiffs also maintained that the defendants knew or should have known that DES contained a cancer-causing agent. Because of the lapse in time from the period when the mothers took DES until the cancer developed in their daughters, many of the plaintiffs could not identify which manufacturer of DES supplied the drug to their mothers. Therefore, the plaintiffs sued all manufacturers of DES that supplied the drug during a specific time period in the area where their mothers lived.

WILLIAMS, C.J.: Defendants correctly assert that the threshold requirement of any products liability action is identification of the injury-causing product and its manufacturer.

The plaintiff must produce evidence of a defect which caused the accident and trace that defect into the hands of the defendant.

It is undisputed that all the plaintiffs in this action will not be able to meet the identification requirement. Paragraph 16 of the Thirteenth Amended Complaint reads: "[S]ome of the plaintiffs will be unable to identify the specific defendant that manufactured the injury-producing drug that was sold to their mothers in spite of all good-faith efforts to determine same."

Despite this hiatus in the pleadings, defendants recognize that plaintiffs would still have set forth a cause of action if their factual situation meets the requirements of the theory of alternative liability. Also called "clearly established double fault and alternative liability," this procedural device shifts the burden of proof on the element of causation in fact to the defendants once an innocent plaintiff demonstrates that all defendants acted tortiously, but only one unidentifiable defendant caused plaintiff's injury. If the defendants cannot meet this burden and exculpate themselves, joint and several liability will be imposed.

Defendants assert that plaintiffs' reliance on alternative liability is totally unsupportable by the pleaded facts of the present case. In order to evaluate this claim, we must explore the theory of alternative liability as it has developed in the jurisprudence of this state.

The doctrine of alternative liability first received formal recognition in the case of *Summers v. Tice.* . . . In that case, plaintiff was injured by one shot during a hunting expedition. Plaintiff sued both of his hunting companions, claiming that both negligently shot at him, although he was unable to determine which one fired the specific shot that injured him.

The *Summers* court agreed, as a preliminary matter, that both defendants were at fault in having acted negligently toward the plaintiff. The court also recognized that plaintiff had failed to meet his traditional burden regarding cause in fact. Only one shot had injured plaintiff; both defendants could not have shot it. Since the most the plaintiff could prove was a 50% probability that either one of the defendants was more likely than the other to have caused the injury, plaintiff had failed to establish that either one of the defendants was more likely than the other to have caused the injury.

The court then decided—as a matter of policy—that it was preferable that the two wrongdoers, both of whom had acted negligently toward the plaintiff and had created the situation wherein plaintiff was injured, should bear the burden of absolving themselves rather than leaving the innocent plaintiff remediless. Therefore, the court placed the burden of proof on the issue of causation in fact upon the defendants.

This rule is now embodied in 2 Restatement Torts, 2d 433B(3), pp. 441–442. Commentary to the Restatement agrees that the reason for the exception to traditional rules is

to prevent the injustice of allowing proved wrongdoers to escape liability for an injury inflicted upon an innocent plaintiff "merely because the nature of their conduct and the resulting harm has made it difficult or impossible to prove which of them has caused the harm. . . ."

[T]he policy underlying the theory of alternative liability has been adopted in this state. We now formally express our approval of the theory of alternative liability. . . .

In sum, alternative liability will be applied in cases in which all defendants have acted tortiously, but only one unidentifiable defendant caused plaintiff's injury. If a plaintiff brings all the possible defendants into court and establishes the other elements of the underlying cause of action, the court should equitably shift an onerous burden of causation in fact to the defendants. If the defendants are unable to exonerate themselves, joint and several liability results.

Plaintiffs, [also] seek to proceed on the traditional theory of concert of action. This theory, although not developed to ease plaintiff's traditional burden of proof of causation, may have that effect. If plaintiffs can establish that all defendants acted tortiously pursuant to a common design, they will all be held liable for the entire result.

The concept is perhaps most clearly illustrated in the racing context. If three drivers join in a drag race, as a result of which one pedestrian is injured, all three may be held liable. Thus a legal fiction is created: all three drivers are found to be the cause in fact, although only one driver may have actually struck the pedestrian. . . .

Unlike the procedural device of alternative liability, a concert of action case does not require that the plaintiff be unable to identify the specific defendant who caused his injury in fact. The plaintiff is usually able to make that determination. Such identification does not preclude liability on a concert of action theory.

Here plaintiffs have alleged that defendants acted together in negligently manufacturing and promoting drugs which were ineffective and dangerous, were inadequately tested, and were distributed without sufficient warnings. These allegations are sufficient to withstand summary judgment. . . . Those plaintiffs who have alleged that a specific manufacturer caused their injuries are not precluded from this cause of action. [*Affirmed.*]

Other courts have handled DES cases differently. In *Sindell v. Abbott Laboratories* the California Supreme Court adopted what it called the *"market share theory."* When the plaintiff could not identify which defendant in fact manufactured the DES which injured her, the court held all defendants liable according to the percentage of the market they had at the time the plaintiff's mother took the drug.

17. Proximate Causation

It is not enough that a plaintiff suing for negligence prove that the defendant caused an injury in fact. The plaintiff also must establish **proximate causation.** "Proximate cause" is, perhaps, more accurately termed "legal cause." It represents the proposition that those engaged in activity are legally liable only for the *foreseeable* risk which they cause.

Defining proximate causation in terms of foreseeable risk creates further problems about the meaning of the word "foreseeable." In its application, foreseeability has come to mean that the plaintiff must have been one whom the defendant could reasonably expect to be injured by a negligent act. For example, it is reasonable to expect, thus foreseeable, that a collapsing hotel walkway should injure those on or under it. But many courts would rule as unforeseeable that someone a block away, startled upon hearing the loud crash of the walkway, should trip and stumble into the path of an oncoming car. The court would likely dismiss that person's complaint against the hotel as failing to show proximate causation.

Another application of proximate cause doctrine requires the injury to be caused *directly* by the defendant's negligence. Causes of injury which intervene between the defendant's negligence and the plaintiff's injury can destroy the necessary proximate causation. Some courts, for instance, would hold that it is not foreseeable that an owner's neegligence in leaving keys in a parked car should result in an intoxicated thief who steals the car crashing and injuring another motorist. These courts would dismiss for lack of proximate cause a case brought by the motorist against the car's owner.

The torts scholar William Prosser urges that we not try to force the doctrine of proximate causation into a rigid logical structure. He says that at the basis of the doctrine is "social policy": the view of nineteenth-century courts that economic activity was valuable and that those engaged in it required insulation from liability for all but the most direct and immediate consequences of their negligence.

Although tort law still requires that the plaintiff prove proximate causation, courts today treat the doctrine somewhat differently than they did a hundred years ago. Today the trend is for courts not to dismiss cases on the basis of lack of proximate cause. The trend is to let plaintiff-sympathetic juries determine this issue.

18. Defenses to Negligence

There are two principal defenses to an allegation of negligence: contributory negligence and assumption of risk. Both these defenses are **affirmative defenses**, which means that the defendant must specifically raise these defenses to take advantage of them. When properly raised and proved, these defenses limit or bar the plaintiff's recovery against the defendant. The defenses are valid even though the defendant has actually been negligent.

CONTRIBUTORY NEGLIGENCE

As originally applied, the contributory negligence defense absolutely barred the plaintiff from recovery if the plaintiff's own fault contributed to the injury "in any degree, however slight." The trend today, however, in the great majority of states is to offset the harsh rule of contributory negligence with the doctrine of comparative responsibility (also called "comparative negligence" and "comparative fault"). Under comparative principles, the plaintiff's contributory negligence does not bar recovery. It merely compares the plaintiff's fault with the defendant's and reduces the damage award proportionally. Under comparative responsibility, injury damages of $100,000 would be reduced by the jury to $80,000 if the jury determined that the plaintiff's own fault contributed 20 percent to the injury.

The following case illustrates contributory negligence and comparative responsibility. Can you tell from the Florida Supreme Court's decision why contributory negligence is an affirmative defense?

INSURANCE COMPANY OF NORTH AMERICA v. PASAKARNIS
415 So.2d 447 (Fla. 1984)

John Menninger ran a red light and caused an accident hitting Richard Pasakarnis' jeep. Pasakarnis was thrown from the jeep and injured. He sued Menninger. The defendant argued, as an affirmative defense, that the injury would not have occurred if Pasakarnis had used his seat belt. The trial court granted the plaintiff's motion to strike the "seat belt defense," and the jury found the defendant 100 percent responsible for the accident.

ALDERMAN, C.J.: [The issue to be decided is] whether Florida courts should consider seat belt evidence as bearing on comparative negligence or mitigation of damages.

In *Hoffman v. Jones*, we decided that contributory negligence as a complete bar to a plaintiff's action was unjust. We reasoned that contemporary conditions must be met with contemporary standards which are realistic and better calculated to obtain justice among all parties involved, based upon the circumstances, and stated that it was inequitable to vest an entire accidental loss on one of the parties whose negligent conduct combined with the negligence of another to produce the loss. The best argument in favor of comparative negligence we found was that it simply provided a more equitable system of determining liability. We stated that in the field of tort law, the most equitable result to be achieved is to equate liability with fault. In adopting the doctrine of comparative negligence, we explained that under this theory a plaintiff is prevented from recovering *"only that proportion of his damages for which he is responsible."*

[We] hold that the "seat belt defense" is viable in Florida. The seat belt has been proven to afford the occupant of an automobile a means whereby he or she may minimize his or her personal damages prior to occurrence of the accident.

As we have already expressly acknowledged . . . , automobile collisions are foreseeable as are the so-called "second collisions" with the interior of the automobile. The seat belt has been a safety device required by the federal government for nearly twenty years. In a 1982 study by the United States Department of Transportation, National Highway Safety Administration Technical Report en-

titled the "Effectiveness and Efficiency of Safety Belt and Child Restraining Usage," it is reported that the evidence for the effectiveness of safety belts in reducing deaths and injury severity is substantial and unequivocal. In view of the importance of the seat belt as a safety precaution available for a plaintiff's protection, failure to wear it under certain circumstances may be a pertinent factor for the jury to consider in deciding whether plaintiff exercised due care for his or her own safety. We agree . . . that:

[T]he failure to expend the minimal effort required to fasten an available safety device which has been put there specifically in order to reduce or avoid injuries from a subsequent accident is, on the very face of the matter, obviously pertinent and thus should be deemed admissible in an action for damages, part of which would not have been sustained if the seat belt had been used.

Those jurisdictions adopting the "seat belt defense" have considered three different approaches: (1) plaintiff's nonuse is negligent per se; (2) in failing to make use of an available seat belt, plaintiff has not complied with a standard of conduct which a reasonable prudent man would have pursued under similar circumstances, and therefore he may be found contributorily negligent; and (3) by not fastening his seat belt, plaintiff may, under the circumstances of a particular case, be found to have acted unreasonably and in disregard of his or her best interests and, therefore, should not be able to recover those damages which would not have occurred if his or her seat belt had been fastened.

Because Florida does not by statute require the use of available seat belts, we reject the rule that failure to wear a seat belt is negligence per se as have the majority of jurisdictions. We also reject the second approach because contributory negligence is applicable only if plaintiff's failure to exercise due care causes, in whole or in part, the accident rather than enhancing the severity of the injuries. Rather, we adopt the third approach. Nonuse of the seat belt may or may not amount to failure to use reasonable care on the part of the plaintiff. Whether it does depends on the particular circumstances of the case. Defendant has the burden of pleading and proving that the plaintiff did not use an available and operational seat belt, that the plaintiff's failure to use the seat belt was unreasonable under the circumstances, and that there was a causal relationship between the injuries sustained by the plaintiff and plaintiff's failure to buckle up. If there is competent evidence to prove that the failure to use

an available and operational seat belt produced or contributed substantially to producing at least a portion of plaintiff's damages, then the jury should be permitted to consider this factor, along with all other facts in evidence, in deciding whether the damages for which defendant may otherwise be liable should be reduced. Nonuse of an available seat belt, however, should not be considered by the triers of fact in resolving the issue of liability unless it has been alleged and proved that such nonuse was a proximate cause of the accident. . . . [*Remanded.*]

Adoption of the comparative negligence principle seems to lead to more frequent and larger awards for plaintiffs. A study of the Illinois Insurance Information Service reaches this conclusion for the year following that state's adoption of comparative negligence.

ASSUMPTION OF RISK

If contributory negligence involves failure to use proper care for one's own safety, the assumption of the risk defense arises from the plaintiff's knowing and willing undertaking of an activity made dangerous by the negligence of another. When professional hockey first came to this country, many spectators injured by flying hockey pucks sued and recovered for negligence. But as time went on and spectators came to realize that attending a hockey game meant that one might occasionally be exposed to flying hockey pucks, courts began to allow the defendant owners of hockey teams to assert that injured spectators had assumed the risk of injury from a speeding puck.

Assumption of the risk may be implied from the circumstances, or it can arise from an express agreement. Many businesses attempt to relieve themselves of potential liability by having employees or customers agree contractually not to sue for negligence, that is, to assume the risk. Some of these contractual agreements are legally enforceable, but many will be struck down by the courts as being against public policy, especially where a business possesses a vastly more powerful bargaining position than does its employee or customer.

It is important to a successful assumption of the risk defense that the assumption was voluntary. Entering a hockey arena knowing the risk of flying pucks is a voluntary assumption of the risk. Courts have often ruled, however, that persons who imperil themselves while attempting to rescue their own or others' property from a risk created by the defendant have not assumed the risk voluntarily. A plaintiff who is injured while attempting to save his possessions from a fire negligently caused by the defendant is not subject to the assumption of the risk defense.

A voluntary assumption of the risk usually bars the plaintiff from any recovery for the defendant's negligence. Contrast this with the situation in many states where the plaintiff's contributory negligence merely reduces the recovery for negligent injury. Because assumption of the risk and contributory negligence defenses in practical application frequently are very similar, this result appears unfair.

STRICT LIABILITY IN TORT

Strict liability is a catchall phrase for the legal responsibility for injury-causing behavior which is neither intentional nor negligent. There are various types of strict liability torts, some of which are more "strict" than others. What ties them together is that they all impose legal liability regardless of the intent or fault of the defendant. The next two sections discuss these torts and tort doctrines.

19. Respondeat Superior

Any time an employee is liable for tortious acts in the "scope of employment," the employer is also liable. This is because of the tort doctrine of **respondeat superior** ("let the master reply").

The reason for respondeat superior is that the employee is advancing the interests of the employer when the tortious act occurs. If the employee were not doing the work, the employer would have to do it. Therefore, the employer is just as liable as the employee when the employee acts tortiously in carrying out the work. In a sense, the employer has set the employee in motion and is responsible for the employee's acts.

Most respondeat superior cases involve employee negligence. Note, however, that the employer is strictly liable once the employee's fault is established. And it does not matter that the employer warned the employee against the tortious behavior. Because Mary's employer told her to be careful while delivering pizzas does not prevent him from being liable when Mary runs a red light and has an accident.

Some respondeat superior cases involve an employee's intentional tort. If a store's service representative strikes a customer during an argument over the return of merchandise, the store will be liable under respondeat superior. But if the argument concerns football instead of the return of merchandise, the store will not be liable. The difference is that the argument over football is not within the scope of employment.

The primary defense the employer has to the strict liability of respondeat superior is that the employee was outside the scope of employment. Sometimes this defense is made using the language *frolic and detour*. An employee who is on a frolic or detour is no longer acting for the employer. If Mary has delivered her employer's pizzas and is driving to see a friend when an accident occurs, the employer is not liable.

An employer who must pay for an employee's tort under respondeat superior may legally sue the employee for reimbursement. In practice this seldom happens because the employer carries insurance. Occasionally, an insurer who has paid a respondeat superior claim will sue the employee who caused the claim.

20. Other Strict Liability Torts

In most states the courts impose strict liability in tort for types of activities they call *ultrahazardous*. Transporting and using explosives and poisons fall under this category, as does keeping dangerous wild animals. Injuries caused from artificial storage of large quantities of liquid also can bring strict liability on the one who stores. In one unfortunate instance, a 2-million-gallon vat of molasses burst and drowned a number of passers-by in a nearby street. Regardless of whose fault or intent it was, the vat owner is strictly liable in this situation because of ultrahazardous activity.

The majority of states impose strict liability upon tavern owners for injuries to third parties caused by their intoxicated patrons. The acts imposing this liability are called *dram shop acts*. Because of the public attention given in recent years to intoxicated drivers, there has been a tremendous increase in dram shop act cases.

Common carriers, transportation companies licensed to serve the public, are also strictly liable for damage to goods being transported by them. Common carriers, howwever, can limit their liability in certain instances through contractual agreement, and they are not liable for (1) acts of God, such as natural catastrophies; (2) action of an alien enemy; (3) order of public authority, such as authorities of one state barring potentially diseased fruit shipments from another state from entering their state; (4) the inherent nature of the goods, such as perishability of vegetables; and (5) misconduct of the shipper, such as packaging improperly.

A major area today of strict liability law is strict tort liability for defective products. Sellers of such products are liable without fault to any injured user. Chapter 7 covers product liability in detail. Note that many scholars do not consider this liability as being *strict,* in the truest legal sense of the word.

Under workers' compensation statutes, employers are strictly liable for accidental injuries their employees suffer which arise "out of and in the course of employment." Chapter 14 discusses the workers' compensation system.

In the following case the Maryland Supreme Court became the first court in the nation to apply strict liability against manufacturers for the criminal use of their products, cheap handguns. Although several other state courts have refused to apply liability against handgun manufacturers in such situations, the *Kelly* case could start a trend. Think of this case in terms of deterrence, distributive justice, and judicial creation of new law.

KELLEY v. R.G. INDUSTRIES, INC.
497 A.2d 1143 (1985)

The plaintiff Kelley was injured when an armed robber shot him in the chest at the grocery store where he worked. The robber used a handgun, known as a "Saturday Night Special," manufactured by Rohm Gesellschaft and designed and marketed by R.G. Industries. Kelley sued both these parties.

ELDRIDGE, J.: Kelley maintains that a manufacturer and marketer of a handgun which inflicts injuries such as his should be held liable under either of two strict liabilities theories. First, Kelley asserts that the manufacturer or marketer is strictly liable because the manufacturing or marketing of handguns is an "abnormally dangerous activity." Second, Kelley argues that the manufacturer or marketer is strictly liable because handguns are "abnormally dangerous products". . . . However, neither of these two doctrines, nor any of the other previously recognized strict liability principles, could properly be applied to hold, in general, the manufacturer or marketer of a handgun liable to a person injured by the handgun during the course of a crime.

The fact that a handgun manufacturer or marketer generally would not be liable for gunshot injuries resulting from a criminal's use of the product, under previously recognized principles of strict liability, is not necessarily dispositive. This court has repeatedly said that "the common law is not static; its life

and heart is its dynamism—its ability to keep pace with the world while constantly searching for just and fair solutions to pressing societal problems." The common law is, therefore, subject to judicial modification in light of modern circumstances or increased knowledge. Indeed, we have not hesitated to change the common law to permit new actions or remedies where we have concluded that such course was justified.

On the other hand, we have consistently recognized that common law principles should not be changed contrary to the public policy of the state set forth by the General Assembly of Maryland. . . .

The express statutory provisions allowing persons to possess and carry handguns in certain specified instances demonstrate that not all handguns or handgun usage is inconsistent with Maryland public policy. In our view, generally to impose strict liability upon the manufacturers or marketers of handguns for gunshot injuries resulting from the misuse of handguns by others, would be contrary to Maryland public policy as set forth by the Legislature.

There is, however, a limited category of handguns which clearly is not sanctioned as a matter of public policy. To impose strict liability upon the manufacturers and marketers of these handguns, in instances of gunshot wounds caused by criminal use, would not be

The Legal Environment of Business   166

contrary to the policy embodied in the enactments of the General Assembly. This type of handgun, commonly known as a "Saturday Night Special," presents particular problems for law enforcement officials. Saturday Night Specials are generally characterized by short barrels, light weight, easy concealability, low cost, use of cheap materials, poor manufacture, inaccuracy and unreliability. These characteristics render the Saturday Night Special particularly attractive for criminal use and virtually useless for the legitimate purposes of law enforcement, sport, and protection of persons, property and businesses.

The legislative policies of both the United States Congress and the Maryland General Assembly reflect the view that "Saturday Night Specials" comprise a distinct category of handguns that, because of their characteristics. . . . should be treated differently from other handguns. Moreover, the manufacturer or marketer of a Saturday Night Special knows or ought to know that he is making or selling a product principally to be used in criminal activity. For example, a salesman for R.G. Industries, describing what he termed to be a "special attribute" of a Rohm handgun, was said to have told a putative handgun marketer, "If your store is anywhere near a ghetto area, these ought to sell real well. This is most assuredly a ghetto gun." The R.G. salesman allegedly went on to say about another R.G. handgun, "This sells real well, but, between you and me, it's such a piece of crap I'd be afraid to fire the thing."

[T]he manufacturer or marketer of a Saturday Night Special knows or ought to know that the chief use of the product is for criminal activity. Such criminal use, and the virtual absence of legitimate uses for the product, are clearly foreseeable by the manufacturers and sellers of Saturday Night Specials.

Moreover, as between the manufacturer or marketer of a Saturday Night Special who places among the public a product that will be used chiefly in criminal activity, and the innocent victim of such misuse, the former is certainly more at fault than the latter.

For the above reasons, we conclude that it is entirely consistent with public to hold the manufacturers and marketers of Saturday Night Special handguns strictly liable to innocent persons who suffer gunshot injuries from the criminal use of their products. Furthermore, in light of the ever growing number of deaths and injuries due to such handguns being used in criminal activity, the imposition of such liability is warranted by today's circumstances.

While the fact that a handgun is a Saturday Night Special may not bring its manufacturer or marketer within any of the previously existing theories of strict liability . . . , we have repeatedly pointed out that the common law adapts to fit the needs of society. Consequently, we shall recognize a separate, limited area of strict liability for the manufacturers, as well as all in the marketing chain, of Saturday Night Specials.

Finally, once the trier of facts determines that a handgun is a Saturday Night Special, then liability may be imposed against a manufacturer or anyone else in the marketing chain, including the retailer. Liability may only be imposed, however, when the plaintiff or plaintiff's decedent suffers injury or death because he is shot with the Saturday Night Special. In addition, the shooting must be a criminal act. The shooting itself may be the sole criminal act, or it may occur in the course of another crime where the person firing the Saturday Night Special is one of the perpetrators of the crime. Although neither contributory negligence nor assumption of the risk will be recognized as defenses, nevertheless the plaintiff must not be a participant in the criminal activity. If the foregoing elements are satisfied, then the defendant shall be liable for all resulting damages suffereed by the gunshot victim, consistent with the established law concerning tort damages. [*So ordered.*]

---

21. Damages

A noted legal scholar concludes that "the crucial controversy in personal injury torts today" is in the area of damages. This is because the average personal injury award has been increasing at nearly double the rate of inflation. For dramatic examples of the size of awards or settlements in some recent cases, take note of Table 6-5. The size of damage awards is largely determined by juries, but judges also play a role in damages, especially in damage instructions to the jury and in deciding whether to approve substantial damage awards.

Most damages awarded in tort cases compensate the plaintiff for injuries suffered. The purpose of damages is to make the plaintiff whole again, at least financially. There are three major types of loss which potentially follow tort injury and which are called *compensatory damages*. They are (1) past and future medical expenses, (2) past and future economic loss (including property damage and loss of earning power), and (3) past and future pain and suffering. Compensatory damages may also be awarded for loss of limb, loss of consortium (the marriage relationship), and mental distress.

Calculation of damage awards creates significant problems. Juries frequently use state-adopted life expectancy tables and present-value discount

TABLE 6-5   Recent Damage Awards or Settlements in Tort Cases

Defendant Company	Event Causing Injury	Award or Settlement in Millions of Dollars
A.H. Robins	Product (Dalkon Shield)	233
Arco	Ship sinking	51
Cargill Inc.	Interference with contractual relations	16
Cessna Aircraft Corp.	Product (airplane)	29
Chevron	Toxic fumes	15
Dow Chemical	Product (Bendectine)	120
Dresser Industries	Patent infringement	121
Hyatt Corp.	Skywalk collapse	120
MGM	Hotel fire	75
Seven chemical companies	Product (Agent Orange)	180
Stouffer Corp.	Hotel fire	48
Texaco	Interference with contractual relations	10,530
Wyeth Laboratories	Drug (suppository)	22

tables to help them determine the amount of damages to award. But uncertainty about the life expectancy of injured plaintiffs and the impact of inflation often makes these tables misleading. Also, awarding damages for pain and suffering is an art rather than a science. These awards measure jury sympathy as much as they calculate compensation for any financial loss. The recent dramatic increases in the size of damage awards helps underline the problems in their calculation. One result is that many individuals and businesses are underinsured for major tort liability.

Compensatory damages are not the only kind of damages. There are also **punitive damages**. By awarding punitive damages, courts or juries punish defendants for committing intentional torts and for negligent behavior considered "gross" or "willful and wanton." The key to the award of punitive damages is the defendant's motive. Usually the motive must be "malicious," "fraudulent," or "evil." Increasingly, punitive damages are also awarded for dangerously negligent conduct which shows a conscious disregard for the interests of others. These damages punish those who commit aggravated torts, and act to deter future wrongdoing. Because they make an example out of the defendant, punitive damages are sometimes called "exemplary" damages.

Presently, there is much controversy about how appropriate it is to award punitive damages against corporations for their economic activities. Especially when companies fail to warn of known danger created by their activities, or when cost-benefit decisions are made at the risk of substantial human injury, courts are upholding substantial punitive damage awards against companies. Yet, consider that these damages are a windfall to the injured plaintiff who has already received compensatory damages. And instead of punishing guilty management for wrongdoing, punitive damages may end up punishing innocent shareholders by reducing their dividends. In the next case, however, the Maine Supreme Court reaffirms the remedy of punitive damages, yet increases the plaintiff's burden of proof in obtaining them.

TUTTLE v. RAYMOND
494 A.2d 1353 (1985)

VIOLETTE, J.: On July 6, 1977 the plaintiff, Hattie Tuttle, was seriously injured when a Lincoln driven by the defendant, Ralph Raymond III, struck the Plymouth in which she was a passenger. The force of the impact sheared the Plymouth in half. Based on the evidence presented at trial, the jury could have found that the defendant was driving at an excessive speed in a 25 mile per hour zone when he struck the Plymouth, and that the defendant went through a red light just before the impact.

The defendant conceded liability at trial and focused instead on the amount of damages the jury should properly award. From the outset of the litigation, the defendant asserted both that punitive damages should not be recognized under the law of Maine and that, in any event, the facts of this case did not generate the issue of punitive damages. Nevertheless, the trial court submitted this issue to the jury, and refused to disturb the jury's decision to award $22,000 in exemplary damages.

Vigorous criticism of the doctrine of punitive damages is hardly a recent development in the field of jurisprudence. Arguments against the availability of such awards have been circulating for one hundred years and longer. During those hundred years, commentators have exhaustively analyzed the doctrine. Nonetheless, a substantial majority of jurisdictions today allow common law punitive damages in appropriate cases as recovery beyond the amount necessary to compensate the plaintiff, for the purpose of deterrence or punishment or both.

The defendant in the case at bar contends that we should nevertheless abandon the judicially created rule of punitive damages in this state. In support of this position, the defendant proffers several arguments. . . .

One objection raised by the defendant is that the civil law is ill-suited to accomplish the goals that purportedly justify the doctrine of punitive damages. The defendant contends that the proper function of the civil tort law is to make plaintiffs whole, and that grave problems arise when it is used to extract from defendants something beyond full compensation for the victim. The defendant asserts that the primary purpose allegedly served by the doctrine of punitive damages, deterrence through punishment, is more properly left to the criminal law with its attendant procedural safeguards.

The bright line that the defendant attempts to interpose between the civil and the criminal law is in fact artificial. The courts of

this country historically have not restricted the civil law to a compensatory function. In 1851, the United States Supreme Court, relying on over a century of judicial precedent, observed: "By the common as well as by statute law, men are often punished for aggravated misconduct or lawless acts, by means of a civil action, and the damages, inflicted by way of a penalty or punishment, given to the party injured." Use of the civil law to shape social behavior is both logical and desirable. There are many instances where the criminal law alone is inadequate to achieve the desired deterrent effect. Another objection to punitive damages raised by the defendant is that they bestow a windfall upon the plaintiff. As the defendant observes, such damages are awarded in Maine in excess of any amount necessary to compensate the plaintiff.

We find, however, that the extra recovery afforded to plaintiffs by punitive damages, rather than constituting a "windfall," serves a useful purpose. The potential for recovering an exemplary award provides an incentive for private civil enforcement of society's rules against serious misconduct. As noted earlier, the civil law effectively augments the criminal law in deterring intolerable conduct. The doctrine of punitive damages encourages the use of civil actions by private parties in response to such conduct, especially when the prospective compensatory recovery is low or the expected cost of litigation is high.

The defendant next argues that the doctrine of punitive damages invites abuse because there is no objective standard by which to determine the amount of a proper award. According to the defendant, the jury is left to speculate concerning the appropriate amount of punitive damages in a given case, with the result of arbitrary and excessive awards. The defendant contends that this is a flaw in the doctrine that outweighs any justification for allowing exemplary awards.

In fact, however, the lack of any precise

formula by which punitive damages can be calculated is one of the important assets of the doctrine. "Punitive damages . . . can be individualized to provide a deterrent that will be adequate for each case." Such flexibility can ensure a sufficient award in the case of a rich defendant and avoid an overburdensome one where the defendant is not as wealthy.

Although we reject the defendant's contention that we should abolish common law punitive damages in Maine, we perceive cogent reasons for avoiding an overbroad application of the doctrine. Notions of fairness and efficiency weigh against allowing exemplary awards where the stated goal of deterring reprehensible conduct would be furthered only marginally or not at all.

We therefore determine that a new standard is needed in Maine. "If one were to select a single word or term to describe [the] essense [of conduct warranting punitive damages], it would be 'malice.'"

This requirement of malice will be most obviously satisfied by a showing of "express" or "actual" malice. Such malice exists where the defendant's tortious conduct is motivated by ill will toward the plaintiff. Punitive damages will also be available, however, where deliberate conduct by the defendant, although motivated by something other than ill will toward aany particular party, is so outrageous that malice toward a person injured as a result of that conduct can be implied. We emphasize that, for the purpose of assessing punitive damages, such "implied" or "legal" malice will not be established by the defendant's mere reckless disregard of the circumstances.

In the case at bar, the evidence shows that the plaintiff was seriously injured by the defendant's reckless operation of an automobile. The plaintiff contends that such conduct on the part of the defendant is sufficient to support an award of punitive damages.

Under the standard we announce today, it clearly is not. We certainly do not condone the defendant's conduct; nor do we fail to appreciate the tragic injuries imposed upon the plaintiff as a result of that conduct. We have determined, however, that deterrence—recognized by this Court as "the proper justification" for punitive damages—cannot justify imposing an exemplary award in addition to compensatory damages and possibly criminal sanctions based solely upon a defendant's reckless disregard of the circumstances. Because the defendant's conduct was not accompanied by malice, either express or implied, we vacate the award of punitive damages.

Our stated goal of avoiding an overbroad application of the doctrine of punitive damages leads us to consider another issue raised bby the defendant, namely, the standard of proof that should govern a claim for an exemplary award. Presently in Maine, a plaintiff must prove his case for punitive damages by a preponderance of the evidence. The defendant urges us to abandon that rule, and to impose instead the more stringent proof requirement of cleaar and convincing evidence upon a plaintiff seeking an exemplary award.

We conclude that such a higher standard of proof is appropriate for a claim for punitive damages. It should be obvious from our discussion . . . that, although punitive damages serve an important function in our legal system, they can be onerous when loosely assessed. The potential consequences of a punitive damages claim warrant a requirement that the plaintiff present proof greater than a mere preponderance of the evidence. Therefore, we hold that a plaintiff may recover exemplary damages based upon tortious conduct only if he can prove by clear and convincing evidence that the defendant acted with malice. [*Judgment amended by vacating award of punitive damages; as so amended, judgment affirmed.*]

The *Tuttle* decision overlooks a very important consideration about punitive damages. Most companies carry liability insurance policies which reimburse them for "all sums which the insured might become legally obligated to pay." This includes reimbursement for punitive damages. Instead of punishing guilty companies, punitive damages may punish other companies who have to pay increased insurance premiums, and may punish consumers, who ultimately pay higher prices. As a matter of public policy, several states prohibit insurance from covering punitive damages, but the great majority of states permit such coverage. This fact severely undermines arguments for awarding punitive damages against companies for their economic activities.

Consider also that an award of punitive damages greatly resembles a criminal fine. Yet the defendant who is subject to these criminal-type damages lacks the right to be indicted by a grand jury and cannot assert the right against self-incrimination. In addition, the defendant is subject to a lower standard of proof than in a criminal case. Might a defendant in a tort suit challenge an award of punitive damages on a constitutional basiis?

Finally, note that the United States is the only country in the world where punitive damages are regularly awarded.

STRUCTURED SETTLEMENTS

A major response to the growing size of damage awards is the rapid spread of *structured settlements* of damages in personal injury cases. For example, a Florida court awarded two children $18 million. Negligent derailment of several tank cars had released poisonous gases which injured the children and killed their parents. Instead of paying the children a lump sum, the railroad negotiated a structured settlement for them. Also known as a periodic payment or protected settlement, the structured settlement usually takes the form of a guaranteed annuity for the plaintiff's lifetime. The annuity purchased for the children in the Florida case could be worth as much as $52 million during their lives, although it only cost the railroad $11.5 million.

Structured settlements protect plaintiffs who may not know how to handle large sums of money. There is also a tax advantage. The Internal Revenue Service regards annuity payments as a nontaxable damage award. When the award has been made in a lump sum, however, any investment return from it can be taxed at unearned income rates as high as 70 percent.

Defendants and their insurers benefit from structured settlements because these settlements can be negotiated at a lower cost than the payment of a lump sum. Since 1979, the use of structured settlements by insurers has more than tripled. There are also a number of states which permit judges to direct structured settlements in malpractice cases, and there are various proposals for uniform state law on such settlements for all personal injury cases.

22. Policy Trends

The distribution of losses due to tort-related injuries has shifted dramatically in this century. In general, the development of tort law has shifted loss from

TABLE 6-6 Developments in Tort Law Illustrating Redistribution of Tort Losses from Plaintiff to Defendant.

1 Increasing submission of proximate cause issue to juries.
2 Expansion of scope of duty.
3 Development of strict liability for defective products.
4 Development of comparative negligence doctrine.
5 Passage of workers' compensation statutes.
6 Growing use of constitutional tort liability under section 1983.
7 Development of res ipsa loquitur.
8 Liability of certain defendants, even when plaintiff cannot prove which specific defendant caused plaintiff's injury.
9 Average personal injury awards growing at twice the rate of inflation.

injured accident victims and placed it on those sued, especially where insurance or increased prices ultimately can spread the loss to society as a whole. The trend is most visible in business-related accidents, because businesses have "deep pockets" and are able to spread injury losses more easily than can injured individuals. Table 6-6 summarizes tort law changes that illustrate this trend.

Of course, businesses are greatly concerned about the rising number of tort lawsuits, the increasing size off damage awards, and other evidences of this trend. A significant problem is that tort litigation itself eats up 30 to 50 percent of all money that defendants pay due to tort suits. Lawyers' fees, discovery costs, lengthy trials and appeals—all create enormous costs even before the plaintiff receives a cent.

One response to litigation expense, discussed in a previous chapter, has been the attempt to manage litigation costs. For instance, attorneys are beginning to use "discovery banks" which centralize and streamline the discovery process in complex tort cases. Likewise, to avoid full-blown, costly trials, many companies are experimenting with using the "mini-trial," especially in patent infringement cases. Companies are also increasingly using salaried in-house counsel to replace the expense of outside law firms who charge by the hour.

Other responses have included proposals to remove most accidental injuries from the tort litigation process. Tort litigation could be replaced by a compensation system based on insurance. Workers' compensation is such a system. No-fault insurance for automobile accidents is another. New Zealand has entirely replaced tort litigation with a no-fault compensation system for accidental injuries.

Whether no-fault compensation will ever substantially replace tort litigation in the United States remains to be seen. What is likely is that if tort law and litigation continue to grow and become more expensive, there will be pressure to reform the way tort law distributes wealth in society. It is a situation which students today will face tomorrow.

REVIEW QUESTIONS

1 Explain the distinction between a tort and a breach of contract.

2 Discuss the basic change in accident loss distribution in the twentieth century.

3 A store manager thinks he sees a customer shoplifting. He screams "Stop, thief!" and grabs the customer roughly. It turns out that the manager made a mistake and that the customer had not shoplifted. Discuss the potential liability of the store manager and the store.

4 The quarterback Joe Montana discovers that a shoe manufacturer is selling "Montana" athletic shoes. Joe has not granted the manufacturer permission to use his name on the shoe. Is the manufacturer liable to Joe? How might the manufacturer defend itself?

5 Acme Airlines attempts to get control of Free Fall Airways by making a public offer to buy its stock from shareholders. Free Fall's president advises the shareholders in a letter that Acme's president is "little better than a crook" and "can't even control his own company." Analyze the potential liability of Free Fall's president for these remarks.

6 Professor McLegal reproduces newspaper accounts of torts for use by the students in her class. Does this practice violate copyright law? Discuss.

When employee Ivey fails to appear for work, his manager, Jones, goes looking for him. There is no answer when Jones knocks at Ivey's home. There is Ivey lying on the floor, passed out in a drunken stupor. Later, Jones fires Ivey and tells him why. What legal action does Jones risk by what he has done?

8 In Texas, a student rents an automobile for a weekend trip. The rental contract contains a clause which limits driving the automobile to "the continental United States." The student drives the car into Mexico. While the student is watching a bullfight, the automobile is stolen. Now the rental agency sues the student. Who will win? Why?

9 PainKill, an aspirin substitute, advertises that it "kills pain" more quickly and effectively than "common aspirin." In fact, the substitute relieves pain no better than aspirin. The Aspirin Association is considering taking legal action against the manufacturer of PainKill. Upon what legal grounds might such action be taken? Discuss.

10 Describe the legal requirements for obtaining a patent on an invention.

11 An equipment manufacturer learns that a former employee has begun a competing business. Many of the same processes used by the manufacturer are also being used by the new business. Further, many of the manufacturer's customers are being contacted by the former employee. The manufacturer desires to sue its former employee. What must it prove in order to maintain a successful suit? Discuss.

12 State Realty owns a large apartment complex. One of its tenants has been robbed and badly beaten in the unlighted parking lot of the complex. The tenant now sues State Realty for negligently failing to maintain adequate security. Describe the basic elements of negligence and discuss how they might apply to these facts.

13 Discuss how comparative negligence principles have modified the contributory negligence doctrine. What is the significance of this development to the business community?

14 How does the "market share" theory modify traditional rules of tort causation?

15 Discuss the pros and cons of punitive damage awards against corporations.

Chapter
7
Products and Service Liability

1. Introduction

In the past twenty years the number of lawsuits brought against businesses has exploded. No area of the law is more responsible for this explosion than products and service liability. Between 1984 and 1985, for example, the number of products liability cases filed in federal courts increased 26 percent. During this period even more substantial increases were recorded in some state court systems: Massachusetts, 47 percent; Ohio, 51 percent; and Texas, 62 percent.

Malpractice suits against those who provide services have increased in a similar dramatic fashion. Products and service liability is of special importance to managers, marketers, product designers, insurers, engineers, attorneys, accountants, health care specialists, and many other members of the business and professional communities.

As with other torts, evidence of the significance of this topic appears regularly in the news media. Plaintiffs have filed over 30,000 lawsuits against asbestos manufacturers. Hundreds of additional cases are initiated monthly. Women suffering from toxic shock syndrome have sued Procter & Gamble and other manufacturers, seeking over $4 billion in damages. In a single suit a Pennsylvania jury awarded $18 million to a man who lost both legs in a forklift accident. Several major states, including California and New York, now permit plaintiffs to recover their damages against all companies in an industry when it is difficult to prove which individual company manufactured a defective product. The physicians in one western state made headlines by going out on strike to protest soaring malpractice insurance rates.

We can identify several effects of the current liability situation. First, overall rates for products liability and malpractice insurance have risen rapidly. In some high-risk industries, companies pay as much as 10 percent of sales for products liability insurance. Second, high insurance premiums have forced some members of the professional and business communities to drop their liability coverage, a risky step known as "going bare." Third, fear of liability has inhibited new product development in certain instances, especially in the pharmaceuticals industry.

Responsibility for the present situation cannot be attributed to any single cause. A variety of factors have led to it. Among them has been the increase in the number of suits brought due to the growing public awareness of the right to sue for injuries arising from defective products and carelessly rendered services. This awareness is likely related to certain changes in the law, which have made it easier for injured parties to recover, and to the resulting widespread coverage in the media of extraordinarily large recoveries received by plaintiffs in some lawsuits.

The Federal Interagency Task Force on Product Liability has also pinpointed the growth in number and complexity of products on the market as a reason for the increase in products liability suits. Uninformed use of such products frequenttly causes injury, which in turn leads to litigation. Another factor increasing costs to products and service sellers has been insurance industry ratemaking practices. Failure by the industry in the 1970s to collect specific data on products liability and malpractice claims often made it difficult to justify large rate hikes. Further, omission to set premium rate levels according to the incidence of actual claims mmade by an insured caused many careful products and service sellers to have to pay for the disproportionately large number of injuries inflicted by a relatively careless few.

An even greater responsibility for the current problems of product and service sellers lies in the tort litigation system itself. Litigation costs make up the largest part of every insurance dollar—nearly 40 percent. The lengthy formal proceedings required by the traditional adversary process are in great measure responsible for this situation. The eroding of many products liability defenses in recent years and the knowledge of the jury that most corporations carry liability insurance have also contributed to higher jury verdicts and thus greater overall costs in that area.

Unfortunately, unsafe manufacturing practices and inadequate professional services also bear responsibility for the current problems. For example, until recently many companies did not have product safety committees or officers whose principal duties involved the preproduction testing, rigorous quality control, and recall contingency planning that is so vital in reducing products liability suits. As a result, many unsafe products entered the marketplace, products which continue to injure consumers and workers.

To avoid future liability suits, managers, marketers, professionals, and others need to understand the political and judicial climate out of which product and service liability has risen, the emerging legal rules of liability, legislative alternatives to judicially imposed legal principles, and planning techniques which can help reduce liability suits. These topics are the subject of the chapter which follows. The chapter first develops products liability and then turns to the liability of those who provide services.

2. Historical Development of Products Liability

Chapter 6 discussed how tort law moved away from strict liability to embrace negligence in the 1800s. This movement was significant for the developing law of liability for injury due to defective products.

The new doctrine of negligence almost totally insulated manufacturers and retailers from being sued successfully. This result occurred because judges ruled that sellers of products owed the "reasonable man" duty only to persons with whom they had actually dealt. For a manufacturer to be liable, the manufacturer must have sold the defective product directly to the injured party. If the injured party were not the purchaser, or if the injured party had purchased the product from a retailer, the manufacturer was not liable for the defects. This aspect of negligence, which limited liability of sellers to those persons with whom they had entered into a contract, was called the privity doctrine. Although the doctrine originally arose out of contract law, it now came to be applied as well in tort cases.

The **privity** doctrine protected retailers in addition to manufacturers. Even if the injured party had purchased the product directly from the retailer, the retailer could seldom be found negligent. The defective product, which was frequently packaged, was the fault not of the retailer but of the manufacturer. The retailer had therefore acted as a "reasonable man." And so moral attitudes and economic conditions became embodied in law which assisted the growing industries of the nineteenth century. With the exception of cases involving "inherently dangerous" products (guns, drugs, and so on), the law placed the risk of loss upon the injured party in most instances. It was truly a time of **caveat emptor,** "let the buyer beware."

In the twentieth century the pendulum began to swing slowly back toward strict liability. As infant industries grew into healthy maturity, as the country became economically prosperous, and as products became increasingly more numerous and complex, the courts began dismantling the legal structure of products liability which had been raised in the preceding century. In its place rose the condition of *caveat venditor,* "let the seller beware."

First to go was the privity doctrine as applied to negligence law. In the famous case of *MacPherson v. Buick* in 1916, Justice Benjamin Cardozo ruled that a plainntiff could sue an automobile company even though the plaintiff had not purchased the defective automobile from the company and was not in privity of contract. Cardozo noted that the automobile company knew that the buyer (the retailer) would resell the automobile to someone like the plaintiff.

He argued that "precedents drawn from the days of travel by stagecoach" must not control the "needs of life in a developing civilization."

It took nearly fifty years following the *MacPherson* case for the privity doctrine as used in negligence to collapse completely. But today no state applies privity in negligence law.

Around the time of *MacPherson,* state courts across the couuntry also began to abandon the concepts of "fault" and the "reasonable man" and to find sellers strictly liable when defective food and drink damaged consumers. Rather than use a strict liability in tort, the courts used a type of strict liability based on an "implied" warranty or guarantee which manufacturers and sellers supposedly made to those who might be affected by the food and drink. Although "warranty" and "guarantee" are words based in contract law, the courts generally did not require the presence of privity of contract between plaintiff and defendant in these cases. Instead, the courts, and in some instances the legislatures, imposed such warranties by law.

During the next half century, as the privity doctrine collapsed in negligence law, it collapsed as well in implied warranty cases involving food, drink, and drugs, imposing strict liability for defects in these products in increasing numbers of states. Finally, in the late 1950s and early 1960s the implied warranty doctrine expanded to cover all types of products. And in the famous case of *Henningsen v. Bloomfield Motors* in 1960, the New Jersey Supreme Court made it clear that the implied warranty could not be disclaimed by the manufacturer in an express contract where the manufacturer's bargaining power was so much greater than the purchaser's that the disclaimer could be presented on a take-it-or-leave-it basis. Other states swiftly followed this reasoning, and throughout the cases the courts continually made reference to "modern marketing conditions" and "the needs of the community."

Still, the close connection of implied warranty to contract law prevented many plaintiffs from suing successfully. The difficulty of meeting various technical requirements of contract law kept many product-injured plaintiffs out of the courts. One last step remained before the full circle of products liability could be completed. The law would have to return to strict liability in tort. Then came the following case.

GREENMAN v. YUBA POWER PRODUCTS, INC.
377 P.2d 897 (Calif. 1963)

TRAYNOR, J.: Plaintiff brought this action for damages against the retailer and the manufacturer of a Shopsmith, a combination power tool that could be used as a saw, drill, and wood lathe. He saw a Shopsmith demonstrated by the retailer and studied a brochure prepared by the manufacturer. He decided he wanted a Shopsmith for his home workshop, and his wife bought and gave him one for Christmas in 1955. In 1957 he bought the necessary attachments to use the Shopsmith as a lathe for turning a large piece of wood he wished to make into a chalice. After he had worked on the piece of wood several times without difficulty, it suddenly flew out of the machine and struck him on the forehead, inflicting serious injuries. About ten and a half months later, he gave the retailer and the manufacturer written notice of claimed breaches of warranties and filed a complaint against them alleging such breaches and negligence.

After a trial before a jury, the court ruled that there was no evidence that the retailer was negligent or had breached any express warranty and that the manufacturer was not liable for the breach of any implied warranty. Accordingly, it submitted to the jury only the cause of action alleging breach of implied warranties against the retailer and the causes of action alleging negligence and breach of express warranties against the manufacturer. The jury returned a verdict for the retailer against plaintiff and for plaintiff against the manufacturer in the amount of $65,000. The trial court denied the manufacturer's motion for a new trial and entered judgment on the verdict. The manufacturer and plaintiff appeal. Plaintiff seeks a reversal of the part of the judgment in favor of the retailer, however, only in the event that the part of the judgment against the manufacturer is reversed.

Plaintiff introduced substantial evidence that his injuries were caused by defective design and construction of the Shopsmith. His expert witnesses testified that inadequate set screws were used to hold parts of the machine together so that normal vibration caused the tailstock to the lathe to move away from the piece of wood being turned permitting it to fly out of the lathe. They also testified that there were other more positive ways of fastening the parts of the machine together, the use of which would have prevented the accident. The jury could therefore reasonably have concluded that the manufacturer negligently constructed the Shopsmith. The jury could also reasonably have concluded that statements in the manufacturer's brochure were untrue, that they constituted express warranties, and that the plaintiff's injuries were caused by their breach.

The manufacturer contends, however, that plaintiff did not give it notice of breach of warranty within a reasonable time and that therefore his cause of action for breach of warranty is barred by section 1769 of the Civil Code. Since it cannot be determined whether the verdict against it was based on the negligence or warranty cause of action or both, the manufacturer concludes that the error in presenting the warranty clause of action to the jury was prejudicial.

Section 1769 of the Civil Code provides: "In the absence of express or implied agreement of the parties, acceptance of the goods by the buyer shall not discharge the seller from liability in damages or other legal remedy for breach of any promise or warranty in the contract to sell or the sale. But, if, after acceptance of the goods, the buyer fails to give notice to the seller of the breach of any promise or warranty within a reasonable time after the buyer knows, or ought to know of such breach, the seller shall not be liable therefor."

Like other provisions of the uniform sales act, section 1769 deals with the rights of the parties to a contract of sale or a sale. It does not provide that notice must be given of the breach of a warranty that arises independently of a contract of sale between the parties. Such warranties are not imposed by the sales act, but are the product of common-law decisions that have recognized them in a variety of situations.

The notice requirement of section 1769, however, is not an appropriate one for the court to adopt in actions by injured consumers against manufacturers with whom they have not dealt. "As between the immediate parties to the sale [the notice requirement] is a sound commercial rule, designed to protect the seller against unduly delayed claims for damages. As applied to personal injuries, and notice to a remote seller, it becomes a boobytrap for the unwary. The injured consumer is seldom 'steeped in the business practice which justifies the rule,' and at least until he has had legal advice it will not occur to him to give notice to one with whom he has had no dealings." We conclude, therefore, that even if plaintiff did not give timely notice of breach of warranty to the manufacturer, his cause of action based on the representations contained in the brochure was not barred.

Moreover, to impose strict liability on the manufacturer under the circumstances of this case, it was not necessary for plaintiff to establish an express warranty as defined in section 1732 of the Civil Code. A manufacturer is strictly liable in tort when an article he places on the market knowing that it is to be used without inspection for defects, proves to have a defect that causes injury to a human being. Recognized first in the case of unwholesome food products, such liability has now been extended to a variety of other products that create as great or greater hazards if defective.

Although in these cases strict liability has usually been based on the theory of an express or implied warranty running from the manufacturer to the plaintiff, the abandonment of the requirement of a contract between them, the recognition that the liability is not assumed by agreement but imposed by law . . . and the refusal to permit the manufacturer to define the scope of its own responsibility for defective products . . . make clear that the liability is not one governed by the law of contract warranties but by the law of strict liability in tort. Accordingly, rules defining and governing warranties that were developed to meet the needs of commercial transactions cannot properly be invoked to govern the manufacturer's liability to those injured by their defective products unless those rules also serve the purposes for which such liability is imposed.

The purpose of strict liability is to insure that the costs of injuries resulting from defective products are borne by the manufacturers that put such products on the market rather than by the injured persons who are powerless to protect themselves. Sales warranties serve this purpose fitfully at best. In the present case, for example, plaintiff was able to plead and prove an express warranty only because he read and relied on the representations of the Shopsmith's ruggedness contained in the manufacturer's brochure. Implicit in the machine's presence on the market, however, was a representation that it would safely do the jobs for which it was built. Under these circumstances, it should not be controlling whether plaintiff selected the machine because of the statement in the brochure, or because of the machine's own appearance of excellence that belied the defect lurking beneath the surface, or because he merely assumed that it would safely do the jobs it was built to do. It should not be controlling whether the details of the sales from manufacturer to retailer and from retailer to plaintiff's wife were such that one or more of the implied warranties of the sales act arose. "The remedies of injured consumers ought not to be made to depend upon the intricacies of the law of sales." To establish the manufacturer's liability it was sufficient that plaintiff proved that he was injured while using the Shopsmith in a way it was intended to be used as a result of a defect in design and manufacture of which plaintiff was not aware that made the Shopsmith unsafe for its intended use. [*Judgment affirmed.*]

TABLE 7-1   Arguments Made for Adoption of Strict Tort Liability

1 When sellers promote mass consumption, injured product users should not have to bear financial losses caused by defective products.
2 Sellers are better able than injured product users to spread liability losses by raising the price of products and obtaining insurance.
3 Strict tort liability will provide manufacturers with incentives for more careful product design and quality control.

With Justice Roger Traynor's decision in the *Greenman* case, the law in California returned to strict tort liability. State after state has followed the reasoning of this case. Today, strict tort liability is nearly universal in its application to product-related injuries. And underlying the widespread adoption of strict liability are social and economic considerations. (See Table 7-1.)

THE BASIC THEORIES OF LIABILITY

3. Introduction

To many sellers of products it must seem as though they are liable anytime someone is injured by one of their products. This, however, is untrue. Sellers are not insurers in the sense that they guarantee no injury will befall those who come into contact with the seller's products. Another way of putting it is to say that sellers are not absolutely responsible for all harm which follows the use of their products. Instead, they are liable only when they have breached some *legal duty* which is owed to any injured party. Such legal duties may arise (1) because of the conduct of the seller, especially that of the manufacturer; (2) because of the quality of the product; and (3) because of promises or representations the seller has made.

4. Duty Based upon Conduct of the Seller: Negligence

The concepts of negligence discussed in the torts chapter apply in products liability cases. The conduct of sellers must fulfill the duty of "ordinary and reasonable" care. Otherwise, sellers must answer in damages for negligence to those injured by their conduct.

In products liability law, sellers owe the duty of reasonable care to all those who may come in contact with the sellers' products. This duty exists because of the sellers' act in placing their products into the stream of commerce. It is the legal reflection of society's judgment that those who make a profit by selling products must bear the expense of harm when by fault of their conduct they cause injury.

Under negligence law, however, not every sale of a defective product, or of one capable of causing injury, constitutes a failure to use reasonable care. For instance, in today's era of prepackaged goods, a retail seller of a defective product can usually not be found liable for negligence. It is not legally "reasonable" to expect that a retailer will open every can of peas to discover whether or not there is a nail in them. Nor can the manufacturing seller always be held liable for negligence for placing a defective product into the stream of commerce. An injured plaintiff must show how the manufacturer was at fault for using unreasonable design, production, or inspection standards. In light of the complexity of modern production processes, it is frequently difficult for the plaintiff actually to show this unreasonableness.

Over the years plaintiffs have used the negligence doctrine of *res ipsa loquitur* in appropriate circumstances to assist them in establishing breach of the duty of reasonable care. Recall that this doctrine applies when a plaintiff can prove that the "thing" causing harm was within the sole control of the defendant and that the injury would not typically have happened unless the defendant were negligent (see Chapter 6). In products liability cases, which apply res ipsa loquitur, the plaintiff must show that the product defect occurred while the product was within a defendant's sole control. This may not be difficult to show if the defect is a mouse in a soft-drink bottle. But if the defect is a crack in the bottle, a specific defendant's sole control may be harder to prove. For example, did the crack in the soft-drink bottle which exploded occur during the manufacturing process or the bottling process? Or did the retailer drop the bottle on the floor prior to shelving it?

Proximate causation is also important in products liability cases. Negligent products sellers (and those who are strictly liable) are liable only for injuries that are "foreseeable." Thus, when a defective soft-drink bottle explodes in a grocery store and puts out the eye of the shopper who has just picked it up, the bottler, if at fault, will be liable, since such an injury is foreseeable. But as to the store manager who was also injured by the same explosion when the loud noise caused him to slip from a chair in which he was standing to replace a light bulb on the other side of the store, he will not likely recover from the bottler. The court will probably rule that his injury was not foreseeable and therefore that there was no proximate cause between the negligent conduct and the injury. Proximate causation also applies to products liability in cases in which a purchaser has misused a product. The question rises as to whether the misuse was foreseeable. In the next case should the removal of ductwork be considered a misuse? Is it unforeseeable? How do you explain the result in this case?

WINGETT v. TELEDYNE INDUSTRIES, INC.
479 N.E.2d 51 (Ind. 1985)

The appellant Wingett was injured while engaged in removing ductwork from a manufacturing plant. Appellant was following the normal procedure of sitting on the ductwork and cutting the aluminum hangers when the ductwork and he fell to the floor.

The accident was caused by a defective connection. The appellant sued Ramsey, the manufacturer, and Severs, the installer, for products liability.

GIVEN, J.: Appellant's claim against Ramsey and Severs was premised on a theory of strict liability in tort. He contends Ramsey and Severs manufactured and installed a product with a dangerously hidden defect and failed to warn him of the danger presented by his reasonably foreseeable use of the product.

In a products liability case, recovery for a plaintiff requires proof that the product defect was the proximate cause of his injury. Liability will be attributed to the manufacturer only if the product contains a defective condition rendering it unreasonably dangerous for its intended use. The applicable statute addressing liability in tort reads in part:

(a) One who sells any product in a defective condition unreasonably dangerous to any user or consumer or to his property is subject to liability for physical harm thereby caused to the user or consumer if he or she is in the class of persons that the seller should reasonably foresee as being subject to the harm caused by the defective condition, and if:

(1) the seller is engaged in the business of selling such a product, and

(2) the product is expected to and does reach the user or consumer without substantial change in the condition in which it is sold.

We cannot agree with appellant's apparent contention that a person who dismantles or demolishes a product be deemed a "user" or "consumer" within the meaning of the statute. Further, there is no authority to support his corollary contention that dismantling or demolishing a product be recognized as an intended use of the product within the scope of products liability law. We hold that a manufacturer's potential liability for products placed in the stream of commerce does not extend to the demolition of the product.

It is uncontroverted that the ductwork was manufactured and installed solely for the purpose of collecting sand and dust from machinery used in the foundry. There is nothing to indicate any risk inherent in the intended use of the ductwork.

While the question of foreseeability is generally one of fact for the jury, we hold that appellant's "use" of the ductwork was not reasonably foreseeable as a matter of law, notwithstanding appellant's allegation that he was employing the standard trade procedure for duct removal. Because the dismantling and demolition of the ductwork was not a reasonably foreseeable use of the product, Ramsey and Severs owed no duty to appellant to work as part of the demolition crew. A manufacturer need only warn of reasonably foreseeable dangers. [*Affirmed.*]

5. Duty Based upon Quality of the Product

If negligence law in products liability is founded upon fault in the conduct of the seller, then strict liability principles come from defects in the quality of the product. The focus in negligence is upon the behavior of the seller; in strict liability, it is upon the behavior of the product in the environment of its use. Because it is far easier to prove a product defect than it is to establish unreasonable human behavior, the enormous explosion in products liability suits during recent times can be explained in large part by the development of strict liability doctrines.

In strict products liability the duty of the commercial seller is to avoid placing defective products into the stream of commerce. As it is currently expressed, such liability can be imposed in virtually every state under tort law or through breach of the implied warranty of merchantability, a contract doctrine.

STRICT LIABILITY IN TORT

Since the *Greenman* decision in 1963, strict products liability in tort has swept the country. In many states the courts have declared this doctrine to be law. In other states the legislatures have imposed strict tort liability on sellers. There is considerable variation in the mannner and extent of application of the doctrine from state to state, but the majority of states have applied strict tort liability as it is found in the Second Restatement of Torts. Students should recall that the restatement was prepared by the American Law Institute, a national body of lawyers, judges, and legal scholars whose pronouncements of the law are very influential, even though they have no official legal weight until courts or legislatures decide to apply them.

Section 402A of the Second Restatement of Torts says that anyone engaged in the business of selling a product who sells it in a *"defective condition unreasonably dangerous* to the user or consumer or to his property" is liable for injuries caused to the user or his property by the defect. The section emphasizes that such liability results even if "the seller has exercised all possible care" and despite the fact that the injured party is not in privity of contract with the seller.

The effect of 402A is to open up all sellers in the distribution chain—manufacturer, wholesaler, distributor, and retailer—to liability to the injured user or consumer. No longer can the retailer successfully defend the suit involving the nail in the can of peas by asserting the reasonableness of his or her behavior. Any seller in the chain of distribution is liable without fault for sale of a defective product causing injury.

The Second Restatement does not take a position, however, on whether or not strict tort liability extends to protect parties other than consumers or users. Does strict liability act to protect an injured pedestrian who is hit by a car which is out of control due to a defective steering column? The definite trend among the states is to extend strict liability in tort to such *bystanders*, but several states have chosen not to protect these individuals through strict liability. In states which have not so extended strict liability, bystanders are covered only by negligence law.

Once the plaintiff establishes strict products liability in tort, the question arises as to the extent to which the plaintiff can recover damages. Presently, the majority of states permit injured parties to recover personal damages that compensate for bodily harm and property damages which compensate for property other than the defective product itself, but they do not allow injured parties to recover for *economic damages,* such as harm to profits or loss of goodwill. Thus, in most states a restaurant owner cannot recover from a food supplier in strict tort liability when restaurant customers suffer food poisoning from spoiled fish, even though the incident deprives the restaurant of goodwill and future profits.

IMPLIED WARRANTY OF MERCHANTABILITY

Another theory of strict products liability arises from the *implied warranty of merchantability* which accompanies every sale of *goods* by a *merchant*. This warranty is implied by law into every contract for the sale of goods by one who is in the business of selling such goods, and it is imposed on sellers by Section 2-314 of the Uniform Commercial Code (UCC). Every state has adopted the UCC with the exception of Louisiana, and Louisiana recognizes law similar to Section 2-314.

Under the implied warranty of merchantability, it is the seller's duty to provide the buyer with a product which is *"fit for the ordinary purposes for which such goods are used."* If the product is not fit for its ordinary use, the seller is strictly liable for injury to person, property, or the product itself. This warranty also guarantees that the goods sold are properly packaged and conform to the class of goods (Grade A, Grade B, and so on) of which they are members. Such guarantees are especially important to commercial buyers who purchase for industrial use or resale. Products liability law is by no means limited only to consumer application.

The UCC permits sellers to disclaim the implied warranty of merchantability. In a written contract, in order for the disclaimer to be binding, the seller must either use the term "merchantability," that is, "seller disclaims all warranties of merchantability," or else use language such as "with all faults" or "as is." Language which recites merely that the seller disclaims "all warranties" does not exclude the implied warranty of merchantability.

It is important, also, to note that presently under federal law a seller cannot disclaim the implied warranty of merchantability as to the product itself in any written consumer warranty or service contract made by the seller. The disclaimer permitted by the UCC still applies in the commercial setting and in consumer transactions in which the seller is not offering a written warranty or a service contract. The UCC, however, does not permit disclaimers to limit damages for personal injuries. Nor does it allow disclaimer of damages in any situation where the court decides the disclaimer is *unconscionable.* In reading the following case, note the similarity between the doctrine of unconscionability and the doctrine of contractual illegality discussed in Chapter 5.

HANSON v. FUNK SEEDS INTERNATIONAL
373 N.W.2d 30 (S.D. 1985)

Larry Hanson purchased sseed corn from Funk Seeds International. Hanson's agent took delivery of the fifty-five bags of corn and signed a delivery receipt that stated in part:

"By acceptance and use of the seed, Buyer agrees that the Company's liability and the Buyer's exclusive remedy for breach of any warranty . . . shall be limited in all events to a return of the purchase price of the seed." This provision was also contained on a tag attached to each bag of corn. When some of the fields planted with corn failed to grow properly, Hanson sued Funk.

HENDERSON, J.: At trial, appellant Funk attempted to introduce delivery receipts and a tag which was attached to the bags of seed delivered to appellee Hanson. These exhibits contained the warranty disclaimer and limitation of remedy provisions outlined in the facts above. The trial court, however, denied admission of these exhibits and found the provisions in question to be unconscionable. Appellant here asserts that such a determination was in error. We disagree.

The exclusion or modification of warranties and the contractual modification or limitation of remedies is permitted under SDCL 57A-2-316 and SDCL 57A-2-719, respectively. In sum, a seller may use a disclaimer clause to control his liability by reducing the manner in which he can be found to have breached; and, also, a seller may attempt to restrict the type of remedy available once a breach occurs. However, the trial court may refuse to enforce such provisions if it finds them to have been unconscionable when made and if it affords the parties a reasonable opportunity to present evidence concerning its commercial setting, purpose, and effect so as to aid the court's decision. The trial court properly followed these procedural requirements by accepting pretrial memoranda and offers of proof at trial and correctly excluded the exhibits, determining their provisions to be unconscionable.

In reaching our determination, we are most persuaded by our past decision in *Durham v. Ciba-Geigy Corp.*, . . . In *Durham*, this Court stated:

To permit the manufacturer of the pesticide to escape all consequential responsibility for the breach of contract by inserting a disclaimer of warranty and limitation of consequential damages clause, such as was used herein, would leave the pesticide user without any substantial recourse for his loss. One-sided agreements whereby one party is left without a remedy for another party's breach are oppressive and should be declared unconscionable.

In this case, loss of the intended crop due to ineffectiveness of the herbicide is inevitable and potential plaintiffs should not be left without a remedy. Furthermore, the purchasers of pesticides are not in a position to bargain with chemical manufacturers for contract terms more favorable than those listed on the preprinted label, nor are they in a position to test the effectiveness of the pesticide prior to purchase. . . .

[P]ublic policy should not allow a chemical manufacturer to avoid responsibility for the ineffectiveness of a product which was offered for one purpose, the effective control of corn rootworm larvae.

Although the product in *Durham* was manufactured and the product here in question, to wit, corn seed, is a product of nature, the process used in marketing both products is nearly identical so as to permit application of the considerations found relevant in *Durham*.

Appellee Hanson, like most farmers, was not in a position to bargain for more favorable contract terms, nor was he able to test the seed before the purchase. A crop failure is inevitable if the corn seed is ineffective and to enforce the provisions here in question, which would only allow the return of the purchase price, would leave appellee without any substantial recourse for his loss. In essence, appellee would be left without a remedy for another's breach. The trial court's determination that these provisions were unconscionable is therefore not in error and we uphold its decision in this regard. [*Affirmed.*]

The implied warranty of merchantability applies only to sales of *goods*, that is, tangible, movable personal property. In recent years, however, many courts have applied the implied warranty concept by analogy to home builders who are sued by home buyers. The courts call the new legal theory the *implied warranty of habitability*. Under this theory, buyers can sue commercial builder-sellers who sell houses with major construction defects.

Of the jurisdictions adopting the warranty, the majority have ruled that it applies only to sales of new housing. Most courts have also imposed privity of contract requirements on the enforceability of the warranty. Thus, only the original buyer may hold the builder-seller to the warranty.

6. Duty Based upon Promises or Representations

A seller has an absolute duty of performance for any promises or representations he or she makes about a product when such statements become part of the basis for the bargain with the buyer. Several theories of law apply to this duty, which is of particular significance in commercial dealings.

EXPRESS WARRANTY

Section 2-313 of the UCC creates an *express warranty* for any promises the seller makes about a product's performance, such as "the transmission of this tractor is guaranteed against mechanical defect for five years." This UCC section also establishes an express warranty for any factual statements describing the product. ("All moving parts are made of stainless steel.") Similarly, the seller is held to warrant expressly that a final shipment of goods will conform to any sample or model which has been furnished the buyer. None of these express warranties need use the words "warranty" or "guarantee," and express warranties cannot be disclaimed by the seller. Special federal law applies to the making of written warranties to consumers. This law is covered in Chapter 15.

Note that an express warranty places upon the seller an absolute duty of performance. That he or she has acted reasonably or that the product is fit for its ordinary use and is not defective does not protect the maker of an express warranty. If the product is not as described or if it does not perform as promised, the seller is liable.

MISREPRESENTATION

A duty of performance which overlaps that of express warranty places tort liability on anyone who misrepresents to the public a material fact about the character or quality of a product through advertising or labeling. This doctrine of **misrepresentation** also imposes a duty of absolute performance upon the seller. A good example of this absolute duty involves a pharmaceutical laboratory. The laboratory advertised its painkilling product as being "nonaddictive." When a patient, whose doctor prescribed the drug freely, became addicted and later died, his widow sued the drug maker. Although the court found that the laboratory was not negligent, that the product was neither defective nor unreasonably dangerous, and that the laboratory honestly believed the drug to be non-addictive, it held the laboratory liable. The description of the drug contained the misrepresentation of a material fact and created absolute liability for the manufacturer. The doctrines of express warranty and misrepresentation warn manufacturers not to oversell products by describing them beyond their capabilities of performance.

IMPLIED WARRANTY OF FITNESS FOR A PARTICULAR PURPOSE

In addition to the doctrines of express warranty and misrepresentation, the law imposes absolute liability on sellers through the *implied warranty of fitness for a particular purpose*. Under UCC Section 2-315, if a purchaser relies upon a seller's skill and judgment to select a product to serve a particular mentioned purpose, the seller is liable if the product fails the purpose. At the basis of this doctrine is the purchaser's describing the purpose to the seller and the subsequent reliance upon the seller to select the proper product. Thus, if a contractor asks a manufacturer to furnish a digging machine which is capable of digging through a certain rocky soil, the manufacturer who supplies a digger is liable if it fails to cleave the soil. This is true even though the machine is not defective and is capable of digging in other kinds of softer soil. To avoid problems in which a piece of equipment is required for a particular purpose, however, the purchaser must make sure that the seller does not disclaim the implied warranty of fitness. The UCC permits such disclaimer.

THE PLAINTIFF'S CASE

In most instances, a plaintiff must prove certain things in order to hold the defendant liable for products that injure. (See Table 7-2.) The plaintiff must prove these things whether the case involves negligence, strict tort liability, or the implied warranty of merchantability.

7. Product Defect

Except where there is an absolute duty of performance (such as in express warranty), the plaintiff must establish that the product causing injury is

TABLE 7-2   Necessary Elements of the Plaintiff's Products Liability Case

1 Defect must be in production or design.
2 Defect must be at the hands of the defendant.
3 Defect must have caused the harm.
4 Defect must make the product unreasonably dangerous.

defective before recovery is permitted. Since the great majority of plaintiffs in product liability suits cannot rely upon express warranties or similar legal theories, they must prove that the product contains a *defect*. Such proof is required whether the lawsuit focuses upon the unreasonableness of the defendant's conduct (negligence), the unreasonable dangerousness of a defect (strict tort liability), or the lack of fitness for ordinary use (implied warranty of merchantability). How the law identifies a defect assumes considerable significance to both plaintiff and defendant.

A number of factors enter into the determination of a defect. Probably the best way to summarize these factors is to say that a *product becomes defective when it does not meet the standard of safety society expects.* That the blade of a kitchen knife may slice a person's thumb, even in normal use, is to be expected, and the law does not regard the knife as defective for doing so. On the other hand, for the sharp blades of a self-propelled power mower to slice the foot of a user is a different matter. If such injury could have been avoided by adding a safety guard, the law may regard lack of the guard as a defect in the mower.

For convenience, product defects can be divided into two categories: production defects and design defects. *Production defects* are generally easy to identify. The product does not meet the manufacturer's own internal production standards. Although the manufacturer may not be negligent simply because there is a production defect, such a defect usually allows the plaintiff to rely upon strict tort or implied warranty of merchantability theories of liability.

In contrast to the case of production defect, the *design defect* case does not involve a deviation from the manufacturer's own standards. Indeed, the product acts just as the manufacturer intended it should. Still, it has injured a plaintiff who sues. In such a case might the manufacturer be liable because of the product's design? Here the expectations of the user and society become important.

One significant cause of product liability suits is the breakdown of products toward the end of their useful lives. Products, especially complex machinery, are hardly expected to last forever, yet when older products break down, causing injury, they are frequently considered "defective" by those injured. Lawsuits ensue.

The issue of whether product breakdown after long use means the product is defective is presently of primary concern to manufacturers. Obviously, if the breakdown, even after long product life, is due to a production flaw, the manufacturer is likely to be found liable for injuries which arise. Many manufacturers, however, have also been held liable in cases of breakdown for design defects. Courts and juries usually determine such cases on the basis of whether or not the breakdown has been premature. The prematurity question relates directly back to the reasonable expectations users have for products they purchase.

Manufacturers can often protect themselves in cases involving the performance life of products by issuing appropriate warnings which cover both the expected duration of product use and proper maintenance procedures.

In some states the legislatures have set *statutes of limitations* for the bringing of product liability suits which permit a suit to be filed, such as, only within six years following purchase. After six years the manufacturer is not liable for injuries arising out of product use. Such statutes eliminate the long "tail" of many tort statutes of limitation which run not from the time of purchase but from the time of injury.

8. Defect in the Hands of the Defendant

Just because a product user has been injured by a defect in the product does not mean that the manufacturer, or any particular party in the chain of distribution, is liable. A vital fact which the plaintiff must prove in order to win a products liability case is that the defect occurred or existed while in the hands of the defendant. As we previously mentioned, a defective crack in a beverage bottle may have occurred during manufacture or distribution, while being shelved, or when the injured user placed the warm bottle in the freezer to chill.

Engineering consultants and other expert witnesses can frequently provide testimony which will fix at what point the product became defective. Sometimes, however, expert witnesses for the plaintiff and for the defendant disagree and contradict each other. In such cases the jury must decide whom to believe, bearing in mind that it is the obligation of the plaintiff to prove his or her case by the preponderance of the evidence.

9. The Defect Must Have Caused the Harm

Chapter 6 discussed the requirement of proof of causation in a successful tort action. The same requirement applies in product liability cases based either on tort or in contract. To win a products liability case, the plaintiff must do more than establish merely that a defect in the product existed at the time of the accident. To win, the plaintiff must show a causal link between the defect and the harm. An inability to do so will usually defeat the claim. For instance, an automobile crash can hardly be attributed to a defective transmission when the automobile turned over after hitting a pothole in the road, even though the defect may have been present when the accident occurred.

In more subtle cases, however, the causation issue can be extremely difficult to unravel. A dramatic example of this was the tragic crash of a DC-10 jetliner immediately after takeoff. Authorities initially assigned responsibility for the accident to a sheared wing-mounting bolt found in the grass near the runway. Only after several days had passed did they change their minds and place the cause for the crash elsewhere. Instead of being defective, the bolt had merely broken under the great pressure put upon it by another mechanical failure.

As among manufacturers, parts makers, and various subcontractors, it is extremely important to place causation for an accident like the DC-10 crash as precisely as possible. Tens of millions of dollars may be involved. Even experts, however, often disagree on whether a particular defect has caused a particular harm.

10. Defect Must Make the Product Unreasonably Dangerous

Closely tied to the concept of the product defect is that the defect must make the product *unreasonably dangerous.* This "unreasonably dangerous" element of the plaintiff's proof in strict liability cases merges completely with the proof of defect when a production flaw causes the injury. The defectively produced product *is* unreasonably dangerous if the defect causes injury.

In cases which involve charges of unsafe design, however, the "unreasonably dangerous" doctrine becomes important. Since the injury-causing item contains no production defect, it will create liability for the manufacturer only if the court determines that the design is unreasonably dangerous. To this extent, strict liability and negligence liability for defectively designed products are very similar. Both theories focus on whether or not it is unreasonable for a product to be sold in the marketplace.

Proper warnings which accompany a potentially dangerous product can go far toward reducing the possibility that a court might find the product unreasonably dangerous. Although many products, such as drugs, can be dangerous under certain conditions or to certain groups, these products are often useful and valuable to society. Hence, when accompanied by a warning, they can be used without risk of unreasonable danger.

In deciding whether or not a warning is necessary or how to word a warning, manufacturers often face two undesirable alternatives. The dramatic impact of a warning may affect product marketability. On the other hand, the failure to warn may subject the manufacturer to multimillion-dollar products liability suits. A company's legal staff, as well as its marketing division, must be consulted in weighing these alternatives.

When a manufacturer decides to warn about product features or side effects, the statement must be worded precisely, or the manufacturer may be held liable even though a warning has been made. In one noted case the label of a cleaning solvent cautioned users not to breathe the solvent's fumes and to make sure that the place of use was adequately ventilated. Nonetheless, a court held the manufacturer liable when several people were injured by the fumes. The court stated that the warning should have said explicitly that the fumes must be vented to the outside air. The people had been injured because the ventilating system was a closed circulation system which had recycled fumes back into the room. Recently, a trial court awarded $8 million against a pesticide manufacturer in the death of Superman. Superman was a prize bull who died after being sprayed by the pesticide. The manufacturer failed to warn strongly enough about the potentially fatal results of improper pesticide application.

In planning for product safety, manufacturers frequently seek to avoid products liability problems by ensuring that their products meet all relevant government standards and industry practices. Although courts will take such steps into their deliberations, many courts have ruled that the meeting of standards and industry practices by no means will bar the courts from determining products to be unreasonably dangerous. The likelihood of a product being called unreasonably dangerous is, of course, substantially less when the product meets relevant standards than when it does not.

THE DEFENDANT'S CASE

11. Parties

In today's highly complex marketplace, seldom does a single firm or company bear complete responsibility for the manufacture, distribution, and sale of a product to the ultimate user. As a result, when someone's person or property is injured through use of a defective product, the damage will usually create potential liability for a number of parties (see Figure 7-1). The plaintiff in these cases usually sues all such parties to increase the chances of recovery against a guilty party which is financially able to pay the judgment. It becomes important, then, to know who may be a defendant in a products liability lawsuit.

LESSORS
The principles of products liability had their beginnings in regular sales transactions. Conditions of the modern marketplace, however, have now led other groups besides those in the normal distribution chain of sale to be

1   Liable only in negligence or for express warranties.
2   Usually not liable for negligence; may seek indemnification from
    preceeding seller; some states do not permit products liability
    actions against these parties if the manufacturer is solvent.
3   Liable only when the product defect is caused by the parts and
    materials supplied or the work performed by these parties.

FIGURE 7-1
Possible Defendants in Product Liability.

pulled within the controlling influence of these principles. Commercial lessors are one such group.

Using the rules of strict tort and warranties of merchantability or fitness for a particular purpose, courts in most jurisdictions presently impose strict liability on commercial lessors of defective products. In 1982 the Supreme Court of Rhode Island imposed strict liability on a commercial lessor. The court noted that such lessors "stand in a far better financial and technical position than lessees to insure against, prevent, or spread the costs of product-related injuries."

Note that in a technical sense both Section 402A of the Restatement and the warranty sections of the UCC apply only to the *sale* of products. In extending strict liability to commercial lessors the courts have analogized to these rules rather than relied upon them in any absolute fashion. Thus courts make new law, stretch old rules, and fill in existing legal gaps and ambiguities to meet what they see as changing needs of society.

FRANCHISORS

One of the most significant developments in marketing during the past twenty-five years has been the growth of franchising. The franchisor grants the franchisee the right to manufacture, distribute, or sell a product using the trademark and name of the franchisor. As a result, almost inevitably, franchisors have become the target of products liability suits based on theories of strict tort and implied warranty. Although franchisors may not manufacture, handle, design, or require the use of a product, they frequently do retain the right to control or approve the design, and they may specify quality-control standards and conduct advertising for the trademark.

SELLERS OF USED PRODUCTS

Sellers of used products are liable for negligence when they fail to use reasonable care in selling defective products that cause injury. However, it is not clear that they may be held strictly liable. Courts in some states favor strict liability for injury-causing, defective used products. Courts in other states do not.

As the following case illustrates, courts are more likely to impose strict liability on a seller of a used product when the product has been rebuilt or reconditioned.

CRANDELL v. LARKIN AND JONES APPLIANCE CO., INC.
334 N.W.2d 31 (S.D. 1983)

Gloria Crandell purchased a used clothes dryer from the defendant, Larkin and Jones Appliance Company, Inc. The dryer had a tag describing the machine as a "Quality Reconditioned Unit" that was "Tag-Tested" and "Guaranteed." Two weeks after the purchase, the dryer caused a fire in Crandell's house and resulted in $25,000 fire and smoke damages. The trial court dismissed the strict products liability action because it was against a commercial seller of used products. The court also ruled that there were no applicable warranties.

DUNN, J.: We adopted the strict liability theory, as set forth in Restatement of Torts (Second) Section 402A and thereby created a new cause of action in tort. Restatement of Torts (Second) Section 402A neither expressly includes nor excludes commercial sellers of used products from its coverage. Rather, its coverage applies to "one who sells any product." We have not determined whether the strict liability doctrine should be broadened to cover the commercial sale of used products. We now undertake that inquiry.

Courts and commentators disagree as to whether strict liability should apply to a commercial seller of used products. Courts rejecting strict liability for used products have primarily dealt with fact patterns which did not involve guarantees of reconditioned, rebuilt, or recapped products. In a case involving the sale of a used wheel, the court specifically limited its holding when it stated: "By used products we do not refer to products rebuilt by a manufacturer, nor do we mean to imply that there is never any liability when used products are sold."

More recently the Oregon Supreme Court came to the same conclusion in a case involving the sale of a used crane "as is" which was inspected and approved by the purchaser. There, the court was reluctant to hold every commercial used-goods dealer responsible for injuries caused by defects in its goods. The court stated:

We conclude that holding every dealer in used goods responsible regardless of fault for injuries caused by defects in his goods would not only affect the prices of used goods; it would work a significant change in the very nature of used goods markets. Those markets, generally speaking, operate on the apparent understanding that the seller, even though he is in the business of selling such goods, makes no particular representation about their quality simply by offering them for sale. *If a buyer wants some assurance of quality, he typically either bargains for it in the specific transaction or seeks out a dealer who routinely offers it* **(by, for example, providing a guarantee, limiting his stock of goods to those of a particular quality, advertising that his used goods are specially selected, or in some other fashion). The flexibility of this kind of market appears to serve legitimate interests of buyers as well as sellers. We are of the opinion that the sale of a used product, without more, may not be found to generate the kind of expectations of safety that the courts have held are justifiably created by the introduction of a new product into the stream of commerce.**

We agree with the rationale provided by these courts to the extent it applies to the broad commercial used-product market. We believe, however, that those used-product merchants who rebuild or recondition goods are subject to the strict liability doctrine. The application of strict liability to sellers of used products, who rebuild or recondition those products, helps to protect the reasonable expectations of consumers . . . [*Reversed.*]

Whether or not courts apply strict tort liability or implied warranties of merchantability in used-product cases, sellers of such products will quickly be held liable if a used product does not live up to an express warranty. For example, in the *Crandell* case the court also found that the defendant had given the plaintiff a ninety-day express warranty on the clothes dryer.

12. Defendant's Defenses

As we mentioned previously, the defendant in products liability cases usually will not be held absolutely liable for injuries caused to the plaintiff. There are still certain burdens of proof, such as "defect," "unreasonable dangerousness," or "fault," which the plaintiff must meet to win the lawsuit. Also, the defendant can raise and prove various defenses, which will defeat a plaintiff's recovery. (See Table 7-3.) Some of the defenses can be raised only to defeat causes of action based on negligence. Other defenses also apply in strict liability cases.

As it is modified by comparative fault principles, **contributory negligence** can be a defense in a products liability negligence action. Chapter 6 discusses this defense in its general tort context. Specifically, products liability defendants are concerned with whether or not they can raise this defense when the plaintiff attempts to hold them strictly liable. Some states do not recognize contributory negligence as a defense to strict tort or warranty liability. However, the trend is to allow defendants to raise comparative fault versions of the contributory negligence defense in product liability actions.

Although states disagree over whether or not carelessness may bar a plaintiff's recovery in strict liability cases, most states permit defendants to claim that the plaintiff voluntarily assumed the risk of a defective product or that injury resulted from the plaintiff's misuse of the product. These defenses are available to defendants in negligence, strict tort, and warranty cases. For the defense of assumption of the risk to succeed, the defendant must show that the plaintiff understood the nature of the risk and voluntarily and unreasonably assumed it. This defense is frequently used in industrial accident cases in which the plaintiff argues defective design (for example, lack of a safety guard on a machine), and the defendant can prove that the plaintiff knew the risk and assumed it.

Another defense is the so-called *state-of-the-art defense.* Product manufacturers, especially machine makers, frequently find themselves sued for injuries which occur during the use of a product which is twenty years old or more. Since the time an older product has been manufactured, the state of technological art may have progressed until it is now possible to manufacture a product considerably safer than the older product. Products liability defendants in situations involving older products raise the state-of-the-art defense usually when the plaintiff has alleged a defective design. The state-of-the-art defense requires that juries judge defendants by the technology feasible at the

TABLE 7-3 Defendant's Product Liability Defenses

1 Contributory negligence (comparative fault type)
2 Assumption of risk
3 State-of-the-art
4 Misuse

time the defendants manufactured the products in question. Not all jurisdictions recognize this defense.

The defendant may also avoid liability by showing that the plaintiff deliberately misused the product. The misuse defense might apply when a plaintiff is injured while using a frying pan as a hammer or a power lawnmower as a hedge trimmer. Courts, however, have been reluctant to bar the plaintiff's recovery when the misuse is foreseeable by the manufacturer. Even when foreseeable misuse is possible, manufacturers can gain some degree of protection from liability by issuing clear warnings about the consequences of misuse.

13. Industrial Accidents Involving Products

When workers suffer job-related injuries, they receive workers' compensation from their employers. Chapter 14 discusses this workers' compensation law in detail. This chapter, however, stresses that workers' compensation is the only amount which an injured employee can get from an employer. Usually, it is only a small fraction of what a jury may have given an employee for the same injury.

As might be expected, injured employees often look to parties other than the employer in an attempt to escape the limitations of workers' compensation. Since many employees are injured while using industrial machinery, they turn to the manufacturers and sellers of this equipment for legal satisfaction of their injury claims. Products liability suits are the result.

Claims by injured employees against the manufacturers and sellers of industrial equipment now constitute a significant portion of total products liability costs. Work-related accidents account for almost half the amount paid to satisfy products liability claims. Furthermore, in many states the employer who has paid workers' compensation to an employee because of a product-related injury has the right to recover the entire amount from the manufacturer or seller if a products liability claim can be made. This right is the right of **subrogation.** Under the principles of subrogation, the employer stands in the place of the employee for the purposes of exercising the legal claim.

14. Indemnification

As we discussed previously, a large group of defendants may be potentially liable in products liability cases. This group ranges from the retail seller all the way back to the manufacturer or even to the raw materials supplier. To establish the basis for liability, however, the plaintiff must be able to prove that the defect existed while the product was in the hands of a particular seller. Because several sellers in the chain of distribution may be liable to the plaintiff, what is their relationship to one another? If one seller pays the entire claim, can that seller seek recovery from other sellers in the distribution chain?

The law answers these questions through the principles of **indemnification**. As they are applied in products liability, these principles permit any seller who is compelled to pay the injured plaintiff to obtain full recovery from the party that sold the defective product to him or her. For instance, a retailer who is held liable can get indemnification from the manufacturer, provided that the defect can be traced back to the manufacturer and the retailer is without fault for failing to conduct a reasonable inspection of the product.

15. The Risk Retention Act

The passage of the *Risk Retention Act of 1981* heralds closer federal involvement in current problems created by products liability laws. This act facilitates the formation of "captive" insurance companies and also permits group purchase of standard product liability insurance.

During times of rapid change in products liability law, it is difficult for insurers to predict the timing and amount of the liability for which they may bear responsibility. Hence, they sometimes overrate the risks. As premium costs soar, manufacturers and other product sellers search for alternatives to standard liability insurance. One alternative is self-insurance. There are advantages to this approach, namely that the self-insured firm pays only for its actual liabilities, and it can earn income from reserves which it sets aside. Drawbacks, however, are that reserve contributions are not deductible for tax purposes, and that failure to keep adequate reserves invites potentially serious impacts on earnings and cash flow when liability losses occur.

Another alternative to purchasing standard liability insurance is participating in the risk retention program of a captive insurer. A captive insurer is one formed by a large company or a group of companies to insure against certain risks (in this case products liability risks). Advantages in using captive insurers are (1) that members are frequently able to evaluate their risks better than are underwriters of standard insurers; (2) that through a captive insurer, an insured company can control the defense of a products liability action; and (3) that the insured company can participate in profits realized by the captive insurer.

The Risk Retention Act advances the formation of captive insurers by legislating that only the state which charters a captive insurer can regulate its formation and operations. This act limits other states to imposing minimal requirements on captives, such as assessing nondiscriminatory premium taxes and requiring the submission of certain reports. Although large standard insurers are subjected to different admission, qualification, and regulatory requirements for each state in which they do business, such a burden would be fatal to small captive insurers.

A number of states have passed the necessary enabling legislation for formation of captive insurers. Major independent insurance brokerage firms usually assist in organizing captive insurers for the risk retention group members.

A second provision of the Risk Retention Act permits manufacturers and other product sellers to group for the purpose of acquiring standard products liability insurance. Before passage of the act, approximately forty-five states had laws limiting or prohibiting the formation of such groups. Now, not only must states allow the formation of these groups but also they can neither impose group size requirements nor prohibit insurers from offering discounts to the groups.

One potential problem faced by members of risk retention and insurance purchase groups involves possible violations of antitrust law. Members of these groups must be aware that exchange of sensitive pricing data among members could lead to unreasonable restraints on competition. Members should arrange for an independent third party to collect sensitive data, or take some other step to minimize antitrust difficulties.

16. Legislative Revision of Products Liability

Traditionally, products liability law has been largely judge-made. It emerged out of common law in a case-by-case process over the last 150 years. Since the early 1950s the pace of its development has accelerated. There has been much "judicial activism" as courts evolve products liability law to accommodate what they believe are changing needs in society. Many commentators applaud this evolutionary process and view the judicial system as a "laboratory of ideas" where courts can develop new concepts and modify old ones in the best interests of society.

However, this case-by-case development imposes costs on manufacturers, insurers, and consumers. Manufacturers face uncertainty about product design and safety standards. Uncertainty also deters new product development. For insurance companies, it makes difficult rate-setting for product liability insurance. Ultimately, the costs arising from uncertainty are passed on to consumers.

Responding to rapidly changing judge-made law and the uncertainty it creates, approximately half the states have enacted statutes revising products liability laws. From the viewpoint of the business community, however, these revisions have not produced satisfactory results. The problem is that product manufacturers and sellers often do business in many states. Even where states have revised products liability laws, their revisions have not been uniform on a state-by-state basis. Moreover, much reform has been on a piecemeal basis. Uncertainty still results, and businesses frequently find themselves forced to set marketing policies or insurance rates on a "worst case" basis, that is, on what the current law is in the strictest jurisdiction. But since the law is still evolving, even that approach cannot always be depended upon for long.

As of this writing, many trade association groups are lobbying Congress to enact federal products liability law to help bring uniformity and certainty to this area. Some consumer groups and most attorney associations oppose federal enactment as an attempt to roll back the rights of injured parties, kill the "laboratory of ideas," and deprive the states of their traditional role in setting products liability policies.

We can identify several key areas of products liability revision that proponents and opponents of federal adoption are debating. (See Table 7-4.) In these areas some state revision has already occurred and other state revision is possible if federal reform efforts fail.

17. Management Planning for Products Liability

The best solution for a company's anxieties concerning products liability is not in legislative reform of existing laws. It lies in placing concern for products liability prevention into every phase of manufacturing, from initial design through production and final sale. (See Table 7-5.) Until recently few companies formally evaluated the dangers of products liability and then followed procedures to lessen them. A Conference Board study concluded that fewer than 30 percent of nearly 300 companies surveyed had full-time products liability managers at the corporate level. Yet, management planning is one of the most crucial components in reducing a manufacturer's products liability.

Although all departments of a company, especially marketing and engineering, should share an interest in the problems of potential products liability, management ultimately is the one to deal effectively with these problems. For instance, a company's engineers may bear the responsibility for designing a product and developing standards for its parts, but management should decide whether to incorporate certain safety features into the product or to rely upon warnings about possible product hazards. This evaluation and decision-making process must not be too informal. A formally constituted committee or products safety officer who reports to top management is desirable.

TABLE 7-4 Possible Products Liability Reforms

1 Reduce the various products liability theories that apply against manufacturers to one theory similar to strict liability.
2 Permit only negligence actions against retailers and wholesalers unless the product manufacturer is insolvent.
3 Eliminate strict liability recovery for defective product design.
4 Establish comparative negligence (fault) principles in all products liability actions.
5 Bar products liability claims against sellers if products have been modified or altered by a user.
6 Provide for the presumption of defense in product-design cases in which the product meets the "state-of-the-art," that is, the prevailing industry standards, at the time of product manufacture.
7 Create a **statute of repose** which would specify a period (such as twenty-five years) following product sale after which plaintiffs would lose their rights to bring suits for product-related injuries.
8 Reduce or eliminate punitive damage awards in most products liability cases.
9 Reduce products liability awards by the amount of workers' compensation the product-injured employees have received.
10 Create a no-fault alternative to litigation for injured product users who do not wish to sue.
11 Eliminate joint and several liability.

TABLE 7-5 Products Liability Prevention

1. Management involvement at all levels of planning and production
2. Formal product-safety policies
3. Product-safety officers or committees
4. Preproduction safety testing
5. Production quality controls and safety audits
6. Thorough legal review of product documents, such as labeling, warranties, and advertising
7. Product monitoring of actual consumer use
8. Product recall plans

Many potential product defects can be eliminated prior to the time actual production builds up sales inventories. Thus, management must consider the extent to which preproduction testing is necessary. Lack of proper testing as well as faulty design contributes to the creation of defective products. Also, before production begins, management should be aware of what dangers may arise from product use and of how purchasers will be safeguarded from or warned about them.

Of course, quality control during production is central to preventing product defects, but merely setting standards is not enough. Management must make sure it constantly audits production to determine that standards are being observed. The key to products safety is supervision.

Before a product is released into the marketplace, management must carefully review all support documents related to the product. Such documents include buyer instructions, labeling, warranties, and even advertising. Legal advice is particularly important at this step. Leaving the review to the marketing department is risky, since that department may be more concerned with sales than with liability prevention.

Persons in management must realize that products liability prevention does not stop with sale of the product. Buyer experience with the product must be monitored. To this end, consumers might be provided with a toll-free number to call if they encounter problems in product use. Sales representatives should be instructed to forward complaints concerning product defects directly to the products safety committee or officer. The company should also make plans for product recall in case that becomes necessary.

Finally, from the beginning to the end of the manufacturing and sales processes, management must convey to all departments that the high quality of company products is a primary company objective. One way to convey this is through a formal statement of company policy, as the following excerpt from the Caterpillar Code of Ethics illustrates:

PRODUCT QUALITY

A major Caterpillar objective is to design, manufacture, and market products of superior quality. We aim at a level of quality which, in particular, offers superiority for demanding applications. . . .

Products are engineered to exacting standards to meet users' expectations for performance, reliability, and life. Throughout the world, products are manufactured to the highest quality level commensurate with value. . . .

Product quality is constantly monitored. Our policy is to offer continuing product improvemments in response to needs of customers and requirements of the marketplace.

Products liability prevention efforts should represent more than a practical business response to dealing with the cost of products liability and its effect on the profitability of the business. By satisfying society's ethical expectation that marketed products will be safe, a business can demonstrate that it also cares about human life and safety.

SERVICE LIABILITY

18. Overview

Another component of the liability explosion in the business and professional communities is service liability. Providers of services frequently become defendants in lawsuits when the services they render cause personal or property injuries. Unlike defective products cases, however, strict liability does not generally reach cases that involve only the sale of services. For instance, the South Carolina Supreme Court ruled that strict liability did not apply in a case in which the defendant failed to remove a deteriorating valve stem from an automobile tire he installed. And an Illinois court held that an injured plaintiff could not sue in strict liability an installer of an elevator furnished by another company.

Most defective service cases are tried under negligence concepts of ordinary and reasonable care. But there are some instances in which courts have found defendants strictly liable when they sell a product and a service together. Plaintiffs have successfully sued under strict liability hairdressers who sell, then apply a hair product which causes injury. Such cases resemble those in the food preparation area where restauranteurs are subject to strict liability for injuries arising from the food they prepare and serve.

Lawyers, accountants, doctors, dentists, hospital administrators, realtors, engineers, and other professionals are held to special standards for defective services. Instead of the duty of the "reasonable person," providers of professional services must observe a higher duty—the duty of the "reasonable professional." Those who breach this duty are guilty of *malpractice*. The chief concept of malpractice, then, is professional negligence, although it also includes breach of contract (including the breach of confidential relationship) and even fraud.

Who determines the nature of the duty owed by professionals? Although standards of professional practice set or followed by professional groups are persuasive in determining this duty, the courts ultimately define its nature and extent. In several instances courts have imposed liability even when the conduct of defendants was acceptable by professional standards.

The number of malpractice suits filed has grown rapidly in recent years. Many of the same factors discussed before are responsible for the rise in litigation in each area, principally the heightened awareness of potential plaintiffs of their rights to sue and the increased willingness of such parties to sue. Due to the lobbying pressure of various professional groups, several states have taken steps to limit the effects of excessive numbers of malpractice suits against one profession or another. Usually, these steps center upon submitting malpractice claims to arbitration rather than to the formal courtroom process. Some professional organizations have taken internal steps to understand the causes of and to reduce the numbers of malpractice suits. For instance, the American Bar Association funded a multiyear project to study legal malpractice insurance claims. Other professional organizations present seminars aimed at reducing malpractice claims.

The next section considers what constitutes malpractice in one particular profession.

19. Malpractice and the Accounting Profession

The federal securities laws are the source of much potential liability for the accounting profession. Chapter 16 examines these laws. What follows here is a discussion of the common law liability of the accountant for malpractice.

In the conduct of their profession, accountants must exercise that degree of care and competence reasonably expected of members of their profession. Failure to exercise this care renders them liable for malpractice. As Table 7-6 shows, malpractice can cost accounting firms dearly. When they are guilty of malpractice against their clients, accountants are liable either for breach of contract or, in tort, for negligence or fraud. All such actions, however, are based on the injury-causing lapse of proper professional care.

TABLE 7-6 Out-of-Court Malpractice Settlements by "Big Eight" Accounting Firms, 1980–1985

Firm	Settlement Total
Arthur Andersen	$137,089,359
Peat Marwick Mitchell	19,400,000
Ernst & Whinney	6,020,500
Deloitte Haskins & Sells	4,997,585
Coopers & Lybrand	4,375,850
Price Waterhouse	3,500,000
Touche Ross	2,250,000
Arthur Young	1,490,000

Accounting malpractice toward a client can arise, for instance, when accountants present a <u>negligently</u> prepared financial statement to the client, and the client relies on it and is injured. Malpractice also results during an audit when accountants fail to pursue evidence that a client's employee is defrauding the client.

A frequent issue in accounting malpractice cases involves the accountants' liability to parties other than their clients for breach of the duty of professional care. The starting point from which to consider this issue is the famous decision in *Ultramares Corp. v. Touche.* In that case, Justice Cardozo ruled that an accountant did not owe a duty to all parties that might foreseeably rely upon the accountant's negligent work. To hold otherwise would be to expose accountants "to a liability in an indeterminate amount for an indeterminate time to an indeterminate class."

Most jurisdictions, however, impose liability on an accountant for negligence when the accountant "knows specifically" that a certain third party will be relying on the work prepared by the accountant for the client. An example would be the accountant negligently preparing a financial statement knowing that the client will use it in obtaining a loan at the bank. Some jurisdictions go a step further and extend an accountant's liability for negligence to parties who, although not known, are members of a "limited class" whose reliance on the accountant's work is "specifically foreseen." Suppliers who sell inventory on credit to a retailer fit the definition of a limited class. Finally, as the next case shows, a growing number of jurisdictions impose malpractice liability on accountants with regard to third parties under general negligence standards. Accountants are held liable for all "foreseeable injuries."

CITIZENS STATE BANK v. TIMM, SCHMIDT & CO.
335 N.W.2d 361 (Wis. 1983)

Timm, Schmidt & Co. [Timm], an accounting firm, prepared financial statements for Clintonville Fire Apparatus, Inc. (CFA) for the years 1973 to 1976. Each year, Timm also sent a letter to CFA stating that the financial statements fairly presented the financial condition of CFA and that the statements were prepared in accordance with generally accepted accounting principles. CFA used the statements in connection with a loan application to Citizens State Bank [Citizens]. After reviewing these financial statements, Citizens made several loans to CFA amounting to

$380,000. In 1977, Timm discovered an error in the 1974 and 1975 financial statements totalling $400,000. When Citizens received notice of this error, it called all of CFA's loans due. CFA went out of business and still owed Citizens $152,214.44. Citizens sued Timm and its malpractice insurance company. The trial court decided that Timm had no liability to Citizens and granted Timm's motion for summary judgment.

DAY, J.: The question on review is whether accountants may be held liable for the negligent preparation of an audit report to a third party not in privity who relies on the report. . . .

Accountants have long been held not liable for their negligence to relying third parties not in privity under an application of Judge Cardozo's decision in *Ultramares v. Touche.* In *Ultramares,* Judge Cardozo absolved the defendant accountants from liability for overvaluing the assets of a company in an audit report to a plaintiff who had loaned money in reliance on a certified balance sheet in the report. Judge Cardozo expressed the concern that "if liability exists, a thoughtless slip or blunder . . . may expose accountants to a liability in an indeterminate amount for an indeterminate time to an indeterminate class."

According to Associate Justice Howard Wiener of the California Court of Appeals, *Ultramares* was relied on by every jurisdiction to consider this question to deny accountant liability to third parties. However, in recent years, *Ultramares* has received new attention and courts have started to find accountants liable to third parties. . . .

In this state, although the liability of accountants to third parties not in privity has been examined, the liability of an attorney to one not in privity was recently examined in *Auric v. Continental Casualty Co.* . . . This court concluded that an attorney may be held liable to a will beneficiary not in privity for the attorney's negligence in supervising the execution of a will. Part of the rationale for this decision was that the imposition of liability would make attorneys more careful in the execution of their responsibilities to their clients.

That rationale is applicable here. Unless liability is imposed, third parties who rely upon the accuracy of the financial statements will not be protected. Unless an accountant can be held liable to a relying third party, this negligence will go undeterred.

There are additional policy reasons to allow the imposition of liability. If relying third parties, such as creditors, are not allowed to recover, the cost of credit to the general public will increase because creditors will either have to absorb the costs of bad loans made in reliance on faulty information or hire independent accountants to verify the information received. Accountants may spread the risk through the use of liability insurance.

We conclude that the absence of privity alone should not bar negligence actions by relying third parties against accountants.

Although the absence of privity does not bar this action, the question remains as to the extent of an accountant's liability to injured third parties. . . .

The fundamental principle of Wisconsin negligence law is that a tortfeasor is fully liable for all foreseeable consequences of his act except as those consequences are limited by policy factors. . . .

We conclude that accountants' liability to third parties should be determined under the accepted principles of Wisconsin negligence law. According to these principles, a finding of non-liability will be made only if there is a strong public policy requiring such a finding. Liability will be imposed on these accountants for the foreseeable injuries resulting from their negligent acts unless, under the facts of this particular case, as a matter of policy to be decided by the court, recovery is denied on grounds of public policy.

This court has set out a number of public policy reasons for not imposing liability despite a finding of negligence causing injury:

(1) The injury is too remote from the negligence; or (2) the injury is too wholly out of proportion to the culpability of the negligent tortfeasor; or (3) in retrospect it appears too highly extraordinary that the negligence should have brought about the harm; or (4) because allowance of recovery would place too unreasonable a burden on the negligent tortfeasor; or (5) because allowance of recovery would be too likely to open the way for fraudulent claims; or (6) allowance of recovery

would enter a field that has no sensible or just stopping point.

Although in some cases this court has decided at the motion-to-dismiss stage that policy factors preclude the imposition of liability for negligent acts, it has generally been found to be better practice to have a full factual resolution before evaluating the public policy considerations involved.

In this case we conclude that a determin-ation of the public policy questions should be made after the facts of this case have been fully explored at trial. The question of the proper scope of these accountants' liabilities to the third party bank cannot be determined upon the information contained in the record. A full factual resolution is necessary before it can be said that public policy precludes Timm's liability for its allegedly negligent conduct. . . . [*Reversed.*]

If they have been hesitant to expose accountants to the possibility of third-party liability for negligence, many courts have been willing to allow *any* injured third party, foreseen or not, to sue accountants who are party to a *fraud.* Moreover, some courts do not require a showing of *intentional* misrepresentation before assessing fraud liability. They hold that gross negligence or even "blindness to the obvious" may provide sufficient evidence upon which to sustain a finding of fraud. This blurring of the distinction between professional negligence and fraud in accounting malpractice cases has helped further extend accountants' malpractice liability to third parties.

Frauds can involve not only misrepresentation of facts but also, under certain circumstances, the failure to disclose facts. In one instance an accounting firm was held liable in fraud for failing to disclose newly learned information which changed the implications of a previously released financial statement. Highly controversial at present is whether accounting firms must disclose the problems of one client to another client who does business with the first client.

REVIEW QUESTIONS

1 For each term in the left-hand column, match the most appropriate description in the right-hand column:

(1) Caveat emptor
(2) Production defect
(3) Merchant
(4) Implied warranty of
merchantability

(a) Professional negligence
(b) A contractual connection
(c) Let the buyer beware
(d) Legislation establishing a legal date after which no lawsuit may be begun

(5) Indemnification

(6) Malpractice

(7) Privity

(8) State-of-the-art defense

(9) Subrogation

(10) Statute of repose

(e) A difference between the way a manufacturer intended a product to be and the way it actually is

(f) One who ordinarily sells goods in the course of business

(g) An insurer's right to be put into the legal position of an insured to whom it has paid benefits

(h) The right to recover from someone based on payment of that person's legal obligation

(i) Requires that juries judge products by the technology feasible at the time of manufacture

(j) The guarantee that a product is fit for ordinary use

2 Discuss the development of product liability from the early 1800s until today.

3 Explain the arguments made for adoption of strict tort liability.

4 Acme Tiller Company sells a tiller to Whole Earth Wholesalers, which resells the tiller to Ralph's Retail. Ralph's Retail sells the tiller to Mr. Smith. While using the tiller, Mr. Smith's assistant is injured when a defective blade bolt breaks. Discuss the potential liability of the various sellers to the assistant.

5 Assume that when the defective blade bolt in question 4 breaks, the tiller blade flies through the window of a passing car, injuring its driver, Ms. Jones. The car then runs off the road and hits Billy Bystander. Under these facts, who will be liable to whom and under what legal theories?

6 When Roger uses a frying pan to hammer a nail into the wall, the handle snaps off, and the heavy pan drops on Roger's foot, permanently injuring it. Is it likely Roger can recover from the manufacturer? Why, or why not?

7 Discuss the variety of possible defendants to a products liability suit.

8 While driving under the influence of alcohol, Joe College runs off the road and wrecks his car. As the car turns over, the protruding door latch hits the ground and the door flies open. Joe, who is not wearing his seat belt, is thrown from the car and badly hurt. Joe sues the car manufacturer, asserting that the door latch was defectively designed. Discuss the legal issues raised by these facts.

9 Discuss the controversy surrounding the application of products liability law in industrial accident cases.

10 After being hit with several products liability suits, your company has asked you to design a management program to help it avoid such suits in the future. Design and discuss such a program.

11 What are some of the legislative revisions to products liability law currently being proposed or enacted?

12 Your company is being sued by an injured plaintiff who alleges that the company's widget is defectively designed. Your company is able to prove that the widget meets all current government standards for widgets. The widget is also as well-designed as any other company's widget. Will your company likely win the lawsuit? Discuss.

13 Does strict liability apply to the selling of services? Explain.

14 What steps have been taken in recent years to help control the effects of rising numbers of malpractice suits?

15 As president of the City National Bank, you are notified that a major borrower has defaulted on repayment of a $5 million loan and is declaring bankruptcy. Investigation uncovers that the borrower's certified financial statement, upon which City National relied in extending the loan, contains a major misstatement as to both assets and liabilities of the borrower. You now consider the possibility of a lawsuit against the accounting firm which certified the financial statement. Discuss the theories upon which such a suit might be based, and indicate what proof is needed to support each theory.

Part Three
PUBLIC LAW AND BUSINESS

Chapter
8

The Constitution and Business

1. Organization

The Constitution, as originally enacted, contained seven articles and a preamble. The Preamble sets forth the purposes of the Constitution, which include such general goals as the establishment of justice and the promotion of general welfare.

Article I establishes the legislative branch of government and defines its functions, powers, method of conducting business, and limitations on its powers, as well as the manner of election and removal of its members. Section 8 of Article I grants Congress numerous powers, including the power to tax and the power to regulate commerce. These powers will be discussed later in this chapter. Some of the other enumerated powers relate to external affairs and the power to wage war. Of special importance to business is the power to enact uniform laws on the subject of bankruptcy and laws that promote the progress of science and useful arts, by securing for limited times to authors and inventors the exclusive right to their writings and discoveries.

Article II vests the executive power in the President. It defines his term of office, qualifications for office, and manner of election. This latter provision, together with the Twelfth Amendment, which concerns the electoral college, is currently the subject of much criticism, with many people advocating election by popular vote. Article II also makes the President the Commander in Chief of the Armed Forces and authorizes him to enter into treaties with the advice and consent of the Senate. It is this article that requires the annual State of the Union message by the President.

Article III creates the judicial branch of government. It defines the original jurisdiction of the Supreme Court and authorizes Congress to create other federal court systems as discussed in Chapter 3. This provision underlies recent attempts to deny courts the power to decide cases involving abortions, school prayer, and busing to achieve integration. Article III also defines treason.

Article IV contains several provisions dealing with relationships between the states. It is often referred to as "the states' relation article," and is discussed in section 8 of this chapter.

Article V sets forth methods for amending the Constitution. To date, there have been twenty-six amendments approved by one of the authorized methods. The proposed equal rights for women amendment was adopted by Congress and ratified by thirty-five states before the time for ratification expired. Proposed amendments on abortion and school busing are also pending.

Article VI contains the supremacy clause, which means that federal laws and treaties are the supreme law of the land. The supremacy clause frequently comes into play when states attempt to regulate a business activity that the federal government also regulates. It will be discussed further in section 3 of this chapter.

2. Separation of Powers

One of the most important of our constitutional law concepts is the doctrine of **separation of powers**. It arose out of the strong fear the founders of this country had that too much power might be concentrated in one branch of government. This doctrine has both horizontal and vertical aspects. First, the horizontal aspect describes the theory that each of three branches of government (executive, legislative, and judicial) has a separate function to perform. Each is not to perform the functions of the others because no one person may exercise the powers of more than one branch at the same time. As the Supreme Court has stated in several cases:

> Each branch shall by the law of its creation be limited to the exercise of the powers appropriate to its own department and no other . . . As a general rule . . . the powers confided by the Constitution to one of these departments cannot be exercised by another.

One facet of this functional aspect of separation of powers is that each branch has the capacity or power to limit the other branches in the performance of their respective functions. For example, courts exercising the power of judicial review may limit the actions of the executive and the legislative branches of government. The legislative branch may determine the jurisdiction of federal courts and may limit the powers of the executive. The executive appoints the judiciary with the advice and consent of the Senate. Therefore, although each branch of government has a separate function to perform, these branches are closely interrelated and each has some control over the others. No branch of government is free to act with total independence of the others. Although the separation of powers concept admits that each branch has some control and influence over the others, it recognizes that each branch of government is to be free from the *coercive* influence of the others. Congress should not interfere with the President as he carries out his duty to "take care that the Laws be faithfully executed." The converse is also true. The President should not interfere with Congress as it performs its constitutional responsibilities.

The vertical aspect of separation of powers is *federalism* or dual federalism. This aspect recognizes that we have two levels of government—a federal level and a state and local level. Each has a separate and distinct role to play. The federal government must recognize that it was created by the states and that states have some sovereignty. The Tenth Amendment reserves some powers to the states and to the people. Congress may not impair the ability of state government to function in the federal system. Likewise, state government may not curtail in any substantial manner the exercise of powers granted by states to the federal government. Thus, the doctrine of separation of powers has both vertical and horizontal aspects.

Former Justice John M. Harlan, in discussing the reasons of our government of divided powers, concluded that in such a government lay the best promise for realizing a free society. In explaining the doctrine of separation of powers he observed:

> The matter has a double aspect: *first,* the division of governmental authority between the states and the central government; *second,* the distribution of power within the federal establishment itself. The former, doubtless born not so much of political principle as of the necessity for achieving a more perfect union than had proved possible under the Articles of Confederation, was solved by making the authority of the Federal Government supreme within the sphere of powers expressly or impliedly delegated to it and reserving to the states all other powers—a reservation which subsequently found express protection in the Bill of Rights through the provisions of the Tenth Amendment. The second aspect of the governmental structure was solved, purely as a matter of political theory, by distributing the totality of federal power among the legislative, executive and judicial branches of the government, each having defined functions. Thus eventuated the two great constitutional doctrines of federalism—often inaccurately referred to as the doctrine of states' rights—and separation of powers.

3. The Supremacy Clause

Closely related to the doctrine of separation of powers is the **supremacy clause.** This clause makes the federal law supreme over a state law if the two are in conflict. This specific clause guarantees federal supremacy even though the states created the federal government.

When courts are called upon to decide if a state law is invalid under the supremacy clause because it conflicts with a federal law, they must construe or interpret the two laws to see if they are in conflict. A conflict exists if the state statute would prevent the accomplishment and execution of the full purposes and objectives of Congress. It is immaterial that a state did not intend to frustrate the federal law if the state law in fact does so. In the case which follows, keep in mind that arbitration is a procedure for submitting controversies to a person or persons other than a court for a binding decision.

SOUTHLAND CORP. v. KEATING
104 S. Ct. 852 (1984)

BURGER, C.J.: . . . We noted probable jurisdiction to consider whether the California Franchise Investment Law, which invalidates certain arbitration agreements covered by the Federal Arbitration Act, violates the Supremacy Clause. . . .

Appellant The Southland Corporation is the owner and franchisor of 7-Eleven convenience stores. Southland's standard franchise agreement provides each franchisee with a license to use certain registered trademarks, a lease or sublease of a convenience store owned or leased by Southland, inventory financing, and assistance in advertising and merchandising. The franchisees operate the stores, supply bookkeeping data, and pay Southland a fixed percentage of gross profits. The franchise agreement also contains the following provision requiring arbitration:

Any controversy of claim arising out of or relating to this Agreement or the breach thereof shall be settled by arbitration in accordance with the Rules of the American Arbitration Association . . . and judgment upon any award rendered by the arbitrator may be entered in any court having jurisdiction thereof.

Appellees are 7-Eleven franchisees. Between September 1975 and January 1977, several appellees filed individual actions against Southland in California Superior Court alleging, among other things, fraud, oral misrepresentation, breach of contract, breach of fiduciary duty, and violation of the disclosure requirements of the California Franchise Investment Law. Southland's answer . . . included the affirmative defense of failure to arbitrate, . . .

The California Court of Appeal . . . interpreted the arbitration clause to require arbitration of all claims asserted under the Franchise Investment Law, and construed the Franchise Investment Law not to invalidate such agreements to arbitrate. Alternatively, the court concluded that if the Franchise Investment Law rendered arbitration agreements involving commerce unenforceable, it would conflict with § 2 of the Federal Arbitration Act and therefore be invalid under the Supremacy Clause . . . The California Supreme Court interpreted the Franchise Investment Law to require judicial consideration of claims brought under that statute and concluded that the California statute did not contravene the federal Act. . . .

The California Franchise Investment Law provides: "Any condition, stipulation or provision purporting to bind any person acquiring any franchise to waive compliance with any provision of this law or any rule or order hereunder is void." The California Supreme Court interpreted this statute to require judicial consideration of claims brought under the State statute and accordingly refused to enforce the parties' contract to arbitrate such claims. So interpreted, the California Franchise Investment Law directly conflicts with § 2 of the Federal Arbitration Act and violates the Supremacy Clause.

In enacting § 2 of the federal Act, Congress declared a national policy favoring arbitration and withdrew the power of the states to require a judicial forum for the resolution of claims which the contracting parties agreed to resolve by arbitration. . . .

The Federal Arbitration Act rests on the authority of Congress to enact substantive rules under the Commerce Clause. . . . The Arbitration Act creates a body of federal substantive law (which is) . . . applicable in state and federal courts. . . . The problems Congress faced were . . . twofold: the old common law hostility toward arbitration, and the failure of state arbitration statutes to mandate enforcement of arbitration agreements. To confine the scope of the Act to arbitrations sought to be enforced in federal courts would frustrate what we believe Congress intended to be a broad enactment appropriate in scope to meet the large problems Congress was addressing. . . .

We are unwilling to attribute to Congress the intent, in drawing on the comprehensive powers of the Commerce Clause, to create a right to enforce an arbitration contract and yet make the right dependent for its enforcement on the particular forum in which it is asserted. And since the overwhelming proportion of all civil litigation in this country is in the state courts, we cannot believe Congress intended to limit the Arbitration Act to disputes subject only to *federal* court jurisdiction. Such an interpretation would frustrate Congressional intent to place an arbitration agreement upon the same footing as other contracts, where it belongs.

In creating a substantive rule applicable in state as well as federal courts, Congress intended to foreclose state legislative attempts to undercut the enforceability of arbitration agreements. We hold that § 31512 of the California Franchise Investment Law violates the Supremacy Clause. . . . [*Reversed.*]

Sometimes a federal law is said to preempt an area of law. If a federal law preempts a subject, then any state law is unconstitutional under the supremacy clause. The conflict is apparent, and the evidence of it is conclusive. This is true not only of federal statutes but also applies to the rules and regulations of federal administrative agencies, as the case which follows illustrates.

FIDELITY FEDERAL SAVINGS AND LOAN ASSOCIATION v. REGINALD D. DE LA CUESTA
102 S. Ct. 3014 (1982)

The Federal Home Loan Bank Board (Board) regulates federal savings and loan associations. In 1976, the Board became concerned about the increasing controversy over "due-on-sale" clauses in mortgages. A due-on-sale clause permits a lender to declare the entire balance of a loan immediately due and payable if the property securing the loan is sold or otherwise transferred. The controversy had arisen because the courts of several states including California had declared such clauses to be illegal as against public policy unless a transfer had impaired the security for a loan. If the reason for acceleration was simply to increase the rate of interest, the clause was illegal.

To end the controversy, the Board issued a regulation which provided:

[A federal savings and loan] association continues to have the power to include, as a matter of contract between it and the borrower, a provision in its loan instrument whereby the association may, at its option, declare immediately due and payable sums secured by the association's security instrument if all or any part of the real property securing the loan is sold or transferred by the borrower without the association's prior written consent. Except as [otherwise] provided in . . . this section . . . , exercise by the association of such option (hereafter called a due-on-sale clause) shall be exclusively governed by the terms of the loan contract, and all rights and remedies of the association and borrower shall be fixed and governed by that contract.

In the preamble of the due-on-sale regulation, the Board explained its intent that the due-on-sale practices of federal savings and loans be governed "exclusively by Federal law." The Board emphasized that "[f]ederal associations shall not be bound by or subject to any conflicting State law which imposes different . . . due-on-sale requirements."

A federal savings and loan association in California sought to enforce its due-on-sale clause. The mortgagor contended that under California law the clause was unenforceable. The trial court upheld the clause and the California court of appeals reversed, finding no intent to supersede state law.

BLACKMUN, J.: . . . At issue in this case is the pre-emptive effect of a regulation, issued by the Federal Home Loan Bank Board (Board), permitting federal savings and loan associations to use "due-on-sale" clauses in their mortgage contracts. Appellees dispute both the Board's intent and its statutory authority to displace restrictions imposed by the California Supreme Court on the exercise of these clauses.

The pre-emption doctrine, which has its roots in the Supremacy Clause, requires us to examine congressional intent. Pre-emption may be either express or implied, and "is compelled whether Congress' command is explicitly stated in the statute's language or implicitly contained in its structure and purpose." Absent explicit pre-emptive language, Congress' intent to supersede state law altogether may be inferred because "[t]he scheme of federal regulation may be so pervasive as to make reasonable the inference that Congress left no room for the States to supplement it," because "the Act of Congress may touch a field in which the federal interest is so dominant that the federal system will be assumed to preclude enforcement of state laws on the same subject," or because "the object sought to be obtained by federal law and the character of obligations imposed by it may reveal the same purpose."

Even where Congress has not completely displaced state regulation in a specific area, state law is nullified to the extent that it actually conflicts with federal law. Such a conflict arises when "compliance with both federal and state regulations is a physical impossibility," or when state law "stands as an obstacle to the accomplishment and execution of the full purposes and objectives of Congress." These principles are not inapplicable here simply because real property law is a matter of special concern to the States: "The relative importance to the State of its own law is not material when there is a conflict with a valid federal law, for the Framers of our Constitution provided that the federal law must prevail."

Federal regulations have no less pre-emptive effect than federal statutes. Where Congress has directed an administrator to exercise his discretion, his judgments are subject to judicial review only to determine whether he has exceeded his statutory authority or acted arbitrarily. When the administrator promulgates regulations intended to preempt state law, the court's inquiry is similarly limited:

If [h]is choice represents a reasonable accommodation of conflicting policies that were committed to the agency's care by the statute, we should not disturb it unless it appears from the statute or its legislative history that the accommodation is not one that Congress would have sanctioned. . . .

A pre-emptive regulation's force does not depend on express congressional authorization to displace state law; moreover, whether the administrator failed to exercise an option to promulgate regulations which did not disturb state law is not dispositive. Thus, the Court of Appeal's narrow focus on Congress' intent to supersede state law was misdirected. Rather, the questions upon which resolution of this case rests are whether

the Board meant to pre-empt California's due-on-sale law, and, if so, whether that action is within the scope of the Board's delegated authority. . . .

(The court then found a clear intent to preempt state law on the part of the Board. Such clauses were declared to be legal if a Federal Savings & Loan Association wanted to use them. The preamble made it clear that such clauses were to be governed *exclusively* by Federal law without regard to any limitations imposed by state law.)

The question remains whether the Board acted within its statutory authority in issuing the pre-emptive due-on-sale regulation. The language and history of the Home Owner's Loan Act convince us that Congress delegated to the Board ample authority to regulate the lending practices of federal savings and loans so as to further the Act's purposes, and that (this regulation) is consistent with those purposes. Accordingly, we hold that the Board's due-on-sale regulation bars application of the (state law) to federal savings and loan associations. The judgment of the Court of Appeals is reversed. [*It is so ordered.*]

There are numerous additional examples of state laws which are unconstitutional under the supremacy clause. For example, a Virginia statute prohibited nonresidents of Virginia from catching certain fish in the Virginia portion of Chesapeake Bay and from obtaining commercial fishing licenses. There was a federal enrollment and licensing law which authorized federal licensing of fishing boats. The Supreme Court held the state law to be unconstitutional under the supremacy clause. Virginia could not prevent federally licensed fishing vessels from fishing in Chesapeake Bay.

Some of the violations of the supremacy clause are not quite so obvious. Arizona had a statute which provided for the suspension of licenses of drivers who could not satisfy judgments arising out of auto accidents, even if the driver was bankrupt. The statute was unconstitutional since it was in conflict with the federal law on bankruptcy. The purpose of the Bankruptcy Act is to give debtors new opportunity unhampered by the pressure and discouragement of pre-existing debt. The challenged state statute hampers the accomplishment and execution of the full purposes and objectives of the Bankruptcy Act enacted by Congress.

4. External Affairs

The President has the power to make treaties, with the advice and consent of the Senate, as is stated in Article II, Section 2 of the Constitution. This power has grown in its importance to the economic life and defense of the nation, as the United States has become a leader in world affairs.

The treaties of most countries affect only their external relations with other countries. The United States is unique in that its treaties are part of the "supreme Law of the Land," and thus have the internal force of the Constitution and laws enacted by Congress. Article VI of the Constitution provides in part: "This Constitution, and the Laws of the United States which shall be made in Pursuance thereof; and all Treaties made, or which shall be made, under the Authority of the United States, shall be the supreme Law of the Land; and the Judges in every State shall be bound thereby, any Thing in the Constitution or Laws of any State to the Contrary notwithstanding." Note that the language employed makes the laws enacted by Congress binding only if made within the limitations of the Constitution. It apparently provides no such restriction on the effect of treaties made "under the Authority of the United States." Therefore, business is subject to the provisions of all treaties entered into by the President which are ratified by the Senate. They are the supreme Law of the Land.

5. The Contract Clause

Section 10 of Article I of the United States Constitution says in part that no state shall pass any law impairing the obligation of contracts. This provision does not apply to the federal government, which does in fact frequently enact laws and adopt regulations that affect existing contracts. For example, the Department of Agriculture from time to time embargoes grain sales to foreign countries, usually as a result of problems in foreign affairs.

The limitation on state action impairing contracts has not been given a literal application. As a result of judicial interpretation, some state laws which affect existing contracts have been approved, especially when the law is passed to deal with a specific emergency situation. On the other hand, this constitutional provision does generally limit alternatives available to state government and prevents the enactment of legislation that changes vested contract rights. The case that follows, while declaring a state statute unconstitutional for violating the contract clause, does indicate those areas in which a literal application will not result.

ALLIED STRUCTURAL STEEL CO. v. SPANNAUS

98 S. Ct. 2716 (1978)

Plaintiff, an Illinois corporation, maintained an office in Minnesota with thirty employees. It had a pension plan, adopted in 1963 and qualified under Section 401 of the Internal Revenue Code, under which employees were entitled to retire and receive a pension at age 65 regardless of length of service. An employee's pension right became vested if he or she satisfied certain conditions as to length of service and age. Plaintiff, the sole contributor to the pension trust fund, each year made contributions to the fund based on actuarial predictions of eventual payout needs. The plan neither required contributions nor imposed any sanction on it for failure to make adequate contributions. Plaintiff retained not only a right to amend the plan but also to terminate it any time and for any reason.

In 1974, Minnesota enacted the Private Pension Benefits Protection Act (Act), under which a private employer of 100 employees or more (at least one of whom was a Minnesota resident) who provided pension benefits under a plan meeting the qualifications of Section 401 of the Internal Revenue Code, was subject to a "pension funding charge" if he terminated the plan or closed a Minnesota office. The charge was assessed if the pension funds were insufficient to cover full pensions for all employees who had worked at least 20 years, and if periods of employment prior to the effective date of the Act were to be included in the 20-year employment criterion. Shortly thereafter, in a move planned before passage of the Act, plaintiff closed its Minnesota office, and several of its employees, who were then discharged, had no vested pension rights even though they had worked for 20 years or more, thus qualifying as pen-

sion obligees under the Act. Subsequently, the State sought to collect a pension funding charge of $185,000.

Plaintiff then brought suit in Federal District Court for injunction and declaratory relief, claiming that the Act unconstitutionally impaired its contractual obligations to its employees under its pension plan. The lower court upheld the law and the plaintiff appealed.

STEWART, J.: . . . The issue in this case is whether the application of Minnesota's Private Pension Benefits Protection Act to the appellant violates the Contract Clause of the United States Constitution. . . .

There can be no question of the impact of the Minnesota Private Pension Benefits Protection Act upon the company's contractual relationships with its employees. The Act substantially altered those relationships by superimposing pension obligations upon the company conspicuously beyond those that it had voluntarily agreed to undertake. But it does not inexorably follow that the Act, as applied to the company, violates the Contract Clause of the Constitution.

The language of the Contract Clause appears unambiguously absolute: "No state shall . . . pass any . . . Law impairing the Obligation of Contracts." The Clause is not, however, the draconian provision that its words might seem to imply. As the Court has recognized, "literalism in the construction of the contract clause . . . would make it destructive of the public interest by depriving the State of its prerogative of self-protection." . . .

First of all, it is to be accepted as a commonplace that the Contract Clause does not operate to obliterate the police power of the states. . . .

If the Contract Clause is to retain any meaning at all, however, it must be understoood to impose some limits upon the power of a State to abridge existing contractual relationships, even in the exercise of its otherwise legitimate police power. The existence and nature of those limits were clearly indicated in a series of cases in this Court arising from the efforts of the States to deal with the unprecedented emergencies brought on by the severe economic depression of the early 1930's.

In *Home Building & Loan Assn. v. Blaisdell*, 290 U.S. 398, the Court upheld against a Contract Clause attack a mortgage moratorium law that Minnesota had enacted to provide relief for homeowners threatened with foreclosure. Although the legislation conflicted directly with lenders' contractual foreclosure rights, the Court there acknowledged that, despite the Contract Clause, the States retain residual authority to enact laws "to safeguard the vital interests of (their) people." In upholding the state mortgage moratorium law, the Court found five factors significant. First, the state legislature had declared in the Act itself that an emergency need for the protection of homeowners existed. Second, the state law was enacted to protect a basic societal interest, not a favored group. Third, the relief was appropriately tailored to the emergency that it was designed to meet. Fourth, the imposed conditions were reasonable. And, finally, the legislation was limited to the duration of the emergency.

The *Blaisdell* opinion thus clearly implied that if the Minnesota moratorium legislation had not possessed the characteristics attributed to it by the Court, it would have been invalid under the Contract Clause of the Constitution. . . .

In applying these principles to the present case, the first inquiry must be whether the state law has, in fact, operated as a substantial impairment of a contractual relationship. The severity of the impairment measures the height of the hurdle the state legislation must clear. Minimal alteration of contractual obligations may end the inquiry at its first stage. Severe impairment, on the other hand, will push the inquiry to a careful examination of the nature and purpose of the state legislation.

The severity of an impairment of contractual obligations can be measured by the factors that reflect the high value the Framers placed on the protection of private contracts. Contracts enable individuals to order their personal and business affairs according to their particular needs and interests. Once arranged, those rights and obligations are binding under the law, and the parties are entitled to rely on them.

[The court then reviewed the effect of the state law on the pension plan.] Thus, the statute in question here nullifies express terms of the company's contractual obligations and imposes a completely unexpected liability in potentially disabling amounts. . . . Yet there is no showing in the record before us that this severe disruption of contractual expectations was necessary to meet an important general social problem. . . . This law can hardly be characterized, as one enacted to protect a broad societal interest rather than a narrow class.

Moreover, in at least one other important respect the Act does not resemble the mortgage moratorium legislation whose constitutionality was upheld in the *Blaisdell* case. This legislation, imposing a sudden totally unanticipated, and substantial retroactive obligation upon the company to its employees, was not enacted to deal with a situation remotely approaching the broad and desperate emergency economic conditions of the early 1930's—conditions of which the Court in *Blaisdell* took judicial notice.

Entering a field it had never before

sought to regulate, the Minnesota Legislature grossly distorted the company's existing contractual relationships with its employees by superimposing retroactive obligations upon the company substantially beyond the terms of its employment contracts. And that burden was imposed upon the company only because it closed its office in the State.

This Minnesota law simply does not possess the attributes of those state laws that in the past have survived challenge under the Contract Clause of the Constitution. The law was not even purportedly enacted to deal with a broad, generalized economic or social problem. It did not operate in an area already subject to state regulation at the time the company's contractual obligations were origi-

nally undertaken, but invaded an area never before subject to regulation by the State. It did not effect simply a temporary alteration of the contractual relationships of those within its coverage, but worked a severe, permanent, and immediate change in those relationships—irrevocably and retroactively. And its narrow aim was levelled not at every Minnesota employer, not even at every Minnesota employer who left the State, but only at those who had in the past been sufficiently enlightened as voluntarily to agree to establish pension plans for their employees. . . .

We do hold that if the Contract Clause means anything at all, it means that Minnesota could not constitutionally do what it tried to do to the company in this case. [*Reversed.*]

---

6. The Taxing Power

The taxing power is the power by which government raises revenue to defray its expenses. It apportions the cost of government among those who receive its benefits. The purpose of taxation and the purposes and function of government are coextensive, in that the taxing power, in the broad sense, includes all charges and burdens imposed by government upon persons or property for the use and support of government.

The taxing power can be exercised only for public purposes. A tax is not a contract based on assent but is a statutory liability based on force and authority. A tax is not a debt in the usual sense of the word, and the constitutional prohibitions against imprisonment for debt are not applicable.

The theory supporting taxation is that since governmental functions are a necessity, the government has the right to compel persons and property within its jurisdiction to defray the costs of these functions. The payment of taxes gives no right to the taxpayer. The privilege of enjoying the protection and services of government is not based on taxes paid. As a matter of fact, there are many examples which illustrate that those who receive the most from the government pay the fewest taxes.

Taxes are paid by those able to do so, in order that all persons may share in the general benefits resulting from government. Thus, property can be taxed without an obvious personal benefit to the property owner.

The power of taxation is in theory exclusively exercised by the legislative branch of the government. The only limitations on the exercise of the taxing power are found in federal and state constitutions and the political power of the electorate to replace the legislators. Since the power of taxation is a legislative function, statutes dealing with taxation must be complete as to both the method of ascertaining the tax and its collection. The fact that a tax may destroy a business or the value of property is no basis for a judicial determination that the tax is unconstitutional. The court must find that the tax violates some specific provision of the Constitution before it can be held invalid. The decision as to the wisdom or propriety of the tax is left to the legislature.

The taxing power is used to accomplish many goals other than raising revenue. Taxation is a very important form of regulation. Tax policy is a major ingredient in government efforts to regulate the economy. For example, depreciation allowances have been accelerated in recent years to bolster the economy by making additional cash available for business investment. The gasoline tax has been substantially increased to raise the price of gasoline and thus reduce consumption.

Tax laws are also used by the federal government to equalize competition among different businesses. For example, the gasoline tax is an important part of the equalization of costs between truckers and other forms of transportation. The taxing power has been used to encourage uniform legislation among the states. States were encouraged to adopt inheritance taxes by a federal law which gave persons an 80 percent credit on the federal estate tax for death taxes paid to states. Similar pressure was put on the states by the Unemployment Compensation Act which allows, as a credit against the federal tax, a certain portion of the tax paid to states.

The federal taxing power is also used to implement social policies. For example, the federal estate tax and the graduated income tax were in part adopted to break up large accumulations of wealth. In addition, the federal government pays money to the states to encourage certain activities such as education, road building, and slum clearance. Persons in one part of the country may pay for social improvements in another as a direct result of the exercise of the taxing and spending power of the federal government. An examination of the implementation policies of the federal government will reveal that many of them are tied directly to taxation.

Few questions are raised today concerning the *validity* of a federally imposed tax. The Sixteenth Amendment to the Constitution and the broad scope of the federal taxing power which has been approved by the courts eliminates most such issues. Of course, there is a considerable amount of litigation involving the *interpretation* and *application* of the federal tax laws and regulations. Great deference is given to the position taken by the Commissioner of Internal Revenue in such cases. Courts tend to hold that federal taxing laws are valid unless there is some clear constitutional infirmity in them.

7. The Import-Export Clause

A provision closely connected with the taxing power is the *Import-Export Clause*. This clause prohibits states from taxing imports. It prohibits both the federal and state governments from directly taxing exports. Difficult questions often arise regarding when property ceases to be an import or when it becomes an export and thus comes within the protection of the constitutional guarantee. At one time it was thought that goods remained imports so long as they were in their original package. Today, the original-package doctrine is not followed. If goods have lost their status as imports, the clause does not prevent state taxation of them. The case that follows discusses the reasons for the constitutional provision and indicates the narrow scope of its application today.

MICHELIN TIRE CORP. v. WAGES
96 S. Ct. 535 (1976)

The state of Georgia assessed a non-discriminatory ad valorem property tax against Michelin's (petitioners') inventory of imported tires and tubes. The tires were in a Georgia warehouse from which petitioner as a wholesaler sold them to franchised dealers in six southeastern states.

Some 25 percent of the tires and tubes were manufactured in and imported from Nova Scotia. They were brought to the United States in tractor-driven, over-the-road trailers packed and sealed at the Nova Scotia factory. The remaining 75 percent of the imported tires and tubes were brought to the United States by sea from France and Nova Scotia in sea vans packed and sealed at the foreign factories. Upon arrival of the ship at the United States' port of entry, the vans are unloaded, the wheels are replaced, and the vans are tractor-hauled to petitioner's distribution warehouse.

The imported tires were packed in bulk into the trailers and vans, without otherwise being packaged or bundled. When unloaded, they are sorted by size and style, stacked on wooden pallets each bearing four stacks of five tires of the same size and style, and stored in pallet stacks of three pallets each.

This is the only processing required or performed to ready the tires for sale and delivery to the franchised dealers.

Sales of tires and tubes from the warehouse are filled without regard to the shipments in which the tires and tubes arrived in the United States or the place of their manufacture. Delivery to the franchised dealers is by common carrier or customer pickup.

Petitioner filed suit to have the assessment declared to be unconstitutional under the Import-Export Clause which provides: "No state shall, without the consent of the Congress, lay any Imposts or Duties on Imports or Exports, except what may be absolutely necessary for executing its inspection laws. . . ."

The Supreme Court of Georgia upheld the tax, and the petitioner sought review from the Supreme Court of the United States.

BRENNAN, J.: . . . The only question presented is whether the Georgia Supreme Court was correct in holding that the tires were subject to the ad valorem property tax. . . . We hold that . . . Georgia's assessment of a nondiscriminatory ad valorem property tax against the imported tires is not within the constitutional prohibition against laying "any Imposts or Duties on Imports. . . ."

One of the major defects of the Articles of Confederation, and a compelling reason for the calling of the Constitutional Convention of 1787, was the fact that the Articles essentially left the individual States free to burden commerce both among themselves and with foreign countries very much as they pleased. Before 1787 it was commonplace for seaboard States to derive revenue to defray the costs of state and local governments by imposing taxes on imported goods destined for customers in inland States. At the same time, there was no secure source of revenue for the central government. . . .

The Framers of the Constitution thus sought to alleviate three main concerns by committing sole power to lay imposts and duties on imports in the Federal Government, with no concurrent state power: the Federal Government must speak with one voice when regulating commercial relations with foreign governments, and tariffs, which might affect foreign relations, could not be implemented by the States consistently with that exclusive power; import revenues were to be the major source of revenue of the Federal Government and should not be diverted to the States; and harmony among the States might be disturbed unless seaboard States, with their crucial ports of entry, were prohibited from levying taxes on citizens of other States by taxing goods merely flowing through their ports to the inland States not situated as favorably geographically.

Nothing in the history of the Import-Export Clause even remotely suggests that a nondiscriminatory ad valorem property tax which is also imposed on imported goods that are no longer in import transit was the type of exaction that was regarded as objectionable by the Framers of the Constitution for such an exaction, . . . was not regarded as an impediment that severely hampered commerce or constituted a form of tribute by seaboard States to the disadvantage of the interior States.

It is obvious that such nondiscriminatory property taxation can have no impact whatsoever on the Federal Government's exclusive regulation of foreign commerce, probably the most important purpose of the clause's prohibition. By definition, such a tax does not fall on imports as such because of their place of origin. . . .

Nor will such taxation deprive the Federal Government of the exclusive right to all revenues from imposts and duties on imports and exports, since that right by definition only extends to revenues from exactions of a particular category; if nondiscriminatory ad valorem taxation is not in that category, it deprives the Federal Government of nothing to which it is entitled. Unlike imposts and duties, which are essentially taxes on the commercial privilege of bringing goods into a country, such property taxes are taxes by which a State apportions the cost of such services as police and fire protection among the beneficiaries according to their respective wealth; there is no reason why an importer should not bear his share of these costs along with his competitors handling only domestic goods. The Import-Export Clause clearly prohibits state taxation based on the foreign origin of the imported goods, but it cannot be read to accord imported goods preferential treatment that permits escape from uniform taxes imposed without regard to foreign origin for services which the State supplies. . . .

Finally, nondiscriminatory ad valorem property taxes do not interfere with the free flow of imported goods among the States. . . . To be sure, allowance of nondiscriminatory ad valorem property taxation may increase the cost of goods purchased by "inland" consumers. But as already noted, such taxation is the quid pro quo for benefits actually conferred by the taxing State.

. . . An evil to be prevented by the Import-Export Clause was the levying of taxes which could only be imposed because of the peculiar geographical situation of certain States that enabled them to single out goods destined for other States. In effect, the clause was fashioned to prevent the imposition of exactions which were no more than transit fees on the privilege of moving through a State. A nondiscriminatory ad valorem property tax obviously stands on a different footing. . . .

. . . [S]ince prohibition of nondiscriminatory ad valorem property taxation would not further the objectives of the Import-Export Clause, only the clearest constitutional mandate should lead us to condemn such taxation. The terminology employed in the clause—"Imposts or Duties"—is sufficiently ambiguous that we decline to presume it was intended to embrace taxation that does not create the evils the clause was specifically intended to eliminate. . . .

Petitioner's tires in this case were no longer in transit. They were stored in a distribution warehouse from which petitioner operated a wholesale operation, taking orders from franchised dealers and filling them from a constantly replenished inventory. The warehouse was operated no differently than would be a distribution warehouse utilized by a wholesaler dealing solely in domestic goods, and we therefore hold that the nondiscriminatory property tax levied on petitioner's inventory of imported tires was not interdicted by the Import-Export Clause of the Constitution. [*The judgment of the Supreme Court of Georgia is accordingly Affirmed.*]

8. States' Relation Article

Article IV is sometimes referred to as the states' relation article. It contains provisions for the admission of new states and authorizes Congress to make rules governing territories and property of the United States. Section 4 of the article guarantees every state a republican form of government and imposes upon the federal government the duty to protect the states from invasion. It also guarantees each state protection against domestic violence.

Section 2 of Article IV contains the so-called *privileges and immunities clause*. This clause provides that "the Citizens of each State shall be entitled to all Privileges and Immunities of Citizens in the several States." This clause assures equality of treatment for all citizens. The clause places the citizens of each state on the same footing as citizens of other states concerning the advantages of citizenship. It relieves them from the disabilities of alienage in other states. It inhibits discriminating legislation against them by other states; it gives them the right of free ingress into other states, and egress from them; it ensures to them while in other states the same freedom possessed by the citizens of those states in acquisition and enjoyment of property and in the pursuit of happiness; and it secures to them while in other states equal protection of their laws. No provision in the Constitution tends so strongly to constitute the citizens of the United States one people as this provision, because it <u>prevents a state from discriminating</u> against citizens of other states in favor of its own. A municipality is a subdivision of the state, and municipal ordinances may be challenged as a violation of the privileges and immunities clause.

Many attempts to favor local citizens over citizens of other states arise from attempts to benefit local residents economically. For example, Alaska passed a local hire act that required that oil and gas leases to which the state was a party contain a provision requiring the employment of qualified Alaskan residents in preference to nonresidents. The act violated the privileges and immunities clause. Alaska's ownership of the oil and gas was insufficient justification for the discrimination.

The case which follows is typical of those dealing with attempts to favor citizens of one state over the citizens of another state.

SUPREME COURT OF N.H. v. PIPER
105 S. Ct. 1272 (1985)

POWELL, J.: . . . The Rules of the Supreme Court of New Hampshire limit bar admission to state residents. We here consider whether this restriction violates the Privileges and Immunities Clause of the United States Constitution, Art. IV, § 2.

Kathryn Piper lives in Lower Waterford, Vermont, about 400 yards from the New Hampshire border. In 1979, she applied to take the February 1980 New Hampshire bar examination. Piper submitted with her application a statement of intent to become a New Hampshire resident. Following an investigation, the Board of Bar Examiners found that Piper was of good moral character and met the other requirements for admission. She was allowed to take, and passed, the examination. Piper was informed by the Board that she would have to establish a home address in New Hampshire prior to being sworn in.

On May 7, 1980, Piper requested from the Clerk of the New Hampshire Supreme Court a dispensation from the residency requirement. Although she had a "possible job" with a lawyer in Littleton, New Hampshire, Piper stated that becoming a resident of New Hampshire would be inconvenient. Her house in Vermont was secured by a mortgage with a favorable interest rate, and she and her husband recently had become parents. According to Piper, these "problems peculiar to [her] situation . . . warrant[ed] that an exception be made."

On May 13, 1980, the Clerk informed Piper that her request had been denied. She then formally petitioned the New Hampshire Supreme Court for permission to become a member of the bar. She asserted that she was well qualified and that her "situation [was] sufficiently unique that the granting of an exception . . . [would] not result in the setting of any undesired precedent."

The Supreme Court denied Piper's formal request on December 31, 1980.

On March 22, 1982, Piper filed this action in the United States District Court for the District of New Hampshire. She named as defendants the State Supreme Court, its five Justices, and its Clerk. She alleged that Rule 42 of the New Hampshire Supreme Court, that excludes nonresidents from the bar, violates the Privileges and Immunities Clause of the United States Constitution, Art. IV, § 2. . . .

Article IV, § 2 of the Constitution provides that the "citizens of each State shall be entitled to all Privileges and Immunities of Citizens in the several States." This clause was intended to "fuse into one Nation a collection of independent, sovereign States." Recognizing this purpose, we have held that it is "[o]nly with respect to those 'privileges' and 'immunities' bearing on the vitality of the nation as a single entity" that a State must accord residents and nonresidents equal treatment. In *Baldwin,* for example, we concluded that a State may charge a nonresident more than it charges a resident for the same elk-hunting license. Because elk-hunting is "recreation" rather than a "means of a livelihood," we found that the right to a hunting license was not "fundamental" to the promotion of interstate harmony.

Derived, like the Commerce Clause, from the fourth of the Articles of Confederation, the Privileges and Immunities Clause was intended to create a national economic union. It is therefore not surprising that this Court repeatedly has found that one of the privileges which the Clause guarantees to citizens of State A is that of doing business in State B on terms of substantial equality with the citizens of that State.

In *Ward v. Maryland,* 12 Wall. 418, 449 (1871), the Court invalidated a statute under which nonresidents were required to pay $300 per year for a license to trade in goods not manufactured in Maryland, while resident traders paid a fee varying from $12 to $150. Similarly, in *Toomer,* the Court held that nonresident fishermen could not be required to pay a license fee of $2,500 for each shrimp boat owned when residents were

charged only $25 per boat. Finally, in *Hicklin v. Orbeck,* 437 U.S. 518, 397 (1978), we found violative of the Privileges and Immunities Clause a statute containing a resident hiring preference for all employment related to the development of the State's oil and gas resources.

There is nothing in *Ward, Toomer,* or *Hicklin* suggesting that the practice of law should not be viewed as a "privilege" under Article IV, § 2. Like the occupations considered in our earlier cases, the practice of law is important to the national economy. As the Court noted in *Goldfarb,* the "activities of lawyers play an important part in commercial intercourse."

The lawyer's role in the national economy is not the only reason that the opportunity to practice law should be considered a "fundamental right." We believe that the legal profession has a noncommercial role and duty that reinforce the view that the practice of law falls within the ambit of the Privileges and Immunities Clause. Out-of-state lawyers may—and often do—represent persons who raise unpopular federal claims. In some cases, representation by nonresident counsel may be the only means available for the vindication of federal rights. The lawyer who champions unpopular causes surely is as important to the "maintenance or well-being of the Union," as was the shrimp fisherman in *Toomer,* or the pipeline worker in *Hicklin.* . . .

We therefore conclude that the right to practice law is protected by the Privileges and Immunities Clause.

The conclusion that Rule 42 deprives nonresidents of a protected privilege does not end our inquiry. The Court has stated that "[l]ike many other constitutional provisions, the Privileges and Immunities Clause is not an absolute." The Clause does not preclude discrimination against nonresidents where: (1) there is a substantial reason for the difference in treatment; and (ii) the discrimination practiced against nonresidents bears a substantial relationship to the State's objective. In deciding whether the discrimination bears a close or substantial relationship to the State's objective, the Court has considered the availability of less restrictive means.

The Supreme Court of New Hampshire offers several justifications for its refusal to admit nonresidents to the bar. It asserts that nonresident members would be less likely: (i) to become, and remain, familiar with local rules and procedures; (ii) to behave ethically; (iii) to be available for court proceedings; and (iv) to do *pro bono* and other volunteer work in the State. We find that none of these reasons meets the test of "substantiality," and that the

means chosen do not bear the necessary relationship to the State's objectives. . . .

We conclude that New Hampshire's bar residency requirement violates Art. IV, § 2, of the United States Constitution. The nonresident's interest in practicing law is a "privilege" protected by the Clause. Although the lawyer is an officer of the court, he does not hold a position that can be entrusted only to a full-fledged member of the political community. A State may discriminate against nonresidents only where its reasons are "substantial," and the difference in treatment bears a close or substantial relation to those reasons. No such showing has been made in this case. Accordingly, we affirm the judgment of the Court of Appeals. [*It is so ordered.*]

The clause does not prevent state citizenship from being used to distinguish among persons, however. A state may limit the right to vote and to hold office to its citizens. The same is true of the right to pay resident tuition to a state university. It is only with respect to those privileges and immunities bearing upon the vitality of the nation as a single entity that the state must treat all citizens, resident and nonresident, equally.

Article IV also contains the so-called *full faith and credit clause*. It provides that "Full Faith and Credit shall be given in each State to the public Acts, Records, and judicial proceedings of every other State. . . ." This does not mean that the precedent in one state is binding in other states, but only that final decisions or judgments rendered in any given state shall be enforced as between the original parties in other states. Full faith and credit applies to a specific decision as it affects the rights of the parties, and not to the reasons or principles upon which it was based. A court judgment in one state is conclusive upon the merits of the issues in another state only if the court in the first state had power to pass on the meritss—that is, had jurisdiction over the subject matter and the relevant parties. The first court's decision on jurisdiction, if that is an issue, is res judicata if the issue of jurisdiction was fully considered by the first court deciding the controversy. A party with a judgment or decree from the courts of one state may obtain enforcement through proper proceedings in other states without relitigating the issues of the original case.

Finally, the states' relation article provides for extradition of those accused of crime from one state to another. This is accomplished by judicial proceedings with the consent of the governor of the surrendering state.

THE COMMERCE CLAUSE

9. Introduction

The power of the federal government to regulate business activity is found in the so-called **commerce clause** of the Constitution. The commerce clause states: "Congress shall have power . . . to regulate Commerce with foreign Nations, and among the several States, and with the Indian Tribes. . . ." This grant of power has been broadly interpreted to give the federal government broad power to regulate business. This power to regulate is the power to prescribe the rules by which commerce is to be conducted. The actual extent of this power will be discussed in subsequent sections.

The commerce clause has been interpreted as imposing limitations on the power of state government to regulate business under the state police power. The *police power* of state and local governments is the inherent power to control persons and property within the jurisdiction of the state to promote the general welfare. General welfare includes the public health, safety, and morals. The inherent police power of the states was reserved to them by the Constitution. The effect of the commerce clause on the police power will be discussed in section 12 of this chapter.

10. Foreign Commerce

The commerce clause has three parts. The first grants the federal government power to regulate foreign commerce. The power to regulate foreign commerce is vested exclusively in the federal government, and it extends to all aspects of foreign trade. In other words, the power extends to all aspects of foreign commerce. The power is total. The federal government can prohibit foreign commerce entirely. For example, in recent years the federal government has imposed trade embargoes on countries such as the Soviet Union. It can also allow commerce with restrictions.

To state that federal power to regulate foreign commerce is exclusive means that state and local governments may not regulate such commerce. However, state and local governments sometimes attempt directly or indirectly to regulate imports or exports to some degree. Such attempts are unconstitutional. State or local laws which regulate or interfere with federal regulation of commerce with foreign nations are invalid as violations of the commerce and supremacy clauses.

The right to import includes the right to sell goods imported. States may not prohibit the sale of imported goods any more than they can prohibit their import. The exclusive federal power over imported goods continues until the goods are mingled with and become a part of the general property of the country, so that for all purposes the imported product is given similar treatment with other property. In most cases, imported goods become a part of internal commerce when the importer or wholesaler disposes of them to retail dealers in local communities. However, if a state or local law tends to continue to distinguish the goods from a point of origin, the foreign-commerce aspect continues, and the law is invalid. For example, a city required that all goods sold at retail originating behind the Iron Curtain be so labeled. This law was unconstitutional.

11. Interstate Commerce

The second component of the commerce clause is the power to regulate commerce "among the several states." At first, this phrase was interpreted to mean interstate commerce as contrasted with intrastate commerce. Later, in a long series of judicial decisions, the power was expanded through interpretation to include not only the channels and instrumentalities of interstate commerce but also activities affecting interstate commerce.

The power of Congress over commerce being plenary, it extends to all commerce, be it great or small. Labeling an activity a "local" or "intrastate" activity does not resolve the question of whether Congress may regulate it under the commerce clause. The commerce power extends to those intrastate activities which so affect interstate commerce, or the exertion of the power of Congress over it, as to make regulation of them appropriate. Regulation is appropriate if it aids in the effective regulation of interstate commerce. Even activity that is purely intrastate in character may be regulated by Congress, when the activity, combined with like conduct by others similarly situated, affects commerce among the states or with foreign nations. The effect on interstate commerce may be positive or negative in the sense that regulated economic activity encourages commerce or hinders it. The effect on interstate commerce to warrant the application of a federal law may be established by the activity itself. It need not result from a violation of the law. The unlawful conduct itself need not have an effect on interstate commerce.

The case which follows traces the history of the expansion of the commerce clause and its extension to activities beyond interstate commerce.

PEREZ v. UNITED STATES
91 S. Ct. 1357 (1971)

The defendant was convicted of violating the "loan sharking" provisions of the Federal Consumer Credit Protection Act. It was proved beyond any doubt that the defendant as a part of organized crime had used extortion in collecting illegal rates of interest. He challenged the constitutionality of the statute on the ground that Congress has no power to control the local activity of loan sharking.

DOUGLAS, J.: . . . The constitutional question is a substantial one. . . .

The Commerce Clause reaches in the main three categories of problems. First, the use of channels of interstate or foreign commerce which Congress deems are being misused, as for example, the shipment of stolen goods or of persons who have been kidnapped. Second, protection of the instrumentalities of interstate commerce, as for example, the destruction of an aircraft, or persons or things in commerce, as for example, thefts from interstate shipments. Third, those activities affecting commerce. It is with this last category that we are here concerned.

Chief Justice Marshall in *Gibbons v. Ogden*, 9 Wheat. 1, 195, 6 L.Ed. 23, said:

The genius and character of the whole government seems to be, that its action is to be applied to all the external concerns of the nation, and to those internal concerns which affect the states generally; but not to those which are completely within a particular state, which do not affect other states, and with which it is not necessary to interfere, for the purpose of executing some of the general powers of the government. The completely internal commerce of a state, then, may be considered as reserved for the state itself. . . .

Chief Justice Stone wrote for a unanimous Court in 1942 that Congress could provide for the regulation of the price of intrastate milk, the sale of which, in competition with interstate milk, affects the price structure and federal regulation of the latter. The commerce power, he said, "extends to those activities intrastate which so affect interstate commerce, or the exertion of the power of Congress over it, as to make regulation of them an appropriate means to the attainment of a legitimate end, the effective execution of the granted power to regulate interstate commerce."

Wickard v. Filburn, 317 U.S. 111, soon followed in which a unanimous Court held that wheat grown wholly for home consumption was constitutionally within the scope of federal regulation of wheat production because, though never marketed interstate, it supplied the need of the grower which otherwise would be satisfied by his purchases in the open market. We said:

. . . even if appellee's activity be local and though it may not be regarded as commerce, it may still, whatever its nature, be reached by Congress if it exerts a substantial economic effect on interstate commerce, and this irrespective of whether such effect is what might at some earlier time have been defined as 'direct' or 'indirect.'

As pointed out in *United States v. Darby*, 312 U.S. 100, the decision sustaining an Act of Congress which prohibited the employment of workers in the production of goods "for interstate commerce" at other than prescribed wages and hours—a *class of activities*—was held properly regulated by Congress without proof that the particular intrastate activity against which a sanction was laid had an effect on commerce. A unanimous Court said:

. . . Congress has sometimes left it to the courts to determine whether the intrastate activities have the prohibited effect on the commerce, as in the Sherman Act. It has sometimes left it to an administrative board or agency to determine whether the activities sought to be regulated or prohibited have such effect, as in the case of the Interstate Commerce Act, and the National Labor Relations Act, or whether they come within the statutory definition of the prohibited Act, as in the Federal Trade Commission Act. And sometimes Congress itself has said that a particular activity affects the commerce, as it did in the present Act, the Safety Appliance Act and the Railway Labor Act. In passing on the validity of legislation of the class last mentioned the only function of courts is to determine whether the particular activity regulated or prohibited is within the reach of the federal power.

That case is particularly relevant here because it involved a criminal prosecution, a unanimous Court holding that the Act was "sufficiently definite to meet constitutional demands." Petitioner is clearly a *member of the class* which engages in "extortionate credit transactions" as defined by Congress and the description of that class has the required definiteness.

It was the "class of activities" test which we employed in *Heart of Atlanta Motel, Inc. v. United States*, 379 U.S. 241, to sustain an Act of Congress requiring hotel or motel accommodations for Negro guests. The Act declared that "any inn, hotel, motel, or other establishment which provides lodging to transient guests' affects commerce *per se*." That exercise of power under the Commerce Clause was sustained. . . . In a companion case, *Katzenbach v. McClung*, 379 U.S. 294, we ruled on the constitutionality of the restaurant provision of the same Civil Rights Act which regulated the restaurant "if . . . it serves or offers to serve interstate travelers or a substantial portion of the food which it serves . . . has moved in commerce." Apart from the effect on the flow of food in commerce to restaurants, we spoke of the restrictive effect of the exclusion of Negroes from restaurants on interstate travel by Negroes. In emphasis of our position that it was the *class of activities* regulated that was the measure, we acknowledged that Congress ap-propriately considered the "total incidence" of the practice on commerce.

Where the *class of activities* is regulated and that *class* is within the reach of federal power, the courts have no power "to excise, as trivial, individual instances" of the class.

Extortionate credit transactions, though purely intrastate, may in the judgment of Congress affect interstate commerce. In an analogous situation, Mr. Justice Holmes, speaking for a unanimous Court, said ". . . when it is necessary in order to prevent an evil to make the law embrace more than the precise thing to be prevented it may do so." . . .

In the setting of the present case there is a tie-in between local loan sharks and interstate crime.

The findings by Congress are quite adequate on that ground . . .

"Even where extortionate credit transactions are purely intrastate in character, they nevertheless directly affect interstate and foreign commerce." . . .

It appears . . . that loan sharking in its national setting is one way organized interstate crime holds its guns to the heads of the poor and the rich alike and syphons funds from numerous localities to finance its national operations. [*Affirmed.*]

Today, legislative acts adjusting the benefits and burdens of economic life are presumed to be constitutional. A court may invalidate legislation enacted under the commerce clause only if it is clear that there is no rational basis for a congressional finding that the regulated activity affects interstate commerce, or that there is no reasonable connection between the regulatory means selected and the asserted ends. The judicial task ends once the court determines that Congress acted rationally in adopting a particular regulatory scheme. Of course, the power of Congress under the commerce clause is subject to other constitutional limitations such as those contained in the Bill of Rights.

Keep in mind that while Congress has the power to regulate certain activities, it may decide not to exercise it. There are activities that the federal government could regulate but that it has chosen not to. It should also be kept in mind that not all business or commercial activity is commerce. For example, it has been held that the activity of accrediting institutions of higher learning is not commerce. Professional baseball has repeatedly been held to be a "sport" and not a business. As a practical matter, the trend is to consider that almost every business activity is a part of commerce, but there are still some noncommercial pursuits.

12. The Commerce Clause and the State Police Power

The grant of power to Congress over commerce does not contain any provision which expressly excludes states from exercising authority over commerce. The Supreme Court in *Cooley v. The Board of Wardens of Port of Philadelphia*[1] held that the nature of the commerce power did not by *implication* prohibit state action and that some state power over commerce is compatible with the federal power. Nevertheless, there are definite limitations on the state powers over commerce because of the commerce clause.

The decisions of the Court have established three distinct subject areas of governmental regulation of commerce, as shown in Table 8-1. Some areas are exclusively federal, some are said to be exclusively local, and still others are such that regulation of them may be dual.

The subject area which is exclusively federal, in addition to foreign commerce, concerns those internal matters where uniformity on a nationwide basis is essential. Any state regulation of such subjects is void whether Congress has entered the field or not. In theory, those matters which are exclusively within the states' power are intrastate activities which do not have a substantial effect on interstate commerce. As noted in the previous section, it is becoming more and more difficult, if not impossible, to find a subject matter which is truly exclusively local in the sense that it does not affect interstate commerce.

The third subject area between the above two extremes, where joint regulation is permissible, can be divided into three subparts. The first concerns those subjects over which the federal government has preempted the field. By express language or by comprehensive regulation Congress has shown that it intends to exercise exclusive dominion over the subject matter. When a federal statute has thus preempted the field, *any* state or local law pertaining to the same subject matter is unconstitutional under the commerce clause and the supremacy clause, and the state regulation is void.

The net effect of a law that preempts the field makes the subject matter of the law exclusively federal. To determine whether or not federal law preempts the field, the courts follow certain guidelines. First of all, the state law cannot be an obstacle to the accomplishment and execution of the full

---

[1]53 U.S. 299 (1851).

TABLE 8-1   Possible Subjects for Government Regulation

Exclusively Federal Subjects	Possible Dual Regulation Subjects	Exclusively Local Subjects
I. Any state regulatory law is unconstitutional under supremacy and commerce clauses.	II. Federal Law preempts the field—moves the subject matter to area No. I. III. Federal law does not preempt the field. A state law is unconstitutional if it: 1 Is in irreconcilable conflict with federal law 2 Constitutes an *undue* burden on interstate commerce 3 Discriminates against interstate commerce in favor of intrastate commerce IV. No federal law/state law is unconstitutional if it: 1 Constitutes an undue burden on interstate commerce 2 Discriminates against interstate commerce in favor of intrastate commerce	V. The Impact on state and local government of laws based on the commerce clause is very limited. Very few subjects are exclusively local.

purposes and objectives of Congress. If it is, the courts will hold that the federal law preempted the field. Another key guideline is found in examining the purposes of both laws. If the objectives are virtually identical, then the courts attempt to reconcile the laws and enforce both. If the purposes are in conflict, chances are that the state law cannot be enforced.

The second division of the area of possible joint regulation includes situations in which the federal regulation of a subject matter is not comprehensive enough to preempt the field. Here state regulation is permitted, but when state law is inconsistent or conflicts irreconcilably with the federal statute, it is unconstitutional and void. Irreconcilable conflicts exist when it is not possible for a business to comply with both statutes. If compliance with both is not possible, the state law must fall under the supremacy clause and the commerce clause. If compliance with both is reasonably possible, dual compliance is required. This usually has the effect of forcing business to meet the requirements of the law with the greatest burden. For example, if the state minimum wage is $4.00 per hour and the federal is $3.35, employers would be required to pay $4.00 since the conflict can be reconciled.

The commerce clause also invalidates state laws imposing an undue burden on interstate commerce. The commerce clause does not prohibit the imposing of burdens on interstate commerce—only the imposition of undue burdens. Every regulatory measure is a burden to some degree. Many laws have the effect of discouraging or impeding commerce among the states. If a local law furthers a legitimate public interest, it is valid unless the burden on interstate activities is undue. Burdens are undue if uniformity of regulation is necessary. Courts frequently are required to balance competing interests, but in many cases incomparables exist which cannot be weighed. In the weighing process, the court examines the goal of the state legislation and weighs it against the burden imposed on business. Although doubts are resolved in favor of state laws, many are held to be unconstitutional, such as the one in the case which follows.

KASSEL v. CONSOLIDATED FREIGHTWAYS CORP., ETC.
101 S. Ct. 1309 (1981)

POWELL, J.: The question is whether an Iowa statute that prohibits the use of certain large trucks within the State unconstitutionally burdens interstate commerce.

Respondent, Consolidated Freightways Corporation of Delaware (Consolidated) is one of the largest common carriers in the country. It offers service in 48 states. Among other routes, Consolidated carries commodities through Iowa on Interstate 80, the principal east-west route linking New York, Chicago, and the West Coast, and on Interstate 35, a major north-south route.

Consolidated mainly uses two kinds of trucks. One consists of a three-axle tractor pulling a 40-foot two-axle trailer. This unit, commonly called a single, or "semi" is 55 feet in length overall. Consolidated also uses a two-axle tractor pulling a single-axle trailer which, in turn, pulls a single-axle dolly and a second single-axle trailer. This combination,

known as a double, or twin, is 65 feet long overall. Many trucking companies, including Consolidated, increasingly prefer to use doubles to ship certain kinds of commodities. Doubles have larger capacities, and the trailers can be detached and routed separately if necessary. Consolidated would like to use 65-foot doubles on many of its trips through Iowa.

The State of Iowa, however, by statute restricts the length of vehicles that may use its highways. Unlike all other States in the West and Midwest, Iowa generally prohibits the use of 65-foot doubles within its borders. Instead, most truck combinations are restricted to 55 feet in length. Doubles, mobile homes, trucks carrying vehicles such as tractors and other farm equipment, and singles hauling livestock, are permitted to be as long as 60 feet. . . .

Because of Iowa's statutory scheme, Consolidated cannot use its 65-foot doubles to move commodities through the State. Instead, the company must do one of four things: (i) use 55-foot singles; (ii) use 60-foot doubles; (iii) detach the trailers of a 65-foot and shuttle each through the State separately; or (iv) divert 65-foot doubles around Iowa.

Dissatisfied with these options, Consolidated filed this suit in the District court averring that Iowa's statutory scheme unconstitutionally burdens interstate commerce. Iowa defended the law as a reasonable safety measure enacted pursuant to its police power. The State asserted that 65-foot doubles are more dangerous than 55-foot singles and, in any event, that the law promotes safety and reduces road wear within the State by diverting much truck traffic to other States.

In a 14-day trial, both sides adduced evidence on safety, and on the burden on interstate commerce imposed by Iowa's law. On the question of safety, the District Court found that the "evidence clearly establishes that the twin is as safe as the semi."

"There is no valid safety reason for barring twins from Iowa's highways because of their configuration.

"The evidence convincingly, if not overwhelmingly, establishes that the 65-foot twin is as safe as, if not safer than, the 60-foot twin and the 55-foot semi. . . .

"Twins and semis have different characteristics. Twins are more maneuverable, are less sensitive to wind, and create less splash and spray. However, they are more likely than semis to jackknife or upset. They can be backed only for a short distance. The negative characteristics are not such that they render the twin less safe than semis overall. Semis are more stable but are more likely to rear end another vehicle."

The District Court . . . concluded that the state law impermissibly burdened interstate commerce. . . . The Court of Appeals for the Eighth Circuit affirmed.

It is unnecessary to review in detail the evolution of the principles of Commerce Clause adjudication. The Clause is both a "prolific source of national power and an equally prolific source of conflict with legislation of the state(s)." The Clause permits Congress to legislate when it perceives that the national welfare is not furthered by the independent actions of the States. It is now well established, also, that the Clause itself is a limitation upon state power even without congressional implementation. The Clause requires that some aspects of trade generally must remain free from interference by the States. When a state ventures excessively into the regulation of these aspects of commerce, it "trespasses upon national interests," and the courts will hold the state regulation invalid under the Clause alone.

The Commerce Clause does not, of course, invalidate all state restrictions on commerce. It has long been recognized that, "in the absence of conflicting legislation by Congress, there is a residuum of power in the State to make laws governing matters of local concern which nevertheless in some measure affect interstate commerce or even, to some extent, regulate it." The extent of permissible state regulation is not always easy to measure. It may be said with confidence, however, that a State's power to regulate commerce is never greater than in matters traditionally of local concern. For example, regulations that touch upon safety—especially highway safety—are those that "the Court has been most reluctant to invalidate." Indeed, "if safety justifications are not illusory, the Court will not second guess legislative judgment about their importance in comparison with related burdens on interstate commerce." Those who would challenge such bona fide safety regulations must overcome a "strong presumption of validity."

But the incantation of a purpose to promote the public health or safety does not insulate a state law from Commerce Clause attack. Regulations designed for that salutary purpose nevertheless may further the purpose so marginally, and interfere with commerce so substantially, as to be invalid under the Commerce Clause. In the Court's recent unanimous decision in *Raymond,* we declined to "accept the State's contention that the inquiry under the Commerce Clause is ended without a weighing of the asserted safety purpose against the degree of interference with interstate commerce." This "weighing" by a court requires—and indeed the constitutionality of the state regulation depends on— "a sensitive consideration of the weight and nature of the state regulatory concern in light of the extent of the burden imposed on the course of interstate commerce."

The State failed to present any persuasive evidence that 65-foot doubles are less safe than 55-foot singles. Moreover, Iowa's law is now out of step with the laws of all other midwestern and western States. Iowa thus substantially burdens the interstate flow of goods by truck. In the absence of congressional action to set uniform standards, some burdens associated with state safety regulations must be tolerated. But where, as here, the State's safety interest has been found to

be illusory, and its regulations impair significantly the federal interest in efficient and safe interstate transportation, the state law cannot be harmonized with the Commerce Clause. . . .

Consolidated, meanwhile, demonstrated that Iowa's law substantially burdens interstate commerce. Trucking companies that wish to continue to use 65-foot doubles must route them around Iowa or detach the trailers of the doubles and ship them through separately. Alternatively, trucking companies must use the smaller 55-foot singles or 60-foot doubles permitted under Iowa law. Each of these options engenders inefficiency and added expense. The record shows that Iowa's law added about $12.6 million each year to the costs of trucking companies. Consolidated alone incurred about $2 million per year in increased costs. . . .

Because Iowa has imposed this burden without any significant countervailing safety interest, its statute violates the Commerce Clause. The judgment of the Court of Appeals is affirmed. [*Affirmed.*]

Among examples of state laws found to be constitutional through the balancing or weighing process are (1) a Minnesota law which banned retail sale of milk in plastic, nonreturnable and nonrefillable containers, but permitted such sale in other nonreturnable, nonrefillable containers such as paperboard milk cartons; (2) a New Hampshire law requiring aircraft used for hunting to display large registration numbers; and (3) a Virginia statute which required all stockbrokers to register with the state. In all three cases the court held that the burden was not excessive in relation to the local benefits.

Finally, the commerce clause has been construed as prohibiting discrimination against interstate commerce in favor of intrastate commerce. State and local governments frequently attempt by legislation to aid local business in its competition with interstate business. The commerce clause requires that all taxes and regulations be the same for local businesses as for businesses engaged in interstate commerce. While interstate commerce is required to pay its fair share of all taxes, it must be placed on a plane of equality with local trade or commerce. A state may not place itself in a position of economic isolation from other states.

The third area of possible joint regulation exists where there is no federal law at all. When there is no federal regulation of a subject, state regulation of interstate commerce is permissible, providing, of course, that it does not discriminate against interstate commerce in favor of local business and does not impose an undue burden on interstate commerce.

13. The Commerce Clause and Taxation

Taxation is a primary form of regulation. Therefore, taxes imposed by state and local governments are subject to the limitations imposed by the commerce clause. The commerce clause limits property taxes, income taxes, and sales or use taxes levied by state and local governments on interstate commerce. Since taxation distributes the cost of government among those who receive its benefits, interstate commerce is not exempt from state and local taxes. The purpose of the commerce clause is to ensure that it only pays its fair share.

In *Northwestern States Portland Cement Co. v. Minnesota,* 358 U.S. 450 (1959), the Supreme Court, speaking through Justice Clark, reviewed some of the general principles regarding limitations placed on state taxing power by the commerce clause. He stated in part:

> It has long been established doctrine that the Commerce Clause gives exclusive power to the Congress to regulate interstate commerce, and its failure to act on the subject in the area of taxation nevertheless requires that interstate commerce shall be free from any direct restrictions or impositions by the States. . . . In keeping therewith a State "cannot impose taxes upon persons passing through the state, or coming into it merely for a temporary purpose" such as itinerant drummers. . . . Moreover, it is beyond dispute that a State may not lay a tax on the "privilege" of engaging in interstate commerce. . . . Nor may a State impose a tax which discriminates against interstate commerce either by providing a direct commercial advantage to local business . . . or by subjecting interstate commerce to the burden of "multiple taxation." . . . Such impositions have been stricken because the States, undder the Commerce Clause, are not allowed "one single tax-dollar worth of direct interference with the free flow of commerce."
>
> On the other hand, it has been established since 1918 that a net income tax on revenues derived from interstate commerce does not offend constitutional limitations upon state interference with such commerce. . . . [T]he entire net income of a corporation, generated by interstate as well as intrastate activities, may be fairly apportioned among the States for tax purposes by formulas utilizing in-state aspects of interstate affairs. . . . [A] tax on net income from interstate commerce, as distinguished from a tax on the privilege of engaging in interstate commerce, does not conflict with the commerce clause. . . . It is axiomatic that the founders did not intend to immunize . . . [interstate] commerce from carrying its fair share of the costs of the state government in return for the benefits it derives from within the State. . . . "It is too late in the day to find offense to that [commerce] clause because a state tax is imposed on corporate net income of an interstate enterprise which is attributable to earnings within the taxing state. . . ."

The foregoing summary indicates that several distinct constitutional problems exist when a state seeks to tax business engaged in interstate commerce. These issues are: (1) Is the tax properly apportioned? (2) Is there a sufficient minimum connection (*nexus*) between the activity being taxed and the tax to satisfy due process? (3) Does the tax discriminate against interstate commerce? And (4) does the tax impose an unconstitutional burden on interstate commerce?

The concept of apportionment is used to prevent multiple taxation of the same property or income of interstate businesses. Apportionment formulas are used to allocate the tax burden of an interstate business among the states entitled to tax it. The commerce clause requires states to use reasonable formulas when more than one state is taxing the same thing.

The term *nexus* describes the requirement of some sufficient contact, connection, tie, or link to the taxing state to justify the tax. In other words, there must be sufficient local activities to justify the tax in a constitutional sense. A business operating in a state directly benefits from its police and fire protection, use of its roads, and the like. Indirectly it will be able to recruit employees more easily if they have easy access to good schools, parks, and civic centers. If the state gives anything for which it can reasonably expect payment, then the tax has a sufficient nexus. In cases involving property taxes, the term *taxable situs* is used in place of nexus, but each is concerned with the adequacy of local activities to support the tax.

The concepts of undue burdens against interstate commerce and discrimination against interstate commerce through taxation are the same as these concepts are applied to other forms of regulation. Taxes which are different from those levied on intrastate commerce cannot be levied on interstate commerce. The case which follows is typical of those cases holding a tax to be unconstitutional under the commerce clause.

ARMCO INC. v. HARDESTY
104 S. Ct. 2620 (1984)

POWELL, J.: . . . In this appeal an Ohio corporation claims that West Virginia's wholesale gross receipts tax, from which local manufacturers are exempt, unconstitutionally discriminates against interstate commerce. We agree and reverse the state court's judgment upholding the tax.

Appellant Armco Inc. is an Ohio corporation qualified to do business in West Virginia. Its primary business is manufacturing and selling steel products. From 1970 through 1975, the time at issue here, Armco conducted business in West Virginia through five divisions or subdivisions. Two of these had facilities and employees in the State, while the other three sold various products to customers in the State only through franchisees or nonresident traveling salesmen.

West Virginia imposes a gross receipts tax on persons engaged in the business of selling tangible property at wholesale. For the years 1970 through 1975 Armco took the position that the gross receipts tax could not be imposed on the sales it made through franchisees and nonresident salesmen. In addition, because local manufacturers were exempt from the tax, Armco argued that the tax discriminated against interstate commerce. . . .

The West Virginia Supreme Court of Appeals . . . held that the tax did not discriminate against interstate commerce; while local manufacturers making sales in the State were exempt from the gross receipts tax, they paid a much higher manufacturing tax. . . .

It long has been established that the Commerce Clause of its own force protects free trade among the States. One aspect of this protection is that a State "may not discriminate between transactions on the basis of some interstate element." That is, a State may not tax a transaction or incident more heavily when it crosses state lines than when it occurs entirely within the State.

On its face, the gross receipts tax at issue here appears to have just this effect. The tax provides that two companies selling tangible property at wholesale in West Virginia will be treated differently depending on whether the taxpayer conducts manufacturing in the State or out of it. Thus, if the property was manufactured in the State, no tax on the sale is imposed. If the property was manufactured out of the State and imported for sale, a tax of 0.27% is imposed on the sale price. . . .

The court below was of the view that no such discrimination in favor of local, intrastate commerce occurred because taxpayers manufacturing in the State were subject to a far higher tax of 0.88% of the sale price. This view is mistaken. The gross sales tax imposed on Armco cannot be deemed a "compensating tax" for the manufacturing tax imposed on its West Virginia competitors.

[M]anufacturing and wholesaling are not "substantially equivalent events" such that the heavy tax on in-state manufacturers can be said to compensate for the admittedly lighter burden placed on wholesalers from out of state. Manufacturing frequently entails selling in the State, but we cannot say which portion of the manufacturing tax is attributable to manufacturing, and which portion to sales. The fact that the manufacturing tax is not reduced when a West Virginia manufacturer sells its goods out of state, and that it is reduced when part of the manufacturing takes place out of state, makes clear that the manufacturing tax is just that, and not in part a proxy for the gross receipts tax imposed on Armco and other sellers from other States.

Moreover, when the two taxes are considered together, discrimination against interstate commerce persists. If Ohio or any of the other 48 States imposes a like tax on its manufacturers—which they have every right to do—then Armco and others from out of state will pay both a manufacturing tax and a wholesale tax while sellers resident in West Virginia will pay only the manufacturing tax. For example, if Ohio were to adopt the precise scheme here, then an interstate seller would pay the manufacturing tax of 0.88% *and* the gross receipts tax of 0.27%; a purely intrastate seller would pay only the manufacturing tax of 0.88% and would be exempt from the gross receipts tax.

Appellee suggests that we should require Armco to prove actual discriminatory impact on it by pointing to a State that imposes a manufacturing tax that results in a total burden higher than that imposed on Armco's competitors in West Virginia. This is not the test. . . . [A] tax must have what might be called internal consistency—that is the tax must be such that, if applied by every jurisdiction, there would be no impermissible interference with free trade. . . . Any other rule would mean that the constitutionality of West Virginia's tax laws would depend on the shifting complexities of the tax codes of 49 other States, and that the validity of the taxes imposed on each taxpayer would depend on the particular other States in which it operated. . . . [*Reversed.*]

REVIEW QUESTIONS

1 The Montana statutory elk-hunting license scheme imposed substantially higher (seven and a half times) license fees on nonresidents of the state than on residents. It also required nonresidents (but not residents) to purchase a general hunting license in order to be able to obtain a single elk. Out-of-state hunters challenged the constitutionality of the Montana hunting license law. Is the Montana law constitutional? Why, or why not?

2 Montana imposes a severance tax on each ton of coal mined in the state, including coal mined on federal lands. Ninety percent of the coal is shipped to other states. Coal producers and their out-of-state utility company customers sought refunds of the taxes paid, contending that the tax was invalid under the commerce and supremacy clauses. Is the state tax constitutional? Why, or why not?

3 Maryland enacted a statute providing that producers or refiners of petroleum products could not operate any retail service station in Maryland. Oil companies challenged the statute under the commerce clause alleging that the statute imposed an undue burden on interstate commerce and that it discriminated against interstate commerce in favor of intrastate commerce. Is the Maryland law constitutional? Why, or why not?

4 National Cash Register Company manufactures cash registers and other machines. It built certain cash registers to foreign buyers' specifications. They were manufactured to register in foreign currency, and they could not be used in the United States. These were warehoused in Ohio awaiting shipment abroad. Title and possession remained with the manufacturers. The state of Ohio assessed an ad valorem personal property tax on the machines. The manufacturers contended that such a tax was a violation of the Import-Export Clause of the Constitution. What was the result? Why?

5 The City of Camden, New Jersey, adopted an ordinance requiring that at least 40 percent of the employees of contractors working on city construction projects be Camden residents. The constitutionality of the ordinance was challenged under the privileges and immunities clause of Article IV of the United States Constitution. The city contended that the clause only applied to state laws and not local ordinances. Is the local ordinance constitutional? Why, or why not?

6 A Florida county adopted an ordinance regulating blood plasma centers in that county. It required that donors take a test for hepatitus and a breath analysis test for alcohol. The Food and Drug Administration (FDA) has promulgated federal regulations establishing minimum standards for the collection of blood plasma. An operator of a blood plasma center filed suit challenging the constitutionality of the ordinances on the ground that they violated the supremacy clause. Decide the case, and give reasons for your decision.

7 A Virginia statute prohibited federally licensed vessels owned by nonresidents of Virginia from fishing in Chesapeake Bay. There were no similar restrictions on Virginia citizens. Is the Virginia law constitutional? Why, or why not?

8 The federal government enacted a statute requiring all automobiles sold in interstate commerce to be equipped with "air bags" in the front passenger compartment. A state has a statute requiring all motor vehicles sold in the state to be equipped with three sets of seat belts in the front seat. The auto manufacturers indicate that both laws can be complied with, but only at extra expense to the manufacturer. Are both laws enforceable? Explain.

9 New Jersey passed a law which prohibited the importation of most solid or liquid waste which originated or was collected outside New Jersey. Does the law violate the commerce clause? Why, or why not?

10 New Hampshire by statute sought to prevent the out-of-state sale of hydroelectric power generated within the state. Electric utilities challenged the constitutionality of the statute. What was the result? Why?

11 A Maine statute imposed a tax on trucks. The tax required owners and operators of foreign-based (out-of-state) trucks using Maine highways to purchase either an annual highway use permit or a one-trip permit. Trucks based in-state were exempt. An out-of-state trucker challenged the constitutionality of the statute. What was the result? Why?

12 A barge company towed barges to and from the state, as well as through and in-between points within it. The state sought to impose a gross income tax on all transactions beginning or ending with the state. May it do so? Explain.

13 A class action suit was filed charging two real estate trade associations and six named real estate firms with violating the federal antitrust laws. It alleged a conspiracy to fix prices in the purchase and sale of residential real estate by the systematic use of fixed commission rates, widespread fee splitting, and the suppression of market information from buyers and sellers. The defendants contended that the law could not cover their activities, which were local and not in interstate commerce. Does the power of the federal government extend to this local activity? Explain.

14 Goldkist had entered into a contract to sell 50 million chickens to Russia. When the Russians invaded Afghanistan, President Carter imposed an embargo on the sale of food to Russia. Did his action violate the contract clause? Explain.

15 A manufacturer of rope, in filing its Ohio personal-property tax return, deducted from the total value of its inventory the value of imported fibers. These were stored in their original packages for future use in the manufacturing process. Are goods exempt from state taxation so long as they remain in the original package? Explain.

16 Illinois enacted a statute which prohibited transporting into the state for purposes of disposal or storage spent nuclear fuel that was used by out-of-state electric utilities. Illinois has the only away-from-site facility in the United States that is accepting spent fuel for storage. Is this statute constitutional? Why, or why not?

17 Japanese vessels carry cargo containers which are owned by companies based, registered, and taxed in Japan. They are used exclusively in foreign commerce. A number of containers were temporarily present in California. May California levy a property tax on the containers? Why, or why not?

Chapter
9

The Bill of Rights and Business

1. Introduction

Perhaps no part of the U.S. Constitution is so well known or held as sacred as the so-called Bill of Rights, the first ten amendments to the Constitution. Most of us are acquainted to some degree with the freedoms of speech, press, religion, and assembly. Usually we do not think of these matters in a business context; we think of them more as dealing with personal rights of individuals in a free society. There are, however, very important aspects of these freedoms relating to economic opportunity and business activity.

As the materials dealing with the Bill of Rights are studied, three important aspects should be kept in mind. First of all, constitutional rights are not absolutes. They are limited to some degree. Mr. Justice Black, dissenting in *Tinker v. Des Moines Independent Community School Dist.*, 89 S. Ct. 733 (1969), noted this fact when he stated:

> The truth is that a teacher of kindergarten, grammar school, or high school pupils no more carries into a school with him a complete right to freedom of speech and expression than an anti-Catholic or anti-Semitic carries with him a complete freedom of speech and religion into a Catholic church or Jewish synagogue. Nor does a person carry with him into the United States Senate or House, or to the Supreme Court, or any other court, a complete constitutional right to go into those places contrary to their rules and speak his mind on any subject he pleases. It is a myth to say that any person has a constitutional right to say what he pleases, where he pleases, and when he pleases.

The same sense of limitation applies to all basic constitutional protections, although certain people (including some Supreme Court justices) from time to time contend to the contrary.

Second, the extent of any limitation on a basic constitutional guarantee depends upon the nature of the competing public policy in a given case. Cases involving the Bill of Rights almost always require courts to strike a balance either between some goal or policy of society and the constitutional protection involved or between competing constitutional guarantees. For example, such cases may involve conflict between the goal of deterring or preventing crime and the rights of the accused, or between freedom of the press and the rights of one on trial. The courts are continually involved in a weighing process to determine the extent of constitutional protections.

Third, constitutional guarantees exist in order to remove certain issues from the political process and the ballot box. They exist to protect the minority from the majority. Freedom of expression (press and speech) protects the unpopular idea or viewpoint. Freedom of assembly allows groups with ideologies foreign to most of us to meet and express their philosophy. Even the most dangerous criminal is entitled to an attorney and is protected from illegal searches and seizures of evidence. The Bill of Rights protects the "worst" among us even more than it does the "best."

Finally, as previously noted, constitutional rights vary from time to time. The doctrine of constitutional relativity especially applies to the Bill of Rights. Not only do the rights change, they are affected by emergencies such as war or civil strife. Constitutional principles are constantly reapplied and reexamined.

THE FIRST AMENDMENT

2. Freedom of Religion

The First Amendment gives us our basic freedoms, commonly known as (1) freedom of religion, (2) freedom of speech, (3) freedom of the press, (4) freedom of assembly, and (5) the right to petition the government for a redress of grievances. These freedoms are intimately connected with the conduct of business as well as with all other aspects of our daily lives.

Freedom of religion is sometimes referred to as the separation of church and state. The First Amendment provisions on freedom of religion have two aspects or are based on two clauses. The First Amendment bans any law "respecting an establishment of religion" (the *establishment clause*) or prohibiting the free exercise thereof (the *free exercise clause*). Cases involving school prayer and tax aid to parochial schools are examples of cases arising under the establishment clause. Cases under this clause usually involve aid to religious organizations or the intrusion of religion into government activities.

Most business-related freedom of religion cases involve the free exercise clause. Religious principles are cited in attempts to prevent the application of a state law or regulation to religious organizations; thus, religion is often asserted as the basis for an exemption to a law. In such cases, courts are called upon to weigh the free exercise of religion against a compelling state interest. A burden upon religion exists where the state conditions receipt of an important benefit upon conduct proscribed by a religious belief, or where it denies such a benefit because of conduct mandated by religious belief, thereby putting substantial pressure on an adherent to modify his or her behavior and to violate his or her beliefs. The state may justify an inroad on religious liberty by showing that it is the least restrictive means of achieving a compelling state interest. However, only those interests of the highest order can overbalance legitimate claims to the free exercise of religion. For example, a Jehovah's Witness could not be denied unemployment compensation when he quit his factory job because it started making turrents for army tanks. His religious beliefs were a good cause for quitting. The following case illustrates that religious liberty may be limited if the limitation proves to be essential to accomplish an overriding governmental interest.

UNITED STATES v. LEE
102 S. Ct. 1051 (1982)

Plaintiff, a self-employed farmer and carpenter, is a member of the Old Order Amish. He believes that there is a religiously based obligation to provide for his fellow members the kind of assistance contemplated by the social security system. During certain years when he employed other Amish to work on his farm and in his carpentry shop, he failed to withhold social security taxes from his employees or to pay the employer's share of such taxes. He believed that payment of the taxes and receipt of benefits would violate the Amish faith. The Internal Revenue Service assessed him for the unpaid taxes, a portion of which he paid. He then sued for a refund, claiming that imposition of the taxes violated his First Amendment free exercise of religion rights and those of his employees. The trial court found for the plaintiff, and the government appealed.

BURGER, J.: . . . The preliminary inquiry in determining the existence of a constitutionally-required exemption is whether the payment of social security taxes and the receipt of benefits interferes with the Free Exercise rights of the Amish. . . .

We . . . accept appellee's contention that both payment and receipt of social security benefits is forbidden by the Amish faith. Because the payment of the taxes or receipt of benefits violates Amish religious beliefs, compulsory participation in the social security system interferes with their Free Exercise rights.

The conclusion that there is a conflict

between the Amish faith and the obligations imposed by the social security system is only the beginning, however, and not the end of the inquiry. Not all burdens on religion are unconstitutional. The state may justify a limitation on religious liberty by showing that it is essential to accomplish an overriding governmental interest.

Because the social security system is nationwide, the governmental interest is apparent. The social security system in the United States serves the public interest by providing a comprehensive insurance system with a variety of benefits available to all participants, with costs shared by employers and employees. . . . The design of the system requires support by mandatory contributions from covered employers and employees. This mandatory participation is indispensable to the fiscal vitality of the social security system. "[W]idespread individual voluntary coverage under social security . . . would undermine the soundness of the social security program." . . . Thus, the government's interest in assuring mandatory and continuous participation in and contribution to the social security system is very high.

The remaining inquiry is whether accommodating the Amish belief will unduly interfere with fulfillment of the governmental interest. . . . To make accommodation between the religious action and exercise of state authority is a particularly delicate task because resolution in favor of the State results in the choice to the individual of either abandoning his religious principle or facing prosecution. The difficulty in attempting to accommodate religious beliefs in the area of taxation is that we are a cosmopolitan nation made up of people of almost every conceivable religious preference. The Court has long recognized that balance must be struck between thee values of the comprehensive social system, which rests on a complex of actuarial factors, and the consequences of allowing religiously based exemptions. To maintain an organized society that guarantees religious freedom to a great variety of faiths requires that some religious practices yield to the common good. Religious beliefs can be accommodated, but there is a point at which accommodation would radically restrict the operating latitude of the legislature.

. . . [I]t would be difficult to accommodate the comprehensive social security system with myriad exceptions flowing from a wide variety of religious beliefs. The obligation to pay the social security tax initially is not fundamentally different from the obligation to pay income taxes; the difference—in theory at least—is that the social security tax revenues are segregated for use only in furtherance of the statutory program. There is no principled way, however, for purposes of this case, to distinguish between general taxes and those imposed under the Social Security Act. If, for example, a religious adherent believes war is a sin, and if a certain percentage of the federal budget can be identified as devoted to war-related activities, such individuals would have a similarly valid claim to be exempt from paying that percentage of the income tax. The tax system could not function if denominations were allowed to challenge the tax system because tax payments were spent in a manner that violates their religious belief. Because the broad public interest in maintaining a sound tax system is of such a high order, religious belief in conflict with the payment of taxes affords no basis for resisting the tax. . . .

Congress and the courts have been sensitive to the needs flowing from the Free Exercise Clause, but every person cannot be shielded from all the burdens incident to exercising every aspect of the right to practice religious beliefs. When followers of a particular sect enter into commercial activity as a matter of choice, the limits they accept on their own conduct as a matter of conscience and faith are not to be superimposed on the statutory schemes which are binding on others in that activity. Granting an exemption from social security taxes to an employer operates to impose the employer's religious faith on the employees. . . . The tax imposed on employers to support the social security system must be uniformly applicable to all, except as Congress provides explicitly otherwise. . . . [*Reversed and remanded.*]

Freedom of religion has been used to challenge Sunday closing legislation. Although the motive for such legislation may in part be religious, there are also economic reasons for suchh legislation. As a result, if law is based on economic considerations, it may be upheld if its classifications are reasonable and in the public interest. However, many such laws have been held invalid as a violation of the First Amendment.

There are other examples of freedom of religion cases that concern business. For example, it has been held that laws relating to unionization may not apply to and protect parochial school teachers. If the National Labor Relations Board (NLRB) were to conduct a union certification election for such teachers, it would violate the doctrine of separation between church and state. In a different type of case, the courts have held that states may restrict religious sects such as the Hare Krishna from soliciting donations and distributing literature in airports. They may not be banned, but may be restricted to a stall or booth.

3. Freedom of the Press

The publishing business is the only organized private business given explicit constitutional protection. Freedom of the press as guaranteed by the First Amendment authorizes a private business to provide organized scrutiny of government. Yet freedom of the press is not absolute. The press is not free to print anything it wants without liability. Rather, freedom of the press is usually construed to prohibit *prior restraints* on publication. If the press publishes that which is improper, mischievous, illegal, or libelous, it has liability for doing so. This liability may be either criminal or civil for damages.

There are many examples of limitations on freedom of the press. For example, television coverage of a human cannonball's entire act was not privileged news. A performer has a right to be paid for the broadcast of his or her act. Also, courts have allowed the Federal Communications Commission to censor "filthy" words on television. The power of the Commission extends to upholding the public's interest in responsible broadcasting.

One of the ongoing debates among legal scholars and jurists is whether the press has rights greater than other citizens. The press frequently asserts greater rights for its members than those possessed by citizens unconnected with the media. For example, members of the press frequently assert the existence of privileged communications between informants and members of the press. They contend that members of the press have a constitutional right to protect the confidential identity of their sources of information. Without such a constitutional privilege, they argue that their sources would dry up and the public's right to know would be jeopardized.

On the other hand, the courts have usually held that no such privileged communication exists. Chief Justice Burger in one case took direct issue with the idea that the institutional press has any freedom beyond or different from the public generally. He concluded that since the Constitution does not create such a privileged communication, unless a statute creates a "shield" for reporters, none exists. Although there is no federal "shield" law, some states have enacted them. Even where a statute creates such a privilege, the rights of the press must be balanced with the rights of others, and the shield law may or may not protect reporters who wish to keep their sources confidential.

The special status of the press has been at issue in other factual situations. Most of these have held that the press has no special status. For example, a reporter's telephone records may be subpoenaed from the telephone company the same as those of anyone else. A newspaper may be searched pursuant to a search warrant the same as any other business. Newspapers have tort liability for invasion of privacy the same as other defendants.

A major area of litigation involving freedom of the press is defamation. The tort theory known as libel is used to recover damages as a result of printed defamation of character. Libel cases compensate individuals for harm inflicted by defamatory printed falsehoods. Since the threat of a libel suit could have a chilling effect on freedom of the press and on the public's rights to information, the law has a different standard for imposing liability when the printed matter concerns an issue of public interest and concern. In such cases, if the person involved is a public official or public figure, a plaintiff seeking damages must prove actual *malice* in order to recover. "Actual malice" includes knowledge that the printed statements were false, or circumstances showing a reckless disregard for whether they were true or not. If the plaintiff is not a public figure or public official, there is liability for libelous statements without a proof of malice.

In a landmark decision concerning the rights of journalist-defendants in libel cases, a plaintiff sought by use of discovery techniques to ascertain the state of mind of the journalist at the time of publication. Since the plaintiff was required to prove malice, he sought to do so with the defendant's own testimony obtained by deposition. The journalist claimed that the First Amendment prohibited such questioning and that discovery procedures could not be used to ascertain the state of mind of a journalist. In rejecting the contentions of the defendant-journalist, the court held that the First Amendment does not protect journalists from having to testify on opinions, judgments, and convictions they held while preparing stories. As a result of this and other decisions, it seems clear that freedom of the press allows the publication of almost anything. However, liability may result if the published matter should not have been published, and the press as a defendant usually has no special status.

4. Freedom of Speech

Freedom of speech is sometimes referred to as freedom of expression. This freedom covers both verbal and written communications. In addition it covers conduct or actions considered symbolic speech. While freedom of speech is not absolute, it is as close to being absolute as any constitutional guarantee. It exists to protect the minority from the majority. It means freedom to express ideas antagonistic to those of the majority. Freedom of speech exists for thoughts many of us hate and for ideas that may be foreign to us. It means freedom to express the unorthodox, and recognizes that there is no such thing as a false idea.

Freedom of speech protects corporations as well as individuals. The public interests served by freedom of expression protect the listener as well as the speaker. Freedom of expression includes freedom of information or the rights of the public to be informed. Since corporations may add to the public's knowledge and information, they also have the right to free speech. While it may not be coextensive with the right of an individual, it may not be limited without a compelling state interest in doing so.

CONSOL. EDISON CO. v. PUBLIC SERVICE COM'N
100 S. Ct. 2326 (1980)

POWELL, J.: . . . The question in this case is whether the First Amendment, as incorporated by the Fourteenth Amendment, is violated by an order of the Public Service Commission of the State of New York that prohibits the inclusion in monthly electric bills of inserts discussing controversial issues of public policy.

The Consolidated Edison Company of New York . . . placed written material entitled "Independence Is Still a Goal, and Nuclear Power Is Needed To Win The Battle" in its January 1976 billing envelope. The bill insert stated Consolidated Edison's views on "the benefits of nuclear power," saying that they "far outweigh any potential risk" and that nuclear power plants are safe, economical, and clean. The utility also contended that increased use of nuclear energy would further this country's independence from foreign energy sources.

[In 1977 the Public Service Commission of the State of New York issued an order which] . . . prohibited "utilities from using bill inserts to discuss political matters, including the desirability of future development of nuclear power." . . . The Commission concluded that Consolidated Edison customers who receive bills containing inserts are a captive audience of diverse views who should not be subjected to the utility's beliefs. Accordingly, the Commission barred utility companies from including bill inserts that express "their opinions or viewpoints on controversial issues of public policy." The Commission did not, however, bar utilities from sending bill inserts discussing topics that are not "controversial issues of public policy." . . .

Consolidated Edison sought review of the Commission's order in the New York state courts. . . . The Court of Appeals held that the order did not violate the Constitution because it was a valid time, place, and manner regulation designed to protect the privacy of Consolidated Edison's customers. . . .

The First and Fourteenth Amendments guarantee that no State shall abridge the freedom of speech. Freedom of speech is indispensable to the discovery and spread of political truth and the best test of truth is the power of the thought to get itself accepted in the competition of the market. The First and Fourteenth Amendments remove governmental restraints from the arena of public discussion, putting the decision as to what views shall be voiced largely into the hands of each of us, in the hope that use of such freedom will ultimately produce a more capable citizenry and more perfect polity.

This Court has emphasized that the First Amendment embraces at the least the liberty to discuss publicly and truthfully all matters of public concern. In the mailing that triggered the regulation at issue, Consolidated Edison advocated the use of nuclear power. The Commission has limited the means by which Consolidated Edison may participate in the public debate on this question and other controversial issues of national interest and importance. Thus, the Commission's prohibition of discussion of controversial issues strikes at the heart of the freedom to speak.

The Commission's ban on bill inserts is not, of course, invalid merely because it imposes a limitation upon speech. We must consider whether the State can demonstrate that its regulation is constitutionally permissible. . . . (as) a reasonable time, place, or manner restriction . . . or a narrowly tailored means of serving a compelling state interest.

This Court has recognized the validity of reasonable time, place, or manner regulations that serve a significant governmental interest and leave ample alternative channels for communication. . . . Various methods of speech, regardless of their content, may frustrate legitimate governmental goals. No matter what its message, a roving soundtrack that blares at 2 A.M. disturbs neighborhood tranquility.

A restriction that regulates only the time, place or manner of speech may be imposed so long as it's reasonable. But when regulation is based on the content of speech, governmental action must be scrutinized more carefully to ensure that communication has not been prohibited merely because public officials disapprove the speaker's views.

As a consequence, we have emphasized that time, place, and manner regulations must be applicable to all speech irrespective of content. Governmental action that regulates speech on the basis of its subject matter "slips from the neutrality of time, place, and circumstance into a concern about content." Therefore, a constitutionally permissible time, place, or manner restriction may not be based upon either the content or subject matter of speech.

The Commission does not pretend that its action is unrelated to the content or subject matter of bill inserts. Indeed, it has undertaken to suppress certain bill inserts precisely because they address controversial issues of public policy. The Commission allows inserts that present information to consumers on certain subjects, such as energy conservation measures, but it forbids the use of inserts that discuss public controversies. The Commission, with commendable candor, justifies its ban on the ground that consumers will benefit from receiving "useful" information, but not from the prohibited information. The Commission's own rationale demonstrates that its action cannot be upheld as a content-neutral time, place, or manner regulation.

Where a government restricts the speech of a private person, the state action may be sustained only if the government can show that the regulation is a precisely drawn means of serving a compelling state interest.

. . . The Commission argues that its prohibition is necessary (i) to avoid forcing Consolidated Edison's views on a captive audience, (ii) to allocate limited resources in the public interest, and (iii) to ensure that ratepayers do not subsidize the cost of the bill inserts.

Even if a short exposure to Consolidated Edison's views may offend the sensibilities of some consumers, the ability of government to shut off discourse solely to protect others from hearing it is dependent upon a showing that substantial privacy interests are being invaded in an essentially intolerable manner. A less stringent analysis would permit a government to slight the First Amendment's role in affording the public access to discussion, debate and the dissemination of information and ideas. Where a single speaker communicates to many listeners, the First Amendment does not permit the government to prohibit speech as intrusive unless the captive audience cannot avoid objectional speech.

Passengers on public transportation or residents of a neighborhood disturbed by the raucous broadcasts from a passing sound-truck, may well be unable to escape an unwanted message. But customers who encounter an objectionable billing insert may effectively avoid further bombardment of their sensibilities simply by averting their eyes. The customer of Consolidated Edison may escape exposure to objectionable material simply by transferring the bill insert from envelope to wastebasket. . . .

The Commission's suppression of bill inserts that discuss controversial issues of public policy directly infringes the freedom of speech protected by the First and Fourteenth Amendments. The state action is neither a valid time, place, or manner restriction, . . . nor a narrowly drawn prohibition justified by a compelling state interest. Accordingly, the regulation is invalid. [*Reversed.*]

Freedom of speech is involved in many business situations. For example, freedom of speech may be an issue in cases involving picketing, expecially by unions. The right to picket peacefully for a lawful purpose is well recognized today. Courts may limit the number of pickets to preserve order and promote safety, but the right to express opinions in a picket line cannot be denied. For example, a court order preventing a client from picketing her lawyer was held to be a violation of the First Amendment. Freedom of speech even extends to boycotts of a business for a valid public purpose such as the elimination of discrimination.

Freedom of expression does not protect obscene materials. Pornography is not entitled to First Amendment protection. In the case of pornography involving children, the material is not protected by the First Amendment even if it is not legally obscene. The community's interest in banning such material outweighs any First Amendment interests. Persons who sell obscene materials or child pornography are frequently prosecuted for doing so. The difficult issues in obscenity cases are in defining obscenity and in determining whether or not items involved are obscene. Today, this decision—as to whether a book, magazine, or movie is obscene—is to be determined generally by the standards of the community involved. A movie that is not obscene by New York City standards may be obscene by the standards of "Smalltown, U.S.A." However, courts still hold that some matters found obscene by juries are not legally so, and so the problem of definition continues.

Obscenity cases based on past conduct are much less difficult than those involving a prior restraint. While freedom of speech does not protect obscenity, it does prevent most attempts to censor speech in advance. Prior restraints, while not illegal per se, must have safeguards to protect First Amendments rights.

5. Commercial Speech

Historically, commercial speech was not protected by the First Amendment. However, in the 1970s the Supreme Court began to recognize that free commercial speech was essential to the public's right to know. Several cases established that commercial speech was protected.

VA. ST. BD. OF PHARM. v. VA. CIT. CONS. COUNCIL
96 S. Ct. 1817 (1976)

The plaintiffs were consumers of prescription drugs who claimed that they would benefit from advertising of prescription drugs. They brought suit against the Virginia State Board of Pharmacy challenging the constitutionality of a Virginia statute declaring it unprofessional conduct for a licensed pharmacist to advertise the price of prescription drugs. The Board was empowered to revoke a license for a violation as well as to impose monetary penalties. As a result of the statute, all advertising of the price of prescription drugs was effectively forbidden. The lower court held the law to be in violation of the First and Fourteenth Amendments. The Board appealed.

BLACKMUN, J.: . . . Freedom of speech presupposes a willing speaker. But where a speaker exists, as is the case here, the protection afforded is to the communication, to its source and to its recipients both. . . . If there is a right to advertise, there is a reciprocal right to receive the advertising, and it may be asserted by these appellees. . . . The appellants contend that the advertisement of prescription drug prices is outside the protection of the First Amendment because it is "commercial speech." . . .

Last term, in *Bigelow v. Virginia*, 421 U.S. 809, (1975), the notion of unprotected "commercial speech" all but passed from the scene. We reversed a conviction for violation of a Virginia statute that made the circulation of any publication to encourage or promote the processing of an abortion in Virginia a misdemeanor. . . . We rejected the contention that the publication was unprotected because it was commercial. . . . We concluded that "the Virginia courts erred in their assumptions that advertising, as such, was entitled to no First Amendment protection," and we observed that the "relationship of speech to the marketplace of products or of services does not make it valueless in the marketplace of ideas." . . .

Here, . . . the question whether there is a First Amendment exception for "commercial speech" is squarely before us. Our pharmacist does not wish to editorialize on any subject, cultural, philosophical, or political. He does not wish to report any particular newsworthy fact, or to make generalized observations even about commercial matters. The "idea" he wishes to communicate is simply this: "I will sell you the X prescription drug at the Y price." Our question, then, is whether this communication is wholly outside the protection of the First Amendment.

We begin with several propositions that already are settled or beyond serious dispute. It is clear, for example, that speech does not lose its First Amendment protection because money is spent to protect it, as in a paid advertisement of one form or another. Speech likewise is protected even though it may involve a solicitation to purchase or otherwise pay or contribute money. . . .

Our question is whether speech which does "no more than propose a commercial transaction," is so removed from any "exposition of ideas," and from " 'truth, science, morality, and arts in general, in its diffusion of liberal sentiments on the administration of Government,' " that it lacks all protection. Our answer is that it is not.

Focusing first on the individual parties to the transaction that is proposed in the commercial advertisement, we may assume that the advertiser's interest is a purely economic one. That hardly disqualifies him from protection under the First Amendment. . . .

As to the particular consumer's interest in the free flow of commercial information that interest may be as keen, if not keener by far, than his interest in the day's most urgent political debate. Appellees' case in this respect is a convincing one. Those whom the suppression of prescription drug price information hits the hardest are the poor, the sick, and particularly the aged. A disproportionate amount of their income tends to be spent on prescription drugs; yet they are the least able to learn, by shopping from pharmacist to pharmacist, where their scarce dollars are best spent. When drug prices vary as strikingly as they do, information as to who is charging what becomes more than a convenience. It could mean the alleviation of physical pain or the enjoyment of the basic necessities.

Generalizing, society also may have a strong interest in the free flow of commercial information. Even an individual advertisement, though entirely "commercial," may be of general public interest. . . . Obviously, not all commercial messages contain the same or even a very great public interest element. There are few to which such an element, however, could not be added. Our pharmacist, for example, could cast himself as a commentator on store-to-store disparities in drug prices, giving his own and those of a competitor as proof. We see little point in requiring him to do so, and little difference if he does not.

Moreover, there is another consideration that suggests that no line between publicly "interesting" or "important" commercial advertising and the opposite kind could ever be drawn. Advertising, however tasteless and excessive it sometimes may seem, is nonetheless dissemination of information as to who is producing and selling what product, for what reason, and at what price. So long as we preserve a predominately free enterprise economy, the allocation of our resources in large measure will be made through numerous private economic decisions. It is a matter of public interest that those decisions, in the aggregate, be intelligent and well informed. To this end, the free flow of commercial information is indispensable. And if it is indispensable to the proper allocation of resources in a free enterprise system, it is also indispensable to the formation of intelligent opinions as to how that system ought to be regulated or altered. Therefore, even if the First Amendment were thought to be primarily an instrument to enlighten public decision making in a democracy, we could not say that the free flow of information does not serve that goal. . . .

In concluding that commercial speech, like other varieties, is protected, we of course do not hold that it can never be regulated in any way. Some forms of commercial speech regulation are surely permissible. . . . [For example] untruthful speech, commercial or otherwise, has never been protected for its own sake. . . . The First Amendment as we construe it today, does not prohibit the State from insuring that the stream of commercial information flow cleanly as well as freely. . . .

What is at issue is whether a State may completely suppress the dissemination of concededly truthful information about entirely lawful activity, fearful of that information's effect upon its disseminators and its recipients. Reserving other questions, we conclude that the answer to this one is in the negative. [*Affirmed.*]

Commercial speech is not protected to the same extent as noncommercial speech. In a case involving a billboard ordinance which banned all billboards, the Supreme Court held the law unconstitutional because it banned noncommercial billboards. The court stated that the Constitution accords a lesser protection to commercial speech than to other forms of speech. Commercial speech is protected only if it concerns a lawful activity and is not misleading. A restriction on commercial speech is valid if it seeks to implement a substantial governmental interest, directly advances that interest, and reaches no farther than necessary to accomplish the objective. If a publication is only partially commercial, such as a newspaper containing ads, the publication is entitled to the full protection of the First Amendment.

In commercial speech cases, the courts are involved in the weighing process previously noted. "For sale" signs cannot be banned in residential areas, but "adult entertainment" businesses may be restricted to certain areas. Universities may ban sales by outsiders in residence halls, but all live entertainment may not be banned from a community. Many commercial speech cases involve attempts by government to regulate morality. These attempts often fail in the weighing process because of the overwhelming importance of freedom of speech.

6. Assembly and Association

The First Amendment includes the right to assemble and associate. The right of association is more than the right to attend a meeting. It includes the right to express an attitude or philosophy by being a member of a group. It also includes the right *not* to join a group. For example, lack of political party affiliation by certain employees may not be a ground for discharging them.

BRANTI v. FINKEL
100 S. Ct. 1287 (1980)

STEVENS, J.:The question presented is whether the First and Fourteenth Amendments to the Constitution protect an assistant public defender who is satisfactorily performing his job from discharge solely because of his political beliefs. . . .

The critical facts can be summarized briefly. The Rockland County Public Defender is appointed by the County Legislature for a term of six years. He in turn appoints nine assistants who serve at his pleasure. The two respondents have served as assistants since their respective appointments in March 1971 and September 1975; they are both Republicans.

Petitioner Branti's predecessor, a Republican, was appointed in 1972 by a Republican-dominated County Legislature. By 1977, control of the legislature had shifted to the Democrats and petitioner, also a Democrat, was appointed to replace the incumbent when his term expired. As soon as petitioner was formally appointed on January 3, 1978, he began executing termination notices for six of the nine assistants then in office. Respondents were among those who were to be terminated. With one possible exception, the nine who were to be appointed or retained were all Democrats and were all selected by Democratic legislators or Democratic town chairmen on a basis that had been determined by the Democratic caucus.

The District Court found that Finkel and Tabakman had been selected for termination solely because they were Republicans and thus did not have the necessary Democratic sponsors. . . .

Having concluded that respondents had been discharged solely because of their politi-cal beliefs, the District Court held that those discharges would be permissible under this Court's decision in *Elrod v. Burns*, 427 U.S. 347, only if assistant public defenders are the type of policymaking, confidential employees who may be discharged solely on the basis of their political affiliations. He concluded that respondents clearly did not fall within that category. Although recognizing that they had broad responsibilities with respect to particular cases that were assigned to them, the court found that respondents had "very limited, if any, responsibility" with respect to the overall operation of the public defender's office. They did not "act as advisors or formulate plans for the implementation of the broad goals of the office" and, although they made decisions in the context of specific cases, "they do not make decisions about the orientation and operation of the office in which they work."

Petitioner advances two principal arguments for reversal: first, that the holding in *Elrod v. Burns* is limited to situations in which government employees are coerced into pledging allegiance to a political party that they would not voluntarily support and does not apply to a simple requirement that an employee be sponsored by the party in power; and, second, that even if party sponsorship is an unconstitutional condition of continued public employment for clerks, deputies, and janitors, it is an acceptable requirement for an assistant public defender.

In *Elrod v. Burns* the Court held that the newly elected Democratic sheriff of Cook County, Ill., had violated the constitutional rights of certain non-civil service employees by discharging them "because they did not support and were not members of the Democratic Party and had failed to obtain the sponsorship of one of its leaders." . . .

Writing for the plurality, Mr. Justice Brennan identified two separate but interrelated reasons supporting the conclusion that the discharges were prohibited by the First and Fourteenth Amendments. First, he analyzed the impact of a political patronage system on freedom of belief and association. Noting that in order to retain their jobs, the sheriff's employees were required to pledge their allegiance to the Democratic party, work for or contribute to the party's candidates, or obtain a Democratic sponsor, he concluded that the inevitable tendency of such a system was to coerce employees into compromising their true beliefs. . . .

If the First Amendment protects a public employee from discharge based on what he has said, it must also protect him from discharge based on what he believes. Under this line of analysis, unless the Government can demonstrate "an overriding interest of vital importance," requiring that a person's private beliefs conform to those of the hiring authority, his beliefs cannot be the sole basis for depriving him of continued public employment. . . .

In sum, there is no requirement that dismissed employees prove that they, or other employees, have been coerced into changing, either actually or ostensibly, their political allegiance. To prevail in this type of an action, it was sufficient, as *Elrod* holds, for respondents to prove that they were discharged "solely for the reason that they were not affiliated with or sponsored by the Democratic Party."

Both opinions in *Elrod* recognize that party affiliation may be an acceptable requirement for some types of government employment. Thus, if an employee's private political beliefs would interfere with the discharge of his public duties, his First Amendment rights may be required to yield to the State's vital interest in maintaining governmental effectiveness and efficiency.

In *Elrod* it was clear that the duties of the employees—the chief deputy of the process division of the sheriff's office, a process server and another employee in that office, and a bailiff and security guard at the Juvenile Court of Cook County—were not of that character, for they were, as Mr. Justice Stewart stated, "nonpolicymaking, nonconfidential" employees.

As Mr. Justice Brennan noted in *Elrod,* it is not always easy to determine whether a position is one in which political affiliation is a legitimate factor to be considered. Under some circumstances, a position may be appropriately considered political even though it is neither confidential nor policymaking in character. As one obvious example, if a State's election laws require that precincts be supervised by two election judges of different parties, a Republican judge could be legitimately discharged solely for changing his party registration. That conclusion would not depend on any finding that the job involved participation in policy decisions or access to confidential information. Rather, it would simply rest on the fact that party membership was essential to the discharge of the employee's governmental responsibilities.

It is equally clear that party affiliation is not necessarily relevant to every policymaking or confidential position. The coach of a state university's football team formulates policy, but no one could seriously claim that Republicans make better coaches than Democrats, or vice versa, no matter which party is in control of the state government. On the other hand, it is equally clear that the governor of a state may appropriately believe that the official duties of various assistants who help him write speeches, explain his views to the press, or communicate with the legislature cannot be performed effectively unless those persons share his political beliefs and party commitments. In sum, the ultimate inquiry is not whether the label "policymaker" or "confidential" fits a particular position; rather, the question is whether the hiring authority can demonstrate that party affiliation is an appropriate requirement for the effective performance of the public office involved.

Having thus framed the issue, it is manifest that the continued employment of an assistant public defender cannot properly be conditioned upon his allegiance to the political party in control of the county government. The primary, if not the only, responsibility of an assistant public defender is to represent individual citizens in controversy with the State. . . .

Thus, whatever policymaking occurs in the public defender's office must relate to the needs of individual clients and not to any partisan political interests. Similarly, although an assistant is bound to obtain access to confidential information arising out of various attorney-client relationships, that information has no bearing whatsoever on partisan political concerns. Under these circumstances, it would undermine, rather than promote, the effective performance of an assistant public defender's office to make his tenure dependent on his allegiance to the dominant political party.

Accordingly, the entry of an injunction against termination of respondents' employment on purely political grounds was appropriate and the judgment of the Court of Appeals is. . . . [*Affirmed.*]

The freedom of assembly and association protection is relevant to many cases involving unpopular groups such as Nazis and Communists. For example, some cases concern the issuance of passports to Communists, and others involve laws prohibiting Communists from holding certain positions, such as officers in labor unions or jobs in defense plants.

The guarantee of freedom of assembly and association prevents guilt by association. It also ensures privacy in one's association. For example, it has been held that state law may not compel the disclosure of membership lists of a constitutionally valid association. Such a disclosure implies likelihood of a substantial restraint upon the member's right to freedom of association. Protection also extends to forms of association that are not political, such as the social, legal, and economic benefits of membership in groups. For example, the First Amendment right to associate and to assemble prevents a state from denying a license to practice law to a Communist. It also prevents a state from denying a group such as the South African rugby team the right to play a match in the United States.

The right to assemble extends to all people irrespective of their race or ideology. The right of "association," like the right of belief, is more than the right to attend a meeting; it includes the right to express one's attitudes or philosophies by membership in a group, or by affiliation with it, or by other lawful means. Association is a form of expression of opinion. However, keep in mind that the right to associate and to express collective opinions does not mean that government or anyone else must follow those opinions.

7. Other First Amendment Freedoms

Finally the First Amendment includes the right to petition the government for a redress of grievances. In addition, the specifics of the Bill of Rights have additional implied rights, such as the right of privacy, the right to knowledge, and the right to one's beliefs. These rights are derived from the others actually specified. For example, the right of freedom of speech and press has been held to include not only the right to utter or to print, but the right to distribute, the right to receive, and the right to read. Freedom of expression includes freedom of inquiry, freedom of thought, and freedom to teach. The case which follows illustrates that even the right to petition is not an absolute and that it is closely connected with other First Amendment guarantees.

McDONALD v. SMITH
105 S. Ct. 2787 (1985)

BURGER, J.: We granted certiorari to decide whether the Petition Clause of the First Amendment provides absolute immunity to a defendant charged with expressing libelous and damaging falsehoods in letters to the President of the United States.

In July 1981, respondent commenced a libel action against petitioner in state court under the common law of North Carolina. Respondent alleged that while he was being considered for the position of United States Attorney, petitioner wrote two letters to President Reagan. The complaint alleges that these letters "contained false, slanderous, libelous, inflammatory and derogatory statements" concerning respondent. In particular, the complaint states that the letters falsely accused respondent of "violating the civil rights of various individuals while a Superior Court Judge," "fraud and conspiracy to commit fraud," "extortion or blackmail," and "violations of professional ethics." Respondent alleged that petitioner knew that these accusations were false, and that peti-

tioner maliciously intended to injure respondent by undermining his prospect of being appointed United States Attorney.

The complaint alleges that petitioner mailed copies of the letters to Presidential adviser Edwin Meese, Senator Jesse Helms, Representative W. E. Johnston, and three other officials in the executive and legislative branches. It further alleges that petitioner's letters had their intended effect: respondent was not appointed United States Attorney, his reputation and career as an attorney were injured, and he "suffered humiliation, embarrassment, anxiety and mental anguish." Respondent sought compensatory and punitive damages of $1 million.

Petitioner removed the case to the United States District Court on the basis of diversity of citizenship. He then moved for judgment on the pleadings on the ground that the Petition Clause of the First Amendment provides absolute immunity. The District Court agreed with petitioner that his communications fell "within the general protection afforded by the petition clause," but held tthat the Clause does not grant absolute immunity from liability for libel. The Fourth Circuit, . . . affirmed.

The First Amendment guarantees "the right of the people . . . to petition the Government for a redress of grievances." The right to petition is cut from the same cloth as the other guarantees of that Amendment, and is an assurance of a particular freedom of expression. In *United States v. Cruikshank,* the Court declared that this right is implicit in "[t]he very idea of government, republican in form." And James Madison made clear in the congressional debate on the proposed amendment that people "may communicate their will" through direct petitions to the legislature and government officials. . . .

Although the values in the right of petition as an important aspect of self-government are beyond question, it does not follow that the Framers of the First Amendment believed that the Petition Clause provided absolute immunity from damages for libel. . . .

In *White v. Nicholls,* 3 How. 266, 11 L. Ed. 591 (1845), this Court dealt with the proper common-law privilege for petitions to the Government. The plaintiff in *White* brought a libel action based on letters written by Nicholls urging the President of the United States to remove him from office as a customs inspector. The Court, after reviewing the common law, concluded that the defendant's petition was actionable if prompted by "express malice," which was defined as "falsehood and the absence of probable cause." Nothing presented to us suggests that the Court's decision not to recognize an absolute privilege in 1845 should be altered; we are not prepared to conclude, 140 years later,

that the Framers of the First Amendment understood the right to petition to include an unqualified right to express damaging falsehoods in exercise of that right.

Nor do the Court's decisions interpreting the Petition Clause in contexts other than defamation indicate that the right to petition is absolute. For example, filing a complaint in court is a form of petitioning activity; but "baseless litigation is not immunized by the First Amendment right to petition."

Similarly, petitions to the President that contain intentional and reckless falsehoods do not enjoy constitutional protection, and may . . . be reached by the law of libel.

To accept petitioner's claim of absolute immunity would elevate the Petition Clause to special First Amendment status. The Petition Clause, however, was inspired by the same ideals of liberty and democracy that gave us the freedoms to speak, publish, and assemble. These First Amendment rights are inseparable, and there is no sound basis for granting greater constitutional protection to statements made in a petition to the President than other First Amendment expressions.

Under state common law, damages may be recovered only if petitioner is shown to have acted with malace; "malace" has been defined by the Court of Appeals of North Carolina, as "knowledge at the time that the words are false, or . . . without probable cause or without checking for truth by the means at hand."

We hold that the Petition Clause does not require the State to expand this privilege into an absolute one. The right to petition is guaranteed; the right to commit libel with impunity is not. The judgment of the Court of Appeals is therefore [*Affirmed.*]

OTHER PROVISIONS

8. The Fourth Amendment

The Fourth Amendment protects individuals and corporations from unreasonable searches and seizures. It primarily protects persons from unwarranted intrusions into their individual privacy.

Fourth Amendment issues usually arise in criminal cases. Among typical issues are (1) the validity of searches incident to an arrest, (2) the validity of search warrants—the presence of probable cause to issue the warrant, (3) the validity of consents to searches, and (4) the extent to which property such as automobiles may be searched without a warrant. In addition, electronic surveilance often raises Fourth Amendment issues. For example, the Omnibus Crime Control and Safe Streets Act authorizes the electronic interception of communications pursuant to a court-authorized order. A "bug" was placed in a building by covert entry. The Supreme Court held that such surveillance does not violate the Fourth Amendment.

In recent years, the protection of the Fourth Amendment often has been narrowed by court decisions. To protect police officers, it has been held that they may search someone being arrested and the immediate area around them for weapons. Officers searching an automobile are given far more latitude than when searching a person, a home, or a building. Persons lawfully arrested may be convicted of other crimes with evidence obtained as the result of valid searches which are an incident of a lawful arrest. The right to search for evidence extends to the premises of persons not suspected of criminal conduct. Such premises may include offices of operating newspapers and attorneys. In addition, one who does not own a vehicle may not object to its search even if the person has property physically present in the vehicle.

Fourth Amendment protection extends to civil matters as well as to criminal cases. For example, in a case involving the right of a counselor to visit the home of a welfare recipient, it was held that such home visits did not violate the Fourth Amendment. In another case, it was held that building inspectors do not have the right to inspect for building code violations without a warrant, if the owner of the premises objects. The Fourth Amendment protection has also been applied to prevent aerial surveillance by Environmental Protection Agency inspectors. The Fourth Amendment has also been used to prevent the Securities and Exchange Commission (SEC) from using confidential reports obtained in the course of its function to establish a violation of federal law. The reports cannot be required for one purpose and then used for another without running afoul of the Fourth Amendment.

The case which follows is typical of those extending Fourth Amendment protection to business is a noncriminal matter.

MARSHALL v. BARLOW'S, INC.

98 S. Ct. 1816 (1978)

WHITE, J.: . . . Section 8 (a) of the Occupational Safety and Health Act of 1970 (OSHA) empowers agents of the Secretary of Labor (the Secretary) to search the work area of any employment facility within the Act's jurisdiction. The purpose of the search is to inspect for safety hazards and violations of OSHA regulations. No search warrant or other process is expressly required under the Act.

On the morning of September 11, 1975, an OSHA inspector entered the customer service area of Barlow's, Inc., an electrical and plumbing installation business located in Pocatello, Idaho. The president and general manager, Ferrol G. "Bill" Barlow, was on hand; and the OSHA inspector, after showing his credentials, informed Mr. Barlow that he wished to conduct a search of the working areas of the business. Mr. Barlow inquired whether any complaint had been received about his company. The inspector answered no, but that Barlow's, Inc. had simply turned up in the agency's selection process. The inspector again asked to enter the nonpublic area of the business; Mr. Barlow's response was to inquire whether the inspector had a search warrant. The inspector had none. Thereupon, Mr. Barlow refused the inspector admission to the employee area of his business. He said he was relying on his rights as guaranteed by the Fourth Amendment of the United States Constitution.

[The Secretary sought a court order compelling Mr. Barlow to admit the inspector. The court refused holding that the Fourth Amendment required a warrant and that the law authorizing "warrantless searches" was unconstitutional. The Secretary appealed.]

The Secretary urges that warrantless inspections to enforce OSHA are reasonable within the meaning of the Fourth Amendment. Regretfully, we are unable to agree.

The Warrant Clause of the Fourth Amendment protects commercial buildings as well as private homes. To hold otherwise would belie the origin of that Amendment, and the American colonial experience.

This Court has already held that warrantless searches are generally unreasonable and that this rule applies to commercial premises as well as homes.

. . . (T)he Fourth Amendment prohibition against unreasonable searches protects against warrantless intrusions during civil as well as criminal investigations. The reason is found in the basic purpose of this Amendment . . . (which) is to safeguard the privacy and security of individuals against arbitrary invasions by governmental officials. If the government intrudes on a person's property, the privacy interest suffers whether the government's motivation is to investigate violations of criminal laws or breaches of other statutory or regulatory standards. . . .

The Secretary nevertheless stoutly argues that the enforcement scheme of the Act requires warrantless searches, and that the restrictions on search discretion contained in the Act and its regulations already protect as much as a warrant would. The Secretary thereby asserts the actual reasonableness of OSHA searches, whatever the general rule against warrantless searches might be. Because reasonableness is still the ultimate standard, the Secretary suggests that the Court decide whether a warrant is needed by arriving at a sensible balance between the administrative necessities of OSHA inspections and the incremental protection of privacy of business owners a warrant would afford. He suggests that only a decision exempting OSHA inspections from the Warrant Clause would give "full recognition to the competing public and private interests here at stake."

The Secretary submits that warrantless inspections are essential to the proper enforcement of OSHA because they afford the opportunity to inspect without prior notice and hence to preserve the advantages of surprise. While the dangerous conditions outlawed by the Act include structural defects that cannot be quickly hidden or remedied, the Act also regulates a myriad of safety details that may be amenable to speedy alteration or disguise. The risk is that during the interval between an inspector's initial request to search a plant and his procuring a warrant following the owner's refusal of permission, violations of this latter type could be corrected and thus escape the inspector's notice.

We are unconvinced, however, that requiring warrants to inspect will impose serious burdens on the inspection system or the courts, will prevent inspections necessary to enforce the statute, or will make them less effective. In the first place the great majority of businessmen can be expected in normal course to consent to inspection without warrant; the Secretary has not brought to this Court's attention any widespread pattern of refusal. . . .

Whether the Secretary proceeds to secure a warrant or other process, with or without prior notice, his entitlement to inspect will not depend on his demonstrating probable cause to believe that conditions in violation of OSHA exist on the premises.

Probable cause in the criminal law sense is not required. For purposes of an administrative search such as this, probable cause justifying the issuance of a warrant may be based not only on specific evidence of an existing violation but also on a showing that "reasonable legislative or administrative standards for conducting an . . . inspection are satisfied with respect to a particular (establishment)." A warrant showing that a specific business has been chosen for an OSHA search on the basis of a general administrative plan for the enforcement of the Act derived from neutral sources such as, for example, dispersion of employees in various types of industries across a given area, and the desired frequency of searches in any of the lesser divisions of the area, would protect an employer's Fourth Amendment rights. We doubt that the consumption of enforcement energies in the obtaining of such warrants will exceed manageable proportions. . . .

Nor do we agree that the incremental protections afforded the employer's privacy by a warrant are so marginal that they fail to justify the administrative burdens that may be entailed. The authority to make warrantless searches devolves almost unbridled discretion upon executive and administrative officers, particularly those in the field, as to when to search and whom to search. A warrant, by contrast, would provide assurances from a neutral officer that the inspection is reasonable under the Constitution, is authorized by statute, and is pursuant to an administrative plan containing specific neutral criteria. Also, a warrant would then and there advise the owner of the scope and objects of the search, beyond which limits the inspector is not expected to proceed. These are important functions for a warrant to perform, functions which underlie the Court's prior decisions that the Warrant Clause applies to inspections for compliance with regulatory statutes. We conclude that the concerns expressed by the Secretary do not suffice to justify warrantless inspections under OSHA or vitiate the general constitutional requirement that for a search to be reasonable a warrant must be obtained.

We hold that Barlow was entitled to a declaratory judgment that the Act is unconstitutional insofar as it purports to authorize inspections without a warrant or its equivalent and to an injunction enjoining the Act's enforcement to that extent. [*Affirmed.*]

9. The Fifth Amendment

The Fifth Amendment is best known for its protection against compulsory self-incrimination. People frequently plead "the Fifth," and almost everyone knows they are exercising their right to its protection. The Fifth Amendment goes much further, however. It contains other protections, and, more specifically, it (1) requires indictment by a *grand jury* for a capital offense or infamous crime, (2) prohibits **double jeopardy**, (3) requires just compensation in eminent domain proceedings, and (4) contains a due process clause.

A grand jury must decide whether there is sufficient evidence of guilt to justify the accused's standing trial. Grand juries are usually made up of twenty-three persons, and it takes a majority vote to indict a defendant. It takes less proof to indict a person and to require him or her to stand trial than it does to convict. The grand jury provision contains an exception for court-martial proceedings.

Proper functioning of the grand jury system depends upon secrecy of the proceedings. This secrecy protects the innocent accused from disclosure of the accusations made against him or her before the grand jury. However, transcripts of grand jury proceedings may be obtained if necessary to avoid possible injustice in judicial proceedings. For example, a litigant may use a grand jury transcript at a trial to impeach a witness, to refresh the witness's recollection, to test his or her credibility, and the like. The disclosure of a grand jury transcript is appropriate only in those cases where the need for it outweighs the public interest in secrecy, and the burden of demonstrating this balance rests upon a private party seeking disclosure.

Protection against double jeopardy means that a person cannot be tried twice by the same governmental body for the same offense. The double jeopardy clause protects corporations as well as individuals. "Eminent domain" is used by governmental bodies to acquire real property for public purposes. The Fifth Amendment requires just compensation. This is a question of fact for a jury if the property owner and the condemning governmental unit cannot agree on a fair market value of the property taken.

The Fifth Amendment protects life, liberty, and property from deprivation by the federal government without due process of law. The Fourteenth

Amendment contains an identical provision which applies to the states. Although due process is difficult to define, it basically amounts to "fundamental fairness." Since interpretations of the due process clauses of the Fifth and Fourteenth Amendments are for all practical purposes identical, the discussion of due process later in this chapter under the Fourteenth Amendment and the cases included there also illustrate due process under the Fifth Amendment.

Protection against compulsory self-incrimination is subject to several limitations. It does not apply to corporations. Although corporations are citizens for most purposes, they are not citizens for this purpose. However, corporate officials retain their personal privilege against compulsory self-incrimination. As a result, corporate officials cannot be required to testify, but they may be required to deliver all corporate records since they are not privileged.

The privilege against compulsory self-incrimination is to protect individuals against compelled self-incrimination. It does not protect against voluntary acts such as the preparation of records in the ordinary course of business. Since the production of records does not compel oral testimony, the Fifth Amendment does not prevent the use of evidence including documents in the hands of an accused or in the hands of someone else such as an accountant. All that is protected is extortion of information from the accused. However, as the case which follows shows, the act of producing the document may be privileged. If the act of producing a business document has testimonial aspects which may have an incriminating effect, the Fifth Amendment protection may be asserted.

UNITED STATES v. DOE
104 S. Ct. 1237 (1984)

POWELL, J.: This case presents the issue whether, and to what extent, the Fifth Amendment privilege against compelled self-incrimination applies to the business records of a sole proprietorship.

Respondent is the owner of several sole proprietorships. In late 1980, a grand jury, during the course of an investigation of corruption in the awarding of county and municipal contracts, served five subpoenas on respondent. The first two demanded the production of the telephone records of several of respondent's companies and all records per-

taining to four bank accounts of respondent and his companies. The subpoenas were limited to the period between January 1, 1977 and the dates of the subpoenas. The third subpoena demanded the production of a list of virtually all the business records of one of respondent's companies for the period between January 1, 1976, and the date of the subpoena. The fourth subpoena sought production of a similar list of business records belonging to another company. The final subpoena demanded production of all bank statements and cancelled checks of two of respondent's companies that had accounts at a bank in the Grand Cayman Islands.

Respondent filed a motion in federal district court seeking to quash the subpoenas. The District Court for the District of New Jersey granted his motion except with respect to those documents and records required by law to be kept or disclosed to a public agency. . . .

The Court of Appeals for the Third Circuit affirmed. It first addressed the question whether the Fifth Amendment ever applies to the records of a sole proprietorship. After noting that an individual may not assert the Fifth Amendment privilege on behalf of a corporation, partnership, or other collective entity under the holding of *Bellis v. United States,* 417 U.S. 85 (1974), the Court of Appeals reasoned that the owner of a sole proprietorship acts in a personal rather than a representative capacity. As a result, the court held that respondent's claim of the privilege was not foreclosed by the reasoning of *Bellis.*

The Court of Appeals next considered whether the documents at issue in this case are privileged. The court noted that this Court held in *Fisher v. United States,* 425 U.S. 391 (1976), that the contents of business records ordinarily are not privileged because they are created voluntarily and without compulsion. The Court of Appeals nevertheless found that respondent's business records were privileged under either of two analyses. First, the court reasoned that, notwithstanding the holdings in *Bellis* and *Fisher,* the business records of a sole proprietorship are no different from the individual owner's personal records. Noting that Third Circuit cases had held that private papers, although created voluntarily, are protected by the Fifth Amendment, the court accorded the same protection to respondent's business papers. Second, it held that respondent's act of producing the subpoenaed records would have communicative aspects of its own.

The turning over of the subpoenaed documents to the grand jury would admit their existence and authenticity. Accordingly, respondent was entitled to assert his Fifth Amendment privilege rather than produce the subpoenaed documents. . . .

The Court in *Fisher* expressly declined to reach the question whether the Fifth Amendment privilege protects the contents of an individual's tax records in his possession. The rationale underlying our holding in that case is, however, persuasive here. As we noted in *Fisher,* the Fifth Amendment protects the person asserting the privilege only from *compelled* self-incrimination. Where the preparation of business records is voluntary, no compulsion is present. A subpoena that demands production of documents "does not compel oral testimony; nor would it ordinarily compel the taxpayer to restate, repeat, or affirm the truth of the contents of the documents sought." Applying this reasoning in *Fisher,* we stated:

[T]he Fifth Amendment would not be violated by the fact alone that the papers on their face might incriminate the taxpayer, for the privilege protects a person only against being incriminnated by his own compelled testimonial communications. The accountant's workpapers are not the taxpayer's. They were not prepared by the taxpayer, and they contain no testimonial declarations by him. Furthermore, as far as this record demonstrates, the preparation of all of the papers sought in these cases was wholly voluntary, and they cannot be said to contain compelled testimonial evidence, either of the taxpayers or of anyone else. The taxpayer cannot avoid compliance with the subpoena merely by asserting that the item of evidence which he is required to produce contains incriminating writing, whether his own or that of someone else.

This reasoning applies with equal force here. Respondent does not contend that he prepared the documents involuntarily or that the subpoena would force him to restate, repeat, or affirm the truth of their contents. The fact that the records are in respondent's possession is irrelevant to the determination of whether the creation of the records was compelled. We therefore hold that the contents of those records are not privileged.

Although the contents of a document may not be privileged, the act of producing the document may be. A government subpoena compels the holder of the document to perform an act that may have testimonial aspects and an incriminating effect. As we noted in *Fisher:*

Compliance with the subpoena tacitly concedes the existence of the papers demanded and their possession or control by the taxpayer. It also would indicate the taxpayer's belief that the papers are those described in the subpoena. The elements of compulsion are clearly present, but the more difficult issues are whether the tacit averments of the taxpayer are both 'testimonial' and 'incriminating' for purposes of applying the Fifth Amendment. These questions perhaps do not lend themselves to categorical answers. Their resolution may instead depend on the facts and circumstances of particular cases or classes thereof.

In *Fisher,* the Court explored the effect that the act of production would have on the taxpayer and determined that the act of production would have only minimal testimonial value and would not operate to incriminate the taxpayer. Unlike the Court in *Fisher,* we have the explicit finding of the District Court that the act of producing the documents would involve testimonial self-incrimination. The Court of Appeals agreed. The District Court's finding essentially rests on its determination of factual issues. . . .

We decline to overturn the finding of the District Court in this regard, where, as here, it has been affirmed by the Court of Appeals.

We conclude that the Court of Appeals erred in holding that the contents of the subpoenaed documents were privileged under the Fifth Amendment. The act of producing the documents at issue in this case is privileged and cannot be compelled without a statutory grant of use immunity . . . [*Affirmed in part and reversed in part.*]

10. The Sixth Amendment

The Sixth Amendment, like the Fifth, provides multiple protection in criminal cases. Essentially, its protections give one the right (1) to a speedy and public trial, (2) to a trial by jury, (3) to be informed of the charge against him or her, (4) to confront one's accuser, (5) to subpoena witnesses in one's favor, and (6) to have the assistance of an attorney.

The American concept of a jury trial contemplates a jury drawn from a fair cross section of the community. The jury guards against the exercise of arbitrary power by using the commonsense judgment of the community as a hedge against the overzealous or mistaken prosecutor. The jury's perspective of facts is used in preference to the professional or perhaps overconditioned, or biased response of a judge.

Community participation in administering criminal law is not only consistent with our democratic heritage, it is also critical to public confidence in the fairness of the criminal justice system. Therefore, a state may not restrict jury service only to special groups or exclude identifiable segments playing major roles in the community. For example, a Missouri law which excluded females who requested an automatic exemption from jury duty was unconstitutional as violating the "cross-section" concept. Likewise, minorities may not be systematically excluded from jury duty.

The right to a trial by jury does not require twelve-person juries nor does it require unanimous verdicts. However, if the jury is less than twelve, the verdict must be unanimous. A person may not be convicted by a nonunanimous six-person jury.

The right to a jury trial does not extend to state juvenile court delinquency proceedings because they are not criminal prosecutions. However, juveniles do have the right to counsel, to confront the witnesses against them, and to cross-examine them.

The right to an attorney exists in any cases where incarceration is a possible punishment. It exists at every stage of the proceeding, commencing with an investigation that centers on a person as the accused. Thus, it can be seen that there are many technical aspects to the Sixth Amendment, and numerous cases still arise concerning it.

11. The Seventh Amendment

The Seventh Amendment guarantees the right to a trial by jury in suits at common law where the amount in controversy exceeds $20. (This amount obviously has not been changed to keep up with inflation.) There is no right to a trial by jury in suits in equity or chancery. Likewise, there is no right to a trial by jury when the proceedings did not exist at common law but where they have been created by legislation. For example, in suits against the United States where Congress has waived governmental immunity, there is no right to a trial by jury unless the statute waiving the immunity specifically grants it. This concept was recently reaffirmed in a suit by a government employee alleging age discrimination. There is a right to trial by jury in age discrimination cases against private employers, but no such right exists in cases against the government, because the Seventh Amendment does not apply in suits against the government.

There is also no right to a jury trial in cases brought before administrative agencies. These agencies did not exist at common law. The Seventh Amendment does not prohibit Congress from assigning the fact-finding function and initial judicial decision to an administrative forum. The jury would be incompatible with this. Fact finding was never the exclusive province of the jury. The Seventh Amendment does not make the jury the exclusive mechanism for fact finding. Much of it is done by administrative agencies such as the National Labor Relations Board, the Equal Employment Opportunity Commission, and the Occupational Health and Safety Administration. The case which finally established this important principle is a part of the next chapter on Administrative Agencies.

THE FOURTEENTH AMENDMENT

12. Introduction

Section 1 of the Fourteenth Amendment contains four provisions. First, it establishes that all persons born or naturalized in the United States are citizens of both the United States and of the state in which they reside. This provision was designed to establish state citizenship as well as United States citizenship for the slaves freed by the Emancipation Proclamation and by the Thirteenth Amendment.

To further establish rights of all citizens, including freed slaves, the Fourteenth Amendment contains three clauses commonly referred to as (1) the privileges and immunities clause, (2) the due process clause, and (3) the equal protection clause. The exact language is as follows:

> No State shall make or enforce any law which shall abridge the privileges or immunities of citizens of the United States; nor shall any State deprive any person of life, liberty or property, without due process of law, nor deny to any person within its jurisdiction the equal protection of the laws.

While all three clauses play a significant role in constitutional law, the due process clause and the equal protection clause have been involved in more significant litigation than has the privileges and immunities clause. The due process clause has played a unique role in constitutional development—one that was probably not anticipated at the time of its ratification. This significant role has been to make most of the provisions of the Bill of Rights applicable to the states. The first phrase of Article I of the Bill of Rights commences: "*Congress* shall make no law. . . ." How then are state and local governments prohibited from making such a law? Some jurists have argued that the due process clause of the Fourteenth Amendment "incorporates" or "carries over" the Bill of Rights and makes its provisions applicable to the states. Starting in 1925, a majority of the Supreme Court started applying various portions of the first eight amendments to the states using the due process clause of the Fourteenth Amendment as the vehicle establishing applicability.

Some justices have argued that all the provisions of the Bill of Rights are incorporated, while others have strongly rejected the incorporation theory. In 1937, Justice Benjamin Cardozo contended that those basic human rights "implicit in the concept of ordered liberty" were incorporated by the due process clause, but all other rights were not. In the latter group at this time were such protections as the Fifth Amendment's safeguard against double jeopardy. As time went by, piecemeal incorporation or absorption of the Bill of Rights continued. For example, the doctrine of separation of church and state was picked up in 1947; the requirement of public trials, in 1948; the Fourth Amendment protection against unreasonable searches and seizures, in 1961; the Eighth Amendment's guarantee against cruel and unusual punishment, in 1962; the Sixth Amendment's right to counsel, in 1963; and the Fifth Amendment's safeguard against compulsory self-incrimination, in 1964. Although justices used different theories and argued about the wisdom of allowing federal courts to use the due process clause to invalidate any state legislative act which they found offensive, the steady march of incorporation continued in the 1960s and 1970s. Cases have held that the Fourteenth Amendment incorporated the right to trial by an impartial jury, the right to a speedy trial, and the protection against double jeopardy. Only a few provisions of the first ten amendments, such as a grand jury indictment, a jury trial in civil cases, and excessive bail, are not yet picked up or incorporated by the due process clause.

The following sections discuss the other aspects of due process and the meaning of the equal protection clause.

13. Due Process of Law

The term *due process of law,* which is probably involved in more litigation than any other constitutional phrase, cannot be narrowly defined. The term describes fundamental principles of liberty and justice. Simply stated, due process means "fundamental fairness and decency." It means that *government* may not act in a manner that is arbitrary, capricious, or unreasonable. The clause does not prevent private individuals or corporations, including public utilities, from acting in an arbitrary or unreasonable manner. The due process clause only applies to state action.

The issues in due process cases are usually divided into questions of *procedural due process* and *substantive due process.* Substantive due process issues arise when property or other rights are directly affected by governmental action. Procedural due process cases often are concerned with whether proper notice has been given and a proper hearing has been conducted. Such cases frequently involve procedures established by state statute. However, many cases involve procedures which are not created by statute. For example, the due process clause has been used to challenge the procedure used in the dismissal of a student from a university medical school.

Due process issues have been discussed previously in other chapters. For example, the validity of long-arm statutes and the minimum contact required is a due process issue. The clause is invoked any time procedures are questioned. The case which follows typifies those challenging state procedures as a denial of due process of law.

DIXON v. LOVE
97 S. Ct. 1723 (1977)

Love, a truck driver, had his driver's license revoked for being "repeatedly convicted of offenses against laws and ordinances regulating the movement of traffic, to a degree which indicates disrespect for the traffic laws." He had been convicted of three traffic offenses within twelve months. The revocation was based on administrative regulations which did not require a hearing prior to the revocation. A hearing was available after the revocation. He challenged the revocation as a denial of due process. The lower court upheld the challenge.

BLACKMUN, J.: . . . The issue in this case is whether Illinois has provided constitutionally adequate procedures for suspending or revoking the license of a driver who repeatedly has been convicted for traffic offenses. The statute and administrative regulations provide for an initial summary decision based on official records, with a full administrative hearing available only after the suspension or revocation has taken effect. . . .

It is clear that the Due Process Clause applies to the deprivation of a driver's license by the State. . . .

It is equally clear that a licensee in Illinois eventually can obtain all the safeguards procedural due process could be thought to require before a discretionary suspension or revocation becomes final. . . . The only question is one of timing. This case thus presents an issue similar to that considered only last Term in *Mathews v. Eldridge*, 424 U.S. 319, 333 (1976), namely, "the extent to which due process requires an evidentiary hearing prior to the deprivation of some type of property interest even if such a hearing is provided

thereafter." We may analyze the present case too, in terms of the factors considered in *Eldridge*:

[I]dentification of the specific dictates of due process generally requires consideration of three distinct factors: first, the private interest that will be affected by the official action; second, the risk of an erroneous deprivation of such interest through the procedures used, and probable value, if any, of additional or substitute procedural safeguards; and finally the Government's interest, including the function involved and the fiscal and administrative burdens that the additional or substitute procedural requirement would entail.

The private interest affected by the decision here is the granted license to operate a motor vehicle. Unlike the social security recipients in *Eldridge*, who at least could obtain retroactive payments if their claims were subsequently sustained, a licensee is not made entirely whole if his suspension or revocation is later vacated. On the other hand, a driver's license may not be so vital and essential as are social insurance payments on which the recipient may depend for his very subsistence. The Illinois statute includes special provisions for hardship and for holders of commercial licenses, who are those most likely to be affected by the deprival of driving privileges. We therefore conclude that the nature of the private interest here is not so great as to require us "to depart from the ordinary principle, established by our decisions, that something less than an evidentiary hearing is sufficient prior to adverse administrative action."

Moreover, the risk of an erroneous deprivation in the absence of a prior hearing is not great. Under the Secretary's regulations, suspension and revocation decisions are largely automatic. Of course, there is the possibility of clerical error, but written objection will bring a matter of that kind to the Secretary's attention. In this case appellee had the opportunity for a full judicial hearing in connection with each of the traffic convictions on which the Secretary's decision was based. Appellee has not challenged the validity of those convictions or the adequacy of his procedural rights at the time they were determined. Since appellee does not dispute the factual basis for the Secretary's decision, he is really asserting the right to appear in person only to argue that the Secretary should show leniency and depart from his own regulations. Such an appearance might make the licensee feel that he has received more personal attention, but it would not serve to protect any substantive rights. We conclude that requiring additional procedures would be unlikely to have significant value in reducing the number of erroneous deprivations.

Finally, the substantial public interest in administrative efficiency would be impeded by the availability of a pretermination hearing in every case. Giving licensees the choice thus automatically to obtain a delay in the effectiveness of a suspension or revocation would encourage drivers routinely to request full administrative hearings. Far more substantial than the administrative burden, however, is the important public interest in safety on the roads and highways, and in the prompt removal of a safety hazard. . . .

We conclude that the public interests present under the circumstances of this case are sufficiently visible and weighty for the State to make its summary initial decision effective without a predecision administrative hearing.

The present case is a good illustration of the fact that procedural due process in the administrative setting does not always require application of the judicial model. When a governmental official is given the power to make discretionary decisions under a broad statutory standard, case-by-case decisionmaking may not be the best way to assure fairness. Here the Secretary commendably sought to define the statutory standard narrowly by the use of his rulemaking authority. The decision to use objective rules in this case provides drivers with more precise notice of what conduct will be sanctioned and promotes equality of treatment among similarly situated drivers. The approach taken by the District Court would have the contrary result of reducing the fairness of the system, by requiring a necessarily subjective inquiry in each case as to a driver's "disrespect" or "lack of ability to exercise ordinary and reasonable care." . . . [*Reversed.*]

During the early part of this century, the due process clauses of the Fifth and the Fourteenth Amendments were used by the Supreme Court to guard the sanctity of private property. Legislative attempts to regulate the economy by laws such as those imposing minimum wages or maximum hours for women and children were held to be unconstitutional as a denial of "substantive due process of law." During this period, if the substance of a law deprived persons of property, the law usually would be declared unconstitutional by the courts as a denial of "due process." If a federal law were under attack, the Fifth Amendment was cited as the ground; and if a state law were involved, the protection of the Fourteenth was invoked.

After the mid-1930s and President Roosevelt's attempt to pack the Supreme Court, the judicial attitude toward the application of the due process clause to economic legislation changed dramatically. The Supreme Court refused to find such legislation unconstitutional on the ground of infringement of "substantive due process," and substantive due process as a bar to economic legislation tended to pass into oblivion.

After the 1930s, the due process clause was most frequently invoked in cases involving individual liberties and civil rights. In the latter area, it was used by courts in seeking a balance between the basic civil rights of individuals and the interests of society as a whole. These cases frequently dealt with "procedural" issues rather than with "substantive" issues. Many of the "noneconomic" issues were raised in criminal cases, while others concerned state action that affected such basic rights as freedom of speech, press, and religion.

Since the change of attitude by at least a majority of the court toward the "due process clause," there is in effect a double standard in the application of the clause. Legislation in the economic sector is presumed to be constitutional, and few challenges on the due process ground can expect to be successful. On the other hand, when basic human freedoms are involved, the courts regard any legislation tending to curb or limit them to be suspect. As a result courts do not hesitate to declare legislation dealing with fundamental human rights such as freedom of speech, press, assembly, worship, or petition to be unconstitutional as a denial of due process of law. In other words, today there is a presumption of constitutionality of economic legislation, but legislation which tends to restrict fundamental rights is suspect and subject to more exacting judicial scrutiny under the Fourteenth Amendment. This double standard is often justified because of the crucial importance of these basic freedoms, which must be protected by the judiciary from the "vicissitudes" of political action. As a result, the due process clause prohibits experimentation with the basic fundamental liberties by the legislative and executive branches of government. It places the judiciary in the role of guarding these rights. Courts are thus the guardians of fundamental liberty; but, at least today, they are not part of the administration of our economic system.

14. Equal Protection

Almost no law treats all persons equally. Laws draw lines and treat people differently. Therefore, almost any state or local law imaginable can be challenged under the equal protection clause. It is obvious that the equal protection clause does not always deny states the power to treat different persons in different ways. Yet the equal protection clause embodies the ethical idea that law should not treat people differently without a satisfactory reason making such treatment fair under the circumstances. In deciding cases using that clause to challenge state and local laws, courts use two distinct approaches. One is the traditional or "minimum rationality" approach, and the other is called the "strict scrutiny" approach. (See Table 9-1.)

TABLE 9-1 Equal Protection Analysis

Standard	Minimun Rationality	Quasi-Strict Scrutiny	Strict Scrutiny
Classifications must be	Rationally connected to a permissible or legitimate government objective	Substantially related to an important government interest	Necessary to a compelling state interest
Examples	**Presumed Valid** Height Weight Age Testing School desegregation Veteran's preference Marriage	**Quasi-Suspect Classes** Sex Gender Legitimacy Affirmative action	**Suspect Classes** Race National origin Alienage **Fundamental Rights** To vote To travel

Whether the approach determines the result of a case or whether the desired result dictates the approach to be used is not always clear. As a practical matter, if the traditional (minimum rationality) approach is used, the challenged law and its classifications are usually found *not* to be a violation of equal protection. On the other hand, if the "strict scrutiny" test is used, the classifications are usually found to be unconstitutional under the equal protection clause.

Under the minimum rationality approach, a classification will survive an equal protection challenge if it has a *rational* connection to a *permissible* state end. A permissible state end is one that is not prohibited by another provision of the Constitution. It qualifies as a legitimate goal of government. The classification must have a reasonable basis (not wholly arbitrary), and the courts will assume any state of facts that can be used to justify the classification. These laws often involve economic issues such as mandatory retirement ages or social legislation such as welfare laws.

Such laws are presumed to be constitutional because courts recognize that the legislature must draw lines creating distinctions and that such tasks cannot be avoided. Further, courts in applying this standard admit that perfection in making classifications is neither possible nor necessary. Only when no rational basis for the classification exists is it unconstitutional under the equal protection clause. A classification judged by this standard must be rationally related to the state's objectives. The classification may be imperfect and may not be the best to accomplish the purpose, yet it is still constitutional if there is a rational basis for the classification. For example, a state law imposing mandatory retirement of police at age fifty was held valid when the rational basis test was applied to it.

Under the strict scrutiny test, a classification will be a denial of equal protection unless the classification is necessary to a *compelling* state end. It is not enough that a classification be rational, it must be necessary. It is not enough that a classification be permissible to a state end, it must be a compelling state objective. To withstand constitutional challenge when this test is used, the law must serve important governmental objectives and the classification must be substantially related to achieving these objectives.

The strict scrutiny test is used if the classification involves either (1) a suspect class, or (2) a fundamental constitutional right. A suspect class is one that has such disabilities, has been subjected to such a history of purposeful unequal treatment, or has been relegated to such a position of political powerlessness that it commands extraordinary protection from the political process of the majority. For example, classifications directed at race, national origin, and alienage are clearly suspect. As a result, the judiciary strictly scrutinizes laws directed at them. Unless the state can prove that its statutory classifications have a compelling state interest as a basis, the classifications will be considered a denial of equal protection. Classifications which are subject to strict judicial scrutiny are presumed to be unconstitutional. The state must convince the court that the classification is fair, reasonable, and necessary to accomplish the objective of legislation that is compelling to a state interest.

Strict judicial scrutiny is applied to a second group of cases, those which involve classifications directed at fundamental rights. If a classification unduly burdens or penalizes the exercise of a constitutional right, it will be stricken unless it is found to be necessary to a compelling state interest. Among such rights are the right to vote and the right to travel. Doubts about such laws result in their being stricken by the courts as a denial of equal protection.

Some cases actually fall between the two tests previously discussed. These cases use what it sometimes called "quasi strict scrutiny" tests because the classifications are only partially suspect or the rights involved are not quite fundamental. For example, classifications directed at sex and legitimacy are partially suspect. In cases involving classifications based on sex or gender, the courts have taken this position between the two tests or at least have modified the strict scrutiny approach. Such classifications are unconstitutional unless they are *substantially* related to an *important* government objective. This modified version of strict scrutiny has resulted in holdings which find laws to be valid as well as unconstitutional.

Equal protection cases run the whole spectrum of legislative attempts to solve society's problems. For example, a major use of the equal protection clause by courts has been to require the integration of public schools. In addition, the meaning and application of the equal protection clause have been central issues in cases involving (1) apportionment of legislative bodies, (2) racial segregation in the sale and rental of real estate, (3) laws distinguishing between the rights of legitimates and illegitimates, (4) the makeup of juries, (5) voting requirements, (6) welfare residency requirements, (7) rights of aliens, and (8) the use of property taxes as the means of financing public schools. The equal protection clause is the means to the end, or goal, or equality of opportunity. As such, it may be utilized by anyone claiming unequal treatment in any case. To be successful, a party alleging discrimination must not only prove unequal treatment, it must prove discriminatory intent by a governmental body if the minimum rationality standard is used. The case which follows is typical of those using this standard.

VIL. OF ARLINGTON HTS. v. METRO. HOUSING DEV.
97 S. Ct. 555 (1977)

Respondent, Metropolitan Housing Development Corporation (MHDC), contracted too purchase a tract of land within the boundaries of petitioner village in order to build racially integrated low- and moderate-income housing. The contract was contingent upon securing rezoning as well as federal housing assistance. MHDC applied to the village for the necessary rezoning from a single-family to a multiple-family (R-5) classification. At a series of Village Plan Commission public meetings, both supporters and opponents touched upon the fact that the project would probably be racially integrated. Opponents also stressed that the location had always been zoned single-family, and that the village's apartment policy called for limited use of R-5 zoning, primarily as a buffer between single-family development and commercial or manufacturing districts, none of which adjoined the project's proposed location. After the village denied the rezoning, MHDC and individual minority respondents filed this suit for injunctive and declaratory relief, alleging that the denial was racially discriminatory and violated the Equal Protection Clause of the Fourteenth Amendment. The district court upheld the zoning board, but the Court of Appeals reversed holding that the ultimate effect of the rezoning denial was racially discriminatory because of a disproportionate impact on blacks.

POWELL, J.: . . . [O]fficial action will not be held unconstitutional solely because it results in a racially disproportionate impact. Disproportionate impact is not irrelevant, but it is not the sole touchstone of an invidious racial discrimination. Proof of racially discriminatory intent or purpose is required to show a violation of the Equal Protection Clause.

[The Law] does not require a plaintiff to prove that the challenged action rested solely on racially discriminatory purposes. Rarely can it be said that a legislature or administrative body operating under a broad mandate made a decision motivated solely by a single concern, or even that a particular purpose was the "dominant" or "primary" one. In fact, it is because legislators and administrators are properly concerned with balancing numerous competing considerations that courts refrain from reviewing the merits of their decisions, absent a showing of arbitrariness or irrationality. But racial discrimination is not just another competing consideration. When there is a proof that a discriminatory purpose has been a motivating factor in the decision, this judicial deference is no longer justified.

Determining whether invidious discriminatory purpose was a motivating factor demands a sensitive inquiry into such circumstantial and direct evidence of intent as may be available. The impact of the official action—whether it "bears more heavily on one race than another"—may provide an important starting point. Sometimes a clear pattern, unexplainable on grounds other than race, emerges from the effect of the state action even when the governing legislation appears neutral on its face. The evidentiary inquiry is then relatively easy. But such cases are rare. Absent a pattern, impact alone is not determinative, and the Court must look to other evidence.

This historical background of the decision is one evidentiary source, particularly if it reveals a series of official actions taken for invidious purposes. The specific sequence of events leading up to the challenged decision also may shed some light on the decision-makers' purposes. For example, if the property involved here always had been zoned R-5 but suddenly was changed to R-3 when the town learned of MHDC's plans to erect integrated housing, we would have a far different case. Departures from the normal procedural sequence also might afford evidence that improper purposes are playing a role. Substantive departures too may be relevant, particularly if the factors usually considered important by the decision-maker strongly favor a decision contrary to the one reached.

The legislative or administrative history may be highly relevant, especially where there are contemporary statements by members of the decision making body, minutes of its meetings, or reports. In some extraordinary instances the members might be called to stand at trial to testify concerning the purposes of the official action, although even then such testimony frequently will be barred by privilege.

The foregoing summary identifies, without purporting to be exhaustive, subjects of proper inquiry in determining whether racially discriminatory intent existed. With these in mind, we now address the case before us.

[The court reviewed the findings of the lower courts which were that the zoning policies were not administered in a discriminatory manner.]

We also have reviewed the evidence. The impact of the Village's decision does arguably bear more heavily on racial minorities. Minorities comprise 18% of the Chicago area population, and 40% of the income groups said to be eligible for Lincoln Green. But there is little about the sequence of events leading up to the decision that would spark suspicion. The area around the property has been zoned R-3 since 1959, the year when Arlington Heights first adopted a zoning map. Single-family homes surround the 80-acre site, and the Village is undeniably committed to single-family homes as its dominant residential land use. The rezoning request progressed according to the usual procedures. The Plan Commission even scheduled two additional hearings, at least in part to accommodate MHDC and permit it to supplement its presentation with answerss to questions generated at the first hearing.

The statements by the Plan Commission and Village Board members, as reflected in the official minutes, focused almost exclusively on the zoning aspects of the MHDC petition, and the zoning factors on which they relied are not novel criteria in the Village's rezoning decisions. There is no reason to doubt that there has been reliance by some neighboring property owners on the maintenance of single-family zoning in the vicinity. The village originally adopted its buffer policy long before MHDC entered the picture and has applied the policy too consistently for us to infer discriminatory purpose from its application in this case. Finally, MHDC called one member of the Village Board to the stand at trial. Nothing in her testimony supports an inference of invidious purpose.

In sum, the evidence does not warrant overturning the concurrent findings of both courts below. Respondents simply failed to carry their burden of proving that discriminatory purpose was a motivating factor in the Village's decision. This conclusion ends the constitutional inquiry. The Court of Appeals' further finding that the Village's decision carried a discriminatory "ultimate effect" is without independent constitutional significance. . . . [*Reversed and remanded.*]

REVIEW QUESTIONS

1 Thornton, a manager of a department store, refused to work on Sundays. A state statute provided Sabbath observers with an absolute and unqualified right not to work on their Sabbath. Is the state law constitutional? Why, or why not?

2 Plaintiff, a promoter of theatrical productions, applied to a municipal board charged with managing a city-leased theater for a license to stage the play *Hair*. Relying on outside reports that because of nudity the production would not be in the best interests of the community, the board rejected the application. Plaintiff sought an injunction permitting it to use the auditorium. What was the result? Why?

3 A federal statute prohibits the mailing of unsolicited advertisements for contraceptives. When the manufacturer of contraceptives proposed to mail to the public unsolicited advertisements including informational pamphlets discussing family planning and venereal disease, the United States Postal Service claimed that the mailings would violate the statute. The company contended that the law violated the First Amendment. Is the law constitutional? Why, or why not?

4 A village passed a zoning ordinance which prohibited all live entertainment, including nonobscene nude dancing, in any business establishment in the village. The owners of an adult book store which contained coin-operated devices for showing adult films challenged the constitutionality of the ordinance. What was the result? Why?

5 Indiana requires government officials to post notice at the courthouse of the sale of real property for nonpayment of taxes. Notice must also be given for three weeks in a newspaper, and notice by certified mail must be given the property owner. Notice to mortgagees is not required. After the tax sale, the owner has two years in which to redeem the property. If there is no redemption, the purchaser at the tax sale may apply for a deed provided notice is once again given to the property owner. Notice need not be given the mortgagee. A mortgagee challenged a tax deed, asserting a denial of due process. Does the Indiana law violate due process? Why, or why not?

6 A restaurant was refused a liquor license because of opposition by a church located within 10 feet of the restaurant. A state statute gives churches and schools veto power over liquor licenses if a church or school is within 100 feet of the establishment seeking the license. Is the state law constitutional? Why, or why not?

7 Charges were filed against a judge by a commission on judicial conduct. The judge sought to take the deposition of a newspaper reporter in order to question him about persons he had interviewed and the information obtained. The newspaper reporter claimed a privilege of confidential communications and refused to reveal his sources. He was held in contempt. On appeal, what would be the result? Why?

8 A Florida statute required newspapers which assail the character of political candidates to afford free space to the candidate for reply. Is the law constitutional? Why, or why not?

9 The Jaycees had a policy of excluding females from membership. Minnesota adopted a law prohibiting discrimination in places of public accommodation. The law by definition applied to the Jaycees. The Jaycees contended that the state law violated the First Amendment right to freedom of association. Was the law constitutional? Why, or why not?

10 The state of Virginia followed the common law doctrine under which a husband was liable for necessaries such as food, lodging, and medical care furnished the wife, but a wife did not have a similar obligation on behalf of the husband. A hospital sought to collect from a husband for his wife's hospital bill. He contended that the doctrine violated the equal protection clause of the Fourteenth Amendment. Was he correct? Why, or why not?

11 The Federal Mine and Safety Health Act of 1977 authorizes mine inspectors to conduct unannounced inspections of mines and quarries. When an inspector appeared at the Wait Rock Quarry, the president of the Wait Co. refused to allow the inspection until the inspector obtained a warrant. Was the president's action illegal? Why?

12 P brought suit against D, a privately owned and operated public utility, for damages. D had terminated P's electric service because she failed to pay her bills. P alleged that she had not been given any notice and that there was no hearing before her service was discontinueed; therefore, she contended, there was a denial of property without due process of law contrary to the Fourteenth Amendment. D contended that its action was not "state action," and therefore the traditional requirements of due process did not need to be met. What was the result? Why?

13 Under a state workers' compensation law, a widower is denied benefits for his wife's work-related death unless he is mentally or physically incapacitated or proves dependence on his wife's earnings. However, the statute grants death benefits to a widow without such restrictions. When Wengler's wife died in a work-related accident, a claim for death benefits was denied. He contended that the statute was unconstitutional. What was the result? Why?

14 The state of Connecticut enacted a statute, under which, for tuition purposes, the status of state university students as nonresidents at time of application for admission was, in effect, conclusively and irrebuttably presumed to continue for the entire period of attendance. A suit was filed challenging the statute under the due process clause of the Fourteenth Amendment. What was the result? Why?

Chapter

10

Administrative Law

1. Introduction

As our industrial society grows and becomes more complex, the social and
economic problems that confront society multiply fantastically. Not only do
these issues increase in number, but interrelationships and conflicting social
goals complicate their solution. Also, advances in technology require special
training and experience for us to attempt an intelligent solution of problems
in many areas.

   To solve these problems our society turns to the methodology referred to
as the **administrative process**. This administrative process relies upon independent regulatory agencies, bureaus, and commissions to develop laws and
enforce them. In a real sense, these independent regulatory agencies constitute a fourth branch of government.

   The direct day-to-day legal impact on business of the rules and regulations adopted and enforced by these agencies is probably greater than the
impact of the courts or other branches of government. Administrative agencies create and enforce the majority of all laws constituting the legal environment of business. Almost every business activity is regulated to some degree
by the administrative process at either the state or federal level. Table 10-1
lists thirteen of the more important federal agencies and briefly describes
their functions. The functions of most of these agencies will be discussed in
detail in later chapters. For example, the National Labor Relations Board
(NLRB) is discussed in Chapter 18, the Environmental Protection Agency
(EPA) in Chapter 22, the Federal Trade Commission (FTC) with the materials

on antitrust in Chapter 21, and the Equal Employment Opportunity Commission (EEOC) in Chapter 17.

Although we focus on federal agencies in this chapter, keep in mind that state and local governments also have many agencies. For example, cases involving industrial accidents and injuries to employees are heard by state workers' compensation boards, and most local governments have zoning boards which make recommendations on zoning laws. State governments usually license and regulate intrastate transportation in a manner similar to the Interstate Commerce Commission's (ICC) regulation of interstate ground

TABLE 10-1   Major Federal Agencies

Name	Functions
Consumer Product Safety Commission (CPSC)	Protects the public against unreasonable risks of injury associated with consumer products
Environmental Protection Agency (EPA)	Administers all laws relating to the environment, including laws on water pollution, air pollution, solid wastes, pesticides, toxic substances, etc.
Federal Aviation Administration (FAA) (Part of the Dept. of Transportation)	Regulates civil aviation to provide safe and efficient use of airspace
Federal Communications Commission (FCC)	Regulates interstate and foreign communications by means of radio, television, wire, cable, and satellite
Federal Reserve Board (FRB)	Regulates the availability and cost of money and credit; the nation's central bank
Federal Trade Commission (FTC)	Protects the public from anticompetitive behavior and unfair and deceptive business practices; law-enforcement agency
Food and Drug Administration (FDA)	Administers laws to prohibit distribution of adulterated, misbranded, or unsafe food and drugs
Equal Employment Opportunity Commission (EEOC)	Seeks to prevent discrimination of employment based on race, color, religion, sex, or national origin and other unlawful employment practices
Interstate Commerce Commission (ICC)	Regulates interstate surface transportation
National Labor Relations Board (NLRB)	Conducts union certification elections and holds hearings on unfair labor practice complaints
Nuclear Regulatory Commission (NRC)	Licenses and regulates the nuclear energy industry
Occupational Safety and Health Administration (OSHA)	Ensures all workers a safe and healthy work environment
Securities and Exchange Commission (SEC)	Enforces the federal securities laws which regulate sale of securities to the investing public

transportation. In addition, state boards usually get rates for local utilities supplying gas and electricity. The principles and problems discussed in this chapter generally apply to the state and local administrative process as well as to the federal. It is clear that almost every aspect of our daily lives is regulated to a substantial degree by the administrative process.

2. Reasons for the Use of Administrative Agencies

Early in our history it was necessary to create a fourth branch of government possessing the powers and functions of the other three branches. There are many reasons why we needed to create administrative agencies to have a more effective government. First, the legislative branch apparently could not legislate in sufficient detail to cover all aspects of a problem. Congress cannot possibly legislate in minute detail and, as a consequence, it uses more and more general language in stating its regulatory aims and purposes. For example, Congress cannot enact a tax law that would cover every possible issue that might arise. Therefore, it delegates to the Internal Revenue Service (IRS) the power to make rules and regulations to fill in the gaps and create the necessary details to make tax laws workable. In many areas an agency has had to develop detailed rules and regulations to carry out a legislative policy.

Courts also cannot handle all disputes and controversies that may arise. For example, each year tens of thousands of industrial accidents cause injury or death to workers. If each of these industrial accidents resulted in traditional litigation, the courts simply would not have the time nor the personnel to handle the multitude of cases. Therefore, workers' compensation boards decide such claims. Likewise, most cases involving alleged discrimination in employment are turned over to agencies for decision.

Another reason many agencies are created is to refer a problem or area to experts for solution and management. The Federal Reserve Board, the Nuclear Regulatory Commission, and the Food and Drug Administration are examples of agencies with expertise beyond that of Congress or the executive branch. The development of sound policies and proper decisions in many areas requires expertise, and thus we tend to resort to administrative agencies for this expertise. Similarly, administrative agencies are often desirable because they provide needed continuity and consistency in the formulation, application, and enforcement of rules and regulations governing business.

Many governmental agencies exist to protect the public, especially from the business community. Business has often failed to regulate itself, and the lack of self-regulation has often been contrary to the public interest. For example, the failure of business to voluntarily refrain from polluting many streams and rivers as well as the air led to the creation of the Environmental Protection Agency (EPA). The sale of worthless securities to the investing public was a major force behind the creation of the Securities and Exchange Commission (SEC). The manufacture and the sale of dangerous products led to the creation of the Consumer Product Safety Commission (CPSC). It is our practice to turn to a governmental agency for assistance whenever a business or business practice may injure significant numbers of the general public. The prevailing attitude is that the government's duty is to protect the public from harm.

Agencies are often created to replace competion with regulation. When a firm is given monopoly power, it loses its freedom of contract, and a governmental body is given the power to determine the provisions of its contracts. For example, electric utility companies are usually given a monopoly in the geographic area in which they serve. A state agency such as a public service commission then has the power to set the rate structure for the utility. Similar agencies have regulated transportation and banking because of the disparity of bargaining power between the business and the public. Regulation is often a substitute for competition.

Of course, many agencies were created simply out of necessity. If we are to have a mail service, a post office is necessary. Welfare programs require government personnel to administer them. The Social Security concept dictates that there be a federal agency to determine eligibility and pay benefits. The mere existence of most government programs automatically creates a new agency or expands the functions of an existing one.

Almost every governmental agency has been created because of a recognized problem in society and from the belief that an agency may be able to help solve the problem. Governmental agencies usually have laudable goals and noble purposes, such as the elimination of discrimination, the providing of a safe and healthy workplace, or the protection of consumers. These agencies allow other branches of government to determine policy while giving those carrying out the policy a significant degree of flexibility and discretion.

3. Functions

As previously noted, administrative agencies tend to possess functions of the other three branches of government. These functions are generally described as (1) rule making, (2) adjudicating, (3) prosecuting, (4) advising, (5) supervising, and (6) investigating. These functions do not concern all administrative agencies to the same degree. Some agencies are primarily adjudicating bodies, such as industrial commissions that rule on workers' compensation claims. Others are primarily supervisory, such as the SEC, which oversees the issue and sale of investment securities. To be sure, most agencies perform all the foregoing functions to some degree in carrying out their responsibilities. Figure 10-1 explains how these functions have been delegated to these agencies.

Agencies exercise their quasi-legislative power by issuing rules and regulations that have the force and effect of law. These rules and regulations may be used to resolve an issue if they are relevant to any issue involved in an adjudicative proceeding. Before rules and regulations are adopted, interested parties are given an opportunity to be heard on the desirability and legality of the proposals.

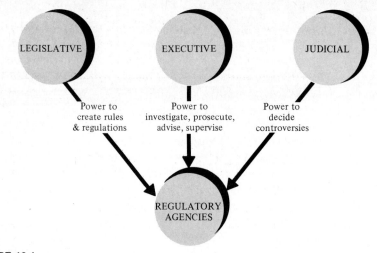

FIGURE 10-1
Administrative Agencies

Guidelines are also issued by agencies to supplement rules. Guidelines are administrative interpretations of the statutes which a commission is responsible for enforcing, and they provide guidance in evaluating the legality of certain practices. They deal with a particular practice and may cut across industry lines.

Rules and regulations may apply to a business practice irrespective of the industry involved, or they may apply only to an industry. For example, Occupational Safety and Health Administration (OSHA) rules may cover anyone using certain equipment, or a rule may be drafted so that its coverage is limited to an industry such as a drug manufacturing one.

The advisory function may be accomplished by making reports to the President or to Congress. For example, the FTC may propose new legislation to Congress, or it may inform the Attorney General of the need for judicial action due to violations of the law. Agencies also report information to the general public that should be known in the public interest, and they publish advisory opinions. For example, a commission may give advice as to whether a firm's proposed course of action might violate any of the laws which that commission administers. Advisory opinions are not as binding as formal rulings, but they do give a business an indication of the view an agency would take if the practice in question were challenged formally. The advisory opinion is a unique device generally not available in the judicial system, as courts deal only with actual cases and controversies.

One of the major functions of all agencies is to investigate activities and practices that may be illegal. Because of this investigative power, agencies can gather and compile information concerning the organization and business practices of any corporation or industry engaged in commerce to determine whether there has been a violation of any law. In exercising their investigative functions, agencies may utilize the subpoena power and require reports, examine witnesses under oath, and examine and copy documents, or they may obtain information from other governmental offices.

There is a federal law which makes it a crime to make any false or fraudulent statement in any matter within the jurisdiction of a federal agency. A person may be guilty of a violation without proof that he or she had knowledge that the matter was within the jurisdiction of a federal agency.

UNITED STATES v. YERMIAN

104 S. Ct. 2936 (1984)

POWELL, J.: . . . It is a federal crime under 18 U.S.C. § 1001 to make any false or fraudulent statement in any matter within the jurisdiction of a federal agency. To establish a violation of § 1001, the Government must prove beyond a reasonable doubt that the statement was made with knowledge of its falsity. This case presents the question whether the Government also must prove that the false statement was made with actual knowledge of federal agency jurisdiction.

Respondent Esmail Yermian was convicted . . . on three counts of making false statements in a matter within the jurisdiction of a federal agency, in violation of § 1001. The convictions were based on false statements respondent supplied his employer in connection with a Department of Defense security questionnaire. Respondent was hired in 1979 by Gulton Industries, a defense contractor. Because respondent was to have access to classified material in the course of his employment, he was required to obtain a Department of Defense Security Clearance. To this end, Gulton's security officer asked respondent to fill out a "Worksheet For Preparation of Personnel Security Questionnaire."

In response to a question on the worksheet asking whether he had ever been charged with any violation of law, respondent failed to disclose that in 1978 he had been

convicted of mail fraud, in violation of 18 U.S.C. § 1341. In describing his employment history, respondent falsely stated that he had been employed by two companies that had in fact never employed him. The Gulton security officer typed these false representations onto a form entitled "Department of Defense Personnel Security Questionnaire." Respondent reviewed the typed document for errors and signed a certification stating that his answers were "true, complete, and correct to the best of [his] knowledge" and that he understood "that any misrepresentation or false statement . . . may subject [him] to prosecution under section 1001 of the United States Criminal Code."

After witnessing respondent's signature, Gulton's security officer mailed the typed form to the Defense Industrial Security Clearance Office for processing. Government investigators subsequently discovered that respondent had submitted false statements on the security questionnaire. Confronted with this discovery, respondent acknowledged that he had responded falsely to questions regarding his criminal record and employment history. On the basis of these false statements, respondent was charged with three counts in violation of § 1001.

At trial, respondent admitted to having actual knowledge of the falsity of the statements he had submitted in response to the Department of Defense Security Questionnaire. He explained that he had made the false statements so that information on the security questionnaire would be consistent with similar fabrications he had submitted to Gulton in his employment application. Respondent's sole defense at trial was that he had no actual knowledge that his false statements would be transmitted to a federal agency.

Consistent with this defense, respondent requested a jury instruction requiring the Government to prove not only that he had actual knowledge that his statements were false at the time they were made, but also that he had actual knowledge that those statements were made in a matter within the jurisdiction of a federal agency. The District Court rejected that request and instead instructed the jury that the Government must prove that respondent "knew or should have known that the information was to be submitted to a government agency." Respondent's objection to this instruction was overruled, and the jury returned convictions on all three counts charged in the indictment.

The Court of Appeals for the Ninth Circuit reversed, holding that . . . the government must prove beyond a reasonable doubt that the defendant knew at the time he made the false statement that it was made in a matter within the jurisdiction of a federal agency. . . .

The only issue presented in this case is whether Congress intended the terms "knowingly and willfully" in § 1001 to modify the statute's jurisdictional language, thereby requiring the Government to prove that false statements were made with actual knowledge of federal agency jurisdiction. The issue thus presented is one of statutory interpretation. Accordingly, we turn first to the language of the statute.

The relevant language of § 1001 provides:

Whoever, in any matter within the jurisdiction of any department or agency of the United States knowingly and willfully . . . makes any false, fictitious or fraudulent statements or representations, . . . shall be fined. . . .

The statutory language requiring that knowingly false statements be made "in any matter within the jurisdiction of any department or agency of the United States" is a jurisdictional requirement. Its primary purpose is to identify the factor that makes the false statement an appropriate subject for federal concern. Jurisdictional language need not contain the same culpability requirement as other elements of the offense. Indeed, we have held that "the existence of the fact that confers federal jurisdiction need not be one in the mind of the actor at the time he perpetrates the act made criminal by the federal statute." Certainly in this case, the statutory language makes clear that Congress did not intend the terms "knowingly and willfully" to establish the standard of culpability for the jurisdictional element of § 1001. The jurisdictional language appears in a phrase separate from the prohibited conduct modified by the terms "knowingly and willfully." Any natural reading of § 1001, therefore, establishes that the terms "knowingly and willfully" modify only the making of "false, fictitious or fraudulent statements," and not the predicate circumstance that those statements be made in a matter within the jurisdiction of a federal agency. Once this is clear, there is no basis for requiring proof that the defendant had actual knowledge of federal agency jurisdiction. The statute contains no language suggesting any additional element of intent, such as a requirement that false statements be "knowingly made in a matter within federal agency jurisdiction," or "with the intent to deceive the federal government." On its face, therefore, § 1001 requires that the Government prove that false statements were made knowingly and willfully, and it unambiguously dispenses with any requirement that the Government also prove that those statements were made with actual knowledge of federal agency jurisdiction. Respondent's argument that the legislative history of the statute supports a contrary interpretation is unpersuasive. . . .

There is no support in the legislative history for respondent's argument that the terms "knowingly and willfully" modify the phrase "in any matter within the jurisdiction of a [federal agency]."

Both the plain language and the legislative history establish that proof of actual knowledge of federal agency jurisdiction is not required under § 1001. Accordingly, we reverse the decision of the Court of Appeals to the contrary. [*It is so ordered.*]

This power of investigation complements the exercise of the other powers such as giving advice, prosecuting violations, issuing rules, and entering cease and desist orders.

The quasi-judicial function involves both fact finding and applying law to the facts. If violations of the law are found, sanctions, such as a fine or other penalty, may be imposed. In addition, an agency may issue a cease and desist order to prevent further violations. Violations of cease and desist orders are punishable by fine.

Quasi-judicial proceedings usually begin with a complaint filed by the agency. The complaint contains allegations of fact concerning the alleged illegal conduct. After the formal complaint is served, the respondent files an answer to the charges and allegations. The case is then assigned to an administrative law judge. At the hearing, counsel for the agency and the respondent produce evidence to prove or disprove the allegations of fact in the complaint and answer. The judge rules on the admissibility of evidence, rules on motions made by counsel, and renders an initial decision that includes a statement of findings and conclusions, along with reasons for them, as to all material issues of fact and law. The ruling also includes an order the judge deems appropriate in view of the evidence in the record. This order becomes final if not challenged within thirty days after it is filed. On the appeal, the agency, board, or commission reviews the record of the initial decision and has all the powers it could have exercised if it had rendered that decision itself.

In reviewing the evidence, the agency uses the preponderance of the evidence standard rather than the clear and convincing proof or beyond a reasonable doubt standard of the criminal law. (Refer to the discussions of burden of proof in Chapter 4.)

Many cases before agencies are settled by agreement before a final decision, just as most lawsuits are settled. Such a settlement results in the issuance of a "consent order" which states that the respondent admits to the jurisdiction of the agency and waives all rights to seek a judicial review. However, a respondent does not have to admit it has been guilty of a violation of the law; but it does agree that it will not engage in the business activities which were the subject of the complaint. A consent order has the same legal force and effect as a final cease and desist order issued after a full hearing. Consent orders save considerable expense; the business involved is not found guilty, but only agrees that it will not do the act complained of in the future.

4. Organization

Administrative agencies, boards, or commissions usually have a chairperson and four other members. Laws creating the regulatory body usually specify that no more than three of the five members may belong to the same political party. Appointments require Senate confirmation, and appointees are not permitted to engage in any other business or employment during their terms. They may be removed from office by the President only for inefficiency, neglect of duty, or malfeasance in office.

Regulatory agencies require staffs to carry out their duties. While each agency has its own distinctive organizational structure to meet its responsibilities, most agencies have persons performing certain functions common to all agencies. Most agencies have quasi-legislative and quasi-judicial functions as well as the usual executive ones. Therefore, the organizational chart of an agency usually contains all the usual duties of government. Figure 10-2 shows an organizational chart outlining the usual functions and duties of most agencies.

The chairperson is designated by the President and is the presiding officer at agency meetings. The chairperson usually belongs to the same political party as the President, and while an equal in voting, is somewhat more important than the other members because of visibility and the power to appoint staff. For example, the chairman of the Federal Reserve Board is often in the news while the other members are relatively unknown.

The secretary is responsible for the minutes of agency meetings and is legal custodian of its records. The secretary usually signs orders and official correspondence and is responsible for publication of all actions in the Federal Register. The secretary also coordinates the activities of the agency with others involved in the regulatory process.

Advisory counsels are persons not employed by the agency but interested in its mission. Persons serving on councils are usually selected because of their expertise. For example, the Consumer Product Safety Commission has an advisory council in poison-prevention packaging and another on flammable fabrics. These councils provide for interaction between regulators and regulatees.

The office of general counsel is so important in many agencies that the appointment usually requires Senate approval. The general counsel is the chief law officer and legal adviser. He or she represents the agency in court and often makes the decision as to whether or not a suit will be filed, or what other remedies will be pursued. The general counsel has significant impact on policy and is often as powerful as a commissioner or board member.

FIGURE 10-2
Organizational Chart of Typical Agency, Board, or Commission

The executive director for administration is the chief operating official of an agency, and supervises usual administrative functions such as acccounting, budgeting, and personnel. Research and planning are usually supervised by the executive director, also. Since agencies spend a great deal of time lobbying with Congress, most of them have a legislative liaison which is under the executive director for administration.

Administrative law judges perform the adjudicative fact-finding functions. They hear cases of alleged law violations and apply the law to the facts. The members of the agency board or commission only hear appeals from the decisions of the administrative law judges. The judges are organizationally separate from the rest of the agency so that the quasi-judicial function will be performed impartially. Administrative law judges use prior decisions or precedent. In addition, they must follow the procedural rules of the agency as well as its policy directives.

The duties and suborganization of the director of operations vary greatly from agency to agency. These operating bureaus are assigned specific areas of activity. For example, at the EPA, one group will be concerned with clean air and another with water problems.

Regional offices investigate alleged violations of the law. In addition, they usually have an educational function. Many regional offices have their own administrative law judges and special legal counsel.

5. Influencing Agency Decisions

As discussed in section 3, agencies adopt rules and regulations as part of their quasi-legislative function and decide controversies in the performance of the quasi-judicial function. Due process of law requires that before a rule or regulation may be adopted by an agency, interested parties be given notice of the proposed rules and an opportunity to express their views on them. Statutes require that agencies give public notice of proposed rules and that they hold public hearings on them.

At public hearings, interested parties are allowed to present evidence in support of, or in opposition to, a proposed rule or regulation. As a result, the best means of influencing a quasi-legislative decision of an administrative agency is to participate in the adoption process.

What alternatives are available to a party unhappy with either rules and regulations that have been adopted or with the quasi-judicial decisions? What are the powers of courts in reviewing decisions of administrative agencies? What chance does one aggrieved by an agency's decision have in obtaining a reversal of the decision? How much deference is given to an agency's decisions? Answers to these questions must be clearly understood if one is to really appreciate the role of administrative agencies in our system. The principles and issues are somewhat different depending upon whether the court is reviewing either a rule or a regulation or a quasi-judicial decision. Judicial review of agency decisions is discussed in the sections that follow. However, it should be recognized that judicial review may sometimes be available even in cases where there was no hearing before the administrative agency. A federal statute known as the Hobbs Act grants judicial review in the Courts of Appeal from all final orders of federal administrative agencies.

In addition to the direct court-imposed constraints on agency action, more subtle ones exist. These include potential lawsuits against individual administrators, and political pressures. The subject of lawsuits against agency personnel is discussed in section 11.

Agencies are not politically responsible, in the sense that they are elected by the people. However, it is clear that they react, sometimes dramatically, to the force of public opinion. For example, in the late 1970s OSHA changed much of its emphasis and efforts from nit-picking safety concerns to major health problems because of public criticism.

Letters designed to obtain action or a change in policy to agencies from citizens may be effective. These are probably even more effective if directed to a member of Congress, who in turn asks the agency for an official response or explanation. At various times, a given agency may find itself bombarded with official congressional hearings inquiring into its activities. Such investigations may actually result in a budget cutback or change in the agency's authority. Just the threat of such a proceeding is often sufficient to cause a review of administrative policy. Finally, even without hearings, it is evident that agencies have often reevaluated policies and changed their posture due to adverse criticism from the media.

FLORIDA POWER & LIGHT CO. v. LORION
105 S. Ct. 1598 (1985)

The Hobbs Act provides that the Courts of Appeals have exclusive jurisdiction to review "all final orders" of the Nuclear Regulatory Commission. The Hobbs Act governs proceedings for the granting, suspending, or amending of any license. It provides for a hearing upon the request of any person whose interest may be affected by the proceeding.

Respondent Lorion (hereafter respondent) wrote a detailed letter to the Commission expressing fears about potential safety threats at Florida Power & Light Co.'s nuclear reactor near her home, and she urged the Commission to suspend the reactor's operating license. Following its rules (Section 2-206), the Commission treated the letter as a citizen's petition requesting the institution of administrative proceedings to suspend a license. The Commission denied the request and in so doing responded to all points made in Lorion's letter. The respondent petitioned the Court of Appeals for review. The court decided that it lacked initial subject-matter jurisdiction to review the Commission's denial of respondent's citizen petition, concluding that such a denial was not an order in a "proceeding" of the Commission because no hearing was held. It held that the review must occur in the district court.

BRENNAN, J.: . . . The issue before us is whether the Commission's denial . . . should be considered a final order initially reviewable exclusively in the Court of Appeals. . . . This issue requires us to decide whether such an order is issued in a "proceeding . . . for the granting, suspending, revoking, or amending of any license." . . . Our task therefore is to decide whether Commission denials of § 2.206 petitions are final orders of the kind Congress intended to be reviewed initially in the Court of Appeals. . . .

Because we find the statute ambiguous on its face, we seek guidance in the statutory structure, relevant legislative history, congressional purposes expressed in the choice of Hobbs Act review, and general principles respecting the proper allocation of judicial authority to review agency orders. We conclude that these sources indicate that Congress intended to provide for initial Court of

Appeals review of all final orders in licensing proceedings whether or not a hearing before the Commission occurred or could have occurred.

Relevant evidence of congressional intent in the legislative history, though fragmentary, supports this interpretation. The legislative metamorphoses of the various bills that eventually became the Atomic Energy Act of 1954 strongly suggest that Congress intended to define the scope of initial Court of Appeals review according to the subject matter of the Commission action and not according to whether the Commission held a hearing. . . .

The evolution of the judicial review provision reveals a congressional intent to provide for initial Court of Appeals review of all final orders in licensing proceedings. When Congress decided on the scope of judicial review, it did so solely by reference to the subject matter of the Commission action and not by reference to the procedural particulars of the Commission action. . . .

Whether subject-matter jurisdiction over denials of § 2.206 petitions properly lies in the district courts or the Courts of Appeals must also be considered in light of the basic congressional choice of Hobbs Act review. The Hobbs Act specifically contemplated initial Court of Appeals review of agency orders resulting from proceedings in which no hearing took place. One purpose of the Hobbs Act was to avoid the duplication of effort involved in creation of a separate record before the agency and before the district court.

Given the choice of the Hobbs Act as the primary method of review of licensing orders, we have no reason to think Congress in the Atomic Energy Act would have intended to preclude initial court of appeals review of licensing proceedings in which a Commission hearing did not occur when the Hobbs Act specifically provides for such review and the consequence of precluding it would be unnecessary duplication of effort.

The legislative history and the basic congressional choice of Hobbs Act review lead us to conclude that Congress intended to vest in the Courts of Appeals initial subject-matter jurisdiction over challenges to Commission denials of § 2.206 petitions. An examination of the consequences that would follow upon adoption of the contrary rule proposed by the Court of Appeals in this case confirms the soundness of this conclusion. . . .

If initial review in the Court of Appeals hinged on whether a hearing before the agency *actually occurred,* then some licensing proceedings will be reviewed in the Courts of Appeals while others will not depending on whether a hearing is requested.

This . . . would result in some final orders in licensing proceedings receiving two layers of judicial review and some receiving only one. Absent a far clearer expression of congressional intent, we are unwilling to read the Act as creating such a seemingly irrational bifurcated system.

In these cases, the indications of legislative intent we have been able to discern suggest that Congress intended to locate initial subject matter jurisdiction in the Courts of Appeals. This result is in harmony with Congress' choice of Hobbs Act review for Commission licensing proceedings and is consistent with basic principles respecting the allocation of judicial review of agency action. We therefore hold that 42 U.S.C. § 2239 vests in the Courts of Appeals initial subject-matter jurisdiction over Commission orders denying § 2.206 citizen petitions.

Whether initial subject-matter jurisdiction lies initially in the Courts of Appeals must of course be governed by the intent of Congress and not by any views we may have about sound policy. [*Reversed and remanded.*]

JUDICIAL REVIEW OF AGENCY DECISIONS

6. Introduction

Each branch of government has some control over the administrative process. The executive branch normally appoints the top officials of an agency with the advice and consent of the legislative branch. In addition, the executive branch makes budget recommendations to the legislature and has veto power over its statutes. The legislature can review and control administrative activity by abolishing the agency, enacting specific legislation contrary to rules adopted by the agency, more explicitly defining limitations on the agency's activities, providing additional procedural requirements for the agency's adjudications, or limiting appropriations of funds to the agency.

The courts also check on administrative bodies by using judicial review of their actions. Just as laws enacted by the legislature must be within its power as established by the Constitution or be void, rules and regulations promulgated by an administrative body must be within the confines of its grant of power from the legislature, or a court will find them void. However, once having determined that an act of the legislature is constitutional or a rule of an agency is authorized, the courts will not inquire into its wisdom or effectiveness. An unwise or ineffectual law may be corrected by political action at the polls; an unwise rule or regulation adopted by an agency may be corrected by the legislature that gave the agency power to make the rule in the first place. In the sections which follow, court functions in reviewing agency activities will be discussed in more detail. Keep in mind that the principles and issues differ somewhat depending upon whether the court reviews either a rule or regulation or a quasi-judicial decision.

7. Judicial Review of Agency Rule Making

The rule-making function in the administrative process is essentially legislative in character. Administrative agencies are usually created by enactments of the legislature in which the legislative branch is generally said to delegate certain responsibility or quasi-legislative power to the agency. Some courts have taken the view that the legislature cannot delegate its lawmaking function at all, but have concluded that authorizing an administrative agency to "fill in the details" of legislation is valid as not being an exercise of the legislative power. Other courts have stated that the legislature can delegate part of its function to an agency as long as certain constitutional safeguards are met. The difference is largely a matter of semantics.

There are two basic issues in litigation challenging the validity of a rule made by an administrative agency. First, is the delegation valid, and second, has the agency exceeded its authority? Delegations of quasi-legislative authority to administrative agencies are subject to two constitutional limitations. First, a delegation must be definite, or it will violate due process. Definiteness means that the delegation must be set forth with sufficient clarity so that all concerned, and especially reviewing courts, will be able to ascertain the extent of the agency's authority. For many reasons, broad language has been held sufficiently definite to meet this test. For example, the term "unfair methods of competition" has been held to be sufficiently definite to meet the requirements of due process.

A very similar limitation to the definiteness requirement on the exercise of quasi-legislative authority is the requirement that the power of administrative agencies to make rules be limited. The limited-power concept means that delegations must contain standards by which a court can determine whether the limitations have been exceeded. The standards set must meet certain minimum requirements before the agency in question is validly empowered to act in a certain area, and the rules promulgated by the agency must follow these standards and limitations imposed by the law establishing the agency, if they are to be upheld. Also, procedural safeguards must exist to control arbitrary administrative action and any administrative abuse of discretionary power.

Just as broad language has been approved as being sufficiently definite for a delegation to be valid under the due process clause, so also have broad standards been approved to meet the limited-power test since the 1930s. Today, it is generally agreed that delegations of authority to make rules may be in very broad language. For example, the delegation of authority to make such rules as the "public interest, convenience and necessity" may require is subject to a valid standard. Delegations that include criteria that are as concrete as the field and factors involved permit will be held valid, since the law now recognizes that practical considerations often make definite standards impossible. In fact, some cases have held that on a challenge of unconstitutional delegation of legislative authority, the court's inquiry should focus on procedural safeguards rather than on statutory standards.

Although it is highly unlikely that a court would hold a delegation invalid because of indefiniteness or lack of standards, courts do find that agencies have exceeded their authority from time to time. Delegation of quasi-legislative power usually involves grants of substantial discretion to the board or agency involved. It must be kept in mind that the delegation of discretion is to the agency and not the courts. Therefore, courts cannot interfere with the discretion given to the agency and cannot substitute their judgment for that of the agency. Courts will hold that an agency has exceeded its authority if an analysis of legislative intent confirms the view that the agency has gone beyond that intent.

FCC v. MIDWEST VIDEO CORP.
99 S. Ct. 1435 (1979)

The Federal Communications Commission (FCC) promulgated rules requiring cable television systems that have 3,500 or more subscribers and carry broadcast signals to develop, at a minimum, a twenty-channel capacity by 1986, to make four channels available for access by public, educational, local governmental, and leased access users, and to furnish equipment and facilities for access purposes. Under the rules, cable operators are deprived of all discretion regarding who may exploit their access channels and what may be transmitted over such channels. During the rule-making proceedings, the FCC rejected a challenge to the rules on jurisdictional grounds. It was contended that the rules amounted to an attempt to impose common-carrier obligations on cable operators, and thus ran counter to the command of Section 3(h) of the Communications Act of 1934 that "a person engaged in . . . broadcasting shall not . . . be deemed a common carrier." The FCC rejected the challenge, maintaining that the rules would promote "the achievement of long-standing communications regulatory objectives by increasing outlets for local self-expression and augmenting the public's choice of programs."

The Court of Appeals held that the FCC had exceeded its jurisdiction, and the FCC was granted a writ of certiorari.

WHITE, J.: . . . The Commission derives its regulatory authority from the Communications Act of 1934. The Act preceded the advent of cable television and understandably does not expressly provide for the regulation of that medium. But it is clear that Congress meant to confer "broad authority" on the Commission, so as "to maintain, through appropriate administrative control, a grip on the dynamic aspects of radio transmission." To that end, Congress subjected to regulation "all interstate and foreign communication by wire or radio." We (have previously) construed Section 2(a) as conferring on the Commission a circumscribed range of power to regulate cable television. The question now before us is whether the Act authorizes the capacity and access regulations that are here under challenge. . . . [The court then re-

viewed two prior CATV cases known as *Southwestern Cable Co.* and *Midwest Video.*]

Because its access and capacity rules promote the long-established regulatory goals of maximization of outlets for local expression and diversification of programming—the Commission maintains that it plainly had jurisdiction to promulgate them. Respondents, in opposition, view the access regulations as an intrusion on cable system operations that is qualitatively different from the impact of the rule upheld in *Midwest Video.* Specifically, it is urged that by requiring the allocation of access channels to categories of users specified by the regulations and by depriving the cable operator of the power to select individual users or to control the programming on such channels, the regulations wrest a considerable degree of editorial control from the cable operator and in effect compel the cable system to provide a kind of common-carrier service. Respondents contend, therefore, that the regulations are not only qualitatively different from those heretofore approved by the courts but also contravene statutory limitations designed to safeguard the journalistic freedom of broadcasters, particularly the command of Section 3(h) of the Act that "a person engaged in . . . broadcasting shall not . . . be deemed a common carrier."

We agree with respondents that recognition of agency jurisdiction to promulgate the access rules would require an extension of this Court's prior decisions.

With its access rules, the Commission has transferred control of the content of access cable channels from cable operators to members of the public who wish to communicate by the cable medium. Effectively, the Commission has relegated cable systems, pro tanto, to common-carrier status. A common-carrier service in the communications context is one that "makes a public offering to provide communications facilities whereby all members of the public who choose to employ such facilities may communicate or transmit intelligence of their own design and choosing." A common carrier does not "make individualized decisions, in particular cases, whether and on what terms to deal."

The access ruless plainly impose common-carrier obligations on cable operators. Under the rules, cable systems are required to hold out dedicated channels on a first-come, nondiscriminatory basis. Operators are prohibited from determining or influencing the content of access programming. And the rules delimit what operators may charge for access and use of equipment. Indeed, in its early consideration of access obligations—whereby "CATV operators would furnish studio facilities and technical assistance but have no control over program content except as may be required by the Commission's rules and applicable law"—the Commission acknowledged that the result would be the operation of cable systems "as common carriers on some channels." In its 1976 Order, the Commission did not directly deny that its access requirements compelled common carriage, and it has conceded before this Court that the rules "can be viewed as a limited form of common carriage-type obligation." But the Commission continues to insist that this characterization of the obligation imposed by the rules is immaterial to the question of its power to issue them; its authority to promulgate the rules is assured, in the Commission's view, so long as the rules promote statutory objectives.

Congress, however, did not regard the character of regulatory obligations as irrelevant to the determination of whether they might permissibly be imposed in the context of broadcasting itself. The Commission is directed explicitly by Section 3(h) of the Act not to treat persons engaged in broadcasting as common carriers. . . . The language of Section 3(h), . . . consistently with the policy of the Act to preserve editorial control of programming in the licensee, forecloses any dis-

cretion in the Commission to impose access requirements amounting to common-carrier obligations on broadcast systems. The provision's background manifests a congressional belief that the intrusion worked by such regulation on the journalistic integrity of broadcasters would overshadow any benefits associated with the resulting public access. It is difficult to deny, then, that forcing broadcasters to develop a "nondiscriminatory system for controlling access . . . is precisely what Congress intended to avoid through Section 3(h) of the Act." . . .

In determining then, whether the Commission's assertion of jurisdiction is "reasonably ancillary to the effective performance of its responsibililties for the regulation of television broadcasting," we are unable to ignore Congress' stern disapproval—evidenced in Section 3(h)—of negation of the editorial discretion otherwise enjoyed by broadcasters and cable operators alike. Though the lack of congressional guidance has in the past led us to defer—albeit cautiously—to the Commission's judgment regarding the scope of its authority, here there are strong indications that agency flexibility was to be sharply delimited. . . .

In the light of the hesitancy with which Congress approached the access issue in the broadcast area, and in view of its outright rejection of a broad right of public access on a common-carrier basis, we are constrained to hold that the Commission exceeded those limits in promulgating its access rules. The Commission may not regulate cable systems as common carriers, just as it may not impose such obligations on television broadcasters. We think authority to compel cable operators to provide common carriage of public originated transmissions must come specifically from Congress. [*Affirmed.*]

8. Review of Adjudications: Procedural Aspects

The exercise of quasi-judicial functions by administrative agencies is very common. Critics say that an agency acts as prosecutor, finder of facts, and judge. However, similar to the current attitude on delegation of legislative power, judicial power may be generally granted to an administrative agency if the power is restricted by procedural safeguards preventing its abuse. The right to a jury trial does not exist in either formal or informal hearings conducted by administrative bodies.

ATLAS ROOFING COMPANY INC. v. OCCUPATIONAL SAFETY, ETC.

97 S. Ct. 1261 (1977)

In 1970, Congress enacted the Occupational Safety and Health Act (OSHA). The law was designed to protect employees from death and injury due to unsafe working conditions. The law provided two new administrative remedies. It allows the federal government proceeding administratively to (1) obtain abatement orders requiring employers to correct unsafe working conditions, and (2) impose civil penalties on any employer maintaining unsafe working conditions. If an employer contests a penalty or abatement order, an evidentiary hearing is then held before an administrative law judge of the Occupational Safety Health Review Commission (Commission), who is empowered to affirm, modify, or vacate the proposed abatement order and penalty. The judge's decision is subject to review by the full Commission. If such review is granted, the Commission's subsequent order directing abatement and payment of a penalty becomes final unless the employer petitions for judicial review in the appropriate Court of Appeals. On appeal, the Commission's findings of fact, if supported by substantial evidence, are conclusive. If the employer fails to pay the

assessed penalty, the Secretary may commence a collection action in a federal district court in which neither the fact of the violation nor the propriety of the penalty assessed may be retried.

In this case, abatement orders were issued and penalties proposed against petitioners for violations of safety standards. The case proceeded through the various review procedures, with the Commission affirming the violations and penalties. Petitioners sought judicial review challenging the constitutionality of OSHA's enforcement procedures, contending that the procedures violated the Seventh Amendment. The Court of Appeals affirmed, and the Supreme Court granted certiorari.

WHITE, J. . . . The issue in this case is whether, consistent with the Seventh Amendment, Congress may create a new cause of action in the Government for civil penalties enforceable in an administrative agency where there is no jury trial. . . .

The Seventh Amendment provides that "in Suits at common law, where the value in controversy shall exceed twenty dollars, the right of trial by jury shall be preserved. . . ." The phrase "suits at common law" has been construed to refer to cases tried prior to the adoption of the Seventh Amendment in courts of law in which jury trial was customary as distinguished from courts of equity or admiralty in which jury trial was not. Petitioners claim that a suit in federal court by the Government for civil penalties for violation of a statute is a suit for a money judgment which is classically a suit at common law and that the defendant therefore has a Seventh Amendment right to a jury determination of all issues of fact in such a case. Petitioners then claim that to permit Congress to assign the function of adjudicating the Government's rights to civil penalties for violation of the statute to a different forum—an administrative agency in which no jury is available— would be to permit Congress to deprive a defendant of his Seventh Amendmennt jury right. We disagree. At least in cases in which "public rights" are being litigated—e.g., cases in which the Government sues in its sovereign capacity to enforce public rights created by statutes within the power of Congress to enact—the Seventh Amendment does not prohibit Congress from assigning the factfinding function and initial adjudication to an administrative forum with which the jury would be incompatible.

Congress has often created new statutory obligations, provided for civil penalties for their violation, and committed exclusively to an administrative agency the function of deciding whether a violation has in fact occurred. These statutory schemes have been sustained by this Court, albeit often without express reference to the Seventh Amendment. Thus taxes may constitutionally be assessed and collected together with penalties, with the relevant facts in some instances being adjudicated only by an administrative agency. . . . Similarly, Congress has entrusted to an administrative agency the task of adjudicating violations of the customs and immigration laws and assessing penalties based thereon.

In *NLRB v. Jones & Laughlin Steel Corp.*, 301 U.S. 1, (1937), the Court squarely addressed the Seventh Amendment issue involved when Congress commits the factfinding function under a new statute to an administrative tribunal. Under the Labor Act, Congress had committed to the NLRB, in a proceeding brought by its litigating arm, the task of deciding whether an unfair labor practice had been committed and of ordering back pay where appropriate. The Court stated:

The instant case is not a suit at common law or in the nature of a such a suit. The proceeding is one unknown to the common law. It is a statutory proceeding. Reinstatement of the employee and payment for time lost are requirements administratively imposed for violation of the statute and are remedies appropriate to its enforcement. The contention under the Seventh Amendment is without merit. . . .

. . . In sum, it is asserted that when Congress creates new statutory "public rights," it may assign their adjudication to an administrative agency with which a jury trial would be incompatible, without violating the Seventh Amendment's injunction that jury trial is to be "preserved" in "suits at common law." Congress is not required by the Seventh Amendment to choke the already crowded federal courts with new types of litigation nor prevented from committing some new types of litigation to administrative agencies with special competence in the relevant field. This is the case even if the Seventh Amendment would have required a jury where the adjudication of those rights is assigned instead to a federal court of law instead of an administrative agency . . .

It is apparent from the history of the jury trial in civil matters that factfinding which is the essential function of the jury in civil cases, was never the exclusive province of the jury under either the English or American legal system at the time of the adoption of the Seventh Amendment; and the question whether a fact would be found by a jury turned to a considerable degree on the nature of the forum in which a litigant found himself. Critical factfinding was performed without juries in suits in equity, and there were not juries in admiralty, neither was there in the military justice system. The jury was the factfinding mode in most suits in the common law courts, but it was not exclusively so; condemnation was a suit at common law but constitutionally could be tried without a jury. Many civil as well as criminal proceedings at common law were without a jury. The question whether a particular case was to be tried in a court of equity—without a jury—or a court of law—with a jury—did not depend on whether the suit involved factfinding or on the nature of facts to be found. Factfinding could be a critical matter either at law or in equity. Rather, as a general rule, the decision turned on whether courts of law supplied a cause of action and an adequate remedy to the litigant. If it did, then the case would be tried in a court of law before a jury. Otherwise the case would be tried in a court of equity sitting without a jury. Thus, suits for damages for breach of contract, for example, were suits at common law with the issues of the making of the contract and its breach to be decided by a jury; but specific performance was a remedy unavailable in a court of law and where such relief was sought the case would be tried in a court of equity with the facts as to making and breach to be ascertained by the court.

The Seventh Amendment was declaratory of the existing law, for it required only that jury trial in suits at common law was to be "preserved." It thus did not purport to require a jury trial where none was required before. Moreover, it did not seek to change the factfinding mode in equity or admiralty nor to freeze equity jurisdiction as it existed in 1789, preventing it from developing new remedies where those available in courts of law were inadequate.

The point is that the Seventh Amendment was never intended to establish the jury as the exclusive mechanism for factfinding in civil cases. It took the existing legal order as it found it, and there is little or no basis for concluding that the Amendment should now be interpreted to provide an impenetrable barrier to administrative factfinding under otherwise valid federal regulatory statutes. We cannot conclude that the Amendment rendered Congress powerless—when it concluded that remedies available in courts of law were inadequate to cope with a problem within Congress' power to regulate—to create new public rights and remedies by statute and commit their enforcement, if it chose, to a tribunal other than a court of law—such as an administrative agency—in which facts are not found by juries. Indeed, the "settled judicial construction" was to the contrary "from the beginning."

Thus, history and our cases support the proposition that the right to a jury trial turns not solely on the nature of the issue to be resolved, but also on the forum in which it is to be resolved. Congress found the common law and other existing remedies for work injuries resulting from unsafe working conditions to be inadequate to protect the Nation's working men and women. It created a new cause of action, and remedies therefor, unknown to the common law, and placed their enforcement in a tribunal supplying speedy and expert resolutions for the issued involved. The Seventh Amendment is no bar to the creation of new rights or to their enforcement outside the regular courts of law. [*Affirmed.*]

Judicial review of agencies' adjudications by its very nature is quite limited. Legislatures have delegated authority to agencies because of their expertise, knowledge, and so on, and courts usually exercise restraint and resolve doubtful issues in favor of an agency. For example, courts reviewing administrative interpretations of law do not always decide questions of law for themselves. It is not unusual for a court to accept an administrative interpretation of law as final if it in the record is warranted and has a rational basis in law. Administrative agencies are frequently called upon to interpret the statute governing an agency, and an agency's construction is persuasive to courts. However, courts frequently replace administrative holdings with their own interpretations of law.

Administrative agencies develop their own rules of procedure unless mandated otherwise by an act of the legislature. These procedures are far less formal than judicial procedures, because one of the functions of the administrative process is to decide issues expeditiously. To proceed expeditiously usually means, for example, that administrative agencies are not restricted by the strict rules of evidence used by courts. Such agencies cannot ignore all rules, but they can use some leeway. They cannot, for example, refuse to permit any cross-examination or unduly limit it. Because an agency "is frequently the accuser, the prosecutor, the judge and the jury," it must remain alert to observe accepted standards of fairness. Reviewing courts are, therefore, alert to ensure that the true substance of a fair hearing is not denied to a party to an administrative hearing. However, the inordinate delay common in administrative hearings is a legitimate cause of public concern.

In reviewing the procedures of administrative agencies, courts are not empowered to substitute their judgment or their own procedures for those of the agency. Judicial responsibility is limited to ensuring consistency with statutes and compliance with the demands of the Constitution for a fair hearing. The latter is based on the due process clause. Due process usually requires a hearing by an agency, but on occasion sanctions may be imposed prior to the hearing.

The principle that federal administrative agencies should be free to fashion their own rules of procedure and pursue methods of inquiry permitting them to discharge their duties grows out of the view that administrative agencies and administrators will be familiar with the industries they regulate. Thus, they will be in a better position than courts or legislative bodies to design procedural rules adapted to the peculiarities of the industry and the tasks of the agency involved.

Important procedural aspects of the broad area of judicial review of administrative action are those of standing to sue and exhaustion of remedies. Standing to sue involves two important issues. First, is the action or decision of the agency subject to judicial review? Not all administrative decisions are reviewable. The Federal Administrative Procedure Act provides for judicial review except where "(1) statutes preclude judicial review or (2) agency action is committed to agency discretion by law." Few statutes actually preclude judicial review, and preclusion of judicial review by inference is rare. It is most likely to occur when an agency decides not to undertake action to enforce a statute. For example, prison inmates ask the Food and Drug Administration (FDA) to ban the use of lethal injections to carry out the death penalty. It refused to do so. The Supreme Court held that this decision of the FDA was not subject to judicial review. Congress may commit an issue only to an agency's discretion by failing to include a meaningful standard against which courts may judge the agency's exercise of discretion.

The second issue is whether or not the plaintiff in any particular case is able to obtain judicial review. It is generally required that the plaintiff be "an aggrieved party" before he or she is allowed judicial review. This subject was discussed as a part of Chapter 4 on page 74. It is clear that persons who may suffer economic loss due to an agency's action have standing to sue. Recent decisions have expanded the group of persons with standing to sue to include those who have noneconomic interests such as First Amendment rights. The second procedural aspect, exhaustion of remedies, is discussed in the next section.

9. Exhaustion of Remedies

The doctrine of *exhaustion of remedies* recognizes that in reviewing administrative decisions, courts should not decide in advance of a hearing that it will not be conducted fairly by the agency in question. In general (although there are exceptions), courts refuse to review administrative actions until a complaining party has exhausted all the administrative remedies and procedures available to him or her for redress. Judicial review is only available for final actions by an agency. Preliminary orders such as a decision to file a complaint are not reviewable. Otherwise, the administrative system would be denied important opportunities to make a factual record, to exercise its discretion, or to apply its expertise in its decision making. Also, exhaustion allows an agency to discover and correct its own errors, and thus it helps to dispense with any reason for judicial review. Exhaustion clearly should be required in those cases involving an area of the agency's expertise or specialization; it should require no unusual expense. It should also be required when the administrative remedy is just as likely as the judicial one to provide appropriate relief. The doctrine of exhaustion of remedies avoids the premature interruption of the administrative process. In general, it is probably more efficient for that purpose to go forward without interruption.

However, when there is nothing to be gained from the exhaustion of administrative remedies, and when the harm from the continued existence of the administrative ruling is great, the courts have not been reluctant to discard this doctrine. This is especially true when very fundamental constitutional guarantees such as freedom of speech or press are involved or when the administrative remedy is likely to be inadequate. Also, probably no court would insist upon exhaustion when the agency is clearly acting beyond its jurisdiction (because its action is not authorized by statute, or the statute authorizing it is unconstitutional), or where it would result in irreparable injury (such as great expense) to the petitioner. Finally, an exception to the doctrine is fraud.

SMITH v. JONES
474 N.E.2d 415 (Ill. App. 3 Dist. 1985)

STOUDER, J.: This suit was brought by the plaintiffs-appellants, John Smith and Dale Livingood, against the defendants-appellees, Michael Jones, Director of the Illinois State Lottery, and the Illinois State Lottery. The Circuit Court of Peoria County granted defendants' motion to dismiss plaintiffs' . . . complaint which sought declaratory and injunctive relief in connection with the alleged breach of contract and fraud of the defendants in the sale of Illinois State Lottery tickets.

. . . On June 18, 1983, each plaintiff purchased tickets for the "Lotto" drawing to be held that day. Each plaintiff correctly picked the winning numbers as did seventy-six other people. The defendants offered to pay each plaintiff $9,544.50 representing 1/78 of $744,471. Plaintiffs allege in substance that the defendants represented there would be a minimum grand prize each week of at least $1,000,000 to be paid to the winner or divided among the winners. The drawing in issue was actually alleged to be worth $1,750,000 because there had been no winner the previous week. The plaintiffs filed this complaint and petition for a temporary restraining order alleging breach of contract and fraud by the defendants for failure to pay each plaintiff 1/78 of $1,750,000. It is the representation concerning dividing the grand prize among multiple winners which the plaintiffs allege is fraudulent.

The defendants' motion to dismiss plaintiffs' cause of action . . . (was) granted . . . based solely on plaintiffs' failure to exhaust their administrative remedies. . . .

Section 7.3 of the Illinois Lottery Law provides for hearings upon complaints charging violations of this Act or of regulations thereunder. Section 25 of the Act allows any party adversely affected by a final order or determination to seek judicial review pursuant to the Administrative Review Law. The general rule is judicial review of an administrative decision may not be had until the aggrieved party has exhausted all administrative remedies. The purpose underlying the doctrine of exhaustion of administrative remedies is to allow administrative agencies to correct their own errors, clarify policies, and reconcile conflicts before resorting to judicial relief. In this manner, the aggrieved party may succeed before the agency, rendering judicial review unnecessary. An exception to the doctrine of exhaustion of administrative remedies is fraud.

A review of the record in the present case discloses that the gist of plaintiffs' cause of action is generally grounded in fraud. We find, therefore, that the theory of plaintiffs' failure to exhaust administrative remedies relied on by the trial court is erroneous. . . . [*Reversed and remanded.*]

A doctrine similar to exhaustion of remedies is known as *primary jurisdiction.* "Exhaustion" applies where a claim is cognizable in the first instance by an administrative agency alone. "Primary jurisdiction" applies where a claim is originally cognizable in the courts. It comes into play whenever enforcement of the claim requires the resolution of issues which, under a regulatory scheme, have been placed within the special competence of an administrative body. In such a case, the judicial process is suspended pending referral of such issues to the administrative body for its views. Primary jurisdiction ensures uniformity and consistency in dealing with matters entrusted to an administrative body. The doctrine is invoked when referral to the agency is preferable because of its specialized knowledge or expertise in dealing with the matter in controversy. Statutes such as those guaranteeing equal employment opportunity that create a private remedy for dollar damages sometimes require resort to an administrative agency as a condition precedent to filing suit. Some of these are federal statutes which require referral to state agencies. In these cases, referral must occur, but the right to sue is not limited by the results of the administrative decision.

10. Review of Agency's Determination of Facts

When it reviews the findings of fact made by an administrative body, a court presumes them to be correct. A court of review examines the evidence by analyzing the record of the agency's proceedings. It upholds the agency's findings and conclusions on questions of fact if they are supported by substantial evidence in the record. In other words, the record must contain material evidence from which a reasonable person might reach the same conclusion as did the agency. If substantial evidence in support of the decision is present, the court will not disturb the agency's findings, even though the court itself might have reached a different conclusion on the basis of other conflicting evidence also in the record. The determination of credibility of the witnesses who testify in quasi-judicial proceedings is for the agency to determine and not the courts.

Thus, it is apparent that on review courts do not (1) reweigh the evidence, (2) make independent determinations of fact, and (3) substitute their view of the evidence for that of the agency. However, courts do determine if there is substantial evidence to support the action taken. But in their examination of the evidence, all that is required is evidence sufficient to convince a reasonable mind to a fair degree of certainty. Thus, substantial evidence is that which a reasonable mind might accept as adequate to support the conclusion. When a case involves the special expertise of the agency, even more deference is paid to the agency's decisions.

BALTIMORE GAS & ELEC. v. NATURAL RES. DEF. COUNCIL
103 S. Ct. 2246 (1983)

The National Environmental Policy Act (NEPA) requires federal agencies to consider the environmental impact of any major

federal action. The Nuclear Regulatory Commission (NRC) adopted a series of generic rules relating to the environmental effect of a nuclear power plant's fuel cycle. In these rules, the NRC decided that licensing boards should assume that the permanent storage of certain nuclear wastes would have no significant environmental impact (the so-called zero-release assumption) and thus should not affect the decision whether or not to license a particular nuclear power plant. The NRC had computed the resources used by nuclear power plants (front-end activities) and the effluents released by them (back-end activities) in making the zero-release assumption. These computations were set forth in a table, Table S-3, adopted by the NRC.

The Court of Appeals held that the rules were arbitrary and capricious and inconsistent with NEPA because the NRC had not factored the consideration of uncertainties surrounding the zero-release assumption into the licensing process in such a manner that the uncertainties could potentially affect the outcome of any decision to license a plant.

O'CONNOR, J.: . . . We are acutely aware that the extent to which this Nation should rely on nuclear power as a source of energy is an important and sensitive issue. Much of the debate focuses on whether development of nuclear generation facilities should proceed in the face of uncertainties about their long-term effects on the environment. Resolution of these fundamental policy questions lies, however, with Congress and the agencies to which Congress has delegated authority, as well as with state legislatures and, ultimately, the populace as a whole. Congress has assigned the courts only the limited, albeit important, task of reviewing agency action to determine whether the agency conformed with controlling statutes. . . .

[A]dministrative decisions should be set aside in this context, as in every other, only for substantial procedural or substantive reasons as mandated by statute—not simply because the court is unhappy with the result reached.

The controlling statute at issue here is the National Environmental Policy Act. NEPA has twin aims. First, it places upon an agency the obligation to consider every significant aspect of the environmental impact of a proposed action. Second, it ensures that the agency will inform the public that it has indeed considered environmental concerns in its decisionmaking process. Congress in enacting NEPA, however, did not require agencies to elevate environmental concerns over other appropriate considerations. Rather, it required only that the agency take a "hard look" at the environmental consequences before taking a major action. The role of the courts is simply to ensure that the agency has adequately considered and disclosed the environmental impact of its actions and that its decision is not arbitrary or capricious.

In its Table S-3 Rule here, the Commission has determined that the probabilities favor the zero-release assumption, because the Nation is likely to develop methods to store the wastes with no leakage to the environment. . . . The Commission recognized, however, that the geological, chemical, physical and other data it relied on in making this prediction were based, in part, on assumptions which involve substantial uncertainties. Again, no one suggests that the uncertainties are trivial or the potential effects insignificant if time proves the zero-release assumption to have been seriously wrong. After confronting the issue, though, the Commission has determined that the uncertainties concerning the development of nuclear waste storage facilities are not sufficient to affect the outcome of any individual licensing decision.

It is clear that the Commission, in making this determination, has made the careful consideration and disclosure required by NEPA. The sheer volume of proceedings before the Commission is impressive. Of far greater importance, the Commission's Statement of Consideration announcing the final Table S-3 Rule shows that it has digested this mass of material and disclosed all substantial risks. The Statement summarizes the major uncertainty of long-term storage in bedded-salt repositories, which is that water could inflitrate the repository as a result of such diverse factors as geologic faulting, a meteor strike, or accidental or deliberate intrusion by man. The Commission noted that the probability of intrusion was small, and that the plasticity of salt would tend to heal some types of intrusions. The Commission also found the evidence "tentative but favorable" that an appropriate site could be found. . . .

Given this record and the Commission's statement, it simply cannot be said that the Commission ignored or failed to disclose the uncertainties surrounding its zero-release assumption.

Congress did not enact NEPA, of course, so that an agency would contemplate the environmental impact of an action as an abstract exercise. Rather, Congress intended that the "hard look" be incorporated as part of the agency's process of deciding whether to pursue a particular federal action. . . .

. . . NEPA does not require agencies to adopt any particular internal decisionmaking structure. Here, the agency has chosen to evaluate generically the environmental impact of the fuel cycle and inform individual licensing boards, through the Table S-3 rule, of its evaluation. The generic method chosen by the agency is clearly an appropriate method of conducting the hard loook required by NEPA. The environmental effects of much of the fuel cycle are not plant specific, for any plant, regardless of its particular attributes, will create additional wastes that must be stored in a common long-term repository. Administrative efficiency and consistency of decision are both furthered by a generic determination of these effects without needless repetition of the litigation in individual proceedings, which are subject to review by the Commission in any event.

The Court of Appeals . . . concluded that the Commission . . . violated NEPA by failing to factor the uncertainty surrounding long-term storage into Table S-3 and precluding individual licensing decisionmakers from considering it.

The Commission's decision to affix a zero value to the environmental impact of long-term storage would violate NEPA, however, only if the Commission acted arbitrarily and capriciously in deciding generically that the uncertainty was insufficient to affect any individual licensing decision. In assessing whether the Commission's decision is arbitrary and capricious, it is crucial to place the zero-release assumption in context. Three factors are particularly important. First is the Commission's repeated emphasis that the zero-risk assumption—and, indeed, all of the Table S-3 rule—was made for a limited purpose. . . .

Second, the Commission emphasized that the zero-release assumption is but a single figure in an entire Table, which the Commission expressly designed as a risk-averse estimate of the environmental impact of the fuel cycle. . . . A reviewing court should not magnify a single line item beyond its significance as only part of a larger Table.

Third, a reviewing court must remember that the Commission is making predictions, within its area of special expertise, at the frontiers of science. When examining this kind of scientific determination, as opposed to simple findings of fact, a reviewing court must generally be at its most deferential.

With these three guides in mind, we find the Commission's zero-release assumption to be within the bounds of reasoned decisionmaking required by the APA. . . .

In sum, we think that the zero-release assumption—a policy judgment concerning one line in a conservative Table designed for the limited purpose of individual licensing decisons—is within the bounds of reasoned decisionmaking. It is not our task to determine what decision we, as Commissioners, would have reached. Our only task is to de-termine whether the Commission has consid-ered the relevant factors and articulated a rational connection between the facts found and the choice made. Under this standard, we think the Commission's zero-release as-sumption, within the context of Table S-3 as a whole, was not arbitrary and capricious. . . . [*Reversed.*]

The findings of an administrative body are not set aside unless the record clearly precludes the decision of the administrative body. The decision of an agency will be affirmed even if the court believes it to be erroneous, if a reasonable person could have reached the conclusion stated. It is the function of an agency to pass upon the weight to be accorded to the evidence and to make the choice, if necessary, between varying inferences which might be drawn therefrom. The possibility of drawing either of two inconsistent in-ferences from the evidence does not prevent an agency from drawing one of them. Courts, however, do not always agree with the administrative determin-ation, and sometimes they set aside a finding because it is not supported by substantial evidence.

For the courts to exercise their function of limited review, an agency must provide a record which sets forth the reasons and basis for its decision. If this record shows that the agency did not examine all relevant data and that it ignored issues before it, a court may set aside the agency's decision because such a decision is arbitrary and capricious. Agencies cannot assume their decisions. They must be based on evidence, and the record must support the decision.

11. Agency Personnel and Damage Suits

In a litigious society such as ours, it is not surprising that often administrators are sued for dollar damages by parties subject to administrative rules, regula-tions, and decisions. Such suits may involve allegations that government officials have violated the constitutional rights of citizens. For example, it has been held that a violation of the Fourth Amendment by federal agents gives rise to a cause of action for damages because of the unconstitutional conduct. However, it should be recognized that government officials are not liable for mere mistakes in judgment, whether the mistake is one of fact or one of law. Damage suits cannot be used as a means to review an agency's decisions.

Government officials faced with damage suits usually assert the defense of **immunity** or contend that they cannot be sued. The courts have recognized that in certain situations some government officials are absolutely immune from suit. They have no liability even if an act performed is unconstitutional. In other cases, the courts have held that there is only a limited or qualified immunity. The immunity defense is usually limited because government officials should not with impunity ignore the limitations which controlling law places on their powers. Immunity only protects officials from conduct that is within the scope of their duties and responsibilities. In most cases, if a government official does an unconstitutional act or one that is clearly beyond his or her legal authority, there is no defense of immunity from suit. For example, in 1971, the Supreme Court held that federal narcotics agents could be sued for conducting illegal searches. If an act is constitutional and is authorized, the defense of immunity is available irrespective of the motive of the official doing the act. Even proof of malice will not overcome the immunity defense for authorized acts.

Immunity is granted to public officials for two reasons: (1) It would be an injustice, particularly in the absence of bad faith, to subject a public official to liability for discretion poorly exercised if his or her position requires exercising discretion. (2) The threat of liability would deter public officials in the performance of their duties and they would not act with the decisiveness required by the public. The law recognizes that public officials must often act swiftly and on the basis of information supplied by others. The extent to which an immunity is qualified or limited is determined by the extent to which the aforesaid reasons apply. In certain cases, they dictate that the immunity be absolute; in others they dictate that it be limited. Officials who seek immunity have the burden of proving that public policy requires it.

As a general rule, executive officials are entitled to only qualified immunity. An important exception exists for hearing examiners and administrative law judges. Judges and justices in our judicial system have almost absolute immunity because of the special nature of their responsibilities. (The only exception is that judges have been held liable for the attorney's fees of persons clearly wronged by them. There is no liability for damages.) Hearing examiners and administrative judges serve a similar function. They exercise independent judgment on the evidence, and they must be free from pressures from the parties. Therefore, persons performing in adjudicatory functions within a government agency are entitled to immunity from damage suit liabilities.

Public prosecutors also have been granted absolute immunity because of the importance of their function and the need to prevent harassment of them by persons charged with crime. The prosecutor's role would likely provoke retaliation unless the immunity were absolute. Therefore, the courts have concluded that an agency's officials who perform functions analogous to those of a prosecutor and who are responsible for the decision to initiate or to continue a proceeding are also entitled to absolute immunity from damage claims. In addition, an agency's attorney who presents evidence in an agency hearing has absolute immunity from suits based on the introduction of such evidence. Legal remedies are available within the agency and within the courts to provide a sufficient check on the activities of such officials of agencies. The quasi-judicial function of government agencies shares enough of the characteristics of the judicial process so that those who participate in it have the same immunity as their counterparts in the judicial process. The risk of an unconstitutional act by those involved in such agency proceedings is clearly outweighed by the importance of preserving the independent judgment of those involved.

12. Equal Access to Justice

The Equal Access to Justice Act which took effect October 1, 1982, requires Uncle Sam to pay the legal costs of small businesses, nonprofit groups, and most individuals who can show they were unjustly treated by the federal government. Prior to the enactment of this law, small companies often were reluctant to take on the U.S. government because of litigation costs. The government was at a great advantage because of the number of attorneys and other resources it has. The law enables the "little guy" to fight the bureaucracy. It should be recognized that awards for legal expenses aren't available to just anyone. Congress limited eligibility to persons whose net worth doesn't exceed $1 million and businesses with no more than $5 million net worth and 500 employees. Charitable and religious tax-exempt organizations qualify if they have 500 or fewer employees. Also, the law grants legal fees only to parties that overcome the government's position in court, administrative proceedings, or in a settlement. Even then, the government agency isn't required to pay if it can show that its original decision was substantially justified.

The Equal Access to Justice Act is not being used very extensively. During the first nineteen months under the law, the government lost 12,000 lawsuits, but there were only thirty applications for legal fees. Under the law, courts may order the federal government to pay attorneys' fees and other legal costs if the agency has acted without "substantial justification." Most of the time the government's position usually meets this test.

PROBLEM AREAS

13. Common Criticisms

The independent regulatory agencies and the administrative process are subjected to a great deal of criticism. They are often charged with being inefficient and ineffective. Many complaints about the administrative process are directly related to its vastness and size. This vastness permeates all levels of government—federal, state, and local. In a real sense, bureaucracy and bureaucrats are the actual rulers of the country.

The administrative process is so extensive it is almost impossible for the business community to be aware of all the rules adopted by the various agencies. Even though agencies planning to promulgate rules and regulations must give public notice of such plans and hold public hearings before rules and regulations are adopted, business is often unaware of all of the rules regulating it.

Not only are there so many rules and regulations that it is impossible to know them or sometimes find them, but rules and regulations of various agencies are frequently in conflict with one another. The regulatory system cannot intelligently address the problems of trade-offs between the goals and objectives of different regulatory bodies. One agency often does not know what others are doing, and there is today a tremendous overlapping of responsibilities. A major criticism of the bureaucracy is that it includes too many unqualified people operating at low levels of efficiency.

The *Peter principle*—that many persons are promoted to their level of incompetency—clearly applies to many bureaucrats. On the other hand, some people are underemployed for their skills, and this also causes job dissatisfaction and reduced efficiency. At top levels, the compensation is probably too low to attract and retain the very best people. At lower levels, employees are sometimes overcompensated if compensation is related to productivity.

The low efficiency levels in many agencies may be attributed to excessive paperwork and to too many meetings. The bureaucracy is literally drowning in paperwork. Many people spend their workday attending committee meetings and arranging others. The status of many employees is determined by the level of meetings attended rather than by accomplishment. It is frequently observed that the administrative process is the classic example of Parkinson's law—doing less and less work with more and more people. Some agencies have been accused of devoting the major part of their time to trivia while ignoring the more important aspects of their mission. Moreover, agencies also have been accused of lack of enforcement and follow-up to ensure compliance with their rules and orders after they have been issued. Many agencies operate without clearly defined goals and priorities.

Bias and lack of political accountability are two of the more often voiced complaints about employees of certain agencies. Bias is almost always present to some degree. Agencies tend to attract people who believe in the goals of the agency. The personnel of EEOC are likely to believe in equal employment opportunity, and are not likely to belong to the Ku Klux Klan or the Nazi Party. Likewise, the personnel of the NLRB are likely to believe in labor unions. Job dissatisfaction would exist at intolerable levels if the people working for an agency did not support the concept of regulation and the general goals of the employing agency or commission.

Lack of political accountability means that voters cannot directly express their dissatisfaction with an agency's rule or position. Occasionally, the legislature responds to public criticism and takes steps to change an agency's rule or limit its appropriations in order to cause a change of attitude. While the executive has the power of appointment, most appointees become quite "independent" of the executive upon confirmation. As a matter of fact, the term "independent regulatory agency" is most descriptive of the attitude of many regulators. Most Presidents have tried to deal with the bureaucracy and control policy and its implementation in some way, but they have generally failed to have much impact, and thus there is little political accountability in most agencies.

14. Procedural Problems

The most often voiced criticism of many agencies is that there is unnecessary delay rendering decisions and providing service. The delay may be a backlog due to overload (compounded by an archaic organization or procedures), inefficiency, or even intentional foot dragging. Many agencies are unable to resolve controversies efficiently even though they were created because of the inability of courts to decide cases quickly. For example, in one recent year, the backlog of unresolved charges of discrimination at EEOC was over 500,000.

Some agencies have been criticized for weaknesses in their enforcement procedures, which may amount to little more than a slap on the wrist. The FTC and SEC, for example, make widespread use of the consent order, in which a respondent agrees or consents not to continue doing an act that has been charged as a violation of the law, without actually admitting or denying a violation. Whereas this method reduces the backlog of cases, many feel that it is not a proper sanction and does not serve justice. Some cases drag on for years. At the same time, social, economic, and technological changes are occurring faster than the agencies are able to respond to them.

The language used by many agencies in preparing rules and regulations is frequently a cause of concern. Such rules tend to be written by lawyers in technical legal words that people cannot understand. There is a frequent call for bureaucrats to use "plain" English in everything they do.

A very serious complaint about the administrative process is that it can be dictatorial—that there is too much discretionary power, often unstructured and unchecked, placed in many bureaucratic hands. For example, the IRS has had sweeping power to seize without a court order the assets of allegedly delinquent taxpayers. It has taken their cars, bank accounts, and attached their wages until it was proved that the IRS was wrong and they did not owe the taxes claimed. Formal as well as informal administrative action can amount to an abuse of power, affecting our daily lives.

15. Cost of Regulation

Regulation is a form of taxation. It directly increases the cost of government. It is estimated that over 3 million people are involved in the regulation of business at a direct cost of over $6 billion per year. But these direct costs of regulation are only a small fraction of the total cost. Regulation significantly adds to the cost of doing business, and these costs are passed on to the taxpaying, consuming public. It should not be overlooked that the consumer for whose protection many regulations are adopted pays the direct cost of regulation in taxes, and the indirect cost when products and services are purchased. The total direct and indirect cost of regulation exceeds $100 billion per year. This cost exceeds 5 percent of the GNP. Regulation is clearly one of the causes of inflation.

The existence of a government agency regulating a designated activity usually forces a company subject to the agency's jurisdiction to create a similar bureaucracy within its own organization to deal with the agency. For example, the existence of the Equal Employment Opportunity Commission (EEOC) has caused most large corporations to designate affirmative action employees who assist the company in complying with the laws, rules, and regulations enforced by EEOC. Whenever a bureaucracy exists, firms dealing with it must spend time and money interacting with the agency. Corporations today tend to have internal groups with responsibilities that are the mirror image of the agency. Government bureaucracy creates a costly private bureaucracy most of the time.

Other costs the public must absorb result from agency regulations that inhibit competition and innovation. Regulation has protected existing companies by creating a barrier to entry into a market. Regulation tends to protect "cozy competition" to the extent that, quite often, the parties that object the most to deregulation are the businesses being regulated.

The financial burden of complying with many regulations is high because it requires new equipment or additional personnel. Perhaps the most disturbing additional cost to the business community is the cost of paperwork. The burden of the paperwork involved in filing applications, returns, reports, and forms alone is overwhelming and a major cost of doing business. In a recent year, it was estimated that 2 billion forms had to be filled out and filed by business due to bureaucratic red tape—at a cost in excess of $20 billion. Some authorities have said that a minimum of 20 percent of the costs incurred in the transportation industries are due to the cost of regulation.

In the past, there has been little or no cost-benefit analysis when new rules and regulations were proposed. Government has tended only to assess the benefits accruing from a cleaner environment, safer products, healthier working conditions, and so on, in deciding to embark upon vast new regulatory programs. The primary focus of policy making by way of such social regulations has not been on balancing the costs of the programs with their potential benefits. The public, and especially consumers, have frequently been forced to pay for many things they did not want or need in the sense that the cost far exceeded the benefits. Moreover, the law does not generally require cost-benefit analysis, as the case which follows illustrates.

AMERICAN TEXTILE MANUFACTURERS INSTITUTE, INC. v. DONOVAN
101 S. Ct. 2478 (1981)

OSHA promulgated a standard strictly limiting occupational exposure to cotton dust, an airborne particle produced during the manufacture of cotton products, exposure to which induces a serious and potentially disabling disease, byssinosis, also known as "brown lung" disease. Petitioners, representing the interests of the cotton industry, challenged the validity of the "cotton dust standard" in the Court of Appeals. They contended that the Occupational Safety and Health Act requires OSHA to demonstrate that its standard reflects a reasonable relationship between the costs and benefits associated with the Standard. The Court of Appeals upheld the Standard and ruled that the Act does not require OSHA to compare costs and benefits. The U.S. Supreme Court granted certiorari.

BRENNAN, J.: . . . The principal question presented in this case is whether the Occupational Safety and Health Act requires the Secretary, in promulgating a standard pursuant to Section 6(b)(5) of the Act, to determine that the costs of the standard bear a reasonable relationship to its benefits. Relying on Sections 6(b)(5) and 3(8) of the Act, petitioners urge not only that OSHA must show that a standard addresses a significant risk of material health impairment, but also that OSHA must demonstrate that the reduction in risk of material health impairment is significant in light of the costs of attaining that reduction. Respondents on the other hand contend that the Act requires OSHA to promulgate standards that eliminate or reduce such risks "to the extent such protection is technologically and economically feasible." To resolve this debate, we must turn to the language, structure, and legislative history of the Occupational Safety and Health Act.

The starting point of our analysis is the language of the statute itself. Section 6(b)(5) of the Act provides:

The Secretary, in promulgating standards dealing with toxic materials or harmful physical agents under this subsection, shall set the standard which most adequately assures, *to the extent feasible*, on the basis of the best available evidence, that no employee will suffer material impairment of health or functional capacity even if such employee has regular exposure to the hazard dealt with by such standard for the period of his working life.

Although their interpretations differ, all parties agree that the phrase "to the extent feasible" contains the critical language in Section 6(b)(5) for purposes of this case.

The plain meaning of the work "feasible" supports respondents' interpretation of the statute. According to Webster's Third New International Dictionary of the English Language, "feasible" means "capable of being done, executed, or effected." Thus, Section 6(b)(5) directs the Secretary to issue the standard that "most adequately assures . . . that no employee will suffer material impairment of health," limited only by the extent to which this is "capable of being done." In effect then, as the Court of Appeals held, Congress itself defined the basic relationship between costs and benefits, by placing the "benefit" of worker health above all other considerations save those making attainment of this "benefit" unachievable. Any standard based on a balancing of costs and benefits by the Secretary that strikes a different balance than that struck by Congress would be inconsistent with the command set forth in Section 6(b)(5). Thus, cost-benefit analysis by OSHA is not required by the statute because feasibility analysis is. . . .

The legislative history of the Act, while concededly not crystal clear, provides general support for respondents' interpretation of the Act. The congressional reports and debates certainly confirm that Congress meant "feasible" and nothing else in using that term. Congress was concerned that the Act might be thought to require achievement of absolute safety, an impossible standard, and therefore insisted that health and safety goals be capable of economic and technological accomplishment. Perhaps most telling is the absence of any indication whatsoever that Congress intended OSHA to conduct its own cost-benefit analysis before promulgating a toxic material or harmful physical agent standard. The legislative history demonstrates conclusively, that Congress was fully aware that the Act would impose real and substantial costs of compliance on industry, and believed that such costs were part of the cost of doing business. . . .

Not only does the legislative history confirm that Congress meant "feasible" rather than "cost-benefit" when it used the former term, but it also shows that Congress understood that the Act would create substantial costs for employers, yet intended to impose such costs when necessary to create a safe and healthful working environment. Congress viewed the costs of health and safety as a cost of doing business. Senator Yarborough, a cosponsor of the Williams bill, stated: "We know the costs would be put into consumer goods but that is the price we should pay for the 80 million workers in America."

Other members of Congress voiced similar views. Nowhere is there any indication that Congress contemplated a different balancing by OSHA of the benefits of worker health and safety against the costs of achieving them. Indeed Congress thought that the *financial costs* of health and safety problems in the workplace were as large or larger than the *financial costs* of eliminating these problems. In its statement of findings and declaration of purpose encompassed in the Act itself, Congress announced that "personal injuries and illnesses arising out of work situations impose a substantial burden upon, and are a hindrance to, interstate commerce in terms of lost production, wage loss, medical expenses, and disability compensation payment."

When Congress passed the Occupational Safety and Health Act in 1970, it chose to place pre-eminent value on assuring employees a safe and healthful working environment, limited only by the feasibility of achieving such an environmentt. We must measure the validity of the Secretary's actions against the requirements of that Act. For "[t]he judicial function does not extend to substantive revision of regulatory policy. That function lies elsewhere—in Congressional and Executive oversight or amendatory legislation." Accordingly, the judgment of the Court of Appeals is . . . [*Affirmed.*]

Shortly after taking office, President Reagan issued an executive order requiring executive agencies to apply cost-benefit analysis before creating "significant" new regulations. The order has had only limited impact for several reasons. It did not apply to independent regulatory agencies, since they are not under the President's direct control. Many regulations escaped the analysis because a "significant" regulation had to have an "annual effect on the economy of $100 million or more." Finally, as the *American Textile* case illustrates, some enabling legislation for executive agencies does not require and may not allow the use of cost-benefit analysis.

Although it seems sensible to require the government to weigh the costs and benefits of its proposed action, a number of practical and ethical criticisms have been leveled at this approach. Formal cost-benefit analysis is itself costly and often slow. Critics claim there is no satisfactory way either to decide how far into the future consequences should be considered or to prevent an unpredictable future from invalidating the analysis. Some argue that the focus of cost-benefit analysis, if it amounts only to a mechanistic toting of predetermined dollar values, can cause options either to be ignored or to be improperly compared to proposed regulation. There are no inherent standards, it is argued, for deciding whose values count in assessing harms and benefits. And some social regulation, especially that dealing with the environment, safety, and health, may be morally right notwithstanding high cost exceeding "benefits."

How do you apply cost-benefit analysis to a rule dealing with human life? How much dollar benefit is to be assigned to a life in measuring it against the cost? Assume that a Department of Transportation rule requiring air bags in all new automobiles sold adds a cost of $800 to each car. Assume also that it saves 50,000 lives per year. Is the cost worth the benefit? Your answer may depend on whether you are one of the 50,000 or not. Cost-benefit analysis becomes ethically awkward when there is an attempt to place a dollar value on things not usually bought and sold, such as life, health, or mobility. Cost-benefit analysis is not possible, appropriate, or suitable for many government rules and regulations. This is not to say that the cost of many agencies cannot be compared with tangible benefits. Cost-benefit analysis applied to some agencies and some rules will clearly point toward deregulation, but its use is obviously limited. Moreover, the debate over cost-benefit analysis may eventually lead to greater use of cost-effectiveness analysis, that is, the "right" social goal being decided in advance of a search for the least expensive means of achieving it.

16. Personnel and Ethical Considerations

It has been charged that too often agencies favor the industries being regulated rather than the public as a result of the cozy relationship that can exist between agencies and industry. One reason for friendship between the two is the so-called "revolving door"—regulators are often persons with high executive positions in the industries they regulate. This is justified by the argument that such persons possess the expertise required to understand the technical problems of the field and to perform their jobs properly. For the same reason, often key staff members are recruited from the regulated industry. Also, it has been common for the reverse to occur. Upon termination of government service, commissioners and staff members have frequently gone into high-paying jobs in the industries they had been regulating. "Sweetheart" regulation sometimes leads agency personnel to become so closely identified with the interests they regulate that eventually they become spokespersons for the interest groups. At least one study also has found that a large number of regulatory agency employees have financial interests such as stockholdings which appear to conflict with their regulatory responsibilities.

Dealing with such conflicts of interest, whether real or only apparent, has not been an easy task for government. Since the late 1950s, there has been a

Federal "Code of Ethics for Government Services." The code states that any person in government service should:

1   Put loyalty to the highest moral principles and to country above loyalty to persons, party, or government department.

2   Uphold the Constitution, laws, and legal regulations of the United States and of all governments therein and never be a party to their evasion.

3   Give a full day's labor for a full day's pay; giving to the performance of duties one's earnest effort and best thought.

4   Seek to find and employ more efficient and economical ways of getting tasks accomplished.

5   Never discriminate unfairly by dispensing special favors or privileges to anyone, whether for remuneration or not; and never accept, for oneself or family, favors or benefits under circumstances which might be construed by reasonable persons as influencing the performance of governmental duties.

6   Make no private promises of any kind binding upon the duties of office, since a government employee has no private word which can be binding on public duty.

7   Engage in no business with the government, either directly or indirectly, which is inconsistent with the conscientious performance of governmental duties.

8   Never use any information received confidentially in the performance of governmental duties as a means for making private profit.

9   Expose corruption wherever discovered.

10   Uphold these principles, ever conscious that public office is a public trust.

The major problem with the code is that it was created by a concurrent resolution of Congress and therefore is not law. Lacking enforcement, the code is really a statement of aspirations. Some recent presidents have attempted to head off potential conflicts of interest by use of internal executive policy or executive order. In 1978, Congress passed the Ethics in Government Act to discourage former government employees from taking unfair advantage of their government service. It was believed that former officials should not be permitted either to exercise undue influence over former colleagues still in government service, or to use information on specific cases gained during government service for their own benefit and that of private clients or employers. The ethics law limits officials' private employment opportunities by placing a minimum two-year prohibition on aiding private parties in matters in which the officials were closely involved while in office. In some instances, the prohibition is a permanent one against both the former official and his or her partners. To avoid even the appearance of impropriety, the law also prevents all business contact between the former official and his or her agency for one year. Not only is the law a criminal statute, but administrative sanctions also may be taken against violators, including barring a violator from contact with the agency for up to five years. The agency itself may make the determination administratively whether a violation has occurred and impose the sanction without the necessity of a criminal prosecution.

While attempting to prevent corruption and other official misconduct, the Ethics in Government Act wisely sets a standard for proper ethical conduct by former government officials. However, the prohibitions of the law may adversely affect the government's ability to recruit and retain experienced personnel. It may become necessary, as has often been suggested, to substantially increase the pay of top administrators to attract highly qualified persons to the jobs and cut the rate of their resignations.

17. Regulatory Reform

Although its faults make the administrative process easy to criticize, it is clear that we cannot do without it. There have been numerous recommendations to "deregulate" this or that activity or industry. There have been calls to substantially cut back on the number of government programs by reorganizing agencies and by paring down their functions. There is a constant demand for cost-benefit analysis of most agency programs and for a reduction in the paperwork required by all agencies. A commission on paperwork was created to assist in this reduction. It has had limited success due in part to too much paperwork!

Proponents of deregulation argue that we should replace rigid and unnecessary regulation with the free play of competitive market forces. They believe that competition and the market can allocate resources and achieve efficiency better than government fiat, resulting in lower prices to consumers. Deregulation would reduce the size of the bureaucracy and the direct cost of maintaining it.

President Reagan's most effective techniques for reducing the impact of government regulations were to cut budgets and to appoint critics of various agencies to them. He sought reform through ideology. If a commissioner or board member does not believe in certain regulatory activities, chances are that they will not be carried out even if the law would allow the agency to do so.

Even with the many problems inherent in the process, it is clear that administrative law and the fourth branch of government are here to stay. The reasons given in section 1 for their creation and existence remain valid. In fact, the trend is toward more regulation and more agencies. For example, one of President Reagan's first acts was to appoint a Task Force on Regulatory Relief—another agency. Our technique for solving society's problems is to turn to an agency for solutions. This is true at both the federal and state levels of government. Even the business community advocates resort to the administrative process when difficult problems face society. There may be increased public participation in the process but it is not likely that there will be a reduction in its size or in the scope of its activities.

What is needed is not the elimination of regulation, but the elimination of bad and excessive regulation. Most agencies exist for valid reasons, and they have proper goals and important roles to play in aiding the legitimate needs of society. They exist because business will not always respond to the needs of society. For example, business did not seriously attempt to clean up the environment until the EPA was created. What is needed is a balanced approach—free enterprise with effective regulation to protect the public interest.

Additional matters concerning the administrative process and administrative law will be further illustrated in subsequent chapters concerned with labor law, antitrust law, securities regulation, the law and the environment, and other areas of business regulation. This source of law comprises a substantial and probably the major portion of the legal environment of business.

REVIEW QUESTIONS

1 For each term in the left-hand column, match the most appropriate description in the right-hand column:

(1) CPSC   (a) Protects the public from anticompetitive behavior and unfair and deceptive business practices; a law enforcement agency

(2) EPA   (b) Licenses and regulates the nuclear energy industry
(3) FCC   (c) Protects the public against unreasonable risks of injury associated with consumer products

(4) FTC   (d) Seeks to prevent discrimination in employment based on race, color, religion, sex, or national orgin, and other unlawful employment practices

(5) FDA   (e) Regulates interstate and foreign communications by means of radio, television, wire, cable, and satellite

(6) EEOC   (f) Ensures all workers a safe and healthy work environment

(7) NLRB   (g) Enforces the federal securities laws which regulate sale of securities to the investing public

(8) NRC   (h) Administers laws to prohibit distribution of adulterated, misbranded, or unsafe food and drugs

(9) OSHA   (i) Conducts union certification elections and holds hearings on unfair labor practice complaints

(10) SEC   (j) Administers all laws relating to the environment, including laws on water pollution, air pollution, solid wastes, pesticides, toxic substances, etc.

2 A liquor control board suspended a liquor license because a clerk sold a twelve-pack of beer to a sixteen-year old. The customer looked "old," and the drinking age was eighteen. There was no evidence of previous violations. Will a court reverse the decision? Why, or why not?

3 The FTC issued an administrative complaint against several major oil companies alleging unfair methods of competition. After failing to get the FTC to dismiss the complaint, the oil companies brought a separate action against the FTC in federal court asserting that the FTC had issued the complaint without having reason to believe that the companies were violating the law. They sought an order to require the FTC to withdraw the complaint. The gist was that political pressure for a public explanation of the gasoline shortages of 1973 forced the FTC to issue the complaint despite insufficient investigation. Should the case be dismissed? Why?

4 Harvey, a school teacher of limited means, had a dispute with a federal administrative agency. When the matter was not resolved before the agency, Harvey appealed to a federal court. The court found all of the issues for Harvey satisfactorily and observed that the government officials had been arbitrary and capricious. Harvey paid his attorney $10,000 to handle the case. Is he entitled to recover this loss from the government? Explain.

5 The EPA discovered that a chemical company was dumping toxic waste into a local river. The agency conducted a hearing with proper notice to the chemical company and found the company to be in violation of EPA's regulations. A heavy fine was imposed. The company appealed to the court, contending that the hearing had denied it its right to a trial by jury. Is it correct? Why, or why not?

6 Leonard's, Inc., was charged with violating a rule of an administrative agency. A hearing was conducted by an administrative law judge. The judge found the company guilty. The rules of the agency provided for a review by the full commission, but rather than seek such a review, Leonard's filed a case in the courts to enjoin further agency action. Is Leonard's entitled to an injunction? Why, or why not?

7 Joe owned a tract of real estate across the street from a major shopping center. The lot was at an intersection of a main road leading to the shopping center, and Joe wanted to build a service station on the property. The property was zoned for single-family residences. Joe filed a request to have the zoning classification changed to commercial. The zoning board denied the request, and Joe filed suit. He contended that the present and best use of the property was for commercial purposes. The zoning board contended that there needed to be a buffer between the shopping center and the residential area, and the only appropriate buffer was the street. What was the decision? Why?

8 Lawyers and legally trained persons are highly visible and important in most administrative agencies. Why do these agencies require so many legally trained personnel to accomplish their goals? Explain.

9 The law creating the EPA states that its purpose is to establish rules and regulations to "promote a healthful environment." Pursuant to this delegation of authority, the agency adopted a regulation that made it unlawful to manufacture or to utilize power plant equipment that allowed emmissions "detrimental to the atmosphere." Consumers Power Company was charged with violating the agency rule. It challenged the constitutionality of the rule. What was the result? Why?

10   Hershel filed a claim for workers' compensation, alleging that he received a knee injury which arose out of and in the course of his employment. The employer contended that Hershel's knee had been hurt in a touch football game. The hearing examiner denied the claim. Hershel then filed suit against the employer and the hearing examiner, contending that there was collusion between them in the denial of his claim. The hearing examiner moved to dismiss the lawsuit. What was the result? Why?

11   Discuss five of the more commonly voiced complaints about the independent regulatory agencies.

12   What steps has the federal government taken to achieve ethical conduct by its employees?

13   What are the advantages and disadvantages of requiring government agencies to employ cost-benefit analysis to justify their regulations?

Part Four
CONDUCTING BUSINESS

Chapter
11

Selecting the Form of Business Organization

1. Introduction

As we continue to focus on the law and business portion of the legal environment of business, it is appropriate that we examine some of the fundamental legal aspects of business organizations. These aspects fall into two categories: (1) legal issues relating to setting up various forms of business organizations, and (2) issues of liability. The liability of the business organization and its owners will be discussed in the next chapter. In this chapter we will discuss the types of business organizations, their operational advantages and disadvantages, and the factors to consider when selecting one of these organizational forms.

This question of selecting the best-suited organization for a business' purpose is of vital importance when a business is being started or when it encounters a substantial change, such as rapid growth. Therefore, the factors used to select a form or organization need to be reviewed periodically. This review should be in consultation with close advisers such as attorneys, accountants, and bankers. These people weigh the factors and costs involved and then select the organizational form deemed most suitable to the business' needs at that time. Because this selection process balances advantages against disadvantages, the decision often is to choose the least objectionable form of organization.

Prior to examining this chapter in depth, you should understand that the discussion throughout this chapter is based on the presumption that the business being analyzed is closely held. In other words, a limited number of owners of the business are involved in this selection decision. When a business is publicly held by an unlimited number of owners, the form of organization almost always is a corporation. The reason for this corporate form being utilized is that shareholders can transfer their ownership interests without interfering with the organization's management.

2. Alternatives

Business is conducted under a variety of legal forms. The three basic forms are sole proprietorships, partnerships, and corporations. Many hybrid forms take on the form of both a partnership and a corporation. These forms include the limited partnership, the professional corporation, and the subchapter S corporation.

As the name implies, a *sole proprietorship* is a business owned by only one person. The business' property belongs to the proprietor, and any income or losses are added to or deducted from that individual's personal income for tax purposes. Any debts incurred by the organization actually are obligations of the proprietor. Because of its inherent limitation to one owner, a sole proprietorship cannot be a possible choice when more than one person wants to co-own a business.

In general, a *partnership* is created by an agreement between two or more persons to operate a business and to share profits and losses. A *corporation* is an artificial, intangible person or being, which is created under the authority of a state's law. When a partnership allows some of the partners to be treated like corporate shareholders for liability purposes, these partners are said to have limited liability. They are limited partners in a **limited partnership**. The law also allows shareholders of a corporation to elect to have their organization taxed like a partnership. Such an election creates a *subchapter S corporation*. The law also permits the formation of *professional corporations* when the owners are performing professional services such as practicing law, medicine, and dentistry.

3. Partnerships Versus Corporations

Before examining in detail the legal aspects involved in selecting the best form of organization, the general advantages and disadvantages of each form of organization should be recognized. This may be done by comparing the basic characteristics of partnerships with those of corporations.

The basic law relating to partnerships is found in the Uniform Partnership Act, which has been adopted by every state except Louisiana. According to this statute, the partnership form of organization generally has the following advantages:

1 A partnership is easily formed because it is based on a contract among persons.

2 Costs of formation are not significant.

3 Partnerships are not tax-paying entities but allocate income or losses among the parties.

4 Each partner has an equal voice in management, unless there is a contrary agreement.

5 A partnership may operate in more than one state without obtaining a license to do business.

6 Partnerships generally are subject to less regulation and less governmental supervision than are corporations.

Offsetting these advantages, the following aspects of partnerships have been considered disadvantages:

1 For practical reasons, only a limited number of people can be partners.

2 A partnership is dissolved any time a partner ceases to be a partner, regardless of whether the reason is withdrawal or death.

3 Each partner's personal liability is unlimited, contrasted with the limited liability of a corporate shareholder.

4 Partners are taxed on their share of the partnership's profits, whether the profits are distributed or not. In other words, partners often are required to pay income tax on money they do not receive.

The usual advantages of the corporate form of organization include the following:

1 This form is the best practical means of bringing together a large number of investors.

2 Control can be vested in those with a minority of the investment.

3 Ownership may be divided into many unequal shares.

4 Shareholders' liabilities are limited to their investment.

5 This organization can have perpetual existence.

6 In addition to being owners, shareholders may be employees entitled to benefits such as workers' compensation.

Among the frequently cited disadvantages of the corporate organization are the following:

1   The cost of forming and maintaining a corporation, with its formal procedural requirements, is significant.

2   License fees and franchise taxes often are assessed against corporations but not partnerships.

3   Corporate income may be subject to double taxation.

4   A corporation must be qualified in all states where it is conducting local or intrastate business.

5   Generally, corporations are subject to more governmental regulation at all levels than are other forms of business.

6   A corporation, as a legal entity, is required to be represented by an attorney in any litigation.

The case that follows provides the reasoning behind the requirement that corporations must be represented by an attorney-at-law in litigation.

LAND MANAGEMENT v. DEPARTMENT OF ENVIR. PROTEC.

368 A.2d 602 (Me. 1977)

ARCHIBALD, J.: . . . The sole issue raised by this appeal is whether the presiding Justice acted properly in dismissing the plaintiff's complaint on the ground that the plaintiff was a corporation not represented by a duly admitted attorney. We conclude that the Justice below correctly dismissed the complaint, and we therefore deny the plaintiff's appeal.

The plaintiff, Land Management, Inc., is a corporation doing business in the State of Maine. On April 9, 1976, it commenced an action in the Superior Court seeking declaratory and injunctive relief against the defendants. Throughout the proceedings in the Superior Court the plaintiff was represented by its president who, admittedly, is not an attorney admitted to practice law in Maine.

All of the defendants filed motions to dismiss the plaintiff's complaint. . . . [These were granted] solely on the basis

that the Plaintiff Land Management, Inc. is not entitled to proceed in this action *pro se* by and through a person who is not an attorney licensed to practice law.

In support of its position that a corporation may represent itself in Maine courts through a corporate officer who is not a duly admitted attorney, the plaintiff relies upon language found in 4 M.R.S.A. §§ 807 and 811.

4 M.R.S.A. § 807 provides:

Unless duly admitted to the bar of this State, no person shall practice law or any branch thereof, or hold himself out to practice law or any branch thereof, within the State or before any court

therein, or demand or receive any remuneration for such services rendered in this State. Whoever, not being duly admitted to the bar of this State, shall practice law or any branch thereof, or hold himself out to practice law or any branch thereof, within the State or before any court therein, or demand or receive any remuneration for such services rendered in this State, shall be punished by a fine of not more than $500 or by imprisonment for not more than three months, or by both. This section shall not be construed to apply to practice before any Federal Court by any person duly admitted to practice therein nor to a person pleading or managing his own cause in court. . . .

4 M.R.S.A. § 811 defines a "person" as "any individual, corporation, partnership or association."

On the basis of these statutory provisions, the plaintiff contends that since a corporation can only act through its agents, it may authorize a non-attorney to represent it in court. We do not agree with the plaintiff's assertion that the Legislature, in enacting §§ 807 and 811, intended to permit a corporation to be represented before the courts of this State by a person who is not authorized to practice law. To accept plaintiff's argument would require us to hold that a corporation may authorize a non-attorney to represent it in court, while an individual may not. We do not believe that the Legislature intended such an illogical result. The purpose of § 811 for including a corporation within the definition of the word "person" was to make it clear that a corporation, as well as anyone else, is prohibited from engaging in the unauthorized practice of law. This section modified the § 807 prohibition against unauthorized practice rather than expanding the right of indi-

viduals to represent themselves in either the Federal or State courts.

The rule that a corporation may appear in court only through a licensed attorney was stated succinctly in *Paradise v. Nowlin*, 86 Cal. App.2d 897, 195 P.2d 867 (1948):

A natural person may represent himself and present his own case to the court although he is not a licensed attorney. A corporation is not a natural person. It is an artificial entity created by law and as such it can neither practice law nor appear or act in person. Out of court it must act in its affairs through its agents and representatives and in matters in court it can act only through licensed attorneys. A corporation cannot appear in court by an officer who is not an attorney and it cannot appear in *propria persona*.

Sound public policy reasons also require such a rule. As stated by the Ohio Supreme Court:

To allow a corporation to maintain litigation and appear in court represented by corporate officers or agents only would lay open the gates to the practice of law for entry to those corporate officers or agents who have not been qualified to practice law and who are not amenable to the general discipline of the court.

There is abundant authority, both state and federal, rejecting the argument, as advanced by the plaintiff, that a corporation has the right to appear in court without the aid of a licensed attorney.

Since the plaintiff was not represented by counsel licensed to practice law, its complaint was a nullity and was propperly dismissed by the presiding Justice. [*Appeal denied.*]

4. Legal Capacity

When considering which organizational alternatives are best suited for a new or changing business, the following factors should be considered: (1) legal capacity, (2) cost and manner of creation, (3) continuity, (4) liability, (5) taxation, and (6) operation. The relative importance of each of these independent factors will vary from business to business depending upon the goals and interests of its owners.

The first consideration, "legal capacity," refers to the capacity of an organization to sue and be sued in its own name. It also refers to the organization's power to own and dispose of property as well as to enter into contracts in its own name. When an organization lacks this legal capacity, it must act through its owners as represenatatives of the organization rather than as a legal entity itself.

In early law, a corporation was considered a legal entity, but a partnership was not. Being a legal entity usually meant that capacity was present to sue and be sued and to hold title to and convey real and personal property in the name of the business instead of the names of the individual owners. Modern statutes on procedure allow suits by and against a partnership in the firm name. They also allow a partnership to own and dispose of real estate and personal property in the firm name. To this extent, a partnership is treated as a legal entity. Because of this modern view of partnerships, the importance of considering this factor has diminished.

GOING INTO BUSINESS

5. Creating Partnerships

A partnership, which is an association of two or more persons who co-own a business for profit, is created by an agreement of the parties who are to be the owners and managers. This agreement, usually known as "Articles of Copartnership," creates the partnership as between the partners. A partnership may also arise by implication from the conduct of the parties. Conduct may create a partnership even though the parties do not call themselves partners or understand the consequences of their conduct.

LUPIEN v. MALSBENDEN
477 A.2d 746 (Me. 1984)

Plaintiff, Lupien, contracted with Cragin, who did business as York Motor Mart, for the construction of a Bradley automobile from a kit. Plaintiff paid down $4,450 of the $8,020 price. He periodically visited York Motor Mart to check on his car. Plaintiff generally dealt with the defendant Malsbenden, because Cragin was seldom present. On one occasion, Malsbenden told plaintiff to sign over ownership of his pickup truck so that the proceeds from its sale could be applied to the purchase price of the car. Malsbenden had provided plaintiff with a rental car and later with a "demo" model of the Bradley. When the plaintiff did not receive the Bradley, he sued Malsbenden for a refund of the purchase price.

Malsbenden asserts that his interest in York Motor Mart was only that of a banker. He had lent $85,000 to Cragin, without interest, to finance the Bradley portion of York Motor Mart's business. The loan was to be repaid from the proceeds of each car sold. Malsbenden testified that Bradley kits were purchased with his personal checks and admitted that he had also purchased equipment for York Motor Mart. After Cragin disappeared, the defendant had physical control of the premises of York Motor Mart. The trial court held that Malsbenden was liable as a partner.

McKUSICK, J.: . . . The Uniform Partnership Act defines a partnership as "an association of 2 or more persons . . . to carry on as co-owners a business for profit." . . . Whether a partnership exists is an inference of law based on established facts. . . . A finding that the relationship between two persons constitutes a partnership may be based upon evidence of an agreement, either express or implied,

to place their money, effects, labor, and skill, or some or all of them, in lawful commerce or business with the understanding that a community of profits will be shared. . . . No one factor is alone determinative of the existence of a partnership. . . .

. . . If the arrangement between the parties otherwise qualifies as a partnership, it is of no matter that the parties did not expressly agree to form a partnership or did not even intend to form one:

It is possible for parties to intend no partnership and yet to form one. If they agree upon an ar-

rangement which is a partnership in fact, it is of no importance that they call it something else, or that they even expressly declare that they are not to be partners. The law must declare what is the legal import of their agreements, and names go for nothing when the substance of the arrangement shows them to be inapplicable. . . .

Here the trial justice concluded that, notwithstanding Malsbenden's assertion that he was only a "banker," his "total involvement" in the Bradley operation was that of a partner. The testimony at trial, both respecting Malsbenden's financial interest in the enterprise and his involvement in day-to-day business operations, amply supported the Superior Court's conclusion. Malsbenden had a financial interest of $85,000 in the Bradley portion of York Motor Mart's operations. Although Malsbenden termed the investment a loan, significantly he conceded that the "loan" carried no interest. His "loan" was not made in the form of a fixed payment or payments, but was made to the business, at least in substantial part, in the form of day-to-day purchases of Bradley kits, other parts and equipment, and in the payment of wages. Furthermore, the "loan" was not to be repaid in fixed amounts or at fixed times, but rather only upon the sale of Bradley automobiles.

The evidence also showed that, unlike a banker, Malsbenden had the right to participate in control of the business and in fact did so on a day-to-day basis. According to Urbin Savaria, who worked at York Motor Mart from late April through June 1980, Malsbenden during that time opened the business establishment each morning, remained present through part of every day, had final say on the ordering of parts, paid for parts and equipment, and paid Savaria's salary. On plaintiff's frequent visits to York Motor Mart, he generally dealt with Malsbenden because Cragin was not present. It was Malsbenden who insisted that plaintiff trade in his truck prior to the completion of the Bradley because the proceeds from the sale of the truck were needed to complete the Bradley. When it was discovered that the "demo" Bradley given to plaintiff while he awaited completion of his car actually belonged to a third party, it was Malsbenden who bought the car for plaintiff's use. As of three years after the making of the contract now in litigation, Malsbenden was still doing business at York Motor Mart, "just disposing of property."

Malsbenden and Cragin may well have viewed their relationship to be that of creditor-borrower, rather than a partnership. At trial Malsbenden so asserts, and Cragin's departure from the scene in the spring of 1980 deprives us of the benefit of his view of his business arrangement with Malsbenden. In any event, whatever the intent of these two men as to their respective involvements in the business of making and selling Bradley cars, there is no clear error in the Superior Court's finding that the Bradley car operation represented a pooling of Malsbenden's capital and Cragin automotive skills, with joint control over the business and intent to share the fruits of the enterprise. As a matter of law, that arrangement amounted to a partnership. . . . [*Judgment affirmed.*]

The sharing of the net profits of a business enterprise by two persons gives rise to a presumption that a partnership exists between them, except when the share of profits is received by one of them for a special reason such as for wages of an employee, for rent to a landlord, or as interest on a loan. A partnership may be considered to be between the partners and third persons when a person by his or her conduct leads third persons to believe a partnership exists and the third person acts in reliance on this conduct (partnership by estoppel). This is true even though there is in fact no partnership between the alleged partners.

A partnership is easily formed, since all that is required is an agreement between partners. The cost of formation is minimal, and the business need not qualify to do business in foreign states. One problem which frequently is a major concern in the creation of a business entity is the name to be used. Since a partnership is created by an agreement, the parties select the name. This right of selection is subject to two limitations in many states. First, a partnership may not use any word in the name, such as "company," that would imply the existence of a corporation. Second, if the name is other than that of the partners, they must give notice as to the actual identity of the partners. Failure to comply with a state's assumed-name statutes may result in the partnership's being denied access to courts, or it may result in criminal actions being brought against those operating under the assumed name.

6. Creating Corporations

A corporation is created by a state issuing a charter upon the application of individuals known as *incorporators*. In comparison with partnerships, corporations are more costly to form. Among the costs of incorporation are filing fees, license fees, franchise taxes, attorneys' fees, and the cost of supplies, such as minute books, corporate seals, and stock certificates. In addition to these costs of creation, there also are annual costs in continuing a corporation's operation. These recurring expenses include annual reporting fees and taxes, the cost of annual shareholders' meeting, and ongoing legal-related expenses.

The application for corporate charter, which is called the "Articles of Incorporation," must contain the proposed name of the corporation. So that persons dealing with a business will know that it is a corporation, the law requires that the corporate name include one of the following words or end with an abbreviation of them: "corporation," "company," "incorporated," or "limited." In addition, a corporate name must not be the same as, or deceptively similar to, the name of any domestic corporation or that of a foreign corporation authorized to do business in the state to which the application is made. Courts of equity may enjoin the use of deceptively similar names, and charters will be refused if the state believes that the names are deceptively similar. The corporate name is an asset and a part of goodwill. As such, it is legally protected.

In addition to the proposed corporate name, the Articles of Incorporation usually will include the proposed corporation's period of duration, the purpose for which it is formed, the number of authorized shares, and information about the initial corporate officials. Typically, a corporation will apply for a perpetual duration; however, a corporation can legally be created for a stated number of years. The corporate purpose stated in the Articles of Incorporation usually is very broad. For example, it would be better to say that a corporation is in the business of selling goods, rather than to limit this activity to either the retail or wholesale level. Stating the purpose very specifically may prohibit a growing corporation from expanding into related areas of operations.

With respect to authorized shares of stock, these Articles of Incorporation must indicate the class and value of stock and the number of shares of each class that will be sold. For example, incorporators may request that the state authorize 250,000 shares of $5 per value common stock of which 100,000 shares will be sold during the first year of operation. A corporation must pay taxes on the shares actually sold rather than on the shares authorized. If additional stock is sold after these initial 100,000 shares, the corporation must file a report and pay the extra taxes or fees.

Finally, the Articles of Incorporation must indicate the names and addresses of the initial board of directors. In other words, these directors are appointed by the incorporators until such time as the shareholders can elect a board. Also appointed and specifically named in the application is the person serving as the corporation's agent to whom legal papers, such as complaints in lawsuits, may be served. Usually, the names and addresses of those persons acting as incorporators also must be included in the Articles of Incorporation.

Once drafted, these papers are sent to the appropriate state official (usually the secretary of state) who approves them and issues a corporate charter. Notice of this incorporation usually has to be advertised in the local newspaper in order to inform the public that a new corporation has been created. The initial board of directors then meets, adopts the corporate bylaws, and approves the sale of stock. At this point, the corporation becomes operational. Sections 15 and 16 discuss issues relating to operating a corporation.

If a corporation wishes to conduct business in states other than the state of incorporation, that corporation must be licensed in these foreign states. The process of qualification usually requires payment of license fees and franchise taxes above and beyond those paid during the initial incorporation process. If a corporation fails to qualify in states where it is conducting business, the corporation may be denied access to the courts as a means of enforcing its contracts.

7. Creating Limited Partnerships

A limited partnership is a hybrid between a general partnership and a corporation. This special organization has at least one general partner with unlimited liability and one or more limited partners who are comparable to shareholders of a corporation. The general partners manage the daily operations of the organization, and they are personally liable for the business' debts. The limited partners also contribute capital and share in the profits or losses, but they are not allowed to control the organization's operations. In return for foregoing this control, these limited partners incur no personal liability beyond their capital contribution with respect to the partnership's debts. It is from this limited liability of the limited partners that the organization gets its name.

Like a general partnership, a limited partnership is created by agreement. However, as in the case of a corporation, state law requires that the contents of a certificate must be recorded in a public office so that everyone may be fully advised as to the details of the organization. This certificate contains, among other matters, the following information: the name of the partnership, the character of the business, its location, the name and place of residence of each member, those who are to be the general partners and those who are to be the limited partners, the length of time the partnership is to exist, the amount of cash or the agreed value of property to be contributed by each partner, and the share of profit or compensation each limited partner shall receive.

The limited-partnership certificate is required to be recorded in the county where the partnership has its principal place of business. An additional copy has to be filed in every community where the partnership conducts business or has an office. Whenever there is a change in the information contained in the filed certificate, a new certificate must be prepared and recorded. If an accurate certificate is not on record and if the limited partnership continues its operation, the limited partners become liable as general partners. Substantial compliance with all the technical requirements of the limited-partnership law is essential if the limited partners are to be assured of their limited liability. Moreover, a limited partner may not seek to protect her or his investment through devices such as security agreements, as the following case makes clear.

KRAMER v. McDONALD'S SYSTEM, INC.
396 N.E.2d 504 (Ill. 1979)

Kramer was a limited partner in a McDonald's franchise, which was organized as a limited partnership. To secure his $90,000 investment, he took a security interest from the franchisee covering all of its equipment, inventory, and receivables. When the business failed, there was a public sale of the assets, which McDonald's, the franchisor, bought. Kramer sued McDonald's for conversion of the property in which he claimed a security interest. The lower court held for the franchisor, and Kramer appealed.

CLARK, J.: . . . The issue herein is not whether a limited partner may secure a loan but whether a limited partner may secure his capital contribution. . . .

A limited partner is prohibited from taking collateral to secure repayment of his capital contribution. To do so would give him an unfair priority over the creditors of the partnership contrary to the express provisions of section 16(1) of the ULPA:

(1) A limited partner shall not receive from a general partner or out of partnership property any part of his contribution until (a) All liabilities of the partnership, except liabilities to general partners and to limited partners on account of their contributions, have been paid or there remains property of the partnership sufficient to pay them.

(b) The consent of all members is had, unless the return of the contribution may be rightfully demanded under the provision of paragraph (2), and
(c) The certificate is cancelled or so amended as to set forth the withdrawal or reduction.

A limited partnership interest is in the nature of an investment. Through his contribution, the limited partner becomes entitled to share in the profits and losses of the partnership, though his share of the losses will not exceed the amount of capital initially contributed to the enterprise. However, when the limited partner makes the contribution, he is placing that amount at risk. He is not permitted to insure that risk or to guarantee a return to himself by taking some form of security. He may not vie with creditors for the assets available to pay the partnership's obligations. [The ULPA] was designed to prevent illegal competition between the limited partner and creditors of the partnership for the assets of the partnership. It would therefore defeat the purpose of the ULPA to permit Kramer to enforce a security interest against the property purchased by the partnership to operate the restaurant.

We therefore hold that Kramer is prohibited by the express provisions of section 16 of the ULPA from accepting collateral as security for his capital contribution. . . . [Affirmed.]

8. Continuity of Organizations

One factor that should be considered when selecting the best form of organization for your business purpose is the degree to which an organization's existence is tied to its owners. In essence, this factor concerns how stable is an organization's independent continuity. In this section, the dissolution of organizations is examined. This term **dissolution** refers to the legal existence of the organizational form. The following paragraphs include general principles about dissolutions and statements about the impact of a dissolution on a business.

A general partnership is dissolved any time there is a change in the partners. For example, if a partner dies, retires, or otherwise withdraws from the organization, the partnership is dissolved. Likewise, if a person is added as a new partner, there is a technical dissolution of the organization. Therefore, it generally is said that the partnership organization is easily dissolved. Even if the partnership agreement provides that the partnership will continue for a stated number of years, any partner still retains the power to dissolve the organization. In other words, although liability may be imposed on the former partner for wrongful dissolution in violation of the agreement, the partnership nevertheless is dissolved. [Note: the principles stated in this paragraph are applicable to limited partnerships if there is a change in the general partners. A limited partner may assign his or her interest to another without dissolving the limited partnership.]

In contrast to the easily dissolved nature of a partnership, a corporation usually is formed to have perpetual existence. The law treats a corporation's existence as distinct frrom its owners' status as shareholders. Thus, a shareholder's death or sale of her or his stock does not affect the organizational structure of a corporation. This ability to separate management from ownership is an often cited advantage of the corporation.

To rely on the general principles of a partnership's continuity being much more unstable than a corporation's is to be short-sighted. The more important question is: How will a dissolution of an organization affect the business of that organization? A dissolution does not necessarily destroy the business of a partnership. Dissolution is not the equivalent of terminating an organization's business activity. Termination involves the winding up or liquidating of a business; dissolution simply means the legal form of organization no longer exists. Likewise, the death of a major shareholder of a corporation has no impact on the organization's existence. However, such an event may have an adverse influence on that corporation's ability to keep old customers or attract new ones.

The solution to problems arising when a partner dies or withdraws from a partnership, or when a shareholder dies or desires to withdraw from a closely held corporation, is a "buy and sell" agreement. These agreements, which need to be entered into when the business entity is *created*, provide for the amount and manner of compensation for the interest of the deceased or withdrawing owner. In a partnership, the buy and sell provisions are usually contained in the Articles of Copartnership. In a corporation, the agreement may be between shareholders or between shareholders and the corporation itself. In the latter case, the corporation redeems the stock of the withdrawing or deceased shareholder. Buy and sell agreements frequently use formulas to compute the value of the withdrawing owner's interest and provide for the time and method of payment. In the case of death, the liquidity needed is often provided by the cash proceeds from life insurance which was taken out on the life of the deceased and made payable to the business or to the surviving partner or shareholder. Upon payment of the amount required by the buy and sell agreement to the estate of the deceased, the interest of the deceased ends, and the surviving owners continue the business. A buy and sell agreement should specify whether the agreement is a right of first refusal or whether the surviving or remaining owners must purchase the interest of the deceased or withdrawing owner.

RENBERG v. ZARRO
667 P.2d 465 (Okla. 1983)

In 1963, the shareholders of a closely held corporation executed an agreement which provided that upon the death of any shareholder, the survivors had an option for one year from the date of death to buy a deceased shareholder's shares at a price set by the majority shareholders each year. If no price was established for a given year, the most recently set price prevailed.

Dorothy Renberg died April 22, 1978. During April of 1979, the surviving shareholders notified Dorothy's husband that they wished to purchase her shares pursuant to the buy and sell agreement. The husband refused to sell and initiated this suit to prevent the transfer of stock. The trial court enforced the agreement, and the plaintiff appealed.

HODGES, J.: . . . Absolute restrictions forbidding the alienation of corporate stock are invalid, but reasonable restrictions are not. The usual purpose of shareholders' agree-

ments which restrict the sale of corporate stock is to prevent transfers to outsiders without first providing an opportunity for the shareholders to acquire the stock. The agreement evolved as a device to assure the succession in interest of persons most likely to act in harmony with the other stockholders. Stock in a corporation creates a personal relationship analogous to a partnership, and shareholders in a close corporation should have the same right to choose one's associates in a corporation as in a firm. Restrictive agreements designed to prevent sale of stock to outsiders must be strictly construed and cannot be applied to transactions which are not expressly mentioned in the agreement; nor can they be enlarged by implication.

A basic reason for buy-sell agreements is to provide methodology to determine the value of the stock. The difficulty of determining the price to be paid arises because shares of a close corporation are not traded on the open market and, therefore, the value cannot be readily ascertained. To induce shareholders to purchase decedents' shares and to provide a market for the stock, the price must be attractive. A great deal of leeway is permitted because the shares represent more than a mere interest in property.

The Sooner shareholders considered several factors other than income tax implications in the periodic revaluation of the option price. These included: the ability of the surviving shareholders to pay the purchase price; maintenance of the option price at a level which would be attractive enough to the survivors to exercise their options; and provision of a market for the shares.

Buy-sell agreements are construed to comply with the manifest intent of the parties. After parties in a close corporation agree on a price formula, the validity of the restriction on transfer does not rest on any abstract notion of intrinsic fairness of price. Before the restriction can be declared invalid, it must be shown that there is more than a mere disparity between option price and current market value. In the absence of fraud, overreaching, or bad faith, an agreement between the stockholders that upon the death of any of them, the stock may be acquired by the corporation is binding. Even a great disparity between the price specified in a buy-sell agreement and the actual value of the stock is not sufficient to invalidate the agreement. Although this agreement inured to the benefit of the Zarrows, it might very well have resulted in benefit to Dorothy had she survived. Under the actuarial tables in effect at the time of the 1963 Agreement, Dorothy stood to gain most by the agreement; she was consistently advised of the value of the stock; she and her attorney had access to Sooner's financial records; and could have called a shareholders' meeting to reassess the stock had she so desired. . . . The language of a written contract governs the rights and obligations of the contracting parties. The courts may not rewrite a shareholders' agreement

under the guise of relieving one of the parties from the apparent hardship of an improvident bargain; nor may the courts rewrite an agreement which is clear and unambiguous on its face. We agree with the trial court's finding that the stipulated price provision wherein no one knows for certain at the time the price is set whether he is to be a buyer or a seller is inherently fair and provides mutuality of risk. . . .

A court of equity will not enforce stock transfer restrictions adopted under circumstances which indicate bad faith and inequitable treatment of stock purchasers. Because close corporations are usually family affairs, a special relationship may exist between the majority shareholder of a close corporation and a minority shareholder. If a fiduciary relationship exists, and circumstances result in the enhancement of the value of the stock which are known to the officers, directors or the majority shareholders because of their position in the corporation, but which are unknown to the minority, the officers, directors, or the majority shareholders are required to make a full disclosure to the minority. Failure to do so may amount to fraud or deceit sufficient to vitiate a sale, and entitle the minority to relief for unjust enrichment.

The relationship of brother and sister does not of itself create a fiduciary relationship between the parties. However, a majority shareholder has a fiduciary duty not to misuse his power by promoting his personal interests at the expense of the corporation, and the majority shareholder has the duty to protect the interests of the minority. Unless minority shareholders have been systematically excluded from directors and shareholders' meetings, minority stockholders in a close corporation usually have access, apart from the corporate records, to inside information which may affect the value of the stock. It has been held that absent circumstances from which fraud or unfair dealing may be inferred, an officer or director of a close corporation has no duty to volunteer information to a stockholder from whom he purchases stock.

There is no evidence that there was fraud or overreaching in connection with the buy-sell agreement. It operated equally con-

cerning all shareholders. The fact that surviving shareholders were allowed to purchase Dorothy's shares on stated terms and conditions which resulted in purchase for less than actual value of the stock does not subject the agreement to attack as a breach of the relation of trust and confidence. . . .[*Affirmed.*]

LIABILITY FACTORS

9. Liability Factors: Partnerships

All partners in a general partnershhip and the general partners in a limited partnership are treated the same for liability purposes. These partners have unlimited liability for their organization's debts. In other words, these partners' personal assets, which are not associated with the partnership, may be claimed by the partnership's creditors. From a creditor's perspective, this personal liability of each partner extends to the organization's entire debt, not just to a pro rata share. These partners are *jointly and severally liable* for the partnership's obligations. For example, assume that a general partnership has three partners and that it owes a creditor $300,000. If it is necessary to collect the debt, this creditor can sue all three partners jointly for thhe $300,000. As an alternative, the creditor can sue any one partner or any combination of two for the entire $300,000. Between the partners, anyone who has to pay the creditor more than her or his pro rata share of the liability usually can seek contribution from the remaining partners.

A more in-depth discussion of partners' liability is presented in the next chapter. There you will see that personal liability may arise from (1) breach of a contract, (2) commitment of a tort, (3) failure to perform a public duty, or (4) violation of a statute. The degree of liability placed on the individual partner may vary depending on the occurrence of each of these events.

The limited partnership as a hybrid for liability purposes has been mentioned previously. The Uniform Limited Partnership Act, which has been adopted or revised by every state except Louisiana, governs the rights and duties of the general and limited partners. Under this statute, a limited partner is viewed as lending money to the business organization for a percentage of the profits rather than for a fixed return such as interest. Because the limited partner is treated as a creditor, there are several restrictions placed on the activities of this party. For example, contributions to the firm may be in cash or property but not services. Surnames of the limited partner may not be used in the partnership's name unless there is a general partner with the same name. If a limited partner's name is used in the firm's name, that partner will become personally liable to unsuspecting creditors. Also, limited partners may not participate in management without incurring unlimited liability. In some states, this participation may not even be indirect, as by managing the partnership through a corporate general partner. However, limited partners do not lose their limited liability by showing an interest in the firm or by making suggestions.

TRANS-AM BUILDERS, INC. v. WOODS MILL, LTD.
210 S.E.2d 866 (Ga. 1974)

STOLZ, J.: . . . The litigation before us arose out of the construction of an apartment complex involving Trans-Am Builders, Inc., as general contractor (appellant) and Woods Mill, Ltd., a limited partnership (appellee) with a number of individuals as limited partners and The Baier Corporation as the general partner. . . .

During the construction of the project, financial difficulties arose, resulting in appellant's either abandoning or being removed from the project. Suits and countersuits were filed. However, there is but one issue before us, that is, have the limited partners conducted themselves in such a manner as to "take part in the control of the business" and thus become liable as a general partner? . . .

Code Ann. § 75-411 provides as follows: (1) A limited partner shall have the same rights as a general partner to (a) Have the partnership books kept at the principal place of business of the partnership, and at all times to inspect and copy any of them. (b) Have on demand true and full information of all things affecting the partnership, and a formal account of partnership affairs whenever circumstances render it just and reasonable. (c) Have dissolution and winding up by decree of court. (2) A limited partner shall have the right to receive a share of the profits or other compensation by way of income, and to the return of his contribution. . . .

The evidence before us reveals that the limited partners (with one exception) held at least two meetings after it became apparent that the project was in financial difficulty. At these meetings the situation was presented by a representative of the general partner, discussions were participated in, and additional money was raised to meet financial obligations. At least one of the limited partners went to the project and went over it with the appellant's superintendent, and "obnoxiously" complained and objected to the way the work was being conducted, but there is nothing to indicate that he gave any directions which may have been followed by the plaintiff's superintendent. . . . The appellant contends that these actions violated Code Ann. § 75-411, *supra,* and that the limited partners thus became general partners. The trial judge held otherwise and sustained the limited partners' motion for summary judgment, from which judgment the plaintiff appeals. . . .

It is well established that just because a man is a limited partner in an enterprise he is not by reason of that status precluded from continuing to have an interest in the affairs of the partnership, from giving advice and suggestions to the general partner or his nominees, and from interesting himself in specific aspects of the business. Such casual advice as limited partners may have given to [the employees] can hardly be said to be interference in day-to-day management. Certainly common sense dictates that in times of severe financial crisis all partners in such an enterprise, limited or general will become actively interested in any effort to keep the enterprise afloat and many abnormal problems will arise that are not under any stretch of the imagination mere day-to-day matters of managing the partnership business. This is all that occurred in this instance. . . .

It would be unreasonable to hold that a limited partner may not advise with the general partner and visit the partnership business, particularly when the project is confronted with a severe financial crisis. [*Judgment affirmed.*]

In an attempt to modernize and clarify the law of limited partnership, a Revised Uniform Limited Partnership Act has been prepared and proposed to the states for adoption. At least ten states (Arkansas, Colorado, Connecticut, Maryland, Minnesota, Montana, Nebraska, Washington, West Virginia, and Wyoming) have adopted this revised act. In these states there is a substantial change in the liability of a limited partner who participates in control of the business. The liability of a general partner is imposed on a limited partner who participates in the control of the business only if the third party has had knowledge of the participation. In addition, this revised act clarifies that a limited partner does not participate in the control of the business by (1) being an agent or employee of the business, (2) consulting with or advising a partner with respect to the partnership, (3) acting as surety of the limited partnership, (4) approving or disapproving of an amendment to the certificate, and (5) voting on matters such as dissolution, sale of assets, or a change of name.

10. Liability Factors: Corporations

Traditionally, it has been said that the investors in a corporation have limited liability but those in a partnership have unlimited liability. This generalization is too broad and needs qualification. To be sure, someone investing in a company listed on the New York Stock Exchange will incur no risk greater than the investment, and the concept of limited liability certainly applies. However, if the company is a small, closely held corporation with limited assets and capital, it will be difficult for it to obtain credit on the strength of its own net worth standing alone. As a practical matter, shareholders will usually be required to add their own individual liability as security for debts. For example, if the XYZ Company seeks a loan at a local bank, the bank often will require the owners, X, Y, and Z, to personally guarantee repayment of the loan. This is not to say that shareholders in closely held corporations do not have some degree of limited liability. Shareholders have limited liability for contract-like obligations which are imposed as a matter of law (such as taxes).

Liability also is limited when the corporate obligation results from torts committed by company employees while doing company business.

Even in these situations, the mere fact of corporate existence does not mean the shareholders will have liability limited to their investment. When courts find that the corporate organization is being misused, the corporate entity can be disregarded. This event has been called "piercing the corporate veil." When this veil of protection has been pierced, the shareholders are treated like partners who have unlimited liability for their organization's debts.

Courts have identified several situations in which the corporate veil can be pierced. First, the corporate entity may be used to defraud or avoid an otherwise valid obligation. For example, if A sold B a business and A agreed not to compete with B for two years, but if, in violation of the contract, A organized a corporation and competed with B, the contract would have been breached. Second, the corporation may be used to evade a statute. For example, if a state law provides that a person may not hold more than one liquor license at a time, this law cannot be circumvented by forming multiple corporations. Third, the corporate entity may be disregarded when one corporation is organized, controlled, and conducted in a manner that makes it an instrument of another corporation. In such circumstances, one corporation is said to be the "alter ego" of another. It must be recognized that the mere relationship of a parent corporation with a subsidiary is not enough by itself to justify piercing the corporate veil. Subsidiaries are often formed in order to limit the liability of the parent corporation. The alter-ego theory, by which the corporate veil can be pierced, may also be used to impose personal liability upon corporate officers and stockholders. If the corporate entity is disregarded by the principals themselves, so that there is such a unity of ownership and interest that separateness of the corporation has ceased to exist, the alter-ego doctrine will be followed and the corporate veil will be pierced. The following case illustrates that courts are not limited to these three factors when they decide whether or not to disregard a corporation's separate identity. If there is, in fact, no separate personality for the corporation, the corporate veil may be pierced.

READER v. DERTINA & ASSOCIATES MARKETING
693 P.2d 398 (Colo. App. 1984)

PIERCE, J.: Defendants, Dertina and Associates Marketing, Inc. (Dertina), and David Dertina, individually, appeal from a trial court judgment entered against both the corporation and David Dertina in favor of plaintiffs, Richard Reader, Robert Kruse, and Styles Adamson. We affirm.

During 1978, while operating as a sole

proprietorship, David Dertina hired Adamson, Reader, and Kruse to perform services for the company in return for commissions, bonuses, and overrides. In 1979, the business was incorporated with David Dertina as the sole stockholder.

After being discharged from their employment, plaintiffs sued defendants for commissions and bonuses due and owing for services rendered in 1978 and 1979. Dertina counterclaimed, arguing plaintiffs had breached their contract by neglecting their duties. The trial court found that plaintiffs had worked diligently, faithfully, and satisfactorily and awarded monetary damages for services rendered for management overrides, consulting fees, and bonuses.

David Dertina first argues that the trial court improperly pierced the corporate veil to find him personally liable to plaintiffs for sums due after the corporation was formed. We disagree.

If the corporate veil is pierced by application of the alter ego doctrine, stockholders may be held personally liable for corporate obligations. This doctrine arises in cases where the corporate entity has been used to defeat public convenience, or to justify or protect wrong, fraud, or crime, or in other similar situations where equity requires.

Here, the testimony showed that the business had been incorporated as a mere formality for IRS purposes; that no director's meetings were held; that David Dertina retained total control of company operations; that David Dertina set the commission structures; that he took money from the corporate account for personal purchases; that ample earnings were made after incorporation; that plaintiffs performed valuable services for the corporation; and that Dertina made promises of possible ownership sharing and future benefits to the plaintiffs. Thus, there is a sound basis for the conclusion that David Dertina used the corporate entity principally as an instrumentality for the transaction of his own affairs; that there was a unity of interest in ownership such that separate personalities of the corporation and David Dertina himself did not exist; and that adherence to the corporate entity would promote injustice. The trial court's finding that the corporation was operated as the alter ego of David Dertina, therefore, is justified. . . . [*Affirmed.*]

TAXATION FACTORS

11. Taxation Factors: Partnerships

A partnership, whether of a general or limited nature, is not a taxable entity. The fact that this type of organization pays no income tax does not mean that the profits of the partnership are free of income tax. A partnership files an information return which allocates to each individual partner his or her proportionate share of profits or losses from operations, dividend income, capital gains or losses, and other items which would affect the income tax owned by a partner. Partners then report their share of such items on their individual income tax returns, irrespective of whether they have actually received the items.

This aspect of a partnership becomes advantageous to the partners if the organization suffers a net loss. The pro rata share of this loss is allocated to each partner, and it can be used to reduce these partners' personal taxable income. However, by this same reasoning the partnership organization becomes disadvantageous if any profits made are retained by the organization for expansion purposes. Suppose a partnership which has three equal partners has $30,000 in net income. If this money is kept by the partnership, there still is a constructive distribution of $10,000 to each partner for tax purposes. Assuming that these partners are in a 40 percent personal income tax bracket, they each would have to pay $4,000 in taxes even though they actually received nothing from the partnership.

12. Taxation Factors: Corporations

Unlike partnerships, corporations must pay income taxes on their earnings. The corporate tax rates may be changed by Congress. These changes relate to the condition of our economy and the impact desired on employment and economic growth. In August 1986, Congress considered a tax reform law designed to lower significantly both individual and corporate tax rates. The lower rates would be offset by the elimination of certain deductions and credits such as the investment tax credit. The following tables compare the 1985 rate structure with the tax reform proposed legislation:

1985 Rates

$ of Income	Tax Rate
0– 25,000	15 percent
25– 50,000	18 percent
50– 75,000	30 percent
75–100,000	40 percent
over 100,000	46 percent

1986 Proposed Rates

$ of Income	Tax Rate
0–50,000	15 percent
25–75,000	25 percent
over 75,000	34 percent

The fact that there is a separate corporate income tax may work as an advantage. For example, if the corporation makes a profit which is to be retained by the corporation for growth needs, no income is allocated to the shareholders. In other words, these shareholders will not have their personal taxable income increased as would a partner in a similar situation. Also, the corporate rate may be lower than the individual rates.

In the past, the most often cited advantage of the corporate organizational form was the sheltering of taxable income. In general, the employees of a corporation could defer from taxes much more income than could employees of a proprietorship, partnership, or limited partnership. Therefore, whenever a business became very successful, there were strong incentives to become a corporation. As of 1984, these incentives have been removed by Congress. Indeed, for the purposes of sheltering income from taxes, all business organizations are treated essentially equally. Thus, the factor of the amount that can be paid into profit-sharing and pension plans is no longer of major importance when deciding which organization is the best for a particular business.

Now we turn to some tax disadvantages of the corporation. Suppose a corporation suffers a loss during a given tax year. The existence of the corporate tax works as a disadvantage, since this loss cannot be distributed to the shareholders in order to reduce their personal tax liability. Indeed, a net operating loss to a corporation can be used only to offset corporate income earned in other years. And the allocation of such a loss can be carried back only for three years and carried forward for fifteen years. [Note: There are many different rules concerning specialized carryover situations. The Internal Revenue Code should be examined prior to relying on the general rule just stated.] Perhaps a greater disadvantage of the corporate tax occurs when a profit is made and the corporation wishes to pay a dividend to its shareholders. The money used to pay this dividend will have been taxed at the corporate level. It is then taxed again because the shareholder must take the amount of the dividend into his or her own personal income. The rate of this second tax depends on the personal tax rate of the shareholder receiving the dividend. This situation has been called the "double tax" on corporate income. A similar situation of "double taxation" occurs when a corporation is dissolved and its assets are distributed to shareholders as capital gains. This next section presents a discussion which indicates that the "double tax" may not be as big a disadvantage as it first seems.

13. Avoiding Double Taxation

There are at least four techniques for avoiding at least part of the problem caused by the "double taxation" of corporate income. First of all, reasonable salaries paid to corporate officials may be deducted in computing the taxable income of the business. Thus, in a closely held corporation in which all or most shareholders are officers or employees, this technique may avoid double taxation of substantial portions of income. As might be suspected, the Internal Revenue Code disallows a deduction for excessive or unreasonable compensation and treats such payments as dividends. Therefore, the determination of the reasonableness of corporate salaries is often a tax problem in that form of organization.

Second, the capital structure of the corporation may include both common stock and interest-bearing loans from shareholders. For example, assume that a company needs $100,000 cash to go into business. If $100,000 of stock is issued, no expense will be deducted. However, assume that $50,000 worth of stock is purchased by the owners, and $50,000 is lent to the company by them at 10 percent interest. In this case, $5,000 interest each year is deductible as an expense of the company and thus subject to only one tax as interest income to the owners. Just as in the case of salaries, the Internal Revenue Code has a counteracting rule relating to corporations that are undercapitalized. If the corporation is undercapitalized, interest payments will be treated as dividends and disallowed as deductible expenses.

The third technique for avoiding double taxation, at least in part, is simply not to pay dividends and to accumulate the earnings. After the earnings have been accumulated, the shareholders can sell their stock or have the company dissolved. In either case, the difference between the original investment and the amount received upon dissolution is given capital gains treatment. [A taxpayer who has held a capital asset, such as stock, for longer than the long-term holding period (currently six months) needs to recognize only 40 percent of the gain as taxable income. In other words, 60 percent of the long-term capital gain is tax-free.] Once again, tax laws exist that are designed to counteract this accumulated-earnings technique. The Internal Revenue Service seeks to compel corporations to distribute those profits not needed for a business purpose, such as growth. When a corporation retains earnings in excess of $250,000, there is a presumption that these earnings are being accumulated to avoid a second tax on dividends. If the corporation cannot rebut this presumption, an additional tax of 27½ percent is imposed on the first $100,000 unreasonably accumulated in excess of $250,000. For undistributed earnings above this amount, the penalty tax equals 38½ percent of the unreasonable accumulation. [Note: These taxes are in addition to the income taxes already paid on these earnings. As you can see, a misuse of this accumulated-earnings technique can be very costly.]

Fourth, there is a special provision in the Internal Revenue Code that allows small, closely held business corporations to be treated as partnerships for income tax purposes and thereby avoid having a tax assessed on the corporate income itself. These Subchapter S corporations cannot have over thirty-five shareholders, each of whom must elect to be taxed as a partnership, that is, to have the corporate income allocated to the shareholders annually in computing their income for tax purposes, whether actually paid out or not. The permissible number of shareholders has been increased in recent years from ten to thirty-five in order to encourage greater use of the Subchapter S election. There are many technical rules of tax law involved in Subchapter S corporations, but as a rule of thumb, this method of organization has distinct advantages for a business operating at a loss, because the loss is shared and immediately deductible on the returns of the shareholders. It is also advantageous for businesses capable of paying out net profits as earned. In the latter case, the corporate tax is avoided. If net profits must be retained in the business, Subchapter S tax treatment is disadvantageous because income tax is paid on earnings not received, and there is a danger of double taxation to the individual because undistributed earnings which have been taxed once are taxed again in the event of the death of a shareholder. Thus, it is evident that the theoretical advantage of using the Subchapter S corporation to avoid double taxation of corporate income must be heavily qualified.

CONTROL

14. In Partnerships

In every business organization, some individual or group of people will make decisions or possess control of the business. In a general partnership, unless the agreement provides to the contrary, each partner has an equal voice in the firm's affairs, with an equal right to possess partnership property for business purposes. In a limited partnership, the general partner or partners with unlimited liability are in control. Limited partners have no right to participate in management.

Partners are liable for all transactions entered into by any partner in the scope of the partnership business and are similarly liable for any partner's torts committed while she or he is acting in the course of the firm's business. Each partner is in effect both an agent of the partnership and a principal, being capable of creating both contract and tort liability for the firm and for her or his copartners, and likewise being responsible for her or his own acts. There are many technical rules concerning what acts of a partner are within the scope or course of the partnership. One such special rule is worthy of mention. A partner in a trading partnership, that is, one engaged in the business of buying and selling commodities, has the implied authority to borrow money in the usual course of business and to pledge the credit of the firm; but a partner in a nontrading partnership, such as an accounting firm, has no implied power to borrow money. In the latter case, such authority must be actual before the firm will be bound. A further discussion of the partnership's operation and liability of the partners is presented in the next chapter.

15. Of Large Corporations

In the corporate form of organization, legal problems created by persons in control and by those seeking control are quite numerous. In very large corporations, control by management is maintained with a very small percentage of stock ownership through the utilization of corporate records and funds to solicit proxies. Management can, at corporate expense, solicit the right to vote the stock of shareholders unable to attend the meetings at which the directors of the company are elected. An outsider must either own sufficient stock to elect the directors or must solicit proxies at his or her own expense. Although there are a few proxy fights, the management of a large corporation usually can maintain control with only a small minority of actual stock ownership.

In corporations having several hundred shareholders or more, a number of techniques are used to gain control without having a majority of the total investment. One technique is to issue classes of stock. In some states there can be nonvoting stock—the group seeking to keep control will buy voting stock while selling nonvoting stock to others. Preferred stock may be used to increase capital without losing control. For example, a group may invest $100,000 in common stock of $1 par value each. Then they will sell another $100,000 of the same common stock, requiring that for each share of common stock purchased, a $5 share of nonvoting preferred stock must be purchased. Thus, the corporation would raise $700,000, and the $100,000 original investment made by the organizing individuals would have 50 percent of the voting power. There are other schemes which can be used, such as selling some stock to the organizers for 10 cents per share and selling later shares for $1 to outsiders. Another method of gaining and keeping control is to pool the stock of several shareholders into a voting trust so that one person gains the power, by contract, to vote all the shares in the trust.

Once again, other issues concerning corporate operations are discussed in the next chapter on liability and in Chapter 16 on investor protection. An understanding of these securities laws really is essential when a corporation's stock is being publicly traded.

16. Of Closely Held Corporations

Unlike the situation with a large, publicly held corporation, one shareholder (or at least a small group of shareholders) may be able to control a closely held corporation. This can result because this individual (or the group) can own an actual majority of the issued shares. This majority can control the election of a board of directors. In fact, the shareholders with the largest amount of stock often are elected to this board of directors. The directors, in turn, elect officers, who again may be the shareholders with the largest interests. The directors also establish important corporate policies, such as declaring dividends and amending the bylaws. In a very real sense, those who own a majority of a closely held corporation can rule with near absolute authority.

What then are the rights of those who do not possess control in a closely held corporation—the so-called "minority interest"? To a very large degree, the owners of the minority interest are subject to the whim or caprice of the majority. The majority may pay themselves salaries which use up profits and may never declare a dividend. However, the minority interest is not without some rights, because the directors and officers stand in a fiduciary relation to the corporation and to the minority shareholders if the corporation is closely held. This relation imposes a duty on directors to act for the best interests of the corporation rather than for themselves individually.

If the majority are acting illegally or are oppressive of the rights of the minority shareholders, a lawsuit known as a *derivative action* may be brought by a minority shareholder on behalf of the corporation. Such suits may seek to enjoin the unlawful activity or to collect damages for the corporation. For example, contracts made between the corporation and an interested director or officer may be challenged. The burden is on the director or officer (who may be the majority shareholder) to prove good faith and inherent fairness in such transactions if a suit is commenced.

A derivative suit cannot be used as a means of harassing management. Therefore, these actions generally cannot begin until all possible means to solve the problem within the corporate organization have been exhausted. Generally, a minority shareholder must first demand that the board of directors institute a suit to protect the corporation. However, a formal demand on the board is excused if the demand would be futile, such as when the directors are accused of the wrongdoing. In these situations, companies may appoint a disinterested committee to decide when a derivative suit filed on behalf of the company is in the organization's best interest. An independent committee balancing between the rights of the aggrieved shareholders and the needs of management may be subject to judicial review.

The basic difficulty of owning a minority interest in a closely held corporation arises from the fact that there is no ready market for the stock should the shareholder desire to dispose of it. Of course, if there is a valid buy and sell agreement, then there is a market for the stock. Thus, buy and sell agreements are absolutely essential in closely held corporations. Although shareholders have the right to attend meetings and vote for directors, they may be constantly outvoted. They have a right to any dividends that are declared but no right to have them declared. They also have a preemptive right, which is to purchase their proportionate share of any new stock issue, but they may not be interested in investing more money when no dividends are being paid. Therefore, as a practical matter, the majority may be able to increase their percentage of ownership further.

The minority shareholder has a right to inspect the books and records of the company, but at a proper time and place; and the books may not have much meaning without entries and account balances being analyzed by an expert.

Finally, minority shareholders have the right to their proportionate share of assets on dissolution, but they have no right to dissolution, except that they may seek it in a court of equity under circumstances that will cause a court to step in to protect creditors and the corporation.

REVIEW QUESTIONS

1 Identify the terms in column A by matching each with the appropriate statement in column B.

A	B
(1) Partnership	(a) A business owned by one person who is personally liable for all losses
(2) Proprietorship	(b) An artificial being created by a state
(3) Limited partnership	(c) Imposed when a corporation fails to justify not paying dividends from earnings

(4) Corporation

(d) Created when shareholders elect to be treated as partners for tax purposes

(5) Legal capacity

(e) Created by an agreement between two or more persons who agree to share profits and losses

(6) Buy and sell agreement

(f) Provides for compensation to a deceased or withdrawing owner of a business in return for that owner's interest

(7) Subchapter S corporation

(g) The ability of an organization to sue or to own property

(8) Accumulated earnings tax

(h) Exists when some partners are treated like shareholders for liability purposes

2 The You-Can-Be-Rich Corporation sells products for resale to citizens in Texas. You-Can-Be-Rich is a Delaware corporation with its principal place of business in Chicago, Illinois. Although it is not licensed to do business in Texas, it has sold its products through sales representatives who have operated out of their own homes. One customer in Texas has failed to pay the money owed, and the corporation has filed suit to collect the debt. What defense, if any, is available to the customer? Explain.

3 Curtis sold feed to a corporation. He was given a corporate check that was returned by the bank for insufficient funds. When the corporation failed to cover the check, he sued the directors and sought to hold them personally liable for the check. Give examples of factors that would justify a decision for the plaintiff.

4 Beck and Kirk entered into a "land development agreement" that provided that Beck would contribute land and Kirk would furnish her expertise to create a residential housing development to be called "Beckhaven Estates." Beck and Kirk agreed to divide any profits. Kirk employed the plaintiff, Indiana Surveying, to plot the development.

When Kirk failed to pay for the survey, a suit was instituted against Beck and Kirk as partners to collect. Beck denied liability. What was the result? Why?

5 Lewis and Tabor signed a written agreement to operate a dairy farm. This contract required Tabor to furnish the cows and the labor and Lewis to provide the land and the milking equipment. These parties also agreed to share the proceeds or losses equally. Their agreement specifically stated that these parties were not partners but that Tabor was leasing Lewis's land and equipment. Are these parties actually partners? Why, or why not?

6 An office manager of a corporation filed suit to collect an account in a small-claims court. The office manager was not an attorney. The defendant moved to dismiss. What result? Why?

7 You and a friend are considering forming a business organization to manufacture and sell widgets. You suspect that the company will show a loss during its first two years of operation. You also know that another manufacturer of widgets has suffered three product liability lawsuits totaling $300,000 within the past year. What form of business organization should be selected under these circumstances? Why?

8 Libby and Gloria have formed a limited partnership, with Gloria agreeing to be the general partner. This partnership has purchased supplies from Carl. Carl has received a promissory note signed on behalf of the partnership as payment. If the partnership is unable to pay this note, can Carl hold Gloria personally liable? Explain.

9 The plaintiffs entered into a series of contracts involving coal excavations with Doral Coal Company and Dean Coal Company. Robert W. William, defendant, was president of both coal companies. When royalty payments owed were not made by the corporations as agreed, plaintiffs canceled the agreements and filed suit against the defendant individually. They contended that the defendant was personally liable because he was the sole shareholder of each corporation. Is the defendant liable? Why, or why not?

10 List and explain four techniques used to avoid the double taxation of corporate income in closely held corporations.

11 X, Y, and Z wish to go into the television sale and repair business. X will contribute $20,000 and work in the business as the chief repairperson. Y will contribute $30,000. She will be employed as manager in charge of buying and selling new television sets. Z will contribute $60,000. Whereas Z will not actively engage in the operations of the business, before he contributes any money he wants to be assured that he will have the final say on all matters other than the day-to-day operations of the business. What form of business organization should be selected to accomplish these objectives? Explain.

12 Albert Anderson and Barbara Brinson wish to enter into the business of manufacturing fine furniture. Which form of business organization would you recommend in each of the following situations? Explain each of your answers.

   a Brinson is a furniture expert, but she has no funds. Anderson knows nothing about such production, but he is willing to contribute all the money needed to start the business.

   b The furniture manufacturing process requires more capital than either Anderson or Brinson can raise together. However, they wish to maintain control of the business.

   c The production process can be very dangerous, and a large tort judgment against the business is foreseeable.

   d Sales will be nationwide.

   e A loss is expected for the first several years.

Chapter
12

Liability of Business Organizations and Managers

1. Introduction

When a contract is breached, a tort committed, or a law violated, issues of liability immediately arise. Is the business entity liable? Is the person involved liable? If there is liability, to whom? If payment is made to one person, is there a right of contribution or indemnity from another? These issues are in part answered by the law of agency. Other answers are found in the law of partnerships and corporations. Still others are found in various statutes and in case law. The sections which follow will discuss some of the more important legal theories used to impose liability on various kinds of businesses and those who operate them.

LIABILITY BASED ON CONTRACT LAW

2. Principals

Businesses obviously have liability on authorized contracts entered into on their behalf. However, questions of contractual liability often arise when an alleged agent enters into a contract with a third party on behalf of a purported principal. The general rule is that a principal has liability on all contracts entered into by the agent within the scope of the actual or apparent authority of the agent. Actual authority includes that expressly given and all that is necessarily implied to carry out the express authority. The principal may be a corporation, a partnership, or a sole proprietorship. Before the person dealing with the agent can hold the principal to the contract, he or she must prove the existence of this authority of the agent, although such factors as trade custom and emergencies may be used to establish it. Actual authority is that which is expressly given and all that is necessarily incidental to or implied in the express authority.

The term "apparent authority," sometimes called "ostensible authority," refers to situations in which no actual authority exists, but in which the law binds the principal as if it did because, by his or her conduct, he or she has led third persons to believe that the agent has authority and that they should rely on the belief. Ostensible authority is when a principal, intentionally or through carelessness, causes or allows another to believe the agent possesses authority. Liability of the principal for the ostensible agent's acts rests on the doctrine of estoppel. Its essential elements are representation by the principal, justifiable reliance thereon by the third party, and change of position or injury resulting from such reliance.

VICKERS v. NORTH AM. LAND DEVELOPMENT
607 P.2d 603 (N.M. 1980)

Plaintiff sued to enforce a land sales contract. The contract provided that the plaintiff would be allowed to trade one purchased lot for a 2-acre parcel of the plaintiff's choice as soon as the property was developed for sale. Defendant refused to allow the exchange, contending that its salesperson, Walsh, lacked authority to agree to trade commercial property for residential property. The trial court held for the defendant.

FEDERICI, J.: . . . We are cognizant of the fact that the record supports the court's conclusion that Walsh lacked actual authority to bind the appellee.

However, the record unequivocally establishes that Walsh had apparent authority to bind appellee. The Doctrine of Apparent Authority has long been established in New Mexico. A principal is bound by the apparent authority of his agent, irrespective of whether he has actual authority, if the agent is placed in a position which would lead a reasonably prudent person to believe that the agent did indeed possess that apparent authority. . . .

If the principal puts one into, or knowingly permits him to occupy, a position in which, according to the ordinary experience and habits of mankind, it is usual for the occupant to have authority of a particular kind, anyone having occasion to deal with one in that position is justified in inferring that the person in question possesses such authority, unless the contrary is then made known.

In this case appellee knowingly placed Walsh in a position and gave him a title and power that would lead a reasonably prudent person to believe that he did have authority to enter into the Contract and Trade Agreement in question.

The Doctrine of Apparent Authority is based upon an estoppel theory: [T]he principal will not be permitted to establish that the agent's authority was less than what was apparent from the course of dealing for when one of two innocent parties must suffer, the loss must fall upon the party who created the enabling circumstances.

Here, Walsh made no oral or written disclaimer of his authority prior to consummating the transaction with appellants. . . .

Inherent in an estoppel theory is the factor of detrimental reliance. The detriment suffered here is in the nature of a loss of the benefit of the bargain, as both parties were in agreement that the property to be traded for . . . would be more valuable than the original parcel acquired. . . . North American Land Development Co., created the enabling circumstances by placing Walsh in a position which would lead a reasonably prudent person to believe that he possessed the power to consummate transactions of the type in question through execution of the agreements, by failing to post or give notice of any limitations on his authority prior to consummation of the transaction, and by cashing the $5,000 check which appellants gave as downpayment, creating an inference of ratification of Walsh's action. In view of these circumstances, we hold that appellee placed Walsh in a position of authority and should now be estopped from disavowing authority on the part of Walsh to bind it on a contract of sale and trade agreement. . . . [*Reversed.*]

In addition to being the basis of liability when an agent lacks actual authority, apparent authority can expand an actual agent's authority beyond that granted by the principal. In other words, apparent authority may exist in a person who is not an agent, or it may increase the actual authority of an agent. In either of these situations, remember that an agent cannot create her or his own apparent authority. This type of authority must be based on the principal's words or conduct; it cannot be based on anything the agent says or does.

Probably the typical situation in which apparent authority is found to exist is when the actual authority is terminated, but notice of this fact is not given to third parties. Cancellation of actual authority does not automatically terminate the apparent authority created by prior transactions. Because apparent authority may survive the termination of an agency relationship, the principal should give notice of termination to third parties.

A principal is also liable for unauthorized contracts if he or she is found to have ratified the contract. Conduct that indicates an intention to adopt an unauthorized transaction will constitute ratification. For example, an expression of approval to the agent or performance of the contract will constitute a ratification. In order for a valid ratification to occur, the principal must (1) have capacity to do what the agent has done, (2) be known to the third party, and (3) have full knowledge of the facts.

First, since ratification relates to the time of the agent's actions, both the principal and agent must be capable of that action at that time. Furthermore, they must maintain their capacity until the ratification actually occurs.

Second, an agent's act may be ratified only when the agent has acted as an agent. A person who professes to act for himself in his own name does nothing that can be ratified, even though he intends at the time to let another have the benefit of his acts. In other words, the third party has to have known about the existence of the principal at the time the unauthorized actions have occurred.

Third, in general, a principal cannot be held to have ratified an agent's unauthorized acts if he lacks full knowledge of all the material facts associated with the agent's actions. When the principal expressly ratifies unauthorized acts and shows no desire to learn all the facts, he may not deny liability on the ground that he has been ignorant of all important information. However, when ratification is implied from the principal's conduct, a lack of full knowledge may become a defense against liability.

A ratification may be expressed by the principal, or it may be implied from the principal's conduct. Any conduct that clearly indicates the principal's intention to approve the agent's actions will be a ratification. Accepting the benefits of the unauthorized acts definitely is a ratification. If the principal knows what the agent has done and if she or he makes no objection within a reasonable time, a ratification results by operation of law. The issue of what is a reasonable time is a factual one for a jury to resolve.

3. Agents

In contractual situations, the ultimate purpose of an agency is to have the agent negotiate and reach an agreement with the third party. Although the contract is made by these two parties, typically they each desire to have the liability run between the principal and third party. That is, in general it is desirable and the expectation of all parties involved for the principal to be substituted for the agent. In other words, if everything works according to plan, the principal and third party become liable to one another, and the agent is not liable on the contract.

EPPLER, GUERIN & TURNER, INC. v. KASMIR
685 S.W.2d 737 (Tex.App. 5 Dist. 1985)

GUITTARD, J.: Eppler, Guerin and Turner, Inc., appeals from a summary judgment that it take nothing on its claim for appraisal fees against the appellees C.D. Kasmir, Esq., and Kasmir, Willingham & Krage, attorneys at law. We hold that the summary judgment evidence established as a matter of law defendants' affirmative defense that they were only acting as agents for a disclosed principal. Therefore, we affirm.

Plaintiff, an investment banking firm, was hired by defendants to render an opinion on the value of certain securities that were the subject of a suit between defendants' client, Intercontinental Industries, Inc., and the Internal Revenue Service. It is undisputed that plaintiff knew at the time it was hired by defendants that defendants were attorneys representing Intercontinental Industries in the pending suit. Plaintiff prepared a letter agreement addressed to defendants outlining the details of its employment. This letter is styled "Re: Intercontinental Industries vs. The Internal Revenue Service." In part, it provides: (1) that plaintiff shall render a valuation opinion on specified securities "to be received and ultimately received by Intercontinental Industries, Inc.," and (2) that the billings for this opinion and for testimony in court "shall be rendered to your firm" (the defendants' firm). In addition, this letter agreement contains the following acknowledgment by defendants:

Agreed and Accepted this
30th day of June 1982
KASMIR WILLINGHAM AND KRAGE
by /s/ Cyril David Kasmir

Plaintiff contends that this letter agreement establishes that defendants undertook personal liability for the payment of its professional fees and that the trial court, therefore, erred in granting the defendants' motion for summary judgment and in denying its motion for summary judgment. We disagree.

Except in the case of negotiable instruments, the general rule is that when an agent contracts for the benefit of a disclosed principal, the agent is not liable on the contracts he makes. Of course, the parties to a contract can alter this general rule by agreement so that the agent will be liable on the contract. The agent may bind himself to such a con-

tract by expressly or impliedly agreeing either to substitute his own responsibility for that of his principal or to add his personal responsibility. Thus, it is clear that if an agent is liable on a contract he has made for the benefit of a disclosed principal, his liability is predicated upon his specified contractual obligation and not upon his agency relationship.

Accordingly, we hold that when an attorney contracts with a third party for the benefit of a client for goods or services to be used in connection with the attorney's representation of a particular client and the third party is aware of these facts, the attorney is not liable on the contract unless he either expressly or impliedly assumes some type of special liability. . . .

Plaintiff argues that defendants' express or implied assumption of liability is established by the letter agreement because it was signed by defendant Kasmir without disclosing an intent to sign only in a representative or agency capacity. In other words, plaintiff argues that the defendants are personally liable on the letter agreement because they did not place the word "agent" or "attorney" after their respective typed or manually signed names. In support of this argument, the plaintiff cites *Seale v. Nichols*, 505 S.W.2d 251 (Tex. 1974), which states:

Texas law provides that in order for an agent to avoid liability for his signature on a contract, he must *disclose* his intent to sign as a representative to the other contracting party. Uncommunicated intent will not suffice.

We do not regard *Seale* as controlling here because in *Seale* the agency relationship was not disclosed on the face of the contract or by extrinsic circumstances. The opinion shows that the only evidence of Seale's agency was his affidavit stating his undisclosed subjective intent to sign the promissory note in question as agent for a corporate principal. Here the letter on its face establishes plaintiff's knowledge that defendants were acting as counsel for a particular client in pending litigation. *Seale* does not require every contract signed by a lawyer for a disclosed client to contain explicit language negating his personal liability. Rather, such contracts are governed by the rule already stated that an agent who signs a contract for the benefit of a disclosed principal is not liable on the contract unless there is an express or implied agreement for specially imposing personal liability.

We hold that defendants have established their affirmative defense of agency. Plaintiff has failed to raise a disputed fact issue upon whether the defendants undertook a special obligation to assume liability for the payment of the plaintiff's fees. Therefore, the trial court properly granted the defendants' motion for summary judgment and denied the plaintiff's motion for summary judgment. [*Affirmed.*]

As the foregoing case illustrates, the general rule is that agents do not become personally liable to third parties, since with regard to liability the principal is substituted for the agent. However, there are three situations in which an agent and third party are contractually bound to one another. First, if the agent fails to disclose the identity of the principal, the agent is personally liable. A person who fails to identify the principal and the fact of the agency relationship is liable as a principal on the contract. This rule seems logical, since the third party has no one other than the agent to hold liable. The agent remains liable to the third party until that time when the principal is disclosed and the third party elects to hold the principal, and not the agent, liable.

The second situation involving the agent's liability to third parties arises whenever the agent agrees to be personally liable or when the agent has failed to sign a document in a representative capacity. When an agent works for a truly undisclosed principal, no representative capacity will be indicated. However, if the agent for a disclosed or partially disclosed principal fails to indicate clearly his agency capacity, that agent becomes personally liable to the third party.

A third instance of an agent's becoming personally bound to a third party occurs when the agent has exceeded actual and apparent authority. In essence, whenever a person as an agent negotiates with a third party, that agent implicitly promises she or he has authority to make the contract involved. If that promise is breached, the agent is liable to the third party.

LIABILITY BASED ON TORT LAW

4. Basic Concepts

The typical situation involving tort liability occurs when an employment arrangement results in injury to a third party. The issue usually involves determining who is liable for the third party's injury—the employee (servant) or the employer (master). The following general statements present the guidelines used in determining tort liabililty:

1   The party committing the tort (wrong) is liable for the damage done.

2   A master is liable for the torts of servants who were acting within the scope of their employment.

3   The party hiring an independent contractor usually is not liable for the torts of that independent contractor.

An employee is always liable for his or her own torts. The fact that the employer may also be liable does not excuse the employee.

SANFORD v. KOBEY BROS. CONST. CORP.
689 P.2d 724 (Colo. App. 1984)

BERMAN, J.: Plaintiffs, Andrew M. and Olivia M. Sanford, appeal the judgment of the trial court holding defendant Kobey Brothers Construction Corp. (Kobey Brothers) liable to plaintiffs in the amount of $8,905.59 and holding co-defendant Harris Kobey not jointly or severally liable. . . .

Kobey Brothers constructed a home for the plaintiffs in the Cherry Hills North area of Englewood, Colorado. For various reasons, the foundation was incompatible with the soil, resulting in heaving and damage to the home. Plaintiffs sued both Harris Kobey and Kobey Brothers for negligent construction and breach of express and implied warranties. The trial court found no individual liability on the part of Harris Kobey, but found Kobey Brothers liable for damages arising from the negligent reduction of the "void space" between the foundation and interior basement walls, as well as from certain other work negligently performed. The trial court measured plaintiffs' damages by the cost to repair the injuries caused by the improperly reduced void space and other errors attributable to Kobey Brothers.

Plaintiffs first contend that the trial court erred in not finding Harris Kobey personally liable for his allegedly negligent acts. They argue the trial court improperly applied the doctrine of *respondeat superior* as a shield barring personal liability and *sua sponte* looked unsuccessfully for reasons to "pierce the corporate veil" instead of simply attributing to Harris Kobey personal responsibility for his negligent acts. We agree that Kobey should be held personally liable.

Neither the doctrine of *respondeat superior* nor the fiction of corporate existence bars imposition of individual liability for individual acts of negligence, even when the individual is acting in a representative capacity. Rather, a servant may be held personally liable for his individual acts of negligence, as also may an officer, director, or agent of a corporation for his or her tortious acts, regardless of the fact that the master or corporation also may be vicariously liable. Thus, if Harris Kobey personally committed any negligent act, judgment should also have entered against him personally.

The record reveals that Harris Kobey

did personally commit the negligent act causing the major portion of damages attributable to Kobey Brothers. The trial court found that the reduction in size of the "void space" from the specified three inches to the improper one and one-half inches constituted negligence. Harris Kobey admitted three times on the witness stand that he personally and solely authorized the reduction, and in fact did so arbitrarily. Accordingly, joint and several liability for the entire judgment should have entered against Harris Kobey. . . . [*Reversed.*]

A principal is vicariously liable for the torts of an agent, and an employer is liable for the torts of an employee if the agent or employee acts within the scope of his or her employment or is working for the employer. Likewise, a partnership and the individual parties have tort liability for torts of a partner or of an employee of the partnership committed within the scope of the partnership business. This liability is created by a doctrine known as *respondeat superior*.

The doctrine of *respondeat superior* imposes vicarious liability on those (masters) who actually have not committed any tort. This concept of vicarious liability is based on the public policy of placing responsibility on the party who is most capable of paying for the damage done. This principle has been referred to as the *deep pocket* theory of liability. In essence, the doctrine of *respondeat superior* provides that the cost of doing business should include liability for injuries to persons and property which are caused by employees within the scope of employment. Thus, the business bears the cost of these injuries rather than having the injured victim or the employee bear the burden alone.

The concept of vicarious liability is an expanding one. In the twentieth century, juries and courts have enlarged the definition of scope of employment and thus have increased the total risk of businesses of all types. This is especially true now that the automobile and truck play a major role in the conduct of business.

STANFIELD v. LACCOARCE
588 P.2d 1271 (OR.) 1978

HOWELL, J.: Plaintiff brought this action for damages arising out of an accident in which the defendant Roy Laccoarce's truck collided with an automobile in which plaintiff was a passenger. The jury returned a verdict for plaintiff, and defendants appeal.

The accident occurred on November 26, 1975, at the crest of Camas Mountain in

Douglas County. Roy Laccoarce was returning from a trip to Roseburg to his home in Camas Valley. The time was late afternoon, it was dark, and light rain was falling. Roy had passed two or three other vehicles going up the grade, and his speed was estimated at 70 miles per hour. Despite the fact that his view was obstructed by a curve, Roy attempted to pass another vehicle 800 to 1,000 feet from the scene of the accident. There was evidence that his vehicle began sliding on the curve, entered the opposite lane, and struck the vehicle in which plaintiff was riding. . . .

There was conflicting evidence with respect to the primary purpose of Roy's trip to Roseburg, but there was evidence from which the jury could reasonably conclude that at least one purpose was to pick up supplies for various businesses owned by Roy's parents in Camas Valley.

Plaintiff sued Roy Laccoarce and his parents, James and Pauline Laccoarce, contending that Roy was negligent and that at the time of the accident Roy was acting as an employee of his parents.

The Laccoarces ran a grocery store, cafe, and ambulance service in Camas Valley. They also owned a service station that was operated by one Hiram Cunningham for a percentage. Mrs. Laccoarce testified that Roy worked at the grocery store and cafe as a "part time cook and part time was available if I needed him and he's helped stock on the heavier stuff and occasionally did chores in town."

After arriving in Roseburg on the date of the accident, Roy picked up an order from a grocery wholesaler and an order from a candy company for his parents' store. He also picked up some automotive parts for his parents' service station. He went to the bank where his parents maintained their checking account, made a deposit for his parents, and picked up change for them. . . .

Under the doctrine of respondeat superior, an employer is liable for the torts of his employee when the employee is acting within the scope of his employment. In deciding whether an employee was acting within the scope of his employment, the factors to be considered are whether the act in question is of a kind the employee was hired to perform, whether the act occurred substantially within the authorized limits of time and space, and whether the employee was motivated, at least in part, by a purpose to serve the employer. The scope of employment limitation is designed to ensure that employers will be held liable only for harm resulting from activity from which they were receiving the benefit. [T]he ultimate question is whether or not it is just that the loss resulting from the servant's acts should be considered as one of the normal risks to be borne by the business in which the servant is employed. Consequently, we have held that the question of whether or not an employee has acted within the scope of his employment at any given time is normally a question for the jury, except in cases where only one reasonable conclusion can be drawn from the facts. This is not a case in which only one reasonable conclusion can be drawn from the facts.

The jury could . . . have concluded that the trip Roy made to Roseburg was "of a kind the employee was hired to perform" and that he was operating "within the authorized limits of time and space" at the time the accident occurred.

Defendants argue that there was no evidence that they had any "right to control" the conduct of Roy at the time of the accident. We have recognized, particularly in automobile cases, that the "right to control" test is often of no assistance in deciding whether an employee is acting within the scope of his employment. No employer can "control" the manner in which an employee drives or other details of his trip. In reality, the question of whether the employer had a "right to control" the employee is merely another way of asking whether the activity in question occurred within the authorized limits of time and space, so that it is fair to make the employer vicariously liable for the conduct of the employee. Viewed in this manner, there was evidence, from which the jury could conclude that defendants had a "right to control" Roy's trip to Roseburg.

Defendants' principal contention is that the primary purpose of Roy's trip was personal and that he was not motivated by a desire to serve his parents. We think there was ample evidence from which the jury could have reached the opposite conclusion.

On the basis of the evidence reviewed above, we conclude that the court did not err in denying defendants' motion for a directed verdict. . . . [*Affirmed.*]

Principals may also have tort liability based on apparent authority. For example, a trade association was held to have liability under the antitrust laws if its personnel were involved in the violations. Likewise, a principal is liable for an agent's fraud even though the agent acts solely to benefit himself or herself, if the agent has apparent authority.

Under the apparent authority theory, liability is based upon the fact that the agent's position facilitates the consummation of the fraud, in that from the point of view of the third person the transaction seems regular on its face and the agent appears to be acting in the ordinary course of business.

It should be noted that everyone performing a service is not necessarily a servant or agent of an employer. Work is sometimes performed by an independent contractor. Whether a person is a servant or an independent contractor is determined by the degree of control the employing party exercises. More control indicates a master-servant relationship. Less control is associated with a proprietor-independent contractor relationship. In essence, an independent contractor has the power to control the details of the work performed.

As a general rule, the person hiring an independent contractor is not personally liable for the contracts or torts of the independent contractor. In other words, general agency principles, including the doctrine of *respondeat superior,* are not applicable in the typical situation involving an independent contractor.

Liability based on tort theories is so important that it was the subject matter of Chapter 6.

5. Illegal Conduct

A business may owe dollar damages to injured parties because of illegal conduct by its officers, agents, or other employees. Conduct may be illegal either because it violates a statute or because it is contrary to public policy. Many statutes provide legal rights to injured parties to recover the damages caused by a business organization. In a civil action, investors can seek to recover their investment when the organization has violated any of the securities laws (Chapter 16), labor laws (Chapters 18 and 19), or antitrust laws

(Chapters 20 and 21). The law of employment also provides for civil remedies if a worker is discharged in violation of equal employment opportunities (Chapter 17). Indeed, a breach of any contract by a business can result in the wronged party seeking monetary damages.

In recent years, courts increasingly have imposed liability upon a business even though the organization has not violated a statute. The basis of this liability is the fact that a business may have acted contrary to public policy. For example, such issues have arisen in cases concerned with the right of an employer to discharge an employee. Public-policy considerations are very important when an employee is not protected by either a collective bargaining agreement or another contract that provides a stated term of employment. Employees who lack these protections traditionally have been called *employees at will*, since the employer can terminate the employment relationship at any time for any reason.

Although the employment-at-will doctrine still exists today, there is a growing movement by courts to vest workers with certain rights and to require business organizations to justify firing a worker. This justification requirement is especially important when the discharge appears to deny an employee the opportunity to exercise a legal right. Such rights may include (1) serving on a jury, (2) filing a workers' compensation claim, (3) refusing to give perjured testimony, (4) refusing to commit an illegal or unethical act, and (5) assisting in the investigation of the organization's wrongful acts.

PALMATEER v. INTERNATIONAL HARVESTER CO.
421 N.E.2d 876 (Ill.) 1981

SIMON, J.: The plaintiff, Ray Palmateer, complains of his discharge by International Harvester Company (IH). He had worked for IH for 16 years, rising from a unionized job at an hour rate to a managerial position on a fixed salary. Following his discharge, Palmateer filed a . . . complaint against IH, alleging . . . that he had suffered a retaliatory discharge. According to the complaint, Palmateer was fired both for supplying information to local law-enforcement authorities that an IH employee might be involved in a violation of the Criminal Code of 1961 and for agreeing to assist in the investigation and trial of the employee if requested. The circuit court of Rock Island County ruled the com-

plaint failed to state a cause of action and dismissed it; the appellate court affirmed. . . . We granted Palmateer leave to appeal to determine the contours of the tort of retaliatory discharge approved in *Kelsay v. Motorola, Inc.* (1978), 74 Ill.2d 172.

In *Kelsay* the plaintiff was discharged in retaliation for filing a worker's compensation claim. The court noted that public policy strongly favored the exercise of worker's compensation rights; if employees could be fired for filing compensation claims, that public policy would be frustrated. . . .

With *Kelsay*, Illinois joined the growing number of States recognizing the tort of retaliatory discharge. The tort is an exception to the general rule that an "at-will" employment is terminable at any time for any or no cause. This general rule is a harsh outgrowth of the notion of reciprocal rights and obligations in employment relationships—that if the employee can end his employment at any time under any condition, then the employer should have the same right. . . .

Recent analysis has pointed out the shortcomings of the mutuality theory. With the rise of large corporations conducting specialized operations and employing relatively immobile workers who often have no other place to market their skills, recognition that the employer and employee do not stand on equal footing is realistic. In addition, unchecked employer power, like unchecked employee power, has been seen to present a distinct threat to the public policy carefully considered and adopted by society as a whole. As a result, it is now recognized that a proper balance must be maintained among the employer's interest in operating a business efficiently and profitably, the employee's interest in earning a livelihood, and society's interest in seeing its public policies carried out.

By recognizing the tort of retaliatory discharge, *Kelsay* acknowledged the common law principle that parties to a contract may not incorporate in it rights and obligations which are clearly injurious to the public. . . . But the Achilles heel of the principle lies in the definition of public policy. When a discharge contravenes public policy in any way the employer has committed a legal wrong. However, the employer retains the right to fire workers at will in cases "where no clear mandate of public policy" is involved: But what constitutes clearly mandated public policy?

There is no precise definition of the term. In general, it can be said that public policy concerns what is right and just and what affects the citizens of the State collectively. It is to be found in the State's constitution and statutes and, when they are silent, in its judicial decisions. Although there is no precise line of demarcation dividing matters

that are the subject of public policies from matters purely personal, a survey of cases in other States involving retaliatory discharges shows that a matter must strike at the heart of a citizen's social rights, duties, and responsibilities before the tort will be allowed. Thus, actions for retaliatory discharge have been allowed where the employee was fired for refusing to violate a statute. It has also been allowed where the employee was fired for refusing to evade jury duty, for engaging in statutorily protected union activities, and for filing a claim under a worker's compensation statute.

The action has not been allowed where the worker was discharged in a dispute over a company's internal management system, where the worker took too much sick leave, where the worker tried to examine the company's books in his capacity as a shareholder, where the worker impugned the company's integrity, where the worker refused to be examined by a psychological-stress evaluator, where the worker was attending night school, or where the worker improperly used the employer's Christmas fund.

The cause of action is allowed where the public policy is clear, but is denied where it is equally clear that only private interests are at stake. Where the nature of the interest at stake is muddled, the courts have given conflicting answers as to whether the protection of the tort action is available. . . .

It is clear that Palmateer has here alleged that he was fired in violation of an established public policy. The claim is that he was discharged for supplying information to a local law-enforcement agency that an IH employee might be violating the Criminal Code, for agreeing to gather further evidence implicating the employee, and for intending to testify at the employee's trial, if it came to that. . . . There is no public policy more basic, nothing more implicit in the concept of ordered liberty than the enforcement of a State's criminal code.

There is no public policy more important

or more fundamental than the one favoring the effective protection of the lives and property of citizens.

Public policy favors the exposure of crime and the cooperation of citizens possessing knowledge thereof is essential too effective implementation of that policy. Persons acting in good faith who have probable cause to believe crimes have been committed should not be deterred from reporting them by the fear of discharge. Public policy favors Palmateer's conduct in volunteering information to the law-enforcement agency. Once the possibility of crime was reported, Palmateer was under a statutory duty to further assist officials when requested to do so. Public policy thus also favors Palmateer's agreement to assist in the investigation and prosecution of the suspected crime.

The foundation of the tort of retaliatory discharge lies in the protection of public policy, and there is a clear public policy favoring investigation and prosecution of criminal offenses. Palmateer has stated a cause of action for retaliatory discharge. . . . [*Reversed.*]

LIABILITY BASED ON THE CRIMINAL LAW

6. Business Organizations

Most statutes provide for penalties to be imposed upon those who violate their provisions. If a statute imposes fines or incarceration as a penalty, the law is criminal, and for a court to find a violation there must be proof beyond a reasonable doubt.

In addition to criminal sanctions, many statutes impose civil liability upon wrongdoers as a result of illegal conduct. For example, the antitrust laws allow victims of price-fixing to collect triple damages from those violating the law. These damages are to deter wrongful conduct as well as to compensate the injured parties.

The fiction of the corporate entity creates some difficult problems insofar as criminal law is concerned. A corporation cannot be imprisoned, although in theory a death penalty of sorts could be imposed simply by the domiciliary state's dissolving it. Corporations act only through agents, and while it is possible to imprison the agents in many instances, this would not be satisfactory punishment for the corporate entity. It is, of course, possible to punish a corporation by imposing a fine.

Proving the commission of a crime by a corporation is often as difficult as imposing a meaningful penalty. "Crime" is usually defined in terms of intentional commission of some prohibited act, often with the *specific* intent to do so. How can an artificial being with no mind have criminal intent? The law has generally resolved this problem by imputing to the corporation the guilty intent of an agent, if the agent was authorized and acting within the scope of his or her employment at the time he or she committed the crime. Many cases have equated "acquiescence" by the company in the wrongful conduct with authority to commit the illegal act.

One of the more important laws imposing criminal liability on business is the Foreign Corrupt Practices Act of 1977. This act makes it a criminal offense for any United States business enterprise—whether or not incorporated or publicly held—to offer a bribe to a foreign official, foreign political party, party official, or candidate for foreign political office to obtain, retain, or direct business to any person. Companies violating the act can be fined up to $1,000,000. Individuals convicted of violating the law may be fined up to $10,000 and imprisoned for up to five years. The act prohibits the fine imposed on the individual from being paid directly or indirectly by the company on whose behalf he or she acted.

The Foreign Corrupt Practices Act also establishes certain standards for business records and internal controls for businesses subject to the reporting requirements of the Securities Exchange Act of 1934. As a practical matter, companies doing business in foreign countries must have corporate codes of conduct which prevent bribery of foreign officials and maintain adequate internal controls to monitor and enforce codes of conduct. They must maintain reasonably detailed, complete, and accurate books and records which will reveal any bribery or attempted bribery. Businesses subject to the act must devise sufficient systems of internal accounting control to provide reasonable assurances that the following four objectives have been met:

1 All transactions must be executed in accordance with management's authorization.

2 All transactions are recorded as necessary (a) to permit preparation of financial statements in conformity with generally accepted accounting principles, and (b) to maintain accountability for assets.

3 Access to assets is permitted only to those authorized.

4 The recorded accountability for assets is compared with existing assets at reasonable intervals and appropriate action taken with respect to any differences.

7. Corporate Executives

Just as employees are liable for their own torts, they are responsible for their own crimes. And, as employers are liable for torts committed while employees are acting in the course of their employment, employers may also be held culpable for the business-related crimes of their employees. For example, suppose that the chief of marketing of ABC, Inc., enters into a price-fixing arrangement with two major competitors of ABC. Clearly both the chief and ABC are guilty of a violation of the Sherman Act, discussed in Chapter 20 and both could be fined. The chief also could be imprisoned. But what about the officers of ABC who are superiors of the chief of marketing, who have no knowledge of the chief's wrongdoing, and who are only indirectly connected to it by reason of their executive position and overall company responsibilities? Are they also guilty? Technically, such persons are not the employer of the chief of marketing—ABC is. Therefore, it would appear that the doctrine of *respondeat superior* would not apply to such top officials. However, they sometimes are prosecuted criminally. The issue in the following case was whether the chief executive officer of a corporation was properly convicted of a crime when he had no direct connection with its commission.

UNITED STATES v. PARK
95 S.Ct. 1903 (1975)

Acme Markets, Inc., a large national retail food chain, and Park, its chief executive officer, were charged with violating the Federal Food, Drug and Cosmetic Act. They had allegedly allowed interstate food shipments being held in their Baltimore warehouse to be exposed to contamination by rodents. While Acme pleaded guilty, Park entered a plea of not guilty.

Park admitted that all of Acme's employees were in a sense under his general direction but contended that the company had an "organizational structure for responsibilities for certain functions according to which different phases of its operations were assigned to individuals who, in turn, have staff and departments under them." He identified those persons responsible for sanitation and claimed that he had been informed that a vice president was investigating the situation in Baltimore when it was called to the company's attention by FDA. Park stated that he did not "believe that there was anything [he] could have done more constructively than what [he] found was being done." However Park admitted that providing sanitary conditions for food was something that he was "responsible for" but argued that it was one of many phases of the company that he assigned to "dependable subordinates."

The court instructed the jury that it was not necessary for Park to have personally participated in the situation to be convicted, so long as he had "a responsible relationship to the issue." The conviction was reversed by the Court of Appeals on the ground that the jury instructions should have required a finding of "wrongful action." The Supreme Court granted certiorari.

BURGER, J.: . . . The question presented [is] whether "the manager of a corporation, as well as the corporation itself, may be prosecuted under the Federal Food, Drug, and Cosmetic Act of 1938 for the introduction of misbranded and adulterated articles into interstate commerce." In *Dotterweich* a jury . . . had convicted Dotterweich, the corporation's president and general manager. The Court of Appeals reversed the conviction on the ground that only the drug dealer, whether corporation or individual, was subject to the criminal provisions of the Act, and that where the dealer was a corporation, an individual connected therewith might be held personally only if he was operating the corporation "as his 'alter ego.'"

In reversing the judgment of the Court of Appeals and reinstating Dotterweich's conviction, this Court looked to the purposes of the Act and noted that they "touch phases of the lives and health of the people which, in the circumstances of modern industrialism, are largely beyond self-protection." It observed that the Act is of "a now familiar type" which "dispenses with the conventional requirement for criminal conduct—awareness of some wrongdoing. In the interest of the larger good it puts the burden of acting at hazard upon a person otherwise innocent but standing in responsible relation to a public danger."

Central to the Court's conclusion that individuaals other than proprietors are subject to the criminal provisions of the Act was the reality that "the only way in which a corporation can act is through the individuals who act on its behalf."

[T]he cases reveal that in providing sanctions which reach and touch the individuals who execute the corporate mission—and this is by no means necessarily confined to a single corporate agent or employee—the Act imposes not only a positive duty to seek out and remedy violations when they occur but also, and primarily, a duty to implement measures that will insure that violations will not occur. The requirements of foresight and vigilance imposed on responsible corporate agents are beyond question demanding, and perhaps onerous, but they are no more stringent than the public has a right to expect of those who voluntarily assume positions of authority in business enterprises whose services and products affect the health and well-being of the public that supports them. . . .

[The Court then turned to respondent's argument that the instructions to the jury were defective because they suggested that a finding of guilt could be justified solely because of respondent's corporate position.]

Reading the entire charge satisfies us that the jury's attention was adequately focused on the issue of respondent's authority with respect to the conditions that formed the basis of the alleged violations. Viewed as a whole, the charge did not permit the jury to find guilt solely on the basis of respondent's position in the corporation; rather, it fairly advised the jury that to find guilt it must find respondent "had a responsible relation to the situation," and "by virtue of his position . . . had authority and responsibility" to deal with the situation. The situation referred to could only be "food . . . held in unsanitary conditions in a warehouse with the result that it consisted, in part, of filth or . . . may have been contaminated with filth." . . .

The record in this case reveals that the jury could not have failed to be aware that the main issue for determination was not respondent's position in the corporate hierarchy, but rather his accountability, because of the responsibility and authority of his position, for the conditions which gave rise to the charges against him.

We are satisfied that the Act imposes the highest standard of care and permits conviction of responsible corporate officials who, in light of this standard of care, have the power to prevent or correct violations of its provisions. . . . [*Reversed.*]

In one recent case, the officers of a corporation were convicted of murder. The company used cyanide in its processes, and steps had not been taken to protect workers from cyanide poisoning. From these cases it is clear there is a trend toward holding top company officials responsible for crimes, even though they are only indirectly involved. This is particularly true when public welfare statutes are violated, making certain acts criminal because they endanger the public health, safety, or general welfare. Conviction of such crimes usually does not require proof of an intent to commit the acts outlawed.

SPECIAL ASPECTS OF MANAGERIAL LIABILITY

8. Partners

The general laws of agency apply to partnerships. Each partner, in effect, is an agent of the organization and both a principal and an agent with respect to all fellow partners. As such, every partner owes the duty of loyalty to the partnership and to the other partners. When conducting business, each partner is obligated to exercise good faith and to contemplate the well-being of the organization and the partners. Any time one partner tries to take advantage of a business opportunity for his own personal benefit, he becomes personally liable for damages, since he has broken his fiduciary duty.

With respect to contractual liability, the principles of authority and ratification are applicable to the partnership and its partners. In general, the implied authority of a partner is greater than that of a general agent. Among the common implied powers are the following: to compromise, adjust, and settle claims or debts owed by or to the partnership; to sell goods in the regular course of business and to make warranties; to buy property within the scope of the business for cash or upon credit; to buy insurance; to hire employees; to make admissions against interest; to enter into contracts within the scope of the partnership; and to receive notices. A partner in a trading partnership, i.e., one engaged in buying and selling commodities, has the implied authority to borrow money in the usual course of business and to pledge the credit of the firm; but a partner in a nontrading partnership, such as an accounting firm, has no implied power to borrow money. In the latter case, such authority must be actual before the firm will be bound. A partner entering into such a contract is personally liable on it.

With respect to torts, a partner has the power to impose liability on the partnership through the doctrine of *respondeat superior*. As we discussed in the previous chapter, partners are jointly and severally liable for the debts of their partnership. Therefore, each partner potentially is liable for the torts of every other partner. If a partnership has liability because of a tort of a partner, the organization has the right to collect its losses from the partner at fault. Likewise, any partner who has liability due to another partner's tort can seek contribution from the partner at fault. However, if the injured third party collects directly from the guilty partner, that partner cannot seek contribution from the other partners.

In addition to the agency principles, creating contract and tort liability on partners, an act in violation of a statute or an act contrary to public policy may make the partners liable for monetary damages to third parties. Criminal liability may be imposed on the individual partners as well.

9. Corporate Officers and Directors

The officers and directors of a corporation may have personal liability both in tort and in contract. Liability is based on common law theories and is also created by statutes. The liability is usually to the corporation. It may also extend to shareholders and to third parties. The tort liability of corporate officers and directors is predicated upon basic principles of fault. For example, a director who participates in fraudulent conduct by the corporation has personal liability to the third party on the usual common law tort theories just as does any other agent or servant. Moreover, the director need not personally commit fraud. He or she is liable if the director sanctions or approves it.

The liability of corporate directors is most frequently based on a violation of the fiduciary duty of loyalty owed to the corporation. A director occupies a position of trust and confidence in the corporation and cannot, by reason of his or her position, directly or indirectly derive any personal benefits not enjoyed by the corporation or the shareholders. The duty of loyalty and the duty to act in good faith prohibit directors from acting with a conflict of interest. The most common violation of this duty occurs when a director enters into a contract with or personally deals with the corporation. Since all officers enter into contracts of employment, alleged violations of this duty are quite common. In all circumstances, the director or officer must fully disclose his or her conflict of interest to the corporation. If he or she fails to do so, the contract may be rescinded.

At common law, such a contract was voidable unless it was shown to be (1) approved by a disinterested board, and (2) "fair" to the corporation, in that its terms were as favorable as those available from any other person. Under some modern statutes, the transaction is valid if (1) it is approved, with knowledge of the material facts, by a vote of disinterested directors or shareholders; and (2) the director can show it to be "fair."

The good-faith requirement is also lacking when a director or officer takes an opportunity for him or herself that the corporation should have had. A director is required to first present all possible corporate opportunities to the corporation. Only after an informed determination by the disinterested directors that the corporation should not pursue such opportunities can a director pursue them for personal benefit. In a closely held corporation, this fiduciary duty of loyalty and good faith extends to the other shareholders and even to the other officers, as the case that follows illustrates.

SAMPSON v. HUNT
564 P.2d 489 (Kan. 1977)

There were two shareholders of Bonanza, Inc., and each owned 50 percent of the stock. The defendant, Hunt, was president, and he managed the business. The plaintiff was secretary but inactive. The business operated a shopping center.

The defendant purchased the plaintiff's stock for $75,000. At the time of the sale, the defendant did not inform the plaintiff of (1) additional leases that had been obtained, (2) a commitment for financing of a third phase of the development, and (3) sale of part of the stock to three doctors. When the plaintiff learned these facts, he sued to recover the difference between the selling price and the fair market value of the stock at the time of the sale, alleging a breach of fiduciary duties. The lower court awarded the plaintiff $93,000, and the defendant appealed.

PRAGER, J.: . . . Hunt's appeal raises a question of law involving the duty of a director or managing officer of a corporation to disclose to another stockholder material information as to the status of the corporation's affairs prior to a sale and purchase of corporate stock. It is the established rule in this state that a director of a corporation owes a high fiduciary duty to the other stockholders of the corporation. The Kansas rule is exemplified by *Stewart v. Harris*, 69 Kan. 498 (1904), where we held:

The managing officers of a corporation are not only trustees of the corporate entity and the corporate property, but they are to some extent, and in many respects, trustees for the corporate shareholders.

When two parties occupy to each other a confidential or fiduciary relation, and a sale is made by one to the other, equity raises a presumption against the validity of the transaction. To sustain it the buyer must show affirmatively that the transaction was conducted in good faith, without pressure or influence on his part, and with express knowledge of the circumstances and entire freedom of action on the part of the seller.

A director or managing officer of a corporation having knowledge of the condition of its affairs, because of the trust relation and the superior opportunities afforded for acquiring information, must inform a stockholder not actively engaged in the management of the true condition of the corporation before he can rightfully purchase his stock.

The defendant Hunt on this appeal concedes that such a fiduciary relationship exists where a director or managing officer of a corporation seeks to purchase the corporate shares of a stockholder not actively engaged in the management of a corporation. He maintains, however, that such a fiduciary relationship does not exist where the stockholder who sold his shares is another director or officer of the corporation as is true in the present case where the plaintiff was both a director and secretary of Bonanza, Inc. Although the majority of the earlier cases held to the contrary, the more recent cases hold that in a closely held corporation where one director or officer has a superior knowledge of corporate affairs because he is intimately involved in the daily operations of the corporation while the other director or officer has only a limited role in corporate management, the fiduciary duty is the same as if the latter were a stockholder not actively engaged in corporate affairs.

We hold that the rule of law to be followed in Kansas is that where knowledge of facts affecting the value or price of stock comes to an officer or director of a corporation by virtue of his office or position, he is under a fiduciary duty to disclose such facts to other stockholders before dealing in company stock with them, even if they too are directors or officers, and regardless of whether these facts pertain to intracompany matters, such as the value of assets, or relate to events "outside" the corporation, such as the existence of favorable contracts, the availability of additional financing, or any other matters which would tend to increase the value of the corporation's stock. Applying this rule to the facts and circumstances of the present case we must conclude that the defendant Hunt, as president and director of Bonanza, Inc., breached his fiduciary duty to the plaintiff Sampson, a director and secretary of the corporation, by Hunt's failure to disclose material information affecting the value of the stock of Bonanza, Inc. before contracting to purchase Sampson's shares. [*The judgment of the district court is affirmed.*]

Directors are also liable for failure to exercise due care. In its simplest terms, the duty of care is synonymous with a duty not to be negligent. The standard may be stated in a variety of ways, but the most common says that a director must exercise that degree of care that an ordinarily prudent person would exercise in managing his or her own personal affairs.

Since many directors are not actively engaged in the day-to-day operation of the business, the law recognizes that they must rely on others for much of the information used in decision making. In performing duties, a director is entitled to rely on information, opinions, reports, and statements of others. These include officers and employees whom the director reasonably believes to be reliable and competent in the matters presented. A director may also rely on legal counsel, public accountants, and other expert professionals. Finally, a director may also rely on committees of the board if they act within the designated authority and if he or she reasonably believes they merit confidence. A director does not fulfill his or her duties and does not act in good faith if he or she has knowledge that would cause the reliance to be unwarranted.

These requirements allow directors to use their best business judgment without incurring liability for honest mistakes. Directors must make difficult policy decisions, and they should not have liability if their decisions are based on information that later turns out to be false.

The liability of directors for negligence in the management of the corporation is to the corporation. Since no duty runs to third-party creditors, there is no liability to them or to shareholders. Of course, a shareholder may enforce this liability through a derivative suit—one brought by a shareholder on behalf of the corporation.

The Caterpillar code recognizes that the duties owed by the board of directors is to the company and to shareholders. However, all decisions are to take the public interest into account. The code provides:

BOARD STEWARDSHIP

Law and logic support the notion that boards of directors are constituted to represent share-holders—the owners of the enterprise. We have long held the view that Caterpillar board members can best meet their responsibilities of stewardship to shareholders if they are elected solely by them—and not appointed by governments, labor unions, or other non-owner groups.

Board composition and board deliberations should be highly reflective of the public interest. We believe that is a basic, inseparable part of stewardship to shareholders.

There are several statutes that impose liability on directors and officers. For example, directors or officers may be liable for failure to pay federal withholding and social security taxes for corporation employees if they have responsibility in that area. Likewise, a director or officer is subject to third-party liability for aiding a corporation in such acts as patent, copyright, or trademark infringements, unfair competition, antitrust violations, violation of laws relating to discrimination, or violations of securities laws. Many of these matters are covered in subsequent chapters.

10. Liability of Agents to Principals

Agents owe various duties to their principals. Many of these duties are based on the contract of employment, and others are implied by law from the nature of the relationship. Since the relationship is a fiduciary one, there is an implied duty of loyalty to the principal. This duty of loyalty requires that agents avoid conflicts of interest. A conflict of interest exists if an agent uundertakes a business venture that competes or interferes in any manner with the business of the employer. In addition, an agent may not make a contract for himself or herself that should have been made for the principal. Agents cannot enter into contracts on behalf of the principal with themselves as the other party. Agents may deal with themselves only if they obtain permission of the principal, after full disclosure of all facts materially influencing the situation. Transactions violating the duty of loyalty may always be rescinded by the principal, even if the agent acted for the best interests of his or her principal and the contract was as favorable as could be obtained elsewhere. If an agent violates this duty of loyalty through a conflict of interest, the principal may rescind the contract. Moreover, a principal is entitled to treat any profit realized by the agent in violation of this duty as belonging to the principal. Such profits include rebates, bonuses, commissions, or divisions of profits received by the agent.

Violations of the duty of loyalty often involve <u>improper use of confidential information</u>. Confidential information or trade secrets may include formulas, customer lists, processes, and business data. Trade secrets are known only to a few persons, and efforts to protect them are required if they are to be protected by law. The law prohibits employees from using trade secrets in competition with the employer or from making them public. Industrial espionage is a major problem for high-technology industries. The law in all its aspects is available to assist employers in protecting these trade secrets. Theft of them is a crime. Courts will enjoin the improper use of them and may award damages for violations of the duty of loyalty. Of course, many important property interests are also protected by laws on patents and copyrights. Infringement suits are common, and there is extensive litigation to protect property rights based on the creation of new products and ideas.

J & K COMPUTER SYSTEMS, INC., v. PARRISH
642 P.2d 732 (Utah 1982)

HOWE, J.: Plaintiff, J & K Computer Systems, Inc., brought this action seeking to recover damages from and enjoin its former employees Douglas T. Parrish and A. Chris Chlarson, and a corporation formed by them, Dynamic Software Corporation, from using or disclosing certain of plaintiff's confidential computer programs. . . .

The trial court found for the plaintiff, awarded it $7,500 damages and enjoined the defendants and all persons associated with them from further use of the computer programs. . . . Defendants appeal.

J & K was originally formed . . . by John Robertson and Keith Blake in 1976 to develop, market and install computer software. In March 1978, they hired Parrish as a computer programmer.

In the months that followed, Parrish developed an open-item/balance forward accounts receivable program which would be usable on the IBM System 34. After the program was developed, it was installed by Parrish at the Arnold Machinery Company in Salt Lake City. . . .

In May 1979, Parrish's brother-in-law, Chlarson, was hired as a trainee by J & K and was assigned to work under his direction. Chlarson also entered into an employment agreement similar to the contract between Parrish and J & K prohibiting the disclosure of J & K's computer programs. Two months later, in May 1979, Parrish voluntarily left the employ of J & K and entered into an agreement with Arnold Machinery Company whereby Parrish would provide Arnold Machinery with programming services. . . .

In June 1979, Chlarson voluntarily left J & K and began working with Parrish. Later that month, they formed Dynamic Software Corporation with Parrish as president and Chlarson as secretary-treasurer. The record shows that in July 1979, Parrish made an electronic copy of the accounts receivable program which J & K had installed at Arnold Machinery Company. This copy was made on a magnetic disk which Parrish then gave to Chlarson so that Chlarson could become familiar with it. Chlarson took the disk to the IBM 34 Computer workroom in the IBM building in Salt Lake City, and there began to work with the programs contained thereon. While Chlarson was working with the disk, an employee of J & K saw one of its programs displayed on the screen of the computer terminal. The employee then advised his employer who thereafter, upon advice of legal counsel, went back to the computer room at IBM. Plaintiff retrieved from the garbage can two printouts of the programs which had been displayed and discarded by Chlarson. Those programs were similar to the J & K accounts receivable program and serve as the basis for this lawsuit.

Defendants assail the judgment of the trial court awarding the plaintiffs damages and injunctive relief claiming that the accounts receivable programs were not confidential or trade secrets. There is no dispute that the plaintiff regarded the programs which it developed and used in its business as proprietary. The employment contracts which Parrish and Chlarson signed specified that the computer programs were "valuable, special and unique assets" of plaintiff's bussiness. An expert witness . . . gave testimony which supports the finding that the programs are trade secrets. . . .

A trade secret includes any formula, patent, device, plan or compilation of information which is used in one's business and which gives him an opportunity to obtain an advantage over competitors who do not know it.

It is a well recognized principle that our law will afford protection to the inventor of a special process or trade secret. With the evidence recited above before it, the trial court could have reasonably determined that J & K's accounts receivable program was secret and worthy of protection by the law. Defendants assert that the accounts receivable program was revealed to certain customers and therefore not protectable. The record, however, shows that the plaintiff endeavored to keep its accounts receivable program secret. Plaintiff's employees and customers were informed of the secret nature of the program. The program was marked with the following legend: "Program Products Proprietary To-J & K Computer Systems,Inc., Salt Lake City, Utah. Authorized Use By License Agreement Only." That a few of the plaintiff's customers had access to the program does not prevent the program from being classified as a trade secret where the plaintiff was attempting to keep the secret and the program is still unavailable to the computer trade as a whole.

Defendants next contend that it is unlawful to enjoin them from using their skills, training and experience which they have gained in the computer programming business. . . . Defendants were not enjoined by the order of the trial court from using their general knowledge, skills, memory or experience. They were, however, enjoined from using the proprietary accounts receivable program which the plaintiff had developed. . . . [*Affirmed.*]

11. Ethical Considerations

The fiduciary duties which the director, officer, or other employee owes the corporation—especially the duty of loyalty—can often present difficult ethical as well as legal questions.

In the past, it has been all too common for corporate officers to engage in bribery, price-fixing, illegal campaign contributions, tax evasion, fraud, kickbacks, and bid rigging to further their business interests. Obviously, such blatant illegality could not hide behind any "duty of loyalty," for it violates not only the law, but also contemporary ethical ideas of what is "right" and "good." True loyalty to a corporation would entail seeing that the corporation operated within the law. Often, ethical standards are embodied in the law, thus ensuring that the principled corporation is not put at a disadvantage in competing with those less scrupulous. For example, every United States firm doing business in a foreign country is prohibited from bribing public officials. Each corporate management has a responsibility under the Foreign Corrupt Practices Act, as discussed in section 6, to ensure adequate internal controls to prevent business bribes to foreign officials. Management further must take corrective action if violations are discovered. Various laws prohibit bribes and kickbacks in the United States. Caterpillar's Code of Ethics regarding these matters is consistent with both the statutes and generally accepted ethical norms.

RELATIONSHIPS WITH PUBLIC OFFICIALS

In dealing with public officials, as with private business associates, Caterpillar will utilize only ethical commercial practices. We won't seek to influence sales of our products (or other events impacting on the company) by payments of bribes, kickbacks, or other questionable inducements.

Caterpillar employees will take care to avoid involving the company in any such activities engaged in by others. We won't advise or assist any purchaser of Caterpillar products, including dealers, in making or arranging such payments. We will discourage dealers from engaging in such practices.

Payments of any size to induce public officials to fail to perform their duties—or to perform them in an incorrect manner—are prohibited. Company employees are also required to make good faith efforts to avoid payment of gratuities or "tips" to certain public officials, even where such practices are customary. Where these payments are as a practical matter unavoidable, they must be limited to customary amounts; and they may be made only to facilitate correct performance of the officials' duties.

A more difficult ethical problem to come to grips with is any subtle form of self-dealing by corporate executives. Is an executive being "loyal" to the corporation and its shareholders by negotiating a lavish salary or extravagant employment guarantees (often called "golden parachutes")? It is argued that the executive has the right to demand what he or she is worth and that the corporation has to pay "good money" to get the best people. But consider the so-called golden parachute. This is a special employment contract protecting key executives if corporate control changes hands. The "protection" requires that hefty sums of money be paid to executives, usually over a period of years. In an era of mergers, golden parachutes to protect corporate managers are becoming more common.

Without doubt, golden parachutes arranged in the heat of corporate takeover attempts raise serious ethical questions. During the Bendix–Martin

Marietta merger battle, sixteen Bendix officers arranged for the company to pay $4.7 million annually should they be fired or demoted after a takeover. Martin Marietta followed suit, securing agreements covering twenty-eight executives, ensuring employment or compensation if Bendix was successful in its tender offer for Martin Marietta. One respected business publication editorialized that this practice amounted "to an outrageous misuse of stockholders' assets and an abuse of management prerogatives." Although approved by the corporations' boards of directors, golden parachutes were compared ethically to an executive stuffing a suitcase of company money under the bed as an insurance policy against losing the job in a takeover (clearly an outright theft). Golden parachutes arranged at the time of employment, rather than in the heat of battle, may not be subject to the same strong criticism. Yet the nagging problem of overcompensation remains. As is often the case, the courts will soon have the opportunity to decide the legal question of whether (or when) a golden parachute is a waste of corporate assets.

12. Making Ethical Business Decisions

Much of the focus of ethical problems in business today is on the corporation and how it deals with ethical dilemmas. In the condensed article that follows, Laura Nash details an approach for examining the ethics of a business decision by the corporation.

Ethics without the Sermon[1]

The trend toward focusing on the social impact of the corporation is an inescapable reality that must be factored into today's managerial decision making. But for the executive who asks, "How do we as a corporation examine our ethical concerns?" the theoretical insights currently available may be more frustrating than helpful.

What is needed is a process of ethical inquiry that is immediately comprehensible to a group of executives and not predisposed to the utopian, and sometimes anticapitalistic, bias marking much of the work in applied business philosophy today. So I suggest, as a preliminary solution, a set of 12 questions that draw on traditional philosophical frameworks but that avoid the level of abstraction normally associated with formal moral reasoning.

The Twelve Questions for Examining the Ethics of a Business Decision

1   Have you defined the problem accurately?

How one assembles the facts weights an issue before the moral examination ever begins, and a definition is rarely accurate if it articulates one's loyalties rather than the facts. The importance of factual neutrality is readily seen, for example in assessing the moral implications of producing a chemical agent for use in warfare. Depending on one's loyalties, the decision to make the substance can be described as serving one's country, developing products, or killing babies. All of the above may be factual statements, but none is neutral or accurate if viewed in isolation.

One simple test of the initial definition is the question:

2   How would you define the problem if you stood on the other side of the fence?

There is a power in self-examination: with an exploration of the likely consequences of a proposal, taken from the viewpoint of those who do not immediately benefit, comes a discomfort or an embarrassment that rises in proportion to the degree of the likely injury and its articulation. The discomfort of the alternative definition is meant to prompt a disinclination to choose the expedient over the most responsible course of action.

3 How did this situation occur in the first place?

A full examination of how the situation occurred and what the traditional solutions have been may reveal a more serious discrepancy of values and pressures, and this will illuminate the real significance and ethics of the problem. It will also reveal recurring patterns of events that in isolation appear trivial but that as a whole point up a serious situation.

Such a mechanism is particularly important because very few executives are outright scoundrels. Rather, violations of corporate and social values usually occur inadvertently because no one recognizes that a problem exists until it becomes a crisis. This tendency toward initial trivialization seems to be the biggest ethical problem in business today. Articulating answers to my first three questions is a way of reversing that process.

4 To whom and what do you give your loyalties as a person and as a member of the corporation?

Every executive faces conflicts of loyalty. The most familiar occasions pit private conscience and sense of duty against corporate policy, but equally frequent are the situations in which one's close colleagues demand participation (tacit or explicit) in an operation or a decision that runs counter to company policy. To whom or what is the greater loyalty—to one's corporation? superior? family? society? self? race? sex?

How does one probe into one's own loyalties and their implications? A useful method is simply to play various roles out loud, to call on one's loyalty to family and community (for example) by asking, "What will I say when my child asks me why I did that?" If the answer is "That's the way the world works," then your loyalties are clear and moral passivity inevitable. But if the question presents real problems, you have begun a demodulation of signals from your conscience that can only enhance corporate responsibility.

5 What is your intention in making this decision?

6 How does this intention compare with the likely results?

Two things to remember in comparing intention and results are that knowledge of the future is always inadequate and that overconfidence often precedes a disastrous mistake.

These two precepts, cribbed from ancient Greece,

may help the corporation keep the disparities between intent and result a fearsome reality to consider continuously. The next two questions explore two ways of reducing the moral risks of being wrong.

7 Whom could your decision or action injure?

In an integrated society where business and government share certain values, possible injury is an even more important consideration than potential benefit. In policymaking, a much likelier ground for agreement than benefit is avoidance of injury through those "universal no's"—such as no mass death, no totalitarianism, no hunger or malnutrition, no harm to children.

8 Can you engage the affected parties in a discussion of the problem before you make your decision?

If the calculus of injury is one way of responding to limitations of knowledge about the probable results of a particular business decision, the participation of affected parties is one of the best ways of informing that consideration.

The issue of participation affects everyone. (How many executives feel that someone else should decide what is in their best interest?) And yet it is a principle often forgotten because of the pressure of time or the inconvenience of calling people together and facing predictably hostile questions.

9 Are you confident that your position will be as valid over a long period of time as it seems now?

As anyone knows who has had to consider long-range plans and short-term budgets simultaneously, a difference in time frame can change the meaning of a problem as much as spring and autumn change the colors of a tree. The ethical coloring of a business decision is no exception to this generational aspect of decision making. Time alters circumstances, and few corporate value systems are immune to shifts in financial status, external political pressure, and personnel.

10 Could you disclose without qualm your decision or action to your boss, your CEO, the board of directors, your family, or society as a whole?

The old question, "Would you want your decision to appear on the front page of *The New York Times?*" still holds. A corporation may maintain that there's really no problem, but a survey of how many "trivial" actions it is reluctant to disclose might be interesting. Disclosure is a way of sounding those submarine depths of conscience and of searching out loyalties.

11 What is the symbolic potential of your action if understood? if misunderstood?

The Greek root of our word symbol means both signal and contract. A business decision—whether it is the use of an expense account or a corporate donation— has a symbolic value in signaling what is acceptable behavior within the corporate culture and in making a tacit contract with employees and the community about the rules of the game. How the symbol is actually perceived (or misperceived) is as important as how you intend it to be perceived.

12 Under what conditions would you allow exceptions to your stand?

If we accept the idea that every business decision has an important symbolic value and a contractual nature, then the need for consistency is obvious. At the same time, it is also important to ask under what conditions the rules of the game may be changed. What conflicting principles, circumstances, or time constraints would provide a morally acceptable basis for making an exception to one's normal institutional ethos?

The Good Puppy Theory

The 12 questions are a way to articulate an idea of the responsibilities involved and to lay them open for examination.

What exactly do we expect of the "ethical," or "good," corporation? Three examples of goodness represent prevailing social opinions, from that of the moral philosopher to the strict Friedmaniac.

1 The most rigorous moral analogy to the good corporation would be the "good man." An abstract, philosophical ideal having highly moral connotations, the good man encompasses an intricate relation of abstractions such as Plato's four virtues (courage, godliness or philosophical wisdom, righteousness, and prudence). The activities of this kind of good corporation imply a heavy responsibility to collectively know the good and to resolve to achieve it.

2 Next, there is the purely amoral definition of good, as in a "good martini"—an amoral fulfillment of a largely inanimate and functional purpose. Under this definition, corporate goodness would be best achieved by the unadorned accrual of profits with no regard for the social implications of the means whereby profits are made.

3 Halfway between these two views lies the good as in "good puppy"—here goodness consists primarily of the fulfillment of a social contract that centers on avoiding social injury. Moral capacity is perceived as present, but its potential is limited. A moral evaluation of the good puppy is possible but exists largely in concrete terms; we do not need to identify the puppy's intentions as utilitarian to understand and agree that its "ethical" fulfillment of the social contract consists of not soiling the carpet or biting the baby.

It seems to me that business ethics operates most appropriately for corporate man when it seeks to define and explore corporate morality at the level of the good puppy. The good corporation is expected to avoid perpetrating irretrievable social injury (and to assume the costs when it unintentionally does injury) while focusing on its purpose as a profit-making organization. Its moral capacity does not extend, however, to determining by itself what will improve the general social welfare.

The good puppy inquiry operates largely in concrete experience; just as the 12 questions impose a limit on our moral expectations, so too they impose a limit (welcome, to some) on our use of abstraction to get at the problem.

[1]Reprinted by permission of the *Harvard Business Review*. "Ethics without the Sermon" by Laura L. Nash (November/December 1981). Copyright © 1981 by the President and Fellows of Harvard College; all rights reserved.

REVIEW QUESTIONS

1 Test your knowledge and understanding by matching the term in column A with the appropriate statement in column B.

	A		*B*
(1)	Implied authority	(a)	Approval of an agent's unauthorized acts
(2)	Apparent authority	(b)	Doctrine that creates vicarious liability on the master
(3)	Ratification	(c)	Standard by which managers' decisions are judged
(4)	Undisclosed principal	(d)	A type of actual authority
(5)	*Respondeat superior*	(e)	The fundamental obligation owed by all agents to their principals
(6)	Fiduciary	(f)	The authority that is created by the principal from the third party's perspective
(7)	Business judgment rule	(g)	Exists when a third party does not know of a principal's existence
(8)	Duty of loyalty	(h)	Type of relationship based on trust and confidence

2 Plaintiffs, residents of a housing development built by Milzoco Builders, Inc., sued the president, vice president, and secretary of the corporation as individuals. The plaintiffs allege that due to faulty planning, their homes were built in an area that is often flooded by the drainage of the other areas of the development and that the defendants were negligent in constructing the development. Can these officers be held personally liable? Why, or why not?

3 Klepp Wood Flooring is a contractor engaged in the business of installing wood floors in gymnasiums. Butterfield, an architect, invited Klepp to bid on a job. After the bid was received, Butterfield accepted the bid, but no formal contract was signed. Klepp completed the work and billed Butterfield. Butterfield refused to pay and told Klepp for the first time that the gym was owned by an undisclosed principal. Klepp sued Butterfield for the work performed. What was the result? Why?

4 Taylor and Terry agreed to operate a business called the Christian Book Center, Inc. Each owned 50 percent of the corporate stock. From the business' inception, Taylor was the corporate president. An argument

occurred over the operations of the business. Thereafter, Taylor told Terry that he was "out of business." A short time later, a promissory note that the corporation owed became due. Rather than discussing a possible extension of this note with Terry, Taylor allowed the corporation to default. At a foreclosure sale, Taylor purchased the assets of the corporation and continued the operation in his own name. Terry was not informed of the default or foreclosure sale. When he learned of Taylor's actions, he sued. What was the result? Why?

5 Ann seeking automobile insurance contacted the Wills Insurance Agency. It was an independent insurance agent and broker for several companies. Mr. Wills told Ann that she had full coverage with the defendant insurance company and accepted her premium check. Later, she had an accident, and the defendant company denied that she was insured. Wills had never applied for the insurance and had kept the premium. Is the defendant company liable? Why, or why not?

6 David purchased a new car and called the Prestige Insurance Company's main office to transfer the insurance from his old car to his new one. He spoke to several employees before being transferred to Agnes. Although she had no actual authority to do so, Agnes told David, "Okay, your new car is covered." David had an accident the next day. The insurance company denied the existence of any coverage. If David sues Prestige, should he win? Explain.

7 For several years, Albert acted as a collection agent for Paulette. Recently, Paulette revoked Albert's authority to collect payments from customers. However, neither Paulette nor Albert told any customers of Albert's termination. Yesterday, Deana, one of Paulette's customers, paid Albert the money owed to Paulette. Albert never gave this money to Paulette. Is Deana liable to pay Paulette? Why, or why not?

8 Scott, a truck driver for Matthew Co., decided to detour seven blocks and stop by his sister's house for a visit. Twenty minutes later, Scott headed back to the Matthew Co.'s garage. He was driving faster than the speed limit when he struck and injured Theresa.

    a What are Theresa's rights, if any, against Scott?

    b Assuming Matthew Co. had instructed its drivers to obey all traffic laws, what are Theresa's rights, if any, against the company?

9 Tammy was shopping in Save-a-Lot Grocery Store when Stewart, an employee, brushed Tammy's ankle with a grocery cart. A short time later, while still shopping, Tammy told Stewart that he should say "Excuse me," and then people would get out of his way. Stewart then punched Tammy in the face, knocking her to the floor. If Tammy sues Save-a-Lot, should she collect for her injuries? Explain.

10 A patient sued Dr. Flynn for medical malpractice. Dr. Flynn, who is a partner in a medical partnership, sought contributions from his partners. He contended that his negligence, if any, occurred in the course of the partnership's business. Is Dr. Flynn entitled to contributions from his partners? Why, or why not?

11 Phil sued the Dallas Company for breach of contract. He was director of the company, and his presence and vote were necessary to the approval of the contract with him. Dallas Company contends that the contract is not binding. Is the company correct? Explain.

12 R. J. owned a majority of the stock of U-Wing Oil Company, and he ran the corporation by himself. The balance of the stock was owned by R. J.'s brother and sister, who agreed to sell their stock to him. At the time of the purchase, R. J. was negotiating a sale of the company, but he did not reveal this fact to his brother and sister. The sale of the company resulted in a great profit to R. J. The brother and sister brought suit to recover the difference. Should the brother and sister succeed? Why?

13 Carr, the president of D Corp., entered into a contract to purchase the stock of P Corp. from Ostrich, its sole shareholder, and to hire Ostrich at a compensation exceeding $100,000. On learning of the transaction, D Corp.'s board of directors discharged Carr as president and renounced the contract. D Corp. contended that Carr lacked authority to make the contract. Did Carr have any authority to make the contract? Why, or why not?

14 One of several owners of a parcel of real estate granted an option to Bell to buy the land. The party granting the option claimed to be the sole owner and did not purport to be the agent of anyone. The other owners refused to go along with the sale when Bell exercised the option. The option consideration had benefited all the owners in that it had been used to pay expenses connected with the land. Are the other owners bound to the contract? Why, or why not?

15 Parents of a deceased child brought a wrongful death action against a company whose employee collided with the deceased when the employee was driving home in an intoxicated condition from the employer's Christmas party. Is the employer liable under the doctrine of *respondeat superior?* Why, or why not?

16 An injured workman brought an action to enforce a worker's compensation award against a bankrupt corporation. The corporation failed to carry workers' compensation insurance. Since the employee was unable to recover from the bankrupt corporation, he brought an action against the officers and directors of the corporation. What was the result? Why?

Chapter

13

International Transactions

1. INTRODUCTION

The education of business students is not complete without some understanding of, and appreciation for, the complexities of the international legal environment. Individuals and firms that engage in transactions across national borders confront legal issues that differ significantly from those in purely domestic transactions.

The recognition of global markets for goods and services has contributed to the increase in international activities by U.S. firms, as have many other factors. In the last two decades, availability of raw materials from foreign countries, access to their labor markets (typically ones in which lower wages are paid), less stringent environmental and other regulatory standards, and incentives offered by other countries to attract business operations have all played a role in dramatically increasing the level of U.S. firms' international business activities. In this chapter the topic of international transactions is presented from the perspective of a U.S. (domestic) firm that conducts business in other countries. Sales of goods or services abroad, purchases of goods or services from abroad, international transportation and communication, currency exchange, international securities transactions, and other forms of international investment illustrate the range of activities that may be affected by international law.

International business activities generate more than one-third of the U.S.

gross national product (GNP); thus, their influence on the U.S. economy is profound. The global impact of international business is also staggering. More than two hundred multinational businesses have sales in excess of $1 billion per year. Virtually all Fortune 500 companies are engaged in international trade, as are most major foreign business enterprises and many smaller domestic firms.

The need for businesses to know and obey local law was discussed in Chapter 1. This need is even more pressing when companies conduct business internationally. Domestically, there may be significant differences in the laws among states. Internationally, not only may the law of one country differ from the law of another, but also fundamental variations may exist in the basic structure of the legal systems. Common law, civil (or code) law, socialist law, Muslim law, and tribal law systems exist throughout the world. Most countries' legal systems are not purely one or another of these but involve mixtures of two or more. Therefore, obtaining knowledge of the legal environment in which one is conducting business will often be extraordinarily difficult. Yet, the need to know and comply with foreign legal requirements is of paramount importance.

The relevant international legal environment does not consist of a cohesive body of uniform principles. It contains elements of U.S. domestic law, law of other countries, bilateral and regional agreements or conventions (treaties), and "customary international law." The entire international legal environment is not summarized here; instead, selected aspects of important issues for firms engaging in international business transactions are presented. These issues include: (1) alternative methods of conducting international business, (2) the legal institutions and agreements affecting international business, and (3) domestic laws having international trade consequences.

ALTERNATIVE METHODS OF CONDUCTING INTERNATIONAL BUSINESS

2. Overview

A U.S. firm that wants to engage in business activities abroad is presented with an almost limitless array of possiblities regarding the manner in which it can do business. Choosing a method of doing business in other countries requires considering not only the factors involved in operating domestically (such as who is in control, what the potential liabilities are, how capital may be raised, how continuity can be maintained, and what the income tax consequences are) but also other factors. Determining the most appropriate form for conducting international operations involves assessing marketing and finance factors as well as international law issues.

3. Direct Sales Abroad

The simplest, least risky approach for a manufacturer to use when trying to penetrate foreign markets is to sell goods directly to buyers located in other countries. However, with foreign sales, increased uncertainty over the ability to enforce the buyer's promise to pay for goods often requires that more complex arrangements for payment be made than with the usual domestic sale. Commonly, an **irrevocable letter of credit** is used to ensure payment. Transactions using such a letter involve, in addition to a seller and buyer, an **issuing bank** in the buyer's country. The buyer obtains a commitment from the bank to advance (pay) a specified amount (i.e., the price of the goods) upon receipt from the carrier, of a **bill of lading**, stating that the goods have been shipped. The issuing bank's commitment to pay is given, not to the seller directly, but to a **confirming bank** located in the United States from which the seller obtains payment. The confirming bank forwards the bill of lading to the issuing bank in order to obtain reimbursement of the funds that have been paid to the seller. The issuing bank releases the bill of lading to the buyer after it has been paid, and with the bill of lading the buyer is able to obtain the goods from the carrier. Use of a letter of credit in the transaction thus reduces the uncertainties involved. The buyer need not pay the seller for goods prior to shipment, and the seller can obtain payment for the goods immediately upon shipment.

Relatively few risks are involved in direct sales abroad. The exports may be subject to tariffs or other fees, but there is no foreign presence by the domestic firm, so the transaction does not usually subject the seller to foreign taxation. Note that both U.S. laws and the laws of other countries may prohibit the sale (export) of certain types of goods. For example, the **Export Administration Act** authorizes the President to prohibit the export of certain goods or technology. In 1980, the export of computer parts and technology to the Soviet Union was prohibited. The **Trading with the Enemy Act** prohibits exports to certain specified countries. Among foreign countries, Syria has prohibited the import of air conditioners, cigarettes, cosmetics, peanuts, and perfume.

4. Use of Foreign Agents

Domestic sellers of goods may be better able to locate potential buyers in other countries by using representatives or **agents** within those countries. Designation of agents with contractual authority is considered by most countries to constitute "doing business" within them, thus subjecting a selling firm to taxation, fees for doing business, and potential lawsuits in foreign courts. Further, principles of agency law in many foreign countries are significantly different from principles of agency law in the United States. In some countries, an agency's relationships may be irrevocable regardless of the principal's dissatisfaction with performance rendered by an agent. In other countries, especially Middle Eastern ones, a company's appointment of a local agent may be possible only if it uses an approved "model contract of agency," which includes provisions giving exclusive distribution rights to the agent. It is extremely important for local companies to retain counsel when dealing with unfamiliar legal systems.

5. Licensing of Technology

In appropriate circumstances, a domestic firm may choose to grant a foreign firm the rights to produce and sell a product. **Licensing** concerns the transfer of intangible property rights, such as patents, trademarks, or manufacturing processes, in exchange for the payment of royalties, which are usually based upon the quantity of goods manufactured or sold. Licensing is often used as a transitional technique for firms expanding international operations, since the risks are greater than with exporting but considerably less than with direct investment abroad. A variation of licensing which is becoming an increasingly favored technique for firms entering foreign markets is franchising of trademarks, trade names, or copyrights.

The international licensing of intangible intellectual property rights presents the need for international protection of these rights. Under national law, owners are provided with exclusive rights to patents, copyrights, trademarks, and trade names after they are registered in the United States. Foreign violations cannot be prohibited unless these rights are also registered in other countries, many of which have differing attitudes toward providing protection. International counterfeiting and piracy of intellectual property have become, during the last decade or so, a monumental problem. Cartier watches, Apple computers, designer jeans, books, movies, videotapes, computer software, and many other products are being produced and sold in violation of the patent, trademark, or copyright owner's rights. Three major **conventions** (agreements) exist that provide some copyright protection on an international scale, but major gaps in protection still exist. The United States is actively seeking diplomatic and political resolution of these serious deficiencies.

6. Foreign Subsidiaries

As their level of involvement in foreign activities increases, domestic firms may find that creation of foreign subsidiaries is necessary. Most countries will permit a foreign firm to conduct business only if a national (individual or firm) of the host country is designated as its legal representative. This designation may create difficulties in control and result in unnecessary expense, so the usual practice for multinational corporations is to create a foreign subsidiary in the host country. The form of subsidiary most closely resembling a U.S. corporation is known as a **societe anonyme (S.A.)** or, in German-speaking countries, an **Aktiengesellschaft (A.G.)**. Other forms of subsidiaries may also exist that have characteristics of limited liability of the owners and fewer formalities in their creation and operation.

Creation of a foreign subsidiary may pose considerable risk to the domestic parent firm. The 1983 incident in Bhopal, India, whereby hundreds of people were killed and thousands injured as a result of toxic gas leaks from a chemical plant, resulted in lawsuits against both the Indian subsidiary corporation and the parent firm in the United States, Union Carbide. Such is the magnitude of the problem that Union Carbide offered $350 million to settle these claims.

As with all forms of international activities, the establishment of contractual provisions between the parties in a licensing arrangement is critically important. Some aspects of all agreements between parties from different countries that merit consideration include:

1 **Language**. Language and translation problems are especially important in the international legal environment. In addition to the usual difficulties associated with all translation, the translation of legal terms often creates additional uncertainty because many terms do not have precise counterparts in other languages. Many legal terms also convey concepts or principles much broader than the words themselves. The language used in contracts and other legal instruments as well as the interpretation given to the words in all relevant languages should be agreed upon before the documents are finalized.

2 **Choice of law**. Disputes are inevitable. The parties in an international transaction may be able to reduce time, expense, and delay in resolving disputes by providing a clause in the contract designating the law which will be used to determine their rights and obligations. Such a provision is known as a "choice-of-law" clause. Commonly, the law of New York is used, but the law, say, of Sri Lanka, Nebraska, or France may be as appropriate.

3 **Arbitration**. Increasingly, parties in international transactions recognize the advantages that arbitration of disputes has over litigation. The International Chamber of Commerce has well-developed rules for arbitration of international disputes. A contractual provision calling for arbitration under these (or other) rules should be considered.

7. Joint Ventures

In many instances, the only legally or politically feasible means a firm has to directly invest in a foreign country is to engage in a joint venture with an entity from that host country. Actually, joint ventures can be constituted by partners from two (or more) countries carrying on operations in a third country, but these types of ventures will not be discussed. A host country's participant may be a private enterprise or, especially in developing countries, a government agency or government-owned corporation. In many countries, for example, mineral resources are considered to be owned by the state; thus, extraction or production of these resources depends upon participation of a state agency.

Among industrialized countries, Japan most notably restricts foreign investment to joint ventures. Indeed, in many industries in Japan the foreign partner may participate only as minority owner. In developing countries such as India and most of South America, joint venture participation is also increasingly required.

8. Risks of Direct Investment

If a domestic firm is involved in a foreign country to the extent of locating assets there (whether through branches, subsidiaries, joint venturers, or otherwise), it may be subject to the ultimate legal and political risk of international business activity—expropriation. **Expropriation**, as used in the context of international law, is the seizure of foreign-owned property by a government. When the owners are not fairly compensated, the expropriation is also considered to be a **confiscation** of property. Usually, the expropriating government also assumes ownership of the property, so the process includes **nationalization** as well. In the United States, the counterpart of expropriation is called the power of **eminent domain**. This power of all governments to take private property is regarded as inherent, yet it is subject to restraints upon its exercise. Our Constitution (as well as the constitutions of most states) prohibits the government from seizing private property except for "public purposes" and upon the payment of "just compensation." These Constitutional safeguards are limited, however, to the taking of property by the states or the federal government. Questions arise, then, as to the legal recourse against a foreign government that has taken over ownership of property within its jurisdiction.

Of course, constitutional or statutory safeguards against expropriationn may exist in other countries as well as in the United States. However, the extent of such protection varies widely. Treaties (or other agreements) between the United States and other countries may provide additional protection against uncompensated takings of property. It is customary for international law to recognize the right of governments to expropriate the property of foreigners only when accompanied by "prompt, adequate and effective compensation." This standard is followed by most industrialized countries; however, developing countries and socialist countries have increasingly rejected this standard in favor of a *national* standard whereby absolute supremacy is asserted with regard to nationalizations in general and compensation in particular.

Nationalization of U.S. firms accompanied by unsatisfactory offers of compensation has led companies to file lawsuits in U.S. courts that seek more satisfactory compensation. Two distinct but related doctrines pose serious obstacles for recovery in these situations: the act-of-state doctrine and the sovereign immunities doctrine.

ACT-OF-STATE DOCTRINE

The classic statement of the act-of-state doctrine provides that, "the courts of one country will not sit in judgment on . . . the acts of the government of another. . . ." Thus, claims that an expropriation by one country violates U.S.

or international law simply cannot be adjudicated in U.S. courts if the doctrine is accepted in an absolute fashion.

Several exceptions to the doctrine have been recognized. The Restatement (2d) of Foreign Relations law of the United States implies that the doctrine applies only when the foreign state has acted "to give effect to its public interest." This interpretation recognizes that governments may also act in a private or commercial capacity and, when so doing, will be subject to the same rules of law as are applicable to private individuals. Of course, a nationalization of assets will almost certainly be considered an act in the "public interest."

Congress expressed its interpretation of the doctrine in an amendment to the **Foreign Assistance Act of 1964**. This act directs that the act-of-state doctrine shall *not* be applied by the courts in cases when property is confiscated in violation of international law, unless the President advises that application of the doctrine is required. Federal courts, however, have narrowly construed this provision and applied it only in cases when the property has somehow found its way back into the United States.

A foreign sovereign may waive the right to assert the act-of-state doctrine, for example, by using a clause in a treaty to this effect. Complications with waiving include whether an express waiver may be retracted and whether an implied waiver will be recognized.

As the following case demonstrates, the doctrine is not compelled by the Constitution but finds its justification in the notion of separation of government powers.

WILLIAMS v. CURTISS-WRIGHT
694 F.2d 300 (3rd Cir. 1982)

The parties were competitors in the business of selling surplus jet engines and parts to foreign governments. Plaintiff brought suit, alleging that Curtiss-Wright monopolized the market, engaged in unfair competition, and committed other wrongs. Defendant moved for a judgment on the ground that the act-of-state doctrine prohibited the court from examining the motives of foreign governments for refusing to purchase engines and parts from plaintiff. The district court denied the motion, and the defendant appealed.

WEIS, Circuit Judge: The act of state doctrine requires evaluation whenever adjudication of a controversy might hinder the executive department in the conduct of foreign relations. . . . Here, defendant moved for judgment on the pleadings on the ground that the act of state doctrine makes the case nonjusticiable. The district court denied the motion, which it treated as one for summary judgment, and certified the order to this court under 28 U.S.C. 1292(b). . . .

The act of state doctrine is a policy of judicial abstention from inquiry into the validity of an act by a foreign state within its own territory and within the scope of its sovereignty. Because the doctrine may be invoked by private litigants, it differs from sovereign immunity, which may be pleaded only by the foreign state itself. The doctrine also differs from the defense of governmental compulsion, which is available only when the offending action was mandated by a foreign sovereign.

The act of state doctrine once rested on the inherent nature of sovereign authority and principles of international law. Now, in this country at least, the doctrine's foundation has shifted to the interest in preserving the separation of powers between the branches of government. A court declines to exercise jurisdiction over a case that may hinder or embarrass the executive in the conduct of foreign affairs in deference to the proper distribution of functions between the judicial and the political branches in the area of international relations. . . . The act of state doctrine is "not lightly to be imposed." To determine whether it applies in a given factual setting, "the court must analyze the nature of the questioned conduct and the effect upon the parties in addition to appraising the sovereign's role."

Here, the litigation is between two private American citizens, on allegations that American antitrust law was violated by defendant's actions in this country and abroad. The thrust of plaintiff's complaint is that Curtiss-Wright dominates the world-wide market in J-65 engines and parts as a result of monopolistic practices that exclude other competitors. There are allegations, for example, that defendant threatened Williams in the United States with economic sanctions, and pressured the United States Navy into refusing his request to recondition certain parts.

The complaint treats the foreign governments, not as wrongdoers against plaintiff, but as fellow victims of Curtiss-Wright. Williams alleges that defendant threatened to terminate warranties and technological support agreements with customers who dealt with him. It may be seen that plaintiff's challenges are aimed at the anticompetitive effect of Curtiss-Wright's activities, not the validity of the decisions by foreign governments to boycott him.

Defendant contends, however, that the act of state doctrine necessarily forbids a court from scrutinizing the reasons for the military procurement decisions of foreign countries. Hence, the argument goes, plaintiff cannot prove a causal connection between his lost sales and defendant's activities. . . .

The act of state doctrine should not be applied to thwart legitimate American regulatory goals in the absence of a showing that adjudication may hinder international relations. As we have said before, in antitrust litigation there is a public interest in clearing monopolistic activities from the channels of American commerce, even though some of the conduct occurred in foreign countries.

On the present state of the record, we do not find that litigation of this case would hinder the conduct of foreign relations by the United States government. Hence, the act of state doctrine is not a barrier. We do not rule out the possibility that significant developments may occur as the case proceeds that might require the district court to reconsider applicability of the doctrine. . . . [*Affirmed.*]

SOVEREIEGN IMMUNITY DOCTRINE
This judicially developed doctrine provides that a foreign sovereign is immune from suit in the United States. Until approximately 1952, this notion was absolute. From 1952 until 1976, U.S. courts adhered to a "restrictive

theory" under which immunity existed with regard to sovereign or public acts but not with regard to private or commercial acts. In 1976, Congress enacted the **Foreign Sovereign Immunities Act** that codifies this restrictive theory and rejects immunity for commercial acts carried on in the United States or having direct effects in this country. The case which follows illustrates the application of a foreign sovereign's immunity from suit in this country.

CAREY v. NATIONAL OIL CORPORATION
453 F. Supp. 1097 (U.S.D.C., S.D.N.Y. 1978)

Plaintiffs brought suit against the Libyan Arab Republic and National Oil Corporation (NOC), a corporation wholly owned by the Libyan government, to recover $1.6 billion in damages for alleged breach of contract to supply them with oil. NOC had entered into contracts to sell oil to plaintiffs. In 1973, oil-producing nations of the Middle East, including Libya, imposed an embargo on petroleum exports to the United States. NOC was ordered not to fulfill its contractual obligations.

DUFFY, District Judge: . . . The question when a foreign state may be sued in a United States Court has been given a comprehensive statutory answer by the Foreign Sovereign Immunities Act of 1976. Jurisdictional immunity to suit is extended to foreign states in all cases save those specifically enumerated in the Act, or covered by an existing international agreement. Since I find that none of the claims against Libya or NOC fall within the enumerated exceptions, I must dismiss this suit as being outside the jurisdiction of the Court. . . .

The only exception to immunity that could even arguably apply to the transactions here is that found in 28 U.S.C.A. 1605(a)(2): "an act outside the territory of the United States in connection with a commercial activity of the foreign state elsewhere . . .

[which] act causes a direct effect in the United States." . . .

These claims, asserted against Libya alone, allege in effect that Libya induced NOC's breach of the 1973 oil contracts. This refers, presumably, to the orders that franchisees cut back their production. It is beyond cavil that these actions by Libya were no part of a commercial undertaking; rather, they were deliberate weapons of foreign policy, aimed at influencing the conduct of other nations, or at least punishing undesirable conduct.

The structure of the Foreign Sovereign Immunities Act leaves no question that noncommercial activities of a foreign state will be treated with the same deference to which they were entitled before 1976. The distinction between acts of a sovereign nature and act of a commercial nature is one dating back to antiquity, and one which was recognized in the famous "Tate letter" to Acting Attorney General Perlman. Sovereigns are "traditionally . . . quite sensitive" about external inquiries into the way in which they conduct their foreign policy. Therefore, I conclude that this was not the kind of act to which the exceptions in 28 U.S.C.A. 1605 were meant to apply. . . .

I am constrained, therefore, to dismiss the action. [*So ordered.*]

It is often difficult to distinguish between government and commercial acts and to determine whether such acts have direct effects in this country. With regard to nationalization, however, one court has stated flatly that "nationalization is the quintessentially sovereign act, never viewed as having a commercial character."

These two doctrines of judicial restraint present serious obstacles to recovery by a domestic owner of nationalized property. Before concluding that the risks are too great for direct investment abroad, however, refer to the section in the text (§ 16) discussing the **Overseas Private Investment Corporation (OPIC)**.

LEGAL INSTITUTIONS AND AGREEMENTS

9. The United Nations (UN)

The **United Nations** (UN) is the paramount international political organization in terms of representation and scope of activities.

The **International Court of Justice** (ICJ), or "World Court," is the judicial branch of the UN. It sits at The Hague in the Netherlands and consists of fifteen judges representing all of the world's major legal systems. The judges are elected by the UN's General Assembly and the Security Council after having been nominated by national groups, not governments. No more than one judge may be a national of any country. Since it began functioning in 1946, the ICJ has rendered, on average, only one contested decision per year and one advisory opinion every two years. Obviously, there has been widespread reluctance to resort to the ICJ as a forum for resolving international disputes. An often misunderstood aspect of the ICJ's jurisdiction to hear and decide disputes is the provision that only *countries* have access to the court. Private persons or corporations may not directly present claims before the court. Further, only countries that have submitted to the jurisdiction of the court may be parties.

In some instances, countries have presented claims to the ICJ on behalf of their aggrieved nationals but no device exists in U.S. law by which a firm or individual can compel the U.S. government to press a claim on its behalf before the ICJ.

The **United Nations Commission on International Trade Law** (UNCITRAL) was created in 1966 in an effort to develop standardized commercial practices and agreements. It has achieved moderate success in a limited number of areas involving international trade, such as sale of goods, shipping, commercial arbitration, and payments. The U.S. Congress is considering adopting a **Convention on the International Sale of Goods** (CISG), drafted by UNCITRAL. The CISG applies to international transactions, much as Article 2 of the Uniform Commercial Code applies to domestic transactions. Ratification of the CISG by the United States would eliminate some of the uncertainties associated with international sales.

The **United Nations Conference on Trade and Development** (UNC-TAD) is a permanent organ of the General Assembly. It was created in 1964 to deal with international trade reform and redistribution of income through trade. It works primarily on behalf of developing countries; to date, UNC-TAD has achieved little notable success.

10. European Community (EC, or "Common Market")

In 1957, the **Treaty of Rome** created the **European Economic Community** (EEC), later renamed the **European Community**, (EC, or "Common Market"). Membership now includes Belgium, Denmark, France, West Germany, Greece, Ireland, Italy, Luxembourg, the Netherlands, Portugal, Spain, and the United Kingdom. The EC has proven to be an unrivaled international organization for promoting and achieving economic unity.

In seeking to achieve its goal of political as well as economic integration, the EC has in its treaty provided for the implementation of free flow of goods, persons, services, and capital among its members; the establishment of common commercial policies toward third-world countries; and the inauguration of common agricultural and transport policies. Further, the treaty calls for enactment of a system to ensure that competition shall not be distorted in the Community. This latter objective is achieved under Articles 85 and 86 of the treaty, which are roughly equivalent to Sections 1 and 2 of the Sherman Act. The EC has the equivalent of its own legislature, executive, and judiciary. EC law, when conflicting with national law of a member state, is supreme; the courts of member states are expected to enforce the Community's law.

11. Other Organizations

The **Council for Mutual Economic Aid** (COMECON) is the Soviet-bloc counterpart to the EC. COMECON members include Bulgaria, Cuba, Czechoslovakia, East German, Hungary, Poland, Rumania, and the Soviet Union. The stated purpose of COMECON is to coordinate the development efforts of its members, raise the standard of industrialization and increase the productivity of its members, and further economic cooperation among its members. Dominated by the Soviet Union, COMECON has been weakened in its supranational structure by the increasing unwillingness of some member countries to accept the roles delegated to them.

A number of other regional organizations exist that have not achieved the degree of success of the EC or COMECON. They include the Latin America Free Trade Association, the Central American Common Market, the East African Economic Community, and the Economic Community of West African States. In addition, many narrowly based international organizations exist, such as the International Labour Organization, the International Monetary Fund, the International Civil Aviation Organization, and the Organization of Petroleum Exporting Countries.

12. General Agreement on Tariffs and Trade (GATT)

The **General Agreement on Tariffs and Trade** (GATT) is a series of over 100 international agreements and protocols, subscribed to by approximately ninety countries, including the United States, that attempts to prohibit discrimination in import regulations and prevent the establishment of import quotas. GATT seeks to implement these goals through the mechanism of **"most-favored nation"** status. Under this provision, each member of GATT is obligated to treat all other GATT members at least as well as it treats the country that receives the most favorable treatment regarding imports or exports. In other words, no country is to give special trading advantages to others. An additional provision specifies that imports will be treated no worse than domestic products with regard to internal taxation or regulation. Under special circumstances, exceptions to these principles may be allowed; they may apply to regional trading organizations such as the EC or to developing countries. Such exceptions may involve temporary restraints being imposed on imports when they are causing serious injury to a domestic industry or quotas being implemented in the event of a domestic balance-of-payments crisis.

DOMESTIC LAWS HAVING SIGNIFICANT INTERNATIONAL TRADE CONSEQUENCES

13. Antidumping Laws

"Dumping" is the practice of selling foreign goods in one country at less than the comparable price in the country from which the goods are being exported. Since the practice of dumping may potentially create an unfair economic advantage (especially when a foreign market may be protected against reciprocal competition from domestic firms), Congress has limited it through several antidumping statutes. Current antidumping legislation is found in the **Trade Agreements Act of 1979**. This statute establishes a two-part test for triggering additional import duties on the goods being dumped. First, the Secretary of the Treasury must determine that a class or kind of merchandise is being or is likely to be sold in the United States at **"less than fair value"** (LTFV). In LTFV determinations, the price for which the goods are being sold in the United States is compared with the price for which the goods are being sold in the country of origin. The second provision requires that the International Trade Commission (part of the Department of Commerce) determine that a domestic industry is being materially injured or threatened or that establishment of domestic industry is being materially retarded. When both determinations prove affirmative, an additional duty will be imposed upon the goods in an amount by which their foreign value exceeds the domestic price. Obviously, the question of what is "material" is crucial to these determinations, but the statute does not define the term.

14. Antitrust

Perhaps no other aspect of our legal system has generated as much recent controversy and ill will abroad as the application of our antitrust law to conduct occurring beyond the borders of the United States. Such activity seems to interfere with the general international agreement that countries are free to regulate economic conduct within their borders. However, economic activities which are prohibited in the United States, such as price-fixing, may actually be encouraged in foreign countries. The U.S. attitude toward the extraterritorial application of domestic antitrust law is that conduct that has a "direct, substantial and foreseeable effect" on domestic trade or commerce, no matter where it occurs, will be subject to scrutiny. In other words, domestic firms, foreign subsidiaries of domestic firms, and foreign firms that violate domestic antitrust law in the United States or abroad may be subject to antitrust enforcement actions. In instances when the required effect on domestic commerce is found but when a foreign state also has an interest in regulating the conduct, a "**jurisdictional rule of reason**" may be applied. This rule involves balancing the interests of the United States along with those of the foreign state to determine whether application of our law is warranted. The elements to be considered include the relative significance of the domestic and foreign effects, the nationality or allegiance of the parties involved, the locations of the parties' principal places of business, and the extent to which enforcement by either nation can be expected to achieve compliance. One can gain insight into the complex question of extraterritorial application of our antitrust law in the following case.

IN RE URANIUM ANTITRUST LITIGATION
617 F.2d 1248 (7th Cir. 1980)

In 1976, Westinghouse filed a complaint alleging antitrust violations against twenty-nine foreign and domestic uranium producers. All of the defendants were served with process; however, nine foreign defendants chose not appear. Default judgments were entered against these defendants. On subsequent appeals, briefs filed by the governments of several countries where the alleged violations occurred as amici curiae (friends of the court) contended that the courts of the United States did not have jurisdiction over conduct occurring outside this country.

CAMPBELL, Senior District Judge.: . . . The governments of Austria, Canada, South Africa and the United Kingdom of Great Britain and Northern Ireland have filed briefs as amici curiae. The principal thrust of the amici's briefs is to call into question the jurisdiction of the United States District Court over this controversy. We view the jurisdictional issue as two-pronged: (1) does subject matter jurisdiction exist; and (2) if so, should it be exercised?

The jurisdictional reach of the Sherman Act to conduct outside the United States was not favorably received at the outset. However, that view was later eroded, and the Act was applied to conduct outside the United States so long as some of the acts occurred within the United States and the parties were American. In *United States v. Aluminum Co. of America (Alcoa)*, Judge Learned Hand articulated what is known as the "intended effects" test. In *Alcoa* Judge Hand reasoned that agreements made outside of the United States which restrain trade or commerce within the United States have the same effect as similar agreements entered into within our borders. Since "any state may impose liabilities, even upon persons not within its allegiance, for conduct outside its borders that has consequences within its borders which the state reprehends," he concluded that Congress did intend to apply the Act to conduct abroad so long as the intended effect of that conduct is prohibited by the Act. Since *Alcoa*, United State Courts have exercised jurisdiction over antitrust activity outside the United States so long as there is an intended effect on American commerce. . . .

The amici, in particular the United Kingdom, contend that Alcoa is "no longer to be accepted by United States Courts as 'settled in law' ", in light of the recent opinions of the United States Courts of Appeals in *Timberlane Lumber Co. v. Bank of America* and *Mannington Mills, Inc. v. Congoleum Corporation*. . . .

The United Kingdom relies primarily on the comment in *Timberlane* that "[t]he effects test by itself iss incomplete because it fails to consider other nations' interests." This amicus curiae contends the critical discussion of the *Alcoa* effects test has undermined its continuing viability as the standard of extraterritorial jurisdiction of the Sherman Act. We do not read *Timberlane* so broadly. The "jurisdictional rule of reason" espoused in *Timberlane* is that while an effect on American commerce is the necessary ingredient for extraterritorial jurisdiction, considerations of comity and fairness require a further deter-

mination as to "whether American authority should be asserted in a given case." The clear thrust of the *Timberlane* Court is that once a District Judge has determined that he has jurisdiction, he should consider additional factors to determine whether the exercise of the jurisdiction is appropriate.

We conclude that nothing in *Timberlane* is inconsistent with our determination that Westinghouse's allegations of concerted conduct by foreign and domestic corporations are sufficient to confer jurisdiction on the District Court, under *Alcoa*. We turn now to the question of whether jurisdiction should be exercised in the present case.

In this case, unlike the situation in *Timberlane* and *Mannington Mills*, there has been a determination by the District Court as to whether jurisdiction should be exercised. In the order of January 3, 1979, and the order of September 17, 1979, the District Judge considered the unique circumstance presented in this case, and determined, in the exercise of his discretion, to proceed. Our task is to decide whether he abused his discretion in reaching that conclusion. We find that he did not.

In granting the requested default judgment, the District Court considered three factors: the complexity of the present multinational and multi-party action; the seriousness of the charges asserted; and the recalcitrant attitude of the defaulters. The District Judge concluded that those factors all weighed heavily in favor of proceeding to judgment and damages. . . . In the present case, the defaulters have contumaciously refused to come into court and present evidence as to why the District Court should not exercise its jurisdiction. They have chosen instead to present their entire case through surrogates. Wholly owned subsidiaries of several defaulters have challenged the appropriateness of the injunctions, and shockingly to us, the governments of the defaulters have subserviently presented for them their case against the exercise of jurisdiction. If this Court were to remand the matter for further consideration of the jurisdictional question, the District Court would be placed in the impossible position of having to make specific findings with the defaulters refusing to appear and participate in discovery. We find little value in such an exercise.

We conclude that given the posture of this case, and the circumstances before the District Court, the Judge did not abuse his discretion in proceeding to exercise his jurisdiction. We therefore decline to remand the case to the District Court as requested by the amici curiae. . . .

The extraterritorial application of U.S. antitrust law can be defended by the act-of-state and sovereign immunity doctrines, discussed previously, and the **doctrine of sovereign compulsion**. This latter doctrine allows the defendant in an antitrust action to assert, in its defense, that its conduct was compelled by a foreign country.

In order to enable domestic exporters to compete better on an international level, the **Webb-Pomerene Act** exempts from appplication of the Sherman Act conduct by associations of export traders that would otherwise violate antitrust law so long as the conduct does not restrain trade within the United States or with domestic competitors of the export associations. Anticompetitive conduct such as price-fixing or dividing markets may thus be allowed.

15. Foreign Corrupt Practices Act (FCPA)

In 1977, following widespread disclosure of scandalous payments by domestic firms to officials of foreign governments, Congress enacted the **Foreign Corrupt Practices Act** (FCPA). This statute has two main provisions: (1) financial records and accounts must be kept "which, in reasonable detail, accurately and fairly reflect the transactions and disposition of assets" of the firm, and (2) firms must "devise and maintain a system of internal accounting controls sufficient to provide reasonable assurances" that transactions are being carried out in accordance with management's authorization. The general language of these "accounting provisions" has resulted in some uncertainty as to the requirements for compliance. These provisions are intended to correct the previously widespread practice of accounting for bribes as commission payments, payments for services, or other normal business expenses, and illegally deducting the payments on income tax returns. Further, they state that investors or potential investors are deemed entitled to disclosure of the financial information. Cynics have referred to the accounting provisions of the FCPA as the "Accountants Full Employment Act," and some domestic criticism of the provisions has occurred, but these features of the FCPA have generated little international comment.

Much more international controversy has arisen over the so-called anti-bribery provisions of the FCPA. These provisions declare that it shall be unlawful for any "domestic concern" (i.e., *any* business) or its officers, directors, employees, or agents to give or pay "anything of value" to "any foreign official for the purpose of influencing any act or decision of such foreign official." Payments to foreign officials who will use their influence to assist firms in obtaining business in their countries are also prohibited, as are payments to "any person" when the payer knows or has reason to know that all or part of the payment will be given to a foreign official. Firms are subject to fines of up to $1 million, and individuals may be fined up to $10,000 and imprisoned up to five years for violations. In the statute, foreign officials are defined as excluding employees of foreign governments whose duties are "essentially ministerial or clerical."

The controversy over the antibribery provisions stems from two main considerations. First, in many parts of the world, under-the-table payments to government officials are an accepted practice. Indeed, civil servants may be expected to supplement their salaries in this manner. The U.S. prohibition of such payments is perceived as an attempt to impose American standards of morality in other parts of the world, and it has caused resentment or discrimination against our businesses. A second objection to the FCPA comes from domestic firms that contend the prohibition of bribes, especially in countries where they are expected, put U.S. firms at a competitive disadvantage. Competitors from other countries are not likely to be operating under similar constraints.

The following case is one of the very few appellate decisions which discusses the FCPA. Note the overlap with the act-of-state doctrine which is also discussed.

CLAYCO PETROLEUM CORP. v. OCCIDENTAL PETROLEUM CORP.
712 F.2d 404 (9th Cir. 1983)

PER CURIAM.: . . . The crux of the complaint is that Occidental conspired to make and made secret payments in England and Switzerland totaling $417,000 to Sheikh Sultan bin Ahmed Muallah (Sultan), Umm Al Qaywayn's Petroleum Minister and son of its ruler, Sheikh Ahmed al Muallah (Ahmed). The complaint further alleges that only through these unlawful and anti-competitive actions did defendants secure the valuable off-shore oil concession. More specifically, plaintiffs allege that in September 1969, Ahmed agreed that Clayco would receive the concession, but instead, on November 18, 1969, he awarded the concession to defendant Occidental of Umm Al Qaywayn, Inc., Occidental Petroleum's subsidiary. . . .

In 1977, the Securities and Exchange

Commission (SEC) commenced an action against Occidental alleging violations of the Securities Exchange Act of 1934 and rules promulgated thereunder, based on illegal or questionable payments made by Occidental. Occidental consented to the entry of a permanent injunction and agreed to conduct an internal investigation of the alleged illegal payments and to prepare for the SEC and Occidental's stockholders a special report describing such payments.

The Payments Report was filed and revealed various illegal payments. . . .

Plaintiff's allege that these $417,000 in payments plus "entertainment" expenses constituted bribes to induce Sultan and his father to award the concession to Occidental. . . .

For the purpose of reviewing the district court's dismissal for failure to state a claim, we must assume that the facts alleged in the complaint are true. . . .

The district court granted defendants' motion to dismiss, based on the act of state doctrine. The courts stated that an exercise of sovereignty—the award of the offshore oil concession—was implicated in the case, and that adjudication would interfere with United States foreign policy. . . .

The appellants raise numerous challenges to the district court's application of the act of state doctrine. In essence, appellants argue first that this case is outside the purview of the act of state doctrine; and second, that the foreign sovereign action involved fits within "corruption" or "commercial" exceptions to the doctrine. . . .

We address appellants' claim that the complained of actions in this case do not include a sovereign policy decision. We cannot agree. We acknowledge that without sovereign activity effectuating "public" rather than private interests, the act of state doctrine does not apply. That test is met here.

Appellants also contend that the passage of the Foreign Corrupt Practices Act of 1977 (FCPA), created an exception to the act of state doctrine which should apply in this case.

The FCPA prohibits bribery of a foreign official for the purpose of obtaining or retaining business. The Act provides for severe criminal penalties including fines and imprisonment. In addition, the Attorney General may bring a civil action to enjoin impending violations.

The FCPA was intended to stop bribery of foreign officials and political parties by domestic corporations. Bribery abroad was considered a "severe" United States foreign policy problem; it embarasses friendly governments, causes a decline of foreign esteem for the United States and casts suspicion on the activities of our enterprises, giving credence to our foreign opponents. The FCPA thus represents a legislative judgment that our foreign relations will be bettered by a strict anti-bribery statute. There is also no question, however, that any prosecution under the Act entails risks to our relations with the foreign governments involved.

The Justice Department and the SEC share enforcement responsibilities under the FCPA. They coordinate enforcement of the Act with the State Department, recognizing the potential foreign policy problems of these actions. Executive bodies have discretion in bringing any action. Therefore, any governmental enforcement represents a judgment on the wisdom of bringing a proceeding, in light of the exigencies of foreign affairs. Act of state concerns are thus inapplicable since the purpose of the doctrine is to prevent the judiciary from interfering with the political branch's conduct of foreign policy.

Here, however, we are faced with a private lawsuit, rather than a public enforcement action. It is the screening of governmental proceedings, with State Department consultation, which distinguishes FCPA enforcement from private suits. Hence, in private suits, the act of state doctrine remains necessary to protect the proper conduct of national foreign policy. We therefore reject appellants' contention, which is not supported by the legislative history, that in enacting the FCPA, Congress intended to abrogate the act of state doctrine in private suits based on foreign payments.

For the reasons above, we hold that the act of state doctrine applies, and that appellants do not come within any exception to the doctrine. The decision of the trial court dismissing the action is therefore [*Affirmed.*]

16. Overseas Private Investment Corporation (OPIC)

The **Overseas Private Investment Corporation** (OPIC) is a hybrid, public and private agency that began functioning in 1971. All of the stock of OPIC is owned by the United States, and eight of the fifteen members of the board of directors are appointed by the President. The other directors are government officials. The general charge given to OPIC is to encourage and support qualified, private investments in developing countries that maintain friendly relations with the United States. Preferential consideration is given to investment projects in countries having per capita income below a specified amount, currently $680 (measured in 1979 dollars). Although OPIC offers several investment incentives, the program having the most significance for domestic firms is the Investment Insurance Program. This program provides domestic investors with coverage for the political risks of expropriation and confiscation, war, revolution, insurrection, civil strife, and inconvertibility of currency. Criteria for eligibility include:

1 The investor must be a U.S. citizen or a firm owned by a substantial number (at least 51 percent) of U.S. citizens.

2 The investment must be in a developing country that has entered into an investment guaranty agreement with the United States. (More than 115 countries have such agreements with the United States.)

3 The foreign host government must approve the project.

4 The project must obtain OPIC approval for serving the host country's economic and social needs.

OPIC has broad discretion to approve projects; preferential consideration is given to small businesses.

The bilateral investment guaranty agreements referred to previously provide that, in the event payment is made by the United States under the insurance contract, the foreign government will recognize the subrogation to the United States government of any claim that the investor might have against the foreign government. Upon receipt of payment under the insurance contract, the investor must transfer any claim against the foreign government to the U.S. federal government. Before making payment under any claim, OPIC requires that the investor exhaust all local remedies in the country where the claim arose.

17. Other Problem Areas

When resolving interstate domestic disputes, courts are often confronted with the problem of which state's law to apply to a case. Recall that this issue, the conflicts-of-law principle, was discussed in Chapter 1. On an international scale, the "conflicts" problem may be even more complex, because the transaction crosses national borders. For example, suppose a Minnesota seller contracts to sell goods to a French buyer. In the event of a lawsuit claiming breach of contract, should the court apply Minnesota law or French law? As explained in the earlier conflict-of-law discussion, a court in the United States would probably base its determination of which law governed this transaction upon either the place where the contract was made, the place of performance, or the place with the most substantial contact with the contract. Further, suppose that the court concludes that the law of France should govern. A court in Minnesota probably could locate French legal materials so as to be able to determine how the case should be decided under French law. If, however, the buyer is from Cameroon, Yugoslavia, or Iceland, it is questionable whether the substantive law of these places could be obtained. Many of these problems can be avoided by inclusion of a choice-of-law clause in the agreement between the parties. This clause contractually specifies which country's law to apply if litigation arises.

A related problem in international law is the enforceability of a judgment obtained in one country by the courts of another country. In the previous example, assume that the French buyer filed suit in France against the Minnesota seller and obtained a judgment ordering the seller to pay damages. To what extent would courts in the United States enforce the foreign judgment? Judgments obtained in one state are enforceable in the other states under the full faith and credit clause of the U.S. Constitution; however, the clause does not apply to judgments from other countries. In general, such foreign judgments may be enforceable if obtained under fair proceedings (i.e., the defendants were afforded essentially the same rights which would have been available in a proceeding in the United States) and if enforcement of the judgment does not offend the public policy of the United States. The likelihood of successfully enforcing a foreign judgment will be enhanced if reciprocity, or comity, exists, that is, if the country which renders the judgment would enforce a similar judgment coming from a U.S. court.

18. Arbitration

The advantages of arbitration in domestic transactions are discussed in Chapter 4. These advantages may be more pronounced in international transactions because of differences among legal systems and the additional expenses and delays involved in international litigation. Arbitration is increasingly used as a method of resolving international business disputes. Several organizations, including the International Chamber of Commerce, the American Arbitration Association, and UNCITRAL have developed sets of rules for international commercial arbitration. In addition, an "ad hoc" arbitration process is available under which the proceedings are conducted in a manner prescribed by the parties.

The case which follows illustrates some of the complexities of international commercial arbitration.

MITSUBISHI MOTORS v. SOLER CHRYSLER-PLYMOUTH
105 S.CT. 3346 (1985)

Petitioner, a Japanese corporation that manufactures automobiles, is the product of a joint venture between Chrysler International; S.A. (CISA), a Swiss corporation; and another Japanese corporation. The petitioner's aim is to distribute through Chrysler dealers outside the continental United States automobiles manufactured by Mitsubishi. Respondent, a Puerto Rican corporation, entered into distribution and sales agreements with CISA. The sales agreement contained a clause providing for arbitration by the Japan Commercial Arbitration Association of all disputes arising out of certain articles of the agreement or for the breach thereof. Thereafter, when attempts to work out disputes arising from a slackening of the sale of new automobiles failed, petitioner withheld shipment of automobiles to respondent, which disclaimed responsibility for them. Petitioner then brought an action in federal district court under the federal Arbitration Act seeking an order to compel arbitration of the disputes in accordance with the arbitration clause. Respondent filed an answer and counterclaims, asserting causes of action under the Sherman Act and other statutes. The district court ordered arbitration of most of the issues, including the federal antitrust issues, raised in the complaint and counterclaims. Despite the doctrine uniformly followed by the Courts of Appeals, that rights

conferred by the antitrust laws are inappropriate for enforcement by arbitration, the district court held that the international character of the undertaking in question required enforcement of the arbitration clause even as to the antitrust claims. The Court of Appeals reversed insofar as the District Court ordered submission of the antitrust claims to arbitration.

BLACKMUN, J.: . . . The first task of a court asked to compel arbitration of a dispute is to determine whether the parties agreed to arbitrate that dispute. The court is to make this determination by applying the "federal substantive law of arbitrability, applicable to any arbitration agreement within the coverage of the Act." And that body of law counsels

that questions of arbitrability must be addressed with a healthy regard for the federal policy favoring arbitration. . . . The Arbitration Act establishes that, as a matter of federal law, any doubts concerning the scope of arbitrable issues should be resolved in favor of arbitration. . . .

That is not to say that all controversies implicating statutory rights are suitable for arbitration. . . . By agreeing to arbitrate a statutory claim, a party does not forego the substantive rights afforded by the statute; it only submits to their resolution in an arbitral, rather than a judicial, forum. It trades the procedures, and opportunity for review of the courtroom for the simplicity, informality, and expedition of arbitration. . . . Having made the bargain to arbitrate, the party should be held to it unless Congress itself has evinced an intention to preclude a waiver of judicial remedies for the statutory rights at issue. Nothing, in the meantime, prevents a party from excluding statutory claims from the scope of an agreement to arbitrate. . . .

We now turn to consider whether Soler's antitrust claims are nonarbitrable even though it has agreed to arbitrate them. . . . We conclude that concerns of international comity, respect for the capacities of foreign and transnational tribunals, and sensitivity to the need of the international commercial system for predictability in the resolution of disputes require that we enforce the parties' agreement, even assuming that a contrary result would be forthcoming in a domestic context.

. . . [T]his Court had recognized the utility of forum-selection clauses in international transactions. In *The Bremen*, an American oil company, seeking to evade a contractual choice of an English forum and, by implication, English law, filed a suit in admiralty in a United States District Court against the German corporation which had contracted to tow its rig to a location in the Adriatic Sea. Notwithstanding the possibility that the English court would enforce provisions in the towage contract exculpating the German party which an American court would refuse to enforce, this Court gave effect to the choice-of-forum clause. It observed:

The expansion of American business and industry will hardly be encouraged if, notwithstanding solemn contract, we insist on a parochial concept that all disputes must be resolved under our laws and in our courts. . . . We cannot have trade and commerce in world markets and international waters exclusively on our terms, governed by our laws, and resolved in our courts. . . .

Again, the Court emphasized:

A contractual provision specifying in advance the forum in which disputes shall be litigated and the law to be applied is . . . an almost indispensable precondition to achievement of the orderliness and predictability essential to any international business transaction. . . .

A parochial refusal by the courts of one country to enforce an international arbitration agreement would not only frustrate these purposes, but would invite unseemly and mutually destructive jockeying by the parties to secure tactical litigation advantages. . . . [It would] damage the fabric of international commerce and trade, and imperil the willingness and ability of businessmen to enter into international commerical agreements. . . .

The judgment of the Court of Appeals is affirmed in part and reversed in part, and the cases are remanded for further proceedings consistent with this opinion. [*So ordered.*]

---

19. Conclusion

International business transactions have become such a pervasive component of the global economy that no businessperson can afford to be uninformed as to the international legal environment. Enhanced communications and transportation will undoubtedly result in an increased level of international economic linkages. The laws applicable to international transactions will continue to evolve and adapt to the "shrinking" earth. This evolution and adaptation will likely result in continued efforts at cooperation through greater participation in international conventions, standardization of legal norms, and familiarity with the law of other countries.

This chapter has provided a broad overview of selected topics of importance to the conduct of international business. Many other topics might also have been included, such as international income tax law, countertrade, the law pertaining to ocean beds and their underlying minerals, international financial institutions, and the selection of legal counsel in other countries. A subsequent edition of this text may even discuss the next horizon for legal development—the legal environment of space.

REVIEW QUESTIONS

1 Define the following terms.
  a Expropriation
  b Confiscation
  c Nationalization
  d Dumping

2 Draw a diagram (or flowchart) explaining the use of an irrevocable letter of credit. Use arrows to and from each party and indicate what document(s) each party gives and receives.

3 Explain the act-of-state doctrine.

4 Explain the doctrine of sovereign immunity.

5 You are the sole owner of a sewing-machine factory located in the country of Utobania. The government of Utobania nationalizes the factory and all equipment, using as its reason the assertion that you have exploited its citizens by paying them less than they deserved. The government refuses to pay you any compensation because, it claims, you have not reinvested enough of your profits in Utobania. Can you sue Utobania in the International Court of Justice? Why, or why not? Explain.

6 What are the main provisions of the Foreign Corrupt Practices Act? Explain each.

7 What is the Overseas Private Investment Corporation? What does it do? Explain.

8 Describe several ways in which a firm in the United States might conduct business abroad.

9 What is the European Community? What does it do? Explain.

10 Two Swedish sandal manufacturers enter into an agreement in Sweden that one will sell its products in the United States only east of the Mississippi River and the other will sell only west of the river. Does this agreement violate U.S. antitrust law? If so, would the Swedish firms be subject to punishment by the U.S. government? Explain.

11 When do the antidumping provisions of United States law apply? Explain

12 When will foreign judgments be enforced by courts of the United States? Explain.

13 What is the United Nations Commission on International Trade Law? What does it do? Explain.

14 What is the United Nations Conference on Trade and Development? What does it do? Explain.

15 How can international conflict-of-law problems be minimized? Explain.

Part Five
PROTECTING THE INDIVIDUAL

Chapter
14

Workers' Protection

1. Introduction

In Illinois, three corporate executives are convicted of murder and receive twenty-five-year sentences in the death of an employee who they failed to warn was handling dangerous chemicals. A California grand jury has indicted an employer for involuntary manslaughter in a helicopter crash that killed film star Vic Morrow and two children. In Ohio, operators of a fireworks factory face manslaughter charges after an explosion that killed nine employees. Around the country, prosecutors have brought a number of criminal cases against employers who do not protect employees adequately from hazardous job conditions. These cases reflect a recent trend in the rapidly developing law of worker protection.

Worker protection laws developed chiefly in this century. Prior to 1900, workers had little or no protection from dangerous job conditions, low pay, and the risk of firing. Today, many laws protect workers. In major part, these laws are statutes passed by Congress and state legislatures in response to political pressure from worker-voters. During this century, the organized power of unions has played an important role in generating political pressure. Unions lobbied strongly for passage of the laws discussed in this chapter: the Occupational Safety and Health Act, the Fair Labor Standards Act, the Social Security Act, the Employee Retirement Income Security Act, and the workers' compensation laws.

Many laws serve to allocate and reallocate economic wealth in society. That is certainly true of the laws discussed in this chapter. When reading, consider how the various laws affect the distribution of wealth. Are they or are they not in the best interest of employers? Do worker protection laws hurt private enterprise, or do they help preserve it? Are they part of the same wealth redistribution trend mentioned in Chapter 6, the chapter on torts? In thinking about such questions, which have no fixed answers, use your education to gain deeper insight into the legal environment of business.

This chapter addresses two major issues of worker protection: <u>job safety</u> (including the handling of work-related injuries) <u>and financial security.</u>

2. The Occupational Safety and Health Act

Congress adopted the *Occupational Safety and Health Act* (OSHA) in 1970 to ensure safe and healthful working conditions for practically every employee in the United States. Special health and safety laws in such industries as construction, maritime, and coal mining had been previously adopted, but such far-reaching legislation as OSHA, with an impact of such magnitude on business, had never been considered at the national level.

OSHA requires that employers furnish to each employee a place of employment that is free from recognized hazards that are causing or are likely to cause death or serious physical harm to the employee. It also requires that the employer comply with occupational safety and health standards established under the act by the secretary of labor. This is done through an agency called The Occupational Safety and Health Administration (also known as OSHA). In order to accomplish its mission, OSHA investigators conduct unannounced inspections. During any investigation, an employer as well as an employee has the right to accompany the inspectors or have a representative do so. Remember that the Supreme Court has ruled that employers can require OSHA inspectors to produce a search warrant before they begin an inspection. Employers also must keep and preserve records relating to accidents and injuries as required by regulations.

OSHA regulates employees as well as employers. It requires that each employee comply with occupational safety and health standards and all rules, regulations, and orders issued under it which are applicable to his or her own actions and conduct.

The secretary of labor issues standards for healthful and safe employment. The Occupational Safety and Health Review Commission reviews citations of violations and proposed penalties. Orders of this commission are, of course, reviewable by a federal Court of Appeals, as in the case of other federal administrative agencies.

The most significant aspect of OSHA is its approach to enforcement by unannounced inspections. Over 70,000 such inspections were made in 1985. Inspections of businesses may be made either on the initiative of the department itself or upon the request of an employee or employee's representative. Inspections must be made during regular working hours and at other reasonable times within reasonable limits and in a reasonable manner. No advance notice of inspections can be given. Employees' representatives have the right to participate in walk-around inspections, and such representatives get compensation from the employer for the time involved. If an inspection reveals a violation, the employer receives a citation. If the violation presents a threat of serious or immediate harm, the secretary of labor can go into a federal district court and get a temporary injunction to restrain the danger. Having received a citation, the employer is next informed of the penalty. If the employer decides to contest the citation or penalty, it may appeal through the review commission and then into the federal court system.

In certain cases, OSHA regulations permit employees a right of "self-help." Because the act itself does not mention a self-help remedy, the following case challenged the remedy's legality:

WHIRLPOOL CORPORATION v. MARSHALL
100 S.Ct. 883 (1980)

STEWART, J.: The Occupational Safety and Health Act of 1970 (Act) prohibits an employer from discharging or discriminating against any employee who exercises "any right afforded by" the Act. The Secretary of Labor (Secretary) has promulgated a regulation providing that, among the rights that the Act so protects, is the right of an employee to choose not to perform his assigned task because of a reasonable apprehension of death or serious injury coupled with a reasonable belief that no less drastic alternative is available. The question presented in the case before us is whether this regulation is consistent with the Act.

The petitioner company maintains a manufacturing plant in Marion, Ohio, for the production of household appliances. Overhead conveyors transport appliance components throughout the plant. To protect employees from objects that occasionally fall from these conveyors, the petitioner has installed a horizontal wire mesh guard screen approximately 20 feet above the plant floor.

Maintenance employees of the petitioner spend several hours each week removing ob-

jects from the screen, replacing paper spread on the screen to catch grease drippings from the material on the conveyors, and performing occasional maintenance work on the conveyors themselves. To perform these duties, maintenance employees usually are able to stand on the iron frames, but sometimes find it necessary to step onto the steel mesh screen itself.

In 1973 the company began to install heavier wire in the screen because its safety had been drawn into question. Several employees had fallen partly through the old screen, and on one occasion an employee had fallen completely through to the plant floor below but had survived.

On June 28, 1974, a maintenance employee fell to his death through the guard screen in an area where the newer, stronger mesh had not yet been installed. Following this incident, the petitioner effectuated some repairs and issued an order strictly forbidding maintenance employees from stepping on either the screens or the angle-iron supporting structure.

On July 7, 1974, two of the petitioner's

maintenance employees, Virgil Deemer and Thomas Cornwell, met with the plant maintenance superintendent to voice their concern about the safety of the screen. The superintendent disagreed with their view. . . . Later, . . . Deemer contacted an official of the regional OSHA office and discussed the guard screen.

The next day, Deemer and Cornwell reported for the night shift at 10:45 P.M. Their foreman, after himself walking on some of the angle-iron frames, directed the two men to perform their usual maintenance duties on a section of the old screen. Claiming that the screen was unsafe, they refused to carry out this directive. The foreman then sent them to the personnel office, where they were ordered to punch out without working or being paid for the remaining six hours of the shift. The two men subsequently received written reprimands, which were placed in their employment files.

A little over a month later, the Secretary filed suit in the United States District Court for the Northern District of Ohio, alleging that the petitioner's actions against Deemer and Cornwell constituted discrimination in violation of . . . the Act.

Following a bench trial, the District Court found that the two employees had "refused to perform the cleaning operation because of a genuine fear of death or serious bodily harm," that the danger presented had been "real and not something which [had] existed only in the minds of the employees," that the employees had acted in good faith, and that no reasonable alternative had realistically been open to them other than to refuse to work. The District Court nevertheless denied relief, holding that the Secretary's regulation was inconsistent with the Act and therefore invalid.

The Court of Appeals for the Sixth Circuit reversed the District Court's judgment. . . . [The] question, as stated at the onset of this opinion, is whether the Secretary's regulation authorizing employee "self-help" in some circumstances is permissible under the Act. . . .

The Act itself creates an express mechanism for protecting workers from employment conditions believed to pose an emergent threat of death or serious injury. . . .

[T]he Secretary is obviously correct when he acknowledges in his regulation that, "as a general matter, there is no right afforded by the Act which would entitle employees to walk off the job because of potential unsafe conditions at the workplace." By providing for prompt notice to the employer of an inspector's intention to seek an injunction against an imminently dangerous condition, the legislation obviously contemplates that the employer will normally respond by voluntarily and speedily eliminating the danger. And in the few instances where this does not occur, the legislative provisions authorizing prompt judicial action are designed to give employees full protection in most situations from the risk of injury or death resulting from an imminently dangerous condition at the worksite.

As this case illustrates, however, circumstances may sometimes exist in which the employee justifiably believes that the express statutory arrangement does not sufficiently protect him from death or serious injury. Such circumstances will probably not often occur, but such a situation may arise when (1) the employee is ordered by his employer to work under conditions that the employee reasonably believes pose an imminent risk of death or serious bodily injury, and (2) the employee has reason to believe that there is not sufficient time or opportunity either to seek effective redress from his employer or to apprise OSHA of the danger. . . .

[T]he Secretary has exercised his rulemaking power . . . and has determined that, when an employee in good faith finds himself in such a predicament, he may refuse to expose himself to the dangerous condition, without being subjected to "subsequent discrimination" by the employer. . . .

The regulation clearly conforms to the fundamental objective of the Act—to prevent occupational deaths and serious injuries. . . . The Act does not wait for an employee to die or become injured. It authorized the promulgation of health and safety standards and the issuance of citations in the hope that these will act to prevent deaths or injuries from ever occurring. . . .

The regulation accords no authority to government officials. It simply permits private employees of a private employer to avoid workplace conditions that they believe pose grave dangers to their own safety. The employees have no power under the regulation to order their employer to correct the hazardous condition or to clear the dangerous workplace of others. Moreover, any employee who acts in reliance on the regulation runs the risk of discharge or reprimand in the event a court subsequently finds that he acted unreasonably or in bad faith. . . .

For these reasons we conclude that [the regulation] was promulgated by the Secretary in the valid exercise of his authority under the Act. Accordingly, the judgment of the Court of Appeals is affirmed. [*Affirmed.*]

---

3. OSHA Trends

In the 1970s, OSHA came under much criticism from industry groups. Its safety regulations were long and difficult to understand and apply. Many people reviewed OSHA inspectors as biased against business and too quick to issue citations. The number of workers injured annually failed to go down and in some instances actually rose.

OSHA has tried a different approach in the 1980s. Its focus has changed somewhat from safety to health. Instead of an inflexible concern over the number of knotholes in ladders and the height of fire extinguishers from the floor, OSHA has devoted attention to workers' exposure to chemical and other health hazards. It has issued regulations limiting exposure to lead, asbestos, cotton dust, noise, and other potential causes of disability and disease. For example, in 1986, OSHA put into effect a hazardous substance "right-to-know" standard. The rule requires chemical manufacturers, distributors, and importers to assess the hazards of their chemicals and to pass along that information to their buyers. Employers receiving such notice must label the chemicals with appropriate warnings and train employees in their use.

A second change in OSHA has been a careful targeting of its resources. It presently concentrates inspections on industries which offer the greatest threat to workers' health and safety (see Table 14-1). It has virtually eliminated inspections of certain employers, including insurance companies, retail stores, and other white-collar and service businesses, where the potential for danger to employees is low. To increase operating efficiency, OSHA has begun a program which allows approved labor-management committees to conduct workplace inspections and keep records. These committees free agency inspectors for other duties.

TABLE 14-1 Most and Least Dangerous Industries According to Days Lost to Occupational Injury or Illness*

Most Dangerous	Least Dangerous
1. Truck transportation	1. Communications
2. Railroad equipment	2. Chemical products
3. Meat packing	3. Aircraft
4. Lumber and wood products	4. Electrical equipment
5. Newspapers	5. Petroleum refining
6. Rail transportation	6. Textile products
7. Water transportation	7. Apparel making
8. Paper products	8. Pipeline transportation
9. Government	9. Motor-vehicle products
10. Air transportation	10. Natural gas production

*Data from National Safety Council.

A final change in OSHA has been the effort to be seen as a helper of business, rather than its enemy. OSHA inspectors have been ordered to offer more help in correcting workplace hazards. The agency has also begun programs which exempt certain employers from regular OSHA inspections when they maintain exceptional safety records.

There are critics of the changes in OSHA. Union leaders have criticized OSHA as attempting to accommodate businesses instead of protecting workers. They point to a decline in the number of OSHA inspections initiated by workers' complaints. They view the significant reduction in the number of employers who contest OSHA complaints as evidence that OSHA is not pursuing cases concerning serious safety violations.

4. Workers' Compensation Acts: Introduction

In the workplace around the turn of the century, the tort system was largely replaced by a series of workers' compensation acts. These statutes were enacted at both the state and federal level, and they imposed a type of strict liability on employers for accidental workplace injuries suffered by their employees. The clear purpose of these statutes was to remove financial losses of injury from workers and redistribute them onto employers and ultimately onto society. The following two sections examine present workers' compensation acts.

Workers' compensation laws are state statutes designed to protect employees and their families from the risks of accidental injury, death, or disease resulting from their employment. They were passed because the common law did not give adequate protection to employees from the hazards of their work. At common law, anyone was liable in tort for damages resulting from injuries caused to another as a proximate result of negligence. If an employer acted unreasonably and his or her carelessness was the proximate cause of physical injury suffered by an employee, the latter could sue and recover damages from the employer. However, the common law also provided the employer with the means of escaping this tort liability in most cases. It provided three defenses: (1) assumption of the risk, (2) contributory negligence, and (3) the **fellow-servant doctrine**.

For example, assume that employer E knowingly instructed workers to operate dangerous machinery not equipped with any safety devices, even though it realized injury to them was likely. W, a worker, had his arm mangled when it was caught in the gears of one of these machines. Even though E was negligent in permitting this hazardous condition to persist, if W were aware of the dangers which existed, he would be unable to recover damages because he knowingly *assumed the risk* of his injury. In addition, if the injury were caused by contributory negligence of the employee, as well as the negligence of the employer, the action would be defeated. And if the injury occurred because of the negligence of another employee, the negligent employee rather than the employer would be liable because of the fellow-servant doctrine.

The English Parliament passed a workers' compensation statute in 1897. Today all states have such legislation, modeled to a greater or lesser degree on the English act. These laws vary a great deal from state to state as to the industries subject to them, the employees they cover, the nature of the injuries or diseases which are compensable, the rates of compensation, and the means of administration. In spite of wide variances in the laws of the states in this area, certain general observations can be made about them.

5. The Workers' Compensation System

State workers' compensation statutes provide a system to pay workers or their families if the worker is accidentally killed or injured or incurs an occupational disease while employed. To be compensable, the death, illness, or injury must arise out of and in the course of the employment. Under these acts, the negligence or fault of the employer in causing an on-the-job injury is not an issue. Instead, these laws recognize the fact of life that a certain number of injuries, deaths, and diseases are bound to occur in a modern industrial society as a result of the attempts of businesses and their employees to provide the goods and services demanded by the consuming public.

This view leads to the conclusion that it is fairer for the consuming public to bear the cost of such mishaps rather than to impose it on injured workers. Workers' compensation laws create strict liability for employers of accidentally injured workers. Liability exists regardless of lack of negligence or fault, provided the necessary association between the injuries and the business of the employer is present. The three defenses the employer had at common law are eliminated. The employers, treating the costs of these injuries as part of the costs of production, pass them on to the consumers who created the demand for the product or service being furnished.

Workers' compensation acts give covered employees the right to certain cash payments for their loss of income due to accidental on-the-job injuries.

In the event of a married employee's death, benefits are provided for the surviving spouse and minor children. The amount of such awards usually is subject to a stated maximum and is calculated by using a percentage of the wages of the employee. If the employee suffers permanent partial disability, most states provide compensation both for injuries which are scheduled in the statute and those which are nonscheduled. As an example of the former, a worker who loses a hand might be awarded 100 weeks of compensation at $95 per week. Besides scheduling specific compensation for certain specific injuries, most acts also provide compensation for nonscheduled ones based upon the earning power the employee lost due to his or her injury. In addition to the above payments, all statutes provide for medical benefits.

As a result of inflation, many states have increased the amounts payable as workers'compensation benefits. However, the amounts paid in most states are substantially inadquate to provide a decent standard of living for injured workers. For example, even some of the more generous of these provide only about $100 per week for periods of temporary total disability and around $25,000 for death benefits.

In some states, employers have a choice of covering their workers' compensation risk with insurance or of being self-insured (that is, paying all claims directly) if they can demonstrate their capability to do so. Approximately 20 percent of compensation benefits are paid by self-insurers. In other states, employers pay into a state fund used to compensate workers entitled to benefits. In these states, the amounts of the payments are based on the size of the payroll and the experience of the employer in having claims filed against the system by its employees.

Workers' compensation laws are usually administered exclusively by an administrative agency, called the industrial commission or board, which has quasi-judicial powers. Of course, the ruling of such boards is subject to review by the courts of the jurisdiction in the same manner as the actions of other administrative agencies.

TESTS FOR DETERMINING WORKERS' COMPENSATION

The tests for determining whether an employer must pay workers' compensation to an employee are simply (1)"*Was the injury accidental?*" and (2) "*Did the injury rise out of and in the course of employment?*" Because workers' compensation laws benefit workers, courts interpret them liberally to favor workers. In recent years, cases have tended to expand employers' liability.

For instance, courts have held that heart attacks (as well as other common ailments in which the employee has had either a preexisting disease or a physical condition likely to lead to the disease) are compensable as "accidental injuries." One ruling approved an award to a purchasing agent who became mentally ill because she was exposed to unusual work, stresses, and strains. Her "nerve-racking" job involved a business whose sales grew over sixfold in ten years. Factors contributing to her "accidental injury" included harsh criticism by her supervisor, long hours of work, and inability to take vacations due to the requirements of her position.

Likewise, the courts have been liberal in upholding awards which have been challenged on the ground that the injury did not arise "out of and in *the course of employment*." Courts routinely support compensation awards for almost any accidental injury which employees suffer while traveling for their employers. A recent Minnesota Supreme Court decision upheld a lower court award of compensation to a bus driver. On a layover during a trip, the driver had been shot accidentally in a tavern parking lot following a night on the town.

However as the following case shows, not every workplace injury arises out of the scope of employment.

SCHULTHEIS v. INDUSTRIAL COMMISSION

449 N.E.2d 1341 (Ill. 1983)

Schultheis, a jeep driver for Johnson Outboards, had a disagreement with one of the company's supervisors. After the argument, he enlisted the help of a union shop steward who also agreed with the supervisor. Schultheis and the shop steward then went to the union office which was located in a trailer on the company premises. As Schultheis entered the office, the union president assaulted him. Schultheis brought a claim for workers' compensation for his injuries. The arbitrator and reviewing Commission denied Schultheis' claim.

CLARK, J.: On appeal before this court [is] . . . whether the Commission's finding that the petitioner's injuries did not arise out of and in the course of his employment because they were the result of a union dispute is against the manifest weight of the evidence. . . .

We turn now to the issue of whether the Commission's finding that the petitioner's injury did not arise out of and in the course of his employment is against the manifest weight of the evidence. In a case like the instant one, the petitioner bears the evidenti-

ary burden of establishing that his injury "arose out of" and "in the course of" his employment. If an injury occurs during working hours, at a place where an employee can reasonably be expected to be in the performance of those duties or something incidental thereto, the injury is said to have occurred in the course of his employment. Since the assault in question in this case took place during working hours, on the employer's premises, while the petitioner was going to speak with a union representative regarding a disagreement he had had with a company supervisor, there seems to be no dispute between the parties that the injury occurred in the course of petitioner's employment. What is disputed, however, is whether petitioner has met his burden of establishing that the injury inflicted by McDonald "arose out" of employment as a jeep driver for Johnson Outboards.

In order to establish that an injury arose out of one's employment, a claimant must make a "showing that the injury resulted from some hazard or risk inherent in the employment situation; i.e.,, there must be a causal connection between the nature of the employment and the resulting injury."

The issue of compensability for injuries resulting from assaults has arisen on numerous occasions before this court. In these cases, this court has cconsistently held that injuries suffered by employees resulting from assaults were not compensable if there was evidence to sustain a finding by the Industrial Commission that the motive was personal to the victim rather than work related or if claimant could not demonstrate a reason for the assault.

In the instant case, the Commission denied compensation because it found that petitioner's injuries were "the result of a union dispute." While we believe that simply because an assault results from a union dispute does not necessarily preclude recovery, the Commission here apparently determined that the assault in this case was not work related. . . .

Since the petitioner had the evidentiary burden of establishing that his injury arose out of and in the course of his employment and he did not provide sufficient evidence to establish the role of the union in this case, we believe that he has failed to meet his burden of establishing that his injury "arose out of" his employment. [*Affirmed.*]

EXCLUSIVE REMEDY RULE

Recently, some courts have been liberal in their interpretations of the *exclusive remedy rule*. This rule, which is written into all compensation statutes, states that an employee's sole remedy against an employer for workplace injury or illness shall be workers' compensation. In the past few years, courts in several important jurisdictions have created exceptions to this rule (see Table 14-2). Note that these exceptions recognize in part the workers' compensation laws do not adequately compensate badly injured workers.

Since workers' compensation laws apply only to accidentally injured workers, the exclusive remedy rule does not protect employers who intentionally injure workers. But the issue arises as to how "intentional" such an injury has to be. What if an employer knowingly exposes employees to a chemical which may cause illness in some employees over a long term? Consider the next case.

TABLE 14-2 Exceptions to the Exclusive Remedy Rule*

1. Employee sues manufacturer of a product which causes work-related injury.
2. Employee sues fellow employee who causes work-related injury.
3. Employee sues insurer who breaches a duty to warn employer of dangerous work conditions.
4. Employee sues employer who intentionally inflicts injury, including mental distress, or who intentionally conceals a dangerous work condition.
5. Employee sues employer who is in a "dual capacity" with employee. Example: Employer manufactured product which injured employee in the workplace.

*Not all exceptions exist in all states.

BLANKENSHIP v. CINCINNATI MILACRON CHEMICALS
69 Ohio St. 2d 608 (1982)

Eight plaintiffs sued the defendant for illness and disability arising from their exposure to certain chemical fumes in the workplace. The plaintiffs maintained that the defendant knew of the danger caused, but chose not to warn them and not to report the conditions to appropriate state and federal agencies. The complaint alleged that the defendant's omissions were "intentional, malicious and in willful and wanton disregard" of the plaintiffs' health. Upon the defendant's motion, the trial court dismissed the complaint due to the exclusive remedy rule. The plaintiffs appealed.

BROWN, J.: [T]he purpose of this appeal is not to try the factual issues presented by this complaint, but rather to determine whether the facts alone are sufficient to withstand a motion [to dismiss]. After carefully reviewing the complaint and seriously considering the arguments presented, this court, for the reasons stated hereinafter, finds that the complaint in question is sufficient to withstand such a challenge.

The primary focus of the dispute between the parties centers upon the question of whether the Workers' Compensation Act [the Act] is intended to cover an intentional tort committed by employers against their employees.

[The Act provides:] "Employers who comply with [the Act] shall not be liable to respond in damages at common law or by statute for any injury, or occupational disease, or bodily condition, received or contracted by any employee in the course of or arising out of his employment. . . ."

Clearly, . . . the pertinent statutory language [does not] expressly extend the grant of immunity to actions alleging intentional tortious conduct by employers against their employees. The General Assembly, however, established a rule of construction which is clearly of assistance in determining the scope of employer immunity. This section provides that: "[The Act] shall be liberally construed in favor of employees and the dependents of deceased employees."

In this regard, this court agrees that where an employee asserts in his complaint a claim for damages based on an intentional tort, "the substance of the claim is not an 'injury . . . received or contracted by an employee in the course of or arising out of his employment' within the meaning of [The Act]." No reasonable individual would equate intentional and unintentional conduct in terms of the degree of risk which faces an employee nor would such individual contemplate the risk of an intentional tort as a natural risk of employment. Since an employer's intentional conduct does not arise out of employment, [the Act] does not bestow upon employers immunity from civil liability for their intentional torts and an employee may resort to a civil suit for damages.

The workers' compensation system is based on the premise that an employer is protected from a suit for negligence in exchange for compliance with the Workers' Compensation Act. The Act operates as a balance of mutual compromise between the interests of the employer and the employee whereby employees relinquish their common law remedy and accept lower benefit levels coupled with the greater assurance of recovery and employers give up their common law defenses and are protected from unlimited liability. But the protection afforded by the

Act has always been for negligent acts and not for intentional tortious conduct. Indeed, workers' compensation acts were designed to improve the plight of the injured worker, and to hold that intentional torts are covered under the Act would be tantamount to encouraging such conduct, and this clearly cannot be reconciled with the motivating spirit and purpose of the Act.

It must also be remembered that the compensation scheme was specifically designed to provide less than full compensation for injured employees. Damages such as pain and suffering and loss of services on the part of a spouse are unavailable remedies to the injured employee. Punitive damages cannot be obtained. Yet, these damages are available to individuals who have been injured by intentional tortious conduct of third parties, and there is no legitimate reason why an employer should be able to escape from such damages simply because he committed an intentional tort against his employee.

In addition, one of the avowed purposes of the Act is to promote a safe and injury-free work environment. Affording an employer immunity for his intentional behavior certainly would not promote such an environment, for an employer could commit intentional acts with impunity with the knowledge that, at the very most, his workers' compensation premiums may rise slightly.

Moreover, as this court noted in *State v. Indus. Comm.*, workers' compensation "is founded upon the principle of insurance. . . ." An insurance policy does not protect the policy holder from the consequences of his intentional tortious act. Indeed, it would be against public policy to permit insurance against the intentional tort.

The use of the element of intent in workers' compensation is in no way novel. Under [the Act] an employee is denied benefits when he inflicts an injury upon himself intentionally. This section thus illustrates that intent plays an important role in the determination of whether an injury is compensable.

In conclusion, it is for the trier of fact to initially determine whether the alleged conduct constitutes an intentional injury. In the instant case, the facts will demonstrate whether an intentional tort occurred or whether the injuries received by appellants were incurred in the course of and arising from appellants' employment such that the worker's compensation remedy would be exclusive. These questions of fact, however, are not properly determinable by a motion to dismiss, for the lower court had before it insufficient facts to determine as a matter of law that appellants' complaint was barred. Appellants should be given an opportunity to prove their injury. [*Judgment reversed.*]

In 1984, a jury awarded $3.75 million to one of the *Blankenship* plaintiffs.

EXCLUSIONS FROM WORKERS' COMPENSATION COVERAGE

Even though all states have some form of workers' compensation, the statutes exclude certain types of employment from their coverage. Generally, domestic and agricultural employees are not covered. In addition, the law may not provide compensation for specified kinds of accidents or diseases. In about one-half the states the statutes are compulsory. In the other half, employers may elect to be subject to the act or to lawsuits by employees or their survivors for damages. If the latter course is chosen, an employee seeking compensation for injuries must prove they resulted proximately from the negligence of the employer, as at common law, however, the case is *not* subject to the common law defenses. In negligence, there is no statutory limit to the amount of damages recoverable.

6. The Future of Workers' Compensation

Currently, many problems confront the state workers' compensation system. Fifty separate nonuniform acts make up the system. Many acts exclude from coverage groups such as farm workers, government employees, and employees of small businesses. Many state legislatures have enacted changes in their compensation laws. However, states which have broadened coverage and increased benefits have greatly boosted the cost of doing business within their borders. This discourages new businesses from locating within these states and encourages those already there to move out.

In the last decade, workers' compensation payments have tripled. Many workers exaggerate their injuries in order to get compensation. On the other hand, compensation payments to seriously injured workers are often inadequate, and this has led to attempts to get around the exclusive remedy rule.

Many states presently grant workers' compensation to employees who develop mental job stress. For instance, a Raytheon Co. employee received compensation in Massachusetts for a nervous breakdown suffered when told she was being transferred. In California, the number of stress-related injuries reported more than tripled in a recent three-year period. Such injuries are difficult to verify and to relate to job conditions as opposed to some other cause.

A major problem concerns slowly developing, occupational diseases. Many toxic chemicals cause cancer and other diseases only after workers have been exposed to them over many years. Often it is difficult or impossible for workers or their survivors to recover workers' compensation for such diseases. A university-conducted study released in 1984 showed that only about one-third of the average losses caused by asbestos diseases was compensated.

One solution to the problems confronting the workers' compensation system would be federal reform. Those advocating such reform have put forth several plans, but Congress has shown little inclination so far to adopt a uniform federal act. But as the next section reveals, there are already federal compensation acts covering certain segments of the work force.

7. Federal Compensation Acts

Congress has enacted several statutes which extend liability to certain kinds of employers for injuries, diseases, and deaths arising out of the course of employment. Railroad workers and other transportation workers are covered by the Federal Employers Liability Act (FELA). This statute does not provide for liability without fault, as in the case of workers' compensation, but it greatly increases the chances of a workers's winning a lawsuit against his or her employer by eliminating the defenses the employer would have had at common law. In a suit for damages based upon the negligence of the officers, agents, or employees of an employer, the contributory negligence of the injured employee does not prevent recovery. If it is present, however, the comparative-responsibility rule reduces damages in proportion to the amount of the employee's negligence. This rule does not apply when the employer's violation of a statute enacted for the safety of the employee has contributed to the injury. Also, the common law defense of assumption of the risk is not available to an employer.

The act further provides that a term in a contract of employment which attempts to exempt a covered employer from liability or to prevent enforcement of the FELA is void. In addition, the legal rights of a deceased employee which are created by the statute survive for the benefit of the surviving spouse and children. Although fault of the employer must be proved for an employee to recover for injuries under the FELA, and a regular lawsuit must be filed in court, the act provides the workers with a distinct advantage over many workers' compensation systems. There is no limit or ceiling to the amount an employee can recover for injuries. It is clear that juries are often sympathetic to the injured worker, and verdicts in six or seven figures are not unusual. The Jones Act gives maritime employees the same rights against their employers as railway workers have against theirs under the FELA.

Other federal statutes require awards for on-the-job injuries or deaths of certain employees without regard to the fault of the employer in the manner of state workers' compensation laws. These provide formulas to use in computing the amounts of the awards for various kinds and degrees of disability, along with upper and lower limits for such awards. One statute is the Longshoremen's and Harbor Workers' Compensation Act. Congress extended this act to cover workers of private employers on United States defense bases.

8. Wages and Hours of Work

Statutes setting *minimum wages* per hour and maximum hours of work exist on both the state and the federal level. Early state legislation of this type mainly applied to labor by children and women. At first, employers successfully attacked such legislation as being an unconstitutional invasion of the freedom of contract. Today we recognize that state governments possess the power to enact statutes of this type for social and economic purposes. Approximately 70 percent of the states have minimum-wage laws.

The federal government also regulates wages and hours. The Fair Labor Standards Act (FLSA), which was originally enacted in 1938, has been amended several times to increase the minimum wage, to decrease maximum hours, and to broaden its coverage. Originally, the FLSA required covered employers to pay their employees at least 25 cents an hour for a regular workweek of forty-four hours, to pay such employees at least time and one-half for all work performed over the forty-four-hour week, and to keep certain records for each worker which would demonstrate compliance or noncompliance with the act. It also restricted the use of child labor. The Supreme Court held the statute to be a constitutional exercise of the power of Congress under the commerce clause.

At the time of this book's writing, the minimum hourly wage is generally $3.35. The standard workweek is forty hours, with overtime pay at a rate of not less than one and one-half times the employee's regular rate of pay. Although this regular rate may not be less than the minimum wage, it can be and usually is more. If it is, the time and one-half is the higher rate. For example, an employee whose hourly rate is $4 receives $6 per hour for overtime. The wage and overtime provisions apply whether an employee is paid on a time, piece, job, incentive, or other basis. The FLSA does *not* require sick pay, holidays off, vacations, overtime pay for weekend or holiday work, or a limit on the hours of work for employees who are sixteen years of age or older.

Not all types of employment were covered by the original FLSA, nor are they today. However, the amendments have expanded coverage greatly along with the minimum wage, so that now it protects most workers. Although there are still some exempt businesses, their number is decreasing, and the trend is to require the minimum wage for all. Categories of persons who are presently not covered include many who do not need the protection, such as those engaged in the practice of a profession, managerial and supervisory personnel, and outside salespeople. Most of the time, persons engaged in such employment earn incomes far in excess of the FLSA minimums, anyway. Also not covered are certain workers employed by small farms and small businesses such as "mom and pop" retail establishments and other small independent stores which are intrastate in operation.

In addition, messengers, handicapped workers, and full-time students employed in similar service operations, institutions of higher education, or agriculture may be paid lower minimum wages, provided the employer first obtains special certificates from the administrator of the Wage and Hour Division of the Department of Labor. As the next case shows, the minimum wage also does not apply to individuals in training when the employer gains no benefit from the training itself.

DONOVAN v. TRANS WORLD AIRLINES, INC.
726 F.2d 415 (1984)

PER CURIAM: The Secretary of Labor appeals from a final judgment entered in the District Court for the Western District of Missouri ruling that flight attendant trainees who had trained at Trans World Airlines, Inc.'s (TWA) Breech Training Academy were not "employees" for the purposes of the Fair Labor Standards Act (FLSA) during the first four weeks of training and, consequently, were not covered by the minimum wage and reporting provisions of the FLSA. We affirm.

For many years TWA, a major commercial air carrier, chose to train all TWA flight attendants at its Breech Training Academy (Academy) located in Overland Park, Kansas. Flight attendant positions were highly desirable and TWA received literally thousands of applications each year. In an effort to keep the cost of training flight attendants down, TWA tried to predict the number of flight attendant vacancies that would arise. Based on those determinations, TWA carefully selected its prospective trainees from a large group of applicants.

Although not officially required to do so, most flight attendant trainees resided in dormitory-like accommodations located on the Academy grounds. During the disputed four-week training periood, the trainees neither received nor expected any wages or monetary compensation from TWA. However, TWA did provide meals, lodging, ground transportation, and health and accident insurance during the training periods.

Trainees attended approximately forty hours of classes per week. About one-half of the training was devoted to the safety and emergency instruction required by the Federal Aviation Administration. TWA also provided instruction in subjects such as aviation history, grooming, personal and public communications, physical fitness, foreign currencies, and food and liquor preparation. The District Court found that although much of this instruction was geared to TWA passenger service and equipment, "much of that training could be utilized in service on other airlines and in other fields of endeavor."

At no time prior to completion of the training course were trainees permitted to work on regular commercial flights or to supplement the work of regular flight attendants. Although completion of the training course qualified trainees as flight attendants, TWA did not guarantee that all successful trainees would be hired upon graduation.

The District Court concluded that TWA flight attendant trainees were not "employees" within the meaning of the relevant provisions of the FLSA because TWA received no immediate benefit from their efforts during training.

Whether or not an individual is an "employee" within the meaning of the FLSA is a legal determination rather than a factual one.

After careful examination of the record, we conclude that the district court's determination is correct. Accordingly, we affirm on the basis of the district court's analysis.

One proposal to amend minimum-wage coverage applies to teenagers. It would allow employers to pay teenagers less than minimum wage. This proposal is in response to widespread teenage unemployment, especially in the cities. The theory is that if employers could pay less than minimum wage, they would hire more teenagers. Unions oppose a reduction in the minimum wage.

CHILD LABOR

Besides having wage and hour provisions, the FLSA contains sections which regulate the employment of child labor outside agriculture. Under these, eighteen is the minimum age for employment in occupations which are declared *hazardous* by the secretary of labor. These include such jobs as working in areas that involve exposure to radioactivity, operating various kinds of dangerous machinery, mining, and roofing. Otherwise, the basic minimum age for employment is sixteen, at which age children may be employed in any nonhazardous work.

The employment of fourteen- and fifteen-year-olds is limited to certain occupations such as sales and clerical work, under specific conditions of work, for limited hours, and outside school time only. Children under fourteen may not be employed, except for a few jobs which are specifically exempt. For example, children employed in agriculture outside of school hours, children employed by their parents in nonhazardous occupations, child actors, and newspaper deliverers are exempt. State laws on child labor must also be followed if they are more strict than the federal standards.

PENALTIES AND REMEDIES

One who willfully violates the provisions of the Fair Labor Standards Act may be prosecuted criminally by the attorney general and, if found guilty, may be punished by a fine of up to $10,000 for the first offense and, for subsequent offenses, a fine of up to $10,000 or imprisonment for up to six months, or both. Violators of the child-labor provisions can be fined a civil money penalty of up to $1,000 for each violation. The act also empowers the federal district courts to issue injunctions restraining violations of it.

Finally, employees who are injured by a violation may bring a civil suit against their employer and recover unpaid wages or overtime compensation and an equal amount as "liquidated" damages, plus reasonable attorneys' fees and costs of the action. However, if the employer shows the court that she or he was not violating the law, the court may, in its discretion, award no liquidated damages, or limit them. The administrator of the Wage and Hour Division of the Department of Labor may supervise the payment of back wages, or the secretary of labor may, upon the written request of an employee, bring suit himself for back pay due the employee.

9. Unemployment Compensation

Unemployment compensation is a federal-state program which provides for payment for temporary periods to workers who are unemployed through no fault of their own. It is a classic example of the use of the federal taxing power as a tool to pressure the states into adopting legislation deemed desirable by the federal government. The Social Security Act of 1935 imposed a federal tax on the wages paid by all employers who were not exempt. However, the act provided that taxed employers were entitled to a credit of up to 90 percent of this tax for any contributions they made to an approved state unemployment insurance plan. Although only Wisconsin had an unemployment compensation law in 1935, all the states enacted such statutes shortly after the Social Security Act.

The federal policy to encourage state unemployment insurance was a result of the mass unemployment in the depression during the 1930s. Then, millions were out of work for long periods, with about 25 percent of the labor force being unemployed. Partly, this mass unemployment was due to a self-feeding cycle. As workers were laid off, they lost their purchasing power and could consume less. Less consumption meant less need for production, so employers had to lay off more workers who lost their purchasing power and could consume less. Production continued to fall, so more workers became unemployed. A major goal of unemployment compensation, besides the humanitarian one, was to break this vicious cycle.

Today, the basic standard of the federal unemployment law imposes a tax on any person who pays $1,500 of wages during any three-month period of the current or preceding year. The tax is on the first $7,000 of wages at a 1985 rate of 6.2 percent. Up to 90 percent of this tax may be deducted for amounts paid to a state unemployment compensation fund.

The federal law grants a series of exemptions from the unemployment tax. Among the exempted are agricultural labor for certain small farming operations, family labor, labor for the United States government or for a state, and labor for a religious, charitable, or educational organization. The states may provide for wider coverage if they desire.

Only workers in a covered business can collect unemployment compensation, and then only if they meet certain tests. If they qualify, they draw payments as a matter of right, regardless of financial position, since need is not a factor. The laws require them either to have worked for a certain minimum number of weeks in a covered industry or to have earned a certain minimum amount of wages. These times and amounts vary from state to state. Generally, a worker must wait one week before applying and must register with the state employment agency and be ready, willing, and able to undertake suitable employment.

The maximum period during which benefits are payable varies from state to state and generally has ranged from twenty-six to thirty-nine weeks. The maximum amount of weekly payments for unemployment also varies widely. Usually it is computed as a percentage of the highest quarterly earnings in a base period.

All states have adopted *experience rating systems* which excuse employers who have a good record of maintaining stable employment from paying part or all of the state unemployment tax. Such systems have been adopted as a result of the provision which allows employers a credit against the federal tax not only for amounts paid the state but also for such amounts as they are excused from paying because of a good experience rating. Thus, businesses with a good rating pay less unemployment taxes than the ones with a higher unemployment experience.

As a result of the credit permitted by the experience rating system, the average unemployment tax rate nationwide has been considerably less than that provided for in the law. Experience rating has given employers the incentive to attempt to control their unemployment record and to detect fraudulent claims filed by former employees. On the minus side, it means that taxes will be lower during times when the economy is in good condition and higher when general conditions are bad.

Generally, a worker is disqualified for unemployment compensation if he or she refuses other work which is suitable, was *discharged for proper cause*, or *quit work voluntarily*. In one case, an employee had been discharged for refusing to obey his employer's orders to get a haircut and shave his beard and sideburns. A court held that the employee did not disqualify himself from receiving unemployment compensation by refusing the employer's offer to rehire him on condition that he observe the hairstyle rules in the future. In the next case the court considers whether refusal to perform "grosscutting" was misconduct which constituted a "proper cause" for discharge.

AMADOR v. UNEMPLOYMENT INSURANCE APPEALS BOARD
677 P.2d 224 (Cal. 1984)

Amador is a histotechnician. Histotechnicians prepare tissue samples for microscopic analysis by pathologists. Two doctors asked Amador to perform "grosscutting" which is the procedure of removing small tissue samples from organs temporarily removed by a doctor from a live patient. Amador refused. She believed that, as a histotechnician, she did not have the skill to perform grosscutting and that such a procedure should be handled only by physicians or specially trained technicians. Other histotechnicians at the hospital, however, did perform grosscutting. Because Amador refused to perform this job, she was discharged.

BIRD, J.: Is a worker disqualified from collecting unemployment insurance benefits when she has been discharged for wilfully refusing to perform work which she reasonably and in good faith believed would jeopardize the health of others?

"An individual is disqualified for unemployment compensation benefits if the director finds that he or she left his or her most recent work voluntarily without good cause or that he or she has been discharged for misconduct connected with his or her most recent work."

The term "misconduct," as used in the code, is limited to "conduct evincing such wilful or wanton disregard of an employer's interests as is found in deliberate violations or disregard of standards of behavior which the employer has the right to expect of his employee, or in carelessness or negligence of such degree or recurrence as to manifest equal culpability, wrongful intent or evil design, or to show an intentional and substantial disregard of the employer's interests or of the employee's duties and obligations to his employer. On the other hand mere inefficiency, unsatisfactory conduct, failure in good performance as the result of inability or incapacity, inadvertencies or ordinary negligence in isolated instances, or good faith errors in judgment or discretion are not to be deemed "misconduct" within the meaning of the statute."

The determination of fault is not concluded by a finding that the discharge was justified. The claimant's conduct must evince culpability or bad faith. "The conduct may be harmful to the employer's interests and justify the employee's discharge; nevertheless, it evokes the disqualification for unemployment insurance benefits only if it is wilful, wanton or equally culpable."

A claimant may not be denied benefits solely on the basis of a "good faith error in judgment."

Although this case involves a discharge for "misconduct," the law concerning voluntary terminations for "good cause" is also relevant. If a claimant's reasons for refusing work constitute "good cause" sufficient to justify resignation, it follows that they should also justify the less drastic step of refusing a work assignment.

In view of the statutory objective of "reducing the hardship of unemployment" "the concept of 'good cause' cannot be arbitrarily limited; the board must take account of 'real circumstances, substantial reasons, objective conditions, palpable forces that operate to produce correlative results, adequate excuses that will bear the test of reason, just grounds for action, and always the element of good faith.' "

The trial court denied the writ based on its finding that Amador had repeatedly and wilfully refused to obey a reasonable directive of the employer. However, such a finding does not conclude the issue. An employee may violate an employer's reasonable rule "as a good faith error in judgment rather than as misconduct."

Further, as courts interpreting similar statutes of other states have recognized, "[t]he refusal to comply with a reasonable work assignment can constitute 'willful misconduct [,]' . . . [but a]n employee's conduct will not . . . be deemed to be disqualifying 'willful misconduct' if he establishes good cause for his actions."

This rule follows from the interrelationship between the statutory disqualifica-

tions for discharges due to misconduct for voluntary terminations without good cause. Because section 1256 does not disqualify employees who leave employment voluntarily with good cause, it can scarcely have been intended to disqualify those who take the less drastic step of refusing a work assignment for good cause. Accordingly, once the employer has proven that the worker wilfully refused a reasonable order, the worker has an opportunity to show that her refusal was for good cause.

Here, Amador presented uncontroverted evidence both as to her reasons for refusing to perform grosscutting and as to the factual and logical basis of those reasons. She testified that, as a histotechnician, she felt unqualified for such an important task. She refused the work "[b]ecause . . . , through my normal training, I know the big responsibility handling these organs, and I know the life and health of the patient depends on this duty, which was given to me."

Her decision was also grounded on her previous work experience at Oxford and Stanford, where histotechnicians had not been permitted to perform grosscutting. Finally, prior to the incidents which precipitated her discharge, she had consulted three doctors, whom she respected as "big authorities in pathology." All three supported her opinion. Her testimony on this point was corroborated by statements signed by two of those pathologists.

The question remains whether this court should rule as a matter of law that Amador's concern for the patients' health was a "reasonable, good faith and honest" one and that she is entitled to benefits. . . .

The essential facts surrounding Amador's discharge are not in dispute. Amador wilfully refused to perform a work order because her past experience and her consultations with outside authorities led her to conclude that the health of patients would be jeopardized. These facts compel the conclusion that Amador refused to perform grosscutting because—from her standpoint in the light of the circumstances facing her and the knowledge posssessed by her at the time—she reasonably and in good faith feared harm to others. Accordingly, she is entitled to benefits.

10. Social Security

Social Security is a federal program for providing income when a family's earnings are reduced or stopped because of retirement, disability, or death. Under Social Security's Medicare provisions, hospital and medical insurance help protect persons who are sixty-five and older from high health-care costs. Every month, 36 million people receive Social Security benefits, which represent 27 percent of all expenditures made by the federal government.

Congress enacted the first Social Security Act in 1935. At first, it covered only certain workers in commerce and industry and provided them only with retirement benefits. Since then, a number of amendments have increased the kind and dollar amount of benefits to what they are today. These amendments have also greatly increased the number of persons covered so that now most self-employed persons, employees of nonprofit corporations, household and farm employees, federal employees, members of the armed forces, the clergy, and others are included also. Currently, nine out of ten workers in the United States are earning Social Security protection, and approximately one out of seven persons receives monthly Social Security checks.

The Social Security law requires that during their working years, covered employees, their employers, and self-employed persons pay Social Security taxes to the federal government. Employers must deduct their employees' share of the contribution to the Social Security system from their wages, match those payments, and send the combined amount to the IRS. Self-employed persons pay their tax each year when filing their individual income returns. Generally, employers must file an Employer's Quarterly Tax Return with the IRS and deposit Social Security taxes with an authorized commercial bank or Federal Reserve Bank at various times, usually at least once per month, depending on the amount of undeposited taxes at the time. A penalty is imposed for failure to make required deposits when due, without reasonable cause. Earnings of those covered are taxable despite age, and even if they are receiving Social Security benefits at the time.

Employers must keep all records pertaining to employment taxes for inspection by the IRS for a period of at least four years after the taxes are due or are paid. These records must include such things as the names, addresses, occupations, and Social Security numbers of the employees paid; the amounts and dates of the payments made to them; the period of their employment; duplicate copies of tax returns filed and the dates and amounts of deposits made.

CRITICISMS AND PROBLEMS OF THE SOCIAL SECURITY SYSTEM

In recent years concern has grown over the financial health of the Social Security system. It appears underfunded, in spite of the fact that the amount of wages subject to Social Security tax, as well as its rates, have increased dramatically. In 1984, the tax was paid on the first $37,800 of personal income, an amount that was $29,700 in 1981. For 25 percent of all employees, Social Security tax is larger than federal income tax, and for small businesses it is the largest federal tax. The rates of taxation will rise gradually, at least through 1990 (see Table 14-3).

Critics of the system point to the fact that much of the burden of paying for increasing Social Security benefits is being imposed on the younger workers of today, at a time when many of them are raising families and attempting to purchase homes. The work force appears to be leveling off due to the trend toward zero population growth in the country. However, the number of Social Security beneficiaries will be increasing due to longer life expectancies and, at the turn of the century, to the retirement of persons born during the period after World War II, that is, the "baby boom" generation.

In 1983, Congress amended the Social Security Act to raise the retirement age for receiving full benefits. Beginning in the year 2000, the current retirement age of 65 will begin to rise. For persons born in 1960 and later, the retirement age will be 67. However, early retirement at reduced benefits will be available. That option may also be exercised at present.

Congress also has made taxable up to 50 percent of Social Security benefits for those whose incomes in retirement exceed a certain amount. Previously, all Social Security benefits were nontaxable. Even with these changes, however, there is still concern about the solvency of the Social Security system. In light of soaring medical costs, the Medicare trust fund of the Social Security system, which pays for retirement health costs, faces severe financial problems in the near future.

11. Private Pension Plans: Introduction

Economic security in retirement has been a national policy goal for much of this century. The Social Security system is a good example. Encouragement of

TABLE 14-3 Rates of Social Security Taxation through 1990*

Year	Employee and Employer, Each	Self-Employed
1986	7.15%	14.30%
1987	7.15%	14.30%
1988	7.51%	15.02%
1989	7.51%	15.02%
1990	7.65%	15.30%

*The amount of income to which the tax applies will also likely rise, but Congress has not yet set it.

private pension plans is another part of this policy. In the past decade the number of employer-established private retirement plans has more than doubled. Some 60 million employees are currently covered by private plans.

The law provides incentives for businesses and individuals to create private pension plans. It also protects employees who are part of such plans.

There are many types of pension plans (as well as profit-sharing arrangements). One of the motivations for such plans, of course, is a genuine interest by a business in the retirement future of all its employees, along with a desire to attract and retain high-quality workers. Some plans have resulted mainly from union pressure and collective-bargaining agreements. In addition, those in control of a business have a personal interest in assuring their own financial futures.

A major financial incentive to the formation of private pension plans is favorable income tax treatment. If an employer has instituted a "**qualified pension plan**," as defined by the Internal Revenue Code, it can claim income tax deductions from contributions made to fund the plan, and fund earnings from investments are not taxable. Employees need pay personal income tax only on payments received after retirement. Such payments often receive special retirement income treatment and come at a time when other sources of income are lower, putting the retired person in a lower tax bracket. Basically, to qualify for this special treatment, a plan must cover either a certain percentage of all employees (usually 70 percent) or cover classifications of employees which do not discriminate in favor of management (officers or highly compensated employees) or shareholders, as determined by the IRS.

12. Employee Retirement Income Security Act

Qualification of a pension plan by the IRS does not ensure that it is a good plan for employees. Prior to 1974, plans were sometimes improperly funded, and the money in them were irresponsibly invested. In other cases, many employees lacked *vested rights* (rights which cannot be taken away) in their company's pension plan. If they were discharged prior to retirement, they received no pension.

In 1974, Congress passed the Employee Retirement Income Security Act (ERISA) to protect employee rights in private pension plans. The act applies to both **defined benefit plans** and **defined contribution plans** (often called money-purchase plans). Defined benefit plans usually guarantee employees a certain retirement income based on years of service and salary or wage level. Actuarial calculations determine employers' funding obligations with such a plan. Under a defined contribution plan, employers contribute a percentage of an employee's pay (often 5 to 10 percent) to the pension fund. Retirement income is determined by the total of these contributions plus investment return.

The defined contribution plan allows employers to budget pension costs in advance. Because of this and because ERISA regulates funding requirements for defined benefit plans very heavily, the majority of employers favor defined contribution plans.

An important provision of ERISA requires *plan termination insurance coverage* for all defined benefit plans. The idea is to make the plans pay annual premiums to insure the benefits to participants in the event that the plan is terminated and its assets are not sufficient to meet its obligations. The act creates the Pension Benefit Guaranty Corporation (PBGC) to provide this insurance. It ensures that vested benefits will be paid up to established maximums. The employer (not just the separate pension plan itself) is also made liable to reimburse PBGC for the insured benefits it pays, up to 30 percent of the employer's net worth. Without this requirement, claims could be made only against the pension trust's assets but not against the employer when the pension trust failed.

Another aspect of ERISA is also designed to protect the assets of pension plans. Strict rules require plan *fiduciaries* (those who are placed in a position of trust and confidence with regard to another's assets) to exercise the degree of care that a prudent person would in handling his or her own affairs in the management of a fund's assets. Anyone who has any such control, as well as one who gives investment advice for a fee, is included in the act's definition of a fiduciary. Also, transactions between the plan and a party with a conflicting interest, like the employer, are forbidden. Under this rule, a loan between the plan and employer is prohibited, as is a sale of property between them. Investments by a plan in the securities of the employer are generally limited to 10 percent.

ERISA also ensures employees' rights to benefits under pension plans. The law states that benefits from an employee's own contributions (if any) to a plan are fully and immediately vested when the contributions are made. Benefits from an employer's plan contributions must begin vesting before retirement under one of several ERISA standards. The most common standard selected by employees provides for full employee vesting after ten years of service. Another standard establishes a gradual five- to fifteen-year vesting.

The record-keeping and reporting requirements under ERISA are substantial. The years of service and percentage of vesting of benefits of each participant must be recorded. If vested employees terminate before retirement, the plan administrator must furnish both the IRS and the Department of Labor with information on their vested benefits. A booklet (approved by the Department of Labor) must be prepared for distribution to plan participants. It must include a detailed plan description and a summary, understandable by the average participant. A very detailed annual report must be filed with the department and made available for examination by plan participants and for public inspection. The plan report generally must include financial statements, an opinion on them by an independent certified accountant, information on the plan's investments, assets, and transactions, and other data which are specified in great detail by the act.

SIMPLIFIED EMPLOYEE PENSIONS

The Revenue Act of 1978 permits employers to set up *simplified employee pensions*. This change was designed to appeal to employers, particularly smaller businesses, who do not wish to set up a full-blown pension plan of their own because of the expense and complications involved. Under this plan, employers can contribute up to a specified amount of an employee's income to an *individual retirement account* (IRA) for each employee. The contributions (including interest or other income from their investment) are not taxable to the employees until they begin drawing from their account in retirement, which can start anytime after age fifty-nine and one-half without penalty. Employees select their own investment vehicle when they open their IRAs. The approved list includes banks, savings and loans, credit unions, insurance companies, and mutual funds. The fact that the employee decides where the IRA is invested should result in greatly reduced liability risk on the part of the employer. The IRA belongs to the employee, so it vests immediately. Also, the fund goes along with the employee who changes jobs, and it continues to accumulate.

Businesses that adopt the simplified employee pensions plan may deduct contributions from their income tax. However, to qualify they must meet certain requirements. For example, all covered employees must receive the same *percentage* contribution. The percentage rate of contribution may be changed from year to year (for all workers), or, in a bad year, the employer may decide to make no contributions at all.

INDIVIDUAL RETIREMENT ACCOUNTS

Individual retirement accounts encourage retirement savings by individuals. Under ERISA, IRA contributions are deductible from presently taxable income, and investment earnings are tax-free until distributed. (However, as of this writing, a current proposal before Congress would remove the tax deductibility of IRA contributions for individuals also covered under an employer's pension plan.)

Any person under age seventy and one-half can contribute up to $2,000 annually to establish and fund an IRA. Within limits set by ERISA, the person can invest the IRA funds. Because the purpose of IRAs is to provide retirement income, there are substantial penalties for early withdrawal of funds. Withdrawals can be made without penalty beginning at age fifty-nine and one-half. If death occurs prior to that age, distributions can also be made to survivors without penalty. Only when distributions occur are IRA funds taxable.

A person can establish an IRA even though he or she also participates in an employer-established pension plan. Along with pension plans, IRAs have helped reduce demands for an expanded Social Security program.

13. ERISA Trends

Most observers consider ERISA a success. Over half of the work force, both male and female, participate in private pension plans. Because of its success,

ERISA might be amended to include retirement medical insurance. This step would help prop up the Social Security Medicare program, which could become insolvent if medical costs continue to rise and Congress fails to provide additional funding.

Even with its success ERISA also faces problems. More than 1,000 private pension plans have fallen into insolvency, and the PBGC is operating at a deficit to meet the obligations of these plans to retired employees. One solution, which PBGC has proposed to Congress, is to raise the annual insurance premium which employers with defined benefit plans currently pay to PBGC.

Employees may also be affected when pension plans are overfunded instead of underfunded. During periods of economic growth, investments made by employers can earn far in excess of the amount necessary to fund pension obligations. In 1985, the nation's 200 largest corporations had $73 billion in liquid pension assets that were not needed to fund promised benefits. A number of companies have terminated employee pension plans in order to capture these excess funds. Congress may place a special tax on such funds.

A major problem of ERISA is the amount of paperwork required of employers who maintain pension plans. These employers must keep records and make reports to three separate governmental agencies: PBGC, the Labor Department, and the Treasury Department (IRS). Many smaller businesses cannot afford to do this and do not have pension plans. A proposed solution would centralize authority in one agency, probably PBGC, thus reducing the paperwork burden.

14. Trends in Worker Protection: Limitations on Employment at Will

Historically, unless employees contracted for a definite period of employment (such as for one year), employers were able to discharge them without reason at any time. This is called the *employment-at-will* doctrine.

During the 1930s, employers began to lose this absolute right to discharge employees whenever they desired. The Labor-Management Relations Act prohibited employers from firing employees for union activities. Now many federal laws limit employers in their right to terminate employees, even at-will employees (see Table 14-4). Some states have also prohibited employers by statute from discharging employees for certain reasons, such as for refusing to take lie-detector examinations.

Courts, too, have begun limiting the at-will doctrine. Under contract theory, several courts have stated that at-will employment contracts (which are not written and are little more than the agreement to pay for work performed) contain an implied promise of good faith and fair dealing by the employer. This promise, implied by law, can be broken in certain cases by unjustified dismissal of employees. Other courts have allowed employees to sue employers for tort in similar cases.

Both contract and tort exceptions have generally involved one of three

TABLE 14-4 Federal Statutes Limiting Employment-at-Will Doctrine

Statute	Limitation on Employee Discharge
1 Labor-Management Relations Act	Prohibits discharge for union activity or for filing charges under the act
2 Fair Labor Standards Act	Forbids discharge for exercising rights guaranteed by minimum-wage and overtime provisions of the act
3 Occupational Safety and Health Act	Prohibits discharge for exercising rights under the act
4 Civil Rights Act	Makes illegal discharge based on race, sex, color, religion, or national origin
5 Age Discrimination in Employment Act	Forbids age-based discharge of employees aged forty to seventy
6 Employee Retirement Income Security Act	Prohibits discharge in order to prevent employees from getting vested pension rights
7 Clean Air Act	Prevents discharge of employees who cooperate in proceedings against employer for violation of the act
8 Clean Water Act	Prevents discharge of employees who cooperate in proceedings against employer for violation of the act
9 Consumer Credit Protection Act	Prohibits discharge of employees due to garnishment of wages for any one indebtedness
10 Judiciary and Judicial Procedure Act	Forbids discharge of employees for service on federal grand or petit juries

types of employer behavior: (1) discharge of employee for performance of an important public obligation (such as jury duty); (2) discharge of employee for reporting employer's alleged violations of law (called "whistle blowing"); and (3) discharge of employee for exercising statutory rights. The next case illustrates this last type of behavior. Note that the court talks about "public policy." Most of the cases that limit at-will employment state that the employer has violated public policy.

FIRESTONE TEXTILE COMPANY v. MEADOWS
666 S.W.2d 730 (Ky. 1984)

Meadows suffered a back injury while working at Firestone Textile Company. After he filed for workers' compensation benefits, the company fired him. Meadows sued Firestone for wrongful discharge.

LEIBSON, J.: The issue is does a complaint seeking damages for wrongful discharge because an employee was terminated for pursuing a claim under KRS Chapter 342 for workers' compensation state a cause of action?

Meadows concedes that ordinarily an employer may discharge his at-will employee for good cause, for no cause, or for a cause that some might view as morally indefensible. But the question before us is not whether the "terminable at-will" doctrine should be discarded. It is much narrower: (1) should there be any exceptions, and, (2) if so, is the Workers' Compensation Act grounds for recognizing such an exception?

Brockmeyer v. Dun & Bradstreet . . . is an excellent treatise on the first question, whether to permit "any judicial exceptions to the employment at-will doctrine." The Wisconsin Supreme Court concludes "that in the interests of employees, employers and the public, a narrow public policy exception should be adopted," and then adopts the following rule:

(A)n employee has a cause of action for wrongful discharge when the discharge is contrary to a fundamental and well-defined public policy as evidenced by existing law. . . . The public policy must be evidenced by a constitutional or statutory provision. An employee cannot be fired for refusing to violate the constitution or a statute. Employers will be held liable for those terminations that effectuate an unlawful end.

Implicit in these sections, and in the Act as a whole, is a public policy that an employee has a right to be free to assert a lawful claim for benefits without suffering retaliatory discharge. Speaking through Judge Wilhoit, the Court of Appeals states:

If it were otherwise, the beneficient purposes of the Act could often be effectively frustrated by merely threatening employees with discharge. A statute need not expressly state what is necessarily implied.

Employers as a group have a legitimate interest to protect by having the cause of action for wrongful discharge clearly defined and suitably controlled. Therefore, we adopt this further from the decision of the Wisconsin Supreme Court in *Brockmeyer v. Dun & Bradstreet:*

The determination of whether the public policy asserted is a well defined and fundamental one is an issue of law and is to be made by the . . . court.

When a discharged employee seeks to establish a cause of action for wrongful discharge, it is a question of law for the court to decide whether the reason for discharge is unlawful because of a constitutionally protected right or a right implicit in a statute.

Should courts judicially recognize a cause of action for wrongful discharge where an employee at-will has been discharged solely because he filed a workers' compensation claim? Indiana so held in *Frampton v. Central Indiana Gas Co.* Though there was no statute expressly prohibiting discharge of an employer because he filed a compensation claim, the Indiana Supreme Court held:

If employers are permitted to penalize employees for filing workmen's compensation claims, a most important public policy will be undermined. The fear of being discharged would have a deleterious effect on the exercise of a statutory right.

Cases from Illinois, Kansas, Michigan, New Jersey, Oregon, Missouri, California, and the United States Fifth Circuit Court of Appeals have reached a similar result. The public policy considerations expressed by the Workers' Compensation Act are no longer subject to debate.

In enacting KRS Chapter 342 of the Kentucky Revised Statutes, the legislature set forth a comprehensive scheme for compensating employees injured on the job. It is an important public interest that injured employees shall receive, and employers shall be obligated to pay, for medical expenses, rehabilitative services and a portion of lost wages. Injured employees should not become public charges. If that is the public policy of Kentucky, and it is, then action on the part of an employer which prevents an employee from asserting his statutory right to medical treatment and compensation violates that policy. The only effective way to prevent an employer from interfering with his employees' rights to seek compensation is to recognize that the latter has a cause of action for retaliatory discharge when the discharge is motivated by the desire to punish the employee for seeking the benefits to which he is entitled by law. [*Affirmed.*]

What does it mean to say that an employer has violated public policy? Is it a court's way of saying that most people no longer support the employer's right to do what it did?

Limitations on employment-at-will doctrine show continued development of workers' protection. Instead of dealing with workers' safety and financial security, they concern a related issue: job security. It may be part of a trend which could ultimately lead to some type of broad, legally guaranteed job security. Many nations have much stricter laws promoting an employee's right to job security than does the United States. In recent years, unions have increasingly focused on job security issues in their bargaining with employers.

15. Workers' Privacy

Individual privacy is such an important part of individual freedom that both legal and ethical questions regarding privacy are bound to multiply in the computer age. While debate continues concerning the need for further federal privacy legislation, many states have passed their own privacy-related statutes. Several states guarantee workers access to their job personnel files and restrict disclosure of personal information to third parties. Almost half the states forbid businesses from requiring lie-detector tests as a condition of employment, although employers can still ask job applicants to submit voluntarily to the tests.

Responding to privacy issues, hundreds of companies have adopted privacy sections in their codes of ethics. Most of these sections concern personnel information. The following is an example from the Caterpillar Code of Ethics.

PRIVACY OF INFORMATION ABOUT EMPLOYEES

Information needed for administration of payrolls, benefit plans, and labor agreements—and for compliance with laws—has resulted in collection, by Caterpillar, of an increasing amount of personal data. We seek to minimize intrusiveness, and maximize fairness and confidentiality of such data.

Personal data will contain only such individually identifiable information as is necessary for business purposes and compliance with law. Such information is to be handled confidentially and securely.

Company access to such information is limited to those who have legitimate, pertinent business purposes.

Entries to employee data files are to be factual, job-related, and accurate. Any information found to be in error will be corrected or eliminated: Company data about an employee will be made available, on request, to that employee . . . excepting for special, sensitive files such as those pertaining to career planning and litigation.

REVIEW QUESTIONS

1 For each term in the left-hand column, match the most appropriate description in the right-hand column:

(1)	Course of employment	(a)	The law which states that an employee may only recover workers' compensation against an employer for an accidental injury
(2)	Defined benefit plan	(b)	A common law doctrine which held that an employer was not liable when one employee injured another
(3)	Defined contribution plan	(c)	The legal concept that an employer may fire at any time an employee who is not under contract
(4)	Discharge for proper cause	(d)	A pension system which guarantees employees a certain retirement income based on years of service and salary
(5)	Employment-at-will	(e)	A pension system under which an employer pays a certain percentage of an employee's wage or salary to a fund but does not guarantee a certain level of retirement income
(6)	Exclusive remedy rule	(f)	The pursuing of the employer's interest under the employer's direction
(7)	Fellow-servant rule	(g)	The firing of someone for failing to follow orders, tardiness, and so on, which makes that person ineligible for unemployment compensation
(8)	Minimum wage	(h)	Rights which cannot legally be taken away

(9) Qualified pension plan

(10) Vested rights

(i) The lowest legal pay an employer can give for certain types of employment

(j) A retirement income program under which employers can claim income tax deductions for contributions made to fund the program

2 Discuss recent changes in OSHA enforcement of safety and health regulations.

3 Why did the common law of negligence not give employees adequate protection from the hazards of their work?

4 If Corgel fails to wear a hard hat as required by his employer and is injured by a falling screwdriver, can he recover workers' compensation from the employer?

5 Discuss exceptions to the exclusive-remedy rule. Why are ever greater numbers of injured employees trying to avoid the impact of the rule?

6 A railroad employee falls from a moving train and suffers back injury. Can the employee recover under workers' compensation? Explain.

7 Dodson works for Cartwright Industries as a welder for $8 an hour. One week she works sixty hours. What are her legal wages for the week?

8 How old must an individual be before he or she can work as a miner?

9 What is the advantage of an experience rating system for an employer who has a low turnover of employees?

10 Claudia's employer fired her for theft of office supplies. Marco quit his job in hopes of becoming a writer. Are either of these persons entitled to unemployment compensation?

11 In spite of dramatic increases in the rate of Social Security taxation and the amount taxed, the Social Security system continues to be financially unstable. Why?

12 Consider defined benefit pension plans and defined contribution pension plans. From a financial viewpoint, which type will an employer usually prefer? An employee? Discuss.

13 Weitz, a retired industrial worker, gets $750 monthly under a defined benefit pension plan. He learns that his former employer is bankrupt and that there is not enough money in the pension plan to continue paying his benefits. What will likely happen to Weitz's retirement income?

14 Roebuck Manufacturing, a small equipment firm, has only thirty-five employees. Because of the expense and complication of setting up a regular defined benefit or contribution plan, it has not set up a pension plan for its employees. Then it learns of the "simplified employee pension." Discuss the advantages of this type of pension plan for a firm like Roebuck Manufacturing.

15 What are the limitations on the employment-at-will doctrine?

Chapter
15

Consumer Protection

1. Introduction

There have been more consumer protection laws passed since World War II than in the 175 years preceding the war. Two key factors seem primarily responsible for this rapid expansion of legal regulation. First, most of the past several decades has been a time of rising affluence, when the public has been willing to absorb costs of individual legal regulation, which inevitably come in the form of higher prices for goods and services. Second, the organization of well-financed consumer lobbying groups has led to legislative responses favorable to consumer interests.

Recent trends toward a more cautious federal approach to consumer protection reveal the conservative, market-oriented philosophy of the Reagan administration. At the state level, however, consumer protection regulation continues to be increasingly active. Even at the federal level, there are a great number of existing laws that continue to be enforced. Many provide remedies allowing injured consumers to sue law violators.

Consumer protection laws achieve their purposes by affecting contractual relationships. Underlying the economic practice of private enterprise is its legal support structure: the right of contract. The buying and selling of raw materials, labor, land, services, and products would hardly be possible without a legal system that supports the enforceability of privately arranged contracts and allows considerable freedom in the agreement of contractual terms. Since the right of contract is the legal basis for the activities of private enterprise, it is perhaps natural that consumer protection laws intervene in the contractual relationships that consumers have with business. Whether legal intervention into the private right of contract between sellers and consumers achieves a fair purpose in an efficient way is the subject of considerable debate. The continuing reality of such intervention, however, cannot be denied.

This chapter divides consumer protection into federal and state laws. As you read, consider how consumer protection laws affect the private right of contract.

2. Who is a Consumer?

The laws discussed in this chapter protect consumers. Who is a consumer? Consider the following case:

ANDERSON v. FOOTHILL INDUSTRIAL BANK
674 P.2d 232 (Wyo. 1984)

Appellants, Glen and Marlene Anderson contracted with the United States Postal Service to deliver mail on a route. The Andersons borrowed $27,500 from appellee Foothill Industrial Bank for start-up expenses in establishing the mail delivery route. The Andersons sued the Foothill Industrial Bank while refinancing the loan, claiming that the bank had failed to comply with Wyoming's Uniform Consumer Credit Code (UCCC) and the federal Truth-in-Lending Act by misrepresenting the annual percentage rate of the loan and other acts.

ROONEY, C.J.: These allegations of appellants are premised on the fact of the loan being a consumer loan and not a commercial loan. The U.C.C.C. applies only to consumer loans and not to commercial loans. A consumer loan is defined in 40-14-304, W.S. 1977, as follows:

(a) Except with respect to a loan primarily secured by an interest in land, 'consumer loan' is a

loan made by a person regularly engaged in the business of making loans in which:
(i) The debtor is a person other than an organization;
(ii) The debt is incurred primarily for a personal, family, household or agricultural purpose;
(iii) Whether the debt is payable in installments or a loan finance charge is made; and
(iv) Either the principal does not exceed twenty-five thousand dollars ($25,000.00) or the debt is secured by an interest in land.

Considering the evidence in this case in accordance with the foregoing, we find that it established the loan to be a commercial loan and not a consumer loan as a matter of fact. Appellant Glen Anderson inquired of three lendors in an attempt to secure the money for his mail route business. He told the loan officer at Person-to-Person that the money was to be used to "buy a mail route." At First Wyoming Bank, he said that it was to be used to operate a truck or otherwise engage in the mail route. He told the representative of appellee Foothill Industrial Bank that it was for a down payment on a truck and for start-up expenses. He did not require a loan until he decided to go into the mail route business. The debt was not "incurred primarily for a personal, family, household . . . purpose" as required by 40-14-304, W.S. 1977, supra. Although part of the proceeds of the loan were used to pay off that due on a second mortgage on appellants' residence, the testimony was that prudent lending practice would require such pay off with transfer of the collateral if the loan were made for the purpose of financing another enterprise. The thrust of all of the evidence was that the debt was "incurred primarily" for the purpose of entering a mail route business and not for a personal family or household purpose. It was not a consumer loan. . . . [*Affirmed.*]

According to the *Anderson* case, <u>consumers are natural</u> (rather than corporate) <u>persons who incur debt "primarily for personal, family, or household purposes.</u>" Most of the statutes in this chapter define "consumer" similarly.

Although the Federal Trade Commission Act protects businesses as well as consumers, the consumer protection mission of the Federal Trade Commission (FTC) is promoted by a special bureau called The Bureau of Consumer Protection. This body within the FTC is the regulatory center for federal consumer protection. The next section begins the topic of federal consumer protection by examining activities of the FTC and the Bureau of Competition.

FEDERAL CONSUMER PROTECTION

3. The Federal Trade Commission

Created in 1914, the FTC is an "independent" regulatory agency charged with keeping competition free and fair and with protecting consumers. The FTC obeys its mandate to promote competition through enforcement of the antitrust laws discussed in Chapter 20. It achieves its consumer protection goal by trade practice regulation under that section of the FTC Act which prohibits using "unfair or deceptive acts or practices in commerce." It also administers several other consumer protection acts covered in this chapter. (See Table 15-1.) In the final analysis, promoting competition and protecting consumers overlap considerably. A highly competitive economy produces better goods and services at lower prices, while trade practice regulation ensures fair competition by preventing those who would deceive consumers from diverting trade from those who compete honestly.

The FTC furthers consumer protection through *trade practice regulation* in several ways. For instance, it advises firms that request it as to whether a proposed practice is unfair or deceptive. Although not legally binding, an *advisory opinion* furnishes a good idea about how the FTC views the legality of

TABLE 15-1 Consumer Protection Laws the FTC Administers

Laws	Duties
FTC Act	To regulate unfair or deceptive acts or practices
Fair Packaging and Labeling Act	To prohibit deceptive labeling of certain consumer products and to require disclosure of certain important information
Equal Credit Opportunity Act	To prevent discrimination in credit extension based on sex, age, race, religion, national origin, marital status, and receipt of welfare payments
Truth-in-Lending Act	To require that suppliers of consumer credit fully disclose all credit terms before an account is opened or a loan made
Fair Credit Reporting Act	To regulate the consumer credit reporting industry
Magnuson-Moss Warranty Act	To require the FTC to issue rules concerning consumer product warranties
Fair Debt Collection Practices Act	To prevent debt collection agencies from using abusive or deceptive collection practices

a given trade practice. Sometimes the FTC also issues *industry guides*, which specify the agency's view of the legality of a particular industry's trade practices. Like advisory opinions, industry guides are informal and not legally binding. The Bureau of Consumer Protection plays the major role in issuing advisory opinions and industry guides on trade regulation issues.

In its function of protecting consumers, however, the FTC goes far beyond merely advising businesses about the legality of trade practices. It also prosecutes them for committing unfair or deceptive trade practices. Such prosecutions arise in one of two related ways. First, the Bureau of Consumer Protection may allege that an individual or company, called a **respondent**, has violated Section 5 of the FTC Act, which prohibits *"unfair or deceptive acts or practices."* Over the years, the FTC's administrative law judges, and the commissioners who review decisions of the judges, have derived a body of quasi-judicial interpretations as to what constitutes unfair and deceptive acts.

Prosecutions may also arise from allegations under Section 5 that a respondent's actions violate a trade regulation rule of the FTC. At the recommendation of the Bureau of Consumer Protection, the five-member Commission adopts trade regulation rules in exercising its quasi-legislative power. These rules are formal interpretations of what the FTC regards as unfair or deceptive, and they have the force and effect of law. The rules usually deal with a single practice in a single industry, and they cover all firms in the affected industry. Examples of trade regulation rules include required disclosures of the "R" value for siding and insulation, and the familiar warning on cigarette packages and in ads.

Alleged trade practice violations may come to the attention of the Bureau of Consumer Protection in a variety of ways. A business executive may complain about another's acts that injure competition, or a consumer may direct the attention of the Bureau to unfair or deceptive acts of a business.

Such complaints are filed informally, and the identity of the complainant is not disclosed. A letter signed by a complaining party provides a basis for proceedings if it identifies the offending party, contains all the evidence which is the basis for the complaint, and states the relief desired. Of course, other government agencies, Congress, or the FTC itself may discover business conduct alleged to be illegal. For instance, the Bureau of Consumer Protection maintains a special media monitoring unit which examines the media for trade practice violations.

The chief legal tools of the Bureau are the *consent order* and the **cease and desist order**. As discussed in Chapter 10, under the consent order procedure, a party "consents" to sign an order which restrains the promotional activity deemed offensive and agrees to whatever remedy the Bureau imposes, if any. Most cases brought by the Bureau are settled by this procedure.

If a party will not accept a consent order, it will be prosecuted before an administrative law judge. If the party is found guilty, the judge will enter a cease and desist order prohibiting future violations. Parties may appeal cease and desist orders to the full five-member commission and from there to the Court of Appeals if legal basis for further appeal is present.

4. FTC Penalties and Remedies

The basic penalty for trade practice violations under the FTC Act is a civil fine of not more than $10,000 per violation. The punishment function of fining violators is only an incidental one, as the FTC's main purpose is to prevent and deter trade practice violations.

To obtain fines, either the FTC or the Justice Department must ask the federal court to assess them. The exception is when companies agree to fines as part of a consent order. Fines may be assessed in three distinct situations: (1) for a violation of a consent or cease and desist order, (2) for a violation of a trade regulation rule, and (3) for a knowing violation of prior FTC orders against others.

This last situation requires some explanation. In 1975, Congress amended the FTC Act to permit the FTC to assess fines against parties who knowingly did what others in the past had been ordered to stop. The main purpose in this change in the law was to be fair to firms who had been ordered to stop a certain practice but whose competitors continued to do it. As changed, the law allows assessment of fines against such competitors once they know of the illegality of their practice. To establish knowledge, the FTC can mail copies of its orders against a respondent to other firms in a respondent's industry. Then, any further instance of the practice would be a knowing violation. In one penalty action, the FTC assessed a $100,000 fine against a toy manufacturer who knowingly continued a practice which the FTC had ordered another manufacturer to cease.

The FTC Act provides that "each separate violation of . . . an order shall be a separate offense." It also states that in the case of a violation through continuing failure to obey an order, each day the violation continues is a separate offense. Because of these provisions, the total fine against a violator may be considerably more than $10,000. The Reader's Digest Association, Inc., was once assessed a fine of $1,750,000 for violating a consent order.

In addition to assessing penalty fines, the FTC has broad powers to fashion appropriate remedies to protect consumers in trade regulation cases. One remedy the FTC uses to accompany some of its orders is **corrective advertising**.

When a company has advertised deceptively, the FTC can require it to run ads that admit the prior errors and correct the erroneous information. The correction applies to a specific dollar volume of future advertising. The theory is that the future advertising, however truthful itself, will continue to be deceptive unless the correction is made because it will remind consumers of the prior deceptive ads. Corrective ads have forced admissions that a mouthwash does not reduce cold symptoms or prevent sore throats, that an oil treatment product cannot decrease gasoline consumption, and that an aspirin-based drug cannot relieve tension.

Other remedies the FTC may use in its orders, or may seek to impose by court action under certain circumstances, include (1) recission of contracts (each party must return what has been obtained from the other), (2) refund of money or return of property, (3) payment of damages to consumers, and (4) public notification of trade practice violations. When it is in the public interest, and when harm from an illegal practice is substantial and likely to continue, the FTC may ask the federal court to grant temporary or even permanent injunctions to restrain violators.

5. Traditional Trade Practice Regulation

The FTC conducts trade practice regulation under its power to determine "unfair or deceptive acts or practices in commerce." Most of its cases have focused on deceptive practices. Often, as the following discussion reveals, proof of traditional deception relies more on a showing of legalistically inaccurate promotional language, rather than on consumer injury.

One common type of advertising traditionally attacked by the FTC makes prospective purchasers believe they will be getting a "good deal" in terms of price if they buy the product in question. For example, a seller of goods was ordered to refrain from advertising its products for sale using a price comparison in which its actual price was compared to a higher "regular" price or a manufacturer's list price. The Commission ruled that it was deceptive to refer to "regular price" unless the defendant had usually sold the items at the price recently in the regular course of business. Also, it was held deceptive to refer to the "manufacturer's list price" when that list price was not the ordinary and customary retail sales price of the item in the locality. This was in spite of the fact that manufacturers themselves had suggested the retail prices to which the seller compared its lower selling price. In ordering enforcement of the Commission's cease and desist order, the Court of Appeals said, "We do not understand the Commission to hold that use of the term 'manufacturer's list price' is unlawful per se; rather it is unlawful only if it is not the usual and customary retail price in the area."

Similar to price representations which offer "free" goods for the purchase of others is a **bait-and-switch promotion**. Here, the seller intends to use a product advertised at a low price only as bait to capture the interest of consumers and then switch their attention from it to products which the baiter really desired to sell from the beginning.

Besides involving misleading price representations, deceptive practices may result from fraudulent, false, or misleading advertising or other representations concerning the performance capability of goods or services being sold. False representations of the composition, quality, character, or source of products, by misbranding or otherwise, have been barred as deceptively misleading. For example, lumber dealers have been barred from advertising under names such as "California white pine" and "Western white pine" when their products were inferior to genuine "white pine," even though these terms were accepted and understood in the trade. Other cases falling into this category violation are ones in which a seller suggested that a beauty aid "restored natural moisture necessary for a lively healthy skin," a claim which was false, and one in which cigars made of domestic tobacco were labeled "Havana."

False statements which misrepresent neither a product nor its price have also been ruled unfair or deceptive. Typical of these is one in which a product is endorsed by one who is misrepresented to be a "doctor" or "scientific expert." Disparaging the goods of others in an attempt to promote the sale of one's own is also an unfair practice. For example, the FTC restrained a manufacturer of stainless-steel cooking utensils from publishing questions like "Do you know that aluminum pans may be full of the most deadly bacteria known to science?" And "Did you ever find maggots in your aluminum pans?"

Other cases have involved no actual misstatement but representations which, while true in themselves, were intended to mislead. Using a word while having a hidden or unusual interpretation in mind for the purpose of promoting sales is an example. If a manufacturer states that its product is "guaranteed for life," most persons would probably believe that the guarantee was to run for the life of the purchaser. However, Parker Pen Company used this phrase in its advertising with the undisclosed intention that the lives in question were those of the pens they manufactured, thus making the guarantee worthless. Parker was restrained from making such "guarantees."

Using the technique of product name simulation is also unfair. This occurs when a manufacturer or seller uses either the same name or one that is deceptively similar to another product of another manufacturer which has required consumer acceptance. This conduct, whether undertaken with the intent of exploiting the goodwill of a competitor or not, may confuse consumers. If the name selected is close enough to that of the established product, its use may be restrained by the FTC as being deceptive.

Even silence by a seller may result in deception of consumers, and the Commission may require that positive disclosures be made before further sales of the goods in question are permissible. For example, nondisclosure that books published were abridged or condensed was ruled as deceptive. In addition, distributing secondhand or rebuilt goods without indicating them as such and selling foreign goods without disclosing their origin have been restrained by the Commission in its efforts to protect consumers from unfair or deceptive trade practices.

Table 15-2 gives recent examples of FTC deceptive trade practice cases. Most of these cases are "traditional" in nature.

6. Policy Trends at the FTC

After the 1970s, the consumer activist decade at the FTC, the 1980s promise a more restrained effort at consumer protection by the agency. During the 1970s, the FTC began broad-scale use of its rule-making powers. It passed or

TABLE 15-2   Recent FTC Deceptive Practice Cases

Company	Order
American Home Products	Must not give the impression that pain relievers are something other than aspirin when they are not. Must disclose presence of aspirin when company's product is contrasted with another product containing aspirin. Required to prove claims of product superiority with two controlled clinical studies.
California-Texas Oil Co.	Must not make unsubstantiated claims about gasoline additives improving fuel mileage. Cannot use language that additives improve mileage "up to" 15 percent unless an appreciable number of consumers can achieve that performance under normal conditions.
Meredith Corp.	Company must stop misleading potential home buyers and sellers by ads which allege that obtaining a Better Homes real estate franchise is more difficult than it actually is.
Champion Home Builders Co.	Must pay $550,000 to consumers who purchased solar furnaces in which ad claims misrepresented amount of heat the furnaces would produce.
Heatcool	Company must run twelve months of corrective ads stating that its products "do not insulate better than comparable glass storm windows."
Sears	Must cease and desist from making claims that Lady Kenmore dishwashers eliminate the need for scraping and prerinsing dishes. Cannot make claims for *any* major home appliance unless reliable substantiating evidence is available.
Sunbeam Corp.	Must not misrepresent the ability of electric air cleaners to eliminate indoor pollutants. Must have competent and reliable evidence for future performance claims.
Weider Health and Fitness	Must halt claims that nutrient supplements will promote muscle development in a unique way. Must refund $400,000 to users.

proposed sweeping rules on thermal insulation, eyeglasses, the funeral industry, franchising, business opportunities, vocational schools, food labeling,
used cars, and children's advertising. These rules threw many affected businesses into such turmoil that Congress, prompted by heavy lobbying, acted to
restrain the FTC.

In the 1980s, the FTC has backed away from its earlier enthusiasm for
rule making. Prior to final adoption, the proposed food labeling and children's advertising rules were withdrawn from consideration. Under the Reagan FTC, the Bureau of Consumer Protection has focused its enforcement
efforts on a case-by-case approach to regulation, rather than on rule making.
And in line with the theory that the marketplace itself can cure many types of
deceptive practices, the Reagan FTC has substantially reduced the number of
deceptive trade practice cases from the levels of previous administrations.

Another development of the past decade which has continued vitality in
the 1980s is the FTC's *ad substantiation program.* It is now an unfair and
deceptive trade practice for sellers to make affirmative claims about their
products which they cannot prove. The claims themselves may even be true,
but it is illegal to make them if there is no proof to support them. Thus, the
FTC required a manufacturer of weight-loss tablets to prove claims that
consumers could lose weight without restricting caloric intake. When the
manufacturer could not substantiate the ads, it had to discontinue them.
Occasionally, the FTC has applied ad substantiation to claims by an entire
industry, rather than to the claims of a specific advertiser.

One 1970s trend at the FTC which continues into the 1980s is the trade
regulation emphasis on disclosure to consumers. For instance, the Commission forced a major encyclopedia company to disclose in its advertising that
salespersons would call on anyone who returned response coupons. The
Commission termed it "deceptive" for the company to fail to make this
disclosure. The emphasis on disclosure underscores the belief that informed
consumers can "regulate" many trade practices by voting with their dollars, if
they possess sufficient information.

In recent years, the FTC has grappled with advertising problems presented by radio and television. The following casse illustrates that in electronic
media ads the FTC can go beyond words to analyze "aural-visual" imagery.

AMERICAN HOME PRODUCTS CORP. v. F.T.C.
695 F.2d 681 (1982)

The Federal Trade Commission (FTC) ruled
that American Home Products (AHP) engaged in deceptive advertising in violation of
the Federal Trade Commission Act. AHP
falsely claimed that Anacin had a unique
pain-killing formula that was superior in effectiveness to all other nonprescription anal-
gesics, when, in reality, Anacin's sole pain-
killing component was merely aspirin. AHP
appealed the Commission's ruling.

ADAMS, J.:

A. The Standard of Review of Findings of Deceptiveness

The Federal Trade Commission Act directs that "[t]he findings of the Commission as to the facts, if supported by evidence, shall be conclusive." It is "clear that properly interpreted, the statute requires review by the substantial evidence in the record as a whole standard." This standard "does not permit the reviewing court to weigh the evidence, but only to determine that there is in the record 'such relevant evidence as a reasonable mind might accept as adequate to support a conclusion.' "

This deferential standard with respect to Commission findings of fact applies to the findings here. Although "in the last analysis the words 'deceptive practices' set forth a legal standard and they must get their final meaning from judicial construction," a Commission finding that advertisements are deceptive or tend to mislead "is obviously an impressionistic determination more closely akin to a finding of fact than a conclusion of law."

Colgate-Palmolive explained that the "Commission is often in a better position than are courts to determine when a practice is deceptive within the meaning of the Act. This Court has frequently stated that the Commission's judgment is to be given weight by reviewing courts. This admonition is especially true with respect to allegedly deceptive advertising since the finding of a section 5 violation in this field rests so heavily on inference and pragmatic judgment."

The Commission's familiarity with the expectations and beliefs of the public, acquired by long experience, is especially crucial when, as with the advertisements proscribed by Parts I(B) and III of the Order in this case, "the alleged deception results from an omission of information instead of a statement."

B. How Advertising is to be Interpreted

"[T]he tendency of the advertising to deceive must be judged by viewing it as a whole, without emphasizing isolated words or phrases apart from their context." The impression created by the advertising, not its literal truth or falsity, is the desideratum. . . .

In the present proceeding, the Commission analyzed not only the words used, but also, with respect to the television advertisements, the messages conveyed through the "aural-visual" pattern. The Commission's right to scrutinize the visual and aural imagery of advertisements follows from the principle that the Commission looks to the impression made by the advertisements as a whole. Without this mode of examination, the Commission would have limited recourse against crafty advertisers whose deceptive messages were by means other than, or in addition to, spoken words. In *Standard Oil Co. of California v. FTC*, the court upheld a Commission finding "that the predominant visual message was misleading, and that it was not corrected or contradicted by the accompanying verbal message in advertisements." *Colgate-Palmolive* also supports the Commission's right to look beyond spoken words to the message conveyed visually. According to *Colgate-Palmolive*, "even if an advertiser has himself conducted a test, experiment or demonstration which he honestly believes will prove a certain product claim, he may not convey to television viewers the false impression that they are seeing the test, experiment or demonstration for themselves, when they are not because of the undisclosed use of mock-ups." . . . [*Modified.*]

NEW DECEPTION GUIDELINES

Traditionally, the concept of deceptive trade practices includes all practices which have a "tendency or capacity" to mislead consumers. No actual harm to any specific group of consumers need be shown. As of this writing, the courts have not changed the "tendency or capacity standard." However, the FTC has.

In its new standard, the FTC has said that it will use three tests to determine whether to take action against trade practices. First, the FTC must conclude that the ad is "likely to mislead consumers." Second, misled consumers must be "acting reasonably in the circumstances." Third, the practice must be "material," that is, it must potentially affect consumer purchasing decisions.

In explaining its new standard, the FTC noted that certain practices are unlikely to deceive consumers acting reasonably. Generally, the FTC will not bring advertising cases based on subjective claims (taste, feel, appearance, smell) or on correctly stated opinion claims. It will also not pursue cases involving obviously exaggerated or puffing claims.

Under the guidelines the FTC will likely ignore technically deceptive practices which cannot be shown to affect consumer purchase decisions, such as an ad which falsely claims the "best prices in town." Although the FTC retains the authority to conclude on its own evaluation whether a practice affects consumer decision making (is material), the new guidelines will probably cause it to turn increasingly to outside evidence provided by consumer testing.

7. Introduction to Federal Credit Regulations

As the large number of credit cards in the average consumer's wallet indicates, credit buying has truly become a national pastime. Credit financing of consumer contracts has jumped astronomically in recent years. At the close of World War II, consumer credit outstanding amounted to only $2.5 billion, a figure which had changed little since the 1920s. Today, however, consumer credit debt has soared above the $350 billion mark. Both in absolute terms and as a percentage of GNP, credit debt has grown steadily since World War II. Considering the importance of credit buying to the consumer and to business, it is no surprise that a number of laws regulating credit extension have been passed. The laws discussed in the following sections cover non-discrimination in credit extension, the collection of information for credit reports, and the standardized disclosure of credit charges. Note that the FTC has the power to bring consumer protection cases under these statutes, as well as under the other federal consumer protection laws discussed in this chapter. Unlike the FTC act, however, which grants power only to the FTC, these statutes also give rights and remedies that consumers themselves can exercise.

8. Equal Credit Opportunity Act

In 1975, Congress passed the Equal Credit Opportunity Act (ECOA). The ECOA's purpose is to prevent discrimination in credit extension. In an economy in which credit availability is so important, the ECOA is a logical extension in a vital consumer area of the antidiscrimination laws found in the employment field.

This act prohibits discrimination based on sex, marital status, race, color, age, religion, national origin, or receipt of welfare in any respect of a consumer credit transaction. Although the ECOA forbids discrimination on the basis of all these different categories, it is aimed especially at preventing sex discrimination. As the divorce rate climbs, the age of first marriage grows later, and more women enter the work force, it is expected that sex discrimination in credit extension will increasingly become a subject for litigation.

The law prohibits one to whom the act applies from discouraging a consumer from seeking credit based on sex, marital status, or any other of the enumerated categories. A married woman, for example, cannot be denied the right to open a credit account separate from her husband's or in her maiden name. Unless the husband will be using the account or the consumer is relying on her husband's credit, it is illegal even to ask if the consumer is married. It is also illegal to ask about birth-control practices or childbearing plans or to assign negative values on a credit checklist to the fact that a woman is of childbearing age.

The ECOA applies to all businesses which regularly extend credit, including financial institutions, retail stores, and credit-card issuers. It also affects automobile dealers, real estate brokers, and others who steer consumers to lenders. And as the following case indicates, many courts are ruling that ECOA covers consumer leasing situations, which may substitute in place of credit/based sales.

BROTHERS v. FIRST LEASING
724 F.2d 789 (1984)

Patricia Ann Brothers attempted to lease an automobile in her own name from the defendant, First Leasing. Even though Brothers did not intend to lease the car jointly with her husband, First Leasing required her to provide information concerning her husband's financial history and required him to sign the application. First Leasing rejected Brothers' application because her husband had previously filed for bankruptcy. Brothers sued First Leasing, claiming the denial of her application constituted discrimination on the basis of sex or marital status under the Equal Credit Opportunity Act (ECOA). The federal district court held that the lease was not covered by the ECOA, and it dismissed the action.

REINHARDT, J.: The issue, then, is whether the ECOA applies only to the Truth in Lending Act or to the Consumer Leasing Act as well. . . .

Preliminarily, we note that there is nothing in the literal language or the legislative history of the CLA, or of the ECOA, including the 1976 amendments, that suggests that the ECOA does not apply to the CLA. We also note that in interpreting other titles of the Consumer Credit Protection Act, we have found an examination of the purpose of the particular title to be crucial to our decision.

"The purpose of the ECOA is to eradicate credit discrimination waged against women, especially married women whom creditors traditionally refused to consider for individual credit." Congress reaffirmed the goal of antidiscrimination in credit in the 1976 amendments to the ECOA by adding race, color, religion, national origin, and age to sex and marital status as characteristics that may not be considered in deciding whether to extend credit.

In enacting and amending the ECOA, Congress recognized that a prohibition against discrimination in credit provides a much-needed addition to the previously existing strict prohibitions against discrimination in employment, housing, voting, education, and numerous other areas. The ECOA is simply one more tool to be used in our vigorous national effort to eradicate invidious discrimination "root and branch" from our society.

In view of the strong national commitment to the eradication of discrimination in our society, we see no reason why Congress would have wanted to subject the leasing of durable consumer goods to regulation under the disclosure provisions of the Consumer Credit Protection Act, but to exclude those transactions from the scope of the antidiscrimination provisions of that Act. Certainly, abolishing discrimination in the affording of credit is at least as important as compelling the disclosure of information regarding finance charges. To conclude that discrimination in consumer leasing transactions is exempt from the ECOA simply because Congress did not add express language covering consumer leases when it amended the ECOA for entirely unrelated reasons would be inconsistent with the broad purpose of the statute and the liberal construction we must give it. It is far more reasonable to conclude that Congress thought that an express amendment was unnecessary because the ECOA on its face applies to all credit transactions and, therefore, the language already in the Act was broad enough to cover consumer leases.

In enacting the Consumer Leasing Act [CLA], Congress explicitly recognized the "recent trend toward leasing automobiles and other durable goods for consumer use as an alternative to installment credit sales." Prospective lessors run extensive credit checks on consumer lease applicants just as they do in the case of credit sales applicants. The problems of persons discriminated against with respect to credit under the Truth in Lending Act and the CLA are for the most part identical. Therefore, interpreting "credit transactions" so that the ECOA applies to lease transactions, as well as to credit sales and loans, is essential to the accomplishment of the Act's antidiscriminatory goal.

We turn now to an analysis of the statutory scheme. The CLA is a part of a comprehensive act regulating numerous financial transactions. The ECOA is a later part of that same comprehensive statute. We must view the umbrella act, the Consumer Credit Protection Act, as a whole and not as separate unrelated parts. We must also treat the amendments to the statute as if they were adopted as part of the original enactment. When the ECOA is examined in that light, it becomes evident that it applies to all transactions covered by Title I of the Consumer Credit Protection Act. The statutory scheme is wholly inconsistent with the view that the ECOA applies to one part of Title I, the Truth in Lending Act, but not to another, the CLA. Moreover, any doubt as to this point is removed when we consider the fact that the CLA was enacted and codified as a subchapter of the Truth in Lending Act, and not as a separate measure.

Finally, to interpret the term "credit transactions" narrowly, so as to exclude consumer leases would nullify Congress' use of flexible language necessary "to insure the effective application of legislative policy to changing circumstances." We hold only that Congress intended to make the ECOA's antidiscrimination provisions applicable to all transactions covered by the Consumer Credit Protection Act, whether those transactions were covered under the initial form of the Act or as a result of the subsequent amendments. . . .[*Reversed and remanded.*]

In basing a credit decision on the applicant's income, the credit extender must consider alimony, child support, and maintenance payments as income, although the likelihood of these payments being actually made may be considered as well. The credit extender must also tell an applicant that she need not disclose income from these sources unless she will be relying on that income to obtain credit. In calculating total income those subject to the law must include income from regular part-time jobs and public assistance programs.

Information on accounts used by both spouses must be reported to third parties, such as credit reporting agencies, in the names of both spouses. This provision of the law helps women establish a credit history and enables a woman who separates from her husband to obtain credit in her own right.

To date, much of the litigation surrounding the ECOA concerns the requirement that *specific* reasons be given a consumer who is denied credit. Several cases have imposed liability upon credit extenders who have failed to provide any reasons for credit denial or who merely informed the consumer that she had failed to achieve a minimum score on a credit rating system. Other cases have dealt with age and race discrimination. The government filed an action recently against a large consumer finance company which made extension of credit to the elderly conditional upon their obtaining credit life insurance. It has also been established that the practice of **redlining**, that is, refusing to make loans at all in certain areas where property values are low, can discriminate on the basis of race in granting mortgage credit.

Private remedies for violation of the ECOA are recovery of actual damages, punitive damages up to $10,000, and attorney's fees and legal costs. Actual damages can include recovery for embarrassment and mental distress. Punitive damages can be recovered even in the absence of actual damages. In addition to private remedies, the government may bring suit to enjoin violations of the ECOA and to assess civil penalties. In one case, the FTC assessed a $200,000 civil penalty against a major national oil company. The FTC charged that the company practiced race and sex discrimination by using ZIP codes as a factor in deciding whether to extend credit and by failing to consider women's alimony and child support income.

9. The Fair Credit Reporting Act

The Fair Credit Reporting Act (FCRA) applies to anyone who prepares or uses a credit report in connection with (1) extending credit, (2) selling insurance, or (3) hiring or discharging an employee. It covers credit reports on consumers but not those on businesses. The purpose of the law is to prevent unjust damage to an individual because of inaccurate or arbitrary information in a credit report. It is also designed to prevent the undue invasion of individual privacy in the collection and selling of information about a person's credit record.

The law gives individual consumers certain rights whenever they are rejected for credit, insurance, or employment because of an adverse credit report. These rights include (1) the right to be told the name of the agency making the report, (2) the right to require the agency to reveal the information given in the report, and (3) the right to correct the information or at least to give the consumer's version of the facts in dispute.

This law does have one important limitation. It provides that a report containing information solely as to transactions or experiences between the consumer and the person making the report is not a "consumer report" covered by the act. To illustrate this limitation, assume that a bank is asked for information about its credit experience with one of its customers. If it reports only as to its own experiences, the report is not covered by the act. The act is designed to cover credit reporting agencies which obtain information from several sources, compile it, and furnish it to potential creditors. If the bank passed along any information it had received from an outside source, then its credit report would be subject to the provisions of the act. Also, if the bank gave its opinion as to the creditworthiness of the customer in question, it would come under the act. The limitation is restricted to information relating to transactions or experiences, and the information furnished must be of a factual nature if the exception in the law is to be applicable.

Many businesses can avoid the pitfalls of being a credit reporting agency, but most businesses will be subject to the "user" provisions of this law. The "user" provision requires that consumers who are seeking credit for personal, family, or household purposes be informed if their application is denied because of an adverse credit report. They must also be informed of the source of the report and of the fact that they are entitled to make a written request within sixty days as to the nature of the information received. If they request the information in the report, they are entitled to receive it so that they may challenge the accuracy of the negative aspects of its contents.

The act also contains a provision on *investigative consumer reports*. These are reports on a consumer's character, general reputation, mode of living, and so on, obtained by personal interviews in the consumer's community. No one may obtain such a report unless at least three days' advance notice is given the consumer that such a report will be sought. The consumer has the right to be informed of the nature and scope of any such personal investigation.

Reports which are intended to be covered by this act are those usually conducted for insurance companies and employment agencies.

In making investigations and collecting information, credit reporting agencies must observe *reasonable procedures*, or they will be liable to consumers. For example, when a consumer investigative report contained false information about a consumer's character—including rumored drug use, participation in demonstrations, and eviction from prior residences—a court found liability against the credit reporting agency. The agency's investigator had obtained the information from a single source, a person with a strong bias against the consumer, and he failed to double-check it. However, if an agency follows reasonable procedures, it is not liable to a consumer, even if it reports false information. Furthermore, several courts have ruled that the FCRA preempts state law. This prevents consumers from filing libel actions against agencies which report false information.

Anyone who violates the FCRA is civilly liable to an injured consumer. The government may also assess civil and criminal penalties in certain instances. For example, one company agreed to pay $122,000 in civil penalties to settle a case. The government had charged that the company had failed to tell certain credit applicants that they were denied credit because of an adverse credit report.

10. The Truth-in-Lending Act

The Truth-in-Lending Act authorizes the Federal Reserve Board to adopt regulations "to assure a meaningful disclosure of credit terms so that the consumer will be able to compare more readily the various credit terms available to him and avoid the uniformed use of credit." As previously mentioned, the FTC enforces these regulations.

The Truth-in-Lending Act covers all transactions in which (1) the lender is in the business of extending credit in connection with a loan of money, a sale of property, or the furnishing of services; (2) the debtor is a natural person as distinguished from a corporation or business entity; (3) a finance charge may be imposed; and (4) the credit is obtained primarily for personal, family, household, or agricultural purposes. It covers loans secured by real estate, such as mortgages, as well as unsecured loans and loans secured by personal property. Disclosure is necessary whenever a buyer pays in four installments or more.

Truth-in-Lending imposes a duty on all persons regularly extending credit to private individuals to inform them fully of the cost of the credit. It does not regulate the charges which are imposed.

The Truth-in-Lending philosophy of full disclosure is accomplished through two concepts, namely, the *finance charge* and the *annual percentage rate* (APR). The borrower uses these two concepts to determine the amount he or she must pay for credit and what the annual cost of borrowing will be in relation to the amount of credit received. Theoretically, a debtor armed with this information will be better able to bargain for credit and to choose one creditor over the other.

The finance charge is the sum of all charges payable directly or indirectly by the debtor or someone else to the creditor as a condition of the extension of credit. Included in the finance charge are interest, service charges, loan fees, points, finder's fees, fees for appraisals, credit reports or investigations, and life and health insurance required as a condition of the loan.

Among the costs frequently paid by debtors which are not included in the finance charge are recording fees and taxes, such as a sales tax, which are not usually included in the listed selling price. These are items of a fixed nature, the proceeds of which do not go to the creditor. Other items of cost not included are title insurance or abstract fees, notary fees, and attorney's fees for preparing deeds.

The law requires that the lender disclose the finance charge, expressing it as an annual percentage rate, and specifies the methods for making this computation. The purpose is to ensure that all credit extenders calculate their charges in a uniform fashion. This enables consumers to make informed decisions about the cost of credit.

The finance charge and annual percentage rate are made known to borrowers by use of a financing statement. This statement must be given to the borrower before credit is extended and must contain in addition to the finance charge and the annual percentage rate the following information:

1   Any default or delinquency charges that may result from a late payment

2   Description of any property used as security

3   The total amount to be financed, including a separation of the original debt from finance charges

As the following case indicates, refinancing of loans also imposes duties on credit extenders.

WISE FURNITURE v. DEHNING
343 N.W.2d 26 (Minn. 1984)

Dehning purchased consumer goods on credit from Wise on four separate occasions. With the purchases on April 2 and October 22, each contract refinanced the previous contract and Wise retained a security interest in all of the goods purchased by Dehning.

Dehning defaulted on the last contract still owing $811.23. He sued Wise for violating the Truth-in-Lending Act (TILA). The trial court ruled that Wise violated TILA.

AMDAHL, C. J.: The express purpose of

TILA is: "[T]o assure a meaningful disclosure of credit terms so that the consumer will be able to compare more readily the various credit terms available to him and avoid the uninformed use of credit, and to protect the consumer against inaccurate and unfair credit billing and credit card practices."

Under TILA the Board of Governors of the Federal Reserve System is empowered to promulgate regulations that effectuate the purpose of TILA. TILA and its regulations create a comprehensive scheme governing consumer credit transactions and impose a system of strict liability in favor of consumers. Protection of unsophisticated consumers is the overriding purpose of TILA and consequently creditors are required to comply with both the letter and spirit of the law.

Under TILA an "open end credit plan" is defined as a credit arrangement "prescribing the terms of credit transactions which may be made thereunder from time to time and under the terms of which a finance charge may be computed on the outstanding upaid balance from time to time thereunder." Although the transactions between Dehning and Wise appear to be closed end credit transactions, i.e., the amount of debt being fixed at the time of purchase, the transactions also have open end characteristics. The carrying forward of the balance due on each previous contract resembles a revolving charge. The disclosures required for open end credit transactions are more stringent than those for closed end transactions. Notwithstanding of the transaction, the intent of the parties appears to have been to create a closed end consumer credit transaction. . . . This is consistent with the trial court's conclusion. The parties' intent to create closed end transactions will govern our characterization of these contracts.

Regulation Z applies to individuals or businesses that extend credit when the following four conditions are satisfied:

(i) The credit is offered or extended to consumers; (ii) the offering or extension of credit is done regularly; (iii) the credit is subject to a finance charge or is payable by a written agreement in more than 4 installments; and (iv) the credit is primarily for personal, family or household purposes.

The facts in the instant case fulfill these requirements. Moreover, Majorie Dehning was the archetype of the unsophisticated consumer TILA was designed to protect.

Section 1638 of Title 15 requires that the finance charge be accurately and fairly disclosed. When there is a refinancing transaction, Regulation Z requires that new disclosures be made to the consumer. "A refinancing occurs when an existing obligation [like the April 2, 1979, contract] . . . is satisfied and replaced by a new obligation undertaken by the same consumer." The April 2, 1979, contract clearly does not disclose whether the balance forward from February 9, 1979, was refinanced; whether the finance charge was subtracted from that contract so that a new finance charge could be computed; or whether the February 9, 1979, balance (including the finance charge) was included in the computation of the new finance charge that, in effect, resulted in a charging of interest twice for part of the items purchased on February 9, 1979. If the financing charges of the first two agreements were in fact incorporated into the final agreement, then this, alone, constitutes a violation of TILA.

Security interests retained by a seller of goods, even though enforceable under state law, are required to be disclosed "on the same side as and above or adjacent to the place for the customer's signature." TILA and its regulations mandate that the description of the security interest retained by the seller be clear and unequivocal. In the instant case, the security interest retained by Wise continued to intend to hold a security interest in goods purchased under the February 9 and April 2 agreements by referring to the "old contract" even though Dehning had paid a total of $946.55 is uncertain. The descriptions of the security interests held by Wise are not clear and unequivocal. The trial court's conclusion that Wise violated TILA and Regulation Z is not clearly erroneous. [*Affirmed.*]

There are both civil and criminal penalties for violation of Truth-in-Lending. The civil liability provisions make creditors liable to debtors for an amount equal to twice the finance charge but not less than $100 nor more than $1,000, plus the costs and attorney's fees required to collect it. Creditors may avoid liability in the event they make an error, provided they notify the debtor within sixty days after discovering the error and also correct the error. In this connection, the law allows for corrections in favor of the debtor only. Creditors cannot collect finance charges in excess of those actually disclosed.

The Truth-in-Lending Act also gives debtors the right to rescind or cancel certain transactions for a period of three business days from the date of the transactions or from the date they are given the notice of their right to rescind, whichever is later. For example, consumers may generally cancel transactions in which they give a security interest on their principal residence if they do so within the three-day period. If the transaction is rescinded, the borrower has no liability for any finance charge, and the security which he or she has given is void.

TRUTH-IN-LENDING TRENDS

In 1980, Congress passed the Truth-in-Lending Simplification Act. Two changes from the original act stand out. First, the law eliminates statutory penalties based on purely technical violations of the act. It restricts such penalties to failures to disclose credit terms that are of *material* importance in credit comparisons. Second, the Simplification Act requires the Federaal Reserve Board to issue model disclosure forms. These are particularly important to small businesses that cannot afford legal counsel to help prepare such forms. Proper use of the forms proves compliance with the Simplification Act.

Studies conducted by the FTC show that many of those involved in credit extension, such as home builders and realtors, fail to make required Truth-in-Lending disclosures in their advertising. In several instances, the FTC has successfully undertaken programs to educate these businesses about their disclosure obligations under Truth-in-Lending.

11. The Magnuson-Moss Warranty Act

Not all federal consumer protection laws involve deceptive trade practices or credit abuses. This section concerns federal regulation of express warranties. Remember from Chapter 7 that an express warranty makes a statement about a product or a promise about its performance. Many, perhaps most, problems that consumers have with the products they buy come from breaches of warranty.

Historically, one of the major problems with consumer warranties was that they contained highly technical legal language. Consumers did not understand that this language often placed severe limitations on their rights to exercise warranties. Many express warranties even actually deprived consumers of rights, such as the rights furnished by implied warranties. Yet at the same time, manufacturers used consumer warranties promotionally to show that their products were "guaranteed."

In 1975, Congress passed the Magnuson-Moss Warranty Act to help correct warranty problems with consumer products. The law covers *express consumer warranties*. Warranties on such goods must disclose the terms of the warranty in simple and readily understood language. If a product costs more than $10, the warranty must be labeled "full" or "limited." The FTC has the responsibility to prepare regulations to accomplish the goals of the law.

Products covered by a *full* warranty must be repaired or replaced by the seller without charge and within a reasonable time in the event there is a defect. Manufacturers cannot impose requirements on buyers to obtain the repairs or replacements unless the requirements are reasonable. The law does not require manufacturers to give any warranty, but if one is given, its nature and extent must be in language that can be understood by the buyer. If a warranty is to be *limited*, the limitation must be conspicuous so that buyers are not misled. If a written warranty is given, there can be no disclaimer of implied warranties, although consequential damages may be limited.

To aid consumers in making intelligent purchase selections, sellers must make warranty information available to buyers prior to purchase. The information must be conspicuously displayed in association with the warranted product. The FTC has taken action against several selllers who have failed to observe this requirement.

The Magnuson-Moss Act also encourages sellers to set up informal dispute settlement procedures to handle complaints made under the warranty. Although not requiring such procedures, the act requires that if they exist, consumers must pursue them prior to filing a lawsuit.

As a result of the law, many sellers have eliminated their warranties or have opted for the limited warranty. Some companies, rather than become involved with all the law's requirements, have stopped giving warranties. But the warranties which remain are more useful to consumers than before Magnuson-Moss.

A much-used section of the act allows consumers to recover attorneys' fees and costs from merchants in a successful lawsuit for breach of an express or implied warranty or of a service contract. This section permits consumers to sue merchants when otherwise they could not because of high legal costs. Remember that usually plaintiffs must pay their own attorneys' fees and costs. This means that in cases involving only a few hundred (or even a few thousand) dollars, it is hardly worthwhile for a plaintiff to file a lawsuit because of the expense involved.

Now under Magnuson-Moss, consumers are much more willing to bring certain lawsuits because they can recover attorneys' fees and costs. These lawsuits usually involve automobiles or major appliances which consumers have purchased and find unsatisfactory.

12. Debt Collection

In a consumer-credit-oriented economy, the collection of bad debts is very important. At present, there are more than five thousand collection agencies in the United States engaged in collecting unpaid accounts, judgments, and other bad debts. Annually, creditors turn over bills totaling more than $5 billion for collection to such agencies.

Due to complaints that some debt-collection agencies used techniques of harassment, deception, and personal abuse to collect debts, Congress in 1978 passed the Fair Debt Collection Practices Act (FDCPA). The act applies only to consumer debt collections. It also applies only to agencies and individuals whose primary business is the collection of debts for others. Creditor collection efforts are exempt from the act since it is assumed that most creditors will avoid using harrassment in order to retain the debtor's goodwill. Attorneys who collect for clients and government officers who make collections in the course of their official duties are exempt as well. However, the law requires the IRS to comply with the FDCPA.

One of the first actions of a debt collector will usually be to locate the debtor. This action, known as "skip-tracing," may require that the collector contact third parties who know of the debtor's whereabouts. The FDCPA permits the collector to contact third parties, such as neighbors, or employers, but it limits the way in which this contact may be carried out. The collector may not state that the consumer owes a debt nor contact any given third party more than once except in very limited circumstances. When the collector knows that an attorney represents the debtor, the collector may not contact any third party, except the attorney, unless the attorney fails to respond to the collector's communication.

Having located the debtor, the collector will next seek to get payment on the overdue account. However, the FDCPA restricts methods that can be used in the collection process. Table 15-3 outlines these restrictions.

If the consumer debtor desires to stop the debt collector from repeatedly contacting him or her about payment, the debtor need only notify the collector in writing of this wish. Any further contact by the collector following such notification violates the act. The collector's sole remedy now is to sue the debtor. Violations of the FDCPA entitle the debtor to sue the debt collector for actual damages, including damages for invasion of privacy and infliction of mental distress, plus court costs and attorney's fees. In the absence of actual

TABLE 15-3 FDCPA's Restrictions on Collection Methods of Collection Agencies

The collector cannot
1. Physically threaten the debtor
2. Use obscene language
3. Represent himself or herself as an attorney unless it is true
4. Threaten the debtor with arrest or garnishment unless the collector can legally take such action and intends to do so
5. Fail to disclose his or her identity as a collector
6. Telephone before 8:00 A.M. or after 9:00 P.M. in most instances
7. Telephone repeatedly with intent to annoy
8. Place collect calls to the debtor
9. Use any "unfair or unconscionable means" to collect the debt

damages, the court may still order the collector to pay the debtor up to $1,000 for violations. Class action suits, as well as individual ones, are permitted under the act.

In recognition that many states also have laws regulating debt collections, Congress specified that the FDCPA does not preempt such laws as long as they are more stringent than the FDCPA. Some states have laws which regulate collections by the creditor as well as collections by outside agencies. In addition, the FDCPA does not preempt state common law actions for invasion of privacy and intentional infliction of mental distress. These tort actions apply to creditors as well as to collection agencies.

The FTC also enforces the FDCPA. It has assessed one New York chain of collection agencies a $90,000 civil penalty for, among other things, falsely threatening the arrest of consumers.

13. Bankruptcy

Another federal consumer protection statute is the Bankruptcy Act. In 1978, Congress revised the federal bankruptcy laws, marking the first time in over fifty years that these laws have been substantially revised. Since the 1978 Bankruptcy Act became effective, the number of bankruptcies has sky-rocketed. Personal bankruptcies climbed from 228,000 in 1979 to over twice that number in 1984. Although a recession prompted part of that increase, the Federal Reserve Board of Atlanta estimated that, nationwide, as much as 75 percent of the increase was due to the liberal provisions of the new law. Annually, the courts discharge more than $6 billion of nonmortgage consumer debt.

Although the force of the consumer movement helped prompt the new changes in the bankruptcy laws, the laws apply both to consumers and to businesses. Under the present laws, corporations and partnerships cannot be discharged of their debts, but all individuals, whether consumers or entrepreneurs, can be.

A principal change in the new laws has been the institution of a bankruptcy court. Previously, most bankruptcy proceedings were handled by legal officials appointed under the authority of the federal district court.

BANKRUPTCY PROCEEDINGS

Bankruptcy proceedings begin upon the filing of either a voluntary or involuntary petition to the court. A *voluntary petition* is one filed by the debtor; an *involuntary petition* is filed by one or more creditors of the debtor. The creditors who sign the involuntary petition must be owed at least $5,000. If the court finds in an involuntary proceeding that the debtor is *unable to pay his or her debts as they mature,* the court will order "relief" against the debtor. Relief may also be ordered if someone has been appointed to control the debtor's property (for example, a receiver) within the previous 120 days for the purpose of satisfying a judgment or other lien.

Two alternatives are possible in a bankruptcy proceeding against an individual. The individual's property will be either *liquidated* and the debts discharged, or the debts will be *adjusted.* An individual who has secured debts (mortgages, security interests against personal property, and so on) of less than $350,000 and unsecured debts of under $100,000 can have his or her debts adjusted by the court. The amount and repayment schedule of the debts will be arranged by the court to permit the debtor to repay the creditors. Creditors cannot require the court to adjust the debts. The decision must be that of the debtor. Most debtors choose to have their debts discharged and their property liquidated, rather than to seek an adjustment, since they remain obligated to pay a portion of adjusted debts.

Even when a debtor's property is liquidated, federal law exempts a substantial portion of the property from the liquidation process. Individual states, however, may reduce the amounts of the federal exemptions through legislation.

Corporations and partnerships can also have all their assets liquidated and distributed to creditors. However, especially for large businesses, an alternative to liquidation is **reorganization**. A main part of the reorganization is a plan which is proposed by the businesses and considered by a committee of creditors prior to court approval. The plan rearranges the businesses' liabilities and equities (ownership assets). Parts of the business may be sold, and always the existing ownership interests in the business are reduced. In effect, the creditors often become owners in the business.

The **trustee in bankruptcy** is an important person in the bankruptcy proceeding. The trustee is someone elected by the creditors to represent the debtor's estate in taking possession of and in liquidating (selling off) the debtor's property. Broad powers are granted the trustee. The trustee can (1) affirm or disaffirm contracts with the debtor which are yet to be performed; (2) set aside fradulent conveyances, that is, transfers of the debtor's property for inadequate consideration or for the purpose of defrauding creditors; (3) void certain transfers of property by the debtor to creditors which prefer some creditors over others; (4) sue those who owe the debtor some obligation; and (5) set aside statutory liens against the debtor's property which take effect upon the beginning of bankruptcy proceedings. With the court's authorization, the trustee can also run the debtor's business during the liquidation process.

Under bankruptcy laws, certain creditors receive priority over others in the distribution of a debtor's assets. The law divides creditors into priority classes, as set forth in Table 15-4. The amounts owing to each creditor class must be satisfied fully before the next lower class of priority can receive anything. Note that secured creditors who hold mortgages or security interests in the debtor's property usually have priority over the bankruptcy creditor classes.

From the debtor's point of view, the purpose of bankruptcy is to secure a *discharge* of further obligation to the creditor. Certain debts, however, cannot be discharged in bankruptcy. They include those arising from taxes, alimony and child support, intentional torts (including fraud), breach of fiduciary duty, liabilities arising from drunken driving, government fines, and debts not submitted to the trustee because the creditor has lacked knowledge of the proceedings. Education loans which become due within five years of the filing of the bankruptcy petition are also nondischargeable. As the following case indicates, an exception to this rule exists when repayment of the loan constitutes an "undue hardship." Consider the difference the court makes between "hardship" and "undue hardship."

TABLE 15-4   Priority of Bankruptcy Creditors

1. Creditors with claims that arise from the costs of preserving and administering the debtor's estate (such as the fee of an accountant who performs an audit of the debtor's books for the trustee)
2. Creditors with claims that occur in the ordinary course of the debtor's business after a bankruptcy petition has been filed
3. Employees who are owed wages earned within ninety days, or employee benefits earned within 180 days of the bankruptcy petition (limited to $2,000 per employee)
4. Consumers who have paid deposits or prepayments for undelivered goods or services (limited to $900 per consumer)
5. Government (for tax claims)
6. Creditors who have other claims (general creditors)

MATTER OF TOBIN
18 B. R. 560 (1982)

MARTIN, Bankruptcy Judge: The sole issue at trial was whether the repayment of student loans made to the defendant constituted an undue hardship to the defendant or his dependents so as to make the debt dischargeable in bankruptcy. . . . In deciding whether the repayment of a student loan would constitute undue hardship, the court is to consider the facts and circumstances of each individual debtor to determine "whether there are such unique circumstances as to render it less likely or likely only with extreme difficulty, or unlikely at all that the bankrupt will within the foreseeable future be able to honor his commitment."

The evidence showed that the defendant is a young man (age 27) without dependents, who at the time of trial was employed by Crown Auto Parts on a probationary basis in the area of sales. He was paid weekly at a rate of $3.25 per hour for a regular service of 40 hours per week. His net take-home pay was approximately $432.00 per month. He anticipated a small raise at the end of his probationary period and annual adjustments thereafter. In addition to working at Crown Auto Parts, Mr. Tobin was attending Metropolitan State University as a full-time student and anticipated receiving a diploma in 2 to 3 years.

Mr. Tobin testified that he had monthly expenses including:

1 rent $280.00

2 gas and electricity $50.00 to $60.00

3 telephone $20.00

4 renter's insurance $20.00

5 food $200.00

6 laundry $20.00

7 transportation $100.00

In addition he had nondischargeable debts surviving his bankruptcy for income taxes and La Crosse telephone service. He also owed attorney's fees in connection with this action.

Mr. Tobin testified that he was receiving help in paying the expenses which exceeded his monthly income from a woman described as his fiancee. His monthly food expenses included food for his fiancee, and his rent was for an apartment they shared.

Mr. Tobin's prospects for future employment are limited by his 1976 arrest and conviction on controlled substances charges. His probation required a monthly appearance in La Crosse to report to a probation officer. He believed his problem in getting jobs subsequent to 1976 was caused by his record and lack of references available from the La Crosse area. He had moved to the Twin Cities to avoid his reputation as a convicted felon but his employment future remained clouded. Mr. Tobin was trained as a diesel mechanic and previously employed as a hypnotist but saw no future for himself in either field. Other than the assistance he was receiving from his fiancee, Mr. Tobin anticipated no available support from friends or relatives. His fiancee was employed as a travel consultant and received take-home pay of approximately $110.00 per week. Her expenses included repayments on a car loan, payments of car insurance and doctors' bills.

Although he hopes to earn a B.A. degree in business and go into business or law, Mr. Tobin has no certainty of improved future employment. He was optimistic that in 3 to 4 years his financial circumstances would be considerably improved.

On the foregoing I find that it would unquestionably be a hardship for the defendant to pay his indebtedness to the Wisconsin Higher Educational Aids Board of $1,828.00. He had at the time of trial no present source from which to make payments. However, undue hardship is the standard to be applied in determining dischargeability of student loans. Mr. Tobin's relocation in the Twin Cities, his continued education and his prospects for the future indicated that the situation may in the future be less severe. No dependents would be affected by the requirement that Mr. Tobin complete payments on his education loans. Therefore, it appears that while repayment of the loans would be a hardship, it would not be an undue hardship justifying the conclusion that the debt should be discharged. [*Judgment may be entered accordingly.*]

In addition to having certain debts denied discharge, the debtor may fail to receive a discharge from *any* of his or her debts if the courts find that the debtor has concealed property, falsified or concealed books of record, refused to obey court orders, failed to explain satisfactorily any losses of assets, or been discharged in bankruptcy within the prior six years. As mentioned previously, corporations and partnerships as legal entities cannot receive a discharge of their debts. Of course, the individuals behind these businesses can always form a new corporation or partnership.

TRENDS IN BANKRUPTCY

A major bankruptcy trend in recent years has been the increasing frequency with which large businesses have gone through bankruptcy reorganization. Some see this trend as a management strategy of even financially healthy businesses for avoiding potential liabilities or forcing renegotiation of burdensome contracts. For instance, the Manville Corporation entered bankruptcy reorganization to attempt to force a favorable settlement of the thousands of asbestos-related lawsuits which it faces.

Other companies have sought reorganization to relieve themselves of obligations imposed by collective-bargaining contracts with unions. After the Supreme Court ruled in 1984 that bankruptcy did affect performance of collective-bargaining contracts, Congress changed the law. Now bankruptcy reorganization can reject a collective-bargaining contract only if the union has refused to accept necessary contractual modifications "without good cause," and on balance the court decides that the situation "clearly favors" rejection.

Another important bankruptcy development affects a consumer's ability to get a discharge of debts through liquidation. Congress amended the law in 1984 to give courts power to refuse to allow consumers to seek the relief of discharge when relief would amount to a "substantial abuse" of the bankruptcy process.

This change in the law recognizes a problem of the bankruptcy process. Historically, consumers with few assets but a well-paying job could get discharged of their debts by surrendering their few assets to liquidation. Creditors argued that debt discharge was unfair in this situation since credit is usually extended to consumers based on their ability to repay out of future earned income.

With the change in the law, courts can deny consumers a discharge of debts through liquidation. When liquidation and discharge relief would be a "substantial abuse," a consumer's only bankruptcy relief will be an adjustment of debts. In this type of relief, the court can consider a consumer's future earning power in deciding what percentage of the consumer's debts must be repaid. It is likely that courts will find that a substantial abuse exists when consumers can reasonably pay for debts out of future income.

14. Additional Federal Protection for Consumers

A lawsuit is not always an adequate remedy for an injured party to a contract. For instance, it is usually not practical for consumers to sue a seller of goods or services over breaches of contract involving only a few hundred dollars. Attorney's fees are high, and small claims court awards are difficult to enforce. From consumers' viewpoints, it would be better if they could simply refuse to pay for unsatisfactory products or services. However, many times consumers have already paid for what they obtained or have promised to pay.

If consumers have already paid for products or services, they have little recourse except to initiate legal proceedings when others refuse to perform their contractual obligations properly. But what occurs in a situation in which consumers have signed credit agreements and have merely *promised* to pay? It appears that consumers can simply refuse to pay until the obligations owed them have been performed satisfactorily. In the past, however, this was not usually the case.

THE HOLDER IN DUE COURSE DOCTRINE AND ITS ABOLISHMENT

Until fairly recently, most credit contracts contained clauses which stated that consumers agreed not to assert any contractual defenses against third parties. These clauses meant that if a merchant sold a consumer's credit contract to a collection agency, the agency could legally collect the contract price from the consumer in spite of the fact that the merchant had breached the contract, or had even defrauded the consumer. In addition to a credit agreement, many times the consumer had also signed a promissory note. (A promissory note is an easily transferrable, special type of commercial instrument or paper.) Because of the **holder in due course** doctrine, third parties who bought notes and other forms of commercial paper could usually enforce them free of all personal defenses the consumer might have against the merchant, such as that purchased goods were defective or were never delivered.

In the mid-1970s, the FTC acted to protect consumers who made purchases on credit. It adopted a rule which abolishes the holder in due course concept and which declares illegal contract provisions cutting off defenses against third parties. The rule applies only to *consumer transactions*. The rule also specifies that the consumer-debtor's right to assert claims and defenses against collection agencies, banks, and other third parties must actually be set forth in any installment credit contract used to finance retail purchases.

REJECTION OF DISPUTED CREDIT CARD CHARGES

A related law now protects consumers in instances in which credit-card charges have been made and contractual disputes arise. Under the federal

Fair Credit Billing Act, a consumer can withhold from any credit-card payments the amount of a disputed charge made to a seller of goods or services. This right applies to any charge of more than $50 when the charge is made in the consumer'ss home state or within 100 miles of his or her home. The procedure requires that the consumer first attempt to resolve the contractual dispute with the seller. When this fails, the consumer can send the bank which issues the credit card a written notice of the problem stating the negotiations have been unfruitful. The consumer can then withhold the amount of the disputed charge from credit-card payments to the bank.

As a practical matter, banks recredit a consumer's account for the amount of a disputed charge (if it has been already deducted) and charge back against the seller's bank. The seller's bank then charges back against the seller. The seller might sue the consumer, but once again, litigation costs make such a course of action unlikely in cases which involve relatively small amounts of money.

STATE CONSUMER PROTECTION

15. State Consumer Fraud Legislation

A Justice Department study released in 1982 identifies fraud as a major problem in our economic system. "Consumer fraud is a serious and pervasive phenomenon which continues to plague the American marketplace," the study stated. In the last twenty-five years, all states have passed legislative acts to help deal with this problem.

Generally termed Unfair and Deceptive Acts and Practices (UDAP) statutes, these acts often resemble the FTC Act. They prohibit fraudulent, deceptive, and unconscionable trade practices. They seek to deter merchants from engaging in such practices and to provide remedies to ensure that consumers will recover for damages and suffering.

Typically, a state's attorney general will administer a UDAP statute, although special agencies are sometimes used. These public authorities often have power to make rules and conduct investigations. If they uncover fraudulent activities, they can impose a variety of remedies (see Table 15-5). Remedies imposed by public authorities (public remedies) constitute the basic means of UDAP enforcement in most states.

To assist state enforcement efforts through public remedies, UDAP statutes provide a number of private remedies that injured consumers themselves can seek from dishonest merchants (see Table 15-6). Private litigation offers a powerful deterrent to consumer fraud and allows consumers to gain compensation for their injuries.

STATE REGULATION OF SPECIFIC BUSINESSES

Recently, states have begun amending UDAP statutes or passing new legislation to regulate specific businesses. For instance, several states specifically regulate the auto repair industry. This regulation came as a result of a United

TABLE 15-5 Public UDAP Remedies*

1. *Injunctions* prohibiting offensive practices
2. *Restitution* forcing fraudulent merchants to reimburse their victims
3. *Civil penalties* which must be paid to the state
4. *Revocation* of licenses and other forms of permission to do business within a state
5. Court appointment of a *receiver* who handles the defendant's assets and runs the defendant's business to benefit injured consumers
6. *Criminal fines* and/or *imprisonment*
7. *Assessment* of court costs or cost of the fraud investigation

*Not all states permit every remedy.

States Department of Transportation undercover study which concluded that consumers waste 53 percent of every dollar spent on auto repairs.

Another specific business targeted by state consumer protection statutes is apartment leasing. A number of states prohibit lessors from retaining consumers' security deposits on apartments unless they follow clearly outlined procedures. Door-to-door sales firms and health spas are also regulated in many states.

States have imposed a variety of procedures for controlling fraud in specific businesses. *Escrow accounts* restrict a seller's ability to get or keep money until he or she has given satisfactory performance. Failure to perform means that the escrow agent (frequently a bank) will return part or all of a consumer's payment. *Bonding* provides a compensation fund for consumers. *Industry pools,* adopted in Hawaii for travel agencies, establish an industry-funded "pool," which is used to compensate defrauded consumers. *Registration* permits easy location of firms by public authorities. *Licensing* requires special training or competence before doing business.

Still other consumer protection regulations serve to prevent fraud or to limit losses in specific situations. *Mandatory disclosures* require merchants to provide certain written information before a sale becomes final. *Plain English* rules require consumer contract provisions to be written in a simply understood fashion. *Cooling-off periods* allow consumers a few days to cancel door-to-door sales agreements. *Limited duration* establishes a maximum length for service contracts and thus limits a consumer's future financial obligations. *Limited pre-payments* limit the amount a merchant can require consumers to pay in advance.

TABLE 15-6 Private UDAP Remedies*

1. Recovery of *actual losses*
2. Recovery of *triple damages* or a *set minimum amount*
3. Assessment of *punitive damages*
4. Assessment of *attorneys' fees* and *costs*
5. Authorization of *class actions* by injured consumers
6. *Injunctions* prohibiting offensive practices
7. *Rescission* freeing consumers from deceptive arrangements and requiring reimbursement of deposits or prepayments

*Not all states permit every remedy.

Increasingly, state (and federal) pressure on specific businesses is forcing them to adopt procedures for mediating or arbitrating disputes with dissatisfied consumers. For instance, consumers who have engine problems with General Motors cars can turn to their local Better Business Bureau for arbitration. Arbitration decisions are binding on GM, although consumers retain the right to go into court if they disagree with the decisions. Most other car manufacturers also have arbitration-type procedures to resolve consumer dissatisfaction problems.

16. Usury

State law has traditionally attempted to protect debtors by limiting the amount of interest that may be charged upon borrowed money or for the extension of the maturity of a debt. Contracts under which the lender is to receive more than the maximum legal rate of interest are *usurious*. **Usury** laws usually provide for criminal penalties and, in addition, may deny a lender the right to collect any usurious interest. However, a few states permit recovery of interest at the legal rate.

The usury laws of most states are better known for permitting exceptions to the general principles than for applying them. Debtors who need the protection of usury laws usually find that their creditors are legally entitled to charge far in excess of the stated legal maximum rate because of some statutory exception. For example, it is not usurious in most states to collect the legal maximum interest in advance or to add a service fee that is no larger than reasonably necessary to cover the costs of making the loan—such as inspection, legal, and recording fees. Both of these practices have the effect of increasing the actual rate of interest paid.

A seller of goods may also add a finance or carrying charge on long-term credit transactions in addition to the maximum interest rate. A different means of avoiding usury is to have a "credit" price that differs from the "cash" price. Another is to charge extra interest for delinquent payments. Some states permit special lenders such as pawnshops, small loan companies, or credit unions to charge in excess of the otherwise legal limit.

When usury is suspected, courts examine very carefully the details and true intent of a transaction. For example, a court may decide that a transaction is a usurious "sale," even though the contract calls it a "lease."

Supporters of an unrestricted marketplace advocate legislation to abolish interest rate limits on consumer credit. They have proposed several plans to Congress.

CONSUMER PRIVACY AND THE FUTURE OF CONSUMERISM

17. Consumer Privacy

As society becomes more complex, as population creates overcrowding, and as the technology of information gathering becomes more sophisticated, the need for privacy increases. In recent years the law has come to recognize the invasion of privacy as a tort (see Chapter 14) and even to extend a constitutional right of privacy. For example, a constitutional right of privacy has been asserted by the Supreme Court under the First and Fourth Amendments in cases involving the freedom of association, the possession in the home of pornographic materials, and the use of contraceptive devices. Most of the laws and cases which apply the concepts of privacy protect the individual from being overwhelmed by the intrusive power of the government and other large organizations, including businesses. Many laws directly affect us as "consumers," and almost all apply to protect us in our personal, rather than public, lives. Consumer protection regulation and privacy laws, then, have very much in common.

Several of the consumer protection laws discussed in this chapter contain provisions protecting personal privacy. Under the Fair Credit Reporting Act, for example, a potential employer, insurer, or creditor must inform the consumer that an investigative report is being obtained on him or her. This notice allows the consumer to terminate the contemplated transaction, thus ending the legitimate business reason for the report and preventing the report from being obtained legally.

One of the chief threats to individual privacy comes from the government and governmental agencies which investigate individuals or which collect information from individuals. Several federal statutes are directed specifically at this problem. The Privacy Act of 1974 places constrains on how certain kinds of information collected by the federal government can be used and limits those to whom the information may be released. It also provides a tort cause of action against those who violate the act. A second statute, the Right to Financial Privacy Act of 1978, requires all government agencies seeking depositors' records from banks and other financial institutions to notify depositors of this fact. The individual depositor then has fourteen days to challenge an agency's legal basis for seeking the records. Depositors are allowed to sue the government agencies or financial institutions which fail to comply with the statute for actual and punitive damages, plus attorney's fees.

18. Policy Trends: The Future of Consumerism

Consumerism and the litigation it breeds seem to be here to stay. The slowdown in the appearance of new consumer protection regulation should by no means, however, be taken as an end to the importance of consumer protection in general. As the laws discussed in this chapter indicate, there is substantial consumer regulation already enacted. And, as these existing laws are further implemented, their impact on the business community will likely continue to grow.

In a quiet way, a recent change in the marketing of legal services may also give a boost to the consumer movement. Low-cost assistance provided by *legal clinics* which specialize in routine, high-volume services is enabling many individuals to pursue consumer complaints which would previously have been too expensive for them to pursue. Hyatt Legal Services, the largest legal clinic, had 117 offices in 1983 and projected 400 to 500 offices by 1988.

Large chains like Sears and H&R Block are also beginning to open their facilities for use by attorneys in providing inexpensive legal advice. In addition, legal advertising is on the increase and will probably constitute significantly to the public's awareness of the availability of legal remedies for common consumer problems.

Increasing numbers of lawyers is one factor which will ensure that consumer litigation does not diminish. There are now approximately 600,000 lawyers in the United States, twice as many as practiced twenty years ago. We have three times as many lawyers per capita as England and twenty times as many as Japan.

Prepaid legal plans for workers and other developments will also help ensure a healthy future for consumerism. Millions of workers and their dependents are presently covered by prepaid legal plans. General Motors has recently covered its 400,000 employees with a legal services plan called for in a collective-bargaining contract.

Finally, the number of legal "hotlines," which provide legal advice by telephone, is growing rapidly. In several states, CIGNA Corp. offers credit-card holders unlimited telephone consultations for a low monthly fee.

REVIEW QUESTIONS

1 The Mosquito-No Company claims that its electronic mosquito repellent will "eliminate all mosquito problems within a one-half acre area." The Federal Trade Commission doubts that this claim is correct. What will the FTC likely demand that the company do?

2 How does FTC regulation of trade practices under the Reagan administration differ from trade practice regulation under other recent administrations?

3 List the goals of and reasons for the passage of each of the following laws:
  a Fair Credit Reporting Act
  b Equal Credit Opportunity Act
  c Truth-in-Lending Act
  d Magnuson-Moss Warranty Act

4 The ABC Department Store refused credit to Mary Jane. Mary Jane has a good job and no debts. She cannot understand the re-

fusal. What would you suggest Mary Jane do? Explain.

5 Describe the responsibility of a manufacturer who gives a "full warranty" under the Magnuson-Moss Warranty Act.

6 Today, penalties under the Truth-in-Lending Act apply only when a failure to disclose is of "material" importance. Why is this important?

7 Under the Truth-in-Lending Act, what is a "finance charge?" What charges are and are not included as finance charges?

8 In the past twenty-five years, what have states done to combat consumer fraud?

9 Mr. Jones, a black school principal, applies for a mortgage loan at a bank. After examining the application, the bank politely but firmly refuses the loan, explaining that property values in Mr. Jones's neighborhood are too low to support the amount he is seeking. Might Mr. Jones have some course of action against the bank? Under what law?

10 Discuss why concern over consumer privacy is growing.

11 Jan has a problem with the engine of his new Chevrolet. If the car dealer refuses to take care of the problem under the warranty, what can Jan do? Consider that he cannot afford to hire an attorney.

12 The Zenith Credit Bureau telephones Dan and his family almost daily about payment of a $3,500 debt which Dan owes to Equipment Suppliers, Inc. The phone calls are causing stress for Dan's family. Dan cannot afford to pay the debt at present, and he needs a listed telephone number for his busi-

ness. Is there anything Dan can do legally to stop the calls from Zenith?

13 Some of Dan's creditors want to petition him into involuntary bankruptcy. What requirements or proof must the creditors meet in order to obtain an order of relief?

14 Under what circumstances can a court refuse to allow consumers to seek the bankruptcy relief of debt discharge through liquidation? Explain.

15 Susan joins a newly opened exercise spa. She pays the annual $200 membership fee with her bank credit card. One week later, the spa locks its doors and goes out of business. Repeated phone calls and letters to the spa's management, which demand a refund of her money, go unanswered. What is now Susan's best course of legal action for getting back her $200?

Chapter

16

Investor Protection

1. Introduction

Since the great depression of the 1930s, government has attempted to protect investors through various laws that regulate the sale of securities. These laws seek to ensure that investors are provided with sufficient accurate information to enable them to make intelligent investment decisions. Violations of these laws are usually crimes, and, in addition, the investors are provided with remedies designed to recover losses on investments. The laws regulating the sale of securities also seek to guarantee the public faith in the stock market. It does so in part with provisions that protect stockbrokers as well as investors.

To provide basic background material on the regulation of securities, this chapter examines the broad legal meaning given to the word *security*. In addition, federal and state securities laws are discussed. Such laws at the federal level regulate the sale of securities in interstate commerce as well as the operation of national securities exchanges. The following sections should give the reader an understanding of two major federal securities laws—the 1933 Securities Act and the 1934 Securities Exchange Act. Included are sections on civil and criminal liability that may occur when either of these laws are violated. At the end of the chapter, states' security laws, often called "blue sky" laws, are described. These laws regulate the sale of securities in intrastate commerce.

2. Definition of Security

Because the objective of securities laws is to protect uninformed people from investing their money without sufficient data, the term *security* has a very broad definition. Indeed, the federal securities laws provide the following definition:[1]

> "Security" means any note, stock, treasury stock, bond, debenture, evidence of indebtedness, certificate of interest of participation in any profit-sharing agreement, collateral-trust certificate, preorganization certificate or subscription, transferable share, investment contract, voting-trust certificate, certificate of deposit for a security, fractional undivided interest in oil, gas, or other mineral rights, or in general, any interest or instrument commonly known as a "security", or any certificate of interest or participation in, temporary or interim certificate for receipt for, guarantee of, or warrant or right to subscribe to or purchase, any of the foregoing.

As this definition indicates, the term *security* includes much more than corporation stock. A security exists when one person invests money and looks to others to manage the money for profit. The securities laws apply to every investment contract in which a person receives some evidence of indebtedness or a certificate of interest or participation in a profit-sharing agreement. As a result, sales of oil-well interests, whiskey receipts, interests in limited partnerships, margin sales of coins, and even savings and loan investments come within the scope of securities laws, Courts seek positive answers to the following three questions when determining whether a person has purchased a security. (1) Is the investment in a common venture? (2) Is the investment premised on a reasonable expectation of profits? (3) Will these profits be derived from the entrepreneurial efforts of others?

The following case has become known as a landmark Supreme Court decision on the issue of what is a security. A careful reading of this interesting factual situation indicates the breadth of the definition of security.

---

[1] 15 U.S.C.A. § 77b(1).

SEC v. W. J. HOWEY CO.
328 U.S. 293 (1946)

MURPHY, J.: . . . This case involves the application of § 2(1) of the Securities Act of 1933 to an offering of units of a citrus grove development coupled with a contract for cultivating, marketing and remitting the net proceeds to the investor.

The Securities and Exchange Commission instituted this action to restrain the respondents from using the mails and instrumentalities of interstate commerce in the offer and sale of unregistered and nonexempt securities . . . The District Court denied the injunction, and the Fifth Circuit Court of Appeals affirmed the judgment.

Most of the facts are stipulated. The respondents, W. J. Howey Company and

Howey-in-the-Hills Service, Inc., are Florida corporations under direct common control and management. The Howey Company owns large tracts of citrus acreage in Lake County, Florida. During the past several years it has planted about 500 acres annually keeping half of the groves itself and offering the other half to the public "to help us finance additional development." Howey-in-the-Hills Service, Inc., is a service company engaged in cultivating and developing many of these groves, including the harvesting and marketing of the crops.

Each prospective customer is offered both a land sales contract and a service contract, after having been told that it is not feasible to invest in a grove unless service arrangements are made. While the purchaser is free to make arrangements with other service companies, the superiority of Howey-in-the-Hills Service, Inc., is stressed. Indeed, 85% of the acreage sold during the 3-year period ending May 31, 1943, was covered by service contracts with Howey-in-the-Hills Service, Inc. . . . Upon full payment of the purchase price the land is conveyed to the purchaser by warranty deed. Purchases are usually made in narrow strips of land arranged so that an acre consists of a row of 48 trees. During the period between February 1, 1941, and May 31, 1943, 31 of the 42 persons making purchases bought less than 5 acres each. The average holding of these 31 persons was 1.33 acres and sales of as little as .065, 0.7 and 0.73 of an acre were made. . . . The service contract, generally of a 10-year duration without option of cancellation, gives Howey-in-the-Hills Service, Inc., a leasehold interest and "full and complete" possession of the acreage. For a specified fee plus the cost of labor and materials, the company is given full discretion and authority over the cultivation of the groves and the harvest and marketing of the crops. The company is well established in the citrus business and maintains a large force of skilled personnel and a great deal of equipment, in-cluding 75 tractors, sprayer wagons, fertilizer trucks and the like. Without the consent of the company, the land owner or purchaser has no right of entry to market the crop, thus there is ordinarily no right to specific fruit. The company is accountable only for an allocation of the net profits based upon a check made at the time of picking. All the produce is pooled by the respondent companies, which do business under their own names.

The purchasers for the most part are non-residents of Florida. They are predominantly business and professional people who lack the knowledge, skill and equipment necessary for the care and cultivation of citrus trees. They are attracted by the expectation of substantial profits. It was represented, for example, that profits during the 1943–1944 season amounted to 20% and that even greater profits might be expected during the 1944–1945 season, although only a 10% annual return was to be expected over a 10-year period. . . .

It is admitted that the mails and instrumentalities of interstate commerce are used in the sale of the land and service contracts and that no registration statement or letter of notification has ever been filed with the Commission in accordance with the Securities Act of 1933 and the rules and regulations thereunder. . . .

The legal issue in this case turns upon a determination of whether, under the circumstances, the land sales contract, the warranty deed and the service contract together constitue an "investment contract" within the meaning of § 2(1). An affirmative answer brings into operation the registration requirements of § 5(a), unless the security is granted an exemption under § 3(b). The lower courts, in reaching a negative answer to this problem, treated the contracts and deeds as separate transactions involving no more than an ordinary real estate sale and an agreement by the seller to manage the property for the buyer.

The term "investment contract" is undefined by the Securities Act or by relevant legislative reports. But the term was common in many state "blue sky" laws in existence prior to the adoption of the federal statute and, although the term was also undefined by state laws, it had been broadly construed by state courts so as to afford the investing public a full measure of protection. Form was disregarded for substance and emphasis was placed upon economic reality. An investment contract thus came to mean a contract or scheme for "the placing of capital or paying out of money in a way intended to secure income or profit from its employment." This definition was uniformly applied by state courts to a variety of situations where individuals were led to invest money in a common enterprise with the expectation that they would earn a profit solely through the efforts of the promoter or of some one other than themselves.

By including an investment contract within the scope of § 2(1) of the Securities Act, Congress was using a term the meaning of which has been crystallized by this prior judicial interpretation. It is therefore reasonable to attach that meaning to the term as used by Congress, especially since such a definition is consistent with the statutory aims. In other words, an investment contract for purposes of the Securities Act means a contract, transaction or scheme whereby a person invests his money in a common enterprise and is led to expect profits solely from the efforts of the promoter or a third party, it being immaterial whether the shares in the enterprise are evidenced by formal certificates or by nominal interests in the physical assets employed in the enterprise. Such a definition . . . embodies a flexible rather than a static principle, one that is capable of adaptation to meet the countless and variable schemes devised by those who seek the use of the money of others on the promise of profits.

The transactions in this case clearly involve investment contracts as so defined. The respondent companies are offering something more than fee simple interests in land, something different from a farm or orchard coupled with management services. They are offering an opportunity to contribute money and to share in the profits of a large citrus fruit enterprise managed and partly owned by respondents. They are offering this opportunity to persons who reside in distant localities and who lack the equipment and experience requisite to the cultivation, harvesting and marketing of the citrus products. Such persons have no desire to occupy the land or to develop it themselves; they are attracted solely by the prospects of a return on their investment. Indeed, individual development of the plots of land that are offered and sold would seldom be economically feasible due to their small size. Such tracts gain utility as citrus groves only when cultivated and developed as component parts of a larger area. A common enterprise managed by respondents or third parties with adequate personnel and equipment is therefore essential if the investors are to achieve their paramount aim of a return on their investments. Their respective shares in this enterprise are evidenced by land sales contracts and warranty deeds, which serve as a convenient method of determining the investors' allocable shares of the profits. The resulting transfer of rights in land is purely incidental.

Thus all elements of a profit-seeking business venture are present here. The investors provide the capital and share in the earnings and profits; the promoters manage, control and operate the enterprise. It follows that the arrangements whereby the investors' interest are made manifest involve investment contracts, regardless of the legal terminology in which such contracts are clothed. The investment contracts in this instance take the form of land sales contracts, warranty deeds and service contracts which respondents offer to prospective investors. And respondents' failure to abide by the statutory and administrative rules in making such offerings, even though the failure result from a bona fide mistake as to the law, cannot be sanctioned under the Act.

This conclusion is unaffected by the fact that some purchasers choose not to accept the full offer of an investment contract by declining to enter into a service contract with the respondents. The Securities Act prohibits the offer as well as the sale of unregistered, non-exempt securities. Hence it is enough that the respondents merely offer the essential ingredients of an investment contract.

We reject the suggestion of the Circuit Court of Appeals that an investment contract is necessarily missing where the enterprise is not speculative or promotional in character and where the tangible interest which is sold has intrinsic value independent of the success of the enterprise as a whole. The test is whether the scheme involves an investment of money in a common enterprise with profits to come solely from the efforts of others. If that test be satisfied, it is immaterial whether the enterprise is speculative or non-speculative or whether there is a sale of property with or without intrinsic value. The statutory policy of affording broad protection to investors is not to be thwarted by unrealistic and irrelevant formulae. [*Reversed.*]

Despite this broad definition of a security, the Supreme Court has made it clear that federal securities laws are not designed to provide a remedy for all fraudulent transactions. In recent years, the Court has held that securities laws do not necessarily apply (1) to a compulsory pension plan into which the employee is not required to make contributions, or (2) to certificates of deposit insured by the federal government. In the first instance, the Court found that the employee was protected by the Employee Retirement Income Security Act, and in the second situation it found that the customer was insured by the Federal Deposit Insurance Corporation. In these areas where "an investor" is protected by other means, protection provided by the securities laws is less essential.

3. Securities and Exchange Commission

The Securities and Exchange Commission (SEC), which was created in 1934, is responsible for administering the federal securities laws. The materials discussed in Chapter 10 on administrative agencies generally apply to the SEC. The SEC consists of five commissioners appointed by the President for a five-year term. In addition to these commissioners, the SEC employs staff personnel such as lawyers, accountants, security analysts, security examiners, and others.

The SEC has both quasi-legislative and quasi-judicial powers. Using its quasi-legislative power, it has adopted rules and regulations relating to financial and other information which must be furnished to the Commission. It also has rules prescribing information which must be given to potential investors. The SEC also regulates the various stock exchanges, utility holding companies, investment trusts, and investment advisers.

The SEC is involved in a variety of investigations and rule-making activities. Typical of these are the following:

1   An investigation of inside trading and stock manipulation, especially that connected with takeover attempts and rumors.

2   An investigation of the leakage of information (factual and false) that can significantly affect stock prices.

3   An ongoing study and investigation of numerous examples of suspected inside trading.

4   Adopting rules that govern stock-market newsletters published by brokerage firms. (The Supreme Court held that it could not regulate newsletters published independently of brokerage firms.)

5   Examining annual reports to ensure that proper accounting practices are followed and that the companies do not have "cooked books" that either puff earnings or exaggerate net worth.

6   Adopting rules that govern which shareholder-proposed resolutions must be submitted for a vote at corporate annual meetings. For example, the SEC requires that a shareholder must have invested $1,000 for at least one year before submitting a proposal. A proposal must get at least 5 percent of the vote the first time before it can be resubmitted.

FEDERAL SECURITIES ACT OF 1933: GOING PUBLIC

4. General Provisions

The Federal Securities Act of 1933 was enacted by Congress to regulate the initial sale of securities to the public. This law makes it illegal to use the mails or any other interstate means of communication or transportation to sell securities without disclosing certain financial information to potential investors. The following sections discuss several aspects of the Federal Securities Act of 1933 in detail, including who is regulated, what documents are required, which transactions are exempted, when civil and criminal liability exists, and what defenses are available. As you read, remember that this law applies only to the initial sale of the security. Subsequent transfers of securities are governed by the Federal Securities Exchange Act of 1934, discussed in sections 12 through 17.

In essence, the 1933 act requires the disclosure of information to the potential investor or other interested party. The information given must not be untrue or even misleading. If this information is not accurate, liability is imposed upon those reponsible. The Federal Securities Act of 1933 recognizes three sanctions for violations. There is the criminal punishment, the equitable remedy of an injunction, and civil liability, which may be imposed in favor of injured parties in certain cases. Proof of an intentional violation usually is required before criminal or civil sanctions are imposed. However, proof of negligence will support an injunction.

5. Parties Regulated

The Federal Securities Act of 1933 regulates anyone who is involved with or who promotes the initial sale of securities. Typically, involved parties may include issuers, underwriters, controlling persons, and sellers. An *issuer* is the individual or business organization offering a security for sale to the public. An *underwriter* is anyone who participates in the original distribution of securities by selling such securities for the issuer or by guaranteeing their sale. (Often, securities brokerage firms or investment bankers have acted as underwriters with respect to a particular transaction.) A *controlling person* is one who controls or is controlled by the issuer, such as a major stockholder of a corporation. Finally, a *seller* is anyone who contracts with a purchaser or who exerts a substantial role which causes the purchase transaction to occur.

These parties who participate in or promote a sale of securities from an issuer to the public are subject to the Federal Securities Act of 1933, which protects a person from being defrauded by false or nonexistent information. The initial reading of the previous paragraph may not indicate the broad meaning given to the words "issuer," "underwriter," "controlling person," and "seller." However, the following case illustrates the wide application of the 1933 act.

JUNKER v. CRORY
650 F.2d 1349 (5th Cir. 1981)

James Junker owned 162 shares of stock in Reco Investment Corporation. These shares were equal to 16.2 percent of the 1,000 shares Reco had outstanding. Reco became heavily indebted to another corporation known as Road Equipment Company, Inc. In order to resolve Reco's poor financial condition, Frederick Heisler, a lawyer for Reco, suggested and strongly recommended that Reco be merged into Road. Due to what he believed

was an unreasonably low appraised value of Reco's stock, Junker voted against the proposed merger. However, the remaining shareholders of Reco approved the merger plan, and it was accomplished. Later, Junker discovered some negative news about Road's financial condition. This information was not revealed at the shareholders' meeting when the merger vote was taken. Junker sued Frederick Heisler, alleging a violation of the 1933

Securities Act. Heisler defended the suit by arguing he had no duty to reveal additional information. The district court ruled in Junker's favor, and Heisler appealed.

RUBIN, J.: . . . Heisler . . . was not an officer, director or shareholder in either Reco or Road. According to the trial court's findings, he acted as attorney or agent for both corporations. . . . Finding no state law cause of action on which to ground Heisler's liability to Junker, we turn to the federal securities law claims.

The trial court held Heisler liable for violation of the 1933 Act. . . .

To recover . . . , the plaintiff must establish that the defendant as a seller of a security misrepresented or failed to state material facts to the plaintiff in connection with the sale. . . .

A merger may amount to a purchase or sale of a security for purposes of the federal securities laws. Thus, the exchange of Junker's Reco shares for stock in Road pursuant to the merger qualifies Junker as a purchaser of Road stock.

Because a purchaser may recover . . . only from his immediate seller, our inquiry focuses on whether Heisler's role in the merger transaction constituted him a seller for purposes of that section. Mere participation in the events leading up to the transaction is insufficient to constitute one a seller of a security. Only those in privity with the purchaser or those "whose participation in the buy-sell transaction is a substantial factor in causing the transaction to take place" are classified as sellers. . . .

[W]e held in *Croy v. Campbell*, 624 F.2d 709 (5th Cir. 1980), that an attorney whose connection with the sale was limited to advising the purchaser on its tax consequences was not a seller. The attorney in *Croy* did not attempt to persuade the plaintiffs to make the purchase; he made no representations to

them concerning the operational aspects of the project in which the plaintiffs ultimately invested. In determining that his involvement was insufficient to constitute a proximate cause of the sale, we noted, "[t]his conclusion should not be interpreted to mean that a lawyer who participates in the transaction can never be a seller. . . ."

Heisler's role in bringing about the merger in this case differed significantly from the relatively inactive part played by the lawyer in *Croy*. According to Heisler's testimony, he initially suggested the possibility of a merger. The minutes of the Reco shareholders' meeting at which the merger was discussed reflect that Heisler attended as . . . proxy and advanced the merger as the solution to Reco's financial problems. He also prepared the merger documents. Thus, unlike the attorney in *Croy*, Heisler did attempt to persuade the Reco shareholders to make the purchase of Road stock pursuant to the merger. He also made representations at the Reco shareholders' meeting regarding his investigation into possible sales of Reco property and the feasibility of a liquidation of Reco as compared with the merger. The evidence of Heisler's involvement in the effort to bring about the merger supports the trial court's finding that he was a key participant in the transaction. His role was not that of a passive advisor as was that of the attorney in *Croy*; rather, he was an active negotiator in the transaction, acting as agent-in-fact as well as attorney-at-law, implementor not counsellor. Therefore, we agree with the trial court's conclusion that Heisler's actions brought him within the scope of the seller definition. . . .

Having determined that Heisler's actions constituted him a seller . . . we also conclude that his representations made to the Reco shareholders at the shareholders' meeting amounted to an oral communication containing misstatements or omissions of material facts relevant to the merger transaction. . . .

Therefore, we conclude that Heisler did not satisfy the burden of proof required to establish that, exercising reasonable care, he could not have been aware of the material misstatements and omissions in his presentation at the Reco shareholders' meeting. . . .

For these reasons the judgment in Junker's favor is [*Affirmed.*]

6. Documents Involved

In regulating the initial sale of securities, the Federal Securities Act of 1933 should be viewed as a disclosure law. In essence, this law requires that securities subject to its provisions be registered prior to any sale and that a prospectus be furnished to any potential investor prior to any sale being consummated. Thus, an issuer of securities who complies with the federal law must prepare (1) a *registration statement,* and (2) a *prospectus*.

REGISTRATION STATEMENT

The Federal Securities Act of 1933 contains detailed provisions relating to the registration of securities and describes which selling activities are permitted at the various stages of the registration process. There are three distinct periods during the registration process: (1) the pre-filing period, (2) the waiting period, and (3) the posteffective period. A registration becomes effective twenty days (the waiting period) after it is filed, unless the SEC gives notice that it is not in proper form or unless the SEC accelerates the effective date. Any amendment filed without the Commission's consent starts the twenty-day period running again.

During the pre-filing period, it is legal for the issuer of a security to engage in preliminary negotiations and agreements with underwriters. It is illegal to sell a covered security during this period. Offers to sell and offers to buy securities also are prohibited during this pre-filing period.

During the waiting period, it is still illegall to sell a security subject to the act. However, it is not illegal to make an offer to buy or an offer to sell. Written offers to sell must conform to the prospectus requirements, but oral offers are permissible. Since contracts to sell are still illegal, offers cannot be accepted during the waiting period. As a result of these waiting periods, sellers may solicit offers for later acceptance also.

Many offers during the waiting period are made in advertisements called "tombstone ads." These ads are brief announcements identifying the security and stating its price, by whom orders will be executed, and from whom a prospectus may be obtained. Almost any issue of *The Wall Street Journal* contains such ads. Offers may also be made during the waiting period by use of a statisical summary, a summary prospectus, or a preliminary prospectus. These techniques alllow dissemination of the facts that are to be ultimately disclosed in the formal prospectus.

PROSPECTUS

During the posteffective period, securities may be sold. A prospectus must be furnished to any interested investor, and it must conform to the statutory requirements. Like the registration statement, the prospectus contains financial information related to the issuer. Indeed, the prospectus contains the same essential information contained in the registration statement. The prospectus supplies the investor with sufficient facts (including financial information) so that he or she can make an intelligent investment decision. The SEC has adopted rules relating to the detailed requirements of the prospectus. The major requirements are detailed facts about the issuer and financial statements, including balance sheets and statements of operations of the issuer.

Theoretically, any security may be sold under the act, provided the law and the rules and regulations enacted under it are followed. The law does not prohibit the sale of worthless securities. An investor may "foolishly" invest his or her money, and a person may legally sell the blue sky if the statutory requirements are met. In fact, the prospectus must contain the following in capital letters and boldface type:

THESE SECURITIES HAVE NOT BEEN APPROVED OR DISAPPROVED BY THE SECURITIES AND EXCHANGE COMMISSION NOR HAS THE COMMISSION PASSED UPON THE ACCURACY OR ADEQUACY OF THIS PROSPECTUS. ANY REPRESENTATION TO THE CONTRARY IS A CRIMINAL OFFENSE.

7. Shelf Registration

Regarding initial sale of securities to the public, the most significant development in some time has been the SEC's relaxation of disclosure requirements. This trend is not a change in the 1933 law, but it is a new direction for the rules and regulations issued by the SEC pursuant to the federal securities laws.

Rule 415, which provides for *shelf registration* of securities, was approved in February 1982 on a temporary basis. This regulation allows companies to submit a single, comprehensive disclosure statement describing their long-term financing plans. These disclosure statements permit companies to sell securities whenever rapidly changing market conditions appear most favorable. Through Rule 415, the issuer of securities to the public no longer has to prepare a prospectus for the SEC's review every time it plans to sell securities.

Several major companies have submitted shelf registration statements which allow them to sell a variety of security devices. These companies have advocated Rule 415's permanent adoption, since they would gain flexibility in raising captial. At the same time, many traditional securities firms and investment bankers argued against Rule 415. They said it decreases the role of the underwriters and the syndicates that traditionally have distributed new issues of securities to the public. Despite this controversy during the initial trial period, the SEC has allowed a modified Rule 415 to become permanent.

Companies with less than $150 million in stock held by investors unaffiliated with the company can no longer use the shelf registration method of selling securities to the public. This revised Rule 415 intends to protect investors who may not be able to get adequate financial data about these smaller, little-known companies in the short time between the announcement of a shelf issue and its sale. This modification does not prohibit all companies from using Rule 415 procedures for employee stock ownership plans, dividend reinvestment plans, and similar transactions that do not involve a conventional distribution of securities to the general public.

8. Exemptions

Some statutory provisions exempt certain transactions, and others exempt certain securities from registration requirements. Provisions that exempt certain transactions limit the application of the law to transactions in which a security is sold in a public offering by the issuer, an underwriter, a controlling person, or a seller. Transactions by a securities dealer (as distinguished from an issuer or an underwriter) are exempt after forty days have elapsed from the effective date of the first public offer. If a company offers the security with no prior registration statements, this period is ninety days. This exemption allows a dealer to enter into transactions in securities after a minimum period has elapsed. In addition, brokers' transactions executed on any exchange or in the over-the-counter market are exempt.

PRIVATE SALES TRANSACTIONS

Perhaps the most difficult issue in determining whether a sale is an exempt transaction is the concept of a public offering. Private sales are exempt. Sales to the general public are not. In determining whether or not a sale is being made to the general public, the SEC will examine (1) the number of offerees, (2) their knowledge about the company in which they are investing, (3) the relationship between the offeror and offeree, (4) whether the security remains in the hands of the offeree or is resold, and (5) the amount of advertising involved. The issuer has the burden of proof to show that the sale is private and not public.

SPECIALIZED SECURITIES

The law also exempts certain securities from its coverage. These include securities subject to regulation by governmental agencies other than the SEC, such as securities of banks and savings and loan institutions and intrastate offerings. The intrastate exemption covers securities that are offered and sold only to persons who reside within the state of incorporation. If the issuer is unincorporated, the purchasers must reside within the state of its residence and place of business. If the sale is to a resident planning to resell to a nonresident, the intrastate exemption is lost. The same is true if the mails or interstate systems of communication are used to sell the security. Remember that even if the sale is exempt under federal law, it is probably subject to a similar state law. Commercial paper arising out of current transactions with a maturity not exceeding nine months and securities issued by not-for-profit corporations are also exempt.

SIZE OF OFFERING

The SEC can create additional exemptions. Typically, these exemptions depend on the dollar amount of securities sold and on who the investor-purchasers are. Furthermore, the exemptions change from time to time. In recent years, the SEC's trend has been to exempt larger offerings in order to help businesses raise capital. Currently, any business may sell up to $500,000 in securities during a twelve-month period without registering the offering, according to the 1933 act's requirements. The amount of this exemption increases to $5 million if the issuer believes that there are no more than thirty-five investor-purchasers who lack the sophistication to acquire and evaluate information about the security being sold.

9. Criminal Liability

Under the Federal Securities Act of 1933, both civil and criminal liability may be imposed for violations. Criminal liability results from a willful violation of the act, or fraud in *any* offer or sale of securities. Fraud also occurs when any material fact is omitted, causing a statement to be misleading. The penalty is a fine up to $10,000 or five years in prison or both. Fraud in the sale of an exempt security is also a criminal violation if the mail is used or if an instrumentality of interstate commerce such as the telephone has been used.

The law requires that violations be willful. "Willful" means with intent to defraud. The government can meet its burden by proving that a defendant deliberately closed his or her eyes to facts he or she had a duty to see, or recklessly stated as facts things of which he or she was ignorant. The willfulness requirement can be satisfied by mere "proof of representation which due diligence would have shown to be untrue." In discussing the state of mind required for a criminal conviction of a lawyer or an accountant under the statute, one court observed:

> In our complex society the accountant's certificate and the lawyer's opinion can be instruments for inflicting pecuniary loss more potent than the chisel or the crowbar. Of course, Congress did not mean that any mistake of law or misstatement of fact should subject an attorney or an accountant to criminal liability simply because more skillful practitioners would not have made them. But Congress equally could not have intended that men holding themselves out as members of these ancient professions should be able to escape criminal liability on a

plea of ignorance when they have shut their eyes to what was plainly to be seen or have represented a knowledge they knew they did not possess.

A person accused of intentionally violating the 1933 act usually cannot escape criminal liability by arguing that a nonexempt transaction involving the exchange of misinformation technically was outside the 1933 act's scope. For example, the Supreme Court held that a pledge of stock as collateral for a bank loan was a sale of a security, and if the value of the stock was misrepresented, the person pledging the stock could be found guilty of a crime under the statute. A pledge of stock as security for a loan is a disposition of a security for value.

10. Civil Liability

This portion of the chapter discusses three sections of the Federal Securities Act of 1933 that directly apply to civil liability of parties involved in issuing securities. The first section of importance (Section 11 of the act) deals with registration statements; the second (Section 12 of the act) relates to prospectuses and oral and written communication; and the third (Section 17 of the act) concerns fraudulent interstate transactions.

The civil liability provision dealing with registration statements imposes liability on the following persons in favor of purchasers of securities:

1 Every person who signed the registration statement

2 Every director of the corporation or partner in the partnership issuing the security

3 Every person who, with his or her consent, is named in the registration statement as about to become a director or partner

4 Every accountant, engineer, or appraiser who assists in the preparation of the registration statement or its certification

5 Every underwriter

SECTION 11: REGISTRATION STATEMENT

The persons mentioned in the preceding paragraph are liable if the registration statement (1) contains untrue statements of material facts, (2) omits material facts required by statute or regulation, or (3) omits information which if not given makes the facts stated misleading. This latter situation describes the factual situation of a statement containing a half-truth, which has the net effect of being misleading. The test of accuracy and materiality is as of the date the registration statement becomes effective.

The SEC and the courts have attempted to define materiality. The term *material* limits information concerning those matters as to which an average prudent investor ought reasonably to be informed before purchasing the security registered. What are "matters as to which an average prudent investor ought reasonably to be informed?" They are matters which such an investor needs to know before he or she can make an intelligent, informed decision whether or not to buy the security. As a result, a material fact is one which if correctly stated or disclosed would have deterred or tended to deter the average prudent investor from purchasing the securities in question. The term does not cover minor inaccuracies or errors in matters of no interest to investors. Facts that tend to deter a person from purchasing a security are those that have an important bearing upon the nature or condition of the issuing corporation or its business.

A plaintiff-purchaser need not prove reliance on the registration statement in order to recover, but proof of actual knowledge of the falsity by the purchaser is a defense. Knowledge of the falsity by a defendant need not be proved, but except for an issuer, reliance on an expert such as an accountant is a defense. For example, a director may defend a suit based on a false financial statement by showing reliance on a CPA.

SECTION 12: PROSPECTUS

The separate provision relating to liability in connection with prospectuses and communications imposes liability on sellers who fail to comply with the registration requirements of the act. This liability is imposed regardless of wrongful intent or conduct of those who fail to comply with the law. It also imposes liability on sellers who use a prospectus or make communications (by mail, telephone, or other instrumentalities of interstate commerce) that contain an untrue statement of material facts required to be stated or necessary to make statements not misleading. Purchasers of such securities may sue for their actual damages or to rescind the purchase and obtain a refund of the price. Used when the purchaser still owns the security, this latter remedy requires privity of contract. There is no liability for aiding and abetting someone who violates these provisions.

SECTION 17: FRAUDULENT TRANSACTIONS

This provision concerning fraudulent interstate transactions prohibits the use of any instrument of interstate communication in the offer or sale of any securities when the result is (1) to defraud, (2) to obtain money or property by means of an untrue or misleading statement, or (3) to engage in a business transaction or practice that may operate to defraud or deceive a purchaser.

The requirement that a defendant-seller must act with the intent (**scienter**) to deceive or mislead in order to prove a Section 17 violation has caused much controversy over the years. In 1980, the Supreme Court resolved this issue by announcing the following decision with respect to the SEC seeking injunctive relief. You should realize that this decision is limited to the remedy of an injunction, since Section 17 does not explicitly provide for the private remedy of monetary damages. Note that the 1, 2, 3 referred to in this case is the same 1, 2, and 3 as mentioned above.

AARON v. SECURITIES AND EXCHANGE COMMISSION
100 S.Ct. 1945 (1980)

Peter Aaron was the managerial employee of a registered broker-dealer firm. Two employees of this firm, Schreiber and Jacobson, gave false information about Lawn-A-Mat Chemical & Equipment Corporation in order to induce clients to invest in Lawn-A-Mat common stock. After being informed of his brokers' wrongful actions, Aaron failed to prevent these brokers, under his direct supervision, from continuing to make false and misleading statements in promoting Lawn-A-Mat common stock.

The SEC filed a complaint seeking to enjoin Aaron from aiding and abetting continuous violations of Section 17(a) of the 1933 Securities Act.

STEWART, J.: The issue in this case is whether the Securities and Exchange Commission (Commission) is required to establish scienter as an element of a civil enforcement action to enjoin violations of § 17(a) of the Securities Act of 1933 (1933 Act). . . .

Following a bench trial, the District Court found that the petitioner had violated and aided and abetted violations of 17(a) . . . and enjoined him from future violations of these provisions. The District Court's finding of past violations was based upon its factual finding that the petitioner had intentionally failed to discharge his supervisory responsibility to stop Schreiber and Jacobson from making statements to prospective investors that the petitioner knew to be false and misleading. . . .

The Court of Appeals for the Second Circuit affirmed the judgment. Declining to reach the question whether the petitioner's conduct would support a finding of scienter, the Court of Appeals held instead that when the Commission is seeking injunctive relief,

"proof of negligence alone will suffice" to establish a violation of § 17(a). . . .

We granted certiorari to resolve the conflict in the federal courts as to whether the Commission is required to establish scienter—an intent on the part of the defendant to deceive, manipulate, or defraud—as element of a Commission enforcement action to enjoin violations of § 17(a). . . .

Section 17(a), which applies only to sellers, provides:

It shall be unlawful for any person in the offer or sale of any securities by the use of any means or instruments of transportation or communication in interstate commerce or by the use of the mails, directly or indirectly—

(1) to employ any device, scheme, or artifice to defraud, or

(2) to obtain money or property by means of any untrue statement of a material fact or any omission to state a material fact necessary in order to make the statements made, in the light of the circumstances under which they were made, not misleading, or

(3) to engage in any transaction, practice, or course of business which operates or would operate as a fraud or deceit upon the purchaser. . . .

The issue here is whether the Commission in seeking injunctive relief . . . for violations of § 17(a) . . . is required to establish scienter. Resolution of that issue could depend upon (1) the substantive provisions of § 17(a) . . . or (2) the statutory provisions authorizing injunctive relief "upon a proper showing" . . .

In determining whether proof of scienter is a necessary element of a violation of § 17(a), there is less precedential authority in this Court to guide us, but the controlling principles are well settled. Though cognizant that "Congress intended securities legislation enacted for the purpose of avoiding frauds to be construed 'not technically and restrictively but flexibly to effectuate its remedial purposes,' " the Court has also noted that "generalized references to the 'remedial purposes' " of the securities laws "will not justify reading a provision 'more broadly than its language and the statutory scheme reasonably permit.' " Thus, if the language of a provision of the securities laws is sufficiently clear in its context and not at odds with the legislative history, it is unnecessary "to examine the additional considerations of 'policy' . . . that may have influenced the lawmakers in their formulation of the statute."

The language of § 17(a) strongly suggests that Congress contemplated a scienter requirement under § 17(a)(1), but not under § 17(a)(2) or § 17(a)(3). The language of § 17(a)(1), which makes it unlawful "to employ any device, scheme, or artifice to defraud," plainly evinces an intent on the part of Congress to proscribe only knowing or intentional misconduct. Even if it be assumed that the term "defraud" is ambiguous, given its varied meanings at law and in equity, the terms "device," "scheme" and "artifice" all connote knowing or intentional practices. . . .

By contrast, the language of § 17(a)(2), which prohibits any person from obtaining money or property "by means of any untrue statement of a material fact or any omission to state a material fact," is devoid of any suggestion whatsoever of a scienter requirement. . . .

Finally, the language of § 17(a)(3), under which it is unlawful for any person "to engage in any transaction, practice, or course of business which *operates* or *would operate* as a fraud or deceit," (emphasis added) quite plainly focuses upon the *effect* of particular conduct on members of the investing public, rather than upon the culpability of the person responsible. . . .

It is our view, in sum, that the language of § 17(a) requires scienter under § 17(a)(1), but not under § 17(a)(2) or § 17(a)(3). Although the parties have urged the Court to adopt a uniform culpability requirement for the three subparagraphs of § 17(a), the language of the section is simply not amenable to such an interpretation. This is not the first time that this Court has had occasion to emphasize the distinctions among the three subparagraphs of § 17(a). In *United States v. Naftalin*, 99 S.Ct. 2077, the Court noted that each subparagraph of § 17(a) "proscribes a distinct category of misconduct. Each succeeding prohibition is meant to cover additional kinds of illegalities—not to narrow the reach of the prior sections." Indeed, since Congress drafted § 17(a) in such a manner as to compel the conclusion that scienter is required under one subparagraph but not under the other two, it would take a very clear expression in the legislative history of congressional intent to the contrary to justify the conclusion that the statute does not mean what it so plainly seems to say. . . .

Accordingly, when scienter is an element of the substantive violation sought to be enjoined, it must be proven before an injunction may issue. But with respect to those provisions such as § 17(a)(2) and § 17(a)(3), which may be violated even in the absence of scienter, . . . there is nothing in the legislative history of either provision to suggest a contrary legislative intent.

This is not to say, however, that scienter has no bearing at all on whether a district court should enjoin a person violating or about to violate § 17(a)(2) or § 17(a)(3). In cases where the Commission is seeking to enjoin a person "*about* to engage in any acts or practices which . . . *will* constitute" a violation of those provisions, the Commission must establish a sufficient evidentiary predicate to show that such future violation may occur. An important factor in this regard is the degree of intentional wrongdoing evident in a defendant's past conduct. Moreover, as the Commission recognizes, a district court may consider scienter or lack of it as one of the aggravating or mitigating factors to be taken into account in exercising its equitable discretion in deciding whether or not to grant injunctive relief. And the proper exercise of equitable discretion is necessary to ensure a "nice adjustment and reconciliation between the public interest and private needs."

For the reasons stated in this opinion, we hold that the Commission is required to establish scienter as an element of a civil enforcement action to enjoin violations of § 17(a)(1) of the 1933 Act. . . . We further hold that the Commission need not establish scienter as an element of an action to enjoin violations of § 17(a)(2) and § 17(a)(3) of the 1933 Act. The Court of Appeals affirmed the issuance of the injunction in this case in the misapprehension that it was not necessary to find scienter in order to support an injunction under any of the provisions in question. Accordingly, the judgment of the Court of Appeals is vacated, and the case is remanded to that court for further proceedings consistent with this opinion. [*So ordered.*]

11. Defenses

The Federal Securities Act of 1933 recognizes several defenses that may be used to avoid liability. Lack of materiality is a common defense. Determining whether or not a particular fact is material depends on the facts and the parties involved.

The statute of limitations is a defense for both civil and criminal liability. The basic period is one year. The statute does not start to run until the discovery of the untrue statement or omission. Or it does not start to run from the time such discovery would have been made with reasonable diligence. In no event may a suit be brought more than three years after the sale.

A defense similar to the statute of limitations is also provided. This statute provides that if the person acquiring the security does so after the issuer has made generally available an earnings statement covering at least twelve months after the effective date of the registration statement, then this person must prove actual reliance on the registration statement. However, this defense has little applicability in most cases.

A very important defense for experts such as accountants is the "due diligence" defense. The law provides that no person is liable who shall sustain the burden of proof that "as regards any part of the registration statement purporting to be made upon his authority as an expert that he had, after reasonable investigation, reasonable ground to believe and did believe, at the time such part of the registration statement became effective, that the statements therein were true and that there was no omission to state a material fact required to be stated therein or necessary to make the statements therein not misleading." In determining whether or not an expert such as an accountant has made a reasonable investigation, the law provides that the standard of reasonableness is that required of a prudent person in the management of his or her own property. The burden of proof of this defense is on the expert, and the test is as of the time the registration statement became effective. The due diligence defense, in effect, requires proof that a party was not guilty of fraud or negligence.

In order to better understand the materials concerning civil liability under the Federal Securities Act of 1933, study Table 16-1. It is intended as a summary of Sections 11, 12, and 17.

TABLE 16-1   Civil Liability Under the 1933 Act

Section of 1933 Act	Purpose of Section	Plaintiff's Required Proof of Defendant's Scienter	Defendant's Defense
Section 11	Creates liability for false or misleading registration statements	Not required to prove defendant's intent to deceive	1. Proof of no false or misleading information is a defense. 2. Proof that plaintiff knew of false or misleading nature of information is a defense. 3. Except for issuer, proof of reliance on an expert (attorney, accountant, etc.) is a defense. 4. Proof of good faith is not a defense.
Section 12	Creates liability for false or misleading prospectus	Not required to prove defendant's intent to deceive	Same as above
Section 17	In an interstate transaction, it is unlawful: 1. to employ device, scheme, or artifice to defraud. 2. to obtain money or property by untrue statement or omission of material fact. 3. to engage in events which operate or would operate as a fraud or deceit.	1. <u>Required to prove defendant's intent to deceive</u> 2. Not required to prove defendant's intent to deceive 3. Not required to prove defendant's intent to deceive	1. Proof of no intent to deceive is a defense. Good faith is a defense. 2. Proof of no material misstatement or omission is a defense. Good faith is not a defense. 3. Proof of no involvement in unlawful activities is a defense. Good faith is not a defense.

FEDERAL SECURITIES EXCHANGE ACT OF 1934: BEING PUBLIC

12. General Coverage

Whereas the Federal Securities Act of 1933 deals with original offerings of securities, the Federal Securities Exchange Act of 1934 regulates transfers of securities after the initial sale. The 1934 act, which created the SEC, also deals with regulation of security exchanges, brokers, and dealers in securities.

It is illegal to sell a security on a national exchange unless a registration is effective for the security. Registration under the 1934 act differs from registration under the 1933 act. Registration under the former requires filing prescribed forms with the applicable stock exchange and the SEC. As a general rule, all equity securities held by 500 or more owners must be registered if the issuer has more than $1 million in gross assets. This rule picks up issues traded over the counter and applies to securities that might have qualified under one of the exemptions under the 1933 act.

Provisions relating to stockbrokers and dealers prohibit the use of the mails or any other instrumentality of interstate commerce to sell securities unless the broker or the dealer is registered. The language is sufficiently broad to cover attempted sales as well as actual sales. Brokers and dealers must keep detailed records of their activities and file annual reports with the SEC.

The SEC requires that issuers of registered securities file periodic reports as well as report significant developments which would affect the value of the security. For example, the SEC requires companies to disclose foreign payoffs or bribes to obtain or retain foreign business operations. Businesses must disclose their minority hiring practices and other social data that may be of public concern. Business has been forced by the SEC to submit certain shareholder proposals to all shareholders as a part of proxy solicitation. When a new pension law was enacted, the SEC required that financial reports disclose the law's impact on the reporting business. SEC activity concerning information corporations must furnish to the investing public is almost limitless. As a result, SEC regulations are of paramount significance to all persons concerned with the financial aspects of business. This area of regulation directly affects the accounting profession. Since the SEC regulates financial statements, the Commission frequently decides issues of proper accounting and auditing theory and practices.

How the Federal Securities Exchange Act of 1934 affects the business person, the accountant, the lawyer, the broker, and the investor is seen in the following sections. These sections cover some fundamental concepts of this law, such as civil liability in general and insider transactions in particular, as well as criminal violations and penalties under the 1934 act.

13. Section 10(b) and Rule 10b-5

Most of the litigation under the Federal Securities and Exchange Act of 1934 is brought under Section 10(b) of the act and Rule 10b-5 promulgated by the

SEC pursuant to the act. Section 10(b) and Rule 10b-5 declare that it is unlawful to use the mails or any instrumentality of interstate commerce or any national securities exchange to defraud *any person* in connection with the *purchase or sale* of any security. They provide a private remedy for defrauded investors. This remedy may be invoked against "any person" who indulges in fraudulent practices in the purchase or sale of securities. In actual practice, defendants in such cases tend to fall into four general categories: (1) insiders; (2) broker-dealers; (3) corporations whose stock is purchased or sold by plaintiffs; and (4) those, such as accountants, who "aid and abet" or conspire with a party who falls into one of the first three categories.

Section 10(b) and Rule 10b-5 are usually referred to as the antifraud provisions of the act. A plaintiff seeking damages under the provisions must establish (1) the existence of a material misrepresentation or omission made in connection with the purchase or sale of a security, (2) the culpable state of mind of the defendant, (3) his or her reliance and due diligence, and (4) damage as a result of the reliance. Materiality under the 1934 act is the same as materiality under the 1933 act. Liability under Rule 10b-5 requires proof of scienter and not proof of simple negligence. It also requires proof of a practice that is manipulative and not merely corporate mismanagement.

SANTA FE INDUSTRIES, INC. v. GREEN
97 S.Ct. 1292 (1977)

Santa Fe sought to merge under the Delaware "short-form" merger statute and obtained independent appraisal values of the stock. The company complied with the statute and sent to each minority shareholder an information statement containing the appraisal values of the assets. It offered the minority shareholders $150 per share (the appraisal value was $125) for their stock. Respondents, minority shareholders, did not pursue their appraisal remedy in the state courts. Instead, they filed suit under Rule 10b-5, claiming that Santa Fe used a device to defraud and that the information statement failed to reveal that the stock was actually worth $772 per share. The district court dismissed the complaint, holding that it failed to state a cause of action. The Court of Appeals reversed.

WHITE, J.: . . . We granted the petition for certiorari challenging this holding because of the importance of the issue involved to the administration of the federal securities laws. . . .

Section 10(b) of the 1934 Act makes it "unlawful for any person . . . to use or employ . . . any manipulative or deceptive device or contrivance in contravention of [Securities and Exchange Commission rules]"; Rule 10b-5, promulgated by the SEC under § 10(b), prohibits, in addition to nondisclosure and misrepresentation, any "artifice to defraud" or any act "which operates or would operate as a fraud or deceit."

. . . [I]n deciding whether a complaint states a cause of action for "fraud" under Rule 10b-5, "we turn first to the language of § 10(b), for '[t]he starting point in every case involving construction of a statute is the language itself.' " . . .

The language of § 10(b) gives no indication that Congress meant to prohibit any conduct not involving manipulation or deception. Nor have we been cited to any evidence in the legislative history that would support a departure from the language of the statute. "When a statute speaks so specifically in terms of manipulation and deception, . . . and when its history reflects no more expansive intent, we are quite unwilling to extend the scope of the statute. . . . " Thus the claim of fraud and fiduciary breach in this complaint states a cause of action under any part of Rule 10b-5 only if the conduct alleged can be fairly viewed as "manipulative or deceptive" within the meaning of the statute.

It is our judgment that the transaction, if carried out as alleged in the complaint, was neither deceptive nor manipulative and therefore did not violate either § 10(b) of the Act or Rule 10b-5.

As we have indicated, the case comes to us on the premise that the complaint failed to allege a material misrepresentation or material failure to disclose. The finding of the District Court, undisturbed by the Court of Appeals, was that there was no "omission" or "misstatement" in the information statement accompanying the notice of merger. On the basis of the information provided, minority shareholders could either accept the price offered or reject it and seek an appraisal in the Delaware Court of Chancery. Their choice was fairly presented, and they were furnished with all relevant information on which to base their decision. . . .

We thus adhere to the position that "Congress by § 10(b) did not seek to regulate transactions which constitute no more than internal corporate mismanagement. There may well be a need for uniform federal fiduciary standards to govern mergers such as that challenged in this complaint. But those standards should not be supplied by judicial extension of § 10(b) and Rule 10b-5 to "cover the corporate universe."

The judgment of the Court of Appeals is reversed, and the case is remanded. . . . [*So ordered.*]

The concept of fraud under Section 10(b) encompasses not only untrue statements of material facts, but also the failure to state material facts necessary to prevent statements actually made from being misleading. In other words, a half-truth that misleads is fraudulent. Finally, failure to correct a misleading impression left by statements already made, or silence where there is a duty to speak, gives rise to a violation of Rule 10b-5 because it is a form of "aiding and abetting." Although there is no general duty on the part of all persons with knowledge of improper activities to report them, a duty to disclose may arise from the fact of a special relationship or set of circumstances, such as an accountant certifying financial statements.

The application of Section 10(b) and Rule 10b-5 applies to all sales of any security if the requisite fraud exists and the interstate aspect is established. The rule requires that those standing in a fiduciary relationship disclose all material facts before entering into transactions. This means that an officer, a director, or a controlling shareholder has a duty to disclose all material facts. Failure to do so is a violation and, in effect, fraudulent. Privity of contract is not required for a violation, and lack of privity of contract is no defense.

Liability under Rule 10b-5 may be imposed on an accountant even though he or she performs only an unaudited write-up. An accountant is liable for errors in financial statements contained in a prospectus or other filed report even though unaudited if there are errors he or she knew or should have known. Even when performing an unaudited write-up, an accountant must undertake at least a minimal investigation into the figures supplied to him or her, and cannot disregard suspicious circumstances.

A plaintiff in a suit under Rule 10b-5 must prove damages. The damages of a defrauded purchaser are usually "out-of-pocket" losses or the excess of "what was paid" over the value of "what was received." Courts in a few cases have used the "benefit of the bargain" measure of damages and awarded the buyer the difference between what he or she paid and what the security was represented to be worth. A buyer's damages are measured at the time of purchase.

Computation of a defrauded seller's damages is more difficult. A defrauding purchaser usually benefits from an increase in the value of the securities, while the plaintiff seller loses this increase. Courts do not allow defrauding buyers to keep these increases in value. Therefore, the measure of the seller's damages is the difference between the fair value of all that the seller received and the fair value of what he or she would have received had there been no fraud, except where the defendant received more than the seller's loss. In this latter case, the seller is entitled to the defendant's profit. As a result, defendants lose all profits flowing from the fraudulent conduct.

Plaintiffs under Rule 10b-5 are also entitled to consequential damages. These include lost dividends, brokerage ffees, and taxes. In addition, courts may order payment of interest on the funds. Punitive damages are not permitted as they are in cases of common law fraud based on state laws. This distinction results from the language of the statute which limits recoveries to "actual damages."

As a general rule, attorneys' fees are not recoverable. This is consistent with the rule in most litigation. However, in class action suits, the attorneys can collect their fees out of the recovery. These fees in a class action suit will often exceed the usual hourly rate and will often be close to or equal to the contingent fee rate (one-third of the recovery).

14. Insider Transactions

Section 16, one of the most important provisions of the Federal Securities Exchange Act of 1934, concerns insider transactions. An *insider* is any person (1) who owns more than 10 percent of any security, or (2) who is a director or an officer of the issuer of the security. Section 16 and SEC regulations require that insiders file, at the time of the registration or within ten days after becoming an insider, a statement of the amount of such issues of which they are the owners. The regulations also require filing within ten days after the close of each calendar month thereafter, if there has been any change in such ownership during such month (indicating the change). There are exemptions to the insider rules for executors or administrators of estates, and odd-lot dealers are also generally exempt.

The reason for prohibiting insiders from trading for profits is to prevent the use of information that is available to an insider but not to the general public. Because the SEC cannot determine for certain when nonpublic information is improperly used, Section 16 creates a presumption that any profit made within a six-month time period is illegal. These profits are referred to as "short-swing profits." Thus, if a director, officer, or principal owner realizes profits on the purchase and sale of a security within a six-month period, the profits inure and belong to the company or to the investor who purchased it from or sold it to an insider, resulting in the insider's profit and investor's loss. The order of the purchase and sale is immaterial. The profit is calculated on the lowest price in and highest price out during any six-month period. Unlike the required proof of intent to deceive under Section 10(b), the short-swing profits rule of Section 16 does not depend on any misuse of information. In other words, short-swing profits by insiders, regardless of the insiders' state of mind, are absolutely prohibited.

15. Nonpublic Information

The SEC's concern for trading based on nonpublic information goes beyond the Section 16 ban on short-swing profits. Indeed, a person who is not technically an insider but who trades securities without disclosing nonpublic information may violate Section 10(b) and Rule 10b-5. The SEC takes the position that the profit obtained as the result of a trader's silence concerning information that is not freely available to everyone is a manipulation or deception prohibited by Section 10(b) and Rule 10b-5. In essence, the users of nonpublic information are treated like insiders if they can be classified as a *tippee,* or a *temporary insider.*

A tippee is a person who learns of nonpublic information from an insider. A tippee is liable for the use of nonpublic information, because an insider should not be allowed to do indirectly what he cannot do directly. In other words, a tippee is liable for trading or passing on information that is nonpublic.

A person who learns of nonpublic information from a source other than an insider is not required to reveal that information prior to trading. In one case, a financial printer had been hired to print corporate takeover bids. An employee of the printer was able to deduce the identities of both the acquiring companies and the companies targeted for takeover. Without disclosing the knowledge about the prospective takeover bids, the employee purchased stock in the target companies and then sold it for a profit immediately after the takeover attempts were made public. He was indicted and convicted for having violated Section 10(b) and Rule 10b-5. The Supreme Court reversed, holding that the defendant had no duty not to reveal the nonpublic information, since he was not in a fiduciary position with respect to either the acquiring or the acquired companies.

In another case the United States Supreme Court further narrowed a tippee's liability. The Court ruled that a tippee becomes liable under Section 10(b) only if the tipper breaches a fiduciary duty to the business organization or fellow shareholders. Therefore, if the tipper communicated nonpublic information for reasons other than personal gain, neither the tipper nor the tippee could be liable for a securities violation.

DIRKS v. SECURITIES AND EXCHANGE COMMISSION
103 S.Ct. 3255 (1983)

POWELL, J. Petitioner Raymond Dirks received material nonpublic information from "insiders" of a corporation with which he had no connection. He disclosed this information to investors who relied on it in trading in the shares of the corporation. The questions is whether Dirks violated the antifraud provisions of the federal securities laws by this disclosure.

In 1973, Dirks was an officer of a New York broker-dealer firm who specialized in providing investment analysis of insurance company securities to institutional investors. On March 6, Dirks received information from Ronald Secrist, a former officer of Equity Funding of America. Secrist alleged that the assets of Equity Funding, a diversified corporation primarily engaged in selling life insurance and mutual funds, were vastly overstated as the result of fraudulent corporate practices. Secrist also stated that various regulatory agencies had failed to act on similar charges made by Equity Funding employees. He urged Dirks to verify the fraud and disclose it publicly.

Dirks decided to investigate the allegations. He visited Equity Funding's headquarters in Los Angeles and interviewed several officers and employees of the corporation. The senior management denied any wrongdoing, but certain corporation employees corroborated the charges of fraud. Nei-

ther Dirks nor his firm owned or traded any Equity Funding stock, but throughout his investigation he openly discussed the information he had obtained with a number of clients and investors. Some of these persons sold their holdings of Equity Funding securities, including five investment advisers who liquidated holdings of more than $16 million. . . .

During the two-week period in which Dirks pursued his investigation and spread word of Secrist's charges, the price of Equity Funding stock fell from $26 per share to less than $15 per share. This led the New York Stock Exchange to halt trading on March 27. Shortly thereafter California insurance authorities impounded Equity Funding's records and uncovered evidence of the fraud. Only then did the Securities and Exchange Commission (SEC) file a complaint against Equity Funding and only then, on April 2, did the *Wall Street Journal* publish a front-page story based largely on information assembled by Dirks. Equity Funding immediately went into receivership.

The SEC began an investigation into Dirks' role in the exposure of the fraud. After a hearing by an administrative law judge, the SEC found that Dirks had aided and abetted violations of § 17(a) of the Securities Act of 1933, § 10(b) of the Securities Exchange Act of 1934, and SEC Rule 10b-5, by repeating the allegations of fraud to members of the investment community who later sold their Equity Funding stock. The SEC concluded: "Where 'tippees'—regardless of their motivation or occupation—come into possession of material 'information that they know is confidential and know or should know came from a corporate insider,' they must either publicly disclose that information or refrain from trading." Recognizing, however, that Dirks "played an important role in bringing [Equity Funding's] massive fraud to light," the SEC only censured him.

Dirks sought review in the Court of Appeals for the District of Columbia Circuit. The court entered judgment against Dirks. . . .

In view of the importance to the SEC and to the securities industry of the questions presented by this case, we granted a writ of certiorari. . . .

We were explicit in *Chiarella* in saying that there can be no duty to disclose where the person who has traded on inside information "was not [the corporation's] agent . . . was not a fiduciary, [or] was not a person in whom the sellers [of the securities] has placed their trust and confidence." . . . This requirement of a specific relationship between the shareholders and the individual trading on inside information has created analytical difficulties for the SEC and courts in policing tippees who trade on inside information. Unlike insiders who have independent fiduciary duties to both the corporation and its shareholders, the typical tippee has no such relationships. In view of this absence, it has been unclear how a tippee acquires the duty to refrain from trading on inside information.

The SEC's position, as stated in its opinion in this case, is that a tippee "inherits" the obligation to shareholders whenever he receives inside information from an insider. . . .

In effect, the SEC's theory of tippee liability appears rooted in the idea that the antifraud provisions require equal information among all traders. This conflicts with the principle set forth in *Chiarella* that only some persons, under some circumstances, will be barred from trading while in possession of material non-public information. . . . We reaffirm today that "[a] duty [to disclose] arises from the relationship between parties . . . and not merely from one's ability to acquire information because of his position in the market." . . .

The conclusion that recipients of inside information do not invariably acquire a duty to disclose or abstain does not mean that such tippees always are free to trade on the information. The need for a ban on some tippee trading is clear. Not only are insiders forbidden by their fiduciary relationship from personally using undisclosed corporate information to their advantage, but they may not give such information to an outsider for the same improper purpose of exploiting the information for their personal gain. . . . Thus, the tippee's duty to disclose or abstain is derivative from that of the insider's duty. . . .

[A] tippee assumes a fiduciary duty to the shareholders of a corporation not to trade on material nonpublic information only when the insider has breached his fiduciary duty to the shareholders by disclosing the information to the tippee and the tippee knows or should know that there has been a breach. . . .

In determining whether a tippee is under an obligation to disclose or abstain, it thus is necessary to determine whether the insider's "tip" constituted a breach of the insider's fiduciary duty. All disclosures of confidential corporate information are not inconsistent with the duty insiders owe to shareholders. . . . In some situations, the insider will act consistently with his fiduciary duty to shareholders, and yet release of the information may affect the market. . . . This standard was identified by the SEC itself: a purpose of the securities laws was to eliminate "use of inside information for personal advantage." Thus, the test is whether the insider personally will benefit, directly or indirectly, from his disclosure. Absent some personal gain, there has been no breach of duty to stockholders. And absent a breach by the insider, there is no derivative breach.

Determining whether an insider personally benefits from a particular disclosure, a question of fact, will not always be easy for courts. But it is essential, we think, to have a guiding principle for those whose daily activities must be limited and instructed by the SEC's inside-trading rules, and we believe that there must be a breach of the insider's fiduciary duty before the tippee inherits the duty to disclose or abstain. . . .

Under the inside-trading and tipping rules set forth above, we find that there was no actionable violation by Dirks. It is undisputed that Dirks himself was a stranger to Equity Funding, with no pre-existing fiduciary duty to its shareholders. He took no action, directly or indirectly, that induced the shareholders or officers of Equity Funding to repose trust or confidence in him. There was no expectation by Dirk's sources that he would keep their information in confidence.

Nor did Dirks misappropriate or illegally obtain the information about Equity Funding. Unless the insiders breached their duty to shareholders in disclosing the nonpublic information to Dirks, he breached no duty when he passed it on to investors as well as to the *Wall Street Journal.*

It is clear that neither Secrist nor the other Equity Funding employees violated their duty to the corporation's shareholders by providing information to Dirks. The tippers received no monetary or personal benefit for revealing Equity Funding's secrets, nor was their purpose to make a gift of valuable information to Dirks. As the facts of this case clearly indicate, the tippers were motivated by a desire to expose the fraud. In the absence of a breach of duty to shareholders by the insiders, there was no derivative breach by Dirks. Dirks therefore could not have been "a participant after the fact in [an] insider's breach of a fiduciary duty."

We conclude that Dirks, in the circumstances of this case, had no duty to abstain from use of the inside information that he obtained. The judgment of the Court of Appeals therefore is [*Reversed.*]

Despite this apparent loophole in the use of nonpublic information, it now appears that a person will be considered to be a temporary insider if the insider conveyed nonpublic information which was to be kept confidential. The following case illustrates the logic of finding a temporary insider liable under Section 10(b) even though there was no breach of a fiduciary duty.

SECURITIES AND EXCHANGE COMMISSION v. LUND
570 F.Supp. 1397 (C.D.Cal. 1983)

Lund was the chief executive officer and chairman of the board of Verit Company.

Horowitz was the chief officer and chairman of the board of P&F. In order to solicit investment funds, Horowitz told Lund about P&F's opportunity to participate in a Las Vegas gambling casino. Horowitz sought investment capital from Verit. After learning of these unannounced plans, Lund purchased 10,000 shares of P&F's stock. Three days later, P&F's plans to participate in the casino joint venture was announced, and the stock doubled in price. Lund sold his shares at a substantial profit. The SEC sued Lund for violating Section 10(b) of the l934 Securities Exchange Act.

LUCAS, J.: . . . The Court must now address the . . . difficult issue raised by this litigation: Lund's contention that under these facts his failure to disclose the information he received or to refrain from trading in P&F stock does not constitute a violation of § 10(b).

The scope of liability under § 10(b) has received much attention in recent years. In particular, the Supreme Court's decisions in *Chiarella v. United States,* 100 S. Ct. 1108 (1980) and *Dirks v. SEC,* 103 S. Ct. 3255 (1983), have significantly clarified the parameters of such liability.

It has long been established that, under certain circumstances, a "tippee" may be held liable under § 10 for trading on material, non-public information. However, the precise contours of tippee liability were unclear until *Dirks.* Under *Dirks* tippee liability cannot be imposed unless the "tipper" has breached a fiduciary duty to the shareholders by disclosing the information to the tippee and the tippee knows or should know that there has been a breach.

Following the publication of *Dirks,* plaintiff correctly abandoned its argument that Lund could be held liable under § 10(b) on a theory of tippee liability. It is clear in this case that Horowitz did not breach his fiduciary duty to P&F or its shareholders by disclosing information concerning the Jockey Club joint venture to Lund. His disclosure of this infor-

mation was within the scope of his authority as an officer and director of the corporation. Absent a breach of a fiduciary duty by Horowitz, Lund cannot be liable under § 10(b) as a tippee.

This determination does not end the Court's inquiry, however. In addition to "tippee" liability discussed above, courts have long imposed liability under § 10(b) in cases of "insider" trading. Although corporate insiders are traditionally defined as officers, directors and controlling shareholders of the corporation, a consistent body of case law makes clear that the scope of the concept "insider" is flexible. In one of the earliest "disclose or abstain" cases, the Commission specifically stated that these three groups "do not exhaust the classes of persons upon whom there is [an obligation to disclose or abstain.]" The commission stated that the scope of the disclose or abstain rule is not "circumscribed by fine distinctions and rigid classifications." Rather, the prohibition against insider trading is directed at "those persons who are in a special relationship with the company and privy to its internal affairs."

This flexible understanding of the scope of the concept "insider" for the purposes of § 10(b) has been confirmed by this Circuit. . . .

Similarly, in *Dirks,* the Supreme Court noted that "outsiders" may, under certain circumstances, become fiduciaries of shareholders and, thus become subject to the same duty to disclose or abstain as an insider. . . .

Persons who, although not traditional "insiders", nevertheless become fiduciaries of the corporation and the shareholders could be called "temporary insiders." They assume the duties of an insider temporarily, by virtue of a special relationship with the corporation. A temporary insider is subject to liability under § 10(b) for trading on the basis of non-public material information received in the context of the special relationship.

The Court has concluded that Lund was

a temporary P&F insider when he traded on the basis of the information concerning the Jockey Club project. Lund and Horowitz were long time friends and business associates. They often exchanged information about their corporations. Horowitz sat on the Board of Verit. Horowitz told Verit, through Lund, of the Jockey Club joint venture because of this special relationship. The information was made available to Lund solely for corporate purposes. It was not disclosed in idle conversation or for some other purpose. The relationship between Horowitz and Lund was such as to imply that the information was to be kept confidential. Horowitz clearly did not expect Lund to make the information public or to use the information for his personal gain. Lund knew or should have known that the information he received was confidential and that it had been disclosed to him solely for legitimate corporate purposes.

Under these circumstances, Lund became a temporary P&F insider upon receipt of the information concerning the Jockey Club project and assumed an insider's duty to "disclose or abstain" from trading based on that information. Lund's breach of that duty is actionable under § 10(b). [*So ordered.*]

Insider rules are rigidly applied in ordinary sale and purchase transactions. However, courts have held that the provisions do not apply to certain "unorthodox" transactions that are not within the intent of the law. For example, it has been held that if a purchaser did not own 10 percent of the total stock prior to the purchase, then the purchase and later sale within six months was not subject to the law.

The SEC has been trying to curb "insider" transactions, but historically it has been difficult because of a limited civil sanction. Historically, the "insider" has been liable only to return the profit illegally gained. In 1984, President Reagan signed into law authority for the SEC to seek a civil penalty of three times the illegal profits. It is anticipated that the SEC will use this increased penalty to further its campaign against the use of inside information.

Because of the increased SEC enforcement, corporations' interest in insiders' use of nonpublic information is very high. The following statement from Caterpillar's Code of Ethics illustrates an appropriate corporate policy on the use and nonuse of inside information.

INSIDE INFORMATION

Inside information may be defined as information about Caterpillar which isn't known to the investing public. Such information may have value—for example, certain financial data, technical materials, and future plans. Those with access to such information are expected to treat it confidentially, and in a fashion which avoids harm to Caterpillar.

Inside information may or may not be "material". Information is "material" if there is substantial likelihood that a reasonable investor would consider it important in making an investment decision about Caterpillar.

Those who have "material" inside information are expected to refrain from using it for personal gain. For example, they are required to refrain from personal trading of Caterpillar stock until the information has become public . . . or until it's no longer "material."

The preceding pertains to both: (1) all corporate officers; and (2) those who, by reason of their jobs, possess such information.

While Caterpillar may hire individuals who have knowledge and experience in various technical areas, we don't wish to employ such persons as a means of gaining access to trade secrets of others. New employees are asked not to divulge such trade secrets.

The concept of "inside information" extends outside the company, and requires ethical judgments by people involved. Beyond other conflict of interest rules which may apply, a Caterpillar employee having access to confidential company information that could affect the price of a supplier's, customer's or customer's stock shouldn't trade in such stock.

16. Additional Civil Liability

Section 18 of the Securities Exchange Act of 1934 imposes liability on a theory of fraud on any person who shall make or cause to be made any false and misleading statements of material fact in any application, report, or document filed under the act. This liability favors both purchasers and sellers. Plaintiffs must prove scienter (knowingly making a false statement), reliance on the false or misleading statement, and damage. Good faith is a defense. Good faith exists when a person acts without knowledge that the statement is false and misleading. In other words, freedom from fraud is a defense under an action predicated on Section 18. There is no liablity under this section for simple negligence.

In addition to Section 18, the securities laws include many provisions that require reports to be filed with the SEC. These reporting provisions do not lead to a civil remedy for inaccurate reporting. This result is due in part to the specific civil remedy provided in Section 18.

Section 14(e) of the Act prohibits fraudulent, deceptive, or manipulative acts or practices in connection with tender offers. This provision has been interpreted in the same way as Section 10(b). For a violation to occur, there must be a misrepresentation or nondisclosure of a material fact—in other words, fraud must be proven. Unfairness is not a violation.

SCHREIBER v. BURLINGTON NORTHERN, INC.
105 S.Ct. 2458 (1985)

In December, 1982, Burlington Northern, Inc., made a hostile tender offer for El Paso Gas Co. Although a majority of El Paso's shareholders subscribed, Burlington did not accept the tendered shares. In January 1983, Burlington and El Paso announced "a new and friendly takeover agreement." Burlington rescinded the December tender offer and substituted a new tender offer. This January tender offer was soon oversubscribed by the shareholders. The rescission of the first tender offer caused a reduced payment to those shareholders who had tendered during the first offer, because those shareholders who retendered were subject to substantial proration. Plaintiff (petitioner) filed suit on behalf of herself and similarly situated shareholders, alleging that Burlington, El Paso, and members of El Paso's board had violated Section 14(e) of the Securities Exchange Act of 1934, which prohibits "fraudulent, deceptive or manipulative acts or practices . . . in connection with any tender offer." She alleged that Burlington's withdrawal of the first tender offer, coupled with the substitution of the January offer, was a "manipulative" distortion of the market for El Paso stock. The District Court dismissed the suit, and the Court of Appeals affirmed

BURGER, J.: . . . We are asked in this case to interpret § 14(e) of the Securities Exchange Act. The starting point is the language of the statute. Section 14(e) provides:

It shall be unlawful for any person to make any untrue statement of a material fact or omit to state any material fact necessary in order to make the statements made, in the light of the circumstances under which they are made, not misleading, or to engage in any fraudulent, deceptive or manipulative acts or practices, in connection with any tender offer or request or invitation for tenders, or any solicitation of security holders in opposition to or in favor of any such offer, request, or invitation. The Commission shall, for the purposes of this subsection, by rules and regulations define, and prescribe means reasonably designed to prevent, such acts and practices as are fraudulent, deceptive, or manipulative.

Petitioner relies on a construction of the phrase, "fraudulent, deceptive or manipulative acts or practices." Petitioner reads the phrase "fraudulent, deceptive or manipulative acts or practices" to include acts which, although fully disclosed, "artificially" affect the price of the takeover target's stock. Petitioner's interpretation relies on the belief that § 14(e) is directed at purposes broader than providing full and true information to investors.

Petitioner's reading of the term "manipulative" conflicts with the normal meaning of the term. We have held in the context of an alleged violation of § 10(b) of the Securities Exchange Act:

Use of the word 'manipulative' is especially significant. It is and was virtually a term of art when used in connection with the securities markets. It connotes intentional or willful conduct *designed to deceive or defraud* investors by controlling or artificially affecting the price of securities.

Other cases interpreting the term reflect its use as a general term comprising a range of misleading practices:

The term refers generally to practices, such as wash sales, matched orders, or rigged prices, that are intended to mislead investors by artificially affecting market activity. . . . Section 10(b)'s general prohibition of practices deemed by the SEC to be 'manipulative'—in this technical sense of artificially affecting market activity in order to mislead investors—is fully consistent with the fundamental purpose of the 1934 Act ' "to substitute a philosophy of full disclosure for the philosophy of *caveat emptor*. . . ." ' . . . Indeed, nondisclosure is usually essential to the success of a manipulative scheme. . . . No doubt Congress meant to prohibit the full range of ingenious devices that might be used to manipulate securities prices. But we do not think it would have chosen this 'term of art' if it had meant to bring within the scope of § 10(b) instances of corporate mismanagement such as this, in which the essence of the complaint is that shareholders were treated unfairly by a fiduciary.

The meaning the Court has given the term "manipulative" is consistent with the use of the term at common law, and with its traditional dictionary definition.

She argues, however, that the term manipulative takes on a meaning in § 14(e) that is different from the meaning it has in § 10(b). Petitioner claims that the use of the disjunctive "or" in § 14(e) implies that acts need not be deceptive or fraudulent to be manipulative. But Congress used the phrase "manipulative or deceptive" in § 10(b) as well, and we have interpreted "manipulative" in that context to require misrepresention. . . .

All three species of misconduct, *i.e.*, "fraudulent, deceptive or manipulative," listed by Congress are directed at failures to disclose. The use of the term "manipulative" provides emphasis and guidance to those who must determine which types of acts are reached by the statute; it does not suggest a deviation from the section's facial and primary concern with disclosure or Congressional concern with disclosure which is the core of the Act.

Our conclusion that "manipulative" acts under § 14(e) require misrepresentation or nondisclosure is buttressed by the purpose and legislative history of the provision. Section 14(e) was originally added to the Securities Exchange Act as part of the Williams Act. "The purpose of the Williams Act is to insure that public shareholders who are confronted by a cash tender offer for their stock will not be required to respond without adequate information." . . .

Nowhere in the legislative history is there the slightest suggestion that § 14(e) serves any purpose other than disclosure, or that the term "manipulative" should be read as an invitation to the courts to oversee the substantive fairness of tender offers; the quality of any offer is a matter for the marketplace.

To adopt the reading of the term "manipulative" urged by petitioner would not only be unwarranted in light of the legislative purpose but would be at odds with it. Inviting judges to read the term "manipulative" with their own sense of what constitutes "unfair" or "artificial" conduct would inject uncertainty into the tender offer process. An essential piece of information—whether the court would deem the fully disclosed actions of one side or the other to be "manipulative"—would not be available until after the tender offer had closed. This uncertainty would directly contradict the expressed Congressional desire to give investors full information.

Congress' consistent emphasis on disclosure persuades us that it intended takeover contests to be addressed to shareholders. In pursuit of this goal, Congress, consistent with the core mechanism of the Securities Exchange Act, created sweeping disclosure requirements and narrow substantive safeguards. The same Congress that placed such emphasis on the shareholder choice would not at the same time have required judges to oversee tender offers for substantive fairness. It is even less likely that a Congress implementing that intention would express it only through the use of a single word placed in the middle of a provision otherwise devoted to disclosure.

We hold that the term "manipulative" as used in § 14(e) requires misrepresentation or nondisclosure. It connotes "conduct designed to deceive or defraud investors by controlling or artificially affecting the price of securities." Without misrepresentation or nondisclosure, § 14(3) has not been violated.

Applying that definition to this case, we hold that the actions of respondents were not manipulative. The amended complaint fails to allege that the cancellation of the first tender offer was accompanied by any misrepresentation, nondisclosure or deception. The District Court correctly found, "All activity of the defendants that could have conceivably affected the price of El Paso shares was done openly." . . . [*Affirmed.*]

17. Criminal Liability

The 1934 act provides for criminal sanctions for willful violations of its provisions or the rules adopted under it. Liability is imposed for false material statements in applications, reports, documents, and registration statements. The penalty is a fine not to exceed $100,000 or five years in prison, or both. Failure to file the required reports and documents makes the issuer subject to a $100 forfeiture per day. A person cannot be convicted if he or she proves that he or she has no knowledge of a rule or regulation, but of course lack of knowledge of a statute is no defense.

Criminal liability is important for officers and directors. It is also important for accountants. Accountants have been found guilty of a crime for failure to disclose important facts to shareholder-investors. Compliance with generally accepted accounting principles is not an absolute defense. The critical issue in such cases is whether the financial statements as a whole fairly present the financial condition of the company and whether they accurately report operations for the covered periods. If they do not, the second issue is whether the accountant acted in good faith. Compliance with generally accepted accounting principles is evidence of good faith, but such evidence is not necessarily conclusive. Lack of criminal intent is the defense usually asserted by accountants charged with a crime. They usually admit mistakes or even negligence but deny any criminal wrongdoing. Proof of motive is not required.

In the case of *United States v. Natelli,* 527 F.2d 311 (1975), the U.S. Court of Appeals for the Second Circuit had occasion to discuss the element of criminal intent and the role of the jury in deciding if it exists. It noted that the failure to follow sound accounting practice is evidence that may prove criminal intent. It said in part:

> It is hard to prove the intent of a defendant. Circumstantial evidence, particularly with proof of motive, where available, is often sufficient to convince a reasonable man of criminal intent beyond a reasonable doubt. When we deal with a defendant who is a professional accountant, it is even harder, at times, to distinguish between simple errors of judgment and errors made with sufficient criminal intent to support a conviction, especially when there is no financial gain to the accountant other than his legitimate fee. . . .
>
> . . . The arguments Natelli makes in this court as evidence of his innocent intent were made to the jury and presented fairly. There is no contention that Judge Tyler improperly excluded any factual evidence offered. . . .
>
> . . . We reject the argument of insufficiency as to Natelli, our function being limited to determining whether the evidence was sufficient for submission to the jury. We hold that it was.
>
> . . . There are points in favor of Natelli, to be sure, but these were presented to the jury and rejected.

From the foregoing, it is clear that great deference is given to the findings of fact by the jury in criminal cases.

As with issues of civil liability, most cases involving potential criminal liability are litigated under Section 10(b) and Rule 10b-5.

CONSIDERATIONS BEYOND THE FEDERAL SECURITIES LAWS

18. State "Blue Sky" Laws

In addition to understanding the federal securities laws discussed in the previous sections, every person dealing with the issuance of securities should be familiar with state securities regulations. Throughout their history, these laws commonly have been referred to as **"blue sky" laws**—probably because they were intended to protect the potential investor from buying "a piece of the attractive blue sky" (worthless or risky securities) without financial and other information about what was being purchased. The "blue sky" laws can apply to securities subject to federal laws as well as those securities exempt from the federal statutes. It is clearly established that the federal laws do not preempt the existence of state "blue sky" laws. Due to their broad application, any person associated with issuing or thereafter transferring securities should survey the "blue sky" laws passed by the various states.

Although the existence of federal securities laws has influenced state legislatures, enactment of "blue sky" laws has not been uniform. Indeed, states typically have enacted laws that contain provisions similar to either (1) the antifraud provisions, (2) the registration of securities provisions, (3) the registration of securities brokers and dealers provisions, or (4) a combination of these provisions of the federal laws. To bring some similarity to the various "blue sky" laws, a Uniform Securities Act was proposed for adoption by all states beginning in 1956. Since that time, the Uniform Securities Act has been the model for "blue sky" laws. A majority of states have used the uniform proposal as a guideline when enacting or amending their "blue sky" laws.

REGISTRATION REQUIREMENTS

Despite the trend toward uniformity, state laws still vary a great deal in their methods of regulating both the distribution of securities and the practices of the securities industry within each state. For example, state regulations concerning the requirements of registering securities vary widely. States have chosen one of the following types of regulations: (1) registration by notification or (2) registration by qualification. Registration by notification allows issuers to offer securities for sale automatically after a stated time period expires, unless the administrative agency takes action to prevent the offering. This is very similar to the registration process under the Federal Securities Act of 1933. Registration by qualification usually requires a more detailed disclosure by the issuer. Under this type of regulation, a security cannot be offered for sale until the administrative agency grants the issuer a license or certificate to sell securities.

In an attempt to resolve some of this conflict over the registration procedure, the drafters of the Uniform Securities Act may have compounded the problem. This act adopts the registration by notification process for an issuer who has demonstrated stability and performance. Registration by qualification is required by those issuers who do not have a proven record and who are not subject to the Federal Securities Act of 1933. In addition, the Uniform Securities Act created a third procedure—registration by coordination. For those issuers of securities who must register with the SEC, duplicate documents are filed with the state's administrative agency. Unless a state official objects, the state registration becomes effective automatically when the federal registration statement is deemed effective.

EXEMPTIONS

To further compound the confusion about "blue sky" laws, various exemptions of the securities or transactions have been adopted by the states. Four basic exemptions from "blue sky" laws have been identified. Every state likely has enacted at least one and perhaps a combination of these exemptions. Among these common four are the exemption (1) for an isolated transaction, (2) for an offer or sale to a limited number of offerees or purchasers within a stated time period, (3) for a private offering, and (4) for a sale if the number of holders after the sale does not exceed a specified number.

This second type of exemption probably is the most common exemption since it is part of the Uniform Securities Act. Nevertheless, states vary on whether the exemption applies to offerees or to purchasers. There also is great variation on the maximum number of such offerees or purchasers involved. That number likely ranges between five and thirty-five, depending on the applicable "blue sky" law. The time period for the offers or purchases, as the case may be, also may vary; however, twelve months seems to be the most common period.

Usually the applicable time limitation is worded to read, for example, "*any* twelve-month time period." In essence, this language means that each day starts a new time period running. For example, assume a security is exempt from "blue sky" registration requirements if the issuer sells (or offers to sell) securities to no more than thirty-five investors during any twelve-month period. Furthermore, assume the following transactions occur, with each investor being a different person or entity:

On February 1, 1986, issuer sells to five investors.

On June 1, 1986, issuer sells to ten investors.

On September 1, 1986, issuer sells to ten investors.

On December 1, 1986, issuer sells to five investors.

On March 1, 1987, issuer sells to five investors.

On May 1, 1987, issuer sells to ten investors.

Only thirty investors are involved during the twelve-month period following February 1, 1986. However, forty investors are purchasers during the twelve months following June 1, 1986. Therefore, this security and the transactions involved are not exempt from the "blue sky" law. Civil as well as criminal liability may result for failure to comply with applicable legal regulations.

Although "blue sky" laws may cause confusion due to their variation, ignorance of the state legal requirements is no defense. This confusion is furthered when the business person considers the applicability of federal securities laws as well as the variety of "blue sky" laws. To diminish this confusion, any person involved in the issuance or subsequent transfer of securities should consult with lawyers and accountants as well as other experts who have a working knowledge of securities regulations.

19. Ethical Considerations

Because of the importance of complying with the financial reporting and disclosure requirements of the securities laws, many companies have developed explicit policies recognizing the legal and social obligations involved. Caterpillar's Code of Ethics, for example, includes the following statements:

ACCOUNTING RECORDS AND FINANCIAL REPORTING

Accounting is called the "universal language" of business. Therefore, those who rely on the company's records—investors, creditors, and other decision makers and interested parties—have a right to information that is timely and true.

The integrity of Caterpillar accounting and financial records is based on validity, accuracy, and completeness of basic information supporting entries to the company's books of account. All employees involved in creating, processing, or recording such information are held responsible for its integrity.

Every accounting or financial entry should reflect exactly that which is described by the supporting information. There must be no concealment of information from (or by) management, or from the company's independent auditors.

Employees who become aware of possible omission, falsification, or inaccuracy of accounting and financial entries, or basic data supporting such entries, are held responsible for reporting such information. These reports are to be made as specified by corporate procedure.

A basic premise of Caterpillar's financial reporting is that conservatism in determining earnings is in the best long-term interests of the company and its shareholders. This means the accounting practices followed by Caterpillar are those which minimize: (1) the possibility of overstating reported earnings; and (2) the likelihood of having unexpected or extraordinary adjustments in future periods.

DISCLOSURE OF INFORMATION

In a free society, institutions flourish and businesses prosper not only by customer acceptance of their products and services, but also by public acceptance of their conduct.

Therefore, the public is entitled to a reasonable explanation of operations of a business, especially as those operations bear on the public interest. Larger economic size logically begets an increased responsibility for such public communication.

In pursuit of these beliefs, the company will:

1 Respond to public inquiries—including those from the press and from governments—with answers that are prompt, informative, and courteous.

2 Keep investors, securities trading markets, employees, and the general public informed about Caterpillar on a timely, impartial basis.

REVIEW QUESTIONS

1 Identify the terms in column A by matching each with the appropriate statement in column B.

A		*B*
(1) Registration statement	(a)	An advertisement made during the waiting period. It announces the security, its price, by whom orders will be executed, and from whom a prospectus may be obtained
(2) Prospectus	(b)	A participant in the distribution of a security who guarantees the sale of an issue
(3) Tombstone ad	(c)	The individual or business organization that offers a security for sale
(4) Insider	(d)	The document that contains financial and other information. It must be filed with the SEC prior to any sale of a security
(5) Issuer	(e)	A party who controls or is controlled by the issuer
(6) Controller person	(f)	A person who owns more than 10 percent of a security of an issuer or who is a director of an officer of an issuer
(7) Underwriter	(g)	Any person who contracts with a purchaser or who exerts a substantial role which causes a purchase transaction to occur
(8) Seller	(h)	A document or pamphlet that includes the essential information contained in the registration statement. It is filed with the SEC and made available to potential investors.

2   Give four examples of transactions other than the sale of stocks or bonds that involve the sale of a security.

3   To secure a loan, Rubin pledged stock which he represented as being marketable and worth approximately $1.7 million. In fact, the stock was nonmarketable and practically worthless. He was charged with violating the Federal Securities Act of 1933. He claims that since no sale occurred, he is not guilty. Is he correct? Why, or why not?

4   Under the provisions of the Federal Securities Act of 1933, there are three important time periods concerning when securities may be sold or offered for sale. Name and describe these three time periods.

5   In an attempt to increase issuers' flexibility in raising capital, the SEC has adopted Rule 415 on shelf registration. Explain the meaning and purpose of shelf registration. What is the applicability of Rule 415?

6   Patrick, a promoter for a newly organized corporation, began to solicit purchasers of the corporation's stock. The corporation did not limit the number of potential shareholders, but it did not plan to sell more than $400,000 worth of securities. What is Patrick's responsibility under the provisions of the Federal Securities Act of 1933 with respect to registering this offering?

7   Betty, a buyer of unregistered securities from the "U-2-Can-B-Rich Co.," lost all her investment when the company filed for bankruptcy. What civil remedies does Betty have if these securities are subject to the Federal Securities Act of 1933?

8   Section 10(b) of the Federal Securities Exchange Act of 1934 and Rule 10b-5 are of fundamental importance in the law of securities regulations. What is the main purpose of this section and rule?

9   Donna, a corporate director, sold 100 shares of stock in her corporation on June 1, 1985. The selling price was $10.50 a share. Two months later, after the corporation had announced substantial losses for the second quarter of the year, Donna purchased 100 shares of the corporation's stock for $7.25 a share. Are there any problems with Donna's sale and purchase? Explain.

10   David, the president of a large corporation, participated in a managerial decision to expand business operations in the near future. Anticipating that the corporation's financial status would improve because of this decision, David purchased stock from Sandra, a shareholder who had no knowledge of the company's plans. The market value of the stock rose immediately after the decision was announced. Is David liable to Sandra for any profits made from this transaction? Why, or why not?

11   The Valley Loan Association (VLA) issued investment notes to various persons. The proceeds were used to make loans to customers of the association. VLA went bankrupt, and its president was charged with a criminal violation of the Federal Securities Law of 1933. He contended that the law was not applicable, because the notes were not securities. Was he correct? Why, or why not?

12   When given an ethical choice, should an executive of a company select the accounting practice that states income conservatively (low) or liberally (high)?

13   Eric Ethan, president of Inside-Outside Sports Equipment Company, had access to information which was not available to the general investor. What standard should Eric Ethan apply in deciding whether this information is so material as to prevent him from investing in his company prior to the information's public release?

Part Six
PROTECTING GROUPS

Chapter
17

Discrimination in Employment

1. Introduction

"That all men are created equal" was one of the "self-evident" truths recognized by the Founding Fathers in the Declaration of Independence. However, equality among all our citizens clearly has been an ideal rather that a fact. The Constitution itself implicitly recognizes slavery by saying that slaves should count as "three-fifths of all other Persons" for determining population in House of Representative elections. And, of course, that all *men* are created equal says nothing about women, who did not even get a constitutionally guaranteed right to vote until 1920.

Nowhere have effects of inequality and discrimination been felt more acutely than in the area of job opportunity. Historically, common law permitted employers to hire and fire virtually at will, unless restrained by contract or statute. Under this system, discrimination was permitted, and white males, the primary economic group, came to dominate the job market in their ability to gain employment and in their salaries and wages, at the expense of minorities and women.

Although the Civil Rights Act of 1866 contains a provision which plaintiffs now widely use in employment discrimination cases, such use is recent.

Passage of labor law in the 1920s and 1930s marks the first significant federal limitation on the relatively unrestricted right of employers to hire and fire. Then, in connection with the war effort, President Roosevelt issued executive orders in 1941 and 1943 requiring a clause prohibiting racial discrimination in all federal contracts with private contractors. Subsequent executive orders in the 1950s established committees to investigate complaints of racial discrimination against such contractors. Affirmative action requirements on federal contracts followed from executive orders of the 1960s.

The most important statute eliminating discriminatory employment practices, however, is the federal Civil Rights Act of 1964, as amended by the Equal Employment Opportunity Act of 1972. The bulk of this chapter focuses on Title VII of the 1964 act, the section which prohibits employment discrimination. We will also discuss the Equal Employment Opportunity Commission and federal laws (1) forbidding employment discrimination against the handicapped or on account of age, (2) mandating equal employment pay for women, and (3) prohibiting other employment-related civil rights violations.

2. The Civil Rights Act: General Provisions

The provisions of Title VII of the Civil Rights Act of 1964 apply to employers with fifteen or more employees. They also cover labor unions and certain others (see Table 17-1). The major purpose of these laws is to eliminate job discrimination against employees, job applicants, or union members based on race, color, religion, sex or national origin. Discrimination for any of these reasons is a violation of the law, except that employers, employment agencies, and labor unions can discriminate on the basis of religion, sex or national origin when these are **bona fide occupational qualifications (bfoq)** reasonably necessary to normal business operations. Title VII also permits discrimination if it results unintentionally from a seniority or merit system.

The types of employer action in which discrimination is prohibited include (1) discharge, (2) refusal to hire, (3) compensation, and (4) terms, conditions, or privileges of employment. The following case establishes that Title VII applies even to partnership promotion at a law firm.

TABLE 17-1 Employers and Others Covered by Title VII

1 Private employers with fifteen or more employees
2 Labor unions with fifteen or more members
3 Employment agencies
4 State and local governments (but elected officials are not covered)
5 Public and private educational institutions
6 Federal government (in most instances)

HISHON v. KING & SPALDING
104 S.Ct. 2229 (1984)

Petitioner Elizabeth Hishon accepted a position with respondent King and Spalding, a large Atlanta law firm in 1972. In 1978, she was considered for admission to the partnership and rejected. One year later, King and Spalding terminated her employment. Hishon sued the respondent, claiming discrimination in her partnership consideration that violated Title VII. The federal district court dismissed the complaint on the ground that Title VII was inapplicable to the selection of partners by a partnership. The federal Court of Appeals affirmed.

BURGER, C. J.: The issue before us is whether petitioner's allegations state a claim under Title VII, the relevant portion of which provides as follows:

"(a) It shall be an unlawful employment practice for an employer—(1) to fail or refuse to hire or to discharge any individual, or otherwise to discriminate against any individual with respect to his compensation, terms, conditions, or privileges of employment, because of such individual's race, color, religion, sex, or national origin." . . .

Because the underlying employment relationship is contractual, it follows that the "terms, conditions, or privileges of employment" clearly include benefits that are part of an employment contract. Here, petitioner in essence alleged that respondent made a contract to consider her for partnership. Indeed, this promise was allegedly a key contractual provision which induced her to accept employment. If the evidence at trial establishes that parties contracted to have petitioner considered for partnership, that promise clearly was a term, condition, or privilege of her employment. Title VII would then bind respondents to consider petitioner for partnership as the statute provides, i.e., without regard to petitioner's sex. The contract she alleges would lead to the same result.

Petitioner's claim that a contract was made, however, is not the only allegation that would qualify respondent's consideration of petitioner for partnership as a term, condition, or privilege of employment. An employer may provide its employees with many benefits that it is under no obligation to furnish by any expressed or implied contract. Such a benefit, though not a contractual right of employment, may qualify as a "privileg[e]" of employment under Title VII. A benefit that is part and parcel of the employment relationship may not be doled out in a discriminatory fashion, even if the employer would be free under the employment contract simply not to provide the benefit at all. Those benefits that comprise the "incidents of employment," or that form "an aspect of the relationship between employer and employees" may not be afforded in a manner contrary to Title VII.

Several allegations in petitioner's complaint would support the conclusion that the opportunity to become a partner was part and parcel of an associate's status as an employee at respondent's firm, independent of any allegation that such an opportunity was included in associates' employment contracts. Petitioner alleges that respondent's associates could regularly expect to be considered for partnership at the end of their "apprenticeships," and it appears that lawyers outside the firm were not routinely so considered. Thus, the benefit of partnership consideration was allegedly linked directly with an associate's status as an employee, and this linkage was far more than coincidental: petitioner alleges that respondent explicitly used the prospect of ultimate partnership to induce young lawyers to join the firm. Indeed, the importance of the partnership decision to a lawyer's status as an associate is underscored by the allegation that associates' employment is terminated if they are not elected to become partners. These allegations, if proved at trial, would suffice to show that partnership consideration was a term, condition, or privilege of an associate's employment at respondent's firm, and accordingly that partnership consideration must be without regard to sex.

Respondent contends that advancement to partnership may never qualify as a term, condition, or privilege of employment for purposes of Title VII. . . . [R]espondent asserts that elevation to partnership entails a change in status from an "employee" to an "employer." However, even if respondent is correct that a partnership invitation is not itself an offer of employment, Title VII would nonetheless apply and preclude discrimination on the basis of sex. The benefits a plaintiff is denied need not be employment to fall within Title VII's protection; it need only be a term, condition, or privilege of employment. It is also of no consequence that employment as an associate necessarily ends when an associate becomes a partner. A benefit need not accrue before a person's employment is completed to be a term, condition, or privilege of that employment relationship. Pension benefits, for example, qualify as terms, conditions, or privileges of employment even though they are received only after employment terminates. . . .

. . . [R]espondent argues that application of Title VII in this case would infringe constitutional rights of expression or association. Although we have recognized that the activities of lawyers may make a "distinctive contribution . . . to the ideas and beliefs of your society," respondent has not shown how its ability to fulfill such a function would be inhibited by a requirement that it consider petitioner for partnership on her merits. Moreover, as we have held in another context, "[i]nvidious private discrimination may be characterized as a form of exercising freedom of association protected by the First Amendment, but it has never been accorded affirmative constitutional protections." . . .

We conclude that petitioner's complaint states a claim cognizable under Title VII. Petitioner therefore is entitled to her day in court to prove her allegations. The judgment of the Court of Appeals is reversed, and the case is remanded for further proceedings consistent with this opinion. [*It is so ordered.*]

Employment *agencies* are prohibited from either *failing to refer* or from *actually referring* an individual for employment on the basis of race, color, religion, sex or national origin. This prohibition differs from the law binding *employers*, where it is unlawful only to fail or refuse to hire on discriminatory grounds—the affirmative act of hiring for a discriminatory reason is apparently not illegal. For example, assume that a contractor with a government contract seeks a qualified black engineer and requests an employment agency to refer such an individual. The agency complies with the request, and a black is referred and hired. Unless a white applicant was discriminated against, the employer probably did not commit an unlawful practice; but the employment agency, by referring an individual on the basis of his color, unquestionably *did* commit a unlawful practice under Title VII.

Employers, unions, and employment agencies are prohibited from discriminating against an employee, applicant or union member because he or she has made a charge, testified, or participated in an investigation or hearing under the act, or otherwise opposed any unlawful practice.

Note that regarding general hiring, referrals, advertising, and admissions to training or apprenticeship programs, Title VII allows discrimination only on the basis of religion, sex or national origin and only where these considerations are bona fide occupational qualifications. For example, it is legal for a Baptist church to refuse to engage a Lutheran minister. EEOC guidelines on sex discrimination consider sex to be a bona fide occupational qualification, for example, where it is necessary for authenticity or genuineness in hiring an actor or actress. The omission of *race* and *color* from this exception must mean that Congress does not feel these two factors are ever bona fide occupational qualifications.

Additional exemptions exist with respect to laws creating preferential treatment for veterans and to hiring based on professionally developed ability tests that are not designed or intended to be used to discriminate. Such tests must bear a relationship to the job for which they are administered, however.

3. Enforcement Procedures

The Civil Rights Act of 1964 created the Equal Employment Opportunity Commission. This agency has the primary responsibility of enforcing the provisions of the act. The EEOC is composed of five members, not more than three of whom may be members of the same political party. They are appointed by the President, with the advice and consent of the Senate, and serve a five-year term. In the course of its investigations, the Equal Employment Opportunity Commission has broad authority to hold hearings, obtain evidence, and subpoena and examine witnesses under oath.

Under the Equal Employment Opportunity Act of 1972, the EEOC can file a civil suit in federal district court and represent a person charging a violation of the act. However, it must first exhaust efforts to settle the claim. Remedies which may be obtained in such an action include reinstatement with back pay for the victim of an illegal discrimination and injunctions against future violations of the act by the defendant. Since discrimination complaints can take years to litigate to a conclusion, the size of back pay awards is often substantial (see Table 17-2). What can an employer accused of discrimination do to limit the amount of back pay awarded? Consider the next case.

TABLE 17-2 Selected Recent Awards in Employee Discrimination Cases

Defendant	Plaintiff(s)	Award or Settlement
University of Minnesota	250 female faculty members	$40 million, plus $2 million attorneys' fees
General Motors	Females and minorities	$42.5 million
Nabisco	8,000 women	$5 million
Leeway Motor Freight	Eighty-two black employees	$2.8 million
Federated Department Stores	Three employees	$2.3 million, plus attorneys' fees
Burlington Northern, Inc.	4,000 black employees	$10 million
Kemper Group	Female employees	$3 million
State Farm	Black employees	$4 million
Northwest Airlines	Female employees	$52.2 million
Geneva Tire and Rubber Company	Two female employees	$118,000, plus $138,000 attorneys' fees
Alabama Power Company	Black employees	$1.7 million

FORD MOTOR CO. v. EQUAL EMPLOYMENT OPPORTUNITY COMM.

102 S.Ct. 3057

In June 1971, three women applied for jobs at a Ford Motor Co. warehouse as "picker-packers." At that time, no woman had ever worked in that capacity at the Ford warehouse. Ford, however, filled its vacant positions with men. The women filed a charge with the EEOC claiming sex discrimination. In July 1973, Ford offered "picker-packer" positions to two of the women, without seniority retroactive to their original applications. They declined, partially because they were unwilling to abandon the seniority they had gained at other employment they held. In 1984, they lost that employment. In 1975, the EEOC sued Ford, seeking injunctive relief and back pay for the women. The district court awarded the women back pay in an amount equal to the "difference between the amount they would have earned had they been hired in August 1971, and the amounts actually earned" between that date and the date of the court's order. Both the district court and, later, the Court of Appeals rejected Ford's contention that two of the women were not entitled to back pay accruing after the dates on which they declined Ford's offer of employment. The Supreme Court granted Ford's petition for certiorari.

O'CONNOR, J.: This case presents the question whether an employer charged with discrimination in hiring can toll the continuing accrual of back pay liability under § 706(g) of Title VII simply by unconditionally offering the claimant the job previously denied, or whether the employer also must offer seniority retroactive to the date of the alleged discrimination.

The question has considerable practical significance because of the lengthy delays that too often attend Title VII litigation. The extended time it frequently takes to obtain satisfaction in the courts may force a discrimination claimant to suffer through years of underemployment or unemployment before being awarded the job the claimant deserves. Court delays, of course, affect all litigants. But for the victim of job discrimination, delay is especially unfortunate. The claimant cannot afford to stand aside while the wheels of justice grind slowly toward the ultimate resolution of the lawsuit. The claimant needs work that will feed a family and restore self-respect. A job is needed—now. In this case, therefore, we must determine how best to fashion the remedies available under Title VII to fulfill this basic need.

In this case, Ford and the EEOC offer competing standards to govern back pay liability. Ford argues that if an employer unconditionally offers a claimant the job for which he previously applied, the claimant's rejection of that offer should toll the continuing accrual of back pay liabililty. The EEOC, on the other hand defends the lower court's rule, contending that back pay liability should be tolled only by the rejection of an offer that includes seniority retroactive to the date on which the alleged discrimination occurred. Our task is to determine which of these standards better coincides with the "larger objectives" of Title VII.

The "primary objective" of Title VII is to bring employment discrimination to an end by "achieving equality of employment opportunities and removing barriers that have operated in the past to favor an identifiable group . . . over other employees." "[T]he preferred means for achieving" this goal is through "[c]ooperation and voluntary compliance."

To accomplish this objective, the legal rules fashioned to implement Title VII should be designed, consistent with other Title VII policies, to encourage Title VII defendants promptly to make curative, unconditional job offers to Title VII claimants, thereby bringing defendants into "voluntary compliance" and ending discrimination far more quickly than could litigation proceeding at its often ponderous pace. Delays in litigation unfortunately are now commonplace, forcing the victims of discrimination to suffer years of underemployment or unemployment before they can obtain a court order awarding them the jobs unlawfully denied them. In a better world, perhaps, law suits brought under Title VII would speed to judgment so quickly that the effects of legal rules on the behavior of the parties during the pendency of litigation would not be as important a consideration. We do not now live in such a world, however, as this case illustrates.

The rule tolling the further accrual of back pay liability if the defendant offers the claimant the job originally sought well serves that objective of ending discrimination through voluntary compliance, for it gives an employer a strong incentive to hire the Title VII claimant. While the claimant may be no more attractive than the other job applicant, a job offer to the claimant will free the employer of the threat of liability for further back pay damages. Since paying back pay damages is like paying an extra worker who never came to work, Ford's proposed rule gives the Title VII claimant a decided edge over other competitiors for the job he seeks.

The rule adopted by the court below, on the other hand, fails to provide the same incentive, because it makes hiring the Title VII claimant more costly than hiring one of the other applicants for the same job. To give the claimant retroactive seniority before an adjudication of liability, the employer must be willing to pay the additional costs of the fringe benefits that come with the seniority that newly hired workers usually do not receive. More important, the employer must also be prepared to cope with the deterioration in morale, labor unrest, and reduced productivity that may be engendered by inserting the claimant into the seniority ladder over the heads of the incumbents who have earned their places through their work on the job. In many cases, moreover, disruptions of the existing seniority system will violate a collective-bargaining agreement, with all that such a violation entails for the employer's labor relations. Under the rule adopted by the court below, the employer must be willing to accept all these additional costs if he hopes to toll his back pay liability by offering the job to the claimant. As a result, the employer will be less, rather than more, likely to hire the claimant.

In sum, the Court of Appeals' rule provides no incentive to employers to hire Title VII claimants. The rule advocated by Ford, by contrast, powerfully motivates employers to put Title VII claimants to work, thus ending ongoing discrimination as promptly as possible.

In conclusion, we find that the rule adopted by the court below disserves Title VII's primary goal of getting the victims of employment discrimination into the jobs they deserve as quickly as possible. The rule, moreover, threatens the interests of other innocent employees by disrupting the established seniority hierarchy, with the attendant risk that an innocent employee will be unfairly laid off or disadvantaged because a Title VII claimant unfairly has been granted seniority.

On the other hand, the rule that a Title VII claimant's rejection of a defendant's job offer normally ends the defendant's ongoing responsibility for back pay suffers neither of these disadvantages while nevertheless adequately satisfying Title VII's compensation goals. Most important, it also serves as a potent force on behalf of Title VII's objective of bringing discrimination to an end more quickly than is often possible through litigation. For these reasons we hold that, absent special circumstances, the rejection of an employer's unconditioned job offer ends the accrual of potential back pay liability. We reverse the judgment of the Court of Appeals and remand for proceedings consistent with this opinion. [*So ordered.*]

In enacting Title VII, Congress made it clear that it did not intend to preempt states' fair employment laws. Where state agencies begin discrimination proceedings, the EEOC must wait sixty days before it starts action. Furthermore, if a state law provides relief to a discrimination charge, the EEOC must notify the appropriate state officials and wait sixty days before continuing action.

An employee must file charges of illegal discrimination with EEOC within 180 days after the alleged unlawful practice occurred. If the EEOC does not act within a certain time period, the employee may personally file a civil action in federal district court against the employer.

A Title VII plaintiff must initially show that actions taken by the employer were likely based on an illegal discriminatory basis, such as race. For example, a Title VII violation may be established by showing that the defendant's employment policies or practices, even though applied equally to all job applicants, were nevertheless discriminatory in effect against a particular group. That is, the defendant selected applicants for hire or promotion in a pattern significantly different from that of racial minorities or women available in the pool of applicants. The employer can defeat the plaintiff's case by showing that the policies used are job-related and based on a legitimate consideration. However, the plaintiff may still prove a violation by showing that other selection devices or practices would serve the employer's legitimate interest in picking the right person for the right job, without having undesirable discriminatory effects.

Even though the employer's practices do not have a disparate impact on minorities, a plaintiff may also prove his or her case by showing (1) that he or she belongs to a minority (2) that he or she applied and was qualified for a job for which the employer was seeking applicants (3) that despite his or her qualifications he or she was rejected and (4) that the job remained open and the employer continued to seek applicants from persons with the plaintiff's qualifications. Here, too, the employer can prevail by showing a legitimate nondiscriminatory reason for the plaintiff's rejection. For example, an employer would not be expected to fill the position of cashier with an applicant who had a prior record of embezzlement.

CURRENT TRENDS

Under Reagan administration appointees, the EEOC has reduced the number of *pattern and practice cases* it chooses to file. Based on statistical profiles of employer work forces by race and sex, these cases show bias through statistical imbalances rather than by proving discriminatory intent. However, the EEOC has continued to prosecute individual complaints vigorously. Note that private plaintiffs can still maintain pattern and practice cases and that a change in presidential administration might induce the EEOC once again to involve itself in such cases on a large scale.

4. Discrimination on the Basis of Race or Color

The integration of blacks into the mainstream of American society was the primary objective of the Civil Rights Act of 1964. Title VII, which deals with employment practices, was recognized by Congress as being the key to achieving this goal. Without equal employment opportunities, blacks can hardly enjoy other guaranteed rights, such as access to public accommodations.

Title VII prohibits discriminatory employment practices based on race or color which involve *recruiting, hiring* and *promotion* of employees. Of course, intentional discrimination in these matters is illegal, but as previously stated, **discrimination-in-effect** is also forbidden. Such discrimination arises from an employer's policies or practices which apply equally to everyone but which discriminate in greater proportion against minorities and have no relation to job qualification. Table 17-3 gives examples of discrimination in effect. Often at issue in discrimination-in-effect cases is whether a discriminatory policy or

TABLE 17-3   Examples of Discrimination in Effect

1 Denying employment to unwed mothers when minorities have a higher rate of illegitimate births than whites
2 Refusing to hire persons because of poor credit rating when minorities are disproportionately affected
3 Refusing to hire persons with arrest records when minorities have higher arrest rates than whites
4 Giving hiring priority to relatives of present employees when minorities are underrepresented in the work force
5 Using discriminatory personnel tests which have no substantial relation to job qualification

practice relates to job qualifications. Courts require proof, not mere assertion, of job relatedness before upholding an employer's discriminatory personnel test or other practice.

The law also prohibits discrimination in *employment conditions* and *benefits*. EEOC decisions have found such practices as the following to be violations: permitting racial insults in the work situation; maintaining all-white or all-black crews for no demonstrable reasons; providing better housing for whites than blacks; and granting higher average Christmas bonuses to whites than blacks for reasons that are not persuasive to the Commission.

5. Discrimination on the Basis of National Origin

Title VII's prohibition against national origin discrimination protects Hispanics and other ethnic groups in the population. Discrimination concerning the speaking of a native language is a frequent source of national origin lawsuits.

For instance, courts have ruled illegal an employer's rule against speaking Spanish during working time without the employer's showing a business need to understand all conversations between Hispanic employees. On the other hand, some courts have held that if jobs require contact with the public, requirements that employees speak some English *may* be a bona fide occupational qualification.

Direct foreign investment in the United States has doubled and redoubled in recent years. This increasing investment has presented some unusual issues of employment discrimination law. For instance, many commercial treaties with foreign countries give foreign companies operating in the United States the right to hire executive-level employees "of their choice." Does this mean that foreign companies in the United States can discriminate as to their managerial employees on a basis forbidden under Title VII? In 1982, the Supreme Court partially resolved this issue by ruling that civil rights laws applied to a Japanese company that did business through a subsidiary incorporated in this country.

6. Discrimination on the Basis of Religion

As was noted, religious corporations, associations, or societies can discriminate in all their employment practices on the basis of religion, but not on the basis of race, color, sex, or national origin. Other employers cannot discriminate on the basis of religion in employment practices, and they must make reasonable accommodation to the religious needs of their employees if it does not result in undue hardship to them. In the following case, the Supreme Court provided guidance on how far employers must go reasonably to accommodate religious needs of their workers.

TRANS WORLD AIRLINES, INC. v. HARDISON
97 S.Ct. 2264 (1977)

WHITE, J.: . . . Petitioner Trans World Airlines (TWA) operates a large maintenance and overhaul base in Kansas City, Mo. . . . [R]espondent Larry G. Hardison was hired by TWA to work as a clerk in the Stores Department at its Kansas City base. Because of its essential role in the Kansas City operation, the Stores Department must operate 24 hours per day, 365 days per year, and whenever an employee's job in that department is not filled, an employee must be shifted from another department, or a supervisor must cover the job, even if the work in other areas may suffer.

Hardison, like other employees at the Kansas City base, was subject to a seniority system contained in a collective-bargaining agreement that TWA maintains with petitioner International Association of Machinists and Aerospace Workers (IAM). . . .

In the spring of 1968 Hardison began to study the religion known as the Worldwide Church of God. One of the tenets of that religion is that one must observe the Sabbath by refraining from performing any work from sunset on Friday until sunset on Saturday. . . . Hardison was asked to work Saturdays when a fellow employee went on vacation. TWA agreed to permit the union to seek a change of work assignments for Hardison, but the union was not willing to violate the seniority provisions set out in the collective-bargaining contract, and Hardison had insufficient seniority to bid for a shift having Saturdays off.

A proposal that Hardison work only four days a week was rejected by the company. Hardison's job was essential and on weekends he was the only available person on his shift to perform it. To leave the position empty would have impaired Supply Shop functions, which were critical to airline operations; to fill Hardison's position with a supervisor or an employee from another area would simply have undermanned another operation; and to employ someone not regularly assigned to work Saturdays would have required TWA to pay premium wages.

When an accommodation was not reached, Hardison refused to report for work on Saturdays. A transfer to the twilight shift proved unavailing since that schedule still required Hardison to work past sundown on Fridays. After a hearing, Hardison was discharged on grounds of insubordination for refusing to work during his designated shift.

Hardison, having first invoked the administration remedy provided by Title VII, brought this action for injunctive relief in the United States District Court against TWA and IAM, claiming that his discharge by TWA constituted religious discrimination in violation of Title VII. . . . Hardison's claim of religious discrimination rested on 1967 EEOC guidelines requiring employers "to make reasonable accommodations to the religious needs of employees" whenever such accommodation would not work an "undue hardship," and on similar language adopted by Congress in the 1972 amendments to Title VII.

After a bench trial, the District Court ruled in favor of the defendants. . . . As the District Court construed the Act, TWA had satisfied its "reasonable accommodation" obligations, and any further accommodation would have worked an undue hardship on the company.

The Eighth Circuit Court of Appeals reversed the judgment for TWA. . . . The Court of Appeals held that TWA had not made reasonable efforts to accommodate Hardison's religious needs under the 1967 EEOC guidelines in effect at the time the relevant events occurred. In its view, TWA had rejected three reasonable alternatives, any one of which would have satisfied its obligation without undue hardship. First, within the framework of the seniority system, TWA could have permitted Hardison to work a four-day week, utilizing in his place a supervisor or another worker on duty elsewhere. That this would have caused other shop functions to suffer was insufficient to amount to undue hardship in the opinion of the Court of Appeals. Second—according to the Court of Appeals, also within the bounds of the collective-bargaining contract—the company could have filled Hardison's Saturday shift with other available personnel competent to

do the job, of which the court said there were at least 200. That this would have involved premium overtime pay was not deemed an undue hardship. Third, TWA could have arranged a "swap between Hardison and another employee either for another shift or for the Sabbath days." In response to the assertion that this would have involved a breach of the seniority provisions of the contract, the court noted that it had not been settled in the courts whether the required statutory accommodation to religious needs stopped short of transgressing seniority rules. . . .

We disagree with the Court of Appeals in all relevant respects. . . . Any shift or change was impossible within the seniority framework and the union was not willing to violate the seniority provision set out in the contract to make a shift or change. As the record shows, Hardison himself testified [TWA] was willing, but the union was not, to work out a shift or job trade with another employee. . . .

Hardison and the EEOC insist that the statutory obligation to accommodate religious needs takes precedence over both the collective-bargaining contract and the seniority rights of TWA's other employees. We agree that neither a collective-bargaining contract nor a seniority system may be employed to violate the statute, but we do not believe that the duty to accommodate requires TWA to take steps inconsistent with the otherwise valid agreement. . . . Without a clear and express indication from Congress, we cannot agree with Hardison and the EEOC that an agreed-upon seniority system must give way when necessary to accomodate religious observances. . . .

Had TWA nevertheless circumvented the seniority system by relieving Hardison of Saturday work and ordering a senior employee to replace him, it would have denied the latter his shift preference so that Hardison could be given his. . . . There were no volunteers to relieve Hardison on Saturdays, and to give Hardison Saturdays off, TWA would have had to deprive another employee of his shift preference at least because he did not adhere to a religion that observed the Saturday Sabbath.

Title VII does not contemplate such unequal treatment. The repeated, unequivocal emphasis of both the language and the legislative history of Title VII is on eliminating discrimination in employment, and such discrimination is proscribed when it is directed against majorities as well as minorities. . . . It would be anomalous to conclude that by "reasonable accomodation" Congress meant that an employer must deny the shift preferences of some employees, as well as deprive some of them of their contractual rights, in order to accommodate or prefer the religious needs of others, and we conclude that Title VII does not require an employer to go that far. . . .

[A]bsent a discriminatory purpose, the operation of a seniority system cannot be an unlawful employment practice even if the system has some discriminatory consequences. . . .

To require TWA to bear more than a [slight] cost in order to give Hardison Saturdays off is an undue hardship. Like abandonment of the seniority system, to require TWA to bear additional costs when no such costs are incurred to give other employees the days off that they want would involve unequal treatment of employees on the basis of their religion. . . . While incurring extra costs to secure a replacement for Hardison might remove the necessity of compelling another employee to work involuntarily in Hardison's place, it would not change the fact that the privilege of having Saturdays off would be allocated according to religious beliefs. . . .

In the absence of clear statutory language or legislative history to the contrary, we will not readily construe the statute to require an employer to discriminate against some employees in order to enable others to observe their Sabbath. [*Reversed.*]

In another case, the Supreme Court let stand a lower court ruling that an employee cannot be required to pay union dues if she or he has religious objections to unions. There, it held that a union had violated the Civil Rights Act by forcing the company to fire a Seventh Day Adventist who did not comply with a collective-bargaining agreement term that all employees must pay union dues. This was despite the union's contention that it had made "reasonable accommodation" to the worker's religious needs by offering to give any dues paid by him to charity.

7. Discrimination on the Basis of Sex

CIVIL RIGHTS ACT
Historically, states have enacted many laws supposedly designed to protect women. For example, many states by statute have prohibited the employment of women in certain occupations such as those which require lifting heavy objects. Others have barred women from working during the night or working more than a given number of hours per week or day. A federal district court held that a California state law which required rest periods for women

only was in violation of Title VII. Some statutes prohibit employing women for a specified time after childbirth. Under EEOC guidelines, such statutes are not a defense to a charge of illegal sex discrimination and do not provide an employer with bona fide occupational qualification in hiring standards. Other EEOC guidelines forbid employers (1) to classify jobs as male or female, and (2) to advertise in help-wanted columns that are designated male or female, unless sex is a bona fide job qualification. Similarly, employers may not have separate male and female seniority lists.

Table 17-4 gives examples of prohibited acts of sex discrimination under Title VII.

Whether sex is a bona fide occupational qualification (and discrimination is thus legal) has been raised in several cases. The courts have tended to consider this exception narrowly. In the following cases involving hiring *no* bona fide occupational qualification was found to exist: a rule requiring airline stewardesses, but not stewards, to be single; a policy of hiring only females as flight cabin attendants; a rule against hiring females with preschool age children, but not against hiring males with such children; and a telephone company policy against hiring females as switchmen because of the alleged heavy lifting involved in the job. In the last case, the court held that for a bona fide occupational qualification to exist, there must be "reasonable cause to believe, that is, a factual basis for believing, that all or substantially all women would be unable to perform safely and efficiently the duties of the job involved." The Supreme Court has indicated that for such a qualification to exist, sex must be provably relevant in job performance.

PREGNANCY DISCRIMINATION ACT

The Pregnancy Discrimination Act amended the Civil Rights Act in 1978. Under it, employers can no longer discriminate against women workers who become pregnant or give birth. Thus, employers with health or disability plans must cover pregnancy, childbirth, and related medical conditions in the same manner other conditions are covered. The law covers unmarried as well as married pregnant women. It also states that an employer cannot force a pregnant woman to stop working until her baby is born, provided she is still

TABLE 17-4 Examples of Illegel Sex Discrimination

1 A radio station's refusing to hire a female newscaster because "news coming from a woman sounds like gossip"
2 A bank's allowing males but not females to smoke at their desks
3 A utility company's allowing women to retire at age fifty, while requiring men to wait until age fifty-five
4 A company's failing to promote women to overseas positions because foreign clients were reluctant to do business with a woman
5 A hospital's firing a pregnant x-ray technician for health reasons instead of giving her a leave of absence
6 A company's failure to stop repeated, offensive sexual flirtations on the part of some of its employees

capable of performing her duties properly. And, the employer cannot specify how long a leave of absence must be taken after childbirth. Coverage for abortion is not required by the statute, unless an employee carries to term and her life is endangered, or unless she develops medical complications because of an abortion. If a woman undergoes an abortion, though, all other benefits provided for employees, such as sick leave, must be provided to her.

Note that sex discrimination applies to discrimination against men as well as against women. Consider the following case decided by the Supreme Court in 1983.

NEWPORT NEWS SHIPBUILDING AND DRY DOCK CO. v. EEOC
103 S.Ct. 2622 (1983)

In 1978, Title VII was amended by the Pregnancy Discrimination Act to prohibit discrimination on the basis of pregnancy. The employer amended its health insurance plan to provide its female employees with hospitalization benefits for pregnancy-related conditions, but the plan provided less extensive pregnancy benefits for spouses of male employees. The EEOC guidelines indicated that the amended plan was unlawful, and the employer filed suit. The federal district court upheld the lawfulness of the amended plan. The Court of Appeals, however, reversed.

STEVENS, J.: Ultimately the question we must decide is whether petitioner has discriminated against its male employees with respect to their compensation, terms, conditions, or privileges of employment because of their sex within the meaning of Title VII. . . .

Section 703(a) makes it an unlawful employment practice for an employer to "discriminate against any individual with respect to his compensation, terms, conditions, or privileges of employment, because of such individual's race, color, religion, sex or na-

tional origin. . . ." Health insurance and other fringe benefits are "compensation, terms, conditions, or privileges of employment." Male as well as female employees are protected against discrimination. Thus, if a private employer were to provide complete health insurance coverage for the dependents of its female employees and no coverage at all for the dependents of its male employees, it would violate Title VII. Such a practice would not pass the simple test of Title VII discrimination for it would treat a male employee with dependents "in a manner which but for that person's sex would be different." The same result would be reached even if the magnitude of the discrimination were smaller. For example, a plan that provided complete hospitalization coverage for the spouses of female employees but did not cover spouses of male employees when they had broken bones would violate the Title VII by discriminating against male employees.

Petitioner's practice is just as unlawful. Its plan provides limited pregnancy-related benefits for employees' wives, and affords more extensive coverage for employees' spouses for all other medical conditions requiring hospitalization. Thus the husbands of female employees receive a specified level of hospitalization coverage for all conditions; the wives of male employees receive such coverage except for pregnancy-related conditions. The 1978 Act makes clear that it is discriminatory to treat pregnancy-related conditions less favorably than other medical conditions. Thus petitioner's plan unlawfully gives married male employees a benefit package for their dependents coverage provided to married female employees.

There is no merit to petitioner's argument that the prohibitions of Title VII do not extend to discrimination against pregnant spouses because the statute applies only to discrimination in employment. A two-step analysis demonstrates the fallacy in this contention. The Pregnancy Discrimination Act has now made clear that, for all Title VII purposes, discrimination based on a woman's pregnancy is, on its face, discrimination because of her sex. And since the sex of the spouse is always the opposite of the sex of the employee, it follows, inexorably, that discrimination against female spouses in the provision of fringe benefits is also discrimination against male employees. By making clear that an employer could not discriminate on the basis of an employee's pregnancy, Congress did not erase the original prohibition against discrimination on the basis of an employee's sex.

. . . The pregnancy limitation in this case violates Title VII by discriminating against male employees. [*Affirmed.*]

EQUAL PAY ACT

Other federal legislation which pertains to sex discrimination in employment includes the *Equal Pay Act of 1963*. Presently administered by the EEOC, the act prohibits an employer from discriminating on the basis of sex in the payment of wages for equal work performed. For jobs to be equal, they must require "equal skill, effort, and responsibility" and must be performed "under similar working conditions." Discrimination is allowed if it arises from a seniority system, a merit system, a piecework production system, or on any factor other than sex.

The focus of Equal Pay Act cases is whether the male and the female jobs being compared involve "equal" work. Courts have recognized that "equal" does not mean "identical," it means "substantially" equal. Thus, courts have ruled "equal" the work of male barbers and female beauticians and of male tailors and female seamstresses. Differences in male and female jobs descriptions will not totally protect employers against charges of equal pay infractions. The courts have held that "substantially equal" work done on different machines would require the employer to compensate male and female employees equally.

In 1983, the Supreme Court ruled that discriminatory male and female pay differences can also be illegal under Title VII. In *County of Washington v. Gunther*, the Court decided that plaintiffs can use evidence of such pay differences to help prove intentional sex discrimination even where the work performed is not "substantially equal." Relying on the *Gunther* case, several

TABLE 17-5 Median Incomes of Male and Female Employees

Occupational Group	Male Median Income	Female Median Income
Managers	$27,994	15,511
Professionals	26,053	15,199
Technical	21,621	13,212
Sales	17,433	14,774
Skilled crafts	17,186	9,333
Clerical	16,050	10,435
Machine operators	15,121	8,309
Service workers	7,344	3,785

Source: *Business and Society Review* (Winter 1985).

lower courts have held that women must be paid equally with men who perform comparable work. For instance, a federal district court ruled that the state of Washington discriminated against secretaries (mostly women) by paying them less than maintenance and other personnel (mostly men). The federal court of appeals reversed. The **comparable worth** theory is highly controversial and has not yet been upheld by the Supreme Court.

In spite of the Equal Pay Act, evidence suggests that there are still substantial differences between what employers pay male and female employees, even in the same occupational groups (See Table 17-5.)

EMPLOYMENT PRACTICES THAT MAY BE CHALLENGED

8. Testing and Educational Requirements

Employers have used a number of tools to help them find the right person for the right job in hiring and promoting employees. Among these are interviews, references, minimum educational requirements (such as a high school diploma), and personnel tests. Obviously, interviewers can be biased, even if they try not to be. One study indicated that interviewers tended to select tall men for sales positions because interviewers *subconsciously* related height with potential sales success. References may not be so reliable, either. A previous employer's letter may reflect personal biases against an applicant that were not related to job performance.

At the other extreme, an employer may give a poor employee a top recommendation due to sympathy or fear of a lawsuit in case the letter is somehow obtained by the employee. Advocates of personnel tests in the selection process feel they are very valuable in weeding out the wrong persons for a job and picking the right ones. They believe reliance on tests results eliminates biases which interviewers or former employers who give references may have. However, as the following case indicates, even where "bottom line" employment practices of the employer favor the group alleging discrimination, test use may be illegal under Title VII.

CONNECTICUT v. TEAL
102 S.Ct. 2525 (1982)

Black employees of a Connecticut state agency were promoted provisionally to supervisors. To attain permanent status as supervisors, they had to pass a written exam as a first step for eligibility. Fifty-four percent of black candidates and 79 percent of the white candidates passed the exam. Respondent black employees failed the exam. They filed suit against petitioners (state of Connecticut and certain state agencies and officials) alleging that the discriminatory test violated Title VII of the Civil Rights Act. Meanwhile, before trial, the petitioners made promotions from the eligibility list, advancing 22.9 percent of the blacks on the list, but only 13.5 percent of the whites. Petitioners urged that this "bottom line" result, more favorable to blacks than to whites, was a complete defense to the suit. The district court agreed. On appeal, the Court of Appeals reversed, holding that the examination results alone established a prima facie case of violation of Title VII. The state of Connecticut petitioned the Supreme Court, which granted certiorari.

BRENNAN, J.: We consider here whether an employer sued for violation of Title VII of the Civil Rights Act of 1964 may assert a "bottom line" theory of defense. Under that theory, as asserted in this case, an employer's acts of racial discrimination in promotions—effected by an examination having disparate impact—would not render the employer liable for the racial discrimination suffered by employees barred from promotion if the "bottom line" results of the promotional process was an appropriate racial balance. We hold that the "bottom line" does not preclude respondent-employees from establishing a prima facie case, nor does it provide petitioner-employer with a defense to such a case.

Respondents base their claim on our construction of this provision in *Griggs v. Duke Power Co.* Prior to the enactment of Title VII, the Duke Power Company restricted its black employees to the labor department. Beginning in 1965, the company required all employees who desired a transfer out of the labor department to have either a high school diploma or to achieve a passing grade on two professionally prepared aptitude tests. New employees seeking positions in any department other than labor had to possess both a high school diploma and a passing grade on these two examinations. Although these requirements applied equally to white and black employees and applicants, they barred employment opportunities to a disproportionate number of blacks. While there was no showing that the employer had a racial purpose or invidious intent in adopting these requirements, this Court held that they were invalid because they had a disparate impact and were not shown to be related to job performance. . . .

Griggs and its progeny have established a three-part analysis of disparate impact claims. To establish a prima facie case of discrimination, a plaintiff must show that the facially neutral employment practice had a significantly discriminatory impact. If that showing is made, the employer must then demonstrate that "any given requirement [has] a manifest relationship to the employment in question," in order to avoid a finding of discrimination. Even in such a case, however, the plaintiff may prevail, if he shows that employer was using the practice as a mere pretext for discrimination.

Petitioners' examination, which barred promotion and had a discriminatory impact on black employees, clearly falls within the literal language of § 703(a)(2), as interpreted by *Griggs*. The statute speaks, not in terms of jobs and promotions, but in terms of *limitations* and *classifications* that would deprive any individual of employment *opportunities*. A disparate impact claim reflects the language of § 703(a)(2) and Congress' basic objectives in enacting that statute: "to achieve equality of employment *opportunities* and remove barriers that have operated in the past to favor an identifiable group of white employees over other employees." When an employer uses a non-job-related barrier in order to deny a minority or woman applicant employment or promotion, and that barrier has a significant adverse effect on minorities or women, then the applicant has been deprived of an employment *opportunity* "because of . . . race, color, religion, sex or national origin." In other words, § 703(a)(2) prohibits discriminatory "artificial, arbitrary, and unnecessary barriers to employment" that "limit . . . or classify . . . applicants for employment . . . in any way which would deprive or tend to deprive any individual of employment *opportunities*." [*Emphasis added.*]

The decisions of this Court following *Griggs* also support respondents' claim. In considering claims of disparate impact under § 703(a)(2) this Court has consistently focused on employment and promotion requirements that create a discriminatory bar to *opportunities*. This Court has never read § 703(a)(2) as requiring the focus to be placed instead on the overall number of minority or female applicants actually hired or promoted. Thus *Dothard v. Rawlinson* found that minimum statutory height and weight requirements for correctional counselors were the sort of arbitrary barrier to equal employment opportunity for women forbidden by Title VII. Although we noted in passing that women constituted 36.89 percent of the labor force and only 12.9 percent of correctional coun-

selor positions, our focus was not on this "bottom line." We focused instead on the disparate effect that the minimum height and weight standards had on applicants: classifying far more women than men as ineligible for employment. Similarly, in *Albemarle Paper Co. v. Moody*, the action was remanded to allow the employer to attempt to show that the tests that he had given to his employees for promotion were job-related. We did not suggest that by promoting a sufficient number of the black employees who passed the examination, the employer could avoid this burden.

In short, the District Court's dismissal of respondents' claim cannot be supported on the basis that respondents failed to establish a prima facie case of employment discrimination under the terms of § 703(a)(2). The suggestion that disparate impact should be measured only at the bottom line ignores the fact that Title VII guarantees these individual respondents the *opportunity* to compete equally with white workers on the basis of job-related criteria. Title VII strives to achieve equality of opportunity by rooting out "artificial, arbitrary and unnecessary" employer-created barriers to professional development that have a discriminatory impact upon individuals. Therefore, respondents' rights under § 703(a)(2) have been violated, unless petitioners can demonstrate that the examination given was not an artificial, arbitrary, or unnecessary barrier, because it measured skills related to effective performance in the role of Welfare Eligibility Supervisor.

In sum, petitioners' nondiscriminatory "bottom line" is no answer, under the terms of Title VII, to respondents' prima facie claim of employment discrimination. Accordingly, the judgment of the Court of Appeals for the Second Circuit is affirmed, and this case is remanded to the District Court for further proceedings consistent with this opinion. [*It is so ordered.*]

As a result of court decisions and government enforcement guidelines, many companies have eliminated or sharply reduced testing as an employment tool, because compliance is too costly and time-consuming. Even if companies obtain what appears to be proper evidence that a given test is valid, the threat of a court challenge with its costs and bad publicity would still exist.

9. Height and Weight Requirements

Minimum or maximum height or weight job requirements apply equally to all job applicants, but if they have the effect of screening out applicants on the basis of race, national origin, or sex, the employer must demonstrate that such requirements are validly related to the ability to perform the work in question. For example, maximum size standards would be permissible, even if they favored women over men, if the available work space were too small to permit larger persons to perform the duties of the job properly. Most size requirements have dictated minimum heights or weights, often based on a stereotyped assumption that a certain amount of strength probably was necessary for the work that smaller persons might not have. In one case, a 5-foot, 5-inch, 130-pound Hispanic won a suit against a police department on the basis that the department's 5-foot, 8-inch minimum height requirement discriminated against Hispanics, who often are shorter than that standard. Later, he was hired when he passed the department's physical agility examination, which included dragging a 150-pound body 75 feet and scaling a 6-foot wall.

In the following case, the Supreme Court considered the legality of Alabama's statutory minimum height and weight requirements for prison guards, along with a Board of Corrections regulation which expressly limited prison jobs to men.

DOTHARD v. RAWLINSON
97 S.Ct. 2720 (1977)

Appellee Rawlinson, a 22-year-old college graduate whose major had been correctional psychology, applied for employment as a "correctional counselor" (prison guard) in Alabama. When her application was rejected because she failed to meet the minimum 120-pound weight requirement of an Alabama Statute, which also established a height minimum of 5 feet, 2 inches, Rawlinson filed a charge with the Equal Employment Opportunity Commission and ultimately brought a class action against appellant corrections officials alleging violations of the Civil Rights Act. The suit challenged: (1) the height and weight requirements of the Alabama Statute; and (2) "Regulation 204" of the Alabama Board of Corrections, which provided that only males could be assigned as correctional counselors to maximum security institutions for "contact positions" (positions requiring close physical proximity to inmates). A three-judge district court decided in appellee's favor, and the Supreme Court agreed to hear the appeal of the correctional officials.

STEWART, J.: . . . Like most correctional facilities in the United States, Alabama's prisons are segregated on the basis of sex. Currently the Alabama Board of Corrections operates four major all-male penitentiaries [T]hese are maximum security institutions. Their inmate living quarters are for the most part large dormitories, with communal showers and toilets that are open to the dormitories and hallways. The Draper and Fountain penitentiaries carry on extensive farming operations, making necessary a large number of strip searches for contraband when prisoners re-enter the prison building.

A correctional counselor's primary duty within these institutions is to maintain security and control of the inmates by continually supervising and observing their activities. . . .

The gist of the claim that the statutory height and weight requirements discriminate against women does not involve an assertion of purposeful discriminatory motive. It is asserted, rather, that these facially neutral qualification standards work in fact disproportionately to exclude women from eligibility for employment by the Alabama Board of Corrections. We dealt in [other cases] with similar allegations that facially neutral employment standards disproportionately excluded Negroes from employment, and those cases guide our approach here. . . .

When the height and weight restrictions are combined, Alabama's statutory standards would exclude 41.13% of the female population while excluding less than one percent of the male population. . . .

[W]e cannot say that the District Court

was wrong in holding that the statutory height and weight standards had a discriminatory impact on women applicants. . . .

We turn, therefore, to the appellants' argument that they have rebutted the prima facie case of discrimination by showing that the height and weight requirements are job related. These requirements, they say, have a relationship to strength, a sufficient but unspecified amount of which is essential to effective job performance as a correctional counselor. In the District Court, however, the appellants produced no evidence correlating the height and weight requirements with the requisite amount of strength thought essential to good job performance. Indeed, they failed to offer evidence of any kind in specific justification of the statutory standards.

If the job-related quality that the appellants identify is bona fide, their purpose could be achieved by adopting and validating a test for applicants that measures strength directly. Such a test, fairly administered, would fully satisfy the standards of Title VII because it would be one that "measure[s] the person for the job and not the person in the abstract." But nothing in the present record even approaches such a measurement.

For the reasons we have discussed, the District Court was not in error in holding that Title VII of the Civil Rights Act of 1964, as amended, prohibits application of the statutory height and weight requirements to Rawlinson and the class she represents.

Unlike the statutory height and weight requirements, Regulation 204 explicitly discriminates against women on the basis of their sex. In defense of this overt discrimination, the appellants rely on § 703(e) of Title VII, which permits sex-based discrimination "in those certain instances where . . . sex . . . is a bona fide occupational qualification reasonably necessary to the normal operation of that particular business or enterprise."

The District Court rejected the bona fide

occupational qualification (bfoq) defense, relying on the virtually uniform view of the federal courts that § 703(e) provides only the narrowest of exceptions to the general rule requiring equality of employment opportunities. . . . The Federal courts have agreed that is it impermissible under Title VII to refuse to hire an individual woman or man on the basis of stereotyped characterizations of the sexes. . . .

In the particular factual circumstances of this case, however, we conclude that the District Court erred in rejecting the State's contention that Regulation 204 falls within the narrow ambit of the bfoq exception.

The environment in Alabama's penitentiaries is a peculiarly inhospitable one for human beings of whatever sex. Indeed, a federal district court has held that the conditions of confinement in the prisons of the State, characterized by "rampant violence" and a "jungle atmosphere," are constitutionally intolerable. The record in the present case shows that because of inadequate staff and facilities, no attempt is made in the four maximum security male penitentiaries to classify or segregate inmates according to their offense or level of dangerousness. . . . Consequently, the estimated 20% of the male prisoners who are sex offenders are scattered throughout the penitentiaries' dormitory facilities. . . .

In the usual case, the argument that a particular job is too dangerous for women may appropriately be met by the rejoinder that it is the purpose of Title VII to allow the individual woman to make that choice for herself. More is at stake in this case, however, than an individual woman's decision to weigh and accept the risks of employment in a "contact" position in a maximum security male prison.

The essence of a correctional counselor's job is to maintain prison security. A woman's relative ability to maintain order in a male, maximum security, unclassified penitentiary of the type Alabama now runs could be directly reduced by her womanhood. . . . In a prison system where violence is the order of the day, where inmate access to guards is facilitated by dormitory living arrangements, where every institution is understaffed, and where a substantial portion of the inmate population is composed of sex offenders mixed at random with other prisoners, there are few visible deterrents to inmate assaults on women custodians. . . .

There was substantial testimony from experts on both sides of this litigation that the use of women as guards in "contact" positions under the existing conditions in Alabama maximum security male penitentiaries would pose a substantial security problem, directly linked to the sex of the prison guard. On the basis of that evidence, we conclude that the District Court was in error in ruling that being male is not a bona fide occupational qualification for the job of correctional counselor in a "contact" position in an Alabama male maximum security penitentiary. [*The judgment is accordingly affirmed in part and reversed in part, and the case is remanded to the District Court for further proceedings consistent with this opinion. It is so ordered.*]

Even though the Supreme Court found that sex was a bona fide occupational qualification in *Rawlinson*, note that the bfoq exception is narrowly interpreted.

10. Appearance Requirements

Employers often have set grooming standards for their employees. Those regulating hair length of males or prohibiting beards or mustaches have been among the most common. Undoubtedly, motivation for these rules stems from the feeling of the employer that the image it projects to the public through its employees will be adversely affected if their appearance is not "proper." It is unclear whether appearance requirements are legal or illegal, since there have been rulings both ways. Refusing to hire applicants because of a company policy prohibiting "handlebar" and "Fu Manchu" mustaches and bushy hairstyles was found illegal. Although the policies appeared neutral on their face, it was held that they had the effect of discriminating against blacks.

In another case, a black employee argued that he was wrongfully fired for breaking a company rule prohibiting beards. Dermatologists testified that the plaintiff had a condition called "razor bumps" (which occurs when the tightly curled facial hairs of black men become ingrown from shaving) and that the only known cure was for him not to shave. Although the federal appeals court found that the plaintiff "was prejudiced by" the employer's regulation, it held in favor of the company, ruling that its "slight racial impact" was justified by the "business purpose" it served. However, a conflicting opinion in still another case upheld an employee's right to wear a beard because of razor bumps.

11. Affirmative Action Programs and Reverse Discrimination

Since the 1940s, a series of presidential executive orders have promoted nondiscrimination and affirmative action by employers who contract with the federal government. The authority for these orders rests with the President's executive power to control the granting of federal contracts. As a condition to obtaining such contracts, employers must agree contractually to take affirmative action to avoid unlawful discrimination in recruitment, employment, promotion, training, rate of compensation, and layoff of workers.

The **affirmative action** requirement means that federally contracting employers must actively recruit members of minority groups being underused in the work force. That is, employers must hire members of these groups when there are fewer minority workers in a given job category than one could reasonably expect, considering their availability. In many instances, employers must develop written affirmative action plans and set goals and timetables for bringing minority (or female) work forces up to their percentages in the available labor pool.

The Labor Department administers executive orders through its Office of Federal Contract Compliance Programs (OFCCP). The OFCCP can terminate federal contracts with employers who do not comply with its guidelines and can make them ineligible for any future federal business. For instance, it required Uniroyal, Inc., to give its female employees an estimated $18 million in back pay to compensate for past employment discrimination. The alternative was elimination of $36 million of existing federal contracts and ineligibility for future federal business.

Not all affirmative action programs are imposed on employers by the government. Many employers have adopted programs voluntarily or through collective-bargaining agreements with unions. Sometimes these affirmative action programs have subjected employers to charges of **reverse discrimination** when minorities or women with lower qualifications or less seniority than white males are given preference in employment or training. Even though such programs are intended to remedy the effects of present or past discrimination or other barriers to equal employment opportunity, white males have argued that the law does not permit employers to discriminate against *them* on the basis of race or sex any more than it allows discrimination against minorities or women.

The employee in the following case challenged his employer's affirmative action plan, relying in part on a 1976 Supreme Court ruling that the 1964 Civil Rights Act prohibits discrimination in private employment against white persons as well as against nonwhites.

UNITED STEELWORKERS OF AMERICA v. WEBER
99 S.Ct. 2721 (1979)

In 1974, petitioners United Steelworkers of America (USWA) and Kaiser Aluminum and Chemical Corporation (Kaiser) entered into a master collective-bargaining agreement covering terms and conditions of employment at 15 Kaiser plants. The agreement included an affirmative action plan designed to eliminate conspicuous racial imbalances in Kaiser's then almost exclusively white craft work forces by reserving for black employees 50 percent of the openings in in-plant craft-training programs until the percentage of black craft workers in a plant was commensurate with the percentage of blacks in the local labor force. Pursuant to the national agreement, *Kaiser*, rather than continuing its practice of hiring trained outsiders, established a training program to train its production workers to fill craft openings, selecting trainees on the basis of seniority, with the proviso that at least 50 percent of the trainees were to be black until the percentage of black skilled craft workers in the plant approximated the percentage of blacks in the local labor force. During the plan's first year of operation, seven black and six white craft trainees were selected from the plant's production work force, with the most junior black trainee having less seniority than several white production workers whose bids for admission were rejected. Thereafter, respondent, one of those white production workers, instituted this class action in federal district court, alleging that because the affirmative action program had resulted in junior black employees receiving training in preference to more senior white employees, respondent Weber and other similarly situated white employees had been discriminated against in violation of the provisions of Title VII of the Civil Rights Act of 1964 that makes it unlawful to "discriminate . . . because of . . . race" in hiring and in the selection of apprentices for training programs. The district court entered judgment in favor of the plaintiff class, and the Court of Appeals affirmed, holding that all employment preferences based upon race, including those incidental to bona fide affirmative action plans, violate Title VII's prohibition against racial discrimination in employment. The Supreme Court granted certiorari.

BRENNAN, J.: . . . The only question before us is the narrow statutory issue of whether Title VII *forbids* private employers and unions from voluntarily agreeing upon bona fide affirmative action plans that accord racial preferences in the manner and for the purpose provided in the Kaiser-USWA plan. That question was expressly left open in *McDonald v. Santa Fe Trail Trans. Co.*, 427 U.S. 273 (1976) which held, in a case not involving affirmative action, that Title VII protects whites as well as blacks from certain forms of racial discrimination.

Respondent argues that Congress intended in Title VII to prohibit all race-conscious affirmative action plans. Respondent's argument rests upon a literal interpretation of Sec. 703(a) and (d) of the Act. Those sections make it unlawful to "discriminate . . . because of . . . race" in hiring and in the selection of apprentices for training programs. Since, the argument runs, *McDonald v. Santa Fe Trans. Co., supra*, settled that Title VII forbids discrimination against whites as well as blacks, and since the Kaiser-USWA affirmative action plan operates to

discriminate against white employees solely because they are white, it follows that the Kaiser-USWA plan violates Title VII.

Respondent's argument is not without force. But it overlooks the significance of the fact that the Kaiser-USWA plan is an affirmative action plan voluntarily adopted by private parties to eliminate traditional patterns of racial segregation. In this context respondent's reliance upon a literal construction of Sec. 703(a) and (d) and upon *McDonald* is misplaced. . . .

It plainly appears from the House Report accompanying the Civil Rights Act that Congress did not intend wholly to prohibit private and voluntary affirmative action efforts as one method of solving this problem. The report provides:

No bill can or should lay claim to eliminating all of the causes and consequences of racial and other types of discrimination against minorities. There is reason to believe, however, that national leadership provided by the enactment of Federal legislation dealing with the most troublesome problems *will create an atmosphere conducive to voluntary or local resolution of other forms of discrimination.* H. R. Rep. No. 914, 88th Cong., 1st Sess. (1963), at 18. [*Emphasis added*]

. . . [W]e cannot agree with respondent that Congress intended to prohibit the private sector from taking effective steps to accomplish the goal that Congress designed Title VII to achieve. The very statutory words intended as a spur or catalyst to cause "employers and unions to self-examine their employment practices and to endeavor to eliminate, so far as possible, the last vestiges of an unfortunate and ignominious page in the country's history," cannot be interpreted as an absolute prohibition against all private, voluntary, race-conscious affirmative action efforts to hasten the elimination of such vestiges. It would be ironic indeed if a law triggered by a

Nation's concern over centuries of racial injustice and intended to improve the lot of those who had "been excluded from the American dream for so long" constituted the first legislative prohibition of all voluntary, private, race-conscious efforts to abolish traditional patterns of racial segregation and hierachy.

. . . Had Congress meant to prohibit all race-conscious affirmative action, as respondent urges, it easily could have answered both objections by providing that Title VII would not require or *permit* racially preferential integration efforts. But Congress added Sec. 703(j) which addresses only the first objection. The section provides that nothing contained in Title VII "shall be interpreted to *require* any employer . . . to grant preferential treatment . . . to any group because of the race . . . of such . . . group on account of" a de facto racial imbalance in the employer's work force. The section does *not* state that "nothing in Title VII shall be interpreted to *permit*" voluntary affirmative efforts to correct racial inbalances. . . .

We therefore hold that Title VII's prohibition against racial discrimination does not condemn all private, voluntary, race-conscious affirmative action plans.

We need not today define in detail the line of demarcation between permissible and impermissible affirmative action plans. It suffices to hold that the challenged Kaiser-USWA affirmative action plan falls on the permissible side of the line. The purposes of the plan mirror those of the statute. Both were designed to break down old patterns of racial segregation and hierachy. . . .

At the same time the plan does not unnecessarily trammel the interests of the white employees. The plan does not require the discharge of white workers and their replacement with new black hires. Nor does the plan create an absolute bar to the advancement of white employees; half of those trained in the program will be white. Moreover, the plan is a temporary measure; it is not intended to maintain racial balance, but simply to eliminate a manifest racial imbalance. Preferential selection of craft trainees at the Gramercy plant will end as soon as the percentage of black skilled craft workers in the Gramercy plant approximates the percentage of blacks in the local labor force.

We conclude, therefore, that the adoption of the Kaiser-USWA plan for the Gramercy plant falls within the area of discretion left by Title VII to the private sector voluntarily to adopt affirmative action plans designed to eliminate conspicuous racial imbalance in traditionally segregated job categories. . . . [*Reversed.*]

The *Weber* case leaves open the question of where the line between legal and illegal affirmative action plans lies. However, a plan patterned closely after Kaiser's apparently would be legal. It would appear, though, that a legal program could not exclude whites altogether, or fire whites to make room for blacks, and it would have to be temporary.

The EEOC has issued guidelines intended to protect employers who set up affirmative action plans. This indicated that Title VII is not violated if an employer determines that there is a reasonable basis for concluding that such a plan is appropriate, and the employer takes "reasonable" affirmative action.

For example, if an employer discovers that it has a job category where one might expect to find more women and minorities employed than are actually in the work force, the employer has a reasonable basis for affirmative action.

In the early 1980s, the Labor Department eased OFCCP regulations on 75 percent of the firms which do business with the federal government. Firms with fewer than 250 employees and federal contracts of under $1 million no longer must prepare written affirmative action plans for hiring women and minorities. The OFCCP has also begun to limit its use of back pay awards to specific individuals who can show an actual loss due to violation of OFCCP guidelines.

In an affirmative action move intended to help minority-owned businesses, Congress passed the 1977 Public Works employment plan. This requires that 10 percent of the work on federally funded local public works projects be performed by minority contractors or subcontractors. Contractor groups attacked the 10 percent requirement as an unconstitutional form of reverse discrimination, in violation of the Fifth and Fourteenth Amendments. However, in 1980 the Supreme Court upheld validity of the requirement.

12. Seniority Systems

Seniority systems give priority to those employees who have worked longer for a particular employer, or in a particular line of employment of the employer. Employers may institute seniority systems on their own, but in a union shop they are usually the result of collective bargaining. Their terms are spelled out in the agreement between the company and the union. Seniority systems often determine the calculation of vacation, pension, and other fringe benefits. They also control many employment decisions such as the order in which employees may choose shifts or qualify for promotions or transfers to different jobs. They also are used to select the persons to be laid off when an employer is reducing its labor force. As a result of seniority, the last hired are usually the first fired. Decisions based on seniority have in recent years been challenged as violating the laws relating to equal employment opportunity. Challenges often arose when recently hired members of minority groups were laid off during periods of economic downturn. Firms with successful affirmative action programs often lost most of their minority employees.

Section 703(h) of the Civil Rights Act of 1964 provides that, notwithstanding other provisions in the act, it is not an unlawful employment practice for an employer to apply different employment standards pursuant to a bona fide (good faith) seniority system if the differences are not the result of an *intention* to discriminate. The issue in the following case is whether a seniority system can be used if it has a discriminatory impact on minorities and if it has been instituted after the adoption of an affirmative action plan.

MEMPHIS FIRE DEPARTMENT v. STOTTS
104 S.Ct. 2576 (1984)

In 1980, the city of Memphis made a settlement in a class action employment discrimination suit in federal district court, and a consent decree was approved. The purpose of the decree was to remedy the hiring and promotion practice of the Memphis Fire Department with respect to blacks. In 1981, the city announced that budget deficits made it necessary to lay off some personnel on a "last hired, first fired" basis under the city-wide seniority plan. The district court ordered the city to modify its layoff plan to protect black employees hired or promoted under the consent decree. The Court of Appeals affirmed.

WHITE, J.: The issue at the heart of this case is whether the District Court exceeded its powers in entering an injunction requiring white employees to be laid off, when the otherwise applicable seniority system would have called for the layoff of black employees with less seniority. We are convinced that the Court of Appeals erred in resolving this issue and in affirming the District Court. . . .

The Court of Appeals held that even if the injunction is not viewed as compelling compliance with the terms of the decree, it was still properly entered because the District Court had inherent authority to modify the decree when an economic crisis unexpectedly required layoffs which, if carried out as the City proposed, would undermine the affirmative action outlined in the decree and impose an undue hardship on respondents. This was true, the court held, even though the modification conflicted with a bona fide seniority system adopted by the City. The

Court of Appeals erred in reaching this conclusion.

Section 703(h) of Title VII provides that is is not an unlawful employment practice to apply different standards of compensation, or different terms, conditions, or privileges of employment pursuant to a bona fide seniority system, provided that such differences are not the result of an intention to discriminate because of race. It is clear that the City had a seniority system, that its proposed layoff plan conformed to that system, and that in making the settlement the City had not agreed to award competitive seniority to any minority employee whom the City proposed to lay off. The District Court held that the City could not follow its seniority system in making its proposed layoffs because its proposal was discriminatory in effect and hence not a bona fide plan. Section 703(h), however, permits the routine application of a seniority system absent proof of an intention to discriminate. Here, the District Court itself found that the layoff proposal was not adopted with the purpose or intent to discriminate on the basis of race. Nor had the City in agreeing to the decree admitted in any way that it had engaged in intentional discrimination. The Court of Appeals was therefore correct in disagreeing with the District Court's holding that the layoff plan was not a bona fide application of the seniority system, and it would appear that the City could not be faulted for following the seniority plan expressed in its agreement with the Union. The Court of Appeals nevertheless held that the injunction was proper even though it conflicted with the seniority system. This was error. . . .

If individual members of a plaintiff class demonstrate that they have been actual victims of the discriminatory practice, they may be awarded competitive seniority and given their rightful place on the seniority roster. It is also clear, however, that mere membership in the disadvantaged class is insufficient to warrant a seniority award; each individual must prove that the discriminatory practice had an impact on him. Even when an individual shows that the discriminatory practice has had an impact on him, he is not automatically entitled to have a non-minority employee laid off to make room for him. He may have to wait until a vacancy occurs, and if there are non-minority employees on layoff, the Court

must balance the equities in determining who is entitled to the job. Here, there was no finding that any of the blacks protected from layoff had been a victim of discrimination and no award of competitive seniority to any of them. Nor had the parties in formulating the consent decree purported to identify any specific employee entitled to particular relief other than those listed in the exhibits attached to the decree. It therefore seems to us that . . . the Court of Appeals imposed on the parties as an adjunct of settlement something that could not have been ordered had the case gone to trial and the plaintiffs proved that a pattern of discrimination existed. [*Reversed.*]

OTHER STATUTES AND DISCRIMINATION IN EMPLOYMENT

13. Civil Rights Act of 1866

An important federal law which complements Title VII of the 1964 Civil Rights Act is the Civil Rights Act of 1866. One provision of that act, known as *Section 1981*, provides that "all persons . . . shall have the same right to make and enforce contracts . . . as enjoyed by white citizens." Since union memberships and employment relationships involve contracts, Section 1981 bans racial discrimination in these areas.

The courts have interpreted Section 1981 as giving a private plaintiff most of the same protections against racial discrimination that the 1964 Civil Rights Act provides. In addition, there are at least two advantages to the plaintiff who files a suit based on Section 1981. First, there are no procedural requirements for bringing such a suit, while there are a number of fairly complex requirements plaintiffs must follow before bringing a private suit under Title VII. For instance, they must file charges of discrimination with the EEOC within 180 days after the illegal practice occurs or lose their rights.

By using Section 1981, a plaintiff can immediately sue an employer in federal court but need not worry about losing rights if he or she fails to do so within 180 days. A second advantage to Section 1981 is that under it the courts can award damages to aggrieved plaintiffs. Although it permits recovery of back pay, Title VII does not allow for the assessment of damages. As a practical matter, parties alleging discrimination usually proceed under both Section 1981 and Title VII.

As interpreted by the courts, Section 1981 applies only to racial discrimination, although there is some authority for the position that it protects all non-citizens. It does not apply to discrimination based on sex, religion, or age. Ethnic groups are also unprotected, except that many courts have considered discrimination against Hispanics as forbidden on racial grounds.

14. Discrimination on the Basis of Age

Neither the Civil Rights Act nor the Equal Employment Opportunity Act forbids discrimination based on age. In 1967, however, Congress passed the Age Discrimination in Employment Act which protects persons between forty and sixty-five years old from job discrimination against them because of age. The act is enforced by the EEOC.

The 1978 amendments to the Age Discrimination in Employment Act prohibit mandatory retirement *before age seventy* for most workers employed by private businesses with over nineteen employees. With the exception of police and firefighters, almost all local and state employees are also protected by the act. And most employees of the federal government cannot be forced to retire at *any* age because of their years. "Bona fide executives" and "high policy makers" of private companies who will have pensions of at least $27,000 per year, however, can be forced into early retirement. The statute invalidates retirement plans and labor contracts which call for retirement before age seventy.

In one case under the act, Standard Oil Company of California agreed to pay $2 million in back wages to 160 employees who had been laid off and were over forty. Thus, if persons over forty are just as qualified as younger workers to handle their jobs, they usually must be kept. This cost-cutting is also illegal. One decision awarded three former department store executives $2.3 million for such discrimination. In another case, a firm transferred a sixty-year-old man to a job that required him to stand for long periods. When he died, his widow, arguing that the transfer was a subterfuge to induce him to retire, obtained a judgment against the firm for $750,000 in damages for illegal discrimination.

An important area of age discrimination litigation exists when age is a bona fide occupational qualification. It is recognized that as people grow older their physical strength, agility, reflexes, hearing, and vision tend to diminish in quality. However, this generally provides no legal reasons for discriminating against older persons as a class. Although courts will uphold job-related physical requirements if they apply on a case-by-case basis, they frequently find as illegal those policies which prohibit the hiring of persons beyond a maximum age, or which establish a maximum age beyond which employees are forced to retire for physical reasons. Thus, one court ruled that a mandatory retirement age of sixty-five was illegally discriminatory as applied to the job of district fire chief. To the contrary, another court ruled that the airlines could impose a maximum age for hiring a new pilot in light of a Federal Aviation Administration mandated retirement age for pilots.

Courts have disagreed on whether remedies for violation of the act include, in addition to reinstatement and wages lost, the psychological trauma of being fired or forced to resign illegally. One federal district court awarded $200,000 to a victim of age discrimination who was an inventor and scientist, for the psychological and physical effects suffered from being forced into early retirement at age sixty. Also awarded were out-of-pocket costs of $60,000 and attorney's fees of $65,000. Note that "willful" violations of the act entitle discrimination victims to _double damages_.

Since the 1978 amendments to the act, age discrimination claims have grown rapidly. In recent years they have more than doubled in number.

15. Discrimination on the Basis of Handicaps

To promote and expand employment opportunities for handicapped persons, both in the public and private sectors, Congress enacted the Rehabilitation Act of 1973. This statute requires each department and agency in the executive branch of the federal government to have an approved affirmative action plan for the hiring, placement, and advancement of qualified handicapped individuals. And under Section 503 of the Rehabilitation Act, every employer doing business with the federal government under a contract for over $2,500, must take affirmative action to hire and advance qualified handicapped persons at all levels, including executive. Section 503 affects about one-half the businesses in the United States and the twelve million or so employable handicapped persons in the population.

A handicapped person protected by the act is anyone with a physical or mental impairment that substantially limits a major life activity, or one who has a _record of_ such an impairment (this would include a rehabilitated mental patient, or a person with a history of cancer or heart condition). _All_ such handicapped persons are not covered, however. An individual must be "qualified," or capable of performing a particular job, with reasonable accommodation to his or her handicap. And an amendment to the act specifically provides that the term "handicapped individual" does not include any individual who is an alcoholic or drug abuser.

Note that employees with certain diseases may qualify as handicapped under the act. One federal Court of Appeals ruled that an employee with tuberculosis was handicapped. Under this reasoning, an AIDS victim would likely be protected by the act.

Both contractors and subcontractors must make "reasonable accommodation" to the physical and mental limitations of handicapped employees or applicants, unless it can be shown that such would involve an "undue hardship" to them. The cost of any necessary workplace accommodation and availability of alternatives bear upon the issue of undue hardship.

The Department of Labor's Office of Federal Contract Compliance Programs can enforce Section 503 of the act by forcing settlements of claims of discrimination by handicapped workers. Claims may be settled by hiring the claimants with payment of back wages and retroactive seniority or the like. In an extreme case, the government contract with the offending employer can be terminated.

16. Other Federal Legislation

Other federal legislation dealing with employment discrimination includes the National Labor Relations Act. The NLRB has ruled that appeals to racial prejudice in a collective-bargaining representation election constitute an unfair labor practice. The NLRB has also revoked the certification of unions which practice discriminatory admission or representation policies. Additionally, employers have an obligation to bargain with certified unions over matters of employment discrimination. Such matters are considered "terms and conditions of employment" and are thus mandatory bargaining issues. Note that the reverse discrimination issue in the *Weber* case arose because of an affirmative action plan in a collective-bargaining contract.

Finally, various other federal agencies may prohibit discriminatory employment practies under their authorizing statutes. The Federal Communications Commission, for example, has prohibited employment discrimination by its licensees (radio and television stations) and has required the submission of affirmative action plans as a condition of license renewal.

17. State Discrimination Laws

Federal laws concerning equal employment opportunity specifically permit state laws which impose additional duties and liabilities. In recent years, fair employment practices legislation has been introduced and passed by many state legislatures. At the time the federal Equal Employment Opportunity Act became effective, forty states had such laws, but their provisions varied considerably. A typical state act makes it an unfair employment practice for any employer to refuse to hire or otherwwise discriminate against any individual because of his or her race, color, religion, national origin, or ancestry. If employment agencies or labor organizations discriminate against an individual in any way because of one of the foregoing reasons, they are also guilty of an unfair employment practice. State acts usually set up an administrative body, generally known as the Fair Employment Practices Commission, which has the power to make rules and regulations and hear and decide charges of violations filed by complainants.

In addition, many states have enacted equal pay statutes similar to the federal one, but these have not proved to be very effective.

18. Avoiding Unfounded Discrimination Claims

Much discrimination in effect, and even intentional discrimination, occurs in employment situations. But most employers strive to obey equal employment laws. These employers still face discrimination claims, however, including many made by unsatisfactory employees who have been discharged or disciplined. How can employers protect themselves from unfounded discrimination claims in such instances? The best protection is a <u>system of adequate documentation</u>. Sometimes called the *paper fortress*, this documentation consists of job descriptions, personnel manuals, and employee personnel files.

Before handing anyone an employment application, the employer should insist that the person carefully study a job description. A <u>well-written job description</u> will help potential applicants eliminate themselves from job situations for which they lack interest or qualification. Applicant self-elimination helps employers later avoid having to dismiss disinterested or unqualified employees, which can lead to discrimination claims.

Once a new employee is hired, the employer should give the employee a <u>personnel manual</u>. This manual should include information about employee benefits and should also outline work rules and job requirements. The employer should go over the manual with the employee and answer any questions. <u>Clear identification of the employer's expectations and policies</u> helps provide a defense against discrimination claims if subsequent discipline or discharge of the employee becomes necessary. The employer should ask that the employee sign a form indicating receipt of the manual and the employer's explanation of its contents.

The employer should enter this form, with all other documentation relevant to an employee's work history, in the <u>employee's personnel file.</u> Regular written evaluations of employee performance should also be entered in the personnel file. A chronological record of unsatisfactory work performance is a very useful defense against an unjustified claim of employment discrimination following discipline or discharge.

Another piece of documentation which helps justify employers' decisions in light of equal employment law is a <u>written warning</u>. Anytime an employee breaks a work rule or performs unsatisfactorily the employer should issue the employee a written warning and should place a duplicate in the personnel file. The warning should explain specifically where the employee went wrong, that is, what work rule the employee violated, and it should give the employee the opportunity to place a letter of explanation in the personnel file. Employers should either have an employee sign that he or she has received a warning, or else note in the personnel file that the employee has received a copy of it.

Congress did not intend for equal employment laws to prevent employers from discharging unsatisfactory employees. Whatever the employee's race, sex, religion, or ethnic background, the employer should not hesitate to terminate the employee for unacceptable performance. In an actual termination conversation, however, the employer should provide the employee with <u>specific reasons for discharge</u>, taken from the personnel file. The employee should also be encouraged to succeed in other employment.

In combating unfounded discrimination claims, an adequate system of documentation is vital. However, other things are also important, such as having a specific company policy coupled with an effective employment program promoting nondiscrimination. Caterpillar has such a policy in its Code of Ethics.

AN EFFECTIVE EMPLOYMENT PROGRAM

We aspire to a high standard of excellence in human relationnships. Specifically, we intend to select and place employees on the basis of qualifications for the work to be performed—without discrimination in terms of race, religion, national origin, color, sex, age, or handicap unrelated to the task at hand.

REVIEW QUESTIONS

1 For each term in the left-hand column, match the most appropriate description in the right-hand column:

(1) Affirmative action

(2) Comparable worth

(3) Paper fortress

(4) Seniority system

(5) Reverse discrimination

(6) Discrimination in effect

(7) Bfoqs

(8) Section 1981

(a) Selection of employees for hire or promotion in a pattern significantly different from that of racial minorities or women available in the pool of job applicants

(b) Documentation including job descriptions, personnel manuals, and employee personnel files

(c) Job-related employment characteristics based on sex or religion

(d) A theory under which employees are paid equally based on jobs which are dissimilar but are rated equally

(e) Taking active steps to seek out and employ groups traditionally underrepresented in the work force

(f) A system to give priority to those employees who have worked longer for a particular employer

(g) Prohibits contractual discrimination based on race

(h) Employment discrimination against white males

2 Smith desires to join the private country club which operated the best golf course in his area. Under its rules, the club admits only persons of Lithuanian descent. If Smith is

refused membership solely because he is of English descent, what are his rights against the club under the Civil Rights Act of 1964?

3 Jennings Company, which manufactures sophisticated electronic equipment, hires its assembly employees on the basis of applicants' scores on a standardized mathematics aptitude test. It has been shown that those who scored higher on the test almost always perform better on the job. However, it has also been demonstrated that the use of the test in hiring employees has the effect of excluding blacks and other minority groups. Is this practice of the Jennings Company prohibited by the Civil Rights Act of 1964?

4 Martel, a competent male secretary to the president of ICU, was fired because the new president of the company believed it would be more appropriate to have a female secretary. (a) Has a violation of the law occurred? (b) Assume that a violation of the law has occurred and Martel decides to take an extended vacation after he is fired. Upon his return seven months later, Martel files suit in federal district court against ICU charging illegal discrimination under the Civil Rights Act of 1964. What remedies will be available to him under the act?

5 The Acme Corporation has a rule requiring all employees to be able to speak English. Is this rule illegal under the Civil Rights Act? Discuss.

6 The Fifth Methodist Church of a large city had two applicants for the job of church custodian. One was a Methodist, the other an atheist. The church hired the Methodist solely because of his religious beliefs and the atheist's lack thereof. Has the church violated the Civil Rights Act of 1964?

7 ADCO, an advertising agency, asked an employment agency to refer females to it who might be suitable to play the role of Mother Nature in a TV commercial ADCO was pre-

paring. The agency referred five women to ADCO, one of whom was selected for the part. Has either ADCO or the employment agency violated the Civil Rights Act?

8 First Bank carries a health insurance plan on all its employees. The insurance does not cover the medical expenses of voluntary pregnancy. Has First Bank violated the law?

9 Ortega, an employee of ABC, Inc., recently joined a church which forbids working on Saturdays, Sundays, and Mondays. Ortega requested that his employer change his work schedule from eight-hour days Monday through Friday to 10-hour days Tuesday through Friday. Ortega's request was refused because the employer was in operation only eight hours per day, five days a week. After a month during which Ortega failed to work on Mondays, he was fired, since the employer said that "only a full-time employee would be acceptable" for Ortega's position. What are Ortega's legal rights, if any?

10 Assume that the degree of job difficulty for secretaries and maintenance personnel is approximately the same. If your state pays secretaries (mostly women) an average salary which is $2,000 below that of maintenance personnel (mostly men), has it violated employment discrimination laws?

11 Tartel, Inc., had been guilty of flagrant discrimination against blacks in its hiring, promotion, and compensation of employees before the Civil Rights Act of 1964 was passed. After the act, Tartel decided to remedy the situation and to place blacks in 50 percent of all new openings created by expansion, or by the retirement, resignation, or death of persons in its almost exclusively white work force. Discuss the legality of Tartel's action.

12 Your company has traditionally hired males to do its assembly-line work. The assembly-line positions include jobs which re-

quire lifting and some that do not. Males are rotated between these jobs, all male workers being on the same pay scale. The company has recently started to hire females for the assembly line, but they only work in nonlifting positions. For this reason they are paid a lower wage scale than the men. The women employees sue. Discuss the considerations a court deciding the case should taken into account.

13 Cantrell, the controller of Xylec's, Inc., was forced to retire at age fifty-eight due to a general company policy. Although Cantrell had a company pension of $50,000 per year, she felt that her lifestyle would soon be hampered due to inflation since the pension provided for no cost-of-living increases. What are Cantrell's rights, if any?

14 A textile company discriminates against Washington, a black female, based on her race. Can she immediately sue the employer in federal district court? Explain.

15 A handicapped person applies for employment on the assembly line of the Johnson Corporation. Does the company violate the law by refusing to hire this person based on her handicap?

16 You have just been hired as personnel manager of a medium-sized corporation. Discuss what steps you can take to shield your company from unfounded claims of employment discrimination.

Chapter
18

Introduction to Labor Law

1. Introduction

Various statutes governing labor-management relations have been enacted by Congress to provide a framework in which management and labor can collectively make decisions on issues of importance to both. Such issues include wages to be paid workers, hours to be worked, and other terms and conditions of employment. This framework also recognizes that the public has an important stake in a workable system of **collective bargaining,** since it benefits not only employers and employees but the public interest as well. Because collective bargaining can only be successful if the bargaining power of the parties is equal, most laws regulating labor-management relations seek to equalize this bargaining power. As a result, some laws add to the bargaining position of labor while others add to that of management.

At the outset, understand that the law encourages workers to join together and bargain as a group with employers. This encouragement of union activity is the logical result of the inequality of bargaining power between any single employee and a business. Unions have had a significant impact on wages, hours, and conditions of employment, not only in unionized industries, but also in those which are not. In the latter, many of the goals of unions have been met in order to avoid unionization. At the present time, approximately 20 percent of the work force is unionized.

The major federal laws which govern labor-management relations are briefly described in Table 18-1. They are discussed in more detail later in this chapter.

TABLE 18-1 Federal Laws Governing Labor-Management Relations

Year	Statute	Summary of Major Provisions
1914	Clayton Act	Exempted union activity from the antitrust laws.
1926	Railway Labor Act	1 Governed collective bargaining for railroads and airlines. 2 Created the National Mediation Board to conduct union elections and mediate differences between employers and unions.
1932	Norris-LaGuardia Act	1 Outlawed yellow-dog contracts. 2 Prohibited federal courts from enjoining lawful union activities including picketing and strikes.
1934	Wagner Act (National Labor Relations Act)	1 Created the National Labor Relations Board (NLRB). 2 NLRB conducts union certification elections. 3 Outlawed certain conduct by management as unfair to labor (unfair labor practices). 4 Authorized NLRB to hold hearings on unfair labor practices and correct wrongs resulting therefrom.
1947	Taft-Hartley Act	1 Outlawed certain conduct by unions as unfair labor practices. 2 Provided for an eighty-day cooling-off period in strikes which imperil national health or safety. 3 Allowed states to enact right-to-work laws. 4 Created the Federal Mediation and Conciliation Service to assist in settlement of labor disputes.
1959	Landrum-Griffin Act (Labor-Management Reporting and Disclosure Act—LMRDA)	1 Bill of Rights for union members. 2 Required reports to the secretary of labor. 3 Added to the list of unfair labor practices.

FEDERAL LAWS BEFORE 1935

2. Clayton Act

The first federal statute of any importance to the labor movement was the Clayton Act of 1914. It contained two sections relating to labor. The first attempted to prohibit federal courts from enjoining activities such as strikes and picketing in disputes over terms or conditions of employment. This provision was narrowly construed by the Supreme Court and has had little impact. The second section stated that antitrust laws regulating anticompetitive contracts did not apply to labor unions or their members in lawfully carrying out their legitimate activities. This exemption covers legitimate union practices. A union that seeks by agreement with a nonlabor party to reduce competition for the benefit of such a party may be guilty of an antitrust violation.

To illustrate the labor union antitrust exemption, assume that a union and several employers enter into a collective-bargaining agreement that restricts the hours of operation of the employers. Such an agreement is immune from attack under the Sherman Antitrust Act. The national labor policy immunizes from the Sherman Act union-employer agreements on when, and on how long, employees must work.

3. Railway Labor Act

In 1926, Congress enacted the Railway Labor Act, which encouraged collective bargaining in the railroad industry to resolve labor disputes that might otherwise disrupt transportation. The act, which provided a means for dealing with labor disputes, was later extended to airlines; it applies to both air and rail transportation today. It established the three-member National Mediation Board, which must designate the bargaining representative for any given bargaining unit of employees in the railway or air transport industries. The Board generally does this by holding representation elections. The Railway Labor Act also outlawed certain *unfair labor practices* such as refusing to bargain collectively.

In 1951, Congress amended the Railway Labor Act to permit the union shop. A union shop permits a union and an employer to require all employees in the bargaining unit to join the union as a condition of continued employment. The act does not permit a union to spend an objecting employee's dues to support political causes, however. The use of money for political purposes is unrelated to the desire of Congress to prevent "free-riders"—those who get the benefits of the union without paying a fair share of the costs. There are other expenditures of dues that are improper. For example, the courts have held that the dues of nonunion members may not be used to pay for (1) litigation that does not involve the negotiation of agreements or the settlement of employee grievances, (2) general organizing efforts, and (3) publications not related to bargaining. The test is whether or not an expenditure is necessarily or reasonably incurred for the purpose of performing the duties of an exclusive representative of the employees in dealing with the employer on labor-management issues.

The National Mediation Board, unlike the National Labor Relations Board (NLRB), has no judicial power to hold hearings and issue cease and desist orders. Willful violations of the Railway Labor Act are punishable through criminal proceedings initiated by the Department of Justice in the regular federal court system. However, convictions are almost impossible to obtain because it is difficult to prove beyond any reasonable doubt that the commission of a given unfair labor practice was intentional.

When the parties to a dispute over proposed contract terms in the transportation industry cannot reach an agreement concerning rates of pay or working conditions, the National Mediation Board must attempt mediation of their differences. If mediation does not resolve their differences, the Board encourages voluntary arbitration. If the parties refuse arbitration and the dispute is likely to disrupt interstate commerce substantially, the Board informs the President, who then appoints a special emergency board. This emergency board also lacks any judicial power, but it encourages the parties to reach agreement by investigating the dispute and publishing its findings of fact and recommendations for settlement. During the investigation, which lasts thirty days, and for an additional thirty days after the report is issued, business is conducted without interruption. The parties, however, have no duty to comply with the special board's proposals. Thus, if no new collective-bargaining agreement is reached after the sixty-day period, lockouts by management and strikes by workers become legal.

In several cases since 1940, the Railway Labor Act has failed to resolve major disputes, necessitating special action by the President or the Congress. The transportation industry frequently has had its labor problems presented to the government for solution because the procedures of the Railway Labor Act were not such that all disputes can be resolved without irreparable damage to the public. It should be noted that the provisions previously discussed apply to assisting employers and unions in arriving at a collective-bargaining agreement where none currently is in force. The act requires compulsory arbitration of disputes concerning interpretation of existing contracts between the parties. This requirement is peculiar to the transportation industry.

4. Norris-LaGuardia Act

In 1932 the Norris-LaGuardia Act was passed by Congress. The first major provision of the Norris-LaGuardia Act made **yellow-dog contracts** (those forbidding union membership) unenforceable. The second listed specific acts of persons and organizations participating in labor disputes which were not subject to federal court injunctions. These included (1) striking or quitting work, (2) belonging to a labor organization, (3) paying strike or unemployment benefits to participants in a labor dispute, (4) publicizing the existence of a labor dispute or the facts related to it (including picketing), (5) peaceably assembling to promote their interests in a labor dispute, and (6) agreeing with others or advising or causing them to do any of the above acts without fraud or violence. These acts are given a liberal interpretation, as is illustrated by the following case which had its roots in international politics rather than in labor relations.

JACKSONVILLE BULK TERMINALS, INC. v. INTERNATIONAL LONGSHOREMEN'S ASSOC.
102 S.Ct. 2673 (1982)

After President Carter announced certain trade restrictions with the Soviet Union because of its intervention in Afghanistan, the defendant union announced that its members would not handle any cargo bound to, or coming from, the Soviet Union. When an affiliated local union refused to load certain goods (not included in the presidential embargo) bound for the Soviet Union, the employer of the union brought suit against the international union, its officers and agents, and the local union. The employer alleged that the union's work stoppage violated the terms of a collective-bargaining agreement which contained a no-strike clause and a provision requiring arbitration of disputes. The district court granted a preliminary injunction pending arbitration. The court reasoned that the political motivation behind the work stoppage rendered inapplicable Section 4 of the Norris-LaGuardia Act, which prohibits injunctions against strikes "in any case involving or growing out of any labor dispute."

MARSHALL, J.: Section 4 of the Norris-LaGuardia Act provides in part:

"No court of the United States shall have jurisdiction to issue any restraining order or temporary or permanent injunction in any case involving or growing out of any labor dispute to prohibit any person or persons participating or interested in such dispute . . . from doing, whether singly or in concert, any of the following acts:

(a) Ceasing or refusing to perform any work or to remain in any relation of employment."

Congress adopted this broad prohibition to remedy the growing tendency of federal courts to enjoin strikes by narrowly construing the Clayton Act's labor exemption from the Sherman Act's prohibition against conspiracies to restrain trade. This Court has consistently given the anti-injunction provisions of the Norris-LaGuardia Act a broad interpretation, recognizing exceptions only in limited situations where necessary to accommodate the Act to specific federal llegislation or paramount congressional policy.

The *Boys Markets* exception, . . . is relevant to our decision today. In *Boys Markets,* this Court . . . held that, in order to accom-

modate the anti-injunction provisions of Norris-LaGuardia to the . . . strong federal policy favoring arbitration, it was essential to recognize an exception to the anti-injunction provisions for cases in which the employer sought to enforce the union's contractual obligation to arbitrate grievances rather than to strike over them. . . .

The Employer argues that the Norris-LaGuardia Act does not apply in this case because the political motivation underlying the Union's work stoppage removes this controversy from that Act's definition of a "labor dispute." . . .

At the outset, we must determine whether this is a "case involving or growing out of any labor dispute" within the meaning of § 4 of the Norris-LaGuardia Act. Section 13(c) of the Act broadly defines the term labor dispute to include "any controversy concerning terms or conditions of employment."

The Employer argues that the existence of political motives takes this work stoppage controversy outside the broad scope of this definition. This argument, however, has no basis in the plain statutory language of the Norris-LaGuardia Act or in our prior interpretations of that Act. Furthermore, the argument is contradicted by the legislative history of not only the Norris-LaGuardia Act but also the 1947 amendments to the National Labor Relations Act (NLRA).

An action brought by an employer against the union representing its employees to enforce a no-strike pledge generally involves two controversies. First, there is the "underlying dispute," which is the event or condition that triggers the work stoppage. This dispute may or may not be political, and it may or may not be arbitrable under the parties' collective-bargaining agreement. Second, there is the parties' dispute over whether the no-strike pledge prohibits the work stoppage at issue. This second dispute can always form the basis for federal court jurisdiction, because § 301(a) gives federal courts jurisdiction over "[s]uits for violation of contracts between an employer and a labor organization."

It is beyond cavil that the second form of dispute—whether the collective-bargaining agreement either forbids or permits the union to refuse to perform certain work—is a "controversy concerning the terms or conditions of employment." This § 301 action was brought to resolve just such a controversy. In its complaint, the Employer did not seek to enjoin the intervention of the Soviet Union in Afghanistan, nor did it ask the District Court to decide whether the Union was justified in expressing disapproval of the Soviet Union's actions. Instead, the Employer sought to enjoin the Union's decision not to provide labor, a decision which the Employer believed violated the terms of the collective-bargaining agreement. It is this contract dispute, and not the political dispute, that the arbitrator will resolve, and on which the courts are asked to rule.

The language of the Norris-LaGuardia Act does not except labor disputes having their genesis in political protests. Nor is there any basis in the statutory language for the argument that the Act requires that *each* dispute relevant to the case be a labor dispute. The Act merely requires that the case involve "any" labor dispute. Therefore, the plain terms of § 4(a) and § 13 of the Norris-LaGuardia Act deprive the federal courts of the power to enjoin the Union's work stoppage in this § 301 action, without regard to whether the Union also has a nonlabor dispute with another entity.

The conclusion that this case involves a labor dispute within the meaning of the Norris-LaGuardia Act comports with this Court's consistent interpretation of that Act. Our decisions have recognized that the term "labor dispute" must not be narrowly construed because the statutory definition itself is extremely broad and because Congress deliberately included a broad definition to

overrule judicial decisions that had unduly restricted the Clayton Act's labor exemption from the antitrust laws. . . .

The criticaal element in determining whether the provisions of the Norris-LaGuardia Act apply is whether "the employer-employee relationship [is] the matrix of the controversy." In this case, the Employer and the Union representing its employees are the disputants, and their dispute concerns the interpretation of the labor contract that defines their relationship. Thus, the employer-employee relationship is the matrix of this controversy. . . .

This case, brought by the Employer to enforce its collective-bargaining agreement with the Union, involves a "labor dispute" within any common-sense meaning of that term. Were we to ignore this plain interpretation and hold that the political motivation underlying the work stoppage removes this controversy from the prohibitions of the Norris-LaGuardiaa Act, we would embroil federal judges in the very scrutiny of "legitimate objectives" that Congress intended to prevent when it passed that Act. The applicability not only of § 4, but of all of the procedural protections embodied in that Act, would turn on a single federal judge's perception of the motivation underlying the concerted activity.

In essence, the Employer asks us to disregard the legislative history of the Act and to distort the definition of a labor dispute in order to reach what it believes to be an "equitable" result. The Employer's real complaint, however, is not with the Union's political objections to the conduct of the Soviet Union, but with what the Employer views as the Union's breach of contract. The Employer's frustration with this alleged breach of contract should not be remedied by characterizing it as other than a labor dispute. . . . In the past, we have consistently declined to constrict Norris-LaGuardia's broad prohibitions except in narrowly defined situations where accommodation of that Act to specific congressional policy is necessary. We refuse to deviate from that path today.

In conclusion, we hold that an employer's § 301 action to enforce the provisions of a collective-bargaining agreement allegedly violated by a union's work stoppage involves a "labor dispute" within the meaning of the Norris-LaGuardia Act, without regard to the motivation underlying the union's decision not to provide labor. [*Affirmed.*]

THE WAGNER ACT

5. General Summary

The labor movement received its greatest stimulus for growth with the enactment in 1935 of the National Labor Relations Act (*Wagner Act*). Noting that a major cause of industrial strife was the inequality of bargaining power between employees and employers, the act stated that its policy was to protect by law the right of employees to organize and bargain collectively and to encourage the "friendly adjustment of industrial disputes."

The Wagner Act accomplishes this policy by providing that the right of employees to bargain collectively is a fundamental right. Section 7 of the law provides:

> Employees shall have the right to self organization, to form, join, or assist labor organizations, to bargain collectively through representatives of their own choosing, and to engage in concerted activities for the purpose of collective bargaining or other mutual aid or protection.

In summary, the Wagner Act:

1 Created the National Labor Relations Board (NLRB), to administer the act.

2 Provided for selection by employees through NLRB-supervised elections of a union with exclusive power to act as their collective-bargaining representative.

3 Outlawed certain conduct by employers which generally had the effect of either preventing the organization of employees or emasculating their unions where they did exist. These forbidden acts were defined as "unfair labor practices," and are discussed in the next chapter (Chapter 19) in detail.

4 Authorized the NLRB to conduct hearings on unfair labor practice allegations and if they were found to exist, to take corrective action including issuing cease and desist orders and awarding dollar damages to unions and employees.

6. The NLRB

Today, the NLRB has five members appointed by the President, with the advice and consent of the Senate, who serve staggered terms of five years each. The President designates one member to serve as chairman. In addition, there is a General Counsel of the Board who supervises Board investigations and serves as prosecutor in cases before the Board. The General Counsel supervises operations of the NLRB so that the Board itself may perform its quasi-judicial function of deciding unfair labor practice cases free of bias. As part of this function, the Board has full authority over the Division of Administrative Law Judges. The administrative law judges are responsible for the initial conduct of hearings in unfair labor practice cases. The General Counsel is appointed by the President with the advice and consent of the Senate for a term of four years. The General Counsel has final authority in investigation of charges, issuance of complaints, and prosecution of such complaints, as well as the dismissal of charges.

The General Counsel also is responsible for the conduct of representation elections, since the Board has delegated this function to its regional directors subject to a review of their actions. (The Board still determines policy questions, such as what types of employers and groups of employees are covered by the labor law.) In addition, the General Counsel is responsible for seeking court orders requiring compliance with the Board's orders, and represents the Board in miscellaneous litigation.

Congress gave the NLRB jurisdiction over any business "affecting commerce," with a few exceptions. However, certain employers and employees are specifically exempt from NLRB jurisdiction. These include employees of federal and state governments, political subdivisions of the states, and persons subject to the Railway Labor Act. Also excluded are independent contractors, individuals employed as agricultural laborers or domestic servants in a home, and those employed by their spouse or a parent. Finally, supervisors are not considered employees. This supervisor exception excludes all employees properly classified as "managerial." For example, university professors who control admissions, hire and fire faculty, and participate in budget preparation are supervisors and not covered by the act. Professors who have no power to act in these areas are covered.

The supervisor or managerial exception raises difficult issues when applied to persons having access to confidential information. The mere fact that a person has access to confidential information of an employer does not make the person a supervisor. Only those persons with access to confidential information of the employer concerning labor relations are exempt. This labor relations connection means that persons who serve in a confidential capacity to persons who formulate, determine, or effectuate labor policy are not covered by the act.

The NLRB has never been able to exercise fully the powers given it, because of budget and time considerations. It has limited its own jurisdiction to cases which it deems to be more significant because they meet certain minimum standards. Under present guidelines, the Board will generally exercise jurisdiction over labor disputes involving the following types of activities:

1   *Nonretail operations* with an annual outflow or inflow across state lines of at least $50,000

2   *Retail enterprises* with a gross volume of $500,000 or more a year

3   *Enterprises operating office buildings* if the gross revenues are at least $100,000 per year

4   *Transportation enterprises* furnishing interstate services

5   *Local transit systems* with an annual gross volume of at least $250,000

6   *Newspapers* which subscribe to interstate news services, publish nationally syndicated features, or advertise nationally sold products with a minimum annual gross volume of $250,000

7   *Communication enterprises* which operate radio or television stations or telephone or telegraph services with a gross volume of $100,000 or more per year

8   *Local public utilities* with an annual gross volume of $250,000 per year, or an outflow or inflow of goods or services across state lines of $50,000 or more per year

9   *Hotel and motel enterprises* serving transient guests which gross at least $500,000 in revenues per year

10   All enterprises whose operations have a substantial impact on *national defense*

11   *Nonprofit hospitals*

12   *Private universities and colleges*

As a result of the foregoing policy, federal labor laws do not cover many small employers, who are subject to any applicable state law on labor relations and to common law principles. Of course the Board may decide to take jurisdiction over any business that affects interstate commerce if it decides to do so.

Each year the NLRB handles over 50,000 cases of all kinds. About two-thirds involve unfair labor practice charges. Most of these are filed by unions or workers against employers, but about one-third involve charges against unions.

7. NLRB Sanctions

The Wagner Act directs the Board, upon finding that a person has committed an unfair labor practice, to issue an order requiring him or her to cease and desist such practices. The Board is also authorized to order corrective action if necessary to overcome any injury caused by the unfair labor practice. Such orders are subject only to limited judicial review. On such a review, the Board's order will not be disturbed unless it can be shown that it is an obvious attempt to achieve ends contrary to the policies of the law. The NLRB has no independent power to enforce its orders. If necessary, it seeks enforcement in the U.S. Courts of Appeal.

To illustrate the corrective action that may be taken, we use the example of an employee who has been discharged wrongfully; the NLRB may order the reinstatement of that employee with back pay and restoration of full seniority rights. In fact, even a purchaser of a business who acquires and operates it knowing that the seller discharged an employee in violation of the Wagner Act may be ordered by the NLRB to reinstate the employee with back pay. The NLRB may require an employer to bargain collectively with the appropriate union, or vice versa. It may order an employer to post notices at the plant assuring employees that it will no longer commit a particular unfair labor practice of which it has been found guilty. If an employer or union has committed an unfair labor practice which may have influenced the outcome of a representation election, the NLRB may set aside the election and hold another one free of such improper pressures on the employees.

At one time, the NLRB was willing to certify a union that lost an election if the employer was guilty of unfair labor practices to such an extent that the employer's conduct could be described as outrageous and pervasive. In 1984, the courts reversed this policy, and today the NLRB will not certify a union that loses an election. It will set aside the election and vote again. The courts have held that a nonmajority bargaining order departs from the national policy of employee free choice. The law requires a union election victory or some other concrete proof of majority assent to union representation. At the present time, unions lose the majority of certification and decertification elections. This negative trend has developed since the late 1970s.

8. NLRB Elections

An employer may voluntarily recognize that its workers desire to have a certain union represent them and agree to bargain with the union. In the absence of such voluntary recognition, the selection of a union as collective-bargaining representative is made by a majority of the employees voting "in a unit appropriate for such purposes." Elections are by secret ballot and supervised by the NLRB. The Board decides what unit of employees is appropriate for purposes of collective bargaining and therefore which employees are entitled to vote in an election. It may select the total employer unit, craft unit, plant unit, or any subdivision of the plant.

Obviously, how the Board exercises its discretion in this regard may be crucial to the outcome of a given election. If all 100 workers at one plant operated by an employer desire to organize, but 400 out of 500 at another of the employer's plants do not, designation of the total employer unit as appropriate would ensure that both plants would remain nonunion. The Board <u>may deny some employees the right to vote,</u> as the case that follows illustrates.

N.L.R.B. v. ACTION AUTOMOTIVE, INC.
105 S.Ct. 984 (1985)

BURGER, C. J.: We granted certiorari to decide whether the National Labor Relations Board may exclude from a collective-bargaining unit employees who are relatives of the owners of a closely held corporation that employs them, without a finding that the employees receive special job-related benefits.

Respondent Action Automotive, Inc., is a retail automobile parts and gasoline dealer with stores in a number of Michigan cities. Action Automotive is a closely held corporation owned equally by three brothers, Richard, Robert, and James Sabo. The Sabo brothers are actively involved in the daily operations of the business. They serve as the corporation's officers, make all policy decisions, and retain ultimate authority for the supervision of every department.

In March 1981, the Retail Store Employees Union, Local 40 (the Union), filed with the Board a petition requesting that a representation election be held among Action Automotive's employees. Action Automotive and the Union agreed to elections in two bargaining units—one consisting of employees at the company's nine retail stores, and the other comprising clerical employees at the company's headquarters. The elections were held on May 29, 1981, and the Union received a plurality of votes in each unit; enough ballots were challenged by each side, however, to place the outcome of the elections in doubt. We are concerned only with the Union's challenge to the ballots of Diane and Mildred Sabo.

Diane Sabo is the wife of Action Automotive's president and one-third owner, Richard Sabo. She works as a general ledger clerk at the company's headquarters in Flint, Michigan. She resides with her husband and both work at the same office. Unlike other clerical workers, she works part-time and receives a salary. She also is allowed to take breaks when she pleases, and she often spends her break in her husband's office.

Mildred Sabo is the mother of the three Sabo brothers who own and manage Action Automotive. She is employed as a full-time cashier at the company's store in Barton, Michigan. Mildred Sabo lives with James Sabo, Secretary-Treasurer of the corporation, and she regularly sees or telephones her other sons and their families. She earns 25 cents per hour more than any other cashier, but she is also one of the company's most experienced cashiers.

In light of these facts, the Board's hearing officer concluded that Diane Sabo's interests are different from those of other clerical employees in the company's headquarters, and that Mildred Sabo's "interests are more closely aligned with management than with the employees of Action Automotive." He reached this conclusion without finding that Diane and Mildred Sabo enjoy special job-related benefits. Believing that such a finding was not a prerequisite to excluding the two women from the bargaining units, the hearing officer recommended that the union's challenge to their ballots be sustained.

The Board adopted the hearing officer's recommendations and, after all qualified votes were counted, certified the Union as the exclusive bargaining representative for the two units. When Action Automotive refused to bargain, the Union filed charges with the Board. The Board . . . ordered the company to bargain with the Union.

The United States Court of Appeals for the Sixth Circuit denied enforcement of the Board's order.

Section 9(b) of the Act vests in the Board authority to determine "the unit appropriate for the purposes of collective bargaining." The Board"s discretion in this area is broad, reflecting Congress' recognition of the need for flexibility in shaping the bargaining unit to the particular case. The Board does not exercise this authority aimlessly; in defining bargaining units, its focus is on whether the employees share a community of interest. A cohesive unit—one relatively free of conflicts of interest—serves the Act's purpose of effective collective bargaining, and prevents a minority interest group from being submerged in an overly large unit.

The Board has long hesitated to include the relatives of management in bargaining units because their interests are sufficiently distinguished from those of the other employees. . . .

. . . [t]he Board considers a variety of factors in deciding whether an employee's familial ties are sufficient to align his interests with management and thus warrant his exclusion from a bargaining unit.

For instance, a relevant consideration is whether the employee resides with or is financially dependent on a relative who owns or manages the business; such an employee is typically excluded from the unit. The greater the family involvement in the ownership and management of the company, the more likely the employee-relative will be viewed as aligned with management and hence excluded. The Board, of course, is always concerned with whether the employee receives special job-related benefits such as high wages or favorable working conditions. When other criteria satisfy the Board that the employee-relative's interests are aligned with management, however, he may be excluded from the unit even though he enjoys no special job-related benefits.

Our review is limited to whether the Board's practice of excluding some close relatives who do not enjoy special job-related benefits has a reasonable basis in law. In reviewing the Board decisions, we consistently yield to the Board's reasonable interpretations and applications of the Act. Indeed, the Board's orders defining bargaining units are "rarely to be disturbed."

The Board's policy regarding family members . . . is a reasonable application of its "community of interest" standard. Close relatives of management, particularly those who live with an owner or manager, are likely to get a more attentive and sensitive ear to their day-to-day and long-range work concerns than would other employees. And it is reasonable for the Board to assume that the family member who is significantly dependent on a member of management will tend to equate his personal interests with the business interests of the employer. The very presence at union meetings of close relatives of management could tend to inhibit free expression of views and threaten the confidentiality of union attitudes and voting. . . .

We are not prepared to second-guess the Board's informed judgment that a bargaining unit's community of interest may be diluted by circumstances other than divergent job-related benefits. . . .

The Board, in applying its general policy to the facts of this case, did not abuse its discretion. Diane Sabo resides with her husband, the president and one-third owner of Action Automotive; Mildred Sabo, the mother of the three owners, lives with one of her sons. All three owners are closely related and actively involved in running the business on a day-to-day basis. Diane Sabo works at the same office with her husband and occasionally takes her coffee breaks in his office. Mildred Sabo has daily contacts with her sons. Certainly their participation in the collective-bargaining units would be viewed with suspicion by other employees. On these facts, the Board could reasonably conclude that Diane and Mildred Sabo's interests are more likely to be aligned with the business interests of the family than with the interests of the employees.

We hold that the Board did not exceed its authority in excluding from collective-bargaining units close relatives of management, without a finding that the relatives enjoy special job-related privileges. The judgment of the Court of Appeals is [*Reversed.*]

PETITIONS

Before a representation election is conducted by the NLRB, a petition for such an election must be filed with the Board of either an employee, labor organization, or employer. If the petition is filed by either an employee or labor organization, it must allege either (1) that a substantial number of employees want a collective-bargaining representative but their employer refuses to recognize their representative, or (2) that a substantial number of employees assert that the union which has been certified by the Board or which the employer currently recognizes as their bargaining representative is no longer such. "Substantial" has been interpreted to mean that at least 30 percent of the employees must support the petition.

An employer may file a petition for selection of an initial representative without making and proving any allegations of fact. However, an employer who files a petition for an election to invalidate certification of an incumbent union must show that it doubts, in good faith, the continued support of the union by a majority of the employees.

The NLRB investigates a petition, and if it determines that there is an issue to be voted upon, it directs that a representation election be held by a secret ballot. After the results are tallied, the Board certifies either that no union has been selected by majority of the employees or that a given one has. In some cases, two or more unions compete to qualify as the legal representative of the bargaining unit.

As was noted, employees may withdraw authority from a previously designated bargaining representative by secret ballot. If at least 30 percent of those in a bargaining unit allege that they desire their union's authority to be rescinded, the Board must hold an election to that effect. However, after any valid election has been conducted by the NLRB, another is not permitted for one year. Also, if an election has resulted in Board certification of a union, no new election may take place within one year of the certification. Also, an election is not allowed within the term of a collective-bargaining agreement or three years after it has been signed, whichever period is shorter.

CARDS

A union seeking to represent employees may solicit cards from them indicating their willingness that the union act in that capacity. The NLRB may issue a bargaining order based on such cards if the cards are unequivocal and clearly indicate that the employee signing the card is authorizing the union to represent him or her. The general counsel of the NLRB is not required to prove that the employees read or understood the cards. If a card states on its face that it authorizes collective bargaining, it will be counted for that purpose unless there is clear proof that the employee was told that it would not be used for that purpose. The employer could have relied upon the cards and agreed to bargain with the union.

Most cards simply request an election because of the belief that peer pressure may cause workers who do not actually favor the union to sign the cards. The secret ballot of the election process ensures freedom of choice for the workers. An employer is entitled to an election. The refusal to accept a union based on cards is not an unfair labor practice.

LINDEN LUMBER DIVISION, SUMMER & CO. v. NLRB
95 S.Ct. 429 (1974)

DOUGLAS, J.: . . . In [this case] respondent union obtained authorization cards from a majority of petitioner's employees and demanded that it be recognized as the collective-bargaining representative of those employees. Linden said it doubted the union's claimed majority status and suggested the union petition the Board for an election. The union filed such a petition with the Board but later withdrew it when Linden declined to enter a consent election agreement or abide by an election on the ground that respondent union's organizational campaign had been improperly assisted by company supervisors. Respondent union thereupon renewed its demand for collective bargaining; and again Linden declined, saying that the union's claimed membership had been improperly influenced by supervisors. Thereupon respondent union struck for recognition as the bargaining representative and

shortly filed a charge of unfair labor practice against Linden based on its refusal to bargain.

There is no charge that Linden engaged in an unfair labor practice apart from its refusal to bargain. The Board held that Linden should not be guilty of an unfair labor practice solely on the basis "of its refusal to accept evidence of majority status other than the results of a Board election." . . .

In [*National Labor Relations Board v. Gissel Packing Co.*] we held that an employer who engages in "unfair" labor practices "likely to destroy the union's majority and seriously impede the election" may not insist that before it bargains the union get a secret ballot election. There were no such unfair labor practices here, nor had the employer . . . agreed to a voluntary settlement of the dispute and then reneged. As noted, we reserved in *Gissel* the questions "whether, absent election interference by an employer's unfair labor practices, he may obtain an election only if he petitions for one himself; whether, if he does not, he must bargain with a card majority if the union chooses not to seek an election; and whether, in the latter situation, he is bound by the Board's ultimate determination of the card results regardless of his earlier good faith doubts, or whether he can still insist on a union-sought election if he makes an affirmative showing of his positive reasons for believing there is a representation dispute."

We recognized in *Gissel* that while the election process had acknowledged superiority in ascertaining whether a union has majority support, cards may "adequately reflect employee sentiment."

Generalizations are difficult; and it is urged by the unions that only the precise facts should dispose of concrete cases. As we said, however, in *Gissel*, the Board had largely abandoned its earlier test that the employer's refusal to bargain was warranted, if he had a good-faith doubt that the union represented a majority. A different approach was indicated. We said:

[A]n employer is not obligated to accept a card check as proof of majority status, under the Board's current practice, and he is not required to justify his insistence on an election by making his own investigation of employee sentiment and showing affirmative reasons for doubting the majority status. . . .

In the present cases the Board found that the employers "should not be found guilty of a violation of Section 8(a)(5) solely upon the basis of [their] refusal to accept evidence of majority status other than the results of a Board election." The question whether the employers had good reasons or poor reasons was not deemed relevant to the inquiry. The Court of Appeals concluded that if the employer had doubts as to a union's majority status, it could and should test out its doubts by petitioning for an election. . . . The Court of Appeals concluded that since Congress in 1947 authorized employers to file their own representation petitions by enacting § 9(c)(1)(B), the burden was on them. But the history of that provision indicates it was aimed at eliminating the discrimination against employers which had previously existed under the Board's prior rules, permitting employers to petition for an election only when confronted with claims by two or more unions. There is no suggestion that Congress wanted to place the burden of getting a secret election on the employer. . . .

The Board has at least some expertise in these matters and its judgment is that an employer's petition for an election, though permissible, is not the required course. It points out in its brief here that an employer wanting to gain delay can draw a petition to elicit protests by the union, and the thought that an employer petition would obviate litigation over the sufficiency of the union's showing of interest is in its purview apparently not well taken. A union petition to be sure must be backed by a 30% showing of employee interest. But the sufficiency of such a showing is not litigable by the parties.

In light of the statutory scheme and the practical administrative procedural questions involved, we cannot say that the Board's decision that the union should go forward and ask for an election on the employer's refusal to recognize the authorization cards was arbitrary and capricious or an abuse of discretion.

In sum, we sustain the Board in holding that, unless an employer has engaged in an unfair labor practice that impairs the electoral process, a union with authorization cards purporting to represent a majority of the employees, which is refused recognition, has the burden of taking the next step in invoking the Board's election procedure. [*Reversed.*]

THE TAFT-HARTLEY ACT

9. Major Provisions

The Wagner Act opened the door for the rapid growth of the union movement. From 1935 to the end of World War II, the strength and influence of unions grew by leaps and bounds. Where, prior to the Wagner Act, employers had the greater advantage in bargaining power, by 1946 many persons felt the pendulum had shifted and that unions with their ability to call nationwide crippling strikes had the better bargaining position.

As an attempt to balance the scale, the Labor-Management Relations Act of 1947 (the *Taft-Hartley Act*) was enacted to amend the Wagner Act. Its purposes were to ensure the free flow of commerce by eliminating union practices which burden commerce and to provide procedures for avoiding disputes which jeopardize the public health, safety, or interest. It recognized that both parties to collective bargaining need protection from wrongful interference by the other and that employees sometimes need protection from the union itself.

In attempting to balance bargaining power, the Taft-Hartley Act:

1 Created the Federal Mediation and Conciliation Service to assist in the settlement of labor disputes.

2 Restricted the right of unions to insist on a union membership.

3 Attempted to give employers freedom of speech in labor-management relations.

4 Provided for an *eighty-day cooling-off period* in strikes which imperil the national health or safety.

5 Allowed suits for breach of contract against a union.

6 Outlawed certain conduct by unions as unfair labor practices (see Chapter 16).

The Federal Mediation and Conciliation Service has a staff of trained specialists who work with the parties to a labor dispute in an attempt to resolve differences. These mediators often become public figures, as in the case of the mediator involved in the baseball strike, and the one involved in the air traffic controller strike.

10. Union Membership

The second major change brought about by the Taft-Hartley Act was its provision which outlawed the *closed shop* but permitted the union shop in those states which did not outlaw it by enacting right-to-work legislation. In a closed-shop contract, the employer agrees that it will *not* hire any person who is *not* a member of the union. In a *union-shop* contract, the employer agrees to require membership in the union after an employee has been hired as a condition of his or her continued employment. Under the Taft-Hartley Act, such a requirement may not be imposed until the thirtieth day after employment begins. In addition, an employer may not compel union membership of an employee (1) if such was not available on the same terms and conditions applicable to other members, or (2) if the employee's membership was denied or terminated for reasons other than failure to pay dues and fees. In states that allow union security agreements, workers must pay dues but they cannot be discharged for failing to abide by union rules or policies.

One of the most distasteful sections of the Taft-Hartley Act to unions is 14(b), which outlaws the union shop in states which have adopted a **right-to-work law**. Right-to-work laws prohibit agreements requiring membership in a labor organization as a condition of continued employment of a person who was not in the union when hired. Approximately twenty states have right-to-work laws today. Workers in these states who do not belong to a union may not be required to pay representation fees to the union that represents the employees. However, such workers are subject to the terms of the collective-bargaining agreement, and the union must handle their grievances, if any, with management.

A union has the power to discipline its members and impose fines. However, unions may not fine employees who are not members or who resign. A union constitution may not prohibit resignations. Taft-Hartley has eliminated compulsory union membership through a closed shop. As a result, a union may not fine former members who have resigned.

PATTERN MAKERS' LEAGUE OF NORTH AMERICA v. N.L.R.B.
105 S.Ct. 3064 (1985)

POWELL, J.: The Pattern Makers' League of North America, AFL-CIO (the League), a labor union, provides in its constitution that resignations are not permitted during a strike or when a strike is imminent. The League fined 10 of its members who, in violation of this provision, resigned during a strike and returned to work. The National Labor Relations Board held that these fines were imposed in violation of § 8(b)(1)(A) of the National Labor Relations Act. We granted a petition for a writ of certiorari in order to decide whether § 8(b)(1)(A) reasonably may

be construed by the Board as prohibiting a union from fining members who have tendered resignations invalid under the union constitution.

The League is a national union composed of local associations (locals). In May 1976, its constitution was amended to provide that:

"No resignation or withdrawal from an Association, or from the League, shall be accepted during a strike or lockout, or at a time when a strike or lockout appears imminent."

This amendment, known as League Law 13, became effective in October 1976, after being ratified by the League's locals. On May 5, 1977, when a collective-bargaining agreement expired, two locals began an economic strike against several manufacturing companies in Rockford, Illinois and Beloit, Wisconsin. Forty-three of the two locals' members participated. In early September 1977, after the locals formally rejected a contract offer, a striking union member submitted a letter of resignation to the Beloit association. He returned to work the following day. During the next three months, 10 more union members resigned from the Rockford and Beloit locals and returned to work. On December 19, 1977, the strike ended when the parties signed a new collective-bargaining agreement. The locals notified 10 employees who had resigned that their resignations had been rejected as violative of League Law 13. The locals further informed the employees that, as union members, they were subject to sanctions for returning to work. Each was fined approximately the equivalent of his earnings during the strike.

The Rockford-Beloit Pattern Jobbers' Association (the Association) had represented the employers throughout the collective-bargaining process. It filed charges with the Board against the League and its two locals, the petitioners. Relying on § 8(b)(1)(A), the Association claimed that levying fines against employees who had resigned was an unfair labor practice. Following a hearing, an Administrative Law Judge found that the petitioners had violated § 8(b)(1)(A) by fining employees for returning to work after tendering resignations. The Board agreed that § 8(b)(1)(A) prohibited the union from imposing sanctions on the 10 employees. . . .

The United States Court of Appeals for the Seventh Circuit enforced the Board's order. . . .

We granted a petition for a writ of certiorari to resolve the conflict between the Courts of Appeals over the validity of restrictions on union members' right to resign. The Board has held that such restrictions are invalid and do not justify imposing sanctions on employees who have attempted to resign from the union. Because of the Board's "special competence" in the field of labor relations, its interpretation of the Act is accorded substantial deference. The question for decision today is thus narrowed to whether the Board's construction of § 8(b)(1)(A) is reasonable. . . .

Section 7 of the Act grants employees the right to "refrain from any or all [concerted] . . . activities. . . ." This general right is implemented by § 8(b)(1)(A). The latter section provides that a union commits an unfair labor practice if it "restrain[s] or coerce[s] employees in the exercise" of their § 7 rights. When employee members of a union refuse to support a strike (whether or not a rule prohibits returning to work during a strike), they are refraining from concerted activity." Therefore, imposing fines on these employees for returning to work "restrains" the exercise of their § 7 rights. Indeed, if the terms "refrain" and "restrain or coerce" are interpreted literally, fining employees to enforce compliance with any union rule or policy would violate the Act.

Despite this language from the Act, the Court in *NLRB v. Allis-Chalmers* held that § 8(b)(1)(A) does not prohibit labor organizations from fining current members. In *NLRB v. Textile Workers*, the Court found as a corollary that unions may not fine former members who have resigned lawfully. . . . We decide today whether a union is precluded from fining employees who have attempted to resign when resignations are prohibited by the union's constitution.

Section 8(b)(1)(A) allows unions to enforce only those rules that "impai[r] no policy Congress has imbedded in the labor laws. . . ." The Board has found union restrictions on the right to resign to be inconsistent with the policy of voluntary unionism implicit in § 8(a)(3). We believe that the inconsistency between union restrictions on the right to resign and the policy of voluntary unionism supports the Board's conclusion that League Law 13 is invalid.

Closed shop agreements, legalized by the Wagner Act in 1935, became quite common in the early 1940's. Under these agreements, employers could hire and retain in their employ only union members in good standing. Full union membership was thus compulsory in a closed shop; in order to keep their jobs, employees were required to attend union meetings, support union leaders, and otherwise adhere to union rules. Because of mounting objections to the closed shop, in 1947—after hearings and full consideration—Congress enacted the Taft-Hartley Act. Section 8(a)(3) of that Act effectively eliminated compulsory union membership by outlawing the closed shop. The union security agreements permitted by § 8(a)(3) require employees to pay dues, but an employee cannot be discharged for failing to abide by union rules or policies with which he disagrees.

Full union membership thus no longer can be a requirement of employment. If a new employee refuses formally to join a union and subject himself to its discipline, he cannot be fired. Moreover, no employee can be discharged if he initially joins a union, and subsequently resigns. We think it noteworthy that § 8(a)(3) protects the employment rights of the dissatisfied member, as well as those of the worker who never assumed full union membership. By allowing employees to resign from a union at any time, § 8(a)(3) protects the employee whose views come to diverge from those of his union.

League Law 13 curtails this freedom to resign from full union membership. Nevertheless, the petitioners contend that League Law 13 does not contravene the policy of voluntary unionism imbedded in the Act. They assert that this provision does not interfere with workers' employment rights because offending members are not discharged, but only fined. We find this argument unpersuasive, for a union has not left a "worker's employment rights inviolate when it exacts [his entire] paycheck in satisfaction of a fine imposed for working." Congress in 1947 sought to eliminate completely any requirement that the employee maintain full union membership. Therefore, the Board was justified in concluding that by restricting the right of employees to resign, League Law 13 impairs the policy of voluntary unionism.

The Board has the primary responsibility for applying "the general provisions of the Act to the complexities of industrial life." Where the Board's construction of the Act is reasonable, it should not be rejected "merely because the courts might prefer another view of the statute." In this case, two factors suggest that we should be particularly reluctant to hold that the Board's interpretation of the Act is impermissible. First, in related cases this Court invariably has yielded to Board decisions on whether fines imposed by a union "restrain or coerce" employees. Second, the Board consistently has construed § 8(b)(1)(A) as prohibiting the imposition of fines on employees who have tendered resignations invalid under a union constitution. Therefore, we conclude that the Board's decision here is entitled to our deference. [*Affirmed.*]

11. Free Speech

Employers had complained that the Wagner Act violated their right of free speech. To meet this objection, Congress added the following provision:

8(c) The expressing of any views, argument, or opinion, or the dissemination thereof, whether in written, printed, graphic, or visual form, shall not constitute or be evidence of an unfair labor practice under any of the provisions of this Act, if such expression contains no threat of reprisal or force or promise of benefit.

This provision gives employers limited free speech, at best. It is difficult to make statements that cannot be construed as a threat or a promise. For example, if an employer predicts dire economic events as a result of unionization, such may be an illegal threat if the employee has it within his or her power to make the prediction come true. Whether particular language is coercive or not often depends on the analysis of the total background of facts and circumstances in which it was uttered. To be forbidden, the statements of an employer need not be proved to have been coercive in fact but only to have had a reasonable tendency to intimidate employees under the circumstances. At the present time, the NLRB takes the position that misleading statements will not automatically cancel election results, nor will inadvertent errors overturn elections. The purpose of this approach is to advance free speech by both sides.

An employer's threats to withdraw existing benefits of employees if they unionize is not speech protected by Section 8(c). For example, in one case the officer of a firm noted in a speech to employees of a plant where an election was forthcoming that the business could supply the same product from one of its nonunion plants. The NLRB held that this statement constituted a threat to provide better and more jobs at nonunion plants, and it set aside the election, which the union had lost. In another case, an illegal threat was ruled to be implied from management comments shortly before a representation election warning that annual pay raises would be subject to collective bargaining and thus delayed by a union victory. However, mere predictions and prophecies are protected. For example, an employer's speeches and handbills during the union's organizational campaign stated its intention to fight the union in every legal way possible and to "deal hard" with the union at arm's length if it were voted in, and warned that employees could be permanently replaced if the union called an economic strike. This language was held to fall within the protection of Section 8(c). The right of free speech guaranteed by the Taft-Hartley Act applies to labor unions as well as employers. However, there is a rule prohibiting either side from making election speeches on company time to massed assemblies of employees within twenty-four hours before an election.

12. Eighty-Day Cooling-off Period

The provision of the Taft-Hartley Act calling for an eighty-day "cooling-off period" after certain procedures that have been followed begins, "Whenever in the opinion of the President of the United States, a threatened or actual strike or lockout affecting an entire industry or substantial part thereof engaged in trade, commerce, transportation, transmission, or communication among the several states or with foreign nations, or engaged in the production of goods for commerce, will, if permitted to occur or to continue, imperil the national health or safety, he may appoint a board. . . ." Thus the procedure starts with the President, recognizing the emergency characteristics of a strike, appointing a board of inquiry to obtain facts about the strike. The board then makes a study of the strike and reports back to the President. If the board finds that the national health or safety is indeed affected by the strike, then the President, through the attorney general, goes to the federal court for an injunction ordering the union to suspend the strike (or company to suspend the lockout) for eighty days. During the eighty-day period, the Federal Mediation Service works with the two parties to try to achieve an agreement. If during this time the reconciliation effort fails, the presidential board holds new hearings and receives the company's final offer. The union members are then allowed to vote on this final proposal by the company. If they vote for the new proposal, the dispute is over and work continues as usual. If they vote against the proposal, the workers may again be called out on strike. At this point, the strike may continue indefinitely until the disagreement causing it is resolved by collective bargaining, or unless there is additional legislation by Congress to solve the problem. Experience has shown that many disputes are settled during the eighty-day period. The injunction provided for in the Taft-Hartley Act may not be used for all strikes but is limited to "national emergency" strikes. These must involve national defense or key industries or must have a substantial effect on the economy.

13. Suits Against Unions

Section 301 of the Taft-Hartley Act provides that suits for breach of a contract between an employer and a labor organization can be filed in the federal district courts, without regard to the amount in question. A labor organization is responsible for the acts of its agents and may sue or be sued. Any money judgment against it is enforceable only against its assets and not against any individual member. Moreover, individuals cannot be sued for actions such as violating no-strike provisions of a collective-bargaining contract. Thus, an employer may enforce a no-strike clause in a collective-bargaining agreement by obtaining an injunction against the union, or it may recover money damages from the union if it breaches such a contract clause. In addition, employees may sue their union and recover the money damages they suffer because of an illegal strike. If a union activity is both an unfair labor practice and a breach of a collective-bargaining agreement, the NLRB's authority is not exclusive and does not destroy the jurisdiction of courts under Section 301 of the Taft-Hartley Act.

THE LANDRUM-GRIFFIN ACT

14. As a "Bill of Rights"

The Landrum-Griffin Act, or Labor-Management Reporting and Disclosure Act (LMRDA) was passed in 1959 as a result of the widespread corruption, violence, and lack of democratic procedures in some labor unions that was revealed in congressional hearings conducted in the 1950s. Its requirements provide for union reform and a "bill of rights" for union members. LMRDA gives union members the following rights:

1   To nominate candidates, to vote in elections, to attend membership meetings, and to have a voice in business transactions, subject to reasonable union rules and regulations.

2   To have free expression in union meetings, business discussions, and conventions subject to reasonable rules and regulations.

3   To vote on an increase of dues or fees.

4   To sue and testify against the union.

5   To receive written, specific charges; to be given a reasonable time for defense; and to be accorded a full and fair hearing before any disciplinary action is taken by the union against them except for nonpayment of dues.

6   To be given a copy of the collective-bargaining agreement that they work under, upon request.

The rights and remedies granted to union members by this statute are in addition to any other rights members may have under other laws or under union constitutions and bylaws. In the event that a member's rights are violated, the statute allows him or her to bring civil actions for damages, including an injunction.

The case which follows is typical of those brought to protect the rights of the rank-and-file union members to control their union. In this case, the secretary of labor filed suit under the Landrum-Griffin Act, challenging the validity of an international union rule which limited eligibility for local union office to certain members.

LOCAL 3489 UNITED STEELWORKERS OF AMERICA v. USERY
97 S.Ct. 611 (1977)

BRENNAN, J.: The Secretary of Labor brought this action in the District Court under § 402(b) of the Labor, Management Reporting and Disclosure Act of 1959 (LMRDA) to *invalidate* the 1970 election of officers of Local 3489, United Steelworkers of America. The Secretary alleged that a provision of the Steelworkers' International constitution, binding on the Local, that limits eligibility for local union office to members who have attended at least one-half of the regular meetings of the Local for three years previous to the election (unless prevented by union activities or working hours), violated § 401(e) of the LMRDA. The District Court dismissed the complaint, finding no violation of the Act. The Court of Appeals for the Seventh Circuit reversed. We granted certiorari to resolve a conflict among Circuits over whether the Steelworkers' constitutional provision violates § 401(e). . . .

The LMRDA does not render unions powerless to restrict candidacies for union office. The injunction in § 401(e) that "every member in good standing shall be eligible to be a candidate and to hold office" is made expressly "subject to reasonable qualifications uniformly imposed." But "Congress plainly did not intend that the authorization . . . of 'reasonable qualifications . . .' should be given a broad reach. The contrary is implicit in the legislative history of the section and in its wording. . . ." The basic objective of Title IV of the LMRDA is to guarantee "free and democratic" union elections modeled on "political elections in this country" where "the assumption is that voters will exercise common sense and judgment in casting their ballots." . . .

Whether a particular qualification is "reasonable" within the meaning of § 401(e) must therefore "be measured in terms of its consistency with the Act's command to unions to conduct 'free and democratic' union elections." . . .

[W]e conclude that here the antidemocratic effects of the meeting-attendance rule outweigh the interests urged in its support. [A]n attendance requirement that results in the exclusion of 96.5% of the members from candidacy for union office hardly seems to be a "reasonable qualification" consistent with the goal of free and democratic elections. A requirement having that result obviously severely restricts the free choice of the membership in selecting its leaders.

Petitioners argue that . . . a member can assure himself of eligibility for candidacy by attending some 18 brief meetings over a three-year period. In other words, the union would have its rule treated not as excluding a category of member from eligibility, but simply as mandating a procedure to be followed by any member who wishes to be a candidate.

Even examined from this perspective, however, the rule has a restrictive effect on union democracy. In the absence of a permanent "opposition party" within the union, opposition to the incumbent leadership is likely to emerge in response to particular issues at different times, and member interest in changing union leadership is therefore likely to be at its highest only shortly before elections. Thus it is probable that to require that a member decide upon a potential candidacy at least 18 months in advance of an election when no issues exist to prompt that decision may not foster but discourage candidacies and to that extent impair the general membership's freedom to oust incumbents in favor of new leadership.

Nor are we persuaded by petitioners' argument that the Secretary has failed to show an antidemocratic effect because he has not shown that the incumbent leaders of the union became "entrenched" in their offices as a consequence of the operation of the attendance rule. The reasons for leaderships becoming entrenched are difficult to isolate. The election of the same officers year after year may be a signal that antidemocratic election rules have prevented an effective challenge to the regime, or might well signal only that the members are satisfied with their stewardship; if elections are uncontested, opposition factions may have been denied access to the ballot, or competing interests may have compromised differences before the election to maintain a front of unity. . . . Congress did not saddle the courts with the duty to search out and remove improperly entrenched union leaderships. Rather, Congress chose to guarantee union democracy by regulating not the results of a union's electoral procedure, but the procedure itself. Congress decided that if the elections are "free and democratic," the members themselves are able to correct abuse of power by entrenched leadership. Procedures that unduly restrict free choice among candidates are forbidden without regard to their success or failure in maintaining corrupt leadership.

Petitioners next argue that the rule is reasonable within § 401(e) because it encourages attendance at union meetings, and assures more qualified officers by limiting election to those who have demonstrated an interest in union affairs, and are familiar with union problems. But the rule has plainly not served these goals. It has obviously done little to encourage attendance at meetings, which continue to attract only a handful of members. Even as to the more limited goal of encouraging the attendance of potential dissident candidates, very few members, as we have said, are likely to see themselves as such sufficiently far in advance of the election to be spurred to attendance by the rule. . . .

We therefore conclude that Congress, in guaranteeing every union member the opportunity to hold office, subject only to "reasonable qualifications," disabled unions from establishing eligibility qualifications as sharply restrictive of the openness of the union political process as is petitioners' attendance rule. . . . [*Affirmed.*]

Some other restrictions relating to union elections have been upheld. In the case which follows, the union was concerned about outside financial support for candidates in union elections. Note that union candidates are given less protection and have more restrictions placed upon them than do candidates for public office.

UNITED STEELWORKERS OF AMERICA v. SADLOWSKI
102 S.Ct. 2339 (1982)

A union amended its constitution to include an "outsider rule." This rule prohibits candidates for union office from accepting campaign contributions from nonmembers. It also creates a committee to enforce the rule and makes the committee's decisions final and binding. Plaintiff is a union member who had been an unsuccessful candidate for union office before adoption of the rule. He had received much of the financial support for his campaign from sources outside the union. He filed suit claiming that the rule violated the "freedom of speech and assembly" provision of Section 101(a)(2) of the LMRDA. The Court of Appeals held that the "outsider" rule was illegal.

MARSHALL, J.: . . . Section 101(a)(2) is contained in Title I of the LMRDA, the "Bill of Rights of Members of Labor Organizations." It provides:

"Freedom of speech and assembly.—**Every member of any labor organization shall have the right to**

meet and assemble freely with other members; and to express any views, arguments, or opinions; and to express at meetings of the labor organization his views, upon candidates in an election of the labor organization or upon any business properly before the meeting, subject to the organization's established and reasonable rules pertaining to the conduct of meetings: *Provided,* That nothing herein shall be construed to impair the right of a labor organization to adopt and enforce reasonable rules as to the responsibility of every member toward the organization as an institution and to his refraining from conduct that would interfere with its performance of its legal or contractual obligations.

We must decide whether this statute is violated by a union rule that prohibits candidates for union office from accepting campaign contributions from individuals who are not members of the union.

At the outset, we address respondents' contention that this case can be resolved simply by reference to First Amendment law. Respondents claim that § 101(a)(2) confers upon union members rights equivalent to the rights established by the First Amendment. They further argue that in the context of a political election, a rule that placed substantial restrictions on a candidate's freedom to receive campaign contributions would violate the First Amendment. Thus, a rule that substantially restricts contributions in union campaigns must violate § 101(a)(2). We are not persuaded by this argument. In light of the legislative history, we do not believe that § 101(a)(2) should be read as incorporating the entire body of First Amendment law, so that the scope of protections afforded by the statute coincides with the protections afforded by the Constitution. . . . There is absolutely no indication that Congress intended the scope of § 101(a)(2) to be identical to the scope of the First Amendment. Rather, Congress' decision to include a proviso covering "reasonable" rules refutes that proposi-

tion. First Amendment freedoms may not be infringed absent a compelling governmental interest. Even then, any government regulation must be carefully tailored, so that rights are not needlessly impaired. Union rules, by contrast, are valid under § 101(a)(2) so long as they are reasonable; they need not pass the stringent tests applied in the First Amendment context.

To determine whether a union rule is valid under the statute, we first consider whether the rule interferes with an interest protected by the first section of § 101(a)(2). If it does, we then determine whether the rule is "reasonable" and thus sheltered by the proviso to § 101(a)(2). In conducting these inquiries, we find guidance in the policies that underlie the LMRDA in general and Title I in particular. First Amendment principles may be helpful, although they are not controlling. We must look to the objectives Congress sought to achieve, and avoid "placing great emphasis upon close construction of the words." The critical question is whether a rule that partially interferes with a protected interest is nevertheless reasonably related to the protection of the organization as an institution.

Applying this form of analysis here, we conclude that the outsider rule is valid. Although it may limit somewhat the ability of insurgent union members to wage an effective campaign, an interest deserving some protection under the statute, it is rationally related to the union's legitimate interest in reducing outsider interference with union affairs.

An examination of the policies underlying the LMRDA indicates that the outsider rule may have some impact on interests that Congress intended to protect under § 101(a)(2). Congress adopted the freedom of speech and assembly provision in order to promote union democracy. It recognized that democracy would be assured only if union members are free to discuss union policies and criticize the leadership without fear of reprisal. Congress also recognized that this freedom is particularly critical, and deserves vigorous protection, in the context of election campaigns. For it is in elections that members can wield their power, and directly express their approval or disapproval of the union leadership.

The interest in fostering vigorous debate during election campaigns may be affected by the outsider rule. If candidates are not permitted to accept contributions from persons outside the union, their ability to criticize union policies and to mount effective challenges to union leadership may be weakened. Restrictions that limit access to funds may reduce the number of issues discussed, the attention that is devoted to each issue, and the size of the audience reached.

Although the outsider rule does affect rights protected by the statute, as a practical matter the impact may not be substantial. Respondents . . . suggest that incumbents have a large advantage because they can rely on their union staff during election campaigns. Challengers cannot counter this power simply by seeking funds from union members; the rank-and-file cannot provide sufficient support. Thus, they must be permitted to seek funds from outsiders. In fact, however, the rank-and-file probably can provide support. The USWA is a very large union whose members earn sufficient income to make campaign contributions. Requiring candidates to rely solely on contributions from members will not unduly limit their ability to raise campaign funds. Uncontradicted record evidence discloses that challengers have been able to defeat incumbents or administration-backed candidates, despite the absence of financial support from nonmembers. . . .

Although the outsider rule may implicate rights protected by § 101(a)(2), it serves a legitimate purpose that is clearly protected under the statute. The union adopted the rule because it wanted to ensure that nonmembers do not unduly influence union affairs. USWA feared that officers who received campaign contributions from nonmembers might be beholden to those individuals and might allow their decisions to be influenced by considerations other than the best interests of the union. The union wanted to ensure that the union leadership remained responsive to the membership. An examination of the policies underlying the LMRDA reveals that this is a legitimate purpose that Congress meant to protect. . . .

We hold that USWA's rule prohibiting candidates for union office from accepting campaign contributions from nonmembers does not violate § 101(a)(2). Although it may interfere with rights Congress intended to protect, it is rationally related to a legitimate and protected purpose, and thus is sheltered by the proviso to § 101(a)(2). We reverse the decision below and remand for further proceedings consistent with this opinion. [*It is so ordered.*]

The LMRDA protects rank and file union members. It does not protect job security or tenure of union officers or employees. For example, the courts have held that after a union election, the winner may remove appointive union officials. Union leaders may select staff members with compatible views.

15. LMRDA Reporting Requirements

The act also contains several provisions concerning the secretary of labor and reports required of unions. The purpose of these reports is to reveal practices detrimental to union members. For example, each union must adopt a constitution and by laws and file them with the secretary of labor, together with the following information:

1 The name and address of the union office and the place where records are kept

2 The names and titles of officers

3 The amount of initiation fees required

4 The amount of dues charged

5 A detailed statement of procedures for (a) qualification for office, (b) levying fees, (c) insurance plans, (d) disbursement of funds, (e) audits, (f) selection of officers, (g) removal of officers, (h) determining bargaining demands, (i) fines, (j) approval of contracts, (k) calling strikes, and (l) issuance of work permits

In addition, yearly financial reports must be filed which indicate:

1 Assets and liabilities

2 Receipts and sources of funds

3 Salaries of officers

4 Loans to members greater than $250

5 Loans to business enterprises

6 Other disbursements

Note that the above reports do not concern the operation of union welfare and pension plan funds, which involve a great deal more money than union treasuries. The Welfare and Pension Plans Disclosure Act of 1958 (as amended in 1962), also known as the Teller Act, governs such funds. This act requires filing with the secretary of labor a description of every employee pension and welfare plan covered by it as well as annual reports detailing the operations of the funds. The act also gives the secretary broad investigative and enforcing powers.

The Landrum-Griffin Act also requires reports on trusteeships. A trusteeship is a method of supervision or control whereby a labor union suspends the automony otherwise available to a subordinate body under its constitution and bylaws. In this report, the union must state the names and addresses of subordinate organizations, the date of establishing trusteeship, and the reasons for establishing the trusteeship.

In addition to the foregoing reports, union employees and officials must file a yearly report with the secretary of labor containing information on possible areas of conflict of interest, such as stock holdings in companies with which the union has dealings and payments personally received from employers. Employers must file yearly reports with the secretary containing information concerning payments made to unions or union officials. An employer must also report on payments made to consultants whom it engages to deal with unions. Reports made to the secretary of labor become public information and may be used as the basis of criminal proceedings.

16. Internal Union Activities

The Landrum-Griffin Act provides an elaborate system of regulation of internal union activities. These regulations cover union election procedures, management of union funds, trusteeships, and union personnel. The secretary of labor is given power to investigate alleged violations of any of the regulations and may institute criminal proceedings through the attorney general.

The act requires that elections be held at minimum regular intervals to promote democracy. National unions must hold elections at least every five years, locals every three years, and intermediate bodies every four years. Elections must be by secret ballot of members, or of delegates who were chosen by secret ballot of members. Every candidate for union office must have access to membership lists. The union must provide adequate safeguards to ensure a fair election, and every candidate is given the right to post observers at the polls and counting place. All candidates must have equal opportunity to run for office without penalty or punishment by the organization. Union funds may not be used by any candidate in his or her campaign.

The act also recognizes the fiduciary responsibility of officers of unions. All clauses in union constitutions which attempt to provide that union officers do not have liability for wrongful conduct are void as against public policy. A member of a union may sue for funds mishandled by union officers after he or she has exhausted union proceedings, and the member will be repaid the cost of bringing suit.

The act makes embezzlement of union funds a federal crime. The penalty is imprisonment for up to five years or a fine of up to $10,000, or both. Every union employee who handles funds must be bonded. No union may lend more than $2,000 to a union employee or official. Any person who willfully violates either of these two provisions is subject to imprisonment for one year or a fine of up to $10,000, or both. Unions are not permitted to pay the fines imposed on their officers or employees who are convicted of violating the act. However, the propriety of payments to cover legal fees in lawsuits is judged on an individual basis.

The Landrum-Griffin Act also makes it a federal offense to engage in extortionate picketing. This is picketing to force an employer to pay money to union officials or other individuals for their own personal use rather than for the benefit of the union membership generally.

17. Labor Law and Government Employees

Perhaps the most difficult problems in the labor field today involve government employees. Should such employees have the right to form unions and to bargain collectively with the government units that employ them? If collective bargaining fails to reach satisfactory agreements, should government employees have the right to strike? The clear-cut trend in the law is to answer the first question affirmatively and the second negatively. Today, unions or employee organizations exist at all levels of government. However, in the absence of a statute giving them the right, there is no right to strike. This was recently reaffirmed when the air controllers who went on strike were discharged and their union decertified. A union without the right to strike is a "paper tiger." Without the right to strike, the power of public employee unions is much less than that of unions in the private sector.

The right to strike is denied government workers because such strikes affect the public more adversely than those by employees in the private sector. Strikes by police, firefighters, teachers, sanitation workers, transportation workers, and other public employees who perform vital services obviously can be directly and immediately detrimental to the health, safety, and welfare of those whom they are supposed to serve.

Collective bargaining in public employment varies throughout the country. States vary from having no laws granting bargaining rights to public employees to having statutes with broad guarantees. A few states even give some public employees the right to strike. Unions of public workers are pressing for legislation that would give them the choice of striking or turning to binding arbitration if a dispute cannot be resolved. Other unions advocate the expansion of the present Wagner and Taft-Hartley Acts to cover state and local employees.

The difficulties of collective bargaining in the public sector are multiplied by the problem of funds needed to meet labor's demands, since one of the most significant differences between public and private labor relations is that there is no "bottom line" for cost in governmental bodies as there is in private corporations. Frequently, public officials have neither the funds to meet labor's demands nor the power to raise taxes without the consent of the voters. A school board may be very willing to grant pay increases, but unless voters will agree to the tax increases required, the money to do so is simply not available. For example, the faculty of Florida's state colleges and universities bargained for a raise of 10 percent. The legislature refused to fund it. In such a case, the collective-bargaining agreement must give way to the constitutional provisions on state funding. A possible solution to this dilemma is to integrate the bargaining process with the budgetary process.

Wisconsin has taken steps toward such integration. There, state employee contracts negotiated by the executive branch are subject to approval by a committee of the legislature, which binds the state if it is given. Rejection by the committee sends a contract back to bargaining.

It is expected that the number of public employees represented by unions will continue to grow. However, few of these will have the right to strike. Employees performing essential services are not likely to be granted this right, even though it is basic to the whole concept of unions. Employees performing nonessential services may acquire the right to strike, or, in some cases, actions will not be taken to stop such strikes even if they are technically illegal. The more important the job, the less likely a strike will be tolerated.

18. Policy Trends and Ethical Considerations

One of the problems facing management today is the mushrooming of fringe benefits for employees demanded and obtained by unions. Among the more familiar of these are longer paid vacations and company-provided benefits such as medical care, life insurance, pensions, and compensation for periods of unemployment during layoffs. One of the latest demands being pushed by unions in bargaining sessions is that for employer-financed group legal plans. Often the expense of fringe benefits is so great to employers that they find it less costly to have a smaller labor force (and pay employees time and one-half for overtime) than to hire additional workers at the regular hourly wage.

Government policy attempts to balance the bargaining power of business and labor so they can settle their disputes themselves by mutual agreement. However, one of the most serious questions involved in labor-management relations today is whether the power to make economic decisions which so greatly affect the public interest can or should be left in the hands of these private parties. It is clear that, with today's competitive threats from foreign industry, it is in the interests of employers and unions as well as the public as a whole that our economy remain viable. But it is doubtful that we can compete effectively and still have the slowdowns, strikes, make-work rules, and restrictions on the use of labor-saving machinery which have been so common in the past. In order to effectively compete with foreign economies with their low wages and high degree of mechanization, we must increase production per labor-hour by utilizing technology. Automation continues to be a major area of disagreement between management and labor. Many contract disputes and difficult bargaining issues center on automation and its effect on employment.

Because of the magnitude of the decisions made at the bargaining table, it is clear that government can no longer simply try to equalize the bargaining position of powerful unions and large corporate employers and sit back neutrally while they make all the decisions. In fact, the status of equality may make long work stoppages more likely, to the public detriment, where giant unions and corporations are in conflict. Each may have the endurance to withstand a long siege. Throughout our history as a country, the people have been wary of bigness and large concentrations of power, first in government, then in business, and finally in the unions which grew to great strength, particularly after the enactment of the Wagner Act. It is likely that the future will bring more government action curbing union power because of public reaction to the wielding of that power, unless restraint is exercised by unions. Many have called for government-imposed compulsory arbitration to take the place of crippling strikes.

One recent suggestion by the Reagan administration's Labor Department, strongly opposed by organized labor, would reduce restrictions on children working. Proposed regulations would allow fourteen-and fifteen-year-olds to work more (and later) hours in more kinds of jobs. Child labor laws preventing exploitation were arduously enacted as a response to often outrageous working conditions imposed on children and teenagers in earlier times. It is natural that many would view a relaxation of child labor laws with alarm. Children aged fourteen and fifteen may already work eighteen hours a week. To increase the number of permissible work hours per week for a high-schooler to twenty-four and to extend work times to nine or ten o'clock at night would certainly appear to create an opportunity for exploitation. This is especially so since small businesses are exempt from the federal minimum wage law, and larger businesses, through a federal exemption procedure, may pay some young workers subminimum wages under present law. One prominent labor union official, pointing out high rates of unemployment, especially among sixteen- to nineteen-year-olds, suggested the proposal would be a "social outrage" even if there were full employment.

Proponents of these proposals argue that these younger teenagers often fill jobs that older workers won't accept (such as sweeping or dishwashing), giving them an opportunity to earn money, gain experience, and learn discipline at the same time. Critics question the educational and developmental impact on a student. Related suggestions to establish a permanent two-tier minimum wage with teenagers being paid less than the standard rate have not met with legislative success. Whether either suggestion would increase teen-age employment (or reduce unemployment) is conjectural. The ultimate ethical question society may have to answer is whether permitting a fourteen-year-old to cook or bake or fold laundry for twenty-four hours a week (till nine o'clock on a school night) is the right step to be taking.

Perhaps the biggest question for United States labor relations in the eighties and beyond is whether the adversarial approach our labor laws provide for has become outmoded. There is much evidence that industry—with or without union participation—is moving to make jobs more satisfying and productive by involving the individual worker more in management decisions. Self-managed work teams, quality circles, labor-management steering committees, and other problem-solving groups are becoming increasingly common in American businesses.

Other capitalist economies are experimenting with mechanisms for greater worker-management cooperation. Co-determination as practiced in western Europe is a prime-example. Since 1976, Germany has required that each publicly held company with at least 2,000 employees have a supervisory board with one-half employee representation, and as well work councils elected by white-collar and blue-collar workers. The supervisory board makes long-term decisions and hires management, while the work councils have an equal voice with management in many more routine decisions such as recruiting, training, compensation, promotion, and discharge policies. Some employers have extended such worker participation to worker ownership and investment in the company. The success of this approach is not universally agreed upon, but many claim this type of industrial democracy has worked well. Variations on the theme of closer business-labor cooperation can be seen in the workings of many Japanese firms.

It is probable that demands for more participatory management and so-called quality-of-work-life programs will increase, thus tempering the traditional adversarial approach, at least on the plant floor. Few expect the bargaining table or the grievance process to be done away with. Yet, greater recognition of mutual interests on the part of management and labor may well influence the tone of bargaining. Revision of the top-to-bottom hierarchical form of management into a more cooperative bottom-up approach may help labor-management relations evolve into a less antagonistic, more participative mode in the future.

REVIEW QUESTIONS

1 Identify the federal statute which accomplished each of the following:

a Exempted union activity from the antitrust laws

b Created the NLRB

c Allowed states to enact right-to-work laws

d Outlawed certain conduct by management as unfair to labor (unfair labor practices)

e Governed collective bargaining for railroads and airlines

f Prohibited federal courts from enjoining lawful union activities, including picketing and strikes

g Bill of rights for union members

h Provided for an eighty-day cooling-off period in strikes which imperil national health or safety

i Outlawed yellow-dog contracts

j Created the Federal Mediation and Conciliation Service to assist in settlement of labor disputes

2 Assume that Z Company has a collective bargaining agreement that includes a no-strike clause during its terms. Despite this, the union, at a time when the contract has over a year to run, calls a strike due to a grievance. No violence results from the strike. Will the Norris-LaGuardia Act prevent a court from issuing an injunction enforcing the contract and ordering the strike to cease? Explain.

3 A musicians' union required orchestra leaders to charge minimum prices, to belong to the union, and to require minimum employment quotas. A suit was filed contending that such requirements violated the antitrust laws. The union contended that it was exempt. Was the union correct? Explain.

4 The United Mine Workers called a nationwide strike. Thirty days later, the issues remained unresolved, and several related industries began laying off thousands of workers. If this strike threatens the nation's security, is there any legal method available to stop the strike? Explain.

5 What position connected with the NLRB, except for direct membership, has the most power and responsibility? Briefly describe these powers and responsibilities.

6 Albert owns a small retail store with seven full- and part-time employees. One employee is fired for advocating that the employees form a union. If the employee files a complaint of an unfair labor practice with the NLRB, what will be the result? Why?

7 Give examples of workers not subject to the jurisdiction of the NLRB.

8 The Yeshiva University Faculty Association filed a representation petition with the NLRB seeking certification as bargaining agent for the full-time faculty. At this private university, the faculty's authority in academic matters at the university was absolute. The university opposed the petition on the ground that all of its faculty members were managerial or supervisory personnel and thus not "employees" within the meaning of the Wagner Act. Is the faculty entitled to conduct a union certification election? Explain.

9 The general counsel of the NLRB issued a bargaining order based on union authorization cards. The authorization cards were unequivocal and clearly stated that the employee authorized the union to represent him or her. The employer contended that the employees were orally told that signing the cards will only result in an election. Will the bargaining order be set aside? Why, or why not?

10 Pat lives in a state that has enacted a right-to-work law. The company which employs her has recognized the United Clerical Workers (UCW) as the bargaining representative of its workers. The union has sought to collect union dues or their equivalent from Pat. Is she required to pay them? Why, or why not?

11 ABC Company's employees voted by 51 percent in an election to have American Confederation act as their collective-bargaining representatives. Only four months later, 60 percent of the employees became disenchanted with American Confederation and wished to oust it. May they do so? Explain.

12 The president of your company is writing a speech to give to the workers prior to a union representation election. What advice would you give relative to the contents of the speech?

13 The Amalgamated Lead Workers' Union suspected that antiunion persons were infiltrating its ranks to overthrow the union. Accordingly, its board proposed a rule, which the membership adopted, that only those who had belonged to the union for at least two years would be eligible for union office. Walter, who had been in AML for only eighteen months, filed a petition to run for president, but it was refused due to the two-year requirement. Walter filed suit, challenging the rule. What was the result? Why?

14 The garbage collectors in Metropolis are city employees. They are represented by a union. Negotiations with the city manager have broken down, and the garbage collectors have gone on strike. The city manager has notified all employees that anyone who does not return to work within twenty-four hours will be discharged. Those who do not return are then replaced with new employees. Will a court order the discharged workers to be rehired? Why, or why not?

Chapter
19

Unfair Labor Practices

1. Introduction

The term "unfair labor practice" was originally used to describe practices by management that were unfair to workers and their unions. The Wagner Act listed five general categories of such violations. A later amendment added a sixth. These are summarized in Table 19-1.

An activity may be, and often is, a violation of more than one of the listed unfair labor practices. Indeed, most violations constitute interference with the right to engage in concerted activity (the first category). For example, retaliation against a union leader for filing charges would constitute a violation of both the first and fourth categories.

If management is guilty of an unfair labor practice, the NLRB has a broad range of remedies to use in eliminating the impact of the violation. If a union has lost a representation election, it may order a new one. If an

TABLE 19-1 Unfair Labor Practices by Employers

1 Interference with efforts of employees to form, join, or assist labor organizations, or to engage in concerted activities for mutual aid or protection
2 Domination of a labor organization or contribution of financial or other support to it
3 Discrimination in hiring or tenure of employees for reason of union affiliation
4 Discrimination against employees for filing charges or giving testimony under the act
5 Refusal to bargain collectively in good faith with a duly designated representative of the employees
6 Agreeing with a labor organization to engage in a secondary boycott

employee has been wronged, for example, by a wrongful discharge, the Board can order the employee rehired with back pay. The NLRB has the capability of righting wrongs that have occurred.

As we noted in the prior chapter, the Taft-Hartley Act declared that certain actions by unions are also unfair labor practices. The Landrum-Griffin Act also expanded the list of unfair labor practices. The sections which follow give examples of violations by both parties—management and labor. The discussion of unfair labor practices by unions begins with section 10 of this chapter.

2. Interference with Efforts of Employees to Form or Join Labor Organizations

In part, the first unfair labor practice listed is for an employer to interfere with the efforts of employees to form, join, or assist labor organizations. This is a catchall intended to guarantee the right to organize and to join a labor union. It clearly prohibits "scare" tactics such as threats by employers to fire those involved in organizing employees, or threats to cut back on employee benefits if employees succeed in unionizing. In addition, less obvious activities are outlawed, such as requiring job applicants to state on a questionnaire whether they would cross a picket line in a strike, unless the questionnaire contains an assurance by the employer against reprisal. In one typical case, the company personnel director questioned two employees on break about both the whereabouts of a union meeting and if the union was paying employees to sign authorization cards. These questions were a coercive interrogation and an unfair labor practice. An employer cannot engage in conduct calculated to erode employee support for the union.

Retaliation for union activity is discussed more fully in section 4 of this chapter. However, keep in mind that not every act of retaliation is an unfair labor practice. For example, the filing of a lawsuit may or may not be an unfair labor practice depending on the outcome of the lawsuit. In the case which follows, the NLRB attempted to stop the lawsuit as an unfair labor practice, but it was not allowed to do so.

BILL JOHNSON'S RESTAURANTS, INC. v. N.L.R.B.
103 S.Ct. 2161 (1983)

Helton, a waitress at Johnson's restaurant, filed unfair labor practice charges with the National Labor Relations Board (Board) alleging that she had been fired because of her efforts to organize a union. Later Helton and other waitresses picketed the restaurant and distributed leaflets. The leaflets accused management of making "[u]nwarranted sexual advances" and maintaining a "filthy restroom for women employees." The restaurant then filed a suit for damages and injunctive relief against Helton and the other demonstrators in an Arizona state court. It alleged that Helton and the other demonstrators had harassed customers, blocked access to the restaurant, created a threat to public safety, and libeled the restaurant by false and outrageous statements in the leaflets.

On the following day, Helton filed a second charge with the Board, alleging that the civil suit was filed in retaliation for the defendant's protected, concerted activities and the filing of charges with the Board. An administrative law judge concluded that filing the suit was an unfair labor practice. He found that the evidence failed to support the allegations of the complaint in the state-court action and that the lawsuit was retaliatory. The Board ordered the restaurant to withdraw its state-court complaint and to reimburse the defendants for their legal expenses.

WHITE, J.: . . . We must decide whether the Board may issue a cease-and-desist order to halt the prosecution of a state court civil suit brought by an employer to retaliate against employees for exercising federally-protected labor rights, without also finding that the suit lacks a reasonable basis in fact or law. . . . The Board does not regard lack of merit in the employer's suit as an independent element of the § 8(a)(1) and § 8(a)(4) unfair labor practice. Rather, it asserts that the *only* essential element of a violation is retaliatory motive.

At first blush, the Board's position seems to have substance. Sections 8(a)(1) and (4) of the National Labor Relations Act (Act) are broad, remedial provisions that guarantee that employees will be able to enjoy their rights secured by § 7 of the Act—including the right to unionize, the right to engage in concerted activity for mutual aid and protec-

tion, and the right to utilize the Board's processes—without fear of restraint, coercion, discrimination, or interference from their employer. The Court has liberally construed these laws as prohibiting a wide variety of employer conduct that is intended to restrain, or that has the likely effect of restraining, employees in the exercise of protected activities. A lawsuit no doubt may be used by an employer as a powerful instrument of coercion or retaliation. As the Board has observed, by suing an employee who files charges with the Board or engages in other protected activities, an employer can place its employees on notice that anyone who engages in such conduct is subjecting himself to the possibility of a burdensome lawsuit. Regardless of how unmeritorious the employer's suit is, the employee will most likely have to retain counsel and incur substantial legal expenses to defend against it. Furthermore . . . the chilling effect of a state lawsuit upon an employee's willingness to engage in protected activity is multiplied where the complaint seeks damages in addition to injunctive relief. Where, as here, such a suit is filed against hourly-wage waitresses or other individuals who lack the backing of a union, the need to allow the Board to intervene and provide a remedy is at its greatest.

There are weighty countervailing considerations, however, that militate against allowing the Board to condemn the filing of a suit as an unfair labor practice and to enjoin its prosecution. . . . The right of access to the courts is an aspect of the First Amendment right to petition the Government for redress of grievances. . . . We should be sensitive to these First Amendment values in construing the NLRA in the present context. As the Board itself has recognized, "going to a judicial body for redress of alleged wrongs . . . stands apart from other forms of action directed at the alleged wrongdoer. The right of access to a court is too important to be called an unfair labor practice solely on the ground that what is sought in court is to enjoin employees from exercising a protected right."

Moreover, in recognition of the States' compelling interest in the maintenance of domestic peace, the Court has construed the Act as not preempting the States from providing a civil remedy for conduct touching interests "deeply rooted in local feeling and responsibility." It has therefore repeatedly been held that an employer has the right to seek local judicial protection from tortious conduct during a labor dispute. . . .

Considering the First Amendment right of access to the courts and the State interests . . . we conclude that the Board's interpretation of the Act is untenable. The filing and prosecution of a well-founded lawsuit may not be enjoined as an unfair labor practice, even if it would not have been commenced but for the plaintiff's desire to retaliate against the defendant for exercising rights protected by the Act.

Although it is not unlawful under the Act to prosecute a meritorious action, the same is not true of suits based on insubstantial claims—suits that lack, to use the term coined by the Board, a "reasonable basis." Such suits are not within the scope of First Amendment protection. . . .

Similarly, State interests . . . do not enter into play when the state-court suit has no basis. Since, by definition, the plaintiff in a baseless suit has not suffered a legally-protected injury, the State's interest in protecting the health and well-being of its citizens is not implicated. States have only a negligible interest, if any, in having insubstantial claims adjudicated by their courts, particularly in the face of the strong federal interest in vindicating the rights protected by the national labor laws.

The right to litigate is an important one, and the Board should consider the evidence with utmost care before ordering the cessation of a state-court lawsuit. In a proper case, however, we believe that Congress intended to allow the Board to provide this remedy. Therefore, we hold that it is an enjoinable unfair labor practice to prosecute a baseless lawsuit with the intent of retaliating against an employee for the exercise of rights protected by § 7 of the NLRA.

To summarize, we hold that the Board may not halt the prosecution of a state-court lawsuit, regardless of the plaintiff's motive, unless the suit lacks a reasonable basis in fact or law. Retaliatory motive and lack of reasonable basis are both essential prerequisites to the issuance of a cease-and-desist order against a state suit. The Board's reasonable basis inquiry must be structured in a manner that will preserve the state plaintiff's right to have a state court jury or judge resolve genuine material factual or state-law legal disputes pertaining to the lawsuit. Therefore, if the Board is called upon to determine whether a suit is unlawful prior to the time that the state court renders final judgment, and if the state plaintiff can show that such genuine material factual or legal issues exist, the Board must await the results of the state-court adjudication with respect to the merits of the state suit. If the state proceedings result in a judgment adverse to the plaintiff, the Board may then consider the matter further and, if it is found that the lawsuit was filed with retaliatory intent, the Board may find a violation and order appropriate relief. In short, then, although it is unfair labor practice to prosecute an unmeritorious lawsuit for a retaliatory purpose, the offense is not enjoinable unless the suit lacks a reasonable basis. . . . [*Reversed and remanded.*]

CONFERRING BENEFITS

Even conferring of benefits by an employer may be an unfair labor practice. In one case, the employer reminded its employees by a letter sent two weeks before a representation election that the company had just instituted a "floating holiday" which they could take on their birthdays. The letter also announced a new system for computing overtime during holiday weeks, which had the effect of increasing wages for those weeks, and a new vacation schedule which let employees extend their vacations by sandwiching them between two weekends. The union lost the election, but the Supreme Court set it aside. It held that it was an unfair labor practice for the employer to engage in conduct immediately favorable to employees which is undertaken with the express purpose of impinging upon their freedom of choice for or against unionization and is reasonably calculated to have that effect. The danger inherent in well-timed increases in benefits is the suggestion of a fist inside the velvet glove. Employees are not likely to miss the inference that the source of benefits now conferred is also the source from which future benefits must flow and which may dry up if it is not obliged.

WORK RULES

Company *work rules* often affect negatively workers' attempts to organize and join a union. These work rules may prohibit wearing buttons or insignia on work clothes. Unless the employer can establish a valid reason for such rules, they cannot be used to stop the wearing of union buttons or insignia. To punish a worker for violating such a work rule would constitute an unfair labor practice. Similarly, "no solicitation on the premises" rules which go beyond the actual necessity of the employer based on health, safety, or the like are not enforceable to stop workers from organizing.

A rule which prohibits solicitation during "working time" is presumptively valid, but a rule which bans solicitation during "working hours" is presumptively invalid. It is an unfair labor practice to prohibit union activity and solicitation on company property during the employees' own time. The employer need not permit it when the employee is supposed to be working.

In one case, the NLRB held that a hospital's rule prohibiting solicitation by its employees at all times "in any area of the hospital which is accessible to or utilized by the public" was presumed to be invalid except in "immediate patient areas." These were defined as places such as patients' rooms, operating rooms, and places where patients receive treatment. The Supreme Court agreed with the Board that the hospital had not justified its rule as applied to its cafeteria, gift shop, and the lobbies and entrances on its first floor. However, union solicitation in the presence or within the hearing of patients in corridors and sitting rooms that adjoined patients' rooms and operating and treatment rooms might have an adverse effect on their recovery. Thus, the no-solicitation rule was not an unfair labor practice as applied to such areas, in addition to the "immediate patient-care areas."

Of course, the Wagner Act does not guarantee the rights of employees to solicit for *any* cause on an employer's property. Solicitation must be protected by Section 7 as involving collective bargaining or an activity engaged in for other mutual aid or protection.

WRITTEN AND ORAL STATEMENTS MADE TO EMPLOYEES

A difficult aspect is presented in those cases in which an employer is accused of an unfair labor practice as a result of something she has said or written. Such allegations may conflict with First Amendment guarantees of freedom of speech and the press. Moreover, as we noted in Chapter 18, the Taft-Hartley Act provides that the expression of views, arguments, or opinions is not evidence of an unfair labor practice if it contains no threats of reprisal or promises of benefits.

An employer may even predict that the consequences of unionization will be unfavorable if she or he does so in a way which contains no threat. The statement that "it is our definite view that if the union were to come in here, it would work to your serious harm" has been held privileged and noncoercive. However, if the employer predicts dire economic events as a result of unionization, such may be an illegal threat if he has it within his power to make the prediction come true.

It is extremely difficult to draw a clear-cut line between those statements of employers which are coercive and those which are noncoercive and thus privileged. Interpretations of the Board have varied with its membership over the years.

3. Interfering with Concerted Activities

The first half of the first unfair labor practice refers to interference with efforts to form, join, or assist labor organizations. The second half covers "*concerted activities* for mutual aid or protection." A violation of the second half does not have to involve a union. It protects any group of employees acting for mutual aid and protection. This protection is limited, however, when an exclusive bargaining representative has already been chosen. It does not protect individuals in other unions.

Concerted activity may directly involve a union and may involve issues of importance to the workers and their union. The phrase is given a liberal interpretation in order to create a climate that encourages unionization, collective bargaining, and all that may flow therefrom. For example, some employees refused to work after a heated grievance meeting. They followed their supervisors onto the workroom floor and continued to argue loudly until they were ordered a second time to resume work. The employer issued letters of reprimand alleging insubordination. This was an unfair labor practice. The employees were engaged in a protected activity. The protection of employee conduct at grievance meetings is extended to a brief "cooling-off period" following an employer's termination of such a meeting. Protection of employees' participation in the meetings themselves would be seriously threatened if the employer could at any point call an immediate halt to the operation of the law simply by declaring the meeting ended.

The case which follows illustrates the extent to which the law protects workers in concerted activities.

EASTEX, INC. v. NLRB
98 S.Ct. 2505 (1978)

Employees of petitioner corporation sought to distribute a four-section union newsletter in nonworking areas of petitioner's plant during nonworking time. The second section encouraged employees to write their legislature to oppose incorporation of the state "right-to-work" statute into a revised state constitution. The third section criticized a presidential veto of an increase in the federal minimum wage and urged employees to register to vote to "defeat our enemies and elect our friends." Representatives of petitioner refused to permit the requested distribution of the newsletter because of the content of its second and third sections. The union then filed an unfair labor practice charge with the NLRB. The Board ruled that petitioner's refusal constituted an unfair labor practice. The Board's cease and desist order was enforced by the Court of Appeals, and the Supreme Court granted certioari.

POWELL, J.: . . . [The question presented here] is whether . . . distribution of the newsletter is the kind of concerted activity that is protected from employer interference by §§ 7 and 8(a)(1) of the National Labor Relations Act. . . .

Section 7 provides that "[e]mployees shall have the right . . . to engage in . . . concerted activities for the purpose of collective bargaining or other mutual aid or protection. . . ." Petitioner contends that the activity

here is not within the "mutual aid or protection" language because it does not relate to a "specific dispute" between employees and their own employer "over an issue which the employer has the right or power to affect." In support of its position, petitioner asserts that the term "employees" in § 7 refers only to employees of a particular employer, so that only activity by employees on behalf of themselves or other employees of the same employer is protected. Petitioner also argues that the term "collective bargaining" in § 7 "indicates a direct bargaining relationship whereas 'other mutual aid or protection' must refer to activities of a similar nature. . . ." Thus, in petitioner's view, under § 7 "the employee is only protected for activity within the scope of the employment relationship." Petitioner rejects the idea that § 7 might protect any activity that could be characterized as "political," and suggests that the discharge of an employee who engages in any such activity would not violate the Act.

We believe that petitioner misconceives the reach of the "mutual aid or protection" clause. The "employees" who may engage in concerted activities for "mutual aid or protection" are defined by the Act to "include any employee, and shall not be limited to the employees of a particular employer, unless the Act explicitly states otherwise. . . ."

This definition was intended to protect employees when they engage in otherwise proper concerted activities in support of employees of employers other than their own. In recognition of this intent, the Board and the courts long have held that the "mutual aid or protection" clause encompasses such activity. Petitioner's argument on this point ignores the language of the Act and its settled construction.

We also find no warrant for petitioner's view that employees lose their protection under the "mutual aid or protection" clause when they seek to improve terms and conditions of employment or otherwise improve their lot as employees through channels outside the immediate employee-employer relationship. The 74th Congress knew well enough that labor's cause often is advanced on fronts other than collective bargaining and grievance settlement within the immediate employment context. It recognized this fact by choosing, as the language of § 7 makes clear, to protect concerted activities for the somewhat broader purpose of "mutual aid or protection" as well as for the narrower purposes of "self-organization" and "collective bargaining." Thus, it has been held that the "mutual aid or protection" clause protects employees from retaliation by their employers when they seek to improve working conditions through resort to administrative and judicial forums, and that employees' appeals to legislators to protect their interests as employees are within the scope of this clause. To hold that activity of this nature is entirely unprotected—irrespective of location or the means employed—would leave employees open to retaliation for much legitimate activity that could improve their lot as employees. As this could "frustrate the policy of the Act to protect the right of workers to act together to better their working conditions," we do not think that Congress could have intended the protection of § 7 to be as narrow as petitioner insists. . . .

The Board determined that distribution of the second section urging employees to write their legislators to oppose incorporation of the state "right-to-work" statute into a revised state constitution, was protected because union security is "central to the union concept of strength through solidarity" and "a mandatory subject of bargaining in other than right-to-work states." The newsletter warned that incorporation could affect employees adversely "by weakening Unions and improving the edge business has at the bargaining table." The fact that Texas already has a "right-to-work" statute does not render employees' interest in this matter any less strong, for, as the Court of Appeals noted, it is "one thing to face a legislative scheme which is open to legislative modification or repeal" and "quite another thing to face the prospect that such a scheme will be frozen in a concrete constitutional mandate." We cannot say that the Board erred in holding that this section of the newsletter bears such a relation to employees' interest as to come within the guarantee of the "mutual aid or protection" clause.

The Board held that distribution of the third section, criticizing a presidential veto of an increase in the federal minimum wage and urging employees to register to vote to "defeat our enemies and elect our friends," was protected despite the fact that petitioner's employees were paid more than the vetoed minimum wage. It reasoned that the "minimum wage inevitably influences wage levels derived from collective bargaining, even those far above the minimum," and that "concern by [petitioner's] employees for the plight of other employees might gain support for them at some future time when they might have a dispute with their employer." We think that the Board acted within the range of its discretion in so holding. Few topics are of such immediate concern to employees as the level of their wages. The Board was entitled to note the widely recognized impact that a rise in the minimum wage may have on the level of negotiated wages generally, a phenomenon that would not have been lost on petitioner's employees. The union's call, in the circumstances of this case, for these employees to back persons who support an increase in the minimum wage, and to oppose those who oppose it, fairly is characterized as concerted activity for the "mutual aid or protection" of petitioner's employees and of employees generally.

In sum, we hold that distribution of both the second and the third sections of the newsletter is protected under the "mutual aid or protection" clause of § 7. . . . [*The judgment of the Court of Appeals therefore is affirmed.*]

WORK RULES

Concerted activities <u>often involve the refusal to follow work rules.</u> If the employer has a rule with which the workers disagree, it is not uncommon for several of them to refuse to comply. Is it permissible to discipline such employees, or is discipline in such cases an unfair labor practice? The answer is often unclear and depends upon the facts in each case.

For example, a typical work rule used in industry is that a worker may not leave work without permission. In one case, the employer discharged seven employees for violating this rule. The employees on a particularly cold day had walked off the job from an uninsulated machine shop which on that day had no heat. On other occasions, protests had been made about the poor heat. The employees claimed to have acted as a group in protest against unfit working conditions, hoping that their concerted action would cause the employer to heat the shop properly. The employer justified the discharge action by claiming that the men left work without permission. The NLRB ruled that the action of the employees was protected concerted activity and that their discharge amounted to an unfair labor practice. The Supreme Court agreed and noted that employees do not

> . . . necessarily lose their right to engage in concerted activities . . . merely because they do not present a specific demand upon their employer to remedy a condition which they find objectionable. The language of [the law] is broad enough to protect concerted activities whether they take place before, after, or at the same time such a demand is made. . . . Having no bargaining representative and no established procedures . . . the men took the most direct course to let the company know they wanted a warmer place in which to work.

However, in another case the Supreme Court held that it was not an unfair labor practice for a company to fire certain employees who picketed the company's store, against union advice. There, the union had investigated charges that the company was racially discriminating against employees and had invoked the contract grievance procedure under the collective-bargaining agreement by demanding that the joint union-management Adjustment Board be convened "to hear the entire case." The discharged employees had begun picketing the company because they felt that the grievance procedure being utilized was inadequate. In upholding the NLRB's decision, the court ruled that the law recognizes the principle of exclusive representation. Therefore, concerted activities by a minority of employees to bargain with their employer over issues of employment discrimination are not protected by the Wagner Act. Such employees may not bypass their exclusive bargaining representative.

INTERVIEWS

The concerted-activity concept has been expanded in recent decisions. In one case, an employer was investigating theft by employees. One employee asked that a union representative be present during her interview. She was refused. The Supreme Court held that the employee had a right to representation when there was a perceived threat to her employment security. The presence of a representative assures other employees in the bargaining unit that they too can obtain aid and protection if they wish when there appears to be a threat to their job security. Refusing the assistance at the interview was an unfair labor practice.

A few years later, a nonunion employee sought to have a union representative present at an investigatory interview. The courts held that the employee had a right to this assistance. Just as a union member has this right, so does a nonunion employee. The right to representation is derived from the protection afforded to concerted activity for mutual aid or protection, not from a union's right to act as an employee's exclusive representative for the purpose of collective bargaining.

SOLE EMPLOYEE AS CONCERTED ACTIVITY

The right to engage in concerted activity has been expanded to cover the actions of a sole employee under certain circumstances. If an employee has a grievance which may affect other workers, that employee has rights protected by the concerted-activity language of the first unfair labor practice.

N.L.R.B. v. CITY DISPOSAL SYSTEMS, INC.
104 S.Ct. 1505 (1984)

James Brown, a truck driver, was employed by City Disposal Systems, Inc., which hauls garbage for the city of Detroit. He was discharged when he refused to drive a truck that he honestly and reasonably believed to be unsafe because of faulty brakes. The collective-bargaining agreement provided: "[t]he Employer shall not require employees to take out on the streets or highways any vehicle that is not in safe operating condition or equipped with safety appliances prescribed by law. It shall not be a violation of the Agreement where employees refuse to operate such equipment unless such refusal is unjustified."

Brown filed a grievance with the union, but the union declined to process it. He then filed an unfair labor practice charge challenging his discharge. The NLRB found that Brown was discharged for refusing to operate the truck and that the discharge was an unfair labor practice. It found that an employee who acts alone in asserting a contract right is nevertheless engaged in concerted activity. He was ordered reinstated with back pay. The Court of Appeals reversed, holding that there was no concerted activity.

BRENNAN, J.: . . . The question to be decided is whether Brown's honest and reasonable assertion of his right to be free of the obligation to drive unsafe trucks constituted "concerted activit[y]" within the meaning of § 7 of the National Labor Relations Act.

The Administrative Law Judge (ALJ) . . . held that an employee who acts alone in asserting a contractual right can nevertheless be engaged in concerted activity within the meaning of § 7:

[W]hen an employee makes complaints concerning safety matters which are embodied in a contract, he is acting not only in his own interest, but is attempting to enforce such contract provisions in the interest of all the employees covered under the contract. Such activity we have found to be concerted and protected under the Act, and the discharge of an individual for engaging in such activity to be in violation of Section 8(a)(1) of the Act.

Section 7 of the NLRA provides that "[e]mployees shall have the right to . . . join or assist labor organizations, to bargain collectively through representatives of their own choosing, and to engage in other concerted activities for the purpose of collective bargaining or other mutual aid or protection." The NLRB's decision in this case applied the Board's longstanding "*Interboro* doctrine," under which an individual's assertion of a right grounded in a collective-bargaining agreement is recognized as "concerted activit[y]" and therefore accorded the protection of § 7. The Board has relied on two justifications for the doctrine: First, the assertion of a right contained in a collective-bargaining agreement is an extension of the concerted action that produced the agreement, and second, the assertion of such a right affects the rights of all employees covered by the collective-bargaining agreement.

The question for decision today is whether the Board's application of § 7 to Brown's refusal to drive truck No. 244 is reasonable. Several reasons persuade us that it is.

Neither the Court of Appeals nor respondent appears to question that an employee's invocation of a right derived from a collective-bargaining agreement meets § 7's requirement that an employee's action be taken "for purposes of collective bargaining or other mutual aid or protection." . . . A single employee's invocation of such rights affects all the employees that are covered by the collective-bargaining agreement. This type of generalized effect, . . . is sufficient to bring the actions of an individual employee within the "mutual aid or protection" standard, regardless of whether the employee has his own interests most immediately in mind. . . .

The invocation of a right rooted in a collective-bargaining agreement is unquestionably an integral part of the process that gave rise to the agreement. That process—beginning with the organization of a union, continuing into the negotiation of a collective-bargaining agreement, and extending through the enforcement of the agreement—is a single, collective activity. Obviously, an employee could not invoke a right grounded in a collective-bargaining agreement were it not for the prior negotiating activities of his fellow employees. Nor would it make sense for a union to negotiate a collective-bargaining agreement if individual employees could not invoke the rights thereby created against their employer. Moreover, when an employee invokes a right grounded in the collective-bargaining agreement, he does not stand alone. Instead, he brings to bear on his employer the power and resolve of all his fellow employees. When, for instance, James Brown refused to drive a truck he believed to be unsafe, he was in effect reminding his employer that he and his fellow employees, at the time their collective-bargaining agreement was signed, had extracted a promise from City Disposal that they would not be asked to drive unsafe trucks. He was also reminding his employer that if it persisted in ordering him to drive an unsafe truck, he could reharness the power of that group to ensure the enforcement of that promise. It was just as though James Brown was reassembling his fellow union members to reenact their decision not to drive unsafe trucks. A lone employee's invocation of a right grounded in his collective-bargaining agreement is, therefore, a concerted activity in a very real sense.

Furthermore, the acts of joining and assisting a labor organization, which § 7 explicitly recognizes as concerted, are related to collective action in essentially the same way that the invocation of a collectivvely bargained right is related to collective action. When an employee joins or assists a labor organization, his actions may be divorced in time, and in location as well, from the actions of fellow employees. Because of the integral relationship among the employees' actions, however, Congress viewed each employee as engaged in concerted activity. The lone employee could not join or assist a labor organization were it not for the related organizing activities of his fellow employees. Conversely, there would be limited utility in forming a labor organization if other employees could not join or assist the organization once it is formed. Thus, the formation of a labor organization is integrally related to the activity of joining or assisting such an organization in

the same sense that the negotiation of a collective-bargaining agreement is integrally related to the invocation of a right provided for in the agreement. In each case, neither the individual activity nor the group activity would be complete without the other.

The *Interboro* doctrine is also entirely consistent with the purposes of the Act, which explicitly include the encouragement of collective bargaining and other "practices fundamental to the friendly adjustment of industrial disputes arising out of differences as to wages, hours, or other working conditions." . . . Moreover, by applying § 7 to the actions of individual employees invoking their rights under a collective-bargaining agreement, the *Interboro* doctrine preserves the integrity of the entire collective-bargaining process; for by invoking a right grounded in a collectivve-bargaining agreement, the employee makes that right a reality, and breathes life, not only into the promises contained in the collective-bargaining agreement, but also into the entire process envisioned by Congress as the means by which to achieve industrial peace. . . .

The NLRB's *Interboro* doctrine recognizes as concerted activity an individual employee's reasonable and honest invocation of a right provided for in his collective-bargaining agreement. We conclude that the doctrine constitutes a reasonable interpretation of the Act. Accordingly, we accept the Board's conclusion tthat James Brown was engaged in concerted activity when he refused to drive truck No. 244. We therefore reverse the judgment of the Court of Appeals and remand the case for further proceedings consistent with this opinion, including an inquiry into whether respondent may continue to defend this action on the theory that Brown's refusal to drive truck No. 244 was unprotected, even if concerted. [*It is so ordered.*]

4. Discharge and Other Forms of Retaliation

One of the primary techniques used by management to discourage unionization and to interfere with the right of workers to engage in concerted union
activity is either to threaten to "fire" the workers or actually to discharge them
if the union wins the election. Retaliation and the threat of retaliation are
clearly unfair labor practices. However, the issues are often much more
complicated. Is it an unfair labor practice to discharge a union organizer who
is also an unsatisfactory employee? What is the effect of an employer's assisting others in making it impossible for the worker to continue his or her
employment?

The latter issue was involved in the following case.

SURE-TAN, INC. v. N.L.R.B.
104 S.Ct. 2803 (1984)

After a union was certified, the employer sent
a letter to the Immigration and Naturalization Service (INS), asking it to check the immigration status of five named employees.
After a short investigation, INS agents discovered that each of the five employees listed
in the letter was a Mexican national working
illegally in the United States. They were arrested and later accepted the INS grant of
voluntary departure as a substitute for depor-
tation. The administrative law judge (ALJ)
and the NLRB found that the employer had
in effect discharged the employees for voting
for and supporting the union. The Court of
Appeals affirmed.

O'CONNOR, J.: . . . We . . . determine
whether the National Labor Relations Board
(NLRB or Board) may properly find that an
employer engages in an unfair labor practice
by reporting to the Immigration and Naturalization Service (INS) certain employees
known to be undocumented aliens in retaliation for their engaging in union activity,
thereby causing their immediate departure
from the United States. . . .

We consider the predicate question
whether the NLRA should apply to unfair
labor practices committed against undocumented aliens. The Board has consistently
held that undocumented aliens are "employees" within the meaning of § 2(3) of the
Act. . . .

Accepting the premise that the provisions of the NLRA are applicable to undocumented alien employees, we must now
address the more difficult issue whether, under the circumstances of this case, petitioners
committed an unfair labor practice by reporting their undocumented alien employees to
the INS in retaliation for participating in
union activities. Section 8(a)(3) makes it an
unfair labor practice for an employer "by discrimination in regard to hire or tenure of
employment or any term or condition of employment to encourage or discourage membership in any labor organization." The
Board . . . has long held that an employer
violates this provision not only when, for the
purpose of discouraging union activity, it directly dismisses an employee, but also when it
purposefully creates working conditions so

intolerable that the employee has no option but to resign—a so-called "constructive discharge."

Petitioners do not dispute that the anti-union animus element of this test was, as expressed by the lower court, "flagrantly met." The record is replete with examples of Sure-Tan's blatantly illegal course of conduct to discourage its employees from supporting the Union. Petitioners contend, however, that their conduct in reporting the undocumented alien workers did not force the workers' departure from the country; instead, they argue, it was the employees' status as illegal aliens that was the actual "proximate cause" of their departure.

This argument is unavailing. According to testimony by an INS agent before the ALJ, petitioners' letter was the sole cause of the investigation during which the employees were taken into custody. This evidence was undisputed by petitioners and amply sup-

ports ALJ's conclusion that "but for [petitioners'] letter to Immigration, the discriminatees would have continued to work indefinitely." . . .

We observe that the Board quite properly does not contend that an employer may never report the presence of an illegal alien employee to the INS. . . . The reporting of any violation of the criminal laws is conduct which ordinarily should be encouraged, not penalized. It is only when the evidence establishes that the reporting of the presence of an illegal alien employee is in retaliation for the employee's protected union activity that the Board finds a violation of § 8(a)(3). Absent this specific finding of anti-union animus, it would not be an unfair labor practice to report or discharge an undocumented alien employee. . . . [*Reversed and Remanded to permit formulation by the Board of an appropriate remedial order.*]

In cases involving mixed motivation for discharge, the NLRB follows a procedure known as the **Wright-Line Doctrine.** Under this doctrine, the NLRB's general counsel first introduces evidence that makes a prima facie showing sufficient to support the inference that the employer's opposition to protected conduct was a "motivating factor" in the employer's discharge decision. The NLRB can find an unfair labor practice based solely on the general counsel's proof of a prima facie case of discrimination. This is possible if the employer does not come forward with any evidence to support its allegations that the discharge has been for legitimate business reasons.

Once this prima facie case is established, the burden shifts to the employer to demonstrate that the same action would have taken place even in the absence of the protected conduct. The Board retains the burden to prove retaliatory discharge by a preponderance of the evidence.

The case which follows is typical of those involving mixed motivation for discharge and the application of the Wright-Line Doctrine. Note that the employer does not have the burden of proving that an unfair labor practice has not occurred. The weighing by the NLRB includes a careful consideration of the employer's "good" reason as well as of the general counsel's evidence of improper motive.

N.L.R.B. v. TRANSPORTATION MANAGEMENT CORP.
103 S.Ct. 2469 (1983)

The National Labor Relations Board found that Transportation Management Corp. (TMC) has discharged Santillo, one of TMC's bus drivers, for union activity. Santillo had attempted to organize TMC drivers and convince them to join the Teamsters' Union. TMC contended that Santillo was dismissed for leaving his keys in the bus and taking unauthorized breaks. The administrative law judge (ALJ) found that the asserted reasons for the discharge could not withstand scrutiny. While acknowledging that Santillo had engaged in some unsatisfactory conduct, the ALJ was not persuaded that Santillo would have been fired had it not been for his union activities.

In conducting the hearing, the Board followed a procedure known as the Wright Line Doctrine. The Court of Appeals held that this doctrine should not be followed.

WHITE, J.: . . . The National Labor Relations Act (NLRA or Act) makes unlawful the discharge of a worker because of union activity, but employers retain the right to discharge workers for any number of other reasons unrelated to the employee's union activities. When the General Counsel of the National Labor Relations Board (Board) files a complaint alleging that an employee was discharged because of his union activities, the employer may assert legitimate motives for his decision. In Wright Line, 251 N.L.R.B. 1083 (1980), the National Labor Relations Board reformulated the allocation of the burden of proof in such cases. It determined that the General Counsel carried the burden of persuading the Board that an anti-union animus contributed to the employer's decision to discharge an employee, a burden that does not shift, but that the employer, even if it failed to meet or neutralize the General Counsel's showing, could avoid the finding that it violated the statute by demonstrating by a preponderance of the evidence that the worker would have been fired even if he had not been involved with the Union. The question presented in this case is whether the burden placed on the employer in Wright Line is consistent with the NLRA which provides that the Board must prove an unlawful labor practice by a "preponderance of the evidence." . . .

Employees of an employer covered by the NLRA have the right to form, join, or assist labor organizations. It is an unfair labor practice to interfere with, restrain, or coerce the exercise of those rights or by discrimination in hire or tenure "to encourage or discourage membership in any labor organization."

Under these provisions it is undisputed that if the employer fires an employee for having engaged in union activities and has no other basis for the discharge, or if the reasons that he proffers are pretextual, the employer commits an unfair labor practice. He does not violate the NLRA, however, if any anti-union animus that he might have entertained did not contribute at all to an otherwise lawful discharge for good cause. . . .

The presence of an anti-union motivation in a discharge case [is] not the end of the matter. An employer [can] escape the consequences of a violation by proving that without regard to the impermissible motivation, the employer would have taken the same action for wholly permissible reasons.

The Board's *Wright Line* decision in 1980 was an attempt to restate its analysis in a way more acceptable to the Courts of Appeals. The Board held that the General Counsel of course had the burden of proving that the employee's conduct protected by § 7 was a substantial or a motivating factor in the discharge. Even if this was the case, and the employer failed to rebut it, the employer could avoid being held in violation . . . by proving by a preponderance of the evidence that the discharge rested on the employee's unprotected conduct as well and that the employee would have lost his job in any event. It thus became clear, if it was not clear before, that proof that the discharge would have occurred in any event and for valid reasons amounted to an affirmative defense on which the employer carried the burden of proof by a preponderance of the evidence. The shifting burden merely requires the employer to make out what is actually an affirmative defense. . . .

The Court of Appeals [held] that . . . had the burden of showing not only that a forbidden motivation contributed to the discharge but also that the discharge would not have taken place independently of the protected conduct of the employee. The Court of Appeals was quite correct, . . . that throughout the proceedings, the General Counsel carries the burden of proving the elements of an unfair labor practice. . . . We are quite sure, however, that the Court of Appeals erred in holding that § 10(c) forbids placing the burden on the employer to prove that absent the improper motivation he would have acted in the same manner for wholly legitimate reasons.

As we understand the Board's decisions, they have consistently held that the unfair labor practice consists of a discharge or other adverse action that is based in whole or in part on anti-union animus—or as the Board now puts it, that the employee's protected conduct was a substantial or motivating factor in the adverse action. The General Counsel has the burden of proving these elements under § 10(c). But the Board's construction of the statute permits an employer to avoid being adjudicated a violator by showing what his actions would have been regardless of his forbidden motivation. It extends to the employer what the Board considers to be an affirmative defense but does not change or add to the elements of the unfair labor practice that the General Counsel has the burden of proving under § 10(c).

We assume that the Board could reasonably have construed the Act in the manner insisted on by the Court of Appeals. We also assume that the Board might have considered a showing by the employer that the adverse action would have occurred in any event as not obviating a violation adjudication but as going only to the permissible remedy, in which event the burden of proof could surely have been put on the employer. The Board has instead chosen to recognize, as it insists it has done for many years, what it designates as an affirmative defense that the employer has the burden of sustaining. We are unprepared to hold that this is an impermissible construction of the Act. [T]he Board's construction here, while it may not be required by the Act, is at least permissible under it and in these circumstances its position is entitled to deference.

The Board's allocation of the burden of proof is clearly reasonable in this context. . . . The employer is a wrongdoer; he has acted out of a motive that is declared illegitimate by the statute. It is fair that he bear the risk that the influence of legal and illegal motives cannot be separated, because he knowingly created the risk and because the risk was created not by innocent activity but by his own wrongdoing.

For these reasons, we conclude that the Court of Appeals erred in refusing to enforce the Board's orders, which rested on the Board's *Wright Line* decision.

The Board was justified in this case in concluding that Santillo would not have been discharged had the employer not considered his efforts to establish a union. . . . The Board's finding that Santillo would not have been fired even if the employer had not had an anti-union animus was supported by substantial evidence on the record considered as a whole.

Accordingly, the judgment is [*Reversed.*]

The NLRB has a rule regarding the discharge of supervisors. Under the rule, the discharge of a supervisor is unlawful only if it interferes with the rights of an employee. Supervisors are excluded from the definition of employee, and the employer is entitled to insist on the loyalty of supervisors. Supervisors are not free to engage in activities which would be protected if engaged in by other employees. The only exceptions to the rule are (1) to discharge a supervisor for testifying before the Board or during the grievance process, (2) to discipline a supervisor for refusing to commit an unfair labor practice, or (3) to discharge a supervisor who has hired his own pro-union crew as a pretext for terminating the former crew.

Retaliation may take other forms than discharge. It may entail a reduction of benefits. For example, several workers were on sick leave when their union commenced a strike. The company discontinued accident and sickness payments to all workers who were sick but continued to make payments to workers who were disabled by job-related injuries. This distinction constituted an unfair labor practice. The sick workers were not required to repudiate the strike, and the employer may not presume support of the strike by silence.

5. Domination of a Labor Organization

Before the Wagner Act was passed, it was a fairly common practice for employers to sidetrack the desires and efforts of employees to organize by forming a "union" which was, in fact, controlled by the employer. The second unfair labor practice prohibits the domination of a labor organization by employers or their contribution of financial or other support to it, and puts an end to the use of such company unions.

Under the Wagner Act, any organization of employees must be completely independent of their employers. Neither they nor their supervisory personnel may promote or sponsor a particular organization for collective bargaining. In the case of a controversy between competing unions, employers must remain strictly neutral, unless they already have a union-shop agreement in force with one of them. This section of the law was violated when it was agreed that an employee representative plan could not be amended if the employer disapproved. Such control of the form and structure of the employees' representative committee deprived them of the guaranteed freedom from control by their employer. It is an unfair labor practice for the employer to support a union by giving it a meeting place, providing refreshments for union meetings, permitting the union to use the employer's telephone, secretary, or copying machine, or allowing the union to keep cafeteria or vending-machine profits.

An employer's agreement to pay initiation fees and dues to a union for member employees is in violation when it is an inducement to join the union. This provision also prevents an employer from recognizing or bargaining with a union before it wins an election if there are two or more rival unions. Even when there is only one union, the employer is in violation by bargaining with it if it does not represent a majority of the employees.

6. Discrimination for Union Affiliation

Under provisions designed to prevent the third unfair labor practice, an employer may neither discharge nor refuse to hire an employee either to encourage or discourage membership in any labor organization. Nor may the employer discriminate regarding any term or condition of employment for such purposes. Thus, discrimination on account of union affiliation concerning wages, hours, work assignments, promotions, vacations, and the like is also forbidden. The law does not oblige an employer to favor union members in hiring employees. It also does not restrict him or her in the normal exercise of any employer's right to select or discharge employees. However, the employer may not abuse that right by discriminatory action based on union membership or activities which encourages or discourages membership in a labor organization. For example, a company may not go partially out of business because some of its employees have organized, nor may it temporarily close that portion of its business that has unionized. If a company closes one plant because a union is voted in, such action discourages union activity at other plants. Partial closings to "chill" unionism are unfair labor practices.

Many other examples of discrimination against union members and especially union leaders exist. In one example, a collective-bargaining agreement contained a no-strike clause, but there was no provision requiring union officials to prevent illegal work stoppages. When union members and leaders refused to cross a picket line (established by a different union), the company suspended employees who were union members for five to ten days. The employees who were union leaders were suspended twenty-five days. The court held that the employer violated Section 8(a)(3) of the Wagner Act. To justify the more severe punishment imposed upon union leaders, there must be an affirmative duty that these leaders prevent illegal work stoppages. Since the contract contained no such duty, the company's action was discriminatory on the basis of an employee's union activity.

In cases such as these, the terms of the collective-bargaining agreement are very important. The union may agree to harsher penalties for union officials as a part of the bargaining process. For example, a wildcat strike was conducted in violation of a collective-bargaining agreement. A union official was suspended for ten days while the rank and file strikers were only suspended for five days. This was not an unfair labor practice. A contract may allow for selective discipline of union officials. The parties to a collective-bargaining agreement may seek to increase the effectiveness of a no-strike clause by providing for heightened efforts on the part of union officials to avoid or reduce the disruptive effects of strikes during the contract term. Provision of harsher penalties for union officials who disobey these duties may spur union officials to honor those duties. Allowing the parties to give effect to such contractual terms furthers the strong national labor policy of substituting peaceful dispute resolution for industrial strife and the equally strong policy of freedom of contract.

7. Discrimination: NLRB Proceedings

Under provisions to prevent the fourth unfair labor practice, employees are protected from being discharged or from other reprisals by their employers because they have sought to enforce their rights under the act. This prevents the NLRB's channels of information from being dried up by employers' intimidation of complainants and witnesses. An employer cannot refuse to hire a prospective employee because charges have been filed by him or her. Although supervisors are not regarded as "employees" within the meaning of the act, they have been held to be protected from discharge or reprisal for testifying in a labor proceeding in which such would coerce those who are employees in the exercise of their rights to organize.

The main defense of any employer accused of reprisal is that he or she discharged or discriminated against the employee for some reason other than filing charges or giving testimony. Thus, most often such cases boil down to trying to prove what motivated the company in pursuing its course of action. If the company can convince the NLRB that the employee was discharged because of misconduct, low production, personnel cutbacks necessitated by economic conditions, or other legitimate considerations, the company will be exonerated. Otherwise, it will be found guilty of this unfair labor practice. Please refer to the discussion in section 4 of this chapter which deals with discharge and other forms of retaliation which constitute violations of the first unfair labor practice provision. Many cases violate more than one provision. Most cases involving the fourth category also involve the first.

8. The Duty to Bargain Collectively in Good Faith

It is now an unfair labor practice for both an employer and the representatives of employees to refuse to bargain collectively with each other. The Wagner Act did not define the term "to bargain collectively." Judicial decisions have added the concept "good faith" to it, so that it actually means to bargain in good faith. Thus, although an employer need not agree to any union demands, such conduct as the failure to make counterproposals to union demands may be evidence of bad faith. To comply with the requirement that they bargain collectively in good faith, employers and unions must approach the bargaining table with fair and open minds and a sincere purpose to find a basis of agreement. Refusing to meet at reasonable times with representatives of the other party, refusing to reduce agreements to writing, and designating persons with no authority to negotiate as representatives at meetings are examples of this unfair labor practice. The employer's duty to bargain collectively includes a duty to provide relevant information needed by a union for the proper performance of its duties as the employees' bargaining representative. For example, data about chemicals used by employees must be furnished so that the union and its members are aware of dangers to health. Companies cannot refuse to provide unions with job-related nonproprietary safety and health information that does not disclose personal medical records. The union has an obligation to safeguard its members' health and safety.

A more fundamental issue than good faith is also inherent in the requirement that parties bargain collectively. That issue, simply stated, is: "About what?" Must the employer bargain with the union about all subjects and all management decisions in which the union or the employees are interested? Are there subjects and issues upon which management is allowed to act unilaterally?

In answering these questions, the law divides issues into two categories—**compulsory bargaining issues** and **voluntary bargaining issues.** Compulsory or mandatory bargaining issues are those concerned with wages, hours, and other terms and conditions of employment. Although the parties may voluntarily consider other issues, the refusal by either to bargain in good faith on such other permissive matters is not an unfair labor practice. Nor is it an unfair labor practice to refuse to bargain over the rights of former employees. For example, an employer eliminated medical benefits to retired workers when Medicare became effective. The union demanded to negotiate. This was not a mandatory bargaining issue. If a matter does not affect employees in a working relationship, it will be a mandatory issue of bargaining only if it vitally affects the terms and conditions of employment for those working.

In recent years, one of the most difficult legal issues in labor-management relations has been the impact on collective-bargaining contracts of bankruptcy proceedings. Employers frequently seek reorganization under Section 11 of the bankruptcy laws. Since collective-bargaining agreements are "executory contracts," the bankruptcy code permits a debtor in possession of its estate or the trustee in bankruptcy to modify or cancel such contracts. The Supreme Court in 1984 in a five-to-four decision held that an employer could unilaterally cancel collective-bargaining agreements and change the wage structure of its employees without committing an unfair labor practice. The Supreme Court decision holding that a unilateral rejection or modification of a labor contract is not an unfair labor practice has been on the premise that such a rejection is a necessary part of reorganization. The dissenting justices believe that the duty to bargain collectively prohibits termination or modification unless the union is given timely notice, there is an order to meet and confer, and the agreement continues for sixty days after notice.

Subsequent to this decision, Congress has amended the bankruptcy laws to give more protection to workers. The law now requires employers filing for bankruptcy to have court approval before they repudiate a labor contract. As a result, employers seeking reorganization may unilaterally change the terms of their collective-bargaining agreement <u>only with court approval</u>. The terms of labor contracts remain compulsory bargaining issues. Courts before approving a petition to modify or reject a labor contract will require reasonable efforts to negotiate a voluntary modification and proof that collective bargaining cannot produce a prompt and satisfactory solution to the problem.

Classifying an issue as <u>*compulsory* or *voluntary*</u> <u>is done on a case-by-case basis.</u> For example, questions relating to fringe benefits are compulsory bargaining issues because they are "wages." The NLRB and the courts are called on to decide whether management and labor must bargain with each other on a multitude of issues, as the case which follows illustrates.

FORD MOTOR COMPANY v. NLRB
99 S.Ct. 1842 (1979)

The petitioner, Ford Motor Company, provided its employees with in-plant cafeteria and vending-machine services. The services were managed by an independent caterer, ARA, but the petitioner had the right to review and approve the quality, quantity, and prices of the food served. When petitioner notified respondent union, which represents the employees, that the cafeteria and vending-machine prices were to be increased, the union requested bargaining over the prices and services. Petitioner refused to bargain, and the union then filed an unfair labor practice charge with the National Labor Relations Board, alleging a refusal to bargain contrary to § 8(a)(5) of the National Labor Relations Act (NLRA). Taking the view that in-plant food prices and services are "other terms and conditions of employment," the NLRB sustained the charge and ordered petitioner to bargain. The Court of Appeals enforced the

order, and the Supreme Court granted certiorari.

WHITE, J.: . . . Because the "classification of bargaining subjects as 'terms or conditions of employment' is a matter concerning which the Board has special expertise," its judgment as to what is a mandatory bargaining subject is entitled to considerable deference. . . .

Of course, the judgment of the Board is subject to judicial review; but if its construction of the statute is reasonably defensible, it should not be rejected merely because the courts might prefer another view of the statute. . . .

Construing and applying the duty to bargain and the language of § 8(d), "other terms and conditions of employment," are tasks lying at the heart of the Board's function. With all due respect to the courts of appeals that have held otherwise, we conclude that the Board's consistent view that in-plant food prices and services are mandatory bargaining subjects is not an unreasonable or unprincipled construction of the statute and that it should be accepted and enforced.

It is not suggested by petitioner that an employee should work a full 8-hour shift without stopping to eat. It reasonably follows that the availability of food during working hours and the conditions under which it is to be consumed are matters of deep concern to workers, and one need not strain to consider them to be among those "conditions" of employment that should be subject to the mutual duty to bargain. By the same token, where the employer has chosen, apparently in his own interest, to make available a system of in-plant feeding facilities for his employees, the prices at which food is offered and other aspects of this service may reasonably be considered among those subjects about which management and union must bargain. The terms and conditions under which food is available on the job are plainly germane to the "working environment." Furthermore, the company is not in the business of selling food to its employees, and the establishment of in-plant food prices is not among those "managerial decisions, which lie at the core of entrepreneurial control." The Board is in no sense attempting to permit the Union to usurp managerial decisionmaking; nor is it seeking to regulate an area from which Congress intended to exclude it. . . .

As illustrated by the facts of this case, substantial disputes can arise over the pricing of in-plant supplied food and beverages. National labor policy contemplates that areas of common dispute between employers and employees be funneled into collective bargaining. The assumption is that this is preferable to allowing recurring disputes to fester outside the negotiation process until strikes or other forms of economic warfare occur.

The trend of industrial practice supports this conclusion. In response to increasing em-ployee concern over the issue, many contracts are now being negotiated that contain provisions concerning in-plant food services. . . . Although not conclusive, current industrial practice is highly relevant in construing the phrase "terms and conditions of employment."

Ford nevertheless argues against classifying food prices and services as mandatory bargaining subjects because they do not "vitally affect" the terms and conditions of employment within the meaning of the standard assertedly established by *Allied Chemical and Alkali Workers v. Pittsburgh Plate Glass Co.*, and because they are trivial matters over which neither party should be required to bargain.

There is no merit to either of these arguments. First, Ford has misconstrued *Pittsburgh Plate Glass*. That case made it clear that while § 8(d) normally reaches "only issues that settle an aspect of the relationship between the employer and employees . . . matters involving individuals outside the employment relationship . . . are not wholly excluded." . . . As for the argument that in-plant food prices and service are too trivial to qualify as mandatory subjects, the Board has a contrary view, and we have no basis for rejecting it. It is also clear that the bargaining unit employees in this case considered the matter far from trivial since they pressed an unsuccessful boycott to secure a voice in setting food prices. They evidently felt, and common sense also tells us, that even minor increases in the cost of meals can amount to a substantial sum of money over time. . . .

Ford also argues that the Board's position will result in unnecessary disruption because any small change in price or service will trigger the obligation to bargain. The problem it is said, will be particularly acute in situations where several unions are involved, possibly requiring endless rounds of negotiations over issues as minor as the price of a cup of coffee or a soft drink. . . .

The Board apparently assumes that, as a

practical matter, requests to bargain will not be lightly made. Moreover, problems created by constantly shifting food prices can be anticipated and provided for in the collective-bargaining agreement. Furthermore, if it is true that disputes over food prices are likely to be frequent and intense, it follows that more, not less, collective bargaining is the remedy. This is the assumption of national labor policy, and it is soundly supported by both reason and experience.

Finally, Ford asserts that to require it to engage in bargaining over in-plant food service prices would be futile because those prices are set by a third-party supplier, ARA. It is true that ARA sets vending machine and cafeteria prices, but under Ford's contract with ARA, Ford retains the right to review and control food services and prices. In any event, an employer can always affect prices by initiating or altering a subsidy to the third-party supplier such as that provided by Ford in this case, and will typically have the right to change suppliers at some point in the future. To this extent the employer holds future, if not present, leverage over in-plant food services and prices.

We affirm, therefore, the Court of Appeals' judgment upholding the Board's determination in this case that in-plant food services and prices are "terms and conditions of employment" subject to the mandatory bargaining under § 8(a)(5) and 8(d) of the National Labor Relations Act. [*Affirmed.*]

A party to labor negotiations may present a demand relating to a non-mandatory bargaining issue as long as its resolution is not a condition precedent to the resolution of mandatory bargaining issues. Tying a voluntary bargaining issue to a compulsory bargaining issue results in a failure to bargain in good faith and is in effect an unfair labor practice.

Courts tend to defer to the special expertise of the NLRB in classifying collective-bargaining subjects, especially in the area of "terms or conditions of employment." The courts have affirmed Board rulings holding that issues such as union dues checkoff, health and accident insurance, safety rules, merit pay increases, incentive-pay plans, Christmas and other bonuses, stock purchase plans, pensions, paid vacations and holidays, the privilege of hunting on a reserved portion of a paper company's forest preserve, proposals for effective arbitration and grievance procedures, and no-strike and no-lockout clauses are compulsory bargaining issues. Industry practice is a major factor in many decisions.

The Board has recently changed its policy on the issue of whether the employer can unilaterally transfer operations from a unionized facility to an unorganized facility during the term of a collective-bargaining agreement. In 1982, the Board held that a unilateral transfer is an unfair labor practice. In 1984, the Board held that an employer does not violate the Wagner Act by relocating the work of a bargaining unit without the union's consent so long as the employer is willing to bargain in good faith over the proposed change. An employer may not unilaterally institute changes before reaching a good-faith impasse in bargaining. Although an employer may not modify the terms and conditions of the contract without the union's consent, if the contract does not specifically prohibit the change, then the only obligation is to bargain in good faith on the issue.

Remember that neither the employer nor the union is required to make concessions to the other concerning a mandatory subject of bargaining. The law only demands that each negotiate such matters in good faith with the other before making a decision and taking unilateral action. If the parties fail to reach an agreement after discussing these problems, each may take steps which are against the wishes and best interests of the other party. For example, the employer may refuse to grant a wage increase requested by the union, and the union is free to strike.

9. Agreeing with a Union to Engage in a Secondary Boycott

The unfair labor practice by employers of a **secondary boycott** was not one of the original five forbidden under the Wagner Act. Taft-Hartley attempted to limit the use by unions of the secondary boycott as an indirect weapon in a campaign to organize employees. It was an unfair labor practice for a union to induce the *employees* of an employer to strike, or engage in a concerted refusal to use, handle, or work on any goods or to perform any services, in order to force the employer to stop doing business with any other person. For example, assume that employer A sells supplies to manufacturer B, which are transported by trucking firm C, whose employees are nonunion. This Taft-Hartley provision makes it illegal for either a union attempting to organize the employees of C or the union representing the employees of A to induce the employees of A to strike or refuse to load C's trucks with supplies in order to require A to stop shipping its goods by C. This represents a swing of the pendulum back from the Norris-LaGuardia Act's liberalization of the use of secondary boycotts toward the policy of the law as it existed before that act. Then, secondary boycotts were viewed as illegal combinations in restraint of trade under the Sherman Act or as illegal conspiracies under the common law.

Taft-Hartley, however, was not successful in eliminating all secondary boycotts. Loopholes appeared in its proscriptions. For example, a **hot-cargo contract** in which an *employer* voluntarily agrees with a union not to handle, use, or deal in non-union-produced goods of another person, was held to be legal. The union was prevented only from inducing the *employees* of the employer to strike or otherwise act to force their employer not to handle such goods. The Landrum-Griffin Act plugged this loophole and outlawed hot-cargo contracts. Its amendment to Taft-Hartley made it an unfair labor practice for any labor organization and any *employer* to enter into any contract or agreement whereby such employer agrees to refrain from handling, using, selling, transporting, or otherwise dealing in any of the products of any other employer, or to cease doing business with any other person. The secondary boycott provisions as they pertain to unions are discussed further in section 12 of this chapter.

UNFAIR LABOR PRACTICES BY UNIONS

10. Introduction

The Wagner Act did not contain any provisions relating to unfair labor practices by labor unions. It was, in effect, one-sided. The Taft-Hartley Act covered the missing side by declaring that certain conduct or activities by labor unions also were unfair labor practices and thus illegal. Six such activities were specified. The Landrum-Griffin Act in 1959 added two additional unfair labor practices by unions to those declared illegal by the Taft-Hartley Act.

The following table summarizes the actions and omissions by unions which are unfair labor practices:

TABLE 19-2   Unfair Labor Practices by Unions

1 Restraining or coercing an employee to join a union or an employer in selecting representatives to bargain with the union
2 Causing or attempting to cause the employer to discriminate against an employee who is not a union member, unless there is a legal union-shop agreement in effect
3 Refusing to bargain with the employer if it is the NLRB-designated representative of the employees
4 Striking, picketing, and engaging in secondary boycotts for illegal purposes
5 Charging new members excessive or discriminatory initiation fees when there is a union-shop agreement
6 Causing an employer to pay for work not performed ("featherbedding")
7 Picketing to require an employer to recognize or bargain with a union which is not currently certified as representing its employees in certain cases
8 Agreeing with an employer to engage in a secondary boycott

Numbers 1, 4, 7, and 8 are discussed in subsequent sections. (Number 3 is the union duty to bargain in good faith. It was discussed in section 8 with the same duty of employers.) The second unfair practice by unions recognizes that if a legal union-shop agreement is in effect, a labor organization may insist that the employer observe its terms. But even when a legal union-shop contract is in effect, this section prohibits a union from attempting to cause an employer to discriminate against an employee who has been denied membership, or had his or her membership terminated, for some reason other than failure to pay the dues and initiation fees uniformly required of all members. And even if an employee is a member, the union may not cause the employer to discriminate against him or her for not following union rules. This prohibition has been designed to prevent the use of the union shop as a means of intimidating employees at odds with union officials over their policies.

Unfair labor practice number 5 exists because employees in a union shop must join the union after they have been employed for a minimum period of thirty days. Since there is unequal bargaining power and the union sets its initiation fee and dues, the law requires that they be neither excessive nor discriminatory against new members.

11. Restraining or Coercing an Employee in Joining a Union

This unfair labor practice includes misconduct by unions directed toward employees and employers. Also forbidden are any attempts by a union to influence an employer in selecting its representatives to bargain with the union. Most allegations of unfair labor practices filed against unions are brought under this provision. The law makes it illegal for a union to restrain or coerce employees in the exercise of their rights to bargain collectively, just as it is an unfair labor practice by employers to interfere with the same rights. Employees also are guaranteed the right to *refrain* from union activities unless required by a legal union-shop agreement in force between their employer and a labor organization. In the following case, the employer refused to bargain with a union which had won a representation election on the grounds that prior to the election the union had violated this provision.

NLRB v. SAVAIR MANUFACTURING COMPANY
94 S.Ct. 495 (1973)

DOUGLAS, J.: The National Labor Relations Board . . . conducted an election by secret ballot among the production and maintenance employees of respondent at the request of the Mechanics Educational Society of America (the Union). . . . The Union won the election by a vote of 22–20.

Respondent filed objections to the election, but . . . the Board certified the Union as the representative of the employees in that unit. Respondent, however, refused to bargain. The Union thereupon filed an unfair labor practice charge . . . alleging that respondent had violated § 8(a)(1) and (5) of the Act. The Board sustained the allegations and ordered respondent to bargain with the Union. The Court of Appeals denied enforcement of the order. . . .

It appeared that prior to the election, "recognition slips" were circulated among

employees. An employee who signed the slip before the election became a member of the union and would not have to pay what at times was called an "initiation fee" and at times a "fine." If the Union was voted in, those who had not signed a recognition slip would have to pay. . . . Under the by-laws of the Union, an initiation fee apparently was not to be higher than $10; but the employees who testified at the hearing (1) did not know how large the fee would be and (2) said that their understanding was that the fee was a "fine" or an "assessment."

One employee, Donald Bridgeman, testified that he signed the slip to avoid paying the "fine" if the union won. He got the message directly from an employee picked by the union to solicit signatures on the "slips." So did Thomas Rice, another employee. . . .

Whatever his true intentions, an employee who signs a recognition slip prior to an election is indicating to other workers that he supports the Union. His outward manifestation of support must often serve as a useful campaign tool in the Union's hands to convince other employees to vote for the Union, if only because many employees respect their co-workers' views on the unionization issue. By permitting the Union to offer to waive an initiation fee for those employees signing a recognition slip prior to the election, the Board allows the Union to buy endorsements and paint a false portrait of employee support during its election campaign.

That influence may well have been felt here for, as noted, there were 28 who signed up with the Union before the election petition was filed with the Board and either seven or eight more who signed up before the election. We do not believe that the statutory policy of fair elections . . . permits endorsements, whether for or against the Union, to be bought and sold in this fashion.

In addition, while it is correct that the employee who signs a recognition slip is not legally bound to vote for the Union and has not promised to do so in any formal sense, certainly there may be some employees who would feel obligated to carry through on their stated intention to support the Union. And on the facts of this case, the change of just one vote would have resulted in a 21–21 election rather than a 22–20 election.

Any procedure requiring a "fair" election must honor the right of those who oppose a union as well as those who favor it.

The Act is wholly neutral when it comes to that basic choice. By § 7 of the Act employees have the right not only to "form, join, or assist" unions but also the right "to refrain from any or all of such activities." An employer who promises to increase the fringe benefits by $10 for each employee who votes against the union, if the union wins the election, would cross the forbidden line under our decisions. . . .

The Board in its supervision of union elections may not sanction procedures that cast their weight for the choice of a union and against a nonunion shop or for a nonunion shop and against a union.

In the *Exchange Parts* case we said that although the benefits granted by the employer were permanent and unconditional, employees were "not likely to miss the inference that the source of benefits now conferred is also the source from which future benefits must flow and which may dry up if it is not obliged." If we respect, as we must, the statutory right of employees to resist efforts to unionize a plant, we cannot assume that unions exercising powers are wholly benign towards their antagonists whether they be nonunion protagonists or the employer. The failure to sign a recognition slip may well seem ominous to nonunionists who fear that if they do not sign they will face a wrathful union regime, should the union win. That influence may well have had a decisive impact in this case where a change of one vote would have changed the result. [*Affirmed.*]

The second part of this provision prohibits a union from restraining or coercing an employer in the selection of its representatives for collective bargaining. It is violated if a union refuses to bargain with a proper representative of an employer and yet threatens a strike if bargaining does not succeed. However, if a strike called by a union is an economic one with the sole objective of obtaining certain contractual terms and is not based on the refusal to deal with the employer's representative, it is not coercion of the employer forbidden by this subsection.

12. Secondary Boycotts and Other Illegal Strikes and Picketing

It is an unfair labor practice for a union to threaten, coerce, or restrain third persons not parties to a labor dispute for the purpose of causing the third person to cease using, selling, handling, transporting, or otherwise dealing in the products of any other producer, or to cease doing business with any other person. The purpose of this law restricting most strikes and picketing to the employer with which the union actually has a labor dispute, protects neutral parties from serious economic injury or even ruin. The case which follows illustrates some situations in which picketing a secondary employer may be legal and some in which it is not. If a foreseeable consequence of a strike, picketing, or boycott is to disrupt the business of a third person, the activity is an unfair labor practice.

NLRB v. RETAIL STORE EMP. UNION, ETC.
100 S.Ct. 2372 (1980)

Safeco Title Insurance Co. does business with several title companies that derive over 90 percent of their gross incomes from the sale of Safeco insurance policies. When contract negotiations between Safeco and respondent union, the bargaining representative for certain Safeco employees, reached an impasse, the employees went on strike. The union picketed each of the title companies, urging customers to support the strike by canceling their Safeco policies. Safeco and one of the title companies filed complaints with the National Labor Relations Board, charging that the union had engaged in an unfair labor practice by picketing in order to promote a secondary boycott against the title companies. The Board agreed and ordered the union to cease picketing. The Court of Appeals set aside the Board's order, and the Supreme Court granted certiorari to consider whether the Court of Appeals correctly applied the decision in *NLRB v. Fruit Packers* (Tree Fruits), 377 U.S. 58(1964).

POWELL, J.: . . . The question is whether § 8(b)(4)(ii)(B) of the National Labor Relations Act, forbids secondary picketing against a struck product when such picketing predictably encourages consumers to boycott a neutral party's business. . . .

Section 8(b)(4)(ii)(B) of the National Labor Relations Act makes it "an unfair labor practice for a labor organization . . . to threaten, coerce, or restrain" a person not party to a labor dispute "where . . . an object thereof is . . . forcing or requiring [him] to cease using, selling, handling, transporting, or otherwise dealing in the products of any other producer . . . or to cease doing business with any other person. . . ."

In *Tree Fruits*, the Court held that § 8(b)(4)(ii)(B) does not prohibit all peaceful picketing at secondary sites. There, a union striking certain Washington fruit packers picketed large supermarkets in order to persuade consumers not to buy Washington apples. Concerned that a broad ban against such picketing might run afoul of the First Amendment, the Court found the statute directed to an " 'isolated evil.' " The evil was use of secondary picketing "to persuade the customers of the secondary employer to cease trading with him in order to force him to cease dealing with, or to put pressure upon, the primary employer." Congress intended to protect secondary parties from pressures that might embroil them in the labor disputes of others, but not to shield them from business losses caused by a campaign that successfully persuades consumers "to boycott the primary employer's goods." Thus, the Court drew a distinction between picketing "to shut off all trade with the secondary employer unless he aids the union in its dispute with the primary employer" and picketing that "only persuades his customers not to buy the struck product." The picketing in that case, which "merely follow[ed] the struck product," did not " 'threaten, coerce, or restrain' " the secondary party within the meaning of § 8(b)(4)(ii)(B).

Although *Tree Fruits* suggested that secondary picketing against a struck product and secondary picketing against a neutral party were "poles apart," the courts soon discovered that product picketing could have the same effect as an illegal secondary boycott. In *Hoffman ex rel. NLRB v. Cement Masons Local 337*, 468 F.2d 1187 (CA9 1972), for example, a union embroiled with a general contractor picketed the housing subdivision that he had constructed for a real estate developer. Pickets sought to persuade prospective purchasers not to buy the contractor's houses. The picketing was held illegal because purchasers "could reasonably expect that they were being asked not to transact any business whatsoever" with the neutral developer. "[W]hen a union's interest in picketing a primary employer at a 'one product' site, [directly conflicts] with the need to protect . . . neutral employers from the labor disputes of others," Congress has determined that the neutrals' interests should prevail. *Cement Masons* highlights the critical difference between the picketing in this case and the picketing at issue in *Tree Fruits*. The product picketed in *Tree Fruits* was but one item among the many that made up the retailer's trade. If the appeal against such a product succeeds, the Court observed, it simply induces the neutral retailer to reduce his orders for the product or "to drop the item as a poor seller." The decline in sales attributable to consumer rejection of the struck product puts pressure upon the primary employer, and the marginal injury to the neutral retailer is purely incidental to the product boycott. The neutral therefore has little reason to become involved in the labor dispute. In this case, on the other hand, the title companies sell only the primary employer's product and perform the services associated with it. Secondary picketing against consumption of the primary product leaves responsive consumers no realistic option other than to boycott the title companies altogether. If the appeal succeeds, each company "stops buying the struck product, not because of a falling demand, but in response to pressure designed to inflict injury on [its] business generally." Thus, "the union does more than merely follow the struck product; it creates a separate dispute with the secondary employer." Such an expansion of labor discord was one of the evils that Congress intended § 8(b)(4)(ii)(B) to prevent.

As long as secondary picketing only discourages consumption of a struck product, incidental injury to the neutral is a natural consequence of an effective primary boycott. But the Union's secondary appeal against the central product sold by the title companies in this case is "reasonably calculated to induce customers not to patronize the neutrals at all." The resulting injury to their businesses is distinctly different from the injury that the Court considered in *Tree Fruits*. Product picketing that reasonably can be expected to threaten neutral parties with ruin or substantial loss simply does not square with the language or the purpose of § 8(b)(4)(ii)(B). Since successful secondary picketing would put the title companies to a choice between their survival and the severance of their ties with Safeco, the picketing plainly violates the statutory ban on the coercion of neutrals with the object of "forcing or requiring [them] to cease . . . dealing in the [primary] product . . . or to cease doing business with" the primary employer. [*Reversed.*]

Another example of illegal secondary activity occurs when a union induces the employees of an employer to strike or engage in a concerted refusal to use, handle, or work on any goods or to perform any services, to force the employer to stop doing business with some third person. For example, assume that employer A sells supplies to manufacturer B, which are transported by trucking firm C, whose employees are nonunion. It is illlegal for either a union attempting to organize the employees of C or the union representing the employees of A to induce the employees of A to strike or refuse to load C's trucks with supplies to require A to stop shipping its goods by C. Similarly, it is forbidden for the union of X's employees in the course of a dispute with X to induce any employees of Y to strike to coerce Y to stop buying the products of X. Likewise, it would be a violation for the union of X's employees to induce them not to work on goods produced by "scab" labor at the nonunion plant of Z, to induce X to use union-made goods instead.

It is also an unfair labor practice for both the employer involved and the union to enter into a hot-cargo contract. A hot-cargo contract is one in which an employer voluntarily agrees with a union that the employees should not be required by their employer to handle or work on goods or materials going to, or coming from, an employer designated by the union as "unfair." Such goods are said to be "hot cargo." These clauses were common in trucking and construction. The law thus forbids an employer and a labor organization to make an agreement whereby the employer agrees to stop doing business with any other employer.

It is also an unfair labor practice for a union to threaten or to coerce an employer to recognize or bargain with one union if another one has been certified as the representative of its employees. This provision was made to protect employers (and their employees) from the destructive rivalry between unions competing to be the bargaining representative of employees in a unit where they had already chosen one. Jurisdictional strikes are also unfair labor practices. A jurisdictional strike is one forcing an employer to assign work to employees in one craft union rather than another. Since the dispute is between the two unions and not with the employer, the law requires that such disputes be submitted to the NLRB by the unions. Note that it is not a violation for a union certified by the Board to represent the employees performing the particular work involved to force the employer to assign it to them.

13. Requiring Employees to Pay Excessive Fees

The unfair labor practice of requiring employees to pay excessive fees was included in the law to protect employees who were required to join a union as a condition of employment by reason of a union-shop agreement. It prohibits the charging of an excessive or discriminatory initiation fee as a requirement of becoming a member of the union.

Since the employees (especially *new* employees) have no choice about membership and no bargaining power, the law requires that the dues and fees be reasonable and not discriminatory. For example, in one case a union raised its initiation fee to $500 from the former $50 for all new employees who received a certain minimum starting salary. This fee was held to be excessive and discriminatory.

14. Causing an Employer to Pay for Work Not Performed

Designating the unfair labor practice of requiring an employer to pay for work that is not performed as illegal was meant to prevent *featherbedding*. It is quite limited in actual operation. The issue is: What are "services not performed or not to be performed"? Make-work rules have been approved by the courts as being outside the prohibition of this provision. It is not violated as long as some services are performed, even if they are of little or no actual value to the employer. In one such case, the Supreme Court held that it was permissible for a musicians' union to require a theater to employ a local orchestra to play overtures and intermissions as a condition of its consent to local appearances of traveling big-name bands. And in another decision, the Court approved the insistence by a union that newspaper publishers who used advertising mats as molds for metal castings from which to print advertisements pay union printers for setting up in type duplicates of these advertisements. The payments were found to be for work actually done, in spite of the fact that the duplicates were not used and ordinarily were just melted down.

15. Picketing When Not Certified

The seventh provision makes it illegal for union picketing to require an employer to recognize or bargain with the union if it is not currently certified as the duly authorized collective-bargaining representative, in certain cases. The purpose is to reinforce the effectiveness of the election procedures employed by the NLRB by outlawing certain tactics used by unions backed by only a minority of the employees of a particular employer. Thus, picketing to force an employer to recognize an uncertified union has become illegal in the following cases:

1 When the employer lawfully has recognized another union as the collective-bargaining representative of its employees

2 When a valid representation election has been conducted by the NLRB within the past twelve months

3 When picketing has been conducted for a reasonable time, not in excess of thirty days, without a petition for a representation election being filed with the NLRB

Under item 3, however, the act does not prohibit so called "informational" picketing. That is, picketing or publicity to truthfully advise the public (including consumers) that an employer has a nonunion business is not prohibited, unless the effect of the picketing is to induce employees of another person to observe the picket line.

Certain kinds of **organizational picketing** have been made unfair by the Landrum-Griffin Act. Before, it was possible for a minority union to picket an employer for recognition as the collective-bargaining representative of its employees, when it was illegal for the employer to accept it as such. Though Congress felt that unions should be able to publicize the fact that certain employers are nonunion, it also felt that unions should not be permitted to attempt to force employers to violate the law. Purely recognitional picketing under the circumstances stated above is illegal. Purely informational picketing probably is legal.

The fact is, however, that often picketing has both purposes. Such dual-purpose picketing under the facts stated in cases 1 or 2 listed above is literally unlawful. However, dual-purpose picketing in case 3 is probably legal unless it inhibits deliveries of goods to the employer being picketed, or the like. Even if it does, the NLRB has ruled that such interruptions must be substantial enough to curtail the employer's business. The rules concerning the application of this provision of the statute have not been clearly enunciated by the NLRB (which has taken several positions) or the courts.

This part of the act also prohibits picketing by an uncertified union (in the situations enumerated) in order to force the *employees* of an employer to select that union as their collective-bargaining representative. When a charge of a violation is filed and there is reasonable cause to believe it is true, the proper officer of the Board must seek a temporary injunction restraining further violation until the NLRB disposes of the matter.

16. The Union's Duty of Fair Representation

None of the federal labor laws contains an *express* provision which requires a union to fairly represent the employees in a collective-bargaining unit after it has been certified as their exclusive bargaining representative. However, Supreme Court rulings have imposed an *implied* duty of fair representation on unions under both the Railway Labor Act and the National Labor Relations

Act. Section 9(a) of the NLRA states the "Representatives designated or selected for the purposes of collective bargaining by the *majority* of the employees in a unit appropriate for such purposes, shall be the *exclusive* representative of *all* the employees in such unit for the purposes of collective bargaining in respect to rates of pay, wages, hours of employment, or other conditions of employment. . . ." [*Emphasis added.*] A similar provision is found in the Railway Labor Act. Thus, bargaining by a single employee with the employer concerning that employee's terms or conditions of employment is not permitted, even if the employee voted against the union. Collectively bargained agreements, through the union and for the benefit of the group, are substituted by the act for employment contracts negotiated separately by individual employees. Because of the union's position as the *exclusive* representative, the Supreme Court has reasoned that the union must exercise fairly the power given it by statute on behalf of all for whom it acts.

In negotiating a collective-bargaining agreement with the employer, the union has an implied "duty of fair representation" to act reasonably, with honesty of purpose, and in good faith. The union can prove that it has met this duty by showing that its motives in settling for the terms in the contract which finally results have not been improper. The union is required to represent all the employees in the bargaining unit, including those who are nonunion, impartially and without hostile discrimination. A union has a great deal of discretion in bargaining and may work to obtain different terms for different employees or subgroups of employees, provided it does not have an improper motive for doing so.

The duty of fair representation not only applies to the *negotiation* of a collective-bargaining agreement, but also to the *administration* of the agreement while it is in effect. That is, unions must also fairly represent employees in disputes with the employer regarding the *interpretation* and *application* of the terms of an existing contract. The law does not grant unions the same exclusive power in the processing of grievances as it does in negotiating contracts. Section 9(a) of the NLRA states that: "any individual employee or a group of employees shall have the right at any time to present grievances to their employer and to have such grievances adjusted, without the intervention of the bargaining representative, as long as the adjustment is not inconsistent with the terms of a collective bargaining contract . . . then in effect: *Provided* . . . , that the bargaining representative has been given an opportunity to be present at such adjustment." However, most collective-bargaining agreements provide that the union has final control over their grievance-arbitration processes.

An employee may file suit in state court against the union and its representatives for damages resulting from breach of their duty of fair rrepresentation in processing his or her grievance against the employer. Unions must act honestly and in good faith in processing grievances as well as in negotiating collective-bargaining agreements. A union may not process a grievance in an arbitrary, indifferent, or careless manner. For example, failure to investigate a grievance probably would be arbitrary. However, even if a union violates its duty of fair representation, the damages attributable solely to the employer's breach of contract are its sole responsibility and are not charged to the union. The union is liable to the employee only for increases (if any) in those damages caused by its refusal to process the grievance. Thus, the award assessed against it may not be substantial. Some authorities feel that the current labor laws do not provide penalties severe enough to deter unions from breaching their duty of fair representation.

The cases in which unions have been found guilty of breaching the duty of fair representation include failing to file a grievance of an employee within the time permitted by a collective-bargaining agreement; failing to present all available evidence in favor of an employee's case; and failure to notify the employee of the time of an arbitration hearing, knowing that no other witnesses would testify in his or her behalf.

REVIEW QUESTIONS

1 A firm parked a cart filled with groceries in the area where employees were casting ballots in a representation election. A sign on the cart said that the value of the food in it was the same as a year's union dues and suggested that the employees vote against the union. Is this an unfair labor practice? Why, or why not?

2 An employer refused to pay vacation benefits to employees who had been on strike on a certain date. No other proof of anti-union motive was offered to the NLRB. Is this sufficient proof that an unfair labor practice had been committed? Explain.

3 Sally, a supervisor for May Candy Company, ordered Will, a worker, to come into her office for an interview regarding alleged serious breaches of company rules. Will complied, and when the interview confirmed Will's misconduct, he was fired. Will and the union filed charges of unfair labor practices with the NLRB against the May Candy Company because a union representative was not present during the interview. What should be the result? Why?

4 Burger King issued a ban on its employees' wearing any button on their uniforms. Only items using the Burger King logo could be worn by employees. Some counter employees wanted to wear union buttons. When they were not allowed to do so, they filed a complaint with the NLRB alleging that an unfair labor practice had been committed. Is the ban on buttons an unfair labor practice? Why, or why not?

5 A corporation refused to permit the union of its employees to circulate a one-page newsletter on company property which was headlined, "Workers of the World Unite!" The newsletter generally discussed the necessity of employees to band together in unions. When the union filed charges with the NLRB, the company defended on the grounds that its employees were already unionized and that the newsletter had no bearing on any dispute between it and its employees or their union. What was the result? Explain.

6 The president of ABC Company learned from one of its supervisors that two of the assembly-line employees were openly advocating unionizing the plant's workers. At an emergency meeting of the board of directors, a sizable wage increase and an additional two days' vacation per year for all ABC employees were approved. Three months later, the employees petitioned for an NLRB representation election. It was held four months later (seven months from the board meeting), and the union lost the election. Was ABC Company guilty of an unfair labor practice? Explain.

7   Some of the employees of a janitorial service business were trying to unionize it. The sole proprietor stated that he would never deal with a union and would go out of the business if his workers voted one in. The union won the representation election, and, true to his word, the owner closed his business and sold all its assets. Was he guilty of an unfair labor practice? Explain.

8   A chemical manufacturer was asked to provide the union representing its employees with the generic names of all substances used and produced at the manufacturer's plant. The union also sought information concerning occupational illness and accident data related to workers' compensation claims. The company refused to furnish the information. Is this refusal an unfair labor practice? Why, or why not?

9   For many years, the employer gave all employees a Christmas turkey. The practice continued after a union was certified. For economic reasons, the employer decided to cancel the practice. The union alleged that cancellation was an unfair labor practice and that it could not be cancelled unilaterally. The turkeys were not mentioned in the collective-bargaining agreement. Is the employer guilty of an unfair labor practice. Why, or why not?

10   A business provided housekeeping and maintenance services for commercial customers, one being a nursing home where it employed about thirty-five workers. Because it was losing money on the nursing-home operation, the business terminated the maintenance contract with the home and discharged the employees working there. When the union requested to bargain about this decision, the petitioner refused and the union filed an unfair labor practice charge. Is this closing a compulsory bargaining issue? Explain.

11   A union prevailed in an NLRB election. The employer challenged it on the ground that a union agent made threatening statements to employees one hour before the election. The evidence established that the union agent said that if anyone helped the employer in a strike, he would be made an example of, and noted that during the last strike an individual who opposed the union was still in the hospital. Should the election be set aside? Why, or why not?

12   A union refused to discuss the inclusion of a clause in the collective-bargaining agreement being negotiated with a corporation whereby the union agreed not to strike during the term of the agreement. Is the union guilty of an unfair labor practice? Why, or why not?

13   XYZ Company has a legal union-shop agreement with the designated collective-bargaining representative of its employees. One of the members, Geraldine, was expelled from the union on a technicality, the real reason being her long-running feud with the union president. May the union require XYZ to fire Geraldine? Why, or why not?

14   A contractor subcontracted construction work to three companies, all of which employed union operating engineers. The union disputed the assignment by one of the subcontractors of an operation involving an

electric welding machine to members of another labor organization. The union demanded jurisdiction over electric welding machines. The union went on strike when the employers neglected the demand, and its members physically prevented operation of the welding machine. Is this an unfair labor practice? Why, or why not?

15 Cosell Manufacturing cancelled all orders for parts that it usually purchased from Madden Corporation, whose employees had no collective-bargaining representative. When asked the reason for the decision, Cosell's purchasing agent stated that her company had agreed with its employees' union that it would only buy its needs from unionized companies in the future. Is this agreement legal? Explain.

16 Ed was discharged for allegedly stealing property from his employer. He asked his union to have him reinstated because his discharge violated the collective-bargaining agreement in force. However, the union did not investigate the incident until it was too late to file a request for arbitration under the collective-bargaining agreement. Assuming that Ed is innocent of the charges, does he have any rights against the union? Explain.

Part Seven
PROTECTING
SOCIETY

Chapter
20

Introduction to Antitrust Law: the Sherman Act

1. The Meaning of Antitrust

A "trust" is a fiduciary relationship concerning property in which one person, known as the trustee, holds legal title to property for the benefit of another, known as the beneficiary. The trustee has the duty to manage and preserve the property for the use and enjoyment of the beneficiary. Trusts are generally legal, and the so-called "antitrust laws" are not aimed at trusts which serve legitimate and socially desirable purposes, such as promoting education or caring for spendthrift or incompetent children.

In the last part of the nineteenth century, the trust device was used extensively to gain monopolistic control of different types of business. Through it, a group of corporations having the same type of business could unite in following common business policies and eliminate competition among themselves by controlling production, dividing the market, and establishing price levels. The trust device allowed all or at least a majority of the stock of several companies to be transferred to a trustee. Stockholders were issued trust certificates, naming them as beneficiaries of the trust and entitling them to dividends declared on the stock they had transferred. The trustee then was in a position to control the operation and policy making of all the companies, since it held the stock and could vote for directors of its own choosing in each. Technically, the companies were still separate businesses, but in substance they were united under one guiding hand.

The first statutes attempting to control monopolistic combinations were enacted about the time this trust device was in vogue; hence these laws came to be known as antitrust laws, although they were aimed at protecting the public from any type of monopoly or activity in restraint of trade. The term *antitrust laws* is used to describe all laws that attempt to regulate competition. The goal of such laws is to ensure that our competitive economic system works and achieves its goals of lower prices, product innovation, and equitable distribution of real income among consumers and the factors of production. In other words, the antitrust laws are designed to ensure a system of workable competition.

This chapter and the next deal with major legislation enacted in the antitrust field. They will examine the roles of the Federal Trade Commission (FTC) and the Justice Department in creating and enforcing antitrust policy, and some typical contemporary problems presented in business operation and decision making resulting from government involvement in regulating competition.

2. Statutes Involved

There are several statutes involved in the field of antitrust law. The basic statute is the **Sherman Antitrust Act** of 1890. Prior to that time, states had enacted the first antitrust laws. These proved to be largely ineffective in preventing monopolistic practices, for a number of reasons. Among these were lack of enforcement facilities and the fact that **monopolies** were really a national problem. The federal government entered the scene in 1887 with the enactment of the Interstate Commerce Act (ICA) to control the railroads, where the obvious danger of monopoly had first appeared. This was followed in 1890 by the Sherman Act, which Congress passed under its constitutional authority to regulate interstate commerce.

The Sherman Act attacks two types of anticompetitive business behavior in order to further the policy of preserving competition. Section 1 covers contracts, combinations, and conspiracies in restraint of trade or commerce. Contracts in restraint of trade usually result from words, but combinations usually result from conduct. A conspiracy is usually established by words, followed by some act carrying out the plan of the conspiracy.

Section 2 of the act is directed at monopoly and at attempts to monopolize any part of interstate or foreign commerce. The law supplies a means to break up existing monopolies and to prevent others from developing. It is directed at single firms and does not purport to cover shared monopolies or oligopolies.

In 1914, Congress decided that the Sherman Act was too general and that it needed to be made more specific. It enacted the Clayton Act, which is actually an amendment to the Sherman Act. The Clayton Act contains several important sections, some of which were later amended.

In 1914, Congress also passed the Federal Trade Commission Act (FTC

Act) which created the Federal Trade Commission (FTC). The FTC was to be an "independent" administrative agency charged with keeping competition free and fair. It enforces the Clayton Act's provisions on price discrimination, tying and exclusive contracts, mergers and acquisitions, and interlocking directorates. In addition, it enforces Section 5 of the Federal Trade Commission Act. This act originally made "unfair methods of competition" in commerce unlawful. The Wheeler-Lea amendments of 1938 added that "unfair or deceptive acts or practices in commerce" were also unlawful under Section 5.

3. Exemptions to the Sherman Act

There are numerous business activities that are exempt from the Sherman Act. Some of these exemptions were created by the original statute, others by the Clayton Act and other amendments, and still others by the courts. Each of these exemptions is based upon another form of regulation and a policy that overrides the goals of the Sherman Act. Among activities and businesses for which there are statutory exceptions are insurance companies, farmers' cooperatives, shipping, milk marketing, and investment companies. Activities required by state law are exempt. In addition, normal activities of labor unions are exempt. These exemptions are narrowly construed and do not mean that every activity of a firm is necessarily exempted simply because most activities are exempted. For example, it has been held that an agreement between an insurance company and a pharmaceutical organization regulating the price of prescription drugs furnished policy holders of the insurance company was not exempt because it was not the business of insurance that was involved in the transaction. It is the business of insurance that is exempt and not the business of insurance companies. Similarly, the courts have eliminated from exemptions persons who belong to organizations but who do not actually participate in the industry declared to be exempt. Likewise, a union would forfeit its exemption when it agrees with one set of employers to impose a certain wage scale on other employers' bargaining units. It is only the usual and legitimate union activity that is exempt.

One exemption from the Sherman Act is known as the **Noerr-Pennington Doctrine.** This doctrine exempts from the antitrust laws concerted efforts to lobby government officials regardless of the anticompetitive purposes. The doctrine is applicable even though the activity to be influenced is a commercial enterprise. The doctrine is based on the First Amendment. For example, Budget Rent-A-Car filed suit against Hertz and National Rent-A-Car because the defendants lobbied officials at three state-owned airports to limit the number of car rental operations. They lobbied for restrictions that would have made it more difficult for Budget to compete. For example, they sought a restriction that would require equal fees for all agencies. They also requested that nationwide reservation systems be required, and that each firm have a specified number of years' experience at a specified number of airports. This lobbying was exempt from the Sherman Act. The Noerr-Pennington Doctrine is based on the free flow of information and the First Amendment right to petition government for a redress of grievances. The doctrine does not have a commercial exception.

4. The State Action Exemption

In a 1943 case known as *Parker v. Brown* the Supreme Court created a **state action exemption** to the Sherman Act. This state action exemption, usually referred to as the doctrine of *Parker v. Brown*, was based on the reasoning that the Sherman Act does not cover state government. Since that time, numerous cases have attempted to define the limits of this exemption. Although the courts are still deciding cases and adding to the body of law applicable to the doctrine of *Parker v. Brown*, several principles limiting its application are evident. First of all, it only covers state action, and the state must act in its sovereign capacity. The state itself and not some private or semipublic group must require the action which constitutes the alleged Sherman Act violation. For example, a state bar association requirement is not a state action, nor is the decision of a state regulatory commission granting an exemption to a public utility. For a private party to be protected by the exemption, it must be complying with a command of the state. The threshold question in state action cases is whether the state required or compelled the challenged activity.

Second, the state action exemption is only available when state action implements an announced or clearly articulated policy of replacing competition with regulation. The mere fact that state or local government is involved is not enough. The Sherman Act may be applied to government entities. For example, a city's operation of a power plant is not automatically exempt from antitrust scrutiny. If a state law is part of a comprehensive and affirmatively expressed regulatory scheme designed to replace business freedom, actions taken pursuant to the law are exempt. Actions by the state such as granting "home rule" to local governments are not such state actions and do not bring the doctrine of *Parker v. Brown* into play.

Third, the state must actively reexamine, supervise, and regulate the anticompetitive conduct. In the case that follows, a California law required resale price maintenance. The law and the contracts made pursuant to it were not exempt under the state action exemption.

Notwithstanding the aforesaid limitations, there are many state laws which do create immunity from antitrust sanctions, not only for the state but also for private parties that comply with state laws. When a state acting in its sovereign capacity seeks to limit competition and replace it with regulations supervised and enforced by the state, *Parker v. Brown* will prevent antitrust liability. For example, Kansas City granted an exclusive license to one company to provide ambulance services. This was held to be a valid state action. The city established the ambulance system pursuant to state authority, and it clearly expressed state policy.

In another case, an unsuccessful candidate for admittance to the Arizona Bar alleged a conspiracy by the Bar examiners in violation of the Sherman Act. He contended that the grading scale was dictated by the number of new attorneys desired rather than the level of competition and answers on the exam. The courts held that this activity was exempt from the Sherman Act. The grading of bar examinations is, in reality, conduct of the Arizona Supreme Court and thus exempt. Action by the courts is just as immune as actions by the legislature.

SANCTIONS

5. The Criminal Sanction

The Sherman Act as amended by the Clayton Act recognizes four separate legal sanctions. First, it is a federal crime to violate the Sherman Act. Second, violations may be enjoined by the courts. Third, injured parties may collect triple damages. Finally, any property owned in violation of Section 1 of the act that is being transported from one state to another is subject to seizure by and forfeiture to the United States. This last remedy has rarely been used.

In addition to these sanctions, the law allows the government to demand information from suppliers, consumers, and target companies in noncriminal investigations. The data obtained may be used to establish proof of market share or other relevant statistics. The information may then be used to obtain injunctions.

The punishment imposed by the criminal law may be a fine or imprisonment or both for any person or corporation that violates its provisions. Although originally such violations were only misdemeanors, today crimes under the Sherman Act are felonies. An individual found guilty may be fined up to $100,000 and imprisoned up to three years. A corporation found guilty may be fined up to $1 million for each offense.

In criminal cases, the defendant has three possible pleas to enter to an indictment charging a violation—"guilty," "not guilty," or "**nolo contendere.**" This last plea of "no contest" allows sentencing just as if the defendant had pleaded or been found guilty. It has the advantage to a defendant of avoiding the cost of trial and the effect of a guilty plea or finding in a subsequent civil suit. Criminal convictions create prima facie cases for triple damages, but this effect can be avoided by the nolo contendere plea. Acceptance of nolo contendere pleas (the plea is not a matter of right but discretionary with the trial court) tends to discourage triple damage suits because of the difficulties private parties face in proving Sherman Act violations. The cost of investigation and preparation of antitrust suits is usually substantial, and therefore private litigants benefit greatly from either a guilty plea or a conviction. As a result, the government today often opposes pleas of nolo contendere.

The criminal sanction is probably the least used of Sherman Act remedies. As a general rule, it is used in price-fixing cases and when there is proof of specific intent to restrain trade or to monopolize. If a firm has been charged civilly and found guilty, the government is required to bring criminal charges if the evidence suggests continuing violations. Many first-offense cases are handled civilly rather than criminally. However, criminal prosecution is likely to result if practices similar to those engaged in have been held to be a violation in a prior case. Action undertaken with knowledge of a prior decision will supply the requisite criminal intent.

Criminal prosecutions under the Sherman Act do require proof of criminal intent. There is no presumption of wrongful intent. The major use of the criminal sanction is in price-fixing cases. For example, criminal cases have been brought against road builders of interstate highways because of rigged bids, and against various real estate firms for fixing the price of real estate commissions. These criminal cases were brought in order to deter others from similar practices.

6. The Injunction

The Sherman Act empowers courts to grant injunctions at the request of the government or a private party that will prevent and restrain violations or continued violations of its provisions. An injunction may prevent anticompetitive behavior or it may even force a breakup of a corporation. For example, it was used to split the former American Telephone & Telegraph Company (Ma Bell) into eight organizations—one national for long-distance and seven regional companies providing local telephone service. The remedy is also used to prevent acquisitions and to stop practices that are deemed to be anticompetitive.

The injunction remedy is frequently used when the success of a criminal prosecution is doubtful. It takes less proof to enjoin an activity (preponderance of the evidence only) than it does to convict of a crime (beyond a reasonable doubt). There have been cases involving this remedy even after an acquittal in a criminal case. In effect, the court ordered the defendant not to do something which it had been found innocent of doing.

Many antitrust cases are settled by agreement of the government and the defendants. In the past, it was sometimes alleged that political considerations played a part in such settlements. Therefore, the law now requires that all contacts between government and company officials, except for those between the lawyers involved, be reported when a proposed negotiated settlement of an antitrust case is made public. In addition, out-of-court settlements must be approved by the court, and the judge must find that the settlement is in the national interest before it can be approved. In the case involving AT&T, the trial judge balked at accepting the settlement agreed upon by the parties. It was later approved after some modifications.

7. Triple Damages

The third remedy (created by the Clayton Act amendment in 1914) affords relief to persons injured by another's violation of the Sherman Act. Such victims are given the right, in a civil action, to collect three times the damages they have suffered, plus court costs and reasonable attorney's fees. Normally, the objective of awarding money damages to individuals in a private lawsuit is to place them in the position they would have enjoyed, as nearly as this can be done with money, had their rights not been invaded. The **triple damage** provisions of the antitrust laws, however, employ the remedy of damages to punish a defendant for a wrongful act in addition to compensating the plaintiff for actual injury. Today it is perhaps the most important remedy of all, because it allows one's competitors as well as injured members of the general public to enforce the law if government fails to do so.

In recent years there have been several developments relating to triple damages. After the Supreme Court held that foreign governments are persons under the Sherman Act, Congress by statute provided that foreign nations may sue only for actual damages when they have purchased products for which prices have been fixed. The Court has held that local governments and nonprofit organizations may be sued under the law when they participate in activities which violate the Sherman Act. Such cases may arise when local government operates a business such as a utility, or when a professional association causes its members to take certain actions. In these cases, liability is imposed by use of the doctrine of respondeat superior and antitrust liability is imposed for unlawful conduct of agents within the scope of their actual or apparent authority.

The law authorizes the attorney general of a state to file triple damage suits on behalf of the citizens of a state. Such suits are similar to a class action suit. For example, either the consumers involved or the attorney general acting on their behalf may sue for triple damages when consumers have paid higher prices for products and when the higher prices have resulted from antitrust violations. Damages under the antitrust laws are not limited to commercial losses or to those of a competitive nature. The term "property" is given a broad definition and includes anything of a material value including money.

The triple damage remedy is perhaps the most important of all the sanctions available. Successful triple damage suits may impose financial burdens on violators far in excess of any fine that could be imposed as a result of a criminal prosecution. This significant liability may be far in excess of the damages caused by any one defendant, because the liability of defendants is based on tort law and is said to be joint and several. For example, assume that ten companies in an industry conspire to fix prices and that the total damages caused by the conspiracy equal $100 million. Also assume that nine of the defendants settle out of court for $25 million. The remaining defendant, if the case is lost, would owe $275 million ($3 \times 100 - 25$). The case which denied any right of contribution in such circumstances follows. It should be noted that Congress is considering legislation to change this decision because of its impact on a few companies which face liabilities approaching a billion dollars.

TEXAS INDUSTRIES, INC. v. RADCLIFF MATERIALS
101 S.Ct. 2061 (1981)

BURGER, C. J.: This case presents the question whether the federal antitrust laws allow a defendant, against whom civil damages, costs, and attorneys' fees have been assessed, a right to contribution from other participants in the unlawful conspiracy on which recovery was based. . . .

Petitioner and the three respondents manufacture and sell ready-mix concrete in the New Orleans, La., area. In 1975, the Wilson P. Abraham Construction Corp., which had purchased concrete from petitioner, filed a civil action . . . naming petitioner as defendant; the complaint alleged that petitioner and certain unnamed concrete firms had conspired to raise prices in violation of § 1 of the Sherman Act. . . . The complaint sought treble damages plus attorneys' fees under § 4 of the Clayton Act. . . .

Through discovery, petitioner learned that Abraham believed respondents were the other concrete producers that had participated in the alleged price-fixing scheme. Petitioner then filed a third-party complaint against respondents seeking contribution from them should it be held liable in the action filed by Abraham. The District Court dismissed the third-party complaint holding that federal law does not allow an antitrust defendant to recover in contribution from co-conspirators. . . .

On appeal, the Court of Appeals for the Fifth Circuit affirmed. . . .

The common law provided no right to contribution among joint tortfeasors. In part, at least, this common-law rule rested on the idea that when several tortfeasors have caused damage, the law should not lend its aid to have one tortfeasor compel others to share in the sanctions imposed by way of damages intended to compensate the victim. Since the turn of the century, however, 39 states and the District of Columbia have fashioned rules of contribution in one form or another, 10 initially through judicial action and the remainder through legislation. Because courts generally have acknowledged that treble-damages actions under the antitrust laws are analogous to common-law actions sounding in tort, we are urged to follow this trend and adopt contribution for antitrust violators. . . .

Proponents of a right to contribution advance concepts of fairness and equity in urging that the often massive judgments in antitrust actions be shared by all the wrongdoers. In the abstract, this position has a certain appeal: collective fault, collective responsibility. But the efforts . . . to invoke principles of equity presuppose a legislative intent to allow parties violating the law to draw upon equitable principles to mitigate the consequences of their wrongdoing. . . .

The proponents of contribution also contend that, by allowing one violator to recover from co-conspirators, there is a greater likelihood that most or all wrongdoers will be held liable and thus share the consequences of the wrongdoing. It is argued that competition would thus promote more vigorous private enforcement of the antitrust laws and thereby deter violations, one of the important purposes of the treble-damages action under § 4 of the Clayton Act. Independent of this effect, a right to contribution may increase the incentive of a single defendant to provide evidence against co-conspirators so as to avoid bearing the full weight of the judgment. Realization of this possibility may also deter one from joining an antitrust conspiracy.

Respondents . . . opposing contribution point out that an even stronger deterrent may exist in the possibility, even if more remote, that a single participant could be held fully liable for the total amount of the judgment. In this view, each prospective co-conspirator would ponder long and hard before engaging in what may be called a game of "Russian roulette." . . .

The parties . . . also discuss at length how a right to contribution should be structured and, in particular, how to treat problems that may arise with the allocation of damages among the wrongdoers and the effect of settlements. Dividing or apportioning damages among a cluster of co-conspirators presents difficult issues, for the participation of each in the conspiracy may have varied. Some may have profited more than others; some may have caused more damage to the injured plaintiff. Some may have been "leaders" and others "followers"; one may be a "giant," others "pygmies." Various formulae are suggested: damages may be allocated according to market shares, relative profits, sales to the particular plaintiff, the role in the organization and operation of the conspiracy, or simply pro rata, assessing an equal amount against each participant on the theory that each one is equally liable for the injury caused by collective action. . . .

The contentions advanced indicate how

views diverge as to the "unfairness" of not providing contribution, the risks and trade-offs perceived by decisionmakers in business, and the various patterns for contribution that could be devised. In this vigorous debate over the advantages and disadvantages of contribution and various contribution schemes, the parties . . . have paid less attention to a very old question: whether courts have the power to create such a cause of action absent legislation and, if so, whether that authority should be exercised in this context.

A right to contribution may arise in either of two ways: first, through the affirmative creation of a right of action by Congress, either expressly or by clear implication; or, second, through the power of federal courts to fashion a federal common law of contribution.

There is no allegation that the antitrust laws expressly establish a right of action for contribution. Nothing in these statutes refers to contribution, and if such a right exists it must be by implication. Our focus, as it is in any case involving the implication of a right of action, is on the intent of Congress. Congressional intent may be discerned by looking to the legislative history and other factors, e.g., the identity of the class for whose benefit the statute was enacted, the overall legislative scheme, and the traditional role of the States in providing relief.

Petitioner readily concedes that "there is nothing in the legislative history of the Sherman Act or the Clayton Act to indicate that Congress considered whether contribution was available to defendants in antitrust actions." Moreover, it is equally clear that the Sherman Act and the provision for treble-damages actions under the Clayton Act were not adopted for the benefit of the participants in a conspiracy to restrain trade. . . . The very idea of treble damages reveals an intent to punish past, and to deter future, unlawful conduct, not to ameliorate the liability of wrongdoers. The absence of any reference to contribution in the legislative history or of any possibility that Congress was concerned with softening the blow on joint wrongdoers in this setting makes examination of other factors unnecessary. We therefore conclude that Congress neither expressly nor implicitly intended to create a right to contribution. If any right to contribution exists, its source must be federal common law.

There is, of course, "no general federal common law." Nevertheless, the Court has recognized the need and authority in some limited areas to formulate what has come to be known as "federal common law." These instances are "few and restricted," and fall into essentially two categories: those in which a federal rule of decision is "necessary to protect uniquely federal interests," and those in which Congress has given the courts the power to develop substantive law. . . .

The antitrust laws were enacted pursuant to the power of Congress under the Commerce Clause, Art. I, § 8, cl. 3, to regulate interstate and foreign trade, and the case law construing the Sherman Act now spans nearly a century. Nevertheless, a treble-damages action remains a private suit involving the rights and obligations of private parties. Admittedly, there is a federal interest in the sense that vindication of rights arising out of these congressional enactments supple-

ments federal enforcement and fulfills the objects of the statutory scheme. Notwithstanding that nexus, contribution among antitrust wrongdoers does not involve the duties of the Federal Government, the distribution of powers in our federal system, or matters necessarily subject to federal control even in the absence of statutory authority. In short, contribution does not implicate "uniquely federal interest" of the kind that oblige courts to formulate federal common law.

[The court then reviewed the Sherman and Clayton Acts and the remedies provided.] We are satisfied that neither the Sherman Act nor the Clayton Act confers on federal courts the broad power to formulate the right to contribution sought here.

The policy questions presented by petitioner's claimed right to contribution are far reaching. In declining to provide a right to contribution, we neither reject the validity of those arguments nor adopt the views of those opposing contribution. Rather, we recognize that, regardless of the merits of the conflicting arguments, this is a matter for Congress, not the courts, to resolve. . . .

Because we are unable to discern any basis in federal statutory or common law that allows federal courts to fashion the relief urged by petitioner, the judgment of the Court of Appeals is . . . [*Affirmed.*]

---

8. The Illinois Brick Doctrine

Who is entitled to collect triple damages? Is everyone in the chain of distribution entitled to use Section 4 of the Clayton Act and recover damages? The leading case on this point involved a company called Illinois Brick. The case has become so well known in antitrust law that the legal principle which it announced is simply referred to as the **Illinois Brick Doctrine.** This doctrine announced that <u>courts generally restrict</u> the recovery of triple damages to direct purchasers, and they do not allow recoveries by indirect purchasers.

ILLINOIS BRICK CO. v. ILLINOIS
97 S.Ct. 2061 (1977)

The state of Illinois and several of its local entities brought suit for triple damages against Illinois Brick Co., a manufacturer of concrete blocks. Illinois Brick sold concrete blocks to many companies who, in turn, had sold them to general contractors from whom the plaintiff had purchased them as part of completed buildings. The complaint alleged that the defendant was a part of a price-fixing conspiracy in violation of Section 1 of the Sherman Act.

The defendant moved for a summary judgment on the ground that indirect purchasers cannot recover triple damages. It relied on the case of *Hanover Shoe, Inc., v. United Shoe Machinery Corp., 392 U.S. 481 (1968)* which had held that a direct purchaser could collect triple damages even though the price increase due to price-fixing had been passed on. The case had held that evidence of injury to indirect purchasers was not admissible or, in other words, there was no pass-on defense in triple damage cases. The district court granted the motion, and the Court of Appeals reversed. The Supreme Court granted certiorari.

WHITE, J.: . . . In this case we once again confront the question whether the overcharged direct purchaser should be deemed for purposes of Section 4 to have suffered the full injury from the overcharge, but the issue is presented in the context of a suit in which the plaintiff, an indirect purchaser, seeks to show its injury by establishing pass-on by the direct purchaser and in which the antitrust defendants rely on Hanover Shoe's rejection of the pass-on theory. Having decided that in general a pass-on theory may not be used defensively by an antitrust violator against a direct purchaser plaintiff, we must now de-

cide whether that theory may be used offensively by an indirect purchaser plaintiff against an alleged violator. (We hold that it may not and we REVERSE).

We reach this result in two steps. First, we conclude that whatever rule is to be adopted regarding pass-on in antitrust damage actions, it must apply equally to plaintiffs and defendants. . . . Second, we decline to abandon the construction given Section 4 in *Hanover Shoe*—that the overcharged direct purchaser, and not others in the chain of manufacture of distribution, is the party "injured in his business or property" within the meaning of the section—in the absence of a convincing demonstration that the Court was wrong in *Hanover Shoe* to think that the effectiveness of the antitrust treble-damage action would be substantially reduced by adopting a rule that any party in the chain may sue to recover the fraction of the overcharge allegedly absorbed by it.

The parties in this case agree that however Section 4 is construed with respect to the pass-on issue, the rule should apply equally to plaintiffs and defendants—that an indirect purchaser should not be allowed to use a pass-on theory to recover damages from a defendant unless the defendant would be allowed to use a pass-on defense in a suit by a direct purchaser . . . We . . . agree for two reasons.

First, allowing offensive but not defensive use of pass-on would create a serious risk of multiple liability for defendants. . . .

Second, the reasoning of *Hanover Shoe* cannot justify unequal treatment of plaintiffs and defendants with respect to the permissibility of pass-on arguments. The principal basis for the decision in *Hanover Shoe* was the Court's perception of the uncertainties and difficulties in analyzing price and out-put decisions "in the real economic world rather than an economists' hypothetical model," and on the costs to the judicial system and the efficient enforcement of antitrust laws of attempting to reconstruct those decisions in the courtroom. This perception that the attempt to trace the complex economic adjustments to a change in the cost of a particular factor of production would greatly complicate and reduce the effectiveness of already protracted treble-damage proceedings applies with no less force to the assertion of pass-on theories by plaintiffs than to the assertion by defendants. However "long and complicated" the proceedings would be when defendants sought to prove pass-on, they would be equally so when the same evidence was introduced by plaintiffs. Indeed, the evidentiary complexities and uncertainties involved in the defensive use of pass-on against a direct purchaser are multiplied in the offensive use of pass-on by a plaintiff several steps removed from the defendant in the chain of distribution. The demonstration of how much of the overcharge was passed on by the first purchaser must be repeated at each point at which the price-fixed goods changed hands before they reached the plaintiff. . . .

We thus decline to construe Section 4 to permit offensive use of a pass-on theory against an alleged violator that could not use the same theory as a defense in an action by direct purchasers. . . .

We are left, then, with two alternatives: either we must overrule *Hanover Shoe* (or at least narrowly confine it to its facts), or we must preclude respondents from seeking to recover on their pass-on theory. We choose the latter course. . . .

Permitting the use of pass-on theories under Section 4 essentially would transform treble-damage actions into massive efforts to apportion the recovery among all potential plaintiffs that could have absorbed part of the overcharge—from direct purchasers to middlemen to ultimate consumers. However appealing this attempt to allocate the overcharge might seem in theory, it would add whole new dimensions of complexity to treble-damage suits and seriously undermine their effectiveness. . . .

It is true that . . . the *Hanover Shoe* rule denies recovery to those indirect purchasers who may have been actually injured by antitrust violations. Of course, as Mr. Justice Brennan points out in dissent, "from the deterrence standpoint, it is irrelevant to whom damages are paid, so long as some one redresses the violation." But Section 4 has another purpose in addition to deterring violators and depriving them of "the fruits of their illegality," it is also designed to compensate victims of antitrust violations for their injuries. *Hanover Shoe* does further the goal of compensation to the extent that the direct purchaser absorbs at least some and often most of the overcharge. In view of the considerations supporting the *Hanover Shoe* rule, we are unwilling to carry the compensation principle to its logical extreme by attempting to allocate damages among all "those within the defendant's chain of distribution," especially because we question the extent to which such an attempt would make individual victims whole for actual injuries suffered rather than simply depleting the overall recovery in litigation over pass-on issues. Many of the indirect purchasers barred from asserting pass-on claims under the *Hanover Shoe* rule have such a small stake in the lawsuit that even if they were to recover as part of a class, only a small fraction would be likely to come forward to collect their damages.

And given the difficulty of ascertaining the amount absorbed by any particular indirect purchaser, there is little basis for believing that the amount of the recovery would reflect the actual injury suffered. [*Reversed.*]

The *Illinois Brick* decision continues to require further interpretation and application. Several courts have held that *Illinois Brick* does not preclude consumers from suing manufacturers who allegedly conspire with middlemen to fix retail prices. These courts recognize that the claim is not based on pass-through damages but is instead a form of retail price-fixing.

Not every case fits into the *Illinois Brick* mold. In one instance, an employee sued for wrongful discharge for refusing to participate in a Sherman Act violation. The employee had standing to sue because the damage problems of the pass-on theory are not present in such cases. The case which follows illustrates another exception to *Illinois Brick*.

BLUE SHIELD OF VIRGINIA v. McCREADY
102 S.Ct. 2540 (1982)

As a county employee in Virginia from 1975 to 1978, McCready received partial compensation in the form of coverage under a pre-paid health plan purchased from Blue Shield. This health plan provided reimbursement for a portion of any outpatient psychotherapy administered by *psychiatrists*. The plan did not reimburse for treatment by *psychologists* unless supervised by and billed through a physician.

McCready submitted several claims to Blue Shield. These claims were denied because they were not billed through a physician. He then filed a class action on behalf of all Blue Shield subscribers denied reimbursement for psychological services, alleging that Blue Shield and the Neuropsychiatric Society of Virginia, Inc., had engaged in unlawful conspiracy to exclude psychologists from receiving compensation under Blue Shield plans in violation of the Sherman Act, Section 1. Plaintiff sought triple damages. Defendants contended that plaintiff was not in the class of persons entitled to triple damages.

The district court held that McCready had no standing under Section 4 to maintain her suit and that only psychologists could sue.

Thus, while McCready clearly had suffered an injury by being denied reimbursement, this injury was "too indirect and remote to be considered 'antitrust injury.'"

The United States Court of Appeals reversed, holding that McCready had alleged an injury within the meaning of Section 4 of the Clayton Act and had standing to maintain the suit. The court recognized that the goal of the alleged conspiracy was the exclusion of clinical psychologists from some segment of the psychotherapy market. But it held that the Section 4 remedy was available to any person "whose property loss is directly or proximately caused by" a violation of the antitrust laws, and that McCready's loss was not "too remote or indirect to be covered by the Act."

BRENNAN, J.: . . . Section 4 of the Clayton Act provides a treble-damages remedy to "*[a]ny person* who shall be injured in his business or property *by reason of anything* forbidden in the antitrust laws." On its face, § 4 contains little in the way of restrictive language. And the lack of restrictive language reflects Congress' "expansive remedial purpose" in enacting § 4: Congress sought to create a private enforcement mechanism that would deter violators and deprive them of the fruits of their illegal actions, and would provide ample compensation to the victims of antitrust violations. As we have recognized, [t]he statute does not confine its protection to consumers, or to purchasers, or to competitors, or to sellers. . . . The Act is comprehensive in its terms and coverage, protecting all who are made victims of the forbidden practices by whomever they may be perpetrated.

Consistent with the congressional purpose, we have refused to engraft artificial limitations on the § 4 remedy. Two recent cases illustrate the point. *Pfizer Inc. v. India* afforded the statutory phrase "any person" its "naturally broad and inclusive meaning," and held that it extends even to an action brought by a foreign sovereign. Similarly, *Reiter v. Sonotone Corp.* rejected the argument that the § 4 remedy is available only to redress injury to commercial interests. In that case we afforded the statutory term "property" its "naturally broad and inclusive meaning," and held that a consumer has standing to seek a § 4 remedy reflecting the increase in the purchase price of goods that was attributable to a price-fixing conspiracy. In sum, in the absence of some articulable consideration of statutory policy suggesting a contrary conclusion in a particular factual setting, we have applied § 4 in accordance with its plain language and its broad remedial and deterrent objectives. But drawing on statutory policy, our cases have acknowledged two types of limitation on the availability of the § 4 remedy to particular classes of persons and for redress of particular forms of injury. We treat these limitations in turn.

In *Hawaii v. Standard Oil Co.*, 92 S. Ct. 885 (1972), we held that § 4 did not authorize a State to sue in its *parens patriae* capacity for damages to its "general economy." Noting that a "large and ultimately indeterminable

part of the injury to the 'general economy' . . . is no more than a reflection of injuries to the 'business or property' of consumers, for which they may recover themselves under § 4," we concluded that "even the most lengthy and expensive trial could not . . . cope with the problems of double recovery inherent in allowing damages" for injury to the State's quasi-sovereign interests.

In *Illinois Brick Co. v. Illinois*, 97 S. Ct. 2061, (1977), similar concerns prevailed. *Hanover Shoe v. United Shoe Mach.*, 88 S. Ct. 2224 (1968), had held that an antitrust defendant could not relieve itself of its obligation to pay damages resulting from overcharges to a direct-purchaser plaintiff by showing that the plaintiff had passed the amount of the overcharge on to its own customers. *Illinois Brick* was an action by an indirect purchaser claiming damages from the antitrust violator measured by the amount that had been passed on to it. Relying in part on *Hawaii v. Standard Oil Co., supra*, the Court found unacceptable the risk of duplicative recovery engendered by allowing both direct and indirect purchasers to claim damages resulting from a single overcharge by the antitrust defendant. The Court found that the splintered recoveries and litigative burdens that would result from a rule requiring that the impact of an overcharge be apportioned between direct and indirect purchasers could undermine the active enforcement of the antitrust laws by private actions. The Court concluded that direct purchasers rather than indirect purchasers were the injured parties who as a group were most likely to press their claims with the vigor that the § 4 treble-damages remedy was intended to promote.

The policies identified in *Hawaii* and *Illinois Brick* plainly offer no support for petitioner here. Both cases focused on the risk of duplicative recovery engendered by allowing every person along a chain of distribution to claim damages arising from a single transaction that violated the antitrust laws. But permitting respondent to proceed in the circumstances of this case offers not the slightest possibility of a duplicative exaction from petitioners. McCready has paid her psychologist's bills; her injury consists of Blue Shield's failure to pay her. Her psychologist can link no claim of injury to himself arising from his treatment of McCready; he has been fully paid for his service and has not been injured by Blue Shield's refusal to reimburse her for the cost of his services. And whatever the adverse effect of Blue Shield's actions on McCready's employer, who purchased the plan, it is not the employer as purchaser, but his employees as subscribers, who are out of pocket as a consequence of the plan's failure to pay benefits.

It is petitioners' position that McCready's injury is too "fortuitous," "incidental," and "remote" from the alleged violation to provide the basis for a § 4 action. . . .

We do not think that because the goal of the conspirators was to halt encroachment by psychologists into a market that physicians and psychiatrists sought to preserve for themselves, McCready's injury is rendered "remote." The availability of the § 4 remedy to some person who claims its benefit is not a question of the specific intent of the conspirators. Here the remedy cannot reasonably be restricted to those competitors whom the conspirators hoped to eliminate from the market. . . .

Section 4 of the Clayton Act provides a remedy to "any person" injured "by reason of" anything prohibited in the antitrust laws. We are asked in this case to infer a limitation on the rule of recovery suggested by the plain language of § 4. But having reviewed our precedents and, more importantly, the policies of the antitrust laws, we are unable to identify any persuasive rationale upon which McCready might be denied redress under § 4 for the injury she claims. The judgment of the Court of Appeals is [*Affirmed.*]

9. The Rule of Reason and Per Se Illegality

The **rule of reason** as applied to the Sherman Act was enunciated in the case of *Standard Oil Co. v. United States.*[1] The court in that case held that contracts or conspiracies in **restraint of trade** were illegal only if they constituted *undue* or *unreasonable* restraints of trade, and that only *unreasonable* attempts to monopolize were covered by the Sherman Act. As a result, acts which the statute prohibits may be removed from the coverage of the law by a finding that they are *reasonable*. The rule of reason gives flexibility and definition to the law. The rule does not open the field of antitrust inquiry to any argument in favor of a challenged restraint that may fall within the realm of reason. Instead, it focuses directly on the challenged restraint's impact on competitive condditions. The fact that prices fixed are reasonable is no defense. Monopolistic practices that promote trade are still illegal.

The *test of reasonableness* is whether challenged contracts or acts are unreasonably restrictive of competitive conditions. Unreasonableness can be based either (1) on the nature or character of the contracts, or (2) on surrounding

[1]221 U.S. 1 (1911).

circumstances giving rise to the inference or presumption that they were intended to restrain trade and enhance prices. Under either branch of the test, the inquiry is confined to a consideration of impact on competitive conditions. If an agreement promotes competition, it may be found legal. If it suppresses or destroys competition, it is unreasonable and illegal.

For purposes of the rule of reason, Sherman Act violations may be divided into two categories. Some agreements or practices are so plainly anticompetitive and so lacking in any redeeming virtues that they are conclusively presumed to be illegal without further examination under the rule of reason. These agreements have such a pernicious effect on competition that elaborate inquiry as to the precise harm they may cause or of a business excuse for them are unnecessary. They are said to be illegal per se. It is not necessary to examine them to see if they are reasonable. They are conclusively presumed to be unreasonable. Of course, the other category consists of agreements and practices that are illegal only if they impose an unreasonable restraint upon competitors.

The concept of **per se illegality** simplifies proof in cases in which it is applied. When an activity is illegal per se, courts are not required to conduct a complicated and prolonged examination of the economic consequences of the activity to determine whether it is unreasonable. If it is illegal per se, proof of the activity is proof of a violation and proof that it is in restraint of trade.

The most common example of an agreement that is illegal per se is one that fixes prices. In other words, an unreasonable contract or combination in restraint of trade is established by simply proving the existence of a price-fixing agreement. Contracts similar to those fixing the price at which conspirators sell their product have been held unreasonable per se. Thus, agreements among competitors to divide up territories, to fix the market price of a product or service they are buying, or to limit the supply of a commodity are outlawed without proof of any unreasonable effects. Group boycotts are usually held to be illegal per se. In the materials that follow, you should note those activities to which the illegal per se concept is applied and those to which the rule of reason is applied. Courts develop this distinction on a case-by-case basis, as is done in the following case:

CATALANO, INC. v. TARGET SALES, INC.
100 S.Ct. 1925 (1980)

Plaintiffs, beer retailers, brought suit alleging that their wholesalers had engaged in an unlawful conspiracy to restrain trade by refusing to sell beer unless plaintiffs paid cash in advance or at the time of the delivery. The wholesalers had an agreement that none of them would grant short-term credit although such credit had been extended in the past.

Plaintiffs requested the trial court to declare the case one of "per se" illegality. The trial court refused and the plaintiffs appealed.

PER CURIAM: In construing and applying the Sherman Act's ban against contracts, conspiracies, and combinations in restraint of trade, the Court has held that certain agreements or practices are so "plainly anticompetitive," and so often lack . . . any redeeming virtue, that they are conclusively presumed illegal without further examination under the rule of reason generally applied in Sherman Act cases.

A horizontal agreement to fix prices is the archetypal example of such a practice. It has long been settled that an agreement to fix prices is unlawful per se. It is no excuse that the prices fixed are themselves reasonable. In *United States v. Socony-Vacuum Oil Co.,* 310 U.S. 150, 60 (1940), we held that an agreement among competitors to engage in a program of buying surplus gasoline on the spot market in order to prevent prices from falling sharply to be unlawful without any inquiry into the reasonableness of the program, even though there was no direct agreement on the actual prices to be maintained. In the course of the opinion, the Court made clear that "the machinery employed by a combination for price-fixing is immaterial."

"Under the Sherman Act a combination formed for the purpose and with the effect of raising, depressing, fixing, pegging, or stabilizing the price of a commodity in interstate or foreign commerce is illegal per se." . . .

It is virtually self evident that extending interest-free credit for a period of time is equivalent to giving a discount equal to the value of the use of the purchase price for that period of time. Thus, credit terms must be characterized as an inseparable part of the price. An agreement to terminate the practice of giving credit is thus tantamount to an agreement to eliminate discounts, and thus falls squarely within the traditional per se rule against price fixing. While it may be that the elimination of a practice of giving variable discounts will ultimately lead in a competitive market to corresponding decreases in the invoice price, that is surely not necessarily to be anticipated. It is more realistic to view an agreement to eliminate credit sales as extinguishing one form of competition among the sellers. In any event, when a particular concerted activity entails an obvious risk of anticompetitive impact with no apparent potentially redeeming value, the fact that a practice may turn out to be harmless in a particular set of circumstances will not prevent its being declared unlawful per se. . . .

Thus, under the reasoning of our cases, an agreement among competing wholesalers to refuse to sell unless the retailer makes payment in cash either in advance or upon delivery is "plainly anticompetitive." Since it is merely one form of price fixing, and since price-fixing agreements have been adjudged to lack any "redeeming virtue," it is conclusively presumed illegal without further examination under the rule of reason.

Accordingly, the judgment of the Court of Appeals is reversed, and the case is remanded for further proceedings consistent with this opinion. [*It is so ordered.*]

10. Proof of Sherman Act Violations

Plaintiffs seeking triple damages must satisfy the interstate commerce element to have a Sherman Act claim. They must allege facts which show that the activity is either in interstate commerce or that it has a substantial effect on interstate commerce. A plaintiff need not allege and prove a change in the volume of interstate commerce but only that the activity had a substantial and adverse or not insubstantial effect on interstate commerce. In a recent case involving the medical profession, it was held that the Sherman Act is applicable to staff privileges at a hospital. The impact on interstate commerce is readily apparent.

Difficulties may arise in proving the existence of a contract, combination, or conspiracy among competitors when they indulge in cooperative action to control the market in some fashion. Must an actual oral or written offer and acceptance be established? If the market behavior of competitors is consciously parallel, will it be implied that they are conspiring together? If one party reacts to another's conduct, does this prove a conspiracy? In the case that follows, there was evidence that a manufacturer terminated a distributor in response to other distributors' complaints about price-cutting. Is this sufficient to prove a conspiracy in violation of Section 1 of the Sherman Act? If there is evidence that tends to prove that a manufacturer and others had a conscious commitment to a common silence designed to achieve an unlawful objective, the issue becomes one of fact for a jury.

MONSANTO CO. v. SPRAY-RITE SERVICE CORP.
104 S.Ct. 1464 (1984)

POWELL, J.: This case presents a question as to the standard of proof required to find a vertical price-fixing conspiracy in violation of Section 1 of the Sherman Act.

Petitioner Monsanto Company manufactures chemical products, including agricultural herbicides. By the late 1960's, the time at issue in this case, its sales accounted for approximately 15% of the corn herbicide market and 3% of the soybean herbicide market. In the corn herbicide market, the market leader commanded a 70% share. In the soybean herbicide market, two other competitors each had between 30% and 40% of the market. Respondent Spray-Rite Service Corporation was engaged in the wholesale distribution of agricultural chemicals from 1955 to 1972. Spray-Rite was essentially a family business, whose owner and president, Donald

Yapp, was also its sole salaried salesman. Spray-Rite was a discount operation, buying in large quantities and selling at a low margin.

Spray-Rite was an authorized distributor of Monsanto herbicides from 1957 to 1968. In October . . . 1968 Monsanto declined to renew Spray-Rite's distributorship. At that time, Spray-Rite was the tenth largest out of approximately 100 distributors of Monsanto's primary corn herbicide. Ninety percent of Spray-Rite's sales volume was devoted to herbicide sales, and 16% of its sales were of Monsanto products. After Monsanto's termination, Spray-Rite continued as a herbicide dealer until 1972. It was able to purchase some of Monsanto's products from other distributors, but not as much as it desired or as early in the season as it needed. Monsanto introduced a new corn herbicide in 1969. By

1972, its share of the corn herbicide market had increased to approximately 28%. Its share of the soybean herbicide market had grown to approximately 19%.

Spray-Rite brought this action under Section 1 of the Sherman Act. It alleged that Monsanto and some of its distributors conspired to fix the resale prices of Monsanto herbicides. Its complaint further alleged that Monsanto terminated Spray-Rite's distributorship, adopted compensation programs and shipping policies, and encouraged distributors to boycott Spray-Rite in furtherance of this conspiracy. Monsanto denied the allegations of conspiracy, and asserted that Spray-Rite's distributorship had been terminated because of its failure to hire trained salesmen and promote sales to dealers adequately.

The case was tried to a jury. The District Court instructed the jury that Monsanto's conduct was *per se* unlawful if it was in furtherance of a conspiracy to fix prices. In answers to special interrogatories, the jury found that the termination of Spray-Rite was pursuant to a conspiracy between Monsanto and one or more of its distributors to set resale prices. . . .

The jury awarded $3.5 million in damages, which was trebled to $10.5 million.

The Court of Appeals for the Seventh Circuit affirmed. It held that there was sufficient evidence to satisfy Spray-Rite's burden of proving a conspiracy to set resale prices. The court stated that "proof of termination following competitor complaints is sufficient to support an inference of concerted action." . . .

In substance, the Court of Appeals held that an antitrust plaintiff can survive a motion for a directed verdict if it shows that a manufacturer terminated a price-cutting distributor in response to or following complaints by other distributors. . . .We reject the statement by the Court of Appeals for the Seventh Circuit of the standard of proof required to submit a case to the jury in dis-

tributor-termination litigation, but affirm the judgment under the standard we announce today.

This Court has drawn two important distinctions that are at the center of this and any other distributor-termination case. First, there is the basic distinction between concerted and independent action—a distinction not always clearly drawn by parties and courts. Section 1 of the Sherman Act requires that there be a "contract, combination . . . or conspiracy" between the manufacturer and other distributors in order to establish a violation. Independent action is not proscribed. A manufacturer of course generally has a right to deal, or refuse to deal, with whomever it likes, as long as it does so independently. (Colgate Doctrine)

Under *Colgate,* the manufacturer can announce its resale prices in advance and refuse to deal with those who fail to comply. And a distributor is free to acquiesce in the manufacturer's demand in order to avoid termination.

The second important distinction in distributor-termination cases is that between concerted action to set prices and concerted action on nonprice restrictions. The former have been *per se* illegal since the early years of national antitrust enforcement. The latter are judged under the rule of reason, which requires a weighing of the relevant circumstances of a case to decide whether a restrictive practice constitutes an unreasonable restraint on competition.

It is of considerable importance that independent action by the manufacturer, and concerted action on non-price restrictions, be distinguished from price-fixing agreements, since under present law the latter are subject to per se treatment and treble damages. On a claim of concerted price-fixing, the antitrust plaintiff must present evidence sufficient to carry its burden of proving that there was such an agreement. If an inference of such an agreement may be drawn from highly ambiguous evidence, there is a considerable danger that the doctrine enunciated in *Colgate* will be seriously eroded.

The flaw in the evidentiary standard adopted by the Court of Appeals in this case is that it disregards this danger. Permitting an agreement to be inferred merely from the existence of complaints, or even from the fact that termination came about "in response to" complaints, could deter or penalize perfectly legitimate conduct. As Monsanto points out, complaints about price-cutters "are natural— and from the manufacturer's perspective, unavoidable—reactions by distributors to the activities of their rivals." Such complaints, particularly where the manufacturer has imposed a costly set of nonprice restrictions, "arise in the normal course of business and do not indicate illegal concerted action." Moreover, distributors are an important source of information for manufacturers. In order to assure an efficient distribution system, manufacturers and distributors constantly must coordinate their activities to assure that their product will reach the consumer persuasively and efficiently. To bar a manufacturer from acting solely because the information upon which it acts originated as a price complaint would create an irrational dislocation in the market. In sum, "[t]o permit the inference of concerted action on the basis of receiving complaints alone and thus to expose the defendant to treble damage liability would both inhibit management's exercise of independent business judgment and emasculate the terms of the statute."

Thus, something more than evidence of complaints is needed. There must be evidence that tends to exclude the possibility that the manufacturer and nonterminated distributors were acting independently. As Judge Aldisert has written, the antitrust plaintiff should present direct or circumstantial evidence that reasonably tends to prove that the manufacturer and others "had a conscious commitment to a common scheme designed to achieve an unlawful objective."

Applying this standard to the facts of this case, we believe there was sufficient evidence for the jury reasonably to have concluded that Monsanto and some of its distributors were parties to an "agreement" or "conspiracy" to maintain resale prices and terminate price-cutters. In fact there was substantial *direct* evidence of agreements to maintain prices. . . .

We conclude that the Court of Appeals applied an incorrect standard to the evidence in this case. The correct standard is that there must be evidence that tends to exclude the possibility of independent action by the manufacturer and distributor. That is, there must be direct or circumstantial evidence that reasonably tends to prove that the manufacturer and others had a conscious commitment to a common scheme designed to achieve an unlawful objective. Under this standard, the evidence in this case created a jury issue as to whether Spray-Rite was terminated pursuant to a price-fixing conspiracy between Monsanto and its distributors. The judgment of the court below is affirmed. [*It is so ordered.*]

ACTIVITIES IN RESTRAINT OF TRADE

11. Introduction

Section 1 of the Sherman Act is directed at contracts, combinations, and conspiracies in restraint of trade. An express agreement is not required to create a contract in restraint of trade. Such contracts may be implied. For example, discussion of price with one's competitors taken together with conscious parallel pricing would establish a violation.

Joint activities by two or more persons that may constitute a contract, combination, or conspiracy in restraint of trade are limitless. The most common form of violation is price-fixing. Agreements relating to territories of operation as well as any other agreement among competitors may be a violation. For example, an agreement by several competitors to buy exclusively from a single supplier is a violation of Section 1. Competition is required when buying as well as when selling. A group boycott may be a violation, even though the victim is just one merchant whose business is so small its destruction makes little difference to the economy. An attempt to extend the monopolistic economic power of a patent or copyright to unrelated products or services may be a violation. Providing credit to one corporation on the condition that products be purchased from a separate corporation likewise may be illegal.

The acceptance of an invitation to participate in a plan that is in restraint of interstate commerce is sufficient to establish an unlawful conspiracy. Circumstantial evidence may be used to prove a conspiracy. For example, the simultaneous price increases by three major cigarette producers at a time of declining sales were admissible evidence without direct proof of communication among them.

The sections which follow illustrate typical Section 1 cases. The usual remedy is a suit for triple damages. However, some of the examples involve criminal violations and others are cases involving injunctions.

12. Price-Fixing

Price-fixing agreements among competitors are illegal per se. The term *price-fixing* is not given a literal interpretation. For example, if partners set the price of their goods or services, they have engaged in price-fixing, but not the type envisioned by the Sherman Act. The price-fixing covered by the Sherman Act is that which threatens free competition. It is no defense to a charge of price-fixing that the prices fixed are fair or reasonable. It also is no defense that price-fixing is engaged in by small competitors to allow them to compete with larger competitors. The per se rule makes price-fixing illegal whether the parties to it have control of the market or not, and whether they are trying to raise or lower the market price. It is just as illegal to fix a low price as it is to fix a high price. It is just as illegal to fix the price of services as it is to fix the price of goods. Maximum fee agreements are therefore just as illegal as minimum fee agreements in the service sector. Price-fixing in the service sector has been engaged in by professional persons as well as by service occupations such as automobile and television repair workers, barbers, and refuse collectors. For many years it was contended that there was a "learned profession" exception to the Sherman Act.

In the mid-1970s, the Supreme Court held that the Sherman Act covered services, including those performed by the learned professions such as lawyers.

GOLDFARB ET UX. v. VIRGINIA STATE BAR ET AL.
95 S.Ct. 2004 (1975)

BURGER, J.: We granted certiorari to decide whether a minimum fee schedule for lawyers published by the Fairfax County Bar Association and enforced by the Virginia State Bar violates § 1 of the Sherman Act, 15 U.S.C. § 1. . . .

In 1971 petitioners, husband and wife, contracted to buy a home in Fairfax County, Virginia. The financing agency required them to secure title insurance; this required a title examination, and only a member of the Virginia State Bar could legally perform that service. Petitioners therefore contacted a lawyer who quoted them the precise fee suggested in a minimum fee schedule published by respondent Fairfax County Bar Association; the lawyer told them that it was his policy to keep his charges in line with the minimum fee schedule which provided for a fee of 1% of the value of the property involved. Petitioners then tried to find a lawyer who would examine the title for less than the fee fixed by the schedule. They sent letters to 36 other Fairfax County lawyers requesting their fees. Nineteen replied and none indicated that he would charge less than the rate fixed by the schedule; several stated that they knew of no attorney who would do so.

The fee schedule the lawyers referred to is a list of recommended minimum prices for common legal services. Respondent Fairfax County Bar Association published the fee schedule although, as a purely voluntary association of attorneys, the County Bar has no formal power to enforce it. Enforcement has

been provided by respondent Virginia State Bar which is the administrative agency through which the Virginia Supreme Court regulates the practice of law in that State; membership in the State Bar is required in order to practice in Virginia. Although the State Bar has never taken formal disciplinary action to compel adherence to any fee schedule, it has published reports condoning fee schedules and has issued two ethical opinions indicating fee schedules cannot be ignored. The most recent opinion states that "evidence that an attorney *habitually* charges less than the suggested minimum fee schedule adopted by his local bar association raises a presumption that such lawyer is guilty of misconduct. . . ."

Because petitioners could not find a lawyer willing to charge a fee lower than the schedule dictated they had their title examined by the lawyer they had first contacted. They then brought this class action against the State Bar and the County Bar alleging that the operation of the minimum fee schedule, as applied to fees for legal services relating to residential real estate transactions, constitutes price fixing in violation of § 1 of the Sherman Act. Petitioners sought both injunctive relief and damages.

[The Court then reviewed the decisions of the lower courts which had resulted in a denial of relief to petitioners.]

We . . . are thus confronted for the first time with the question of whether the Sherman Act applies to services performed by attorneys in examining titles in connection with financing the purchase of real estate. . . .

. . . The County Bar argues that because the fee schedule is merely advisory, the schedule and its enforcement mechanism do not constitute price fixing. Its purpose, the argument continues, is only to provide legitimate information to aid member lawyers in complying with Virginia professional regulations. Moreover the County Bar contends that in practice the schedule has not had the effect of producing fixed fees. The facts found by the trier belie these contentions. . . . The fee schedule was enforced through the prospect of professional discipline from the State Bar, and the desire of attorneys to comply with announced professional norms, the motivation to conform was reinforced by the assurance that other lawyers would not compete by underbidding. This is not merely a case of an agreement that may be inferred from an exchange of price information, for here a naked agreement was clearly shown, and the effect on prices is plain.

Moreover, in terms of restraining competition and harming consumers like petitioners the price-fixing activities found here are unusually damaging. A title examination is indispensable in the process of financing a real estate purchase, and since only an attorney licensed to practice in Virginia may legally examine a title, consumers could not turn to alternative sources for the necessary service. All attorneys, of course, were practicing under the constraint of the fee schedule. . . . These factors coalesced to create a pricing system that consumers could not realistically escape. On this record respondent's activities constitute a classic illustration of price fixing.

The County Bar argues that Congress never intended to include the learned professions within the terms "trade or commerce" in § 1 of the Sherman Act, and therefore the sale of professional services is exempt from the Act. No explicit exemption or legislative history is provided to support this contention, rather the existence of state regulation seems to be its primary basis. Also, the County Bar maintains that competition is inconsistent with the practice of a profession because enhancing profit is not the goal of professional activities; the goal is to provide services necessary to the community. That, indeed, is the classic basis traditionally advanced to distinguish professions from trades, businesses, and other occupations, but it loses some of its force when used to support the fee control activities involved here.

In arguing that learned professions are not "trade or commerce" the County Bar seeks a total exclusion from antitrust regulation. Whether state regulation is active or dormant, real or theoretical, lawyers would be able to adopt anticompetitive practices with impunity. We cannot find support for the proposition that Congress intended any such sweeping exclusion. The nature of an occupation, standing alone, does not provide sanctuary from the Sherman Act, nor is the public service aspect of professional practice controlling in determining whether § 1 includes professions. Congress intended to strike as broadly as it could in § 1 of the Sherman Act, and to read into it so wide an exemption as that urged on us would be at odds with that purpose.

The language of § 1 of the Sherman Act, of course, contains no exception. . . . Indeed, our cases have specifically included the sale of services within § 1. Whatever else it may be, the examination of a land title is a service; the exchange of such a service for money is "commerce" in the most common usage of that word. It is no disparagement of the practice of law as a profession to acknowledge that it has this business aspect, and is subject to § 1 of the Sherman Act. . . . In the modern world it cannot be denied that the activities of lawyers play an important part in commercial intercourse, and that anticompetitive activities by lawyers may exert a restraint on commerce.

In *Parker v. Brown* 317 U.S. 341 (1943), the Court held that an anticompetitive marketing program "which derived its authority and efficacy from the legislative command of the state" was not a violation of the Sherman Act because the Act was intended to regulate private practices and not to prohibit a State from imposing a restraint as an act of government. Respondent State Bar and respondent County Bar both seek to avail themselves of this so-called state action exemption. . . .

The threshold inquiry in determining if an anticompetitive activity is state action of the type the Sherman Act was not meant to proscribe is whether the activity is required by the State acting as sovereign. Here we need not inquire further into the state action question because it cannot fairly be said that the State of Virginia through its Supreme Court Rules required the anticompetitive activities of either respondent. Respondents have pointed to no Virginia statute requiring their activities. . . . [*Reversed and remanded.*]

As a result of the foregoing case, the cost of legal services for real estate transactions was reduced significantly in the area involved. Price competition in the service sector is lowering such prices, and the threat of triple damage suits is forcing the abandonment of price-fixing activities by many groups which had actively engaged in them prior to 1975.

Some professional groups have attempted to avoid laws restricting price-fixing through the use of ethical standards. Others have attempted to determine the price of services indirectly by using formulas and relative value scales. For example, some medical organizations have determined that a given medical procedure would be allocated a relative value on a scale of one to ten. Open-heart surgery might be labeled a nine and an appendectomy a three. All members of the profession would then use these values in determining professional fees. Such attempts have been uniformly held to be illegal.

The case which follows is typical of those in which an ethical standard came into conflict with the Sherman Act's ban on limiting competition. While such ethical standards are not illegal per se, they are nevertheless anticompetitive and a violation of the Sherman Act. While not a form of price-fixing, the ethical standards in this case prevented price competition.

NATIONAL SOCIETY OF PROFESSIONAL ENGINEERS v. UNITED STATES
98 S.Ct. 1355 (1978)

STEVENS, J.: This is a civil antitrust case brought by the United States to nullify an association's canon of ethics prohibiting competitive bidding by its members. The question is whether the canon may be justified under the Sherman Act, 15 U.S.C. Section 1 et. seq., because it was adopted by members of a learned profession for the purpose of minimizing the risk that competition would produce inferior engineering work endangering the public safety. The District Court rejected this justification without making any findings on the likelihood that competition would produce the dire consequences foreseen by the association. The Court of Appeals affirmed. We granted certiorari, . . . we affirm. . . .

The charges of a consulting engineer may be computed in different ways. He may charge the client a percentage of the cost of the project, may set his fee at his actual cost plus overhead plus a reasonable profit, may charge fixed rates per hour for different types of work, may perform an assignment for a specific sum, or he may combine one or more of these approaches. Suggested fee schedules for particular types of services in certain areas have been promulgated from time to time by various local societies. This case does not, however, involve any claim that the National Society has tried to fix specific fees, or even a specific method of calculating fees. It involves a charge that the members of the Society have unlawfully agreed to refuse to negotiate or even to discuss the question of fees until after a prospective client has selected the engineer for a particular project. Evidence of this agreement is found in Section 11(c) of the Society's Code of Ethics, adopted in July 1964.

The District Court found that the Society's Board of Ethical Review has uniformly interpreted the "ethical rules against competitive bidding for engineering services as prohibiting the submission of any form of price information to a prospective customer which would enable that customer to make a price comparison on engineering services." If the client requires that such information be provided, then Section 11(c) imposes an obligation upon the engineering firm to withdraw from consideration for that job. The Society's Code of Ethics thus "prohibits engineers from both soliciting and submitting

such price information," and seeks to preserve the profession's "traditional" method of selecting professional engineers. Under the traditional method, the client initially selects an engineer on the basis of background and reputation, not price.

In 1972 the Government filed its complaint against the Society alleging that members had agreed to abide by canons of ethics prohibiting the submission of competitive bids for engineering services and that, in consequence, price competition among the members had been suppressed and customers had been deprived of the benefits of free and open competition. The complaint prayed for an injunction terminating the unlawful agreement.

In its answer the Society admitted the essential facts alleged by the Government and . . . in defense . . . averred that the standard set out in the Code of Ethics was reasonable because competition among professional engineers was contrary to the public interest. It was averred that it would be cheaper and easier for an engineer "to design and specify inefficient and unnecessarily expensive structures and methods of construction." Accordingly, competitive pressure to offer engineering services at the lowest possible price would adversely affect the quality of engineering. Moreover, the practice of awarding engineering contracts to the lowest bidder, regardless of quality, would be dangerous to the public health, safety and welfare. For these reasons, the Society claimed that its Code of Ethics was not an "unreasonable restraint of interstate trade or commerce." (The lower courts held that the canon was a per se violation of Section 1 and illegal without regard to claimed or possible benefits.)

[After reviewing the rule of reason the court continued.]

Price is the "central nervous system of the economy," and an agreement that "interferes with the setting of price by free market forces" is illegal on its face. In this case we are presented with an agreement among competitors to refuse to discuss prices with potential customers until after negotiations have resulted in the initial selection of an engineer. While this is not price fixing as such, no elaborate industry analysis is required to demonstrate the anticompetitive character of such an agreement. It operates as an absolute ban on competitive bidding, applying with equal force to both complicated and simple projects and to both inexperienced and sophisticated customers. As the District Court found, the ban "impedes the ordinary give and take of the market place" and substantially deprives the customer of "the ability to utilize and compare prices in selecting engineering services." On its face, this agreement restrains trade within the meaning of Section 1 of the Sherman Act. . . .

The Sherman Act does not require competitive bidding; it prohibits unreasonable restraints on competition. Petitioner's ban on competitive bidding prevents all customers from making price comparisons in the initial selection of an engineer, and imposes the Society's views of the costs and benefits of competition on the entire market place. It is this restraint that must be justified under the Rule of Reason, and petitioner's attempt to do so on the basis of the potential threat that competition poses to the public safety and the ethics of its profession is nothing less than a frontal assault on the basic policy of the Sherman Act.

The Sherman Act reflects a legislative judgment that ultimately competition will not only produce lower prices, but also better goods and services. "The heart of our national economic policy long has been faith in the value of competition." The assumption that competition is the best method of allocating resources in a free market recognizes that all elements of a bargain—quality, service, safety, and durability—and not just the immediate cost, are favorably affected by the free opportunity to select among alternative offers. Even assuming occasional exceptions to the presumed consequences of competition, the statutory policy precludes inquiry into the question whether competition is good or bad.

The fact that engineers are often involved in large-scale projects significantly affecting the public safety does not alter our analysis. Exceptions to the Sherman Act for potentially dangerous goods and services would be tantamount to a repeal of the statute. In our complex economy the number of items that may cause serious harm is almost endless—automobiles, drugs, foods, aircraft components, heavy equipment, and countless others, cause serious harm to individuals or to the public at large if defectively made. The judiciary cannot indirectly protect the public against this harm by conferring monopoly privileges on the manufacturers. . . .

In sum, the Rule of Reason does not support a defense based on the assumption that competition itself is unreasonable. . . . [*Affirmed.*]

13. Resale Price Maintenance: Vertical Price-Fixing

Manufacturers frequently seek to control the ultimate retail price for their products. These efforts result in part from the desire to maintain a high-quality product image, the assumption being that a relatively high price establishes quality. These efforts are also based on a desire to maintain adequate channels of distribution. If one retailer is selling a product at prices significantly below those of other retailers, there is a strong likelihood that the other retailers will not continue to carry the product.

At one time, retail price maintenance was based on state fair trade laws. Congress had authorized states to enact fair trade laws as an exception to the Sherman Act. These fair trade laws allowed manufacturers to enter into contracts with one or more retailers, setting the minimum price for products. The provisions of these contracts were then binding on all sellers in that state, and in effect nonsigners of the contract could not sell below the agreed-upon price without being in breach of contract. In the 1970s, the fair trade exception to the Sherman Act was repealed, and state fair trade laws and the contracts entered into pursuant to them were thus illegal.

Although most **resale price-maintenance** schemes run afoul of the Sherman Act, it is possible for a manufacturer to effectively control the resale price of its products. The primary method of legally controlling the retail price is for a manufacturer to simply announce its prices and to refuse to deal with those who fail to comply. This practice is commonly referred to as the **Colgate Doctrine.** The Colgate Doctrine recognizes that independent action by a manufacturer is not a violation. The *Monsanto* case on page 623 illustrated that although price-fixing is illegal per se, there must be concerted action and not simply a refusal to deal with distributors who do not comply with the announced price policy. The Colgate Doctrine will justify resale price maintenance only if there is no coercion or pressure other than the announced policy and its implementation.

Other methods of maintaining retail prices have been attempted. For example, real estate leases and equipment leases sometimes contain provisions allowing the lessor to set the prices to be charged by the lessee. Such leases are illegal because there is usually coercion present. Another example of attempted retail price maintenance is the use of a **consignment** contract. In a consignment, the consignor retains title to the property and the consignee has possession. The consignee is paid a commission if he or she sells the property. Since the property belongs to the consignor, she or he is entitled to determine the price for its product. Art objects and racehorses are frequently sold on consignment. However, the consignment technique may not be used to subvert the antitrust laws.

Whether or not **vertical price-fixing** should be illegal per se is a matter of debate among economists and politicians. The Reagan administration has indicated that it believes that some vertical price-fixing is not anticompetitive, rather it may in fact aid competition. Congress in 1984 adopted a resolution condemning vertical price-fixing and indicating its attitude that vertical price-fixing is just as bad as horizontal price-fixing and therefore should be illegal per se. Since Congress has spoken, vertical price-fixing is just as illegal as horizontal price-fixing.

14. Agreements Relating to Territory

Territorial agreements may be either horizontal or vertical. A horizontal agreement would be entered into by a group of similar businesses for the purpose of giving each an exclusive territory. For example, if all Oldsmobile dealers in state X agreed to allocate each an exclusive territory, a horizontal arrangement would exist. It would be illegal per se under the Sherman Act. This is true even if the arrangement is made by a third party. For example, an agreement among competing cable television operators to divide the market in Houston, Texas, was a per se violation even though the agreement required city council approval.

A vertical agreement is one between a manufacturer and a dealer or distributor. It assigns the dealer or distributor an exclusive territory, and the manufacturer agrees not to sell to other dealers or distributors in that territory in exchange for an agreement by the dealer that it will not operate outside the area assigned. Such agreements are usually part of a franchise or license agreement, and while they are not per se violations, they may nevertheless be illegal. The case which follows explains why such agreements are subject to the rule of reason.

CONTINENTAL T.V., INC. v. GTE SYLVANIA, INC.
97 S.Ct. 2549 (1977)

GTE (Sylvania), in order to improve its market position, limits the number of retail franchises granted for any given area. It requires each franchisee to sell its television sets only from the location or locations at which it is franchised. At one time, Sylvania had distributed its television sets through wholesalers. Its plan to distribute through franchised retailers rather than through wholesalers was developed after it suffered a significant reduction in its market share. It was decided that only aggressive and competent retailers should be allowed to sell its televisions. However, franchisees were not given exclusive territories.

This suit was brought by one of the franchised retailers (Continental) after Sylvania had granted an additional franchise within approximately 1 mile of Continental's place of business. Sylvania had also denied petitioner a franchise in another area. These decisions ruptured the franchiser-franchisee relationship between the parties and ultimately resulted in a lawsuit by Sylvania to recover money owed by Continental. Continental, in defense, alleged a violation of Section 1 of the Sherman Act.

The trial judge rejected Sylvania's jury instruction that the location restriction was illegal only if it unreasonably restrained or oppressed competition. Instead, the court instructed the jury that it was a per se violation if Sylvania attempted to restrict the locations from which the retailers resold merchandise purchased from it. The jury found for Continental and assessed triple damages. The Court of Appeals reversed, holding that the restriction should be judged under the rule of reason. The Supreme Court granted certiorari.

POWELL, J.: . . . Franchise agreements between manufacturers and retailers frequently include provisions barring the retailers from selling franchised products from locations other than those specified in the agreements. This case presents important questions concerning the appropriate antitrust analysis of these restrictions under Section 1 of the Sherman Act . . . and the Court's decision in *United States v. Arnold, Schwinn & Co.,* 388 U.S. 365, (1967).

We turn first to Continental's contention that Sylvania's restriction on retail locations is a per se violation of Section 1 of the Sherman Act as interpreted in Schwinn.

. . . [In Schwinn] the Court proceeded to articulate the following "bright line" per se rule of illegality for vertical restrictions: "Under the Sherman Act, it is unreasonable without more for a manufacturer to seek to restrict and confine areas or persons with whom an article may be traded after the manufacturer has parted with dominion over it." But the Court expressly stated that the rule of reason governs when "the manufacturer retains title, dominion, and risk with respect to the product and the position and function of the dealer in question are, in fact, indistinguishable from those of an agent or salesman of the manufacturer." . . .

In the present case, it is undisputed that title to the television sets passed from Sylvania to Continental. Thus, the Schwinn per se rule applies unless Sylvania's restriction on location falls outside Schwinn's prohibition against a manufacturer's attempting to restrict a "retailer's freedom as to where and to whom it will resell the products." . . . [T]he language of Schwinn is clearly broad enough to apply to the present case. . . .

Both Schwinn and Sylvania sought to reduce but not to eliminate competition among their respective retailers through the adoption of a franchise system. . . . The Schwinn franchise plan included a location restriction similar to the one challenged here. These restrictions allowed Schwinn and Sylvania to regulate the amount of competition among their retailers by preventing a franchisee

from selling franchised products from outlets other than the one covered by the franchise agreement. . . .

Sylvania argues that if Schwinn cannot be distinguished, it should be reconsidered. . . . We are convinced that the need for clarification of the law in this area justifies reconsideration. Schwinn itself was an abrupt and largely unexplained departure from *White Motor Co. v. United States,* 372 U.S. 253, (1963), where only four years earlier the Court had refused to endorse a per se rule for vertical restrictions. Since its announcement, Schwinn has been the subject of continuing controversy and confusion, both in the scholarly journals and in the federal courts. . . . In our view, the experience of the past 10 years should be brought to bear on this subject of considerable commercial importance.

The traditional framework of analysis under Section 1 of the Sherman Act is familiar and does not require extended discussion. Section 1 prohibits "every contract, combination . . . or conspiracy, in restraint of trade or commerce." Since the early years of this century a judicial gloss on this statutory language has established the "rule of reason" as the prevailing standard of analysis. Under this rule, the fact-finder weighs all of the circumstances of a case in deciding whether a restrictive practice should be prohibited as imposing an unreasonable restraint on competition.

Per se rules of illegality are appropriate only when they relate to conduct that is manifestly anticompetitive. As the Court explained in *Northern Pac. R. Co. v. United States,* 356 U.S. 1, 5, (1958), "there are certain agreements or practices which because of their pernicious effect on competition and lack of any redeeming virtue are conclusively presumed to be unreasonable and therefore illegal without elaborate inquiry as to the precise harm they have caused or the business excuse for their use."

In essence, the issue before us is whether Schwinn's per se rule can be justified under the demanding standards of Northern Pac. R. Co. We turn now to consider Schwinn in light of Northern Pac. R. Co. . . .

The market impact of vertical restrictions is complex because of their potential for a simultaneous reduction of intrabrand competition and stimulation of interbrand competition. Significantly, the Court in Schwinn did not distinguish among the challenged restrictions on the basis of their individual potential for intrabrand harm or interbrand benefit. . . . The pivotal factor was the passage of title: All restrictions were held to be per se illegal where title had passed, and all were evaluated and sustained under the rule of reason where it had not.

. . . Nonsale transactions appear to be excluded from the per se rule, not because of a greater danger of intrabrand harm or a greater promise of interbrand benefit, but rather because of the Court's unexplained belief that a complete per se prohibition would be too "inflexible." . . .

Vertical restrictions promote interbrand competition by allowing the manufacturer to achieve certain efficiencies in the distribution of his products. These "redeeming virtues" are implicit in every decision sustaining vertical restrictions under the rule of reason. Economists have identified a number of ways in which manufacturers can use such restrictions to compete more effectively against other manufacturers. For example, new manufacturers and manufacturers entering new markets can use the restrictions in order to induce competent and aggressive retailers to make the kind of investment of capital and labor that is often required in the distribution of products unknown to the consumer. Established manufacturers can use them to induce retailers to engage in promotional activities or to provide service and repair facilities necessary to the efficient marketing of their products. Service and repair are vital for many products, such as automobiles and major household appliances. The availability and quality of such services affect a manufacturer's goodwill and the competitiveness of his product. Because of market imperfections such as the so-called "free rider" effect, these services might not be provided by retailers in a purely competitive situation, despite the fact that each retailer's benefit would be greater if all provided the services than if none did.

Economists also have argued that manufacturers have an economic interest in maintaining as much intrabrand competition as is consistent with the efficient distribution of their products. Although the view that the manufacturer's interest necessarily corresponds with that of the public is not universally shared, even the leading critic of vertical restrictions concedes that Schwinn's distinction between sale and nonsale transactions is essentially unrelated to any relevant economic impact. Indeed, to the extent that the form of the transaction is related to interbrand benefits, the Court's distinction is inconsistent with its articulated concern for the ability of smaller firms to compete effectively with larger ones. Capital requirements and administrative expenses may prevent smaller firms from using the exception for nonsale transactions.

We conclude that the distinction drawn in Schwinn between sale and nonsale transactions is not sufficient to justify the application of a per se rule in one situation and a rule of reason in the other. The question remains whether the per se rule stated in Schwinn should be expanded to include nonsale transactions or abandoned in favor of a return to the rule of reason. We have found no persuasive support for expanding the per se rule. . . .

We revert to the standard articulated in *Northern Pac. R. Co,* and reiterated in *White Motor,* for determining whether vertical restrictions must be "conclusively presumed to be unreasonable and therefore illegal without elaborate inquiry as to the precise harm they have caused or the business excuse for their use." Such restrictions, in varying forms, are widely used in our free market economy. As indicated above, there is substantial scholarly and judicial authority supporting their economic utility. There is relatively little authority to the contrary. Certainly, there has been no showing in this case, either generally or with respect to Sylvania's agreements, that vertical restrictions have or are likely to have a "pernicious effect on competition" or that they "lack . . . any redeeming virtue." Accordingly, we conclude that the per se rule stated in Schwinn must be overruled. . . .

In sum, we conclude that the appropriate decision is to return to the rule of reason that governed vertical restrictions prior to Schwinn. When anticompetitive effects are shown to result from particular vertical restrictions they can be adequately policed under the rule of reason, the standard traditionally applied for the majority of anticompetitive practices challenged under Section 1 of the Act. [*Affirmed.*]

15. Concerted Activities by Competitors

Concerted activities among competitors take a variety of forms and appear in diverse circumstances. Some arise out of a desire to protect a channel of distribution or a marketing system. Others result from attempts to keep marginal competitors in business, which is, in fact, one goal of the antitrust laws. Thus, some cases dealing with concerted activities actually involve conflicts between various competing goals of the antitrust laws.

In the next case, the concerted activity among competitors took the form of an exchange of price information. Economic theory was used to support the assumption that prices would be more unstable and lower if the information had not been exchanged. Conduct directed at price stabilization is per se anticompetitive.

UNITED STATES v. CONTAINER CORPORATION OF AMERICA
89 S.Ct. 510 (1969)

DOUGLAS, J.: This is a civil antitrust action charging a price-fixing agreement in violation of § 1 of the Sherman Act. . . .

The case as proved is unlike any other price decisions we have rendered. There was here an exchange of price information but no agreement to adhere to a price schedule. . . . There was here an exchange of information concerning specific sales to identified customers, not a statistical report on the average cost to all members, without identifying the parties to specific transactions. . . . While there was present here, as in *Cement Manufacturers Protective Assn. v. United States* 268 U.S. 588, an exchange of prices to specific customers, there was absent the controlling circumstance, *viz.*, that cement manufacturers, to protect themselves from delivering to contractors more cement than was needed for a specific job and thus receiving a lower price, exchanged price information as a means of protecting their legal rights from fraudulent inducements to deliver more cement than needed for a specific job.

Here all that was done was a request by each defendant from its competitor for information as to the most recent price charged or quoted, whenever it needed such information and whenever it was not available from another source. Each defendant on receiving that request furnished the data with the expectation that he would be furnished reciprocal information when he wanted it. That concerted action is of course sufficient to establish the combination or conspiracy, the initial ingredient of a violation of § 1 of the Sherman Act.

There was of course freedom to withdraw from the agreement. But the fact remains that when a defendant requested and received price information, it was affirming its willingness to furnish such information in return.

There was to be sure an infrequency and irregularity of price exchanges between the defendants; and often the data was available from the records of the defendants or from the customers themselves. Yet the essence of the agreement was to furnish price information whenever requested.

Moreover, although the most recent price charged or quoted was sometimes fragmentary, each defendant had the manuals with which it could compute the price charged by a competitor on a specific order to a specific customer.

Further, the price quoted was the current price which a customer would need pay in order to obtain products from the defendant furnishing the data.

The defendants account for about 90% of the shipment of corrugated containers from plants in the southeastern United States. While containers vary as to dimensions, weight, color, and so on, they are substantially identical, no matter who produces them, when made to particular specifications. The prices paid depend on price alternatives. Suppliers when seeking new or additional business or keeping old customers, do not exceed a competitor's price. It is common for purchasers to buy from two or more suppliers concurrently. A defendant supplying a customer with containers would usually quote the same price on additional orders, unless costs had changed. Yet where a competitor was charging a particular price, a defendant would normally quote the same price or even a lower price.

The exchange of price information seemed to have the effect of keeping prices within a fairly narrow ambit. Capacity has exceeded the demand from 1955 to 1963, the period covered by the complaint, and the trend of corrugated container prices has been downward. Yet despite this excess capacity and the downward trend of prices, the industry has expanded in the Southeast from 30 manufacturers with 49 plants to 51 manufacturers with 98 plants. An abundance of raw materials and machinery makes entry into the industry easy with an investment of $50,000 to $75,000.

The result of this reciprocal exchange of prices was to stabilize prices though at a downward level. Knowledge of a competitor's price usually meant matching that price. The continuation of some price competition is not fatal to the Government's case. The limitation or reduction of price competition brings the case within the ban, for . . . interference with the setting of price by free market forces is unlawful *per se*. Price information exchanged in some markets may have no effect on a truly competitive price. But the corrugated container industry is dominated by relatively few sellers. The product is fungible and the competition for sales is price. The demand is inelastic, as buyers place orders only for immediate, short-run needs. The exchange of price data tends toward price uniformity. For a lower price does not mean a larger share of the available business but a sharing of the existing business at a lower return. Stabilizing prices as well as raising them is within the ban of § 1 of the Sherman Act. As we said in *United States v. Socony Vacuum Oil Co.*, "in terms of market operations stabilization is but one form of manipulation." The inferences are irresistible that the exchange of price information has had an anticompetitive effect in the industry, chilling the vigor of price competition. . . .

Price is too critical, too sensitive a control to allow it to be used even in an informal manner to restrain competition. [*Reversed.*]

Typical of the cases involving concerted activities was a 1981 suit filed against the National Association of Broadcasters, charging that its "over-commercialization" rules improperly regulated the amount and format of advertising on television in violation of the Sherman Act. The code had the effect of curtailing and restricting the quantity of broadcast time available for television advertising and the number and format of advertisements that could be broadcast. The challenged rules put varying limits on the amount of "nonprogram material" aired every hour. In prime time, the hourly limit was nine and one-half minutes, plus thirty seconds for promotional announcements. At other times, it was generally sixteen minutes; however, children's shows were allowed nine and one-half minutes on weekends and twelve minutes during the week. Other rules limited the number of consecutive announcements and the number of interruptions within programs. A consent decree was entered stopping the practice. The rules on the number of broadcasts were not per se violations. However, a rule prohibiting more than one product being advertised in a commercial lasting less than sixty seconds was a per se violation.

In 1984, the televising of college football games was the subject matter of a significant antitrust suit. It was filed by two football powers, the University of Georgia and the University of Oklahoma, against the National Collegiate Athletic Association (NCAA). The NCAA had adopted a plan to limit television of college football games in order to prevent adverse effect on game attendance. The number of television games was limited, as was the number of appearances by any one school. Television receipts were divided among participating schools. The Supreme Court held that the agreements were a violation of the Sherman Act and a form of price-fixing, as well as a group boycott. The plan raised prices and reduced output without regard to consumer preference. The plan was basically anticompetitive, and there was no evidence to justify its existence.

Competitors sometimes attempt to share some activities or join together in the performance of a function. Joint research efforts to find a cure for cancer or to find substitutes for gasoline would seem to provide significant benefits to society. A sharing of technology may be beneficial also. Joint efforts in other areas may reduce costs and improve efficiency. For example, several professional football teams share the information of a college scouting organization. Joint operations may violate the Sherman Act.

MONOPOLY

16. Section 2: The Rationale

Competition tends to keep private markets working in ways that are socially desirable. It encourages an efficient allocation of resources, stimulates efficiency and product innovation, and may even encourage the conservation of scarce resources. Competition also tends to limit private economic power and substitutes individual decisions for government regulation. Of course, a competitive system that allows easy entry and withdrawal from the marketplace is consistent with individual freedom and economic opportunity. Therefore, it is not surprising that the Sherman Act attacks monopoly and attempts to monopolize.

In *United States v. Aluminum Company of America*[2] Circuit Judge Learned Hand commented on the purposes and philosophy of Section 2 of the Sherman Act. In holding that Alcoa was guilty of a violation of Section 2 for having intentionally acquired and maintained control of over 90 percent of the domestic "virgin" ingot market in aluminum, even though Alcoa had not misused such monopoly power to obtain exorbitant profits, Judge Hand said:

> . . . it is no excuse for "monopolizing" a market that the monopoly has not been used to extract from the consumer more than a "fair" profit. The Act has wider purposes. Indeed, even though we disregard all but economic considerations, it would by no means follow that such concentration of producing power is to be desired, when it has not been used extortionately. Many people believe that possession of unchallenged economic power deadens initiative, discourages thrift and depresses energy; that immunity from competition is a narcotic, and rivalry is a stimulant, to industrial progress; that the spur of constant stress is necessary to counteract an inevitable disposition to let well enough alone. such people believe that competitors, versed in the craft as no consumer can be, will be quick to detect opportunities for saving and new shifts in production, and be eager to profit by them. In any event the mere fact that a producer, having command of the domestic market, has not been able to make more than a "fair" profit, is no evidence that a "fair" profit could not have been made at lower prices. . . . True, it might have been thought adequate to condemn only those monopolies which could not show that they had exercised the highest possible ingenuity, had adopted every possible economy, had anticipated every conceivable improvement, stimulated every possible demand. No doubt, that would be one way of

---

[2]148 F.2d 416 (1945).

dealing with the matter, although it would imply constant scrutiny and constant supervision, such as courts are unable to provide. Be that as it may, that was not the way that Congress chose; it did not condone "good trusts" and condemn "bad" ones; it forbade all. Moreover, in so doing, it was not necessarily actuated by economic motives alone. It is possible, because of its indirect social or moral effect, to prefer a system of small producers, each dependent for his success upon his own skill and character, to one in which the great mass of those engaged must accept the direction of a few. . . .

Judge Hand indicated that, besides the economic reasons behind the Sherman Act's proscription of monopoly,

. . . there are others, based upon the belief that great industrial consolidations are inherently undesirable, regardless of their economic results. In the debates in Congress Senator Sherman himself . . . showed that among the purposes of Congress in 1890 was a desire to put an end to great aggregations of capital because of the helplessness of the individual before them. . . . Throughout the history of these statutes it has been constantly assumed that one of their purposes was to perpetuate and preserve, for its own sake and in spite of possible cost, an organization of industry in small units, which can effectively compete with each other. . . .

In 1958 Justice Black in *Northern Pacific Ry. Co. v. United States*, 356 U.S. 1, discussed the purpose of the Sherman Act. He stated in part:

The Sherman Act was designed to be a comprehensive charter of economic liberty aimed at preserving free and unfettered competition as the rule of trade. It rests on the premise that the unrestrained interaction of competitive forces will yield the best allocation of our economic resources, the lowest prices, the highest quality and the greatest material progress, while at the same time providing an environment conducive to the preservation of our democratic political and social institutions.

17. Section 2—The Approach

Under Section 2, it is a violation for a firm to (1) monopolize, (2) attempt to monopolize, or (3) conspire to monopolize any part of interstate or foreign commerce. Attempts to monopolize cases require proof of intent to destroy competition or achieve monopoly power. This is most difficult and, as a result, there have been few cases concerning attempts to monopolize. A conspiracy to monopolize requires proof of specific intent to monopolize and at least one overt act to accomplish it. Proof of monopoly power or even that it was attainable is not required. This conspiracy theory is usually joined with the allegation of actual monopoly in most cases.

A firm has violated Section 2 if it followed a course of conduct through which it obtained the power to control price or exclude competition. The mere possession of monopoly power is not a violation. There must be proof that the power resulted from a deliberate course of conduct, or proof of intent to maintain the power by conduct. Proof of deliberateness is just as essential as is proof of the power to control price to exclude competition.

Section 2 Sherman Act cases require proof of market power—the power to affect the price of the firm's products in the market. Whether such power exists is usually determined by an analysis of the reaction of buyers to price changes by the alleged monopolist seller. Such cases require a definition of the relevant market and a study of the degree of concentration within the market. Barriers to entry are analyzed and the greater the barriers, the greater the significance of market share. The legal issues in such cases require structural analysis.

In defining the relevant market, the courts examine both product market and geographic market. A relevant market is the smallest one wide enough so that products from outside the geographic area or from other producers in the same area cannot compete with those included in the defined relevant market. In other words, if prices are raised or supply is curtailed within a given area while demand remains constant, will products from other areas or other products from within the area enter the market in enough quantity to force a lower price or increased supply?

Some monopoly cases involve homogeneous products, whereas others involve products for which there are numerous substitutes. For example, aluminum may be considered a product that is generally homogeneous. If a firm has 90 percent of the virgin aluminum market, a violation would be established. However, if a firm had 90 percent of the danish coffee-cake market, the decision is less clear because numerous products compete with danish coffee cakes as a breakfast product. The relevant product is often difficult to define because of differences in products, substitute products, product diversification, and even product clusters.

Section 2 cases may involve a variety of proofs and many different forms of economic analysis. The degree of market concentration, barriers to entry, structural features such as market shares of other firms, profit levels, the extent to which prices respond to changes in supply and demand, whether or not a firm discriminates in price between its customers, and the absolute size of the firm are all factors usually considered by courts in monopoly cases. In addition, courts examine the conduct of the firm. How did it achieve its market share? Was it by internal growth or acquisition? Does the firm's current conduct tend to injure competition? These and other issues are important aspects in any finding of the existence of monopoly power.

As previously noted, proof of monopoly power alone is not enough. Some monopolies are lawful. If monopoly power is "thrust upon" a firm or if it exists because of a patent or franchise, there is no violation of Section 2 if the firm does not engage in conduct that has the effect or purpose of protecting, enforcing, or extending the monopoly power. The power must either have been acquired or used in ways that go beyond normal, honest industrial business conduct. In other words, the power must have been *deliber-*

atively acquired or used. A firm is guilty of monopolization when it acquires or maintains monopoly power by a course of deliberate conduct that keeps other firms from entering the market or from expanding their share of it. Deliberativeness is not difficult to prove in most cases.

Conduct that proves deliberativeness may be anything in restraint of trade. For example, proof of predatory conduct would prove deliberativeness. Conduct which is exclusionary in purpose and effect will also do so. For example, if a firm through its leases tends to exclude its competitors from a market, the case is made, even though the conduct is less than predatory. In some cases, the courts have concluded that proof of monopoly power creates a prima facie case. If the firm seeks to deny that power was deliberately achieved or maintained, it may rebut the presumption by proving that power is attributable solely to a reason that is not illegal or against public policy. For example, proof that power arose from a patent or franchise would rebut the presumption.

Monopolistic conduct is often described as predatory. "Predatory" means that a firm seeks to advance its market share by injuring its actual or potential competitors by means other than improved performance. It may be for the purpose of driving out competitors, for keeping them out, or for making them less effective. Pricing policies are frequently examined for proof of predatory conduct. Profit-maximizing pricing, limit pricing whereby the price is limited to levels that tend to discourage entry, and discriminatory pricing all may tend to prove monopoly power and predatory conduct.

OTHER CONSIDERATIONS

18. Policy Trends

Congress and the courts face numerous difficult problems related to the Sherman Act and its interpretation. The Justice Department has a "hot line" to encourage people to report price-fixing and other antitrust violations. However, under the Reagan administration, attorneys for the Justice Department's Antitrust Division have begun intervening in private suits on behalf of defendants, arguing that the Sherman Act should be given a narrower interpretation. For example, in one case involving a fight between two New England grocery chains, the Justice Department argued that courts should no longer consider it unlawful for a powerful company to insist that, in order to get one of its products, a customer must also agree to purchase another product. In the past, briefs by the Justice Department were on the plaintiff's side, arguing for enhanced antitrust powers.

One suggestion to streamline antitrust enforcement is to create a special court to hear only antitrust cases. This proposal recognizes that antitrust cases are extremely complicated and terribly time-consuming. Cases frequently last several years, and issues are too complex to be objectively considered by a jury. Special pretrial procedures are needed to limit discovery and reduce the cost to the government and to the parties of such litigation.

There is a bill in Congress to reverse the *Illinois Brick* decision and to either give a right of contribution or limit damages that any one defendant may owe for price-fixing. There is also a bill to limit recovery to actual damages rather than triple damages.

Antitrust enforcement by state government is rapidly expanding. As previously noted, a state's attorney general may bring triple damage suits under the Sherman Act as well as suits for an injunction. In addition, state legislators have enacted antitrust laws covering both products and services. These laws cover intrastate activities and are designed to prevent loss of competition in local communities. For example, recent cases have involved agreements by golf course operators to fix the price of green fees and golf cart rentals. Another case involved a real estate subdivider whose contracts of sale required that his real estate firm be used as the broker on a subsequent sale. For several years, the federal government awarded grants to aid state governments in antitrust enforcement. The impact of such local enforcement is likely to be much greater in the future.

19. Ethical Considerations

The antitrust violations discussed in this chapter raise several ethical questions which are coextensive with, or complementary to, the legal issues involved. Is it ethical to develop or enforce a code of professional ethics running counter to the requirements of the law? What are the ethical implications of retaining corporate executive officers found guilty of price-fixing?

FORMAL CODE OF ETHICS

The first question—can a code of ethics be unethical?—must be answered affirmatively. It is clear that law can be unethical, such as one that stated that all people of a certain race may not own property or have civil rights, or one that stated that human slaves may be bought and sold. One can imagine scores of examples of possible laws which would violate commonly accepted ideas of what is right. But one hopes that a democratic approach to creation of law prevents such "unethical" law, or stated another way, that the law encourages or at least tolerates ethical behavior.

A code of ethics derived by any group to affect or control the conduct of group members is akin to private law. It is the group's opinion of proper conduct within the group's domain. It is possible for any code of conduct, even one labeled a code of ethics, to sanction acts contrary to law or the ethics of society as a whole. Thus, we see professional groups in both the *Goldfarb* and *National Society of Professional Engineers* cases discussed in section 12 laying down standards of professional conduct which are anticompetitive in the extreme. By preventing price competition, the conduct encouraged as "ethical" for both attorneys and engineers amounted to unreasonable restraints of trade in violation of Section 1 of the Sherman Act. One suspects that these "ethical" approaches to "professional competition" were designed and used less to protect the public from shoddy work and more to protect the professionals from the rigors of the marketplace. Whether or not a conscious decision has been made to avoid the obligations imposed by law or ethics, a group's code which abrogates standards established by society at large is subject to legal challenge, social criticism, or both.

INFORMAL CODES OF ETHICS

Whether or not a corporation creates a formal code of ethics, it has one. If found nowhere else, a code is established by the activities encouraged (or condoned by inaction) in the corporate hierarchy. The ethical attitudes and sensitivities of the corporation's leaders appear to be crucial in determining the ethical character of a corporation. Consider, for example, why price-fixing has been so common. An alarmingly high percentage of both large and small businesses has engaged in price-fixing at various times in the more than ninety years it has been a crime. Companies prominent both nationally and in their respective industries have been convicted of it. Some have even been regular repeat offenders. It has been estimated that price-fixing costs consumers $60 billion annually. Like other crimes committed for corporate rather than direct personal gain, price-fixing has soiled businesses' general reputation and depressed public confidence in executives. So why have price-fixing violations continued? Until recently, the profits to be made through price-fixing were often high compared to the risks of being caught or the penalties imposed. Today's threat of triple damage actions together with greater criminal fines and the likelihood of prison terms may counterbalance the economic incentives to conspire with competitors. Of course, many factors contribute to price-fixing, including similarities of products sold, degree of price competition, profit margins, the industry's production capacity, character of market demand, and the level in the corporation where prices are determined. The most important determinant may be whether the company treats price-fixing as improper conduct. Is there emphasis on short-run returns and an uncaring attitude about how those profits are achieved? Is there formal, or even informal, training about what market conduct is approved and what is prohibited by the company? Are executives or other employees convicted of price-fixing discharged or allowed to resign, or are they welcomed back to the corporate bosom with open arms? If employees who violate the law "on behalf of" the corporation are treated differently from those who violate the law "against" the corporation (embezzlement), a message is being sent through the corporate structure that criminal conduct on behalf of the company will be tolerated.

INTERNAL SANCTIONS

If a company were serious about not price-fixing, it would act as though it meant it by imposing corporate penalties for price-fixing. Law compliance programs and training to help employees deal with ethical dilemmas would also affirm the corporation's attitude toward misconduct. However, a real threat to job security for price-fixers might go further than any education program or code of ethics ever could. Giving lip service to corporate integrity while at the same time tolerating unlawful conduct to reach a profit on the bottom line signifies either corporate hypocrisy or blindness. Either leads one to the conclusion that the company is ethically insensitive.

20. Caterpillar Code of Competition

As an illustration of a corporate statement concerning competitive conduct, the following detailed provision of the Caterpillar code is included. It should be noted that Caterpillar appears to be using United States law to establish ethical norms for its conduct throughout the world.

COMPETITIVE CONDUCT

Fair competition is fundamental to the free enterprise system. We support laws prohibiting restraints of trade, unfair practices, or abuse of economic power. And we avoid such practices everywhere—including areas of the world where laws don't prohibit them.

In large companies like Caterpillar, particular care must be exercised to avoid practices which seek to increase sales by any means other than fair merchandising efforts based on quality, design features, productivity, price, and product support.

In relationships with competitors, dealers, suppliers, and customers, Caterpillar employees are directed to avoid arrangements restricting our ability to compete with others—or the ability of any other business organization to compete freely and fairly with us, and with others.

There must be no arrangements or understandings, with competitors, affecting prices, terms upon which products are sold, or the number and type of products manufactured or sold—or which might be construed as dividing customers or sales territories with a competitor.

In the course of our business, we may sell engines and other items to companies which are also competitors in other product areas. Related information from such customers will be treated with the same care we would expect Caterpillar data to be accorded, in a similar situation.

Relationships with dealers are established in the Caterpillar dealership agreements. These embody our commitment to fair competitive practices, and reflect customs and laws of various countries where Caterpillar products are sold. Our obligations under these agreements are to be scrupulously observed.

Caterpillar aims to increase its sales—to excel and lead. We intend to do this through superior technical skill, efficient operations, sound planning, and effective merchandising.

We believe that fair competition is good for the marketplace, customers and Caterpillar.

REVIEW QUESTIONS

1 For each term in the left-hand column, match the most appropriate description in the right-hand column:

(1) Nolo contendere

(2) Noerr-Pennington Doctrine

(3) Per se illegality

(4) Price-fixing

(5) State action exemption

(6) The rule of reason

(7) Resale price maintenance

(8) Illinois Brick Doctrine

(a) An agreement or combination by which the conspirators set the market price of a product or service either being sold or purchased, whether high or low

(b) A plea of "no contest" to a charge of a criminal violation of the law

(c) The controlling by a manufacturer of a brand or trade name product of the minimum retail price at which it is sold

(d) A rule that contracts or conspiracies are illegal only if they constitute undue or unreasonable restraints of trade or unreasonable attempts to monopolize

(e) Certain acts in themselves are unreasonable and therefore illegal under the Sherman Act

(f) The antitrust laws do not cover activities mandated by state and local laws

(g) Concerted efforts to lobby governmental bodies are exempt from the antitrust laws

(h) Only direct purchasers from a price-fixer are entitled to collect triple damages

2 A city used federal funds to build a sewage-treatment facility. It refused to supply sewage-treatment services to neighboring towns but did supply services to landowners who agreed to be annexed to the city. Neighboring towns brought suit under the Sherman Act. What was the result? Why?

3 Three rating bureaus representing common carriers in five southeastern states provided a forum for carriers to discuss and agree on rates for intrastate transportation of commodities. These rates are then proposed to the public-service commissions for approval. The United States instituted action to enjoin this activity. The defendants asserted the state action exemption. What was the result? Why?

4 Reiter purchased a hearing aid and filed suit for triple damages alleging price-fixing. Sonotone Corp. contended that Reiter was not injured in her business or property and therefore was not entitled to triple damages. Is she entitled to triple damages? Why, or why not?

5 Doctors in a county medical society fixed *maximum* fees to be charged patients for various medical services. Arizona filed suit to enjoin the use of maximum fee schedules. What was the result? Why?

6 The four largest real estate brokers in Atlanta conspired to fix real estate commissions. They were indicted by a federal grand jury and ultimately entered a plea of nolo contendere. The usual commission rate prior to the conspiracy was 5 percent. The agreed-upon rate was 7 percent.

   a What punishment may be imposed on the individuals involved?

   b If the brokers are incorporated, what punishment may be imposed?

   c If a suit for triple damages is filed, what proof is required? Explain.

   d Assume that you had sold your house for $150,000 during the period the conspiracy was in effect. How much could you collect from your broker who was involved?

7 National associations of repossessors established fee schedules to be used in charging for their services. Repossessors were to be hired by lenders such as automobile dealers to take possession of items that were bought with loans that were later defaulted. The Justice Department sought to enjoin the use of the fee schedules. What was the result? Why?

8 Members of a real estate brokers' association voted to raise their commission rate from 6 to 7 percent. The bylaws of the association provided for expulsion of any member charging less than the agreed-upon commission. If broker X continues to charge 6 percent, can she be expelled legally? Why, or why not?

9 A candy manufacturer had a policy of terminating the supply of its product to retailers who failed to comply with its designated resale prices. Several retailers complained to the FTC, which ordered the manufacturer to cease and desist. On appeal, what was the result? Why?

10 The American Society of Anesthesiologists has an ethical standard which prevents its member doctors from working for salaries at hospitals. It insists on fee-for-service arrangements. Is such a standard a violation of the Sherman Act? Explain.

11 There was a contract between the manufacturer of paint and a retailer of paint in which they agreed not to compete on the retail level. Is this a per se violation of the Sherman Act? Why, or why not?

12 Auto manufacturers entered into contracts with their dealers, who were the only persons eligible to bid on "company cars" (new automobiles which had been used only by manufacturers' employees), that the dealers would not bid on such cars for the purpose of reselling them to used-car dealers in other towns. Are the contracts violations of the Sherman Act? Why, or why not?

13 A shopping center leased a service-station location to a major oil company. The lease contained a provision that the lessor would not lease any other part of the shopping center for use as a service station. Does the lease violate the Sherman Act? Why, or why not?

14 A buying association for small- and medium-sized regional supermarket chains allocated territories to its members in which they had exclusive or de facto exclusive licenses to sell the association's private-label brands, and a veto over admission of new members. No price-fixing was involved. It was contended that such practices actually increase competition by enabling members of the association to compete successfully with larger regional and national chains. Is this arrangement a violation of the Sherman Act? Why, or why not?

15 A newspaper publisher produced the

only paper serving a three-county area. It informed all of its advertisers that they must boycott the local radio station before the newspaper would sell them advertising space. Is this a Sherman Act violation? Why, or why not?

16 The government filed a civil suit under Section 2 of the Sherman Act claiming Grinnell Corporation had a monopoly over the central station hazard-detecting devices. These are security devices to prevent burglary and to detect fires. They involve electronic notification of the police and fire departments at a central location. Grinnell, through three separate companies, controlled 87 percent of that business. It argued that it faces competition from other modes of protection from burglary, and therefore it does not have monopoly power. Did Grinnell violate the Sherman Act? Why, or why not?

17 The *Kansas City Star* publishes the only major daily newspapers in Kansas City. It terminated its existing contracts with independent carriers and used instead its employees who sell and deliver newspapers. No newspapers were sold at wholesale. As a result, the newspaper had a monopoly of the distribution of newspapers. Is this a Sherman Act violation? Why, or why not?

Chapter
21

Additional Antitrust Laws: The Clayton and Federal Trade Commission Acts

1. Introduction

After it had been in effect for a time, the Sherman Act was criticized as being inadequate. For one thing, it did little to prevent practices which only tended to reduce competition or were simply conducive to creating monopolies. As interpreted with the rule of reason, the Sherman Act did not apply to situations likely to lead to the destruction of competition but that fell short of an actual monopoly or combination in unreasonable restraint of trade. Also, the rule of reason and lack of specificity in the Sherman Act practically required that courts decide each alleged violation on its own merits on a case-by-case basis. Also, there were a few interpretations by the courts that were contrary to the will of Congress. For example, the Supreme Court held that the law applied to labor unions.

The foregoing factors led to the passage of the Clayton Act and the Federal Trade Commission Act in 1914. One purpose of the Clayton Act was to exclude labor unions along with nonprofit agricultural organizations from the scope of antitrust legislation. The Federal Trade Commission (FTC) was created as the expert agency in the antitrust field to enforce the antitrust laws.

The Clayton Act was more specific than the Sherman Act in declaring certain enumerated practices in commerce illegal. These were practices that might adversely affect competition but were not themselves contracts, combinations, or conspiracies in restraint of trade; such practices did not go far enough to constitute actual monopolization or attempts to monopolize. Further, the enumerated practices did not have to actually injure competition to be wrongful; they were outlawed if their effect substantially lessened competition or tended to create a monopoly. Thus, the burden of proving a violation was eased. It would be much easier, for example, for a court to find that certain practices tended toward monopoly than to find that they amounted to a monopoly. The Clayton Act made it possible to attack in their incipiency many practices which, if continued, eventually could destroy competition or create monopoly. The idea was to remedy these matters before full harm was done.

The sections of the Clayton Act discussed in detail in this chapter are:

- Section 2—price discrimination

- Section 3—tying and exclusive contracts

- Section 7—mergers and acquisitions

Section 8 of the Clayton Act also has antitrust significance. It is aimed at **interlocking directorates.** It prohibits a person from being a member of the board of directors of two or more corporations at the same time, when one of them has capital, surplus, and undivided profits totaling more than $1 million, where elimination of competition by agreement between such corporations would amount to a violation of any of the antitrust laws.

In recent years there have been numerous Section 8 challenges of outside directors on the boards of many large companies. As corporations have tended to diversify and as the number of conglomerates has increased substantially, it is not difficult to find some form of competition between two companies which are ostensibly involved in quite different fields. For example, a director on the board of a business manufacturing aluminum who also served on the board of a steel company was in violation even though the companies were in different industries, because aluminum and steel compete under certain circumstances.

Violations of the original Clayton Act were not crimes, and the act contained no sanction for forfeiture of property. However, it did provide that the Justice Department might obtain injunctions to prevent violations. Those persons injured by a violation could obtain injunctive relief in their own behalf and, in addition, were given the right to collect three times the damages they suffered plus court costs and reasonable attorney's fees. All discussion in Chapter 20 relating to triple damage suits was based on Section 4 of the Clayton Act.

The Clayton Act expanded Sherman Act provisions by allowing private individuals to obtain injunctions in cases of threatened loss due to violations of any of the antitrust laws. It also greatly eased the burden of proof which normally must be shouldered by a plaintiff in triple damage suits. A final decision in favor of the United States to the effect that a defendant has violated the antitrust laws was made prima facie evidence of such violation. This means that if a business is found to be guilty of a Sherman Act violation, a suit for triple damages need not prove violation of the law other than by showing a copy of the court order finding the defendant guilty.

PRICE DISCRIMINATION—SECTION 2

2. The Original Clayton Act

Section 2 of the Clayton Act as originally adopted in 1914 declared that it is unlawful for a seller to discriminate in the price charged different purchasers of commodities when the effect may be to lessen competition substantially or create a monopoly in any line of commerce. However, "discrimination in price . . . on account of differences in the grade, quality, or quantity of the commodity sold, or that makes only due allowance for differences in the cost of selling or transportation . . ." was not illegal. This latter provision so weakened Section 2 that it was very difficult if not impossible to prevent **price discrimination.**

In the 1920s and early 1930s, various techniques such as quantity discounts were used by large-volume retailers, especially chain stores, to obtain more favorable prices than those available to smaller competitors. In addition to obtaining quantity discounts, some large businesses created subsidiary corporations that received brokerage allowances as wholesalers. Another method used by big business to obtain price advantages was demanding and obtaining larger promotional allowances than were given to smaller businesses. The prevalence of the foregoing practices led to the enactment in 1936 of the **Robinson-Patman amendment** to Section 2 of the Clayton Act. This statute attempted to eliminate the advantage that a large buyer could secure over a small buyer solely because of the large buyer's quantity purchasing ability. The legal principles in the sections which follow are based on the Robinson-Patman amendment to the Clayton Act.

3. Predatory Pricing

The Robinson-Patman amendment made it a crime for a seller to sell at lower prices in one geographic area than elsewhere in the United States in order to eliminate competition or a competitor, or to sell at unreasonably low prices to drive out a competitor. The statutory language declared predatory pricing to be illegal.

Predatory pricing means pricing below marginal cost by a company willing and able to sustain losses for a prolonged period in order to drive out competition. (It is assumed that the price will later be increased when the competitor is destroyed.) It is also predatory pricing to charge higher prices on some products to subsidize below-cost sales of other products or to cut prices on a product below cost in just one area to wipe out a small local competitor.

Historically, price-cutting was generally deemed predatory when a price was below total costs, including long-term fixed costs for basic research and factory buildings. Normally, these costs are allocated to each product, raising total costs for purposes of calculation. However, some economists have argued that pricing is predatory only if companies slash prices below average variable costs—the short-run expenditures, such as for labor and materials needed to produce some more units of a product. With long-term fixed costs excluded, prices llegally could be cut to a much lower level without the price-cutter being guilty of predatory conduct. Those who oppose this variable-cost theory contend that it allows large companies with "deep pockets" to eliminate even efficient competition.

Several jurisdictions have held that a prima facie case of predatory pricing is established by proof that a price is below average variable costs. Such pricing is proof of anticompetitive conduct unless evidence of justification is admitted to show some other reason for the low price. If a price is below average total costs but above average variable costs, a plaintiff must offer proof that the price has been predatory in these jurisdictions. Only when prices are below average variable costs is a prima facie case established.

In those jurisdictions that use the average variable cost test, many cases alleging predatory pricing do not succeed. Usually no other evidence to prove predatory pricing exists, and once a defendant proves that its unit prices exceed variable costs, the cases are often dismissed. The law has not required that all costs be recovered in most jurisdictions.

There are several recognized exceptions to the laws prohibiting sales below cost. For example, sales for legitimate purposes, such as for liquidation of excess, obsolete, or perishable merchandise, may be legal, even if the prices used are below unit cost.

4. Robinson-Patman Provisions

The goal of the Robinson-Patman amendment is to ensure equality of price to all customers of a seller of commodities for resale when the result of unequal treatment may be to lessen competition substantially or to create a monopoly in any line of commerce or injure competition with any person. An injury to competition may be established by showing an injury to a competitor victimized by the discrimination. It is a violation to knowingly receive a benefit of such discrimination. Therefore, the law applies both to buyers and sellers. It is just as illegal to receive the benefit of price discrimination as it is to give a lower price to one of two buyers. In price-discrimination cases, a determination of fact is required as to the relevant market and the probably anticompetitive effects of the discrimination. The relevant market determination has two aspects—product market and geographic market.

The Robinson-Patman amendment forbids any person engaged "in commerce" to discriminate in price when the goods involved are for resale. It does not apply to a sale by a retailer to consumers. The term "commerce" is defined as "trade or commerce among the several states and with foreign nations. . . ." This means that the Clayton Act extends only to transactions in goods in interstate commerce. It does not extend to transactions that only affect interstate commerce.

The law protects competitors from one another. As a general rule there is no exemption for state purchases to compete with private enterprise. However, the Nonprofit Institutions Act provides that the Robinson-Patman Act does not apply to purchases of supplies for their own use by schools, colleges, universities, public libraries, churches, hospitals, and charitable institutions not operated for profit. This exemption is limited to goods purchased for their own use. If the goods are resold, there is no governmental exemption.

JEFFERSON CTY. PHARMACEUTICAL ASS'N v. ABBOTT LABS.

103 S.Ct. 1011 (1983)

POWELL, J.: . . . The issue presented is whether the sale of pharmaceutical products to state and local government hospitals for resale in competition with private retail pharmacies is exempt from the proscriptions of the Robinson-Patman Act.

Petitioner, a trade association of retail pharmacists and pharmacies doing business in Jefferson County, Alabama, commenced this action in 1978 . . . as the assignee of its members' claims. Respondents are 15 pharmaceutical manufacturers, the Board of Trustees of the University of Alabama, and the Cooper Green Hospital Pharmacy. The University operates a medical center, including hospitals, and a medical school. Located in the University's medical center are two pharmacies. Cooper Green Hospital is a county hospital, existing as a public corporation under Alabama law.

The complaint seeks treble damages and injunctive relief . . . for alleged violations of § 2(a) and (f) of the Clayton Act, as amended by the Robinson-Patman Act (the Act). Petitioner contends that the respondent manufacturers violated § 2(a) by selling their products to the University's two pharmacies and to Cooper Green Hospital Pharmacy at prices lower than those charged petitioner's members for like products. Petitioner alleges that the respondent hospital pharmacies knowingly induced such lower prices in violation of § 2(f) and sold the drugs to the general public in direct competition with privately owned pharmacies. . . .

The District Court held that "government purchases are . . . beyond the intended reach of the Robinson-Patman Price Discrimination Act, at least with respect to purchases for hospitals and other traditional governmental purposes." The Court of Appeals affirmed. . . .

The issue here is narrow. We are not concerned with sales to the federal government, nor with state purchases for use in traditional governmental functions. Rather, the issue before us is limited to state purchases for the purpose of competing against private enterprise—with the advantage of discriminatory prices—in the retail market.

The courts below held, and respondents contend, that the Act exempts all state purchases. Assuming, without deciding, that Congress did not intend the Act to apply to state purchases for consumption in traditional governmental functions, and that such purchases are therefore exempt, we conclude that the exemption does not apply where a State has chosen to compete in the private retail market.

The Robinson-Patman Act by its terms does not exempt state purchases. . . . Moreover, as the courts below conceded, [t]he statutory language—"persons" and "purchasers" —is sufficiently broad to cover governmental bodies. . . .

We do not perceive any reason to construe the word "person" in that Act any differently than we have in the Clayton Act, which it amends, and it is undisputed that the Clayton Act applies to states. In sum, the plain language of the Act strongly suggests that there is no exemption for state purchases to compete with private enterprise.

The plain language of the Act is controlling unlesss a different legislative intent is apparent from the purpose and history of the Act. An examination of the legislative purpose and history here reveals no such contrary intention.

Our cases have been explicit in stating the purposes of the antitrust laws, including the Robinson-Patman Act. On numerous occasions, this Court has affirmed the comprehensive coverage of the antitrust laws and has recognized that these laws represent "a carefully studied attempt to bring within [them] every person engaged in business whose activities might restrain or monopolize commercial intercourse among the states."

It has beeen said, of course, that the antitrust laws, and Robinson-Patman in particular, are to be construed liberally, and that the exceptions from their application are to be construed strictly. The Court has recognized, also, that Robinson-Patman "was enacted in 1936 to curb and prohibit all devices by which large buyers gained discriminatory preferences over smaller ones by virtue of their greater purchasing power." Because the Act is remedial, it is to be construed broadly to effectuate its purposes.

The legislative history falls far short of supporting respondents' contention that there is an exemption for state purchases of "commodities" for "resale." . . . [W]e find no legislative intention to enable a State, by an unexpressed exemption, to enter private competitive markets with congressionally approved price advantages.

"A general application of the [Robinson-Patman] Act to all combinations of business and capital organized to suppress commercial competition is in harmony with the spirit and impulses of the times which gave it birth." The legislative history is replete with references to the economic evil of large organizations purchasing from other large organizations for resale in competition with the small, local retailers. There is no reason, in the absence of an explicit exemption, to think that congressmen who feared these evils intended to deny small businesses, such as the pharmacies of Jefferson County, Alabama, protection from the competition of the strongest competitor of them all. To create an exemption here clearly would be contrary to the intent of Congress.

We hold that the sale of pharmaceutical products to state and local government hospi-

tals for resale in competition with private pharmacies is not exempt from the proscriptions of the Robinson-Patman Act. [*Reversed.*]

The Robinson-Patman amendment also has given the FTC jurisdiction and authority to regulate quantity discounts. It also proscribes certain hidden or indirect discriminations by sellers in favor of certain buyers. Section 2(c) prohibits an unearned brokerage or commission related to a sale of goods. For example, it is unlawful to pay or receive a commission or discount on sales or purchases except for actual services rendered. Section 2(d) outlaws granting promotional allowances or payments on goods bought for resale, unless such allowances are available to all competing customers. For example, a manufacturer who gives a retailer a right to purchase three items for the price of two as part of a special promotion must give the same right to all competitors in the market. Section 2(e) prohibits giving promotional facilities or services on goods bought for resale, unless they are made available to all competing customers. The act does not expressly require that any anticompetitive effects be demonstrated to prove a violation of these provisions. Note that the price-discrimination provisions relate to commodities. They do not relate to services or the sale of advertising such as television time.

DEFENSES

The statute recognizes certain exceptions or defenses: (1) Price differentials based on differences in the cost of manufacture, sale, or delivery of commodities are permitted (cost justification defense). (2) Sellers may select their own customers in bona fide transactions and not in restraint of trade. (3) Price changes may be made in response to changing conditions such as actual or imminent deterioration of perishable goods, obsolescence of seasonal goods, distress sales under court process, or sales in good faith in discontinuance of business in the goods concerned (changing conditions defense). (4) A seller in good faith may meet the equally low price of a competitor (**good-faith meeting of competition** defense). The cost justification and good-faith meeting of competition defenses are discussed in detail in later sections.

5. Proof Required

Price discrimination is not illegal per se. Only those differences in prices that may adversely affect competition are prohibited. A plaintiff seeking triple damages because of price discrimination must prove that the effect of the discrimination is to injure, destroy, or prevent competition with any person who grants or knowingly receives the benefit of the discrimination, or with customers of either of them. A plaintiff seeking damages for a Robinson-Patman violation must prove actual injury attributable to the violation. It is not enough to prove a price differential, as there are no automatic damages.

J. TRUETT PAYNE CO. v. CHRYSLER MOTORS CORP.
101 S.Ct. 1923 (1981)

Plaintiff, petitioner, a former automobile dealer, brought suit against Chrysler alleging that defendant's "sales incentive" programs over a certain period violated the Robinson-Patman amendment. Under its programs, defendant paid a bonus to its dealers if they exceeded their sales quotas. Plaintiff alleged that its quotas were higher than those of its competitors and that to the extent it failed to meet its quotas, and to the extent its competitors met their lower quotas it received fewer bonuses. The net effect to plaintiff was that it paid more for its automobiles than did its competitors. Plaintiff sought as damages the amount of the price difference multiplied by the number of petitioner's purchases. The defendant maintained that the sales incentive programs were nondiscriminatory, and that they did not injure petitioner or adversely affect competition. The jury returned a verdict for the plaintiff which the court trebled. The Court of Appeals reversed, finding that the plaintiff had failed to introduce substantial evidence of injury attributable to the programs, much less substantial evidence of the amount of such injury, as was required in order to recover triple damages under § 4 of the Clayton Act.

REHNQUIST, J.: . . . The question presented in this case is the appropriate measure of damages in a suit brought under § 2(a) of the Clayton Act, as amended by the Robinson-Patman Act.

Petitioner first contends that once it has proved a price discrimination in violation of § 2(a) it is entitled at a minimum to so-called "automatic damages" in the amount of the price discrimination. Petitioner concedes that in order to recover damages it must establish cognizable injury attributable to an antitrust violation and some approximation of damage. It insists, however, that the jury should be permitted to infer the requisite injury and damage from a showing of a substantial price discrimination. . . . We disagree.

By its terms § 2(a) is a prophylactic statute which is violated merely upon a showing that "the effect of such discrimination *may be* substantially to lessen competition." As our cases have recognized, the statute does not "require that the discriminations must in fact have harmed competition." Section 4 of the Clayton Act, in contrast, is essentially a remedial statute. It provides treble damages to "any person who *shall be injured* in his business or property by reason of anything forbidden in the antitrust laws. . . ." To recover treble damages, then, a plaintiff must make some showing of actual injury attributable to something the antitrust laws were designed to prevent. . . . It must prove more than a violation of § 2(a), since such proof establishes only that injury may result.

Our decision here is virtually governed by our reasoning in *Brunswick Corp. v. Pueblo Bowl-O-Mat, Inc.*, 97 S. Ct. 690, (1977). There we rejected the contention that the mere violation of § 7 of the Clayton Act, which prohibits mergers which *may* substantially lessen competition, gives rise to a damage claim under § 4. We explained that "to recover damages [under § 4] respondents must prove more than that the petitioner violated § 7, since such proof established only that injury may result."

Likewise in this case, proof of a violation does not mean that a disfavored purchaser has been actually "injured" within the meaning of § 4.

Petitioner next contends that even though it may not be entitled to "automatic damages" upon a showing of a violation of § 2(a), it produced enough evidence of actual injury to survive a motion for a directed verdict. . . . [After reviewing the evidence the court remanded the case so that the Court of Appeals could consider the sufficiency of plaintiff's evidence of injury.] [*So ordered.*]

6. Levels of Competition

Robinson-Patman cases <u>vary somewhat depending on the level of competition</u>. Courts recognize primary level cases (competition among sellers); secondary level cases (competition among customers of sellers); and third level cases (when there is a wholesaler between the manufacturer and the retailer). The chart which follows (Figure 21-1) illustrates these levels.

In primary line cases, proof of an adverse competitive effect is required. <u>Primary line cases usually involve territorial price discrimination</u>—the charging of different prices by a multimarket seller in different geographic areas—

1. X and Y are primary level competitors. Y's sale to B is a primary line violation.

2. A, B, and C are secondary level competitors. Y's sale to B is also a secondary line violation.

3. If the retailers A, B, and C each purchased the goods through a wholesaler, they would be considered third-level competitors, and the price discrimination would be a third-line violation.

FIGURE 21-1
Levels of Competition: Robinson-Patman Violation Analysis

to drive out its direct competitors. For example, a frozen pie maker was sued for triple damages when it sold pies for a lower price to retail outlets only in the Salt Lake City market to increase its share of that market.

In secondary line competition cases, it is presumed that competition is adversely affected if directly competing customers of manufacturers and producers are charged different prices. Note, this establishes the violation but not the injury. Secondary line cases require proof that both buyers compete in the same geographic area.

Cases have expanded the lines of competition to include injuries to competitors of the customer of the buyer. In the case which follows, there were actually four levels in the distribution system.

PERKINS v. STANDARD OIL COMPANY OF CALIFORNIA
89 S.Ct. 1871 (1969)

Plaintiff, Perkins, brought suit for triple damages under Section 2 of the Clayton Act as amended by the Robinson-Patman amendment. He alleged that Standard Oil was guilty of price discrimination in two ways: (1) that it sold gasoline to its own branded dealers at prices lower than it sold to plaintiff and (2) that it sold gasoline at a lower price to another oil company, which in turn sold it to a wholesaler, who in turn sold it to a competitor of the plaintiff at a price that was still lower than the price paid by the plaintiff for similar gasoline. The jury awarded plaintiff $333,404.57, which when tripled gave plaintiff $1,298,213.71. The Court of Appeals reversed. The issue on this appeal is whether or not the second type of price discrimination which was alleged is within the coverage of the act.

BLACK, J.: . . . We disagree with the Court of Appeals conclusion that Sec. 2 of the Clayton Act, as amended by the Robinson-Patman Act, does not apply to the damages suffered by Perkins as a result of the price advantage granted by Standard to Signal,

then by Signal to Western, then by Western to Regal. The Act, in pertinent part, provides:

(a)It shall be unlawful for any person engaged in commerce . . . either directly or indirectly, to discriminate in price between different purchasers of commodities of like grade and quality . . . where the effect of such discrimination may be substantially to lessen competition or tend to create a monopoly in any line of commerce, or to injure, destroy, or prevent competition with any person who either grants or knowingly receives the benefit of such discrimination, or with customers of either of them. . . .

The Court of Appeals read this language as limiting "the distributing levels on which a supplier's price discrimination will be recognized as potentially injurious to competition." According to that court, the coverage of the Act is restricted to injuries caused by an impairment of competition with (1) the seller ["any person who . . . grants . . . such discrimination"], (2) the favored purchaser ["any person who . . . knowingly receives the benefit of such discrimination"] and (3) customers of the discriminating seller or favored purchaser ["customers of either of them"]. Here, Perkins' injuries resulted in part from impaired competition with a customer (Regal) of a customer (Western Hyway) of the favored purchaser (Signal). The Court of Appeals termed these injuries "fourth level" and held that they were not protected by the Robinson-Patman Act. We conclude that this limitation is wholly an artificial one and is completely unwarranted by the language or purpose of the Act.

In *FTC v. Fred Meyer, Inc.*, 390 U.S. 341 (1968), we held that a retailer who buys through a wholesaler could be considered a "customer" of the original supplier within the meaning of § 2(d) of the Robinson-Patman Act, a section dealing with discrimination in promotional allowances which is closely analogous to § 2(a) involved in this case. In *Meyer*, the Court stated that to read "customer" narrowly would be wholly untenable when viewed in light of the purposes of the Robinson-Patman Act. Similarly, to read "customer" more narrowly in this section than we did in the section involved in *Meyer* would allow price discriminators to avoid the sanctions of the Act by the simple expedient of adding an additional link to the distribution chain. Here, for example, Standard supplied gasoline and oil to Signal. Signal, allegedly because it furnished Standard with part of its vital supply of crude petroleum, was able to insist upon a discriminatorily lower price.

Had Signal then sold its gas directly to the Regal stations, giving Regal stations a competitive advantage, there would be no question, even under the decision of the Court of Appeals in this case, that a clear violation of the Robinson-Patman Act had been committed. Instead of selling directly to the retailer Regal, however, Signal transferred the gasoline first to its subsidiary, Western Hyway, who in turn supplied the Regal stations. Signal owned 60% of the stock of Western Hyway; Western in turn owned 55% of the stock of the Regal stations. We find no basis in the language or purpose of the Act for immunizing Standard's price discriminations simply because the product in question passed through an additional formal exchange before reaching the level of Perkins' actual competitor. From Perkins' point of view, the competitive harm done hiim by Standard is certainly no less because of the presence of an additional link in this particular distribution chain from the producer to the retailer. Here Standard discriminated in price between Perkins and Signal, and there was evidence from which the jury could conclude that Perkins was harmed competitively when Signal's price advantage was passed on to Perkins' retail competitor Regal. These facts are sufficient to give rise to recoverable damages under the Robinson-Patman Act. . . . [*Verdict and judgment reinstated.*]

7. The Cost Justification Defense

A company's first defense for a price-discrimination charge is cost justification. When a plaintiff has introduced proof of differential pricing of the same kind of goods by the defendant and proves that requisite injury to competition resulted, he or she has established a prima facie case. The burden of showing cost justification is upon the person charged with a violation. Section 2(a) provides that nothing "shall prevent differentials which make only due allowance for *differences in the cost of manufacture, sale, or delivery* resulting from the differing methods or quantities in which . . . commodities are . . . sold or delivered." [*Emphasis added.*] This would appear to be a significant excuse which would permit cost savings to be passed on to customers.

The cost justification defense has proved largely illusory in practice. Because of the complexities in determining what is "cost," this defense very rarely was successful in the past. One obvious problem is that of bringing forth acceptable evidence of cost. As a practical matter, proof of cost involves both direct costs and indirect costs. Indirect costs are based on assumptions, and accountants may make different ones. Therefore, there are disputes over the technique to determine actual cost, and proof of it is difficult if not impossible. The status of the act is such that only the most prosperous and patient business firms can afford pursuit of this often illusory defense.

8. Good-Faith Meeting of Competition Defense

A very important affirmative defense justifying price discrimination is the good-faith meeting of competition. Section 2(b) of the Robinson-Patman amendment permits a defendant to demonstrate that a given price discrimination was not unlawful by "showing that his lower price or the furnishing of services or facilities to any purchaser or purchasers was made in good faith to meet an equally low price of a competitor, or the services or facilities furnished by a competitor." This defense may be established by proof of a price reduction to meet a competitor's price. It may also be established by proof that price was not increased in one market in order to meet competition in that market when prices were raised in other markets. In other words, the defense may result from active conduct (lowering prices), or it may be passive (not increasing prices).

"Good faith" is not easily defined. It is a flexible and pragmatic, not a technical or doctrinaire concept. The standard of good faith is simply the standard of the prudent businessperson responding fairly to what he or she reasonably believes is a situation of competitive necessity. The facts and circumstances in each case govern its interpretation and application. Thus, the same method of meeting competition may be consistent with an inference of good faith in some circumstances, inconsistent with such an inference in others.

Although the term "good faith" cannot be quantified, it is clear that this defense cannot be established when the purpose of a seller's price discrimination is to eliminate competition. The seller may offer discriminatory prices to customers whether or not it has done business with them in the past, but these discriminatory prices must not knowingly be lower than those offered by competitors.

The timing of the price offers must be such that it is apparent they are made to meet an individual competitive situation and are not part of a general system of competition. The seller must have knowledge of the prices it is meeting, to the extent that a reasonable person would believe a lower price was necessary. Actual knowledge of a competitor's exact price is not required.

The overriding consideration concerning the good-faith requirement is the motive of the discriminating seller. The good-faith concept should be used solely to test the seller's adherence to the basic objectives of the meeting-competition proviso: facilitating price reductions in genuine response to competitive market pressures to equalize a competitive opportunity.

The good-faith meeting of competition defense is available to buyers as well as sellers. The buyers' liability is baased on the sellers' liability, and as the next case shows, if the seller has a defense, so does the buyer.

GREAT ATLANTIC & PACIFIC TEA CO., INC. v. FTC
99 S.Ct. 925 (1979)

STEWART, J.: . . . The question presented in this case is whether the petitioner, the Great Atlantic and Pacific Tea Company (A&P), violated Section 2(f) of the Robinson-Patman Act, by knowingly inducing or receiving illegal price discriminations from the Borden Company (Borden).

The alleged violation was reflected in a 1965 agreement between A&P and Borden under which Borden undertook to supply "private label" milk to more than 200 A&P stores in a Chicago area that included portions of Illinois and Indiana. This agreement resulted from an effort by A&P to achieve cost savings by switching from the sale of "brand label" milk (milk sold under the brand name of the supplying dairy) to the sale of "private label" milk (milk sold under the A&P label).

To implement this plan, A&P asked Borden, its longtime supplier, to submit an offer to supply under private label certain of A&P's milk and other dairy product requirements. After prolonged negotiations, Borden offered to grant A&P a discount for switching to private label milk provided A&P would accept limited delivery service. Borden claimed that this offer would save A&P $410,000 a year compared to what it had been paying for its dairy products. A&P how-

ever, was not satisfied with this offer and solicited offers from other dairies. A competitor of Borden, Bowman Dairy, then submitted an offer which was lower than Borden's.

At this point, A&P's Chicago buyer contacted Borden's chain store sales manager and stated, "I have a bid in my pocket. You [Borden] people are so far out of line it is not even funny. You are not even in the ball park." When the Borden representative asked for more details, he was told nothing except that a $50,000 improvement in Borden's bid "would not be a drop in the bucket."

Borden was thus faced with the problem of deciding whether to rebid. A&P at the time was one of Borden's largest customers in the Chicago area. Moreover, Borden had just invested more than five million dollars in a new dairy facility in Illinois. The loss of the A&P account would result in underutilization of this new plant. Under these circumstances, Borden decided to submit a new bid which doubled the estimated annual savings to A&P, from $410,000 to $820,000. In presenting its offer, Borden emphasized to A&P that it needed to keep A&P's business and was making the new offer in order to meet Bowman's bid. A&P then accepted Borden's bid after concluding that it was substantially better than Bowman's.

[The FTC filed a complaint against A&P charging that it had violated Section 2(f) of the Robinson-Patman Act by knowingly inducing or receiving price discrimination from Borden. The Commission found that Borden had discriminated in price between A&P and its competitors, that the discrimination had been injurious to competition, and that A&P had known or should have known that it was the beneficiary of unlawful price discrimination. The Commission rejected A&P's defenses that the Borden bid had been made to meet competition and was cost justified. The Court of Appeals affirmed holding that as a matter of law A&P could not successfully assert a meeting competition defense because it, unlike Borden, had known that Borden's offer was better than Bowman's. The Supreme Court granted certiorari.]

The Robinson-Patman Act was passed in response to the problem perceived in the increased market power and coercive practices of chain stores and other big buyers that threatened the existence of small independent retailers. Notwithstanding this concern with buyers, however, the emphasis of the Act is in Section 2(a), which prohibits price discriminations by sellers. Indeed, the original Patman Bill as reported by Committees of both Houses prohibited only seller activity, with no mention of buyer liability. Section 2(f) of the Act, making buyers liable for inducing or receiving price discriminations by sellers, was the product of a belated floor amendment near the conclusion of the Senate debates.

As finally enacted, Section 2(f) provides: "That it shall be unlawful for any person engaged in commerce, in the course of such commerce, knowingly to induce or receive a discrimination in price which is prohibited by this section."

Liability under Section 2(f) thus is limited to situations where the price discrimination is one "which is prohibited by this section." While the phrase "this section" refers to the entire Section 2 of the Act, only subsections (a) and (b) dealing with seller liability involved discriminations in price. Under the plain meaning of Section 2(f), therefore, a buyer cannot be liable if a prima facie case could not be established against a seller or if the seller has an affirmative defense. In either situation, there is no price discrimination "prohibited by this section." The legislative history of Section 2(f) fully confirms the conclusion that buyer liability under Section 2(f) is dependent on seller liability under Section 2(a). . . .

Thus, a buyer cannot be held liable under Section 2(f) if the lower prices received are justified by reason of one of the seller's affirmative defenses.

The petitioner, relying on this plain meaning of Section 2(f) argues that it cannot be liable under Section 2(f) if Borden had a valid meeting competition defense. The respondent, on the other hand, argues that the petitioner may be liable even assuming that Borden had such a defense. The meeting competition defense, the respondent contends, must in these circumstances be judged from the point of view of the buyer. Since A&P knew for a fact that the final Borden bid beat the Bowman bid, it was not entitled to assert the meeting competition defense even though Borden may have honestly believed that it was simply meeting competition. Recognition of a meeting competition defense for the buyer in this situation, the respondent argues, would be contrary to the basic purpose of the Robinson-Patman Act to curtail abuses by large buyers.

The short answer to these contentions of the respondent is that Congress did not provide in Section 2(f) that a buyer can be liable even if the seller has a valid defense. The clear language of Section 2(f) states that a buyer can be liable only if he receives a price discrimination "prohibited by this section." If a seller has a valid meeting competition defense, there is simply no prohibited price discrimination. . . .

Because both the Commission and the Court of Appeals proceeded on the assumption that a buyer who accepts the lower of two competitive bids can be liable under Section 2(f) even if the seller has a meeting competition defense, there was not a specific finding that Borden did in fact have such a defense. But it quite clearly did.

The test for determining when a seller has a valid meeting competition defense is whether a seller can "show the existence of facts which would lead a reasonable and prudent person to believe that the granting of a lower price would in fact meet the equally low price of a competitor." "A good faith belief, rather than absolute certainty, that a price

concession is being offered to meet an equally low price offered by a competitor is sufficient to satisfy the Robinson-Patman's Section 2(b) defense." Since good faith, rather than absolute certainty, is the touchstone of the meeting competition defense, a seller can assert the defennse even if it has unknowingly made a bid that in fact not only met but beat his competition.

Under the circumstances of this case, Borden did act reasonably and in good faith when it made its second bid. . . .

Since Borden had a meeting competition defense and thus could not be liable under Section 2(b), the petitioner who did no more than accept the offer cannot be liable under Section 2(f). [*Accordingly, the judgment is Reversed.*]

---

9. The Future of Section 2

The Robinson-Patman amendment has, in the view of many economists, resulted in higher prices than would exist in a more competitive market. Moreover, there is evidence that the statute offers little economic protection to small businesses. The Antitrust Division of the Justice Department from time to time has concluded that the act promotes high prices and restricts entry and inefficiency in the distribution of goods. Since the act does not apply to the offering of services, the Robinson-Patman amendment is not a key factor in preserving efficient small businesses. Some commissioners of the FTC and many staff members also do not believe in the underlying philosophy of the amendment. As a result, enforcement of Section 2 has been limited and sporadic.

On its face, the Robinson-Patman amendment purports to preserve competition. However, in fact, it represents to some degree a withdrawal or modification of that policy. For example, the amendment does not allow a supplier to encourage those who can buy the product in very large quantities by giving them price concessions or discounts. The net result of such provisions partially removes the small, individual business from some of the forces of competition. Partially insulating such businesses from competition and preserving them may effectively reward less efficient operations and keep prices artificially high for the consumer. Thus, higher prices may result from attempts to preserve competition even though one reason for preserving competition is to obtain lower prices for consumers. The Robinson-Patman amendment's purpose of preserving small competitors at the cost of competition may eventually lead to its repeal.

SECTION 3

10. Tying Arrangements

Section 3 of the Clayton Act makes it unlawful for a person engaged in commerce to lease or sell commodities (whether patented or unpatented) or to fix a price charged on the condition that the lessee or purchaser should not use or deal in the commodities of a competitor or competitors of the lessor or seller when the effect may be to substantially lessen competition or tend to create a monopoly in any line of commerce. The same issues concerning the relevant market and probable anticompetitive effects are involved in determining a violation of Section 3 of the Clayton Act as in a case of alleged price discrimination. Under Section 3, the law covers tying contracts, reciprocal dealings, and exclusive arrangements.

A **tying contract** is one in which a commodity is sold or leased for use only on condition that the buyer or lessee purchase a different product or service from the seller or lessor. The arrangement tying a product may even be to a loan of money. Tying arrangements may be violations of both Section 1 of the Sherman Act and Section 3 of the Clayton Act. Although most tying arrangements are subject to the rule of reason, some tying arrangements are illegal without proof of anticompetitive effects. They are unreasonable in and of themselves (a per se violation) whenever (1) a party has sufficient economic power with respect to the tying product to restrain free competition appreciably in the market for the tied product; (2) some coercion is shown; and (3) a "not insubstantial" amount of interstate commerce is affected.

The per se rule for tying contracts does allow a defendant to justify undertaking the tie. A tie-in may be justified if it is implemented for a legitimate purpose and if no less restrictive alternative is available. For example, Baskin-Robbins ice cream may legally require its franchisees to purchase all of their ice cream from Baskin-Robbins. The legitimate purpose is to maintain the image of the franchise and the product. Customers expect the same ice cream from every retail operation.

A common form of tying arrangements is known as "full-line forcing." In full-line forcing, the buyer or lessee is compelled to take a complete product line from the seller. Under these arrangements, the buyer cannot purchase only one product of the line. A typical illegal agreement under this concept is one in which a gasoline company requires its dealers to purchase a stated amount of regular gasoline and premium-priced gasoline in order to obtain no-lead gasoline. Another example is when an automobile manufacturer requires that only its radios be sold with its new cars.

11. Reciprocal Dealings

A **reciprocal dealing arrangement** exists when two parties face each other as both buyer and seller. One party offers to buy the other's goods but only if the second party buys other goods from the first party. For example, if one party is both a food wholesaler and a provider of goods used in processing foods, food processors may be faced by a reciprocal requirement. The first party may agree to buy the processor's products only if the processor buys the processing goods from it.

Reciprocity cases are quite similar to tying cases, and courts treat them in a similar manner. In each case, one side of a transaction has special power in the marketplace. It uses this power to force those with whom it deals to make concessions in another market. In tying arrangements, a seller with economic power forces the purchaser to purchase something else to obtain the desired item. In reciprocal dealings, a buyer with economic power forces a seller to buy something from it to sell its goods. In both cases, the key is the extension of economic power in one market to another market. Thus, the standard for judging reciprocal arrangements is the same as the standard for judging tie-in arrangements, as previously discussed. A reciprocal arrangement may be a per se violation if it is coercive and not justified by legitimate business objectives for which there is no better alternative.

Most cases involving reciprocity threaten foreclosure only of small percentages of any market. Nevertheless, courts apply the per se rule. Reciprocity cases are complicated by the fact that they can occur without an actual agreement. A seller may buy from a would-be customer in the hope that doing so will create goodwill and will lead eventually to sales. It is a natural thing for a seller to show appreciation by purchasing from its buyers.

12. Exclusive Dealings

An **exclusive dealings** contract contains a provision that one party or the other (buyer or seller) will deal only with the other party. For example, a seller of tomatoes agrees to sell only to Campbell Soup. A buyer of coal may agree to purchase only from a certain coal company. Such agreements tend to foreclose a portion of the market from competitors.

A similar arrangement is known as a *requirements contract.* In a requirements contract, a buyer agrees to purchase all of its needs of a given contract from the seller during a certain period of time. The buyer may be a manufacturer who needs the raw materials or parts agreed to be supplied, or it may be a retailer who needs goods for resale. In effect, the buyer is agreeing not to purchase any of the product from competitors of the seller.

Franchise contracts often require that the franchisee purchase all of its equipment and inventory from the franchisor as a condition of the agreement. These provisions are commonly inserted because of the value of the franchiser's trademark and the desire for quality control to protect it. Some courts take the view that a franchiser should not be able to license its trademark in such a manner that it can coerce franchisees to give up alternate supply sources, because such agreements are unreasonable restraints off trade. They argue that the quality-control aspect is not present for items such as packaging materials and food items where special ingredients or secret formulas are not involved, and thus the purpose of the "exclusive source of supply" provision is only to limit competition. Although franchise agreements are not per se violations, they are subject to the rule of reason.

Exclusive contracts and requirements contracts are less likely to harm competition than are tying contracts. Such contracts may add competition by eliminating uncertainties and the expense of repeated contracts. However, the courts tend to give per se violation treatment to exclusive contracts if they substantially affect commerce. In one case involving less than 1 percent of the coal market, the court concluded that the contract was legal because the small percentage of foreclosures did not actually or potentially cause a substantial reduction of competition. As a result of these decisions, we do not have full per se illegality in this area, but neither do we have full economic inquiry as to the impact of a given contract.

13. Ethics and Section 3

Caterpillar has a special part of its ethics code which deals with the relationship with suppliers. Reciprocity is forbidden, and exclusive dealings are rare. The specific statement is as follows. Note that compliance with this standard will probably prevent any legal problems from occurring.

RELATIONSHIPS WITH SUPPLIERS

Caterpillar's superior relationships are a vital, highly valued aspect of our worldwide operations. These relationships are based on a commitment to deal fairly and reasonably.

We aim at creation and maintenance of long-lasting company-supplier relationships. But as a general rule, neither Caterpillar nor a supplier should be overly dependent on the other, from a long-term standpoint.

Selection of suppliers and purchase of materials and services are determined by evaluations of quality, cost/price benefit, delivery capability, service, and maintenance of adequate supply sources. Other things being equal, our intention is to buy from sources as near to the using facility as possible.

Supplier competitiveness for Caterpillar business is encouraged throughout the world . . . as is company-supplier cooperation toward maximizing the value of Caterpillar products. No supplier is asked to buy Caterpillar products in order to compete for business, or continue as a supplier.

Suppliers may trade with Caterpillar's competitors and still merit our purchases. Further, Caterpillar personnel shall avoid arrangements or understandings prohibiting a supplier from selling products in competition with us, except where: (1) the supplier makes the product with tooling or materials owned by Caterpillar; or (2) the product is one in which the company has a proprietary interest which has been determined to be legally protectable. Such an interest might arise from an important contribution by Caterpillar to the concept, design, application, or manufacturing process.

SECTION 7

14. Introduction

A business may acquire other businesses in a variety of ways. For example, two corporations may join together and create a third corporation, with the two original companies being dissolved. This is technically known as a "consolidation." One business may acquire and absorb another business, with the acquired business being dissolved. This is technically known as a "merger." Another method for one company to acquire another is for the former to purchase a controlling interest in the stock of the latter. The subsidiary is controlled by the parent company's electing the board of directors and controlling policy. When the stock of a company is controlled, both companies continue to exist, and no dissolution occurs. A fourth method of acquisition is for one business to purchase the assets of another. The selling company then ceases to continue its former business activities, and the purchased assets are integrated into the buying company.

In the material which follows, technical consolidations, mergers, and other acquisitions are generally referred to as mergers. Mergers are usually classified as *horizontal, market extension, vertical,* or *conglomerate*. A **horizontal merger** usually combines two businesses in the same field or industry. The acquired and acquiring companies have competed with each other, and the merger reduces the number of competitors and leads to greater concentration in the industry. The term **market extension merger** describes an acquisition in which the acquiring company extends its markets. This market extension may be either in new products (product extension) or in new areas (geographical extension). For example, if a brewery which did not operate in New England were to acquire a New England brewery, this would be a geographical market extension merger.

A **vertical merger** brings together a company which is the customer of the other in one of the lines of commerce in which the other is a supplier. Such an integration of production and supply ordinarily removes or has the potential to remove the merged customer from the market as far as other suppliers are concerned. It may also remove a source of supply if the acquiring company is a customer of the acquired one. A **conglomerate merger** is one in which the businesses involved neither compete nor are related as customer and supplier in any given line of commerce. Some people consider product extension and geographic extension mergers to be conglomerate ones with many characteristics of horizontal ones. In any event, there is a great deal of similarity in the legal principles applied to market extension and to conglomerate mergers.

Each year there are thousands of acquisitions which not only tend to increase the concentration of economic power but which also reduce the number of businesses, both large and small, operating in the United States. Since our competitive economic system depends on a large number of competitors, the importance of the law in this area is obvious. It is equally obvious that the application of laws regulating external growth through mergers and acquisitions must reconcile competing goals of society. Freedom of contract, the desire for an economy of abundance, and the need for efficient factors of production suggest that legal constraints on external growth ought to be minimal. At the same time, if our competitive economic system is to deliver the assumed benefits of competition, there must be enough competitors in the various markets to ensure that no one competitor is able to unilaterally determine its prices and levels of production. There must be limitations on the concentration of economic power in a single firm or even in a group of firms. Monopoly must generally be illegal, and oligopoly must at least be highly suspect. Excess concentration must be avoided, and small firms must be protected. The antitrust laws on mergers seek to strike the balances between these competing goals of society and to prevent anticompetitive acquisitions before they occur.

15. Reasons for External Growth

Before we examine further the laws designed to prevent external growth, we should recognize the reasons that business tends to favor external over internal growth and the reasons that such growth may be inimical to the public interest. The goal of growth for a business is almost the equivalent of a human instinct. Though we assume that growth is per se desirable, the actual reasons for this goal need to be examined.

One reason for many acquisitions is that the market price of the stock of many companies is not only below asset value but even below book value. Mergers provide a means of investing in undervalued assets, and buying a company is often much cheaper than building one.

Among the more commonly stated additional reasons for desiring growth and especially external growth are the following: (1) economies of scale, lower costs, and increased efficiency—especially in production, sales, research and development, and finance; (2) all of the advantages that come from diversification, such as reduction of the risk in one industry caused by economic cycles and the ability to deploy capital into new areas which may be developing rapidly; (3) the capacity to join a company with substantial liquid assets with one in need of cash for expansion and growth; (4) the desire of many managers to govern larger enterprises; (5) the potential positive effect on the earnings per share and on the market price of the corporate stock involved in such transactions; and (6) the ability to avoid being a price victim of a monopolist or being dependent upon a questionable source of supply. In addition, the tax laws are a motivating factor to one of the parties to many mergers.

The success of many management teams is judged by market share, earnings per share, and the price of the company stock. Horizontal mergers are an obvious means to a rapid increase in market share. All mergers and accounting principles such as pooling of assets that are used to record such transactions have an immediate impact upon earnings per share and often upon the price of the stock. Internal growth almost always involves expenses without income for a start-up period, thus reducing earnings per share in the short run. Start-up costs are usually significant, and they are avoided if the growth is external rather than internal. A merger usually results in immediate income and a significant increase in assets. Thus, managers faced with an expansion decision often opt for mergers rather than internal growth because of the effect of the latter on the financial ratios by which their performance is judged.

Vertical mergers are often the result of an attempt to integrate production and supply for the purpose of cost reduction and stabilizing the source of supply. Assume that a utility company wants to lower its fuel costs. A logical means to achieve this is to purchase a coal company. Ownership of the coal company should enable the utility to lower its fuel costs and to have a more certain source of supply. Today, many corporations such as airlines would like to own sources of petroleum products simply in order to guarantee adequate supplies.

16. Reasons to Prevent External Growth

Of course, there are many reasons society may oppose external growth and force internal growth through law. Some of these reasons are economic, and others are based on social implications as well as problems inherent for the financial community. Among economic reasons for limiting mergers and acquisitions that do not amount to monopolies are the following.

1 Economies of scale will allow large companies to drive out smaller, less efficient competitors.

2 Diversified companies can absorb losses in some areas of operations while driving out competitors.

3 Large companies serve as a barrier to entry into a market by small companies.

4 Smaller companies will be less competitive in their activities because of fear of retaliation.

5 A potential entrant of an area of competition is eliminated when an industry is entered by acquisition.

6 All the anticompetitive effects of reciprocity are potentially present.

7 Excessive concentrations of economic power with the likelihood of predatory conduct can result.

8 Acquisitions often tend to entrench a dominant firm.

9 Firms with a large share of a market frequently emerge as price leaders.

Many of the foregoing reasons for denying a firm the right to grow externally are based on our desire to keep a large number of small competitors. The goal remains as stated by Justice Learned Hand in *U.S. v. Alcoa*, 148 F.2d 416 (1945): "Throughout the history of these [antitrust] statutes it has been consistently assumed that one of their purposes was to perpetuate and preserve, for its own sake, and in spite of possible cost, an organization of industry in small units which can effectively compete with each other."

17. Tender Offers

It should be recognized that many acquisitions and mergers are not the result of a mutual agreement. Many takeovers are, in fact, hostile, at least insofar as the management of the acquired firms is concerned. Hostile takeovers occur as a result of **tender offers** by the acquiring firm to the shareholders of the acquired firm. The management of the firm to be acquired often objects to the takeover for very obvious reasons. Hostile takeovers usually result in wholesale changes in management, and existing management is simply fighting for survival. Moreover, if roadblocks are placed in the path of a merger, the price may be raised and other offerors may even enter the picture. It is common for existing management to contend that an offering price is too low even though the offering price is substantially in excess of current market price. Existing management frequently raises merger objections to a proposed takeover even though the Justice Department and the FTC do not.

In order to discourage hostile takeovers, a variety of techniques have been developed and are being adopted by various corporations. Among the techniques are the following:

1 Fair pricing bylaws. These require that all shareholders be paid the same price for their stock in the event of a takeover.

2 Staggered terms for directors. These bylaws make it more difficult to gain control of the board of directors. Since fewer directors are elected each year, more votes are required to elect a director.

3 Special stock issues. These give special voting rights to a limited group of shareholders likely to oppose a takeover.

4 Stronger voting guidelines. These require approval of a large percentage of all shareholders before a merger or takeover is approved. Some of these percentages are as high as 95 percent.

5   Golden parachutes. These contracts protect executives by guaranteeing them cash settlements equal to several years' salaries if a takeover occurs.

6   Corporate restructuring. Corporations sometimes take "poison pills" in the form of increased debt to avoid a takeover. The debt may be used to buy back stock. Valuable units are also sometimes sold in order to make a business less attractive.

These techniques have been described as **shark repellents** because the company attempting a hostile takeover is viewed as a shark. They are needed by existing management because the price offered is usually significantly higher than the existing market price of the stock. The fair price bylaw stops someone from buying majority control at one price and paying a lower price or not purchasing the shares of other shareholders. The proposal for staggered terms for directors is designed to prevent someone from buying 5 percent or 10 percent of a company's stock and threatening a proxy fight unless management agrees to buy back the raider's stock at a premium. This latter technique is often described as **greenmail** to indicate that it is, in fact, a form of blackmail by which individuals or companies force someone to pay them off in order to avoid a takeover.

The *golden parachute* phenomenon does not prevent many mergers and acquisitions. However, it does give management the security of knowing that it will be well rewarded financially if a takeover occurs. There have been so many agreements providing golden parachutes in recent months that the SEC is seriously considering rules limiting such agreements. Under the terms of some agreements, a corporate president may receive several million dollars in the event the business is taken over by another organization. Some agreements call for the opening of the parachute on less than a total change of ownership and management.

Another technique used to fight takeovers is often referred to as the *white knight*. The white knight is another firm that makes a competing offer at a price significantly higher than the tender offer. The white knight is a friendly takeover candidate, and its presence creates a bidding war. The use of the white knight is in recognition that the company is likely to lose its independence, and therefore the best arrangement is a friendly rather than a hostile buyer.

Another technique used to discourage hostile takeovers is known as the *lockup*. In a lockup, the target company agrees either to sell part of its stock or part of its company to an acquirer of its choice. The lockup usually involves a white knight and frequently means that the most attractive part of the company is gone, thus discouraging the hostile takeover. The net effect of a lockup is to favor one bidder over another and to stack the deck in favor of one. Sometimes the lockup simply involves an option to someone to purchase a significant portion of the business.

Congress is considering several means of curbing unfriendly takeovers. Some people contend that the antitrust laws should be tightened to restrict unfriendly takeovers as a predatory practice. Others contend that the employees should be given the power to veto unfriendly takeovers. Finally, there is substantial support for new laws prohibiting greenmail. In some recent situations, greenmail has rewarded certain individuals and companies they control with windfall profits of $30 million to $40 million. A buyer can achieve such a windfall by acquiring a substantial block of stock and forcing management to rebuy it at a premium. One of the notable examples of greenmail in recent years involved Walt Disney. In this situation, one group made millions of dollars and significantly depressed the value of Disney stock in the process.

18. Statutes Involved

The law of mergers is based primarily upon three statutes—the Sherman Act, the Clayton Act, and the Bank Merger Act. A horizontal merger would amount to a violation of the Sherman Act if it is a combination in unreasonable restraint of trade, or if it results in monopolization of a line of commerce, or if it is an attempt to monopolize. Most of the suits filed under the Sherman Act to challenge a merger will use Section 1 of the act rather than Section 2.

SHERMAN ACT

The *Sherman Act* forbids any merger between major competitive forces (horizontal) in a relevant market if the effect of the merger is the elimination of significant competition between them. The reason for limiting horizontal mergers is quite simple—it is to protect the public's interest in a workable competitive economic system. Whereas some mergers may be beneficial to the public because of increased efficiencies and economies of scale, there is a limit to such external growth because of the need to maintain a competitive market structure.

The courts in Sherman Act cases determining the legality of horizontal mergers will examine such factors as (1) the market shares of the acquired and acquiring firms, (2) the degree of concentration in the industry. (3) if there is a trend toward concentration in the industry and if other competitors are vulnerable to takeover, (4) the purposes or motives of the parties, (5) the growth history of the firms and the extent to which the growth has been external, and (6) any special characteristics of the firms which may impact on competition. Courts are primarily concerned with the structure of the market and the shares of the firms involved. A horizontal merger is presumed to be illegal under the Sherman Act if it produces a firm controlling an *undue* percentage of the relevant market and results in a *significant* increase in the concentration of firms in that market. Proof of predatory purpose is not required for such mergers to be declared illegal. However, the rule of reason is applied in these cases.

CLAYTON ACT

Section 7 of the Clayton Act as amended provides essentially that no business engaged in commerce shall acquire any of the stock or assets of another such business if the effect may be substantially to lessen competition or to tend to create a monopoly in any line of commerce in any section of the country. Violations of it only require a finding and conclusion that a given acquisition has a reasonable probability of lessening competition or tendency toward monopoly. The sections which follow in this chapter will discuss Section 7 of the Clayton Act in detail.

In Sherman Act cases, proof of the applicable product and geographic markets is not required. If the evidence proves that the acquired and acquiring firms significantly compete, a violation is established. Cases brought under the Clayton Act require proof of the relevant product and geographic markets. However, it should be noted that proof of markets is generally necessary if the required proof of competition is to be made in Sherman Act cases.

The Sherman Act is of special importance when a criminal action is brought, since the Clayton Act does not have a criminal sanction. However, the Clayton Act's merger provisions are the most important ones when the injunction sanction to prevent a merger or to cause a divestiture is used. The Clayton Act burden of proof is generally considered to be less than is required under the Sherman Act.

BANK MERGER ACTS

A great deal of merger litigation involves banks. Such mergers are subject to both the Sherman Act and the Clayton Act. In addition, they are subject to the provision of the *Bank Merger Acts* of 1960 and 1966. Under these laws, bank mergers are illegal unless approved by one of the agencies which regulate banks. If the merger involves a national bank, the approval of the Comptroller of the Currency is required. If the banks are state banks that are members of the Federal Reserve System, the approval of the Federal Reserve Board is necessary. Other mergers of banks insured by the Federal Deposit Insurance Corporation require approval of that agency.

Before the regulatory agencies will approve a bank merger, they will consider the effect of the merger on competition. They are to consider the needs and convenience of the public in obtaining banking services. Bank mergers cannot be approved if the merger will result in a monopoly or if it is part of an attempt to monopolize. In addition, permission to merge will be denied if the merger will substantially lessen competition, tend to create a monopoly, or restrain trade, unless the anticompetitive effects are clearly outweighed by the advantages of the merger in meeting the banking needs of the public.

If a bank merger is approved by one of the three appropriate regulatory agencies, it may nevertheless be challenged under the antitrust laws by the Justice Department within thirty days. The filing of a suit by the Justice Department stops the merger until the case is decided.

19. Section 7—General Principles

As originally enacted in 1914, the Clayton Act covered horizontal mergers. In 1950, Congress passed the Celler-Kefauver amendment which substantially broadened the coverage. First of all, this amendment plugged a loophole in that the original Section 7 only prohibited certain acquisitions of stock by one corporation of another. Technically, the same end could be accomplished and was permitted under it through an acquisition of assets. Therefore, the acquisition of assets was also prohibited. Second, the Celler-Kefauver amendment prohibited all acquisitions where the effect lessened competition substantially in any line of commerce in any section of the country. Thus, the amendment added vertical and conglomerate mergers to the coverage of Section 7. In 1980, Congress expanded coverage by substituting "person" for corporation, and included not only businesses engaged in interstate commerce but businesses engaged in activities which affect commerce. The word "person" includes sole proprietorship and partnerships.

The language of Section 7 neither adopts nor rejects any particular tests for measuring relevant markets. Both the product market and geographic market of the companies involved are factual issues to be considered by the courts. In determining the relevant "line of commerce" (product market) and the relevant "section of the country" (geographic market) affected by the merger in question, the actual outcome of the litigation is frequently decided. The more narrowly the product line or geographic area is defined, the greater the impact a merger or acquisition will have on competition. Thus, the relevant market decision frequently determines the issue as to the probable anticompetitive effects of the merger. It is also obvious that a decision which enlarges the line of commerce may be equally important in establishing that a merger is *not* anticompetitive. Trial courts and reviewing courts frequently disagree as to what constitutes relevant markets in any given case. Reviewing courts today give great deference to trial court findings on these issues.

In addition to determining the relevant market affected by a given merger, courts must also find that within that market the effect of the merger "may be substantially to lessen competition, or to tend to create a monopoly" before a violation is established. Some cases have held that a small percentage increase in market share is sufficient to establish the prohibited effect. The degree of market concentration prior to the merger and the relative position of the merged parties are important factors in such cases. Where there has been a history of tendency toward concentration in an industry, slight increases in further concentration are prohibited because of the policy of the law to curb such tendencies in their incipiency. The following case illustrates the great uncertainty that exists as to the legality of many mergers and acquisitions. Note that the law deals with probabilities and is designed to arrest anticompetitive tendencies at their incipiency.

UNITED STATES v. VON'S GROCERY CO.
384 U.S. 270 (1966)

The United States brought an action which charged that the acquisition by Von's Grocery Company of Shopping Bag Food Stores violated Section 7 of the Clayton Act. After the district court refused the request of the government for a temporary injunction, Von's immediately took over Shopping Bag's capital stock and assets. Then, after hearing the evidence, the district court entered judgment for the defendants, ruling as a matter of law that there was "not a reasonable probability" that the acquisition would tend "substantially to lessen competition" or tend to "create a monopoly." The government appealed.

BLACK, J.: . . . The record shows the following facts relevant to our decision. The market involved here is the retail grocery market in the Los Angeles area. In 1958 Von's retail sales ranked third in the area and Shopping Bag's ranked sixth. In 1960 their sales together were 7.5% of the total two and one-half billion dollars of retail groceries sold in the Los Angeles market each year. For many years before the merger both companies had enjoyed great success as rapidly growing companies. From 1948 to 1958 the number of Von's stores in the Los Angeles area practically doubled from 14 to 27, while at the same time the number of Shopping Bag's stores jumped from 15 to 34. During that same decade, Von's sales increased fourfold and its share of the market almost doubled, while Shopping Bag's sales multiplied seven times and its share of the market tripled. The merger of these two highly successful, expanding and aggressive competitors created the second largest grocery chain in Los Angeles with sales of almost $172,488,000 annually. In addition the findings of the District Court show that the number of owners operating a single store in the Los Angeles retail grocery market decreased from 5,365 in 1950 to 3,818 in 1961. By 1963, three years after the merger, the number of single-store owners had dropped still further to 3,590. During roughly the same period from 1953 to 1962 the number of chains with two or more grocery stores increased from 96 to 150. While the grocery business was being concentrated into the hands of fewer and

fewer owners, the small companies were continually being absorbed by the larger firms through mergers. According to an exhibit prepared by one of the Government's expert witnesses, in the period from 1949 to 1958 nine of the top 20 chains acquired 126 stores from their smaller competitors. Figures of a principal defense witness . . . illustrate the many acquisitions and mergers in the Los Angeles grocery industry from 1953 through 1961 including acquisitions made by Food Giant, Alpha Beta, Fox and Mayfair, all among the 10 leading chains in the area. Moreover, a table prepared by the Federal Trade Commission appearing in the Government's reply brief, but not a part of the record here, shows that acquisitons and mergers in the Los Angeles retail grocery market have continued at a rapid rate since the merger. These facts alone are enough to cause us to conclude contrary to the District Court that Von's Shopping Bag merger did violate § 7. Accordingly, we reverse. . . .

Like the Sherman Act in 1890 and the Clayton Act in 1914, the basic purpose of the 1950 Celler-Kefauver Bill was to prevent economic concentration in the American economy by keeping a large number of small competitors in business. In stating the purposes of the bill, both of its sponsors, Representative Celler and Senator Kefauver, emphasized their fear, widely shared by other members of Congress, that this concentration was rapidly driving the small businessman out of the market. The period from 1940 to 1947, which was at the center of attraction throughout the hearings and debates on the Celler-Kefauver Bill, had been characterized by a series of mergers between large corporations and their smaller competitors resulting in the steady erosion of the small independent business in our economy. . . .

The facts of this case present exactly the threatening trend toward concentration which Congress wanted to halt. The number of small grocery companies in the Los Angeles retail grocery market had been declining rapidly before the merger and continued to decline rapidly afterwards. This rapid decline in the number of grocery store owners moved hand in hand with a large number of significant absorptions of the small companies by the larger ones. In the midst of this steadfast trend toward concentration, Von's and Shopping Bag, two of the most successful and largest companies in the area, jointly owning 66 grocery stores, merged to become the second largest chain in Los Angeles. This merger cannot be defended on the ground that one of the companies was about to fail or that the two had to merge to save themselves from destruction by some larger and more powerful competitor. What we have on the contrary is simply the case of two already powerful companies merging in a way which makes them even more powerful than they were before. If ever such a merger would not violate § 7, certainly it does when it takes place in a market characterized by a long and continuous trend toward fewer and fewer owner-competitors, which is exactly the sort of trend which Congress, with power to do so, declared must be arrested.

Appellee's primary argument is that the merger between Von's and Shopping Bag is not prohibited by § 7 because the Los Angeles grocery market was competitive before the merger, has been since, and may continue to be in the future. Even so, § 7 "requires not merely an appraisal of the immediate impact of the merger upon competition, but a prediction of its impact upon competitive conditions in the future; this is what is meant when it is said that the amended § 7 was intended to arrest anticompetitive tendencies in their 'incipiency.' " It is enough for us that Congress feared that a market marked at the same time by both a continuous decline in the number of small businesses and a large number of mergers would, slowly but inevitably, gravitate from a market of many small competitors to one dominated by one or a few giants, and competition would thereby be destroyed. Congress passed the Celler-Kefauver Bill to prevent such a destruction of competition. Our cases since the passage of that bill have faithfully endeavored to enforce this congressional command. We adhere to them now. . . . Since appellees have been on notice of the anti-trust charge from almost the beginning . . . we not only reverse the judgment below but direct the District Court to order divestiture without delay. [*Reversed.*]

[Two of the Justices issued a strong dissent from the majority opinion above, stating in effect that the court was holding that the existence of certain superficial facts which were unrelated to any actual anticompetitive effects lead to a conclusion that the merger violated Section 7, per se. They argued that there should be demonstrated at least a reasonable probability of a substantial reduction in competition before a merger is outlawed, and that an examination of the economic facts in the relevant market did not establish such a probability in the *Von's Grocery* case.]

20. Special Doctrines

The law recognizes two special doctrines in the merger area. These are commonly referred to as the "potential entrant" and failing company doctrines. The potential-entrant doctrine recognizes that there may be injury to competition as the result of a loss of a potential competitor. Of course, potential competitors that actually join a market increase competition. In addition, the mere presence of a potential competitor may affect a market by influencing the conduct of those actually competing. For example, the existence of a potential entrant may inhibit price increases. Actual competitors may price their goods just below the level that would attract the potential entrants to the market.

The potential-entrant doctrine finds that the prohibited effect may exist when an acquisition or merger involves a potential entrant into a market. An acquisition of a competitor by a potential competitor is thus illegal when the effect may be to substantially lessen competition. The potential-entrant doctrine has been used to prevent product extension mergers as well as geographic extension mergers. The potential-entrant doctrine is applied not only because if entry does occur there is an additional competitor, but also because the mere presence of a potential competitor at the edge of the market has positive effects on those companies actually competing.

In the 1920s, the Supreme Court created a **failing-company exception** to the law restricting mergers. It held that when a company is failing, the statutory prohibitions on anticompetitive mergers are set aside. The company in the case in which the exception was decided had in one year turned a surplus of $4 million into a deficit of $4.4 million.

The failing-company doctrine allows for special approval of mergers that would otherwise be unlawful. There are three general conditions which must be met. First, the acquisition candidate must be on the brink of bankruptcy. Second, corporate reorganization under Chapter 11 of the bankruptcy laws must not be a viable alternative. Finally, the doctrine requires proof that there is no other merger partner that would raise fewer antitrust problems.

Historically, the courts have been quite strict in interpreting the failing-company doctrine. They have required clear and convincing proof of the foregoing conditions. However, the Justice Department and the FTC have been more lenient in deciding which cases to oppose. The Justice Department's attitude has always been to recognize the doctrine and not to challenge those involving companies in serious financial difficulty. It has tended to consider the long-term prospects of a company, and if the future looks bleak, it has tended not to challenge the acquisition of a failing company. For example, the Justice Department approved a merger of LTV Corporation and Republic Steel because there were serious doubts about Republic's ability to survive. The merger significantly increased concentration in steel, but Republic's faltering financial health was a part of the reality of the situation. The Justice Department did not require an extensive search for another buyer, as time was an important factor.

As more and more companies have diversified and acquired subsidiaries, the failing-company doctrine has been applied to failing divisions and failing subsidiaries. If a company is about to close down an operation and a competitor is willing to take it over, society is probably better off if the law allows the sale or divestiture of the division rather than have it no longer exist as an economic unit. A sale which increases concentration is preferable to the death of the unit. At least the employees still have a job, and a new owner may be able to restore the division or organization to a profitable entity.

21. Enforcement

Section 7 of the Clayton Act is enforced by the Justice Department, the FTC, and individuals and affected firms. It is a tool to prevent hostile takeovers as well as a law enforced by government. The basic remedy used by the Justice Department is the *injunction*. The FTC may prevent a merger by use of a cease and desist order or may order a divestiture through a decision finding unfair methods of competition.

The injunction is a major tool sought by government and individuals in the merger field. Preliminary injunctions are used to maintain the status quo while the merging parties are involved in the legal process required to accomplish the merger. The preliminary injunction prevents consummation until legal issues are resolved. Preliminary injunctions will be issued whenever there is a strong likelihood that the merger is illegal, assuming there is potential for serious injury to the public from the proposed merger. After a trial, a preliminary injunction is either made permanent or it is dissolved. If it is dissolved, the parties are free to proceed with the merger.

The injunction remedy is also used after mergers have been consummated. Such mandatory injunctions may require a divestiture of a merged firm or even a sale of stock in the event there is only partial ownership. Sometimes an acquisition or merger is challenged many years after it was consummated. While an acquisition of stock or assets may be perfectly legal at that time, it later may become illegal because it "threatens to ripen into a prohibited effect" of substantially lessening competition. The test of illegality is the time of the challenge.

The remedy of triple damages in effect allows one's competitors and other individuals directly affected to enforce the antimerger provisions of the Clayton Act. There have been numerous triple damage suits brought by one competitor against another and by a takeover candidate against its "suitor." Such suits may seek damages because of inadequate prices or for the costs of fending off a hostile takeover.

The FTC looks at market share as an important indication of anticompetitive effects of mergers. Other factors considered are barriers to entry and technological changes. If the barriers to entry are low, market share is less important. The FTC has indicated that it will give great weight to the Justice Department guidelines, which are discussed in more detail in section 23.

The FTC also examines the companies involved. Market power is more important than market share. Market share may understate competitive significance. For example, a firm with a small market share may have unique competitive potential. Since mergers may improve the efficiency of a firm, this factor is considered in deciding whether or not to challenge an acquisition. However, if the challenge is made, increased efficiency is no defense. The failing division as well as the failing-company doctrine are also considered by the FTC. The fact that a company or part of one may go out of business is obviously a factor to consider unless someone else seeks to take it over and keep it as a competitor.

Most cases involving Section 7 are settled by agreement. Many consent decrees in merger cases contain an arrangement that the company involved will not acquire any other firm for a stated period of time. Such decrees frequently provide that the divesting company will not engage in a certain line of business for a stated period, as well. The usual number of years in such cases is ten, although some have been for as long as twenty.

In recent years, the Justice Department has used Section 7 of the Clayton Act as a basis for attacking foreign acquisitions. For example, it was used to prevent the Gillette Company from acquiring a German manufacturer of electric razors. The theory was that the German company was a potential competitor in the domestic shaving instrument market. Thus, the power of United States courts applies to foreign as well as domestic mergers.

22. FTC Premerger Notification

The application of Section 7 to any given merger is discretionary with the Justice Department and the FTC. Both have issued guidelines as to which mergers are likely to be challenged, but they have reserved the right to bring action against mergers and acquisitions they feel will probably lessen competition or tend to create a monopoly. To assist in enforcement, the FTC, pursuant to a 1976 statute, has adopted a premerger notification rule. This rule requires that prior notice be given to the Justice Department and to the FTC of all pending mergers subject to the rule. Once the notice is given in advance of the acquisition, either agency may institute appropriate action to prevent it.

The application of the premerger notification rules are determined by the size of the firms involved and by the size of the transaction. The rules cover transactions involving at least 15 percent of either the assets or the voting securities of the firm to be acquired when the value of the purchase exceeds $15 million. There is a proposal to raise this purchase value to $25 million. The value of the assets is determined by fair market value and not by book value. The value of the securities is current value and not par value.

If we assume that the transaction is within the required size, we find that the premerger rules are applied if the acquiring party has either annual net sales or total assets of $100 million or more and if the acquired firm is engaged in manufacturing and has annual net sales or total assets of $5 million or more. If the acquired firm is not engaged in manufacturing, the rule applies if the acquired firm has total assets of $5 million, irrespective of the size of sales. In order to prevent avoidance of the rules by having the smaller firm acquire the larger, the rules are also applicable whenever an acquired firm has annual sales of $10 million or more and the acquiring firm has annual sales of $100 million or more.

The notification requires a brief description of the proposed acquisition, the amount of securities or assets being acquired, and the manner of acquisition. It will include the sales information broken down by industry, product class, and product. Copies of all SEC filings together with market information and facts relative to other acquisitions by both firms must be submitted.

23. Justice Department Merger Guidelines

In 1982, the Justice Department issued new **merger guidelines**. The guidelines are designed primarily to indicate when the Justice Department is likely to challenge a merger. These latest guidelines are more permissive than the ones announced in the 1960s, and most of their attention is directed at horizontal acquisitions. Under the new guidelines, the legality of vertical and conglomerate mergers is judged solely on their impact on future direct competition. This examination of horizontal mergers is achieved by examining the post-merger market concentration and the increase in concentration resulting from the merger.

An index known as the **Herfindahl-Hirschman Index** (HHI) is used to test the legality of horizontal acquisitions. The index is computed by squaring the market share of each firm in a market and adding the results. If the sum is 1,000 or less, the merger probably will not be challenged, as the market is considered to be unconcentrated, having the equivalent of at least ten equally sized firms. If the sum is between 1,000 and 1,800, a careful examination of the moderately concentrated market will be made to determine if acquisition is likely to harm competition. Harm will likely be found if the merger adds 100 points to the index. If less than fifty points are added, the Justice Department is unlikely to challenge the merger. The amount a merger will add is equal to twice the product of the merging firms' market share.

Notwithstanding the foregoing use of the HHI, the Justice Department is likely to challenge the merger of any firm with 1 percent of the market with the leading firm if the latter has 35 percent or more of the total market and is approximately twice as large as the second largest firm. In addition to examining market concentration and market share, the Justice Department also examines ease of entry, the nature of the product, conduct of firms in the market, and market performance in deciding if a merger will be challenged. Keep in mind that the HHI is only a guide and a general prediction of which mergers and acquisitions will actually be challenged. A sample HHI calculation is shown in Table 21-1.

In 1984, the Justice Department revised the merger guidelines in order to clarify some aspects of them. The revision explains the techniques to be used in defining and measuring a market. It also lists the factors that may affect the significance of concentration and market share data in evaluating horizontal mergers. The guidelines also indicate that foreign competition will be included in the relevant market data even though there are import quotas. Import quotas are treated as a separate factor to be considered.

The revised guidelines indicate that if entry into a market is so easy that existing competitors could not succeed in raising prices for any significant period of time, the Department is unlikely to challenge mergers in that

TABLE 21-1 Example of HHI Calculation

Assumptions: In a market of ten firms with market shares as stated, Firm No. 4 seeks to merge with Firm No. 8.

Firm No.	Assumed Market Share	Premerger Index	Assumed Merger of No. 4 + No. 8 Index
1	20	400	400
2	18	324	324
3	16	256	256
4	12	144	289
5	10	100	100
6	8	64	64
7	6	36	36
8	5	25	—
9	3	9	9
10	2	4	4
	Increase of +120	1,362	1,482

Note that the increase in the index is equal to the product of the market share of the merging firms times 2 ($12 \times 5 \times 2 = 120$).

market. The Department is more likely to challenge a merger in the following circumstances:

1 Firms in the market previously have been found to have engaged in horizontal collusion regarding price, territories, and customers, and the characteristics of the market have not changed appreciably since the most recent finding.

2 One or more of the following types of practices are adopted by substantially all of the firms in the market: (*a*) mandatory delivered pricing; (*b*) exchange of price or output information in a form that could assist firms in setting or enforcing an agreed price; (*c*) collective standardization of product variables on which the firms could compete; and (*d*) price protection clauses.

3 The firm to be acquired has been an unusually disruptive and competitive influence in the market.

Two other items of the revised guidelines are worthy of note. First, the Department recognizes that increased efficiency is generally desirable. Some mergers that might otherwise be challenged may be reasonably necessary to achieve significant net efficiencies. If the parties to the merger establish by clear and convincing evidence that a merger will achieve such efficiencies, those efficiencies will be considered in deciding whether to challenge the merger. Efficiency claims will be rejected if comparable savings can reasonably be achieved through other means.

Second, the guidelines recognize the failing-company doctrine and note that it has been ambiguous. The guidelines indicate that the Justice Department is unlikely to challenge an anticompetitive merger in which one of the merging firms is allegedly failing when (1) the allegedly failing firm probably would be unable to meet its financial obligations in the near future; (2) it probably would not be able to reorganize successfully in bankruptcy; and (3) it has made unsuccessful good-faith efforts to elicit reasonable acquisition offers that would keep it in the market and pose a less severe danger to competition. Similarly, the "failure" of a division is an important factor affecting the likely competitive effect of a merger.

24. Current Attitudes

The Supreme Court has adopted a narrow view of the application of Section 7. It can be used only against mergers of companies actually engaged in interstate commerce. As a result, most service industries are exempt from the law, because such businesses are usually involved only in intrastate commerce. The Supreme Court also follows a policy of affirming the findings and conclusions of district courts unless they are "clearly erroneous." When the evidence is such that a court can reasonably find that no substantial lessening of competition has occurred or is threatened by an acquisition, the Supreme Court does not change the decision of the lower courts. As a result, there are fewer appeals by the Justice Department of negative lower court decisions.

When President Reagan was elected in 1980, he indicated a desire for less government involvement in economic decisions and for greater reliance on competition to regulate the economy. This shift in policy is very evident in antitrust enforcement and especially in the Justice Department's enforcement of Section 7 of the Clayton Act. Mergers which prior administrations would probably have challenged were routinely approved by the Reagan administration and by Reagan's appointees to the Federal Trade Commission.

The Reagan administration tends to believe that government has no business interfering with mergers except in cases that significantly reduce competition or create economic dislocations. It finds that most mergers do not lessen competition and therefore should not be challenged. It believes that challenging mergers reduces divestitures and that many of these are beneficial to the divesting company. Also, the current attitude is to allow increases in size in order to meet foreign competition. This is especially true in basic industries such as steel.

The Justice Department during the Reagan administration has adopted an attitude of sitting down with merger candidates and examining the market impact of proposed mergers rather than filing a suit to stop an acquisition. If the examination reveals factors that have an anticompetitive impact, it allows the parties to either dispose of the portion of the acquired business creating the conflict or to agree to such a divestiture if the merger is not challenged. This policy has sometimes been described as the "fix-it-first" rule in reviewing mergers.

The lack of enforcement of Section 7 by the Reagan administration is a concern to many economists. They point to the trend toward further concentration and the disruption in the financial markets caused by the very large mergers—especially in petroleum. Although the low level of enforcement today has resulted in a significant increase in concentration in many industries, future administrations may challenge many of the recent acquisitions. More vigorous enforcement is possible if the legality and impact on competition are tested at the time of the challenge and not at the time of the acquisition.

THE FEDERAL TRADE COMMISSION ACT

25. Introduction

The FTC was created in 1914 to have an "independent" administrative agency charged with keeping competition free and fair. It enforces the Clayton Act provisions on price discrimination, tying and exclusive contracts, mergers and acquisitions, and interlocking directorates. In addition, it enforces Section 5 of the Federal Trade Commission Act. This act originally made "unfair methods of competition" in commerce unlawful. The Wheeler-Lea amendments of 1938 added that "unfair or deceptive acts or practices in commerce" were also unlawful under Section 5. The FTC has broad, sweeping powers and a mandate to determine what methods, acts, or practices fall within the vague category of being "unfair or deceptive" and are thus unlawful. Such decisions are made on a case-by-case basis. A discussion of unfair methods of competition follows in the next section. Since unfair or deceptive acts or practices were prohibited to protect consumers and not competition, they were discussed in Chapter 15 which deals with consumer protection. That chapter also discussed many of the other consumer protection statutes for which the FTC has enforcement responsibility.

The FTC issues trade regulation rules dealing with business practices in an industry. For example, the FTC has said the American Medical Association can allow doctors to advertise. The FTC also periodically issues "trade practice rules and guides," sometimes referred to as industry guides. These rules are the FTC's informal opinion of legal requirements applicable to a particular industry's practices. Although compliance with the rules is voluntary, they provide the basis for the informal and simultaneous abandonment by industry members of practices thought to be unlawful. "Guidelines" are administrative interpretations of the statutes which the Commission enforces, and they provide guidance to both the FTC staff and business people evaluating the legality of certain practices. Guidelines deal with a particular practice and may cut across industry lines.

The primary function of the FTC is to prevent illegal business practices rather than to punish violations. It prevents wrongful actions by use of cease and desist orders. Whereas violations of these orders may be punished by a fine of $10,000 per day, with each day being a new violation, the punishment factor is only incidental to the FTC's primary prevention role. As noted in Chapter 10 on administrative law, most FTC cases are settled by consent orders. In such cases, the respondent need not admit a law violation but agrees *not* to do the act complained of in the future.

26. Unfair Methods of Competition

Although the original Section 5 of the FTC Act outlawed unfair methods of competition in commerce and directed the FTC to prevent the use of such, it offered no definition of the specific practices which were unfair. The term "unfair methods of competition" was designed by Congress as a flexible concept, the exact meaning of which could evolve on a case-by-case basis. It can apply to a variety of unrelated activities. It is generally up to the FTC to determine what business conduct is "unfair." Great deference is given to the FTC's opinion as to what constitutes a violation and to the remedies it desires to correct anticompetitive behavior.

Business conduct in violation of any provision of the antitrust laws may also be ruled illegal under Section 5 of the FTC Act. Further, anticompetitive acts or practices which *fall short* of transgressing the Sherman or Clayton Acts may be restrained by the FTC as being "unfair methods of competition." When an unfair trade practice is alleged to exist, the choice of the law under which to proceed will depend upon the nature of the relief being sought, the nature of the violation, and the status of the party seeking it. Thus, if criminal sanctions are desired, the Justice Department must initiate the action in the regular federal courts on behalf of the United States and generally must proceed under the Sherman Act. The burden of proof in such cases is beyond a reasonable doubt. As a result, such cases are successfully brought only when the business practice involved is clearly unfair. On the other hand, if the business practice is a violation of the Clayton Act, such as a tying contract, the Justice Department may seek and obtain an injunction. The proof required in such a case is less than is required for a Sherman Act conviction. If the practice is such that it is not only questionable that the Sherman Act is violated but also doubtful that the proof is sufficient to prove a Clayton Act violation, the FTC may nevertheless proceed and find that the business practice is unfair. Thus, business practices which could not be prevented in a judicial proceeding may be stopped by FTC cease and desist orders.

In the decision which follows, Brown Shoe Company attempted to obtain additional retail outlets that would handle Brown Shoe products exclusively by entering into franchise agreements for the sale of its products. These arrangements were challenged by the FTC under Section 5 of the FTC Act. It may be assumed that the activities in this case would not be a violation of either the Sherman or Clayton Acts.

FTC v. BROWN SHOE CO.
384 U.S. 316 (1966)

BLACK, J.: Section 5(a)(6) of the Federal Trade Commission Act empowers and directs the Commission "to prevent persons, partnerships, or corporations . . . from using unfair methods of competition in commerce and unfair or deceptive acts or practices in commerce." Proceeding under the authority of § 5, the Federal Trade Commission filed a complaint against the Brown Shoe Co., Inc., one of the world's largest manufacturers of shoes with total sales of $236,946,078 for the year ending October 31, 1957. The unfair practices charged against Brown revolve around the "Brown Franchise Stores' Program" through which Brown sells its shoes to some 650 retail stores. The complaint alleged that under this plan Brown, a corporation engaged in interstate commerce, had "entered into contracts or franchises with a substantial number of its independent retail shoe operator customers which require said customers to restrict their purchases of shoes for resale to the Brown lines and which prohibit them from purchasing, stocking or reselling shoes manufactured by competitors of Brown." Brown's customers who entered into these restrictive franchise agreements, so the complaint charged, were given in return special treatment and valuable benefits which were not granted to Brown's customers who did not enter into the agreements. In its answer to the Commission's complaint Brown admitted that approximately 259 of its retail customers had executed written franchise agreements and that over 400 others had entered into its franchise program without execution of the franchise agreement. Also in its answer Brown attached as an exhibit an unexecuted copy of the "Franchise Agreement" which, when executed by Brown's representative and a retail shoe dealer obligates Brown to give to the dealer but not to other customers certain valuable services, including among others, architectural plans, costly merchandising records, services of a Brown field representative, and a right to participate in group insurance at lower rates than the dealer could obtain individually. In return, according to the franchise agreement set out in Brown's answer, the retailer must make this promise:

In return I will:
> **Concentrate my business within the grades and price lines of shoes representing Brown Shoe Company Franchises of the Brown Division and will have no lines conflicting with Brown Division Brands of the Brown Shoe Company.**

Brown's answer further admitted that the operators of "such Brown Franchise Stores in individually varying degrees accept the benefits and perform the obligations contained in such franchise agreements or implicit in such Program," and that Brown refuses to grant these benefits "to dealers who are dropped or voluntarily withdraw from the Brown Franchise Program . . ." The foregoing admissions of Brown as to the existence and operation of the franchise program were buttressed by many separate detailed fact findings of a trial examiner, one of which findings was that the franchise program effectively foreclosed Brown's competitors from selling to a substantial number of retail shoe dealers. Based on these findings and on

Brown's admissions the Commission concluded that the restrictive contract program was an unfair method of competition within the meaning of § 5 and ordered Brown to cease and desist from its use.

On review the Court of Appeals set aside the Commission's order. . . .

. . . Thus the question we have for decision is whether the Federal Trade Commission can declare it to be an unfair practice for Brown, the second largest manufacturer of shoes in the Nation, to pay a valuable consideration to hundreds of retail shoe purchasers in order to secure a contractual promise from them that they will deal primarily with Brown and will not purchase conflicting lines of shoes from Brown's competitors. We hold that the Commission has power to find, on the record here, such an anticompetitive practice unfair, subject of course to judicial review. . . .

. . . The Commission has broad powers to declare trade practices unfair. This broad power of the Commission is particularly well established with regard to trade practices which conflict with the basic policies of the Sherman and Clayton Acts even though such practices may not actually violate these laws. The record in this case shows beyond doubt that Brown, the country's second largest manufacturer of shoes, has a program which requires shoe retailers, unless faithless to their contractual obligations with Brown, to substantially limit their trade with Brown's competitors. This program obviously conflicts with the central policy of both § 1 of the Sherman Act and § 3 of the Clayton Act against contracts which take away freedom of purchasers to buy in an open market. Brown nevertheless contends that the Commission had no power to declare the franchise program unfair without proof that its effect "may be to substantially lessen competition or tend to create a monopoly" which of course would have to be proved if the Government were proceeding against Brown under § 3 of the Clayton Act rather than § 5 of the Federal Trade Commission Act. We reject the argument that proof of this § 3 element must be made for our cases hold that the Commission has power under § 5 to arrest trade restraints in their incipiency without proof that they amount to an outright violation of § 3 of the Clayton Act or other provisions of the antitrust laws. . . .

It is . . . clear that the Federal Trade Commission Act was designed to supplement and bolster the Sherman Act and the Clayton Act . . . to stop in their incipiency acts and practices which, when full blown, would violate those Acts . . . as well as to condemn as "unfair methods of competition" existing violations of them.

We hold that the Commission acted well within its authority in declaring the Brown franchise program unfair whether it was completely full blown or not. [*Reversed.*]

27. Ethical Considerations

Section 5 of the Federal Trade Commission Act prohibits "unfair methods of competition in and affecting commerce, and unfair or deceptive acts or practices in or affecting commerce." To be "unfair," a method of competition or an act or practice does not have to be deceptive. "Unfair" undoubtedly includes deception, but "unfair" also encompasses many other things which could not accurately be described as deceptive. Likewise, violations of the Sherman and Clayton acts may be Section 5 FTC Act violations, but the terms "unfair methods of competition" and "unfair acts or practices" embrace much more conduct than merely violations of those antitrust statutes. To decide whether challenged business conduct is "unfair" as a method of competition or as a commercial practice, the Commission asks three major questions if there is no deception or antitrust violation involved:

1 Does the conduct injure consumers significantly?

2 Does the conduct offend an established public policy? (Conduct may offend public policy even though not previously unlawful.)

3 Is the conduct oppressive, unscrupulous, immoral, or unethical?

Answering any one of these questions affirmatively could lead to a finding of unfairness. The Supreme Court has declared that the Commission can operate "like a court of equity" in considering "public values" to establish what is unfair under Section 5. Unless Congress limits the FTC by more precisely defining what "unfairness" it wants prohibited, the Commission will probably continue to consider public attitudes about what is "right" in deciding what is "unfair." Since unethical or unscrupulous practices also usually injure consumers or violate public policy, there may be little practical value in eliminating the flexibility Section 5 now has to reach whatever creative schemes are devised to take advantage of consumers or competitors.

REVIEW QUESTIONS

1 For each term in the left-hand column, match the most appropriate description in the right-hand column:

(1) Price discrimination	(a) An individual is a member of the board of directors of two or more competing corporations at the same time
(2) Failing-company doctrine	(b) A commodity is sold or leased for use only on condition that the buyer or lessee purchase certain additional products or services from the seller or lessor
(3) Requirements contract	(c) A contract whereby a buyer agrees not to purchase an item or items of merchandise from competitors of the seller
(4) Full-line forcing	(d) A buyer agrees to purchase all his or her business needs of a product from the seller during a certain period

(5) Predatory pricing

(e) A seller charges different purchasers different amounts for the same commodity

(6) Exclusive-dealing contract

(f) A form of tying arrangement in which the buyer or lessee is compelled to take a complete product line from the seller as a condition of being permitted to purchase the main product of the line

(7) Reciprocal dealing

(g) A doctrine which allows an acquisition to proceed because the company to be acquired is likely to go out of business because of financial difficulty

(8) Tying contract

(h) The administrative equivalent of a court injunction which is issued by an administrative agency with quasi-judicial powers to restrain future violations of the law

(9) Cease and desist order

(i) This arrangement exists when two parties face each other as both buyer and seller

(10) Interlocking directorate

(j) Selling at prices below average variable cost to close out competition

2 Copp Paving Company sued Gulford for triple damages, alleging a violation of the Robinson-Patman amendment. Copp operates an asphaltic concrete "hot plant" in California. The plant manufactures asphalt for surfacing highways, including interstate highways in California. Its whole operation is in intrastate commerce. Does the complaint allege a valid claim? Why, or why not?

3 Alice, who recently received a degree in business, has been named general sales manager of a building materials manufacturer. She has called a meeting of the sales force, and among other matters Alice has made the following statement: "We will cut prices so low our competitors will be cut off at the knees." If this policy is carried out, will any law be violated? Explain.

4 In the same situation as question 3, Alice later called on the corporation's most important customer. While informing this customer of its special importance, Alice said: "To you,

Larry, and to you alone, the price we charge will always be below cost." If this policy is carried out, will it be in violation of any law? Explain.

5 A class action suit was brought against defendant corporation for alleged violations of Section 1 of the Sherman Act, stemming from *tying arrangements* included in fast-food franchise agreements. Under the tie-in, potential franchisees were required to purchase a specified amount of cooking equipment and other items at a higher cost than competitors' products. What was the result? Why?

6 Teen-Age Products Corporation is a large conglomerate; it has a subsidiary in the toiletry business. For the past two years, it has been packaging its brand-name men's cologne "Brute" and selling it to retailers for $8 per bottle. However, it has also been selling the same substance to another company for private-brand packaging for $6 per bottle. There is wide customer recognition of Brute and a willingness to pay more for it. Is Teen-Age Products violating any law? Explain.

7 A department store solicited and received contributions from vendors toward the cost of the store's one-hundredth anniversary celebration. The store gave the vendors no direct promotional services for vendors' products. Is the store in violation of Section 2 of the Clayton Act as amended? Why, or why not?

8 Weinberg is on the board of directors of both Sears Roebuck & Company and B.F. Goodrich. Sears and Goodrich each have capital, surplus, and undivided profits in excess of $1 million. They compete with each other on the retail level in ninety-seven communities in the sale of appliances, hardware, automotive supplies, sporting goods, tires, radios, television sets, and toys. Is Weinberg acting illegally? Why, or why not?

9 Standard Oil entered into exclusive supply contracts with the operators of independent retail service stations. In these contracts, the dealers agreed to purchase from Standard Oil not only all of their requirements for petroleum products but also all of their tubes, tires, and batteries. Standard Oil had 6.7 percent of the gasoline market. Are these contracts illegal? Why, or why not?

10 The American Medical Association adopted a code of ethics which prohibited all advertising by physicians. Included in the prohibition were ads indicating that physicians would make house calls. The FTC challenged the ethical rules under Section 5 of the FTC Act. What was the result? Why?

11 The market for lead-based antiknock additives to gasoline is highly concentrated, with four manufacturers controlling all of the market. The two largest manufacturers, Ethyl Corporation and Du Pont, control 70 percent of the market. It is a common practice in the industry to announce publicly price increases through press releases. The FTC

seeks to stop the practice by filing a complaint alleging that the price signaling is an unfair method of competition. It does not contend that the companies are in collusion or that they agree on price increases. What was the result? Why?

12 Du Pont acquired 23 percent of the stock of General Motors in 1917 to 1919. By 1947, Du Pont supplied 67 percent of GM's requirements for finishes and almost 40 percent of its requirements for fabrics. In 1949, the government filed suit, alleging that the acquisition violated Section 7 of the Clayton Act. Must Du Pont dispose of its GM stock? Why, or why not?

13 In an industry, there were ten competitors, each with the following market shares:

1–20%	6–10%
2–18%	7–8%
3–16%	8–5%
4–15%	9–3%
5–12%	10–1%

Number 7 decides to merge with number 9. Will the merger be challenged under the 1982 guidelines? Explain.

14 The FTC challenged the acquisition by Procter & Gamble (P&G) of Clorox. Clorox was the leading manufacturer of liquid bleach at the time of the acquisition, accounting for 48 percent of the national sales. It was the only firm selling nationally, and the top two firms accounted for 65 percent of national sales. P&G is a large, diversified manufacturer of household products, with its primary activity being in the area of soaps, detergents, and cleaners. It accounted for 54 percent of all packaged detergent sales, and the top three firms accounted for 50 percent of the market. P&G is the nation's leading advertiser. What was the result? Why?

15 The Stroh's Brewing Company has made a tender offer of $17 per share for all shares of the Schlitz Brewing Company. Stroh's is the nation's seventh largest brewer, with approximately 5 percent of the United States beer market. Schlitz is the third-ranked beer nationally, with approximately 8 percent of the market. Prior to the Stroh's tender offer, the G. Heilemann Company had attempted to acquire Schlitz. Heilemann had 7.5 percent of the market, and its merger attempt was rejected by the Justice Department.

The beer industry in the United States is dominated by Anheuser Busch and the Miller Brewing Company. Together, they account for approximately 50 percent of the nation's beer sales. Schlitz's beer market has declined in recent years, except in the southeastern states where Schlitz holds 13.5 percent of the market and Stroh's 6.9 percent. Is it likely that the Justice Department will challenge Stroh's tender offer? Explain.

16 The LTV Corporation owns Jones & Laughlin Steel. The Lykes Corporation owns Youngstown Sheet and Tube Company. It is proposed that these two corporations merge, forming a steel company that would rank third in size behind U.S. Steel and Bethlehem Steel. Both companies are major producers of flat-rolled steel. Together, they account for 11 percent of that market. They also hold 19 percent of the tube market and 22 percent of the tin-plate business. The steel industry in the United States has difficulty in competing with cheaper foreign imports. Both LTV and Lykes are operating at significant losses. Is it likely that this merger will be challenged? Explain.

Chapter

22

Environmental Laws and Pollution Control

1. Introduction

Over the next decade, industry will spend several hundred billion dollars on pollution control. Environmental regulation remains the single most expensive area of government's regulation of the business community. As with other regulatory costs, these costs are eventually passed on to consumers. However, a recent Harris poll suggests a strong nationwide support for environmental cleanup. A 70 percent majority favored passing on cleanup costs to everyone, including themselves. They also expressed willingness to pay higher taxes to support cleanup efforts.

Cleanup efforts mean environmental regulation, and after being much criticized in the early 1980s, the EPA has shown renewed commitment to achieving regulatory goals. Criminal prosecutions of environmental law violators have increased. The EPA is paying new attention to the presence of toxic chemicals in the air and water.

Meanwhile, researchers almost daily report new instances of how technological civilization affects life on our planet. For every allegation of pollution-caused environmental harm, however, there are usually countertheories raised, maintaining that the harm is not as significant as alleged, or else arguing that the harm arises from causes unrelated to industrial pollution. Lack of unanimous scientific opinion on many environmental issues underscores their great complexity. It also reveals a key controversy at the heart of environmental regulation: *How much certainty of harm is required to justify regulatory intervention?*

The concern over *acid rain* illustrates the problem. In the eastern United States and Canada, rain with a high acid content is killing fish in lakes and posing a significant threat to forests and certain crops. Considerable theory and research points to midwestern industrial sulfur emissions as causing acid rain problems. Pressure is mounting in Congress to legislate limitations on these emissions. On the other hand, other scientific opinion warns against overly hasty legislative "solutions" to acid rain. It points out that much acid rain is caused naturally.

Overshadowing acid rain as a future pollution concern is increasing atmospheric concentrations of carbon dioxide. The National Academy of Sciences notes that global carbon dioxide levels have increased 6 percent since 1960. The increase is due largely to the burning of fossil fuels such as oil and coal.

Higher carbon dioxide levels could lead to warmer global temperatures, the so-called *greenhouse effect.* Changing climate patterns and rising sea levels could be possible results. But the timing and magnitude of the greenhouse effect is hotly debated. Is regulatory intervention justified? Will the United States join with other nations seeking to limit the growth of fossil fuel consumption? These are some of the questions which the business students of the 1980s will quite possibly face during their business careers. Present answers to these questions are unknown. Only one conclusion is clear-cut: We possess immense technological power today to change the environment for better and for worse, both intentionally and inadvertently.

Three basic areas of environmental regulation are examined in this chapter: (1) the government's regulation of itself, (2) the government's regulation of business, and (3) suits by private individuals. Table 22-1 illustrates this break-down.

GOVERNMENT'S REGULATION OF ITSELF

2. The National Environmental Policy Act

The way government regulates the environmental impact of business's decision making interests the business community greatly. The federal government, for instance, pays private enterprise over $40 billion annually to conduct studies, prepare reports, and carry out projects. In addition, the federal government is by far the nation's largest landholder, controlling one-third the entire area of the United States. Private enterprise must rely on government agencies to issue permits and licenses to explore and mine for minerals, graze cattle, cut timber, or conduct other business activities on government property. Thus, any congressional legislation which influences the decision making concerning federal funding or license granting also

TABLE 22-1   Pollution Control Laws

Government's Regulation of Itself
  National Environmental Policy Act
  State environmental policy acts

Government's Regulation of Business
  Clean Air Act
  Clean Water Act
  Noise Control Act
  Pesticide Control Acts
  Solid Waste Disposal Act
  Toxic Substances Control Act
  Natural Resource Conservation and Recovery Act
  Other federal, state, and local statutes

Suits by Private Individuals
  Public and private nuisance
  Strict liability for ultrahazardous activity
  Negligence
  Trespass
  Citizen enforcement provisions of various statutes

affects business. Such legislation is the *National Environmental Policy Act* (NEPA).

NEPA became effective in 1970. The act is divided into two titles. Title I establishes broad policy goals and imposes specific duties on all federal agencies, and Title II sets up the Council on Environmental Quality (CEQ). As the CEQ's role under NEPA consists mainly in gathering and assessing information, issuing advisory guidelines, and making recommendations to the President on environmental matters, this section will center on Title I.

THE ENVIRONMENTAL IMPACT STATEMENT

Title I of NEPA imposes specific "action-forcing" requirements on federal agencies. The most important requirement demands that all federal agencies prepare an **environmental impact statement** (EIS) prior to taking certain actions. An EIS must be included "in every recommendation or report on proposals for legislation and other major Federal actions significantly affecting the quality of the human environment." This EIS is a "detailed statement" estimating the environmental impact of the proposed action. Any discussion of such action and its impact must contain information on adverse environmental effects which cannot be avoided, any irreversible use of resources necessary, and available alternatives to the action (see Figure 22-1).

There have been hundreds of cases interpreting the EIS requirements. In the following case, the Supreme Court decides whether psychological fear caused by the risk of accident at a nuclear power plant is an "environmental effect."

"Federal action" requirement

"Human environment" requirement

"Detailed statement" requirement

"Major action" requirement

ENVIRONMENTAL IMPACT STATEMENT

Examines adverse environmental effects

Examines alternatives to proposed action

Examines irreversible commitment of resources

FIGURE 22-1

METROPOLITAN EDISON COMPANY v. PEOPLE AGAINST NUCLEAR ENERGY
103 S.Ct. 1556 (1983)

Metropolitan Edison Company decided to re-open its TMI-1 plant at Three Mile Island, Pennsylvania, after it had been shut down when a serious accident damaged the reactor. People Against Nuclear Energy (PANE), an association of Three Mile Island–area residents, sued, claiming that the Nuclear Regulatory Commission failed to consider the psychological harm that reopening the plant and exposing the community to the risk of a nuclear accident might cause.

REHNQUIST, J.: Section 102(C) of NEPA directs all federal agencies to "include in every recommendation or report on proposals for legislation and other major Federal actions significantly affecting the quality of the human environment, a detailed statement by the responsible official on—(i) the environmental impact of the proposed action, [and] (ii) any adverse environmental effects which cannot be avoided should the proposal be implemented. . . ."

To paraphrase the statutory language in light of the facts of this case, where an agency action significantly affects the quality of the human environment, the agency must evaluate the "environmental impact" and any unavoidable adverse environmental effects of its proposal. The theme of section 102 is sounded by the adjective "environmental": NEPA does not require the agency to assess every impact or effect of its proposed action, but only the impact or effect on the environment. If we were to seize the word "environmental" out of its context and give it the broadest possible definition, the words "adverse environmental effects" might embrace virtually any consequence of a governmental action that some one thought "adverse." But we think the context of the statute shows that Congress was talking about the physical environment—the world around us, so to speak. NEPA was designed to promote human welfare by alerting governmental actors to the effect of their proposed actions on the physical environment. . . .

Our understanding of the congressional concerns that led to the enactment of NEPA suggests that the terms "environmental effect" and "environmental impact" in section 102 be read to include a requirement of a reasonably close causal relationship between a change in the physical environment and the effect at issue. The issue before us, then, is how to give content to this requirement. This is a question of first impression in this Court.

The federal action that affects the environment in this case is permitting renewed operation of TMI-1. The direct effects on the environment of this action include release of low-level radiation, increased fog in the Harrisburg area (caused by operation of the plant's cooling towers), and the release of warm water into the Susquehanna River. The NRC has considered each of these effects in its EIS, and again in the EIA. Another effect of renewed operation is a risk of a nuclear accident. The NRC has also considered this effect.

PANE argues that the psychological health damage it alleges "will flow directly from the risk of [a nuclear] accident." But a risk of an accident is not an effect on the physical environment. A risk is, by definition, unrealized in the physical world. In a causal chain from renewed operation of TMI-1 to psychological health damage, the element of risk and its perception by PANE's members are necessary middle links. We believe that the element of risk lengthens the causal chain beyond the reach of NEPA.

Risk is a pervasive element of modern life; to say more would belabor the obvious. Many of the risks we face are generated by modern technology, which brings both the possibility of major accidents and opportunities for tremendous achievements. Medical experts apparently agree that risk can generate stress in human beings, which in turn may rise to the level of serious health damage. For this reason among many others, the question whether the gains from any technological advance are worth its attendant risks may be an important public policy issue. Nonetheless, it is quite different from the question whether the same gains are worth a given level of alteration of our physical environment or depletion of our natural resources. The latter question rather than the former is the central concern of NEPA.

Time and resources are simply too limited for us to believe that Congress intended to extend NEPA as far as the Court of Appeals has taken it. The scope of the agency's inquiries must remain manageable if NEPA's goal of "ensur[ing] a fully informed and well considered decision," is to be accomplished.

If contentions of psychological health damage caused by risk were cognizable under NEPA, agencies would, at the very least, be obliged to expend considerable resources developing psychiatric expertise that is not otherwise relevant to their congressionally assigned functions. The available resources may be spread so thin that agencies are unable adequately to pursue protection of the physical environment and natural resources. As we said in another context "[w]e cannot attribute to Congress the intention to . . . open the door to such obvious incongruities and undesireable possibilities." . . . [*Reversed.*]

Several regulatory guidelines issued by the CEQ have made the EIS more useful. One guideline directs the federal agencies to engage in *scoping*. Scoping requires that even before EIS preparation, agencies must designate which environmental issues of a contemplated action are most significant. It encourages impact statements to focus on more substantial environmental concerns and reduce the attention devoted to trivial issues. It also allows other agencies and interested parties to participate in the scoping process. This helps ensure that formal impact statements will address matters regarded as most important.

Another guideline directs EISs be "clear, to the point, and written in plain English." This deters the use of technical jargon and helps those reading impact statements to understand them. The CEQ has also limited the length of impact statements, which once ran to more than 1,000 pages, to 150 pages except in unusual circumstances.

Critics of NEPA and the CEQ guidelines raise several issues regarding the current EIS process. Some critics point out that the present process fails to consider the economic injury caused by abandoning or delaying projects. They also contend that those preparing EISs are forced to consider far too many alternatives to proposed federal action without regard to their economic reasonableness. Other critics maintain that most impact statements are too descriptive and not sufficiently analytical. They fear that the EIS is "a document of compliance rather than a decision-making tool." A final general criticism of the EIS process notes the limits of its usefulness. As follow-ups on some EISs have shown, environmental factors are often so complex that projections concerning environmental effects amount to little more than guesswork.

Although NEPA applies only to federal actions, numerous states have enacted similar legislation to assist their decision making. Many interpretive problems found on the national level are also encountered at the state level. In addition, as the states frequently lack the resources and expertise of the federal government, state EISs are often even less helpful in evaluating complex environmental factors than are those prepared by federal agencies.

GOVERNMENT'S REGULATION OF BUSINESS

3. Introduction

More and more companies are hiring environmental managers to deal with environmental compliance issues. This trend reflects the continuing importance of the government's regulation of private enterprise and its impact on the environment. Congress may fine-tune environmental acts, but the national commitment to a cleaner environment is here to stay.

For businesses which have borne the enormous expense of environmental cleanup, there is one bright note. When adjusted for inflation, real spending for pollution control is beginning to decline. The reason for the decline is that much of the initial expense of pollution control equipment has already been met.

The modern environmental movement began in the 1960s. As it gained momentum, it generated political pressure which forced government to reassess its role in environmental issues. One of the first steps taken at the federal level in response to this pressure was the establishing of the *Environmental Protection Agency* (EPA) in 1970. At the federal level, the EPA coordinates public control of private action as it affects the environment.

Today, the EPA is an enormous bureaucracy with a number of major responsibilities (see Table 22-2). Most importantly, it administers federal laws concerning pollution of the air and water, solid waste and toxic substance disposal, pesticide regulation, and radiation. The following sections examine these laws.

4. The Clean Air Act: Basic Structure

In 1257, Queen Eleanor of England was driven from Nottingham Castle because of harsh smoke from the numerous coal fires in London. Coal had come into widespread use in England during this time, following the cutting of forests for fuel and agricultural purposes. By 1307, a royal order prohibited coal burning in London's kilns under punishment of "grievous ransoms." This early attempt at controlling air pollution does not appear, however, to have been very effective. As recently as the London smog of 1952, 4,000 people died of air pollution–related causes, including coal smoke.

The key federal legislation for controlling air pollution in the United States is the Clean Air Act. This legislation directs the EPA administrator to establish air quality standards and to see that these standards are achieved according to a definite timetable. So far, the administrator has set primary and secondary air quality standards for particulates, carbon monoxide, sulfur dioxide, nitrogen dioxide, hydrocarbons, and lead. **Primary standards** are those necessary to protect public health. *Secondary standards* guard the public from other adverse air pollution effects such as injury to property, vegetation, and climate, and damage to esthetic values. In most instances, primary and secondary air quality standards are identical.

Government regulation of private action under the Clean Air Act is a

TABLE 22-2 Responsibilities of the EPA

1. Conducting research on the harmful impact of pollution
2. Gathering information about present pollution problems
3 Assisting states and local governments, through grants, technical advice, and other means in controlling pollution
4. Advising the CEQ about new policies needed for protection of the environment
5. Administering federal pollution laws

joint federal and state effort. The EPA sets standards and the states devise implementation plans, which the EPA must approve, to carry them out. The states thus bear principal responsibility for enforcing the Clean Air Act, with the EPA providing standard setting, coordinating, and supervisory functions. However, the EPA may also participate in enforcement. The administrator can require the operator of any air pollution source to keep such records and perform such monitoring or sampling as the EPA deems appropriate. In addition, the EPA has the right to inspect these records and data. Various criminal and civil penalties and fines back up the Clean Air Act. In addition, industries that do not obey cleanup orders face payment to the EPA; payment amounts to the economic savings they realize from their failure to install and operate proper antipollution equipment.

For control purposes, the Clean Air Act amendments divide air pollution sources into two categories: *stationary* and *mobile* (transportation). Under the state implementation plans, major stationary polluters, such as steel mills and utilities, must reduce their emissions to a level sufficient to bring down air pollution to meet primary and secondary standards. Polluters follow time-tables and schedules in complying with these requirements. To achieve designated standards, they install a variety of control devices, including wet collectors (scrubbers), filter collectors, tall stacks, electrostatic precipitators, and afterburners. New stationary pollution sources, or modified ones, must install the best system of emission reduction which has been adequately demonstrated. Under the act's provision, citizens are granted standing to enforce compliance with these standards.

The act requires both stationary and mobile sources to meet a timetable of air pollution standards for which control technology may not exist at the time. This "technology-forcing" aspect of the act is unique to the history of government regulation of business, yet it has been upheld by the Supreme Court.

UNION ELECTRIC CO. v. EPA
427 U.S. 246 (1975)

MARSHALL, J.: Petitioner is an electric utility company servicing the St. Louis metropolitan area, large portions of Missouri, and parts of Illinois and Iowa. Its three coal-fired generating plants in the metropolitan St. Louis area are subject to the sulfur dioxide restrictions in the Missouri implementation plan. Petitioner did not seek review of the Administrator's approval of the plan within 30 days, as it was entitled to do under § 307(b)(1) of the Clean Air Act, but rather applied to the appropriate state and county agencies for variances from the emission limitations affecting its three plants. Petitioner received one-year variances, which could be extended upon reapplication. The variances on two of petitioner's three plants had expired and petitioner was applying for extensions when, on May 31, 1974, the Administrator notified petitioner that sulfur dioxide emissions from its plants violated the emission limitations contained in the Missouri plan. Shortly thereafter petitioner filed a petition in the Court of Appeals for the Eighth Circuit for review of the Administrator's 1972 approval of the Missouri implementation plan.

Section 307(b)(1) allows petitions for review to be filed in an appropriate court of appeals more than 30 days after the Administrator's approval of an implementation plan only if the petition is "based solely on grounds arising after such 30th day." Petitioner claimed to meet this requirement by asserting that various economic and technological difficulties had arisen more than 30 days after the Administrator's approval and that these difficulties made compliance with the emission limitations impossible. . . .

We reject at the outset petitioner's suggestion that claim of economic or technological infeasibility may be considered upon a petition for review based on new information and filed more than 30 days after approval of an implementation plan even if such a claim could not be considered by the Administrator in approving a plan or by a court in reviewing a plan challenged within the original 30-day appeal period. In pertinent part § 307(b)(1) provides:

A petition for review of the Administrator's action in approving or promulgating any implementation plan under section 110 . . . may be filed only in the United States Court of Appeals for the appropriate circuit. Any such petition shall be filed within 30 days from the date of such promulgation or approval, or after such date if such petition is based solely on grounds arising after such 30th day.

Regardless of when a petition for review is

filed under § 307(b)(1), the court is limited to reviewing "the Administrator's action in approving . . . [the] implementation plan. . . ." Accordingly, if new "grounds" are alleged they must be such that, had they been known at the time the plan was presented to the Administrator for approval, it would have been an abuse of discretion for the Administrator to approve the plan. To hold otherwise would be to transfer a substantial responsibility in administering the Clean Air Act from the Administrator and the state agencies to the federal courts.

Since a reviewing court—regardless of when the petition for review is filed—may consider claims of economic and technological infeasibility only if the Administrator may consider such claims in approving or rejecting a state implementation plan, we must address ourselves to the scope of the Administrator's responsibility. The Administrator's position is that he has no power whatsoever to reject a state implementation plan on the ground that it is economically or technologically infeasible, and we have previously accorded great deference to the Administrator's construction of the Clean Air Act. After surveying the relevant provisions of the Clean Air Amendments of 1970 and their legislative history, we agree that Congress intended claims of economic and technological infeasibility to be wholly foreign to the Administrator's consideration of a state implementation plan.

As we have previously recognized, the 1970 Amendments to the Clean Air Act were a drastic remedy to what was perceived as a serious and otherwise uncheckable problem of air pollution. The Amendments place the primary responsibility for formulating pollution control strategies on the States, but nonetheless subject the States to strict minimum compliance requirements. These requirements are of a "technology-forcing character" and are expressly designed to force regulated sources to develop pollution control devices that might at the time appear to be economically or technologically infeasible.

This approach is apparent on the face of § 110(a)(2). The provision sets out eight criteria that an implementation plan must satisfy, and provides that if these criteria are met and if the plan was adopted after reasonable notice and hearing, the Administrator "shall approve" the proposed state plan. The mandatory "shall" makes it quite clear that the Administrator is not to be concerned with factors other than those specified, and none of the eight factors appears to permit consideration of technological or economic infeasibility.

Our conclusion is bolstered by recognition that the Amendments do allow claims of technological and economic infeasibility to be raised in situations where consideration of such claims will not substantially interfere with the primary congressional purpose of prompt attainment of the national air quality standards. Thus, we do not hold that claims of infeasibility are never of relevance in the formulation of an implementation plan or that sources unable to comply with emission limitations must inevitably be shut down.

Perhaps the most important forum for consideration of claims of economic and technological infeasibility is before the state agency formulating the implementation plan. So long as the national standards are met, the State may select whatever mix of control devices it desires, and industries with particular economic or technological problems may seek special treatment in the plan itself. Moreover, if the industry is not exempted from, or accommodated by, the original plan, it may obtain a variance, as petitioner did in this case; and the variance, if granted after notice and a hearing, may be submitted to the EPA as a revision of the plan. . . .

. . . Technology forcing is a concept somewhat new to our national experience and it necessarily entails certain risks. But Congress considered those risks in passing the 1970 Amendments and decided that the dangers posed by uncontrolled air pollution made them worth taking. Petitioner's theory would render that considered legislative judgment a nullity, and that is a result we refuse to reach. [*Affirmed.*]

Technology-forcing does not always succeed. It is neither always possible nor always feasible to force new technological developments. In recognizing this fact, developers of the Clean Air Act have allowed the EPA in many instances to grant *compliance waivers* and *variances* from its standards. As of 1982, for example, more than 60 percent of the automobiles sold in the United States had received at least one pollution compliance waiver.

5. The Clean Air Act: Policy Trends

In the past few years, the EPA has moved to make its regulatory practices more economically efficient. All new pollution control rules are now subjected to cost-benefit analysis. The EPA has also developed specific policies to achieve air pollution control in an economically efficient manner.

THE BUBBLE CONCEPT

Traditionally, the EPA has regulated each individual pollution emission **point source** (such as a smokestack) within an industrial plant or complex. Increasingly, however, the EPA is encouraging the states, through their implementation plans, to adopt an approach called the **bubble concept**. Under the bubble concept, each plant complex is treated as if it were encased in a bubble. Instead of each pollution point source being licensed for a limited amount of pollution emission, the pollution of the plant complex as a whole is the focus of regulation. Businesses may suggest their own plans for cleaning up multiple sources of pollution within the entire complex, as long as the total pollution emitted does not exceed certain limits. This approach permits flexibility in curtailing pollution and provides businesses with economic incentives to discover new methods of control. The following case shows that the Supreme Court has upheld the EPA's authority to approve the bubble concept even in states where pollution exceeds air quality standards.

CHEVRON, U.S.A., INC. v. NATURAL RESOURCES DEFENSE COUNCIL

104 S.Ct. 2778 (1984)

The Clean Air Act Amendments of 1977 impose certain requirements on states that have not achieved the national air quality standards established by the EPA, including the requirement that such "nonattainment" states establish a permit program regulating "new or modified major stationary sources" of air pollution. A permit may be issued only after stringent conditions are met. In 1981, the EPA ruled that the term "stationary source" included treating an entire plant as a single stationary source. Thus, an existing plant could modify the equipment on only one of several pollution-emitting devices in a single plant without meeting the permit conditions as long as the total emissions within the "bubble" did not increase. The National Resources Defense Council filed a petition for a review of the EPA "bubble" policy. The Court of Appeals determined that while the Clean Air Act did not explicitly define "stationary sources," the plantwide or "bubble" definition was "inappropriate" as applied to the nonattainment program.

STEVENS, J.: When a court reviews an agency's construction of the statute which it administers, it is confronted with two questions. First, always, is the question whether Congress has directly spoken to the precise question at issue. If the intent of Congress is clear, that is the end of the matter, for the court, as well as the agency, must give effect to the unambiguously expressed intent of Congress. If, however, the court determines Congress has not directly addressed the precise question at issue, the court does not simply impose its own construction on the statute, as would be necessary in the absence of an administrative interpretation. Rather, if the statute is silent or ambiguous with respect to the specific issue, the question for the court is whether the agency's answer is based on a permissible construction of the statute.

"The power of an administrative agency to administer a congressionally created . . . program necessarily requires the formulation of policy and the making of rules to fill any gap left, implicitly or explicitly, by Congress." If Congress has explicitly left a gap for the agency to fill, there is an express delegation of authority to the agency to elucidate a specific provision of the statute by regulation. Such legislative regulations are given controlling weight unless they are arbitrary, capricious, or manifestly contrary to the statute. Sometimes the legislative delegation to an agency on a particular question is implicit rather than explicit. In such a case, a court may not substitute its own construction of a statutory provision for a reasonable interpretation made by the administrator of an agency. . . .

In light of these well-settled principles it is clear that the Court of Appeals misconceived the nature of its role in reviewing the regulations at issue. Once it determined, after its own examination of the legislation, that Congress did not actually have an intent regarding the applicability of the bubble concept to the permit program, the question before it was not whether in its view the concept is "inappropriate" in the general context of a program designed to improve air quality, but whether the Administrator's view that it is appropriate in the context of this particular program is a reasonable one. Based on the examination of the legislation and its history, we agree with the Court of Appeals that Congress did not have a specific intention on the applicability of the bubble concept in these cases, and conclude that the EPA's use of that concept here is a reasonable policy choice for the agency to make. . . .

Our review of the EPA's varying interpretations of the word "source"—both before and after the 1977 Amendments—convince us that the agency primarily responsible for administering this important legislation has consistently interpreted it flexibly—not in a sterile textual vacuum, but in the context of implementing policy decisions in a technical and complex arena. The fact that the agency has from time to time changed its interpretation of the term source does not, as respondents argue, lead us to conclude that no deference should be accorded the agency's interpretation of the statute. An initial agency interpretation is not instantly carved in stone. On the contrary, the agency, to engage in informed rulemaking, must consider varying interpretations and wisdom of its policy on a continuing basis. Moreover, the fact that the agency has adopted different definitions in different contexts adds force to the argument that the definition itself is flexible, particularly since Congress has never indicated any disapproval of a flexible reading of the statute. . . .

Judges are not experts in the field, and are not part of either political branch of the Government. Courts must, in some cases, reconcile competing political interests, but not on the basis of the judges' personal policy preferences. . . .

When a challenge to an agency construction of a statutory provision, fairly conceptualized, really centers on the wisdom of the agency's policy, rather than whether it is a reasonable choice within a gap left open by Congress, the challenge must fail. In such a case, federal judges—who have no constituency—have a duty to respect legitimate policy choices made by those who do. The responsibilities for assessing the wisdom of such policy choices and resolving the struggle between competing views of the public interest are not judicial ones: "Our Constitution vests such responsibilities in the political branches."

We hold that the EPA's definition of the term "source" is a permissible construction of the statute which seeks to accommodate progress in reducing air pollution with economic growth. . . .

[*The judgment of the Court of Appeals is reversed.*]

EMISSIONS REDUCTION BANKING

A number of states are now developing EPA-approved plans for **emissions reduction banking.** Under such plans, businesses can cut pollution beyond what the law requires and "bank" these reductions for their own future use or to sell to other companies as emission offsets. Eventually, we may be headed for a "marketable rights" approach to pollution control, where the right to discharge a certain pollutant would be auctioned off to the highest bidder. This approach would promote efficiency by offering to those who have the greatest need for pollution rights the opportunity to obtain them by bidding highest for them. Already, thousands of emissions trades have taken place around the country.

PREVENTION OF SIGNIFICANT DETERIORATION

Another important policy of the Clean Air Act is the *prevention of significant deterioration.* Under this policy, pollution emission is controlled even in areas where the air is cleaner than prevailing primary and secondary air quality standards require. In some of these areas, the EPA permits construction of new pollution emission sources according to a strictly limited scheme. In other areas it allows no new pollution emission at all. Critics of this policy argue that it prevents industry from moving into southern and western states where air quality is cleaner than standards require.

THE PERMITTING PROCESS

One of the most controversial issues involving the Clean Air Act concerns the delay and red tape caused by the permitting process. Before a business can construct new pollution emission sources, it must obtain the necessary environmental permits from the appropriate state agency. Today the estimated time needed to acquire the necessary permits to build a coal-fired electrical generating plant is five to ten years. This is nearly twice the length of time it took in the early 1970s. The formalities of the permitting process, the lack of flexibility in state implementation plans, the requirement that even minor variations in state implementation plans be approved by the EPA—all of these factors contribute to delay. Both the EPA and Congress are considering ways to streamline the permitting process.

In spite of the controversy generated by the Clean Air Act, evidence indicates that the overall air quality in the United States is steadily improving. Thus, the 16,000 quarts of air we each breathe daily are cleaner and healthier in most places than they were a decade ago (Figure 22-2). Note, however, that

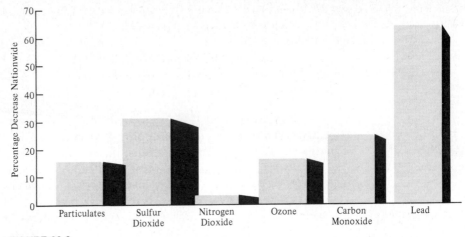

FIGURE 22-2
Emissions Reduction 1975–1982

air pollution is an international problem and that not all countries of the world have, or can afford, our air quality standards. This situation exists especially in developing nations of the world, which are striving to reach our standard of living.

RECOGNITION OF NEW AIR POLLUTANTS

In drawing up air quality standards in the 1970s, the EPA regulated only the six pollutant groups mentioned in Figure 22-2. Since that time, however, environmental scientists have discovered scores of other potentially dangerous air pollutants, including asbestos, formaldehyde, and benzene. Partially in response to lawsuits by environmental organizations, the EPA has been forced to recognize that the Clean Air Act applies to these pollutants. As of this writing, the exact role of the EPA in regulating many of these pollutants has not been determined.

An environmental problem about which there is growing awareness concerns indoor air pollution. Paints, cleaning products, furniture polishes, gas furnaces, and stoves all emit pollutants that can be harmful to human health. Some studies have found that indoor levels of certain pollutants far exceed outdoor levels, whether at work or home. Although the Clean Air Act does not apply to such pollution, the possibility of new regulation covering indoor pollution is always a possibility.

6. The Clean Water Act

Business enterprise is a major source of water pollution in the United States. Almost one-half of all water used in this country is for cooling and condensing purposes in connection with industrial activities. The resulting discharge into our rivers and lakes sometimes takes the form of heated water, called thermal effluents. In addition to thermal effluents, industry also discharges chemical and other effluents into the nation's waterways.

The principal federal law regulating water pollution is the Clean Water Act. As with the Clean Air Act, the Clean Water Act is administered primarily by the states in accordance with EPA standards. If the states do not fulfill their responsibilities, however, the federal government through the EPA can step in and enforce the law. The Clean Water Act applies to all navigable waterways, intrastate as well as interstate. As the following case shows, the term "navigable" has been interpreted quite broadly.

QUIVIRA MINING COMPANY v. EPA
765 F.2d 126 (1985)

The EPA issued permits to Quivira Mining Company and Homestake Mining Company that limited these companies' rights to discharge pollutants into Arroyo del Puerto and San Mateo Creek. The companies challenged the EPA's power to regulate discharges into these nearly dry "gullies," asserting that the EPA could only regulate discharges into "navigable waters" under the Clean Water Act.

SAFFELS, District Judge.: It is the national goal of the Clean Water Act to eliminate the discharge of pollutants into navigable waters. The term "navigable waters" means "the waters of the United States, including the territorial seas." In *United States v. Earth Sciences, Inc.* . . . this court noted that the Clean Water Act is designed to regulate to the fullest extent possible sources emitting pollution into rivers, streams and lakes. "The touchstone of the regulatory scheme is that those needing to use the waters for waste distribution must seek and obtain a permit to discharge that waste, with the quantity and quality of the discharge regulated." It is the intent of the Clean Water Act to cover, as much as possible, all waters of the United States instead of just some.

The extent of the Clean Water Act's coverage of discharges of pollution is illustrated by a review of some of the cases which have been before the United States Court of Appeals for the Tenth Circuit. In *Ward v. Coleman*, . . . the court found that Boogie Creek, a tributary of the Arkansas River, is a navigable water of the United States for purposes of the Clean Water Act because the Arkansas River is navigable in fact. In *United States v. Earth Sciences, Inc.*, . . . the court found the Rito Seco to be a "water of the United States," although it is not navigable in fact nor does it transport any goods or materials, and although it is located entirely in Costilla County, Colorado. There, the facts were that the stream supported trout and some beaver, the water collected in the reservoirs was used for agricultural irrigation, and the resulting products were sold into interstate commerce. The court stated, "It seems clear Congress intended to regulate discharges made into every creek, stream, river or body of water that in any way may affect interstate commerce. Every court to discuss the issue has used a commerce power approach and agreed upon that interpretation." In *United States v. Texas Pipe Line Co.*, the court found that the Clean Water Act covered oil spilled into an unnamed tributary of Caney Creek, which discharges into Clear Boggie Creek, itself a tributary of the Red River.

This court's findings in *Earth Sciences* and *Texas Pipe Line* compel a finding herein affirming the decision of the EPA. Substantial evidence here supports the Administrator's findings that both the Arroyo del Puerto and San Mateo Creek are waters of the United States. Substantial evidence before the Administrator supports his finding that during times of intense rainfall, there can be a surface connection between the Arroyo del Puerto, San Mateo Creek and navigable-in-fact streams. Further, the record supports the finding that both the Arroyo del Puerto and San Mateo Creek flow for a period after the time of discharge of pollutants into the waters. Further, the flow continues regularly through underground acquifers fed by the surface flow of the San Mateo Creek and Arroyo del Puerto into navigable-in-fact streams. The court finds that the impact on interstate commerce is sufficient enough to satisfy the commerce clause. And, as noted above, it was the clear intent of Congress to regulate waters of the United States to the fullest extent possible under the commerce clause. [*Affirmed.*]

The Clean Water Act sets goals to eliminate water pollution. Principally, these goals are to make the nation's waterways safe for swimming and other recreational use and clean enough for the protection of fish, shellfish, and wildlife. The law sets strict deadlines and strong enforcement provisions, which must be followed by industry, municipalities, and other water polluters. Enforcement of the Clean Water Act revolves around its permit discharge system. Without being subject to criminal penalties, no polluter can discharge pollutants from any point source (that is, a pipe) without a permit, and municipal as well as industrial dischargers must obtain permits. The EPA has issued guidelines for state permit programs and has approved those programs that meet the guidelines.

Under the Clean Water Act, industries have a two-step sequence for cleanup of industrial wastes discharged into rivers and streams. The first step requires polluters to install best practicable technology (BPT). The second demands installation of best available technology (BAT). Various timetables apply in achieving these steps, according to the type of pollutant being discharged. In 1984, the EPA announced application of the bubble concept to water pollution from the steel industry.

In addition to the Clean Water Act, two other acts related to water pollution control are administered by the EPA. One, the Marine Protection, Research, and Sanctuaries Act of 1972, requires a permit system for the discharge or dumping of various material into the seas. The other is the Safe Water Drinking Act of 1974, which has forced the EPA to set maximum drinking water contaminant levels for certain organic and inorganic chemicals, pesticides, and microbiological pollutants.

7. The Noise Control Act

The Preamble to the Constitution establishes as a constitutional purpose the assurance of "domestic tranquillity." This phrase has been legally defined as the state or character of being quiet, or "quietness." Nearly 200 years since the Constitution's ratification, however, our society is noisier than ever, despite the fact that excessive noise has been implicated not only in causing deafness but also in contributing to high blood pressure, heart disease, stress, and emotional disturbance. The EPA estimates that some seventy million Americans presently live with neighborhood noise levels sufficiently high to cause annoyance and dissatisfaction. A recent Census Bureau survey reports that street noise was the most frequently mentioned neighborhood problem.

To combat the growing effects of noise pollution, Congress passed the Noise Control Act of 1972. In the opening sections of the act, Congress lists, as the major sources of noise, transportation vehicles and equipment, machinery, appliances, and other products used in commerce. The act aims at controlling the noise emission of these manufactured items rather than at limiting outside noise levels.

Under the act, the EPA must set limits on noise emission for any product which is identified as a major source of noise or which falls into certain specified categories. In setting these standards the EPA must consider the noise levels necessary to protect public health and welfare, the best available technology, and the cost of compliance. The EPA has set or proposed standards for trucks, motorcycles, buses, air compressors, rock drills and pavement breakers, bulldozers, front-end loaders, power mowers, and air conditioners.

Most of the standards will take effect over a several-year period and apply only to new products. Manufacturers of these products are held to warrant to purchasers that its product complies with the standards, and no state or local government may enact or enforce noise emission levels which differ from them. For any product which the EPA determines emits noise capable of adversely affecting the public welfare or which is sold on the basis of its effectiveness in reducing noise, the agency must require that notice of this product's noise level be given to each prospective purchaser.

The act prohibits (1) commercial distribution by a manufacturer of a product not complying with designated noise levels, (2) the removal from a product of a required noise control device, (3) the use of the product after removal, (4) the distribution of a product without a required notice of noise level and removal of this notice, and (5) the importation of a product not in compliance with designated noise levels. The EPA enforces these prohibitions through both criminal and civil remedies. It may also require manufacturers to maintain records and conduct tests of their products.

In the early 1980s, implementation and enforcement of the Noise Control Act slowed considerably. It remains to be seen whether noise control in the future will gain a significant role in environmental regulation.

8. The Pesticide Control Acts

Pests, especially insects and mice, destroy over 10 percent of all crops grown in the United States, causing several billion dollars of damage annually. In many underdeveloped countries, however, a much greater percentage of total crop production is lost to pests, as high as 40 to 50 percent in countries such as India. Perhaps the principal reason for our lower rate of crop loss is that the United States uses more pesticides per acre than any other country.

The widespread, continual application of pesticides presents environmental problems, however. Not only is it dangerous to wildlife, particularly birds and fish, but it may eventually threaten our agricultural capacity itself. Rapidly breeding pests gradually become immune to the application of pesticides, and researchers may not always be able to invent new poisons to kill them.

Federal regulation of pesticides is accomplished primarily through two statutes: the Federal Insecticide, Fungicide, and Rodenticide Act of 1947, as amended, and the Federal Environmental Pesticide Control Act of 1972 (FEPCA). Both statutes require the registration and labeling of agricultural pesticides, although FEPCA coverage extends to the application of pesticides as well.

Under the acts, the administrator of the EPA is directed to register those pesticides which are properly labeled, which meet the claims made as to their effectiveness, and which will not have unreasonable adverse effects on the environment. The phrase "unreasonable adverse effects on the environment" is defined as "any unreasonable risk to man or the environment, taking into account the economic, social, and environmental costs and benefits of the use of any pesticide." In addition to its authority to require registration of pesticides, the EPA classifies pesticides for general use or restricted use. In the latter category, the EPA may impose further restrictions requiring application only by a trained applicator or with the approval of a trained consultant.

The EPA has a variety of enforcement powers to ensure that pesticide goals are met, including the power to deny or suspend registration. For instance, in late 1983 the EPA banned most uses of the controversial pesticide ethylene bromide.

There are two chief criticisms of pesticide control: one coming from affected businesses, the other from the environmental movement. Pesticide manufacturers complain that the lengthy, expensive testing procedures required by the FEPCA registration process delay useful pesticides from reaching the market and inhibit new research. On the other hand, many in the environmental movement contend that our country's pesticide control policy is hypocritical in that the FEPCA does not apply to pesticides which U.S. manufacturers ship to foreign countries. Companies can sell overseas what they cannot sell in this country.

9. The Solid Waste Disposal Act

Pollution problems cannot always be neatly categorized. For instance, solid waste disposal processes often create pollution in several environmentally related forms. When solid waste is burned, it can cause air pollution and violate the Clean Air Act. When dumped into rivers, streams, and lakes, solid waste can pollute the water beyond amounts permitted under the Clean Water Act. Machinery used in solid waste disposal can also be subject to the regulation of the Noise Control Act.

By all accounts, solid waste pollution problems during the last twenty-five years have grown as the population has risen and we have become more affluent and productive. Currently, total solid wastes produced yearly in the United States exceed 5 billion tons, or almost 25 tons for every individual in the population. Half this amount is agricultural waste, another third is mineral waste, and the remainder is industrial, institutional, and residential waste. Some wastes are toxic and hazardous while others stink or attract pests. All present disposal problems of significant proportion.

The Solid Waste Disposal Act represents the primary federal effort in solid waste control. Congress recognized in this act that the main responsibility for nontoxic waste management rests with regional, state, and local management and limited the federal role in this area. Under this act, the federal role in nontoxic waste management is limited mainly to promoting research and providing technical and financial assistance to the states.

In responding to solid waste disposal problems, state and local governments have taken a variety of approaches. These include development of sanitary landfills, requiring that solid waste be separated into categories facilitating disposal and recycling, and granting tax breaks for industries using recycled materials. A report by the Council of State Governments noted that there are over a thousand community recycling centers and that over a hundred cities and counties have waste-to-energy facilities. Nine states with 25 percent of the nation's population have beverage container deposit laws, the so-called "bottle bills."

Some companies have incorporated waste disposal provisions into their codes of ethics, as the following excerpt from the Caterpillar Code of Ethics illustrates.

WASTE DISPOSAL

Proper means for disposal of municipal and industrial wastes are essential to society. For example, continued operation of Caterpillar facilities depends upon availability of landfills and contract services for disposal.

When practical, Caterpillar reuses or recycles byproducts of manufacturing processes. But in some cases, reuse and recycling aren't practical. It then becomes necessary that waste materials be handled and disposed of in a manner consistent with the public interest, as expressed in applicable laws and regulations.

Aside from government regulations, we shall make certain that disposition of Caterpillar wastes is carried out in a manner consistent with the ethical business practices set forth in the Code. When contractors are involved, they should demonstrate necessary technical competence, maintain a high level of performance, and otherwise meet Caterpillar standards regarding long-lasting supplier relationships.

In 1976, Congress amended the Solid Wastes Disposal Act with the National Resource Conservation and Recovery Act. The next section discusses this act and other statutes related to toxic wastes.

10. Toxic and Hazardous Substances: Introduction

According to the opinion research organization Yankelovich, Skelly and White, the control of toxic and hazardous chemicals "ranks first" on the public's list of where the government's regulation of industry is needed. In the last several years, regulation of such chemicals has been expanding rapidly. We can divide the government's regulation of business in this area into three categories: (1) regulation of the use of toxic chemicals, (2) regulation of toxic and hazardous waste disposal, and (3) regulation of toxic and hazardous waste cleanup.

11. Toxic Substances Control Act

Even as the Clean Air and Water Acts are slowly beginning to diminish many types of air and water pollution, attention is being drawn to another environmental problem which is potentially the most serious of all: toxic substances. Hardly a day passes without the news media reporting some new instance of alleged threat to human health and well-being from one or another of the chemical substances so important to manufacturing, farming, mining, and other aspects of modern life.

Threats to human welfare from toxic substances are not new to history. Some people suggest that poisoning from lead waterpipes and drinking vessels may have depleted the ranks of the ruling class of ancient Rome and thus contributed to the downfall of the Roman Empire. More recently, some think that the "mad hatters" of the nineteenth-century fur and felt trades likely suffered brain disorders from inhaling the vapors of mercury used in their crafts. Today, however, the presence of toxic substances in the environment is made more serious by the fact that over 70,000 industrial and agricultural chemical compounds are in commercial use, and new chemicals, a significant percentage of which are toxic, are being introduced into the marketplace at the rate of over 1,000 substances annually.

To meet the special environmental problems posed by the use of toxic chemicals, Congress in 1976 enacted the Toxic Substances Control Act (TSCA). Prior to passage of the TSCA, there was no coordinated effort to evaluate effects of these chemical compounds. Some of these compounds are beneficial to society and present no threat to the environment. Some, however, are both toxic and long-lasting, a fact which in the past has been uncovered only after these compounds were introduced into wide use and became important to manufacturing and farming. The primary purpose of the TSCA is to force an early evaluation of suspect chemicals before they become economically important.

The EPA collects information under TSCA sections which require that manufacturers and distributors report to the EPA any information they possess indicating that a chemical substance presents a "substantial risk" of injury to health or the environment. The TSCA further demands that the EPA be given advance notice before the manufacture of new chemical substances or the processing of any substance for a significant new use. Based on the results of its review, the EPA can take action to stop or limit introduction of new chemicals if they threaten human health or the environment with unreasonable risks.

The law also authorizes the EPA to require manufacturers to test their chemicals for possible harmful effects. Since not all the 70,000 chemicals in commerce can be tested simultaneously, the EPA has developed a priority scheme for selecting substances for testing baased on whether or not the chemicals cause cancer, birth defects, or gene mutations.

In view of the beneficial role which many chemical substances play in all aspects of production and consumption. Congress directed the EPA through the TSCA to consider the economic and social impact of its decisions as well as the environmental one. In this respect, the TSCA is unlike the Clean Air Act, which requires that certain pollution standards be met without regard for economic factors.

12. Natural Resource Conservation and Recovery Act

The congressional Office of Technology Assessment reports that more than a ton of hazardous waste per citizen is dumped annually into the nation's environment. A major environmental problem has been how to ensure that the generators of toxic wastes dispose of them safely. In the past, there have been instances where even some otherwise responsible companies have placed highly toxic wastes in the hands of less-than-reputable disposal contractors.

To help ensure proper handling and disposal of hazardous and toxic wastes, Congress in 1976 amended the Solid Waste Disposal Act by the Resource Conservation and Recovery Act (RCRA). Under the RCRA, a generator of wastes has two primary obligations. The first is to determine whether its wastes qualify as hazardous under RCRA. The second is to see that such wastes are properly transported to a disposal facility which has an EPA permit or license.

The EPA lists a number of hazardous wastes, and a generator can determine if a nonlisted waste is hazardous in terms of several chemical characteristics specified by the EPA. The RCRA accomplishes proper disposal of hazardous wastes through the *manifest system.* This system requires a generator to prepare a manifest document which designates a licensed facility for disposal purposes. The generator then gives copies of the manifest to the transporter of the waste. After receiving hazardous wastes, the disposal facility must return a copy of the manifest to the generator. In this fashion, the generator knows the waste has received proper disposal.

Failure to receive this manifest copy from the disposal facility within certain time limits requires the generator to notify the EPA. Under RCRA, the EPA has various investigatory powers. The act also prescribes various recordkeeping requirements and assesses penalties for failure to comply with its provisions.

In 1984, a coalition of chemical industry executives and environmental leaders formed Clean Sites, Inc. This nonprofit organization proposes to obtain industry know-how and resources to promote voluntary cleanup of toxic dump sites.

13. The Superfund

After passage of TSCA and RCRA in 1976, regulation of toxic and hazardous substances was still incomplete. These acts did not deal with problems of the cleanup costs of unsafe hazardous waste dumps or spills, which are often substantial. Many dump sites are abandoned and date back as far as the nineteenth century. Even current owners of unsafe dump sites are frequently financially incapable of cleaning up hazardous wastes. The same applies to transporters and others who cause spills or unauthorized discharges of hazardous wastes.

In 1980, Congress created the Comprehensive Environmental Response, Compensation, and Liability Act to address these problems. Known as the **Superfund,** this act has allotted billions of dollars for environmental cleanup of dangerous hazardous wastes. Taxes on industry finance most of the fund. The EPA estimates that the Superfund program will eventually have to clean up as many as 2,200 sites. As of 1985, long-term cleanups had begun at only 134 sites.

The act requires anyone who releases unauthorized amounts of hazardous substances into the environment to notify the government. Whether it is notified or not, the government has the power to order those responsible to clean up such releases. Refusal to obey can lead to a suit for reimbursement for any cleanup monies spent from the Superfund plus punitive damages of up to triple the cleanup costs. The government can also recover damages for injury done to natural resources. To date the biggest Superfund case involved Shell Oil and the U.S. Army. These parties agreed to clean up a site outside Denver. Total costs may exceed $1 billion.

TABLE 22-3   Recent Hazardous Waste Settlements

Company	Amount	Location
Alcoa	$5.6 million	Greenup, Ill.
Occidental	$30 million	Niagara Falls, N.Y.
Ten companies	$50 million	Baton Rouge, La.
Waste Management, Inc.	$10.5 million	Vickery, Ohio
Diamond Shamrock	$12 million	Newark, N.J.

The act imposes a type of strict liability on those responsible for unauthorized discharges of hazardous wastes. Thus, no negligence need be proved. An additional strict liability falls on generators of hazardous wastes. They are strictly liable for *any* illegal discharge of hazardous waste as long as they have a contractual relationship with the responsible parties. For example, a chemical company whose transporter of wastes causes an unauthorized release of toxic chemicals, or whose disposal facility dumps chemicals illegally, is strictly liable for any resulting injury.

Finally, take note that both the Clean Air Act and Clean Water Act also contain provisions related to government suits to recover costs related to the cleanup of toxic chemicals. Suits under the Superfund and other acts are growing rapidly (see Table 22-3) and will be a major area of environmental litigation in coming years.

14. Radiation

In 1979, the nuclear power plant accident at the Three Mile Island installation in Pennsylvania focused the nation's attention on the potential hazards of radiation pollution as thousands of nearby residents were evacuated. Although no single piece of legislation comprehensively controls radiation pollution and no one agency is responsible for administering legislation in this technologically complex area, overall responsibility for such control rests with the Nuclear Regulatory Commission. The EPA, however, does have general authority to conduct testing and to provide technical assistance in the area of radiation pollution control. Also, the Clean Air Act, the Federal Water Pollution Control Act, and the Ocean Dumping Act all contain sections applicable to radiation discharges into the air and water.

SUITS BY PRIVATE INDIVIDUALS

15. Introduction

Achieving environmental goals requires coordinated strategy and implementation. As private citizens, individuals and groups of individuals lack both the power and foresight necessary to control pollution on a broad scale. There is a role, however, for the private control of private action in two principal areas.

First, most of the environmental laws, such as the Clean Air and Water Acts, contain "citizen enforcement" provisions. These provisions grant private individuals and groups the standing to sue to challenge failures to comply with the environmental laws. In many instances, private citizens can sue polluters directly to force them to cease violating the law. Private citizens also have standing to sue public agencies (the EPA) to require them to adopt regulations or implement enforcement against private polluters which the environmental laws require.

A second area of private control of private action lies in the common law and its state codifications. When pollution directly injures private citizens, they may sue offending polluters under various theories of tort law. Thus, the traditional deterrence of tort law contributes to private control of private action. The last section further develops the common law's role in pollution control.

16. Common Law Tort Theories and Pollution

Examination of the common law and pollution control reveals little understanding of the interdependence between ourselves and our environment. Instead, common law theories, as they have been applied to environmental problems of pollution and the like, focus mainly on the action of one person as it injures the health, or interferes with the property rights, of another. In other words, the common law attacks the pollution problem by using the traditional theories of tort such as nuisance, negligence, and trespass.

NUISANCE

The principal tort theory used in pollution control has been that of nuisance. The law relating to nuisance is somewhat vague, but in most jurisdictions the common law has been put into statutory form. Several common elements exist in the law of nuisance in most states. To begin with, there are two types of nuisances: public and private.

A *public nuisance* arises from an act which causes inconvenience or damage to the public in the exercise of rights common to everyone. In the environmental area, air, water, and noise pollution can all constitute a public nuisance if they affect common rights. More specifically, industrial waste discharge that kills the fish in a stream may be held a public nuisance since fishing rights are commonly possessed by the public. Public nuisance actions may be brought only by a public official, not private individuals, unless the latter have suffered some special damage to their persons or property as a result of the public nuisance.

Any unreasonable use of one's property so as to cause substantial interference with the enjoyment or use of another's land establishes a common law *private nuisance*. The unreasonableness of the interference is measured by a balancing process in which the character, extent, and duration of harm to the plaintiff is weighed against the social utility of the defendant's activity and its appropriateness to its location. Since society needs industrial activity as well as natural tranquillity, people must put up with a certain amount of smoke, dust, noise, and polluted water if they live in concentrated areas of industry. But what may be an appropriate industrial use of land in a congested urban area may be a private nuisance if it occurs in a rural or residential location.

Take note that the proving of nuisance does not demand that a property owner be found negligent. An unreasonable use of one's land does not mean that one's *conduct* is unreasonable. In the following case, the Rhode Island Supreme Court ruled that the defendants' chemical dump site constituted a nuisance even though the defendants alleged that the plaintiff's case had not established negligence.

WOOD v. PICILLO
443 A.2d 1244 (R.I. 1982)

WEISBERGER, J.: This is an appeal from a judgment of the Superior Court entered after trial without the intervention of a jury. Finding that the defendants created a public and private nuisance in maintaining a hazardous waste dump site on their Coventry farm, the trial justice enjoined further chemical disposal operations at the defendants' property and ordered the defendants to finance cleanup and removal of the toxic wastes. The defendants now contend that the trial justice erred in finding the disposal operation to be a public and private nuisance. We strongly disagree. Accordingly, the judgment of the Superior Court is affirmed.

The testimony elicited during the extensive hearings conducted on this case revealed the following dramatic events. On September 30, 1977, an enormous explosion erupted into fifty-foot flames in a trench on defendants' Coventry property. Firefighters responded to the blaze but could not extinguish the flame. As the fire raged within the trench, additional explosions resounded. From the conflagration billowed clouds of thick black smoke that extended "as far as the eye could see on the eastern horizon."

Not unexpectedly, the extraordinary blaze aroused the interest of various state officials. The state fire marshal declared the dump site a fire hazard and ordered defendants to cease disposal activity and to remove all flammable wastes. . . .Despite the fire marshall's order and the ongoing official investigations the dumping and burying of chemical wastes continued. . . .

Several witnesses testified at trial to the immediate and future effects of the chemical presence. Neighbors of the Picillos reported that in the year preceding the fire, tractor-trailer traffic to and from defendants' property greatly increased. According to the testimony many of the trucks bore "Flammable" warnings and the name of a chemical company. The neighbors also testified that on several occasions during the summer of 1977 pungent odors forced them to remain inside their homes. The odors were described variously as "sickening," "heavy," "sweet," "musky," "terrible," and "like plastic burning." One neighbor testified that the odors induced in her severe nausea and headaches, while another stated that on one occasion fumes from the Picillo property caused her to cough severely and to suffer a sore throat that lasted several days.

According to the experts, the chemicals present on defendants' property and in the marsh, left unchecked, would eventually threaten wildlife and humans well downstream from the dump site. Mr. Frank Stevenson, the principal sanitary engineer for the DEM, and Dr. William Kelly, an Associate Professor of Civil and Environmental Engineering at the University of Rhode Island, testified as experts in soil mechanics and groundwater hydrology. The experts established that the soil at the dump site consisted of an unstratified composition of sand, gravel, and silt of varying sizes. The permeable nature of this soil would allow any liquid or chemical in or on it to percolate down to the water table and to travel with the groundwater in a northerly flow. The opinion of the experts was buttressed by the documented presence of toluene, xylene, chloroform, trichloroethane, and trichloroethylene in the northern marsh and in several monitoring wells. The only possible source of the pollutants, according to Dr. Kelly, was the Picillo dump site.

Expert testimony further revealed that the chemicals had traveled and would continue to travel from the dump site into the marsh at the rate of about one foot per day. From the marsh, predicted the experts, the chemicals would flow in a southwesterly direction into the Quinabog River and its tributaries Moosup River and Roaring Brook, and Wickford Pond. These waters are inhabited by fish and used by humans for recreational and agricultural purposes.

On these and other facts the trial justice determined the dump site to be a public and private nuisance. He found also that the cur-rent danger to the public health and safety posed by the chemical presence would worsen unless effective remedial action was quickly taken. The trial judge thus permanently enjoined disposal operations on defendants' property and ordered that all chemicals and contaminated earth be removed to a licensed disposal facility. Because defendants had in the past displayed an unwillingness or inability to remedy the danger, the Superior Court justice authorized plaintiffs to effectuate cleanup of defendants' property at defendants' expense.

The defendants contend that the evidence adduced at trial was insufficient to support a finding of public and private nuisance. The defendants point to two alleged evidentiary inadequacies: (1) that plaintiffs failed to establish any significant injury to persons or to natural wildlife and (2) that plaintiffs failed to meet their obligation to show that defendants acted negligently in disposing chemical wastes on their property. We find both assertions to be without merit.

In his brief defendant has accurately stated that the injury produced by an actionable nuisance "must be real and not fanciful or imaginary." The defendant next suggests that the injuries in the case at bar are of the insubstantial, unactionable type. It is this statement, however, rather than the purported injuries, that is fanciful. The testimony to which reference is made in this opinion clearly establishes that defendants' dumping operations have already caused substantial injury to defendants' neighbors and threaten to cause incalculable damage to the general public. The Picillos' neighbors have displayed physical symptoms of exposure to toxic chemicals and have been restricted in the reasonable use of their property. Moreover, expert testimony showed that the chemical presence on defendants' property threatens both aquatic wildlife and human beings with possible death, cancer, and liver disease. Thus, there was ample evidence at trial to support the finding of substantial injury implicit in the trial justice's finding of public and private nuisance.

The defendants' remaining contention is that Rhode Island case law requires plaintiffs to prove negligence as an element of the nuisance case and that plaintiffs failed to do so. Generally, this court has not required plaintiffs to establish negligence in nuisance actions. . . . The essential element of an actionable nuisance is that persons have suffered harm or are threatened with injuries that they ought not have to bear. Distinguished from negligence liability, liability in nuisance is predicated upon unreasonable injury rather than upon unreasonable conduct. Thus, plaintiffs may recover in nuisance despite the otherwise nontortious nature of the conduct which creates the injury.

For the reasons stated, the defendants' appeal is denied and dismissed. [*Affirmed.*]

OTHER TORT DECISIONS

Private plaintiffs in pollution cases frequently allege the applicability of other tort doctrines besides that of nuisance. These doctrines, however, do overlap that of nuisance, which is really a field of tort liability rather than a type of conduct.

One such doctrine is that of trespass. A defendant is liable for trespass if without right she or he intentionally enters land in possession of another, or causes something to do so. The entrance is considered intentional if the defendant knew that it was substantially certain to result from her or his conduct. Thus, airborne particles which fall on a plaintiff's property can constitute a trespass. In recent years, many courts have merged the theories of nuisance and trespass to such an extent that before plaintiffs can recover for a particle trespass, they must prove that the harm done to them exceeds the social utility of the defendant's enterprise.

Negligence doctrine is sometimes used by private plaintiffs in environmental pollution cases. The basis for the negligence tort lies in the defendant's breach of his or her duty to use ordinary and reasonable care toward the plaintiff, which proximately (foreseeably) causes the plaintiff injury. A factory's failure to use available pollution control equipment may be evidence of its failure to employ "reasonable care."

Finally, some courts recognize the applicability in pollution cases of *strict liability tort doctrine.* This tort liability arises when the defendant injures the plaintiff's person or property by voluntarily engaging in ultrahazardous activity which necessarily involves a risk of serious harm that cannot be eliminated through the exercise of the utmost care. No finding of fault, or failure of reasonable care, on the defendant's part is necessary. This doctrine has been employed in situations involving the use of poisons, such as in crop dusting and certain industrial work, the storage and use of explosives, and the storage of water in large quantities in a dangerous place.

Increasing numbers of private plaintiffs are suing companies for pollution-related harm. In one recent case, a chemical company settled with three plaintiffs for $2.7 million.

REVIEW QUESTIONS

1 For each term in the left-hand column, match the most appropriate description in the right-hand column:

(1) EIS

(2) Point source

(3) Prevention of significant deterioration

(4) Superfund

(5) Nuisance

(6) Bubble concept

(7) Manifest system

(8) Primary air quality standards

(a) An unreasonable use of one's land which interferes with the use or enjoyment of another's land

(b) Treating several point sources at a plant as one source

(c) A process which must be followed by federal agencies before undertaking major actions which significantly affect the environment

(d) A smokestack, pipe, or other opening which discharges pollution

(e) The Comprehensive Environmental Response, Compensation, and Liability Act

(f) The tracking process for toxic waste disposal

(g) Air pollution levels necessary to protect human health

(h) The policy of preventing additional pollution in certain areas which have air cleaner than required by primary standards

2 Discuss why the way government regulates the environmental impact of its decision making is of significant interest to the business community.

3 Your firm has been hired to build a large government facility near a residential neighborhood. A committee of residents has been formed to oppose the building. You have been asked to assist in writing the EIS. What factors must your EIS take into consideration?

4 Outline criticisms of the EIS process. Why are state EISs often less helpful in evaluating complex environmental factors than are those prepared by federal agencies?

5 The Avila Timber Company has asked for and been granted permission by the Department of the Interior to cut 40 acres of timber from the 10,000-acre Oconee National Forest. Prior to the actual logging, a local environmental group files suit in federal district court contending that the Department of Interior has not filed an EIS. Can the group challenge the department's action? Analyze whether an EIS should be filed in light of the facts given.

6 An EIS prepared for the Army Corps of Engineers by a private consulting firm concludes that the value of the farmland which will be submerged by a proposed dam is greater than the navigational benefits which the dam will bring. Is the Corps prohibited from building the dam because of this conclusion? Discuss.

7 What does it mean to say that the Clean Air Act is "technology-forcing"? What happens when an industry cannot meet the technological standards set by the EPA?

8 The Akins Corporation wishes to build a new smelting facility in Owens County, an area where air pollution exceeds primary air standards. What legal difficulties may they face? What solutions might you suggest for these difficulties?

9 What is the difference between "effluents" and "emissions"?

10 What is the difference between an individual point-source approach and a bubble policy approach to dealing with factory pollution? For the factory owner, what are the advantages of employing the bubble concept?

11 Bug Control Incorporated desires to product a new pesticide for control of fire ants. Before beginning manufacture, it must follow what process under the pesticide control acts?

12 Your company has decided to produce a new chemical which has great promise in manufacture of synthetic fabrics. It is recognized that if this chemical is used incorrectly or disposed of improperly, there may be risk to human health or to the environment. What steps must your company take prior to actual production to avoid legal difficulties with the EPA?

13 As a manufacturer of paints, you need to dispose of certain production byproducts which are highly toxic. Discuss the process which the law requires you to follow in disposing of these products.

14 An abandoned radioactive waste site is discovered by local authorities. The waste came from a company that manufactured radium watch faces and is now out of business. Who will pay to clean up these radioactive wastes? Discuss.

15 Cedar Creek flows into the Lethe River. Cedar Creek is barely 6 feet wide, and the Lethe River is navigable only by raft or canoe. Would the EPA have regulatory authority over pollutants discharged into Cedar Creek? Explain.

Appendix 1

We the People of the United States, in Order to form a more perfect Union, establish Justice, insure domestic Tranquility, provide for the common defence, promote the general Welfare, and secure the Blessings of Liberty to ourselves and our Posterity, do ordain and establish this Constitution for the United States of America.

Article I

SECTION 1
All legislative Powers herein granted shall be vested in a Congress of the United States, which shall consist of a Senate and House of Representatives.

SECTION 2
The House of Representatives shall be composed of Members chosen every second Year by the People of the several States, and the Electors in each State shall have the Qualifications requisite for Electors of the most numerous Branch of the State Legislature.

No Person shall be a Representative who shall not have attained to the Age of twenty five Years, and been seven Years a Citizen of the United States, and who shall not, when elected, be an Inhabitant of that State in which he shall be chosen.

Representatives and direct Taxes shall be apportioned among the several States which may be included within this Union, according to their respective Numbers, which shall be determined by adding to the whole Number of free Persons, including those bound to Service for a Term of Years, and excluding Indians not taxed, three fifths of all other Persons. The actual Enumeration shall be made within three Years after the first Meeting of the Congress of the United States, and within every subsequent Term of ten Years, in such Manner as they shall by Law direct. The Number of Representatives shall not exceed one for every thirty Thousand, but each State shall have at Least one Representative; and until such enumeration shall be made, the State of New Hampshire shall be entitled to chuse three, Massachusetts eight, Rhode Island and Providence Plantations one, Connecticut five, New-York six, New Jersey four, Pennsylvania eight, Delaware one, Maryland six, Virginia ten, North Carolina five, South Carolina five, and Georgia three.

When vacancies happen in the Representation from any State, the Executive Authority thereof shall issue Writs of Election to fill such Vacancies.

The House of Representatives shall chuse their Speaker and other Officers; and shall have the sole Power of Impeachment.

SECTION 3

The Senate of the United States shall be composed of two Senators from each State, chosen by the Legislature thereof, for six Years; and each Senator shall have one Vote.

Immediately after they shall be assembled in Consequence of the Election, they shall be divided as equally as may be into three Classes. The Seats of the Senators of the first Class shall be vacated at the Expiration of the second Year, of the second Class at the Expiration of the fourth Year, and of the third Class at the Expiration of the sixth Year, so that one third may be chosen every second Year; and if Vacancies happen by Resignation, or otherwise, during the Recess of the Legislature of any State, the Executive thereof may make temporary Appointments until the next Meeting of the Legislature, which shall then fill such Vacancies.

No Person shall be a Senator who shall not have attained to the Age of thirty Years, and been nine Years a Citizen of the United States, and who shall not, when elected, be an Inhabitant of that State for which he shall be chosen.

The Vice President of the United States shall be President of the Senate, but shall have no Vote, unless they be equally divided.

The Senate shall chuse their other Officers, and also a President pro tempore, in the Absence of the Vice President, or when he shall exercise the Office of President of the United States.

The Senate shall have the sole Power to try all Impeachments. When sitting for that Purpose, they shall be on Oath or Affirmation. When the President of the United States is tried, the Chief Justice shall preside: And no Person shall be convicted without the Concurrence of two thirds of the Members present.

Judgment in Cases of Impeachment shall not extend further than to removal from Office, and disqualification to hold and enjoy any Office of honor, Trust or Profit under the United States: but the Party convicted shall nevertheless be liable and subject to Indictment, Trial, Judgment and Punishment, according to Law.

SECTION 4

The Times, Places and Manner of holding Elections for Senators and Representatives, shall be prescribed in each State by the Legislature thereof: but the Congress may at any time by Law make or alter such Regulations, except as to the Places of chusing Senators.

The Congress shall assemble at least once in every Year, and such Meeting shall be on the first Monday in December, unless they shall by Law appoint a different Day.

SECTION 5

Each House shall be the Judge of the Elections, Returns and Qualifications of its own Members, and a Majority of each shall constitute a Quorum to do Business; but a smaller Number may adjourn from day to day, and may be authorized to compel the Attendance of absent Members, in such Manner, and under such Penalties as each House may provide.

Each House may determine the Rules of its Proceedings, punish its Members for disorderly Behaviour, and, with the concurrence of two thirds, expel a Member.

Each House shall keep a Journal of its Proceedings, and from time to time publish the same, excepting such Parts as may in their Judgment require Secrecy; and the Yeas and Nays of the Members of either House on any question shall, at the Desire of one fifth of those Present, be entered on the Journal.

Neither House, during the Session of Congress, shall, without the Consent of the other, adjourn for more than three days, nor to any other Place than that in which the two Houses shall be sitting.

SECTION 6

The Senators and Representatives shall receive a Compensation for their Services, to be ascertained by Law, and paid out of the Treasury of the United States. They shall in all Cases, except Treason, Felony and Breach of the Peace, be privileged from Arrest during their Attendance at the Session of their respective Houses, and in going to and returning from the same; and for any Speech or Debate in either House, they shall not be questioned in any other Place.

No Senator or Representative shall, during the Time for which he was elected, be appointed to any civil Office under the Authority of the United States, which shall have been created, or the Emoluments whereof shall have been encreased during such time; and no Person holding any Office under the United States, shall be a Member of either House during his Continuance in Office.

SECTION 7

All Bills for raising Revenue shall originate in the House of Representatives; but the Senate may propose or concur with Amendments as on other Bills.

Every Bill which shall have passed the House of Representatives and the Senate, shall, before it become a Law, be presented to the President of the United States; If he approve he shall sign it, but if not he shall return it, with his Objections to that House in which it shall have originated, who shall enter the Objections at large on their Journal, and proceed to reconsider it. If after such Reconsideration two thirds of that House shall agree to pass the Bill, it shall be sent, together with the Objections, to the other House, by which it shall likewise be reconsidered, and if approved by two thirds of that House, it shall become a Law. But in all such Cases the Votes of both Houses shall be determined by Yeas and Nays, and the Names of the Persons voting for and against the Bill shall be entered on the Journal of each House respectively. If any Bill shall not be returned by the President within ten Days (Sundays excepted) after it shall have been presented to him, the Same shall be a Law, in like Manner as if he had signed it, unless the Congress by their Adjournment prevent its Return, in which Case it shall not be a Law.

Every Order, Resolution, or Vote to which the Concurrence of the Senate and House of Representatives may be necessary (except on a question of Adjournment) shall be presented to the President of the United States; and before the Same shall take Effect, shall be approved by him, or being disapproved by him, shall be repassed by two thirds of the Senate and House of Representatives, according to the Rules and Limitations prescribed in the Case of a Bill.

SECTION 8

The Congress shall have Power to lay and collect Taxes, Duties, Imposts and Excises, to pay the Debts and provide for the common Defence and general Welfare of the United States; but all Duties, Imposts and Excises shall be uniform throughout the United States;

To borrow Money on the credit of the United States;

To regulate Commerce with foreign Nations, and among the several States, and with the Indian Tribes;

To establish an uniform Rule of Naturalization, and uniform Laws on the subject of Bankruptcies throughout the United States;

To coin Money, regulate the Value thereof, and of foreign Coin, and fix the Standard of Weights and Measures;

To provide for the Punishment of counterfeiting the Securities and current Coin of the United States;

To establish Post Offices and post Roads;

To promote the Progress of Science and useful Arts, by securing for limited Times to Authors and Inventors the exclusive Right to their respective Writings and Discoveries;

To constitute Tribunals inferior to the supreme Court;

To define and punish Piracies and Felonies committed on the high Seas, and Offenses against the Law of Nations;

To declare War, grant Letters of Marque and Reprisal, and make Rules concerning Captures on Land and Water;

To raise and support Armies, but no Appropriation of Money to that Use shall be for a longer Term than two Years;

To provide and maintain a Navy;

To make Rules for the Government and Regulation of the land and naval Forces;

To provide for calling forth the Militia to execute the Laws of the Union, suppress Insurrections and repel Invasions;

To provide for organizing, arming, and disciplining, the Militia, and for governing such Part of them as may be employed in the Service of the United States, reserving to the States respectively, the Appointment of the Officers, and the Authority of training the Militia according to the discipline prescribed by Congress;

To exercise exclusive Legislation in all Cases whatsoever, over such District (not exceeding ten Miles square) as may, by Cession of particular States, and the Acceptance of Congress, become the Seat of the Government of the United States, and to exercise like Authority over all Places purchased by the Consent of the Legislature of the State in which the Same shall be, for the Erection of Forts, Magazines, Arsenals, dock-Yards, and othe needful buildings;—And

To make all Laws which shall be necessary and proper for carrying into Execution the foregoing Powers, and all other Powers vested by the Constitution in the Government of the United States, or in any Department or Officer thereof.

SECTION 9

The Migration or Importation of such Persons as any of the States now existing shall think proper to admit, shall not be prohibited by the Congress prior to the Year one thousand eight hundred and eight, but a Tax or Duty may be imposed on such Importation, not exceeding ten dollars for each Person.

The Privilege of the Writ of Habeas Corpus shall not be suspended, unless when in Cases of Rebellion or Invasion the public Safety may require it.

No Bill of Attainder or ex post facto Law shall be passed.

No Capitation, or other direct, Tax shall be laid, unless in Proportion to the Census or Enumeration herein before directed to be taken.

No Tax or Duty shall be laid on Articles exported from any State.

No Preference shall be given by any Regulation of Commerce or Revenue to the Ports of one State over those of another: nor shall Vessels bound to, or from, one State, be obliged to enter, clear, or pay Duties in another.

No Money shall be drawn from the Treasury, but in Consequence of Appropriations made by Law; and a regular Statement and Account of the Receipts and Expenditures of all public Money shall be published from time to time.

No Title of Nobility shall be granted by the United States: And no Person holding any Office of Profit or Trust under them, shall, without the Consent of the Congress, accept of any present, Emolument, Office, or Title, of any kind whatever, from any King, Prince, or foreign State.

SECTION 10

No State shall enter into any Treaty, Alliance, or Confederation; grant Letters of Marque and Reprisal; coin Money; emit Bills of Credit; make any Thing but gold and silver Coin a Tender in Payment of Debts; pass any Bill of Attainder, ex post facto Law, or Law impairing the Obligation of Contracts, or grant any Title of Nobility.

No State shall, without the Consent of the Congress, lay any Imposts or Duties on Imports or Exports, except what may be absolutely necessary for executing its inspection Laws: and the net Produce of all Duties and Imposts, laid by any State on Imports or Exports, shall be for the Use of the Treasury of the United States; and all such Laws shall be subject to the Revision and Controul of the Congress.

No State shall, without the Consent of Congress, lay any Duty of Tonnage, keep Troops, or Ships of War in time of Peace, enter into any Agreement or Compact with another State, or with a foreign Power, or engage in War, unless actually invaded, or in such imminent Danger as will not admit of delay.

Article II

SECTION 1

The executive Power shall be vested in a President of the United States of America. He shall hold his Office during the Term of four Years, and, together with the Vice President, chosen for the same Term, be elected, as follows:

Each State shall appoint, in such Manner as the Legislature thereof may direct, a Number of Electors, equal to the whole Number of Senators and Representatives to which the State may be entitled in the Congress: but no Senator or Representative, or Person holding an Office or Trust or Profit under the United States, shall be appointed an Elector.

The Electors shall meet in their respective States, and vote by Ballot for two Persons, of whom one at least shall not be an Inhabitant of the same State with Themselves. And they shall make a List of all the Persons voted for, and of the Number of Votes for each; which List they shall sign and certify, and transmit sealed to the Seat of the Government of the United States, directed to the President of the Senate. The President of the Senate shall, in the Presence of the Senate and House of Representatives, open all the Certificates, and the Votes shall then be counted. The Person having the greatest Number of Votes shall be the President, if such Number be a Majority of the whole Number of Electors appointed; and if there be more than one who have such Majority, and have an equal Number of Votes, then the House of Representatives shall immediately chuse by Ballot one of them for President; and if no Person have a Majority, then from the five highest on the List the said House shall in like Manner chuse the President. But in chusing the President, the Votes shall be taken by States, the Representation from each State having one Vote; A quorum for this Purpose shall consist of a Member or Members from two thirds of the States, and a Majority of all the States shall be necessary to a Choice. In every Case, after the Choice of the President, the Person having the greatest Number of Votes of the Electors shall be the Vice President. But if there should remain two or more who have equal Votes, the Senate shall chuse from them by Ballot the Vice President.

The Congress may determine the Time of chusing the Electors, and the Day on which they shall give their Votes; which Day shall be the same throughout the United States.

No Person except a natural born Citizen, or a Citizen of the United States, at the time of the Adoption of this Constitution, shall be eligible to the Office of President; neither shall any Person be eligible to that Office who shall not have attained to the Age of thirty five Years, and been fourteen Years a Resident within the United States.

In Case of the Removal of the President from Office, or of his Death, Resignation, or Inability to discharge the Powers and Duties of the said Office, the Same shall devolve on the Vice President, and the Congress may by Law provide for the Case of Removal,

Death, Resignation or Inability, both of the President and Vice President, declaring what Officer shall then act as President, and such Officer shall act accordingly, until the Disability be removed, or a President shall be elected.

The President shall, at stated Times, receive for his Services, a Compensation, which shall neither be encreased nor diminished during the Period for which he shall have been elected, and he shall not receive within that Period any other Emolument from the United States, or any of them.

Before he enter on the Execution of his Office, he shall take the following Oath or Affirmation:—"I do solemnly swear (or affirm) that I will faithfully execute the Office of President of the United States, and will to the best of my Ability, preserve, protect and defind the Constitution of the United States."

SECTION 2

The President shall be Commander in Chief of the Army and Navy of the United States, and of the Militia of the several States, when called into the actual Service of the United States; he may require the Opinion, in writing, of the principal Officer in each of the executive Departments, upon any Subject relating to the Duties of their respective Offices, and he shall have Power to grant Reprieves and Pardons for Offences against the United States, except in Cases of Impeachment.

He shall have Power, by and with the Advice and Consent of the Senate, to make Treaties, providing two thirds of the Senators present concur; and he shall nominate, and by and with the Advice and Consent of the Senate, shall appoint Ambassadors, other public Ministers and Consuls, Judges of the supreme Court, and all other Officers of the United States, whose Appointments are not herein otherwise provided for, and which shall be established by Law: but the Congress may be Law vest the Appointment of such inferior Officers, as they think proper, in the President alone, in the Courts of Law, or in the Heads of Departments.

The President shall have Power to fill up all Vacancies that may happen during the Recess of the Senate, by granting Commissions which shall expire at the End of their next Session.

SECTION 3

He shall from time to time give to the Congress Information of the State of the Union, and recommend to their Consideration such Measures as he shall judge necessary and expedient; he may, on extraordinary Occasions, convene both Houses, or either of them, and in Case of Disagreement between them, with Respect to the Time of Adjournment, he may adjourn them to such Time as he shall think proper; he shall receive Ambassadors and other public Ministers; he shall take Care that the Laws be faithfully executed, and shall Commission all the Officers of the United States.

SECTION 4

The President, Vice President and all civil Officers of the United States, shall be removed from Office on Impeachment for, and Conviction of, Treason, Bribery, or other high Crimes and Misdemeanors.

Article III

SECTION 1
The judicial Power of the United States, shall be vested in one supreme Court, and in such inferior Courts as the Congress may from time to time ordain and establish. The Judges, both of the supreme and inferior Courts, shall hold their Offices during good Behaviour, and shall, at stated Times, receive for their Services, a Compensation, which shall not be diminished during their Continuance in Office.

SECTION 2
The judicial Power shall extend to all Cases, in Law and Equity, arising under this Constitution, the Laws of the United States, and Treaties made, or which shall be made, under their Authority;—to all Cases affecting Ambassadors, other public Ministers and Consuls;—to all Cases of admiralty and maritime Jurisdiction;—to Controversies to which the United States shall be a Party;—to Controversies between two or more States;—between a State and Citizens of another State;—between Citizens of different States;—between Citizens of the same State claiming Lands under Grants of different States, and between a State, or the Citizens thereof, and foreign States, Citizens or Subjects.

In all Cases affecting Ambassadors, other public Ministers and Consuls, and those in which a State shall be Party, the supreme Court shall have original Jurisdiction. In all the other Cases before mentioned, the supreme Court shall have appellate Jurisdiction, both as to Law and Fact, with such Exceptions, and under such Regulations as the Congress shall make.

The Trial of all Crimes, except in Cases of Impeachment, shall be by Jury; and such Trial shall be held in the State where the said Crimes shall have been committed; but when not committed within any State, the Trial shall be at such Place or Places as the Congress may by Law have directed.

SECTION 3
Treason against the United States, shall consist only in levying War against them, or in adhering to their Enemies, giving them Aid and Comfort. No Person shall be convicted of Treason unless on the Testimony of two Witnesses to the same overt Act, or on Confession in open Court.

The Congress shall have Power to declare the Punishment of Treason, but no Attainder of Treason shall work Corruption of Blood, or Forfeiture except during the Life of the Person attainted.

Article IV

SECTION 1
Full Faith and Credit shall be given in each State to the public Acts, Records, and judicial Proceedings of every other State. And the Congress may by general Laws pre-

scribe the Manner in which such Acts, Records and Proceedings shall be proved, and the Effect thereof.

SECTION 2

The Citizens of each State shall be entitled to all Privileges and Immunities of Citizens in the several States.

A Person charged in any State with Treason, Felony, or other Crime. who shall flee from Justice, and be found in another State, shall on Demand of the executive Authority of the State from which he fled, be delivered up, to be removed to the State having Jurisdiction of the Crime.

No Person held to Service or Labour in one State, under the Laws thereof, escaping into another, shall, in Consequence of any Law or Regulation therein, be discharged from such Service or Labour, but shall be delivered up on Claim of the Party to whom such Service or Labour may be due.

SECTION 3

New States may be admitted by the Congress into this Union; but no new State shall be formed or erected within the Jurisdiction of any other State; nor any State be formed by the Junction of two or more States, or Parts of States, without the Consent of the Legislatures of the States concerned as well as of the Congress.

The Congress shall have Power to dispose of and make all needful Rules and Regulations respecting the Territory or other Property belonging to the belonging to the United States; and nothing in this Constitution shall be so construed as to Prejudice any Claims of the United States, or of any particular State.

SECTION 4

The United States shall guarantee to every State in this Union a Republican Form of Government, and shall protect each of them against Invasion; and on Application of the Legislature, or of the Executive (when the Legislature cannot be convened) against domestic Violence.

Article V

The Congress, whenever two thirds of both Houses shall deem it necessary, shall propose Amendments to this Constitution, or, on the Application of the Legislatures of two thirds of the several States, shall call a Convention for proposing Amendments, which, in either Case, shall be valid to all Intents and Purposes, as Part of this Constitution, when ratified by the Legislatures of three fourths of the several States, or by Conventions in three fourths thereof, as the one or the other Mode of Ratification may be proposed by the Congress; Provided that no Amendment which may be made prior to the Year One thousand eight hundred and eight shall in any Manner affect the first and fourth

Clauses in the Ninth Section of the first Article; and that no State, without its Consent, shall be deprived of its equal Suffrage in the Senate.

Article VI

All Debts contracted and Engagements entered into, before the Adoption of this Constitution, shall be as valid against the United States under this Constitution, as under the Confederation.

    This Constitution, and the Laws of the United States which shall be made in Pursuance thereof; and all Treaties made, or which shall be made, under the Authority of the United States, shall be the supreme Law of the Land; and the Judges in every State shall be bound thereby, any Thing in the Constitution or Laws of any State to the Contrary notwithstanding.

    The Senators and Representatives before mentioned, and the Members of the several State Legislatures, and all executive and judicial Officers, both of the United States and of the several States, shall be bound by Oath or Affirmation, to support this Constitution; but no religious Test shall ever by required as a Qualification to any Office or public Trust under the United States.

Article VII

The Ratification of the Conventions of nine States, shall be sufficient for the Establishment of this Constitution between the States so ratifying the Same.

Amendment I [1791]

Congress shall make no law respecting an establishment of religion, or prohibiting the free exercise thereof; or abridging the freedom of speech, or the press; or the right of the people peaceably to assemble, and to petition the Government for a redress of grievances.

Amendment II [1791]

A well regulated Militia, being necessary to the security for a free State, the right of the people to keep and bear Arms, shall not be infringed.

Amendment III [1791]

No Soldier shall, in time of peace be quartered in any house, without the consent of the Owner, nor in time of war, but in a manner to be prescribed by law.

Amendment IV [1791]

The right of the people to be secure in their persons, houses, papers, and effects, against unreasonable searches and seizures, shall not be violated, and no Warrants shall issue, but upon probable cause, supported by Oath or affirmation, and particularly describing the place to be searched, and the persons or things to be seized.

Amendment V [1791]

No person shall be held to answer for a capital, or otherwise infamous crime, unless on a presentment or indictment of a Grand Jury, except in cases arising in the land or naval forces, or in the Militia, when in actual service in time of War or public danger; nor shall any person be subject for the same offense to be twice put in jeopardy of life or limb; nor shall be compelled in any criminal case to be a witness against himself, nor be deprived of life, liberty, or property, without due process of law; nor shall private property be taken for public use, without just compensation.

Amendment VI [1791]

In all criminal prosecutions, the accused shall enjoy the right to a speedy and public trial, by an impartial jury of the State and district wherein the crime shall have been committed, which district shall have been previously ascertained by law, and to be informed of the nature and cause of the accusation; to be confronted with the Witnesses against him; to have compulsory process for obtaining witnesses in his favor, and to have the Assistance of counsel for his defence.

Amendment VII [1791]

In Suits at common law, where the value in controversy shall exceed twenty dollars, the right of trial by jury shall be preserved, and no fact tried by a jury, shall be otherwise re-examined in any Court of the United States, than according to the rules of the common law.

Amendment VIII [1791]

Excessive bail shall not be required, nor excessive fines imposed, nor cruel and unusual punishments inflicted.

Amendment IX [1791]

The enumeration in the Constitution, of certain rights, shall not be construed to deny or disparage others retained by the people.

Amendment X [1791]

The powers not delegated to the United States by the Constitution, nor prohibited by it to the States, are reserved to the States respectively, or to the people.

Amendment XI [1798]

The Judicial power of the United States shall not be construed to extend to any suit in law or equity, commenced or prosecuted against one of the United States by Citizens of another State, or by Citizens or Subjects of any Foreign State.

Amendment XII [1804]

The Electors shall meet in their respective states and vote by ballot for President and Vice-President, one of whom, at least, shall not be an inhabitant of the same state with themselves; they shall name in their ballots the person voted for as President, and in distinct ballots the person voted for as Vice-President, and they shall make distinct lists of all persons voted for as President, and of all persons voted for as Vice-President, and of the number of votes for each, which lists they shall sign and certify, and transmit sealed to the seat of the government of the United States, directed to the President of the Senate;—The President of the Senate shall, in the presence of the Senate and House of Representatives, open all the certificates and the votes shall then be counted;—The person having the greatest number of votes for President, shall be the President, if such number be a majority of the whole number of Electors appointed; and if no person have such majority, then from the persons having the highest numbers not exceeding three on the list of those voted for as President, the House of Representatives shall choose immediately, be ballot, the President. But in choosing the President, the votes shall be taken by states, the representation from each state having one vote; a quorum for this purpose shall consist of a member or members from two-thirds of the states, and a majority of all the states shall be necessary to a choice. And if the House of Representatives shall not choose a President whenever the right of choice shall devolve upon them, before the fourth day of March next following, then the Vice-President shall act as President. The person having the greatest number of votes as Vice-President, shall be the Vice-President, if such number be a majority of the whole number of Electors appointed, and if no person have a majority, then from the two highest numbers on the list, the Senate shall choose the Vice-President; a quorum for the purpose shall consist of two-thirds of the whole number of Senators, and a majority of the whole number shall be necessary to a choice. But no person constitutionally ineligible to the office of President shall be eligible to that of the Vice-President of the United States.

Amendment XIII [1865]

SECTION 1
Neither slavery nor involuntary servitude, except as a punishment for crime whereof the party shall have been duly convicted, shall exist within the United States, or any place subject to their jurisdiction.

SECTION 2
Congress shall have power to enforce this article by appropriate legislation.

Amendment XIV [1868]

SECTION 1
All persons born or naturalized in the United States, and subject to the jurisdiction thereof, are citizens of the United States and of the State wherein they reside. No State shall make or enforce any law which shall abridge the privileges or immunities of citizens of the United States; nor shall any State deprive any person of life, liberty, or property, without due process of law; nor deny to any person within its jurisdiction the equal protection of the laws.

SECTION 2
Representatives shall be appointed among the several States according to their respective numbers, counting the whole number of persons in each State, excluding Indians not taxed. But when the right to vote at any election for the choice of electors for President and Vice President of the United States, Representatives in Congress, the Executive and Judicial officers of a State, or the members of the Legislature thereof, is denied to any of the male inhabitants of such State, being twenty-one years of age, and citizens of the United States, or in any way abridged, except for participation in rebellion, or other crime, the basis of representation therein shall be reduced in the proportion which the number of such male citizens shall bear to the whole number of male citizens twenty-one years of age in such State.

SECTION 3
No person shall be a Senator or Representative in Congress, or elector of President and Vice President, or hold any office, civil or military, under the United States, or under any State, who, having previously taken an oath, as a member of Congress, or as an officer of the United States, or as a member of any State legislature, or as an executive or judicial officer of any State, to support the Constitution of the United States, shall have engaged in insurrection or rebellion against the same, or given aid or comfort to the enemies thereof. But Congress may by a vote of two-thirds of each House, remove such disability.

SECTION 4

The validity of the public debt of the United States, authorized by law, including debts incurred for payment of pensions and bounties for services in suppressing insurrection or rebellion, shall not be questioned. But neither the United States nor any State shall assume or pay any debt or obligation incurred in aid of insurrection or rebellion against the United States, or any claim for the loss or emancipation of any slave; but all such debts, obligations and claims shall be held illegal and void.

SECTION 5

The Congress shall have power to enforce, by appropriate legislation, the provisions of this article.

Amendment XV [1870]

SECTION 1

The right of citizens of the United States to vote shall not be denied or abridged by the United States or by any State on account of race, color, or previous condition of servitude.

SECTION 2

The Congress shall have power to enforce this article by appropriate legislation.

Amendment XVI [1913]

The Congress shall have power to lay and collect taxes on incomes, from whatever source derived, without apportionment among the several States, and without regard to any census or enumeration.

Amendment XVII [1913]

The Senate of the United States shall be composed of two Senators from each State, elected by the people thereof, for six years; and each Senator shall have one vote. The electors in each State shall have the qualifications requisite for electors of the most numerous branch of the State legislatures.

When vacancies happen in the representation of any State in the Senate, the executive authority of such State shall issue writs of election to fill such vacancies: *Provided*, That the legislature of any State may empower the executive thereof to make temporary appointments until the people fill the vacancies by election as the legislature may direct.

This amendment shall not be so construed as to affect the election or term of any Senator chosen before it becomes valid as part of the Constitution.

Amendment XVIII [1919]

SECTION 1

After one year from the ratification of this article the manufacture, sale, or transportation of intoxicating liquors within, the importation thereof into, or the exportation thereof from the United States and all territory subject to the jurisdiction thereof for beverage purposes is hereby prohibited.

SECTION 2

The Congress and the several States shall have concurrent power to enforce this article by appropriate legislation.

SECTION 3

This article shall be inoperative unless it shall have been ratified as an amendment to the Constitution by the legislatures of the several States, as provided in the Constitution, within seven years from the date of the submission hereof to the States by the Congress.

Amendment XIX [1920]

The right of citizens of the United States to vote shall not be denied or abridged by the United States or by any State on account of sex.

Congress shall have power to enforce this article by appropriate legislation.

Amendment XX [1933]

SECTION 1

The terms of the President and Vice President shall end at noon on the 20th day of January, and the terms of Senators and Representatives at noon on the 3d day of January, of the years in which such terms would have ended if this article had not been ratified; and the terms of their successors shall then begin.

SECTION 2

The Congress shall assemble at least once in every year, and such meeting shall begin at noon on the 3d day of January, unless they shall by law appoint a different day.

SECTION 3

If, at the time fixed for the beginning of the term of the President, the President elect shall have died, the Vice President elect shall become President. If a President shall not have been chosen before the time fixed for the beginning of his term, or if the President elect shall have failed to qualify, then the Vice President elect shall act as President until a President shall have qualified; and the Congress may be law provide for the case wherein neither a President elect nor a Vice President elect shall have qualified, declaring who shall then act as President, or the manner in which one who is to act shall be selected, and such person shall act accordingly until a President or Vice President shall have qualified.

SECTION 4

The Congress may by law provide for the case of the death of any of the persons from whom the House of Representatives may choose a President whenever the right of choice shall have devolved upon them, and for the case of the death of any of the persons from whom the Senate may choose a Vice President whenever the right of choice shall have devolved upon them.

SECTION 5

Sections 1 and 2 shall take effect on the 15th day of October following the ratification of this article.

SECTION 6

This article shall be inoperative unless it shall have been ratified as an amendment to the Constitution by the legislatures of three-fourths of the several States within seven years from the date of its submission.

Amendment XXI [1933]

SECTION 1

The eighteenth article of amendment to the Constitution of the United States is hereby repealed.

SECTION 2

The transportation or importation into any State, Territory, or possession of the United States for delivery or use therein of intoxicating liquors, in violation of the laws thereof, is hereby prohibited.

SECTION 3

This article shall be inoperative unless it shall have been ratified as an amendment to the Constitution by conventions in the several States, as provided in the Constitution, within seven years from the date of the submission hereof to the States by the Congress.

Amendment XXII [1951]

SECTION 1

No person shall be elected to the office of the President more than twice, and no person who has held the office of President, or acted as President, for more than two years of a term to which some other person was elected President shall be elected to the office of the President more than once. But this Article shall not apply to any person holding the office of President when this Article was proposed by the Congress, and shall not prevent any person who may be holding the office of President, or acting as President, during the term within which this Article becomes operative from holding the office of President or acting as President during the remainder of such term.

SECTION 2
This article shall be inoperative unless it shall have been ratified as an amendment to the Constitution by the legislatures of three-fourths of the several States within seven years from the date of its submission to the States by the Congress.

Amendment XXIII [1961]

SECTION 1
The District constituting the seat of Government of the United States shall appoint in such manner as the Congress may direct:

A number of electors of President and Vice President equal to the whole number of Senators and Representatives in Congress to which the District would be entitled if it were a State, but in no event more than the least populous State; they shall be in addition to those appointed by the States, but they shall be considered, for the purposes of the election of President and Vice President, to be electors appointed by a State; and they shall meet in the District and perform such duties as provided by the twelfth article of amendment.

SECTION 2
The Congress shall have power to enforce this article by appropriate legislation.

Amendment XXIV [1964]

SECTION 1
The right of citizens of the United States to vote in any primary or other election for President or Vice President, for electors for President or Vice President, or for Senator or Representative in Congress, shall not be denied or abridged by the United States or any State by reason of failure to pay any poll tax or other tax.

SECTION 2
The Congress shall have power to enforce this article by appropriate legislation.

Amendment XXV [1967]

SECTION 1
In case of the removal of the President from office or of his death or resignation, the Vice President shall become President.

SECTION 2

Whenever there is a vacancy in the office of the Vice President, the President shall nominate a Vice President who shall take office upon confirmation by a majority vote of both Houses of Congress.

SECTION 3

Whenever the President transmits to the President pro tempore of the Senate and the Speaker of the House of Representatives his written declaration that he is unable to discharge the powers and duties of his office, and until he transmits to them a written declaration to the contrary, such powers and duties shall be discharged by the Vice President as Acting President.

SECTION 4

Whenever the Vice President and a majority of either the principal officers of the executive departments or of such other body as Congress may by Law provide, transmit to the President pro tempore of the Senate and the Speaker of the House of Representatives their written declaration that the President is unable to discharge the powers and duties of his office, the Vice President shall immediately assume the powers and duties of the office as Acting President.

Thereafter, when the President transmits to the President pro tempore of the Senate and the Speaker of the House of Representatives his written declaration that no inability exists, he shall resume the powers and duties of his office unless the Vice President and a majority of either the principal officers of the executive department or of such other body as Congress may by law provide, transmit within four days to the President pro tempore to the Senate and the Speaker of the House of Representatives their written declaration that the President is unable to discharge the powers and duties of his office. Thereupon Congress shall decide the issue, assembling within forty-eight hours for that purpose if not in session. If the Congress, within twenty-one days after receipt of the latter written declaration, or, if Congress is not in session, within twenty-one days after Congress is required to assemble, determines by two-thirds vote of both Houses that the President is unable to discharge the powers and duties of his office, the Vice President shall continue to discharge the same as Acting President; otherwise, the President shall resume the powers and duties of his office.

Amendment XXVI [1971]

SECTION 1

The right of citizens of the United States, who are eighteen years of age or older, to vote shall not be denied or abridged by the United States or by any State on account of age.

SECTION 2

The Congress shall have power to enforce this article by appropriate legislation.

Appendix 2

THE SHERMAN ACT AS AMENDED (EXCERPTS)

1 Trusts, etc., in Restraint of Trade Illegal; Exception of Resale Price Agreements; Penalty

Every contract, combination in the form of trust or otherwise, or conspiracy, in restraint of trade or commerce among the several States, or with foreign nations, is declared to be illegal. Every person who shall make any contract or engage in any combination or conspiracy declared by sections 1 to 7 of this title to be illegal shall be deemed guilty of a felony, and, on conviction thereof, shall be punished by fine not exceeding one million dollars or by imprisonment not exceeding three years, or by both said punishments, in the discretion of the court.

2 Monopolizing Trade a Felony; Penalty

Every person who shall monopolize, or attempt to monopolize, or combine or conspire with any other person or persons, to monopolize any part of the trade or commerce among the several States, or with foreign nations, shall be deemed guilty of a felony, and, on conviction thereof, shall be punished by fine not exceeding one million dollars if a corporation, or, if any other person, one hundred thousand dollars or by imprisonment not exceeding three years, or by both said punishments, in the discretion of the court.

16 Judgments—Prima Facie Evidence

(a) A final judgment or decree heretofore or hereafter rendered in any civil or criminal proceeding brought by or on behalf of the United States under the antitrust laws to the effect that a defendant has violated said laws shall be prima facie evidence against such defendant in any action or proceeding brought by any other party against such defendant under said laws or by the United States under section 15a of this title, as to all matters respecting which said judgment or decree would be an estoppel as between the parties thereto: *Provided*, That this section shall not apply to consent judgments or decrees entered before any testimony has been taken or to judgments or decrees entered in action 15a of this title.

Appendix 3

Section 2

(a) It shall be unlawful for any person engaged in commerce, in the course of such commerce, either directly or indirectly, to discriminate in price between different purchasers of commodities of like grade and quality, where either or any of the purchases involved in such discrimination are in commerce, where such commodities are sold for use, consumption, or resale within the United States or any Territory thereof or the District of Columbia or any insular possession or other place under the jurisdiction of the United States, and where the effect of such discrimination may be substantially to lessen competition or tend to create a monopoly in any line of commerce, or to injure, destroy, or prevent competition with any person who either grants or knowingly receives the benefit of such discrimination, or with customers of either of them: *Provided,* That nothing herein contained shall prevent differentials which make only due allowance for differences in the cost of manufacture, sale, or delivery resulting from the differing methods or quantities in which such commodities are to such purchasers sold or delivered: *Provided, however,* That the Federal Trade Commission may, after due investigation and hearing to all interested parties, fix and establish quantity limits, and revise the same as it finds necessary, as to particular commodities or classes of commodities, where it finds that available purchasers in greater quantities are so few as to render differentials on account thereof unjustly discriminatory or promotive of monopoly in any line of commerce; and the foregoing shall then not be construed to permit differentials based on differences in quantities greater than those so fixed and established: *And provided further,* That nothing herein contained shall prevent persons engaged in selling goods, wares, or merchandise in commerce from selecting their own customers in bona fide transactions and not in restraint of trade: *And provided further,* That nothing herein contained shall prevent price changes from time to time where in response to changing conditions affecting the market for or the marketability of the goods concerned, such as but not limited to actual or imminent deterioration of perishable goods, obsolescence of seasonal goods, distress sales under court process, or sales in good faith in discontinuance of business in the goods concerned.

BURDEN OF REBUTTING PRIMA-FACIE CASE OF DISCRIMINATION

(b)   Upon proof being made, at any hearing on a complaint under this section, that there has been discrimination in price or services or facilities furnished, the burden of rebutting the prima-facie case thus made by showing justification shall be upon the person charged with a violation of this section, and unless justification shall be affirmatively shown, the Commission is authorized to issue an order terminating the discrimination: *Provided, however,* That nothing herein contained shall prevent a seller rebutting the prima-facie case thus made by showing that his lower price or the furnishing of services or facilities to any purchaser or purchasers was made in good faith to meet an equally low price of a competitor, or the services or facilities furnished by a competitor.

PAYMENT OR ACCEPTANCE OF COMMISSION, BROKERAGE OR OTHER COMPENSATION

(c)   It shall be unlawful for any person engaged in commerce, in the course of such commerce, to pay or grant, or to receive or accept, anything of value as a commission, brokerage, or other compensation, or any allowance or discount in lieu thereof, except for services rendered in connection with the sale or purchase of goods, wares, or merchandise, either to the other party to such transaction or to an agent, representative, or other intermediary therein where such intermediary is acting in fact for or in behalf, or is subject to the direct or indirect control, of any party to such transaction other than the person by whom such compensation is so granted or paid.

PAYMENT FOR SERVICES OR FACILITIES FOR PROCESSING OR SALE

(d)   It shall be unlawful for any person engaged in commerce to pay or contract for the payment of anything of value to or for the benefit of a customer of such person in the course of such commerce as compensation or in consideration for any services or facilities furnished by or through such customer in connection with the processing, handling, sale, or offering for sale of any products or commodities manufactured, sold, or offered for sale by such person, unless such payment or consideration is available on proportionally equal terms to all other customers competing in the distribution of such products or commodities.

FURNISHING SERVICES OR FACILITIES FOR PROCESSING, HANDLING, ETC.

(e)   It shall be unlawful for any person to discriminate in favor of one purchaser against another purchaser or purchasers of a commodity bought for resale, with or without processing, by contracting to furnish or furnishing, or by contributing to the furnishing of, any services or facilities connected with the processing, handling, sale, or offering for sale of such commodity so purchased upon terms not accorded to all purchasers on proportionally equal terms.

KNOWINGLY INDUCING OR RECEIVING DISCRIMINATORY PRICE

(f)   It shall be unlawful for any person engaged in commerce, in the course of such commerce, knowingly to induce or receive a discrimination in price which is prohibited by this section.

Section 3

It shall be unlawful for any person engaged in commerce, in the course of such commerce, to lease or make a sale or contract for sale of goods, wares, merchandise, machinery, supplies, or other commodities, whether patented or unpatented, for use, consumption, or resale within the United States or any Territory thereof or the District of Columbia or any insular possession or other place under the jurisdiction of the United States, or fix a price charged therefor, or discount from, or rebate upon, such price, on the condition, agreement, or understanding that the lessee or purchaser thereof shall not use or deal in the goods, wares, merchandise, machinery, supplies, or other commodities of a competitor or competitors of the lessor or seller, where the effect of such lease, sale, or contract for sale or such condition, agreement, or understanding that the lessee or purchaser thereof shall not use or deal in the goods, wares, merchandise, machinery, supplies, or other commodities of a competitor or competitors of the lessor or seller, where the effect of such lease, sale, or contract for sale or such condition, agreement, or understanding may be to substantially lessen competition or tend to create a monopoly in any line of commerce.

Section 7

No person engaged in commerce or in any activity affecting commerce shall acquire, directly or indirectly, the whole or any part of the stock or other share capital and no person subject to the jurisdiction of the Federal Trade Commission shall acquire the whole or any part of the assets of another person engaged also in commerce or in any activity affecting commerce, where in any line of commerce or in any activity affecting commerce, where in any line of commerce or in any activity affecting commerce in any section of the country, the effect of such acquisition may be substantially to lessen competition, or to tend to create a monopoly.

No person shall acquire, directly or indirectly, the whole or any part of the stock or other share capital and no person subject to the jurisdiction of the Federal Trade Commission shall acquire the whole or any part of the assets of one or more persons engaged in commerce or in any activity affecting commerce, where in any line of commerce or in any activity affecting commerce in any section of the country, the effect of such aquisition, of such stocks or assets, or of the use of such stock by the voting or granting of proxies or otherwise, may be substantially to lessen competition, or to tend to create a monopoly.

This section shall not apply to persons purchasing such stock solely for investment and not using the same by voting or otherwise to bring about, or in attempting to bring about, the substantial lessening of competition. Nor shall anything contained in this section prevent a corporation engaged in commerce or in any activity affecting commerce from causing the formation of subsidiary corporations for the actual carrying on of their immediate lawful business, or the natural and legitimate branches of extensions thereof, or from owning and holding all or a part of the stock of such subsidiary corporations, when the effect of such formation is not to substantially lessen competition.

Nor shall anything herein contained be construed to prohibit any common carrier subject to the laws to regulate commerce from aiding in the construction of branches or short lines so located as to become feeders to the main line of the company so aiding in such construction or from acquiring or owning all or any part of the stock of such branch lines, nor to prevent any such common carrier from acquiring and owning all or any part of the stock of a branch or short line constructed by an independent company where there is no substantial competition between the company owning the branch line so constructed and the company owning the main line acquiring the property or an interest therein, nor to prevent such common carrier from extending any of its lines through the medium of the acquisition of stock or otherwise of any other common carrier where there is no substantial competition between the company extending its lines and the company whose stock, property, or an interest therein is so acquired.

Nothing contained in this section shall be held to affect or impair any right heretofore legally acquired: *Provided,* That nothing in this section shall be held or construed to authorize or make lawful anything heretofore prohibited or made illegal by the antitrust laws, nor to exempt any person from the penal provisions thereof or the civil remedies therein provided.

Nothing contained in this section shall apply to transactions duly consummated pursuant to authority given by the Civil Aeronautics Board, Federal Communications Commission, Federal Power Commission, Interstate Commerce Commission, the Securities and Exchange Commission in the exercise of its jurisdiction under section 79j of this title, the United States Maritime Commission, or the Secretary of Agriculture under any statutory provision vesting such power in such Commission, Secretary, or Board.

Section 8

No private banker or director, officer, or employee of any member bank of the Federal Reserve System or any branch thereof shall be at the same time a director, officer, or employee of any other bank, banking association, savings bank, or trust company organized under the National Bank Act or organized under the laws of any State or of the District of Columbia, or any branch thereof, except that the Board of Governors of the Federal Reserve System may by regulation permit such service as a director, officer, or employee of not more than one other such institution or branch thereof; but the foregoing prohibition shall not apply in the case of any one or more of the following or any branch thereof:

(1)   A bank, banking association, savings bank, or trust company, more than 90 per centum of the stock of which is owned directly or indirectly by the United States or by any corporation of which the United States directly or indirectly owns more than 90 per centum of the stock.

(2)   A bank, banking association, savings bank, or trust company which has been placed formally in liquidation or which is in the hands of a receiver, conservator, or other official exercising similar functions.

(3)   A corporation, principally engaged in international or foreign banking or banking in a dependency or insular possession of the United States which has entered into an agreement with the Board of Governors of the Federal Reserve System pursuant to sections 601 to 604a of Title 12.

(4)   A bank, banking association, savings bank, or trust company, more than 50 per centum of the common stock of which is owned directly or indirectly by persons who own directly or indirectly more than 50 per centum of the common stock of such member bank.

(5)   A bank, banking association, savings bank, or trust company not located and having no branch in the same city, town, or village as that in which such member bank or any branch thereof is located, or in any city, town, or village contiguous or adjacent thereto.

(6)   A bank, banking association, savings bank, or trust company not engaged in a class or classes of business in which such member bank is engaged.

(7)   A mutual savings bank having no capital stock . . .

No person at the same time shall be a director in any two or more corporations, any one of which has capital, surplus, and undivided profits aggregating more than $1,000,000, engaged in whole or in part in commerce, other than banks, banking associations, trust companies, and common carriers subject to the Act to regulate commerce, approved February fourth, eighteen hundred and eighty-seven, if such corporations are or shall have been theretofore, by virtue of their business and location of operation, competitors, so that the elimination of competition by agreement between them would constitute a violation of any of the provisions of any of the antitrust laws. The eligibility of a director under the foregoing provision shall be determined by the aggregate amount of the capital, surplus, and undivided profits, exclusive of dividends declared but not paid to stockholders, at the end of the fiscal year of said corporation next preceding the election of directors, and when a director has been elected in accordance with the provisions of this Act is shall be lawful for him to continue as such for one year thereafter.

When any person elected or chosen as a director or officer or selected as an employee of any bank or other corporation subject to the provisions of this Act is eligible at the time of his election or selection to act for such bank or other corporation in such capacity his eligibility to act in such capacity shall not be affected and he shall not become or be deemed amenable to any of the provisions hereof by reason of any change in the affairs of such bank or other corporation from whatsoever cause, whether specifically excepted by any of the provisions hereof or not, until the expiration of one year from the date of his election or employment.

Appendix 4

THE WAGNER ACT AS AMENDED (EXCERPTS)

Section 7

Employees shall have the right to self-organization, to form, join, or assist labor organizations, to bargain collectively through representatives of their own choosing, and to engage in other concerted activities for the purpose of collective bargaining or other mutual aid or protection, and shall also have the right to refrain from any or all of such activities except to the extent that such right may be affected by an agreement requiring membership in a labor organization as a condition of employment as authorized in section 8(a)(3).

Section 8

(a)   It shall be an unfair labor practice for an employer—

(1)   to interfere with, restrain, or coerce employees in the exercise of the rights guaranteed in section 7;

(2)   to dominate or interfere with the formation or administration of any labor organization or contribute financial or other support to it: *Provided,* That subject to rules and regulations made and published by the Board pursuant to section 6, an employer shall not be prohibited from permitting employees to confer with him during working hours without loss of time or pay;

(3)   by discrimination in regard to hire or tenure of employment or any term or condition of employment to encourage or discourage membership in any labor organization: *Provided,* That nothing in this Act, or in any other statute of the United States, shall preclude an employer from making an agreement with a labor organization (not established, maintained, or assisted by any action defined in section 8(a) of this Act as an unfair labor practice) to require as a condition of employment

membership therein on or after the thirtieth day following the beginning of such employment or the effective date of such agreement, whichever is the later, (i) if such labor organization is the representative of the employees as provided in section 9(a), in the appropriate collective-bargaining unit covered by such agreement when made; and (ii) unless following an election held as provided in section 9(e) within one year preceding the effective date of such agreement, the Board shall have certified that at least a majority of the employees eligible to vote in such election have voted to rescind the authority of such labor organization to make such an agreement: *Provided further,* That no employer shall justify any discrimination against an employee for nonmembership in a labor organization (A) if he has reasonable grounds for believing that such membership was not available to the employee on the same terms and conditions generally applicable to other members, or (B) if he has reasonable grounds for believing that membership was denied or terminated for reasons other than the failure of the employee to tender the periodic dues and initiation fees uniformly required as a condition of acquiring or retaining membership.

(4)   to discharge or otherwise discriminate against an employee because he has filed charges or given testimony under this Act.

(5)   to refuse to bargain collectively with the representatives of his employees, subject to the provisions of section 9(a).

(b)   It shall be an unfair labor practice for a labor organization or its agents—

(1)   to restrain or coerce (A) employees in the exercise of the rights guaranteed in section 7: *Provided,* That this paragraph shall not impair the right of a labor organization to prescribe its own rules with the respect to the acquisition or retention of membership therein; or (B) an employer in the selection of his representatives for the purposes of collective bargaining or the adjustment of grievances;

(2)   to cause or attempt to cause an employer to discriminate against an employee in violation of subsection (a)(3) or to discriminate against an employee with respect to whom membership in such organization has been denied or terminated on some ground other than his failure to tender the periodic dues and the initiation fees uniformly required as a condition of acquiring or retaining membership;

(3)   to refuse to bargain collectively with an employer, provided it is the representative of his employees subject to the provisions of section 9(a);

(4)   (i) to engage in, or to induce or encourage any individual employed by any person engaged in commerce or in an industry affecting commerce to engage in, a strike or a refusal in the course of his employment to use, manufacture, process, transport, or otherwise handle or work on any goods, articles, materials, or commodities or to perform any services; or (ii) to threaten, coerce, or restrain any person engaged in commerce or in an industry affecting commerce, where in either case an object thereof is—

(A)   forcing or requiring any employer or self-employed person to join any labor or employer organization or to enter into any agreement which is prohibited by section 8(e);

(B) forcing or requiring any person to cease using, selling, handling, transporting, or otherwise dealing in the products of any other producer, processor, or manufacturer, or to cease doing business with any other person, or forcing or requiring any other employer to recognize or bargain with a labor organization as the representative of his employees unless such labor organization has been certified as the representative of such employees under the provisions of section 9: *Provided,* That nothing contained in this clause (B) shall be construed to make unlawful, where not otherwise unlawful, any primary strike or primary picketing;

(C) forcing or requiring any employer to recognize or bargain with a particular labor organization as the representative of his employees if another labor organization has been certified as the representative of such employees under the provisions of section 9;

(D) forcing or requiring any employer to assign particular work to employees in a particular trade, craft, or class rather than to employees in another labor organization or in another trade, craft, or class, unless such employer is failing to conform to an order or certification of the Board determining the bargaining representative for employees performing such work:

Provided, That nothing contained in this subsection (b) shall be construed to make unlawful a refusal by any person to enter upon the premises of any employer (other than his own employer), if the employees of such employer are engaged in a strike ratified or approved by a representative of such employees whom such employer is required to recognize under this Act: *Provided further,* That for the purposes of this paragraph (4) only, nothing contained in such paragraph shall be construed to prohibit publicity, other than picketing, for the purpose of truthfully advising the public, including consumers and members of a labor organization, that a product or products are produced by an employer with whom the labor organization has a primary dispute and are distributed by another employer, as long as such publicity does not have an effect of inducing any individual employed by any person other than the primary employer in the course of his employment to refuse to pick up, deliver, or transport any goods, or not to perform any services, at the establishment of the employer engaged in such distribution;

(5) to require of employees covered by an agreement authorized under subsection (a)(3) the payment, as a condition precedent to becoming a member of such organization, of a fee in an amount which the Board finds excessive or discriminatory under all the circumstances. In making such a finding, the Board shall consider, among other relevant factors, the practices and customs of labor organizations in the particular industry, and the wages currently paid to the employees affected; and

(6) to cause or attempt to cause an employer to pay or deliver or agree to pay or deliver any money or other thing of value, in the nature of an exaction, for services which are not performed or not to be performed; and

(7) to picket or cause to be picketed, or threaten to picket or cause to be picketed, any employer where an object thereof is forcing or requiring an employer to recognize or bargain with a labor organization as the representative of his employees, or

forcing or requiring the employees of an employer to accept or select such labor organization as their collective bargaining representative, unless such organization is currently certified as the representative of such employees:

(A) where the employer has lawfully recognized in accordance with this Act any other labor organization and a question concerning representation may not appropriately be raised under section 9(c) of this Act.

(B) where within the preceding twelve months a valid election under section 9(c) of this Act has been conducted, or

(C) where such picketing has been conducted without a petition under section 9(c) being filed within a reasonable period of time not to exceed thirty days from the commencement of such picketing: *Provided,* That when such a petition has been filed the Board shall forthwith, without regard to the provisions of section 9(c)(1) or the absence of a showing of a substantial interest on the part of the labor organization, direct an election in such unit as the Board finds to be appropriate and shall certify the results thereof: *Provided further,* That nothing in this subparagraph (C) shall be construed to prohibit any picketing or other publicity for the purpose of truthfully advising the public (including consumers) that an employer does not employ members of, or have a contract with, a labor organization, unless an effect of such picketing is to induce any individual employed by any other person in the course of his employment, not to pick up, deliver or transport any goods or not to perform any services.

Nothing in this paragraph (7) shall be construed to permit any act which would otherwise be an unfair labor practice under this Section 8(b).

(c) The expressing of any views, argument, or opinion, or the dissemination thereof, whether in written, printed, graphic, or visual form, shall not constitute or be evidence of an unfair labor practice under any of the provisions of this Act, if such expression contains no threat of reprisal or force or promise of benefit.

(d) For the purposes of this section, to bargain collectively is the performance of the mutual obligation of the employer and the representative of the employees to meet at reasonable times and confer in good faith with respect to wages, hours, and other terms and conditions of employment, or the negotiation of an agreement, or any question arising thereunder, and the execution of a written contract incorporating any agreement reached if requested by either party, but such obligation does not compel either party to agree to a proposal or require the making of a concession: *Provided,* That where there is in effect a collective-bargaining contract covering employees in an industry affecting commerce, the duty to bargain collectively shall also mean that no party to such contract shall terminate or modify such contract, unless the party desiring such termination or modification—

(1) serves a written notice upon the other party to the contract of the proposed termination or modification sixty days prior to the expiration date thereof, or in the event such contract contains no expiration date, sixty days prior to the time it is proposed to make such termination or modification;

(2) offers to meet and confer with the other party for the purpose of negotiating a new contract or a contract containing the proposed modifications;

(3) notifies the Federal Mediation and Conciliation Service within thirty days after such notice of the existence of a dispute, and simultaneously therewith notifies any State or Territorial agency established to mediate and conciliate disputes within the State or Territory where the dispute occurred, provided no agreement has been reached by that time; and

(4) continues in full force and effect, without resorting to strike or lock-out, all the terms and conditions of the existing contract for a period of sixty days after such notice is given or until the expiration date of such contract, whichever occurs later:

The duties imposed upon employers, employees, and labor organizations by paragraphs (2), (3), and (4) shall become inapplicable upon an intervening certification of the Board, under which the labor organization or individual, which is a party to the contract, has been superseded as or ceased to be the representative of the employees subject to the provisions of section 9(a), and the duties so imposed shall not be construed as requiring either party to discuss or agree to any modification of the terms and conditions contained in a contract for a fixed period, if such modification is to become effective before such terms and conditions can be reopened under the provisions of the contract. Any employee who engages in a strike within the sixty-day period specified in this subsection shall lose his status as an employee of the employer engaged in the particular labor dispute, for the purposes of section 8, 9, and 10 of this Act, as amended, but such loss of status for such employee shall terminate if and when he is reemployed by such employer.

(e) It shall be an unfair labor practice for any labor organization and any employer to enter into any contract or agreement, express or implied, whereby such employer ceases or refrains or agrees to cease or refrain from handling, using, selling, transporting or otherwise dealing in any of the products of any other employer, or to cease doing business with any other person, and any contract or agreement shall be to such extent unenforcible and void: *Provided,* That nothing in this subsection (e) shall apply to an agreement between a labor organization and an employer in the construction industry relating to the contracting or subcontracting of work to be done at the site of the construction, alteration, painting, or repair of a building, structure, or other work: *Provided further,* That for the purposes of this subsection (e) and section 8(b)(4)(B) the terms "any employer," "any person engaged in commerce or an industry affecting commerce," and "any person" when used in relation to the terms "any other producer, processor, or manufacturer," "any other employer," or "any other person" shall not include persons in the relation of a jobber, manufacturer, contractor, or subcontractor working on the goods or premises of the jobber or manufacturer or performing parts of an integrated process of production in the apparel and clothing industry: *Provided further,* That nothing in this Act shall prohibit the enforcement of any agreement which is within the foregoing exception.

(f) It shall not be an unfair labor practice under subsections (a) and (b) of this section for an employer engaged primarily in the building and construction industry to make an agreement covering employees engaged (or who, upon their employment, will be engaged) in the building and construction industry with a labor organization of which building and construction employees are members (not established, maintained, or assisted by any action defined in section 8(a) of this Act as an unfair labor practice) because (1) the majority status of such labor organization has not been established under the provisions of section 9 of this Act prior to the making of such agreement, or (2) such agreement requires as a condition of employment, membership in such labor organization after the seventh day following the beginning of such employment or the effective date of the agreement, whichever is later, or (3) such agreement requires the employer to notify such labor organization of opportunities for employment with such employer, or gives such labor organization an opportunity to refer qualified applicants for such employment, or (4) such agreement specifies minimum training or experience qualifications for employment or provides for priority in opportunities for employment based upon length of service with such employer, in the industry or in the particular geographical area: *Provided,* That nothing in this subsection shall set aside the final proviso to section 8(a)3 of this Act: *Provided further,* That any agreement which would be invalid, but for clause (1) of this subsection, shall not be a bar to a petition filed pursuant to section 9(c) or 9(e).

Section 14

(b) Nothing in this subchapter (a) shall be construed as authorizing the execution or application of agreement requiring membership in labor organization as a condition of employment in any State or Territory in which such execution or application is prohibited by State or Territorial law.

Glossary

Abatement   Decrease, reduction, or diminution.

Ad infinitum   without limit; endlessly.

Adjudication   The judicial determination of a legal proceeding.

Administrative law   The branch of public law dealing with the operation of the various agency boards and commissions of government.

Ad Valorem   According to value.

Affidavit   A sworn written statement made before an officer authorized by law to administer oaths.

Affirmative action program   A program designed to promote actively the position of minority workers with regard to hiring and advancement.

Affirmative defense   A matter which, assuming the complaint to be true, constitutes a defense to it.

A fortiori   Even more clearly; said of a conclusion that follows with even greater logical necessity from another which is already included in the argument.

Amicus curiae   A friend of the court who participates in litigation though not a party to the lawsuit.

Annuity   A contract by which the insured pays a lump sum to the insurer and later receives fixed annual payments.

Appellant   The party seeking review of a lower court decision.

Appellee   The party responding to an appeal. The winner in the trial court.

Arbitration   Submission of a dispute to an extrajudicial authority for decision.

Arguendo   For the sake of argument.

Artisan's lien   The lien which arises in favor of one who has expended labor upon, or added value to, another's personal property. The lien allows the person to possess the property as security until reimbursed for the value of labor or materials. If the person is not reimbursed, the property may be sold to satisfy the claim.

Assault and battery   Assault: The intentional creation of immediate apprehension of injury or lack of physical safety. Battery; An intentional, unpermitted, offensive contact or touching.

Assumption of the risk   Negligence doctrine which bars the recovery of damages by an injured party on the ground that such party acted with actual or constructive knowledge of the hazard causing the injury.

Attachment   The term *attachment* has three meanings. First, attachment is a method of acquiring in rem jurisdiction of a nonresident defendant who is not subject to the service of process to commence a lawsuit. By "attaching" property of the nonresident defendant, the court acquires jurisdiction over the defendant to the extent of the value of the property attached. Second, attachment is a procedure used to collect a judgment. A plaintiff may have the property of a defendant seized, pending the outcome of a lawsuit, if the plaintiff has reason to fear that the defendant will dispose of the property before the court renders its decision. Third, attachment is the event which creates an enforceable security interest under the Uniform Commercial Code (UCC). In order that a security interest attach, there must be a signed, written security agreement, or possession of the collateral by the secured party; the secured party must give value to the debtor; and the debtor must maintain rights in the collateral.

Bait-and-switch   An illegal promotional practice in which a seller attracts consumer interest by promoting one product, the "bait," then once interest has been attracted switches it to a second, higher-priced product by making the "bait" unavailable or unattractive.

Beneficiary A person entitled to the possession, use, income, or enjoyment of an interest or right to which legal title is held by another; a person to whom an insurance policy is payable.

Beyond a reasonable doubt The burden of proof required in a criminal case. The prosecution in a criminal case has the burden of proving the defendant is guilty, and the jury must have no reasonable doubt about the defendant's guilt. See also *Burden of proof.*

Bilateral contract An agreement which contains mutual promises, with each party being both a promisor and a promisee.

Bill of particulars In legal practice, a written statement furnished by one party to a lawsuit to another, describing in detail the elements upon which the claim of the first party is based.

Biodegradable Capable of being decomposed by organic action.

"Blue sky" laws Statutes designed to protect investors in stock and other securities by the regulation of transactions in securities, generally by requiring registration and disclosure of pertinent financial information.

Bona fide In good faith; innocently; without fraud or deceit.

Brief A written document produced by a party for a reviewing court which contains the facts, propositions of law, and argument of a party. It is in this document that the party argues the desired application of the law and any contentions as to the rulings of the lower court.

"Bubble" concept A procedure by which the Environmental Protection Agency (EPA) allows a business to treat its entire plant complex as though encased in a bubble. The business suggests its own methods of cleanup, provided the total pollution does not exceed certain limits.

Bulk transfer A transfer made outside the ordinary course of the transferor's business involving a major part of the business' inventory. Bulk transfers are subject to Article 6 of the UCC.

Burden of proof The term *burden of proof* has two meanings. It may describe the party at a trial with the burden of coming forward with evidence to establish a fact. The term also describes the party with the burden of persuasion. This party must convince the judge or jury of the disputed facts in issue or else lose that issue. There are various degrees of proof. See also *Beyond a reasonable doubt, Preponderance of the evidence,* and *Clear and convincing proof.*

Cause of action This phrase has several meanings but it is commonly used to describe the existence of facts giving rise to a judicially enforceable claim.

Caveat emptor Let the buyer beware; rule imposing on a purchaser the duty to inform him or herself as to defects in the property being sold.

Cease and desist order   An administrative agency order directing a party to refrain from doing a specified act.

Certiorari   The name of a writ by which an appellate court may exercise discretionary review of the ruling of an inferior tribunal.

Chancery   Court of equity.

Chattel   An item of personal property.

Chose in action   A right to recover personal property not presently in the possession of the owner.

Civil law   That area of law dealing with the rights and duties of private parties as individual entities, to be distinguished from criminal law. Sometimes the phrase refers to the European system of codified law.

Class action suit   An action brought on behalf of other persons similarly situated. For example, a class action may be brought on behalf of all purchasers of a defective product. Class actions are popular because they often involve matters in which an individual would not have a sufficient financial interest to warrant the expense of a lawsuit.

Clear and convincing proof   The burden of proof in a civil suit which requires a party to prove the facts beyond a well-founded doubt. This standard is more than a preponderance of the evidence, but less than beyond a reasonable doubt, which is required in a criminal case.

Colgate doctrine   The doctrine stating that although price-fixing is illegal per se, there still must be a concerted action rather than simply a refusal to deal with distributors who do not comply with the manufacturer's price policy. A seller has the right to select its customers and to refuse to deal with those that do not charge its suggested price.

Collateral estoppel   The doctrine which bars further inquiry into factual matters which have been conclusively adjudicated at a previous trial or hearing.

Collective bargaining   The process of good-faith negotiation between employers and employee representatives concerning issues of mutual interest.

Commerce clause   Article I, Section 8, Clause 3 of the Constitution of the United States, granting Congress the authority to regulate commerce with foreign nations and among the several states.

Common law   That body of law deriving from judicial decisions as opposed to legislatively enacted statutes and administrative regulations.

Comparable worth   Jobs which, although different, produce substantially equal value for the employer.

Comparative negligence   A doctrine which compares plaintiff's contributory fault with the defendant's fault and allows the jury to reduce the plaintiff's verdict by the percentage of plaintiff's fault.

Complaint In legal practice, the first written statement of the plaintiff's contentions, which initiates the lawsuit.

Compulsory bargaining issue Mandatory bargaining issues regarding wages, hours, or other terms or conditions of employment. Refusal to engage in good faith bargaining with regard to these issues is an unfair labor practice.

Condition precedent In the law of contracts, a condition precedent is an event that must occur before a duty of immediate performance of the promise arises. Contracts often provide that one party must perform before there is a right to performance by the other party. For example, completion of a job is often a condition precedent to payment for that job. One contracting party's failure to perform a condition precedent permits the other party to refuse to perform, cancel the contract, and sue for damages.

Conflicts-of-law principles Rules of law the courts use to determine which substantive law applies when there is an inconsistency between laws of different states or countries.

Conglomerate merger The merger resulting when merging companies have neither the relationship of competitors nor that of supplier and customer.

Consideration An essential element in the creation of a contract obligation which creates a detriment to the promisee or a benefit to the promisor.

Consignment A delivery by the owner of goods to another for disposition usually by sale by the latter.

Consolidation The process by which two or more corporations are joined to create a new corporation.

Conspiracy A combination or agreement between two or more persons for the commission of a criminal act.

Consumer investigative report A report on a consumer's character, general reputation, mode of living, etc., obtained by personal interviews in the community where the consumer works or lives.

Contingent fee An arrangement whereby an attorney is compensated for services in a lawsuit according to an agreed percentage of the amount of money recovered.

Contribution The right of one who has discharged a common liability to recover from another also liable, the proportionate share of the common liability.

Contract A legally enforceable promise.

Contributory negligence A failure to use reasonable care by the plaintiff in a negligence suit.

Conversion An unlawful exercise of dominion and control over another's property which substantially interferes with property rights.

Corrective advertising   A Federal Trade Commission (FTC) remedy which requires companies that have advertised deceptively to run ads that admit the prior errors and correct the erroneous information.

Counterclaim   Any claim filed by the defendant in a lawsuit against the plaintiff in the same suit.

Covenant   An agreement or promise in writing by which a party pledges that something has been done or is being done. The term is often used in connection with real estate to describe the promises of the grantor of the property.

Criminal law   That area of law dealing with wrongs against the state as representative of the community at large, to be distinguished from civil law which hears cases of wrongs against persons.

Damages   Monetary compensation recoverable in a court of law.

D.B.A.   Doing business as.

Decree   The decision of a court of equity.

Defined benefit plan   A money-purchase plan which guarantees a certain retirement income based on the employee's service and salary under the Employee Retirement Income Security Act. The benefits are fixed, and the contributions vary.

Defined contribution plan   A money-purchase plan which allows employers to budget pension costs in advance under the Employee Retirement Income Security Act. The contribution is fixed and the benefits vary.

Demurrer   In common law pleading a formal statement by the defendant that the facts alleged by the plaintiff are insufficient to support a claim for legal relief.

Deposition   Sworn written testimony of a witness taken outside of court; a discovery procedure.

Dicta   Statements made in a judicial opinion which are not essential to the decision of the case.

Directed verdict   A motion for a directed verdict requests that the judge direct the jury to bring in a particular verdict if reasonable minds could not differ on the correct outcome of the lawsuit. In deciding the motion, the judge will view in the light most favorable to the nonmoving party, and if different inferences may be drawn by reasonable men, then the court can not direct a verdict. In essence, a directed verdict removes the jury's discretion.

Discovery   Procedures by which one party to a lawsuit may obtain information relevant to the case from the other party or from third persons.

Discrimination in effect   The discriminatory result of policies which appear to be neutral.

Dissolution   Termination of the existence of a business entity.

Divestiture   The antitrust remedy which forces a company to get rid of assets acquired through illegal mergers or monopolistic practices.

Docket   A book containing a brief summary of all acts done in court in the conduct of each case.

Domicile   That place that a person intends as his or her fixed and permanent legal residence; place of permanent abode, as contrasted with a residence, which may be temporary; a person can have a number of residences but only one domicile; the state of incorporation of a corporation.

Double jeopardy   A constitutional doctrine which prohibits an individual from being prosecuted twice in the same tribunal for the same criminal offense.

Due process   Fundamental fairness. As applied to judicial proceedings, adequate notice of a hearing and an opportunity to appear and defend in an orderly tribunal.

Duty   A legal obligation imposed by the law.

Easement   The right of one other than the owner of land to some use of that land.

Ejusdem generis   Of the same kind or class; a doctrine of legislative interpretation.

Embezzlement   The fraudulent appropriation by one person, acting in a fiduciary capacity, of the money or property of another.

Eminent domain   Authority of the state to take private property for public use.

Emissions reduction banking   The policy stating that businesses that lower pollution beyond the requirements of the law may use the additional reductions in the future.

En banc   Proceedings by or before the court as a whole rather than any single judge.

Enjoin   To require performance or abstention from some act through issuance of an injunction.

Environmental impact statement   A filing of documents required by the National Environmental Policy Act which forces governmental agencies to consider the environmental consequences of their actions.

Equal protection   A principle of the Fifth and Fourteenth Amendments to the Constitution that individuals under like circumstances shall be accorded the same benefits and burdens under the law of the sovereign.

Equity   A body of law which seeks to adjust conflicting rights on the basis of fairness and good conscience. Courts of equity or chancery may require or prohibit specific acts where monetary damages will not afford complete relief.

Escrow   A deed, bond, or deposit which one party delivers for safekeeping by a second party who is obligated to deliver it to a third party upon the fulfillment of some condition.

Estoppel   The legal principle that one may not assert facts inconsistent with one's own prior actions.

Exculpatory clause   A provision in a contract whereby one of the parties attempts to relieve itself of liability for breach of a legal duty.

Exclusive dealing contract   A contract under which a buyer agrees to purchase a certain product exclusively from the seller or in which the seller agrees to sell all his product production to the buyer.

Executory contract   An agreement which is not completed. Until the performance required in a contract is completed, it is executory.

Exemplary damages   Punitive damages. Monetary compensation in excess of direct losses suffered by the plaintiff which may be awarded in intentional tort cases where the defendant's conduct deserves punishment.

Failing company doctrine   A merger between a failing company and a competitor may be allowed, although such a merger would be illegal if both companies were viable competitors.

False imprisonment   The tort of an intentional, unjustified confinement of a nonconsenting person who knows of the confinement.

Fee schedule   A plan, usually adopted by an association, which establishes minimum or maximum charges for a service or product.

Fellow-servant doctrine   The doctrine which precludes an injured employee from recovering damages from his employer when the injury resulted from the negligent act of another employee.

Felony   A criminal offense of a serious nature, generally punishable by death or imprisonment in penitentiary; to be distinguished from a misdemeanor.

Fiduciary   One having a duty to act for another's benefit in the highest good faith.

Financing statement   An established form that a secured party files with a public officer such as the Secretary of State to perfect a security interest under the Uniform Commercial Code (UCC). It is a simple form which contains basic information such as a description of the collateral, names, and addresses. It is designed to give notice that the debtor and secured party have entered into a security agreement.

Firm offer   An offer in signed writing by a merchant to buy or sell goods; it gives assurances that the offer will be held open as governed by the Uniform Commercial Code (UCC).

Foreclosure   If a mortgagor fails to perform his or her obligations as agreed, the mortgagee may declare the whole debt due and payable, and she or he may foreclose on the mortgaged property to pay the debt secured by the mortgage. The usual method of foreclosure authorizes the sale of the mortgaged property at a public auction. The proceeds of the sale are applied to the debt.

Forum non conveniens The doctrine under which a court may dismiss a lawsuit in which it appears that for the convenience of the parties and in the interest of justice the action should have been brought in another court.

Fraud A false representation of fact made with intent to deceive another which is justifiably relied upon to the injury of that person.

Full-line forcing An arrangement in which a manufacturer refuses to supply any portion of the product line unless the retailer agrees to accept the entire line.

Garnishment A legal proceeding whereby a creditor may collect directly from a third party who is obligated to the debtor.

Geographic extension merger A combining of companies involved with the same product or service which do not compete in the same geographical regions or markets.

Geographic market The relevant section of the country affected by a merger.

Going bare A professional practicing (in her or his field of expertise) without liability insurance.

Good faith Honesty in dealing; innocence; without fraud or deceit.

Good-faith meeting of competition A bona fide business practice which is a defense to a charge of violation of the Robinson-Patman Act. The Robinson-Patman Act is an amendment to the Clayton Act, which outlaws price discrimination that might substantially lessen competition or tend to create a monopoly. This exception allows a seller in good faith to meet the equally low price, service, or facility of a competitor. The good-faith exception cannot be established if the purpose of the price discrimination has been to eliminate competition.

Greenmail Forcing a corporation to buy its own stock at an inflated price to avoid a takeover.

Guardian One charged with the duty of care and maintenance of another person such as a minor or incompetent under the law.

Guardian ad litem A guardian appointed to prosecute or defend a lawsuit on behalf of an incompetent.

Habeas corpus The name of a writ which orders one holding custody of another to produce that individual before the court for the purpose of determining whether such custody is proper.

Hearsay evidence Evidence of statements made or actions performed out of court which is offered to prove the truth thereof.

Hearsay rule   The exclusion, with certain exceptions, of evidence not within the personal knowledge of the witness.

Herfindahl-Hirschman Index   An index used by the Justice Department to test the legality of horizontal acquisitions. The index is computed by squaring the market share of each firm in a market and adding the results.

Holder in due course   One who has acquired possession of a negotiable instrument through proper negotiation for value, in good faith, and without notice of any defenses to it. Such a holder is not subject to personal defenses which would otherwise defeat the obligation embodied in the instrument.

Horizontal merger   Merger of corporations that were competitors prior to the merger.

Hot-cargo contract   An agreement whereby an employer agrees to refrain from handling, using, selling, transporting, or otherwise dealing in the products of another employer or to cease doing business with any other person.

Illinois brick doctrine   The standing-to-sue requirement of the Sherman Act which requires that the plaintiff be directly injured by the defendant's violation. Damages are not passed through the channels of distribution.

Immunity   Status of exemption from lawsuits or other legal obligations.

Implied in fact contract   A legally enforceable agreement inferred from the circumstances and conduct of the parties.

Indemnify   To reimburse another for a loss suffered.

Indictment   A document issued by a grand jury formally charging a person with a felony.

Industry guide   An issue of the FTC defining the agency's view of the legality of an industry's trade practice.

Infliction of mental distress   An intentional tort to the emotions which causes both mental distress and physical symptoms as a result of the defendant's outrageous behavior.

Injunction   A court order directing a party to do or to refrain from doing some act.

In personam   The jurisdiction of a court to affect the rights and duties of a specific individual.

In rem   The jurisdiction of a court to affect property rights with respect to a specific thing.

Intangible property   Something which represents value but has no intrinsic value of its own, such as a note or bond.

Interference in contractual relations   A business tort in which persons are induced to breach binding agreements.

Interlocking directorates   A situation in which the same persons are members of the board of directors of two or more corporations at the same time.

Interpleader   A legal procedure by which one holding a single fund subject to conflicting claims of two or more persons may require the conflicting claimants to come into court and litigate the matter between themselves.

Interrogatory   A written question propounded by one party to a lawsuit to another; a type of discovery procedure.

Inter se   Between themselves.

Intestate   A person who dies without a will.

Invasion of privacy   A tort based on misappropriation of name or likeness, intrusion upon physical solitude, or public disclosure of objectionable, private information.

Joint tenancy   A form of ownership in which each of two or more owners have an undivided right to possession of the property. Upon the death of an owner his or her interest passes to the surviving owners because of survivorship.

Judicial activist   An activist judge tends to abide by the following judicial philosophies: (1) The political process cannot adequately handle society's difficult issues; (2) the courts can correct society's ills through the decision-making process; (3) following precedent is not crucial; and (4) "judge-made law" is often necessary to carry out the legislative intent of the law. See also *Judicial restraint.*

Judicial restraint   A judge who abides by the judicial restraint philosophy (1) believes that the political process, and not the courts, should correct society's ills, (2) decides an issue on a narrow basis, if possible, (3) follows precedent whenever possible, and (4) does not engage in "judge-made law," but interprets the letter of the law. See also *Judicial activist.*

Judgment   Official adjudication of a court of law.

Judgment notwithstanding the verdict   The decision of a court which sets aside the verdict of a jury and reaches the opposite result.

Judicial restraint   A judicial philosophy. Those following it believe that the power of judicial review should be exercised with great restraint.

Judicial review   The power of courts to declare laws enacted by legislative bodies and actions by the Executive to be unconstitutional.

Jurisdiction   The power and authority of a court or other governmental agency to adjudicate controversies and otherwise deal with matters brought before it.

Jurisprudence   The science of the law; the practical science of giving a wise interpretation of the law.

Jury instruction   A statement made by the judge to the jury informing them of the law applicable to the case which the jury is bound to accept and apply.

Laches   Defense to an equitable action based on the plaintiff's unreasonable delay in bringing the action.

Legacy   Personal property disposed of by a will. Sometimes the term is synonymous with bequest. The word devise is used in connection with real property distributed by will.

Libel   A defamatory written statement communicated to a third party.

Lien   A claim to an interest in property in satisfaction of a debt or claim.

Limited partnership   A partnership in which one or more individuals are general partners and one or more individuals are limited partners. The limited partners contribute assets to the partnership without taking part in the conduct of the business. Such individual are liable for the debts of the partnership only to the extent of their contributions.

Liquidation   The process of winding up the affairs of a business for the purpose of paying debts and disposing of assets. May be voluntary or under court order.

Long-arm statute   A state statute which gives extraterritorial effect to process (summons) in specified cases. It allows state courts to obtain jurisdiction in civil actions over defendants who are beyond the border of the state provided the defendants have minimum contact with the state sufficient to satisfy due process.

Malfeasance   Doing of some wrongful act.

Mandamus   A court order directing the holder of an office perform his or her legal duty.

Market extension merger   An acquisition in which the acquiring company increases its market through product extension or geographical extension.

Material breach   A substantial failure, without excuse, to perform a promise which constitutes the whole or part of a contract.

Mayhem   Unlawfully depriving a human being of a member of his body.

Mechanic's lien   A lien on real estate that is created by statute to assist suppliers and laborers in collecting their accounts and wages. Its purpose is to subject the owner's land to a lien for material and labor expended in the construction of buildings and other improvements.

Merger   The extinguishment of a corporate entity by the transfer of its assets and liabilities to another corporation which continues in existence.

Merger guidelines   Standards issued by the government regarding the combination of two or more unrelated businesses into a single legal entity.

Ministerial duty   An example of a definite duty regarding which nothing is left to discretion or judgment.

Misdemeanor   A criminal offense of less serious nature than a felony, generally punishable by fine or jail sentence other than in a penitentiary.

Misfeasance   A misdeed or trepass.

Misrepresentation   Any untrue manifestation of fact by word or conduct; it may be unintentional.

Monopoly   Exclusive control of a market by a business entity.

Mortgage   A transfer of an interest in property for the purpose of creating a security for a debt.

Motion   The process by which the parties make written or oral requests that the judge issue an order or ruling.

Mutual mistake   A situation in which parties to a contract reach a bargain on the basis of an incorrect assumption common to each party.

Negligence   A person's failure to exercise reasonable care which foreseeably causes another injury.

Nexus   A logical connection.

NLRB   National Labor Relations Board.

Noerr-Pennington doctrine   This doctrine exempts from the antitrust laws concerted efforts to lobby government officials regardless of the anticompetitive purposes. It is based on the First Amendment freedom of speech.

No-fault laws   Laws barring tort actions by injured persons against third-party tort-feasors and requiring such persons to obtain recovery from their own insurers.

Nolo contendere   A plea entered by the defendant in a criminal case which neither admits nor denies the crime allegedly committed but which if accepted by the court permits the judge to treat the defendant as guilty.

Noscitur a sociis   The principle that the scope of general words is delimited by specific accompanying words; a doctrine of legislative interpretation.

Notary public   A public officer authorized to administer oaths and certify certain documents.

Notice   Communication sufficient to charge a reasonable person with knowledge of some fact.

Nuisance   A physical condition constituting an unreasonable and substantial interference with the rights of individuals or the public at large.

Oligopoly   Control of a commodity or service in a given market by a small number of companies or suppliers.

Option   A contractual arrangement under which one party has for a specified time the right to buy certain property from or sell certain property to the other party.

Ordinance The legislative enactment of a city, county, or other municipal corporation.

Organizational picketing Picketing by members of a union seeking to represent workers and to obtain recognition as the exclusive bargaining agent for them. Under the Landrum-Griffin Act, purely recognitional picketing under some circumstances is illegal, while purely informational picketing may be legal.

Ownership The bundle of rights to possess and use property because of title to the property.

Pari materia, in Concerning the same subject matter. A rule of statutory construction that two such statutes will be construed together.

Parker v. Brown doctrine The name given to the state action exemption to the Sherman Act. See *State action exemption*.

Parol evidence Legal proof based on oral statements; with regard to a document, any evidence which is extrinsic to the document itself.

Parol evidence rule Parol evidence is extrinsic evidence. In contracts, the parol evidence rule excludes the introduction of evidence of prior written or oral agreements which may vary, contradict, alter, or supplement the present written agreement. There are several exceptions to this rule. For example, when the parties to an agreement do not intend for that agreement to be final and complete, then parol evidence is admissible.

Patent To be patentable, inventions must be nonobvious, novel, and useful. A patent creates a 17-year protection period during which there is a presumption of validity if the patent is properly registered with the Patent Office.

Per capita By or for each individual.

Per curiam By the court; said of an opinion expressing the view of the court as a whole as opposed to an opinion authored by any single member of the court.

Peremptory challenge The right of the parties to a proceeding to have a specified

Perjury The giving of false testimony under oath.

Per se In itself.

Per se illegal Under the Sherman Act, agreements and practices are illegal only if they are unreasonable. The practices which are conclusively presumed to be unreasonable are per se illegal. If an activity is per se illegal, only proof of the activity is required, and it is not necessary to prove an anticompetitive effect. For example, price-fixing is per se illegal. See also *Rule of reason*.

Peremptory challenge The power granted each party to reject a limited number of potential jurors during voir dire examination. No reason for the rejection need be given.

Personal property Physical or intangible property other than real estate.

Plaintiff The person who initiates a lawsuit.

Pleadings The process by which the parties to a lawsuit present formal written statements of their contentions to create the issues of the lawsuit.

Plenary Entire; complete in all respects.

Point source Any source of air pollution which must be licensed under the Clean Air Act.

Potential entrant doctrine In antitrust law, a doctrine that prohibits mergers and acquisitions by a firm that is only a potential competitor in a market.

Precedent A prior judicial decision relied upon as an example of a rule of law.

Predatory pricing A seller lowering prices in one geographic area in order to eliminate competition.

Prejudicial error An error in judicial proceedings which may have affected the result in the case.

Preponderance Preponderance of the evidence means that evidence, in the judgment of the jurors, has greater weight and overcomes the opposing evidence and presumptions.

Price discrimination A seller charging different purchasers different prices for the same goods at the same time.

Price-fixing An agreement or combination by which the conspirators set the market price of a product or service either being sold or purchased, whether high or low.

Prima facie On the face of it; thus, presumed to be true unless proved otherwise.

Primary air quality standards The standards necessary to protect human health. Secondary air quality standards are stricter standards necessary to protect various environmental amenities.

Privilege A special advantage accorded by law to some individual or group; an exemption from a duty or obligation generally imposed by law.

Privity Interest derived from successive relationship with another part; a contractual connection.

Procedural law The body of rules governing the manner in which legal claims are enforced.

Product extension merger A merger that extends the products of the acquiring company into a similar or related product but one which is not directly in competition with existing products.

Promissory estoppel Court enforcement of an otherwise unbinding promise if injustice can only be avoided by enforcement of the promise. A substitute for consideration.

Pro tanto So far as it goes.

Proximate cause The doctrine which limits an actor's liability to consequences which could reasonably be foreseen to have resulted from the act.

Punitive damages Monetary damages in excess of a compensatory award, usually granted only in intentional tort cases where defendant's conduct involved some element deserving punishment; exemplary damages.

Purchase money security interest A security interest that is taken or retained by the seller of the collateral to secure all or part of the collateral's price.

Qualified pension plan A private retirement plan which gains favorable income tax treatment from the Internal Revenue Service (IRS). A qualified pension plan allows for the deduction of contributions made to fund the plan. Also, earnings from fund investments are not taxable, and employees defer personal income tax liability until payments are received after retirement. To qualify, the plan must cover a high percentage of workers (usually 70 percent) or cover classifications of employees that do not discriminate in favor of management or shareholders.

Quantity discount The practice of giving a lower per unit price to businesses that buy a product in volume than to their competitors that do not.

Quasi-contract A quasi-contract, often referred to as an implied-in-law contract, is not a true contract. It is a legal fiction that the courts use to prevent unjust enrichment and wrongdoing. Courts permit the person who conferred a benefit to recover the reasonable value of that benefit. Nonetheless, the elements of a true contract are not present.

Quasi-judicial Administrative actions involving factual determinations and the discretionary application of rules and regulations.

Quid pro quo The exchange of one thing of value for another.

Quitclaim deed The transfer by deed of all of rights, title, and interest in property.

Quo warranto An action brought by the government to test the validity of some franchise, such as the privilege of doing business as a corporation. By what authority are you acting?

Ratio decidendi Logical basis of judicial decision.

Real property Land and fixtures to land.

Reciprocal agreement A contract in which two parties agree to mutual actions so that each party can act as both a buyer and seller. The agreement violates the Clayton Act if it results in a substantial lessening of competition.

Redlining An act or refusal to act which results in a discriminatory practice. For example, refusing to make loans in low-income areas can discriminate against minorities in granting credit.

Release Relinquishment of a right or claim against another party.

Remand Return of a case by an appellate court for further action by the lower court.

Remedy The action or procedure that is followed in order to enforce a right or to obtain damages for injury to a right; the means by which a right is enforced or the violation of a right is prevented, redressed, or compensated.

Reorganization The legal process of forming a new corporation after bankruptcy or foreclosure.

Replevin An action for the recovery of goods wrongfully taken or kept.

Res A thing, object, or status.

Resale price maintenance Manufacturer control of a brand or trade-name product's minimum resale price.

Rescission The equitable remedy which annuls a contract and returns the parties to the position each occupied before the making of the contract. A party entitled to rescind a contract may choose to affirm it instead. The contract is voidable but not void. A contract which is void doesn't exist, and there is nothing to affirm.

Res judicata The doctrine which deems a former adjudication conclusive and prevents a retrial of matters decided in the earlier lawsuit.

Rescind To cancel or annul a contract and return the parties to their original positions.

Rescission Annulment or cancellation of an obligation so as to return the parties to their status prior to the origin of the obligation.

Respondeat superior The doctrine imposing liability on one for torts committed by another person who is in his or her employ and subject to his or her control.

Respondent The party answering a suit in equity or an appeal.

Restraint of trade Monopolies, combinations, and contracts that impede free competition.

Reverse Overturn or vacate the judgment of a court.

Reverse discrimination The advancement and recruitment of minority workers ahead of similarly qualified nonminority workers.

Right of redemption The right to buy back. A debtor may buy back or redeem his or her mortgaged property when he or she pays the debt.

Right-to-work law A state statute which outlaws a union shop contract—one by which an employer agrees to require membership in the union sometime after an employee has been hired as a condition of continued employment.

Robinson-Patman Act The amendment to Section 2 of the Clayton Act covering price discrimination. As originally adopted, the Robinson-Patman Act outlawed price discrimination in interstate commerce that might substantially lessen competition or tend to create a monopoly.

Rule of reason Under the Sherman Act, contracts or conspiracies are illegal only if they constitute an unreasonable restraint of trade or attempt to monopolize. An activity is unreasonable if it adversely affects competition. An act is reasonable if it promotes competition. The rule of reason requires that an anticompetitive effect be shown. See also *Per se illegal*.

Sanctions Penalties imposed for violation of a law.

Scienter With knowledge; particularly, guilty knowledge.

Secondary boycott Conspiracy or combination to cause the customers or suppliers of an employer to cease doing business with that employer.

Security Under the securities law, an investment in which the investor does not participate in management.

Seniority plan A system giving priority to employees based on the length of time the employee has worked for the employer. An employer may apply different standards pursuant to a good faith seniority system if the differences are not the result of an intention to discriminate.

Separation of powers The doctrine which holds that the legislative, executive, and judicial branches of government function independently of one another and that each branch serves as a check on the others.

Shark repellant Corporate action to make a threatened acquisition unattractive to the acquiring company.

Sherman Act An 1890 Congressional enactment designed to regulate anticompetitive behavior in interstate commerce.

Slander An oral defamatory statement communicated to a third person.

Specific performance Equitable remedy which requires defendants in certain circumstances to do what they have contracted to do.

Standing The doctrine which requires the plaintiff in a lawsuit to have a sufficient legal interest in the subject matter of the case.

Stare decisis The doctrine which traditionally indicates that a court should follow prior decisions in all cases based on substantially similar facts.

State action exemption The Sherman Act exemption of the sovereign action of a state which replaces competition with regulation if the state actively supervises the anticompetitive conduct.

Status quo   The conditions or state of affairs at a given time.

Statute   A legislative enactment.

Statute of frauds   Legislation which states that certain contracts will not be enforced unless there is a signed writing evidencing the agreement.

Strict liability   The doctrine under which a party may be required to respond in tort damages without regard to such party's use of due care.

Subpoena   A court order directing a witness to appear or to produce documents in his or her possession.

Subrogation   The right of a party secondarily liable to stand in the place of the creditor after he or she has made payment to the creditor and to enforce the creditor's right against the party primarily liable in order to obtain indemnity from him.

Substantive law   A body of rules defining the nature and extent of legal rights.

Summary judgment   A judicial determination that no genuine factual dispute exists and that one party to the lawsuit is entitled to judgment as a matter of law.

Summons   An official notice to a person that a lawsuit has been commenced against him or her and that he or she must appear in court to answer the charges.

Superfund   The Comprehensive Environmental Response, Compensation, and Liability Act of 1980.

Supremacy clause   Article VI, U.S. Constitution, which states that the Constitution, laws, and treaties of the United States shall be the "supreme law of the land," and shall take precedence over conflicting state laws.

Surety   One who incurs a liability for the benefit of another. One who undertakes to pay money in the event that his principal is unable to pay.

Tangible property   Physical property.

Tender offer   An invited public offer by a company or organization to buy shares from existing stockholders of another public corporation under specified terms.

Testator   One who has made a will.

Title   Legal evidence of ownership.

Tort   A civil wrong other than a breach of contract.

Treason   Breach of allegiance to one's government, specifically by levying war against such government or by giving aid and comfort to the enemy.

Treble damages   An award of damages allowable under some statutes equal to three times the amount found by the jury to be a single recovery.

Trespass   An act done in an unlawful manner so as to cause injury to another; an unauthorized entry upon another's land.

Trust   A fiduciary relationship whereby one party (trustee) holds legal title for the benefit of another (beneficiary).

Trustee   One who holds legal title to property for the benefit of another.

Truth-in-lending   A federal law which requires disclosure of total finance charges and the annual percentage rate for credit in order that borrowers may be able to shop for credit.

Tying contract   A contract which ties the sale of one piece of property (real or personal) to the sale or lease of another item of property.

Ultra vires   Beyond the scope of corporate powers granted in the charter.

Unconscionable   In the law of contracts, provisions which are oppressive, over-reaching, or shocking to the conscience.

Usury   A loan of money at interest above the legal rate.

Venue   The geographical area over which a court presides. Venue designates the court in which the case should be tried. Change of venue means to move to another court.

Verdict   Findings of fact by the jury.

Vertical merger   A merger of corporations where one corporation is the supplier of the other.

Vertical price-fixing   An agreement between a seller and a buyer (for example, between a manufacturer and a retailer) to fix the resale price at which the buyer will sell goods.

Voidable   Capable of being declared a nullity, though otherwise valid.

Voir dire   The preliminary examination of prospective jurors for the purpose of ascertaining bias or interest in the lawsuit.

Voluntary bargaining issues   Either party may refuse to bargain in good faith regarding matters other than wages, hours, and other terms and conditions of employment. This refusal does not constitute an unfair labor practice. An issue over which parties may bargain if they choose to do so.

Waiver   An express or implied relinquishment of a right.

Warrant   A judicial authorization for the performance of some act.

Warranty of merchantability   A promise implied in a sale of goods by merchants that the goods are reasonably fit for the general purpose for which they are sold.

White knight A slang term which describes the inducement of a voluntary acquisition when an involuntary acquisition is threatened. The voluntary acquisition group is a white knight since it saves the corporation from an unfriendly takeover.

Workers' compensation A plan for the compensation for occupational diseases, accidental injuries, and death of employees which arise out of employment. Compensation includes medical expenses and burial costs and lost earnings based on the size of the family and the wage rate of the employee.

Wright-Line doctrine Establishes procedures for determining the burden of proof in cases involving mixed motivation for discharge.

Writ of certiorari A discretionary proceeding by which an appellate court may review the ruling of an inferior tribunal.

Writ of habeas corpus A court order to one holding custody of another to produce that individual before the court for the purpose of determining whether such custody is proper.

Yellow-dog contract An agreement in which a worker agrees not to join a union and that discharge will result from a breach of the contract.

Index